Religious Organizations in the United States

Religious Organizations in the United States

A Study of Identity, Liberty, and the Law

EDITOR IN CHIEF

James A. Serritella

ASSOCIATE EDITORS

Thomas C. Berg
W. Cole Durham, Jr.
Edward McGlynn Gaffney, Jr.
Craig B. Mousin

CAROLINA ACADEMIC PRESS
Durham, North Carolina

Library of Congress Cataloging-in-Publication Data

Religious organizations in the United States : a study of identity, liberty, and the law /
by James A. Serritella ... [et al.].
   p. cm.
ISBN 1-59460-028-7 (alk. paper)
1. Corporations, Religious--Law and legislation--United States. 2. Religious institutions--United States. I. Serritella, James A. II. Title.

KF4865.R45 2005
  344.73'096--dc22   2005001646

CAROLINA ACADEMIC PRESS
700 Kent Street
Durham, North Carolina 27701
Telephone (919) 489-7486
Fax (919) 493-5668
www.cap-press.com

Printed in the United States of America

We dedicate this book to all who come together in religion and strive to live their beliefs in a free society governed by law.

Contents

Table of Cases   xi

Prologue
James A. Serritella   xvii

Acknowledgments   xxvii

Section I

Definition of Religion
W. Cole Durham, Jr. and Elizabeth A. Sewell   3

Religious Polity
Martin E. Marty and James A. Serritella   85

Religious Diversity, Civil Law, and Institutional Isomorphism
Rhys H. Williams and John P.N. Massad   111

Religious Structures under the Federal Constitution
Thomas C. Berg   129

State Constitutions and Religious Liberty
Craig B. Mousin   167

Section II

Legal Structuring of Religious Institutions
W. Cole Durham, Jr.   213

Associational Structures of Religious Organizations
Patty Gerstenblith   223

Unincorporated Associations and Charitable Trusts
Patricia B. Carlson   253

Religious Organizations and the Law of Trusts
H. Reese Hansen   279

Civil Court Resolution of Property Disputes among Religious Organizations
Patty Gerstenblith   315

Regulation of Religious Organizations via Governmental Financial Assistance
Carl H. Esbeck   349

Appendix: Charitable Choice and the Critics
Carl H. Esbeck   391

Section III

Regulation of Religious Bodies
Edward McGlynn Gaffney, Jr.   405

Exemption of Religious Organizations from Federal Taxation
Edward McGlynn Gaffney, Jr.   409

Exemption of Religious Communities from State and Local Taxation
Edward McGlynn Gaffney, Jr.   459

Appendix: State Constitutions Containing Provisions for Tax Exemption of
Charitable Organizations, Including Religious Bodies
Edward McGlynn Gaffney, Jr.   515

Employment in Religious Organizations
Patrick J. Schiltz and Douglas Laycock   527

Land Use Regulation of Churches
Angela C. Carmella   565

Derivative Liability
Mark E. Chopko   591

How the Legal System's Treatment of Clerical Sexual Misconduct with
Minors Affects Religious Freedom
Stephen J. Pope and Patricia B. Carlson   633

Section IV

Affiliated Ministries: Education, Social Services, Health Care
Thomas C. Berg   671

Religiously Affiliated Education
Thomas C. Berg   675

Appendix: The Supreme Court's Voucher Decision (*Zelman v. Simmons-Harris*)
Thomas C. Berg   719

Religiously Affiliated Health Care Providers: Legal Structures and
Transformations
Donald H.J. Hermann   727

Section V

Constitutional Coherence and the Legal Structures of American Churches
William P. Marshall   759

Full and Free Exercise of Religion
Edward McGlynn Gaffney, Jr.   773

Epilogue
James A. Serritella   811

About the Authors   813

Index   819

Table of Cases

Agostini v. Felton, 521 U.S. 203 (1997), 140-141, 154, 222, 397-398, 465, 478, 482, 502, 552, 711-712, 713

Abortion Rights Mobilization, Inc. v. Regan, 544 F. Supp. 471 (S.D.N.Y. 1982), 454, 456

Africa v. Commonwealth of Pennsylvania, 662 F.2d 1025 (3d Cir. 1981), 25, 27

African Methodist Episcopal Zion Church in America v. Zion Hill Methodist Church, 534 So.2d 224 (Ala. 1988), 340-341

Aguilar v. Felton, 473 U.S. 402 (1985), 465, 478, 498

Alamo Foundation v. Secretary of Labor, 471 U.S. 290 (1985), 157, 164, 768-769

Ambrosio v. Price, 495 F. Supp. 381 (D. Neb. 1979), 607, 608

Anderson v. World Wide Church of God, 661 F. Supp. 1400 (D. Minn. 1987), 619

Arneth v. Gross, 699 F. Supp. 450 (S.D.N.Y. 1988), 386

Atterberry v. Smith, 522 A.2d 683 (Pa. Commw. 1987), 296-297

Ayon v. Gourley, 47 F. Supp.2d 1246 (D. Col. 1998), 649-650

Babcock v. New Orleans Theological Seminary, 554 So.2d 90 (La. App. 1990), 149, 151, 706-707

Barr v. United Methodist Church, 153 Cal. Rptr. 322 (Ct. App. 1979), 192, 274, 277-278, 618, 623-625, 627, 628

Bartling v. Superior Court, 209 Cal. Rptr. 200 (Ct. App. 1984), 753

Basich v. Board of Pensions, Evangelical Lutheran Church in America, 540 N.W.2d 82 (Minn. Ct. App. 1995), 193

Bear v. Reformed Mennonite Church, 341 A.2d 105 (Pa. 1975), 615, 616

Benedictine Society v. National City Bank, 109 F.2d 679 (3d Cir. 1940), 617, 627

Bethel Baptist Church v. United States, 822 F.2d 1334 (3d Cir. 1987), 438-439, 440

Bishop & Diocese of Colorado v. Mote, 716 P.2d 85 (Colo. 1986), 295, 298-299, 332-333, 336

Black v. Snyder, 471 N.W.2d 715 (Minn. Ct. App. 1991), 249

Board of Education of the City of Cincinnati v. Minor, 23 Ohio St. 211 (1872), 182

Board of Education v. Allen, 392 U.S. 236 (1968), 478

Bob Jones University v. United States, 461 U.S. 574 (1983), 452, 453, 483, 488, 704-705

Bowen v. Kendrick, 487 U.S. 589 (1988), 155

Boy Scouts of America v. Dale, 120 S. Ct. 1446 (2000), 137, 684, 724

Brillhart v. Scheier, 758 P.2d 219 (Kan. 1988), 607-608, 628

Brown v. Board of Education, 347 U.S. 483 (1954), 451

Buteas v. Raritan Lodge No. 61 F. & A.M., 591 A.2d 623 (N.J. Super. 1991), 271-272

Candy H. v. Redemption Ranch, Inc., 563 F. Supp. 505 (M.D. Ala. 1983), 616

Cantwell v. State of Connecticut, 310 U.S. 296 (1940), 471, 635-636

Carr v. St. John's University, 231 N.Y.S.2d 410 (App. Div.), aff'd 187 N.E.2d 18 (1962), 706

Chittenden Township School District v. Department of Education, 738 A.2d 539 (Vt. 1994), 202, 204

Christian Echoes National Ministry v. United States, 470 F.2d 849 (1972), 449

Church of Lukumi Babalu Aye v. City of Hialeah, 508 U.S. 520 (1993), 49, 569, 570, 571, 641, 715, 802, 816

Cimijotti v. Paulson, 230 F. Supp. 39 (N.D. Iowa 1964), 654

City of Boerne v. Flores, 521 U.S. 507 (1997), xvii, 142, 143, 184, 194, 196, 569-570, 571, 582, 585, 586, 803, 809, 816

Cocks v. Manners, 4A Scott, The Law of Trusts (4th ed. 1989), 259

Coles v. Wilburn, 245 S.E.2d 273 (Ga. 1978), 273

Committee for the Public Education v. Nyquist, 413 U.S. 756 (1973), 722

Corporation of Presiding Bishop v. Amos, 483 U.S. 327 (1981), 144, 164, 701, 725

Corporation of Presiding Bishop v. City of Porterville, 338 U.S. 805 (1949), 589-590

Corsie v. Campanalonga, 721 A.2d 733 (N.J. Super. 1998), rev'd in part 734 A.2d 788(1999), 654

County of Allegheny v. ACLU, Greater Pittsburgh Chapter, 492 U.S. 573 (1989), 782

Cox v. Thee Evergreen Church, 836 S.W.2d 167 (Tex. 1992), 272, 274, 608, 620

Craigdaillie v. Aikman, 4 Eng. Rep. 435 (1820), 286

Crest Chimney Cleaning Co. v. Ahi Ezer Congregation, 310 N.Y.S.2d 217 (Civ. Ct. 1970), 617-618

Crocker v. Barr, 409 S.E.2d 368 (S.C. 1991), 272

DaCosta v. De Pas, 1 Amb. 228 (1754), 255

Dausch v. Rykse, 52 F.3d 1425 (7th Cir. 1994), 612

Davey v. Locke, 299 F.3d 746 (9th Cir. 2002) rev'd 540 U.S. 712 (2004), 199

Davis v. Beason, 133 U.S. 333 (1890), 797

Daytona Rescue Mission, Inc. v. City of Daytona Beach, 885 F. Supp. 1554 (M.D. Fla. 1995), 578

DeBose v. Bear Valley Church of Christ, 890 P.2d 214 (Co. App. 1995), rev'd 928 P.2d 1315 (Colo. 1997), 634

De LaSalle Institute v. United States, 195 F. Supp. 891 (N.D. Cal. 1961), 617

Destefano v. Grabrian, 763 P.2d 275 (Colo. 1988), 612, 613

Doe v. Norwich Roman Catholic Diocesan Corporation, 268 F. Supp.2d 139 (D. Conn. 2003), 639

Drevlow v. Lutheran Church, Missouri Synod, 991 F.2d 468 (8th Cir. 1993), 541, 542

Eckler v. General Council of Assemblies of God, 784 S.W.2d 935 (Tex. App. 1990, writ denied), 600-601, 603, 625, 628

EEOC v. Kamehameha Schools, 990 F.2d 458 (9th Cir. 1993), 601

Employment Division v. Rogue Valley Youth for Christ, 770 P.2d 588 (Or. 1989), 188

Employment Division v. Smith, 494 U.S. 872 (1990), xvii, xxi, 47, 48, 49, 82, 132, 135-137, 139, 141-143, 145, 149-151, 153, 154, 156, 159-160, 183-184, 187-191, 193, 194, 218-220, 246, 247, 248-250, 496, 498, 506, 528, 543, 549-52, 568-569, 570, 571, 575, 580, 590, 636, 641, 651, 684, 686-687, 715, 724, 790, 800, 802-804, 809

Everson v. Board of Education, 330 U.S. 1 (1947), 198, 463, 479, 480, 495, 762-763, 778, 780, 781, 790, 795

First Covenant Church of Seattle v. Seattle, 840 P.2d 174 (Wash. 1992), 185, 189

First Evangelical Methodist Church v. Clinton, 360 S.E.2d 584 (Ga. 1987), 294

First Methodist Church v. Putnam, 72 N.Y.S.2d 70 (Sup. Ct. 1947), 266-267

First Presbyterian Church v. United Presbyterian Church in the U.S., 464 N.E.2d 454 (N.Y. 1984), 284

Follett v. Town of McCormick, S.C., 321 U.S. 573 (1944), 460, 463, 469-470, 475-478, 486, 488, 491, 492, 495, 496, 511

Folwell v. Bernard, 477 So.2d 1060 (Fla. Dist. Ct. App. 1985), 606-607, 625, 628

Fordham University v. Brown, 856 F. Supp. 684 (D.D.C. 1994), 362-363

Gallo v. Salesian Society, Inc., 676 A.2d 580 (N.J. Super. Ct. App. Div. 1996), 545

George v. International Society of Krishna Consciousness, 571 N.E.2d 340 (Mass. 1991), 620

Gilmour v. Coats, 4A Scott, The Law of Trusts (4th ed. 1989), 259

Gibson v. Brewer, 952 S.W.2d 239 (Mo. 1997), 192, 651

Gonzalez v. Roman Catholic Archbishop, 280 U.S. 1 (1929), 530-531, 534, 537, 539, 646

Grove City College v. Bell, 465 U.S. 555 (1984), 372

Guinn v. Church of Christ, 775 P.2d 766 (Okla. 1989), 614-615

Hadnot v. Shaw, 826 P.2d 978 (Ok. 1992), 654

Hernandez v. Commissioner of Internal Revenue, 490 U.S. 680 (1989), 501-502

Holmes v. Bush, No. CV99-3370, 2002 WL 1809079 (Fla. Cir. Ct., Aug. 5, 2002), 198

Hope Lutheran Church v. Chellew, 460 N.E.2d 1244 (Ind. Ct. App. 1984), 625

Humphries v. Wiley, 76 S.W.2d 793 (Tex. Civ. App. 1934, writ dism'd), 264

Hunt v. McNair, 413 U.S. 734 (1973), 158

Hutchins v. Grace Tabernacle United Pentecostal Church, 804 S.W.2d 598 (Tex. App. 1991, no writ), 270

Hutchinson v. Luddy, 606 A.2d 905 (Pa. Super. 1992), 653

Illinois ex rel. McCollum v. Board of Education, 333 U.S. 203 (1948), 478

In re Carpenter's Estate, 297 N.Y.S. 649 (Sur. Ct. 1937), 256

In re Estate of Muhammad, 520 N.E.2d 795 (Ill. App. Ct. 1987), 254

In re The Bible Speaks, 869 F.2d 628 (1st Cir. 1989), 619

In re Wagners' Will, 148 N.Y.S.2d 110 (Sur. Ct. 1955), 266

Jackson v. Benson, 578 N.W.2d 602 (Wis. 1998), 204

Jeffery v. Ehrhardt, 43 S.E.2d 483 (S.C. 1947), 263-264

Jeffrey Scott E. v. Central Baptist Church, 243 Cal. Rptr. 128 (Ct. App. 1988), 608, 610

Jesus Center v. Farmington Hills Zoning Board of Appeals, 544 N.W.2d 698 (Mich. Ct. App. 1996), 578

Jimmy Swaggart Ministries v. Board of Equalization, 493 U.S. 378 (1990), 135, 136, 141, 145, 451, 461, 468-470, 477, 480, 486-7, 492-495, 496, 500-503, 505

John Doe v. Holy See, Case No. CV.02430 BR (Dir. Or.), 658

Johnson v. Drake, 932 F.2d 975 (10th Cir. 1991), 609

Jones v. Opelika, 316 U.S. 584 (1942), 472-473

Jones v. Watford, 50 A. 180 (N.J. Ch. 1901), modified, 53 A. 397 (N.J. 1902), 255-256

Jones v. Wolf, 443 U.S. 595 (1979), xviii, 98, 146-148, 150-151, 152, 153, 192, 220-221, 254, 281, 282, 286, 290, 295-296, 298, 299, 302, 303, 311, 327, 338, 339, 536, 537, 542, 561, 806, 807

Kedroff v. St. Nicholas Cathedral, 344 U.S. 94 (1952), 135, 145, 146, 191, 531-532, 534, 537, 539

Kelly v. Lutheran Church in America, 589 A.2d (Pa. Super Ct. 1991), 629

Killinger v. Samford University, 113 F.3d 196 (11th Cir. 1997), 702-704

Kotterman v. Killian, 972 P.2d 606 (Ariz. 1999), 203

Larson v. Valente, 456 U.S. 228 (1982), 457-458, 481-482, 501-502

Late Corporation of the Church of Jesus Christ of Latter-Day Saints v. United States, 136 U.S. 1 (1890), 797

LDS Social Service Corp. v. Richins, No. A 89 AO 382, slip op. (Ga. Ct. App. Apr. 28, 1989), 604

Leary v. Geoghan, 2001 WL 1902391 (Mass. App.Ct., Dec. 21, 2001), 653

Lemon v. Kurtzman, 403 U.S. 602 (1971), xvii, 15, 131, 137, 140, 154-155, 186, 202, 222, 397, 464, 479-480, 552, 553, 556, 709-711, 762

Lexington Theological Seminary v. Vance, 596 S.W.2d 11 (Ky. App. 1979), 706

Libhart v. Copeland, 949 S.W.2d 783 (Tex. App. 1997, no writ), 269-270

Little v. Wuerl, 929 F.2d 944 (3d Cir. 1991), 695-696

Living Faith, Inc. v. Commissioner, 60 T.C.M. 710 (1990), 437

Lochner v. New York, 198 U.S. 45 (1905), 470

Locke v. Davey, 540 U.S. 712 (2004), 171, 187, 723, 724

Lunsford, Withrow & Co. v. Wren, 63 S.E. 308 (W. Va. 1908), 269

Lynch v. Donnelly, 465 U.S. 668 (1984), 778

Malicki v. Doe, 814 So.2d 347 (Fla.2002), 634, 647, 650

Malloy v. Fong, 232 P.2d 241 (Cal. 1951), 602-603

Malnak v. Yogi, 592 F.2d 197 (3d Cir. 1979), 25

Marbury v. Madison, 1 Cranch (5 U.S.) 137 (1803), 803

Marshall v. International Longshoremen's and Warehousemen's Union, Local 6, Dist. 1, 371 P.2d 987 (Cal. 1962), 271

Martinelli v. Bridgeport Roman Catholic Diocesan Corporation, 196 F.3d 409 (2nd Cir. 1999), 638-639

Maryland and Virginia Eldership v. Church of God at Sharpsburg, Inc., 396 U.S. 367 (1970), 288-291, 533-544, 536-537

McClure v. Salvation Army, 460 F.2d 553 (5th Cir. 1972), 539, 540, 664

McCulloch v. Maryland, 17 U.S. 316 (1819), 406, 511

Meek v. Pittenger, 421 U.S. 349 (1975), 396-397, 398

Michigan v. Long, 463 U.S. 1032 (1983), 171

Minersville School District v. Gobitis, 310 U.S. 586 (1940), 471-472, 473, 475, 799-800, 802

Minker v. Baltimore Annual Conf. of United Methodist Church, 894 F.2d 1354 (D.C. Cir. 1990), 149, 151

Mitchell v. Helms, 120 S.Ct. 2530 (2000), 141, 222, 396-401, 478, 712-714, 720

Molko v. Holy Spirit Association, 762 P.2d 46 (Cal. 1988), 620

Moses v. Diocese of Colorado, 863 P.2d 310 (Colo. 1993), 638, 646

Mueller v. Allen, 463 U.S. 481 (1986), 488, 713, 816

Murdock v. Pennsylvania, 319 U.S. 105 (1943), 460, 469, 470, 473-478, 488, 489, 491, 492, 494-496, 502, 511

NAACP v. Claiborne Hardware Co., 458 U.S. 886 (1982), 662

Nally v. Grace Community Church, 763 P.2d 948 (Cal. 1988), 613-614

New York East Annual Conference of Methodist Church v. Seymour, 199 A.2d 701 (Conn. 1964), 265

New York Times Co. v. Sullivan, 376 U.S. 254 (1964), 541

N.H. v. Presbyterian Church (U.S.A.), 998 P.2d 592 (Ok. 1999), 660

NLRB v. Catholic Bishop of Chicago, 440 U.S. 490 (1979), 138-139, 156, 545-547, 664, 683, 692-694, 698

NLRB v. Hanna Boys Center, 940 F.2d 1295 (9th Cir. 1991), 694

Ohio Civil Rights Commission v. Dayton Christian Schools, 477 U.S. 619 (1986), 546, 547

Olson v. Magnuson, 457 N.W.2d 394 (Minn. Ct. App. 1990), 601, 659

Paul v. Watchtower Bible and Tract Society, 819 F.2d 875 (9th Cir. 1987), 615, 616

Pierce v. Society of Sisters, 268 U.S. 510 (1925), 682

Ponce v. Roman Catholic Apostolic Church in Porto Rico, 210 U.S. 296 (1908), 267-268

Presbyterian Church v. Mary Elizabeth Blue Hull Memorial Presbyterian Church, 393 U.S. 440 (1969), 192, 280-

282, 286, 289-291, 298, 302, 319, 328, 334, 532-537, 542, 548, 805-806

Presbytery of Donegal v. Calhoun, 513 A.2d 531(Pa. Commw. 1986), 296

Presbytery of Donegal v. Wheatley, 513 A.2d 538 (Pa. Commw. 1986), 295

Pritzlaff v. Archdiocese of Milwaukee, 533 N.W.2d 780 (Wis. 1995), 649

Protestant Episcopal Church in the Diocese of Los Angeles v. Barker, et al., 115 Cal.App.3d 599 (1981), 312-313

Rashedi v. General Board of Church of the Nazarene, 54 P.3d 349 (Ariz. 2003), 657

Rayburn v. General Conference of Seventh-Day Adventists, 772 F.2d 1164 (4th Cir. 1985), 647

Regan v. Taxation with Representation of Washington, 461 U.S. 540 (1983), 487, 488

Reynolds v. United States, 98 U.S. 145 (1878), 796

Robertson v. Bullions, 11 N.Y. 243 (1854), 286-287, 313

Roemer v. Board of Public Works, 426 U.S. 736 (1976), 156, 158

Roman Catholic Archbishop v. Industrial Accident Commission, 230 P. 1 (Cal. 1924), 597, 598, 612, 627

Rosenberger v. Rectors of University of Virginia, 515 U.S. 819 (1995), 154, 499, 715, 724

Rust v. Sullivan, 500 U.S. 173 (1991), 724

Salem Church of United Brethren in Christ v. Numsen, 59 A.2d 757 (Md. 1948), 264

Salem College and Academy, Inc. v. Employment Division, 695 P.2d 25 (Or. 1985), 187-188

Scheidler v. National Organization of Women, 537 U.S. 393 (2003), 662

Schmidt v. Bishop, 779 F. Supp. 321 (S.D.N.Y. 1991), 629-630

Serbian Eastern Orthodox Church v. Milivojevich, 426 U.S. 696 (1976), 139, 150, 289, 303, 320, 328, 534-537, 539, 542

Sherbert v. Verner, 374 U.S. 398 (1963), 134-135, 183-184, 186, 188-190, 528, 542-543, 549, 551, 556, 568-569, 571, 575, 576, 578, 764, 801-802, 808

Siegel v. Truett-McConnell College, 73 F.3d 1108 (11th Cir. 1995), 702-704

Simpson v. Wells Lamont Corp., 494 F.2d 490 (5th Cir. 1974), 539-540

Skelton v. World Chapel, Inc., 637 P.2d 753 (Ariz. Ct. App. 1981), 268-269

Smith v. Employment Division, 721 P.2d 445 (Or. 1986), 188, 189

Smith v. Nelson, 18 Vt. 511 (1846), 286, 313

Smith v. O'Connell, 986 F. Supp. 73 (D.R.I. 1997), 651

Society of Jesus of New England v. Boston Landmarks Comm'n, 564 N.E.2d 571 (Mass. 1990), 191

St. Martin's Evangelical Lutheran Church v. South Dakota, 451 U.S. 772 (1981), 161, 439, 699-700

State of Vermont v. DeLaBruere, 577 A.2d 254 (Vt. 1990), 194, 195

State v. Gunwall, 720 P.2d 808 (Wash. 1986), 173, 184, 190

State v. Hershberger, 462 N.W.2d 393 (Minn. 1990), 185, 193

Stevens v. Roman Catholic Bishop, 123 Cal. Rptr. 171 (Ct. App. 1975), 607-608, 628-629

Stewart v. West Ohio Conference of the United Methodist Church, 2003 WL 21692670 (Ohio App. June 5, 2003), 658

Surinach v. Pesquera de Busquets, 604 F.2d 73 (1st Cir. 1979), 652

Swanson v. The Roman Catholic Bishop of Portland, 692 A.2d 441 (Me. 1997), 649

Terrett v. Taylor, 13 U.S. (9 Cranch) 43 (1815), 760-761, 771

Texas Monthly v. Bullock, 489 U.S. 1 (1989), 144, 157, 460, 468-70, 477, 486-496, 502

Thomas v. Review Board, 450 U.S. 707 (1981), 186, 801, 802, 808

Thornton v. Howe, 62 N.J. Eq. 341, cited in Jones v. Watford, 50 A 180 (N.J. Ch. 1901), 256

Thurmond v. Cedar Spring Baptist
   Church, 36 S.E. 221 (Ga. 1900), 269
Tilton v. Richardson, 403 U.S. 672 (1971),
   395, 709-711
Toney v. Bower, 744 N.E.2d 351 (Ill. App.
   Ct. 2001), 201
Torcaso v. Watkins, 367 U.S. 488 (1961),
   479
Trinity Pentecostal Church v. Terry, 660
   S.W.2d 449 (Mo. Ct. App. 1983), 269
Trustees of Philadelphia Baptist Ass'n. v.
   Hart's Executor, 17 U.S. 1 (1819), 263
Trustees of the General Assembly of the
   Presbyterian Church in the United
   States v. Guthrie, 10 S.E. 318 (Va.
   1889), 264-265

United States v. Ballard, 322 U.S. 78
   (1944), 53, 59, 619, 765-766
United States v. Lee, 455 U.S. 252 (1982),
   439-440, 493
United States v. Seeger, 380 U.S. 163
   (1965), 23, 26, 52

Valley Forge Christian College v. Ameri-
   cans United, 454 U.S. 464 (1982), 395-
   396
Van Schaick v. Church of Scientology of
   California, Inc., 535 F. Supp, 1125 (D.
   Mass. 1982), 663-664

Wallace v. Jaffree, 472 U.S. 38 (1985), 778,
   781
Walz v. Tax Commission of the City of
   New York, 397 U.S. 664 (1970), 406-
   407, 430-432, 460-462, 464-466, 468-
   470, 477-483, 485-490, 495-496, 502,
   503, 505-506, 511, 512, 766-767
Watson v. Jones, 80 U.S. (13 Wall.) 679
   (1871), 45-46, 89-93, 97, 98, 102, 104,
   146, 191-192, 219, 287, 320-321, 324-
   326, 328, 334, 443, 503, 528, 529-542,
   547, 551, 561, 805-808
Weissman v. Congregation Shaare Emeth,
   38 F.3d 1038 (8th Cir. 1994), 545

Welsh v. United States, 398 U.S. 333
   (1970), 23
West Virginia State Board of Education v.
   Barnette, 319 U.S. 624 (1943), 475,
   799-800, 802
Western Presbyterian Church v. Board of
   Zoning Adjustment, 862 F. Supp. 538
   (D.D.C. 1994), 577-578
Wilder v. Bernstein, 499 F. Supp. 980
   (S.D.N.Y. 1980) (Wilder II), and 645 F.
   Supp. 1292 (S.D.N.Y. 1986) (Wilder
   III), 368-369
Wilder v. Sugarman (Wilder I), 385 F.
   Supp. 1013 (S.D.N.Y. 1974), 366, 368
Williams v. United Pentecostal Church In-
   ternational, 115 S.W.3d 612 (Tex.App.
   2003), 658-659
Williamson v. Wallace, 224 S.E.2d 253
   (N.C. Ct. App. 1976), 271
Wilson v. Hinkle, 67 Cal. App. 3d 506 (Cal.
   Ct. App. 1977), 192
Wimmer v. Saint John the Apostle Parish,
   No. 88-1645-K, 1989 WL 145443 (D.
   Kan. Dec. 1, 1989), 269
Wisconsin v. Yoder, 406 U.S. 205 (1972),
   134, 440, 682-684, 686, 688-689, 801-
   802, 808
Witters v. Department of Services for the
   Blind, 474 U.S. 481 (1986), 713
Witters v. State Com'n for the Blind, 771
   P.2d 1119 (Wash. 1989), 141, 186-187,
   201, 204
Wollersheim v. Church of Scientology, 260
   Cal. Rptr. 331 (Ct. App. 1989), 616
Wolman v. Walter, 433 U.S. 229 (1977),
   396-397, 398, 464-465

Zehner v. Wilkinson Memorial United
   Methodist Church, 592 A.2d 1304 (Pa.
   1991), 627-628
Zelman v. Simmons-Harris, 122 S. Ct.
   2460 (2002), xviii, 202, 672, 714, 719-
   725
Zobrest v. Catalina Foothills School District, 509 U.S. 1 (1993), 713

Prologue

James A. Serritella

This book speaks to lawyers and the world of law. It is meant to speak no less to religious leaders and the world of religion and to anyone who is interested in religion and how it functions in our society. It also reflects the authors' desire to plumb a firm and improved foundation of a new jurisprudence for organized religion.

Religion is now at center stage in the United States and the world. Religious leaders and religious organizations have become highly visible and potent advocates in the public discussion of front-page issues as diverse as abortion, educational choice, termination of treatment of the gravely ill, assisted suicide, stem cell research, cloning, welfare reform, health care accessibility and finance, race relations, affirmative action, defense spending, same sex marriage, and so many others. The administration of President George W. Bush has helped fuel this discussion by promoting programs such as "faith-based initiatives" and "charitable choice." Religious organizations themselves have attracted national interest and attention, and their leaders have become lightning rods for widespread debate on issues such as sexual misconduct with minors by some clergy. Religion has also towered on the world scene. It has been a rallying cry for intense conflicts in the Middle East, Africa, Northern Ireland, and elsewhere. Signally, religion has been a dominant focus in the events of September 11, 2001, and their aftermath. Even if one had no interest or inclination at all toward religion, a person living in this country or on this planet would find it almost impossible to avoid being touched by it in some way.

Religion is also the subject of public policy and the law worldwide. Some believe that government and religion should be entirely separate from one another, while others are convinced that there should be an identity between the two. The idea that church and state should be separate is imbedded in the American culture and is both the touchstone and the idiom for any discussion about religion and government in the United States. This does not mean that everyone's beliefs about separation are the same, or even that there is a broad-based understanding of the issues. Almost everyone somehow incorporates the word "separation" in what they say, but despite its omnipresence in the discussion, the meaning and consequences of the term remain, at best, unclear.

The law governing religious organizations in this country is also deficient. Much of it is derived from the law governing commercial organizations, or is imported from the secular not-for-profit world, and does not address religion or religious organizations on their own merits. As a result our law, jurisprudence, and public policy relating to religion misses the mark and is often distorted. Its derivative character is not just a bad fit—it channels religious activity away from religion and toward the secular, commercial world. This result may be unintended but it is nonetheless real. Because this channeling toward the secular may be subtle, gradual, masked by goodwill, and obscured by the meanderings of our culture, its impact often escapes attention and is ignored.

For example, a religious organization may have people who work on its behalf and are compensated for their services. It would seem obvious that one should seek out the terminology and laws that relate to employment in the commercial or secular not-for-profit worlds and apply them to these workers. In some religious traditions the employment concept aptly describes the relation between the church and someone working on its behalf, even a member of its clergy. Nonetheless, for other religious traditions to define or classify a member of the clergy or someone working for the church as an employee entirely misses the point of the person's relation to the church. There are many differences on this issue among religious traditions. In the Roman Catholic world, for example, the term "employee" has very little relevance to the relation between a priest and his diocese. In other traditions many, if not all, of those working on behalf of the church are believed to be ministers or at least to partake of the ministerial status in some sense of that word. Part of the search for a new jurisprudence for religion necessarily requires a search for new words, a new mode of discourse that has meaning in the world of religion as well as the world of law. The corollary for this search for a new language is a search for new, more relevant legal principles.

Thus, a more soundly based jurisprudence would focus on a particular religious organization's understanding of those working on its behalf and their relationship to the church. Instead of simply importing legal terms and principles from the secular world, a better jurisprudence would try to identify a terminology and fashion legal principles that are faithful to this religious understanding. Thus, a Roman Catholic priest is ordained and incardinated into a diocese, not hired. The term "incardination" is very different from the term "hired." It indicates that the priest is made part of the diocese, and that the diocese is obligated to provide for his care and welfare. Neither the priest nor the diocese can escape the obligations signified by "incardination" very easily. The obligations are rooted in the church's mission and are intended to remain in effect for the life of the priest.

Civil law treatment of a priest as "hired" rather than "incardinated" would secularize and distort the relationship and could yield results that reduce both the priest's and the diocese's religious freedom—not because of a faulty interpretation of constitutional principles, but because of a poor understanding of the relationship at issue. Analogizing incardination to employment gives about as accurate an understanding of incardination as analogizing a dog to a table because they both have four legs. For example, application of legal principles relating to employment, such as the civil rights laws, to a church's selection and "hiring" of clergy would restrict its ability to select clergy strictly according to religious criteria. Similarly, applying the laws of contract would intrude on the denomination's own specifications for the relationship by creating the impression that bishops and priests were free to reinvent it. Treating the priest as a common law employee would substitute employment criteria that have evolved in the commercial world for those more appropriate to a religious relationship. Nonetheless, a review of the relevant legal databases reveals hardly a mention of the word "incardination."

Sometimes the law acknowledges the awkward fit of commercial or secular terminology and concepts to religious realities. For example, the courts have consistently held that the civil rights laws do not apply to the selection of clergy, and they frequently enunciate a constitutional rationale for this position. On the other hand, the law sometimes blunders ahead with ill-fitting terminology and principles. Although a Roman Catholic priest is neither an independent contractor nor an employee, the Internal Revenue Service requirement that an independent contractor's compensation be reported on Form 1099 and an employee's compensation be reported on Form W-2 is often enforced as if the priest were an employee. This obscures rather than illuminates the relationship between a priest and his diocese.

In the pages that follow, our authors highlight instances in which legislatures, courts, lawyers, and religious organizations themselves fail to translate a religious organization's self-understanding into legal concepts. No single instance of the law requiring organized religion to endure ill-fitting terminology is likely to destroy or seriously impair religious freedom, but the cumulative effect of dozens if not hundreds of such instances can and does constrict, skew, and otherwise contort a religious organization's ability to pursue its goals in accordance with its self-understanding.

The authors of these essays do not advocate that religious organizations be totally unfettered in living out their self-understanding. Our coming together as a nation and good citizenship provide limits on the conduct of all who live here. Certain particular limiting principles applicable to religious organizations are identified, explained, and tested throughout this volume. For example, respect for a religious organization's self-understanding is limited by what we define as religious. It is also well established that the law should not respect a religious organization's fraudulent portrayal of its self-understanding. At the same time, courts are in the early stages of sorting out new principles to limit government's ability to enforce neutral, generally applicable laws as they may relate to religious organizations. The burden of searching for appropriate limits falls not only on public bodies and scholars but on religious organizations themselves. The courts and other public bodies have the authority to make important decisions, but they are constitutionally restricted in their ability to sift through the religious elements of matters before them. Scholars can pursue a broad and thorough analysis, but their role is limited in that they are not directly involved in legal proceedings. As a result, much of the burden of explaining their self-understanding and even helping to shape limits remains with religious organizations.

If the law sometimes blunders in its dealings with religious organizations, the organizations sometimes are awkward in their dealings with the law. The problem begins with a religious organization's translation of its self-understanding into a civil law identity. Sometimes the organization has a clear and complete image of itself that it can thoughtfully articulate to a civil lawyer who can sensitively and faithfully translate it into civil law language. All too often, though, there are both major and minor failures along the way. The result is that legislatures, courts, government agencies, advocates, and even scholars frequently begin their treatment of the religious organization with a very dim picture of that understanding.

Sometimes the awkwardness results from misconceptions about our legal system. There are more than a few in religious organizations who believe the law to be a matrix that yields ready answers to all questions, rather than an instrument that a skilled and knowledgeable practitioner uses to achieve justice. Others seem to believe that courts are oracles that dispense justice spontaneously without much input from the parties before them. In fact, our courts are very dependent on the parties to present the facts and advocate the legal principles they believe dispositive. Courts make their determination of the operative facts in a case on the basis of the information the parties present to them. The only minor exception is that courts are permitted to take "judicial notice" of certain widely accepted factual generalities, such as "The summers in Chicago can be hot" or "Cars have by and large replaced horses for personal transportation." While courts cannot engage in independent factual research to supplement the parties' factual presentations, they can and do develop their own legal research to check and supplement the parties' legal presentations. Nonetheless, they weigh the parties' presentations of legal principles heavily in formulating their own interpretation of these principles and applying that interpretation to their own determination of the facts. In short, the courts are very much dependent on litigants to describe the facts sensitively and advocate the relevant law clearly. Without such input, courts are not likely to deal with the religious organization's self-understanding in a way that safeguards or enhances religious freedom.

Moreover, many religious organizations have a certain discomfort with dealing with the legal profession and the legal system. They employ a terminology of their own that reflects the fact that they function in this world but have a strong second focus that is, at least in some sense of the word, otherworldly. Meanwhile, lawyers routinely use the commercial terminology they understand, and sometimes provide their input based on a fairly crass version of the here and now. Even lawyers familiar with the secular not-for-profit world do not necessarily find words or concepts to describe religious organizations accurately. Consequently, there may not be a meeting of the words or minds between lawyer and client.

Sometimes the religious organization does not have the resources to secure superior or even adequate advocacy. All too often it is so occupied with its other work that it does not give sufficient attention to selecting and collaborating with legal counsel who will go beyond a commercial or secular analysis and formulate an accurate picture of the religious organization. Despite these difficulties, achieving and safeguarding religious freedom remains in large part the task of religious organizations themselves.

Changing immigration patterns have brought millions of people to the United States who are neither Christians nor Jews but belong to religious traditions and organizations that are relatively new to the American legal environment. These new immigrants provide us with an opportunity to renew and reinvigorate our jurisprudence of religious organizations. One would hope they will not have to endure the ill-fitting commercial language and principles that our legal system has imperfectly adapted to Christian and Jewish organizations. The new realities cry out for a new terminology and new discourse that could open the way to a new jurisprudence. One hopes that all parties to the legal system will be up to the task.

These essays were originally inspired by a study of the civil law structures that religious organizations use to conduct their work. Situations were observed in which a religious organization's choice of a legal structure made for clear but frequently unintended differences in how the law treated that organization. For example, a church that incorporates one of its activities separately from the church's own corporation is likely to experience some unintended consequences. Participants in the legal system such as public agencies, courts, private litigants, and attorneys begin to perceive the newly created separate corporation as something apart from the church. This perception may be exacerbated by the organizers' failure to include in the new corporation's governing documents language and other features that specify its religious character or connection to the church. As a result, participants in the legal system frequently begin treating the two corporations in different ways. The separate corporation, for example, may lose some of the church's exemptions, such as the exemptions from filing Internal Revenue Form 990 and from participating in the unemployment compensation program. Private litigants may insist that the new corporation be treated as separate from the church, or as not even being religious. Courts in turn may defer to this position. In addition, the two corporations may begin to perceive themselves and each other as separate organizations. This perception often grows over time—even a fairly short time—and especially when there are changes in personnel. The separate corporation's identity as part of the church may fade and eventually it may even go its own way. What began as a separation for organizational convenience may end up as separation for its own sake. These consequences do not always occur, but they happen frequently enough to be an important concern.

Commercial organizations may also decide to separately incorporate a portion of their activities. They have to face some of the same organizational psychology as churches do, but they have access to better legal tools to deal with the situation. For example, a commercial corporation can retain control of a separate commercial entity through stock ownership—a device not available to religious organizations. It is not surprising that commercial organizations have better developed legal tools. Commercial law is based on a clear understanding of commercial concepts, and the law and the concepts have evolved together over time. Moreover, commercial organizations almost anywhere in the United States can use the law of Delaware, which is especially well developed and permits them to fashion sophisticated legal structures for their activities. There is no analogue to the law of Delaware for religious organizations. On the other hand, the almost haphazard channeling of a religious organization's legal structure into certain benign and fairly common commercial legal forms may well twist the organization's self-understanding into a new shape. This distortion impinges on constitutional principles of religious freedom.

The original insight for these essays to focus on legal structures was developed into a working hypothesis which was the subject of ongoing discussions between the authors and the editorial team as well as the DePaul University College of Law Center for Church/State Studies Legal Scholars Advisory Board. There were also discussions with experts about religion and the law abroad, because many of the authors had led or participated in consultations about religious freedom in Europe and the former Iron Curtain countries.

In addition, the authors were actively involved in the controversies, litigation, and legislative efforts of the time that stemmed from several important United States Supreme Court cases relating to religious issues. The Court's 1990 decision in *Employment Division v. Smith*[1] was perhaps the most important of these cases. The *Smith* case is understood to severely limit constitutional principles of religious freedom that had been used to evaluate and sometimes invalidate laws believed to impinge on religion. The controversy over this ruling moved Congress to enact the Religious Freedom Restoration Act to reinstate the principles legislatively. This act was challenged in *City of Boerne v. Flores*,[2] which held portions of it unconstitutional. There has been litigation that has dealt with the parameters of the *City of Boerne* case and helped to clarify its meaning. There has also been legislation at the state level to replace the portions of the Religious Freedom Restoration Act which were held unconstitutional.

Some of the authors of this book also participated in several other Supreme Court cases that generated extensive interest and discussion. The 1971 case of *Lemon v. Kurtzman*[3] laid out a test for evaluating programs of financial aid to parochial schools. In the decades that followed, experts and ultimately the Court itself became increasingly critical of this test. The result has been a reorientation of the principles used to evaluate

---

1. 494 U.S. 872 (1990).
2. 521 U.S. 544 (1997).
3. 413 U.S. 602 (1971).

such aid programs, as reflected in the Court's recent decision in *Zelman v. Simmons-Harris*.[4] The 1979 case of *Jones v. Wolfe*[5] enunciated the so-called "neutral principles of law" doctrine as a possible alternative to the well-established "deference to church polity" doctrine for adjudicating church property disputes. The case gave rise to widespread disagreements about how broadly the neutral principles of law doctrine might be extended. Those disagreements are reflected in these pages.

The authors were on all sides of these controversies, and the fullness of their efforts produced an abundance of ideas. For example, during one of the formal conferences about these essays, Carl H. Esbeck surfaced the expression "charitable choice." He has since developed the concept to the point where it has gained enough currency to influence President Bush to advance the "faith-based initiatives" program. This program would open the government's delivery of social services to a whole new group of providers, many of which are very up-front about the religious character and religious mission of their organizations. Some of our authors agree with Esbeck's analysis, while others see questions and even constitutional obstacles to the approach he is advancing. In short, the authors' efforts as scholars and advocates helped reshape and enrich both the original concept for this study and the essays themselves. Their differing insights and viewpoints probe what William P. Marshall refers to as the "conflicting policies and impulses" of law and religion. As a result, the study addresses not only the law's treatment of a religious organization's legal structure but also its treatment of the organization's self-understanding.

Marshall raises questions about whether a religious organization's self-understanding should be a basis for the improvement of our jurisprudence. In the process, he emphasizes what he believes to be the inscrutability of legal issues relating to religion. He also cautions about the need for limitations on deferring to the self-understanding of religious organizations. Finally, referring to some of the religious excesses of our times, he asserts what he believes to be a need for protection from religion. Others, such as Edward McGlynn Gaffney, Jr., view Marshall's position as at least a partial abdication of legal scholars' and advocates' traditional role of trying to sort out the difficult issues and fashion limiting principles that are consistent with our constitution.

While the authors touch on many of the legal topics that are important to religious organizations, this is not a handbook or casebook. The essays explore issues such as the legal definition of religion, the structuring of religious organizations, and the relationship between an organization and those who work on its behalf. They do not, however, catalogue specific measures for addressing those concerns. Instead, they provide the foundation needed to understand the diverse ways in which the law influences how religious organizations function and interact with the greater society. We seek to enhance the discussion of these fundamental issues and to draw not only lawyers but historians, political scientists, ethicists, theologians, and other concerned parties into that discussion. It is hoped that this will help deepen our understanding of these issues and stimulate development of relevant pragmatic measures.

The chapter on sexual misconduct with minors by some clergy is a good example of how a discussion of fundamental issues inherent in a difficult problem can help point the way to practical initiatives for addressing it. Stephen J. Pope and Patricia B. Carlson provide the insights of a distinguished ethicist and a practicing lawyer. They focus on issues which are emerging from court rulings as well as positions advocated by litigants and commentators that have an impact on a religious organization's self-understanding.

---

4. 122 S. Ct. 2460 (2002).
5. 443 U.S. 595 (1979).

Importantly, they point out risks to religious freedom as well as suggest limits on that freedom. Their thoughtful work is an important contribution to the discussion of a topic that will occupy lawyers, courts, scholars, and religious organizations for many years to come.

Viewed as a whole, these essays move the course of the law relating to religious organizations in a new direction. The goal should not be a leveling of religious organizations' self-understanding so that all religious traditions can be described by the same words and forced to fit into the same commercial concepts. Instead, it should be to build a legal language and principles that respect the differences between various religious settings and understandings. For instance, a Roman Catholic priest may be incardinated by a diocese but employed as a teacher in a university, while a congregational church might call and employ a pastor.

A jurisprudence rooted in a religious organization's self-understanding is oriented inductively rather than deductively. Its starting point is the reality of a religious tradition as understood by itself—not a pre-existing secular legal language and principles, and especially not a pre-existing commercial law language and principles. This approach might lead to the use of a pre-existing legal word, like "employment," or of a word that is relatively new to the civil law, like "incardination." These terms, in turn, would help us to fashion more apt legal principles. The outcome would be a jurisprudence that deals with religious organizations as they are, rather than as they may be viewed through commercial or secular lenses.

These seeds of a new jurisprudence do not require sweeping legislative action or a mass expenditure of funds. They require only that the participants in the legal process work at the new jurisprudence day in and day out in their dealings with each other. The misunderstandings in the law today are a necessary starting point, and this book helps develop a sensitivity for them. Religious organizations themselves are not just observers but participants in the legal process, and as such they have a central role to play in the effort to generate a new jurisprudence. They have to articulate their self-understanding in a way that other participants can understand. The other participants—such as legislatures, courts, and government officials—need to listen more sensitively. The dealings include not only litigation and transactions, but also the interaction between the government and religious organizations. The work includes a persistent striving for new and better language to describe the religious organizations, as well as a reshaping of legal principles. Through these efforts a new jurisprudence will gradually displace the old, bringing with it an enhanced religious freedom.

This volume focuses primarily on organized religion, a term used broadly here to mean a religious tradition or, more popularly, a religious denomination or sect. The Roman Catholic Church, the Evangelical Lutheran Church in America, and Reformed Judaism would be examples of particular religious traditions. The term "organized religion" is also used more narrowly to mean a particular organization or institution within a religious tradition. This would include either a subdivision of a religious tradition, such as a diocese or synod, or an institution or activity within a tradition, such as a college, hospital, or social services program.

The nature of a religious tradition may be reflected in a variety of sources. These may include a scripture or other inspired writing, such as the Bible or the Qur'an, as well as oral and written traditions and practices, the teachings of the tradition's scholars, and directives of its leaders. There also may be other sources such as adherents' beliefs and folkways or a tradition's culture, art, and music. These sources may be interpreted by outside experts or by representatives of the tradition. The tradition's understanding of itself may be based on some or all of these sources and perhaps others. It includes the obvious, the subtle, and the otherworldly, and it is usually expressed in words. Descriptions of a religious tradition by someone outside it can seldom match the tradition's own highly nuanced view of itself. This self-understanding is a natural starting point for a thorough analysis of the civil law's treatment of religion. Stated in another way, any civil law treatment of religion that does not respect this self-understanding is suspect, and most likely flies in the face of our constitutional guarantees of religious freedom.

Professor Marshall would remind us that civil law's completely unfettered adoption of a religious organization's self-understanding may run afoul of the Establishment Clause. This is a good caution, but not a good reason to abandon self-understanding as the starting point for a new jurisprudence. It is a reason, however, to have sound limits for the legal treatment of that self-understanding just as we need sound limits for the legal treatment of any other phenomenon. Developing these appropriate limits, and reorienting our law away from secular models and toward religious organizations' self-understanding, remains a challenge for scholars, lawyers, courts, and legislatures. As Gaffney counsels, this effort should not sidestep difficult questions but should engage them with careful and thoughtful scholarship.

Religion stands in two worlds: the visible world and the world of belief. It functions in the world we can see and touch, yet it usually has its origin and reason for being in a world we cannot see and touch. That world of belief can be brushed by reason, but mainly lies beyond it. It may appear irrational, but it has a rationality of its own that sometimes baffles ordinary human reason without violating it. Religious discourse, organizations, and modes of functioning may have many similarities to the kind of human activity that can be seen, touched or measured, while at the same time they extend beyond perception and reason. The confluence of these two worlds invests religion with a certain internal tension and mystery.

While there must be sound limits on the law's treatment of religious organizations' self-understanding, there are also constraints that make it somewhat difficult to establish those limits. For example, the United States Constitution restricts the ability of the courts to delve into that self-understanding and reach conclusions that touch the religious dimension of a religious organization. The courts may not usurp a religious organization's ability to make its own decisions about such matters. Since courts are limited in their ability to probe the religious aspects of such organizations, the organizations themselves must take the initiative and present their self-understanding clearly and persuasively if the courts are to respect it. The courts, in turn, may legitimately check these presentations to make sure they are not tainted by fraud or collusion.

The courts may also check this self-understanding by reference to what the law can identify as being religious or not religious. This identification implies the need for a definition of religion that will work in a legal context. There are constitutional restrictions here as well, because an overly narrow definition would exclude some organizations that are truly religious, while an overly broad definition will fail to separate what is religious from what is not. In these pages W. Cole Durham, Jr. and Elizabeth A. Sewell analyze the complexities of formulating a definition of religion and examine the limits such a definition imposes on a religious organization's self-understanding. They conclude that it is fairly easy to recognize most religious organizations as such because of "family resemblances." On the other hand, as one might expect, the task of separating what is religious from what is not becomes more daunting at the margins. That is why principles for using a definition in a legal context are as important as the definition itself.

Respect for a religious organization's self-understanding should be the starting point of a new jurisprudence, but it does not require courts to abdicate their role of making decisions and setting limits. Instead, it challenges courts and other participants in the legal system to honor that self-understanding while channeling it in ways that are consistent with our constitutional system. The Supreme Court's decision in *Employment Division v. Smith,*[6] and the controversy which has come in its wake, highlights the complexity of this challenge.

The First Congress and the early state legislatures recognized the unique station of religion and quite properly put it in a specially protected category by adopting the First Amendment to the United States Constitution. Religion is also specially addressed in the constitutions of each of the fifty states. The Religion Clauses of the federal Constitution do not stand apart from the balance of our legal system. They infuse the legal system and shape its treatment of religion — or at least they should. The central question addressed in our collection of essays is: How is religious freedom affected by the legal system's treatment of organized religion's self-understanding?

These essays are divided into five main sections, each of which deals with the civil law treatment of a religious tradition in different contexts. In addition to this Prologue, the associate editors have introductory remarks at the beginning of the second, third, and fourth sections.

Sometimes the focus of the chapters is on the religious tradition itself; sometimes it is on a particular kind of activity, organization, or institution. The chapters in the first section lay a foundation for the rest of the book by showing how the law treats religious endeavors differently from other human activities. Durham and Sewell begin with an analysis of the task of defining religion and critical comparisons of the various ways it is defined in the law and other relevant literature. They push this effort to the limits and show the complexities in selecting a definition that is universal yet still helps separate religion from the rest of human experience. In the process, they also explore definitions of related terms such as "church" and "religious organizations."

The next chapter carries forward the effort to distinguish religion from other enterprises, and focuses on religious polity — the governance and structure of religious organizations. The authors discuss the strengths and weaknesses of how the religious understanding of this governance and structure has been translated into civil law terms. They also make suggestions on how to improve the situation, especially in the face of challenges that are confronting religious organizations today.

There follows an empirical study of religious organizations' expressed views on the law's treatment of their self-understanding. This study confirms an important theme that is played out in the other chapters: that the fairly uniform application of the commercial law's language and concepts to religious traditions has a leveling impact on the law's treatment of organized religion. Instead of respecting and reflecting each religious tradition's self-understanding, this approach tends to make all religious traditions appear similar — at least as viewed in a legal context — even when they may actually be very different.

The first section concludes with chapters on the federal Constitution and the constitutions of various states. These chapters highlight the treatment these constitutions give religious organizations.

---

6. 494 U.S. 872 (1990).

The second section is devoted to an analysis of the legal structures available to organized religion and their modes for dealing with their ownership of real estate. Hence the chapters in this section address the matter of corporations, unincorporated associations, trusts, church property disputes, and government finance of religious organizations. Importantly, this segment includes discussion of the often misunderstood "neutral principles of law" concept.

The third section builds on the first two by canvassing some of the substantive areas of the law and how they apply to religious organizations. Accordingly, it includes essays on liability principles, sexual misconduct with minors by some clergy, federal and state taxation, and employment.

The fourth section focuses on some of the activities in which religious traditions engage. These include education and health care.

The fifth section contains two chapters on how constitutional principles that guarantee religious freedom are impacted by the law's treatment of a religious tradition's self-understanding. The authors of these chapters use elements in the previous essays as reference points for their analyses. The volume concludes with an epilogue that addresses some of the thoughts expressed in these chapters.

This book was planned and produced over an extended period of time. Given the number of chapters and authors, different portions of the book were completed at different times and some may be more current than others in some sense of the word "current." A few authors have supplemented their chapters with appendices or footnotes to deal with important new developments. Most do not. More pertinently, this is a book about basic principles governing the relationship between religious organizations and the law in our society, not a catalog of each and every recent legal precedent. As a study of principles, all of the chapters are quite up to date and current, even if they do not mention this or that recent precedent.

It is important to emphasize that this book is a collection of essays by different authors—not the work of a single scholar, which one would expect to be sharply focused throughout and tightly hewn to a central topic or question. The richness of a multi-author work derives from the fact that each author poses and addresses questions in a different way. The questions are matched neither with each other nor with complete answers that neatly dovetail to form an harmonious whole. Instead, the essays reflect differences of opinion in an ongoing discussion. Questions and fragments of questions stand side-by-side with answers, parts of answers, and even misunderstandings and new questions. The goal has not been to bring the discussion to a firm conclusion, but to advance it by exposing it to a broader public and encouraging further inquiry. It is in this spirit that we present this book.

Acknowledgments

This book would not have been completed without the extraordinary efforts of a great many individuals and institutions. We acknowledge the efforts of those who assisted in the research project that resulted in this volume. The administration and faculty of DePaul University, and in particular the College of Law, have been enthusiastic throughout. The project took shape under two DePaul presidents: Rev. John Richardson, C.M., whose vision helped give birth to the College of Law's Center for Church/State Studies, and Rev. John P. Minogue, C.M. Four College of Law deans — Elwood Griffin, John Roberts, Teree Forester, and Glen Weissenberger — and two acting deans — Wayne Lewis and Mark Weber — also supported the project. Faculty advisers Patty Gerstenblith and Katheryn Dutenhaver provided their thoughtful counsel. Each of the Center's executive directors — Rev. Robert Kealy, Rev. John Pollard, Charles Emmerich, and Rev. Craig B. Mousin — helped keep the project moving forward during good and difficult times. In particular, Rev. Pollard spearheaded a yearlong planning process that was central to designing the project, and Rev. Mousin coordinated efforts to bring it to a successful conclusion. During and after the planning process, Donna Ioppolo served as our research coordinator and helped develop the initial editorial notes and bibliographies for each chapter.

The Lilly Foundation provided critical support for the planning and early stages of the project, the McCormick Foundation helped fund its empirical segment, and the Joseph and Jeanne M. Sullivan Foundation provided general support. A number of individuals and law firms also contributed. In this connection, Kirkland & Ellis, Rueben & Proctor, Mayer, Brown & Platt, and Hoogendoorn & Talbot merit special mention. The DePaul University Research Council provided grants for conferences; Marjorie Piechowski and Gene Sterud of DePaul's Office of Sponsored Programs and Research provided important grant-writing assistance. Susan Dvora merits our gratitude for her ideas and assistance in generating financial support for our work. We thank Dennis Conroy and Michael Bates for working with us to identify funding possibilities.

Our national survey of religious denominations and organizations under the leadership of Dr. John Massad calls for thanks to many. Our colleagues at the Northwestern University Survey Laboratory, particularly Paul J. Lavrakas and Judith A. Schejpal, provided able assistance in performing and reporting on the Empirical Survey of Religious Organizations at the National Level. The survey instrument and research were designed in-house by the Center. DePaul faculty members Patty Gerstenblith and Joyce Sweeney deserve special commendation for their early work on the research and instrument design. Dr. Elliott Wright deserves singular acknowledgment for his assistance in revising and operationalizing the instrument. The Center's Legal Scholars Advisory Board — including Elliot M. Abramson, William Baker, Thomas C. Berg, Rodney J. Blackman, Marvin Braiterman, Lynn R. Buzzard, Angela C. Carmella, Wilfred R. Caron, Mark E.

Chopko, Philip E. Draheim, W. Cole Durham, Jr., Katheryn M. Dutenhaver, Grant D. Erickson, Edward McGlynn Gaffney, Frederick Mark Gedicks, Patty Gerstenblith, Steve Greenberger, Rev. James Halstead, O.S.A., David J. Hardy, Phillip H. Harris, Donald H. J. Hermann, Craig R. Hoskins, Norbert S. Jacker, Warren L. Johns, Rev. Robert T. Kennedy, Mary Logan, Robin Lovin, Ira C. Lupu, Michael W. McConnell, William P. Marshall, Michael J. Perry, Rev. John E. Pollard, Steven Resnicoff, Jane Rutherford, Rabbi David Saperstein, Hon. Antonin Scalia, James A. Serritella, Jeffrey M. Shaman, Winifred Fallers Sullivan, Oliver Thomas, Rev. Laurie Tockey, Earl W. Trent, Miriam D. Ukeritis, C.S.J., Rev. Charles M. Whelan, S.J., Jane M. Whicher, and Rev. Elliott Wright—participated in refining the direction of both the survey project and the legal research.

The center conducted two formal conferences to help shape and advance this project. The "Working Conference Examining the Interaction Between Religious Institutions and American Civil Law" on September 30 and October 1, 1994, analyzed feedback from the empirical study. Most of our authors participated in a DePaul conference entitled "Religious Decisions in the Context of American Law" on April 7 and 8, 1995, which facilitated discussion among the authors as well as between them and other experts. Neither conference could have been held without the gracious and generous support of the DePaul University Research Council.

Research coordinator Mieke Holkeboer joined the project at a crucial turning point, moving us from a work of many voices to a coordinated mosaic. Her work ethic and diplomacy saw us through many difficult moments. When Ms. Holkeboer took on added responsibilities, the task of copy editing was ably fulfilled by Renaldo Migaldi. We are also grateful for Randall Newman's thorough work in providing an index to this book. As we have all learned, bringing a project to completion often takes more than expected at first. We could not have tied this book together without the able and energetic work of Maribeth Conley and Mr. Migaldi. Three administrative assistants kept us organized and we are indebted to Amy Cranford, Jennifer Donham, and Jennifer Keplinger, who kept us steady through all our doubts, crises, and successes.

We also acknowledge the many contributions of DePaul law students—Steve Anderson, Patrick Baele, Miriam Barasch, Rachel Calabro Barner, Steve Becker, Attila Bogdan, Mary Anne Boley, James Botana, Thomas Brandon, Joseph Brennan, Annette Cavanaugh, John Corrigan, Maritoni Derecho, Lisa Dooley, Lori Frerichs, Johanna Garton, Gregg George, Jason Gyling, Christine Koman, Michelle McGee, Elissa O'Leary, Kristin Saam, Susan Segebarth, Justin Schwartz, Jennifer Simutis, Mark Tetzlaff, Brandon Thomas, Geri Thomas, Claudia Valenzuela, James Vasselli, and Hannah Yoo—who provided research assistance to the editors and to individual authors.

Several of our authors wish to acknowledge those who have provided particular assistance for their chapters. Mark Chopko acknowledges the attorneys for various denominations who provided him with insights and concrete examples from their wideranging experience. Carl H. Esbeck is indebted to Michael J. Woodruff and the late Rev. Dean M. Kelley for their suggestions. Patty Gerstenblith acknowledges the support of the DePaul Summer Research Program and the assistance of Neil Wolf, Richard Doucher, Sarah Kahn, Anita Bolanos, and Margaret Domin. William Marshall is grateful to Melvyn Durchshag for his comments, and to Brad Winter for research assistance. Donald H.J. Hermann thanks Savi Heller Ratican and W. Patrick Downes. Rev. Craig Mousin thanks Thomas C. Berg, W. Cole Durham, Jr., Gill Gott, and Mieke Holkeboer for their comments and Fred Gedriks, Case Hoogendern, Louis Keating, William P. Marshall, Randy Rapp, Earl Talbot, and Cliff Zimmerman for their advice and encouragement. W. Cole Durham, Jr., thanks Jonathan O. Hafen, Scott M. Ellsworth, Eric P. Myers, Melinda R. Porter, Tim and Amy Bennett Rodriguez, Micah Echols, Shawn Bailey, and Lincoln Peterson for research assistance and Val Ricks, Frederick Mark Gedicks, Brett G. Scharffs, John W. Welch, J. Clifton Fleming, H. Reese Hansen, Jennifer and Keith Lane, Michael W. Durham, and others for helpful comments.

Several chapters in this volume have previously been published in part or in full. Portions of the chapter "Derivative Liability" by Mark E. Chopko appeared in an article entitled "Ascending Liability for the Actions of Others," 17 Am. J. Trial Advoc. 289 (1993). The chapter published in this book revises and updates that article and adds more recent case developments. A partial version of Craig Mousin's chapter, entitled "State Constitutions and the Autonomy of Religious Institutions," was published in *Church Autonomy*, Gerhard Robbers, ed. (2001). Portions of the chapter by Patty Gerstenblith, "Civil Court Resolution of Property Disputes Among Religious Organizations," were previously published under the same title at 39 Am. U. L. Rev. 513 (1990). "Associational Structures of Religious Organizations," also by Gerstenblith, was published at 1995 BYU L. Rev. 439. A portion of Carl Esbeck's chapter on governmental financial assistance to religious organizations was published by the Center for Public Justice in 1996, in an article entitled "The Regulation of Religious Organizations as Recipients of Governmental Assistance." Finally, Esbeck's piece "Charitable Choice" was previously published at 16 Notre Dame J. L. Ethics & Pub. Pol'y 568 (2002) under the title "Statement Before the United States House of Representatives Concerning Charitable Choice and the Community Solutions Act." The authors thank each of these publications for permission to include these chapters in this volume.

A book about church organizations and structure would not be possible without all the many people who have gathered in community and church and who have struggled with the balance of religious organization in the United States. We acknowledge those many lay people and religious leaders who have influenced some of us to write about people gathering in religious ceremony and building parishes, synagogues, mosques, auxiliary organizations, dioceses, and denominations.

I would like to extend my personal gratitude to the associate editors — Thomas Berg, W. Cole Durham, Jr., Edward McGlynn Gaffney, Jr., and Rev. Craig Mousin — for their hard work, brilliant insights, and especially their persistence. Their work has been critical to the completion of this project. Several people have reviewed portions of the text and provided useful comments; I acknowledge the special efforts of John O'Malley, Mark Chopko, Bishop Raymond Goedert, and Bishop Thomas Paprocki. I am also especially grateful to Charles Whalen, S.J., and Martin E. Marty for their assistance and advice, as well as to Bishop Edwin Conway, Rev. William Lion, Jimmy Lago, and Donna Ioppolo for their support and encouragement. Importantly, the help and patience of my wife Ruby and our son Anthony has been essential in helping move this complex, long-term project to completion. In a very special way, I would also like to thank all those others who helped but whom we have neglected to mention by name.

James A. Serritella

Section I

Definition of Religion

W. Cole Durham, Jr. and Elizabeth A. Sewell

> *If any man among you seem to be religious, and bridleth not his tongue, but deceiveth his own heart, this man's religion is vain.*
>
> *Pure religion and undefiled before God and the Father is this, To visit the fatherless and widows in their affliction, and to keep himself unspotted from the world.*[1]

In the beginning comes definition. At first it appears to be a simple and logical preliminary task. If freedom of religion is a fundamental right affording special privileges and protections, then one must start by saying what religion is, in order to divide what is embraced by this freedom from what is not.

Quickly, however, one finds oneself in a dark wood from which no exit seems possible. In addressing the question of the definition of religion, scholars in the field appear to agree only on their disagreement.[2] In fact, the inability to define religion has been de-

---

1. James 1:26–27 (the only passage in Christian scripture defining religion: a reminder of the danger of spending too much time seeking self-consciously to define religion, as opposed to doing unself-consciously that to which religion calls).

2. *See, e.g.,* W. Richard Comstock, Toward Open Definitions of Religion, 52 J. Am. Acad. of Religion 499, 499 (1986); William Herbrechtsmeier, Buddhism and the Definition of Religion: One More Time, 32 J. for the Sci. Study of Religion 1, 1 (1993); Stewart Eliott Guthrie, Religion: What Is it?, 35 J. for the Sci. Study of Religion 412 (1996) ("Writers in every discipline concerned with religion admit that even a definition of the term still eludes consensus.") (citing sociologists, philosophers, religionists and anthropologists); Phillip E. Devine, On the Definition of "Religion," 3 Faith and Phil. 270, 270–71 (1986) (describing the impossibility of a value-free definition of religion); Peter B. Clarke & Peter Byrne, Religion Defined and Explained 5–7, 9–11 (1993) (exploring problems inherent in defining religion); Frederick Ferré, The Definition of Religion, 38 J. of the Am. Acad. of Religion 3 (1970); John Bowker, Religion, in The Oxford Dictionary of World Religions xv (John Bowker ed., 1997); Frederick J. Streng, Studying Religion: Possibilities and Limitations of Different Definitions, 40 J. of the Am. Acad. of Religion 219, 219–223; Russell T. McCutcheon, The Category "Religion" in Recent Publications: A Critical Survey, 42 Numen 284 (1995); Max Weber, The Sociology of Religion 1 (1922) ("To define 'religion' to say what it *is*, is not possible at the start of a presentation such as this. Definition can be attempted, if at all, only at the conclusion of the study").

Debate has continued to rage over whether a definition of religion is even necessary. *See* Richard Machalek, Definitional Strategies in the Study of Religion, 16 J. for the Sci. Study of Religion 395, 395–397 (1977) (describing the debate); Ferré, *supra* note 2, at 3–7 (providing arguments pro and con); Benson Saler, Conceptualizing Religion 1 (1993) ("Although various scholars have questioned the analytical powers of the category religion, and some have proposed that the term religion be dropped from research vocabularies or that employment of it be limited, many academics and the public-at-large continue to talk about religion freely. It seems that we are more or less stuck with religion, both as term and as category, at least for the foreseeable future. That confers a practicality on

scribed as "almost an article of methodological dogma" in the field of religious studies.[3] At first the problem seems to derive from the seemingly endless varieties of religious experience. The term "religion" has been used by scholars and individuals to describe everything from Marxism,[4] sports,[5] and "free market ideology"[6] to mathematics,[7] belief in the possibility of cold fusion,[8] "radical" psychotherapy,[9] use of health food,[10] and nothingness itself.[11] Every definition finds new examples of belief that our equalitarian age cannot exclude.

But the problem runs deeper than mere multiplicity. What begins as a simple Aristotelian task of identifying essence quickly comes unraveled in the constant weaving and reweaving of beliefs that fills all waiting and seeking for answers, as well as efforts to avoid the wrong answer. Each proposed definition reveals itself as one more Sisyphean stone rolled upward only to relapse into a sea of endless deconstruction. The finite world of Aristotelian definition gives way to the infinite universe of possible beliefs, believings, and believers. Different definitions serve different purposes, but the purposes seem incommensurable.[12] There is no Archimedean point from which a neutral definition can be propounded.

The problem is even more convoluted than it at first seems. Definition of religion is not merely a propositional undertaking. It is not simply a matter of dictionaries or grammar. Ultimately it is about the interaction of normative universes which overlap, intertie, sometimes conflict, and inevitably exert gravitational influence on each other. These overlapping universes have common elements which are given meanings that are sometimes similar and sometimes different, depending on the vantage points from which they are viewed. A definition propounded from the perspective of one world—

---

a critical discussion of how religion has been conceptualized—and of how it might be conceptualized for certain purposes.") (also exploring, in chapters 1–2, recommendations that the term "religion" be expunged or that a definition be delayed for further study).

3. Brian C. Wilson, From the Lexical to the Polythetic: A Brief History of the Definition of Religion, in What is Religion? Origins, Definitions, and Explanations 141, 141 (Thomas A. Idinopulos & Brian C. Wilson eds., 1998).

4. See Saler, supra note 2, at 19 (describing Goodenough's claim that Marxism is a religion); Ninian Smart, Theravāda Buddhism and the Definition of Religion, 34 Sophia 161, 163–165 (1995) (suggesting that secular world views such as Marxism could well be considered religions); Guthrie, supra note 2, at 413 (citing to descriptions of communism as a religion and of "civil religion"); Devine, supra note 2, at 277–280 (making the case for Marxism as a religion); Tomis Kapitan, Devine on Defining Religion, 6 Faith and Phil. 207, 212 (1989) (challenging Devine's definition of religion, and making a stronger case for Marxism as a religion).

5. See Sport and Religion (Shirl J. Hoffman ed., 1992).

6. See Devine, supra note 2, at 280–282.

7. See Sarah Voss, Depolarizing Mathematics and Religion, 5 Philosophica Mathematica 129 (1990).

8. See Paul A. LaViolette, 2000 EEOPUB LEXIS 4858 (U.S. Equal Employment Opportunity Commission 2000) (upholding as religious a claimed belief in cold fusion). See also Curt Suplee, EEOC Backs 'Cold Fusion' Devotee, Wash. Post, Aug. 23, 2000, at A23.

9. See Amy B. Siskind, The Sullivan Institute/Fourth Wall Community: "Radical" Psychotherapy as Quasi-Religion," in Between Sacred and Secular: Research and Theory on Quasi-Religion, 51 (Arthur L. Greil & Thomas Robbins eds., 1994) [hereinafter Between Sacred and Secular].

10. See Jill Dubisch, You Are What You Eat: Religious Aspects of the Health Food Movement, in Magic, Witchcraft, and Religion: An Anthropological Study of the Supernatural 69 (Arthur C. Lehman & James E. Myers eds., 2d ed., 1989).

11. See James Davison Hunger et al., Is "Nothing" Sacred?: "Sacred" Cosmology Among the Avant-Garde, in Between Sacred and Secular, supra note 9, at 79.

12. See, e.g., Brett G. Scharffs, Adjudication and the Problems of Incommensurability, 42 Wm. & Mary L. Rev. 1367 (2001).

for example, the secular state—may correspond with some but not all views perceived from within the myriad religious worlds that exist within or without that state. There may well be differences over which normative order can make ultimate claims or final decisions with respect to which spheres of influence. There may also be questions about whether and to what extent different normative orders deserve respect from each other. With respect to such questions, the power to define is the power to confer differential dignity and legitimacy. When backed by state power, it can result in either endorsement or exclusion.

State power in this arena can be and has been exercised in myriad ways. For example, the state can exercise its power to define one and only one form of religion as legitimate while criminalizing or discriminating against all others. That is, a state could create a single established religion,[13] or it might recognize a prevailing religion that tolerates other religions.[14] Another approach would be for the state to define religion in terms that would include "traditional" religions but exclude those that are countercultural, new, or different.[15] A still more flexible approach would be to provide broad, welcoming definitions that make room for a rich array of different systems of belief, subject only to a carefully restricted set of limitations. Modern constitutional democracies tend to opt for variations on this latter theme, recognizing that while there are some limits on what can be done in the name of religion (i.e., what falls within the ambit of the definition of religion), broad respect should generally be granted to the diverse normative claims by which persons and communities feel bound.

The point of linking definition of religion to the state's definition of varying church/state configurations is to emphasize that in the final analysis, the two notions are not discontinuous. Definition of religion is an inherent part of how the church and state mutually determine and structure their relations with each other and with the different normative worlds of religion(s) and the state, with all their institutional and lifestyle manifestations.[16] Similarly, from the vantage point of religion, definition is an assertion of individual and communal autonomy. Manifestations of religion are a way of defining religious beliefs through conduct, both individual and institutional. We define ourselves and our communities not only in words and beliefs, but in actions. Restraints on this power of self-definition are necessarily restraints on religious freedom.

---

13. As the world shrinks and the experience of pluralism becomes more pervasive, a definition of religion limited solely to the religion of the state becomes more difficult to imagine. In theory, however, a theocratic state could define religion in a way that could include only the religion approved by the state.

14. This is typical of most current established church systems, such as those in Norway and the United Kingdom. This was the case for Sweden prior to its disestablishment. *See* U.S. State Department Report on International Religious Freedom (2001), reports on Norway, Sweden, and United Kingdom, available on-line at http://www.religlaw.org/search.html (visited Mar. 14, 2002).

15. The most blatant system of this type is that of China. *See, e.g.,* R. Lanier Britsch, The Current Status of Christianity in China, 1995 BYU L. Rev. 1367. A number of other foreign systems, however, make heightened benefits available to traditional religions. For example, heightened benefits are available in Lithuania for "traditional religions." Law on Religious Communities and Associations of the Republic of Lithuania, Oct. 4, 1995, No. I-1057, available on-line at http://www.religlaw.org/search.html (visited Mar. 14, 2002). *See also* Christopher J. Miner, Losing My Religion: Austria's New Religion Law in Light of International and European Standards of Religious Freedom, 1998 BYU L. Rev. 607.

16. In a related vein, sociologist Eileen Barker has described the social function of the creation of definitions of religion and their use to impart value judgments. Eileen Barker, But Is It a Genuine Religion?, in Between Sacred and Secular, *supra* note 9, at 97 [hereinafter Barker, But Is It a Genuine Religion?].

Not surprisingly, then, the problem of definition of religion cannot be resolved independently of determining the nature and limits of religious freedom.

With these considerations in mind, the aim of this chapter is to move through and beyond many of the classical approaches to the definition of religion to suggest a more dynamic and interactive understanding of what issues of definition are really about. In the first place, this analysis ultimately suggests that the problem should be reconceived as a matter of the extent to which state institutions should defer to self-definitions propounded by believers and their religious communities. In a normative world, self-definition is an inherent part of what we mean by autonomy (the capacity and dignity of imposing self-chosen or self-accepted norms).[17] The problem of definition is not limited to developing verbal tests for what will count as religion. Most fundamentally it is about the extent to which religious self-definition, which is the core of authentic and autonomous religious belief, can be accorded full respect, including space for self-expression through conduct. In this sense, virtually every chapter in this volume is dealing with the definition of religion: to what extent can individuals and religious communities define themselves through the way they own property, establish corporate structures, organize employment relationships, adjust their structures to adapt to the requirements of taxation, and so forth.

Further, the problem of definition is not merely about defining words such as religion, church, and the like. The problem typically discussed under the heading of "definition of religion" affects the use of all kinds of other terms. Different belief communities use religiously freighted terms in very different ways. What it is to be a "priest" or "minister" or even simply a "member" may have very different meanings for different religions. Legal norms used in governing multiple religious communities, if not flexibly construed, can encroach on religious autonomy in just the same way as can an excessively narrow definition of religion. It is not remotely possible to catalogue all the ways in which religiously freighted legal terminology might hamper legitimate autonomy claims of religious communities. The aim in this chapter is to treat a few examples in some detail to show how the problem of definition extends not only to terms such as "religion" and "church," but to a variety of other terms that are found in legislation that affects religious organizations and that have different meanings in different religious communities. Definitional problems of this type also need to be addressed with a deferential approach that accords maximal respect to religious autonomy. To the extent that such autonomy claims are ignored, religious autonomy values are compromised.

The issue of definition of religion is endlessly fascinating from a theoretical perspective. Its perplexities raise central questions about the nature of religious freedom and its place in a just regime. As intricate as the borderline can become, however, it is important to remember that in most cases the definitional questions are easy. While many examples are often cited of borderline cases—nontheistic Buddhism,[18] Transcendental

---

17. *See, e.g.,* the discussion of this point in James A. Serritella's Prologue to this volume.

18. *See* Ninian Smart, Numen, Nirvana, and the Definition of Religion, 160 Church Q. Rev. 216, 222 (1959) [hereinafter Numen, Nirvana, and the Definition of Religion] (citing Buddhism as a "crux" in the comparative study of religion because of its borderline nature); Smart, *supra* note 4, at 162 (arguing that Theravāda Buddhism "represents a possible boundary in the circumscribing of religions"); Herbrechtsmeier, *supra* note 2; Shivesh C. Thakur, Conjecture and Criticism in Religious Belief, 15 Religious Studies, 71, 72 (1979); Clarke & Byrne, *supra* note 2, at 8 (describing the Durkheim-Spiro debate over whether nontheistic traditions like Buddhism count as religions); Kagnam Oh, Is Zen a Religion?, in The Notion of "Religion" in Comparative Research: Selected Pro-

Meditation,[19] Spinozaism,[20] "New Age" beliefs,[21] belief in magic, witchcraft, and ghosts,[22] and Marxism,[23] to name a few—the truth is that usually there is little doubt as to whether a group is religious. The difficulty of resolving cases at the margin should not be mistaken for difficulty in the broad range of cases.

As will become clear in what follows, some of the traditional definitions are too narrow,[24] but religions that fall within them (i.e., most familiar religions) are clearly entitled to religious freedom protections. For example, a definition that refers to belief in a Supreme Being may be narrowly theistic or monotheistic; but clearly, theistic religions pass this test. Recent cases in other countries that have held that groups such as the Jehovah's Witnesses or Salvation Army do not qualify as religions for the purpose of being registered or incorporated[25] ignore this simple reality, and are blatantly discriminatory. Whatever other complexities may be associated with the problem of definition, theoretical complexity should not be allowed to obscure practical entitlement.

In what follows, we attempt to provide some overview of the vast literature, both in the legal field and elsewhere, that addresses the problem of definition of religion. We then attempt to develop and defend our own theory of how the definitional issue should be dealt with in practical settings. As suggested above, we examine such questions not only with a focus on broad terms such as "religion" and "church," but with re-

---

ceedings of the XVIth Congress of the International Association for the History of Religions 583 (Ugo Bianchi ed., 1994) [hereinafter The Notion of Religion].

19. *See* Bertel Wahlstrom, The Indefinability of Religion, 17 Temenos 101, 114 (1981).

20. *See* Devine, *supra* note 2, at 275–77.

21. *See* Hartmut Zinser, Ist das New Age eine Religion? Oder brauchen wir einen neuen Religionsbegriff?, Zeitschrift für Religions-und Geistesgeschichte 33 (1992).

22. *See* Timothy Fitzgerald, Religion, Philosophy, and Family Resemblances, 26 Religion 215, 215 (1996) (listing "an ideology such as Marxism," "magic, witchcraft, belief in ghosts," and "rituals which have no supernatural reference and no stable doctrinal or even mythological representation" as border cases).

23. *See* Devine, *supra* note 2, at 275 (listing Marxism as one of the "problem cases" for the concept of religion); Ninian Smart, The World's Religions 22–26 (2d ed. 1989) (discussing whether secular world views such as Marxism and nationalism can be considered religions). *See also* sources cited *supra* note 4.

24. For example, twentieth-century scholars have repeatedly pointed out that our lexical definitions are vague and based solely on traditional Western religions such as Christianity and Judaism. *See* Herbrechtsmeier, *supra* note 2, (arguing that nontheistic forms of Buddhism are not adequately addressed by traditional western conceptions of religion as a worship of superhuman beings); Thakur, *supra* note 18, at 71 (Western definitions of religion in previous centuries "have tended to be parochial, failing to apply to, say, Eastern religions, not to mention so-called 'primitive' religions; and have often given to what should only have been 'local squabbles' the appearance of universal religious concern"); Ferré, *supra* note 2, at 7 ("Especially in the theistic West there is a tendency to import, at least implicitly, theistic or supernaturalistic characteristics into the list of defining characteristics that determine the essence of a religion"); Winston L. King, Religion, in 12 The Encyclopedia of Religion 282, 282–83 (Mircea Eliade ed., 1987) (explaining the Western biases behind the attempt to define religion and most definitions); see also Saler, *supra* note 2, at 227–64 (recognizing Western bias in lexical definitions of religion and defending their use "as markers that map a productive starting place" if self-reflective monitoring is used).

But see Michael Pye, What is "Religion" in East Asia?, in The Notion of "Religion," *supra* note 18, at 115 (refuting the idea that an abstract concept of religion is purely Western).

For a thoughtful discussion of the issues, see Kurt Rudolph, Inwieweit Ist Der Begriff "Religion" Eurozentrisch?, in The Notion of "Religion," *id.* at 131; and Saler, *supra* note 2, at 227–64.

25. *See, e.g.*, Sharon LaFraniere, In Russia, Regions Curb Spread of Foreign Faiths, Wash. Post Foreign Service, Feb. 8, 2002, at A1.

spect to representative examples of the array of terms often used in legal norms that affect religious believers and belief communities.

Social Science Approaches to the Definition of Religion

Historians, anthropologists, sociologists, psychologists, and religious studies scholars have debated the definition of religion for more than a century. Although no consensus has emerged, the dividing lines and various definitional approaches have been fairly well demarcated.[26] The initial debate raged over whether definitions should be substantive—listing required theological characteristics—or avoid examining the truth claims of religions. In the late nineteenth and twentieth centuries, substantive definitions have largely been abandoned and the discussion has turned to whether non-substantive definitions should be more taxonomic and functional, providing a set list of factors indicative of religion, or should focus instead on Ludwig Wittgenstein's ideas of "family resemblance." Finally, scholars also disagree over whether definitions should be based on an "-emic," or "insider" perspective on religion, or should rely on an "-etic," or "outsider" perspective.

Modern definitional attempts build on social science efforts from the late nineteenth century and early twentieth century. These early definitions can be classified as "cognitive" or "substantive," as they provide a list of required characteristics of a religion. They are seen to be positive real definitions, which presuppose the metaphysical reality of religion,[27] and they are based on the truth claims of the believers, particularly those in the western traditions. An example is E.B. Tylor's early definition of religion as "the belief in Spiritual Beings."[28] R.R. Marett, another anthropologist, attempted a similar but, in his view, more basic definition of religion as a "belief in a supernatural power."[29] In addition to these positive real definitions, other substantive definitions exist that instead define religion in ways that take a negative stand concerning religious truth claims.[30]

Although substantive definitions continue to be advanced by contemporary scholars,[31] they have been widely challenged since the late nineteenth and early twentieth

---

26. For an introduction into the history of the definition of religion, see Saler, *supra* note 2; Wilson, *supra* note 3; Jan Platvoet, The Definers Defined: Traditions in the Definition of Religion, 2 Method and Theory in the Study of Religion 180 (1990); Johannes Irmscher, Der Terminus Religion und Seine Antiken Entsprechungen im Philologischen und Religionsgeschichtlichen Vergleich, in The Notion of "Religion," *supra* note 18, at 63. For useful discussions of the problems of defining religion, see Clarke & Byrne, *supra* note 2, at 3–27; J.A.M. Snoek, Classification and Definition Theory, An Overview, in The Notion of "Religion," *supra* note 18, at 741.

27. *See, e.g.,* Wilson, *supra* note 3, at 148–49. For a more general discussion of theory of definitions, see Richard Robinson, Definition (1954).

28. Edward B. Tylor, 1 Primitive Culture 424 (1891).

29. R.R. Marett, The Threshold of Religion (1919).

30. Examples of this sort include the theories of Marx ("opiate of the masses") and Freud ("the future of an illusion"). *See generally* Daniel L. Pals, Seven Theories of Religion (1996).

31. *See, e.g.,* Robin Horton, A Definition of Religion, and its Uses, 90 J. of the Royal Anthropological Inst. of Gr. Brit. & Ir. 211 (1960) (building on Tylor's definition to define religion as "an extension of the field of people's social relationships beyond the confines of purely human society"); Platvoet, *supra* note 26; Jack Goody, Religion and Ritual: The Definitional Problem, 12 Brit. J. Soc. 142–64 (June 1961) (refining Tylor's definition); Melford E. Spiro, Religion: Problems of Definition and Explanation, in Anthropological Approaches to the Study of Religion, 85–126 (M. Banton ed.,

centuries. Essentialists have charged that they are too doctrinal and fail to reflect the experiential aspects of religion. Functionalists, however, drawing on the materialist assumptions of the social sciences, have attacked substantive definitions as being too bound up with real definitions and insufficiently explanatory. They have felt that by stressing social or psychological functions, they could study religion without giving it a positive or negative definition.

As a reaction to the overly formalistic and doctrinal nature of substantive definitions, some scholars have adopted an essentialist or "-emic" definitional approach in which the nature of religion is the experience of the individual believer, not the doctrines or principles in which he or she believes.[32] Probably the best known definition of this variety is Mircea Eliade's conception of the sacred as a mode of being defined by its opposition to the profane.[33] This tradition traces its roots to Friedrich Schleiermacher's conception of religion as a self-authenticating experience.[34] He defined religion as a "feeling of absolute dependence."[35] One of the earliest attempts to develop this idea was Rudolph Otto's 1917 work, *Das Heilige*, which defined religion as an experience of supernatural power, or "the holy," in contrast to a mere belief in supernatural power.[36] A major modern influence in the essentialist camp is Wilfred Cantwell Smith, who insisted that definitions of religion must reflect its double nature and discuss its internal or personal aspects along with the external or observable ones.[37] Various other similar essentialist definitions have also been offered.[38]

Critics of essentialism question the appropriateness and utility of relying on transcendent experiences in scholarly definitions.[39] For the most part, late nineteenth- and twentieth-century social scientists have been uncomfortable with essentialism's reliance on "real" definitions, which assume the existence or nonexistence of the thing to be defined.[40] Instead, they insist that only an "-etic" or "outsider" approach that relies on observable data can avoid subjectivity and be used across cultural and individual differences.[41]

In an attempt to avoid the question of real definitions of religion, both substantive and essentialist, most social scientists of the late nineteenth and twentieth centuries

---

1966) (defining religion as "an institution consisting of culturally patterned interaction with culturally postulated superhuman beings"); G. E. Swanson, Experience of the Supernatural, in Sociology of Religion: Selected Readings, 237–52 (Roland Robertson ed., 1969); Brian K. Smith, Exorcising the Transcendent: Strategies for Defining Hinduism and Religion, History of Religions 27, 32–55, 53 (1987) (defining religion as "canonicity").

32. For a helpful discussion of the -emic/-etic divide, see Platvoet, *supra* note 26, at 183–187, and McCutcheon, *supra* note 2, at 285–287.

33. *See* Mircea Eliade, The Sacred and The Profane: The Nature of Religion 10 (1959).

34. *See generally* Wilson, *supra* note 3, at 147–48.

35. *See* Friedrich Schleiermacher, The Christian Faith (1928), proposition 4.

36. Rudolph Otto, The Idea of the Holy: An Inquiry Into the Non-Rational Factor in the Idea of the Divine and Its Relation to the Rational (1950); *see generally* Wilson, *supra* note 3, at 148.

37. *See* Wilfred Cantwell Smith, The Meaning and End of Religion (1962).

38. *See generally* chapters 3–4 in Saler, *supra* note 2 (discussing various essentialist definitions and their critics).

39. There is also a tradition following David Hume (including Freud and Marx) that discounts the reality of transcendent experiences. While this tradition is clearly -etic rather than -emic, its followers also often use the experience of believers to define religion. *See generally* Daniel L. Pals, Seven Theories of Religion (1996).

40. To some extent, then, this -emic/-etic debate is merely a variant of the polarity between real and nominal definitions dating back to Aristotle. *See* Robinson, *supra* note 27, at 149–92. *See also* Comstock, *supra* note 2, at 501–2 (criticizing Aristotle and real and essential definitions of religion).

41. *See generally* chapters 3–4 in Saler, *supra* note 2 (discussing various essentialist definitions and their critics).

have taken a functional approach.[42] Functional definitions attempt to define religion by looking at the roles or functions that it plays in society or for individuals. For example, Paul Tillich's popular definition of religion as an individual's "ultimate concern"[43] can be seen as a psychological functional definition.

Sociologists, anthropologists, and religious studies scholars have all tried their hand at drafting functional definitions of religion, with widely varying results.[44] Two of the earliest and most influential thinkers to proffer such definitions were Emile Durkheim and Bronislaw Malinowski. Durkheim, who originated the sacred/profane dichotomy, gave a definition of religion that phrased a substantive definition in social functional terms: "A religion is a unified system of beliefs and practices relative to sacred things, that is to say, things set apart and forbidden—beliefs and practices which unite into one single moral community called a Church, all those who adhere to them."[45] In contrast to Durkheim's focus on the socially unifying force of religion, Malinowski, a psychological functionalist, stressed the function of religion in individuals, arguing that it "saves man from a surrender to death and destruction (and is derived from our instincts)."[46]

---

42. Ironically, as Wilson notes (*see supra* note 3, at 150), some of the most influential functionalists have been "firmly committed to negative real definitions of religion." Saler likewise argues that many functional definitions are essentialist. *See* Saler, *supra* note 2, at 24.

43. Paul Tillich, Dymamics of Faith, 11–12 (1957).

44. *See, e.g.,* J. Milton Yinger, The Scientific Study of Religion 7 (1970) (defining religion as "a system of beliefs and practices by means of which a group of people struggle with the ultimate problems of life"); Jonathan Z. Smith, Map is Not Territory 291 (1978) ("Religion is the quest, within the bounds of the human, historical condition, for the power to manipulate and negotiate one's 'situation' so as to have 'space' in which to meaningfully dwell. It is the power to relate one's domain to the plurality of environmental and social spheres in such a way as to guarantee the conviction that one's existence 'matters'"); J. Paul Williams, The Nature of Religion, 2 J. for the Sci. Study of Religion 3, 8 (1962) (defining religion as "a mental quality which modifies certain aspects of the life of individuals (and through individuals of groups); this quality must have each of the following characteristics in some degree: a belief-attitude that the Ultimate for man exists (however it may be conceived) and that certain aspects of life derive from the Ultimate; a belief-attitude that the derivation (from the Ultimate) of these aspects of life is beyond empirical demonstration; a belief-attitude that these aspects of life are of supreme importance (at least potentially) for the concern of the individual (and perhaps of groups and/or all men)"); Morton B. King, Is Scientific Study of Religion Possible?, 30 J. for the Sci. Study of Religion 108, 109 (1991) (defining religion as "the behavior of human beings patterned on a set of beliefs, usually institutionalized, serving as arbiter of ultimate meanings"); Hideo Kishimoto, An Operational Definition of Religion, 8 Numen 236, 240 (1961) (defining religion as "an aspect of culture centered upon activities which are taken by those who participate in them to elucidate the ultimate meaning of life and to be related to the ultimate solution of its problems. Many religious systems contain the notion of deity and/or holiness in relation with such activities."); Ferré, *supra* note 2, at 11 (defining religion as "one's way of valuing most intensively and comprehensively"); Streng, *supra* note 2, at 235 (defining religious forms as "structural processes of ultimate transformation").

Functional definitions are also occasionally combined with substantive definitions. *See, e.g.,* Devine, *supra* note 2, at 272 (defining religion as something that "affirms the existence of one or more superhuman agents" and "unifies, through a system of symbolic representations, the framework by which an individual or group regulates its thought and life").

45. Emile Durkheim, The Elementary Forms of the Religious Life, 62 (1965). For a fuller discussion of Durkheim's definition and influence, see Brian Morris, Anthropological Studies of Religion 106–40 (1990).

46. Bronislaw Malinowski, The Role of Magic and Religion, 4 Encyclopedia of the Social Sciences 634–42 (Seligman & Johnson eds., 1931). For more discussion of Malinowski's views, see Morris, *supra* note 45, at 148–49.

A more recent and highly influential functional definition was offered by anthropologist Clifford Geertz in the 1960s. He proposed that religion is "(1) a system of symbols which acts to (2) establish powerful, pervasive, and long-lasting moods and motivations in men by (3) formulating conceptions of a general order of existence and (4) clothing those conceptions with such an aura of factuality that (5) the moods and motivations seem uniquely realistic."[47] As this definition indicates, functional definitions sometimes turn into laundry lists of factors inherent in religions. For example, King gives as a definition "the attempt to order individual and societal life in terms of culturally perceived ultimate priorities," and attempts to add substance by listing eight characteristics and structures of religious life.[48]

Although popular, functionalist definitions have also been sharply criticized. One major criticism is that they are over- and under-inclusive when compared against traditional lexical definitions of religion.[49] For example, Tillich's "ultimate concern" could arguably include sports, work, or anything to which a person chose to devote his or her life, but might exclude some forms of Buddhism that do not attempt to address "ultimate concerns" of life, or might at the very least distort the prominence of beliefs within various traditions.[50] When they attempt to avoid these problems through increased generalization, functional definitions raise critiques that they are merely "empty generalit[ies]."[51] They also fail to address the problem that some activities or beliefs traditionally considered religious do not fulfill the functions assigned to them by sociologists or anthropologists.[52] Disagreements among religions or millenialist movements,

---

47. Clifford Geertz, Religion as a Cultural System, in Anthropological Approaches to the Study of Religion 4 (Michael Bainston ed., 1966).

48. King, *supra* note 24 at 286–292 (traditionalism, myth and symbol, concepts of salvation, sacred places and objects, sacred actions or rituals, sacred writings, the sacred community, and the sacred experience). In this regard, Wilson distinguishes between monothetic and polythetic functional definitions: monothetic definitions have a single set of sine qua non characteristics and polythetic definitions have a list of potential factors. *See* Wilson, *supra* note 3, at 158.

49. *See, e.g.,* Comstock, *supra* note 2, at 501–02 (critiquing Geertz's definition as overinclusive and potentially including all other cultural forms such as science, social ideologies, and political discourse); Horton, *supra* note 31, at 201–206 (attacking functionalism's lack of explanatory power). *See also* Voss, *supra* note 7, at 129 (1990) (using Geertz's definition to explain why mathematics is akin to religion).

50. *See, e.g.,* Shirl J. Hoffman, Sport and Religion 1, 1–10, in Sport and Religion, *supra* note 5 (describing how sport fits within functional definitions of religion); Numen, Nirvana, and the Definition of Religion, *supra* note 18, at 222 (detailing how reductionists often misinterpret or distort various forms of Buddhism in order to fit them into generalized categories); Clarke & Byrne, *supra* note 2, at 8 (noting that functionalist definitions are often broad enough to include "baseball or playing the stock market"). *But see* Saler, *supra* note 2, at 108–111 (using citations from Tillich's works to suggest that under his theory there may be false objects of ultimate concern and that the only true object of ultimate concern is "Being Itself" or "the Unconditional," which is best expressed in Protestant Christianity). This critique of functionalism often plays itself out in a debate over whether religion is necessarily universal. *See* Clarke & Byrne, *supra* note 2, at 8–9 (exploring the tension inherent in functionalism between seeking to identify universal characteristics and becoming overbroad in the process); Spiro, *supra* note 31, at 91; Saler, *supra* note 2, at 150–156. In response to the criticism that their definitions lack universality, some have argued that religion is simply not a universal category. Others argue that the characteristics they observe are universal. *See* Wilson, *supra* note 3, at 156.

51. Numen, Nirvana, and the Definition of Religion, *supra* note 18, at 222; Wilson, *supra* note 3, at 155.

52. *See* Wilson, *supra* note 3, at 154–155.

for example, may disrupt rather than serve the end of social cohesion.[53] Finally, functionalist definitions have been criticized for their inability to explain the origin of religious beliefs.[54]

Late twentieth-century reactions to functionalist definitions have included a return to substantive definitions,[55] as well as a new strain of thought that relies on Wittgenstein's idea of creating definitions through identifying "family resemblances,"[56] sometimes referred to as "linguistic" or "open" definition.[57] Followers of this approach generally list a variety of features typical of religions, without requiring that a belief have all listed features in order to be considered a religion.[58] This introduces more flexibility into the cross-cultural application of definitions.[59] As Ninian Smart, one of the earliest

---

53. *See* Allan W. Eister, Religious Institutions in Complex Societies: Difficulties in the Theoretic Specifications of Functions, 22 Am. Soc. Rev. 287 (1957); Wilson, *supra* note 3, at 154–155.

54. *See* Wilson, *supra* note 3, at 155–156; Machalek, *supra* note 2, at 398–400 (summarizing main criticisms of functionalism as: "(1) Functional definitions are too inclusive. (2) Functional definitions create rather than discover reality. (3) Functional definitions are not feasible because religion is a multi-functional phenomenon"). *But see* Machalek, *supra* note 2 (attempting to defend functionalism against these charges).

55. *See* Goody, *supra* note 31, at 142–64; Spiro, *supra* note 31; Swanson, *supra* note 31.

56. Ludwig Wittgenstein, Philosophical Investigations 32e (G.E.M. Anscombe, trans., 1953).

57. *See* Comstock, *supra* note 2; Wahlstrom, *supra* note 19, at 103–114 (explaining the need for an open definition of religion); Wilson, *supra* note 3. This school of thought's additional reliance on a range of postmodern thought is discussed in Comstock, *supra* note 2, at 508–509.

58. *See, e.g.,* Clarke & Byrne, *supra* note 2, at 12–13 (proposing a family resemblance definition through listing characteristic theoretical, practical, social, and experiential dimensions with "characteristic kinds of objects (gods or transcendent things), goals (salvation or liberation) and functions (the provision of meaning and unity to group or individual life"); Saler, *supra* note 2, at 158–226 (discussing numerous Wittgensteinian approaches and advocating a modified Wittgensteinian approach); William P. Alston, Religion, in 7 The Encyclopedia of Philosophy 140, 141–2 (Paul Edwards ed., 1967) (listing nine "religion-making characteristics" that are neither necessary nor sufficient: "1. Belief in supernatural beings (gods). 2. A distinction between sacred and profane objects. 3. Ritual acts focused on sacred objects. 4. A moral code believed to be sanctioned by the gods. 5. Characteristically religious feelings (awe, sense of mystery, sense of guilt, adoration), which tend to be aroused in the presence of sacred objects and during the practice of ritual, and which are connected in idea with the gods. 6. Prayer and other forms of communication with gods. 7. A world view, or a general picture of the world as a whole and the place of the individual therein. This picture contains some of the specification of an over-all purpose or point of the world and an indication of how the individual fits into it. 8. A more or less total organization of one's life based on the world view. 9. A social group bound together by the above"); Numen, Nirvana, and the Definition of Religion, *supra* note 18, at 13–21 (proposing seven nonessential dimensions of religions: the practical and ritual dimension, the experiential and emotional dimension, the narrative or mythic dimension, the doctrinal and philosophical dimension, the ethical and legal dimension, the social and institutional dimension, and the material dimension); Martin Southwold, Buddhism and the Definition of Religion, 13 Man 362 (1978) (requiring some of the following attributes to be religion: "(1) A central concern with godlike beings and men's relations with them. (2) A dichotomisation of elements of the world into sacred and profane, and a central concern with the sacred. (3) An orientation towards salvation from the ordinary conditions of worldly existence. (4) Ritual practices. (5) Beliefs which are neither logically nor empirically demonstrable or highly probable, but must be held on the basis of faith.... (6) An ethical code, supported by such beliefs. (7) Supernatural sanctions on infringements of that code. (8) A mythology. (9) A body of scriptures, or similarly exalted oral traditions. (10) A priesthood, or similar specialist religious elite. (11) Association with a moral community, a church (in Durkheim's sense). (12) Association with an ethnic or similar group").

59. *See* Clarke & Byrne, *supra* note 2, at 13–14 ("The family resemblance approach to the meaning of 'religion' sets boundaries to the application of the word, not by checking off putative examples of religion against an agreed list of determinate properties, but by judging that systems of belief and/or action do or do not contain sufficient of the dimensions and specific distinguishing features of religion.... This will allow us to give the concept of religion boundaries").

proponents of a family-resemblance definition of religion, explained, this sort of definition allows us to "place both early Buddhism and early Islam in the same family, even though they have nothing obvious or important in common."[60]

Family-resemblance definitions have been subject to many of the same critiques as functional and substantive decisions. For example, choosing any set of basic features of a religion opens the door to allegations of ethnocentrism.[61] Further, establishing a set number of minimum requisite characteristics appears arbitrary.[62] If no set number of minimum characteristics is given, then the category becomes infinitely malleable.[63] To advocates of family-resemblance theories, however, these problems can be largely recast as benefits (such as flexibility) or problems to be expected in working with inherently "fuzzy" sets.[64]

Legal Approaches to the Definition of Religion

Definitions of religion in the legal scholarly literature and United States court cases largely follow the types of definitions advanced by social scientists. Early legal definitions, like early anthropological definitions, were largely substantive and Western-based. Substantive definitions, with their focus on a set of required beliefs, have largely been supplanted by functional approaches, such as Tillich's "ultimate concern" theory. These have had a long run of popularity, both with courts and with commentators, but they raise serious problems of excessive breadth and vagueness or under-inclusiveness. Recently, some commentators have also advocated a Wittgensteinian "family resemblances" or "analogical" approach to defining religion. This approach has several significant advantages. It provides a framework that is flexible enough to accommodate new or unusual beliefs without necessarily becoming infinitely malleable.

Other commentators' approaches attempt to avoid a single state-sanctioned definition. While these highlight important religious liberty concerns that are raised by the enterprise of defining, we argue that attempts to solve this problem by eschewing definitions entirely ultimately prove unworkable.

---

60. Numen, Nirvana, and the Definition of Religion, *supra* note 18, at 223.

61. *See* Wilson, *supra* note 3, at 160; Don Wiebe, Problems with the Family Resemblance Approach to Conceptualizing Religion, in Perspectives on Method and Theory in the Study of Religion 314 (Armin W. Geertz and Russell T. McCutcheon eds., 2000) [hereinafter Perspectives on Method and Theory in the Study of Religion]; Russell T. McCutcheon, Taming Ethnocentrism and Trans-Cultural Understandings, in *id.*, at 294.

62. *See* Wilson, *supra* note 3, at 160; Gary Lease, The Definition of Religion: An Analytical or Hermeneutical Task?, in Perspectives on Method and Theory in the Study of Religion, *supra* note 61, at 287.

63. *See* Fitzgerald, *supra* note 22, at 226–28 (challenging family resemblance theories as being unable to distinguish "the family of religion from other close relatives, such as the family of ideologies, or the family of world-views, or the family of symbolic and ritual systems" to the extent that they refuse to identify necessary characteristics); Wilson, *supra* note 3, at 160; Wiebe, *supra* note 61, at 314. *But see* Comstock, *supra* note 2, at 514–15 (1986) (arguing that ambiguity and lack of boundaries are inevitable and can be a virtue); Saler, *supra* note 2, at 217–226 (claiming that specifying necessary and sufficient conditions is not productive, that the best one can do is to "trace diminishing degrees of typicality").

64. *See, e.g.,* Benson Saler, "Conceptualizing Religion": Responses, in Perspectives on Method and Theory in the Study of Religion, *supra* note 61, at 323, 324.

Unitary or dual definitions

Before launching into a more thorough discussion of these various positions, it is important to note a threshold issue raised by legal commentators which does not arise in social-science discussions of religion. The issue is usually phrased as whether the word "religion" in the First Amendment to the United States Constitution should be considered to have a single or dual definition, although the principle of multiple potential definitions of religion clearly applies beyond just the First Amendment. The idea that definitions should reflect their context may not normally be controversial—but in the First Amendment context it is, because the term "religion" is used only once.

One school of thought, advanced primarily by Laurence H. Tribe in the first edition of his treatise on constitutional law,[65] holds that the word "religion" as used in the First Amendment should have two meanings: one that reflects the intent of the Establishment Clause, and one that reflects the intent of the Free Exercise Clause. Tribe argued that an expansive definition of religion is necessary to achieve the purposes of the Free Exercise Clause in a time when "recognizably legitimate" forms of religion are multiplying.[66] Conversely, according to Tribe, a narrower definition of religion is required for purposes of the Establishment Clause "in the age of the affirmative and increasingly pervasive state...lest all 'humane' programs of government be deemed constitutionally suspect."[67] Tribe's solution was to consider anything that is "arguably religious" as religious under the Free Exercise Clause, and anything that is "arguably non-religious" as nonreligious under the Establishment Clause.[68]

Tribe was ultimately persuaded to drop his dual definition approach; he retreated from it in the second edition of his treatise.[69] Proponents of a unitary definition make three principal arguments. First, the text of the First Amendment uses the word "religion" only once: "The word governs two prohibitions and governs them alike. It does not have two meanings, one narrow to forbid 'an establishment' and another, much broader, for securing 'the free exercise thereof.' 'Thereof' brings down 'religion' with its entire and exact content, no more and no less, from the first into the second guaranty."[70] Second, as Stanley Ingber points out, a dual definition creates the potential for conflict.[71] Both Ingber and Carl H. Esbeck suggest that a group that is "arguably religious" would be able to receive free exercise protection under Tribe's approach, but, if also "arguably non-religious," could still be endorsed by the state.[72] This would unfairly privilege the new group as compared to older and better established religious groups.

---

65. Laurence H. Tribe, American Constitutional Law § 14-6, at 826 (1st ed. 1978). *See also* Note, Toward a Constitutional Definition of Religion, 91 Harv. L. Rev. 1056, 1083–86 (1978) (arguing for a dual definition).

66. Tribe, *supra* note 65, at 827.

67. *Id.*

68. *Id.* at 828.

69. Laurence H. Tribe, American Constitutional Law § 14-6, at 1186 (2d ed. 1988).

70. Everson v. Board of Education, 330 U.S. 1, 32 (1946) (Rutledge, J., dissenting).

71. *See* Stanley Ingber, Religion or Ideology: A Needed Clarification of the Religion Clauses, 41 Stan. L. Rev. 233, 288–91 (1989). *See also* Phillip E. Johnson, Concepts and Compromise in First Amendment Religious Doctrine, 72 Cal. L. Rev. 817, 834–35 (1984).

72. *See* Ingber, *supra* note 71, at 288–91; Carl H. Esbeck, The Establishment Clause as a Structural Restraint on Government Power, 84 Iowa L. Rev. 1, 6–7 (1998).

Third, as Jesse H. Choper,[73] Ingber,[74] and Kent Greenawalt[75] have argued, a dual definition may be unnecessary.[76] Greenawalt and Choper both recognize the differences between Free Exercise Clause and Establishment Clause claims but argue, in Greenawalt's words, that a "[f]ocus on the specific purpose of the inquiry permits accommodations of these differences without a rigid distinction between free exercise and establishment cases that both strains the constitutional language and obscures important differences among cases arising under each clause."[77] Or, as Choper puts it, "a dual definition of religion may not be required to avoid the results feared under a unitary version of the term" because the legal tests for each clause differ.[78] The basis of this third argument seems to be that in practice the Supreme Court's legal tests for applying the Establishment Clause do not require a definition of religion because Establishment Clause cases turn on the government's behavior rather than the behavior of religious individuals or organizations.[79]

The latter approach to dismissing the problem that Tribe originally senses may be too quick. It is true that the Supreme Court uses different legal tests in the establishment and free exercise domains. But this merely evades rather than solves the problem. Think for a moment about just one of these tests: the much-criticized but recurrently invoked *Lemon* test. According to it, to withstand Establishment Clause scrutiny, state action must have a secular purpose, a primarily secular effect, and an absence of excessive entanglement.[80] From a definitional standpoint, the "different legal test" merely obscures the definitional problem or begs the question at issue. It assumes that we know what a "secular" as opposed to a "religious" purpose or effect is. But in hard cases, these are merely opposite and contested sides of a disputed boundary. Similarly, whether there is excessive entanglement will obviously depend on the breadth of the definition of religion. If the definition is narrow, entanglement is less likely; if it is broad, entanglement may be pervasive. The difficulty is that equality concerns create strong pressures for an expansive notion of religion for purposes of free exercise, but applying such expansive definitions on the Establishment Clause side would arguably impose excessive constraints on government action. The extreme version of the argument would be that any program that reflected or coincided with strongly held beliefs (e.g., laws against homicide) would constitute an impermissible establishment of religion. This would obviously go much too far.

To observe that the text of the Constitution appears to assume a unitary definition does not get us any closer to identifying an effective unitary definition. Furthermore, the practical requirements of the two Religion Clauses do seem to demand different ways of treating religion. The argument that we can simply apply different legal tests for each clause acknowledges this fact while bypassing the need to find a unitary definition.

---

73. *See* Jesse H. Choper, Defining "Religion" in the First Amendment, 1982 U. Ill. L. Rev. 579, 605–6.

74. *See* Ingber, *supra* note 71, at 288–91.

75. *See* Kent Greenawalt, Religion as a Concept in Constitutional Law, 72 Cal. L. Rev. 753, 769 (1984).

76. *See* Ingber, *supra* note 71, at 288–91; Choper, *supra* note 73, at 828; Greenawalt, *supra* note 75, at 769.

77. Greenawalt, *supra* note 75, at 769.

78. Choper, *supra* note 73, at 605.

79. *See id.* at 606.

80. *See* Lemon v. Kurtzman, 403 U.S. 602, 612–13 (1971).

Indeed, in his most recent work, Choper has emphasized that his proposed definition of religion is intended only for purposes of the Free Exercise Clause.[81] He makes no attempt at a definition that encompasses both Religion Clauses.

One reason the definitional problems remain largely unobserved on the Establishment Clause side is that it is so much less likely that the state will be tempted to support or endorse marginal religious groups. The hazard, rather, is that clearly accepted traditional groups that fall clearly within everyone's conception of religion will exploit their political power to secure benefits, to entrench their position in society, or to assert their preeminence in a variety of symbolic ways. The difficult problems in this area arise when religious groups structure portions of their activities in secular forms in order to be eligible for the same state support that flows to other secular organizations. For example, a religious order may set up a secular nonprofit corporation to establish a hospital eligible for various state grants. Even here, there may be questions about whether the Establishment Clause should be allowed to "pierce the secular veil," and about whether there is too much religious control or religious influence. But there is seldom any real doubt that the sponsoring organization is religious and that the sponsored activity is secular. The hardest definitional problems arise in countercultural domains.

Definitional problems can become even more complicated in legal systems that permit a more extensive array of benefits to flow to dominant religions. In such systems, drafters of legislation and regulations often seek to make the term "religion" (or other terms such as "church" or "sect") do the work of substantive classifications. Narrowing the definition of the term "religion" when the stakes or benefits are higher may be a natural reaction, but it is intellectually and politically dishonest. Eileen Barker gives a memorable account of how easily this happens:

> A university chaplain once told me that he could not call the International Society of Krishna Consciousness a religion because (despite the fact that it would fit all the criteria he would normally use in defining "religion") there were "not enough rooms" — and the University had a rule that each religion should have a room. When I asked whether it might not be more honest to change the rule, he replied in a shocked voice that to do that could be seen as religious discrimination.[82]

While definitions may be context-specific, it is important for religious freedom that they not be used to disguise preferences or policy choices. Hiding value choices under supposedly "neutral" or "scientific" definitions may make them less visible but no less discriminatory.[83] It is inevitable that in the last analysis, definitions of religion will need to take context and purpose into account in giving practical meaning to religion-laden terms, but explicit or tacit reliance on discriminatory purpose is fundamentally inconsistent with canons of religious freedom and equality.

---

81. *See* discussion of Choper's theories in section on modern substantive definitions, *infra*. *See also* Note, Toward a Constitutional Definition of Religion, 91 Harv. L. Rev. 1056 (1978), which recommends dual definitions.

82. Eileen Barker, Why the Cults?: New Religious Movements and Freedom of Religion or Belief, n.1, in Facilitating Freedom of Religion or Belief: A Deskbook (Tore Lindholm, et al., eds., 2004) [hereinafter Barker, Why the Cults?]. For a more extensive account of this encounter, and other similar tales of misuses and abuses of definitions, see Eileen Barker, But Is It A Genuine Religion?, in Between Sacred and Secular, *supra* note 9.

83. Eileen Barker, for example, makes forceful arguments for why social scientists should not succumb to the temptation to mask value judgments in seemingly neutral definitions. *See* Barker, But Is It A Genuine Religion?, in Between Sacred and Secular, *supra* note 9.

Substantive definitions

Legal definitions of religion have largely followed social science trends. Just as substantive definitions have largely given way to functional definitions in the social sciences' study of religion, so too have they generally been replaced by functional definitions in the legal sphere. Functional definitions have the advantage of being open to new or unfamiliar forms of religious belief, but that openness becomes a disadvantage when a definition fails to provide enough guidance to make courts consistent and predictable in their rulings. Functional definitions also tend to be overbroad. An abstract religious "function" is usually so open-ended that some beliefs and practices not ordinarily considered religious can easily fall under the definition. Conversely, substantive definitions tend to provide clearer guidance to courts, but they also create the danger that the law will not recognize emerging religions that depart from the familiar doctrines or practices of more established religions. The definitions of religion that we now consider reflect these strengths and weaknesses to varying degrees—but none, in our opinion, is ultimately successful in providing a workable definition that also addresses religious liberty concerns.

Early substantive definitions

In the vein of the early definitions of religion advanced by anthropologists Tylor ("belief in Spiritual Beings")[84] and Marett ("belief in a supernatural power"[85]), early U.S. Supreme Court cases adopted traditional Western-based substantive definitions. While a majority of the Court has never strictly required a belief in a Supreme Being,[86] it originally used traditional Western Christianity as a benchmark of religion. For example, in 1890 the Court rejected the claim of members of the Church of Jesus Christ of Latter-day Saints that polygamy was a religious practice, explaining:

> The term 'religion' has reference to one's views of his relations to his Creator, and to the obligations they impose of reverence for his being and character, and of obedience to his will.... To call [polygamy's] advocacy a tenet of religion is to offend the common sense of mankind.[87]

A deistic, traditional definition was offered in 1931 in a dissent by Chief Justice Hughes joined by Justice Holmes: "[t]he essence of religion is belief in a relation to God involving duties superior to those arising from any human relation."[88] In recent years, however, the Court has moved decisively away from deistic and traditional Western substantive definitions.[89]

---

84. Tylor, *supra* note 28, at 424.

85. R.R. Marett, *supra* note 29.

86. *See* Greenawalt, *supra* note 75, at 802–03.

87. Davis v. Beason, 133 U.S. 333, 341–42 (1890).

88. United States v. MacIntosh, 283 U.S. 605, 633–34 (1931) (Hughes, C.J., dissenting, joined by J. Holmes).

89. *See, e.g.,* United States v. Seeger, 380 U.S. 163, 166 (1965) (defining religion as "an individual's belief in a relation to Supreme Being involving duties superior to those arising from any human relation, but does not include essentially political, sociological or philosophical views or a merely personal moral code"). *See generally* Greenawalt, *supra* note 75, at 802–03; Anita Bowser, Delimiting Religion in the Constitution: A Classification Problem, 11 Val. U. L. Rev. 163, 215–25 (1977).

Modern substantive definitions

Just as substantive definitions of religion have recently experienced a small flurry of popularity in the social science field,[90] where they have been seen as a corrective to the often overbroad functional definitions, a few substantive legal definitions of religion have also recently reappeared. Choper, for example, argues that religion requires the precision of a substantive definition.[91] He offers two different criteria for defining religion under the Free Exercise Clause: "extratemporal consequences"[92]and "transcendent reality."[93]

Under the "extratemporal consequences" criterion, a person may claim a free exercise exemption from government mandates if he believes that "the effects of actions taken pursuant or contrary to the dictates of a person's beliefs extend in some meaningful way beyond his lifetime."[94] Choper's example uses conscientious objectors to military service. Under the "extratemporal consequences" definition, a conscientious objector would be freed from military service if his religious belief taught that such service would lead to punishment beyond the grave.[95] Those whose objections to military service do not entail extratemporal consequences would not be exempt from service, even if the objections are based on religious belief.[96] Choper argues that those who believe in extratemporal consequences deserve relief because "intuition and experience affirm that the degree of internal trauma on earth for those who have put their souls in jeopardy for eternity can be expected to be markedly greater than for those who have only violated a moral scruple."[97]

The "transcendent reality" criterion is somewhat more inclusive. Although this approach appears to be Choper's second choice, Ingber proposes it as his preferred standard under both of the First Amendment's Religion Clauses.[98] This definition identifies as religious those beliefs that "invoke a transcendent reality," even if the religion does not teach that one's actions have consequences beyond this life.[99] For example, Choper

---

90. *See supra* note 31.

91. *See* Jesse H. Choper, Securing Religious Liberty: Principles for Judicial Interpretation of the Religion Clauses 64–86 (1995) [hereinafter Securing Religious Liberty]; Choper, *supra* note 73, at 597–601.

92. Choper, *supra* note 73, at 597–601.

93. *Id.* at 601–604.

94. *Id.* at 599.

95. *See id.* at 598.

96. *See id.* at 598, n.109.

97. *Id.* at 598.

98. *See* Ingber, *supra* note 71, at 288–91. Ingber does not characterize his approach as either substantive or functional, but he cites the work of both Emile Durkheim and Mircea Eliade—functional theorists—as inspirations for his position. *Id.* at 285. Although Durkheim and Eliade defined religion more functionally than substantively, Ingber's definition of religion does not incorporate the full richness and complexity of Durkheim's and Eliade's work. This is not necessarily a shortcoming in Ingber's proposal; the need to make legal principles efficient and practically applicable may appropriately lead to simplification. We choose to characterize Ingber's position as a substantive definition because he relies on an understanding of "transcendent reality" that in application refers to the content of belief. Similarly, Timothy L. Hall, Note, The Sacred and the Profane: A First Amendment Definition of Religion, 61 Tex. L. Rev. 139 (1982), straddles the line between substantive and functional definitions in its proposal to define religion on the basis of Durkheim's dichotomy of the sacred and the profane; Hall's Note proposes that where a belief system makes a meaningful distinction between the sacred and the profane, the belief system should be recognized as a religion for First Amendment purposes.

99. Choper, *supra* note 73, at 602.

says, Christian teachings such as those of Saint Augustine and John Calvin hold that salvation after this life is a gift of God, not earned by good works.[100] Similarly, the indigenous religion of China, "in which the spirits of dead forebears are regarded as taking an active and continuing role in the well-being of the family[,]...involves strong duties, but does not usually connect them with consequences to follow after death."[101] Ingber says, "Although not necessarily bound by any theistic precept, religious duties must be based in the 'otherworldly' or the transcendent—transcendent not as an abstract concept reachable only by reason and intellect is transcendent, but a transcendent reality."[102] "A religion can be non-anthropomorphic, non-theistic, or even have a membership of one as long as the claimed religious obligations are imposed by or under the influence of some sacred force."[103]

Other commentators have proposed substantive criteria similar to the "transcendent reality" test, based either on the presence of nonrational belief[104] or on the presence of "belief in a nonmaterial reality."[105]

One critique of the "extratemporal consequences" definition focuses on the difficulty of implementation. Ingber notes that this definition would force courts to intrusively examine individual beliefs and make irrational distinctions between almost identical beliefs. For example, if an individual believed that serving in the military was prohibited by his or her religion and that such service would lead to extratemporal consequences, the individual would be exempt. But a similar individual, who also believed that serving in the military was prohibited by his or her religion, but also believed that any extratemporal consequences would be mitigated by God if the action were compelled by law or for other religious reasons, would receive no exemption.[106] Choper responds that the intrusiveness is no greater than that of any other substantive test, and that the distinction between these two conscientious objectors is perfectly rational: exemptions are only made for those who truly feel they need them to avoid more severe extralegal consequences.[107]

Choper's "extratemporal consequences" definition has also been criticized as being "grossly underinclusive," "even by conservative standards," because it relies on Western notions of tying actions to after-death rewards or punishments.[108] Even the "transcendent reality" test, which Greenawalt sees as preferable,[109] has been assailed as underinclusive. Greenawalt argues that it "treats as nonreligious the activities of groups, such as Ethical Culture, that engage in practices closely resembling the worship services of the traditional religions but that do not assert a realm of meaning inaccessible to ordinary

---

100. *See id.* at 601.

101. *Id.* at 602.

102. *Id.* at 285–86.

103. *Id.* at 287.

104. *See* Dmitry N. Feofanov, Defining Religion: An Immodest Proposal, 23 Hofstra L. Rev. 309, 385 (1994) ("Religion is a manifestly non-rational (i.e., faith-based) belief concerning the alleged nature of the universe, sincerely held"); Andrew W. Austin, Faith and the Constitutional Definition of Religion, 22 Cumb. L. Rev. 1, 43 (1991/1992) ("any belief system that is based upon one or more unprovable (as opposed to unproven) assumptions that include a belief in a greater power").

105. Richard O. Frame, Note, Belief in a Nonmaterial Reality: A Proposed First Amendment Definition of Religion, 1992 U. Ill. L. Rev. 819, 838 (1992) ("[A] belief or belief-system is religious if it includes a belief in a non-material reality").

106. *See* Ingber, *supra* note 71, at 276–77.

107. *See* Choper, Securing Religious Liberty, *supra* note 91, at 76–77.

108. Ingber, *supra* note 71, at 276.

109. *See* Greenawalt, *supra* note 75, at 805.

observation."[110] Choper agrees that his definition eliminates some types of practices as nonreligious. "[T]he dominant purpose of the Religion Clauses is to single out 'religion,' as opposed to other systems of belief. This concept must therefore have some minimum content."[111] But this does not mean that beliefs not fitting the "extratemporal consequences" definition are left unprotected. "Rather, all individual concerns, opinions, and beliefs receive substantial protection under other constitutional provisions."[112]

Ingber's defense of the "transcendent reality" definition turns largely on his distinction between religion and ideology.[113] "Ideology" is an Enlightenment concept that "emphasized reason, rationality, and sensory experience" and "from its very inception was biased against religious perspectives and authorities."[114] Ingber argues that the Framers understood well the conflict between religion and ideology, which is why the First Amendment singles out religion for protection.

> The religion clauses represent an acknowledgment of pre-Enlightenment beliefs and a realization that for many there are duties or obligations that precede those made by human beings. The obligations imposed by religion are of a different, higher nature than those derived from human relationships; they are not part of the agenda of public debate.[115]

Thus, Ingber believes, the "transcendent reality" definition follows an authentic historical understanding of religion under the Constitution.

Ingber argues that his definition can "function for legal purposes" without "being too tied to Western religions or forcing courts to get too involved in evaluating religious doctrine."[116] He claims that it can be flexible and yet avoid what he calls the "total vagueness"[117] of an approach like Greenawalt's analogical method.[118] He also believes that it escapes the "problems of either limiting the religious clauses' protection too severely or leaving no meaningful distinction between religions and ideologies"—problems found in some functional definitions.[119]

Ultimately, however, Ingber and Choper's definitions, while certainly preferable to nineteenth-century judicial approaches, suffer the weaknesses of all substantive definitions. Ingber's, for example, is not much different from Marett's early definition of religion as "belief in a supernatural power"[120] and is just as over- and under-inclusive. It would exclude religions that have a strong tradition of understanding divine phenomena through reason, rationality, and sensory experience, such as Christian Science and some strains of Roman Catholic thought, but could easily include a belief in flying saucers or cold fusion, neither of which has been proved by reason, rationality, or sensory experience. By selecting one element of the religious experience, substantive definitions leave little room for new religious movements and tend to distort the importance of beliefs within religious traditions. The legal clarity of substantive definitions may be tempting, but their narrowness becomes a procrustean bed for believers and belief traditions.

---

110. *Id.*

111. Choper, Securing Religious Liberty, *supra* note 91, at 78.

112. *Id.*

113. *See* Ingber, *supra* note 71, at 277–285.

114. *Id.* at 279.

115. *Id.* at 285 (citations omitted).

116. *Id.* at 287.

117. *Id.*

118. *See* discussion of Greenawalt's analogical approach to defining religion, *infra*.

119. Ingber, *supra* note 71, at 287 (citations omitted).

120. *See supra*, text accompanying notes 27–30.

Structural definitions

In his book *Loyalty*,[121] George Fletcher offers an unusual substantive definition. Rejecting a definition based on individual beliefs, he argues that "[w]e need an account of religious commitment that goes beyond the recognition of the psychological weight of these commitments and an explanation of why these commitments should prevail over secular law."[122] Fletcher suggests a definition rooted in communitarian practices. "Religious beliefs, so far as they are to be taken seriously, arise in congregations or communities of believers."[123]

Fletcher distinguishes beliefs held passionately but privately from beliefs and practices that the law should respect as genuinely religious. He suggests that his communitarian approach has two virtues in drawing this distinction in favor of communities. First, "[t]he competing loyalty that religious commitments represent is a loyalty to the group as well as to the divine voice.... Humility requires that one hear the voice of God not as a self-proclaimed prophet but as one member of a congregation that tests its visions over time."[124] Second, "a congregational conception of religion mediates against the excesses of individuals who think they hear the voice of God."[125] Consequently, "[t]he correct interpretation of the free exercise clause...would defer to religious loyalties only if they are founded on a system of beliefs embedded in community practices and tested and refined within a community of believers."[126]

Fletcher recognizes a problem with his definition: "a communitarian approach to the free exercise clause may require the Court to assess whether a particular community really grounds its views in the Bible or whether these views are the product of independently motivated customs and convictions."[127] Fletcher seems not to be deeply troubled by this problem of state assessment of religious views, perhaps because he feels that an open and principled acknowledgment that the Court is classifying certain beliefs as legitimately religious is preferable to the often cursory or insensitive treatment that the Court has given to the beliefs of various minority religious groups.[128]

In reacting to the problems of open-ended functionalist definitions such as "ultimate concern," however, Fletcher's definition goes to the other extreme. His approach embodies the problem inherent in substantive definitions: insensitivity to non-mainstream religious beliefs and traditions. While it is helpful to focus on the rights of groups to preserve their autonomy through associational opportunities and congregational worship, using these aspects to define religion itself becomes problematic. This approach presupposes familiar types of religiosity, and is not sufficiently open to genuine but distinctive religions. Fletcher's approach reflects a clear bias toward existing religions that have already survived long enough to generate entrenched patterns of communal conduct.

---

121. George P. Fletcher, Loyalty: An Essay on the Morality of Relationships 98 (1993).

122. *Id.* at 95.

123. *Id.* at 98.

124. *Id.* at 98–99.

125. *Id.* at 99.

126. *Id.*

127. *Id.* at 99.

128. *See id.* at 92–98. "Despite...favorable treatment of Protestant sects, other religious groups have not received the same deferential recognition. Jews and Moslems have fared badly before the Court. The treatment of Native Americans has been less than respectful. Scientologists received short shrift." *Id.* at 92–93.

Clearly, the focus of this book is the legal structuring of American religious organizations, but a necessary precondition to addressing questions of the shape and nature of those organizations is the legal ability to form such associations. If substantive definitions must of necessity adopt requisite characteristics from existing religions, the most problematic one from the viewpoint of preserving religious freedom is the requirement that the religion have an existing community. This simply creates a catch-22 for those who, like Jesus or Muhammad, would found new religious traditions. They have no protections until they are a community (or a "tested and refined" community), and in many other countries they cannot form a community without legal protections. While this is not the case in the United States, which has extremely liberal standards for the creation of legal entities and protects individual believers as well as belief communities, it is a practical problem in a number of former Communist countries. Several of these countries require a religion to have a large number of adherents before it can obtain legal entity status, but bar any groups or individuals without legal personality from proselytizing or conducting public worship services—actions that might allow them to attract adherents.

Even for existing groups, Fletcher's desire to limit the term religion to communities that are "tested and refined" raises the concern that the definitional issue would become an inquiry into the normative value or antiquity of religious beliefs, something that also has happened in some post-Communist countries. Fletcher's fears of the excesses of individuals may at times be justified. Certainly horrors have been wrought in the name of religion. Yet using this as a reason to narrowly define religion to include only "tested" beliefs of communities is a vastly overbroad limitation. Religious freedom only for traditional religions falls far short of what this fundamental right should provide. As we suggest elsewhere, limitations on free exercise protections should not be smuggled in at the definitional level. Resolving problems that flow from individual excesses in new movements through the application of ordinary criminal law after crimes have been committed, for example, seems much more evenhanded than denying the qualification of "religious" to groups and believers who may not be affiliated with a "tested" or "refined" belief community.

Functional definitions

In the late twentieth century, U.S. courts have largely moved from substantive definitions to use of a functional approach.[129] Instead of making certain requirements of a set of beliefs, functional definitions focus on the role that those beliefs or practices play in an individual's life. "Religion" then becomes anything that fulfills this role in a person's life. One of the most prominent and most criticized of functional definitions is that given by Tillich, that religion is the "ultimate concern"[130] in a person's life. Other functional definitions have been proffered by social scientists,[131] but the legal world has not ventured past the definition in terms of "ultimate concern" that has also been used by the Supreme Court.[132]

---

129. *See, e.g.,* Note, Developments in the Law—Religion and the State: II. The Complex Interaction Between Religion and Government, 100 Harv. L. Rev. 1612, 1622–25 (1987) (summarizing the Supreme Court's transition from substantive definitions to functional definitions).

130. Paul Tillich, Dymamics of Faith 11–12 (1957). *See supra*, text accompanying notes 42–43.

131. *See supra* notes 42–54 and accompanying text.

132. *See, e.g.,* Note, Developments in the Law-Religion and the State: II. The Complex Interaction Between Religion and Government, 100 Harv. L. Rev. 1612, 1622–25 (1987).

The Court first employed Tillich's definition in *United States v. Seeger*.[133] It was asked to determine whether a conscientious objector's beliefs were religious as defined by the Universal Military Training and Service Act.[134] The act used a traditional substantive definition of religion: "an individual's belief in a relation to Supreme Being involving duties superior to those arising from any human relation, but does not include essentially political, sociological or philosophical views or a merely personal moral code."[135] Disregarding the text of the statute, the Court used a functional definition of religion, quoting Tillich.[136] Religion, according to *Seeger*, is determined by

> whether a given belief that is sincere and meaningful occupies a place in the life of its possessor parallel to that filled by the orthodox belief in God of one who clearly qualifies for the exemption.[137]

The broad scope of the Tillichian definition adopted in *Seeger* became clear a few years later in another conscientious objector case, *Welsh v. United States*.[138] In that case, the Supreme Court decided that the Universal Military Training and Service Act covered a person who "originally characterized his beliefs as nonreligious" and later "declared that his beliefs were 'certainly religious in the ethical sense of the word.'"[139] The Court held that the act's definition of religion did not "exclude those who hold strong beliefs about our domestic and foreign affairs or even those whose conscientious objection to participation in all wars is founded to a substantial extent upon considerations of public policy."[140]

Tillich-style functional definitions of religion have also been proposed by commentators.[141] A prominent defense of an "ultimate concern" definition was given in 1978 by a *Harvard Law Review* note, *Toward a Constitutional Definition of Religion*.[142] The note recognizes the most obvious problems in a Tillichian definition—overbreadth and a limitless ability for an individual to define his or her religion[143]—but argues that these are not insurmountable. With regard to overbreadth, the practical problem would be the threat to the effectiveness of government programs. But the "ultimate concern" definition does not eliminate the need for courts to balance religious liberty interests against government interests.[144] Moreover, the law may counter fraudulent claims by considering the claimant's sincerity.[145]

---

133. 380 U.S. 163 (1965).

134. *See* 380 U.S. at 166 (interpreting 50 U.S.C. App. § 456(j) (1958)).

135. 50 U.S.C. App. § 456(j) (1958).

136. *See* 380 U.S. at 187.

137. 380 U.S. at 165–66.

138. 398 U.S. 333, 340–44 (1970).

139. 398 U.S. at 341.

140. 398 U.S. at 342.

141. *See, e.g.,* C. John Sommerville, Defining Religion and the Present Supreme Court, 6 J. Law. & Pub. Pol'y 167, 177 (1994) (Proposing that "[t]he protections guaranteed to religion [be] offered to those with a sincere belief in, or relation to, a power or being to which all else is subordinate, but excluding essentially political, social or philosophical opinions or a moral code involving no transcendent consequences"); John Mansfield, Conscientious Objection—1964 Term, in 1965 Religion & Pub. Ord. 9, 10 (D. Giannella ed., 1966) (religion should provide answers to ultimate questions of life).

142. Note, *supra* note 65, at 1066–75.

143. *See id.* at 1075–79.

144. *See id.* At the time the note was written, the standard was a compelling state interest. This argument is even stronger today in light of *Smith's* greatly reduced governmental burden.

145. *See id.* at 1079–82.

The definition of religion based on Tillich's ideas of "ultimate concern" has come under considerable criticism. Commentators not only have noticed the vagueness and overbreadth recognized by the note,[146] but also have highlighted particular problems raised by use of "ultimate concern" as a legal standard. For example, Choper argues that although Tillich's views "may well be the profound expressions of a radical theologian searching for truth," he "only marginally comprehend[s] 'religion' as that term is understood by most theologians or laymen."[147] Choper sees Tillich's definition as being unworkable in the context of the First Amendment. "Ultimate concern," he points out, can cover matters such as science, politics, economics, and social welfare, which government normally regulates.[148] The point of the First Amendment, on the other hand, is to set aside a realm where government "is incompetent to interfere."[149]

Ingber and Greenawalt point out the central fault with Tillich's definition: the poor fit with a lexical understanding of religion, and the resulting difficulty of practical implementation. Noting that even religious individuals may not have religion as their "ultimate concern," Ingber explains that "[i]n application, the standard is either so demanding as to bestow religious protection upon an extremely limited few or so broad that it leaves no distinction between religion and other value systems, thus becoming insignificant or even meaningless."[150]

Analogical approaches

Greenawalt[151] and George Freeman[152] have advocated what Greenawalt calls an "analogical approach to the constitutional concept of religion"[153] based on Wittgenstein's "family resemblances" theory of language.[154] Freeman argues that "the search for the constitutional definition of 'religion' is misguided. There simply is no essence of religion, no single feature or set of features that all religions have in common and that distinguishes religion from everything else."[155] Greenawalt writes, "[A]ny dictionary approach oversimplifies the concept of religion, and the very phrase 'definition of religion' is potentially misleading."[156]

As an alternative to dictionary-style substantive definitions, Greenawalt suggests an approach that "begins with instances of the indisputably religious, instances about

---

146. *See, e.g.,* Choper, *supra* note 73, at 593–94 ("In fact, a traditional believer's religion does not play a single, ascertainable role in his existence.... Nor needs its influence remain constant; rather, it may change over time"), 597 (vagueness problem); Ingber, *supra* note 71, at 272 (arguing that these definitions succeed "only by being so general as to include nearly all belief systems").

147. Choper, *supra* note 73, at 595.

148. *See id.* at 596.

149. *Id.*

150. Ingber, *supra* note 71, at 268–69. *See also* Greenawalt, *supra* note 75, at 806 ("the approach is marred by the difficulty in rendering any account of ultimate concern that both retains its attractive features and achieves an acceptable degree of coherence for a legal standard"), 808 (arguing that individuals have more than one "ultimate concern").

151. *See* Greenawalt, *supra* note 75.

152. *See* George C. Freeman, III, The Misguided Search for the Constitutional Definition of "Religion," 71 Geo. L.J. 1519 (1983).

153. Greenawalt, *supra* note 75, at 762.

154. *See supra* notes 56–64 and accompanying text.

155. Freeman, *supra* note 152, at 1565.

156. Greenawalt, *supra* note 75, at 763.

which virtually everyone would say, 'This certainly is religion.'"[157] "Instances of the indisputably religious" then become the paradigm cases for determining whether certain borderline beliefs or practices are religious. But because the paradigm embraces diverse religions, it also reflects many possible features of religion, and no religion must include every feature.[158]

Greenawalt believes that the analogical approach is more effective than other approaches because it is applicable in a variety of situations and it fits in with common lexical understandings.[159] He also suggests that definition by analogy is essentially what the courts did in the cases of *Malnak v. Yogi*[160] and *Africa v. Commonwealth of Pennsylvania*.[161] In *Malnak*, the U.S. Court of Appeals for the Third Circuit determined that the Science of Creative Intelligence-Transcendental Meditation was a religion and that teaching it in public schools would therefore violate the Establishment Clause. In *Africa*, the same court determined that the MOVE organization was not a religion and that the plaintiff, a prison inmate, was therefore not entitled to a special diet that satisfied his asserted religious requirements. In his concurring opinion in *Malnak*, Judge Arlin M. Adams described an analogical approach to the problem of defining religion which the court later adopted in *Africa*. Adams proposed three criteria as "'useful indicia' to determine the existence of a religion."[162]

> First, a religion addresses fundamental and ultimate questions having to do with deep and imponderable matters. Second, a religion is comprehensive in nature; it consists of a belief-system as opposed to an isolated teaching. Third, a religion often can be recognized by the presence of certain formal and external signs…that may be analogized to accepted religions. Such signs might include formal services, ceremonial functions, the existence of clergy, structure and organization, efforts at propagation, observance of holidays and other similar manifestations associated with the traditional religions.[163]

For Greenawalt, the important point is that Adams's approach purports to work by analogy and does not tie itself inflexibly to any particular substantive definition. Thus, Greenawalt's proposal is not a radical departure from past practices in the courts. "Far from requiring drastic alteration of what the courts have been doing," he writes, "[the analogical approach] is a method faithful to those efforts."[164]

At the practical level, one response to the underinclusiveness difficulty faced by substantive and functional definitions has been the proposal of multi-factor tests. When

---

157. *Id.* at 767.
158. "Our society identifies what is indubitably religious largely by reference to beliefs, practices, and organizations. These include: a belief in God; a comprehensive view of the world and human purposes; a belief in some form of afterlife; communication with God through ritual acts of worship and through corporate and individual prayer; a particular perspective on moral obligations derived from a moral or from a conception of God's nature; practices involving repentance and forgiveness of sins; 'religious' feelings of awe, guilt, and adoration; the use of sacred texts; and organization to facilitate the corporate aspects or religious practices and to promote and perpetuate beliefs and practices. This list could be expanded or organized differently. The main point is that among religions typical in this society a number of different elements are joined together." *Id.* at 767–68.
159. *See id.* at 802–813.
160. 592 F.2d 197 (3d Cir. 1979).
161. 662 F.2d 1025 (3d Cir. 1981).
162. 662 F.2d at 1032.
163. 662 F.2d at 1032, 1035.
164. Greenawalt, *supra* note 75, at 776.

such tests use various factors to help identify what constitutes religion, but also recognize that many religions will not exemplify all the factors, they constitute a species of the analogical approach. The factors are in effect a list, possibly only a partial list, of the criteria by which the analogy is specified. One well known application of this approach is the set of factors identified by the Internal Revenue Service in determining the meaning of the term "church" in the Internal Revenue Code. Because the IRS list is fairly representative of a multi-factored analogical approach, it is worth setting forth in full. According to the list, a church has:

1. A distinct legal existence
2. A recognized creed and form of worship
3. A definite and distinct ecclesiastical government
4. A formal code of doctrine and discipline
5. A distinct religious history
6. A membership not associated with any other church or denomination
7. An organization of ordained ministers
8. Ordained ministers selected after completing prescribed studies
9. A literature of its own
10. Established places of worship
11. Regular congregations
12. Regular worship services
13. Sunday schools for religious instruction of the young
14. Schools for the preparation of ministers

No single factor is controlling, although all fourteen may not be relevant to a given determination.[165]

Ingber has criticized the Greenawalt/Freeman analogical approach as suffering from the same weakness as the Supreme Court's conclusion in *Seeger*. In that case, "the test for whether a belief was religious is 'whether a given belief that is sincere and meaningful occupies a place in the life of its possessor parallel to that filled by the orthodox belief in God of one who clearly qualifies for the [religious] exemption [from the draft].'"[166] According to Ingber, both Greenawalt and *Seeger* "essentially accept...a totally open-ended perspective."[167] These approaches "are not definitions of religion at all. They merely accept acknowledged religions as yardsticks and ask if the claimed religion is a functional equivalent. But functionally equivalent in what way?"[168] Greenawalt's approach "may suit philosophers, [but] it fails to take into account the responsibility of the legal system for structuring, creating, and fulfilling legal expectations."[169]

But Ingber misunderstands the Wittgensteinian or "analogical" approach, confusing it with a non-multiple factor functional definition. While it is true that both can be open-ended (although a Wittgensteinian definition need not be),[170] analogical defini-

---

165. Richard R. Hammar, Pastor, Church, and Law 124 (1983) (citing Am. Guidance Found. v. United States, 490 F. Supp. 304 (D.D.C. 1980)).

166. Ingber, *supra* note 71, at 273 (quoting United States v. Seeger, 380 U.S. 163, 165–66 (1965)).

167. *Id.* at 273.

168. *Id.*

169. *Id.* at 274.

170. A functional definition is of necessity open-ended, as it focuses on an abstract function that religion (or its equivalents) perform. Wittgensteinian definitions, on the other hand, may be "open polythetic" or "closed polythetic." "Open polythetic" definitions would have an open-ended list of characteristics, any of which or any *x* number of which are necessary, but none of which is sufficient

tions either explicitly or implicitly have a list of characteristics, such that anything satisfying the definition necessarily exhibits at least some of the characteristics. One or a number of factors may be sufficient to confirm analogy to religion, but different grounds of similarity may apply in different cases. This gives more form and substance to the definition, but prevents it from easily earning the criticism that substantive definitions have of being too narrow or too culturally specific.

The analogical approach as articulated by Greenawalt and Freeman has retained much appeal to subsequent commentators, and has been somewhat refined by proposals of additional guidelines or criteria for use in the analogical comparison.[171] Its advantage is that it avoids the under-inclusiveness that bedevils substantive definitions by acknowledging that some religions can be recognized as religions for legal purposes even though they may fail to exemplify some factors of the definition. Of course, the value of an analogical approach is lost if it becomes merely a rote application of a substantive laundry-list definition, as one commentator suggests happened in the *Africa* decision.[172]

Our primary criticism of the analogical approach, despite its many strengths, is that it focuses attention on the wrong question. By asking religious groups to meet an external standard—even a relatively flexible and broad one—and prove that they are "religious" at the outset, the analogical approach fails to give deference to and thus respect the autonomy of religious groups. Greenawalt does allow some deference to individual definitions: "An individual's own idea of religion may show which factors he or she takes as most important, and that may be relevant for a court." But he argues that "[n]evertheless, judicial resolution of what counts as religious should not depend finally on what an individual claimant regards as religious."[173] While we do not argue for complete self-definition, we see a greater role for it than Greenawalt does. We contend, as further spelled out later in this chapter, that the primary question should not be "what counts as religious," but instead what the proper extent of the state's power to constrain self-definitions of religion should be. Shifting the focus to the appropriate limitations on state power provides the greatest possible respect for the autonomy of religious organizations.

Other strategies

Abstention

As more and more thought has been given to the problem of definition of religion and to the implication that an excessively narrow definition may result in practical limi-

---

by itself. "Closed polythetic" definitions would have a closed list of similar characteristics. Closure makes the definition susceptible to critiques of arbitrariness or cultural bias, but these are both mitigated by the fact that none of the characteristics is sufficient by itself. *See supra* note 48, and accompanying text.

171. *See, e.g.,* Paul Horwitz, Scientology in Court: A Comparative Analysis and Some Thoughts on Selected Issues in Law and Religion, 47 DePaul L. Rev. 85, 141–42 (1997); Eduardo Peñalver, Note, The Concept of Religion, 107 Yale L.J. 791, 818–21 (1997); Ben Clements, Note, Defining "Religion" in the First Amendment: A Functional Approach, 74 Cornell L. Rev. 532, 553 (1989).

172. *See* Horwitz, *supra* note 171, at 135. *See also* Note, Developments in the Law-Religion and the State: II. The Complex Interaction Between Religion and Government, 100 Harv. L. Rev. 1612, 1625–31 (1987) (criticizing the *Africa* decision for failure to apply properly the functional approach set forth in *Seeger* and *Welsh*).

173. Kent Greenawalt, Judicial Resolution of Issues about Religious Conviction, 81 Marq. L. Rev. 461, 464 (1998).

tations on religious freedom, a number of commentators have sought other paths out of the thicket. One approach is simply to call for the state to abstain from efforts to define religion. Advocates of abstention share our view that the proper focus is on the extent of governmental power to engage in definition of religion. They simply take a position more radical than the one we take below—namely, that government lacks power in this area altogether. Jonathan Weiss, for example, articulates this position well: "Any definition of religion would seem to violate religious freedom in that it would dictate to religions, present and future, what they must be...."[174] These very real concerns have led Weiss and Kurland to suggest that the U.S. Constitution requires courts to abstain from any definition of religion. For Weiss, this results from the problem of a definition's exclusive quality. "[A]n attempt to define religion, even for purposes of increasing freedom for religions, would run afoul of the 'establishment' clause, as excluding some religions, or even as establishing a notion respecting religion."[175] Kurland, on the other hand, sees abstention from definition as being required by a neutrality principle embedded in the First Amendment. The establishment and free exercise commands "would be impossible of effectuation unless they are read together as creating a doctrine more akin to the reading of the equal protection clause than to the due process clause, *i.e.*, they must be read to mean that religion may not be used as a basis for classification for purposes of governmental action, whether that action be the conferring of rights or privileges or the imposition of duties or obligations."[176]

But the definitional problem cannot be evaded this easily. As at least Kurland implicitly acknowledges, a non-definition still leaves the question to the courts of dividing a religious sphere, where courts should not intrude, from a nonreligious sphere.[177] Weiss would solve this problem partially through self-definition (which he calls "asking for assent") and partially through a fairly traditional substantive definition: "To make a common sense decision whether a movement is a religion and a claim clearly religious, we look in general to: (a) whether the movement claims through an asking for assent (a rigorous proof of religion would probably refer to grounds of assent); (b) 'supernatural' claims traditionally connected with religion; (c) whether the traditional customary activities and trappings of 'religion' are present."[178] Weiss also implicitly defines religion and shows the perils of such definitions when he designates a public sphere in which

---

174. Jonathan Weiss, Privilege, Posture and Protection: "Religion" in the Law, 73 Yale L.J. 593, 604 (1964). *See also* Sharon L. Worthing, "Religion" and "Religious Institutions" Under the First Amendment, 7 Pepp. L. Rev. 313, 314–15 (1980) ("If officials—either elected or appointed—are permitted to construct definitions in those areas where they are forbidden to discriminate, they may impose by definitional form that which they are forbidden to impose by direct decree").

175. Weiss, *supra* note 174, at 604.

176. Philip B. Kurland, Of Church and State and the Supreme Court, 29 U. Chi. L. Rev. 1, 5 (1961).

177. For Kurland, this shows up in a recognition that classifications are not purely nominal: "Not the least of them [questions unanswered by the neutrality principle] flows from the fact that the actions of the state must be carefully scrutinized to assure that classifications that purport to relate to other matters are not really classifications in terms of religion." *Id.* at 5. To go beyond nominal distinctions between religious-based classifications and non-religious-based ones, however, merely begs the original question of defining religion.

178. Weiss, *supra* note 174, at 606. *See also id.* at 604 ("Since religion is traditionally an area of faith and assent, we may say that a religious claim is one which asks for adherence on the grounds of religious truth, or one which is defined or spoken by its author as religious"). *See also* Gail Merel, The Protection of Individual Choice: A Consistent Understanding of Religion Under the First Amendment, 45 U. Chi. L. Rev. 805, 834 (proposing definition of religion as "any multidimensional system of beliefs that an individual claimant sincerely asserts to be religiously held").

only the public standard applies and religion can serve as neither a defense nor a claim. Far from being a non-definition, this definition of religion as "affirmation" of a belief, but not as actions expressing those beliefs,[179] is particularly restrictive. As Greenawalt explains, neutrality "purchases partial avoidance of definitional difficulties at the cost of elimination of free exercise accommodation."[180]

Kurland sagely offers no such definition, suggesting only that his neutral principle "is meant to provide a starting point for solutions to problems brought before the Court, not a mechanical answer to them."[181] He recognizes that courts will be forced to distinguish between unlawful "religious" classifications and "neutral," or nonreligious, classifications, but rejects the action/belief dichotomy.[182] Kurland offers little hope that a definition or distinguishing mechanism is possible.[183] He instead relies on the "genius of the common law, and thus of American constitutional law," or the development of rules in concrete factual scenarios, to develop the distinctions needed." The Kurland approach thus pleads abstention, but ultimately lapses into analogy.

Reductionist approaches

In addition to a neutrality-based abstention principle such as that articulated by Weiss and Kurland, two other strategies have been suggested, and attacked, by commentators. One is what Ingber calls "the reduction principle," giving and allowing no special deference to religious beliefs.[184] The idea is that religion cannot defend the right to be a preferred freedom,[185] or that in any event, any special right to protection is adequately protected by other constitutional claims such as freedom of speech or equal protection.[186] These positions appear to be gathering increasing support in academic settings and cannot be addressed fully here. While they clearly solve the definition problem—essentially by abrogating the need for distinctive legal categories involving religion, thereby eliminating the need for definition—they do so at the cost of requiring a radical break from the tradition of affording religion special protection.[187] The reductionist trend may well reflect powerful trends in political thought associated with the

179. *See* Weiss, *supra* note 174, at 623 ("The task is to discern whether religion forms a variable in the statute's formulation or application by seeing whether an assumption or decision on a perspective or belief is called for. If so, then the statute is unconstitutional. If not, then religion can form neither a defense to its application nor a justification after application for calling the statute unconstitutional").

180. Greenawalt, *supra* note 75, at 811. *See also* Ingber, *supra* note 71, at 246–47 (citing Kurland, *supra* note 176).

181. Kurland, *supra* note 176, at 6.

182. *See id.* at 5 and 96.

183. *See id.* at 96 ("This test is meant to provide a starting point for the solution to problems brought before the Court, not a mechanical answer to them. Perhaps such a search for rules of decision is futile or undesirable").

184. *See, e.g.,* William P. Marshall, Solving the Free Exercise Dilemma: Free Exercise as Expression, 67 Minn. L. Rev. 545, 546 (1983) (proposing that "the Court should review all claims brought by religious proponents seeking exemption from laws of general applicability according to a free expression analysis, not an independent free exercise analysis").

185. *See, e.g.,* Steven D. Smith, The Rise and Fall of Religious Freedom in Constitutional Discourse, 140 U. Pa. L. Rev. 149 (1991); Steven G. Gey, Why Is Religion Special?: Reconsidering the Accommodation of Religion Under the Religion Clauses of the First Amendment, 52 U. Pitt. L. Rev. 75 (1990).

186. *See, e.g.,* Marshall, *supra* note 184; Frederick Mark Gedicks, Towards a Defensible Free Exercise Doctrine, 68 Geo. Wash. L. Rev. 925 (2000).

187. *See* Ingber, *supra* note 71, at 241–46.

rise of equality paradigms, but it neglects the stubborn reality that virtually all legal systems, including our own, do in fact accord special respect to freedom of religion and belief. Once assumed as a matter of course, the unique nature of religion, and thus religious rights, continues to attract explicit justifications.[188] The problem of definition of religion is unlikely to wither away any time soon.

Self-definition

A more sophisticated but still problematic attempt to avoid definitions is what Ingber has referred to as "the self-defining principle"—that is, total deference to a believer's definition of religion.[189] Weiss uses this in part. Similarly, some functional Tillichian definitions verge on it. It is not clear, however, that any legal commentator has explicitly advocated allowing believers the unfettered right to define the scope of their own beliefs for legal purposes. Ingber raises questions of over-inclusiveness and fraud that could be enabled by such openness. Even beyond this, however, it seems logical that any legal protection based on a definition with infinitely malleable borders and no protections against potential strategic behavior would cease over time to have any meaningful substance.

Greenawalt proposes the possibility of using self-definition subject to a test of sincerity.[190] He presents two options: an extreme version, in which courts would accept any claim founded on sincere belief, and a moderate version, in which courts "would decide if some minimum objective requisites were met; if they were met the individual's judgment would be conclusive."[191] Greenawalt opposes the extreme version because "[i]t would be odd to extend the umbrella of free exercise protection to an activity only because the individual who engaged in it has a highly idiosyncratic view of what constitutes religion."[192] The moderate version is likewise rejected, because the fate of a claim would depend on the conceptual borderlines of the person making the claim. "Even assuming that the free exercise clause is meant to safeguard a sense of liberty, a person's feeling that his liberty has been invaded is unlikely to track his conceptualization of what is religion."[193]

While it appears clear that pure self-definition, like other attempts at non-definition, fails to resolve the problems inherent in providing a workable definition of religion, it seems to us that Greenawalt rejects some role for self-definition too quickly. His argument that "the [Free Exercise] clause does not grant or withhold protection based on where a particular individual happens to think the boundaries of the *concept* of religion lie"[194] brushes too quickly past the point that legal protection of religion does indeed depend on where someone, such as a judge or state representative, thinks the boundaries of the concept of religion lie. It is not clear why the views of the believer (or nonbeliever) whose freedom is at stake should have no role in this process.

---

188. *See, e.g.,* Michael W. McConnell, Why is Religious Liberty the "First Freedom"?, 21 Cardozo L. Rev. 1243 (2000) [hereinafter McConnell, Religious Liberty]; Michael W. McConnell, The Problem of Singling Out Religion, 50 DePaul L. Rev. 1 (2000) [hereinafter McConnell, The Problem of Singling Out Religion]; John T. Noonan, Jr., Religious Liberty at the Stake, 84 Va. L. Rev. 459 (1998).
189. *See* Ingber, *supra* note 71, at 247–49.
190. *See* Greenawalt, *supra* note 75, at 812.
191. *Id.*
192. *Id.*
193. *Id.*
194. *Id.*

Interjurisdictional respect

Perry Dane has proposed a different way of conceptualizing the problem of definition. His "model of competing authorities"[195] treats religions as "non-state legal orders."[196] In his view, rules that govern conflicts of laws are a useful model; conflict between the demands of civil law and the requirements of religion should be understood by analogy to the way in which different legal systems treat each other's norms. For the purposes of this chapter, Dane's contribution to the discussion about defining religion is twofold. First, he presents an original theoretical approach to the concept of religion in the constitutional context. Second, he proposes a set of features that the law may use to identify legitimate claims for exemption from legal requirements on the basis of religion.

Dane's theoretical treatment of religion begins with the observation that religions make unique claims of autonomy with regard to secular powers. The confrontation of religious and secular requirements is at times, he suggests, a "challenge to democratic authority posed by the behavioral, authoritative, and transcendent attributes of religious systems of belief."[197] The Constitution's recognition of religious liberty is a recognition that, within limits, the religious challenge to democratic authority is not only legitimate but entitled to protection. We traditionally try to accommodate the demands of religious authority within the liberal theory of rights. The problem with this approach is that "rights-talk comes out of a given legal system,"[198] and tends to "serve the purposes of a legal regime."[199] Thus, the authentic character of a religious system can be distorted if it is required to fit too closely to the same view of the world as the civil authority embodies.

Dane suggests that a more fruitful approach would treat both state legal orders and non-state legal orders (such as religions) as sovereigns. This is of course consistent with a very old tradition of thinking of religions and state institutions as coordinate sovereigns or competences. Sovereignty, as Dane speaks of it, "is not indivisible, or unlimited. Nor is it necessarily homogenous. But, however divided, limited, and heterogeneous it is, it is a dynamic, organic whole."[200] "Sovereignty-talk" does not preclude "rights-talk,"[201] but it forces us to recognize that the language of rights does not fully appreciate the demands of non-state legal orders.

> Religious autonomy is more than a right of free exercise, although it is handy, even sensible, to call it that. Respecting another legal order's autonomy does not require accepting the full extent of its claims. It does require, however, treating the other legal order as a legitimate occupant of sovereign space.... The recognition of another's sovereignty is...mutually empowering. It is, for legal communities, something like a human being's passage out of infancy—not the disintegration of self but its sharper definition in a world of other selves.[202]

---

195. Perry Dane, Note, Religious Exemptions Under the Free Exercise Clause: A Model of Competing Authorities, 90 Yale L.J. 350 (1980) [hereinafter Dane, Note].

196. Perry Dane, The Maps of Sovereignty: A Meditation, 12 Cardozo L. Rev. 959, 965 (1991) [hereinafter Dane, Maps].

197. Dane, Note, *supra* note 195, at 370.

198. Dane, Maps, *supra* note 196, at 967.

199. *Id.* at 970.

200. *Id.* at 967.

201. *Id.* at 972.

202. *Id.* at 966, 970.

Dane argues that once we acknowledge alternatives to what he calls "state exclusivism" (the idea that the world is divided into mutually exclusive territorial states, each of which has exclusive sovereignty within its borders),[203] we can recognize the possibility that we can "in effect carve out a 'territory' for religious concerns and articulate conditions that determine when persons are operating within that territory."[204] The problem then becomes how to reconcile the competing claims of religion and civil authority. Dane suggests that rules governing the conflict of laws provide a useful analogy.

To that end, Dane has suggested a three-step procedure for identifying legitimate claims to religion-based exemptions.[205] First, "In the context of adjudicating exemption claims, religion would be defined as a system of belief, not necessarily theistic or institutional, that contained a source of authority perceived to transcend both the believer and the state. This source of authority must be external to personal belief or philosophy, no matter how strong or sincere, and must have a reality and normative force analogous to that of a foreign government."[206] Second, the court must determine "whether a nexus existed between [the claimant's] particular belief and a general intent to be governed by the religious source of authority."[207] This would also include an evaluation of the sincerity of belief.[208] "Finally, the test would ask whether the specific religious claim fell within the ambit of the religious source of authority."[209]

Dane's definitional approach is thoughtful and unique. Looking at religion's function as sovereignty and authority in the life of a believer provides a uniquely legal approach to defining religion. This, along with his conflict of laws analysis, provides a fairly workable way of respecting the autonomy of believers and communities while reconciling their demands with those of the state. Moreover, it suggests a model for thinking about deference to religious autonomy in the definitional setting. Definition is not so much about identifying substantive or functional features of a religion as it is about identifying an independent locus of normative authority and determining under which conditions state deference to that authority is appropriate. One difficulty with Dane's analysis is that it still shares some of the faults of over- and under-inclusiveness of functional definitions. While many religions do assert an authority and sovereignty over their members that transcends the state, such authority is not exercised only by religions. For example, militia movements, the Ku Klux Klan, or communal independence movements such as the recent "Republic of Texas" may function as sovereigns for those who believe in them, but would not likely consider themselves to be religions. Also, some traditional religions, such as Buddhism and Native American religions, do not comply neatly with the image of religion as a locus of authority. Thus there may be limits to the extent to which the picture of competing competences can provide a totally satisfactory approach to problems of definition, but it provides a very useful model that in our view points in the right direction.

---

203. *See id.* at 973.

204. Dane, Note, *supra* note 196, at 367–68. Esbeck's discussion of the Establishment Clause as a structural restraint on the government's power to regulate certain matters relating to religion appears to rely on a similar understanding. *See* Esbeck, *supra* note 72.

205. *See* Dane, Note, *supra* note 195, at 370–373.

206. *Id.* at 370.

207. *Id.* at 371.

208. *Id.*

209. *Id.* at 372.

The Limited Deference Model

The deferentialist approach

We now turn to elaboration of a deferentialist approach to the problem of definition of religion. A deferentialist looks for the solution to the problem not by looking to criteria that can guide external assessments of what constitutes religion or religiousness, but by conceptualizing the problem, following the lead provided by Dane, as one that concerns interrelations between the normative order of the state and independent normative orders constituted by religious communities. In this context, since the state gives high priority to religious freedom, it must therefore give high deference to the internal self-understanding of groups claiming to be religious. That is, limited deference takes the position that in assessing whether a group, action, or claim is religious, there should be an effort to achieve a sympathetic, fair-minded and nondiscriminatory understanding of how the group making religious claims understands itself from an internal point of view.[210] One powerful argument for this approach is that a sensitive external understanding of a community and its beliefs and practices is parasitic on, and largely meaningless without, an understanding of the beliefs, attitudes, thought, and arguments of the community's members as these are practiced and lived from an internal point of view.[211] Even if this were not the case, however, it is clear that the religious beliefs and actions entitled to protection as a matter of constitutional law are not the beliefs and actions as they are understood by outsiders, or as they are understood by a particular portion of a religious community, but beliefs as held by the very person or persons making the religious claims.[212]

---

210. We have here the kind of contrast between internal and external points of view articulated, for example, by H.L.A. Hart and Ronald Dworkin. *See, e.g.,* H.L.A. Hart, *The Concept of Law* 40, 86–88 (1961), or Ronald Dworkin, *Law's Empire* 45–85 (1986).

211. Ronald Dworkin, *Law's Empire* 62–65 (1986).

212. *See, e.g.,* Thomas v. Review Bd. of the Indiana Employment Sec. Div., 450 U.S. 707, 714 (1981) ("[R]eligious beliefs need not be acceptable, logical, consistent, or comprehensible to others to merit First Amendment protection"). One might maintain that it is still a leap to go from saying that beliefs can only be understood by reference to the internal point of view, and that it is subjective beliefs that are protected constitutionally, to the claim that we are constitutionally obligated to defer, subject to very narrow exceptions, to the internal and subjective point of view about what is religious. The worry from the state's perspective is that this would effectively shift control of the availability of religious freedom claims to the claimant, opening up endless risks of strategic behavior and legal manipulation that could ultimately lapse into anarchy. But there is an equally significant counter-worry from the perspective of the religious claimant: namely, that failure to insist on state deference will give the state unfettered discretion to reject sincerely held claims that beliefs are religious. The question is whether the presumption should run in favor of the state or the believer, or how it should be split. As will become clear in what follows, our view is that those holding that their own views are religious are in a better position to assess religiousness than the state, and that the state's interests are adequately protected by a limited inquiry into sincerity and by the fact that religious liberty claims themselves are not absolute. This approach seems consistent with the Supreme Court's approach in other areas of expressive conduct. Thus, in *Spence v. Washington*, 418 U.S. 405 (1974), while the Court noted that it could not "accept the view that an apparently limitless variety of conduct can be labeled 'speech' whenever the person engaging in the conduct intends thereby to express an idea," it went on to hold that conduct is expressive when an "intent to convey a particularized message [is] present" and when the circumstances are such that the message is likely to be understood. *Id.* at 409–11. That is, courts necessarily defer at least in part to the internal and subjective point of view of the party engaging in the conduct to assess

Total deference

Deference can be either absolute—totally accepting of a religious group's self-conception and self-definition—or limited.[213] The "total deference" view has attracted sub-

---

whether it is constitutionally protected.

Similarly, in *Boy Scouts of America v. Dale,* 530 U.S. 640 (2000), the Court made it very clear, over strenuous dissent (*see id.* at 685–88 (Stevens, J., dissenting)), that it is fundamentally inappropriate for the state to engage in its own assessment of the content of an association's beliefs, the consistency of those beliefs, and how they should be expressed. *Id.* at 650–55. Significantly, the Court granted substantial deference to the Boy Scouts' claim that its action in excluding Dale as a leader was expressive in content and was not merely discriminatory conduct. The point in each of these cases is that even where the state may disagree with the conduct in question, protection of core religious and expressive interests requires the state to respect the claimant's sense of the expressive or religious character of its beliefs and conduct, and clearly does not allow it to be treated as an irrelevancy.

213. Indeed, as Perry Dane has shown, there are many ways in which deference can occur. Taking American church property dispute cases as his starting point, he distinguishes a variety of ways in which state institutions, notably courts, can defer to religious norms. First, they can defer by abstaining from involvement in religious disputes. In this regard, the scope of abstention can vary. A court can defer absolutely by simply refusing to hear or take jurisdiction over religious claims, thereby engaging in what Dane calls "adjudicative abstention." Alternatively, a court may take jurisdiction over a claim but engage in "interpretive abstention." Courts refusing to take positions on religious claims because the "law knows no heresy" are engaged in what Dane calls "substantive interpretive abstention." There is also "jurisdictional interpretive abstention," when courts "decline to try to identify the locus of religious authority within a religious community." "Procedural interpretive abstention" is exemplified by cases such as *Serbian Eastern Orthodox Diocese v. Milivojevich*, 426 U.S. 696 (1976), in which the U.S. Supreme Court held that civil courts may not determine whether the religious community's own procedural requirements have been complied with, even though their application may appear arbitrary when viewed from outside. Second, a court may "recognize" religious norms in various ways. Recognition, for Dane, entails "the willingness of the secular legal system at least to cognize one or another relevant religious norm." But as Dane is quick to point out, "[t]o cognize a norm…is not necessarily to yield to it." Where a secular court seeks "to be guided by a religious community's own first-order norms in deciding a question affecting the internal life of that community," it engages in "substantive deference." Rather than trying to interpret the substantive demands of a religious community on its own, a court might instead engage in "decisional deference," by following the "judgment of some designated decisionmaking organ within the religious community." State institutions engaging in various kinds of deference must also decide the extent to which they will defer to a religious communities' efforts to entrench norms and insulate them against change ("constitutive deference") and, on the other hand, to processes of evolution and change within a community ("dynamic deference"). Third, there are questions of the extent to which religious categories can be "integrat[ed]…into [a secular legal regime's]…own legal understanding." That is, within the general domain of recognizing religious norms, there are questions about whether or not such norms should be integrated into or at least accommodated within the secular legal order. Dane suggests that there are four general possibilities: a secular legal regime can reject the religious norm and refuse to integrate it into the legal system ("non-integrative rejection"), as typically happens in "the most patent cases of religious oppression." It can accept the legal norm in the process of rejecting the religious practice ("integrative rejection"), as when the nineteenth-century Supreme Court accepted the Mormon notion of plural marriage to sustain bigamy prosecutions. It can adopt an attitude of abstention, whereby "secular law neither interferes with, nor makes any effort to give secular significance to, the internal affairs of a religious community ("non-integrative acceptance"). And finally, it can seek to "further religious autonomy by translating religious categories into affirmative, and affirming, secular terms ("integrative acceptance"). Perry Dane, The Varieties of Religious Autonomy [hereinafter Varieties], in Church Autonomy: A Comparative Survey 117, 126–31, 134–36 (Gerhard Robbers ed., 2001) [hereinafter Church Autonomy].

A fuller elaboration of limited deference theory needs to take into account Dane's nuanced analysis of the varieties of state deference to the autonomy of religious communities in greater detail than we can provide here. Dane's approach makes it clear that there are several types of autonomy at

stantial criticism in the literature,[214] but is, in fact, a view that virtually no one has held.[215] Behind the rejection of total deference lies a recognition that there are limits on what can be understood as religious, even if those limits are drawn in a way that maximizes freedom of religious belief. In a pluralistic world, protection of religious freedom requires allocating the ultimate "competence of competences" to the secular state. That is, for a variety of reasons both historical and philosophical, we have come to understand that while both religion and the state should be autonomous within their spheres, the state must have ultimate authority to delimit the boundary between those spheres. This is at least in part because of the inherent risks of allowing any particular religion to be judge in its own case vis-a-vis other religions. More generally, it follows from the idea of liberal democracy and the rule of law: everyone has some say in the rule of all, and no individual or group is categorically exempt from the rule of all others. There is a need for some independent, neutral arbiter. This does not mean that arbitrary authority is allocated to the state. The state is entrusted with the responsibility to protect freedom of conscience and religious autonomy consistent with preserving equal freedom for all. To the extent a state breaches this trust, it becomes unjust.

Limited deference theory

Limited deferentialism recognizes the need for some limits on self-definition, and also recognizes the need to allocate the "competence of competences" to the state. But it rejects the conclusion that this allocation is a total abdication of the right of religious communities to have any say in how the boundary is shaped. For reasons set forth in more detail below,[216] the state is obligated to exercise its ultimate line-drawing authority in ways that are neutral (impartial and nondiscriminatory) and that focus on justifiable state concerns rather than on religiousness per se.

In assessing permissible limitations on belief systems, it is vital to remember that from the standpoint of believers, meta-beliefs about whether particular beliefs or belief systems are religious are themselves religious. They are part of the complex of beliefs that constitute a religious worldview, and are woven together in religious life. They are not merely neutral beliefs about which the state is free to make its own decisions. It is not as though the believer and the state agree about the facts of what the beliefs are, and disagree only about whether they should be evaluated as being religious. When the believer sincerely reports that a belief or activity is religious, she is not making her own dispas-

---

play, and the differences need to be taken into account in working out a complete theory of deference. At the same time, his analysis makes it clear that most types of deference he mentions have been constitutionally condoned. It also recognizes, however, that deference is not unlimited. As he indicates, "no method of resolving intra-church disputes affords complete 'autonomy' to a religious community...." *Id.* at 131. His analysis suggests that deference need not take the form of absolute Adjudicative Abstention; none of the major constitutional theories seems to have gone that far. *Id.* at 130. Ultimately, what is most helpful is Dane's working out of the variety of contexts in which limited deference theory may need to be applied.

214. *See, e.g.,* Ingber, *supra* note 71, at 247–49; Hall, *supra* note 98, at 160–61; Mary Harter Mitchell, Secularism in Public Education: The Constitutional Issues, 67 B.U. L. Rev. 603, 631–33(1987); Alfred G. Killilea, Standards for Expanding Freedom of Conscience, 34 U. Pitt. L. Rev. 531, 538–41 (1973).

215. Val D. Ricks, To God God's, to Caesar Caesar's, and to Both the Defining of Religion, 26 Creighton L. Rev. 1053, 1082 (1993). Ricks cites Alfred Killilea on this point, who only raises the point briefly and does not actually espouse it. *Id.,* citing Alfred G. Killilea, Standards for Expanding Freedom of Conscience, 34 U. Pitt. L. Rev. 531, 538–41 (1973).

216. *See* text accompanying notes 257–355, *infra.*

sionate assessment based on the stipulated facts. Rather, she is reporting that she is bound in a distinctive way to the belief or activity. She is reporting not an arbitrary choice, but a committed condition of life going to the core of human dignity. The mere fact that someone sincerely believes that certain conduct or beliefs are religious, and feels bound by them or feels that they are infused with the sacred, constitutes a strong prima facie showing that they really are so. Thus, belief about whether a particular activity, belief, or system of beliefs is religious is itself entitled to religious freedom protection.

The definition question is not a separable threshold question; the same concerns that apply in determining whether to afford religious freedom protection to conduct also apply in determining whether to protect assertions of religious autonomy involved in asserting sincere beliefs about religiousness of conduct. From the standpoint of the sincere believer or belief community, a state determination that one's belief system is not religious is simply phase one in an official discriminatory practice. Indeed, the state's refusal to accept a sincerely held belief as to religiousness adds secular insult to religious injury. It sets the stage for legal encroachment on a perceived religious right by rolling out props that create the illusion that the refusal to take the sincere claims of believers into account is merely a benign manifestation of secular objectivity.[217] Because of the risk that the state may err, and particularly because the error may be motivated by conscious or unconscious religious discrimination, a sincere claim to religiousness needs to be given at least prima facie respect.

Stated differently, the standard approach assumes that the problem of definition of religion poses a normal subsumption problem. That is, one needs to determine whether a certain set of facts (arguably religious belief or conduct) falls under a certain legal rule (one involving religious freedom). The state needs to know whether the belief or conduct is religious in order to determine whether the facts are properly subsumed. The difficulty is that here, subsumption is not a neutral process of legal interpretation, but constitutes a case of the very problem the subsuming rule is intended to address. The limited deference approach is designed to take this unique feature of the definition-of-religion problem into account by assuring that the same standards of religious freedom that apply to ordinary conduct and beliefs are also applied when the state tackles the subsumption problem posed by defining religion.

Limits on religious beliefs about religiousness are no different in principle from limits on other types of religious beliefs, except that the purpose and context of setting limitations on definitions of religion are somewhat different from those of other types of constraints on religious freedom. At first blush, the difference appears to be that being able to define one's beliefs as a religion is a threshold eligibility requirement for asserting substantive religious liberty claims. Viewed in this way, it appears problematic for the state to defer to a religious group's self-understanding of whether it is religious, because this would allow the group to bootstrap itself into eligibility to assert substantive religious freedom claims.

In reality, this characterization of the definition problem depends in part on unjustified statist assumptions and is in any event an overly simplistic analysis of the situation. The statist assumption is that the religious community is only entitled to prevail on a religious claim if the state determines that it is eligible for the protection or favorable treatment in question. But except with respect to benefits that are totally within the state's discretion to grant,[218] this is not the case. Religious freedom is not something

---

217. As will be explained more fully below, the insincere claimant cannot make the same claim. *See* text accompanying notes 285–306, *infra*.

218. This explains why there are some situations, typically involving access to state benefits that the state is not obligated to provide, in which the state may have some justification to claim that it

given to individuals and religious communities by the state; it is an innate human right. Thus, if the state defines religion too narrowly, it violates religious freedom as surely as it would if it admitted a group was religious but then arbitrarily denied its justified religious freedom claim. Indeed, denial of a group's religious status constitutes an even deeper affront to religious freedom because it is not merely the denial of a particular claim, but an across-the-board denial of the right to assert any religious freedom claims. In addition, it is an official state disavowal of the group's claim to equal treatment. Of course, a sincere religious believer can overvalue a religious claim just as the state can undervalue it. But the risks are not symmetrical. Error on the state side results in violation of a religious freedom right. Error in favor of the believer operates like the presumption of innocence; it provides a margin of safety designed to assure full protection of a fundamental right. Limited deference thus provides a better approach by recognizing claims to religious status as being presumptively valid and allowing them to be rebutted only to the extent necessary to protect the inherent demands of religious freedom or some other legitimate overriding interest.

Significantly, not only does state rejection of meta-beliefs about the religiousness of a larger set of beliefs run inherent risks of discrimination; it also overlooks the fact that such meta-beliefs are *internal* beliefs that individuals are entitled to hold regardless of the attitude of the state. From the perspective of the neutral state, they are presumptively entitled to religious freedom protection unless and until they operate to injure or threaten the concrete rights and interests of others. State action in adopting a definition of religion that holds these meta-beliefs to be nonreligious arguably operates to chill exercise of both the meta-beliefs and the entire belief system held by the meta-beliefs to be religious. If the state adopts a specific position on what counts as religion, this inevitably sends a cultural signal that will reinforce the sense that certain types of conduct or belief are religious, and that will create subtle pressures for groups to adapt to that norm. Either beliefs will change to conform to the norm, or the sense that the beliefs are religious will fade. Moreover, when the state bases a definition of religion purely on external definitional criteria—be they substantive, functional, or analogical—it runs the risk of encroaching on presumptively valid rights to adopt and hold mere beliefs. But, in theory at least, mere beliefs, as opposed to conduct, are entitled to absolute protection under the belief/action distinction.[219] Further, when the state applies these definitions to reject claims relating to *conduct* the group believes to be religious, it risks violating standard religious freedom norms applicable to conduct.

Of course, if the state rejects the self-definition of the individual or group for reasons justifiable in terms of general limitations on the freedom of religion—either on grounds inherent in religious freedom norms themselves or on the basis of social interests of sufficient magnitude to override such a fundamental right[220]—it may do so. The

---

alone should have discretion to decide the threshold eligibility question. But note that even here, benefits must be distributed equally. Equality is not a commodity that the state has the right to allocate in an arbitrary manner. Defining religion in a discriminatory manner will violate this constraint. For a discussion of these issues in the context of taxation, see Edward McGlynn Gaffney, Jr., "Exemption of Religious Organizations from Federal Taxation" and "Exemption of Religious Organizations from State and Local Taxation," in this volume.

219. Reynolds v. United States, 98 U.S. 145 (1878); Cantwell v. Connecticut, 310 U.S. 296 (1940).

220. What are characterized here as two separate types of grounds—those inherent in religious freedom and those that override religious freedom—may in fact simply be two aspects of a single basis for limitations of religious freedom. That is, it may be inherent in the idea of religious freedom that it must have limits, and these limits are defined at least in part in terms of overriding interests.

problem with externally imposed definitional criteria is that they ignore the internally held beliefs, and may reject claims of religiousness purely on the basis of an external judgment, even though there is neither an inherent need nor an overriding ground for doing so. The limited deference approach, in contrast, by its very nature takes into account putative religious beliefs, disclaiming them only when doing so is strictly necessary from the perspective of maintaining a general regime of freedom of religion or belief and protection of other legitimate overriding interests.

Thus, limited deferentialism is simply the practical recognition of religious freedom and of the more general obligation of the state to respect religious freedom in all contexts, including that of defining who or what is entitled to the protection. The contents and religiousness of the belief or practice are to be assessed from the vantage point of the believer. In the last analysis, we believe the most credible approach to this problem takes into account, and accords great deference to, the self-concept of the person or organization as to whether it is religious or religiously motivated—but the deference is not unlimited.[221] Thus, the fact that Scientology regards itself as a religion should count heavily in favor of its being regarded as such by others, whereas the fact that Marxism would be distressed by being labeled as a religion should count against its being so treated. This deference makes even more sense in the U.S. context, where a claim to be a religion as opposed to a worldview comes with definite handicaps as well as benefits.[222] It may well be that worldviews should receive equal treatment whether they are religious or not.[223] But this does not imply that all worldviews are necessarily religious. The state, rather than second-guessing the judgment of religious status (and thus interfering or chilling internal religious beliefs), should focus on things from the vantage point appropriate to it as the state: is there some reason why a presumptively valid claim must be rejected, not because of the state's assessment of religiousness, but in light of the state's role of moni-

---

We find it useful, however, to distinguish the two types of grounds. Thus, one can argue that it is inherent in the notion of religious freedom that there may be multiple belief systems needing protection, and that as between competing belief systems, the state in seeking to protect religious freedom "knows no heresy" and cannot differentiate among groups on the basis of religious beliefs. This leads to an insistence on state neutrality. Similarly, it is inherent in the notion of protecting religious freedom that the beliefs actually held by a group are entitled to protection. This is the basis for taking sincerity into account. Overriding state interests, such as protection of public health, safety, or morals, pose different kinds of issues concerning the legitimate ranking of state priorities. In this ranking, protection of religious freedom holds a very high position, but in some circumstances it may be outweighed by other values.

221. *See* Ricks, *supra* note 215, at 1100–07 (outlining approach that partially defers to organization's characterization of itself while allowing courts to consider other facts if necessary to determine organization's status); Note, Religious Exemptions Under the Free Exercise Clause: A Model of Competing Authorities, 90 Yale L.J. 350, 362–76 (1980) (student note by Perry Dane). For another analysis pointing to the significance of state deference to religious understanding, see Gerhard Robbers, Staat und Religion, 59 Veröffentlichungen der Deutschen Staatsrechtslehrer 231, 237, 256 (2000).

222. *See* McConnell, The Problem of Singling Out Religion, *supra* note 188 (noting, *inter alia*, that religions cannot be taught in public schools, officially promoted by government agencies, or bailed out by the government).

223. For this reason, international instruments speak of "freedom of religion *or belief*." *See, e.g.,* International Covenant on Civil and Political Rights, Dec. 19, 1966, 999 U.N.T.S. 171, 178 (entered into force Mar. 23, 1976) [hereinafter ICCPR]. In a similar vein, article 4 of the German Basic Law provides that "Freedom of faith and conscience as well as freedom of creed, religious *or ideological*, are inviolable." Basic Law for the Federal Republic of Germany (official translation published by the Press and Information Office of the Federal Government, revised and updated 1995) (emphasis added).

toring and enforcing the narrow set of limitations that justify it in encroaching on religious beliefs when such beliefs cross the threshold from belief into action?

Context and state purpose

One important qualification needs to be borne in mind before going further. It is vital to remember that the problem of definition takes on different contours in different contexts where different legal purposes are at play.[224] Legal definitions are not merely abstract verbal signs for all seasons and settings; they serve a practical function in helping those who administer laws to make distinctions that are sensible and fair in various legal contexts. In the context of military conscription, the definition of religion and conscience affects who goes to war and who is exempt or at least eligible for alternative service.[225] In the context of labor law, religious beliefs require accommodations not granted to secular convictions;[226] religious employers can engage in preferential treatment in hiring and other employment practices that would constitute religious discrimination if engaged in by a secular employer.[227] In the tax code, definitions of religion and church play complex roles in determining whether institutions are eligible for various tax benefits.[228] Limited deference theory must ultimately be able to take such concerns into account.

The need for definitions of religion and religion-linked terms runs through every chapter in this volume, and of course the chapters do not begin to exhaust the range of contexts in which definitional issues may arise. The quantum of available benefits or the need to have burdens borne may be different in each context, as may the significance of the personal interests involved. In at least some contexts this tends to require differential strictness in definitions. The challenges of enforcement and policing boundaries may also differ from case to case. The dynamics of tax evasion are different from responses to military conscription. Bright lines may be necessary in some areas, such as taxation; case-by-case analysis seems more feasible and more vital in the field of conscientious objection to military service. The intensity of religious convictions at stake varies in different contexts, subtly altering legal equations.

A full account of the ways in which context and purpose affect definitional issues would yield a much richer understanding of the variegated challenges involved in the interaction between sacred and secular across the topography of law. Our sense is that the apparent differences in definitions necessitated by the wide range of purposes and

---

224. The significance of this point was brought home to us following a presentation of an earlier version of this paper in a work-in-progress session at Brigham Young University. We owe special thanks in this regard to Jack Welch and Cliff Fleming. Space and time constraints prevent us from devoting the full attention to this insight that it deserves.

225. *See, e.g.,* United States v. Seeger, 380 U.S. 163 (1965); Welsh v. United States, 398 U.S. 333 (1970), discussed *supra. See also* José de Sousa e Brito, Conscientious Objection, in Lindholm, *supra* note 82.

226. *See, e.g.,* Thomas v. Review Bd. of the Indiana Employment Sec. Div., 450 U.S. 707 (1981) (holding that denial of unemployment benefits violated First Amendment free exercise guarantee where claimant terminated his job because his religious beliefs forbade participation in the production of armaments).

227. *See* Corp. of the Presiding Bishop of the Church of Jesus Christ of Latter-day Saints v. Amos, 483 U.S. 327 (1987).

228. The definitional issues arising in the tax code are addressed in Edward McGlynn Gaffney, Jr., "Exemption of Religious Organizations from Federal Taxation" and "Exemption of Religious Organizations from State and Local Taxation," in this volume.

contexts in which they must be deployed are best conceived in terms of differing inter-actions between deference to self-conceptions of religiousness on the one hand and the distinct constraints of inherent limitations on religious freedom and overriding state in-terests on the other. This approach is more sensitive to religious differences than the other types of definition discussed thus far, yet it is sufficiently flexible to take differing types of state concerns into account. In this chapter, the best we can do is draw atten-tion to this issue and leave more refined treatment for another day.

The conceptual framework of limited deference theory

As indicated above, the starting intuition for limited deference theory is that the def-inition question is really about the interrelations between different, if overlapping and partially interpenetrating, normative worlds—about how the normative order of a state committed to religious freedom recognizes the norms of a religious nomos. Fun-damentally, the state's commitment to religious freedom implies that the autonomy of the religious nomos should be respected. This will include deference to the entire nor-mative structure of the nomos, including meta-norms about the religiousness of indi-vidual norms and the normative structure of the nomos as a whole. It will also include respect in the form of not imposing unnecessary or undue burdens on the nomos. Be-fore turning to the elaboration of specific limitations, it is helpful to note certain impli-cations of this way of conceptualizing the definition problem.

First, the notion of interacting legal orders contains an implicit recognition that the notion of sovereignty is less exclusivist than inhabitants of modern states tend to as-sume,[229] and that at a minimum, these other orders have juridical dignity[230]—the right to be taken seriously by other normative orders, including the state. The positivist cast of the background legal culture leads us to forget that at most stages of human history, multiple overlapping normative orders have been common.[231] In fact, one of the main criticisms of the modern liberal state is that it "limit[s] the domain of law to the law of the state."[232] In short, there is room in and around the modern state for recognition of other normative orders.

Second, the state would in fact be much weaker without such independent norma-tive orders. The reality is that states are highly dependent on them. If the only source of social order were law, and law depended for its viability on the coercive pressure of the state, the state would collapse under the sheer expense and weight of its enforcement mechanisms. In fact, states are highly dependent on voluntary acceptance of their norms, and on independent overlapping normative orders that support compliance with law. The role of religion in this regard has long been recognized. Before Locke it

---

229. *See* Dane, Maps, *supra* note 196, at 973–991.

230. *Id.* at 965.

231. *Id.* at 974–77. Dane gives several examples. The normative orders of various religious com-munities within (and often extending beyond) the borders of a small state are one example. Claims to use land for certain purposes but not others were common in aboriginal societies. Ideas of per-sonal as opposed to territorial jurisdiction constitute another example. The emergence of the mod-ern state can be understood in part as an effort to level some of the complexities of overlapping feu-dal jurisdictions.

232. *Id.* at 964 & n. 17.

was widely assumed that religious homogeneity was required as a kind of social glue to prevent social disintegration.[233] State preemption of this normative space undercuts and enervates the ability of other normative systems to play this critical role. Moreover, it undermines critical sources of meaning and community by weakening key "mediating institutions" in society.[234]

Third, the state that fails to respect other legitimate normative orders would not only be weaker; it would be unjust. This is the core insight behind the doctrine of the limited state. Rousseau was partially right in understanding that law derives its legitimacy from the fact that it is self-given, but his notion of the general will oversimplified the process by which this happens. The process is not merely an assimilation of all particular wills into a society-wide legislator that is given the right to give a common norm to everyone. It often allows individuals to "give themselves" general norms by accepting them as mediated through other normative orders (for example, those of religious life) to which the individual feels strong loyalty and attachment. Particularly in domains involving religion, the process often involves finding norms that are flexible for society in the same way that religious association laws have proven sufficiently flexible in the legal structures used by religious associations in the United States.[235] That is, legitimacy derives from the fact that religious liberty, as a norm that applies to all, allows religious communities broad deference in structuring their own normative worlds. In Rawlsian terms, the consensus is an overlapping one, grounded in multiple normative worlds.[236]

Of course, in a pluralistic world with multiple overlapping normative orders, it is vital to have a neutral institution that can help resolve disputes between normative orders when they come into conflict. This is the ground of the idea of the liberal state:

> [The state] exists just so that persons with different interests can live together in security and equality. It affords the thin, neutral framework that reconciles or mediates conflicting claims and aspirations. That framework is a system of rights, including the allocation of scarce resources and a guarantee of personal dignity and freedom.[237]

There is, of course, a rich variety of theories on the nature of the liberal state, but at its core liberal theory is committed to affording maximal equal autonomy to individuals and groups, subject to the constraint of maintaining ordered liberty. In general, the state defers to the exercise of liberty by individuals in forming their life plans and acting upon them. Even greater protection is afforded to freedom of religion and belief, in part because (1) religious convictions are linked centrally with the core of human dignity;[238]

---

233. W. Cole Durham, Jr., Perspectives on Religious Liberty: A Comparative Framework, in Religious Human Rights in Global Perspective: Legal Perspectives 1, 7 (Johan D. van der Vyver & John Witte, Jr. eds., 1996).

234. Peter L. Berger & Richard John Neuhaus, To Empower People: From State to Civil Society 157 (Michael Novak ed., 2d ed. 1996); W. Cole Durham, Jr. & Alexander Dushku, Traditionalism, Secularism, and the Transformative Dimensions of Religious Institutions, 1993 BYU L. Rev. 421; Adam Seligman, The Idea of Civil Society 44–58 (1992).

235. Rhys H. Williams and John P.N. Massad describe this as a phenomenon of isomorphism. *See* Williams & Massad, "Religious Diversity, Civil Law, and Institutional Isomorphism," in this volume; *see also* text accompanying note 370, *infra*. Our sense is that there is definitely a convergence on legal structures used, but this is a reflection not of being fit into a procrustean bed, but of religious association structures that are sufficiently flexible to accommodate a broad range of organizations.

236. *See* John Rawls, Political Liberalism 133–72 (1993).

237. Dane, Maps, *supra* note 196, at 984.

238. *See* Second Vatican Ecumenical Council, Dignitatis humanae (Declaration on Religious Liberty), in The Documents of Vatican II 675 (Walter M. Abbott & Joseph Gallagher eds, 1966).

(2) they are experienced as "dictates" of conscience that have a higher-order normative force than other beliefs;[239] (3) the legitimacy and stability of the state are weakened to the extent that the state refuses to respect these higher-order norms;[240] (4) recognizing religious freedom helps confirm the limited nature of the state, thereby preventing totalitarian excesses;[241] and (5) religious groups left alone within their sphere historically have played a strong positive role in societies, particularly when constrained from using the "engine of civil policy"[242] to impose their values on other religious communities.

Conceptualizing the definition-of-religion situation in the context of interjurisdictional respect highlights the notion that definition problems typically involve a collision between the norms of a state and the norms of a religious individual or community (including implicit norms such as protecting religiously-based values). This is obvious when a state norm directly collides with a religious directive, but it is also true when state action imposes a burden on a religious community or religiously motivated activity. In such a case, the state is acting on a norm that holds it permissible to ignore or override religious autonomy in the particular situation or class of situations. To focus on norm collisions in this way is not to say that ethical requirements along the lines of religious commandments and normative prescriptions of the type familiar within the Christian, Judaic, and Muslim traditions are necessary to religiousness. It is well known that some religious traditions, such as those of Native Americans, are more attuned to sacred spaces and sites than to sets of behavioral norms.[243] The point is that from the perspective of the state, problems of religious freedom do not arise except where there is a collision or risk of collision[244] between state and religious normative structures and their associated conduct and values. For example, religious freedom claims of Native Americans with respect to sacred spaces only arise when state norms, including liberty norms that allow secular uses of the spaces involved, collide with Native American beliefs about what is necessary to avoid desecration of those spaces. The point here is obvious: where there is no conflict of norms, there is no need to determine whether the conflict implicates religious norms, and therefore the question of the definition of religion does not arise.

A special but very significant case in this category is the situation in which the religious self-understanding is content to accept secular norms and does not feel compelled to object to their imposition on secular grounds. For example, consider the Jewish doctrine of *dina de-malkhuta dina*, according to which "the law of the kingdom is the

---

239. *See* James Madison, A Memorial and Remonstrance, in 8 The Papers of James Madison 299 (Robert A. Rutland et al. eds., Univ. of Chicago Press 1973) (1785); W. Cole Durham, Jr., Religious Liberty and the Call of Conscience, 42 DePaul L. Rev. 71, 79–85(1992) [hereinafter Conscience].

240. *See* Madison, *supra* note 239, at 299; John Rawls, A Theory of Justice 205–11 (1971).

241. Peter L. Berger, The Serendipity of Liberties, in The Structure of Freedom: Correlations, Causes & Cautions 1, 14–16 (Richard John Neuhaus ed., 1991).

242. Madison, *supra* note 239, at 301. Madison actually uses this phrase in the context of arguing for the inappropriateness of the civil magistrate using religion to advance civil ends, but the concern of religion using the state to promote its ends is equally problematic.

243. *See, e.g.,* Smart, *supra* note 4, at 21; *see also* Joseph Epes Brown with Emily Cousins, Teaching Spirits: Understanding Native American Religious Traditions 9–40 (2001); Joseph K. Olupona, Major Issues in the Study of African Traditional Religion, in African Traditional Religions in Contemporary Society 25, 28 (Joseph K. Olupona, ed., 1991).

244. Establishment Clause requirements do not necessarily involve situations in which state coercion is involved, but the clause is clearly aimed at least in part at protection of the normative space and maneuvering room of religious systems. *See* Esbeck, *supra* note 72, at 42–58; Carl H. Esbeck, The American System of Church-State Relations (and Its Bearing on Church Autonomy), in Church Autonomy, *supra* note 213, at 149.

law."[245] This doctrine constitutes a basis within Jewish law for accepting the law of the secular state within which a Jewish community lives. Many religious traditions have beliefs according to which the rule of the civil magistrate is valid within its own sphere.[246] There is also the notion that many areas of law constitute "matters indifferent," which can be resolved one way or another without making any difference from a religious point of view.[247] With respect to each of these religious notions governing which domains of normative space can be abdicated or turned over to the secular state, there are typically religious assessments of where the limits lie. The important point for our purposes is that the state can take such doctrines into account in determining areas where there is no religious basis for holding that the secular normative order of the state should prevail.

While noting areas in which normative collisions do not occur can greatly simplify the task of drawing boundaries in interjurisdictional disputes, it cannot altogether eliminate the difficult boundary questions that are the substantive core of the definition-of-religion problem. Conventional theories dealing with the definition of religion — whether substantive, functional, or analogical — implicitly recognize the practical necessity for a neutral institution to monitor collisions between differing religious worldviews in society, and to delimit the appropriate sphere of its own activity. However, these theories draw the wrong implication from this necessity. They assume that the need to allocate the "competence of competences" — the "jurisdiction to determine jurisdiction"[248] — to the state implies that the question concerning meta-beliefs about whether particular beliefs are religious must be allocated in its entirety to the state, and that any involvement of religious individuals and communities in this question will ultimately undermine the sovereignty of the state. The worry is that if the state does not retain absolute authority in this area, religious groups will become a "law unto themselves."[249]

But this is simply a version of the more general Hobbesian mistake concerning the nature of sovereignty in the social contract. That is, Hobbes maintained that necessities of self-preservation would drive individuals in the state of nature to enter into a social contract whereby they would convey control of their anarchic individual liberty to the Leviathan state, which consequently would become the absolute repository of all sovereignty.[250] Hobbes thought that if the state did not monopolize sovereignty, including sovereignty over construing the scope of its own sovereignty, it would not truly be sov-

---

245. *See* Dane, Maps, *supra* note 196, at 1000–01.

246. *See, e.g.,* Martin Luther, Temporal Authority: To What Extent It Should Be Obeyed, in Religious Pluralism in the West 86 (David George Mullan ed., Blackwell 1998) (1523) [hereinafter Religious Pluralism]; John Locke, Letter Concerning Toleration, in Religious Pluralism 174 (1685).

247. *See* Thomas Aquinas, Summa Theologica, in Introduction to St. Thomas Aquinas 648 (Anton C. Pegis, ed., 1945) (1266–1273) (Question 95, Art. 2).]

248. Perry Dane, Jurisdictionality, Time, and the Legal Imagination, 23 Hofstra L. Rev. 1, 34 (1994) [hereinafter Jurisdictionality].

249. *See* Employment Div., Dep't of Human Resources of Oregon v. Smith, 494 U.S. 872, 890 (1990) ("It may fairly be said that leaving accommodation to the political process will place at a relative disadvantage those religious practices that are not widely engaged in; but that unavoidable consequence of democratic government must be preferred to a system in which each conscience is a law unto itself or in which judges weigh the social importance of all laws against the centrality of all religious beliefs"); Reynolds v. United States, 98 U.S. 145, 166–67 (1878) ("Can a man excuse his [illegal] practices…because of his religious belief? To permit this would be to make the professed doctrines of religious belief superior to the law of the land, and in effect to permit every citizen to become a law unto himself").

250. Thomas Hobbes, Leviathan (ed. 1914) (1651).

ereign[251] and its ability to lift society out of the state of nature would be compromised. If some other institution or group could second-guess the normative determinations of the state—especially its determinations of the scope of its own sovereignty—then either that other group would become the real sovereign, or the state would not truly have escaped the state of nature since its sovereignty would now be subject to the conflicting claims of other groups also in the state of nature (that is, not subject to a sovereign) who were trying to control it.[252]

But at least since Locke it has been clear that there are also less absolutist and far more limited conceptions of the state. It is from these more limited conceptions that modern constitutional governments have evolved. The fact that the state has some sovereignty does not make that sovereignty boundless or exclusive, and the fact that it must be given some power to police boundaries and prevent parties in the state of nature from being judges in their own cases[253] does not imply that the views of those parties as to the nature of their claims must be left totally out of account. Likewise, the fact that the ultimate responsibility for determining the definition of religion necessarily falls to the state does not imply that the state cannot or should not take the self-understanding of a normative community into account in assessing whether it is religious. On the contrary, the idea of the limited state suggests that the state may violate the conditions of its trust if it exercises its ultimate competence in ways that are not maximally respectful of the beliefs (including meta-beliefs about religiousness) of the individuals and subcommunities within its jurisdiction. There may be limitations on its ability to accept religious self-definitions as they become operative in practice, but such limitations must be narrowly restricted and strictly justified, because of the significance of the rights at stake and because of the risk that the secular state may not understand the importance of the religious values involved or may administer rights in discriminatory ways.

Our view is that limited deference theory helps to explain Greenwalt's intuition that individual views of the nature of religion should be taken into account but not be controlling. Greenwalt states the point as follows:

> One particular question is how much an individual's own view of what is religious and what is nonreligious should matter. I am certain it should not always be controlling; a person should not receive more or less protection because of his or her idiosyncratic view of the boundaries of religion.... In my defense of an "analogical" approach to defining religion, I have claimed that no particular factor, like belief in God or corporate worship, is necessary. An individual's own idea of religion may show which factors he or she takes as most important, and that may be relevant to a court. Nevertheless, judicial resolution of

---

251. *Id.*, chapter XVIII.

252. *See id.*, chapter XVIII ("Eighthly, is annexed to the Soveraigntie, the Right of Judicature; that is to say, of hearing and deciding all Controversies, which may arise concerning Law, either Civill, or Naturall, or concerning Fact. For without the decision of the Controversies, there is no protection of one Subject, against the injuries of another; the Lawes concerning *Meum* and *Tuum* are in vaine; and to every man remaineth, from that naturall and necessary appetite of his own conservation, the right of protecting himselfe by his private strength, which is the condition of Warre; and contrary to the end for which every Common-wealth is instituted").

253. Kant saw the fact that individuals in the state of nature were necessarily judges in their own cases as a critical defect in the state of nature, and the introduction of neutral judicial authority as a key feature of civil society. *See* Immanuel Kant, The Metaphysical Elements of Justice 56–58 (John Ladd trans., Macmillan, 1965) (1797).

what counts as religious should not depend finally on what an individual claimant regards as religious.[254]

In our view, this analysis accurately senses the significance of deferring to religious believers, but it stops short of giving them adequate deference because of a misperception of the demands of the "competence of competence" issue. We agree that self-definition "should not always be controlling," but we do not believe this is because "a person should not receive more or less protection because of his or her idiosyncratic view of the boundaries of religion." Any theory of definition of religion will decide whether or not to give individuals and groups religious freedom protections based on differences of religious belief. The question is whether it is better for the state to decide the standard in terms of what *it* believes religion is, or for it to respect what those making religious freedom claims believe it is, subject to normal constraints on the limits of religious freedom. An unduly narrow state definition of religion is just as much a denial of religious freedom as a state failure to respect religious freedom on any other ground. The appropriate inquiry is not about whose judgment of religiousness is correct, but about whether there is an inherent limit on religious freedom or an overriding state concern that necessitates rejecting the self-definition.

One final aspect of conceptualizing the definition problem in terms of interjurisdictionality involves the possibility of mistakes in determining the content of norms. The point is that "a court with jurisdiction has the right to be wrong and still be authoritative. That is, in a sense, the essence of authority. A court without such authority, without jurisdiction, does not even have the right to be right."[255] Stated differently, a court with jurisdiction "has the right to be wrong, but only while it continues to act within its jurisdiction."[256] The significance for limited deference theory is as follows. There is something profoundly troubling about having the institutions of the secular state making judgements about the nature of religion. There are strong reasons to think this task is beyond the ability of the secular state, both because of the hazards of discrimination against lesser known groups and because of the inability of an outsider to fully understand a religious nomos from the internal point of view. For that reason, there should be limits on the competence (jurisdiction) of the secular state to assess these issues. Attempts to decide the question of religiousness from the external point of view arguably breach this jurisdictional limit. They don't even have the "right to be right," let alone the "right to be wrong." Limited deference theory either entirely obviates or at least radically reduces the need to second-guess religious self-definition. In this sense, it is narrowly tailored to allow maximal protection of religious freedom.

Limited deference theory and the constitutional protection of religious autonomy

At the constitutional level, limited deference theory is the extension of the core principles behind constitutional protection of religious autonomy to the problem of defining religious freedom itself. The principles of religious autonomy are embedded in the long line of American cases stretching back to *Watson v. Jones*[257] regarding the

---

254. Greenwalt, *supra* note 173, at 464.

255. Dane, Jurisdictionality, *supra* note 248, at 23.

256. *Id.* at 49.

257. 80 U.S. (15 Wall.) 679, 725–33 (1872) (rejecting implied trust principles because they required assessment of departure from doctrine).

approach the state should take to resolve various kinds of religious disputes. Case law in this area has established broad protections for religious autonomy by requiring judicial abstention from disputes regarding issues of doctrine,[258] organizational structure,[259] personnel issues,[260] and matters related to membership and discipline.[261] Like limited deference theory, the constitutional doctrine of religious autonomy requires state institutions to defer to religious self-conceptions, particularly in areas going to the core nature and identity of the religious nomos. Also like limited deference theory, it does not leave religious autonomy absolutely unfettered. For example, fraudulent or collusive conduct remains within state purview, although conduct that appears arbitrary from a secular perspective falls within the domain protected by religious autonomy.[262]

As Dane has noted, "[t]he problem of 'religious autonomy' straddles the Establishment and Free Exercise Clauses...."[263] The Supreme Court, in deciding religious autonomy cases, has based its holdings on the First Amendment generally and has avoided stating expressly whether they are based on the Free Exercise or the Establishment Clause.[264] Scholars have argued for both conclusions.[265] Douglas Laycock argued in a 1981 article that it would be mistaken to base the holdings on the Establishment Clause "because that clause forbids support of religion, not interference with religion."[266] Further, in his view, "the right to autonomy exists even if the interference is not accompanied by government support, and even if the government requires church 'entanglement' with a private secular organization instead of with the government itself."[267]

The strength of this position has been weakened in two respects. First, Laycock's interpretation of the Establishment Clause is no longer linked so exclusively to the no-

---

258. *See, e.g.,* Thomas v. Review Bd. of the Indiana Employment Sec. Div., 450 U.S. 707, 715–16 (1981); Maryland & Va. Eldership v. Church of God, 396 U.S. 367, 368 (1970) (courts may not resolve religious controversies).

259. *See, e.g.,* Serbian East Orthodox Diocese v. Milivojevich, 426 U.S. 696, 708–24 (1976); Presbyterian Church v. Mary Elizabeth Blue Hull Memorial Presbyterian Church, 393 U.S. 440, 449–51 (1969); Kreshik v. St. Nicholas Cathedral, 363 U.S. 190, 191 (1960); Kedroff v. St. Nicholas Cathedral, 344 U.S. 94, 119 (1952); Shepard v. Barkley, 247 U.S. 1, 2 (1918).

260. *See, e.g.,* Serbian East Orthodox Diocese v. Milivojevich, 426 U.S. 696, 708–20 (1976); Kedroff v. St. Nicholas Cathedral, 344 U.S. 94, 116 (1952); Gonzalez v. Roman Catholic Archibishop, 280 U.S. 1, 16 (1929); NLRB v. Catholic Bishop, 440 U.S. 490, 501–04 (1979); Cummings v. Missouri, 71 U.S. (4 Wall.) 277 (1872).

261. *See, e.g.,* Watson v. Jones, 80 U.S. (15 Wall.) 679, 733 (1872); *cf.* Order of St. Benedict v. Steinhauser, 234 U.S. 640, 647–51 (1914) (voluntarily accepted vow of poverty not contrary to religious freedom); Bouldin v. Alexander, 82 U.S. (15 Wall.) 131, 139–40 (1872).

262. Jones v. Wolf, 443 U.S. 595, 609 n.8 (1979); Serbian East Orthodox Diocese v. Milivojevich, 426 U.S. 696, 713 (1976); Gonzales v. Roman Catholic Archbishop, 280 U.S. 1 (1929).

263. Dane, Varieties, *supra* note 213, at 121.

264. Esbeck, *supra* note 72, at 50 & n.204. In the *Smith* case, the Court cites the religious autonomy cases in the context of a passage that begins by talking about the content of free exercise, but then shifts to talking about what "[t]he *First Amendment* obviously excludes" before citing the religious autonomy cases. *See* Employment Div., Dep't of Human Resources of Oregon v. Smith, 494 U.S. 872, 877 (1990).

265. That is, some view religious autonomy as fundamentally a matter of free exercise. *See, e.g.,* Erwin Chemerinsky, Interpreting the Constitution 1035 n.113 (1987); Douglas Laycock, Towards a General Theory of the Religion Clauses: The Case of Church Labor Relations and the Right to Church Autonomy: 81 Colum. L. Rev. 1373 (1981) [hereinafter General Theory]. Others, however, see it as an Establishment Clause matter. Esbeck, *supra* note 72, at 44–51; Tribe, *supra* note 69, § 14-11, at 1231–42.

266. Laycock, General Theory, *supra* note 265, at 1416.

267. *Id.* at 1416–17.

support or no-aid view. In a recent article, he has contended that the fundamental Establishment Clause concern is with "minimizing government influence on religious choices...."[268] Protection of religious autonomy can easily be reconciled with this view of the Establishment Clause. Second, the entire lay of the land in First Amendment jurisprudence was shifted seismically by the 1990 *Smith* decision.[269] Laycock's 1981 article assumed a much stronger Free Exercise Clause. It was much easier in 1981 to allocate protection of religious autonomy to that clause, when it appeared that the scope of such protection would be as strong or even stronger under free exercise as under Establishment Clause principles—especially since that allocation would correspond more naturally to an intuitive lay sense of the two clauses' meaning. After *Smith*, however, the attractiveness of an Establishment Clause grounding deserves greater attention.

The alternative view has been argued perhaps most persuasively by Esbeck. In his view, while the Free Exercise Clause is about rights, the Establishment Clause is a structural provision about the limits of state power and jurisdiction.[270] It places matters that are "inherently religious" outside the jurisdiction of the state.[271] Since issues traditionally protected by religious autonomy are all inherently religious, they fall outside state competence. Religious autonomy decisions that have required state abstention from resolution of these issues are best explained, Esbeck maintains, as a reflection of the structural character of the Establishment Clause.[272] This avoids the need to generate complex "group rights" theories to explain what is going on in these cases.[273] The structural interpretation of nonestablishment makes better sense of constitutional text and history, and it squares with the way in which courts tend to defer to religious organizations in recognizing their juridical status.[274] It also helps to explain the ban on judicial inquiry into the centrality of religious doctrines that might be the basis for religious freedom claims.[275]

Note that the structural approach comports naturally with the interjurisdictional approach that lies behind limited deference theory. In Esbeck's words,

> [a]n important consequence of attributing structural characteristics to the Establishment Clause is that it acknowledges the existence of a competency centered in religion that is on a plane with that of civil government. Stated differently, the Establishment Clause presupposes a constitutional model consisting of two spheres of competence: government and religion. The subject matters that the Clause sets apart from the sphere of civil government—and thereby

---

268. Douglas Laycock, The Underlying Unity of Separation and Neutrality, 46 Emory L.J. 43, 70 (1997).

269. Employment Div., Dep't of Human Resources of Oregon v. Smith, 494 U.S. 872, 890 (1990).

270. Esbeck, *supra* note 72, at 2. Historically, it might be more accurate to note that both free exercise and establishment were conceptualized as limitations on Congressional power rather than as rights. When the First Amendment said, "*Congress shall make no law* respecting an establishment of religion or prohibiting the free exercise thereof," it was depriving Congress of power with respect to both dimensions of the Religion Clause. *See* Steven Smith, Foreordained Failure 49 (1995). But it is of course much easier to convert denial of power to prohibit free exercise into a right than to do the same with the clearly much more structural Establishment Clause.

271. *Id.* at 105–09.

272. *Id.* at 44–51.

273. *Id.* at 51–54.

274. *Id.* at 14–25, 54–55.

275. *Id.* at 56–57, relying inter alia on Employment Div., Dep't of Human Resources of Oregon v. Smith, 494 U.S. 872, 887 (1990).

leaves to the sphere of religion—are those topics "respecting an establishment of religion"....[276]

Limited deference theory holds that religious autonomy extends to determining what counts as religious within a religious community. Applying Esbeck's structural view of the Establishment Clause, the state's obligation to defer to a religious community's definition of its own religiousness reflects the fact that meta-beliefs about religiousness lie outside civil jurisdiction, except where there is insincerity or fraud or when other overriding considerations are present. We cannot claim that Esbeck would see the extension of his theory into the definitional realm the same way we do, or that his approach and ours would reach the same result in all cases. But enough has been said to suggest the connection.

Regardless of how one thinks the religious autonomy cases are anchored in the First Amendment—whether in free exercise, nonestablishment, or both—they are clearly moored in the Religion Clauses taken as a whole. The Supreme Court has never suggested that in retrenching from earlier case law in the *Smith* decision it was narrowing its religious autonomy precedents. Indeed, in the *Smith* case itself the Court cites the key religious autonomy cases for the proposition that "government may not...lend its power to one or the other side in controversies over religious authority or dogma."[277] As Dane has noted, religious autonomy claims, unlike exemption claims, "do not depend for their force on the specific norms of a particular religious community,"[278] and accordingly are not problematic in the way that religion-based exemptions were for the *Smith* court.[279] Religious groups may employ their autonomy to structure their affairs in various ways, just as religious individuals may invoke the general right to religious freedom to protect particular practices. In neither case, however, is religious autonomy or religious freedom anything but a general liberty right equally accessible to all. This is part of the structure of liberty norms; they authorize those claiming them to adhere to various values and to engage in various kinds of activities. Similarly, the obligation of the state to defer—within limits—to sincerely held beliefs about religiousness is an obligation that applies across the board to all religious communities. Different religious groups may have slightly different conceptions of religiousness which the state will be obligated to respect, but this does not make each group a "law unto itself." Rather, it reflects the fact that different groups are entitled to lay equal claim to a fundamental law of liberty. Those not recognized by the state as religions are those that either do not consider their own views religious or are excluded because of inherent or overriding limits on religious freedom.

---

276. *Id.* at 10 (footnotes omitted). As a historical matter, the Establishment Clause as originally drafted may have been more about federalism (i.e., about preventing the federal government from interfering with state establishments) than about general constraints on the power of the state to assert jurisdiction over religion. *See, e.g.*, Akhil Reed Amar, The Bill of Rights 32–45 (1998). In the aftermath of incorporation, however, the Establishment Clause has acquired the more generalized jurisdictional meaning.

277. 494 U.S. at 877. Unfortunately, some courts have confused the references to "general and neutral laws" in *Smith* with references to "neutral principles" in *Jones v. Wolf*, 443 U.S. 595 (1979), with the result that courts improperly assume that they are free to override religious autonomy whenever a "general and neutral law" is involved. *See* Frederick Mark Gedicks, Towards a Defensible Free Exercise Doctrine, 69 Geo. Wash. L. Rev. 925, 943 & n.n. 98–99 (2000). This turns the original aim of the never-withdrawn "neutral principles" method of *Jones* on its head. There the aim is to protect religious autonomy by assuring that if religious organizations exercise their autonomy in sufficiently clear language, neutral principles of interpretation drawn from contracts, wills, and the like can be applied to protect the religious autonomy thus exercised.

278. Dane, Varieties, *supra* note 213, at 121; *see id.* at 122 n. 19.

279. *Id.*

Note that particularly where definition of religion is the issue, the relevant inquiry is not whether particular conduct is protected by free exercise rights, but whether a definition that excludes a group or groups claiming religiousness is strictly necessary. That is, the state is proposing a classification that will include some groups within the class of groups entitled to religious freedom protections, and it will exclude others. Even after the *Smith* decision jettisoned the compelling state interest test for most purposes under the Free Exercise Clause, "governmental classifications based on religion" remain subject to strict scrutiny.[280] Laws that target groups on the basis of religion are invalid.[281] A definition of religion that excludes a particular group from the religious category has that as its object; the exclusion is not merely an incidental effect of the legislation.[282] Since those who are excluded are often unpopular, unfamiliar, and lacking in political power, it is particularly important that potential discrimination in this area be subject to strict scrutiny. As the Supreme Court emphasized in *Church of the Lukumi Babalu Aye*, "the Free Exercise Clause protects against governmental hostility which is masked, as well as overt. 'The Court must survey meticulously the circumstances of governmental categories to eliminate, as it were, religious gerrymanders.'"[283] Resolution of the definitional issue itself must be strictly necessary; the question remains subject to strict scrutiny.[284]

At the constitutional level, then, the Court's religious autonomy jurisprudence points toward a limited deference approach to the problem of definition. The relevant case law holds that state institutions may not intervene in matters of doctrine and other areas of religious autonomy. But since definitional claims are themselves part of the belief systems, they qualify as religious and are also entitled to deference (within limits that will be described in more detail below). Limited deference theory thus mirrors in both strategy and substance the constitutional insistence on protection of religious autonomy.

Limitations on the state obligation to defer to religious self-conceptions

Reorientation of the definition of religion problem to focus on permissible state limits on self-definition has the obvious consequence that the functional outcome of the approach will ultimately depend heavily on how the limits are interpreted and applied. In many respects the limits are derived from and interconnected with the general conceptual approach and constitutional considerations described above.[285] We anticipate that there could be variants of the limited deferentialist approach, just as there are vari-

---

280. 494 U.S. at 886 n.3.

281. Church of the Lukumi Babalu Aye, Inc. v. City of Hialeah, 508 U.S. 520, 534 (1993).

282. In contrast, the *Smith* decision reasoned that the ban on prohibiting the free exercise of religion did not extend to legislation that imposed incidental effects on religion; it merely applied to legislative prescriptions or prohibitions that had classification on the basis of discrimination as an objective. 494 U.S. at 878.

283. Church of the Lukumi Babalu Aye, Inc. v. City of Hialeah, 508 U.S. 520, 534 (1993), *citing* Walz v. Tax Comm'n of New York City, 397 U.S. 664, 696 (1970) (Harlan, J., concurring).

284. Strict scrutiny will contribute to affording maximal (but not unlimited) deference by requiring great caution in assessing whether the definition proposed by a group is sincere or dishonest, and whether it is genuinely nondiscriminatory. It can also examine whether, in the particular context, rejecting a particular definition is strictly necessary in terms of the seriousness and imminence of the likely threat of a proposed definition to other necessary responsibilities of the state.

285. *See* text accompanying notes 229–284, *supra*.

ations of substantive, functional, and analogical approaches to the definition problem. Our aim here is to give an overview and general justification for the approach, recognizing that refinements may be necessary and that variants may be developed.

Inherent limitations

We believe that grounds for limiting state deference to putative definitions of religion proposed by religious groups fall into two categories: those inherent in religious freedom and those that override it. To some extent these blend into each other, but it will be helpful to treat them separately. For present purposes, inherent limitations primarily concern constraints relating to the issues of sincerity and fraud, which respectively legitimize or vitiate the right to assert religious claims. Limitations based on overriding state interests constitute either constraints on the way the state can exercise its power based on considerations of justice or assessment of when other state interests override religious freedom claims. We turn first to inherent limitations.

Sincerity

The first of these is sincerity, appropriately understood.[286] Sincerity plays a somewhat different role in limited deference theory than it does with respect to other approaches to definition of religion. Normally, the definition question is resolved as an initial threshold matter, and sincerity arises as an independent secondary issue that affects eligibility to make claims that have been prequalified as religious. There is an obvious logic to this. Sincerity cannot transmute a secular claim into a religious claim, and while insincerity may negate the viability of a religious claim, it does not thereby make the claim nonreligious. But the situation is different in limited deference theory, because the definition itself is left at least partly in the hands of the party claiming religiousness. There is no independent external set of criteria that can be applied to complete the determination of religiousness before the claimant comes into the picture. Deference is accorded not only to the claimant's substantive beliefs, but also to the claimant's meta-beliefs about the religiousness of an entire belief system. Whatever questions may exist about the appropriateness of state inquiry into sincerity in other contexts,[287] the need to take it into account in limited deference analysis in the very process of defining religion is unavoidable.

To see why this is the case, it is necessary to recall that the claims that are to be protected by religious freedom have grown out of the actual normative order adhered to by a religious individual or group.[288] The point from an interjurisdictional perspective is sim-

---

286. Issues of sincerity have posed thorny problems ever since they were first confronted in *United States v. Ballard*, 322 U.S. 78 (1944).

287. Ever since Justice Jackson questioned the appropriateness of engaging in sincerity analysis in religious fraud prosecutions, there have been residual questions about the constitutional permissibility of such inquiry. *See* United States v. Ballard, 322 U.S. 78, 92-93 (1944) (Jackson, J., dissenting); Marjorie Heins, "Other People's Faiths": The Scientology Litigation and the Justiciability of Religious Fraud, 9 Hastings Const. L.Q. 153 (1981); Kent Greenawalt, Five Questions About Religion Judges are Afraid to Ask 10, unpublished manuscript cited by Horwitz, *supra* note 171, at 146. One of the risks in this area is that just as the state can err in making biased assessments of religiousness, so it can make biased findings of insincerity. Theoretically, this might call for a regress of presumptions—presumption of sincerity, of sincerity of profession of sincerity, etc. In the end, one has to rely on the fact that making findings of sincerity is a normal judicial task involving factors sufficiently distinct from religious belief that the margin of judicial error is acceptable.

288. *See* text accompanying notes 257–285, *supra*.

ply that there is no obligation to protect or defer to pseudo-norms or beliefs that a claimant—whether individual or group—does not hold.[289] This reasoning applies to meta-beliefs about whether other norms in a system of beliefs are religious. The state has no obligation to defer, even in part, to claims of religiousness that are not sincerely held.

The issue is somewhat more complex in group settings because the degree of sincerity may vary within the group. Some members may be sincere and others not. Those who are not may be either leaders or peripheral members. There may be individuals who have lapsed entirely from belief, individuals who fall short of the belief system's aspirations, and so forth. Even if the leader is cynical or insincere, followers may believe nonetheless, either because they don't know about the leader's insincerity or because for them the belief system has acquired a life of its own. Such complexities raise the issue of how one assesses the sincerity of an entire group's beliefs,[290] but they are not fundamentally different from those one encounters in ascribing liability to a group. As a practical matter, there ought to be at least prima facie deference to the beliefs of a group, at least where failure to do so could operate to deprive sincere believers of religious freedom rights.

To establish sincerity, a claimant must hold a belief honestly and in good faith.[291] It is reasonable to place the burden of showing sincerity on the claimant. Since fact finders cannot read minds, the claimant needs to provide evidence, many types of which can be used for this purpose.[292] Most obviously, an individual or representatives of a group can testify themselves or provide expert testimony describing the beliefs in question. In the context of defining religion, it is the claimant's reasons for concluding that beliefs are religious that will be critical. To make a credible and sincerely held claim that a particular belief or practice is religious, the claimant will need to explain why these beliefs are similar to others that would be recognized as religious or fit into an underinclusive definition.[293] While the criteria of similarity and analogy can be elaborated, the claimant may not make a belief or practice religious by definitional fiat. Limited deferentialism demands state respect for sincere claims of religiousness, but this is not an open invitation to arbitrarily define anything as religion. At the same time, the state's inquiry into sincerity is independent from, and should not be allowed to collapse into, an assessment of the substance or credibility of the claims of religiousness. Religion is a vague

---

289. Stephen Senn, The Prosecution of Religious Fraud, 17 Fla. St. U.L. Rev. 325, (1990), citing Frazee v. Illinois Dep't. of Employment Sec., 489 U.S. 829 (1989); Patrick v. Le Fevre, 745 F.2d 153, 157 (2d Cir. 1984) ("[B]elief must be sincerely held and religious in nature to be accorded first amendment protection"); Childs v. Duckworth, 705 F.2d 915, 921 (7th Cir. 1983) ("The exercise of beliefs, insincerely held, cannot be used as a masquerade to hold meetings presumably protected by the First Amendment"); International Soc'y for Krishna Consciousness, Inc. v. Barber, 650 F.2d 430 (2d Cir. 1981); Founding Church of Scientology v. United States, 409 F.2d 1146, 1160, 1165 (D.C. Cir.), cert. denied, 396 U.S. 963 (1969); see also Tribe, supra note 69, § 14-12; Note, Burdens on the Free Exercise of Religion: A Subjective Alternative, 102 Harv. L. Rev. 1258, 1271–72 (1989) [hereinafter Note, Burdens on Free Exercise].

290. For discussion of some of these complexities, see Horwitz, supra note 171, at 148.

291. See United States v. Seeger, 380 U.S. 163, 185 (1965) (recognizing that "while the 'truth' of a belief is not open to question, there remains the significant question of whether it is 'truly held.' This is the threshold question of sincerity which must be resolved in every case").

292. For more detailed analysis of the types of factors that have been used to demonstrate or rebut sincerity, many of which are problematic, see Horwitz, supra note 171, at 146–150 (1997); Senn, supra note 289, at 341–42.

293. The Supreme Court has noted that "[o]ne can, of course, imagine an asserted claim so bizarre, so clearly nonreligious in motivation, as not to be entitled to protection under the Free Exercise Clause." Thomas v. Review Bd. of Indiana Employment Sec. Div., 450 U.S. 707, 715 (1981).

term in the natural language of both state and religious normative orders, but the fact that a term is vague does not make it infinitely elastic.

The practical question is how this vague term should be construed and applied. The only feasible starting point for the claimant seeking to show that a borderline belief system is indeed religious is either to show that it fits into an underinclusive substantive or functional definition or to explain how its beliefs are similar to those of acknowledged religions. In doing so, the claimant is free to draw on any of the approaches to definition of religion that have been described in this chapter, or on others that he, she, or it may develop. The claimant needs to show a sincere belief in its belief system, and as a practical matter, this will generally entail demonstrating sincere belief in its being sufficiently similar to other acknowledged religions in at least some respects so as to make it discriminatory for the state to make a determination of nonreligiousness. The state will then need to evaluate the sincerity of these claims on the basis of factors that can be examined without evaluating the truth of the meta-beliefs about religiousness that are involved, as is more fully described in the next section of this chapter. As stated by the Supreme Court in *United States v. Seeger*, the term "religion" — or its adjectival equivalent, "religious" — is to be construed to indicate whether "the beliefs professed by a claimant are sincerely held and whether they are, in [the claimant's] own scheme of things, religious."[294] The need to be able to sincerely explain how the proposed activity or belief can be subsumed under the term "religion" as used in natural language will mean that the limited deference approach will function much like the analogical approach in practice. But it does not simply collapse into the analogical method, because it defers to sincere claims of religiousness held by believers rather than leaving the ultimate decision of religiousness totally in the hands of the state.

Fraud and strategic behavior

In many ways, sincerity and fraud are two sides of the same fundamental issue. If a claim is sincerely held, the scienter requirement of fraud will be negated. If the claim is not sincerely held, making it is inherently a form of fraud, or at least attempted fraud or moral dishonesty. The deference in limited deference theory is to actual beliefs that are actually held, not to putative religious norms advanced on fraudulent or dishonest grounds (except to the extent there is some margin of error to give the benefit of the doubt where there is uncertainty as to sincerity). Efforts to use the "cloak of religion" in support of self-serving strategic behavior are undeserving of protection for the same reason.

Generally speaking, insincerity or fraud can take a number of forms. (1) A claimant may feign belief in the actual norms or other beliefs of an actual normative community. (2) The claims may relate to an authentic norm and community in which the party's claim to membership is really made for strategic reasons.[295] (3) The claimed beliefs may

---

294. 380 U.S. 163, 185 (1965).

295. This is suggested by a hypothetical advanced by Kent Greenawalt, in which a prisoner, whose father was Jewish but who was raised as a Christian by a Christian mother and stepfather, claimed entitlement to a Jewish dinner. Greenawalt uses this as an example indicating that "[l]awyers may need to learn that people can have multiple and shifting identities, that 'sincerity' need not lock them into one religious affiliation and set of doctrinal propositions." Kent Greenawalt, *supra* note 173, at 463. The possibility of "multiple and shifting identities" needs to be taken seriously, but if the individual had expressed no qualms about eating non-kosher food the previous day, had joked about "getting a Jewish meal" with other prisoners in the afternoon, and gave no other indications thereafter of following a Jewish life, one would have a very strong case that the claim of Jewish affiliation was insincere. If the conversation with the other prisoners was a very earnest assertion that, "my father was Jewish, and I'm as entitled to a fancy meal as any other Jewish

relate to an inauthentic religion in which no one sincerely believes, created as a pretext for other strategic purposes such as making a profit, avoiding taxes, etc. (4) An individual could sincerely believe in a norm followed by a religious group, but could know that the particular norm was not one that the group's meta-beliefs qualified as being religious. This last case raises special complexities because it is possible for an individual to have idiosyncratic but sincere convictions about what is religious that diverge from his or her community's meta-beliefs concerning religiousness, just as he or she may have stricter or more liberal beliefs than other members of the community.[296]

Whatever the nature of the fraudulent or insincere beliefs in a particular case, they are not "truly held" and thus are not among those that the state is obliged to respect. The state has a strong interest in rooting out fraudulent claims, both because they result in undeserved favorable treatment and because if fraud is protected, it is likely to attract additional strategic behavior which can ultimately reduce general confidence and detract from the inherent credibility of broad religious freedom protections. Temptations toward strategic behavior can also distort the authenticity of otherwise genuine and genuinely held beliefs.

Since the Supreme Court's decision in *United States. v. Ballard*,[297] however, it has been clear that it is often difficult to ascertain fraud or insincerity in a particular case without assessing the bona fides of the religious belief. In particular, Justice Jackson's dissent contended that judgments about the credibility of a sincerity claim are often linked as a practical matter with assessments of the plausibility of the belief system.[298] As noted above,[299] however, an assessment of sincerity is really unavoidable in limited deference theory. Applying this theory helps reduce the risk of engaging in state assessment of the veracity of beliefs in the guise of making sincerity findings, because the claimant in explaining the religiousness of those beliefs is likely to emphasize their similarity to others that are more familiar, thereby helping to reduce the plausibility gap. Moreover, the very structure of limited deference analysis helps sensitize fact finders to the fact that they should avoid second-guessing religious judgments.

It is true that fact finders will almost unavoidably tend to apply a kind of sliding scale—"the more unusual or self-serving the claim, the greater the scrutiny."[300] But stricter scrutiny of a claim's sincerity does not necessarily mean that the state is questioning the belief itself. While it may be harder to determine whether a less plausible belief is sincerely held, the inquiries into credibility and sincerity are in fact independent of each other. As described in the next paragraphs, several factors that bear on sincerity can be examined without probing the veracity or credibility of beliefs. Even if this were not the

---

prisoner," the case would be closer. In this situation, the individual does not qualify technically as a member of the Jewish community under the norms of the community (his father, not his mother, was Jewish), but he sincerely though mistakenly believes that he can claim membership, and he sincerely believes he is as entitled as other imperfectly faithful Jews (prison is not a normal consequence of strict adherence to Jewish law) to a Jewish meal as a result. But if this line of reasoning were to support a finding of sincerity, a lapsed Jehovah's Witness would be as entitled to make a conscientious claim as the super-believing Jehovah's Witness in *Thomas v. Review Board*, 450 U.S. 707 (1981). At bottom, what one has in this variant is a sincere but secular equal protection claim made by a nonbeliever who happens to be able to invoke a religious characteristic as a basis for inclusion in a class entitled to religious benefits.

296. *See, e.g.,* Thomas v. Review Bd. of the Indiana Employment Sec. Div., 450 U.S. 707 (1981).
297. 322 U.S. 78 (1944).
298. 322 U.S. at 92–93.
299. *See* the preceding section on sincerity, *supra.*
300. Note, Burdens on the Free Exercise of Religion, *supra* note 289, at 1271.

case, the focus on sincerity may be salutary. And even if fact finders take implausibility into account as partial evidence of a claim's insincerity, they will still hesitate to dismiss it because of the possibility that the claim, however implausible, may be sincere. Particularly where the method of analysis itself encourages self-scrutiny designed to avoid discriminatory rejection of beliefs, the valid interest in avoiding fraud affords some latitude for more careful examination of sincerity when circumstances are present that would normally prompt suspicion—for instance, inducement to strategic behavior or unusual conduct. Stricter scrutiny is not the same as state rejection of religious beliefs.

In assessing sincerity in the context of definition of religion, there are many factors that may be examined without evaluating the truth of the substantive beliefs or meta-beliefs of a particular belief system. These are essentially the same as factors that are legitimate in other contexts such as prosecuting religious fraud[301] or assessing eligibility for various types of religious exemptions,[302] taking into account the uniqueness of the definition of religion context and making certain that examination of such factors does not become a cover for discrimination or for inquiry into the veracity of beliefs.

Evidence of inconsistent behavior or statements can be taken into account, though care must be taken to assure that such inconsistency is not the reflection of a sincere change of views.[303] A claimant may also be able to defuse suspicions of secular strategic behavior by demonstrating that denial of a claim of religiousness will result in a substantial burden on belief, or that the claimant if found religious is likely to undertake some kind of alternative service or confer some other social benefit that shows that classification as religious is probably not being sought for strategic reasons.[304] Evidence of secular fraud, such as proof that funds ostensibly meant for a religious purpose are diverted to personal use, obviously raises suspicions. Finally, evidence of "attempts to cover up activities suggesting fraud [may be considered], though mere evidence of an effort to conceal spiritual doubt should not be permitted."[305] This list is not necessarily exhaustive, but it represents the kind of factors that can be used to judge sincerity without second-guessing the veracity of beliefs.

One significant practical consequence of the sincerity constraint is that a religious group will generally need to be consistent in determining whether it is religious for both Free Exercise and Establishment Clause purposes. That is, in the absence of some unique justification that can square canons of sincerity with inconsistent claims, it cannot simultaneously claim to be nonreligious to escape Establishment Clause constraints and religious to claim Free Exercise Clause protections. It can segregate its activities into religious and nonreligious categories, but the activities it conceives as being secular or

---

301. *See* Heins, *supra* note 287; Horwitz, *supra* note 171; Senn, *supra* note 289.

302. *See* Senn *supra* note 289, at 341–42 (giving list of factors considered by courts: "(a) actions inconsistent with professed beliefs; (b) the willingness to bear adverse consequences of the religious belief; (c) an alternative secular purpose; (d) the size and history of the religious organization; (e) the extent to which the claimed beliefs parallel traditional beliefs; (f) the intensity of the believer's devotion; (g) the defendant's testimony and statements relevant to the defendant's religious sincerity; (h) whether the challenged tenet is part of an organized faith of which the defendant is a member; (i) the coexistence of secular fraud; (j) previous case law on the defendant, the religious organization, or the religious belief; and (k) evidence of the defendant's attempts to cover up embarrassing or questionable activities").

303. *See id.*

304. *See id.*

305. Horwitz, *supra* note 171, at 150. The factors listed here reflect the narrowed list endorsed by Horwitz, *id.* at 146–150, after winnowing out other possible factors suggested by Senn, *supra* note 289, at 341–42.

religious for one purpose retain the same character for other purposes. Similarly, as religious institutions become more global, consistency across legal systems may provide added indicia of sincerity, particularly where maintaining the position carries adverse consequences.

Limitations based on grounds overriding religious freedom

In addition to the inherent claimant-oriented constraints identified above, deference to self-definition may also be limited by independent state interests that override religious freedom claims, or by jurisdictional or other limitations on the exercise of state power. Protection of freedom of religion and belief is a high-order responsibility of the state, but it is obviously not the only responsibility. There is a wide range of state activities that are optional, but there are also others usually thought to be of sufficient importance that they may, under appropriate circumstances, override religious freedom claims. Typical examples include legislation in the areas of public safety, order, health, and the rights of third parties. Protecting certain matters of public morality is also often included on this list.[306]

Independent overriding state interests

It is useful to differentiate two situations in which independent overriding factors may set limits on deference. The first is the situation wherein the religious character of a group or belief system is being assessed. Here the question is whether there is an overriding state interest in rejecting a group's claim that it and its beliefs are religious. The state interest in making this assessment will depend to some extent on the context and reasons behind the claim. It could be that the group is attempting to assert a free exercise claim against some burdensome state requirement, that it is trying to be incorporated under a religious corporation law, that it seeks to strengthen individual claims being made by its members, that it seeks to establish eligibility for financial or other benefits, and so forth. A group might also, of course, seek to establish nonreligious status to avoid constraints imposed by the Establishment Clause.

It is important here to remember the uniqueness of the definitional context. The issue is whether the potentially overriding factors justify rejection of a definitional claim in the abstract, not rejection of a particular substantive free exercise claim. In the general inquiry about whether a group or its beliefs are religious, the issue becomes whether there is some overriding reason to impose a total ban on the right of the group or its members to bring their individualized claims, bearing in mind the considerable likelihood that a determination of religiousness in one context will spill over into others. That is, is there some ground for imposing an across-the-board ban on making a particular species of religion-related claims, or for that matter, on making any religion-related claims at all. The types of state interests that are likely to arise are familiar. They are no different in substance from those often mentioned in standard Religion Clause cases. But adverse determination of the religiousness question has broader implications in this context than in a more limited case, so that the over-

---

306. For a further discussion of this point, see text accompanying notes 257–285, *supra,* and notes 355–389, *infra.*

riding state concern needs to be stronger, and special care must be taken to assure that they involve immediate and concrete concerns, not just abstract, speculative, and remote worries.

The second type of situation involves assessment of the religiousness of individualized conduct. In this setting it will typically be difficult to distinguish the grounds for overriding a particular claim from the grounds for overriding its religiousness. Where that is true, there is no real need to get into the question of whether to defer to the claimant's conception of religiousness or not. One can simply assume religiousness (or nonreligiousness) for purposes of analysis, and show why overriding state interests would in any event dictate an outcome adverse to the claimant. This obviates the need for the state to get into the business of second-guessing the claimant's beliefs, but it reaches results consistent with the protection of religious freedom.

Constraints on the exercise of state power
Necessity

State authority to override self-definition claims is itself limited. Flowing from the concept of deferentialism and interjurisdictionality is the requirement that state activities carried out in furtherance of these objectives are strictly necessary. A liberal state that respects the autonomy claims of religious organizations should not be able to override self-definition through just any state action, but should be required to justify such overrides as being necessary for significant or essential state ends.[307] Necessity analysis thus places constraints on determining which of these state objectives have sufficient importance to override religious freedom claims. Moreover, necessity considerations require narrow tailoring to assure that even when there is a sufficiently strong state interest, it is pursued in ways that minimize the adverse impact on religious freedom. If there is a less burdensome alternative, a constraint is not strictly necessary.

Equality and neutrality

Another type of limitation of state action, which arises from the notion of religious freedom and the liberal state, is the idea of neutrality and equal treatment. The interjurisdictional model recognizes that the presence of multiple potentially colliding normative worlds requires a neutral arbiter capable of assuring maximal equal autonomy for each. If the arbiter is guided not by efforts to be neutral and to afford equal treatment among groups, the need for a neutral arbiter has not yet been met. Of course there are questions about whether a perfectly neutral position is strictly possible, but this is a more general problem in human justice systems, and the fact that the ideal cannot be perfectly attained does not in itself cut against limited deference theory. Among other things the state's obligation to treat groups equally and neutrally will support its respect for religious autonomy, which in turn supports maximal deference to religious self-definition, subject to like respect for other religious groups. Note that as a practical matter, one of the key requirements of any method of defining religion is that the definition not be allowed to become a verbal technique for legitimizing discrimination.[308]

---

307. Note that strict scrutiny will apply to an analysis of claims involving definitions of religion, even after *Smith*. *See* the extended discussion on this point at text accompanying notes 280–284.

308. *See* text accompanying notes 82 and 83.

Definitional difficulties

Having described the limited deference approach in some detail, we now address its relevance to a number of recurrent issues in the domain of definition of religion. The aim is not so much to explore the details of resolving concrete cases as to suggest why the limited deference model may be preferred in dealing with certain general difficulties inherent in defining religion. These difficulties, the daunting complexity of which is suggested in the opening sections of this chapter, appear to be theoretically intractable for a number of reasons. Here we focus on a few that seem most significant.

Continuum problems

First, wherever one attempts to set the definitional line, there is always some new group, belief, or activity that falls outside the definition but is functionally analogous to something included within it and cries out for equal treatment.[309] This equalitarian argument is either resisted, in which case one is left with difficult problems of unequal treatment, or it is accepted, in which case the boundary is pushed out farther and farther until almost no group would be excluded.[310] At that point there is a risk that the definition becomes vacuous. "A definition [that does] not exclude, does not define."[311]

As a practical matter, limited deference theory will draw a perimeter wide enough to include those who select themselves into the category of religion, though there will be constraints as described above. A significant point to bear in mind, however, is that there are also many reasons why some individuals may select themselves out. An outsider may be inclined to think of Marxism as the functional equivalent of a religion, but the Marxist herself is likely to disclaim the category. Equal treatment issues will sort themselves out to a considerable extent, taking into account and respecting the views of those most likely to suffer discrimination. Certain further constraints will result from the avoidance of intrusion into non-secular issues by legitimate state inquiries, but these too will be sensitive to equality concerns. The resulting definition of religion may be broader in some ways than what the state might have chosen if left to its own substantive, functional, or analogical devices, but the greater inclusion may pay for itself in dividends of greater social stability and loyalty of those who benefit from the added re-

---

309. Emile Durkheim wrote, "One can define religions such as they are, or such as they have been, but not such as they more or less vaguely tend to become." Emile Durkheim, The Elementary Forms of the Religious Life 62 (1965). Though sociologists like Durkheim have the luxury of modifying their definitions freely to fit changing circumstances, the law cannot escape the burden of erecting a definitional framework which, though it may be modified, is rigid enough to provide some degree of settled predictability in future applications.

310. See, e.g., Washington Ethical Soc'y v. Dist. of Columbia, 249 F.2d 127 (D.C. Cir. 1957) (religious exemption construed to include nontheistic group); Fellowship of Humanity v. County of Alameda, 315 P.2d 394 (Cal. Dist. Ct. App. 1957) (same); Note, Defining Religion: Of God, the Constitution and the D.A.R., 32 U. Chi. L. Rev. 533 (1965); Marc Galanter, Religious Freedom in the United States: A Turning Point?, 1966 Wis. L. Rev. 217, 260 (courts avoid definitional dilemmas by construing religion "broadly in terms of social function of the group rather than the content of its beliefs").

311. Ricks, *supra* note 215, at 1061. We wish to acknowledge both special affinity and special indebtedness to Val Ricks's article. An early version of Ricks's article was written for a seminar taught by Durham at a time when work on this chapter was already in process. The Ricks article obviously appeared much earlier and we have benefited greatly from its effort to work out some shared intuitions that were already under discussion when work on it commenced.

spect provided by limited deference theory. Failure to show respect for religious beliefs is one of the surest ways for the state to provoke passionate opposition and its resulting destabilizing pressures.

The discontinuity of sacred and secular: Incommensurability and transcendence

The second major difficulty derives from the profound discontinuity between sacred and secular. It is fundamentally this discontinuity which makes it inappropriate for secular institutions to make pronouncements about the incommensurable religious realms that lie beyond secular purview.[312] Protection of this divide has a deep historical and constitutional grounding that undergirds the jurisdictional limitations the legal system imposes when the state begins to intrude on matters of religious autonomy. The distinction between what is Caesar's and what is God's[313] has been one of the hallmarks of the West.[314] It lies at the core of Locke's seminal *Letter Concerning Toleration*,[315] which remains one of the classic studies of the place of religion in society. It is of course a central objective of the Religion Clause of the U. S. Constitution, and it lies at the core of the religious autonomy cases themselves—one of the richest strands in Religion Clause jurisprudence.[316] The discontinuity is most striking when it relates to transcendent claims of various kinds, which helps to explain why so many substantive definitions of religion focus on the significance of belief in a Supreme Being or to beliefs with other types of transcendent grounding.

In many ways, the problem of definition amounts fundamentally to marking out the boundaries of this discontinuity. The religious autonomy cases portray in sharp relief the challenges of grappling with it in its transcendent and other varieties. A secular state committed to religious freedom and to respect for manifestations of the sacred must avoid intruding into sacred space while simultaneously keeping manifestations of religion from eroding or circumventing the secular government structures needed to protect distinctive but equal spheres of freedom for all. Limited deference provides the best way of doing this.

Delimitation problems

Third, there are various areas in which the religious shades into the secular, creating difficult problems of delimiting boundaries. As indicated earlier,[317] these become even

---

312. *See* Durham & Dushku, *supra* note 234. For a more general analysis of the incommensurability problem, see Scharffs, *supra* note 12.

313. *See* Matt. 22:21.

314. *See* Harold J. Berman, Law and Revolution: The Formation of the Western Legal Tradition 273–94 (1983).

315. *See* John Locke, Letter Concerning Toleration, in Religious Pluralism, *supra* note 246, at 178 (1685) ("[T]he whole Jurisdiction of the Magistrate reaches only to...Civil Concernments; and...all Civil Power, Right and Dominion, is bounded and confined to the only care of promoting these things; and...it neither can nor ought in any manner to be extended to the Salvation of Souls...").

316. This line of cases is discussed in the text accompanying notes 257–285, *supra*, and at length elsewhere in this volume. *See especially* H. Reese Hansen, "Religious Organizations and the Law of Trusts," and Patty Gerstenblith, "Associational Structures of Religious Organizations," in this volume.

317. *See* text accompanying notes 224–229, *supra*.

more complex when one takes into account the myriad contexts and state purposes that are involved when definitional problems arise.

Religion or fraud

Where is the borderline between religious belief, which is shielded by religious freedom protection, and fraud, which is not?[318] We encountered this problem when dealing with sincerity of meta-beliefs about religiousness,[319] but it recurs at the level of other substantive beliefs as well. What one person takes to be religious truth may appear to another as the height (or depth) of fraudulent hucksterism. Recognizing this dilemma, the Supreme Court has rightly held that "the truth or verity of...religious doctrines or beliefs" cannot be considered in assessing claims of fraud.[320] Yet it is clear that sometimes religious people make misrepresentations on secular grounds or on arguably religious grounds that are not sincerely held. Even here, issues can be difficult. Justice Jackson found it hard in the *Ballard* case to distinguish questions of religious truth from questions of sincerity:

> I do not see how we can separate what is believed from considerations as to what is believable.... [A]ny inquiry into intellectual honesty in religion raises profound psychological problems.... The appeal in such matters is to a very different plane of credulity than is invoked by representations of secular fact in commerce.... [It is difficult] to say how literally one is bound to believe the doctrine he teaches and even more difficult to say how far it is reliance upon a teacher's literal belief which induces followers to give him money.[321]

These are areas in which the state must tread extremely lightly but cannot avoid treading altogether—at least not until it has clearly passed the boundary of its competence. The cloak of religion does not grant unlimited immunity from deceptive practices, and the state must be able to assess where that cloak frays to the vanishing point.

In this area, limited deference theory frankly faces some of the same conundrums as other theories in trying to prevent inquiries into sincerity from turning into state assessment of the veracity of beliefs. At a minimum, however, it helps clarify the distinctive role that sincerity plays at the level of meta-beliefs about religiousness and with respect to substantive religious freedom claims. It also helps focus judicial analysis away from inquiries into belief.

---

318. *See, e.g.*, Weiss, *supra* note 174; Kurland, *supra* note 176.

319. *See* section on inherent limitations of the state's obligation to defer to religious self-conceptions, *supra.*

320. United States v. Ballard, 322 U.S. 78, 86 (1944). As Justice Douglas wrote in the *Ballard* case, freedom of religious belief "embraces the right to maintain theories of life and of death and of the hereafter which are rank heresy to orthodox faiths. Heresy trials are foreign to our Constitution. Men may believe what they cannot prove. They may not be put to the proof of their religious doctrines or beliefs. Religious experiences which are as real as life to some may be incomprehensible to others. Yet the fact that they may be beyond the ken of mortals does not mean that they can be made suspect before the law.... The religious views espoused by respondents might seem incredible, if not preposterous, to most people. But if those doctrines are subject to trial before a jury charged with finding their truth or falsity, then the same can be done with the religious beliefs of any sect. When the triers of fact undertake that task, they enter a forbidden domain." *Id.* at 86–87.

321. *Id.* at 92–94 (Jackson, J., dissenting).

Religion or commerce

Another delimitation problem arises at the boundary of commercial conduct. When is conduct religious and when is it merely commercial? Religious organizations face problems of finance. Space for meetings must be leased or purchased. Employees must be paid. Charitable work may entail purchase or transportation of goods, and both cost money. Jesus cast money changers from the temple,[322] but even his inner circle had a common purse, albeit one carried by Judas—in retrospect the most suspect disciple.[323]

In traditional religions the commercial element is often minimized, but it cannot be eliminated entirely. Voluntary contributions are one type of revenue, but it is not at all unusual to find religious groups raising necessary funds by engaging in behavior that has commercial character. One thinks of everything from church bazaars to operation of agricultural property to service projects (for example, a car wash in the church parking lot) to much more substantial economic enterprises such as hospitals, broadcasting stations, or universities. Assets such as church buildings are really more like liabilities; they generate operational costs that must constantly be paid. Larger religious organizations accordingly need to build up reserves to cover the continuing or even increased costs of providing their services during lean times.

Moreover, while religions often make every effort to minimize the commercial side of their activities, different traditions conceptualize their financial activities in different ways. Luther criticized the practice of paying for indulgences in the Middle Ages, but sometimes penance or religious sacrifice may have a material side. Jesus advised the rich young man to "go thy way, sell whatever thou hast, and give to the poor, and thou shalt have treasure in heaven."[324] Scientologists believe that payments made for "auditing" services should be regarded as donations like tithing;[325] outsiders are often highly critical of this notion.[326] The challenges in this area are in fact more difficult than are often realized. People who clearly understand why the truth of religious beliefs cannot be made a triable issue in an action for fraud often forget that a religious community's temporal management practices may themselves be determined by its religious principles. Such a community is not obligated to be bound by traditional notions of the relation of money and religion. At some level, however, the state may need to distinguish between religious and commercial activity. Distinctions between tax-exempt revenue and unrelated business income are not unreasonable.[327] Denying religious organizations autonomy in managing their financial affairs or other matters, such as labor practices, that have a secular cast[328] may strike at the heart of religious practices. But in other respects, religious believers are ordinary citizens subject to regulatory burdens like anyone else.

How deferential should the state be in this area? Limited deference theory would recognize the importance of controlling for fraud and strategic behavior—for example,

---

322. Matt. 21:12–16; Mark 11:15–19; Luke 19:45–48.

323. John 12:6, 13:29.

324. Mark 10:21; *see* Matt. 19:16–26; Luke 18:18–27.

325. *See* Horwitz, *supra* note 171, at 98.

326. *See id.* at 98–99.

327. *See* Edward McGlynn Gaffney, Jr., "Exemption of Religious Organizations from Federal Taxation" and "Exemption of Religious Organizations from State and Local Taxation," in this volume.

328. *See* Corp. of the Presiding Bishop of the Church of Jesus Christ of Latter-day Saints v. Amos, 483 U.S. 327 (1987). *See also* Patrick J. Schiltz and Douglas Laycock, "Employment in Religious Organizations," in this volume.

where mischaracterization of a commercial transaction as religious could result in financial benefits to the religious organization. But in general it would respect the presumptively valid claims of religious groups. Fraudulent mischaracterizations are likely to be in the distinct minority. If the self-understandings were not presumed to be valid, a cloud would be cast over the validity of all religious transactions. This would operate as a massive limitation on religious freedom in general and religious autonomy in particular. Limited deference to self-understanding is vital. Having said this, we acknowledge that context may be important.

Religion or personal beliefs

Another cluster of delimitation problems centers on sorting out which kinds of beliefs count as religious. How are religious beliefs, which may be eligible for special protections, to be distinguished from beliefs that are merely personal,[329] philosophical,[330] aesthetic,[331] or political?[332] Behind each of these questions lie deeper ones about how freedom of religion differs from general freedom of action, and about why and whether it, along with certain other "first freedoms," should be accorded heightened protection as contemplated by the First Amendment.[333]

There is a growing trend toward doubting the legitimacy of distinctive religious claims. We think these arguments profoundly underestimate religion's significance.[334] In any event, as a practical matter our Constitution and laws do distinguish claims based on religion from those based on other types of beliefs. Accordingly, whatever the ultimate outcome of the philosophical debate, the task of delimiting the two will remain.

Limited deference theory provides some flexibility here by obliging the state to take into account the subjective perspectives of the individuals making claims. Thus, where an individual can claim sincerely that his or her conduct has a sufficient religious dimension, the state will defer in the absence of independent overriding considerations. In many cases, individuals will have a stronger interest in maintaining that their beliefs are not religious, or will have difficulty establishing that they sincerely believe their beliefs are religious. Leaving that aside, however, it should be borne in mind that part of the purpose and force of the heightened protection afforded religious freedom is that within the civil polity, claims of conscience constitute an order of claim different from other claims.[335] At the same time, even when the state is disposed toward deferring to claims of

---

329. *See, e.g.,* Brown v. Pena, 441 F. Supp. 1382, 1384 (S.D. Fla.1977) (refusing to find that an employee's personal belief that eating "Kozy Kitten People/Cat Food...contribut[ed] significantly to his state of well being" constituted a religious belief meriting protection).

330. *See, e.g.,* the cases on conscientious objection to compulsory military service discussed *supra.*

331. A narrative may be taken as literal religious truth by some, as figurative truth by others, and as pure fiction by still others.

332. *See, e.g.,* Ingber *supra* note 71.

333. *See, e.g.,* Smith, *supra* note 185; Gey, *supra* note 185. Lupu and Tuttle have advanced a theory that attempts to mark out the residual place of religion in a world in which it appears to have become harder to distinguish religious beliefs from secular moral commitments. Ira C. Lupu and Robert Tuttle, The Distinctive Place of Religious Entities in Our Constitutional Order, 47 Vill. L. Rev. 37 (2002). While this theory is preferable to more reductionist ones that deny any distinctive position to religion, our sense is that it accords insufficient significance to the distinctive value that the framers correctly saw in protecting religion.

334. *See, e.g.,* McConnell, Religious Liberty, *supra* note 188; McConnell, The Problem of Singling Out Religion, *supra* note 188; Noonan, *supra* note 188.

335. *See, e.g.,* Durham, *supra* note 239.

religiousness, it may have legitimate secular reasons for resisting infinitely elastic definitions. Limited deference provides a vehicle for balancing some of these tensions.

Religion or culture

A parallel set of issues arises not so much at the level of personal conscience but at the level of communal life—at the boundary between religion and culture. Generally, religion is tightly interconnected with culture. The distinctive markers of culture—art, architecture, music, patterns of social interaction, and so forth—are often strongly influenced by religious life. When do the fruits of religious life lose their distinctive religious charge and become simply a part of secular culture? When does a church become a museum or a landmark? When does a religious command become a secular moral or legal imperative?[336] How many reindeer need to be added to a creche before it ceases to be a sacred scene?[337] When does the activity of a public school chorus constitute performance of great music, and when does it veer into worship?[338]

One of the most significant aspects of religion is its ability to generate normative social orders.[339] Over time, this generativity leaves secularized cultural deposits that typically do not deserve the same free exercise protection as living religion itself. Many features of ordinary civil and criminal law can be cited as examples. On the Establishment Clause side, there are settings in which recognition of cultural values no longer constitutes imposition of religion. Holiday celebrations and symbols may, for good or ill, take on a secular cast, at least in part, and may cease to reflect patterns of domination, persecution, or endorsement of religion in society.[340] Requiring a public school to drop study and performance of all religious music would deprive choral music courses of much of their content. Compelling students to perform such music in religious settings would be problematic, but recognizing the music as part of society's cultural heritage should be permissible.[341] Similarly, it should be permissible in history courses to give accounts of the role that religion has played in history.[342]

---

336. Religious norms regarding murder and theft have been secularized, but to what extent are moral considerations concerning abortion now secularized? For a discussion of the significance of allegedly religious motivations behind abortion-related legislation, see *Harris v. McRae*, 448 U.S. 297 (1980) (holding that statute limiting federal funding to reimburse cost of abortions does not violate the Establishment Clause).

337. *See, e.g.,* County of Allegheny v. ACLU Greater Pittsburgh Chapter, 492 U.S. 573 (1989) (holding that display of a nativity scene in a county building violated Establishment Clause where there was no accompanying display of secular Christmas symbols); Lynch v. Connelly, 465 U.S. 668 (1984) (holding that display of a nativity scene on public property did not violate Establishment Clause where secular Christmas symbols were also displayed).

338. *See* Soc'y of Separationists, Inc. v. Whitehead, 870 P.2d 916, 932 (Utah 1993) (discussing the permissibility under the Establishment Clause of public school choir performances of religious music).

339. *See* Robert M. Cover, The Supreme Court, 1982 Term—Foreword: Nomos and Narrative, 97 Harv. L. Rev. 4, 19–25 (1983).

340. *See, e.g.,* County of Allegheny v. ACLU Greater Pittsburgh Chapter, 492 U.S. 573 (1989); Lynch v. Donnelly, 465 U.S. 668 (1984).

341. *See* Soc'y of Separationists, Inc. v. Whitehead, 870 P.2d 916, 932 (Utah 1993) ("When a Christmas carol is sung *as part of a worship service*, it falls within the terms of the Utah Constitution [prohibiting use of public funding to support religious exercise]. But when sung apart from a formalized worship service, on or off church property, carols are simply artistic expressions of a predominantly Christian culture").

342. "Studies have shown that the role of religion in American life and history has received rather short shrift in public school history and social science textbooks.... 'Above all, those who are

A complicating factor here is that the artifacts of culture have symbolic significance which can be read in different ways by different individuals and groups, depending on context. The issue is often not so much whether a particular state activity is religious or not. It is often both, depending on perspective. Moreover, the state never acts in a cultural vacuum, and any position it takes may communicate some orientation toward the religious or cultural activity. The question, then, is how a state can structure its affairs responsibly and sensitively in a cultural environment in which multiple messages are unavoidable and some constitute impermissible endorsement of religion.

In this domain, limited deference theory highlights a dilemma: there are contexts in which the perceptions of individuals and groups as to whether something is religious will simply differ, often in contradictory ways. Any action the state takes will appear to coincide with or presuppose some view or other. The state cannot satisfy everyone, but it can seek a position that will minimize impact on religious beliefs.[343] In following this approach, the state needs to consider, as best it can, the beliefs that are self-consciously religious. Some state positions, such as recognizing the historical realities of the cultural environment, will not have any significant effect on religious belief. History is what it has been for everyone. On the other hand, the state should abstain, to the extent it can, from activities that could reasonably be read as messages of religious endorsement or exclusion. Part of the appeal of Justice O'Connor's endorsement test, which was developed in this cultural domain, is that it wrestles with this difficult problem.[344]

The dialectic of sacred and secular

The problem of delimitation appears, at least initially, to be more complex at the boundary of religion and culture than elsewhere. What is religious at first becomes secular over time, and this is not a uniform or homogeneous process. Things that remain profoundly religious for some may drift into secularity for others. Secularization may proceed more rapidly in some groups than in others. Moreover, the process is neither inevitable nor unidirectional. A cultural residue may reacquire religious charge. Further, the structure of a society's symbolic space, as already noted, may be perceived differently by different groups. What is an innocuous or positive symbol for some groups may invoke memories of persecution in others. The cross, which has played a central and positive role in Christian symbolism, may be a reminder of crusades or pogroms to Muslims or Jews. Delimitation problems in this domain can be particularly complex because of the shifting meanings attached to the artifacts and symbols of culture.

At a deeper level, each of the other areas of delimitation we have described shares this feature, at least to some limited extent. This is because the nature of individual involvement in a religious community and in religious life is constantly shifting and varied. Religious communities draw together individuals with shared values and convictions, but they are not composed of religious clones. What is religious for some

---

committed to their religious tradition—at the very least as an important part of the historical record—are not represented.'" James Davison Hunter, Culture Wars: The Struggle to Define America 204–05 (1991) (citing studies by the National Institute of Education, People for the American Way, and Americans United for the Separation of Church and State).

343. As an attempted way out of the dilemma, we invoke here Laycock's test for "substantive neutrality." *See* Laycock, *supra* note 268, at 70.

344. *See, e.g.,* Lynch v. Donnelly, 465 U.S. 668, 687–694 (1984) (O'Connor, J., concurring). *But see* Steven D. Smith, Symbols, Perceptions, and Doctrinal Illusions: Establishment Neutrality and the "No Endorsement" Test, 86 Mich. L. Rev. 266 (1987).

members may be merely social or communal for others. There are people whose beliefs are very stable over long periods of time, but often there are also people who move closer or further from the ideals of the belief system, in terms of both behavior compliance and degree of conviction. Even for those with long-term stable beliefs and loyalties, religious life is seldom a steady-state experience. As Clifford Geertz has noted,

> The movement back and forth between the religious perspective and the common-sense perspective is actually one of the more obvious empirical occurrences on the social scene, though, again, one of the most neglected by social anthropologists, virtually all of whom have seen it happen countless times. Religious belief has usually been presented as a homogeneous characteristic of an individual, like his place of residence, his occupational role, his kinship position, and so on. But religious belief in the midst of ritual, where it engulfs the total person, transporting him, so far as he is concerned, into another mode of existence, and religious belief as the pale remembered reflection of that experience in the midst of everyday life are not precisely the same thing....[345]

The point is that even the most deeply committed religious believer tends to move back and forth between ordinary secular experience and what is usually for the believer some fundamentally different type of meaning/giving experience associated with the exercise of his or her religious beliefs. The nature of such meaning/giving experiences may vary across traditions, as may the extent of the contrast between the religious and the secular, the sacred and the profane. But there is something profound and powerful about the dialectic process by which religious meaning interacts with ordinary experience to create, strengthen and transform normative worlds.

The reality of this dialectic means that the boundary between the religious and the secular is not a fixed and stable line. It oscillates at differing frequencies and amplitudes at different times with different individuals. Beliefs sincerely held and practiced sometimes slip, resulting in the hypocritical distancing of action from belief. If the distance becomes great enough, insincerity passes over into fraud.[346] The financial side of religious life can be experienced either as consecrated sacrifice or as something merely commercial, like paying dues or insurance premiums.

Aesthetics and philosophy pose more difficult delimitation problems, in part because they often have a dialectical impact similar to that encountered as the believer moves between religious and everyday experience. They can heighten sensitivity, clarify confusion, and deepen normative sensitivity and commitment. This is part of the reason why the Supreme Court ultimately concluded in the draft cases that religion includes sincere beliefs occupying "a place in the life of its possessor parallel to that filled by the orthodox belief in God...."[347] Of course, it is often the case that the philosophy or art in ques-

---

345. Geertz, *supra* note 46, at 119–20.

346. The borderline between fraud and religion is in some ways quite distinct from the other delimitation problems we are describing in this section. The others are aspects of the contrast between sacred and secular in various recurring contexts. Fraud, in contrast, is simply deceptive practice. The difficulty here is that truth is a defense, and beliefs sincerely believed to be true negate scienter. Thus, the difficulty is not distinguishing sacred from secular, but recognizing that freedom of religion requires the state to remain neutral on the issue of religious truth and tolerant of sincerely held beliefs. Even here, however, there is a touch of the moving back and forth between everyday and religious experience, because the sincerity with which beliefs are held shifts. In the end, however, fraud is not simply a relapse into the secular. It is simply wrongdoing.

347. United States v. Seeger, 380 U.S. 163 (1965); *see also* Welsh v. United States, 398 U.S. 333 (1970).

tion is not understood, either by its author or by the individual whose beliefs are affected by it as something religious.

The delimitation of religion from politics has to do with another dimension of the distinction between sacred and secular. The basic intuition here is that religious beliefs (and to some extent conduct) are not subject to state-imposed obligations in the same straightforward way that political obligations are. That is, while political beliefs and their formulation are extremely important to the political process and accordingly should receive the protection that freedom of speech provides,[348] there is no sense that they exempt anyone from obligations to obey the state. One is free to advise or criticize the state, but in the end, once the state has deliberated and passed laws (except, of course, laws impermissibly restraining speech), everyone is bound by the result, even those who have objected. Thus, someone who objects to military service because he is politically opposed to a particular war does not have a claim, once a law imposing an obligation to support the war has been passed, to object on political grounds. In contrast, the structure[349] of conscientious objection arguments is, to use Madison's words, that religious beliefs are "precedent both in order of time and degree of obligation, to the claims of Civil Society."[350] In this argument, religious freedom functions like a reservation clause on the social contract that civil society is obliged to respect.[351] The distinction between religion and politics has a more clearly jurisdictional cast under the Establishment Clause.[352] But the general point is the same: religion stands outside the domain of state jurisdiction in a way that politics does not. Religion and politics have a relationship that mirrors the dialectic of sacred and secular, but the optimal value of the interaction is not likely to be achieved unless the two remain independent in their respective spheres.[353]

While the inevitable oscillations that occur at the various interfaces described above complicate the problem of delimitation, they also help underscore the importance of finding a method of undertaking this task with sensitivity. The oscillations—the movement through recurring contacts with more powerful sources of meaning—are a key aspect of the transformative nomos creating and maintaining power of religion.[354] It is at least in part the capacity to infuse secular phenomena with greater meaning and inspire deeper commitment to conscientiously chosen normative orders that makes religious institutions so significant.[355] Accordingly, it is particularly vital that the method of definition not set unnecessary obstacles in the path of this fragile dialectic. Limited deference theory, by taking religious self-understanding seriously, is in an optimal position to contribute to this end.

---

348. Among other things, this is a major justification for free speech protections. *See, e.g.,* Alexander Meiklejohn, Free Speech and Its Relation to Self-Government (1948); Alexander Meiklejohn, Political Freedom (1960); Tribe, *supra* note 69 § 12-1 at 786.

349. Of course there will be disagreement with the validity of this argument, particularly by those who discount the special claims of conscience in general, or of religious conscience in particular, to exemption from normal political obligations. Our intention here is not to get into that debate, but merely to point out that there is a structural difference between the nature of claims based merely on political beliefs and those placed on religious beliefs or beliefs arguably within the same domain.

350. Madison, *supra* note 239, para. 1.

351. *See* Durham, *supra* note 239, at 79–85.

352. *See generally* Esbeck, *supra* note 72.

353. *Id.*

354. *See* Cover, *supra* note 339.

355. *See* Durham & Dushku, *supra* note 234, at 430.

Limited deference:
The example of international law

Not only is limited deference theory fruitful at the level of theory and application, but it also has significant explanatory value. In our view, a sound interpretation of key international instruments dealing with freedom of religion and belief points to the strategy of deference with appropriate yet narrow constraints that is the core of the limited deference model. Pertinent international norms have elaborated the permissible limitations that would justify rejecting a particular self-definition of religion.

The most significant international treaty provision on this point is Article 18 of the International Covenant on Civil and Political Rights (ICCPR), which protects freedom of religion and belief.[356] The United Nations Human Rights Committee, which is the body charged by the treaty with interpretation of the application of its provisions,[357] has promulgated a General Comment providing the official interpretation of Article 18. This document takes the following approach to the definition question:

> The terms belief and religion are to be broadly construed. Article 18 is not limited in its application to traditional religions or to religions and beliefs with institutional characteristics or practices analogous to those of traditional religions. The Committee therefore views with concern any tendency to discriminate against any religion or belief for any reasons, including the fact that they are newly established, or represent religious minorities that may be the subject of hostility by a predominant religious community.[358]

Obviously, this provision does not provide either a substantive or a functional definition of religion. In a broad sense it does suggest an analogical approach, but particularly when taken in connection with the Human Rights Committee's overall interpretation of Article 18, its approach to the definition question arguably employs something very much like limited deference. It recognizes that the real issue all too often at play in efforts to exclude groups by definition is discrimination. Moreover, by "viewing with *concern* any tendency to discriminate against *any* religion or belief *for any reason*," the committee implicitly uses a presumption approach. That is, while not ruling out the possibility that groups claiming religious status may not deserve the name, it notes that exclusionary definitions are to be viewed skeptically, which is to say there is a presumption in favor of the claim to be religious. This presumption is particularly important where the religion involved is "newly established" or "may be the subject of hostility by a predominant religious community." This approach is obviously vague at the boundaries but relatively clear as a procedural matter. If a group claiming to be religious is a traditional religion, or is similar to a traditional religion, that will generally be a suffi-

---

356. *See* ICCPR, *supra* note 223. The United States ratified this Covenant belatedly in 1992 with reservations designed to assure that the ratification could not be deemed to condone an interpretation of the Covenant that would be inconsistent with the U.S. Constitution, and in particular, the First Amendment. *See* 138 Cong. Rec. S 4783 (1992).

357. *See* ICCPR, *supra* note 223, Article 40(4). For an account of the evolution of the Human Rights Committee's practice of issuing general comments which interpret the Covenant, see Philip Alston, The United Nations and Human Rights: A Critical Appraisal 412–16, 494–6 (1992).

358. United Nations Human Rights Committee, General Comment No. 22 (48), concerning Article 18, adopted July 20, 1993, CCPR/C/21/Rev.1/Add. 4 (1993) [hereinafter General Comment No. 22 (48)].

cient condition for deferring to its claim, presuming that it is religious, and treating it accordingly, in the absence of grounds for rebutting the presumption.

Within the structure of the ICCPR, such a presumption can be rebutted only under a very narrow set of circumstances. Just as U.S. constitutional law recognizes a distinction between belief and action, with the right to belief per se enjoying absolute protection,[359] so the ICCPR protects an absolute right to "have or adopt" inner beliefs and opinions.[360] Both the right to "freedom of thought, conscience and religion" and the right "to hold opinions" are absolute within the "internal forum" of the mind. In this regard, "[e]veryone shall have the right to hold opinions without interference."[361] Similarly, a person's right to "freedom of thought, conscience and religion…shall include freedom to adopt a religion or belief of his choice;"[362] it is only "[f]reedom to *manifest* one's religion or beliefs [that] may be subject…to…limitations."[363]

This absolute, unfettered right to inner freedom of religion and belief includes not only substantive beliefs but meta-religious beliefs. Both are entitled to a strong presumption that actions manifesting them are entitled to the protections afforded freedom of religion or belief. They deserve deference precisely because they arise and are held within the inviolable internal forum. Moreover, since "[n]o one shall be subject to coercion which would impair his freedom to have or to adopt a religion or belief of his choice,"[364] any other presumption by the state would in effect chill their maintenance or adoption, which in turn would constitute impermissible state coercion of internal beliefs.

The ICCPR recognizes—along lines that parallel the American belief/action distinction, albeit with significantly greater precision—that *manifestations* of religion may be subject to limitations, but only if the limitations are "prescribed by law and are *necessary* to protect public safety, order, health, or morals or the fundamental rights and freedoms of others."[365] There is an extensive literature on the strictness of these requirements.[366] For our purposes, it suffices to quote from the paragraph addressing the limitations clause in the Human Rights Committee's General Comment:

> Article 18(3) permits restrictions on the freedom to manifest religion or belief only if limitations are prescribed by law and are necessary to protect public safety, order, health, or morals, or the fundamental rights and freedoms of others. The freedom from coercion to have or to adopt a religion or belief and the liberty of parents and guardians to ensure religious and moral education cannot be restricted. In interpreting the scope of permissible limitation clauses, States parties should proceed from the need to protect the rights guaranteed under the Covenant, including the right to equality and non-discrimination.…

---

359. Reynolds v. United States, 98 U.S. 145, 166 (1878); Cantwell v. Connecticut, 310 U.S. 296, 305–06 (1940) ("[T]he [First] Amendment embraces two concepts,—freedom to believe and freedom to act. The first is absolute but, in the nature of things, the second cannot be"). While we disagree with the blanket acceptance of regulation of religious *activity* espoused by early Supreme Court cases, they point to the fact that religious *belief* has always been considered inviolable.

360. General Comment No. 22(48), *supra* note 358, at para. 3.

361. ICCPR, *supra* note 223, at Article 19(1).

362. *Id.* at Article 18(1).

363. *Id.* at Article 18(3).

364. *Id.* at Article 18(2).

365. *Id.* at Article 18(3) (emphasis added).

366. For an excellent analysis of the narrowness of this so-called "limitations clause," see Manfred Nowak & Tanja Vospernik, Permissible Restrictions on Freedom of Religion or Belief, in Lindholm, *supra* note 82.

Limitations imposed must be established by law and must not be applied in a manner that would vitiate the rights guaranteed in article 18. The Committee observes that paragraph 3 of article 18 is to be strictly interpreted: restrictions are not allowed on grounds not specified there, even if they would be allowed as restrictions to other rights protected in the Covenant, such as national security. Limitations may be applied only for those purposes for which they were prescribed and must be directly related and proportionate to the specific need on which they are predicated. Restrictions may not be imposed for discriminatory purposes or applied in a discriminatory manner.[367]

As the General Comment explains, strong constraints, based on the nature of necessary limitations on religious freedom, restrict the permissible grounds for negating the presumption of religiosity. For example, the state may not invoke a claim that the presumptive religion is false or that its interpretation of scriptures is misguided in order to rebut the claim of religiousness, though it may be able to invoke claims of insincerity. Similarly, it may not delegate to a particular religion or set of religions the task of evaluating whether the presumption is warranted. From the international perspective for which the U.N. interpretation applies, allowing a country's dominant religion to decide whether to recognize another religion would seem an obviously suspect way of trying to delimit religions.[368] Moreover, if a number of countries with acknowledged stature in respecting religious freedom have conceded that a particular organization is religious—particularly those countries that have had substantial experience with the religion in question—then there would seem to be little justification for other countries to withhold similar recognition.

The necessity requirement is without question the most important constraint on limitations. Necessity analysis opens up proportionality concerns, making it possible to examine whether independent state interests are really sufficient to override religious freedom. Discriminatory limitations on freedom of religion or belief are neither permissible nor necessary. Legislation that limits religious freedom must be narrowly tailored in light of the objective it is designed to further.

Countries that dispense subsidies to religious organizations may have legitimate reasons for limiting the range of groups eligible to receive them (although this will obviously raise discrimination issues).[369] Nonetheless, status as a religion eligible for fundamental religious freedom protections should be made widely available, and definitional gambits should not be used to artificially restrict the scope of such protections. Thanks to the strength of the U. S. Constitution's Establishment Clause, many of the questions concerning which groups should be subsidized simply do not arise in American states.

---

367. General Comment No. 22(48), *supra* 358, at para. 8.

368. The Greek Constitution, for example, provides that "[t]here shall be freedom to practice any known religion." Greek Const. art. 13, para. 2. Because of the influence of the Greek Orthodox Church, however, it was quite clear that not many religions were "known" for purposes of this clause. Fortunately, a series of recent cases from the European Court of Human Rights has made it clear that granting religious groups special influence of this type is not compatible with the freedom of religion provisions of the European Convention for the Protection of Human Rights and Fundamental Freedoms. *See, e.g.,* Serif v. Greece, 31 Eur. H.R. Rep. 20 (2001); Hasan and Chaush v. Bulgaria (Eur. Ct. H.R., Oct. 26, 2000), *at* http://www.ehcr.coe.int/; Metropolitan Church of Bessarabia v. Moldova (Eur. Ct. H.R., Dec. 13, 2001), *at* http://www.ehcr.coe.int/.

369. Many European countries with respected traditions of religious freedom have two-tier church/state systems that guarantee broad protections of religious freedom but restrict state cooperation and direct or indirect subsidies in ways that benefit a more restricted subset of religions. *See generally* State and Church in the European Union (Gerhard Robbers ed., 1996).

The stakes of the definitional issue are accordingly much lower. But the same notion—that definitions should not be manipulated to exclude groups that fall within underinclusive definitions or are reasonably close to traditional patterns of religiousness—ought to apply.

Much more could be said about the foregoing provisions, but the analogy to limited deference should be clear. Limited deference does not provide a substantive or functional definition, but it does establish a presumption that those claiming to be religious—including new and unpopular groups—are in fact religious. This deference is not without limits, however. It can be limited by inherent constraints such as sincerity, and by other narrowly tailored and tightly restricted state interests that must be proportional to the ends the state is seeking to further, taking into account its obligation to protect religious freedom.

Practice more workable than theory

It is significant to note that finding a method for resolving the dilemmas of defining religion turns out in many respects to be the obverse of the common saying, "That sounds fine in theory, but doesn't work in practice." There is much in this chapter that suggests just how daunting the problem of definition can be theoretically. But in this area, practice turns out for the most part to be easier and more workable than theory. As difficult as the boundary questions may be, most cases lie far from the boundaries. Thus, the problem is not overly serious for most religious groups as a practical matter, except in political systems that have no scruples about employing definitions to exclude a wide range of social groups that are generally viewed by sociologists, historians, anthropologists, and others as religious. In the overwhelming majority of cases in which courts and administrators face religious claims, there is no serious doubt about the claimant's religious status. This, among other things, is why resolving the definition question does not even warrant mention in the vast majority of cases involving religion and religious rights. The groups or activities involved are so clearly religious that there is simply no plausible ground for doubt.

The point can be broadened to take into account many of the attempts at definition described in earlier sections of this chapter. A recurring problem with many of them is that they are underinclusive in crucial respects. Typically, they make presuppositions based on traditional religions, and fail to take into account cases that do not fit traditional paradigms. The practical point to bear in mind is that most everyday questions of definition will fall within even underinclusive definitions.[370] If a group asserting reli-

---

370. Saler has an extended and useful discussion of the value and limitations of prototypes and prototypicality in a Wittgensteinian definition. *See* Saler, *supra* note 2, at 202–217. Saler proposes "that we formally acknowledge what many of us do informally: that we explicitly recognize our individual idealizations of 'mainstream' Judaisms and Christianities as 'prototypical' in the highest degrees of the category religion. I suggest, moreover, that we enlarge this set of eminently category-fitting phenomena to include that family of religions called 'Islam.'" Saler, *supra* note 2, at 212. Saler warns, however, that use of a prototype should not be used as a scalar comparison, *i.e.*, that the number of characteristics similar to a good exemplar do not always reflect the degree of membership. *Id.* at 215–225. Hence, the fact that a new religious movement may not be monotheist, for example, like main "prototypical" religions, does not necessarily indicate that it does not squarely fall within the designation of a religion. *See id.* at 221–23 (rejecting theism as a necessary element in a definition and discussing problems of defining "theism"). Saler does recognize, however, that the prototypical elements and beliefs will gradually change as the category of analysis is applied in other cultures. *See id.* at 262–264 (suggesting, for example, that *dharma* could be an interesting tool for judging the typicality of religions). For a discussion and critique of Saler's use of prototypes, see

gious status can show that it falls within the range of definitions that are underinclusive, its claims should be vindicated—unless there are reasons deriving from inherent or overriding limits on religious freedom that preclude recognizing them.

Among other things, this means that while belief in a Supreme Being or other divinity and a strong sense of the sacred or transcendent are not necessarily required to qualify as a religion, belief systems with these characteristics clearly qualify.[371] Borderline cases will remain where a definition is arguably overinclusive, but generally they will be few. The fact is that most practical cases will be fairly easy. Officials should not be misled by the theoretical complexity of the borderline cases into thinking and acting as though normal cases were equally problematic. Even more importantly, officials should not use the complexity of theoretical issues as an excuse to discriminate against smaller, less well known groups that are religious by any reasonable tests.

Summary

Limited deference theory, then, defines religion by deferring to a group's own conception regarding whether it is religious or not, subject to general limits on religious freedom. That is, it maintains that the beliefs of an individual, including the meta-religious belief about whether other beliefs are religious, are to be respected to the extent that they are sincerely and conscientiously held. However, the reality implicit in the very idea of religious freedom—that different individuals and groups equally have the right to have, adopt, and maintain different beliefs—means that some limits must be set on the right to manifest these differing beliefs in action, at least to the extent that they collide in society. As a practical matter, this means that there must be some institution (the state) that polices permissible interactions among religious individuals and groups themselves and between them and secular aspects of society, including the state.

To speak more concretely: according to limited deference theory, if a group conceives itself to be a religion, or if it conceives of an action or symbol as being religious, the state obligation to respect and protect religion requires that there be a presumption in favor of the claim that the group, action, or symbol is religious. Like the presumption of innocence, this presumption of religiousness is strong and carries practical consequences. Even when the religion is new and unfamiliar, it should be able to organize and carry out its activities and to avail itself of rights and privileges available to other religious communities—at least until the presumption of religiousness has been rebutted, or until there is a reasonable likelihood that it will be rebutted, and irreversible or significant harm of types sufficient to override religious freedom will occur if the claim of religiousness is allowed to continue. The presumption also recognizes that given the significance of religious freedom, it is better to err on the side of an overinclusive rather than an underinclusive definition—at least until grounds for rebutting the presumption can be fairly evaluated. Only under a narrowly restricted set of circumstances can the presumption be rebutted.

William E. Paden, Prototypes: Western or Cross-Cultural?, in Perspectives on Method and Theory in the Study of Religion, *supra* note 61, at 307.

371. They meet what Ricks, in his version of limited deference theory, has called the "'clearly' standard," according to which clearly nonreligious practices or beliefs cannot be invoked to sustain free exercise claims, and clearly religious claims cannot be used to avoid limitations imposed by the Establishment Clause. Ricks, *supra* note 215, at 1101–02.

Other Problematic Definitions

While much of the scholarly debate, and our response, has centered on the definition of religion itself, definitional problems and strategies are not limited to that term. Issues of definition, self-definition, and religious freedom arise in a host of situations governed by various laws that use terms having different connotations and denotations in different religious traditions. There are countless examples of this type of issue. For example, laws may refer to members of religious organizations, but membership may have different meanings, be marked by different rites, and be conceptualized in different ways. Statutes may, for example, refer to the "clergy," "ministers," and so forth—terms that, while familiar in some churches, may have no applicability in a tradition with a lay clergy. This section attempts to illustrate some examples of such religion-sensitive terms, which can create genuine practical problems for religious traditions. We use the example of state statutes granting confidential communication privileges to explore in some depth how our theory, among other practical alternatives, might solve such recurrent definitional problems.

One prominent example of a key religious term with different meanings in various religious traditions is the term "church." The definition of "church," particularly in the Internal Revenue Code, has generated nearly as much debate as the definition of "religion." Because Edward McGlynn Gaffney, Jr., describes this issue well in his chapter on federal taxation in this volume, we now move to related terms that are equally problematic. The New York code, for example, attempts to define "denomination" with a list of thirty-eight religious organizations.[372] As mentioned in this book's Prologue, the term "incardination" raises another set of difficulties.[373] "Fundamentalism" and "extremism" likewise elude definition.[374] "Clergy "[375] and "confession"[376] are used frequently in connection with the confidential communications privilege or abuse-reporting statutes and prove equally hard to pin down. The term "clergy" is sometimes further qualified as "ordained,"[377] which generates yet more definitional difficulties. The trend is toward more inclusive language, such as "spiritual advisor,"[378] "religious organization,"[379] "de-

---

372. *See* discussion in Patty Gerstenblith, "Civil Court Resolution of Property Disputes Among Religious Organizations," in this volume.

373. *See* James A. Serritella's Prologue to this volume.

374. *See, e.g.,* Peter Antes, Fundamentalism: A Western Term with Consequences, in Perspectives on Method and Theory in the Study of Religion, *supra* note 61, at 260.

375. *See* extended discussion in this section.

376. Ariz. Rev. Stat. Ann. § 13-3620 (A) (Supp. 1996); Idaho Code § 16-1619(a), (c) (Supp. 1997); Mont. Code Ann. §§ 41-3-201(1)–(2), (4) (1997).

377. Ala. Code § 12-21-166 (2001); Idaho Code § 16-1619(a), (c) (Supp. 1997); 23 Pa. Cons. Stat. Ann. §§ 6311(a), (b) (Supp. 1997); Ross v. Ross, 1998 WL 516159 (Conn. Super. Ct. 1998); Newport Church of the Nazarene v. Hensley, 983 P.2d 1072 (Or. Ct. App. 1999). For a further discussion on the problems of requiring formal ordination, see text accompanying *infra* notes 399–403.

378. 735 Ill. Comp. Stat. Ann. 5/8-803 (1996); N.D. Cent. Code § 50-25.1-03 (Bender 2001); Reardon v. Savill, 1999 WL 1063195 (Conn. Super. Ct. 1999); Mullins v. State, 721 N.E.2d 335 (Ind. Ct. App. 1999); State v. Ellis, 756 So.2d 418 (La. Ct. App. 1999); State v. Gooding, 989 P.2d 304 (Mont. 1999); State v. Cary, 751 A.2d 620 (N.J. Super. Ct. App. Div. 2000); R.A. ex rel. N.A. v. First Church of Christ, 748 A.2d 692 (Pa. Super. Ct. 2000); Hodges v. Kleinwood Church of Christ, 2000 WL 994337 (Tex. App. 2000); Kos v. State, 15 S.W.3d 633 (Tex. App. 2000).

379. Cal. Penal Code § 11166(c)(1) (West 2002); Carnesi v. Ferry Pass United Methodist Church, 770 So.2d 1286 (Fla. Dist. Ct. App. 2000).

nomination,"[380] and "penitential communication,"[381] although broader terms can also yield potential problems of definition.

Another problem of terminology arises in so-called charitable choice legislation in the United States, which commonly bars a faith-based service provider from using government funds "for sectarian worship, instruction, or proselytization."[382] These terms are usually not defined,[383] and raise difficult issues concerning when a discussion of religious issues becomes "instruction" or "proselytization."[384] A diverse set of religious, educational, and civil rights organizations have attempted to flesh this and other charitable choice issues out in a document describing areas of consensus and disagreement on government cooperation with faith-based service providers.[385] They acknowledge that "[i]t is difficult, if not impossible, to define these concepts," but also offer a first attempt. They agree that "[t]eaching values or beliefs as religious texts constitutes religious instruction or proselytizing," and then attempt to distinguish between "urging a beneficiary to accept Jesus Christ or some other religious faith as the only way to move from welfare into employment," which would be improper proselytization, and permissible discussion of "commonly held values such as abiding by the law and being honest."[386] The grey areas between these extremes, however, are not hard to imagine. This interpretation further posits that prohibited federally-funded worship would "include...such acts as offering prayers and reading scripture, but observing a neutral moment of silence does not constitute worship."[387] While these are plausible lines to draw, they certainly will not be the only attempts to define "worship," "proselytization," and "instruction." Terms like "prayer" and "scripture" also vary in their meaning across traditions.

Still another sensitive domain has to do with family and marriage law.[388] Some of the complexities that can arise here have become familiar as a result of some of the case law and literature surrounding the problems of obtaining the "get" or "bill of divorcement" that is necessary under Jewish law for a woman to remarry after divorce.[389] Even well-intended legislative efforts to resolve the dilemmas Jewish women may encounter in this

---

380. Cal. Penal Code § 11166(c)(1) (West 2002); Md. Code Ann. Fam. Law § 5-705 (Bender 2001); Md. Code Ann. Cts. & Jud. Proc. § 9-111 (Bender 2001); Metro. Philip v. Steiger, 98 Cal. Rptr. 2d 605 (Cal. Ct. App. 2000); Poe v. Doe, 2000 WL 1228660 (Conn. Super. Ct. 2000); Doe v. Malicki, 771 So.2d 545 (Fla. Dist. Ct. App. 2000).

381. Cal. Penal Code § 11166(c)(1) (West 2002); Cal. Evid. Code § 1032 (1996); State v. Richmond, 590 N.W.2d 33 (Iowa 1999); Gonzalez v. State, 21 S.W.3d 595 (Tex. App. 2000); State v. Martin, 959 P.2d 152 (Wash. C. App. 1998).

382. See, e.g., 42 U.S.C. § 604a(j).

383. See, e.g., 42 U.S.C. § 619 (definitions section).

384. See Carl H. Esbeck, "Charitable Choice and the Critics," in this volume.

385. See Government Cooperation with Faith-based Social Service Providers: A Statement Arising from Discussions Convened by The American Jewish Committee and the Feinstein Center for American Jewish History at Temple University 8 (February 27, 2001), available on-line at http://www.temple.edu/feinsteinctr/pubs.html#papers (last visited Feb. 8, 2002).

386. Id.

387. Id.

388. For a valuable effort to help identify the variety of types of interaction between secular and religious norms in this setting, see Carol Weisbrod, Family, Church and State: An Essay on Constitutionalism and Religious Authority, 26 J. Fam. L. 741 (1987–88).

389. See, e.g., Schwartz v. Schwartz, 153 Misc. 2d 789, 583 N.Y.S.2d 716 (Sup. Ct., Kings Cty. 1992); Irving Breitowitz, Between Civil and Religious Law: The Plight of the Agunah in Modern Society (1993); Susan Metzger Weiss, Sign at Your Own Risk: the "RCA" Prenuptial May Prejudice the Fairness of Your Future Divorce Settlement, 6 Cardozo Women's L.J. 49 (1999). For an extensive bibliography on this topic, consult http://users.aol.com/Agunah/bib-agun.htm (last visited April 5, 2002).

area can lead to unexpected complexities. Some have argued that the New York "get" law[390] may misfire, since a get procured by the force of secular statutes may be involuntary and thus invalid under Jewish law.[391] Similarly, secular efforts to respect and protect "kosher" rules can lead to difficult problems of interpretation of religious language.[392] These issues pose difficult questions of determining how the secular state should intervene to protect against religiously disputed "kosher" claims, and of how religious terminology can be translated into or coordinated with legal terminology.

The range of responses to such definitional dilemmas emerges with particular clarity in exemptions to child-abuse reporting statutes and in statutes granting the confidential communications privilege, both of which must decide who is entitled to the privilege and how to denote the group covered by the privilege. As virtually all states have such laws, and variation in statutory language is substantial, the complexities posed by such definitional problems become obvious in this setting.

One common approach is simply to list the traditional names of clergy from various faith traditions.[393] For example, a Georgia confidential communication statute grants

---

390. N.Y. CLS Dom Rel § 253(3), (6).

391. Weiss, *supra* note 174, at 102 n.40; Dane, Varieties, *supra* note 213, at 143–45.

392. Dane, Varieties, *supra* note 213, at 137–40.

393. *See* Alaska R. Evid. 506(a)(1) ("a minister, priest, rabbi, or other similar functionary of a religious organization, or an individual reasonably believed so to be by the person consulting the individual"); Ariz. Rev. Stat. § 12-2233 (West 2001) ("a clergyman or priest"); Ark. R. Evid. 505(a)(1) ("a minister, priest, rabbi, accredited Christian Science Practitioner, or other similar functionary of a religious organization, or an individual reasonably believed so to be by the person consulting him"); Cal. Evid. Code § 1030 (1996) ("a priest, minister, religious practitioner, or similar functionary of a church or of a religious denomination or religious organization"); Colo. Rev. Stat. § 13-90-107(1)(c) (1999) ("[a] clergyman, minister, priest, or rabbi"); Conn. Gen. Stat. § 52-146b (2001) ("[a] clergyman, priest, minister, rabbi or practitioner of any religious denomination accredited by the religious body to which he belongs who is settled in the work of the ministry"); Del. R. Evid. § 505(a)(1) ("a minister, priest, rabbi, accredited Christian Science practitioner or other similar functionary of a religious organization, or an individual reasonably believed so to be by the person consulting him"); D.C. Code Ann. § 14-309 (1996) ("[a] priest, clergyman, rabbi,…practitioner of Christian Science"); Fla. Stat. § 90.505 (West 2001) ("a priest, rabbi, practitioner of Christian Science, or minister of any religious organization or denomination usually referred to as a church, or an individual reasonably believed so to be by the person consulting him or her"); Ga. Code Ann. § 24-9-22 (1996) ("Protestant minister of the Gospel, any priest of the Roman Catholic faith, any priest of the Greek Orthodox Catholic faith, any Jewish rabbi, or…any Christian or Jewish minister, by whatever name called"); Haw. R. Evid. 506(a)(1) ("a minister, priest, rabbi, Christian Science practioner, or other similar functionary of a religious organization, or an individual reasonably believed so to be by the communicant"); Idaho R. Evid. § 505(a)(1) ("a minister, priest, rabbi, accredited Christian Science Practitioner, or other similar functionary of a religious organization, or an individual reasonably believed to be a clergyman by the person consulting"); 735 Ill. Comp. Stat. Ann. § 5/8-803 (West 1996) ("A clergyman or practitioner of any religious denomination"); Ky. R. Evid. 505(a)(1) ("a minister, priest, rabbi, accredited Christian Science practitioner, or other similar functionary of a religious organization, or an individual reasonably believed so to be by the person consulting him"); La. Code Evid. Ann. art. 511(A)(1) (West 1996) ("a minister, priest, rabbi, or other similar functionary of a religious organization, or an individual reasonably believed so to be by the person consulting him"); Me. R. Evid. 505(a)(1) ("a minister, priest, rabbi, accredited Christian Science practitioner, or other similar functionary of a religious organization, or an individual reasonably believed so to be by the person consulting that individual"); Md. Code Ann. Cts. & Jud. Proc. § 9-111 (1997) ("[a] minister of the gospel, clergyman, or priest of an established church of any denomination"); Mass. Ann. Laws ch. 233 § 20A (1996) ("[a] priest, rabbi or ordained or licensed minister of any church or an accredited Christian Science practitioner"); Mich. Comp. Laws Ann. § 600.2156 (West 2001) ("minister of the gospel, or priest of any denomination whatsoever, or duly accredited Christian Science practitioner"); Miss. Code Ann. § 13-1-22(1)(a) (1996) ("a minis-

the privilege to "any Protestant minister of the Gospel, any priest of the Roman Catholic faith, any priest of the Greek Orthodox Catholic faith, any Jewish rabbi, or any Christian or Jewish minister, by whatever name called."[394] This sort of definition can be either substantive, if merely a list, or an analogical or Wittgensteinian "family resemblance" definition, if it leaves open the possibility of a similar but unlisted type of clergy.

Ostensive definitions of this sort suffer the same problem as all substantive definitions: underinclusiveness. For example, only eighteen of the thirty-four states with a listing approach to defining "clergy" include Christian Science practitioners among the list.[395] As the statutes referred to in the previous note demonstrate, most state defini-

---

ter, priest, rabbi, or other similar functionary of a church, religious organization, or religious denomination"); Mo. Rev. Stat. §491.060(4) (1995) ("[a]ny person practicing as a minister of the gospel, priest, rabbi or other person serving in a similar capacity for any organized religion"); Mont. Code Ann. §26-1-804 (1995) ("[a] clergyman or priest"); Neb. Rev. Stat. Ann. §27-506(1)(a) (Michie 1996) ("a minister, priest, rabbi, or other similar functionary of a religious organization, or an individual reasonably believed so to be by the person consulting him"); Nev. Rev. Stat. Ann. §49.255 (Michie 1995) ("[a] clergyman or priest"); N.H. Rev. Stat. Ann. §516:35 (2001) ("[a] priest, rabbi or ordained or licensed minister of any church or a duly accredited Christian Science practitioner"); N.M. R. Evid. 11-506(A)(1) ("a minister, priest, rabbi, or other similar functionary of a religious organization, or an individual reasonably believed so to be by the person consulting that person"); N.Y. C.P.L.R. 4505 (Consol. 1996) ("a clergyman, or other minister of any religion or duly accredited Christian Science practitioner"); N.C. Gen. Stat. §8-53.2 (West 2001) ("priest, rabbi, accredited Christian Science practitioner, or a clergyman or ordained minister of an established church"); N.D. R. Evid. 505 ("a minister, priest, rabbi, accredited Christian Science practitioner, or other similar functionary of a religious organization, or an individual reasonably believed so to be by the person consulting him"); Okla. Stat. Ann. tit. 12 §2505(A)(1) (West 1996) ("a minister, priest, rabbi, accredited Christian Science practitioner or other similar functionary of a religious organization, or any individual reasonably believed to be a clergyman by the person consulting him"); 42 Pa. Cons. Stat. §5943 (1996) ("clergyman, priest, rabbi or minister of the gospel of any regularly established church or religious organization"); Tenn. Code Ann. §24-1-206(a)(1), (d) (1996) ("minister of the gospel, priest of the Catholic Church, rector of the Episcopal Church, ordained rabbi, or regular minister of religion of any religious organization or denomination usually referred to as a church"); Tex. R. Evid. 505(a)(1) ("a minister, priest, rabbi, accredited Christian Science Practitioner, or other similar functionary of a religious organization or an individual reasonably believed so to be by the person consulting with such individual"); Utah R. Evid. 503(a)(1) ("a minister, priest, rabbi, or other similar functionary of a religious organization or an individual reasonably believed so to be by the person consulting that individual"); Utah Code Ann. §78-24-8(3) (1996) ("a clergyman or priest"); Vt. R. Evid. 505(a)(1) (1996) ("a minister, priest, rabbi, accredited Christian Science Practitioner, or other similar functionary of a religious organization, or an individual reasonably believed so to be by the person consulting him"); Wash. Rev. Code Ann. §5.60.060(3) (West 2001) ("[a] member of the clergy or priest"); W. Va. Code Ann. §57-3-9 (Michie 2001) ("priest, nun, rabbi, duly accredited Christian Science practitioner or member of the clergy authorized to celebrate the rites of marriage in this state"); Wis. Stat. §905.06 (1994) ("a minister, priest, rabbi, or other similar functionary of a religious organization, or an individual reasonably believed so to be by the person consulting the individual").

394. Ga. Code Ann. §24-9-22 (1996).

395. *See* Ark. R. Evid. 505(a)(1) ("a minister, priest, rabbi, accredited Christian Science Practitioner, or other similar functionary of a religious organization, or an individual reasonably believed so to be by the person consulting him"); Del. R. Evid. §505(a)(1) ("a minister, priest, rabbi, accredited Christian Science practioner or other similar functionary of a religious organization, or an individual reasonably believed so to be by the person consulting him"); D.C. Code Ann. §14-309 (1996) ("[a] priest, clergyman, rabbi,…practitioner of Christian Science"); Fla. Stat. Ann. §90.505 (West 2001) ("a priest, rabbi, practitioner of Christian Science, or minister of any religious organization or denomination usually referred to as a church, or an individual reasonably believed so to be by the person consulting him or her"); Haw. R. Evid. 506(a)(1) ("a minister, priest, rabbi, Christian Science practitioner, or other similar functionary of a religious organization, or an individual rea-

tions tend to be analogical, privileging not only ministers, priests, or rabbis, but also "similar functionar[ies] of...religious organization[s]." This seems a workable common-sense approach that would easily include something like a Christian Science practitioner. Of course, even such analogical definitions can be underinclusive if given cramped interpretations or if they, like the previously referenced Georgia statute, limit the range of examples to "Christian or Jewish minister[s]."

One twist on the substantive listing approach is definition by exclusion. This generally, though not always, solves the underinclusiveness problem. For example, Colorado's abuse reporting statute, instead of listing exempt clergy, enumerates those individuals (such as health workers) who are required to report. However, this list includes Christian Science practitioners, thus impliedly defining them as non-clergy and denying them the benefit of an exemption.[396]

The other typical definitional strategy in abuse-reporting statutes, which is sometimes combined with a substantive or analogical listing, is a functional approach.

---

sonably believed so to be by the communicant"); Idaho R. Evid. § 505(a)(1) ("a minister, priest, rabbi, accredited Christian Science Practitioner, or other similar functionary of a religious organization, or an individual reasonably believed to be a clergyman by the person consulting"); Ky. R. Evid. 505(a)(1) ("a minister, priest, rabbi, accredited Christian Science practitioner, or other similar functionary of a religious organization, or an individual reasonably believed so to be by the person consulting him"); Me. R. Evid. 505(a)(1) ("a minister, priest, rabbi, accredited Christian Science practitioner, or other similar functionary of a religious organization, or an individual reasonably believed so to be by the person consulting that individual"); Mass. Ann. Laws ch. 233 § 20A (1996) ("[a] priest, rabbi or ordained or licensed minister of any church or an accredited Christian Science practitioner"); Mich. Comp. Laws Ann. § 600.2156 (West 2001) ("minister of the gospel, or priest of any denomination whatsoever, or duly accredited Christian Science practitioner"); N.H. Rev. Stat. Ann. § 516:35 (1995) ("[a] priest, rabbi or ordained or licensed minister of any church or a duly accredited Christian Science practitioner"); N.Y. C.P.L.R. 4505 (Consol. 1996) ("a clergyman, or other minister of any religion or duly accredited Christian Science practitioner"); N.C. Gen. Stat. § 8-53.2 (1995) ("priest, rabbi, accredited Christian Science practitioner, or a clergyman or ordained minister of an established church"); N.D. R. Evid. 505 ("a minister, priest, rabbi, accredited Christian Science practitioner, or other similar functionary of a religious organization, or an individual reasonably believed so to be by the person consulting him"); Okla. Stat. Ann. tit. 12 § 2505(A)(1) (West 1996) ("a minister, priest, rabbi, accredited Christian Science practitioner or other similar functionary of a religious organization, or any individual reasonably believed to be a clergyman by the person consulting him"); Tex. R. Evid. 505(a)(1) ("a minister, priest, rabbi, accredited Christian Science Practitioner, or other similar functionary of a religious organization or an individual reasonably believed so to be by the person consulting with such individual"); Vt. R. Evid. 505(a)(1) ("a minister, priest, rabbi, accredited Christian Science Practitioner, or other similar functionary of a religious organization, or an individual reasonably believed so to be by the person consulting him"); W. Va. Code Ann. § 57-3-9 (Michie 2001) ("priest, nun, rabbi, duly accredited Christian Science practitioner or member of the clergy authorized to celebrate the rites of marriage in this state").

396. *See, e.g.,* Colo. Rev. Stat. § 19-3-304 (1999), *amended by* 2001 Colo. Legis. Serv. Ch. 68 (S.B. 01-47) (West) ("(2) Persons required to report such abuse or neglect or circumstances or conditions shall include any: (a) Physician or surgeon, including a physician in training; (b) Child health associate; (c) Medical examiner or coroner; (d) Dentist; (e) Osteopath; (f) Optometrist; (g) Chiropractor; (h) Chiropodist or podiatrist; (i) Registered nurse or licensed practical nurse; (j) Hospital personnel engaged in the admission, care, or treatment of patients; (k) Christian science practitioner; (l) Public or private school official or employee; (m) Social worker or worker in a family child care home, foster care home, or child care center as defined in section 26-6-102, C.R.S.; (n) Mental health professional; (o) Dental hygienist; (p) Psychologist; (q) Physical therapist; (r) Veterinarian; (s) Peace officer as defined in section 18-1-901(3)(l), C.R.S.; (t) Pharmacist; (u) Commercial film and photographic print processor as provided in subsection (2.5) of this section; (v) Firefighter as defined in section 18-3-201(1), C.R.S.; (w) Victim's advocate, as defined in section 13-90-107(1)(k)(II), C.R.S; (x) Licensed professional counselors; (y) Licensed marriage and family therapists; (z) Unlicensed psychotherapists").

States define clergy based on their role within a religious organization, often focusing particularly on their authorization or ordination.[397] For example, Ohio exempts reporting of abuse when it has been communicated to a "member of the clergy, rabbi, priest, or regularly ordained, accredited, or licensed minister of an established and

---

397. *See* Ala. Code § 12-21-166 (Michie 1996) ("Any duly ordained, licensed or commissioned minister, pastor, priest, rabbi or practitioner of any bona fide established church or religious organization"); Ariz. Rev. Stat. § 13-3620(A) (2000) ("[a] clergyman or priest...in that person's role as a clergyman or priest in the course of discipline enjoined by the church to which the clergyman or priest belongs"); Cal. Evid. Code § 1032 (1996) ("a clergyman who...is authorized or accustomed to hear such communications"); Conn. Gen. Stat. Ann. § 52-146b (West 2001) ("practitioner of any religious denomination accredited by the religious body to which he belongs"); D.C. Code Ann. § 14-309 (1996) ("duly licensed, ordained, or consecrated minister of a religion authorized to perform a marriage ceremony"); 735 Ill. Comp. Stat. Ann. § 5/8-803 (1996) ("A clergyman or practitioner of any religious denomination accredited by the religious body to which he or she belongs"); Ind. Code Ann. § 34-46-3-1 (West 2001) ("a clergyman...in the course of discipline enjoined by the clergyman's church"); Iowa Code § 622.10 (1995) ("a member of the clergy...in the person's professional capacity"); Kan. Stat. Ann. § 60-429 (1995) ("'duly ordained minister of religion' means a person who has been ordained, in accordance with the ceremonial ritual, or discipline of a church, religious sect, or organization established on the basis of a community of faith and belief, doctrines and practices of a religious character, to preach and to teach the doctrines of such church, sect, or organization and to administer the rites and ceremonies thereof in public worship, and who as his or her regular and customary vocation preaches and teaches the principles of religion and administers the ordinances of public worship as embodied in the creed or principles of such church, sect, or organization; (2) the term 'regular minister of religion' means one who as his or her customary vocation preaches and teaches the principles of religion of a church, a religious sect, or organization of which he or she is a member, without having been formally ordained as a minister of religion, and who is recognized by such church, sect, or organization as a regular minister; (3) the term 'regular or duly ordained minister of religion' does not include a person who irregularly or incidentally preaches and teaches the principles of religion of a church, religious sect, or organization and does not include any person who may have been duly ordained a minister in accordance with the ceremonial, rite, or discipline of a church, religious sect or organization, but who does not regularly, as a vocation, teach and preach the principles of religion and administer the ordinances of public worship as embodied in the creed or principles of his or her church, sect, or organization"); Minn. Stat. § 595.02(c) (West 2001) ("[a] member of the clergy or other minister of any religion...in a professional character, in the course of discipline enjoined by the rules or practice of the religious body to which the member of the clergy or other minister belongs"); N.H. Rev. Stat. Ann. § 516:35 (1995) ("[a] priest, rabbi or ordained or licensed minister of any church or a duly accredited Christian Science practitioner"); N.J. Stat. § 2A:84A-23 (Michie 1996) ("a cleric in the cleric's professional character, or as a spiritual advisor in the course of the discipline or practice of the religion body to which the cleric belongs or of the religion which the cleric professes"); N.C. Gen. Stat. § 8-53.2 (West 2001) ("priest, rabbi, accredited Christian Science practitioner, or a clergyman or ordained minister of an established church"); Ohio Rev. Code Ann. § 2317.02(C) (West 2001) ("[a] member of the clergy, rabbi, priest, or regularly ordained, accredited, or licensed minister of an established and legally cognizable church...in the member of the clergy's, rabbi's, priest's, or minister's professional character"); Or. Rev. Stat. § 40.260(1)(b) (1995) ("a minister of any church, religious denomination or organization or accredited Christian Science practitioner who in the course of the discipline or practice of that church, denomination or organization is authorized"); R.I. Gen. Laws § 9-17-23 (2001) ("duly ordained minister of the gospel, priest or rabbi of any denomination...in his or her professional capacity"); S.C. Code Ann. § 19-11-90 (Law. Co-op. 1995) ("regular or duly ordained minister, priest or rabbi...in his professional capacity"); S.D. Codified Laws § 19-13-17 (Michie 1996) ("a clergyman in his professional character as spiritual adviser"); Va. Code Ann. § 19.2-271.3 (Michie 1996) ("regular minister, priest, rabbi, or accredited practitioner over the age of eighteen years, of any religious organization or denomination usually referred to as a church...in his professional capacity"); W. Va. Code Ann. § 57-3-9 (Michie 2001) ("priest, nun, rabbi, duly accredited Christian Science practitioner or member of the clergy authorized to celebrate the rites of marriage in this state"); Wyo. Stat. Ann. § 1-12-101 (Michie 1996) ("[a] clergyman or priest...in his professional character").

legally cognizable church ... in the member of the clergy's, rabbi's, priest's, or minister's professional character."[398]

One potential problem with such functional definitions is their overly narrow description of a clergy's function. They commonly refer to clergy's "professional" capacity and/or formal ordination, and accordingly fail to address the problem of lay clergy or religious leaders that are not formally ordained or licensed.[399] In Alabama, for example, as in several other states,[400] the confidential communications privilege is "limited to any person who regularly, as a vocation, devotes a substantial portion of his time and abilities to the service of his respective church or religious organization,"[401] thus apparently excluding part-time or lay clergy. The intent presumably is to limit the exemption to primary as opposed to subordinate religious personnel. But the law may totally fail to track the sense within a religious community of who is obliged to keep confidences as a matter of religious belief. Moreover, while it may pick out primary leaders in one tradition, it may totally exclude them in another that has only a lay clergy.

Similarly, the definition of clergy in Kansas's confidential communications provision excludes not only lay and part-time clergy but also those religious leaders who have not been formally ordained. The privilege is limited to "a person who has been ordained, in accordance with the ceremonial ritual, or discipline of a church, religious sect, ... to preach and to teach the doctrines of such church ... and to administer the rites and ceremonies thereof in public worship, and who as his or her regular and customary vocation preaches and teaches the principles of the religion and administers the ordinances of public worship embodied in the creed or principles of such church, sect, or organization...."[402] How does this apply in a religious tradition that does not ordain its leaders? Utah's legislators avoided the problem of excluding lay clergy by making reference to a cleric's "religious capacity" instead of "professional character."[403] Clearly functional definitions, if based on too narrow a conception of function, can severely limit religious expression.

A related concern in some functional definitions of "clergy" is the tendency to incorporate normative judgments about the actions of the clergy member. For example, Rhode Island and South Carolina only privilege communications to clergy if they are "necessary and proper to enable [the clergy member] to discharge the functions of his

---

398. Ohio Rev. Code Ann. § 2317.02(C) (West 2001).

399. This problem also shows up occasionally in statutes that otherwise rely on a list of approved types of clergy. For example, Rhode Island limits privileged statements to those "properly entrusted to [the clergy member] in his or her professional capacity, and necessary and proper to enable him or her to discharge the functions of his or her office in the usual course of practice or discipline...." R.I. Gen. Laws § 9-17-23 (2001).

400. *See, e.g.,* Conn. Gen. Stat. Ann. § 52-146b (West 2001) ("A clergyman, priest, minister, rabbi or practitioner of any religious denomination accredited by the religious body to which he belongs who is settled in the work of the ministry shall not disclose confidential communications made to him in his professional capacity"); Iowa Code § 622.10 (1995) (privileging "confidential communication properly entrusted to the person in the person's professional capacity, and necessary and proper to enable a person to discharge the functions of the person's office according to the usual course of practice or discipline"); Nev. Rev. Stat. Ann. § 49.255 (Michie 2001) (privileging "any confession made to him in his professional capacity").

401. Ala. Code § 12-21-166(a)(1) (1996).

402. Kan. Stat. Ann. § 60-429 (1995).

403. "The term 'in the cleric's religious capacity' was chosen over 'in the cleric's professional character' to avoid an implication that only communications with professional members of the clergy are protected. The privilege applies to confidential communications with lay clerics as well." Adv. Comm. Notes to Utah R. Evid. 503.

office."[404] Other statutes rely on a requirement that the clergy member be bound to confidentiality "under canon law or church doctrine."[405] While it is perhaps understandable that states would want to use this kind of functional definition to limit the privilege to those cases in which such communication is theologically significant, these limitations not only raise additional questions regarding definitions of "church doctrine" or the "functions of [a clergy member's] office," but also highlight serious problems of internal church autonomy, forcing courts to interpret the doctrine, beliefs, or canon law of a religious organization. Moreover, they discriminate against groups that lack a highly articulated doctrine with respect to confidential communications.

An even more problematic approach is some states' use of the phrase "well-recognized religion."[406] Much like the problem many European countries have had in trying (and failing) to define "sect" or "cult,"[407] the use of "well-recognized religion" in statutes is an attempt to transform vague lexical definitions and prejudices into law. Legal privileges should not be tied to how well known a group may be. Even more problematic are attempts to form legal definitions of terms, such as "sect" and "cult," that come fraught with extremely negative connotations.[408] These terms are largely "used to provide an a priori appraising value judgment which will let the inquirer know whether or not the movement is good or bad—despite the fact that it sounds, even to the inquirer, that the inquiry is for purely factual information."[409] Lawyers, like sociologists, "should not be party to a practice in which 'religion' is overtly defined in one (characterizing) way, but covertly (appraisingly) defined in terms of those whom we like and those whom we do not like so that laws and mores applying expressly to 'religion' are applied only to 'religions-of-which-we-approve,' while religions-of-which-we-do-not-approve are defined as 'non-religions'—or, indeed, vice versa."[410]

---

404. R.I. Gen. Laws § 9-17-23 (2001) ("properly entrusted to him or her in his or her professional capacity, and necessary and proper to enable him or her to discharge the functions of his or her office in the usual course of practice or discipline"); S.C. Code Ann. § 19-11-90 (Law. Co-op. 1995) ("necessary and proper to enable him to discharge the functions of his office according to the usual course of practice or discipline of his church or religious body").

405. Utah Code Ann. 62a-4a-403(2)(b) (2000). *See also* Md. Code Ann. Cts. and Jud. Proc. § 9-111 (2001); Md. Code Ann. Fam. Law § 5-705 (2001); Idaho Code § 16-1619(c)(3) (Supp. 1997); Gates v. Seattle Archdiocese, 10 P.3d 435 (Wash. Ct. App. 2000); Leary v. Geoghan, 2000 WL 1473579 (Mass. Super. Ct. 2000).

406. Ohio Rev. Code Ann. § 2317.02(A) (West 2001); Surdel v. Metrohealth Med. Ctr., 733 N.E.2d 281 (Ohio Ct. App. 1999); James v. James, 1999 WL 247320 (Ohio Ct. App. 1999); Universal Life Church, Inc. v. State, 205 Cal. Rptr. 11 (Cal. Ct. App. 1984); Board of Educ. of Mountain Lakes v. Maas, 152 A.2d 394 (N.J. Super. Ct. App. Div. 1959).

407. For example, the Belgian Center for Information and Advice on Harmful Sectarian Organizations and the has struggled to find a definition of "sect." *See* Centre d'Information et d'Avis sur les organisations sectaires nuisibles, Rapport bisannuel, § I.B. (2001). French and Belgian parliamentary commissions have taken a more direct approach, providing a list of 172 "sects" (France) and 189 "harmful sects" (Belgium). This approach has been rejected by the Council of Europe, which determined that "it is unnecessary to define what constitutes a sect or to decide whether it is a religion or not." "Illegal Activities of Sects," section I.5., doc. 8373, Council of Europe Parliamentary Assembly, Committee on Legal Affairs and Human Rights (13 April 1999).

408. In most European languages, the term "sect" carries the negative connotations that the word "cult" does in English. For an in-depth treatment of discrimination against new religious movements, see Eileen Barker, Why the Cults?, *supra* note 82.

409. Barker, But Is It A Genuine Religion?, in Between Sacred and Secular, *supra* note 16, at 102.

410. *Id.*, at 109.

The foregoing examples suggest the wide range of situations arising in one particular domain (clergy confidentiality) in which religious organizations can experience a lack of fit—or, to use the phrase suggested by Williams and Massad in their chapter,[411] "disarticulation"—between legal categories and the requirements of religious beliefs. Once one moves beyond general terms such as "religion" or "church" to the more specific vocabulary used to describe religious roles, organizational features, and other aspects of religious life that have different connotations or denotations in different religions, several things become clear.

First, it is almost inevitable that some such disarticulation will occur. Natural languages have limited numbers of terms and are ordinarily used to describe similar aspects of different traditions. Legislatures have no choice but to resort to natural language, and they reasonably assume that speakers coming from the different normative communities of a pluralistic society will have sufficient ability to understand each other so that all terms do not become incommensurable and untranslatable across traditions. But there will be problems of integrating secular and religious terminology, of translating religious into secular language, and of coordinating different meanings from varying religious traditions with secular terminology.[412]

Second, because different subcommunities may develop separate terminology, or use identical vocabulary in different ways, and these differences often have great significance for religious identity and authentic religious practice, religious freedom requires us to find ways to respect these differences. Third, the problem that arises with respect to this type of disarticulation of concrete terminology is structurally similar to the general problem of definition: in the last analysis, it is not merely a problem of determining meaning of terminology, but rather of how maximal respect can be given to the religious community's self-understanding of the terminology it uses, without violating general outer limits on the freedom of religion or belief available to all.

Consideration of the situations involving clergy confidences has suggested a variety of ways in which concrete problems of disarticulation can arise: (1) omission from a statutory list of the specific nomenclature used by a religious community to designate its leaders; (2) use of terminology that is underinclusive; (3) use of terminology that acknowledges one type of community and ignores others (for example, excessive use of terminology drawn exclusively from Christian sources); (4) use of limiting language that makes it difficult to apply terminology to other traditions by analogy ("Christian or Jewish ministers"); (5) use of discriminatory language ("well-recognized religion"); and so forth.

Were one to focus on other domains, other types of problems would no doubt emerge. Perry Dane has noted, for example, that there may be problems of the meaning or relevance of terminology shifting over time, possibly at different times in different communities and subcommunities.[413] He also notes that the possible permutations of state attitudes toward religion are complex. Typically a secular state engaging in religious oppression will tend to reject the related religious vocabulary. But it also may accept the meaning of the vocabulary in the process of rejecting the related conduct, as when secular courts in the nineteenth century recognized Mormon religious marriages

411. Williams & Massad, *supra* note 235.
412. Dane, Varieties, *supra* note 213, at 140–44.
413. *Id.* at 129.

in order to hold them illegal. The state can simply refuse to give secular significance to religious expression. Or it may try to devise language that accommodates religious meanings under secular or neutral labels.[414]

The question for present purposes is how a limited deferentialist approach would wrestle with such problems. In this regard, the first point to emphasize is that limited deference theory does not require making every religious community a law unto itself. It does not require the state to abrogate its lawmaking functions, or to legislate by delegation or cross-reference to the norms of religious communities. On the contrary, limited deference recognizes that both the state and religious communities are sources of normative order presumptively deserving respect. Part of the idea of having a state in pluralistic society is to provide an institution that can enforce outer limits on the freedom of everyone, including religious communities. Short of those limits, the state should structure its norm-giving capacity in ways that respect the autonomy of religious communities in structuring their own normative worlds. In terms of the conflict-of-laws analogy, the fact that a jurisdiction recognizes and gives force to a norm emanating from another entity does not mean that the jurisdiction has lost its own sovereignty and lawmaking power. Limited deference seeks to give maximum respect to religious communities out of respect for their autonomy.

What does this mean as a practical matter? The issue can be considered at three levels: legislative, judicial, and executive (bureaucratic). At the level of legislation, the effort should be to be maximally respectful of religious difference. When legislation is being drafted, every effort should be made to have open hearings and other processes that can help alert lawmakers to the distinctive meanings and implications that legislation and its terminology will have for different groups. In the nature of things, it will not be possible to take all such variations into account, but often an open and respectful process can help to identify language that is broadly acceptable.

Neutrality in this regard does not necessarily imply sameness of treatment. Language can be neutral and rigid or neutral and flexible. The latter is more likely to accord with limited deferentialism. Often it means finding language that exhibits "noncoercive isomorphism." That is, just as the extremely diverse range of religious organizations in the United States are now organized as religious not-for-profit corporations and exhibit a non-coerced pattern of isomorphism, so legislators should find terminology in other areas that is both neutral and flexible, so that it leaves room for self-understanding to operate. For example, use of the term "confidential communication" instead of "confession" covers the relevant religious practices of virtually all religious groups without invoking particular religious conceptions of any. When burdens are being imposed or benefits are being extended, statutory language should be drafted so that the distribution of burdens and benefits will not hinge on arbitrary differences of terminology reflecting differences across traditions.

Efforts should be made to avoid terminology that expressly or tacitly restricts itself to dominant or traditional religions. Caution should be used in referring to religious rituals (for example, ordination) in describing organizational features of religions; different religions may allocate roles in different ways. Pejorative terms, such as "sect" and "cult," should be avoided, as should language that expressly or implicitly prefers religions (typically, more conventional religions).

At the level of the judiciary, a limited deferentialist approach calls upon judges to construe statutory language in a manner that will afford maximum latitude to religious

---

414. *Id.* at 134–45.

self-understanding, interpreting it reasonably in light of its purpose while ensuring that the law as thus construed does not violate religious freedom rights and that the religious self-understanding in question does not go beyond the permissible outer limits of religious freedom norms. In general, this will call upon judges to invoke broader canons of statutory interpretation. It will also require broad use of analogy to assure that what might otherwise be excessively narrow and underinclusive language will be given sufficient breadth to avoid discriminating against the self-understandings of less familiar religions.

Similar flexibility is called for from individuals in the executive branch, who often have more discretion than the judiciary in finding workable solutions to problems. They too should seek to find interpretations that are open, flexible, and receptive to religious self-understanding. At a minimum, administrative convenience should not be sufficient justification to rule out deference to religious understanding and religious needs.

Conclusion

In his Prologue to this volume, James A. Serritella calls for a more soundly based jurisprudence that would focus on a particular religious organization's self-understanding.[415] The call is a general one that he articulated at the outset of work on this volume, and it echoes through all its chapters. Limited deference theory is an attempt to respond to that call at the threshold level of definition of religion itself.

William P. Marshall, dissenting in part from the call to self-understanding, has noted in his chapter in this book that "a civil law that defers too much to religion's self-understanding may also offend constitutional standards."[416] In particular, in the context of definition of religion he noted that "[t]here are free exercise issues if the religious claimant is improperly adjudicated to be nonreligious, and there are establishment concerns created by a court's or state's improperly granting or denying an 'official' imprimatur of theological legitimacy."[417] He concludes, moreover, that any effort to assess sincerity without inquiring into believability of religious claims is doomed to unintelligibility.[418] The limits articulated in limited deference theory are an attempt to address these and related concerns.

But neither the response to Serritella's call nor the efforts to attend to Marshall's warnings have been fully successful. Despite the length of this chapter, we remain conscious that it is at best an initial effort to help develop a much-needed autonomy-based approach to thinking about the definition question. Two obvious areas for further research have been merely touched upon here: (1) to what extent do the practical contexts of specific legislative settings require definitional adjustments, and (2) what does limited deference require in the context of deferring to religious understanding of other legal terms? Our sense is that interpretation of the limits on deference articulated in limited deference theory will be sufficient to handle the adjustments needed in differing

---

415. Serritella, Prologue to this volume.

416. William P. Marshall, "Constitutional Coherence and the Legal Structure of American Churches," in this volume; *id.* at note 6 and accompanying text.

417. *Id.*, text accompanying note 38.

418. *Id.*, text accompanying notes 39–43.

practical and legislative contexts, but further research and analysis is necessary to validate this hypothesis. Similarly, all we have been able to do here is explore in depth the complexities that arise with respect to terms that laws use to describe religious leaders. This is precisely the kind of problem Serritella was referring to when he wrote:

> No single instance of the law requiring organized religion to endure ill-fitting terminology is likely to destroy or seriously impair religious freedom, but the cumulative effect of dozens if not hundreds of such instances can and does constrict, skew, and otherwise contort a religious organization's ability to pursue its goals in accordance with its self-understanding.[419]

The work to document a larger set of such instances is immense and has barely begun. It includes not only identifying and researching terms that need to be interpreted with more sensitivity to religious difference, but also finding the methods—statutory construction, translation, integration, and abstention, to mention a few[420]—that can be used to open up the necessary flexibility. Still another challenge is that of more fully elaborating the interjurisdictional analogy that lies behind many of aspects of limited deference theory. Pursuing this model in greater depth could refine many of its insights, but could also reveal its limits.

An even deeper difficulty is that the deference model runs against the grain of contemporary Religion Clause analysis in a number of ways. First, in effect it recommends a somewhat more subjectivist approach when much of the history of Religion Clause interpretation has sought to identify objective mechanisms such as the belief/action distinction, external objectivist definitions of religion, and burden analysis in order to counteract what is perceived as a potential flood of litigation and, even more worrisome, the radical subjectivity of religion.[421] The specter behind this trend, quite visible in Justice Scalia's opinion in *Smith*, is one of "anarchy" and of religion being a "law unto itself."[422] Second, despite the fact that we have become accustomed to the idea of a limited sovereign, it remains somewhat alien to think that the "competence of competences" regarding the definition question can in effect be partially shared by state and religion through combining deference with limitations. Third, rights talk has led us to forget the absence-of-power perspective within which the First Amendment was originally framed, so that the jurisdictional approach implicit in Esbeck's structural conception of the Establishment Clause—with which we sympathize—seems somewhat foreign.

Still, despite remaining challenges, we believe there is much to be said for the limited deference approach. On the one hand, its contours are not likely to diverge from earlier definitions in ways that might suggest it is radically unworkable. There are at least two reasons for this. First, the overwhelming majority of cases tend to be fairly clear and to fall within the range of traditional definitions, whether substantive, functional, or analogical. Second, the sincerity constraint will generally require individuals to show how their views on the definition issue fall within or are similar to other definitions that have been developed. They will have broad flexibility in how they articulate these similarities, but they will not be able to merely assign a radically new meaning to the term "religion." While we understand the long-standing worry identified by Marshall—and by

---

419. Serritella, Prologue to this volume.

420. These are some of the approaches to dealing with respect for autonomy in different types of situations noted by Dane. *See generally* Dane, Varieties, *supra* note 213.

421. *See* Note, Burdens on the Free Exercise of Religion, *supra* note 289, at 1260–65.

422. Employment Div., Dep't of Human Resources of Oregon v. Smith, 494 U.S. 872, 879, 888–90 (1990).

Justice Jackson before him[423]—about the practical linkage between sincerity and credibility, sufficient constraints can be put on the sincerity inquiry to prevent it from becoming an assessment of the veracity of beliefs. The fact that a less familiar or strange belief may induce stricter scrutiny of sincerity does not in and of itself mean that the veracity of the belief as such is being called into doubt. These considerations will operate to prevent unduly expansive self-definitions of religion.

In fact, it is likely that the limited deference approach may allow more flexibility at the outer boundary of what counts as religion. Even if it did not, however, use of this approach would still make a significant contribution by sending a symbolic message of inclusion that would be worth any additional costs in what the state might regard as questionable claims in additional borderline cases. Just as the presumption of innocence leads our criminal system to err on the side of acquittal, so the limited deference theory leads to a definition process that errs on the side of protecting religious freedom.

Limited deference analysis focuses attention where it should be focused: not on second-guessing religious judgments, but on assessing whether there are legitimate state factors that justify constraining a particular putative definition. As a practical matter, one of the most significant risks in imposing limits on religious autonomy is that definitions can be manipulated to discriminate against unpopular religious groups. Such dangers are always present, but they increase dramatically when the imposition is disguised as the mere providing of a "neutral" definition. A neutral, scientific definition of religion does not exist. Pretending that it does merely distracts from the real issues, and can be a sleight-of-hand for avoiding scrutiny of discriminatory judgments.

Limited deference theory extends the insights of religious autonomy cases to the problem of definition itself, and enables the state to avoid second-guessing or taking sides. It introduces new complexities, not all of which have been fully worked out here. But in the last analysis, it is maximally protective of the kind of authentic and autonomous religion that is vital to cultivation of the normative worlds in which we live.

---

423. United States v. Ballard, 322 U.S. 78, 92–95 (1944) (Jackson, J., dissenting).

Religious Polity

Martin E. Marty and James A. Serritella

Polity is a word used to describe the mode of governance of a religious organization. It is the organizing principle by which individual believers form a religious body.

When we speak of individuals "forming" such a body, we necessarily are using the language of social science observation and law. If we were called to be faithful to what anthropologists call "agents' description," which means seeing phenomena from the viewpoint of insiders, it would be just as important to note that in the eyes of some groups, it is not they who form a religious body. This community or communion of faith and practice is a given, an object of divine revelation. It is something whose basic structure is prescribed by the very nature of things or by the disclosive act of a suprahuman, supernatural force, "God."

In such cases, if a religious community claims that its form of organization is directly derived from revelation, it dares not tamper with forms or basic restructuring. In this concept, Allah, Yahweh, the Father of Jesus Christ, or the First Cause arranges that a preexisting community of believers exists "in the mind of God" and gives it reality on earth. Humans may then be predestined to find their place in it, to grow in awareness of its reality, and to accept it as the given that it is. Social scientists and historians will not stress this "givenness" so readily as they will notice that such communities are formed purposively.

Thus in a notable essay on denominationalism, the American religious historian Sidney E. Mead has discerned that "purposiveness" characterizes denominations in the United States. "The denomination, unlike the traditional forms of the church, is not primarily confessional, and it is certainly not territorial. Rather it is purposive." Theological interpreters may find this social scientific designation unwelcome. They may chafe to see their divinely ordained church listed on a par with the hundreds of bodies that they would have called "sects." They may resent it that, as Mead puts it, "a church as church has no legal existence in the United States. It is represented legally by a civil corporation," and is "a voluntary association of like-hearted and like-minded individuals, who are united on the basis of common beliefs for the purpose of accomplishing tangible and defined objectives."

According to Mead, these objectives may include the propagation of a view which it in some sense holds to be true. The organization may give impulse to missionary or reform purposes, or it may exist for institutional self-aggrandizement. But no legal or privileged place can be found from which the society determines that the *'umma* of Islam, the *Q'lal Yahweh* of Jews, the body of Christ for all Christians, or the Catholic church for Orthodox or Roman Catholics is a divinely nurtured "given" exempt from human observation and law. They are to be viewed from below, as it were. This doubleness of viewpoints is a fact that creates a disparity among theologians, especially those who begin on idealist bases, and social scientists and legal observers, who see religious bodies all denominationally "on par," and their polities matters of human choice, not divine purpose.[1]

Especially in the area of church property disputes, the mode of governance used by religious organizations has had a strong impact on how courts have dealt with them. Civil courts have often interpreted religious polity rigidly and formalistically, declaring the polity of an individual religious body to be part of a distinct, analytical category (hierarchical, presbyterial, congregational) rather than recognizing that religious polity falls along a continuum, each church having some aspects of the various, distinct polities.

A church's mode of governance has its beginnings in the church's understanding of itself and need to conduct its own affairs. This self-understanding, in turn, is usually tied to the church's religious beliefs as set forth in its doctrine and scripture.[2] In the United States this faith dimension of institutional organization and governance has constitutional implications which set churches apart from other nonprofit organizations. That is, just as individuals have constitutional guarantees of religious freedom, so do the institutions which are the collective expression of those beliefs.[3]

While the basic thrust and dimension of a church's governance may be tied to religious beliefs, other aspects of its governance may be based purely on practical considerations such as ease of administration. What is religious and what is practical may be difficult to discern depending on the church's theology, its history, and the degree to which the religious and the practical have been enmeshed with each other.

The religious organization does not act within a vacuum but as part of society which also has a set of standards and structure by which it operates. In this instance, as in the already noted disparity between theological interpretations of the founding of religious communities and social scientific observations concerning this empirical situation, conceptual and perceptual gaps occur between the claims some church bodies make for their independence from surrounding culture and those that interpreters in other bodies express through a whole range of adaptations. A classic typology of relationships between religious communities and their surroundings—of the efforts of those who stress independence and those who recognize the interpenetration of influences—is H. Richard Niebuhr's *Christ and Culture*.[4]

Niebuhr's mid-century analysis has stood the test of time. He used Christian terminology that can easily be translated for other belief systems. Those who accent independence adhere to the Niebuhrian models of "Christ above culture" or "Christ against cul-

---

1. Sidney E. Mead, The Lively Experiment: The Shaping of Christianity in America, 103–04 (1963).

2. *See* Center for Church/State Studies, DePaul Univ. College of Law, 1994 Report on the Survey of Religious Organizations at the National Level, Q2, Q3 (unpublished survey, on file with the Center for Church/State Studies, DePaul University College of Law) [hereinafter Survey]. For a discussion of the Survey's method and findings, see Rhys H. Williams & John P.N. Massad , "Religious Diversity, Civil Law, and Institutional Isomorphism," in this volume.

3. *See* Thomas C. Berg, "Religious Structures Under the Federal Constitution," in this volume.

4. H. Richard Niebuhr, Christ and Culture (1956). *See, e.g.,* Michael W. McConnell, Christ, Culture, and Courts: A Niebuhrian Examination of First Amendment Jurisprudence, 42 DePaul L. Rev. 191 (1992); *compare* Ira C. Lupu and Robert Tuttle, The Distinctive Place of Religious Entities in Our Constitutional Order, 47 Vill. L. Rev. 37 (2002). *See also* Angela C. Carmella, A Theological Critique of Free Exercise Jurisprudence, 60 Geo. Wash. L. Rev. 782 (1992).

ture." In the former case, the religious community is so pure that it transcends all efforts by mundane agents to connect it with its "corrupting" environment, one made up of outsiders. In the latter case, the religious community recognizes the lures of the surrounding cultures and willfully withstands everything in them that might taint or compromise it.

At the opposite end of the cultural spectrum Niebuhr posed "Christ of culture," in which the religious community of any sort is so much the agent of what is good in the surrounding environment and so much the product of what is productive in that milieu that distances cannot be discerned between the insiders' perceptions or claims and the claims of those who do not belong to the community. Niebuhr offers two other models, "Christ transforming culture" and "Christ and culture in paradox," in which the Christian community or, by analogy, any religious body, is in some sort of tension with the surrounding cultural environment but is neither aloof from it or totally absorbed by it.

These distinctions made by religious bodies are most relevant to our present concerns in the cases where the environment is defined in constitutional and legal terms. In such cases the religious community does not determine its destiny solely in its own terms, but is subject to determinations by external forces. Many are reluctant to acknowledge what they would call "nontheological factors" in their common life. Yet from the legal angle these are inescapable, and members of a society who are also members of a religious communion are given no choice but to live within the boundaries of such factors, however grudgingly.

Few, if any, religious bodies operate outside a civil law structure. Churches and other religious bodies must translate their polity into a civil law structure such as a corporation, trust, or unincorporated association.[5] In addition, courts and government agencies make decisions about churches based on civil legal structures which the law has created, further complexifying the polity issue.

As any linguist can attest, not all concepts translate easily from one language to another. A church's polity can sometimes be difficult to capture in a civil law form. Unlike other types of organizations, a religious body's successful legal structuring depends upon more than purely functional considerations. Numerous complexities intrude upon the attempt to cleanly translate an ecclesiastical body's self-perception as a religiously inspired entity into operations in the civil order. Difficulties occur especially when religious organizations do not have a well developed view of their ecclesiology or when their self-understanding changes.

Some religious communions will utter claims that religious bodies do not or should not have "*self*-understandings." Rather, these bodies are to be receptive of divinely revealed patterns and some consequent understandings associated with them. Among such communions, Eastern Orthodox Christianity is typical. It and others like it are therefore resistant even to the concept of permissible change. They may well make minor adaptations to meet the circumstances of different times and places. For example, the Orthodox related differently to the givens of their environment in the Ottoman Empire, where they were in minority enclaves (following a pattern called the *rum millet*), than they did in situations where they held a religious monopoly and exemplified ways of relating the governments of church and state that are characterized as

5. *See* Patricia B. Carlson, "Unincorporated Associations and Charitable Trusts," Patty Gerstenblith, "Associational Structures of Religious Organizations," and H. Reese Hansen, "Religious Organizations and the Law of Trusts," in this volume.

theocratic, hierocratic, or Erastian.[6] To ecclesiastics who guard the Orthodox tradition, these adjustments would be merely pragmatic and superficial adaptations, and would have nothing to do with the essence of the church's polity, the divinely prescribed form.

It also happens that the civil law structure may not keep up with the changes in a church's governing structure or developments in pertinent law. Improper application of the law or lack of insight about a church's governing structure can lead to serious adverse effects and possibly impair the very mission of the church.

Religious polity has posed a special challenge to civil society. Over the past century courts and administrative agencies have made decisions about churches and their polity which sometimes have gone askew, even to the point of threatening religious freedom. While civil order is hospitable to religious polity, it does not always understand it or sufficiently accommodate it.

What is it to make a theological claim for a particular polity or to web the doctrinal, practical, and behavioral life of a religious body to theological claims in such ways that courts find it difficult to adjudicate when conflict arises? Since most religious groups see theology or some cognate interpretive scheme to be integral to their existence, it puzzles many of them that their disputes, so clearly grounded in their originating scriptures, should not be patent to the courts and thus subject to legal scrutiny and decision. Yet on two sets of grounds described in this chapter the courts do back off from decisions that crack open the whole issue of theology.

What is this "theology" that causes so much difficulty in legal life? Etymologically, of course, it combines the words *theos*, god, with *logos*, word. So it has to do with making words about the reality called God. But since God is not immediately available except in the experience of the mystic, language about God ordinarily refers to language of the believing community that has an experience of God, or reads a scripture revealing God, or *is* a scripture that claims to be revealing God. That language, of course, is available for scrutiny. Scriptural scholars study the texts. Historical theologians follow the trajectory of believing and interpreting communities through history. Philosophical scholars take data deemed revelation by believing communities and appraise it in critical terms.

What none of them do is produce God on stage, as it were, for empirical observation. This poses special problems for law courts which need to evaluate things empirically. What is more, these interpretations of the lives of people, or theologies, come in the plural. In cultures where kingship is endowed with divine right or in theocracies where clergy rule, matters are simpler, especially in precritical eras. But in a culture encompassing hundreds of thousands of congregations and a couple of thousand religious bodies embracing differing and sometimes mutually contradictory scriptures and traditions, the situation is much more complex. It demands that the question be asked, as it was by the founders: Whose claim, which God, which scripture should be taken as true or at least normative?

There was no way to determine this in an era when the church establishments were in the process of yielding monopoly or privilege for their scriptures, communities, in-

---

6. In a theocratic form of governance, God is the immediate ruler and a religious or priestly order serves and administrates as God's agents. The same order serves in a hierocracy, but it is no longer viewed as having agent status with respect to the divine will. The priests or other religious are here the real rulers rather than God Godself. Finally, Erastian governance implies state supremacy in all religious affairs—a complete subordination, in other words, of ecclesial powers to reigning secular ones.

terpreters, and guardians of polity over others. While these founders may have had implied theologies of their own in the name of Nature's God or the God of Reason, they believed that you could not constitute a republic by basing it on transcendental and revealed claims. This republic and its courts never discouraged religious groups from employing theology to determine their own inner life. Yet they could not effectively make theological claims that would be validated in a court of law. Indeed the courts have always kept their distance from interpreting or evaluating theological claims.

A word should be said about nontheistic religions, since they do not profess to relate to *theos.* Among these would be some humanist elements in the Unitarian Universalist Association, those espousing some forms of Buddhism, and the like. They may not revere a God specifically named and defined, but they tend to be drawn to themes that motivate what Paul Tillich called their "ultimate concern." Indeed in the eyes of their theistic competitors, these groups are serious about locating such concern, even if not in a supernatural revelation. The courts are sophisticated about what they cannot know and why and how they cannot know it. So they observe without intervening as religious bodies set up institutional shop with a variety of polities, each of them legally legitimate and each of them having claims that carry them beyond the empirical and thus beyond the courts of law.

This chapter focuses on the following questions: Have the forms of governance recognized by participants in the legal system been overly restrictive, in that alternative forms of governance are either not considered or mislabeled? If so, what other forms of governance should courts recognize? Are there areas other than church property disputes which can be successfully addressed by reference to church governance? For example, are the application of civil rights laws to religious bodies influenced by religious polity? To what extent is the availability of church assets to creditors related to church polity and church structure? How can lawyers, courts (including bankruptcy courts), and legislators work to facilitate better decisions about church governance and assets by public leaders? This chapter holds to the notion that the better decisions are those which enable a religious organization to enjoy the full benefits of religious freedom.

Polity in the Legal Sense

The tension between religious groups and government has been around for as long as religion and government have occupied the same space in history, arguably as long as humans have lived in an organized society. Oddly enough, however, the first significant United States court case dealing with religious polity arose near the end of the nineteenth century. In the 1872 case *Watson v. Jones*[7] the Court grappled with the issue of schismatic control. After the American Civil War ended, the congregation of the Walnut Street Presbyterian Church in Louisville, Kentucky, divided between those who supported the new emancipation of slaves and those who did not. The Walnut Street Church fell under the ecclesiastical jurisdiction of the General Presbyterian Church in the United States which, as a denomination, condemned slavery. In reaction to the emancipation, a significant portion of the congregation, including elders and trustees, dissented from this antislavery doctrine and decided to separate

---

7. 80 U.S. (13 Wall.) 679 (1872).

from the Presbyterian Church. The dissenters then confronted the church hierarchy and claimed the right to the local church property. The general church authorities deemed the dissenters to have voluntarily separated themselves from the Presbyterian church and removed the rebel congregants from control of the Walnut Street Church.

Rather than deciding the case, the Supreme Court deferred to the judgment of the Presbyterian church authorities because the Court determined that the Presbyterian church, and not the Court, had jurisdiction over the ecclesiastical matters of the Walnut Street Church. The Court refused to disturb the ecclesiastical decision of the Presbyterian church which ruled that the dissenters had no ecclesiastical right of control over religious activities of a local congregation. According to the Presbyterian church, only its highest level, the General Assembly of the General Presbyterian Church, had the authority to make decisions affecting local churches.

In this decision the Court adopted a strong deferential stance toward church affairs and religious matters in general. Among the principles established was that the courts are competent to enforce express terms contained in documents governing the use or ownership of property, but may not inquire into religious doctrine in order to determine such ownership.

> That the jurisdiction of civil courts being confined to "civil actions," they may not take cognizance of purely spiritual or ecclesiastical questions, as such; just as they may not take cognizance of any moral or scientific questions for the purpose of determining upon their abstract truth.... In these several cases the exclusive standard of judgment is the CONSTITUTION of the church itself.[8]

When a dispute arises, particularly between subordinate and superior bodies of a hierarchical church:

> the rule of action which should govern the civil courts, founded in a broad and sound view of the relations of church and state under our system of laws, and supported by a preponderating weight of judicial authority is, that, whenever the questions of discipline, or of faith, or ecclesiastical rule, custom, or law have been decided by the highest of these church judicatories to which the matter has been carried, the legal tribunals must accept such decisions as final, and as binding on them, in their application to the case before them.[9]

In the spirit of *Watson*'s expansive deference to ecclesiastical decision makers, the courts have developed two somewhat complementing legal principles to guide their own decisions concerning a religious group. The first principle we shall take up is what we can call the "polity approach," an approach widely used but not always named as such. Secondly, we shall discuss the "neutral principles of law approach," which is frequently misunderstood.[10]

---

8. *Id.* at 710–11.

9. *Id.* at 727.

10. Many of the early cases which followed *Watson* involved denominational disputes over the ownership of church-held property, as *Watson* itself did. Out of these seminal property cases the two basic approaches developed into legal standards. The relationship between the two principles remains ambiguous and the courts have been reluctant to formulate a unified principle.

The polity approach

This legal principle has sometimes been called "ecclesiastical abstention" but "polity approach" more accurately captures what this line of cases advocates—namely, deference to a church's organizational self-understanding and governance. The polity approach is a simple separatist view. It leaves controversies over theology to the theologians, and church practice to the proper church authorities. In short, when a governing religious structure can be identified which has ultimate authority to make decisions concerning an organization, and when it is determined that the governing body has made a decision regarding a dispute, the civil court system has no jurisdiction to evaluate or inquire into the organization's decision in the absence of fraud, collusion, or arbitrariness.[11] Courts have generally followed this approach and avoided interfering with internal church struggles. Consequently a strong line of cases developed in which courts deferred to a church's own conflict-resolution structure.[12]

As an example, if a church encounters schism or an individual church withdraws from a broader body, the courts do not have jurisdiction to evaluate which group practiced or practices the original tenets of the faith. In order to decide which group should prevail, *Watson* and the cases which follow it explicitly reject the line of English common law cases which take an active, intruding role and try to determine which church body departed from the church's doctrine. Under *Watson* the courts should treat schismatic matters or doctrinal challenges as internal church disputes, beyond civil court reach even when property rights and civil rights are affected.[13] The polity approach is available not only for schisms between the local church and its larger denominational body, but for schisms within the local church as well.[14]

Watson is a fascinating case not only for its ruling, but also for its rationale. It is important to note that *Watson* rests its polity approach on common law, not on the First Amendment's Free Exercise Clause. Nevertheless, post-*Watson* courts have grounded the polity approach not in the common law, but rather in a religious body's First Amendment right to free exercise of religion,[15] drawing a broad line separating the court's jurisdiction from the church's. Within the First Amendment context, courts reason that the Constitution prohibits government from making any theological determination because such rulings lie beyond the scope of the state's civil and secular, judicial and legislative, competence.[16]

---

11. *See* Gonzalez v. Roman Catholic Archbishop, 280 U.S. 1, 16 (1929).

12. *See* Kedroff v. St. Nicholas Cathedral, 344 U.S. 94 (1952); Kreshik v. St. Nicholas Cathedral, 363 U.S. 190 (1960); Serbian E. Orthodox Diocese v. Milivojevich, 426 U.S. 696 (1976).

13. *See* Crowder v. Southern Baptist Convention, 828 F.2d 718 (11th Cir. 1987); Nunn v. Black, 506 F. Supp. 444 (W.D. Va.) *aff'd*, 661 F.2d 925 (4th Cir. 1981); Tibbs v. Kendrick, 637 N.E.2d 397 (Ohio Ct. App. 1994); Hines v. Turley, 615 N.E.2d 1251 (Ill. App. Ct. 1993); Allen v. Board of Incorporators, No. 92 C 6098, 1992 WL 390755 (N.D. Ill. Dec. 18, 1992); Fowler v. Bailey, 844 P.2d 141 (Okla. 1992); Alexander v. Shiloh Baptist Church, 592 N.E.2d 918 (Ohio, C.P., Franklin County 1991). *But see* Reid v. Gholson, 327 S.E.2d 107 (Va. 1985).

14. *See* Bishop of Colo. v. Mote, 716 P.2d 85 (Colo. 1986) (en banc); Schismatic and Purported Casa Linda Presbyterian Church in America v. Grace Union Presbytery, Inc., 710 S.W.2d 700 (Tex. App. 1986 writ ref'd n.r.e.); Zaiser v. Miller, 656 S.W.2d 312 (Mo. Ct. App. 1983); Sorrenson v. Logan, 177 N.E.2d 713 (Ill. App. Ct. 1961).

15. *See* Presbyterian Church in United States v. Hull Mem'l Presbyterian Church, 393 U.S. 440 (1969).

16. *See Kedroff*, 344 U.S. 94; *Kreshik*, 363 U.S. 190.

While cases after *Watson* justify the polity approach under the First Amendment rather than under common law, the basic principles of *Watson* remain intact. American courts will defer to the proper religious authority in disputes touching on religious beliefs. This deference to church governance is not limited to property disputes. Basing their rationale on *Watson* and its progeny, courts have held that applying Title VII provisions to the relationship between a church and its ministers would cause an unconstitutional intrusion into church administration.[17]

Nonetheless, the polity approach leaves some issues unresolved. Paramount among these are the determinations of what is a church and what is a church's proper polity. For example, is a church that portion of a religious organization which has a worship function, or does church encompass all ecclesial functions including education, community service, and health care? Even if it is in some sense clear that a given activity is part of a church, how do courts identify the appropriate church body that has the decision-making authority to determine its polity? Further, how much theological analysis are courts permitted to undertake to identify the appropriate church polity? The answers to these questions are dependent on the degree to which the courts will defer to a church's self-understanding.

To contending parties in congregational or denominational schisms, the fact that courts using the polity approach stand back and refuse to make theological judgments is often frustrating. As far as they are concerned, the scriptural or traditional textual prescriptions about polity and doctrine are so patent that all reasonable people ought easily to comprehend them and make judgments in the light of them.

To employ a term theologians welcome, such partisans are not recognizing *hermeneutics*. That is, they see the original documents as being perspicuous, unambiguous, unshrouded by mystery. In theistic traditions this claim translates to the following: if the scripture is the word of a God who wants to be obeyed, then it insults the divine character to suggest that God cannot "get through" clearly to humans. Over against such contentions, those who are committed to hermeneutical approaches assume that all interpreters bring some preunderstandings to their interpreting. They judge the part of a text in the light of a whole, or make much of prejudices and prejudgments that color the claims of believers and interpreters like themselves on all sides.

The courts in such cases cannot make determinations between the literalists, however impassioned and putatively clarifying their expressed self-understandings may be, and the hermeneuticians, who demand complex interpretations. So the same courts that will not make theological judgments will not even make judgments about how theological judgments are made or should be made.

Although the polity approach provides complete deference to the religious organization by claiming incompetence on matters of theology, in practice a pure application of the deference standard is impractical, if not impossible. Even in the same church members may hold differing opinions as to what their church's polity may be.[18] A court must traverse, even if ever so lightly, theological terrain in order to determine a church's self-understanding so that it can defer to the proper church authority. In identifying the

---

17. *See* McClure v. Salvation Army, 460 F.2d 553 (5th Cir. 1972).
18. *See* Grace Evangelical Lutheran Church v. Lutheran Church-Mo. Synod, 454 N.E.2d 1038 (Ill. App. Ct. 1983); Werling v. Grace Evangelical Lutheran Church, 487 N.E.2d 990 (Ill. App. Ct. 1985).

governance structure, courts beginning with *Watson* have tended to group religious polities into one of two types, thinking these would describe the universe—a hierarchical or a congregational form of polity.

Introducing the theology of forms of polity

One reason the courts have often made their judgments as if the categories "hierarchical" and "congregational" exhausted all options has to do with the fact that adherents of these two polity forms tend to be more emphatic and precise about defining and, in many cases, seeing traditional and scriptural warrants for their polity as belonging integrally to the life of their communion. Those who see themselves in mixed polities of the sorts that appear along a spectrum between the courts' two exhaustive extremes are less likely to be literalist about the claims of tradition, more ready to change when necessary, and more able to consider these polities to be products of human invention and not divine prescription. These mixed polities include connectionalism, synodicalism, and presbyterianism (which, as we shall see, is in the courts' eye kin to episcopacy for being hierarchical), and the like. In all these cases, statements of denominational discipline may be extremely prescriptive and may be backed by formal church law. No one can credibly accuse Methodism of being casual about the laws and disciplines of its bodies. Indeed, it tends to be better organized than many hierarchical bodies. Nevertheless, Methodism less readily resorts to ontological and theological claims. Whereas Orthodoxy and Catholicism tend to see hierarchy as integral to the life of the communion, indeed, as belonging to the *esse* of the religious communion, the connectionalists would say that their governing bishops belong to its *bene esse,* or its beneficial core. Thus some Lutherans live with bishops who are in the apostolic succession, but their role, office, and selves are not of the *esse,* the essence of the church. Other Lutherans who do not claim to be in the succession are governed by bishops and see them as being of the *bene esse.* Still others may be governed without bishops and with other forms of government. All of them have equal claims to being authentically Lutheran, because Lutherans were never constituted or defined by polity and they tend to be quite pragmatic about most of their forms.

The hierarchical character of the Roman Catholic church, on the other hand, comes to its originating and summary point in the bishop of Rome, the pope, an office which compels certain absolute doctrinal beliefs not to be bartered away or compromised. Orthodox Catholics contend that from the time of the earliest Christian church to the present, a consistent claim for realizing polity on grounds of divine revelation has characterized their church. Some among them may debate the relative rights and duties of the pope and the council of bishops, who are to relate "collegially." But no outcomes could leave the church describing itself as catholic if the papacy were compromised or if episcopal rights were qualified by equals or "people below." The courts have little trouble with such a concept.

The theological claims need not always be made on such absolute grounds. Thus the Church of Christ, Scientist, has a polity that grants great power to the central authorities at its Mother Church in Boston. Very few deviations from its organizational prescriptions are permitted. Any local Christian Science congregation that patently departed from the norms of church law would be judged critically in any court. Yet in the face of schisms—and there were many in the early years of the Church of Christ, Scientist—partisans will make divine claims for their polity as each of them interprets it. At this level courts cannot enter the scene effectively.

At the other end of the spectrum are "pure" congregationalist polities and individuals to match or counter the "pure" hierarchical bodies. Religious freedom in the United States assures that each church body can choose its polity—or affirm its transcendently mandated polity—without fearing the intervention of civil law. But within the congregationalist bodies schism and disruption of tradition form long traditions of their own—for fairly obvious reasons.

Most advocates of pure congregationalism aver that in divine revelation or church tradition no legitimate, formal authority stands higher than that of the local congregation and its leadership. These proponents insist that divine revelation prescribed this pattern of local authority. So understood, congregationalism—a widespread expression of Protestant life—is easy to define and sustain. Courts can make many kinds of legal rulings on the basis of how various factions live with their claims and self-definitions.

Indeed, the fact that congregationalists make no claims to authority higher than the local is attractive to the courts; contenders in an internal church dispute have to win only local legal favor, without second-guessing or resorting to other ecclesial authority. Claims to prescriptive divine revelation are irrelevant to the court, but may serve as a clarifying element to both sides in a dispute and provide coherent ground rules for the court. This contrasts with those circumstances in which the local congregation as the scene of a conflict not only asks the courts to intervene on its affairs but may also invoke synodical, hierarchical, or national authority to justify claims on any side.

When the mixed and fluid polities between the hierarchical and congregational come into play, advocates for these churches may be just as ready to resort to specification in church law or to make a more immediate appeal to the pragmatic and empirical situation. The congregational and connectional polities are effective for those who would carry out specific denominational purposes. They may claim certain warrants in revelation and will almost certainly become consolidated in church law. Yet the decisions connected with congregationalism tend not to be seen as rooted in anything integral or essential to the churches' life.

In classic terms polity is thus in this case an *adiaphoron,* something arbitrary that can serve as a basis for transaction, the best provision in the eyes of the custodians of the church tradition—but not fixed for the ages. The courts manifest confusion in such situations, not seeing that connectional, synodical, and presbyterial polities may be adhered to as zealously as congregational or hierarchical ones, though only the latter two polity forms claim a governance prescribed by divine revelation.

Forms of polity

Hierarchical churches are organized as one body that holds together many congregations of similar beliefs or heritage under a common ruling ecclesiastical head. In this form of polity, a hierarchy holds authority over all local assemblies or congregations by virtue of a divine right. Local congregations are subordinate to higher church units and ecclesiastical tribunals. The constitutive element of all hierarchical churches is a clearly defined vertical line of authority. Within the hierarchical form courts have recognized two subdivisions: episcopal and presbyteral. Episcopal churches may be ruled by one person or by a specially authorized group. In the United States these religious bodies would include, for example, the Roman Catholic church, the Orthodox churches, and the Protestant Episcopal church. Presbyteral forms of polity, also called *synodal,* include churches which vest authority in the individual members or the congregation for local activities, but offer democratically elected, representative government. Presbyteral forms allow members to choose representatives for decision-making governing bodies, and the local church is then subject to these supreme bodies. The Presbyterian church and the Reformed Church in America are examples of presbyteral polities.

In contrast, congregational forms of polity, each separate assembly or congregation is self-governing and independent. Most commonly, individual congregational churches are governed by their membership or some other local entity like a church board. Congregationalist decisions are typically made by a majority of the local governing entity or membership. Being independent does not preclude a local church from identifying itself with a wider body of believers, but ecclesiastically this body of believers has a radically decentralized governance. The heart of this type of governing structure, which focuses on independence, is rooted in congregationalist theology, its ecclesial self-understanding, and its view of how God works on the local church level. Courts have generally recognized Baptist churches, Disciples of Christ, and the Jewish bodies, among others, as taking this form.

A form of polity not often recognized by the legal system is *connectional*. While this polity may employ a denominational leader for purposes of moderating an annual or quadrennial conference, during most times direction is not centralized but emerges out of a sense of all congregations and agencies being connected through sharing the same beliefs and governing documents. The United Methodist church most clearly mainfests this polity,[19] though its blend of the two major court-approved polity types, hierarchical and congregational, has often caused it to be misconstrued.[20]

Limitations of the polity approach

In using a two-option approach to make determinations of religious polity, courts, albeit with good intention, have tried to fit churches into narrowly defined categories in order to resolve internal ecclesial disputes. If a court can determine a church is clearly hierarchical or congregational, it can, of course, more easily resolve the jurisdictional question, namely, whether a dispute should be settled by a governing body higher in authority than the local church or by a majority vote of the local congregation. When a church defines its polity somewhere along the continuum between the more easily understood endpoints, that jurisdictional issue is more difficult to resolve. In such cases the court may try to force a church into the form of polity under which it believes the church is organized.

Danger looms for religious bodies if courts misinterpret their polity. For example, if a grouping of congregationalist churches shares common doctrines and beliefs and its member congregations voluntarily connect themselves to regional or national bodies, they may be mischaracterized as hierarchical church organizations. Such a mischaracterization could lead a court to usurp the legitimate authority of a local church in favor of the voice of a consortium of similarly believing churches. Likewise, a court could misread an election within a local congregation (whether legitimate or not) as a sign of

---

19. Edward McGlynn Gaffney, Jr., & Philip C. Sorensen, Ascending Liability in Religious and Other Nonprofit Organizations 133–37 (1984).

20. Most courts and commentators have determined that the United Methodist Church is hierarchical. *See* Barr v. United Methodist Church, 153 Cal. Rptr. 322 (Ct. App. 1979); Arlin M. Adams & William R. Hanlon, Jones v. Wolf: Church Autonomy and the Religion Clauses of the First Amendment, 128 U. Pa. L. Rev. 1281, 1292 n.6 (1980) ("Among the principal denominations with an episcopal form of polity are...the Methodist Church"); John Lynch, Church Polity *in* 3 The Encyclopedia of Religion, 477 (Mircea Eliade ed., 1986).

a congregational polity and deprive rightful religious authorities of their power of decision making.[21] This error not only deprives a church of its autonomy; it inappropriately leavens the church's theology with a secular misreading and therein impairs a religious body's constitutionally protected religious freedom.

Mischaracterization, moreover, can lead to confusing decisions. For example, it would be difficult to find the head of the United Methodist Church or its headquarters. Methodists have held that theirs is a connectional church structure, neither hierarchical nor congregational. Nevertheless, the California courts determined that the church was hierarchical and derivatively liable for the actions of retirement homes with a Methodist affiliation.[22] Additionally, different courts looking at the same church have not agreed on the church's polity. For example, the United Presbyterian Church in the U.S.A. has been deemed presbyteral in Maryland[23] and congregational in Pennsylvania.[24] Similarly, the Protestant Episcopal Church in the United States was found to be an episcopal hierarchy in Michigan[25] and a congregational polity in Kentucky.[26]

The polity approach affords great deference and respect for religious bodies, but that deference and respect is always susceptible to ill-informed judicial analysis. The polity approach, in other words, is only as good as a court's understanding of the religious polity and particular faith of the case at hand. As we have seen, not all religious groups fit neatly into one of the two major polity forms. When asked to characterize their own polity, religious organizations in the survey discussed in this volume indicated polity types as follows: about 20% hierarchical, about 40% congregational, about 10% presbyteral, about 10% connectional, about 10% along a continuum of polity types, and about 10% as other polity forms.[27] The courts in the United States have developed their approaches to polity in a culture largely shaped by Judaism and Christianity, so it is legitimate to ask whether the increasing pluralism of an always pluralist society will be likely to change these approaches to adjudication. Since the changes in immigration laws in 1965, great numbers of people from Asia, Latin America, and Africa have made their way into the United States and are in the process of changing its religious complexion. They come from a wide variety of polities, in which religion and regime interact in diverse ways. Thus in much of the Arab Muslim world—not the only Muslim world there is!—nothing equivalent to western Enlightenment-based separations of church and state have occurred. New heirs of these cultures become citizens of the United States, build mosques, gather worshipers, and have their own legal disputes to match those of the Jews and Christians. Will their experiences change the legal situation, and particularly the courts' approach to polity determinations?

Not likely. Other factors may influence the courts' interpretations of communities that live by theological interpretations yet under positive law. But the Christian communities whose cases have made it to the Supreme Court have manifested so much internal variety that it is hard to picture unprecedented types or tests in the legal system.

Hinduism and Buddhism, in any case, live with what Lester Kurtz calls "decentralized structures." Indeed, Kurtz, a scholar at the University of Texas in Austin who has

---

21. *See* Primate and Bishops' Synod of Russian Orthodox Church Outside Russ. v. Russian Orthodox Church of Holy Resurrection, 636 N.E.2d 211 (Mass. 1994).

22. *See Barr*, 153 Cal. Rptr. 322; *see also* Gaffney & Sorensen, *supra* note 19.

23. *See* Babcock Mem'l Presbyterian Church v. Presbytery of Baltimore, 464 A.2d 1008 (Md. 1983).

24. *See* Presbytery of Beaver-Butler v. Middlesex Presbyterian Church, 489 A.2d 1317 (Pa. 1985).

25. *See* Bennison v. Sharp, 329 N.W.2d 466 (Mich. Ct. App. 1982).

26. *See* Bjorkman v. Protestant Episcopal Church in United States, 759 S.W.2d 583 (Ky. 1988).

27. *See* Survey, *supra* note 2, Q1.

also taught in China and India, has noted that "the Hindu system rather resembles American Protestant churches." Ancient texts have an influence, but they do not prescribe a consistent polity. Since between a half million and a million Americans practice the religions of the Asian subcontinent, Hinduism in its various forms being primary, the subject needn't argue its relevance.

"The Hindu solution to questions of ordering the collective life of a highly diverse population is reflected in this religion's theology and its organization.... Respect for authority in general is highly regarded and internalized; Hindus are expected to be submissive to legitimated authorities." Yet any claim to authority has to be proven, and institutional forms are held without rigidity. Therefore, at least with regard to the polity matters at hand, Hindu theology offers no intrinsic novelty.

As for Buddhism, Kurtz observes with other scholars that no one polity prevails; rather, Buddhism has gleaned elements from indigenous cultures in different regions. It gives every sign of doing the same in the United States. As for Islam and Judaism, what Kurtz calls "tribal continuities" do more to link congregations than do any kind of theologically based organizational prescriptions. In Islam conflicts may arise in the case of those who belong to Shi'ite fundamentalist-like movements and want their judicial life to be measured by normative *shari'a,* or Muslim law, since *shari'a* does offer what Kurtz calls "a comprehensive judicial system" and defines the Muslim state. Such comprehensively prescriptive revealed legal systems, Muslim or otherwise, will not take precedence over the United States Constitution in religious matters. The larger, Sunni, branch of Islam more easily admits many kinds of interpretation. Kurtz's summary is apt: "In both Judaism and Islam, the solidarity of socioethnic ties of the community diffuses authority and [gives] religious elites socially derived rather than formal authority of a religious institution."[28]

The diversity of Christian churches—be they hierarchical, connectional, congregational, or any form between these—and the variety of theological options prescribing specific forms or permitting improvisation have been vast, and the experiences in the courts extensive. Consequently, it is not likely that the courts will have to adapt interpretations to accommodate utterly novel groups and cases. Moreover, courts are not likely to begin to evaluate theological judgments on a terrain that grows more complex and more contentious with each passing year.

Following *Watson v. Jones* the Supreme Court's rule of deference to church polity was the governing principle for intrachurch dispute matters. In 1952 the Supreme Court reaffirmed the polity approach and gave it constitutional standing.[29] This approach offered broad deference to religious bodies even when matters touched upon substantive civil issues such as property rights. As cases developed, however, courts, equipped with the polity approach, struggled to determine to which polity and jurisdictional entity they could appropriately defer.

The neutral principles of law approach

Human affairs do not always fit into neat compartments. Accordingly, it is not surprising that not all churches can be classified as either hierarchical or congregational. As

---

28. Lester R. Kurtz, Gods in the Global Village: The World's Religions in Sociological Perspective 85–92 (1995).
29. *See* Kedroff v. St. Nicholas Cathedral, 344 U.S. 94 (1952).

we have said, most fall along a continuum and contain aspects of each type of governance. Nonetheless, disputes are presented to courts even when the polity of the church at issue cannot be readily classified. Faced with the limits of the polity approach in mixed-polity cases, the courts turned to the neutral principles of law approach.

Determining neutral principles

In 1969 the Supreme Court overturned a Georgia decision based on departure from original church doctrine.[30] In so doing the court noted that "there are neutral principles of law, developed for use in all property disputes, which can be applied...."[31] One year later the Court upheld a state court's application of this neutral principles approach.[32] In a concurring opinion Justice Brennan outlined acceptable approaches to intrachurch disputes. "[A] State may adopt *any* one of various approaches for settling church property disputes so long as it involves no consideration of doctrinal matters, whether the ritual and liturgy of worship or the tenets of faith."[33]

Although the neutral principles of law approach had been articulated, the Court continued to find the polity approach an acceptable rationale for adjudicating intrachurch disputes.[34] The Court noted that reliance on neutral principles could not justify a court's substitution of its own interpretation of church rules for that of a church's authoritative body.[35]

In *Jones v. Wolf*[36] the Supreme Court approved an alternative to the polity approach to address church property disputes and modified the long-standing deference rule found in *Watson v. Jones*. The Court noted that the advantages of the neutral principles of law approach

> are that it is completely secular in operation, and yet flexible enough to accommodate all forms of religious organization and polity. The method relies on objective, well-established concepts of trust and property law familiar to lawyers and judges. It thereby promises to free civil courts completely from entanglements in questions of religious doctrine, polity, and practice. Furthermore, the neutral-principles analysis shares the peculiar genius of private-law systems in general — flexibility in ordering private rights and obligations to reflect the intentions of the parties. Through appropriate reversionary clauses and trust provisions, religious societies can specify what is to happen to church property in the event of a particular contingency, or what religious body will determine the ownership in the event of a schism or doctrinal controversy. In this manner, a religious organization can ensure that a dispute over the ownership of church property will be resolved in accord with the desires of the members.[37]

This alternative approach requires courts to focus on deeds, incorporation papers, and similar documents to determine who is entitled to church property. Putting aside

---

30. *See* Presbyterian Church in United States v. Hull Mem'l Presbyterian Church, 393 U.S. 440 (1969).

31. *Id.* at 449.

32. *See* Maryland and Va. Eldership of Churches of God v. Church of God, 396 U.S. 367 (1970) (per curiam).

33. *Id.* at 368 (emphasis in original).

34. *See* Serbian E. Orthodox Diocese v. Milivojevich, 426 U.S. 696 (1976).

35. *See id.* at 721.

36. 443 U.S. 595 (1979).

37. *Id.* at 603–04.

theological or ecclesiological questions, it grounds its query in the "neutral" legal documents. Consequently, the threshold question of this approach is whether the given dispute is resolvable without resorting to theological considerations. If a court cannot determine a church's polity or satisfactorily resolve the dispute by resort to neutral (read secular and civil) principles, then it may not resolve the dispute at all.[38]

It would seem at first that the neutral principles of law approach is harmless to religion, for how can one argue against holding churches accountable for the organizational and property documents they themselves created or maintained? A closer look reveals the pitfalls that attend this seemingly innocent question. The premise of the neutral principles of law approach is that the relevant facts are neutral on their face and contain no theological import. The question that must be asked is: can anything related to the structure of a church be without religious significance? Religious bodies are intentional about their self-understandings and their missions. From carvings in the minbar for Muslims to how the communion bread is served for Christians (whether at the front of the church by a priest or in the pews by fellow lay believers), structures of architecture, time, liturgy, and organization purposefully reflect religious organizations' deeper foundations.

Assuming it is possible to get around this obstacle, another very practical impediment presents itself. A religious organization's documents may not be written clearly or neutrally enough to enable a court to reach a decision. This is particularly true when older documents contain "departure-from-doctrine" language or references to ecclesiastical documents as factors to be considered in determining when local church property reverts to the larger denominational body.

Courts have consistently refused to consider departure-from-doctrine language on grounds that such considerations would require unconstitutional entanglement with religious doctrine. If property decisions were made based on departure from doctrine, it would force the court to determine which body departed from the original doctrine or purposes—the general body or the local congregation. For example, does a decision to ordain women by the general church constitute a departure from doctrine when a local church holds to traditional notions of a male-only clergy?[39] In such a case the local body has a reasonable argument that the general church has departed from original doctrine. To ask the court to decide this controversy is not only unconstitutional, but futile.

It may also be unwise to rely on references to other ecclesial documents to effect the transfer of property ownership to the general church. Under the neutral principles of law approach the court may choose not to look at these documents, or may ascribe to them merely spiritual relevance with nothing bearing on property-dispute resolution.

When you try to extend the neutral principles approach beyond property disputes to disputes regarding personnel, more difficulties arise. For example, menial employment appears neutral, but when encompassed within a church, it can grow a religious dimension. Who changes the light bulbs may look neutral to a court, but for a religious body it may be very important that its work force, down to the last person, has a religious role and so is subject to religious authority.[40]

For a court to characterize such documents or such employment as neutral, it must either ignore the religious character of a religious institution or, while recognizing it,

---

38. *See* Grace Evangelical Lutheran Church v. Lutheran Church-Mo. Synod, 454 N.E.2d 1038 (Ill. App. Ct. 1983).
39. *See* Protestant Episcopal Church v. Barker, 171 Cal. Rptr. 541 (Ct. App. 1981).
40. *See* Corporation of Presiding Bishop v. Amos, 483 U.S. 327 (1987).

determine it to be irrelevant to the question at issue. The term "neutral principles" is so seductive that it is a great source of temptation for courts and governmental bodies to extract from a religious organization that which they determine to be neutral, but what in context is not neutral at all.

Application of the neutral principles of law approach

It is apparent that the civil law tools for dealing with and respecting a church's self-understanding are limited. Deference ought to keep the courts out of theology, but for a court to accord deference it must first inquire into the religious organization by investigating its structure and internal governance.

Problems may be compounded when lawyers and other professionals do not accurately or effectively use available tools to translate a church's polity into civil law terms. No doubt failings sometimes occur because lawyers drafting the church's documents do not adequately understand the church's polity or neglect to change legal documents to reflect changes in a denomination's internal rules, or because the legal structures available do not reflect its particular polity and the most appropriate form of structure is not offered in a particular state. Often the courts are left to deal with a highly ambiguous religious structure which has been translated only imperfectly into legal terms.

Not only can church dispute resolution be affected by the drafting of legal documents, but it also is highly dependent upon how a court chooses to apply the neutral principles approach and which documents the court chooses to examine neutrally. Following the 1976 decision by the Protestant Episcopal church to allow the ordination of women, a number of congregations across the country disaffiliated from the denomination and attempted to take their local church property with them.

In California four parishes withdrew from the Episcopal Diocese of Los Angeles and wanted to retain their property while the diocese asserted that the local property was bound by an implied trust in its favor.[41] In resolving this dispute, the court looked to the holder of legal title to the property, which for all four parishes was the local congregation. Although a 1958 diocesan canon declared that upon dissolution of a parish its property was to be conveyed to the diocese[42] and although all of the parishes' articles of incorporation acknowledged that the diocesan constitution, canons, and discipline would always form a part of their own articles and bylaws,[43] only the most recently organized parish identified itself as a subordinate body of the diocese and contained an express trust conveying property to the diocese upon revocation of its charter.

The court did not consider the diocesan canons in making a determination, but looked to the deeds and incorporation documents. It found the acknowledgment of the diocesan constitution and canons to be expressions of merely present intent at the time of incorporation and not an open-ended agreement to conform to all future changes.[44] Consequently, the court determined that the property of the most recently formed parish reverted to the diocese because it included express language of subordination to the diocese, while the other parishes were allowed to disaffiliate and retain their property.

---

41. *See Protestant Episcopal Church*, 171 Cal. Rptr. 541.
42. *See id.* at 546.
43. *See id.* at 544–45.
44. *See id.* at 554.

The principle that might be gleaned from the California court is the following: For a general church at the regional or national level to include in its own book of discipline or ecclesiastical law that upon disaffiliation or dissolution property reverts to the general church (or statements to the effect that local church property is held in beneficial trust for the general church) is not enough to trigger court resolution in favor of the general church. Reversionary clauses triggered by "upon dissolution" language are not always honored in the manner expected by the general church because courts have secular rules that local congregations which disaffiliate from general church bodies are not "dissolved" as corporate entities.[45] If a polity wishes to insure that local church property is given to the general church if the local body disaffiliates, each and every property document must be amended to contain this language. The courts may not look as far as ecclesiastical law, but may make determinations on the basis of the property document alone.

This rationale extends to any trust theory of property ownership in the name of the general church. If property is not held in trust by the general church or its leader, the court may not find such a trust. The freedom granted to the local congregation for the general church's administrative convenience "carries the risk that congregations which disaffiliate will take their property with them."[46]

A few years after the California case the Colorado court faced a dispute arising out of a similar disaffiliation within the same denomination. In the Colorado case[47] the court decided that neutral principles of law allowed it to look farther than merely the property deed and incorporation documents. The court concluded that the "intent on the part of the local church corporation to dedicate its property irrevocably to the purposes of PECUSA [Protestant Episcopal Church of the USA] was expressed unambiguously in the combination of the 1955 articles of incorporation, the local church bylaws, and the canons of the general church to which the local church acceded in its articles at the time this dispute arose...."[48]

As churches relate to other affiliated or connected organizations, such as national or regional conferences, or their own integrated auxiliaries, such as service corporations, the lack of refinement in property documents only compounds the difficulties. Although all religious bodies are affected, this ambiguity may be especially felt in larger, more complex organizations, such as those which include higher education and health care institutions. The neutral principles approach is supposed to avoid this morass by focusing on the segments of church documents that deal only with secular matters. If these segments are truly representative of the organization as a whole, and if documents are redrawn each time a change in religious or civil law occurs, courts will indeed be able to make appropriate decisions. To the extent that lawyers and courts must wrench neutral segments from a religious context, however, appropriate civil-court decisions become difficult or impossible.

Thus the application of the neutral principles of law approach—not mandated but obviously preferred by the Supreme Court—has proven no easier for courts to use than the polity approach. The mechanistic application of this theory without considering the theological aspects of religious organization can reach results just as questionable as the mischaracterization of polity type does under a deference approach.

---

45. *See* First Presbyterian Church v. United Presbyterian Church in United States, 464 N.E.2d 454, 461 (N.Y. 1984).

46. *Protestant Episcopal Church*, 171 Cal. Rptr. at 553.

47. *See* Bishop of Colo. v. Mote, 716 P.2d 85 (Colo. 1986).

48. *Id.* at 104.

Untangling the Religious Polity Web

Three specific groups in the civil order may be identified which seem to have difficulties in understanding religious polity in the United States: (1) lawyers and other professionals; (2) courts; and (3) legislators.

Legal decisions are further complicated by the fact that those who ground their understanding of polity in divine revelation, especially hierarchical or congregational bodies, or see it as integral to the life of their religious communion adjudicate their internal disputes, in the first instance, by employing theologians and other ecclesiastical thinkers who may use norms uncongenial to attorneys, courts, and legislatures. It is notoriously difficult for these religious organizations to translate their theological claims into precise and incontrovertible legal terms. Given these challenges, they are well advised to engage in anticipatory action when writing about or clarifying the implications of their fundamental grasp of polity.

While we can make some good suggestions as to how courts and legislatures could better deal with these issues, those suggestions will not advance free exercise unless religious bodies themselves act. The most important thing a religious organization can do is to take action to protect itself, and therefore the majority of the following suggestions focus on clarifying the concept of religious polity for the secular world.

Lawyers and other professionals must be sensitive to the religious underpinning of any civil action by a religious group. If a lawyer, accountant, or other professional fails to accurately translate church order into civil order, then a church may be constrained in its ability to move effectively and freely within the civil world. Additionally, the implications for the religious body may spill over far beyond the immediate act.

Take, for example, the ongoing discussion over whether Roman Catholic priests should be classified as employees of their dioceses or as independent contractors.[49] This discussion has centered on these commercial law terms and what the federal government wants. It rarely touches on the word "incardination," which the church uses to describe the relationship. This shortsighted focus on readily available commercial terms rather than on the less familiar religious term distorts the law's treatment of this relationship.

Resolving this controversy pragmatically on commercial law terms without due consideration of the ecclesiastical implications will not by itself destroy the relationship between priest and bishop. Instead, this pragmatic resolution will become one of the descriptors of the relationship between priest and bishop that will haunt the civil law realm and, in an unrelated case, perhaps undermine a more accurate description.

Religion in a pluralistic culture needs a consistent, fair, and respectful treatment, but review of the cases involving religious polity shows that courts have not developed a consistent approach to treating religious groups. Although courts generally operate in the spirit of *Watson,* the polity approach and the neutral principles of law approach can create different results when applied. Courts have been reluctant to acknowledge forms of polity other than the hierarchical and congregational. And perhaps most significantly, courts are understandably reluctant to leave disputes unresolved.

---

49. The implications of the classification are many, but most notably concern how income tax is calculated. *See* J. Massad et al., "Report on the National Survey of Reporting of Clergy Compensation to the Internal Revenue Service" (DePaul College of Law Center for Church/State Studies, 1996.)

Even when lawyers and other professionals prepare a church's civil documents well, treatment of a church consistent with its self-understanding is far from guaranteed when courts ignore the religious dimension rather than deal with it. The simplistic appearance of fairness created by exaggerating the neutrality of the court's approach is an insidious threat to religious freedom.

We have previously discussed the situation of a pluralistic culture, one that is likely to grow ever more diverse. The experiences of what used to be called cults and now are often referred to as NRMs, "New Religious Movements," attest to the fact that the courts have an easier time working with religious groups that have long accommodated themselves to the American legal patterns. And yet even some long-established groups are not accommodated. When Christian Scientists refuse medical care for their children and the state intervenes, two theological systems conflict, the church's and the state's. The same is true when a child is taken from Jehovah's Witnesses parents in order to receive a blood transfusion—something against the Jehovah's Witnesses' belief. It cannot be said that all theology dwells in the arena of particular groups. The state itself is working with interpretations of a civil religion that receives its norms from a generalized metaphysical or metalegal base. In such cases the court justifies its intervention with beliefs and ideas about "compassion," "stewardship," "responsibility," or "the search for the common good." The Christian Scientists or Jehovah's Witnesses may well view the court's intervention as one based on theological norms external and antithetical to their own. Parents in such groups question whether a secular court can pull rank and credibly uphold a claim that runs against those theological interpretations of human nature and destiny that are internal to their respective religious organizations.

Add to the above-mentioned cases the Seventh-day Adventists' legal cases (questioning the civil implications of the Christian transmutation of the Jewish Sabbath into Sunday), and you have only part of the American story. The religious bodies that have been making their presence felt more recently are often the subjects of much bewilderment to their neighbors.

Thus Muslims who live by Qur'an and Shari'a will interpret the *umma* in theologically prescriptive terms that may look abrasive to the uninitiated. Such uninitiated ones will more easily welcome "established" religions—those that have long ago addressed their problems in the terms and courts of our American legal system. And thus Islamic communal practice and law prescribe rites of prayer that may come at hours that conflict with employers' and other employees' rights and conventional practices.

Many traditionally religious Americans and certainly more with a simply secular outlook are critical of other movements, particularly some of the NRMs. They see in the intense efforts to convert, form disciplined community, and inculcate the tenets of the movement what some have called "brainwashing" and "mind control." Yet it is difficult for the law to intervene when such accusations are made. Like the traditional faiths, these movements characteristically ground their patterns and practices in what they conceive of as the teachings of divine revelation.

If legislatures refuse to recognize the unique position and needs of religious groups in American culture, then the most basic principles of religious freedom are threatened. States vary greatly in the legal structures they afford to religious groups and in their criteria for what qualifies as a religious group.[50] From issues of property ownership to cor-

---

50. *See* Patty Gerstenblith, "Associational Structures of Religious Organizations," in this volume.

porate control and marshaling of assets for creditors to exercising the rights of conscience, legislatures play a pivotal role in framing a religious group's playing field.

Returning to supporting the structures of religious polity, *Watson* and the polity approach is an estimable attempt at deference, but falls short of its goals. The precarious-
ness of the *Watson* progeny poses the question: How, if at all, can the polity approach
or the neutral principles of law approach be enhanced so that judicial process offers the
maximum respect and protection for religious polity?

The solution to this question may be far in the future, but for now religious groups
can do several things to insulate themselves from encroachments by the civil order. Religious groups themselves sometimes undermine their religious character or freedom by
allowing their attorneys to neglect the religious issues presented in legal matters. Primarily, religious bodies should not put aside their theology and doctrine when entering
the secular arena, but should instead make sure that their religious polity is internally
clear and in the forefront of considerations when adopting legal structures or drawing
up legal documents. If there are religiously driven ambiguities, then that should be
made clear as well. Churches and other religious organizations should review their documents with sensitivity to structural issues. This is true not only in light of cases divided
on where to draw the line of deference, but also and especially in light of the other legal
complexities which come into play. Perhaps the most important issue for these groups
is the basic question of what civil form most effectively approximates their polity.
Churches should be fully aware of how their attorneys and other professionals in their
employ have described them legally to the world. Religious groups must be vigilant to
ensure that their agents have accurately translated ecclesiastical notions of governance
and accountability into civil law structures. The burden of ensuring a clear translation
from church order to civil order does not fall solely on the civil professionals. If a religious body's founding ecclesiastical documents are unclearly written or have an uniden-
tifiable structure, then there may be little or nothing the civil professionals can do to
help the religious organization avoid pitfalls. The desperate need for adequate translation of ecclesiology into religious polity depends heavily upon a church's own internal
documents. The leaders of religious bodies must make the first move in securing an effective civil form by making the ecclesial form clear and understandable.

It may sound like simply a matter of documentation and tidiness, but it is in times of
crisis that the cracks in the foundation are revealed. The failure to plan properly can result in disaster. In litigation or complex transactions coherency and clarity are of paramount importance as issues of ascending and descending liability bring scrutiny of the
structures.[51] It should be noted that establishing a legal structure is not a simple or one-
dimensional issue; countervailing considerations must be weighed in determining how
a religious group structures itself in the civil order. Control and separate liability, as well
as a host of legal issues which span the range of this volume's chapters, must be thought
through at every juncture. The organization's ability to maintain a structure and keep it
relevant over time must also be weighed. Depending on how a religious organization is
structured, the organization may establish a right to one exemption or create doubt as
to others; it may emphasize one consideration to the detriment of another. In evaluating the host of legal issues in which a church can find itself ensnared, and as one values
and balances these other operational issues, it is apparent that all analysis begins in the
context of the appropriate legal structure. Additionally, while a church's polity must be
carefully understood and communicated, countervailing civil considerations must also

---

51. *See* Mark E. Chopko, "Derivative Liability," in this volume.

be taken into account. A church should not rush into a civil structure without considering how the civil law issues will bear on that structure. For example, when a supralocal governing body uses a reversionary clause to retain accountability and control of a local church, it may bring the implications of ascending liability upon itself as well, a result the governing body may not have intended.[52] Similarly, devices adopted for convenience or to protect control need to be evaluated carefully in light of the full range of legal issues, including the availability of certain assets to satisfy liabilities of the broader organization. Thus a sophisticated review of both a church's polity and this polity's attending civil law implications is essential to a religious body in determining which civil structure and structural features suit its polity best. The value of the selections made may be truly tested when there is a legal challenge to church authority or a claim against certain church assets.

Suggestions to religious bodies and their lawyers

The previous discussion analyzed the precarious situation in which religious bodies sometimes find themselves when operating in the contemporary civil order. At face value, they have a difficult time presenting their religious polity to outsiders in a clear and effective way. What's more, the current state of American jurisprudence, constitutional and otherwise, offers a religious body's civil operations few certainties. Nevertheless, a religious body can take a number of helpful actions to ensure that it has done as much as it can for effective understanding of its polity. We offer the following four suggestions and questions as potentially helpful.

Identify the supreme source of authority

The architects of a church's civil form must be very clear about the appropriate locus of ultimate ecclesial authority. The most critical goal of translating church polity into civil law structure is clarity, particularly about internal decision making, so that courts may easily locate internal governing authority and are not tempted to interpret religious dogma.[53] Embodying religious polity in a civil structure must make unquestionably clear and recognizable who or what is the competent decision maker and what decisions fall under the decision maker's purview. Likewise, the relationship with other ecclesiastical bodies within a denomination must be clearly understood.[54]

The planner must understand the ecclesial implications of the chosen entity

A religious organization's legal structure must be planned carefully so as to reflect the secular needs and religious dimensions of the organization. This process must produce

---

52. *See Id.*

53. *See* Grace Evangelical Lutheran Church v. Lutheran Church-Mo. Synod, 454 N.E.2d 1038 (Ill. App. Ct. 1983); Presbytery of Donegal v. Wheatley, 513 A.2d 538 (Pa. Commw. Ct. 1986).

54. *See* F.E.L. Publications, Ltd. v. Catholic Bishop, 754 F.2d 216 (7th Cir. 1985); Presbytery of Donegal v. Calhoun, 513 A.2d 531 (Pa. Commw. Ct. 1986); Lozanoski v. Sarafin, 485 N.E.2d 669 (Ind. Ct. App. 1985); Presbyter of Elijah Parish Lovejoy v. Jaeggi, 682 S.W.2d 465 (Mo. 1984) (en banc); Babcock Mem'l Presbyterian Church v. Presbytery of Baltimore, 464 A.2d 1008 (Md. 1983); Foss v. Dykstra, 342 N.W.2d 220 (S.D. 1983); Kelley v. Riverside Boulevard Indep. Church of God, 358 N.E.2d 696 (Ill. App. Ct. 1976).

a clearly defined legal structure whose relationship with its religious "shadow" counterpart is also well articulated. For example, if a local church impresses its assets into a trust in favor of a hierarchical church and explicitly restates this preference in its articles of incorporation, it is not entitled to these assets even if it ends this affiliation.[55] Likewise, if a governing body must approve asset transfers by the local church, the civil structures and operations must recognize this relationship.[56] Moreover, if a portion of the church's assets are restricted for a particular purpose, those restrictions should be clearly documented and consistently observed. Religious bodies should understand and identify the ways in which rights and procedures guaranteed under civil law for the civil structure may conflict with religious beliefs.[57]

The religious mission and purpose of related entities must be clearly stated

Although most of the cases we have considered focus on churches and church property, no definitive law explicitly addresses those religious institutions not devoted primarily to serving the function of a church. If a church establishes a related organization to separately perform the church's mission, the church must expressly state the religious connection, purpose, and motivation in all important documents relating to that entity.[58]

If decisions are made pursuant to doctrine, a religious organization should expressly and specifically state that this is the case

Some courts have held that if in matters such as clergy or staff employment, property use, and general administration, it is not clear that religious precepts are motivating and guiding conduct or providing the conduct with a clear religious objective, they will defer to the neutral principles approach.[59] Courts have taken this position even in circumstances where religious intent existed with the church and its representatives.[60]

Suggestions to the courts

The Supreme Court has allowed the states to adopt any approach to resolving intra-church disputes as long as it does not involve a consideration of doctrine or theology. At the same time, the Court has indicated its preference for the neutral principles approach. After more than twenty years of observing the application of this approach and

---

55. *See* Fonken v. Community Church, 339 N.W.2d 810 (Iowa 1983). *But see* York v. First Presbyterian Church, 474 N.E.2d 716 (Ill. App. Ct. 1984).

56. *See* Fluker Community Church v. Hitchens, 419 So. 2d 445 (La. 1982).

57. *See* Ward v. Jones, 587 N.Y.S.2d 94 (Sup. Ct. 1992); Saunders v. Grogans, No. 01-CA-92, 1992 WL 330212 (Ohio Ct. App. Nov. 5, 1992); Barnett v. Hicks, 792 P.2d 150 (Wash. 1990) (en banc); Bethlehem Missionary Baptist Church v. Henderson, 522 So. 2d 1339 (La. Ct. App. 1988); Herning v. Eason, 739 P.2d 167 (Alaska 1987).

58. *See* Barr v. United Methodist Church, 153 Cal. Rptr. 322 (Ct. App. 1979). In addition, see Chopko, *supra* note 51.

59. *See* Dlaikan v. Roodbeen, 522 N.W.2d 719 (Mich. Ct. App. 1994); Mikilak v. Orthodox Church in Am., 513 A.2d 541 (Pa. Commw. Ct. 1986).

60. *See also* Diocese of Galveston-Houston v. Stone, 892 S.W.2d 169 (Tex. App. 1994, no writ.).

the unpredictability of results under it, perhaps the time has come to reconsider a constitutionally permissible way for such disputes to be resolved which neither entangles the court with religion nor ignores the religious component of the entity involved. When any organization cannot reasonably predict the outcome of a disputed case because of the vagaries of judicial application of the law, or is forced to continually reexamine all of its documents to be sure that they will be found to mean what the organization believes they mean, it may be time to restate a constitutional principle in a way that allows for predictable results and a guarantee of religious freedom.

Suggestions to the legislatures

States must evaluate how they can improve the laws and legal tools available to churches, courts, and attorneys. Are there substantive changes that could be made to not-for-profit acts, religious corporation acts, or charitable trusts acts in light of this?

Religious/ecclesiastical corporations

States should allow for more flexible governance within this structure. Some states, such as Pennsylvania, have a statute providing that church property is to be held according to the rules and doctrine of the organization to which that church is a member.[61] In a way, Pennsylvania codifies the security of the polity approach. Moreover, some states like California specifically reference the religious documents and tenets as inclusive of governing bylaws of religious corporations.[62]

This approach depends upon clearly written internal church documents and a clear notion of church governance. If members of a religious body disagree on or have different interpretations of ecclesiastical law without internal resolution of these conflicts, the strength of this legal structure is lost.

Accountability and relationships with state agencies, such as the department of revenue, secretary of state, and attorney general, should be evaluated with sensitivity toward the religious group and the maintenance of its integrity. For example, one court has held that when a religious not-for-profit corporation dissolves, its religious nature terminates and the distribution of its assets may be subject to statutory provisions and civil review, regardless of the group's beliefs about the distribution of money.[63]

In addition, volunteers and lay workers of religious corporations should enjoy the same liability immunity as volunteers under the general not-for-profit corporation acts.

Not-for-profit corporations

The same admonitions regarding religious corporations apply to not-for-profit structural forms. New ideas should be considered that do not put religious organizations in

---

61. *See* Presbytery of Beaver-Butler v. Middlesex Presbyterian Church, 471 A.2d 1271 (Pa. Commw. Ct. 1984), *rev'd*, 489 A.2d 1317 (Pa. 1985).

62. *See* Korean United Presbyterian Church v. Presbytery of the Pacific, 281 Cal. Rptr. 396 (Ct. App. 1991), *disapproved of on other grounds by* Morehart v. County of Santa Barbara, 872 P.2d 143 (Cal. 1994).

63. *See* Prince v. Firman, 584 A.2d 8 (D.C. 1990).

the position of having to repeatedly review their documents to ensure that their rights are properly secured. For example, the members of a not-for-profit corporation could be issued membership certificates as a neutral way of keeping control. The certificates could state that, in addition to the election of the local governing board, the member had certain reserve powers, such as approval of property transfers by the local church. The certificates, of course, would also have to reflect restrictions required by the federal tax laws. They would not be used as vehicles to distribute assets.

Unincorporated associations

Like the statutes for religious corporations and not-for-profit corporations, these statutes should not unduly restrict the decision-making mechanisms and structures of churches formed in this manner. For example, a rule of majority representation for ecclesiastical decisions should only be a presumption or default provision to allow religious expression in governance.[64]

Charitable trusts

For most church groups, the holding and use of money or other assets is a necessary part of their ability to function. All these assets are subject to a charitable trust in some sense of that word. Particular assets or groups of assets may be subject to additional restrictions because of church rules or practices. The civil law rules governing all these assets are often unclear—sometimes very unclear. This lack of clarity leaves religious organizations on very uneasy ground and compromises their religious freedom. Legislatures should act to clarify these rules for the administration and protection of church assets. In the meantime, of course, churches should take measures to make sure their documents reflect their goals.

Conclusion

Religious groups should not have to conform their beliefs about organization and governance to secular models solely in order for the law to recognize or respond to them appropriately. What is needed is greater attention from all those engaged in respecting and protecting religious polity. The churches must carefully analyze what they want from a civil structure, not only thinking through the implications of a particular structure civilly, but also considering how that civil form communicates the church's ecclesiology or philosophy of structure. The legislatures must reevaluate the civil forms they afford religious organizations. After decades of use, is particular legislation effectively allowing churches to exercise their religious freedom in pursuing their perceived mission, or are current structures hampering religion's flourishing? Lastly, courts must pay close attention to the form of polity in which a church governs itself in the secular order and have the courage to recognize when their competence ends.

Religious leaders as a matter of prudence must think through the implications of religious polity. Government bodies, legislators, and courts must—as a matter of justice—

---

64. *See* Bethany Indep. Church v. Stewart, 645 So. 2d 715 (La. Ct. App. 1994); Royal Heights Church of Christ v. Williams, No. 87-60-11, 1987 WL 18670 (Tenn. Ct. App. Oct. 21, 1987).

pay special attention to how a religious body understands itself and its mission in the world. There is much room for improvement in the relationship between law and religious polity. But then again, this is nothing new. We should not expect immediate results, but should hope for constant improvement and reform. It is worth repeating that the give and take between religion and the state has been a constant feature of human affairs for millennia and undoubtedly will continue.

Religious Diversity, Civil Law, and Institutional Isomorphism

Rhys H. Williams and John P.N. Massad

While it seems completely obvious to observe that organized religion requires the existence of formally constituted organizations, the implications for the function and practice of religion are profound. Religion, whatever its transcendent qualities, is an inherently social phenomenon. If it is to have a continuing presence in society, that presence must be organized in some way; in contemporary American society this almost invariably means the founding and maintenance of formal organizations. These are not just necessary evils or incidentals to theology and religious beliefs. Religious adherents must nurture their organizations, devoting time and other resources to them.[1] And, in turn, the organization shapes how religion is both experienced and practiced. In the words of Robert Wuthnow, religious organizations function to "produce the sacred."[2]

However, what religious organization means to adherents and what it means to outsiders, including the state, can be very different things. In response to the ambiguity in the phrase "organizational structure" and recognizing the complexity of contemporary society, this volume develops a careful distinction between a religious organization's *legal structure* and its *religious structure*. The legal structure is the particular corporate form a religious organization takes in the eyes of the law; it is, in other words, the embodiment of the religion as an organization in matters legal and governmental. As a result, some aspects of any given legal structure are not available to the discretion of organizational adherents—religious or otherwise—but are dictated by law. Examples of legal structure include a not-for-profit corporation, a trust, a corporation sole, and an unincorporated association.

The religious structure of a religious organization generally pertains to the group's understanding of its polity and its governance, thus designating a broader range of phenomena than its legal structure. This structure, referred to by such terms as "congregational" or "hierarchical," controls internal organizational governance, in particular the distribution of religious authority and authority over internal organizational decisions

---

1. For an examination of many aspects of religious organizations see Sacred Companies: Organizational Aspects of Religion and Religious Aspects of Organization (N.J. Demerath et al. eds., 1998) [hereinafter Sacred Companies].

2. Robert Wuthnow, Producing the Sacred: An Essay on Public Religion (1994). The argument that the United States is now an "organizational society" can be found in several places. Two good sources are Charles Perrow, A Society of Organizations, 20 Theory & Soc'y 725–62 (1991), and Mayer N. Zald & John D. McCarthy, Social Movements in an Organizational Society (1987).

(such as the distribution and placement of personnel). As a result, religious structure is often considered to be dictated by transcendent rather than human demands. Indeed, its models are often derived directly from scriptural interpretation or theological insight. Because many aspects of a group's religious structure are of little direct concern to the law, they are more or less explicitly protected from state intervention.

This chapter uses empirical data generated by a survey of national-level offices of religious organizations to examine the ways in which legal structure, religious structure, the demands of civil law, and processes of *institutional isomorphism* (a principle drawn from the sociology of organizations)[3] interact in contemporary American society. Our central argument flows along the following lines: The constitutional separation of church and state has traditionally protected many aspects of religious organization from state intervention as forms of religious free exercise. This relatively unregulated condition of American religion has, in turn, been conducive to religious heterogeneity. In terms of how religious groups organize themselves, this diversity is most evident in the religious structures they employ.

However, while the tremendous religious diversity of American society increasingly attracts different religious faiths and organizations into it and thereby into contact with each other and the law, a number of centripetal pressures nonetheless have drawn many different religious groups into using very similar legal structures as organizational tools. Institutional isomorphism helps us understand this apparent contradiction. We find that in this context there exists a potential lack of fit, or *disarticulation,* between the religious structure and the legal structure of religious organizations. Such disarticulation is an underlying theme behind the cases of legal conflict discussed in this volume. Disarticulation may be more severe for some groups than for others, an important consequence of organized religious life.

First we examine the reasons to expect organizational diversity in American religion. Second, we turn to our data to assess whether such diversity indeed exists at the level of legal structure. Finally, we discuss the sociological forces driving organizational change, isomorphism, and disarticulation.

Religion and the American State

The American tradition of the separation of church and state has often been credited, not undeservedly, with creating a legal and political climate in which organized religion can flourish.[4] By officially disestablishing religious faith, the United States severed

---

3. The term was coined in Paul J. DiMaggio & Walter W. Powell, The Iron Cage Revisited: Institutional Isomorphism and Collective Rationality in Organizational Fields, 48 Am. Soc. Rev. 147–60 (1983) [hereinafter DiMaggio & Powell, Iron Cage Revisited]. That article and a number of other pieces focused on institutional dynamics are brought together in The New Institutionalism in Organizational Analysis (Walter W. Powell & Paul J. DiMaggio eds., 1991).

4. See, for example, the arguments in N.J. Demerath III & Rhys H. Williams, Separation of Church and States? A Mythical Past and Uncertain Future, in Church-State Relations: Tensions and Transitions 77–90 (T. Robbins & R. Robertson, eds. 1987); N.J. Demerath III & Rhys H. Williams, A Bridging of Faiths: Religion and Politics in a New England City (1992) [hereinafter Demerath & Williams, A Bridging of Faiths]; Roger Finke & Rodney Stark, The Churching of America (1992); Kenneth Wald, Religion and Politics in the United States (3d ed. 1997).

the tie between religion and state legitimation on the one hand and between religious and political dissent on the other. Religious organizations were freed to follow the dictates of their faith without undue interference; at the same time they no longer had the coercive power of the state to force attendance at worship services or to provide support for organizational maintenance. The result has been, the argument goes, not only a separation of church and state but also a religious climate in which a healthy competition for members and resources have kept organizations vibrant and members involved.[5]

However, the religious pluralism fostered by this competitive climate has also occasionally resulted in clashes between rival organizations and faiths and between religious groups and other civic institutions. These have ranged from legal disputes to political antagonisms to outright violence.[6] Pluralist societies often experience such tension, and as religious organizations operate and thrive in the relatively open "religious market" of the United States, some of that competition has been very antagonistic. In some cases, the state has taken an active role in conflicts, historically supporting majority religious sentiment. This has included actions against Mormons in the nineteenth century, suppression of Native American religious expressions, and other actions that have forced unwilling minorities to conform to the majority will in ways that they have sometimes perceived as being antithetical to their own religious beliefs and practices.[7] More common than overt participation in coercion, however, has been the government's willingness to allow social arrangements that have systematically disadvantaged minority religious groups. For example, pacifist groups such as the Mennonites suffered during the World Wars,[8] Protestant-based school prayers dominated public schools into the 1960s, and anti-Semitic restrictive covenants were tolerated in property contracts until the 1970s.

Protestantism has lost its unofficially established status, however, particularly since World War II. The growth and prosperity of American Catholics fostered a series of church/state legal cases that further separated governmental and religious institutions. In addition, since the 1965 opening of immigration, non-Christian immigrants have become an increasingly large portion of the population and faiths such as Islam and Buddhism have gained sizable American followings. During the postwar period, the state has become less active in religious disputes generally, and has often opted to confine its intervention to the role of mediator.[9]

More recently, the United States has developed an extended, bureaucratized social welfare state. With this development the contact points between government and religion have expanded from the narrowly political realm to the social service sector. While religious organizations continue to provide social services as part of their respective missions, government regulation on many levels has increasingly affected and shaped their efforts. Even as the level of organized, collective conflict between religious groups abates, and liberties for religious minorities are more seriously enforced and less con-

---

5. *See* R. Stephen Warner, Work in Progress Toward a New Paradigm for the Sociological Study of Religion in the United States, 98 Am. J. Soc. 1044–93 (1993).

6. Examples abound, but several are mentioned in John Higham, Strangers in the Land (1973), and David Bennett, The Party of Fear (1988).

7. *See* Rhys H. Williams, Breaching the "Wall of Separation": The Balance Between Religious Freedom and Social Order, in Armageddon in Waco: Critical Perspectives on the Branch Davidian Conflict, 299–322 (Stuart Wright ed., 1995).

8. *See* Fred Kniss, Disquiet in the Land (1997).

9. Those who study so-called new religious movements will still point to notable cases of state coercion, such as the Branch Davidians case.

tested,[10] the state and religious organizations continue to expand the areas in which they have contact. Thus while officially separated, religious organizations and representatives of government have a level of interaction that is arguably higher than ever.

Religious Organizations and Civil Law

The regulation of society through civil law, of course, touches all aspects of life and many different kinds of organizations and associations. We argue, however, that it has a particular impact upon religious organizations. As numerous scholars have observed, religious groups are particularly unlikely to choose their organizational forms through rational calculation of efficient means and alternative arrangements.[11] Rather, religious structure is often invested with a sacred quality and backed by scriptural or theological sanction. Indeed, many denominations in the United States, such as the Episcopalians, Presbyterians, and Congregationalists, actually name themselves in terms of their polity or religious structure. Therefore, changing one's organizational form is not a minor task; it can strike at the heart of a group's religious identity. The rise and fall of the fortunes of different groups in American history testifies to that fact. Groups more adapted to the social context of any given moment flourish; and those using the most flexible organizational forms—such as the Methodists in their use of lightly educated, itinerant circuit riders in the early nineteenth century—have had a competitive advantage and have grown.[12]

But groups less suited to their social environments often face great challenges in trying to adapt. If the religious structure is sacralized, such things cannot easily be adjusted with only a rationale of competitive advantage. Indeed, some religious groups have faced organizational death due to their incapacity to change.[13] Even if such a drastic outcome is not likely, tension and conflict within a group often accompany organizational change. Witness the continuing tension within American Catholicism over the structural changes brought about by the Second Vatican Council.[14] In sum, the history of organizational conflict in American religion, often leading to schism or division, speaks to the saliency of organizational issues. Moreover, it demonstrates that theological and ideological conflict usually has organizational consequences.

Combining the difficulty of changing organizational forms with general expectations that religious institutions should be free of state interference could easily result in a loathing on the part of some religious groups to cooperate with state-mandated guidelines. If regulation at a variety of levels affects religious and legal structures in ways that

---

10. Religious freedom means different things to different people, of course, and remains a contentious issue. The Supreme Court's 1990 *Smith* decision, the Religious Freedom Restoration Act, and the subsequent challenge to its constitutionality all attest to this fact. Nonetheless, we maintain that the current level of religious persecution in this country is low compared both to historical precedents and to the situation in other nations such as Israel, India, Saudi Arabia, and Ulster.

11. *See* James A. Beckford, Religious Organizations (1973); *see also* Sacred Companies, *supra* note 1.

12. *See* Nathan O. Hatch, The Democratization of American Christianity (1989); *see also* Finke & Stark, *supra* note 4.

13. This point is thoroughly documented at the congregational level by Nancy Tatom Ammerman, Congregation and Community (1996).

14. *See* John Seidler & Katherine Meyer, Conflict and Change in the Catholic Church (1989).

require a set of formal changes, we should expect resistance, tension, and perhaps even a fair amount of open conflict from the affected religious institutions.[15] For as we recall, solid theoretical and historical reasons lead us to expect a wide variety of organizational forms within American religion and to think that these forms are relatively sacrosanct and immutable.

The theoretical dilemmas notwithstanding, this research asks how, in fact, religious organizations in the contemporary United States actually interact with the state and the demands of civil law. This interaction takes many forms over a number of different issues. For example, local governments control such things as parking regulations, zoning and land use, and health and safety inspections. State governments license teachers, schools, and health care workers, and have courts for litigating insurance coverage or property ownership disputes. And perhaps most fundamentally, states regulate the actual organizational form—the legal structure—that nonprofit organizations may use to incorporate. This, of course, becomes central to questions of tax exemption and other regulatory effects and, hence, a major issue in resource acquisition and organizational survival.

The Current Study

The DePaul University Center for Church/State Studies undertook a comprehensive survey of national-level religious organizations to investigate how the variety of religious organizations operate and perceive themselves to be treated under American civil law. It is important to note that most of the interactions between religious groups and the state happen without conflict and indeed with cooperation. Many organizations do not perceive themselves as burdened by compliance with the law, but rather accept it as the price of participating in our modern, bureaucratized society. However, it is sociologically useful to look for points of conflict. This is not mere sensationalism; finding occasions or locations of conflict in social life is a way of revealing the unspoken assumptions and unarticulated meanings of day-to-day interactions. Things that usually happen "below" the surface of religious organizations are exposed during periods of tension. Significantly in this regard, many of the landmark cases in church/state law have come "from the margins"; that is, they originated in conflicts involving smaller, nonmainstream groups. Thus, while conflict is not the normal state of human affairs, neither should we necessarily consider it as pathology or aberration. It is a part of social life and analytically useful for what it can reveal about society.

Traditionally, American courts have made decisions regarding the organization and liability of American religious institutions based on hierarchical, congregational, and

---

15. There are many examples of conflict in the sociological and legal literature on church/state relations. *See* Robert Wuthnow, The Restructuring of American Religion (1988); Demerath & Williams, A Bridging of Faiths: Religion and Politics in a New England City, *supra* note 4. Not surprisingly, this is an important topic for those who study marginal religious groups. *See* James T. Richardson, The "Deformation" of New Religions: Impacts of Societal and Organizational Factors, *in* Cults, Culture, and the Law 163–76 (T. Robbins et al. eds., 1985); David G. Bromley & Thomas Robbins, The Role of Government in Regulating New and Unconventional Religions *in* The Role of Government in Monitoring and Regulating Religion in Public Life 205–40 (J.E. Wood, Jr. & D. Davis eds., 1993); Forum: Interpreting Waco, 8 Religion & Am. Culture 1–30 (Conrad Cherry, ed., 1998).

presbyterial models of religious structure. These are models of church polity in which organizational and theological authority are invested in centralized hierarchies, local congregations, and regional judicatories, respectively. Significantly, these models are derived from a characterization of "church" established at the founding of the Republic and are best represented by Christian, particularly Protestant, religious organizations. However, the increased religious pluralism of the twentieth century raises questions as to whether these models still adequately describe the gamut of American religious institutions. While the courts generally try to ignore religious structure — as part of separation — many of their de facto assumptions reflect the historical dominance of certain traditions. Given these observations, the courts may need to recognize additional models of religious organization to address the present institutional diversity. Indeed, judicial decisions and government regulation based strictly on traditional models may have a discriminatory effect, even if unintended, on religious life in America.

Methods

The 1994 Survey of Religious Organizations at the National Level was conducted from September 1993 through April 1994 for the DePaul University Center for Church/State Studies by the Northwestern University Survey Laboratory. The majority of respondents were identified through the standard annual directory of United States religious bodies prepared for the Education, Communication, and Discipleship Unit of the National Council of Churches of Christ in the USA.[16] Additional respondents, identified in Melton,[17] were selected to represent taxonomic families of nonmainstream religious groups that were organized on the national level but not included in the annual directory or directly recognized by the National Council of Churches. The internal files of the Center for Church/State Studies were used wherever possible to identify the legal counsel of specific religious organizations; these representatives were the direct contact for the survey.

Using a population generated from established directories of American religious organizations had theoretical as well as methodological advantages. These directories rely significantly on information provided by groups who self-identify specifically as religious bodies. Thus the survey targeted groups aware of their position within American society as specifically religious entities, formally organized as such, and directly involved in the issues such a position may bring in terms of legal structure. Concomitantly, this method underrepresents storefront and house churches, with both advantages and disadvantages. Small, decentralized, and more informal religious groups may well be less likely to have to interact with government over civil law issues; but their less developed organizational form may also make any given interaction more difficult for them. In all probability they have less access to legal and other professional advice. Further, small and marginal groups may be more likely targets of state action and transgressors of civil law. Added to this, they often have less legitimacy and fewer allies for political protection. We recognize this trade-off and accept it as part of the price of compiling a full sample of national-level organizations.

In all, 261 religious organizations at the national level were contacted through their legal affairs representative or the equivalent. Of those, 170 completed the telephone

---

16. *See* Yearbook of American and Canadian Churches, 1992 (Kenneth Bedell ed., 1992).
17. *See* J. Gordon Melton, The Encyclopedia of American Religions (2d ed. 1986).

component of the survey, a completion rate of 65%. In 64 cases the appropriate representative could not be reached, and 26 organizations declined to participate. The cooperation rate (as compared to declines) was 86%. Of those completing the telephone component, 100% agreed to complete a follow-up self-administered questionnaire by mail. Duplicate questions in the two instruments allowed for cross-checking to ensure the accuracy of responses, and no unresolved deviations were identified. A total of 117 completed questionnaires were returned, which yielded a completion rate of 69% for the mail component and 45% for the survey as a whole. These response rates are considered consistent, if not above, expectations for this type of survey at this level of contact. In order to identify any differences in the substantive data gathered, the group of telephone participants who failed to return a mail instrument was compared to those who completed both. The two groups were statistically more similar than dissimilar; no trends were associated with the few statistically significant differences that were identified.

In toto, the sample was representative of national religious organizations in the United States. These included adherents of Protestant and Orthodox Christianity, Judaism, Islam, Buddhism, and independent groups. They ranged from those listing fewer than 1,000 members to those listing over one million. Respondents were asked to define their membership using their own criteria. Certain major groups responded as umbrella or panchurch organizations, listing their memberships in numbers of local or regional bodies rather than individual adherents. They were, in effect, "organizations of organizations" and were removed from this analysis so as not to skew the effect of size by mixing individuals and organizations in that variable.

Significantly, the Roman Catholic church was not included in the final sample; the church responded through the National Council of Catholic Bishops, which provided information on itself as a single national entity rather than the church as a whole. As noted, the respondents that identified as "organizations of organizations" were processed separately for future reference. Statistical analysis demonstrated that this removal did not significantly effect the measured outcomes. In fact, the 117 completed surveys were found to be proportional to the original sample, capturing the diversity of religious membership in the United States. Furthermore, the particular strength of the data is its inclusion of nonmainstream, but nationally organized, groups who are rarely if ever studied in this manner. In other words, surveys of individuals naturally capture large numbers of members for mainstream Christian denominations; the numbers of members for smaller groups often do not reach statistical significance. We circumvented that problem by surveying the groups themselves.

Findings

Summing for the moment the large number of variables and the many different areas about which questions were asked, the most startling finding emerging from the data is the lack of variation in legal structures and the conformity of organizational responses to the requirements for participating in and interacting with civil society. Whether the issue is the use of the nonprofit corporation as a legal form or the employment of administrative staff professionals to handle such matters as insurance, religious groups of widely varying theological and ideological commitments behave in very similar ways. To repeat, in a country that may be the world's most religiously pluralist, where organi-

TABLE 1
Description and sources of organizational structure

Which one of the following best characterizes the organizational structure of your religious organization?	Telephone respondents	Mail respondents
Hierarchical	21%	22%
Congregational	39%	41%
Presbyterial	11%	11%
Connectional	11%	13%
Continuum of types	8%	7%
Other form	11%	10%
Is the organizational structure prescribed by religious doctrine?		
Yes	67%	62%
No	33%	38%
Is this organizational structure prescribed by scripture?		
Yes	60%	49%
No	40%	51%

zational identities represent fundamental schismatic divisions, and where religious free exercise is interpreted in institutional as well as individual terms, the formal and legal organizational structures among a huge segment of religious groups are strikingly similar. Indeed, when compared to the nation's religious diversity, its organizational homogeneity makes for an ironic reading of *e pluribus unum*. We examine each of these—the diversity and the unexpected homogeneity—in turn.

Potential sources of diversity

Several items on the survey support the idea that religious organizations in the United States should take a variety of forms. For example, table 1 reports respondents' answers to a question asking for a term that best describes their organizational religious structure and whether that structure is prescribed by religious doctrine or scripture. While about three-fifths of the sample declared either a hierarchical or congregational polity, answers of the remaining 40% spread across a number of different forms. More significantly, about three-fifths of the sample considers this aspect of their organizational structure to be prescribed by religious sources, either doctrinal or scriptural. We emphasize that this question taps into the religious structure of these organizations.

Thus the theoretical point made above is confirmed in these data: a substantial number of religious bodies choose their organizational religious structure not because of instrumental commitments to efficiency or efficacy, but according to the religiously prescribed nature of the structure. Indeed, it may be something of a misrepresentation to speak of religious bodies as choosing their polities. For many groups, how they organize themselves is understood as dictated by faith requirements and not really chosen at all. There is always room for interpretation about which exact offices must be contained within a hierarchical form, or how many translocal organizations are legitimate for a congregational polity. However, organizations do not necessarily make these choices on

TABLE 2
Involvement with Government Agencies and Funding

Has your organization recently applied for or received any government funding within the past three years?

Yes	7%
No	93%

[of those who responded "yes" to above]

Has the possibility of government support influenced the choice of legal structure for these activities?

[various activities listed in questionnaire]

Yes	27%
No	73%

Has your organization been involved in any legal matter regarding structural or doctrinal issues, or conflict with any governmental agency which required an attorney's assistance within the last five years?

Yes	17%
No	84%

the basis of strategic calculation. With the variety of religious groups included in the survey, this sign of religious prescription should generate a variety of religious structures and attendant organizational policies and practices.

Another piece of evidence that would suggest relative diversity in organizational forms is the data that show that the sample generally eschews direct involvement with government agencies and their funding. As table 2 demonstrates, the overwhelming majority of the sample had not recently applied for or received government funding; of those few that had, almost three-quarters denied that such support affected their choice of legal structure for these activities. Given that such interaction with the state usually requires of the organization a particular legal structure, the answers to this question indicate either that the groups already had such a structure and thus did not need to adapt, or that they eschewed such entanglements.

In addition, as table 2 shows, 83% of those in the sample reported that they had not had a recent legal matter with any governmental agency that required an attorney. While the history of American religion may be filled with examples of conflict and tension, at least at the time of this survey little evidence of it appears. This overall lack of interaction with government by the clear majority of religious groups should be expected, given the legal and normative separation of organized religion and the state. Logically extending this thesis, one might expect this lack of interaction to preserve whatever diversity in organizational form already exists. Indeed, while we noted above that government/church interaction is increasing over social service delivery and the like, these data remind us that this interaction still shapes, intentionally or unintentionally, a minority of religious organizations, at least at the national level.

In sum, answers to some of the questions in the survey give us reason to expect a fair amount of organizational variation among nationally organized religious bodies. Many religious groups hold aspects of their structure to be religiously mandated. Further, most religious groups do not seek governmental aid, change their organizational forms in response to such funding, or get involved in conflict that requires legal assistance. It is a picture of relative church/state separation, perhaps reflective of the pluralism and diversity our theories would expect. The data support this notion with regard to issues of religious structure. When we turn to issues associated with the legal structures of religious organizations, however, a distinctly different profile emerges.

The religious structure may not affect organizational ability to interact with civil society, but legal structure is the means whereby this interaction takes place. It is at such intersections of the state's interest and the means whereby religious groups organize themselves to interact with civil society that we would expect legal structure to be affected; apparently this has not necessarily affected the religious structure of such organizations.

Signs of organizational conformity

Responses to questions about legal structure undermine the portrait of organizational diversity achieved through *benign separationism*. The most dramatic evidence is presented in table 3; almost nine of every ten organizations have the formal legal structure of a "religious not-for-profit" corporation. This is an astounding piece of nonvariation, given the diversity of structures that could be expected from the data and from the reasoning above. Indeed, we have reason to believe that the homogeneity is even greater than these numbers indicate, as closer inspection of the data reveals that some respondents who answered other than "religious not-for-profit" corporation may have misidentified themselves.

It seems obvious to us that this convergence in legal structure is related to civil law requirements such as those regarding tax-exempt status for nonprofit, religious, and charitable organizations. Tax-exempt status requires particular organizational forms and practices which also show up in data reported in table 3. Almost all the organizations surveyed offer financial contributors the opportunity for tax-exempt contributions, and 85% of them hold IRS 501(c)(3) status (some of the 11% reporting that they were "uncertain" of their status are probably so designated). Five follow-up questions asked about financial accounting and documenting practices; a minimum of 69% of the sample said they participate in such practices. These practices require certain professional expertise, and the overwhelming majority of the sample reported employing legal counsel, insurance advisors, and professional financial personnel in their routine organizational practices.[18] Thus the regulatory environment shapes the legal structures and organizational policies and practices of religious groups despite our theoretical expectations that separationism would lead to diversity in organizational form.

The standardization of legal structures is apparently of relatively long standing. Table 4 demonstrates that few of the respondents had changed their legal structure within the decade prior to the survey (1984–94), and of those that had, more than half had already had one of the two most common organizational structures. More than half of the respondents had had their current structure for at least fifty years (data not shown). Of the 7% that reported changing their legal structure within the preceding decade, eleven of those twelve organizations registered current not-for-profit corporation status. Thus not only is the homogeneity that appears in the data overwhelming, it increased in the decade preceding the survey.

---

18. Data available upon request; *see also* Mark Chaves et al., Are Priests Employees? The State, Professional Networks, and Change in Religious Organizations (presented at the annual meeting of the American Sociological Association, Toronto, 1997).

TABLE 3

Which one of the following would best characterize the formal legal structure of your organization?

An unincorporated association 8%
A Religious Not-for-Profit corporation 87%
A Not-for-Profit corporation 3%
A Charitable or Religious Trust 1%
A Corporation Sole 1%
A For-Profit Corporation 1%
Some other type of legal structure 1%

Are all or some part of private contributions made to your organization tax deductible?

Yes 99%
No 1%

Is your organization an Internal Revenue Code Section 501(c)(3) organization according to the Internal Revenue Service?

Yes 85%
No 4%
Uncertain 11%

[the following apply to those with 501(c)(3) status]

Does your organization provide an annual financial statement to members?

Yes 73%

Does your organization make an annual financial statement available to members?

Yes 92%

Does your organization make an annual financial statement available to the general public?

Yes 69%

Does your organization provide a financial statement to members which specifies how funds have been spent?

Yes 89%

Does your organization regularly undergo an independent outside audit?

Yes 69%

A significant follow-up question, namely, whether the legal change was at the behest of a governmental overture, produced an interesting result. While a vast majority of those organizations who had changed had not done so because of governmental overture, 17% (two) had. Both of these organizations that had changed their legal structure changed it to that of a not-for-profit corporation. So while the numbers are small (because of the already existing conformity), a bit of direct evidence does indicate that government overtures to organized religious groups result in pressures to conform, and thus in an increasingly homogeneous legal organizational climate.

These data on legal structure almost completely reverse the picture drawn from the data on religious structure. Several questions emerge that could guide further research into religious organizations and their relations with their societal (including legal) environment. How can conformity of legal structure coexist with the apparent diversity of religious structure? Is this disarticulation between the two forms of organizational structure of long standing? Does it present problems for organizational functioning and

TABLE 4

Has your organization changed its overall legal structure within the past 10 years?
Yes 7%
No 93%

[asked only of those who answered "yes" above]

What was the prior legal structure of your organization?
An unincorporated association 33%
A Religious Not-for-Profit corporation 25%
A Not-for-Profit corporation 8%
A Charitable or Religious Trust 0%
A Corporation Sole 8%
A For-Profit Corporation 8%
Some other type of legal structure 0%
Uncertain of prior legal structure 17%

Was this change in legal structure the result of overture from government on any level?
Yes 17%
No 83%

In what year did this change occur?
1984 . . . . 9%
1985 . . . . 18%
1986 . . . . 18%
1987 . . . . 9%
1988 . . . . 9%
1990 . . . . 18%
1991 . . . . 9%
1992 . . . . 9%

policy-making? Are these problems differentially distributed? In other words, do some groups find them more difficult than others? While some of these questions go beyond the scope of this chapter, we consider how this organizational conformity came about and what factors continue to maintain it.

Possible explanations

The near uniformity in legal structure presents us with a dilemma in pursuing the logic of our investigation. We cannot examine the sources and causes of variations in legal structure because the survey reveals no effective variation. Indeed, legal structure, at least for national-level religious organizations, is strictly speaking not a variable. As a result, two of the most common variables used in the study of organizations and especially religious organizations—namely, *size* and *time since incorporation*—are clearly not the source of this formal convergence. Scholars of religious organizations often analyze these factors as key organizational variables in shaping the institutional forms assumed by religious groups.[19]

With regards to the current issue, considering size and time since incorporation could lead to opposing expectations. That is, one could imagine that older and larger

19. *See, e.g.,* Sacred Companies, *supra* note 1; Beckford, *supra* note 11.

religious organizations would be less likely to have adopted contemporary forms of legal structure. On one hand, older religious organizations could be expected to be more resistant to change (as argued above); on the other hand, larger and older organizations with more societal resources, such as money, members, and societal legitimacy, might be able to resist any attempt by the state to enforce or shape their legal structures. However, one could also reasonably expect that older and larger groups might be more likely than their smaller and younger counterparts to adopt the legal structures that are favored or mandated by civil law. Larger religious organizations are more likely to be bureaucratized internally and thus be comfortable with the formal structures mandated by a bureaucratic state. Older religious groups may well be more culturally legitimate and mainstream and thus more confident accommodating themselves to the demands of secular society. For example, mainline Protestantism may not have experienced disarticulation between legal and religious structures as its organizations emerged historically with the modern state. Thus they are not burdened by this issue, as their accommodation to society seems natural.

A similar dynamic of accommodation and tension is the central argument in Max Weber's and Ernst Troeltsch's distinction between "church" and "sect."[20] They perceived a division between *churches,* which are culturally central, high status religious groups, and *sects,* which serve disadvantaged populations and are in tension with their cultural environment. This division affects the organization of religious authority, the styles of worship, and the social class base of adherents. In the United States, church/sect theory has developed a cyclical form. In time, all religious organizations are expected to accommodate to the culture and lower their level of tension with their environment. As they do, they no longer appeal to marginalized groups; these groups object to compromise and form schismatic sects that reflect their interests. As the members prosper and become less alienated from society, their preferred forms of religious expression, doctrinally and organizationally, become more accommodating and the cycle repeats itself. Thus, larger groups and those which have been incorporated for a longer period of time would be expected—almost by definition—to handle adaptation to societal demands more easily. Smaller, sectarian off-shoots would experience more tension with civil society, and presumably with the state, and be more likely to resist externally imposed changes.

But whether we expect more established groups to be able to resist the state more effectively or whether we expect them to accommodate to external demands more readily, both perspectives lead us to expect systematic variation among different types of religious organizations. What our data reveal is little variation in legal structure. To the extent that there is a slight tendency not to adopt the not-for-profit corporation form, it is found among congregationally oriented polities—those groups that are more loosely organized at the national level and that often have a more separatist ideology toward worldly forms and government interaction. Additionally, we note again that our sample underrepresents storefront churches and local, small, minority religious groups. Thus church/sect theory may be a slightly better guide to the current situation than explanations based on the size or age of the religious organization.

Nonetheless, the overwhelming tendency among religious organizations that have grown enough to have a national organizational presence is to adopt the not-for-profit

---

20. Max Weber, The Sociology of Religion (The Beacon Press 1963) (1922); Ernst Troeltsch, The Social Teachings of the Christian Churches (Harper and Row 1960) (1931). The classic adaptation of their ideas to the United States is found in H. Richard Niebuhr, The Social Sources of Denominationalism (1929).

corporation legal structure and its attendant policies and practices. This fact cuts across most of the usual sources of religious diversity, including polity differences in the structure of religious authority. Thus while our search for explanation is thwarted by a lack of variation, we argue that this in itself is sociologically interesting and in need of explanation.

Discussion

How can we account for this lack of diversity at the organizational level of legal structure? A theoretical answer coming from the sociology of organizations is that of institutional isomorphism.[21] Institutional isomorphism is the process through which organizations, or more specifically the organizational forms used by different institutions and organizations, come to resemble each other. While a number of mechanisms pressure organizations toward homogeneity, two are particularly pertinent in this case.

The first is a *coercive isomorphism,* in which organizations change according to the dictates of the state. This should be a somewhat problematic process with regard to religious organizations in the United States, given our putative separation. That the government might regulate public institutions, or even aspects of business organizations, is generally accepted. That it might apply direct coercive measures to religious organizations is more controversial. However, our data show that even in a nation where religious organizations have some type of privileged status regarding formal state regulation, the state has some ability to demand conformity. In the absence of direct state support — the mandate of disestablishment — religious organizations must rely on their members for the material resources of institutional survival. Given this state of affairs, a change in the tax exempt status of a religious organization, while perhaps not fatal, could seriously curtail its ability to maintain its current level of programming. In another paper we have demonstrated how powerful tax exemption is as an issue. Indeed, a ruling by the Internal Revenue Service can prompt even large and culturally established churches to change aspects of their internal organization.[22] In sum, while the American state has limited resort to direct coercion, it does have access to indirect coercive measures.

Our data here provide some evidence of isomorphism prompted by the state's actions. Recall that the organizations that reported having changed their legal structures altered them in the direction of conformity with the legal structures of other religious organizations, particularly if they did so while responding to a governmental overture. Also, table 5 reports the results from several questions asking respondents whether their organizations were hindered from engaging in certain activities due to government regulation or tax law. Regarding the political issues listed in table 5, a large number of groups reported feeling constrained. Many of these groups also reported that their organization (or its members or leaders) would engage in activities regarding these issues if government regulation permitted. It is also the case that questions about other issues, such as human rights, antidiscrimination, and voter registration, produced only a few "yes" responses, suggesting a generally low level of perceived constraint. Nonetheless,

---

21. *See* DiMaggio & Powell, Iron Cage Revisited, *supra* note 3.
22. *See* Chaves et al., *supra* note 18. For a more in-depth address of tax-exemption issues, see Edward McGlynn Gaffney, Jr., "Exemption of Religious Organizations from Federal Taxation," in this volume.

TABLE 5

Do you feel current government regulation or tax law prevents or hinders your organization from engaging in activities involving any of the following?

Issues regarding abortion
- Yes 18%
- No 53%
- No Opinion 30%

Political issues in general
- Yes 17%
- No 52%
- No Opinion 31%

Moral issues in general
- Yes 19%
- No 56%
- No Opinion 25%

from this we infer some evidence for indirect coercive isomorphic processes: the demands of the state and its requirements regarding legal structure act as a constraint on actions that religious groups might otherwise take.

A second isomorphic process is called *mimetic isomorphism*. This occurs as organization leaders within a particular "organizational field" adopt a common form in response to an innovative practice developed by one organization within the field.[23] Organizational innovation within a field, such as the development of a new technology or a restructuring of organizational work, is often thought of as improving competitive chances in the market. Other organizations in the field, noticing the innovation, adopt it themselves, often with only minimal evidence that it actually improves those chances.

Nonetheless, the innovation soon becomes normative, and all organizations within the field are then expected to exhibit it in order to be recognized as legitimate actors in their arena. Whether the innovation "works" becomes less an issue of its rational effectiveness than of its ability to signal to organizational partners and competitors within the field that one is to be taken seriously. Accomplishing a goal efficiently may remain the formal rationale, but the diffusion of the innovation depends on its ability to achieve a sense of legitimacy for the organization as an actor within its relevant organizational field. While our data clearly demonstrate this effect, they give little direct evidence of the underlying processes at work; cross-sectional surveys are not really the way to capture it. Also, we should anticipate mimetic isomorphism less among religious organizations than among other types of organizations.[24] Since the former are often developed and justified theologically, we would expect as much diversity in organizational

---

23. An organizational field is "those organizations that, in the aggregate, constitute a recognized area of institutional life." DiMaggio & Powell, Iron Cage Revisited, *supra* note 3, at 148. Thus, a field contains organizations that often come into contact with each other, making the communication and transmission of innovations (or resistance to innovations) relatively easy.

24. Actions by the state can also help prompt mimetic isomorphism. If the regulatory environment is uncertain, leaving organizations unsure what demands might be made of them, mimetic adaptation is one way to anticipate and possibly avoid coercive power. *See* John R. Sutton & Frank Dobbin, The Two Faces of Governance: Responses to Legal Uncertainty in U.S. Firms, 1955 to 1985, 61 Am. Soc. Rev. 794–811 (1996); Chaves et al., *supra* note 18.

forms as in religious philosophies and theologies. However, our data point to a surprising lack of such diversity. We can make some inferences about the process which has led to this isomorphic effect from other literature in the sociology of religion.

A key development in American religion from the middle of the nineteenth century to the late twentieth century has been the rise of national bureaucratic structures.[25] These first emerged among missionary and evangelizing societies and then spread to denominational agencies. Eventually the organizational form spread to judicatories that possessed religious authority as well as those that performed specific functional tasks.[26] The routine areas of religious governance have become more centralized and more bureaucratized throughout the past century. National bureaucratic forms have become so pervasive and standardized that they have developed even among religious groups with histories and theologies of local control. For example, Paul Harrison revealed tensions over bureaucratization among Baptists almost forty years ago.[27] More recently, conflict within the Southern Baptist Convention has revolved around theological issues, but has occurred primarily within the few supralocal organizations legitimate within the SBC—seminaries and the boards that produce Sunday school material.[28] Thus, while Baptists continue to think of themselves as congregationally organized, major national conflict occurs within the available translocal organizational venues.

By the 1960s and 1970s scholars were finding that denominational bureaucrats working in national offices often had more in common with similarly situated professionals in other denominations than they did with local members of their own religious groups (or local-level clergy). The twin developments of bureaucratization and professionalization were affected by both legal and religious structure, but were driven by organizational rather than theological demands.[29] We would expect the greatest effect of this process to appear in changes in legal structure, moving toward homogeneous organizational forms as a means of conforming to the bureaucratic and professional needs of the growing national-level organizations. This is the level most directly addressed by our data. Although the national/local division became a source of tension for a number of denominations during the protests of the 1960s,[30] the isomorphic tendency to develop national-level bureaucracies was apparent among many religious groups and traditions. However, it seemed most pronounced within mainline Protestantism, perhaps reflecting the largely middle-class, middle-management base of its memberships, as well as the theological tendency within liberal Protestantism to accommodate modern secular society.[31] Recently, several Protestant denominations have tried to "de-nationalize" their corporate bureaucracies and make them more responsive to local congregations; for ex-

---

25. *See, e.g.,* Kenneth A. Thompson, Bureaucracy and Church Reform (1970). For historical accounts of the societal processes of large-scale organizing, see Peter Dobkin Hall, The Organization of American Culture, 1700–1900 (1984); Peter Dobkin Hall, Religion and the Organizational Revolution in the United States, *in* Sacred Companies, *supra* note 1, at 99–115.

26. *See* Mark Chaves, Denominations as Dual Structures: An Organizational Analysis, *in* Sacred Companies, *supra* note 1, at 175–94.

27. *See* Paul M. Harrison, Authority and Power in the Free Church Tradition (1959).

28. *See* Nancy Tatom Ammerman, Baptist Battles: Social Change and Religious Conflict in the Southern Baptist Convention (1990).

29. *See* J. Kenneth Benson & James H. Dorsett, Toward a Theory of Religious Organizations, 10 J. Sci. Stud. Religion 138–51 (1971).

30. *See* Jeffrey K. Hadden, The Gathering Storm in the Churches (1969).

31. Good discussions of religious organization, its development, and its scope, are found in N.J. Demerath III & Phillip E. Hammond, Religion in Social Context: Tradition and Transition (1969), and American Denominational Organization: A Sociological View (Ross P. Scherer ed., 1980).

ample, several relocated their denominational headquarters out of New York City's ecumenical organizational center at 475 Riverside Drive. Nonetheless, their denominations remain thoroughly bureaucratized. In sum, the sociological literature on religious organizations highlights the historical processes that have produced the types of institutional isomorphism reflected in the lack of variation in our data set. This is particularly true at the national level of religious organization.

Conclusions

We began this project with a set of assumptions different from that of most research on church/state relations. Rather than focusing on legal rulings, points of conflict, or overt state persecution, we looked at a different dimension of church/state interaction. We were interested in the daily issues of accommodation and adaptation to civil law experienced by American religious groups. Issues of overt conflict and direct persecution are important, and they are as current as each session of the Supreme Court. However, we are asking different questions. We maintain that the contours of civil law have powerful shaping effects on religious organizations and that these effects often occur without overt conflict or even direct legal intervention.

The primary effect, according to our data, is an isomorphic convergence of legal organizational structure. The regulatory environment has pushed religious groups from a literally worldwide assortment of faith traditions and polity forms into a single primary legal form: the religious not-for-profit corporation. That legal structure, in turn, has entailed other organizational commitments: to legal counsel, insurance arrangements, accounting and tax professionals, and particular employment arrangements. In turn, the courts have come to operate on an assumption of homogeneity of legal structure and have tried to ignore issues of religious structure. This reinforces the indirect pressures on religious groups to conform organizationally. The totality of pressure in an "organizational society," it seems, is oriented toward isomorphism.

We note that most of the respondents in our data do not report conflict with the government over their politics, religious practices, or organizational arrangements. And while the state's coercive power has the capacity to enforce a certain structural conformity, we are convinced that it is rather the inducements of the regulatory environment and the mimetic practices of similarly situated religious organizations that prompt many religious groups to assume similar legal structures. That the disarticulation between religious and legal structures is only occasionally reported to be a source of conflict should not lull us into overlooking the potential organizational burdens that it might entail or to ignore that these burdens fall more directly on some groups than on others.

In sum, the distinction with which we begin this volume, namely that between the legal structure and the religious structure, is a vital component of our ability to understand organized American religion. We have found this distinction to be an important source of difference in the empirical world. Religious structures vary by faith tradition and are often created and legitimized through theology and scripture. They reflect the tremendous religious diversity the United States currently contains. Legal structures, by contrast, vary hardly at all and seem driven by the demands of the state for a particular organizational form. This clear difference highlights the utility of conceptualizing religious organizations in terms of their particular religious and legal structures. The particularity of such structural combinations may in fact underscore and define the "religious" in religious organizations. That pluralism and diversity seem to reign in one dimension while isomorphism dominates the other testifies to the importance of understanding the nuances of religious organization.

Religious Structures under the Federal Constitution*

Thomas C. Berg

Churches and other religious organizations are bound to interact with government. The conditions of modern America ensure that. Religious groups engage in a wide range of activities affecting the public; moreover, since the New Deal at least, government has asserted broad power both to regulate private entities and activities and, where it wishes, to encourage them by providing tax-supported assistance. But religious entities are different from their secular counterparts, and the primary legal difference lies in the words of the First Amendment to the Constitution: "Congress shall make no law respecting an establishment of religion, or prohibiting the free exercise thereof."[1] These clauses, free exercise and nonestablishment, clearly place some limits on how and to what extent government and religious institutions can interact—limits that do not apply to secular organizations.

The particular focus of this volume is on how the structures of churches and other religious organizations are affected by legal rules. This chapter concerns the federal Constitution. Its task, therefore, is to discuss how the First Amendment casts its shadow over a religious entity's decisions about its structure, as well as over state actions that interfere with that structure. After defining the concept of "structure," I examine two major questions. First, to what extent do various First Amendment doctrines respect churches' right "to decide for themselves, free from state interference, matters of church government as well as those of faith and doctrine"?[2] After looking at that question in

---

* This chapter incorporates case law and other developments through early 2000. Since that time, there have been two major developments relevant to this chapter. First, the U.S. Supreme Court approved the inclusion of religious schools in elementary and secondary-school voucher programs under the Establishment Clause in *Zelman v. Simmons-Harris*, 536 U.S. 639 (2002). *Zelman* and its implications for constitutional analysis are discussed in detail in Thomas C. Berg, "Appendix: The Supreme Court's School Voucher Decision (*Zelman v. Simmons-Harris*)," in this volume. Second, there has been a great deal of discussion and debate concerning the federal "charitable choice" legislation, first passed in 1996, which allows religious social service providers to benefit from government assistance on roughly the same terms as other providers. Charitable choice is discussed in detail in Carl H. Esbeck, "Appendix: Charitable Choice and the Critics," in this volume.

1. U.S. Const. amend. I. These clauses apply to the states through the Fourteenth Amendment. *See* Cantwell v. Connecticut, 310 U.S. 296 (1940) (incorporating free exercise); Everson v. Board of Educ., 330 U.S. 1 (1947) (incorporating nonestablishment). Although incorporation, especially of the Establishment Clause, remains controversial among scholars (*see, e.g.,* Akhil Amar, The Bill of Rights as a Constitution, 100 Yale L. J. 1131, 1157–1160 (1991)), the Court will not reverse those decisions at any time in the near future.

2. Kedroff v. St. Nicholas Cathedral, 344 U.S. 94, 116 (1952).

general, I consider it in the specific context of "internal" church matters, such as who controls property or who has a claim to be a minister or a member. I then turn to the second major question: to what extent does a religious organization's treatment under the First Amendment depend upon the structure that it has chosen? The organization's structure does make a difference in some ways, both as to its regulation by government and as to its receipt of government assistance. I conclude by making some connections between organizational structure and some general features of jurisprudence under the First Amendment's religion provisions.

Definitions of "Structural" Decisions by Religious Organizations

Before asking how churches' structural decisions relate to the provisions of the Religion Clauses, we need a definition of "structural decisions." As this volume elsewhere makes clear,[3] the concept of structure has several aspects. At its core are decisions concerning the formal legal status that a religious organization will adopt. Will it operate as a voluntary association or will it incorporate (and if the latter, in what form: a corporation sole, a religious corporation, a general nonprofit corporation)? If the activity is not itself a church but is related to a congregation or some higher church body, will it be legally integrated into that body or will it be separately organized (and if the latter, what sort of formal controls, if any, will the church maintain over the separate entity)?

In the broader sense, however, a religious organization's structure includes not just its formal legal status, but also the whole range of policies and practices that the organization adopts to conduct, or structure, its operations. Like their secular counterparts, religious organizations follow policies for hiring, training, or disciplining employees. Social service agencies have policies and practices governing who they will serve and how such choices will be made; analogously, schools have policies for deciding which students to admit. Schools have directives for what they will teach; social service agencies have policies about what services they will provide.[4]

Among other things, such policies and practices determine how "religious" the organization is—how pervasive the religious influence is, or what Carl H. Esbeck calls its

---

3. *See, e.g.*, Thomas C. Berg, "Religiously Affiliated Education," in this volume.

4. In an analysis of religiously based social services, Esbeck has made a similar distinction between *de jure* and *de facto* structures of religious organizations. *See* Carl H. Esbeck, Government Regulation of Religiously Based Social Services: The First Amendment Considerations, 19 Hastings Const. L. Q. 343, 347–348 (1992). Esbeck's category of *de jure* structures corresponds closely to my category of formal decisions; in his words,

> the *de jure* structure entails the jural relationship between the church and the social service agency [, e.g.,] integrated auxiliary of the church; separate but wholly controlled subsidiary, non-profit corporation; corporation sole of an archbishop; separate, non-profit corporation without interlocking directorates; or para-church, non-profit corporation unaffiliated with any denomination.

Id. at 347. But his second category, *de facto* structure, is narrower than mine. It considers "the actual, working relationship between a church and the social ministry." *Id.* I see structural decisions in the broad sense as encompassing not merely the religious organization's relationship (if any) to a church, but more broadly the whole range of ways in which the organization decides to conduct its affairs so as to maintain its identity and pursue its mission.

"relatedness to the core of organized religion."[5] The organization may hire only members of its faith, or accept only members as clients, patients, or students; or it may accept the best qualified employees or the most needy clients without regard to religion. The services it provides—education, food and shelter, counseling, or medical care—may be pervaded by explicit religious teaching and witness, or they may not. The organization makes those choices based on theological, practical, financial, and other considerations, and structures its affairs accordingly.

Because the broader category of structure involves a wider range of organizational features than does formal structure, it is bound to raise more questions concerning contact with government. Most constitutional issues concerning the interaction of religious institutions and the state touch on structure only in the broader sense. But I will also discuss constitutional issues where formal structure is important.

Introduction to First Amendment Principles

The general interpretation of the Religion Clauses is currently in great flux. This is particularly true for the Establishment Clause, where the Court has drifted away from its three-part test of *Lemon v. Kurtzman*[6] for more than a decade[7] but has yet to agree on an alternative.[8] Some patterns, however, can be identified.

General Religion Clause approaches

The basic question of Religion Clause jurisprudence is: what posture do the two clauses, taken together, require government to adopt toward religion? From the late 1940s through the 1970s, the Court interpreted the Religion Clauses together to mandate a fairly strong, although not absolute, separation of church and state.[9] The Court's separationist approach was reflected in a series of decisions interpreting the Establishment Clause to bar most forms of government financial assistance to religiously affili-

---

5. *Id.* at 347.

6. 403 U.S. 602, 612–613 (1971) (requiring that government action have a secular purpose, have a "primary effect that neither advances nor inhibits religion," and not create "excessive entanglement" between church and state).

7. *See, e.g.*, Marsh v. Chambers, 463 U.S. 783 (1983) (disregarding *Lemon* test in upholding legislative prayers based on historical acceptance); County of Allegheny v. ACLU, 492 U.S. 573 (1989) (evaluating government-sponsored religious displays based not on *Lemon* but on whether displays "endorsed" religion); Lee v. Weisman, 505 U.S. 577 (1992) (striking down school-sponsored graduation prayer as an example of "coercion" toward dissenters, without resolving overall Establishment Clause standard).

8. *See, e.g.*, Board of Educ. v. Mergens, 496 U.S. 226 (1990) (upholding equal access for high school student religious clubs, but without any majority analysis).

9. For discussion, see Ira C. Lupu, The Lingering Death of Separationism, 62 Geo. Wash. L. Rev. 230, 233–237 (1993); Thomas C. Berg, Slouching Towards Secularism: A Comment on *Kiryas Joel School District v. Grumet*, 44 Emory L. J. 433, 442–446 (1995). Before the 1940s, there were relatively few Religion Clause cases, in large part because the clauses had not yet been applied to state actions through incorporation in the Fourteenth Amendment.

ated elementary and secondary schools.[10] On the other hand, the Court also read both the Free Exercise and Establishment clauses to shield churches and believers not only from discriminatory regulation, but from general laws that infringed too greatly on religious practice.[11]

In recent years, however, the Court has shifted away from separation and toward two different themes. The most predominant tendency is to give religious individuals and institutions treatment equal to that of other individuals and groups. Thus religious groups have the same rights to speak and assemble on public property that other groups do.[12] And more and more, religious organizations may receive aid from the government, directly or indirectly, on the same terms as comparable secular organizations; such equal aid does not offend the Establishment Clause.[13] On the other hand, a series of recent decisions, culminating in the "peyote" decision of *Employment Division v. Smith*,[14] has held that notwithstanding the Free Exercise Clause, religious activity may be subject to the same regulation that applies to secular activities.[15]

A second theme of recent decisions, though its tones are more muted, is deference to the government. Compared to the separationist model, government has recently been given much more constitutional latitude to aid religion, but also to regulate it. More-

---

10. *See, e.g.*, Lemon v. Kurtzman, 403 U.S. 602 (1971) (salary supplements and payments for teachers in secular classes); Committee for Public Educ. v. Nyquist, 413 U.S. 756 (1973) (grants to parents for tuition reimbursement and to schools for building maintenance); Meek v. Pittenger, 421 U.S. 349 (1975) (provision of public school teachers, materials, and equipment); Wolman v. Walter, 433 U.S. 229 (1977) (provision of materials and equipment); Grand Rapids School Dist. v. Ball, 473 U.S. 373 (1985) (assistance for remedial courses taught by public and religious school teachers); Aguilar v. Felton, 473 U.S. 402 (1985) (provision of public school teachers to teach remedial courses in secular subjects).

11. *See* Sherbert v. Verner, 374 U.S. 398 (1963) (standard for unemployment benefits that required recipient to take available work on Saturday, her sabbath); Wisconsin v. Yoder, 406 U.S. 205 (1972) (educational regulations requiring parents to send children to school beyond age 14); NLRB v. Catholic Bishop of Chicago, 440 U.S. 490 (1979) (application of federal collective-bargaining laws to teachers in parochial schools).

12. *See* Widmar v. Vincent, 454 U.S. 263 (1981) (student religious group meeting in university rooms on same terms as other groups); Board of Educ. v. Mergens, 496 U.S. 226 (1990) (high school student religious club meeting in noninstructional time on same terms as other clubs); Lamb's Chapel v. Center Moriches Sch. Dist., 508 U.S. 384 (1993) (church holding meeting on family issues in school classrooms after hours on same terms as other social and civic groups); Capitol Square Review and Advisory Bd. v. Pinette, 515 U.S. 753 (1995) (privately-erected religious symbol in public square in front of state capitol on same terms as other meetings or displays).

13. *See* Mueller v. Allen, 463 U.S. 388 (1983) (tax credits for parents of children in both public and private schools); Witters v. Washington Dept. of Services, 474 U.S. 481 (1986) (special education grants to students in religious as well as secular colleges); Bowen v. Kendrick, 487 U.S. 589 (1988) (direct grants to religious social service agencies on same terms as to nonreligious counterparts); Zobrest v. Catalina Foothills Sch. Dist., 509 U.S. 1 (1993) (sign language interpreter to deaf student in parochial school on same terms as to students in public schools); Rosenberger v. Rectors of Univ. of Virginia, 515 U.S. 819 (1995) (financial assistance for publication of student religious magazine on same terms as for other student publications); Agostini v. Felton, 521 U.S. 203 (1997) (provision of public school teachers to teach remedial classes in religious schools on same terms as to secular private schools); Mitchell v. Helms, 530 U.S. 793 (2000) (provision of instructional equipment and materials to religious schools on same terms as to other schools).

14. 494 U.S. 872 (1990).

15. *Smith*, 494 U.S. 872 (no free exercise bar when a generally applicable law is applied to religious conduct); Jimmy Swaggart Ministries v. Board of Equalization, 493 U.S. 378 (1990) (no free exercise bar to applying generally applicable sales tax scheme to religious ministry); Alamo Found. v. Sec'y of Labor, 471 U.S. 290 (1985) (no free exercise bar to applying generally applicable labor regulations to religious organization).

over, even though government is not required to give special protection to religious exercise, it may do so if it wishes, at least in many cases. There are counterexamples where the Court has recently struck down government action accommodating or assisting religion; two newer appointees, Justice Souter and Justice Ginsburg, are turning out to be quite activist in policing the line between church and state. But nearly half of the justices—Rehnquist, Scalia, Kennedy, and Thomas—are strongly committed to deferring to the political branches.

How have these general trends affected the constitutional rules concerning the regulation of religious institutions?

Church autonomy and the Free Exercise Clause

If one is looking for places to anchor limits on governmental regulation of religious bodies' structural and organizational decisions, the most logical starting point is the Free Exercise Clause. To begin with, the right to free exercise of religion undoubtedly extends to religious groups and organizations as well as to individuals. As Justice Brennan has written,

> [r]eligion includes important communal elements for most believers. They exercise their religion through religious organizations, and these organizations must be protected by the clause.... Such a community represents an ongoing tradition of shared beliefs, an organic entity not reducible to a mere aggregation of individuals.... [And] furtherance of the autonomy of the autonomy of religious organizations often furthers individual religious freedom as well.[16]

Furthermore, free exercise unquestionably includes the right to be free from coercion of belief or worship,[17] as well as the right to express religious views.[18] These protections may be relevant to some structural decisions made by religious entities. But structural decisions are also forms of behavior or conduct, and the Supreme Court has always asserted that protection of actions cannot be as absolute as protection of belief or speech.[19]

Religious freedom also clearly includes protection from discrimination by the government. It is virtually unquestioned that government may not intentionally prefer one religious group over others unless there is a very strong reason for doing so and the distinc-

---

16. Corporation of Presiding Bishop v. Amos, 483 U.S. 327, 341–42 (1987) (Brennan, J., concurring) (quoting Douglas Laycock, Towards A General Theory of the Religion Clauses: The Case of Church Labor Relations and the Right to Church Autonomy, 81 Colum. L. Rev. 1373, 1389 (1981)). *But see* Ira C. Lupu, Free Exercise Exemption and Religious Institutions: The Case of Employment Discrimination, 67 B.U. L. Rev. 391 (1987) (arguing that religious institutions should have lesser free exercise rights than individuals and should be subject to the same oversight in their employment decisions as are secular organizations).

17. *See* Torcaso v. Watkins, 367 U.S. 488 (1961) (invalidating requirement that state officeholder to swear to belief in God); U.S. Const. art. VI, § 3 (forbidding such oaths at federal level).

18. *See, e.g., Smith,* 494 U.S. at 881. *Smith* cited, for example, some of the many decisions protecting the religious speech of Jehovah's Witnesses during the 1940s and 1950s under both the Free Exercise and Free Speech clauses. *Id.*

19. *See Cantwell,* 310 U.S. at 303–304 ("freedom to believe...is absolute but, in the nature of things,...[c]onduct remains subject to regulation for the protection of society"); Reynolds v. United States, 98 U.S. 145, 164 (1878).

tion is "closely fitted" to that reason.[20] The Court has always assigned this rule of denominational equality to the Establishment Clause,[21] but regulation that discriminates against certain sects should be equally prohibited by the free exercise principle. A particular sect may not be singled out from others for either regulation[22] or benefits;[23] and this rule will be relevant to the question of whether different religious groups may be treated differently based on their formal or broader structure.[24] Free exercise also forbids discrimination against religion in general: if religious entities are singled out for suppression when other entities are left alone, the Free Exercise Clause is clearly violated.[25]

However, in a time of activist government, where private entities are heavily regulated in general, a mere nondiscrimination principle leaves religion exposed to a great deal of unwelcome contact with government. Thus, for many years the Supreme Court, embracing seriously the concept of church/state separation, asserted that the Free Exercise Clause sometimes required that religious entities be free from regulation when secular entities were not. Both *Sherbert v. Verner*[26] and *Wisconsin v. Yoder*[27] held that if government action significantly burdened a sincere religious practice, the action had to be justified by a "compelling" or "overriding" state interest.[28] In practice, the test of *Sherbert* and *Yoder* balanced the intrusion on religion against the government's need to regulate, in a fairly case-specific way: it subsequently produced some decisions where free exercise claims won, but others where they lost.[29] Indeed, after *Yoder* the Court's application of the test was increasingly half-hearted.[30] However, at least the Court continued to require some showing of need before government could inflict even an incidental burden on religious practice.

The special solicitude for religious freedom was clearest in situations where a believer or church was forced by government to violate a specific doctrinal tenet — for example,

---

20. Larson v. Valente, 456 U.S. 228, 244–247 (1982).

21. *See, e.g., id.* at 244–245 (describing the rule as the "[t]he clearest command of the Establishment Clause").

22. *See Larson* (striking down law regulating fundraising activities of only those religious groups that solicited more than fifty percent of their money from nonmembers; law was aimed primarily at Rev. Sun Myung Moon's Unification Church).

23. *See* Kiryas Joel Sch. Dist. v. Grumet, 512 U.S. 687, 114 S. Ct. 2481, 2493 (1994) (striking down school district created to allow disabled children of one insular Hasidic sect to attend classes in their village) (following *Larson*).

24. *See* section on the First Amendment and Internal Church Disputes, *infra*.

25. *See, e.g.,* Church of Lukumi Babalu Aye v. City of Hialeah, 508 U.S. 520 (1993) (invalidating animal-cruelty ordinances directed at Santeria religion); McDaniel v. Paty, 435 U.S. 618 (1978) (invalidating state constitutional provision prohibiting clergy from serving in state legislature).

26. 374 U.S. 398 (1963).

27. 406 U.S. 205 (1972).

28. *Sherbert*, 374 U.S. at 406; *Yoder*, 406 U.S. at 215–216.

29. For catalogs of the results, see James E. Ryan, Note, *Smith* and the Religious Freedom Restoration Act: An Iconoclastic Assessment, 78 Va. L. Rev. 1407, 1418–1420 (1992); Thomas C. Berg, What Hath Congress Wrought? An Interpretive Guide to the Religious Freedom Restoration Act, 39 Vill. L. Rev. 1, 11–12 nn.40–44 (1994); EEOC v. Townley Engineering Co., 859 F.2d 610, 625–29 (9th Cir. 1988) (Noonan, J., dissenting).

30. *See, e.g.,* United States v. Lee, 455 U.S. 252 (1982) (upholding application of social security laws to Amish community); Bob Jones Univ. v. United States, 461 U.S. 574 (1983) (upholding revocation of tax exemptions of racially discriminatory college); Alamo Found. v. Sec'y of Labor, 471 U.S. 290 (1985) (upholding application of minimum wage laws to religiously owned business). The Court also rejected more and more claims as not triggering strict scrutiny in the first place. Bowen v. Roy, 476 U.S. 693 (1986) (claims challenging government's "internal operations"); Goldman v. Weinberger, 475 U.S. 503 (1986) (challenges to military regulations); O'Lone v. Estate of Shabazz, 482 U.S. 342 (1987) (challenges to prison regulations); Lyng v. Northwest Indian Cemetery Protective Ass'n., 485 U.S. 439 (1988) (challenges to government's management of its property).

in *Sherbert v. Verner*, where the eligibility rules for unemployment compensation pressured Mrs. Sherbert to work on a day that her faith commanded was for resting. The unique protection of conduct found in the Free Exercise Clause reflects a special concern for the problems of conscience faced by citizens whose perceived duties to a higher power conflict with the demands made by the state.[31] As James Madison put it in the *Memorial and Remonstrance Against Religious Assessments*, one's duty to the Creator as one understands him "is precedent, both in order of time and degree of obligation, to the claims of Civil Society."[32] These rights of "conscientious objection," as Douglas Laycock calls them,[33] are therefore at the heart of the free exercise guarantee. And they are enjoyed not only by individuals but by organizations, for example if a Catholic church asserted protection against applying a sex discrimination law to force it to hire women as priests.

The Court, however, often went beyond such claims to recognize broader rights of "church autonomy" even when no specific doctrinal tenet was involved.[34] Among these rights of autonomy was the right of a church to decide how to structure its affairs. In *Kedroff v. St. Nicholas Cathedral*,[35] the Court held that the Free Exercise Clause embodies

> a spirit of freedom for religious organizations, an independence from secular control or manipulation, in short, *power to decide for themselves, free from state interference, matters of church governance as well as those of faith and doctrine.*[36]

In a pair of cases in 1990, however, the Supreme Court did away with much of the special protection that the Free Exercise Clause had offered. In other words, the Court moved away from elevating separation and substantive freedom in free exercise cases and embraced the principle that religion may be regulated equally with other activities. *Jimmy Swaggart Ministries v. Board of Equalization*[37] unanimously held that there was no free exercise claim because the government had neither prohibited conduct mandated by, nor required conduct proscribed by, tenets of the faith.[38] As Laycock has observed, this rule, taken seriously, eliminates free exercise claims to church autonomy if the church cannot show that its organizational decisions are mandated by a specific tenet of the faith.[39]

The Court in *Employment Division v. Smith*[40] went further and embraced the "equal treatment" principle explicitly, doing away with special solicitude even for some of the starkest claims of religious conscience. Under *Smith*, if a law is "neutral and generally applicable," courts do not even ask anymore how seriously it burdens religion or

---

31. *See* Timothy L. Hall, Religion, Equality, and Difference, 65 Temp. L. Rev. 1, 32–36 (1992); Michael W. McConnell, The Origins and Historical Understanding of Free Exercise of Religion, 103 Harv. L. Rev. 1409, 1452–1455 (1990).

32. Memorial and Remonstrance Against Religious Assessments, §1, *in* Appendix to *Everson v. Board of Education*, 330 U.S. 1, 63, 64 (1947) (Rutledge, J., dissenting).

33. Laycock, *supra* note 16, at 1388–90.

34. For discussion, see *id.* at 1388–1402.

35. 344 U.S. 94 (1952).

36. *Id.* at 116 (emphasis added).

37. 493 U.S. 378 (1990) (holding that religious group had no right to be free from general sales tax as applied to its sales of evangelistic tracts).

38. *Id.* at 391–392. *Cf.* Ira C. Lupu, Where Rights Begin: The Problem of Burdens on the Free Exercise of Religion, 102 Harv. L. Rev. 933 (1989) (discussing how, even before Swaggart, the Court limited free exercise claims by narrowing the category of cognizable burdens on religion).

39. *See* Douglas Laycock, The Remnants of Free Exercise, 1990 Sup. Ct. Rev. 1, 26.

40. 494 U.S. 872 (1990).

whether there is any justification for imposing that burden.[41] If *Smith* is followed rigidly, then the Free Exercise Clause, in Laycock's words, permits churches to be regulated as heavily as General Motors is: that is, in the welfare state, a good deal.[42]

What free exercise protection is left for church structural and polity decisions after *Smith* and *Swaggart*? Some of a church's choices about how to organize its affairs could be seen as matters of conscience, doctrinally commanded. For Catholics, for example, papal authority is not just efficient; it is the way Christ commanded his followers to "build my church."[43] And for many churches, polity decisions have expressive implications: "What we do and the way we do it," says the Presbyterian Church (U.S.A.), "is an expression of how we understand our faith."[44]

When structure is understood in the broad sense defined earlier in this chapter, it can encompass a host of decisions that a church might view as religiously commanded: for example, a policy of hiring only fellow adherents might be seen as following from the command to avoid being "yoked with unbelievers."[45] Other polity decisions, however, are not to be tied directly to any specific command or tenet, although they are important decisions about how to proclaim the faith or minister to the community. *Swaggart* indicates that these will receive no free exercise protection. For example, some courts have held after *Swaggart* that no free exercise issues are raised by architectural preservation laws that prevent a church from expanding or reconfiguring its buildings to meet its needs when no doctrinal tenet of the church is directly involved.[46]

Moreover, even an institutional practice mandated by the tenets of the faith can often be subjected to regulation, under the *Smith* rule, if the law is neutral and generally applicable. Still, *Smith* did set forth at least three potentially relevant exceptions and limitations to that principle. First, it reaffirmed previous holdings that courts should continue to refrain from "lend[ing] its power to one or the other side in controversies over religious authority or dogma"[47]—even, apparently, pursuant to a general law. Although the scope of this doctrine (which will be examined in greater detail below) is uncertain, it could protect religious institutions from government interference in their internal affairs. A number of currently pressing issues could be characterized as "internal" controversies over authority and dogma: certainly, for example, the question of whom to hire as a minister or church leader, and possibly even the whole range of labor and employment decisions (from whom to hire for various positions to what the terms of employment will be).

Second, a religious institution's challenge to regulation may involve a combination of free exercise and some other constitutionally recognized interest, such as

---

41. *Id.* at 877 (holding that no free exercise issue was raised by criminal prosecution of Native Americans for sacramental use of peyote, the central ritual of their Native American Church faith).

42. Laycock, *supra*, note 39.

43. *See* Matt. 16:18 ("You are Peter; and on this rock I will build my church").

44. 195th General Assembly of the Presbyterian Church in the U.S.A., Historic Principles, Conscience, and Church Government (1983), *quoted in* McCarthy, The Emerging Importance of Presbyterian Polity, in the Organizational Revolution: Presbyterians and American Denominationalism at 279, 302 (1992). *See id.* ("Our polity is not just a convenient way of getting things done.") *See* Brief of Amici Curiae at 9, Primate and Bishop's Synod of Russian Orthodox Church Outside Russia v. Russian Orthodox Church of Holy Resurrection, Inc., 630 N.E.2d 603, *aff'd* 636 N.E.2d 211 (Mass. 1994)).

45. 2 Cor. 6:14 (New King James Bible)

46. *See, e.g.*, Rector of St. Bartholomew's Church v. City of New York, 914 F.2d 348, 355 (2d Cir. 1990) (citing *Swaggart*).

47. *Smith*, 494 U.S. at 877.

freedom of speech, freedom of association, or the freedom of parents to direct the upbringing and education of their children.[48] This exception for what the *Smith* Court called "hybrid" claims, if it were generously interpreted, could preserve protection for religious institutions in important areas. The selection, assignment, and discipline of ministers and parochial school teachers, for example, implicates rights not only of free exercise but of free speech (who will speak for the church?) and freedom of association (the right to control personnel in the most intimate, core ideological functions of the institution).[49] A school's autonomy over its selection of teachers would be bolstered in particular by the Supreme Court's recent decision in *Boy Scouts of America v. Dale*,[50] holding that to force the Boy Scouts to accept an openly gay man as a scoutmaster violated the organization's right of "expressive association." An even broader range of activities of religiously affiliated schools could be protected by a combination of rights of religious exercise and of parental control over education—another "hybrid" constitutional claim mentioned by the *Smith* opinion.

Third, *Smith*'s constitutional approval is limited to laws that are "neutral and generally applicable." If a law or regulation covers religious entities but exempts a significant number of other entities or activities, the Court may find that it flunks the test of general applicability and that religious exercise, a constitutionally recognized interest, should receive no less protection than the other exempted activities. An easy case was the Court's ruling that a city could not draft its animal-cruelty ordinances so as to permit numerous kinds of killing of animals but not ritual animal sacrifice.[51] Harder cases involve legal schemes where some but not all other activities are exempted: for example, the bankruptcy laws, which allow debtors to spend money before their bankruptcy petitions on a variety of consumption goods but which at one time were interpreted to allow the overturning of tithes made by the debtor to her church.[52]

Although each of these exceptions and limitations to *Smith* might preserve significant protection from regulation for religious institutions, such protection is uncertain. The Court may follow the theories that underlie *Smith*—equal treatment between religion and nonreligion and deference to majoritarian decisions—and thus recognize such protection sparingly.

Nonentanglement and church autonomy

Although one might expect most protections against regulation of religious institutions to stem from the Free Exercise Clause, the Court in its separationist years also read the Establishment Clause to protect against such regulation. The *Lemon* test required not only that a law have a secular purpose and effect, but also that it not create "exces-

---

48. 494 U.S. at 881–82.

49. *See, e.g.*, Roberts v. United States Jaycees, 468 U.S. 609 (1984) (recognizing freedom of association claims for intimate associations and ideologically oriented organizations, though not for large commercially oriented clubs such as the Jaycees). The *Smith* Court cited *Roberts* in its brief reference to freedom of association claims. 494 U.S. at 882 (citing *Roberts*, 468 U.S. at 622).

50. 530 U.S. 640 (2000).

51. Church of Lukumi Babalu Aye v. City of Hialeah, 508 U.S. 520 (1993).

52. *See, e.g.*, *In re* Young, 82 F.3d 1407 (8th Cir. 1996), *vacated and remanded sub nom.* Christians v. Crystal Evangelical Free Church, 521 U.S. 1114 (1997), *reaffirmed on remand*, 141 F.3d 854 (8th Cir. 1998).

sive entanglement" between church and state.[53] Some historical basis can be found for assigning this value of institutional separation to the Establishment Clause as well as the Free Exercise Clause.[54] One of the objections to the Church of England and to colonial established churches was that they were tightly controlled by the state, producing, in Madison's words, "pride and indolence in the Clergy [and] ignorance and servility in the laity."[55]

The first use of the entanglement test, ironically, was to strike down funding that religious entities desired, on the ground that the accompanying regulation would interfere with their autonomy.[56] But later in *NLRB v. Catholic Bishop of Chicago*,[57] the Court turned the entanglement factor to uphold the arguments of religious entities, ruling that application of the federal collective bargaining laws to teachers in those schools would create a "significant risk" of serious and continuing government intrusion into the management of the schools.[58] Accordingly, the Court refused to apply the laws to parochial school teachers until Congress explicitly indicated its intent to do so.[59]

Catholic Bishop, however, was the high-water mark of protection against regulation on the basis of entanglement; as with free exercise, courts have retreated and have tended to allow churches to be regulated as much as other entities. Federal courts in later decisions have usually found a way to distinguish *Catholic Bishop*. Various other schemes of regulation have been found to create less entanglement than the collective bargaining laws, which empower the Labor Board to exercise continuing oversight over all "terms and conditions of employment." The Supreme Court concluded that both minimum-wage laws and sales-tax laws created only "routine regulatory interaction" such as the occasional filing of reports.[60] And a number of courts have said that discrimination claims by non-clergy employees do not create excess entanglement because they require only a limited investigation into that claim.[61] Other courts have limited *Catholic Bishop* to teachers, noting the Court's emphasis there on the central role of the teacher in the parochial school.[62] And courts applying state labor laws and other regulations have sidestepped *Catholic Bishop* by concluding that the statute before them did

---

53. *Lemon*, 403 U.S. at 613.

54. For arguments in support of this use, see Carl H. Esbeck, Establishment Clause Limits on Governmental Interference with Religious Organizations, 41 Wash. & Lee L. Rev. 347 (1984); James A. Serritella, Tangling With Entanglement: Toward a Constitutional Evaluation of Church-State Contacts, Spring, L. & Contemp. Probs. at 143 (1981); Michael W. McConnell, Accommodation of Religion: An Update and a Response to the Critics, 60 Geo. Wash. L. Rev. 685, 725–726 (1992). *Contrast* William P. Marshall and Douglas Blomgrem, Regulating Religious Organizations Under the Establishment Clause, 47 Ohio St. L. J. 293 (1986) (largely rejecting special protection for religion from regulatory entanglement).

55. Madison, Memorial and Remonstrance, §7 (1785) *reprinted in Everson*, 330 U.S. at 67 (adding that "ecclesiastical establishments, instead of maintaining the purity and efficacy of Religion, have had a contrary operation").

56. *See* discussion of *Lemon* and other decisions involving aid to schools, *infra*.

57. 440 U.S. 490 (1979).

58. *Id.* at 502–504.

59. *Id.* at 504–07.

60. *See* Alamo Found. v. Sec'y of Labor, 471 U.S. 290, 305–306 (1985) (minimum wages); *Swaggart*, 493 U.S. at 392 (taxation).

61. *See* DeMarco v. Holy Cross High Sch., 4 F.3d 166, 169–70 (2d Cir. 1993) (collecting cases).

62. *Catholic Bishop*, 440 U.S. at 501. *See, e.g.*, NLRB v. Hanna Boys Ctr., 940 F.2d 1295 (9th Cir. 1991) (refusing to block application of collective bargaining laws to maintenance staff and even child-care workers at church-owned residential school).

clearly extend to religious schools and essentially dismissing *Catholic Bishop* as merely an exercise in the interpretation of the federal labor laws.[63]

However, the nonentanglement principle has remained fairly strong in two classes of cases, which often overlap. First, courts may not resolve disputes involving churches by making decisions concerning the meaning or significance of religious concepts or doctrines. Second, courts may not become involved in controversies over who is the proper church authority. In both of these situations, the nonentanglement principle requires deference by the civil government to whatever resolution has been reached within the church—for example, deference to the resolution by the church's highest tribunal. These related prohibitions reflect the fact that for many centuries, a classic feature of European religious establishments was the authority of the state to decide doctrinal questions, determine church leadership and membership, and decide which members of the established church were faithful to its tenets.

The constitutional bar on such interference was preserved by *Employment Division v. Smith* when it again forbade involvement in "controversies over religious authority and dogma,"[64] citing several previous decisions. One of the decisions cited by *Smith* barred courts from awarding church property to a local congregation on the basis of interpretation of doctrine—in particular, on the basis that the broader denomination had committed "a 'substantial departure' from the tenets of faith and practice existing at the time of the local churches' affiliation."[65] Another decision, *Serbian Eastern Orthodox Church v. Milivojevich*,[66] barred a state court from stopping the defrocking of an Orthodox bishop. The Supreme Court held that the state court, in overturning the church's removal of the bishop, had impermissibly (i) passed on theological and not just secular questions and (ii) resolved a dispute over who would exercise pastoral authority in the church.[67]

These decisions, especially *Milivojevich*, have been important in preventing government intervention in the selection and handling of clergy. Numerous decisions have found excessive entanglement in the church/clergy relationship from various regulatory schemes, and as applied to a number of positions that could be classified as "clergy."[68]

Overall, the nonentanglement principle remains a shield for churches even after the Court's recent shrinking of free exercise protections. But it has not been a very strong

---

63. *See, e.g.*, Catholic High Sch. Ass'n. v. Culvert, 753 F.2d 1161, 1163 (2d Cir. 1985) (state labor laws); *In re* Hill-Murray Fed'n of Teachers, 487 N.W.2d 857, 861–62 (Minn. 1992) (same).

64. *Smith*, 494 U.S. at 877.

65. Presbyterian Church v. Hull Church, 393 U.S. 440, 449–450 (1969). *Accord* Jones v. Wolf, 443 U.S. 595, 602, 604 (1979); Watson v. Jones, 80 U.S. (13 Wall.) 679 (1871) (same rule against interpretation of doctrine, though under federal common law before incorporation of Religion Clauses against states).

66. 426 U.S. 696 (1976).

67. *Milivojevich* involved a dispute over church property as well, but the control of property was incidental to the question of who would speak for the church. *Id.* at 709; *see also, e.g.*, *Kedroff*, 344 U.S. at 96–97 (control of cathedral depended on who was valid archbishop in America for the Russian Orthodox Church).

68. *See, e.g.*, Rayburn v. General Conference of Seventh-Day Adventists, 772 F.2d 1164 (4th Cir. 1985) (sex discrimination claim by minister); McClure v. Salvation Army, 460 F.2d 553 (5th Cir. 1972) (sex discrimination claim by Salvation Army evangelists); EEOC v. Southwestern Baptist Theological Seminary, 651 F.2d 277 (5th Cir. 1981) (inquiry into sex discrimination barred as to ordained theology teachers); Dole v. Shenandoah Baptist Church, 899 F.2d 1398 (4th Cir. 1990) (clergy exempted from federal minimum-wage laws); Maguire v. Marquette Univ., 627 F. Supp. 1499 (E.D. Wis. 1986) (sex discrimination claim by theology professor), *aff'd in part, vacated in part*, 814 F.2d 1213 (7th Cir. 1987).

shield in other than core religious areas such as the selection and handling of clergy and certain parochial school teachers.

Aid to religiously affiliated institutions

The Court's overall move toward the principle of equal treatment will allow substantially greater government regulation of religious institutions and correspondingly greater interference in their autonomy. But when we turn to the side of government assistance, the move toward equal treatment analysis and away from separation is likely to have more mixed effects on religious institutions' autonomy. Religious institutions will be better able to participate in general programs of public benefits; this will remove a burden that the activist state places on religious activity, and will also reduce the pressure on potential clients (such as parents of schoolchildren) to receive social services from secular entities rather than from religious ones. However, with the additional aid may come regulatory conditions that will limit the institutions' autonomy. Some such conditions may be appropriate limits on the expenditure of government funds; others, however, may create pressure on religious entities to become just like their secular counterparts in order to receive aid.

As already noted, the nonentanglement prong of the Establishment Clause first was used to enforce the separation principle against providing aid to religiously affiliated organizations. In *Lemon v. Kurtzman* itself, the Court held that the state could not supplement the salaries of teachers in parochial elementary schools, even in secular subjects. The Court ensnared such aid in a catch-22: to pay teachers in schools pervaded by religion would have the impermissible "primary effect" of advancing religious teaching unless the state monitored against such uses; but such monitoring would in turn produce a "comprehensive, discriminating, and continuing state surveillance" that excessively entangled church and state.[69] The Court refused to extend this strict prohibition on aid to religiously affiliated colleges and universities, reasoning that they were not as pervasively religious.[70] But it continued to apply it for many years to elementary and secondary schools.[71]

However, separation is giving away noticeably to equal treatment in evaluating government aid as well as regulation. Retreating from the strict rules that governed aid to schools, the Court held that religious social service agencies were less pervasively religious as a group and could receive government aid unless those challenging the aid could prove that the particular agency actually used the money to teach religion.[72] Even more importantly, the Court has allowed several programs that provided neutral benefits to individuals who could then choose to use the benefits at any school they wished.[73] And in recent decisions, the Court has approved forms of aid that go more directly to schools: the provision of public school teachers for remedial classes in inner-city private schools in *Agostini v. Felton*,[74] and most recently the provision of instructional materials

---

69. *Lemon*, 403 U.S. at 618–620. *See also, e.g.*, Aguilar v. Felton, 473 U.S. 402, 414 (1985).
70. See the more detailed discussion *infra* in notes 154–168 and accompanying text.
71. See cases cited *supra* in note 10.
72. Bowen v. Kendrick, 487 U.S. 589 (1988).
73. *See Zobrest*, 509 U.S. 1; *Witters*, 474 U.S. 481; *Mueller*, 463 U.S. 388.
74. 521 U.S. 203 (1997). The *Agostini* Court emphasized the program's neutrality toward religion—teachers were provided to secular private schools as well—and it overruled its previous decision striking down the same program (Aguilar v. Felton, 473 U.S. 402 (1985)), as well as much of the separationist reasoning found in *Aguilar*.

and equipment to religious schools, as well as other private schools, in *Mitchell v. Helms.*[75]

In decisions concerning educational aid, the Court increasingly has deemed it irrelevant how religious is the school chosen by the recipient. In rulings on aid provided to individuals, it has emphasized that a decision to use the aid at a religious school is the individual's, not the government's,[76] thus making it irrelevant how "sectarian" the school in question may be (indeed, one of the decisions, *Witters,* involved a pervasively religious bible college training students for Christian missions). And the court in *Mitchell* refused to ask how "pervasively sectarian" the school in question was, even when the school was the direct recipient of government aid. Four justices vigorously attacked the concept that courts should identify "pervasively sectarian" schools and bar them from receiving aid, and the crucial concurring opinion implicitly rejected the concept as well.[77] After *Mitchell,* the chief limit on a program of direct aid given equally to religious schools is that the aid must not be divertible to religious uses.[78] The next logical step is for the Court to approve a properly crafted program of vouchers for parents to use at public, secular private, or religious schools.[79]

Still, such aid might come with a host of strings attached. That the Court would approve considerable regulation monitoring the use of government money is foreshadowed both by the weakening of the nonentanglement prong, mentioned above, and by developments in other areas. For example, the Court permitted the federal government to exercise substantial control over private agencies receiving federal grants for pregnancy-related services; the Court upheld restrictions on grantees' mentioning abortion services, even in programs that arguably were not closely related to the programs that directly received the grants.[80]

Nonconstitutional accommodations: The Religious Freedom Restoration Act and legislative exemptions from regulation

If the *Smith* and *Swaggart* decisions were the end of the matter, religious organizations might find it difficult to block state regulation except at the very core of their religious activities. However, as *Smith* itself suggested,[81] exemptions may still be granted by legislative or administrative grace rather than by constitutional right.

---

75. 120 S. Ct. 2530 (2000).

76. *See, e.g., Witters,* 474 U.S. 481 (approving use of aid by blind student preparing for ministry at a pervasively religious bible college). See appendix on *Zelman v. Simmons-Harris,* in this volume.

77. *See Mitchell,* 120 S. Ct. at 2551–52 (plurality opinion of Thomas, J., for four justices); *id.* at 2558–60 (O, Connor, J., joined by Breyer, J., concurring in the judgment).

78. This is the key concept of Justice O'Connor's crucial concurring opinion in *Mitchell. Id.* at 2562.

79. For discussion of the law on vouchers, both in the Supreme Court and in state and lower federal courts, see Thomas C. Berg, "Religiously Affiliated Education" and appendix on *Zelman,* in this volume.

80. Rust v. Sullivan, 500 U.S. 173 (1991). For detailed discussion of the extent and kinds of regulation that accompany government funding, see Carl H. Esbeck, "Regulation of Religious Organizations via Governmental Financial Assistance," in this volume.

81. 494 U.S. at 890.

Such "permissive" exemptions are often included in the statute that regulates the religious entity; by this means, churches and religious organizations are exempted from a variety of taxes, labor and employment laws, education regulations, and so forth. These statute-specific exemptions will likely continue to be a significant source of protection for religious exercise.

In addition, Congress in late 1993 restored the general rule mandating exemptions in some cases, this time as a matter of statutory right. The Religious Freedom Restoration Act (RFRA)[82] provided that government could not impose a "substantial burden" on religious exercise, even through application of a general law, unless applying the law was the least restrictive means of accomplishing a compelling governmental interest.[83] RFRA returned free exercise analysis to the kind of balancing of religious and governmental interests that existed before *Smith*, and that was a significant development for churches' freedom from intrusive regulation. Courts interpreted RFRA to shield a religious university from a professor's sex discrimination claim,[84] confessions to a Catholic priest from discovery by state prosecutors,[85] churches from having to return tithes made by members who later went bankrupt,[86] and church-run homeless shelters from zoning restrictions that would have forced them to cease operating.[87]

However, the Supreme Court in *City of Boerne v. Flores*[88] struck down RFRA as unconstitutional, at least as applied to state and local laws, on the ground that it exceeded Congress's power to legislate to enforce the guarantees of the Fourteenth Amendment. The majority held that the enforcement power, found in section 5 of the amendment, only authorized Congress to design remedies for violations of a constitutional standard announced by the Court, and not to adopt a broader substantive reading of the amendment.[89] Thus when Congress legislated to protect free exercise, a right incorporated in the Fourteenth Amendment, it could only act to enforce the principles of the Free Exercise Clause set forth in *Smith*; it could not legitimately reject the *Smith* standard of nondiscrimination, as it did in RFRA, in favor of a broader substantive principle of religious accommodations.[90]

Because of *Boerne*, there now is no broad-ranging federal statutory right to exemption from state and local laws that are generally applicable. However, RFRA may remain

---

82. 42 U.S.C. § 2000bb (enacted November 16, 1993).

83. 42 U.S.C. § 2000bb-3(b). I discuss the statute in this chapter on the Federal Constitution because it obviously sought to restore a once constitutionally-based norm by legislation. In Professor Lupu's suggestive metaphor, it is a "statute[] revolving in [a] constitutional law orbit[]." Ira C. Lupu, Statutes Revolving in Constitutional Law Orbits, 79 Va. L. Rev. 1 (1993).

84. E.E.O.C. v. Catholic Univ., 83 F.3d 455 (D.C. Cir. 1996).

85. Mocklaitis v. Harcelroad, 104 F.3d 1522 (9th Cir. 1997).

86. *In re* Young, 82 F.3d 1407 (8th Cir. 1996), *vacated on other grounds and remanded sub nom.* Christians v. Crystal Evangelical Free Church, 521 U.S.1114 (1997), *reaffirmed on remand*, 141 F.3d 854 (8th Cir. 1998).

87. *See, e.g.,* Stuart Circle Parish v. Bd. of Zoning Appeals, 946 F. Supp. 1225 (E.D. Va. 1996); Jesus Center v. Farmington Hills Zoning Bd., 544 N.W.2d 698 (Mich. Ct. App. 1996) (holding that denial of permit to operate homeless shelter substantially burdened church's religious exercise under RFRA even though shelter could be located elsewhere); Western Presbyterian Church v. Board of Zoning Adjustment, 849 F. Supp. 77 (D.D.C. 1994) (issuing preliminary injunction after RFRA against zoning board's exclusion of a soup kitchen that had operated safely for ten years). For a catalog of RFRA's results, and a more skeptical view of its accomplishments, see Lupu, The Failure of RFRA, 20 U. Ark. Little Rock L. J. 575 (1998).

88. 521 U.S. 557, 117 S.Ct. 2157 (1997).

89. *Id.* at 2162–2168.

90. *Id.* at 2168–2171.

valid as applied to federal laws and regulations, as one federal court of appeals has held.[91] With respect to RFRA's application to federal law, Congress was not acting under its section 5 power to impose a rule on the states; it was acting, presumably, under its Article I powers to ensure that religion would not be unduly or unnecessarily burdened by the Article I statutes it has enacted. (For example, as applied to modify federal employment discrimination laws, RFRA would be an exercise of the Commerce Power, the same basis on which the employment discrimination laws themselves were enacted.)[92] Some critics of RFRA, however, assert that the statute is invalid as applied to federal law as well because it does not rest on any single enumerated power and because, by displacing the standard set forth in *Smith*, it intrudes on the Court's authority to interpret the Free Exercise Clause and thereby violates the separation of powers.[93] Congress has failed to pass broad new legislation protecting religious practices against state and local laws, although it did enact heightened scrutiny for religious freedom claims against zoning and architectural preservation laws and against prison regulations.[94]

If RFRA remains valid as applied to federal law, then federal legislation will continue to provide protection for some religious practices, of institutions and individuals, even against generally applicable laws. But uncertainties will remain even in those situations where such legislation applies. Courts may be less than vigorous in enforcing the requirement that government prove a compelling interest, just as decisions before *Smith* had sometimes enforced that standard halfheartedly.[95] The threshold that the burden on religion be "substantial" to trigger the statute might be interpreted to preserve the rule that a free exercise claimant must demonstrate that a law forces her to violate a specific religious tenet[96]—a rule that, as noted above, eliminates many claims based on church autonomy.[97] Before *Boerne*, several courts of appeals inter-

---

91. *Christians*, 141 F.3d 854; *see also Catholic University*, 83 F.3d 455 (upholding RFRA as applied to a federal law before *Boerne*); *but cf.* Popovich v. Cuyahoga County Court of Common Pleas, 227 F.3d 627, 635 (6th Cir. 2000) (questions whether RFRA is constitutional, but avoids deciding).

92. *Christians*, 141 F.3d 854; *Catholic University*, 83 F.3d at 457–58. For elaboration of this argument, see Thomas C. Berg, The Constitutional Future of Religious Freedom Legislation, 20 U. Ark. Little Rock L. J. 715 (1998).

93. *See, e.g.*, Eugene Gressman and Angela C. Carmella, The RFRA Revision of the Free Exercise Clause, 57 Ohio St. L. J. 65 (1996) (emphasizing the separation-of-powers challenge); Marci A. Hamilton, The Religious Freedom Restoration Act: Letting the Fox Into the Henhouse Under Cover of Section 5 of the Fourteenth Amendment, 16 Cardozo L. Rev. 357 (1994) (emphasizing the enumerated-powers challenge); Christopher L. Eisgruber and Lawrence G. Sager, Why the Religious Freedom Restoration Act is Unconstitutional, 62 N.Y.U. L. Rev. 437 (1994); Edward J. Blatnik, Note, No RFRAF Allowed: The Status of the Religious Freedom Restoration Act's Federal Applications in the Wake of *City of Boerne v. Flores*, 98 Colum. L. Rev. 1410 (1998).

94. Religious Land Use and Institutionalized Persons Protection Act, 42 U.S.C.A. 2000cc ("RLUIPA," signed into law Sept. 22, 2000).

95. *See* cases cited *supra* note 30; Lupu, *supra* note 9, at 274 (noting that "post-*Yoder* federal court rulings very much tended to dilute the rigors of *Yoder*"). For other, more religion-protective views of the proper meaning of "compelling interest" under RFRA, see, e.g., Oliver Thomas and Douglas Laycock, Interpreting the Religious Freedom Restoration Act, 73 Tex. L. Rev. 209, 222–27 (1994) (arguing for stringent interpretation of the test); Berg, *supra* note 29, at 31 & ff. (arguing for "a less-than-absolute approach that gives careful scrutiny to the government's asserted interests but acknowledges real limits on religious freedom").

96. *See, e.g.*, Goodall v. Stafford County Sch. Bd., 60 F.3d 168 (4th Cir. 1995) (finding no burden from denial of speech translator to deaf student in religious school).

97. *See supra* notes 37–46 and accompanying text. For arguments that the statute should not be so narrowly construed, see Thomas and Laycock, *supra* note 95, at 228–33; Berg, *supra* note 29, at 52–57. The 2000 RLUIPA statute makes clear that religious exercise is protected "whether or not [it

preted the statute generously to cover any practice that is "religiously motivated," not just those compelled by a specific tenet; but others interpreted the burden requirement restrictively.[98]

In addition, both the general accommodation of RFRA and more case-specific legislative accommodations have been challenged as "favoring" or "promoting" religion in violation of the Establishment Clause. If the Free Exercise Clause does not mandate any exemptions, opponents say, then the legislature may not go further and give special protection to religion.[99] The Supreme Court has not yet given clear guidance on how far the legislature may go in accommodating religion. It has repeatedly affirmed that special protection for religious freedom is permissible in some cases.[100] But it has also struck down several religion-specific exemptions, especially where it believed that the exemption placed burdens on other citizens that were more serious than the burdens it removed from religion,[101] or that it discriminated unjustifiably between religious sects.[102] In *Texas Monthly v. Bullock*,[103] for example, a fragmented Court struck down an exemption from state sales taxes limited to religious publications. A plurality opinion, written by Justice Brennan, concluded that the exemption unduly favored religious practice because there was no showing that religious publications were seriously burdened by sales taxes and because the exemption forced other publications to pay more in order to maintain the tax base.[104] The plurality distinguished the previous decision of *Corporation of Presiding Bishop v. Amos*,[105] which had upheld the Title VII exemption permitting religious organizations to engage in religious employment preferences, on the ground that requiring religious organizations to hire nonadherents imposed a much greater burden than did the application of sales taxes.[106] This line of reasoning was not

---

is] compelled by, or central to, a system of religious belief," 42 U.S.C. §2000cc-5(7)(A); this provision also applies to religious exercise under RFRA. 42 U.S.C. §2000bb-2(4).

98. *Compare, e.g., Young*, 82 F.3d at 1418–19 (practice of tithing was protected by RFRA even if it was not religiously compelled); Mack v. O'Leary, 80 F.3d 1175, 1179 (7th Cir. 1996) (Posner, C.J.) (various practices of Muslim prisoners were protected even if they were not "actually obligatory for Muslims"); with Lupu, *supra* note 87, at 601–616 (listing decisions in which courts rejected RFRA claims on ground of no substantial burden on religion).

99. *See, e.g.*, Mark Tushnet, Of Church and State and the Supreme Court: *Kurland* Revisited, 1989 Sup. Ct. Rev. 373, 388–389; Steven G. Gey, Why Is Religion Special? Reconsidering the Accommodation of Religion Under the Religion Clauses of the First Amendment, 52 U. Pitt. L. Rev. 75 (1990); Lupu, Reconstructing the Establishment Clause: The Case Against Discretionary Accommodation of Religion, 140 U. Pa. L. Rev. 555 (1991) (arguing that religion-specific exemptions are unconstitutional unless required by the Free Exercise Clause).

100. *See, e.g.*, Corporation of Presiding Bishop v. Amos, 483 U.S. 327 (1987) (upholding Title VII's exemption of religious organizations from the rule against religious discrimination in employment); Gillette v. United States, 401 U.S. 437 (1971) (upholding exemptions from draft for religious objectors to all wars); Zorach v. Clauson, 343 U.S. 306 (1952) (upholding release time program allowing public school students to attend religious classes off school grounds). *See also, e.g., Smith*, 494 U.S. at 890 (encouraging "nondiscriminatory religious-practice exemptions" by legislatures).

101. *See, e.g.*, Texas Monthly v. Bullock, 489 U.S. 1 (1989) (striking down sales-tax exemption for religious publications, in part because it imposed greater tax burden on competing publications); Estate of Thornton v. Caldor, 472 U.S. 703 (1985) (striking down law giving employee absolute right to day off on his designated sabbath, in part because it imposed burdens on other, nonreligious employees).

102. *See Kiryas Joel*, 114 S. Ct. at 2493; *see supra* notes 20–24 and accompanying text.

103. 489 U.S. 1 (1989).

104. *Id.* at 15, 18.

105. 483 U.S. 327 (1987).

106. *Texas Monthly*, 489 U.S. at 18 n.8 (plurality opinion).

adopted by a majority of the Court, but it does reveal the fine distinctions that some of the justices are willing to adopt in cases involving legislative accommodations.

The divided results in these cases show the post-separationist Court hedging between a rule of equal treatment for religion (which would forbid most legislative accommodations) and a posture of deference to the political branches (which, as in *Smith*, would affirm accommodations by the legislature while refusing to mandate accommodations under the Constitution).

Under current conditions in America, permitting legislative accommodations is vital to maintaining religious freedom. Given the pervasiveness of government regulation generally, activity by religious institutions will be heavily regulated unless it is given specific protection. After *Smith* and *Swaggart's* weakening of federal constitutional standards, legislative accommodations—whether in specific statutes like Title VII or through general statutes like RFRA—must play a key role in preserving the autonomy of religious institutions.

The First Amendment and Internal Church Disputes

The preceding discussion suggests that although courts have sometimes given constitutional protection to church autonomy, they have just as often not done so, especially in recent years. But one area remains where courts give greater deference to a church's organization and structure: the category of "internal" disputes between members or factions of a religious community.[107] In such cases—which include litigation over matters such as who controls the church property, who can serve as a minister or other authority, or whether a member may remain in good standing—courts generally seek to reach a decision according to the rules that the parties have adopted for themselves, respecting the community's right, emphasized in *Kedroff v. St. Nicholas Cathedral* and subsequent decisions, to decide matters of church governance. This does not mean that courts should simply refuse to hear such disputes: churches, like other organizations, need to have recourse to a court where necessary to resolve internal disputes, and society too has an interest in ensuring peaceful resolutions of such disputes.[108] But both the "no preference between religions" rule and basic free exercise principles of autonomy demand that in deciding these disputes, courts not unfairly favor one faction over the other and also not distort the organizational rules that members of a community have agreed upon for themselves.

---

107. Believers are often commanded to resolve disputes between themselves without resorting to civil courts. *See, e.g.,* I Cor. 6:6 (NEB) ("Must Christian go to law with Christian—and before unbelievers at that?"). But that injunction seems to be regularly ignored. *See* Arlin M. Adams and William R. Hanlon, *Jones v. Wolf:* Church Autonomy and the Religion Clauses of the First Amendment, 128 U. Pa. L. Rev. 1291, 1291 (1980) (reporting significant rise in filing of civil actions concerning internal church disputes).

108. Presbyterian Church v. Hull Church, 393 U.S. 440, 445 (1969); Ira Mark Ellmann, Driven from the Tribunal: Judicial Resolution of Internal Church Disputes, 69 Cal. L. Rev. 1378, 1383 (1981) ("Immunity from judicial dispute resolution may...burden the organizational efforts of religious groups by denying them the benefit of secular rules that facilitate the creation and growth of private, voluntary associations").

For many years, the means that courts used to try to follow a church's own rules was to identify who held authority within the church's organizational structure and then defer to the decision of that authority. Under this approach, in other words, the court tries to identify the church's polity in order to determine whose verdict within the organization is final. Decisions under this approach, beginning with the Supreme Court's early ruling in *Watson v. Jones*,[109] tend to group church polities into two categories. In the hierarchical church, authority is lodged in an ascending series of officers or tribunals. When those higher authorities have spoken, their decisions must "be binding in all cases of ecclesiastical cognizance, subject only to such appeals as the organism itself provides for."[110] On the other hand, congregational churches, where local congregations affiliate in looser organizations but without creating authority in the central entity, are governed by the ordinary legal principles governing voluntary associations. In disputes between a local congregation and the larger organization, this usually leads to awarding property or other spoils to the local body.[111]

The polity approach obviously embodies the *Kedroff* right to decide internal matters of church governance. The court identifies the structure of decision making within the church and then defers to that structure. But although the polity approach was the law for more than a century, it received strong criticisms. Commentators have complained that it unduly favors the church hierarchy. Even if a church is hierarchical in its overall structure, control over some particular issue (for example, a certain piece of property) might be given by the parties to some lower body (such as the local congregation) through a deed, conveyance, or other instrument. In that case, critics argue, deference to the hierarchy upsets the arrangements made within the community and violates the free exercise rights of the local body.[112] The Supreme Court added a second criticism in *Jones v. Wolf*:[113] in some religious bodies, "the locus of control would be ambiguous" and the court would have to make theological decisions based on "a searching and therefore impermissible inquiry into church polity."[114]

Based on these misgivings about the polity approach, the Court in *Jones v. Wolf* approved another means of resolving disputes over church property: the application of "neutral principles" of trust or property law that are used in property litigation between secular parties.[115] To decide who owns the property when a split occurs, courts may examine "the language of the deeds, the terms of the local church charters, the state statutes governing the holding of church property, and the provisions in the constitution of the general church concerning the ownership and control of church prop-

---

109. 80 U.S. (13 Wall.) 679 (1871).

110. *Watson*, 80 U.S. at 729. The classic examples among Christian groups are the episcopal churches: Roman Catholic, Orthodox, and Episcopal. But more complicated polities, such as those of the various Presbyterians denominations, were usually held to be hierarchical as well. *See, e.g., Watson*, 80 U.S. at 729; Calvary Presbyterian Church v. Presbytery of Lake Huron, 384 N.W.2d 92, 94–95 (Mich. App. 1986).

111. Giovan Harbour Venable, Note, Courts Examine Congregationalism, 41 Stan. L. Rev. 719, 726–727 & n.44 (1989) (citing cases). Baptists are the primary example in America.

112. *See, e.g.*, Patty Gerstenblith, Civil Court Resolution of Property Disputes Among Religious Organizations, 39 Am. U. L. Rev. 513, 519–21 (1990); William G. Ross, The Need for an Exclusive and Uniform Application of "Neutral Principles" in the Adjudication of Church Property Disputes, 32 St. Louis U. L.J. 263, 305–15 (1987); Adams and Hanlon, *supra* note 107, at 1335–39.

113. 443 U.S. 595 (1979).

114. *Id.* at 605 (quotation omitted).

115. *Id.* at 602–603; *accord Hull Church*, 393 U.S. at 449 (suggesting approval of "neutral principles of law, developed for use in all property disputes").

erty."[116] Reading secular documents in the light of neutral principles of law may produce quite a different result in a hierarchical church. The Massachusetts state courts, for example, recently allowed a parish congregation that broke away from a Russian Orthodox denomination—a hierarchical body if there ever was one—to take the church building and land because of the language in the property deeds and the parish bylaws.[117]

At first glance, it might seem that if courts can apply the same trust and property rules to churches as to other organizations, then the First Amendment right to decide matters of church governance is lost. The internal affairs of commercial businesses, after all, are constantly interfered with by government regulation. But *Jones v. Wolf*, if read properly, does not go that far.

As Ira Ellman has pointed out in this context, legal rules do not always impose an absolute policy judgment on the regulated party; many rules are simply "gap fillers" that come into play only when the parties to a dispute have not provided for the resolution of a matter by contract or other instrument.[118] Gap-filling rules—otherwise referred to as default rules—are often designed to facilitate the parties' intent by "express[ing] the understanding that the parties probably would have had, if only they had considered the point."[119] Even if a default rule reflects an independent societal judgment rather than a guess about the parties' likely intent, the key is that such a rule can be overridden by the parties. Thus, gap fillers "are usually flagged by clauses that allow a different result if corporate articles or bylaws so provide."[120]

On the other hand, some legal rules impose certain results or procedures on the parties regardless of their agreements. Such "policy based" rules "impose a policy favored by the government, such as that corporate directors be chosen by cumulative voting, or that interest rates not exceed eighteen percent."[121] Policy-based rules that commonly affect churches include requirements of majority voting control, as well as federal and state laws prohibiting employment discrimination and requiring payment of minimum wages. Policy-based rules raise the clearest religious freedom issues, because in them "the state imposes its own values on a religious organization."[122] For example, if state law provides that the majority of an entity's trustees must approve major decisions, it infringes on the First Amendment right of church governance to apply that rule to a Catholic entity that is organized to give the diocesan bishop veto power over decisions.

---

116. *Id.* at 603.

117. Primate and Bishops' Synods, Russian Orthodox Church Outside of Russia v. Church of the Holy Resurrection, 617 N.E.2d 1031 (1993), *aff'd*, 636 N.E.2d 211 (Mass. 1994).

118. Ellman, *supra* note 108, at 1406–1407, 1422–1423.

119. *Id.* at 1422. It is prohibitively costly for parties to consider and resolve all questions that might arise, so gap filling rules facilitate agreements by providing missing terms rather than letting the agreement collapse. *See, e.g.*, Richard A. Posner, Economic Analysis of Law 92–93 (4th ed. 1992); Ian Ayres and Robert Gertner, Filling Gaps in Incomplete Contracts: An Economic Theory of Default Rules, 99 Yale L.J. 87, 87 (1989).

120. Ellman, *supra* note 108, at 1422. A default rule, instead of seeking the parties' likely intent, might, for example, put the burden on the better-informed or more sophisticated party to draft explicit provisions in its favor. *See* Ayres and Gertner, *supra* note 119, at 97–98. I do not take a position here on whether default rules as applied to religious internal disputes must seek only to effectuate the parties' likely intent. The main point is that rules applied to internal disputes must be default rules or gap fillers; that is, the parties must be able to override them through explicit terms.

121. Ellman, *supra* note 108, at 1422.

122. *Id.*

The reasoning in *Jones v. Wolf* provides a justification only for gap-filling or default rules. The Court answered the charge that the use of neutral property laws infringed on religious freedom by arguing that such laws are designed to "order[] private rights and obligations to reflect the intentions of the parties" and are "flexible enough to accommodate all forms of religious organization."[123]

> Through appropriate reversionary clauses and trust provisions, religious societies can specify what is to happen to church property in the event of a particular contingency, or what religious body will determine the ownership in the event of a schism or doctrinal controversy. In this manner, a religious organization can ensure that a dispute over the ownership of church property will be resolved in accord with the desires of the members....
>
> Under the neutral-principles approach, the outcome of a church property dispute is not foreordained. At any time before the dispute erupts, the parties can ensure, if they so desire, that the faction loyal to the hierarchical church will retain the church property.... And the civil courts will be bound to give effect to the result indicated by the parties, provided it is embodied in some legally cognizable form.[124]

This argument, that churches will be able to use neutral laws to order their operations as they wish, has some force. In the wake of *Jones*, denominations that had once relied on their judicially declared status as "hierarchical" churches to ensure control over church property began to amend their constitutions to include explicit trusts giving local church property to the denomination if the local congregation broke away.[125] In disputes that arose after those amendments were effective, several courts gave effect to them under the neutral principles approach.[126]

In other words, the neutral principles approach can be seen as seeking to determine and enforce the church's authority structure, just as the polity approach seeks to do. It is simply that in the neutral principles approach the court looks for secular legal terms as the expression of that structure. To be sure, the initial default allocation of rights and duties can be crucial to the parties' relative position in bargaining with each other; but the option to bargain around the rules remains. In fact, the use of general contract, property, or trust laws may give a church greater flexibility in reflecting the nuances of its polity than does the polity approach with its tendency to pigeonhole churches as purely hierarchical or purely congregational. But this is only so when the laws applied are gap fillers that can be overridden by specific language. Neutral rules that do not allow a church to contract around them are not supported by *Jones*'s rationale, which expressly argued that neutral legal principles help a religious community facilitate its

---

123. *Jones*, 443 U.S. at 603.

124. *Id.* at 603–604, 606. See also Perry Dane, "Omalous" Autonomy, 2004 B.Y.U. L. Rev. 1715, 1742–44.

125. *See, e.g.*, PC(USA) Book of Order G-8.0201 (1994) ("[a]ll property held by or for a particular church...is held in trust nevertheless for the use and benefit of the Presbyterian Church (U.S.A.)"); Episcopal Church Canons and Constitutions Title I, Canon 7, §§ 3–4 (1985) ("[a]ll real or personal property held by or for the benefit of any Parish...is held in trust for the [Episcopal] Church and the Diocese thereof").

126. *See, e.g.*, Rector, Wardens, and Vestrymen v. Episcopal Church, 620 A.2d 1280, 1292 (Conn. 1993) (trust in Episcopal Church Constitution); Bishop and Diocese of Colorado v. Mote, 716 P.2d 85, 105–107 (Colo. 1986) (same); Babcock Mem'l Presbyterian Church v. Presbytery of Baltimore, 464 A.2d 1008, 1016–1017 (Md. 1983) (trust in Presbyterian Church Book of Order). But for courts that failed to give these provisions effect, see *infra* notes 143–144, and accompanying text.

collective intent and understandings. At the least, the government should have a compelling reason before it overrides the internal arrangements of an organization.

Employment lawsuits by ministers against their churches also show that the government cannot override the parties' intent in internal disputes. Laws against employment discrimination or wrongful discharge are, in Ellman's terms, policy-based rules that do not give a church room to effectuate a contrary intent. That is one reason why such claims have always been barred on constitutional grounds, clearly under the Free Exercise Clause before *Employment Division v. Smith*,[127] but even after that decision as well under additional principles of free speech, nonentanglement, and freedom of association.[128] However, if the church makes an explicit commitment to a minister, it may well be held to that commitment through a claim based on contract—that is, a claim that seeks to effectuate the parties' intent. The distinction is illustrated in *Minker v. Baltimore Annual Conf. of United Methodist Church*:[129] the court dismissed a minister's Title VII and wrongful-discharge claims, but permitted a breach-of-contract count to proceed based on his allegation that church authorities had promised and failed to find him "a congregation more suited to his training and skills."[130] Similarly, in *Babcock v. New Orleans Baptist Seminary*,[131] a Louisiana court ruled that a seminary could not expel a ministerial student, even though he had separated from his wife (after allegedly beating her) in clear violation of the church's standards, because the school had failed to follow the pretermination procedures set forth in its handbook. "[B]y describing its due process procedures in the handbook," the court said, "the Seminary has taken the issue of a student's dismissal out of the arena of a religious controversy and into the realm of a contract dispute."[132]

---

127. *See, e.g.*, Rayburn v. Gen. Conf. of Seventh-Day Adventists, 772 F.2d 1164 (4th Cir. 1985); EEOC v. Southwestern Bapt. Theol. Seminary, 651 F.2d 277 (5th Cir. 1981) (treating seminary professors as ministers); McClure v. Salvation Army, 460 F.2d 553 (5th Cir. 1972).

128. *See, e.g.*, EEOC v. Catholic Univ., 83 F.3d 455, 461–63 (D.C. Cir. 1996); EEOC v. Roman Catholic Diocese of Raleigh, 213 F.3d 795 (4th Cir. 2000); Combs v. Cent. Texas Annual Conf. of United Methodist Church, 173 F.3d 343, 347–50 (5th Cir. 1999); Gellington v. Christian Methodist Episcopal Church, 203 F.3d 1299, 1302–04 (11th Cir. 2000).

129. 894 F.2d 1354 (D.C. Cir. 1990).

130. *Id.* at 1355. As discussed *infra* in text following note 131, I think permitting this particular contract claim was wrong. For another example of a court permitting a contract claim, see *Alicea v. New Brunswick Theol. Seminary*, 581 A.2d 900 (N.J. Super. 1990) (rejecting all claims by seminary professor who was denied tenure, except for claim that school failed to follow "clear" procedures in faculty handbook for tenure evaluation).

131. 554 So. 2d 90 (La. App. 1989).

132. *Id.* at 95. The approach suggested here is heavily consent-based: if the parties within a religious community agree to certain arrangements by contract, a court is bound to respect and enforce those arrangements even in the face of a contrary general rule. This does not mean, however, that every such agreement should be enforceable. Contract-law doctrines, or similar trust-law doctrines, concerning the requisites for enforcing an agreement or instrument may still apply—doctrines such as the requirement of consideration, or the vitiating of an agreement by fraud or mistake. Application of such "neutral principles" does not in itself generally invade religious autonomy, since the purpose is generally to ensure that the parties truly agreed or intended their agreements to be binding. Thus, the constitutionally required "opt out" I have been defending would not, for example, necessarily make enforceable a member's donation pledge that is otherwise unenforceable under contract law (because of a lack of consideration or a lack of the reliance required by promissory estoppel).

On the other hand, a member of a religious community could not argue that the terms of her arrangement with the community should be overridden because the terms were substantively unfair (what, in contract terms would be called "substantively unconscionable").

Moreover, some such contract doctrines would require the court to inquire into and make judgments about religious matters. If a member's donation pledge was otherwise enforceable, for ex-

The proposition that courts may not impose policy-based rules on religious institutions' internal decisions without a compelling reason might seem inconsistent with the holding in *Employment Division v. Smith* that generally applicable laws may be applied to religious practices without violating the Free Exercise Clause. But as has already been noted, *Smith* explicitly reaffirmed previous rulings that courts should not interfere in internal "controversies over religious authority or dogma."[133] One of those rulings, the *Milivojevich* decision, had held that courts could not interfere in an internal matter (the defrocking of a bishop) even in the face of a claim that the decision violated generally applicable legal standards because it was arbitrary and beyond the church tribunal's jurisdiction.[134] Thus the best reading of *Smith* is that it does not increase the government's authority to interfere in the internal governance of a religious institution by imposing a policy-based rule, even if that rule is generally applicable to nonreligious entities and activities—at least not in the absence of a truly compelling reason for such interference.

If a distinct kind of analysis is required in cases of "internal" religious disputes, then the line between these and "external" disputes must be defined. Even a conservative reading of the former term would define disputes over the employment terms of ministers and clergy as "internal" and would require deference to a church's own rules for resolving the disputes. (Of course, a church's control over a minister is limited to the terms of her employment and her relation to the church; a church could not hire someone to physically assault a minister and then claim it was a purely internal matter.) The extent to which courts must defer concerning other employees is a key issue. Some employees, such as parochial school teachers, are also close enough to the core of an organization's religious identity that the state must defer to the church's employment rules concerning them.

Indeed, one might argue that any employment practice of a religious institution is an internal matter because employees have voluntarily chosen to work at the institution and because their loyalty is crucial to the institution's mission.[135] Similarly, one might argue that students who choose to attend a religious college have consented to its rules and the matter is therefore solely internal. Courts, however, have never been willing to go that far. While they are quite willing to stay out of disputes over ministerial authority and other core positions in a church, they are much more likely to allow regulation of employment relationships in positions that seem to be further from the religious and ideological core of the organization. In other words, the courts have not given sufficient scope to the autonomy of religious institutions. Nevertheless, the arguments I have just made do provide a basis for limiting the "neutral principles of law" approach of *Jones v.*

---

ample, she could not avoid the obligation by claiming that the church had defrauded her about the spiritual benefits she would thereby receive, or that she had been mistaken about the hope of such benefits. Such claims would require courts to determine the truth or the reasonableness of religious beliefs—a fundamental intrusion of the government into religious matters. *See* United States v. Ballard, 322 U.S. 78 (1944). However, as the prosecution of televangelist Jim Bakker shows, some claims of fraud or mistake can be examined and decided. If a church fraudulently induced a donation by promising to use the money for one purpose and then diverted it to another, the court need not make religious judgments, and the contract should be vitiated.

   133. 494 U.S. at 877.

   134. *Milivojevich*, 426 U.S. at 713.

   135. As Laycock has argued,

     The free exercise of religion includes the right to run large religious institutions...[, which] can only be run through employees. It follows that...the churches are entitled to insist on undivided loyalty from these employees.... When an employee agrees to do the work of the church, he must be held to submit to church authority in much the same way as a member.

Laycock, *supra* note 16, at 1408–09.

Wolf and *Employment Division v. Smith* so as to preserve substantial control by an organization over its internal structure and governance.

Even so, however, difficulties with the neutral principles approach remain. First, even *Jones* recognized that however "neutral" is the governing legal principle, it is inappropriate for the judge applying it to decide questions that turn on theological tenets; when interpretation of such tenets arises, the court must defer to the church authority's interpretive ruling.[136] Employment disputes with ministers often raise such theological issues, since the qualifications and performance of the minister are typically at issue; courts commonly dismiss lawsuits on this ground.[137] Even a contract claim is impermissible when the terms incorporate subjective or theological concepts. Therefore the claim in *Minker*, discussed above, should probably have been dismissed: what secular standards would a court use to decide whether a "suitable" congregation existed for the plaintiff to serve as spiritual overseer?

As is shown by *Babcock v. New Orleans Seminary* and other decisions cited above, a contract claim will more likely be permitted when the terms involve no religious content—as is often the case, for example, with the procedures for discipline or termination.[138] But even contract claims based on clear secular language should be viewed with caution. Suits by ministers still involve free speech issues because they concern who will speak for the church. It is unacceptable, therefore, to grant the relief of reinstatement;[139] and even a damage or back-pay award will deter the church from acting and thus impinge on its right to select who will speak for it in religious matters.

Even in property cases, moreover, the use of neutral principles may not give the church sufficient room to organize itself according to its own polity. *Jones* recognized that the neutral principles approach would force churches to express their structure explicitly in secular legal terms, but the Court was confident that "[t]he burden involved in taking such steps will be minimal."[140] That seems entirely too sanguine. Sometimes theological concepts concerning polity and governance cannot be translated wholly into secular terms.

Moreover, even if such translation is possible, the increased legalization of structural arrangements can distract churches from their religious mission, as Justice Powell pointed out in his dissent in *Jones v. Wolf*.[141] The burden falls disproportionately on small denominations or independent congregations, which lack access to specialized legal counsel. Given their relative lack of legal sophistication and their focus on religious rather than legal priorities, churches as a class can be expected to leave many issues unresolved. Judges may have to do a great deal of gap filling, often with very little raw information from church documents and with even less understanding for the

---

136. *See supra* notes 63–66 and accompanying text; *Jones*, 443 U.S. at 604; *Milivojevich*, 426 U.S. at 713; *Watson*, 80 U.S. at 729.

137. *See* cases cited in note 67, *supra*.

138. *See Babcock*, 464 A.2d 1008; *Alicea*, 581 A.2d 900 (both noting that procedures in handbooks were defined in wholly secular terms).

139. The *Babcock* decision ultimately imposed the shocking remedy of forcing the seminary to grant the ministerial student a degree, and thus essentially certify him as fit for the ministry, in spite of what the school regarded as his serious personal misconduct. Such a remedy was only justified, if at all, because of singular circumstances: the school had earlier settled his suit by agreeing to allow him to stay in school and then, months later, claimed that that did not mean it had to graduate him or give him a degree.

140. *Jones*, 443 U.S. at 606.

141. *Id.* at 614 (Powell, J., dissenting) (neutral principles approach "imposes on the organization of churches additional legal requirements which in some cases might inhibit their formation by forcing the organizers to confront issues that otherwise might never arise").

terms used in those documents.[142] With little to go on, courts might be forced back into broad generalizations such as hierarchical or congregational structure—the very stereotypes that the neutral-principles approach sought to avoid.

These difficulties are magnified when, as is often the case, courts applying neutral principles concentrate on reading the familiar secular documents, such as deeds, leases, or conveyances, rather than the church's constitution and other ecclesiastical documents. For example, in the Russian Orthodox dispute mentioned above, the general church canons explicitly provided "that the Bishop have authority over the property of the church"; but the Massachusetts courts overrode this on the basis of property deeds as well as evidence that other parishes had left the denomination and "t[aken] with them their own property without claim by the church."[143] Other courts have focused on the deeds and dismissed trusts or other property provisions in general church constitutions as "of moral value only and without legal effect."[144] If a general church body cannot rely on overarching provisions in its constitutions and canons, then it must adjust the language of the particular instruments for each individual piece of property—an impossibly burdensome task. Thus even if the neutral principles approach is acceptable in theory, its actual application has often been grossly insensitive to the rights of religious bodies to organize themselves as they see fit.

In short, although the use of neutral principles of law has some advantages over the polity approach in disputes over church property, it also poses significant risks. Perhaps, then, *Jones v. Wolf* was right when it treated both approaches as constitutionally permissible in property disputes and neither as required.[145] Unfortunately, leaving the choice to the states has meant, inevitably, that different states have chosen different rules.[146] Like any other patchwork of state regulation, this presents particular difficulties for interstate entities—in this instance national religious denominations.

The Effect of Church Structure
on Constitutional Rules

Finally, it is important in this chapter to ask generally to what extent a church's structure does, or should, affect its treatment under the First Amendment. The previous sec-

---

142. Ellman, *supra* note 108, at 1420 & n.127 (recognizing that "[i]nternal church agreements may be ambiguous more often than commercial contracts," and that judges familiar with commercial practices "may be entirely off the mark in ascertaining the intentions of the parties to a church dispute").

143. *Primate and Bishops' Synod*, 617 N.E.2d at 1033–35 (quoting but not following Apostolic Canon concerning church property).

144. Bjorkman v. Protestant Episcopal Church, 759 S.W.2d 583, 586 (Ky. 1988); *accord* Presbytery of Beaver-Butler v. Middlesex Presbyterian Church, 489 A.2d 1317, 1325 (Pa. 1985) (looking solely at deeds and dismissing general church documents as merely "overseeing the spiritual development of member churches").

145. *Jones*, 443 U.S. at 602.

146. As Gerstenblith has shown, at least seven states continue to give automatic deference to the authoritative church body; a larger group of decisions apply the same neutral principles as would apply to a secular organization; and a large number of courts apply neutral principles but temper them with presumptions unique to religious organizations, such as a presumption that ambiguous documents are to be construed to create a trust in favor of a national church. Gerstenblith, *supra* note 112, at 529–550.

tion addressed that question with respect to disputes "internal" to the religious community. With respect to internal disputes, I argued, the courts must seek to decide according to the rules that the religious organization has adopted for itself. There, the First Amendment requires that the church's chosen polity be controlling. And as I argued, even the neutral principles approach approved in *Jones v. Wolf* was approved only on the premise that it would allow the church to translate its chosen polity into legal terms through use of the facilitative and gap-filling rules of property, contract, and trust law.

As has already been mentioned, however, many governmental actions toward religious organizations do not seek to resolve disputes that are purely internal to the organization. Rather, they seek to impose some government policy on the organization concerning those of its operations that arguably have some effect on the broader society. These range from zoning rules concerning uses of church's property to state regulations concerning teacher and curriculum qualifications in parochial schools, as well as to (arguably) employment laws as they apply to employees who are not at the core of an entity's religious identity. In these cases, the courts have not applied the framework of the internal-dispute cases; their aim in applying the First Amendment has not been simply to enforce the structure of decision making that the organization has adopted.[147] In these cases, how (if at all) does the entity's structure influence its constitutional treatment?

Answering that question requires going back to the overarching approaches to the First Amendment discussed earlier. If the governing norm for Religion Clause analysis is equal treatment between religious and other entities—as is increasingly the case under both the Free Exercise and Establishment clauses—then a particular religious entity's structure should not matter in the analysis. Under the Free Exercise Clause as interpreted in *Employment Division v. Smith*, for example, religious entities can (for the most part) be regulated as much as secular ones: all a court does to apply the constitutional rule is to ask whether every entity is being regulated in the same degree and manner, and there is no need (or warrant) to treat any particular religious entity differently because of its structure (or indeed for any other reason). The same is true with respect to government aid under the Establishment Clause. If, as recent decisions indicate, the government can constitutionally provide funds to families to use at any school, then a school's structure or organizational practices will not affect its ability to receive aid as far as the First Amendment is concerned.[148]

Suppose, however, the rule is to some degree one of church/state separation rather than equal treatment: that is, that government must sometimes treat religious entities differently from secular ones, either exempting them from general regulation or denying them aid provided to other organizations, in order to preserve separation between church and state. If that is the rule, the nature of the religious entity may matter in the analysis whether the First Amendment forbids government to regulate it or assist it. Even when the Court was at its most separationist, it never prohibited all regulation of religious entities or all assistance to them. It has always recognized that "[s]ome rela-

---

147. In fact, I would see many of these matters as primarily internal, so that courts should give the religious entity autonomy—especially in matters concerning employment in the entity's ministries. But courts in fact have tended to use the internal-dispute analysis only in cases involving ministers or their functional equivalent.

148. If the government program itself purposefully or explicitly distinguishes between religions—for example, if it exempts only one sect or groups of sects while leaving others covered—the Constitution will require the government to produce a strong reason for the differential treatment. *See supra* notes 20–24 and accompanying text; for discussion of the implications of this point, see section on distinctions between organizations based on formal structure, *infra*.

tionship between government and religious organizations is inevitable."[149] On both regulation and aid, the Court has tried to draw lines to accommodate conflicting interests and separate permissible from impermissible involvement. As I will try to show, sometimes such lines have been drawn according to the nature of the religious organization being assisted or regulated. A religious entity's structure and organization is an important part of its overall nature. Thus, the entity's structure may matter to its constitutional status. In this section I will try to explain how.

Regulation, funding, and the broad nature of the institution under the separation approach

The separation model is still relevant to First Amendment analysis in certain places, even though the Court has moved noticeably toward the equality model in *Employment Division v. Smith* and the recent financial-aid decisions. Under the separation model, the nature of the religious institution in question is relevant to whether it should be treated distinctively as a matter of the Religion Clauses: that is, whether the institution may be regulated by a generally applicable law and whether it may receive financial assistance from the government.

On the question of government aid, the equality model has not yet entirely displaced the separation model. To be sure, the Court has followed the equality model in approving forms of aid given to individual beneficiaries who then may use it at religious institutions. Moreover, two recent aid decisions, *Rosenberger v. Rectors of University of Virginia*[150] and *Agostini v. Felton*,[151] both followed the equality approach in holding, respectively, that a state university could pay the bills for a student religious magazine on the same terms as for other student publications, and that the government could provide public school teachers to conduct remedial education classes in parochial schools on the same terms as in public schools. However, *Rosenberger* went on to say, citing the line of separationist decisions epitomized by *Lemon v. Kurtzman*, that there were "special Establishment Clause dangers where the government makes direct money payments to sectarian institutions."[152] And *Agostini* emphasized that the form of aid approved there—the provision of public school teachers to teach secular classes—was extremely unlikely to result in religious indoctrination, no matter how pervasively religious was the private school to which the teachers were sent. These qualifying passages in the two opinions suggest that at least for now, principles of separation may continue to govern the analysis of many forms of direct aid to religious institutions.

The separationist analysis of direct aid to religiously affiliated entities long ago settled into a familiar pattern.[153] The Court did not prohibit all such aid. For example, the possibility that aid to secular aspects of a church school might indirectly free up money for building a sanctuary does not bar the aid. But the Court has required the state "to

---

149. *Lemon*, 403 U.S. at 614 (adding that "total separation is not possible in an absolute sense").

150. 515 U.S. 819 (1995).

151. 521 U.S. 203 (1997).

152. *Rosenberger*, 515 U.S. at 841 (distinguishing those decisions on the ground that the university had paid no money to the student religious magazine).

153. The analysis might change in the near future toward equality or neutrality analysis even in direct-aid cases. But see *Mitchell v. Helms*, 530 U.S. 793, 842–44 (O'Connor, J., concurring in the judgment).

guarantee the separation between secular and religious educational functions [in the school] and to ensure that State financial aid supports only the former."[154] In short, one must not be able to trace directly the flow of funds to activities with religious teaching mixed in them. As the Court applied this tracing analysis, however, the most important question became whether the schools receiving aid are "pervasively sectarian": that is, whether they are set up such that "education is an integral part of the dominant sectarian mission and…an atmosphere dedicated to the advancement of religious belief is constantly maintained."[155] If so, then the Court assumes that most aid will end up supporting activities with religious teaching intermixed. The state might avoid that impermissible effect by monitoring the aid, but that lands it in the catch-22 set forth in *Lemon*: given the pervasiveness of religion throughout a school, the monitoring necessary to prevent religious uses will have to be so "comprehensive, discriminating, and continuing" that it will violate the nonentanglement prong.[156] This analysis has sunk the large majority of forms of direct aid to religious elementary and secondary schools or their employees.

However, the Court simultaneously held that a number of religiously affiliated colleges and universities could receive direct aid that would be barred to lower-level schools.[157] The key, of course, was that the colleges were not "pervasively sectarian." Thus, there was "little risk that religion would seep into the teaching of secular subjects, and the state surveillance necessary to separate the two, therefore, was diminished."[158] The majority opinions in these cases stated that "the character of the aided institutions" was the "most impressive" factor distinguishing the forbidden aid to lower-level schools from the permissible aid to colleges.[159]

The character of the institutions was also important to the reasoning in *Bowen v. Kendrick*,[160] where the Court upheld a facial validity of a grant program that included religious social service agencies, on the ground that "of the eligible religious institutions, many will not deserve the label 'pervasively sectarian.'"[161] Although the statute survived the facial challenge, the Court strongly suggested that funds would be barred, on an as-applied basis, to those agencies that were pervasively sectarian—again because the secular and religious activities of the agency could not be separated without continuous and intrusive government intervention.[162]

To the extent that separationism still applies under federal or state constitutions, the character of the institution receiving aid can be important. But how specifically, under this analysis, does the institution's structure play a role? Recall the dual definitions described above: an organization's structure encompasses not just the narrow concept of formal legal status, but also the broader concept of how the institution organizes its af-

---

154. *Lemon*, 403 U.S. at 613. *See also* Roemer v. Bd. of Public Works, 426 U.S. 736, 765 (1976) (requiring that the program "identify…separate secular functions" to receive aid).

155. Grand Rapids Sch. Dist. v. Ball, 473 U.S. 373, 388 (1985) (quoting Meek v. Pittenger, 421 U.S. 349, 371 (1975)).

156. *Lemon*, 403 U.S. at 619; *Meek*, 421 U.S. at 370; *Aguilar*, 473 U.S. at 414.

157. Tilton v. Richardson, 403 U.S. 672 (1971) (building construction grants); Hunt v. McNair, 413 U.S. 734 (1973) (building construction loans); *Roemer*, 426 U.S. 736 (1976) (broader cash grants).

158. *Roemer*, 426 U.S. at 762; *Hunt*, 413 U.S. at 743; *Tilton*, 403 U.S. at 686–687.

159. *Roemer*, 426 U.S. at 766, 764 (giving this the "dominant emphasis").

160. 487 U.S. 589 (1988).

161. *Id.* at 610.

162. *Id.* at 621.

fairs.[163] The organizational features broadly defined as "structural" decisions are very similar to the features that the Court has examined to gauge how pervasively sectarian a school is. The "profile" of a pervasively religious school in aid cases typically includes religious preferences in employment and admissions, required religious exercises (chapel or morning prayers), required classes in doctrine, religiously based codes of conduct, and a religious viewpoint throughout the curriculum, as well as some relation with a sponsoring church or churches.[164] By contrast, the colleges in *Roemer v. Board of Public Works*[165] had "a high degree of institutional autonomy" from their churches, treated chapel services as optional, used few or no religious considerations in admissions and faculty hiring, and afforded academic freedom to faculty at least in nonreligion courses.[166]

The nature of the religious institution may still be relevant not only to the permissibility of government assistance, but also to the limits on government regulation. If the Religious Freedom Restoration Act remains valid in cases involving federal law (and even more if new legislation passes to shield religion from state laws),[167] then to that extent free exercise analysis will return to at least the mild separationism of pre-*Smith* law, under which religious practices are shielded from substantial burdens imposed by generally applicable laws unless the state has a compelling interest in regulation. The same is true for those cases involving "hybrid" rights of free exercise combined with free speech, freedom of association, or parental control over education.

In determining how substantial a burden on a religious institution is, courts under the pre-*Smith* regime were influenced by the religious nature of the institution—in particular, how religious the institution appeared in the court's eyes. For example, parochial schools, as "pervasively sectarian" institutions, were exempted from unionization of teachers in *NLRB v. Catholic Bishop* for the same reasons that they could not receive many forms of government aid.[168] Lower court decisions held that pervasively religious schools and other institutions were constitutionally exempt from some other forms of regulation.[169] These rulings indicated—some explicitly, some implicitly—that an institution was more likely to be "substantially" burdened by regulation if religious

---

163. *See* Definitions of "Structural" Decisions by Religious Organizations, *supra.*

164. The profile in PEARL v. Nyquist, 413 U.S. 756, 767 (1973), described schools that (a) impose religious restrictions on admission; (b) require attendance of pupils at religious activities; (c) require obedience by students to the doctrines and dogmas of a particular faith; (d) require pupils to attend instruction in the theology or doctrine of a particular faith; (e) are an integral part of the religious mission of the church sponsoring it; (f) have as a substantial purpose the inculcation of religious values; (g) impose religious restrictions on faculty appointments; and (h) impose religious restrictions on what or how the faculty may teach.
For similar descriptions, see *Ball*, 473 U.S. at 379 (quoting school handbook); *Meek*, 421 U.S. at 356; *Lemon*, 403 U.S. at 615–616.

165. 426 U.S. 736.

166. *Id.* at 755–756; for similar descriptions of colleges in other decisions upholding aid, see *Hunt*, 413 U.S. at 746; *Tilton*, 403 U.S. at 681–682, 685–687.

167. *See supra* notes 85–87 and accompanying text.

168. *Catholic Bishop*, 440 U.S. at 501 (recognizing that, as with schools barred from receiving aid, " '[r]eligious authority necessarily pervades the school system' ") (quoting *Lemon*, 403 U.S. at 617).

169. *See, e.g.*, Little v. Wuerl, 929 F.2d 944, 946 (3d Cir. 1991) (freeing school from employment discrimination claim by teacher; noting that school "took very seriously its mission to be a Catholic presence in a secular world"); Dayton Christian Schools v. Ohio Civil Rights Comm., 766 F.2d 932 (6th Cir. 1985), *vacated on abstention grounds*, 477 U.S. 619 (1986) (employment discrimination claim by teacher); Miller v. Catholic Diocese, 728 P.2d 794 (Mont. 1986) (same); Feldstein v. Chris-

elements pervaded all of its operational decisions. Conversely, the more commercial the activities of a religiously affiliated organization, the less likely it was to be constitutionally protected from regulation, as the Court indicated concerning minimum wage laws in *Alamo Foundation v. Sec'y of Labor*.[170]

Similar questions may arise under the Court's analysis of legislative accommodations of religious practice. The permissibility of such exemptions under the Establishment Clause also appears to depend on a weighing process in which the strength of an institution's religious interest (and hence the nature of the institution) is important. As noted earlier, a plurality of the Court in the *Texas Monthly* decision indicated that the permissibility of a legislative accommodation should turn on comparing the burden that the accommodation removes from religious practice—a factor to which the nature of the practice or institution will be relevant—against the burden that the accommodation imposes on others.[171]

In short, to the extent that separation continues to be a part of Religion Clause decision making, the nature of the religious institution, including its structure in the broad sense, will be relevant. Under the separationist approach, the more an entity appears pervasively religious from its structural decisions, broadly defined, the more a court is likely to keep it strictly separate from the state: no regulation, no aid. On questions of both aid and regulation, the nature of the institution is not the only factor,[172] but it is highly important.[173]

---

tian Science Monitor, 555 F. Supp. 974 (D. Mass. 1983) (employment discrimination claim by reporter at religious newspaper).

170. *Alamo Foundation*, 471 U.S. at 305 (noting that minimum-wage laws apply only to "commercial activities undertaken with a 'business purpose'" and would not cover organization's "evangelical activities").

171. *Texas Monthly*, 489 U.S. at 15, 18 & n.8 (plurality opinion of Brennan, J.); *see supra* notes 97–100 and accompanying text.

172. For example, even highly religious schools might face regulation in other jobs besides the central and sensitive one of teacher. *Hanna Boys Center*, 940 F.2d 1295 (child-care workers at religious residential school could unionize); EEOC v. Southwestern Baptist Theol. Sem., 651 F.2d 277 (5th Cir. 1981) (seminary forbidden to discriminate on basis of gender in non-faculty jobs). And under the separationist analysis, religious elementary schools can receive some limited forms of aid (*see, e.g., Agostini*, 521 U.S. 203; Wolman v. Walter, 433 U.S. 229 (1977)), while even significantly secularized religious colleges cannot use aid for religious purposes such as constructing or maintaining chapels (*Tilton*, 403 U.S. at 682–83).

173. The notion of separation between church and state, of course, can be criticized as an overall model for Religion Clause jurisprudence. Some of the difficulties with the model will be discussed below. But more broadly, separation might be challenged by other overarching visions of the First Amendment. One, already noted and now influential on the Supreme Court, is the principle of equality of treatment among religions and between religious and nonreligious activity. Another vision, consistent with some but not all recent Court decisions, emphasizes religious liberty and government accommodation of religious practice: this approach leads to a strong theory of exemption from regulation and to approval of the participation of religious entities in neutral programs of government aid. According to this approach, equality theory fails to acknowledge religion's constitutional distinctiveness and, in particular, the importance of religious institutions' autonomy. On the other hand, the accommodation approach asserts, the separation model treats religion distinctively but only a cost of isolating serious religious activity from participating in public life. Indeed, as a prime example of this improper isolation, accommodationists cite the line of decisions preventing seriously (that, is "pervasively") religious schools from receiving government assistance even for the secular services they provide. For fuller discussion of these three visions, see Thomas C. Berg, The State and Religion in a Nutshell 13–25 (West, 1998); Berg, *supra* note 9, at 441–55. Separationists respond that if religious activity is to be given special protection from regulation, it is only fair that it be specially barred from receiving direct government support.

Whatever criticisms can be made of the separationist model, it is still worth tracing how the distinctive treatment it gives to religious institutions depends on the institution's structural features, in both the narrow (formal) and broad sense.

Formal, de jure structure has typically played only a limited role in determining how religious an institution is. Direct legal control by a church, order, diocese, or denomination makes the entity look more religious; but it is only one factor among many.[174] The Catholic colleges in *Roemer* and the Baptist college in *Hunt v. McNair* were officially controlled by a convention of churches or by an order—for example, their trustee boards were substantially controlled by such bodies—but in practice each enjoyed substantial autonomy of operations.[175] The Court therefore permitted direct financial assistance to them even under the separationist approach.

It is obvious why courts have wanted to look at many factors to decide how pervasively religious an entity is, and why they have been reluctant to categorize the entity based only on one feature such as formal relationship to a church. To distinguish between religious entities based on formal structure is distinction among sects, which must be closely fitted to accomplish an important goal.[176] Under the separationist analysis, the goal is to determine which entities have the strongest religious interest in freedom from regulation—or conversely, which ones are more likely to use funding to teach religion. Given this goal, it seems arbitrary for courts to look at just one factor (particularly a legal fiction) and not to examine the totality of an institution's characteristics. A deeply religious social service agency, for example, may have no ties to a church, while an agency that is formally church-related might be highly commercial and have few distinctively religious elements. The more factors a court considers in each case, the more it can fine-tune its results.

Yet such fine tuning also brings problems with it. First, like any multifactor standard, it gives judges little guidance and considerable discretion.[177] Moreover, it gives them discretion to decide a question that is highly sensitive and subjective: how religious is the entity before them?

In this case, particularly, the operation of subjective discretion may produce a tendency to devalue the religious interest, especially if the entity does not behave in ways that judges think of as distinctively "religious." Angela C. Carmella points out that courts often fail to give protection to religiously motivated conduct that "appropriate[s] from the [broader] culture those methods and techniques that [the adherents] consider consistent with their faith and most effective in their ... ministries."[178] She suggests that judges often do not think an activity is religious unless it is somehow "countercultural," different from the mainstream, strange to the outside observer. In her prime example, an ecumenical counseling center run by a mainline Protestant seminary was denied a religious-use zoning permit because the court said its activities were predominantly secular rather than religious; the court pointed out that the center served people of all faiths, did not attempt to convert its counselees, and used tech-

---

174. *Aguilar*, 473 U.S. at 412; *Meek*, 421 U.S. at 356; *Lemon*, 403 U.S. at 617 (all noting this factor). *See also Kendrick*, 487 U.S. at 620 n.16 (whether institution has "explicit corporate ties to a particular religious faith" is "relevant to the determination of whether [it] is 'pervasively sectarian'" but is "not conclusive").

175. *Roemer*, 426 U.S. at 755; *Hunt*, 413 U.S. at 746; *see also Tilton*, 403 U.S. at 681 (although "institutional documents" at Catholic colleges "stated certain religious restrictions on what could be taught, other evidence showed that these restrictions were not in fact enforced").

176. *See* notes 20–24, *supra* (discussing Larson v. Valente, 456 U.S. 228 (1982)).

177. *See, e.g.*, Antonin Scalia, The Rule of Law as a Law of Rules, 56 U. Chi. L. Rev. 1175 (1989) (arguing against open-ended standards on this ground).

178. Angela C. Carmella, A Theological Critique of Free Exercise Jurisprudence, 60 Geo. Wash. L. Rev. 782, 790 (1992).

niques prevalent in modern secular psychology.[179] As Carmella points out, the court overlooked the clear religious motivation behind the activity because the activity did not appear religiously distinctive.

There are other examples. Maryland's highest court held that a Lutheran high school was not "operated primarily for religious purposes," and so was not exempt from federal requirements for paying unemployment taxes, even though the school mandated chapel services and religion courses and sought to integrate Christian teaching into other courses.[180] The court held that the school failed to show that religion courses "'were devoted to deepening religious experiences in the particular faith rather than teaching a range of human religious experiences as an academic discipline'";[181] and had failed to show that in other classes, "intellectual or academic freedom was overwhelmed by religious pressure."[182] In other words, for an institution to be religious, the judges said, it must be set up so that religious pressure overwhelms the intellect. Again, the sense is that if an entity undertakes any sort of harmonious contact with secular culture, it forfeits its claim to be called religious. Indeed, by making such a move toward acculturation in just a few areas, the entity loses its right to assert its distinctiveness in other areas.

Facing such uncomprehending attitudes on the courts toward religious self-definition, a religious institution might well be tentative about a great many organizational steps. I sat for a number of years on the Religious Affairs Committee of my former employer, Samford University, and one year we were discussing a reworking of the mandatory chapel services for undergraduates. Some sentiment was expressed that mandating chapel attendances was inconsistent with the Baptist commitment to purely voluntary faith.[183] We did not vote to make chapel voluntary; but if we had, would a court using the "profile" of a pervasively religious school have viewed our move as evidence that the university was becoming predominantly secular in its orientation—and thus ineligible for various exemptions from regulation?

Finally, the multifactor approach requires a detailed inquiry into the nature of an institution to decide whether it is religious or not. The very inquiry itself might be seen as objectionable. As the Court has stated in another context, "[t]he prospect of church and state litigating in court about what does or does not have religious meaning touches the core of the constitutional guarantee against religious establishment."[184]

The Court in *Employment Division v. Smith* was bothered by this dynamic concerning the analysis of when exemptions from regulation are proper. The Court objected to the very process of case-by-case balancing under which it compared the burden on the religious interest against the strength of the state interest; the process involved the courts in, among other things, "[j]udging the centrality of different religious practices" and "'evaluating the relative merits of differing religious claims.'"[185] The holding in

---

179. Needham Pastoral Counseling Ctr. v. Board of Appeals, 557 N.E.2d 43, 46–47 (Mass. App. 1990), discussed in Carmella, *supra* note 178, at 788–90.

180. Baltimore Lutheran High School Ass'n. v. Employment Security Admin., 490 A.2d 701 (Md. 1985).

181. *Id.* at 705 (quotation omitted).

182. *Id.* at 707.

183. *See* Dictionary of Baptists in America 279–80 (Bill J. Leonard ed. 1995) (discussing Baptist commitment to voluntarism).

184. New York v. Cathedral Academy, 434 U.S. 125, 133 (1978).

185. *Smith,* 494 U.S. at 887 (quoting *United States v. Lee,* 455 U.S. 252, 263 n.2 (1982) (Stevens, J., concurring)). See also *Mitchell,* 530 U.S. at 826–29 (Thomas, J.) (criticizing "pervasively sectarian" analysis on this and other grounds).

Smith escaped the process, of course, by simply refusing to grant exemptions from generally applicable laws. The Court's discomfort with evaluating different religious claims drove it toward treating all claims, religious or nonreligious, equally.

The same discomfort with evaluating different religious claims has, in all likelihood, contributed to the move toward an "equal treatment" approach in other areas as well. The recent line of financial aid decisions, which approves aid channeled through individuals no matter how sectarian is the entity that ultimately receives the aid, allows the courts to avoid inquiring into the nature of the recipient institution.[186] Moreover, even where the Court has inquired into the "sectarian" nature of schools, it often has done so mechanistically rather than searchingly: with little further analysis, elementary and secondary schools were often presumed to be pervasively sectarian, and colleges and universities have been presumed not to be, "sometimes despite quite persuasive evidence" to the contrary.[187] The break between higher and lower education avoids the process of fine tuning case by case.[188]

The impulse to avoid searching, case-by-case examination of religious institutions is powerful. But the Court's actual responses have often been misguided. *Smith* avoids distinguishing between religious claims only at the cost of permitting a very great reduction in the scope of constitutionally protected religious liberty. Denying all direct government aid to pervasively religious organizations puts up a barrier to the participation of serious religion in public life; it also arguably infringes on the liberty and equality rights of citizens who choose religious schools or agencies to receive education or other services.

Can distinctions between organizations be based on formal structure?

Problems remain, then, with the broad, multifactor analysis of the nature of an institution as a way of deciding whether it may constitutionally be regulated or receive government aid. Can a way be found to avoid such problems without altogether eliminating distinctive protection for religious institutions? If the broad definition of structural decisions is not a perfect tool for differentiating between religious claims, might it turn out that the narrower concept of formal structure could actually play some role?

Formal structure has one advantage as a differentiating tool: it is likely to provide clearer lines for deciding which entities may be regulated or funded than is the multifactor inquiry that focuses on a much wider range of organizational decisions. The very nature of formal legal vehicles is to provide clear lines that do not require detailed examination in order to be applied in particular cases.

Nevertheless, it still does not seem likely that formal structure will be much more than one factor in deciding whether an institution should be treated specially under

---

186. *See* notes 72–73, *supra*, and accompanying text.

187. Michael W. McConnell, Political and Religious Disestablishment, 1986 B.Y.U. L. Rev. 405, 422.

188. It remains to be seen what will develop in the area of direct aid to social service entities, where such bright lines between different kinds of programs are not immediately apparent. *See* Timothy S. Burgett, Note, Government Aid to Religious Social Services Providers: The Supreme Court's "Pervasively Sectarian" Standard, 75 Va. L. Rev. 1077, 1093–1096 (1989).

the religion provisions. Distinctions based on formal legal structure are too likely to produce arbitrary results that fail to capture the degree to which a particular religious institution is really religious in nature. A focus on an organization's formal structure seems legitimate when the purpose is to permit the organization to enforce that structure in its internal governance: that is the point of the argument in the third part of this chapter. But when the goal is to decide the external rights and duties of religious organizations—to what extent they should be treated specially in regulation of their relations with the broader society—then any differential treatment based on the organization's formal legal structure is likely to produce unjustified discrimination between religious groups.

The federal unemployment tax exemption: A troublesome preference based on formal structure

The clearest case of differential treatment among religious organizations based on de jure or formal legal structure is found in the Federal Unemployment Tax Act (FUTA),[189] a portion of the social security laws. FUTA generally requires employers to pay taxes, calculated according to the salaries and wages they pay to employees, so as to help fund the provision of benefits to employees who become unemployed. However, FUTA exempts an organization from paying taxes as to service performed:

> in the employ of (A) a church or convention or association of churches; or (B) an organization which is operated primarily for religious purposes and which is operated, supervised, controlled, or principally supported by a church or convention or association of churches.[190]

The exemption distinguishes between a school, social service, or other entity that is integrated into a church's legal structure and one that is separately incorporated. The former is exempt from FUTA under clause (A) without further inquiry, as the Supreme Court held in *St. Martin's Evangelical Lutheran Church v. South Dakota*.[191] But an entity that is "separately incorporated" must meet the additional requirements of clause (B) in order to be exempt.[192] Thus, an entity that is highly religious but is largely independent from the control or support of any church or group of churches must pay taxes, under the plain language of the exemption.

These distinctions, based on legal or other affiliation with a "church," discriminate on their face among religious organizations and thus are quite likely unconstitutional, since no compelling reason for the differential treatment is apparent.[193] Different agencies can be equally devoted to religion in their teaching and operations, even though one is "operated by church officials, another by persons separately appointed by a church congregation to conduct [the agency], and the third by persons independent of

---

189. 26 U.S.C. § 3301-3311.

190. 26 U.S.C. § 3309(b).

191. 451 U.S. 772, 782–83 & n.12 (1981) (stating that "schools that have no legal identity separate from a church" are "uniformly...excluded from coverage by § 3309(b)(1)(A)").

192. *Id.* at 782–83 & n.12.

193. *See supra* notes 20–24 and accompanying text (discussing, e.g., *Larson*, 456 U.S. 228). *See* Esbeck, *supra* note 54, at 404 ("Statutory exemptions based on the distinction of whether a religious organization is church-affiliated or an independent, nondenominational ministry discriminate in a manner contrary to the Establishment Clause").

any organization describing itself as a church."[194] The FUTA exemption is thus an unconstitutional preference for some religious polities over others.[195]

The FUTA exemption creates two unacceptable distinctions. First, while an organization that is integrated into a church's legal structure is automatically exempt from the tax, an organization with a less formal relationship of control or support by a church must prove that it is "operated primarily for religious purposes." This added burden is not terribly great if courts are sensitive to an organization's religious self-understanding; but many courts are not. As has just been discussed, courts often think that if the entity they are examining does the same sort of things as a secular entity, then it is not really religious.[196] Thus courts have held that a Lutheran high school failed the religious-purposes test because it allowed its teachers academic freedom,[197] and that a nursing home run by an evangelistic association was a secular activity because it accepted persons of all faiths.[198]

The refusal to recognize an organization's religious character is a common problem. But the FUTA exemption raises a more serious discrimination: it flatly excludes scores of independent and parachurch organizations that have no relationship with any single congregation or group of churches. Indeed, parachurch organizations are among the fastest growing categories of religious activity in the nation.[199] An example is Young Life, a freestanding evangelical Christian agency that seeks to convert and minister to high school and college students. It is subject to paying unemployment taxes,[200] while a youth evangelism ministry set up by a Baptist congregation or a city association of evangelical churches would be exempt.[201]

The Colorado Supreme Court held that this differential treatment between church and parachurch organizations was sufficiently justified to satisfy the strict scrutiny applied to denominational preferences by the Establishment Clause; but the court's reasons were obscure. It noted that many of Young Life's employees carried out "administrative" functions comparable to those in secular organizations, such as accounting, data processing, and fundraising,[202] but the same could be said of employees in entities formally or informally tied to a church. The court also found it a "valid basis" for distinction that "Young Life would be less likely than church organizations to provide on a voluntary basis a continuing means of support for Young Life workers who leave the organization and remain unemployed."[203] But it seems doubtful that an organization is more likely to give support to its former workers merely because it has some relation to a congregation or group of congregations; and the court gave no evidence to support its generalization.

194. Salem College Academy v. Employment Div., 695 P.2d 25, 37 (Or. 1985).

195. *See* Christian School Ass'n. v. Commwlth. Dept. of Labor, 423 A.2d 1340, 1347 (Pa. Commw. Ct. 1980) (striking down organizational distinction under Free Exercise Clause); *Salem Academy*, 695 P.2d at 40 (striking down distinction under state constitution).

196. *See supra* notes 172–76 and accompanying text.

197. Baltimore Lutheran High Sch. Ass'n. v. Employment Security Admin., 302 Md. 649, 490 A.2d 701 (Md. 1985). For further discussion of this case, see Berg, *supra* note 79.

198. Alton Newton Evangelistic Ass'n. v. South Carolina Employment Security Comm., 326 S.E.2d 165, 167 (S.C. 1985).

199. Larry Eskridge, More Money, More Ministry: Money and Evangelicals in Recent North American History (2000).

200. Young Life v. Division of Employment and Training, 650 P.2d 515 (Colo. 1982).

201. Another example would be an independent liberal arts college with strong and pervasive religious commitment but with no formal relation to any denomination or religious body.

202. *Young Life*, 650 P.2d at 522.

203. *Id.*

Other courts have more sensibly held that the term "church" must be broadly construed to include parachurch entities in order to avoid an unconstitutional denominational preference.[204]

However, even if a legislature or court decides that the exemption in FUTA is unconstitutionally discriminatory, it might react not by extending the exemption to independent and parachurch organizations, but by eliminating the exemption for everyone. The FUTA standard sets a floor for the states' own provisions on unemployment taxes and benefits; states lose their own federal tax credit if they give less protection against unemployment than FUTA provides, but they are free under FUTA to give greater unemployment protection.[205] For example, the Oregon Supreme Court, after criticizing the FUTA exemption as discriminatory, decided it was less risky to interpret the state's statute to exempt no one and tax all religious schools:

> If FUTA validly requires coverage of independent religious schools, a holding that excludes them from coverage under ORS chapter 657 would have consequences directly contrary to the legislature's dominant objective of maintaining Oregon's conformity with FUTA. In a choice between exempting independent religious schools and losing conformity with FUTA or maintaining that conformity and extending coverage to all religious schools, the legislature in 1977 [when the state statute was amended] surely would have chosen the latter course.[206]

The FUTA exemption is an example of a legal rule based on an entity's structure or polity that does not serve as a good proxy for gauging the strength of the religious interest in the entity. It points up the dangers of making legal treatment turn solely on church structure: such treatment will often favor familiar forms of polity and discriminate against equally sincere religious activity by organizations with less familiar structures.

For-profit vs. nonprofit status: A less troublesome basis for distinction?

There is another distinction based on formal structure that arguably is less arbitrary, a better proxy for the strength of the religious interests in a case involving the freedom of religious institutions from general regulation. It is the for-profit or nonprofit status of a religious organization. One might argue, for example, that while nonprofit activities of religious organizations should often be protected from general regulation, for-profit activities should not be exempted. Under such a view, exemption of commercial entities would not be required by the Free Exercise Clause and might in many circumstances violate the Establishment Clause.

The fundamental problem concerning exemptions from regulation is how to separate valid accommodations of religion from actions that slide into impermissible fa-

---

204. *See, e.g., Christian Jew Foundation*, 653 S.W.2d 607, 617 (Tex. Civ. App. 1983); Young Life Campaign v. Patino, 122 Cal. App. 3d 559 (1981); *see* Esbeck, *supra* note 54, at 404–405 & nn.346–347. *But see* State Dept. of Employment v. Idaho Allied Christian Forces, 669 P.2d 201 (Idaho 1983) (holding that religious organization that received eighty-five percent of its funds from various churches was not controlled or supported by an "association of churches," and not addressing the Establishment Clause issue).

205. *Salem Academy*, 695 P.2d at 29.

206. *Id.*

voritism for religion.[207] The analysis seeks to distinguish situations in which exemption removes a serious government-imposed burden on religion from those in which it works to give religious activities a disproportionate or unnecessary advantage over competitors. There is no perfect line to be drawn here, but the profit/nonprofit distinction responds to some of the core concerns. On one side of the ledger, the degree of regulatory burden, a money-making activity seems to have a relatively attenuated connection to the core free exercise concern of conscientious obligations, and even to other religiously motivated activities of caring for others (which are done by nonprofit entities). Moreover, for-profit entities suffer less from regulation than nonprofits do, because nonprofits are more limited in raising their prices to absorb regulatory costs.[208]

On the other side of the ledger (the effect of exemption on others), for-profit activities of religious organizations almost always place them in direct competition with some secular entity; thus exemptions usually give the religious entity a direct competitive advantage. One might also be concerned about the government regulating other entities' employment decisions but standing by while religious entities use purely secular economic power over employees to ensure conformance by the general population to religious standards.

The structure-based distinction between nonprofit and for-profit entities has appeared in Supreme Court decisions recently. In *Alamo Foundation v. Secretary of Labor*, the Court noted that the religious entity had no legitimate free exercise objection to application of the minimum-wage statute because the statute applied only to "commercial" activities.[209] The fullest discussion of the issues, however, is in *Corporation of Presiding Bishop v. Amos*,[210] where the Court unanimously upheld the Title VII provision that exempted religious institutions from liability for religious discrimination—that is, hiring exclusively or predominantly members of the faith—in secular as well as religious activities. The majority pointed out that by exempting all activities, not just "religious" ones, the statute avoided making courts do a detailed examination of the structure, nature, and mission of an organization to determine which activities were "religious." The Court explained:

> It is a significant burden on a religious organization to require it, on pain of substantial liability, to predict which of its activities a secular court will consider religious. The line is hardly a bright one, and an organization might understandably be concerned that a judge would not understand its tenets and sense of mission.[211]

Justice Brennan's concurrence agreed with the majority that limiting Title VII's religious exemption to "religious" activities, defined by a case-by-case examination of all the facts, "would both produce excessive government entanglement with religion and create the danger of chilling religious activity."[212] Yet, on the other hand, a limitless exemption for even the most secular and commercial activities "puts at the disposal of the religion the added advantages of economic leverage in the secular realm."[213]

Faced with the problems in a case-by-case distinction between religious and secular activities, Justice Brennan turned to the bright-line distinction between nonprofit and

---

207. *See, e.g., Amos*, 483 U.S. at 334–35 (distinguishing legitimate accommodations from actions that "devolve into 'an unlawful fostering of religion'") (quoting Hobbie v. Unemployment Appeals Comm'n, 480 U.S. 136, 145 (1987)).
208. *See* Laycock, *supra* note 39, at 55–56 & n.219.
209. *Id.* at 303–304.
210. 483 U.S. 327 (1987).
211. *Amos*, 483 U.S. at 336.
212. *Id.* at 343–344 (Brennan, J., concurring).
213. *Id.* at 343.

profit-making activities. He concluded that "a categorical exemption for [nonprofit] enterprises appropriately balances the...competing concerns," but that the constitutionality of exempting for-profit activities remained open.[214] The rest of the Court seemed to agree, either explicitly or implicitly.[215]

In short, it might be argued that the for-profit/nonprofit distinction is a relatively bright line that avoids detailed, uncertain inquiries into the nature of an organization—and yet is at the same time more closely tailored to the underlying principles of accommodation and nonfavoritism than is the FUTA exemption. The latter arbitrarily distinguishes between church-related and independent religious organizations without regard to the strength of the organization's religious interest.

Even the for-profit/nonprofit distinction is problematic in many important cases. Usually we can expect that a commercial business will not have a religiously grounded conscientious objection to legal regulation. After all, the primary purpose of a commercial business is to make a profit. Consider as a counterexample, however, the recurring situation of a landlord who objects on religious grounds to renting to unmarried, sexually active couples, heterosexual or homosexual, on the ground that she would thereby be assisting sinful practices.[216] When such landlords have raised free exercise objections to obeying state or local ordinances forbidding discrimination in housing because of marital status, most courts have held that the antidiscrimination ordinance prevails, in large part because the landlords have chosen to engage in commercial activity.[217] Yet the landlords raise much more serious free exercise issues than most for-profit entities. The nature of their business involves them more intimately and directly than most businesses in the conduct to which they object: they are forced to provide their property for acts they believe to be sinful. Moreover, their refusal to rent to unmarried couples is unlikely to give them a competitive advantage over other landlords (indeed, quite the opposite). The landlord cases show, once again, that no single factor is likely to capture all of the interests at stake in a clash between religious exercise and government regulation.

Another problem with the for-profit/nonprofit distinction is that it answers only a limited range of questions, since relatively few religious organizations operate for profit. Under what circumstances must nonprofit religious organizations be freed from regulation, and under what circumstances may the legislature do so? To the extent the Court permits or requires exemptions in some cases, the determination cannot be solely on the basis of formal structure, but must take into account other factors. Looking at other factors does lead to greater uncertainty and to more searching case-by-case examination of an organization's nature. Still, that is far preferable both to eliminating all special protection for religious organizations and to making discriminations based on poorly tailored features such as formal legal structure.

In the end, therefore, it seems unlikely that a religious organization's formal legal structure—structure in the "narrow" sense identified earlier—will ever play a major role in determining how the organizational is treated in constitutional decisions concerning government regulation and assistance. Indeed, if the Court continues its trend to-

---

214. *Id.* at 345–346.

215. *See* 483 U.S. at 337 (majority opinion); *id.* at 346 (Blackmun, J., concurring); *id.* at 348–349 (O'Connor, J., concurring).

216. *See, e.g.,* Smith v. Fair Employment and Housing Comm'n, 913 P.2d 909 (Cal.Ct. App. 1996); Swanner v. Anchorage Equal Rights Comm'n, 874 P.2d 274 (Alaska 1994); Attorney General v. Desilets, 636 N.E.2d 233 (Mass. 1994).

217. *See id.*

ward treating both religious and nonreligious institutions the same under both Religion Clauses, inquiries into the nature of the institution may become largely unnecessary. But to the extent that constitutional decisionmaking continues to be affected by the value of church/state separation—with its requirement that religious institutions be treated distinctively in some cases—courts will continue to be concerned with just how seriously or pervasively religious an organization is. And that question implicates the whole host of operational practices that we have defined as structural in the broad sense.

State Constitutions and Religious Liberty

Craig B. Mousin

Since colonial times, state constitutions have provided fertile ground for development of theories of governance, for allocation of rights, and for institutionalizing of classical republican thought in America. The first two hundred years of colonial and early United States history generated novel understandings of how religious life in the colonies and newly formed states interacted with government. Moreover, the experiences of the states and the early protections of religion found in their constitutions influenced the First Amendment's protection of religion and religious institutions.[1] Initially, state constitutions permitted different understandings of religious freedom. This period was followed by a century of convergence between government and religion in which only entities that were predominantly Protestant were offered significant autonomy.[2] During the nineteenth century and the first part of the twentieth, however, state constitutional jurisprudence left little ground for the freedom of other religious groups. Since 1990 some states have opened tantalizing possibilities for expanded religious freedom, but that goal remains elusive.[3]

---

1. The First Amendment of the Constitution states, in relevant part, "Congress shall make no law respecting an establishment of religion or prohibiting the free exercise thereof...." U.S. Const., amend. I. Since the middle of the twentieth century, the United States Supreme Court, by means of the doctrine of incorporation of the Fourteenth Amendment's protections, has held that the protection and restrictions of the First Amendment applies to all government activity, not just congressional legislation. *See* Cantwell v. Connecticut, 310 U.S. 296 (1940) (holding the free exercise provisions of the First Amendment binding on all state and local government activity), *and* Everson v. Board of Educ., 330 U.S. 1 (1947) (similarly holding the Establishment Clause binding on state and local governments).

2. For a more thorough history and description of specific state constitutional jurisprudence, see generally, Thomas M. Cooley, Constitutional Limitations (8th ed. 1927); Carl Zollman, American Civil Church Law (photo. reprint 1969) (1917); Chester James Antieau, Phillip Mark Carroll, and Thomas Carroll Burke, Religion Under the State Constitutions (1965); Daniel A. Crane, Beyond RFRA: Free Exercise of Religion Comes of Age in the State Courts, 10 St. Thomas L. Rev. 235 (1998); G. Alan Tarr, Church and State in the States, 64 Wash. L. Rev. 73 (1989); Angela Carmella, State Constitutional Protection of Religious Exercise: An Emerging Post-*Smith* Jurisprudence, 1993 BYU L. Rev. 275 (1993).

3. In part, this movement reflects developments in First Amendment jurisprudence since 1990. In addition, for more than twenty years scholars and commentators have proclaimed a new federalism in which civil and individual rights will receive state recognition and protection beyond the scope of the federal Constitution. *See generally* William J. Brennan, Jr., State Constitutions and the Protection of Individual Rights, 90. Harv L. Rev. 489 (1977); Hans A. Linde, First Things First: Re-

The thirteen original colonies, the fifty states, Puerto Rico,[4] and other territories[5] have drafted, enacted, amended, and changed their constitutions ever since the 1600s.[6] Given that every state has adopted language protecting religious liberty, this chapter asks questions similar to those just posed by Thomas C. Berg with respect to the First Amendment: Do the states, through their constitutions, treat religious institutions differently from other corporations and associations? If so, how do the religion clauses of state constitutions respect religious institutions' right to decide matters of internal government free from state interference? Secondly, to what extent does a religious organization's freedom under state constitutions depend upon the structure it has chosen for its ministries?[7] The question is not necessarily whether state constitutions offer greater religious liberty to religious institutions, but whether the distinctive histories, texts, traditions, and laws of the states offer religious institutions an autonomy distinct from that permitted under the federal Constitution.[8]

In this book's Prologue and Epilogue, James A. Serritella suggests that there is a need for greater clarity and specificity in developing a jurisprudence for religious institutions.[9] Joining the debate, William P. Marshall despairs of any unified theory of institutional autonomy being derived from the First Amendment's language or jurisprudence. Edward McGlynn Gaffney, Jr., on the other hand, argues that history does provide helpful guidelines.[10] Although federal constitutional protection controls any state understanding of the federal law, it does not preclude states from granting greater liberty under their respective charters as long as they do not trespass on any other federal constitutional rights. This raises the question of whether the states can offer an alternate approach to dealing with the Serritella-Gaffney/Marshall divide.

---

discovering the States' Bill of Rights, 94 U. Balt. L. Rev. 379 (1980); Hans A. Linde, E Pluribus, 18 Ga. L. Rev. 165 (1984); Tarr, *supra* note 2; Carmella, *supra* note 2; *but see* Daniel O. Conkle, The Free Exercise Clause: How Redundant, and Why?, 30 Loy. U. Chi. L.J. 95, 118, n.120 (2001); James A. Gardner, The Failed Discourse of State Constitutionalism, 90 Mich. L. Rev. 761 (1992); and James A. Gardner, What is a State Constitution?, 24 Rutgers L. J. 1025 (1993).

4. *See* Asociacion de Maestros de Puerto Rico v. Torres, 1994 WL 780744 (P.R. Nov. 30, 1994) (interpreting Article II, sections 3 and 5 of the Commonwealth Constitution). Section 3 "establishes a complete separation of Church and State," and section 5 "bars the use of public property or public funds for the support of schools other than of the state." *Id.* at 2.

5. *See, e.g.,* Guam v. Guerrero, 290 F.3d 1210 (9th Cir. 2002) (holding that the highest tribunal in Guam could not interpret its "bill of rights" as providing broader rights in its religious freedom provisions). *Id.* at 1217.

6. Edmund Morgan claims that the compact drafted by John Winthrop provided the first written constitution for Massachusetts, recognizing the start of a continuous government under a written constitution from as early as 1622. Edmund S. Morgan, The Puritan Dilemma, The Story of John Winthrop 91 (1958); *see also* Charles H. Baron, The Supreme Judicial Court in its Fourth Century: Meeting the Challenge of the "New Constitutional Revolution," 77 Mass. L. Rev. 35 (1992).

7. *See* Thomas C. Berg, "Religious Structures Under the Federal Constitution," in this volume, *citing* Kedroff v. St. Nicholas Cathedral of Russian Orthodox Church in North America, 344 U.S. 94, 116 (1952).

8. In describing this dual system of law, former Supreme Court Justice Brennan wrote, "This is both necessary and desirable under our federal system—state courts no less than federal are and ought to be the guardians of liberties." Brennan, *supra* note 3, at 491.

9. *See* James A. Serritella's Prologue and Epilogue to this volume; *see also* Ira C. Lupu & Robert Tuttle, The Distinctive Place of Religious Entities in Our Constitutional Order, 47 Vill. L. Rev. 37 (religious institutions face "uncertain place in our polity"). *Id.* at 39.

10. *See* William P. Marshall, "Constitutional Coherence and the Legal Structures of American Churches," in this volume; and Edward McGlynn Gaffney, Jr., "Full and Free Exercise of Religion," in this volume.

Trends in federal law and in the sociology of religious institutions also raise the question of whether examination of state constitutions will yield new and different approaches to religious liberty and autonomy. Other authors in this book point to the federal trend to treat religious institutions the same as other nongovernment organizations, thus undercutting Serritella's vision of a distinct jurisprudence.[11] Rhys H. Williams and John P.N. Massad suggest that religious institutions may mimic some of those same legal trends.[12] Sociologist Steven Warner finds that despite the plurality of religious cultures in the United States, there is now a "convergence across religious traditions toward de facto congregationalism, more or less on the model of reformed Protestant tradition of the congregation as a voluntary gathered community."[13] Both law and culture, therefore, seem to hold out little hope that religious organizations may soon benefit from a distinctive jurisprudence. Although it shows more potential than actuality, the diversity of state protection for religious institutions offers at least one alternative to this federal trend.

This chapter examines these state constitutional experiments in providing conceptions of religious autonomy that are significantly different from those set forth under the First Amendment of the Constitution. In plumbing those possibilities, this chapter first explains when state constitutional law can provide results different from those derived from First Amendment jurisprudence, and includes a discussion of the different ways state courts have sought either identical or different treatment. It then explores some of the ways religious institutions have been treated differently. The space constraints of this book do not permit a full exploration of the developments in every state, but this chapter will explore some illustrative examples.[14] It will then examine how states have failed to offer a jurisprudence that is fully distinct from the federal protections. It will also set forth some reasons why state constitutional protection has promised more real differences from First Amendment analysis than it has delivered. Given the federal trends described in this book, this chapter, however, concludes that religious leaders and attorneys cannot ignore specific state constitutional provisions in their efforts to protect the autonomy of religious institutions.

---

11. *See also* Frederick Mark Gedicks, Towards a Defensible Free Exercise Doctrine, 68 Geo. Wash. L. Rev. 925, 926–7 (2000); *but see* Michael W. McConnell, The Problem of Singling Out Religion, 50 DePaul L. Rev. 1 (2000) (suggesting that "'singling out religion' for special constitutional protection is fully consistent with our constitutional tradition"). *Id.* at 3.

12. *See* Rhys H. Williams and John P.N. Massad, "Religious Diversity, Civil Law, and Institutional Isomorphism," in this volume, discussing this as a process of institutional isomorphism.

13. Stephen R. Warner, The Place of Congregations in the Contemporary American Religious Configuration, *in* James P. Wind and James Lewis, American Congregations, Volume 2, New Perspectives in the Study of Congregations 54 (1954). Warner also suggests that his term "de facto congregationalism" shares many similarities with the term "institutional isomorphism." *Id.* at 82.

14. For further elaboration, see note 3, *supra*, and sources cited therein; *see also* Jennifer Friesen, State Constitutional Law: Litigating Individual Rights, Claims, and Defenses 199 *passim* (2d. ed. 1996).

The Right to Be Different under State Constitutions

The Federal Constitution

The Supremacy Clause of the United States Constitution makes the First Amendment the minimum standard for protection, but does not prevent a state from granting greater protection so long as in so doing it does not infringe another constitutional right.[15] Thus, litigants have often challenged state courts to hold that the state language provides protection greater than that provided under the First Amendment.[16] Greater protection, however, does not automatically result in greater religious liberty or religious involvement in state affairs. Indeed, any state court that finds its free exercise equivalent provides greater religious freedom must be careful to avoid violating the Constitution's Establishment Clause restrictions. Conversely, state charters that restrict the use of state funds for sectarian religious purposes could lead state courts to limit government far more than the federal Constitution permits, thus arguably restricting institutional autonomy more than would the federal Constitution.[17]

The ninth circuit recently held that a state constitutional prohibition against appropriating state money for religious education did not provide a compelling state interest sufficient to excuse the state from offering a scholarship to a student majoring in theology.[18] Joshua Davey, who was pursuing a joint degree in theology and business, had persuaded the ninth circuit that the state of Washington had violated the First Amendment when it withdrew a college scholarship pursuant to the state constitu-

---

15. U.S. Const. art. VI, § 2:

This Constitution, and the Laws of the United States which shall be made in pursuance thereof; and all Treaties made, or which shall be made, under the authority of the United States, shall be the supreme Law of the Land; and the judges in every State shall be bound thereby, any Thing in the Constitution or laws of any State to the Contrary notwithstanding.

Justice Thomas stated "[T]he states may pass laws that include or touch on religious matters so long as these laws do not impede free exercise rights or any other individual religious liberty issue." *See* Zelman v. Simmons-Harris, 122 S.Ct. 2460, 2481 (2002) (Thomas, J., concurring). *See also* Marbury v. Madison, 5 U.S. 137 (1803).

16. *See, e.g.,* State v. Gunwall, 720 P.2d 808, 811 (Wash. 1986) (en banc), *citing* Pruneyard Shopping Ctr. v. Robins, 447 U.S. 74, 81 (1980).

17. *See* Carl Esbeck, *The Establishment Clause As a Structural Restraint on Government*, 84 Iowa L. Rev. 1 (1998). Esbeck contends that the Establishment Clause restrains governmental power, not individual liberty. While states must provide at least as much religious liberty as the federal government to comply with constitutional free exercise protections, they may place greater restrictions on government support or "establishment" of religion than the federal government without running afoul of the Supremacy Clause. The Supreme Court held it unnecessary to decide whether a stricter state constitutional provision prohibiting even indirect support to religion would provide a compelling reason that "could ever outweigh" First Amendment rights. *Id.* In the case, the Supreme Court held that the state of Missouri had a compelling interest in justifying content-based discrimination against religious speech. Widmar v. Vincent, 454 U.S. 263, 275 (1981). *See, e.g.,* Holmes v. Bush, No. CV99-3370, 2002 WL 189079 (Fla. Dist. Ct. Aug. 5, 2002) (state constitution barred funding of private religious schools even though law was constitutional under the First Amendment).

18. Davey v. Locke, 299 F.3d 748, 760 (9th Cir. 2002), *rev'd*, 540 U.S. 712 (2004).

tion's provision banning public money for religious worship, exercise, or instruction.[19] After holding that the scholarship program had unconstitutionally singled out religion, the ninth circuit further held that the state constitution's establishment clause did not excuse the state from excluding Davey from the scholarship.[20] The Supreme Court, however, reversed, holding that the state plan did not violate Davey's free exercise in *Locke v. Davey*.[21] Writing for the Court, Chief Justice Rehnquist held that the state, "pursuant to its own constitution which has been authoritatively interpreted as prohibiting even indirectly funding religious instruction that will prepare students for ministry," could choose not to fund the religious education of a future minister.[22] The Chief Justice added that the program neither imposed criminal or civil sanctions on religious behavior nor required students to choose between religious beliefs and receiving a government benefit.[23] Because the Court held that the program was not presumptively unconstitutional, it did not directly address whether the state constitutional provision could ever override a free exercise violation, but instead added that the "state's interest in not funding the pursuit of devotional degrees is substantial and the exclusion of such funding places a relatively minor burden" on the students.[24] The Court thus left room for states to continue to look to their state constitutions for a distinctive religious liberty jurisprudence within the overarching parameters of the federal Constitution.

Given the potential differences in state constitutional jurisprudence, two federalism guidelines—one federally driven, the other chosen by the states—temper how state supreme courts address state constitutional claims in light of the First Amendment. First, in *Michigan v. Long*,[25] the U.S. Supreme Court chartered the parameters for judicial review of state court decisions. Under the Supremacy Clause, the Court has the authority and the responsibility for reviewing all federal questions. Thus, if a state supreme court were to decide an issue under federal precedent, its decision would be subject to federal review. If, conversely, the decision were clearly based on an independent analysis under state law, then it would be immune from federal review.[26] Ambiguity in the decision would leave it open to federal review, but a clear statement of the grounds for the holding would suffice to preclude review.[27] Thus, under *Michigan v. Long*, state supreme courts can determine issues under their state constitutions without fear of review if the decisions clearly reveal independent and adequate analysis.[28]

---

19. *Id.*

20. *Id.*

21. 540 U.S. at 715.

22. *Id.*

23. *Id.*

24. *Id.* at 5.

25. 463 U.S. 1032 (1983).

26. Justice O'Connor wrote: "If the state court decision indicates clearly and expressly that it is alternatively based on bona fide separate, adequate, and independent grounds, we, of course, will not undertake to review the decision." *Id.* at 1040–41.

27. If a state decision is based on federal law, "interwoven with the federal law," or predicated on an ambiguous rationale, it will be subject to federal Supreme Court review. *Id.* The Court can then decide the case or, if the decision is ambiguous, remand it for the state supreme court to make clear whether it is based on state constitutional law or federal law. In *Bush v. Palm Beach Cty. Canvassing Bd.*, 531 U.S. 70 (2000), the Court remanded a voting rights case back to the Florida court stating, "[w]e find 'that there is considerable uncertainty as the precise grounds for the decision;'" *Id.* at 77, *quoting* Minnesota v. Nat'l Tea Co., 309 U.S. 551, 555 (1940).

28. *See, e.g.*, State v. Hershberger, 462 N.W.2d 393, 396 (Minn. 1990) (holding that it is unnecessary to rest decision on uncertain developments in federal law when the Minnesota constitution al-

State models of interpretation

Not all states have accepted the invitation to decide religious liberty cases independently on state grounds. This raises the question of how each state decides what relevance it gives to the jurisprudence of the respective federal and state constitutions. In examining their own constitutions within the federal system, state courts have developed distinct theories to guide them in their selection and interpretation of federal and state law. Commentators and courts have described this process in many different ways, but most have tended to group the various approaches into three categories: primacy,[29] dual sovereignty,[30] and lockstep.[31] Primacy involves examining the state constitution first and ignoring federal precedents if state constitutional analysis results in protecting the specific liberty interest addressed by the state constitution. Dual sovereignty calls for examination of both constitutions. Lockstep typically looks to federal jurisprudence for an appropriate understanding of the state constitution. Of course, regardless of the analysis applied, the Supremacy Clause necessitates that no state's protection fall short of that provided by the federal Constitution. Accordingly, federalism permits but does not require a separate state analysis of religious freedom under state constitutions. As will be discussed below, however, choice of the theory applied does not automatically predict the outcome.

---

ready provides an independent and adequate basis to protect Amish religious beliefs that result in practices contrary to state law).

29. *See, e.g.,* Salem College & Academy, Inc. v. Employment Div., 695 P.2d 25 (Or. 1985) (Oregon courts should "determine the state's own law before deciding whether the state falls short of the federal constitutional standard.") *Id.* at 34. *See also* Friesen, *supra* note 14, at 43–48.

30. *See* First Covenant Church v. Seattle, 840 P.2d 174 (Wash. 1992). *See also,* State v. Fuller, 374 N.W.2d 722, 726 (Minn. 1985):

> It is axiomatic that a state supreme court may interpret its own state constitution to offer greater protection of individual rights than does the federal constitution. Indeed, as the highest court of this state, we are "'independently responsible for safeguarding the rights of [our] citizens.'"
>
> State courts are, and should be, the first line of defense for individual liberties within the federalist system. This, of course, does not mean that we will or should cavalierly construe our constitution more expansively than the United States Supreme Court has construed the federal constitution. Indeed, a decision of the United States Supreme Court interpreting a comparable provision of the federal constitution that, as here, is textually identical to a provision of our constitution, is of inherently persuasive, although not necessarily compelling force. [Footnote and citations omitted.]

See also Holmes v. Bush, No. CV99-3370, 2002 WL 1809079 (Fla. Dist. Ct. Aug. 5, 2002).

31. *See, e.g.,* People v. Falbe, 727 N.E.2d 200, 207 (Ill. 2000) ("any statute which is valid under the first amendment is also valid under the Constitution of Illinois"). *See also In re* Springmoor, Inc., 498 S.E.2d 177 (N.C. 1998); Board of Educ. v. Bakalis, 299 N.E.2d 737 (Ill. 1973). *See also* Michael S. Seng, Freedom of Speech, Press and Assembly, and Freedom of Religion Under the Illinois Constitution, 21 Loy. U. Chi. L.J. 91 (1989). Some courts have looked to federal jurisprudence for guidance in interpreting their state constitutions. *See* McKelvey v. Pierce, 776 A.2d 903 (N.J. Super. Ct. App. Div. 2001), *rev'd on other grounds,* 800 A.2d 840 (N.J. 2002), where the court stated, "[b]ecause the Religion Clause in the New Jersey Constitution is 'less pervasive' than the federal provision, our courts have not interpreted the State Constitution more broadly; the interpretation of our constitutional standard is informed by understanding of federal constitutional doctrine." *Id.* at 910.

Distinctive Protections State Constitutions Provide

Notwithstanding the judicial interpretation of the federal Constitution, state constitutions reveal distinctive ways in which the fifty different sovereignties seek to interpret the relationship between government and religion. State courts often fail to indicate clearly when or how they will choose which theory of priority to use in determining a case. Further complicating the matter, some states have, for example, chosen to analyze one provision of a state constitution under independent theory while analyzing another provision under a different theory such as lockstep. This is particularly true with religion clauses, where some state courts have followed lockstep for Establishment Clause equivalents while pursuing a more independent analysis for free exercise equivalents.[32] The Washington Supreme Court has been one of the most active in articulating a factor analysis to determine whether it should apply an independent interpretation of the Washington constitution. In *State v. Gunwall*, it held that Washington courts should not even engage in independent analysis unless the parties plead and persuade the court that the following six nonexclusive factors require such analysis.

1. Textual language of the state constitution
2. Significant differences in the texts of parallel provisions of federal and state constitutions
3. State constitutional and common law history
4. Preexisting bodies of state law, including statutory law
5. Differences in structure between the federal and state constitutions
6. Matters of particular state interest or local concern[33]

Religion and the rights of religious institutions often present persuasive grounds for using these nonexclusive factors, along with others recognized by other state courts, as a guide for considering protection of religious liberty distinct from that provided by the First Amendment.[34] This chapter will review factors one and two together, followed by

32. *See, e.g.*, Minnesota Fed'n of Teachers v. Mammenga, 500 N.W.2d 136 (Minn. Ct. App. 1993) (Minnesota Supreme Court's treatment of Minnesota's free exercise clause, art. I, sec.16, not binding on analysis of state constitutional establishment-type clauses prohibiting benefits and support to schools that teach distinct religious doctrines); Humphrey v. Lane, 728 N.E.2d 1039, 1043, 1047 (Ohio 2000), *cert. denied sub nom.* Fink v. Ohio, 121 S.Ct. 263 (2000).

33. 720 P.2d 808, 812–13 (Wash. 1986); *Accord*, People v. Catania, 398 N.W.2d 343, 352, n12 (Mich. 1987), citing the *Gunwall* factors as relevant in Michigan court determinations. The Washington courts, for the most part, have held litigants to that requirement. In *Malyon v. Pierce Cty.*, 935 P.2d 1272, 1277 (Wash. 1997) (en banc), the court noted that Washington courts followed the *Gunwall* test, but recognized its own inconsistency in *Witters v. State Com'n. for the Blind*, 771 P.2d 1119 (Wash. 1989), in which the Washington supreme court held "without any *Gunwall* analysis, the state provision, in the educational context, to be 'far stricter'" than the federal provision. *Malyon*, 935 P.2d at 1278, n. 10. *See also* Gallwey v. Grimm, 48 P.3d 274, 289–93 (Wash. 2002) (Johnson, J., concurring).

34. *See also* Steve McAllister, Interpreting The State Constitutions: A Survey and Assessment Of Current Methodology, 35 U. Kan. L. Rev. 593, 610 (1987) (also noting vagueness or confusion of federal guidelines as an additional consideration in independent state constitutional analysis).

discussion of the historical understandings of religion under state constitutions, of differences in the structure of constitutions, of matters of particular local concern, and finally of federal uncertainties in examining how state courts have differentiated between federal and state protection of religious liberty.

Textual differences between federal and state constitutions

The brevity of the sixteen-word First Amendment contrasts dramatically with the length and diversity of state constitutional texts that address religion or religious issues. This chapter will mention briefly some of the variations in state provisions, but it will specifically address only the Free Exercise Clause equivalents that provide expansive state protection of worship and conscience, as well as the Establishment Clause equivalents that absolutely or partially ban funding for religious institutions.

Neither religion nor God receive significant attention within the federal Constitution.[35] In contrast, a simple reading of state constitutions might lead one to presume that the realm of God can be found alive and well within the vast majority of states. While sharing the stated aim of the Constitution to "secure the blessings of liberty," most states in the preambles to their respective constitutions also expressly seek the help of God or a Supreme Being to meet those goals for a good society.[36] From preambles and clauses protecting religious liberty to clauses precluding state funding of private, sectarian, or religious education, state constitutional language betrays the early republican theories of governance by recognizing the participation of divine authority in the

---

35. The First Amendment protects religious exercise and prohibits religious establishment. In addition, Article VI, section 3 prohibits a religious test for public office. According to John Wilson, Article VI contains everything the founders believed necessary to be said about federal control of religion. John Wilson, Religion, Political Control, and the Law, 41 DePaul L. Rev. 821, 822 (1992). *See also* Steven D. Smith, Foreordained Failure, The Quest for a Constitutional Principle of Religious Freedom (1995); and Robert N. Bellah, The Broken Covenant: American Civil Religion in a Time of Trial 4 (1971). Gordon Wood writes that "When Alexander Hamilton was asked why the members of the Philadelphia Convention had not recognized God in the constitution, he allegedly replied, speaking for many of his colleagues, 'We forgot.'" Wood, The Radicalism of the American Revolution 330 (1992).

36. Compare, for example, the preamble of Maine's constitution:

> We the people of Maine, in order to establish justice, insure tranquility, provide for our mutual defense, promote our common welfare, and secure to ourselves and our posterity the blessings of liberty, acknowledging with grateful hearts the goodness of the SOVEREIGN Ruler of the Universe in affording us an opportunity, so favorable to the design; and, imploring GOD'S aid and direction in its accomplishment....

to that of the U.S. Constitution:

> We the People of the United States, in Order to form a more perfect Union, establish Justice, insure domestic Tranquility, provide for the common defense, promote the general Welfare, and secure the Blessings of Liberty to ourselves and our Posterity, do ordain and establish this Constitution for the United States of America.

In *State v. Hershberger*, 462 N.W.2d 393, 398 (Minn. 1990), the Minnesota court also noted that the state constitution's preamble opened with "We the people of the State of Minnesota, grateful to God for our civil and religious liberty," thus revealing the Minnesota framers' designation of "religious liberty as coequal with civil liberty."

daily lives of each state's citizens. God or the Supreme Being is acknowledged as a transcendent force, alive and sovereign, in at least forty-seven state constitutions,[37] several of which mandate that citizens have the "duty to worship God" while others simply acknowledge that public worship constitutes a necessary condition to the overall good of the state and its citizens.[38] Many states' clauses bar or limit funding to sectarian institutions.[39] The very presence of these clauses acknowledges that religious institutions have a role in society—necessarily a voluntary and privately funded one. Several states also specifically warn that no preference shall be given to any denomination or religion—providing, at least textually, equal footing for all of them.[40] Some states protect not just

---

37. *See* Carmella, *supra* note 2, at 287.

38. An example of such a provision is found in the Massachusetts constitution, Article 3, which provides that:

> As the public worship of God and instruction in piety, religion and morality, promote the happiness and prosperity of a people and the security of a republican government;—therefore, the several religious societies of this commonwealth, whether corporate or unincorporate, at any meeting legally warned and holden for that purpose, shall ever have the right to elect their pastors or religious teachers, to contract with them for their support....

39. Thirty-four states have enacted provisions that prohibit gifts, funds, or appropriations to churches, religious schools, or religious institutions. Examples include:

Ariz. Const. art. II, § 12 (Arizona constitution):

> No public money or property shall be appropriated for or applied to any religious worship, exercise, or instruction, or to support of any religious establishment.

Ill. Const. art. X, § 3 (Illinois constitution):

> Neither the General Assembly nor any county, city, town, township, school district, or other public corporation, shall ever make any appropriations or pay from any public fund whatever, anything in aid of any church or sectarian purpose, or to help support or sustain any school, academy, seminary, college, university, or other literary or scientific institution, controlled by any church or sectarian denomination whatever; nor shall any grant or donation of land, money, or other personal property ever be made by the State, or any such public corporation, to any church, or for any sectarian purpose.

N.Y. Const. art. XI, § 3 (New York state constitution):

> Neither the state nor any subdivision thereof shall use its property or credit or any public money, or authorize or permit either to be used, directly or indirectly, in aid or maintenance, other than for examination or inspection, of any school or institution of learning wholly or in part under the control or direction of any religious denomination, or in which any denominational tenet or doctrine is taught, but the legislature may provide for the transportation of children to and from school or institution of learning.

40. Thirty-two state constitutions contain provisions that forbid giving preference to one religious denomination over another. Examples of such state constitutional provisions are found in the Minnesota state constitution, Article I, section 16: "nor shall any control of or interference with the rights of conscience be permitted, or any preference be given by law to any religious establishment or mode of worship" (Minn. Const. art. I, § 16). Another example is the New Jersey constitution, which provides that "There shall be no establishment of one religious sect in preference to another." N.J. Const. art. I, § 4.

Two commentators have suggested that this nonpreference understanding of the state's relationship to religion influenced delegates in voting for the establishment language found in the First Amendment. *See, e.g.*, Chester James Antieau, et.al, Freedom From Federal Establishment Formation and Early History of the First Amendment Clauses 132 (1964) ("It is highly plausible that the men in the First Congress from New Jersey, Delaware, North Carolina, New York, and Pennsylvania brought with them this same idea, namely, that 'no establishment' meant 'no preference'"); *see also* Friesen, *supra* note 14, at 204. *But see* Thomas J. Curry, Farewell to Christendom, The Future of Church and State in America 33–41 (2001), for a discussion minimizing the impact of the nonpreference language in the states during the debate and implementation of the First Amendment.

the free exercise of religion, but "conscience,"[41] the "exercise of conscience," "worship,"[42] "public worship,"[43] and "dictates of conscience."[44] Among others, ten states emulate the federal Constitution's "establishment" language, leaving forty others the textual independence to formulate distinctive understandings of the state's recognition and support of religion.[45] Many limit the protection of religious liberty by stating that liberty of conscience is not an excuse for acts of licentiousness or for practices inconsistent with peace and safety of the state.[46]

The wide range of language, moreover, presents a more complex understanding of government's protection and limitations on its interference with religious autonomy than that represented by the two poles of free exercise and nonestablishment under the First Amendment. The specificity of state language has also led courts to view the issue without immediately labeling a given case as either a Free Exercise or Establishment Clause case.[47] The absence of such pigeonholing gives courts and litigants an additional opportunity to provide distinctive analysis of the relationship between government and religion.

State constitutional and common law history

The history of state constitutional protection of religion begins with the pre-federal period, during which colonial governments engaged in constitution making and first grappled with the problems of balancing rights and understanding the impact of estab-

---

41. An example of such a provision is in Arizona's constitution:

The liberty of conscience secured by the provisions of this Constitution shall not be so construed as to excuse acts of licentiousness, or justify practices inconsistent with the peace and safety of the State.

Ariz. Const. art. II, §12.

Thirty-seven other states also provide for freedom of "conscience" from official interference. *See, e.g.,* Cal. Const. art. I, §4; N.Y. Const. art. I, §3.

For arguments regarding conscience under the First Amendment, see Rodney K. Smith, Converting the Religious Equality Amendment Into a Statute With a Little "Conscience," 1996 BYU L. Rev. 645, 657, n 42, *citing* Michael J. Perry, Religion in Politics 28 (1997).

42. "All men shall be secure in their Natural right, to worship Almighty God...." Or. Const. art. I, §2 (freedom of worship provision).

43. The "public worship" provision is illustrated in the Massachusetts constitution, Article 3.

44. The right to worship according to one's "dictates of conscience" is guaranteed in twenty-seven different states. An example of such language is found in the Minnesota constitution which states "The right of every man to worship God according to the dictates of his own conscience shall never be infringed." Minn. Const. art. I, §16.

45. *See* Tarr, *supra* note 2, at 85–88. *See, e.g.,* Mont. Const. art. II, §5: "The state shall make no law respecting an establishment of religion or prohibiting the free exercise thereof."

46. The many provisions including this public health and safety language also demonstrate another way in which state constitutions have influenced judicial interpretation of the First Amendment. In *City of Boerne v. Flores,* 521 U.S. 507 (1997) (Scalia, J., concurring in part), Justice Scalia pointed out that the public safety language in state constitutions supported the Court's decision in *Smith. Compare* Michael W. McConnell, Freedom from Persecution or Protection of the Rights of Conscience?: A Critique of Justice Scalia's Historical Arguments in *City of Boerne v. Flores,* 39 Wm. & Mary L. Rev. 819 (1998), *with* Philip A. Hamburger, A Constitutional Right of Religious Exemption: An Historical Perspective, 60 Geo. Wash. L. Rev. 915 (1992).

47. *See, e.g.,* Holmes v. Bush, No. CV99-3370, 2002 WL 1809079 at *2 (Fla. Dist. Ct. Aug. 5, 2002). *See also* Carmella, *supra* note 2, at 321, *citing* Fox v. City of Los Angeles, 587 P.2d 663 (Cal. 1978).

lishment, freedom of religion, and freedom of conscience.[48] Within the United States, state constitutions have governed colonies and states for more than three hundred years. For the last two hundred years, the Constitution has been the foundation of a federal system, establishing a national jurisprudence while allowing the states to interpret their respective laws. During that time, however, the federal government has delineated the relationship between the federal and state courts as well as between the respective sovereignties of a national government and its now fifty states.

The federal and state constitutions differ substantively in how they protect religious autonomy. When the thirteen colonies achieved independence from Great Britain and transformed themselves into sovereign states, many had already developed sophisticated understandings of how constitutional law would come to bear on the relationship between the people and the states, and subsequently between the states and a new federal government.[49] Indeed, many states had operated under their own constitutions for years prior to the drafting of the federal Constitution and Bill of Rights. The citizens of Massachusetts have been governed for a longer period of self-rule under a written constitution than any other people in the world.[50] Massachusetts has thus provided a model for many of the other states during the last two centuries.[51] Donald Lutz has calculated that prior to 1776, the colonists had developed and were governed under at least ninety-five documents that included thirty-six charters and forty-one colonial documents similar to constitutions.[52] Between 1776 and the ratification of the Constitution in 1789, the original thirteen states and Vermont drafted and ratified eighteen state constitutions.[53]

A remarkable convergence of events at the time of the drafting of the first state constitutions led to a radical "new world" understanding of the relationship between religion and government. At that time, the Bible still remained the primary source book for understanding life and society. God and the Bible were the main reference points in life.[54] Political and religious discourse began with the premise not of a free human, but of a free God.[55] H. Richard Niebuhr suggests that in colonial days, the Kingdom of God was understood as the sovereignty of God, in accord with Reformation understandings of the "present sovereignty and initiative" of God in daily life.[56]

Especially in the New England colonies, the earliest colonists saw themselves as first building a church, not a government.[57] But that quickly raised the question of how to constrain the radical freedom unleashed by the Reformation. Niebuhr calls this the "Protestant dilemma," moving newly emancipated persons and institutions into a constructive life that provided more order than would come from simply relying on the be-

---

48. *See* Michael McConnell, The Origins and Historical Understanding of Free Exercise of Religion, 103 Harv. L. Rev. 1409, 1421 (1990) ("If the states can be laboratories of democracy (New State Ice Co. v. Lieberman, 285 U.S. 262, 311 (1932) (Brandeis, J., dissenting)), the American colonies surely served as laboratories for the exploration of different approaches to religion and government" (footnote omitted)). *But see* Crane, *supra* note 2, at 265, suggesting that because of the unifying force of the federal Constitution, it may be heretical to permit states to experiment with such fundamental rights as religious liberty.

49. Donald Lutz, Popular Consent and Popular Control 31, 50, 61 (1980).

50. Id. at 84; *see also* Baron, *supra* note 6.

51. *See* Lutz, *supra* note 49.

52. *Id.* at 31.

53. *Id.* at 43.

54. Christopher Hill, The English Bible and Seventeenth-Century Revolution 7, 34 (1994).

55. H. Richard Niebuhr, The Kingdom of God in America 24 (1988).

56. *Id.* at 17.

57. *Id.* at 68; *see also* Perry Miller, Errand Into the Wilderness 38 (1956).

lief in a sovereign God.[58] Anarchy threatened if new disciplines were not developed. Balancing these new freedoms with the presence of God active in daily life led to the adoption of colonial and state constitutions of the type that have been called "biblical commonwealth"[59] and "constructive Protestantism."[60] Perry Miller warns, however, that these constitutions and compacts do not readily fit modern political definitions and instead contain contradictory elements of democracy, aristocracy, and hierarchy.[61] These contradictions were to be carried over into new understandings of republican theories of government.

State constitutional language frequently recalls the classic biblical covenants that were based on a societal thanksgiving for God's saving role and promise of benefits for continuing that life.[62] Grounded in biblical understanding, the earliest state constitutions reflect the immediacy of the relationship with God and the unequal covenantal relationship between humans and divine authority.[63] Such language does not simply suggest the rule of society by an established church. Rather, its key point is the recognition of a complete dependence on God. Niebuhr points out that this means no human plan can be identified with a universal kingdom; the human tendency to act in one's own self-interest necessitates that all attempts at governance, either by the state or by religion, will be undermined by human finitude and corruption.[64]

Simultaneously with the development of this language, republican political theory developed first in response to the colonies' attempts to understand their place in the British Empire, and later in resonance with the currents of rebellion and self-rule. Although adoption of the federal Constitution resulted in the triumph of the Federalists and a national government, state constitutions drafted before the adoption of the federal Constitution were essentially the triumph of Whig and radical Whig political theory,[65] which located authority and sovereignty in the people and emphasized the ability to amend constitutions.[66] Whereas Federalists saw self-interest as the guiding principle and check on any one faction gaining too much power, Whigs believed in the ideal of the homogeneous community in which each member knew and agreed upon the rules. Community rights could trump individual rights because in a homogenous community they were virtually identical.[67] Even under Whig political philosophy, however, religious rights—especially the right to worship and respond to God—were considered inalienable.[68] The state could not control religious beliefs, which were only accountable to the creator.[69] But in an interesting convergence of interests, Puritan theological understandings of the Reformation came together with

---

58. Niebuhr, *supra* note 55, at 51.

59. Miller, *supra* note 57, at 53.

60. Niebuhr, *supra* note 55, at 51.

61. Miller, *supra* note 57, at 53.

62. Gerhard von Rad, Old Testament Theology, Vol. I 130 (1962); *see also* Lutz, *supra* note 42, at 226–27.

63. *Id.* at 129.

64. Niebuhr *supra* note 55, at 51 *passim. See also* Robert T. Handy, The Voluntary Principle in Religion and Religious Freedom in America, in Voluntary Associations, A Study of Groups in Free Societies, Essays in Honor of James Luther Adams 131 (1966).

65. Lutz, *supra* note 49, at 10; *see also* Gordon Wood, The Radicalism of the American Revolution (1992).

66. Lutz, *supra* note 49, at 8.

67. *Id.* at 50.

68. *Id.*

69. *Id.*

Whig political thinking in early state constitutions.[70] Whigs could believe that homogenous communities could succeed, again because of the belief that a transcendent God active in daily life could constrain conscience. According to James Washington, the prevailing view was that the "existence of God was the ultimate constraint on the great engine of humanity."[71] Democracy was subject to the Kingdom of God.[72]

These beliefs, along with the tremendous changes in colonial life caused by the American Revolution, helped precipitate the end of establishment under state constitutions. Of the nine states that had constitutionally established religions prior to the revolution, five quickly moved to disestablish religion.[73] After the ratification of the federal Constitution, which at that time only prohibited federal establishment, Connecticut (1818) and Massachusetts (1833) became the last two states to disestablish religion under their constitutions.[74] Significantly, it was often institutional autonomy more than the force of law that led to disestablishment. Mark DeWolfe Howe suggests that disestablishment at this time arose from an increased tolerance for new faith communities that allowed individuals to respond freely to God's grace.[75] Before the revolution, town and parish were coterminous, both in legal structure and in use of the same physical structure. The church building was also the town hall, and membership in the congregation coincided with membership in the town.[76] Although some towns gave tax exemptions to those belonging to other faiths, those exemptions precluded their recipients from voting in parish affairs.[77] When this practice proved unworkable, new faith communities developed as typically American responses to restrictions on liberty. Dissenters could leave the homogenous communities and either seek other communities more aligned with their beliefs or start new communities or religious traditions.[78] Gordon Wood notes that one of the most overlooked facts of the early republic was the tremendous social dislocation caused by vast migrations of people, both internally and from immigration.[79] Social institutions based on homogenous communities could not long withstand the constant change in membership.

In contrast to some contemporary critics of federal Establishment Clause jurisprudence, Alan Tarr argues that state constitutional language, while being more detailed

---

70. *Id.* at 10.

71. James Washington, The Crisis in Sanctity of Conscience in American Jurisprudence, 42 DePaul L. Rev. 11, 12 (1992). For example, see the Vermont constitution which guarantees "That all persons have a natural and unalienable right, to worship Almighty God, according to the dictates of their own consciences and understandings, *as in their opinion shall be regulated by the word of God....*" Chap. I, art. 3 (emphasis added).

72. *See* Washington, *supra* note 71.

73. John K. Wilson, Religion Under the State Constitutions 1776–1800, 32 J. Church & State 753, 755 (1990).

74. *Id.* at 754; *see also* Curry, *supra* note 40, at 41–45.

75. Mark DeWolfe Howe, The Garden and the Wilderness 88 (1965).

76. Milford v. Godfrey, 1822 WL 1537 (Mass. 1822) at 5–6. *See also* Zollman, *supra* note 2, at 39 *citing* Alna v. Plummer, 3 Me. 88 (1824); *accord*, Curry, *supra* note 40, at 31; *see* Edward McGlynn Gaffney, Jr., "Exemption of Religious Organizations From Federal Taxation," in this volume.

77. *Milford*, 1822 WL 1537, at 7.

78. Lutz, *supra* note 49, at 56 (the religious pluralism of society allowed settlements, homogenous in themselves, to differ from other settlements, offering religious dissidents alternative places to live).

79. Wood, *supra* note 65, at 125–128, stating that "the basic fact of early American history was the growth and movement of people" and that the population outran society's political and religious institutions. *Id.* at 125, 128, 131.

than that of the First Amendment, "did not move to secularize society."[80] Instead, it gave all citizens freedom to choose their beliefs unfettered by state restriction or the influence of state funding.[81]

Religious life in the new United States took advantage of this freedom in conjunction with the freedom to expand into the new settlements that had arisen since the revolution. Nathan Hatch suggests that new communities tasting the freedom to think for themselves about issues of freedom, sovereignty, and representation contributed to the growth of evangelical fervor and popular sovereignty.[82] This accelerated the Christianization of American society while simultaneously "allowing indigenous expressions of faith to take hold among ordinary people, both white and black."[83] Hatch concludes that it also led to a democratization of Christianity that had less to do with polity or governance than with "the very incarnation of the church into popular culture."[84]

By the late nineteenth century and early into the twentieth, Protestant culture dominated government and society. Carl Zollman pointed out that Christianity became part of the law of the land.[85] This was often recognized, implicitly and explicitly, by most state courts. Niebuhr suggests that Christians, while still employing the metaphor of the Kingdom of God, changed their interpretation of that language to mean the Kingdom of Christ and saw nothing wrong with the state regulating the moral code of the land, imbued as it was with Christian values.[86] Significantly, the loss of a belief in God's divine activity in daily life coincided with a loss of belief in conscience as a tool for social control or moral guidance.[87]

With the substantial overlay of Protestant culture upon the law, few in power saw state enforcement of Protestant norms as a hindrance on religious liberty. Nowhere was that more obvious than in the funding of education. As early as 1780, the adoption of the Massachusetts constitution required the state to provide public Protestant teachers of piety, religion, and morality.[88] Before education was considered a responsibility of

---

80. Tarr, *supra* note 2, at 87–88. *See also* Wilson, *supra* note 66, at 831.

81. *See, e.g.,* Locke v. Davey, 540 U.S. 712 (2004) at 722 (quoting F. Lambert, "Americans in all regions found that Radical Whig ideas best framed their argument that state-supported clergy undermined liberty of conscience and should be opposed"). *Id.*

82. Nathan O. Hatch, The Democratization of Christianity and the Character of American Politics, *in* Religion in American Politics 93–94 (1990).

83. *Id.* at 95.

84. *Id.* at 96.

85. Zollman, *supra* note 2, at 12–15. Robert Handy notes that it was a time when the United States was "a state without a church, but not without a religion," and that the religion was predominantly Protestant. Robert Handy, Undermined Establishment 25 (1977).

86. Niebuhr, *supra* note 55, at 170. *See, e.g.,* People v. Ruggles, 1811 WL 1329 (N.Y. Sup. 1811) ("Though the constitution has discarded religious establishments, it does not forbid judicial cognisance of those offences against religion and morality which have no reference to any such establishment, or to any particular form of government, but are punishable because they strike at the root of moral obligation, and weaken the security of the social ties").

87. Washington, *supra* note 71, at 28. "By the end of the nineteenth century, it was evident that the juridical use of conscience had been diminished by the decline of its authority. It was no longer considered by some to be a transcendent reality brokered by the human will. It had been reduced to a state of individual consciousness." *But see* Mark Modak-Truran, Habermas Discourse Theory of Law and the Relationship Between Law and Religion, 26 Cap. U. L. Rev. 461 (1997).

88. Thomas James, Rights of Conscience and State School Systems in Nineteenth Century America, *in* Paul Finkleman and Stephen E. Gottlieb, Toward a Useable Past: Liberty Under State Constitutions 122 (1991).

the state, clergy frequently served as both teacher and religious leader.[89] Given the congruity of congregation and town in early colonial society, education naturally was seen as part of the clergy function.[90] Moreover, state funding of these schools was not considered unconstitutional until the states had disestablished religion.[91] With the growth of republican ideals of individual freedom and thought and the subsequent disestablishment of state churches in the colonies and new states of the republic, education soon became the responsibility of the common school.[92] Republican thought necessitated that every citizen be educated,[93] but its emphasis on individual enlightenment and piety rather than on mediation through an established church also fed the perception that established churches could not exist in the states.[94] Seventeen states enacted constitutional language precluding any funding of sectarian schools as states adopted new constitutions that eliminated establishment.[95] This also led to confusion about how common schools could teach morality and citizenship without formal establishment.[96]

The solution that appeared to work for most of the nineteenth century was a curriculum drawn from Protestant values that held little tolerance for other beliefs.[97] The forces of migration within the nation and immigration from abroad worked against that solution, however. Educators and political leaders recognized that increasing immigration required common schools not only to assimilate thousands of newcomers to the nation, but also to inculcate the morality and virtue required for a flourishing democracy.[98]

But increased immigration by those who found Protestant culture difficult if not impossible to accept led to challenges to the imposed Protestant views.[99] In Cincinnati,

---

89. Joseph P. Viteritti, Blaine's Wake: School Choice, The First Amendment, and State Constitutional Law, 21 Harvard J. L. & Pub. Pol'y 657, 662 (1998).

90. Zollman, *supra* note 2, at 39, *citing* Alna v. Plummer, 3 Me. 88 (1824).

91. *See* Viteritti, *supra* note 89, at 663. *See also* Chittenden Town Sch. Dist. v. Dept. of Educ., 738 A.2d 539 (Vt. 1999) (as early as 1777, towns in Vermont had power to tax to support church-based education. Id. at 552); Steven K. Green, The Blaine Amendment Reconsidered, XXXVI The Am. J. Legal Hist. 38, 44 (1992).

92. *See* Thomas C. Berg, "Religiously Affiliated Education," in this volume.

93. Wood, *supra* note 65, at 349.

94. Peter S. Onuf, State Politics and Republican Virtue: Religion, Education and Morality in Early American Federalism, *in* Finkleman & Gottlieb, *supra* note 88, at 98, 101. Of course, this led to great stress for republican theorists who anticipated that organized religious communities would be among the homogenous communities that educated citizens about virtue and morality. *Id.* at 101; *see also* Joseph P. Viteritti, Choosing Equality: Religious Freedom and Educational Opportunity Under Constitutional Federalism, 15 Yale L. & Pol'y Rev. 113, 123 (1996).

95. *Chittenden*, 738 A.2d at 556 (noting that Vermont's constitutional provision banning public aid to religious organizations had its earliest antecedent in 1682 in Pennsylvania, and that it was first adopted in Vermont when the common school was established with the adoption of the state constitution of 1777).

96. Onuf, *supra* note 94, at 107.

97. Viteritti, *supra* note 89, at 666. *See also* Zollman, *supra* note 2, at 32–33; Handy, *supra* note 85, at 11, 12, 37–38.

98. *See* Donahoe v. Richards, 38 Me. 379 (1854), stating that "Large masses of foreign population are among us, weak in the midst of our strength. Mere citizenship is of no avail, unless they imbibe the liberal spirit of our laws and institutions, unless they become citizens in fact as well as in name. In no other way can the process of assimilation be so readily and thoroughly accomplished as through the medium of the public schools, which are alike open to the children of the rich and the poor, of the stranger and the citizen. It is the duty of those to whom this sacred trust is confided, to discharge it with magnanimous liberality and Christian kindness."

99. In the thirty years between 1815 and 1845, almost one million Irish immigrated to America. At the start of the 1800s, about 50,000 Roman Catholics resided in the United States. By 1850, they

what have been described as the "Cincinnati Bible Wars" broke out when several proposed solutions to address the competing needs of a large Catholic population and the Protestant culture all failed.[100] In 1869, the Cincinnati school board tried to merge public and Catholic schools at public expense. Although the Catholic archbishop did not favor the merger, the publicity led to a greater awareness of religious pluralism within the city. Subsequently, the school board decided to end the reading of the King James Bible in the public schools. A lawsuit overturned the school board's action, but the Ohio Supreme Court unanimously reversed the superior court's decision in *Board of Education of the City of Cincinnati v. Minor*.[101] While deciding the case on whether the superior court had the authority to enjoin the school board, the supreme court, in dicta, also discussed religious pluralism under the Ohio constitution. The court acknowledged its belief that although religion furthered republican government, no religion, not even the majority Christian faith, could be secured by law. Significantly, notwithstanding the inclusion of language from the Northwest Ordinance that "religion, morality and knowledge are essential to good government,"[102] the court interpreted the Ohio constitution as securing the role of religion by a "hands off" policy.[103] The court, citing true republican doctrine, stated:

> It means a free conflict of opinions as to things divine; and it means masterly inactivity on the part of the state, except for the purpose of keeping the conflict free, and preventing the violation of private rights or the public peace. Meantime, the state will impartially aid all parties in their struggles after religious truth, by providing the means for the increase of general knowledge, which is the handmaid of good government, as well as of true religion and morality."[104]

The court emphasized the state constitution's protection of religious minorities and the full and unrestricted right of parents to impart religious convictions to their children.[105] The toleration in Cincinnati was emulated in a few other cities but not broadly across the nation, as many state courts saw nothing incongruous or unconstitutional in denying claims for religious exemptions from mandatory Bible reading in public classrooms.[106]

Instead, increasing waves of nativism encouraged Congressman James Blaine of Maine to seek to cut off all funding of religious schools by state tax money by amending the federal Constitution pursuant to the Blaine Amendment in 1876. The amendment passed the House of Representatives but failed by four votes in the Senate.[107] Undeterred, nativists throughout the country adopted similar amendments in many state

---

constituted the largest church in the United States. Martin M. Marty, Pilgrims in Their Own Land, 500 Years of Religion in America 272 (1985).

100. Handy, *supra* note 85, at 40. I have based this account primarily on Handy's history.

101. 23 Ohio St. 211 (1872).

102. The Ohio state constitution had incorporated the provisions of the Northwest Ordinance when the state entered the Union. *Id.* at 222, 224; *see also* Green, *supra* note 91, at 46.

103. *Minor*, 23 Ohio St. at 250 ("Let the state not only keep its own hands off, but let it also see to it that religious sects keep their hands off [the state]").

104. *Id.* at 251.

105. *Id.*

106. The Chicago school board suspended reading of the Bible shortly thereafter. *See* Green, *supra* note 91, at 47. *See, e.g.*, Kaplan v. Indep. Sch. Dist. of Virginia, 214 N.W. 18 (Minn. 1927) (no constitutional right is infringed by requiring teachers to read extracts from the Bible) ("liberty of conscience, whatever else it may mean, does not include license to remain wholly ignorant") (Stone, J. concurring). For other cases, see Cooley, *supra* note 2, at 969–974, and Zollman, *supra* note 2, at 32.

107. Viteritti, *supra* note 89, at 672.

constitutions, while Congress eventually required all territories seeking statehood to include similar provisions within their new state constitutions. By 1890, twenty-nine states had adopted constitutional requirements prohibiting state funds for private or religious schools.[108]

Outside of concerns over education and prior to incorporation of the First Amendment, state courts were the final arbiter for state regulation of religion. In 1845, the Supreme Court held, "The Constitution makes no provisions for protecting the citizens of the respective states in their religious liberties; that is left to the state constitutions and law."[109] Most state courts in the early twentieth century invoked the provisos of public safety, health, and restrictions against licentiousness in their decisions regarding religious liberty.[110] During most of the nineteenth and twentieth centuries, under the Protestant consensus requests for exemptions from laws were routinely denied on the basis of public safety language in the state constitutions.[111]

With the Supreme Court's decision in *Sherbert v. Verner*[112] in 1963, however, the simple acceptance of the public safety clauses came under attack. For free exercise claims, many state courts adopted the *Sherbert* analysis with its strict scrutiny standard and its recognition that exemptions were constitutionally permissible.[113] Both the strict scrutiny test and the power of federal doctrine led to a period during which state constitutional standards were neglected as state courts applied *Sherbert*'s analysis to federal and state constitutions with little or no regard for the distinction between the two.

Employment Div. v. Smith[114] led to a reawakening in some courts, requiring them to analyze claims under both the federal and their own state constitutions. In *Smith*, the Supreme Court held that *Sherbert* and its exemptions had never been the law of the land, but had been limited to isolated administrative hearings and hybrid cases involving other constitutional rights. Thus, neutral laws of general applicability that burdened religious behavior were not unconstitutional, having only an incidental impact on such conduct.[115] After *Smith*, few claimants could show that the government actions were aimed specifically at their religious practice, and therefore, few were able to prevail.[116] Although most state courts continued to follow the federal precedent and readily adopted the *Smith* decision as being consistent with their own state law, a few states engaged in independent analysis to find heightened protection under the state constitu-

---

108. *Id.*; *see also* Tarr, *supra* note 2, at 95; *see generally* Antieau, *supra* note 2 for a review of how the states have analyzed this language. *See also* Kotterman v. Killian, 972 P.2d 606 (Ariz. 1999) (en banc), and Frank R. Kemerer, State Constitutions and School Vouchers, 120 Ed. L. Rep. 1 (1977).

109. Permoli v. City of New Orleans, 44 U.S. 589, 609 (1845); *see also* Barron v. Baltimore, 32 U.S. 243 (1833).

110. *See* Carmella, *supra* note 2, at 294.

111. *See, e.g.*, People v. Brossard, 33 N.Y.S.2d 369 (1942); Lyon v. Strong, 6 Vt. 219 (1834); *but cf.* Ferriter v. Tyler, 48 Vt. 444 (1876).

112. 374 U.S. 398 (1963); *see also* Thomas C. Berg, "Religious Structures Under the Federal Constitution," in this volume.

113. Carmella, *supra* note 2, at 306. *Sherbert*'s strict scrutiny test was invoked when a claimant alleged that government had burdened a religious belief. The government then had the burden of showing that a compelling interest necessitated the government action, and also that there was no less restrictive means to accomplish the same end. *Sherbert*, 374 U.S. at 406–08.

114. 494 U.S. 872 (1990). *See* Thomas C. Berg, "Religious Structures Under the Federal Constitution," in this volume.

115. *Smith*, 494 U.S. at 881–83.

116. *But see* Church of the Lukumi Babalu Aye v. City of Hialeah, 508 U.S. 520 (1993) (city specifically discriminated against the religious practices of the church, and therefore violated the Constitution).

tions that was now lacking under First Amendment analysis. As Thomas C. Berg more fully describes in the previous chapter, *Smith*'s legacy only increased federal uncertainty. Congress enacted the Religious Freedom Restoration Act (RFRA) in 1993, restoring the *Sherbert* test.[117] The Supreme Court held RFRA unconstitutional in *City of Boerne v. Flores*.[118] Subsequently, Congress restored the *Sherbert* test for limited governmental action involving land use and incarcerated persons.[119] As discussed below, this rapidly evolving federal law has militated against consistent state court responses.[120]

Structural differences

The federal Constitution defines itself as one of enumerated powers, allowing the federal government to exercise only those constitutionally delegated powers expressly granted by the states.[121] States possess sovereignty, including police powers that are neither given to the federal government through adoption of the federal Constitution, denied by that document to the states, nor reserved to the people.[122] State sovereignty had predated federal sovereignty and would not be yielded lightly.[123] Through the ratification process, the existing states transferred significant responsibilities of their respective sovereignties to the federal government, but not without retaining certain powers for themselves. The Washington supreme court, in *State v. Gunwall*, contrasted the federal Constitution's limited enumerated powers with the state constitution's understanding of sovereign power inherent directly in the people, concluding that "[t]he explicit affirmation of fundamental rights in our state constitution may seem as a guarantee of those rights rather than as a restriction on them."[124] Religion, based on its historical importance within the states, therefore, suggests that religious liberty should be treated differently under a state constitution.

---

117. 42 U.S.C.A. §§2000bb et seq.; *see* Thomas C. Berg, "Religious Structures Under the Federal Constitution," in this volume.

118. 521 U.S. 507 (1997).

119. Religious Land Use and Institutionalized Persons Act, 42 U.S.C.A. §§200cc–200cc-5; *see also* Thomas C. Berg, "Religious Structures Under the Federal Constitution," in this volume.

120. See text at footnotes 190–202.

121. McCulloch v. Maryland, 17 U.S. (1 Wheat.) 316, 405 (1819); U.S. v. Cruikshank, 92 U.S. 542, 551 (1875). For an example of how one state supreme court enunciated this distinction, see *First Covenant Church v. Seattle*, 840 P.2d 174, 186 (Wash. 1992):

> The United States Constitution is a grant of limited power, authorizing the federal government to exercise only those constitutionally enumerated powers that the States expressly delegate to it. Our state constitution imposes limitations on the otherwise plenary power of the State to do anything not expressly forbidden by the state constitution or federal law.

122. *See* Cooley, *supra* note 2, at 81–82.

123. *See generally* Patrick T. Conley & John P. Kaminiski, The Constitution and the States (1988).

124. 720 P.2d 808, 812 (Wash. 1986). *See also* Malyon v. Pierce County, 935 P.2d. 1272, 1277 (Wash. 1997); State v. Hershberger, 462 N.W.2d 393, 397 (Minn. 1990) ("the state Bill of Rights expressly grants affirmative rights in the area [ ] of * * * religious worship while the corresponding federal provision simply attempts to restrain governmental action"); *Citing* Fleming & Nordby, The Minnesota Bill of Rights: Wrapt in the Old Miasmal Mist, 7 Hamline L. Rev. 51, 67 (1984). In *Malyon*, the court noted that structural differences between the federal and state constitutions will "always favor an independent state interpretation." *Malyon*, 935 P.2d at 1280 (citation ommitted).

The importance of local issues

Given the freedom to interpret their own state constitutions, state courts are not shackled by the same concerns about federalism that the Supreme Court faces in determining federal constitutional principles. Indeed, Judge Hans Linde suggests that the essence of federalism requires state courts to "divine different answers in state constitutions."[125] The Supreme Court must identify constitutional principles that will be applied across all the states, and this requires consideration of how they will affect all citizens.[126] Specifically, the Supreme Court must also balance the separation of powers principle at the federal level with the impact of its decisions in all fifty states. State courts, when solely examining rights under their respective state constitutions, may take only the local state considerations into account, which thus permits some flexibility in articulating state constitutional rights.[127]

In addition, local histories and reasons for textual differences may lead a court to a different understanding of religious liberty. In *Hershberger*, the Minnesota Supreme Court noted that Minnesota had been founded by "early settlers...of varied sects" who "may have endured religious intolerance in their native countries and were thus sensitive to religious differences among them."[128] Similarly, in *First Covenant Church of Seattle v. Seattle*, while recognizing that religious liberty is not a local concern, the Washington court pointed out that courts in that state had emphasized that the state had a local interest in broader protection than would be provided by the federal government.[129]

The uncertainty of federal law

Even if a state supreme court wants to follow federal law to guide its interpretation of the state constitution, the federal Constitution's imprecision regarding protections may give it pause.[130] As Berg and Marshall suggest, nowhere is the confusion and uncertainty greater in federal jurisprudence than in the Religion Clauses.[131] The Vermont Supreme Court cited this uncertainty in deciding a school funding case on its own interpretation of its state constitution, stating that "when faced with a choice between deciding a constitutional case on state grounds—yielding a final answer in the form of 'adequate and independent state grounds to support our judgment'—and a construction of the fed-

---

125. Hans Linde, Are State Constitutions Common Law?, 34 Ariz. L. Rev. 215, 228 (1992).

126. *See, e.g.,* Robert F. Williams, Methodology Problems in Enforcing State Constitutional Rights, 3 Ga. St. U. L. Rev. 143, 161 (1986–87).

127. Antony B. Klapper, Finding a Right in State Constitutions for Community Treatment of the Mentally Ill, 142 U. Pa. L. Rev. 739, 790 (1993).

128. *Hershberger*, 462 N.W.2d at 398. *But see* Garrett Epps, To an Unknown God: The Hidden History of *Employment Division v. Smith*, 30 Ariz. St. L.J. 953, 968 (1998), suggesting that although Oregon was founded by ethnically diverse settlers, religious and racial beliefs merged to seek a "white Protestant paradise" that excluded nonwhites and sought state neutrality towards religion.

129. 840 P.2d 174, 186–87 (Wash. 1992) (en banc).

130. *See, e.g.,* Steve McAllister, Interpreting the State Constitution: A Survey of Current Methodology, 35 U. Kan. L. Rev. 593, 610 (1987).

131. *See* Thomas C. Berg, "Religious Structures Under the Federal Constitution," in this volume; William P. Marshall, "Constitutional Coherence and the Legal Structures of American Churches," in this volume. *See also* Smith, *supra* note 35. *But see* Carl H. Esbeck, The Establishment Clause as a Structural Restraint on Governmental Power, 84 Iowa L. Rev. 1 (1998).

eral constitution that faces an uncertain future given the state of applicable federal principles, out duty is to choose the former course of action."[132] Federal uncertainty provides a strong reason for state supreme courts to consider their constitutions independently from federal law.

Thus text, history, tradition, state jurisprudence, and lack of a national focus or concern would cause one to predict that states could develop an independent and distinct protection for institutional religious liberty. Despite all of those factors, however, this goal has been more anticipated than attained.

The Failure to Develop Independent Protection of Religious Liberty

One hallmark case that demonstrates the independent and distinctive stance of a state supreme court, as well as the nearly universal disregard of that decision outside of the state, occurred when the Washington Supreme Court accepted the U.S. Supreme Court's invitation to review a religious liberty issue in Witters v. State of Washington Commission for the Blind.[133] In *Witters*, a visually handicapped student sought state aid for attending a bible college. On the basis of the three-part test established by the U.S. Supreme Court in *Lemon v. Kurtzman*, the state supreme court initially held that Larry Witters was ineligible for vocational rehabilitation funds because he was studying to become a religious leader.[134]

The first time the Washington court addressed this issue, it failed to analyze Witters's rights on state constitutional grounds.[135] The Supreme Court reversed and remanded the case, stating that "on remand, the state court is of course free to consider the applicability of the 'far stricter' article of the Washington State Constitution."[136] In accepting that invitation, the Washington court found that Inland Empire School of the Bible was a Christian college and that Witters had chosen courses to prepare for his career "promoting Christianity," and therefore providing him with vocational rehabilitation funds would violate the "sweeping comprehensive" prohibition of Article 1, section 11 of the Washington state constitution, which prohibits the application of public money for religious instruction or religious institutions. Despite having prevailed under the federal Constitution, Mr. Witters found himself denied funds by the state court pursuant to the state constitution. The state court held that this denial did not violate his First Amendment free exercise rights, and it relied on *Sherbert* and *Thomas* to also hold that the denial did not force him to give up or violate any tenet of his faith.[137]

Witters exemplifies an independent stance by a state court that results in less freedom for religious institutions to access public funds than is permitted under the Establishment Clause. It also demonstrates the extent to which courts ignore state constitutional

---

132. *Chittenden*, 738 A.2d at 547.
133. 711 P.2d 1119 (Wash. 1989).
134. Witters v. State Commission for the Blind, 689 P.2d 53 (Wash. 1984).
135. *Id.*
136. Witters v. Department of Services for the Blind, 474 U.S. 481, 489 (1986).
137. *Witters*, 771 P.2d at 1122–23; *See also,* Locke v. Davey, 540 U.S. 712 (2004) at 719.

law. Most cite the Supreme Court's holding in *Witters* for allowing indirect public funding for religious schools, but few acknowledge that Witters resided in a state that, through strict construction of its own constitution, deprived him of that very aid.[138] In *Locke v. Davey*, the Supreme Court again upheld Washington's refusal to fund a college student's pursuit of a theology degree under the Washington state constitution.[139]

The lack of distinctive jurisprudence

Even when a court determines that it can engage in independent analysis, that decision does not dictate the outcome or lead to greater protection.[140] Ironically, Oregon, the state that led the nation in advocating for a state-first interpretation of its constitution, actually started the line of cases that led to the federal retrenchment in *Smith*. Justice Hans Linde of the Oregon Supreme Court has long been regarded as one of the leading proponents of the primacy theory—that is, of interpreting the state constitution first before analyzing federal constitutional rights. Writing for the majority in *Salem College & Academy, Inc. v. Employment Div.*,[141] he articulated the primacy approach as "the judicial responsibility to determine the state's own law before deciding whether the state falls short of federal constitutional standard."[142]

In *Salem College*, a nondenominational school had requested exemption from Oregon unemployment tax requirements, arguing that its free exercise guarantees had been violated because churches and other religious organizations that were operated, supervised, controlled, or principally supported by churches or conventions of churches were receiving the exemption while Salem College was not. The parties agreed that even though Salem College was religiously oriented, it did not meet the state's definition of a religious organization. The college officials sought the freedom from control that nondenominational status provided. They claimed, therefore, that "the distinction made by the unemployment compensation law between church-related and independent religious schools in effect compels the Academy to 'reorganize as a church' or affiliate with a church in order to avoid liability for unemployment compensation."[143] Noting that Oregon's religious freedom clauses neither defined religion nor specifically named any churches, but instead referred generally to rights to worship and enjoyment of religious opinions, the court emphasized Oregon's religious pluralism, recognizing that the state

---

138. *See* Zelman v. Simmons-Harris, 122 S.Ct. 2460, 2466–67 (2002); Jackson v. Benson, 578 N.W.2d 602 (Wis. 1998).

139. *Locke*, 540 U.S. at 725.

140. See, e.g., Catholic Charities of Sacramento v. Superior Court, 85 P.3d 67 (Ca. 2004). The California Supreme Court recognized that it had the authority to pave an independent path for free exercise under the state constitution, but over time had not faced a case that required it to do so. *Id.* at 20. With regards to individual religious free exercise, state courts have occasionally found greater protection for the individual asserting the right than the federal Constitution. In *Hershberger*, the Minnesota court applied strict scrutiny to protect the right of an Amish individual to not place a bright traffic safety symbol on his slow-moving buggy. *Hershberger*, 462 N.W.2d 393. In Oregon, the court permitted an employer to raise free exercise defense to the state antidiscrimination statute. Meltebeke v. Bureau of Labor Industries, 903 P.2d 351 (Or. 1995). In *Humphrey v. Lane*, the Ohio Supreme Court permitted a prison guard to receive an exemption from normal prison regulations regarding length of hair based on his religious practices. *Humphrey*, 728 N.E.2d 1039 (Ohio 2000), *cert. denied* 121 S.Ct. 263 (2000).

141. 695 P.2d 25, 34 (Or. 1985).

142. *Id.* at 34.

143. *Id.* at 36.

had been settled by pioneers of every opinion on the subject of religion from "half-crazed fanatic to the unbelieving atheist."[144] The court refused to rule on whether religious institutions should be treated differently than other not-for-profits, and instead held that the unemployment compensation tax should be extended to all schools, religious or otherwise, thus avoiding the discriminatory distinction and upholding religious pluralism.[145]

Subsequently, in *Employment Div. v. Rogue Valley Youth for Christ*,[146] the Oregon Supreme Court faced a similar issue of how to define a church, stating:

> It may be possible to expound a judicial test for "church" consistent with both the intent of the Oregon legislature and with FUTA. Any such definition, however, would still face the problem discussed in *Salem College*—that is, Oregon would still be put in the position of treating unequally what, at least for Oregon constitutional purposes, are religious organizations. Creating such a "distinction contravenes the equality among pluralistic faiths and kinds of religious organizations embodied in the Oregon Constitution's guarantees of religious freedom." *Salem College & Academy, Inc. v. Emp. Div.*, *supra*, 298 Or. at 495, 695 P.2d 25. Therefore, we hold that Oregon must treat all religious organizations similarly whether or not they would qualify as churches under FUTA or OAR 471-31-090(1)(a).[147]

The court resolved the problem by taxing all religious organizations. Primacy theory, therefore, does not necessarily free religious institutions from governmental regulation or other restrictions on autonomy.

Within this context, the Oregon Supreme Court took its first look at whether discharge of an employee for religious use of peyote amounted to discharge for misconduct and therefore was grounds for ineligibility for unemployment compensation benefits in *Smith v. Employment Div.*[148] When *Smith* was first heard in Oregon, the supreme court denied Alfred Smith relief under the state constitution, but granted relief under the *Sherbert* analysis of First Amendment protection.[149] The court first examined Smith's claims under the Oregon constitution, which includes free exercise language that on its face is broader than the First Amendment's protections,[150] stating: "The statute and the

---

144. *Id.* at 37, quoting Carey, A History of the Oregon Constitution 300–301 (1926).

145. *Id.* at 40–41. Justice Linde avoided the question posed in this book of whether the actual structure of the institution's ministry made a difference: "Whether a religious institution may, with respect to functions other than worship, be afforded privileges or immunities not extended to otherwise similar secular institutions is a thorny problem not presented in this case." *Id.* at 37.

146. 770 P.2d 588 (Or. 1989).

147. *Id.* at 591. *Compare* St. John's Lutheran Church v. State Comp. Ins. Fund, 830 P.2d 1271 (Mont. 1992) (both federal and state constitutions considered simultaneously whether a pastor was a church employee for purposes of workers compensation coverage) *with* Young Life v. Div. of Employment and Training, 650 P.2d 515 (Colo. 1982) (despite differences in their language, the federal and state constitutions "embody the same values of free exercise and governmental non-involvement"; therefore, the Christian youth organization Young Life is neither a denomination nor a mode of worship protected by the state constitution, and can be included in the state unemployment compensation tax program). *Id.* at 525.

148. 721 P. 2d 445 (Or. 1986), *rev'd*, Employment Div. v. Smith, 494 U. S. 872 (1990), *remanded to*, Smith v. Employment Div., 799 P. 2d 148 (1990). For a fascinating explanation of the story behind the *Smith* case, see Epps, *supra* note 128, at 953.

149. *Smith*, 721 P.2d at 448–449.

150. Or. Const., art. I, §§ 2–5:

All men shall be secure in the Natural right, to worship Almighty God according to the dictates of their own consciences.

No law shall in any case whatever control the free exercise, and enjoyment of relegeous [sic]

rule are completely neutral toward religious motivations for misconduct. If the statute or the rule did discriminate for or against claimants who were discharged for worshiping as they chose, we would be faced with an entirely different issue…"—but here, "[c]laimant was denied benefits through the operation of a statute that is neutral both on its face and as applied."[151] Because the law did not violate Oregon's constitution, the court then examined federal law under the First Amendment. Applying the *Sherbert* test, it held that Smith had been improperly denied employment benefits. His expanded protection under the First Amendment proved to be short-lived, however, given the subsequent Supreme Court decision;[152] his case was remanded to the Oregon court and he lost under both the federal and state constitutions.[153]

In contrast, state cases involving land use regulation have emphasized religious institutional autonomy through a separate state analysis. In Massachusetts, for example, the Jesuits sought to renovate the interior of a large urban cathedral that Boston had designated as a historical landmark. Recognizing that declining attendance had caused the cathedral to seem empty and inhospitable for worship, the Jesuits wanted to change the interior to provide a smaller, more intimate space. The landmark designation, however, restricted the Jesuits' ability to define the manner of their own worship. In deciding the case solely on the Massachusetts constitution, the court recognized that the constitution's language and original intent recognized "the right freely to exercise one's religion to an uncompromising principle."[154] The court further noted that the text of the constitution protected not only belief but also religious practice, contemplating "broad protection for religious worship."[155]

Similarly in another post-*Smith* case, *First Covenant Church v. Seattle*,[156] the supreme court of Washington faced the issue of whether Seattle's landmarks ordinance was unconstitutional as applied to First Covenant Church, which owned and used its church building exclusively for religious purposes. The ordinance allowed churches to be nominated for landmark designation, and in cases where alteration of a building's exterior was required for liturgical reasons, it mandated that the owner discuss alternative design solutions with the Landmarks Preservation Board.[157] The church sought a declaratory judgment that such application violated its religious freedom under the state constitution.[158] The Washington court initially held that the landmark-preservation

---

opinions, or interfere with the rights of conscience.

No religious test shall be required as a qualification for any office of trust or profit.

No money shall be drawn from the Treasury for the benefit of any religeous [sic], or theological institution, nor shall any money be appropriated for the payment of any religeous [sic] services in either house of the Legislative Assembly.

art. I, § 20:

No law shall be passed granting to any citizen or class of citizens privileges, or immunities, which, upon the same terms, shall not equally belong to all citizens.

151. 721 P.2d at 448.

152. Smith v. Employment Div., 494 U.S. 872 (1990), *remanded to* 799 P.2d 148 (Or. 1990).

153. *Smith*, 799 P.2d at 149.

154. Society of Jesus of New England v. Boston Landmarks Comm'n, 564 N.E.2d 571, 573 (Mass. 1990).

155. *Id.*

156. 840 P.2d 174 (Wash. 1992).

157. *Id.* at 178.

158. Article 1, section 11, of the Washington State Constitution provides that:

Absolute freedom of conscience in all matters of religious sentiment, belief, and worship, shall be guaranteed to every individual, and no one shall be molested or disturbed in person or property on account of religion; but the liberty of conscience hereby secured shall

ordinance violated both the First Amendment and Article 1, Section 11 of the state constitution,[159] but in light of *Smith*, the Supreme Court remanded the case back to the Washington court.[160]

On remand, the court again held the ordinance unconstitutional, but engaged in an independent analysis under both *Smith* and its understanding of the First Amendment and the Washington state constitution. The court stated: "Washington, like all the states, may provide greater protection for individual rights, based on its 'sovereign right to adopt in its own Constitution individual liberties more expansive than those conferred by the Federal Constitution.'"[161]

In analyzing the *Gunwall* factors, the court held that Article 1 clearly protects both belief and conduct, in contrast to the First Amendment in *Smith*.[162] While holding that the protections in the state constitution could be more expansive than those in the federal Constitution, the majority decision analyzed Article 1, section 11 under a compelling-interest and least-restrictive-means test, chose to appropriate the earlier *Sherbert* test, and held the ordinance unconstitutional.[163]

In his concurrence, Justice Utter complained that the majority had failed to "devote enough attention to the unique language of our state constitution."[164] Fearing that an independent state analysis could not occur when the court "reverts" to federal First Amendment jurisprudence, Utter suggested some alternate ways of examining the language. He noted that the Washington constitution protected both belief and conduct, the two being closely related.[165] Moreover, with respect to issues of structural freedom Utter stated, "Religion is to some extent a communal matter. Ritual in many religions is inseparable from one's spiritual experience in faith."[166] He also stressed that only the government's interest in peace and safety or in preventing licentious acts can excuse an imposition on religious belief or practice.

In its majority decision, the court adopted the language of a compelling interest and least-restrictive-means test, but seemed intent on modifying the federal meaning, providing a state definition saying that a "compelling interest is one that has a 'clear justification...in the necessities of national or community life'...that prevents a 'clear and present, grave and immediate' danger to public health, peace, and welfare."[167] The court's decision required the state to "demonstrate that the means chosen to achieve its compelling interest are necessary and the least restrictive available."[168] In a subsequent case, the same court held that traditional zoning regulations frequently are enough to satisfy a state's compelling interest in regulating religious institutions.[169]

---

not be so construed as to excuse acts of licentiousness or justify practices inconsistent with the peace and safety of the state.

159. *First Covenant Church*, 787 P.2d 1352 (Wash.1990).

160. 499 U.S. 901 (1991), *remanded to* 840 P.2d 174 (1992).

161. *First Covenant Church*, 840 P.2d at 185.

162. *Id.* at 186.

163. *Id.* at 187.

164. *Id.* at 191.

165. *Id.* at 192.

166. *Id.*

167. *First Covenant Church*, 840 P.2d at187.

168. *Id.*; *see* Humphrey v. Lane, 728 N.E.2d 1039 (Ohio 2000), *cert. denied*, 121 S. Ct. 263 (2000).

169. Open Door Baptist Church v. Clark Cty., 995 P.2d 33, 46 (Wash. 2000) (en banc); *see also* Douglas Laycock, State RFRAs and Land Use Regulation, 32 U. C. Davis L. Rev. 755 (1999).

States may also enact landmark legislation that accommodates religious institutions. In California, the supreme court upheld a landmark preservation statute that gave religiously-affiliated institutions the opportunity to opt out of landmark status should such designation cause substantial hardship measured in terms of economic loss or deprivation of reasonable or appropriate use of the property "in furtherance of its religious mission."[170] Looking to both federal law and the state constitution, the court upheld the statute, holding that the California equivalent of the Establishment Clause coincided with the intent of the First Amendment.[171] Moreover, since the statute did not violate the Establishment Clause, the court reasoned that it could violate neither California's no-preference provision nor its no-aid-to-religion clause. Judge Stanley Mosk wrote a strong dissent, contending that "state law and state constitutional principles should be our first and sole referent...."[172]

Massachusetts, Minnesota, and Oregon have developed truly independent state analyses, but their results lead to vastly different regulation of religious institutions. Certainly, in addressing religious pluralism, Oregon foreshadowed the equality-of-religion issues in *Smith* that resulted in treating religious institutions the same as other not-for-profit institutions. *Society of Jesus* does indeed carve out a special place for protecting worship, but even that court limited its discussion to the interior of the worship space. In Minnesota, the supreme court adopted the strict-scrutiny test previously followed by the federal courts for free exercise claims, but continued to follow the federal lead on establishment-type issues. Thus, independent analysis does not in itself lead to a distinctive religious liberty jurisprudence.

State constitutional and common law emulation of Supreme Court lead

As demonstrated by almost every chapter in this book, when courts undertake to resolve disputes within religious organizations or claims against them by former members, they hold themselves divested of jurisdiction to make ecclesiastical or theological decisions. Under First Amendment jurisprudence, however, they can resolve such cases if they are able to employ neutral principles.[173] Under *Watson v. Jones*,[174] prior to incorporation of the First Amendment, the Supreme Court first enunciated a rule based on common law. In *Kedroff v. St. Nicholas Cathedral*, the Court recognized that this rule of deference was "founded in a broad and sound view of the relations of church and state

---

170. East Bay Asian Local Dev. Corp. v. California, 13 P.3d 1122, 1128 (Cal. 2000), *cert. denied*, 532 U.S. 1008 (2001).

171. *Id*. at 1138. In *Catholic Charities of Sacramento v. Superior Court,* the California Supreme Court recently held that although many of its previous decisions had "applied the federal and state free exercise clauses interchangeably, without ascribing any independent meaning to the state clause," it nonetheless retained the ability to find independent meaning of the state language. *Id*. 85 P.3d at 90. It further held that no case yet, including the *Catholic Charities* case, required it to exercise its authority to determine an independent meaning for the state clause.

172. *East Bay Asian Local,* 13 P.3d at 1141 (Mosk, J., dissenting).

173. *See* Thomas C. Berg, "Religious Structures Under the Federal Constitution," H. Reese Hansen, "Religious Organizations and the Law of Trusts," and James A. Serritella's Prologue, in this volume.

174. 80 U.S. (13 Wall.) 679 (1872). *See also* Presbytery of Elijah Parish Lovejoy v. Jaeggi, 682 S.W.2d 465, 468 (Mo. 1984) (en banc).

under our system of laws."[175] In *Jones v. Wolf,* the Court held *Watson's* principles to be rooted in the First Amendment as applied to the states through the Fourteenth Amendment.[176]

The neutral principles rule has remained impervious to change in state constitutional litigation. The state provisions have added nothing to the federal law already in place. Most state cases involving intrareligious disputes simply examine the parties' rights under the First Amendment with no mention of any state constitutional principles.[177] The Missouri Supreme Court acknowledged in *Gibson v. Brewer* that the parties themselves had failed to cite or plead that the Missouri constitution's religion clauses made any substantive difference.[178] A Colorado court recognized that its own interpretation of the Colorado religion clauses would not produce a resolution any different than would result from an analysis under the First Amendment.[179] In one intrachurch dispute in California, *Wilson v. Hinkle,* the plaintiffs contended that the state constitution required the court to examine whether the defendant church and its minister had departed from doctrine, thus enabling the plaintiffs to prevail in seeking the return of the church.[180] The court noted that the departure from doctrine test had been ruled unconstitutional under the First Amendment by *Presbyterian Church v. Hull Church,* 393 U.S. 440 (1969).[181] It refused to accept the plaintiff's invitation to rely on the state constitution while delving into the question of whether the defendants had departed from doctrine, because that would unavoidably have resulted in religious institutions receiving less protection under the state constitution than under the federal Constitution.[182] Later, however, in a much-criticized case, *Barr v. United Methodist Church,* a California court permitted residents from fourteen Methodist retirement homes to sue the denomination over a "continuing care agreement."[183] After examining the defendant church's argument that both the First Amendment and the California constitution divested the court of jurisdiction, the court first characterized the Methodists' provision of retirement care as a "secular activity" and then held that "To apply a different standard to determine the jural status of religious organizations as opposed to non-religious organizations in purely secular suits might very well constitute a preference for religion in violation of the establishment clause."[184] Relying

---

175. 344 U.S. 94 (1952).

176. 443 U.S. 595 (1979).

177. *See, e.g.,* First Presbyterian Church of Schenectady v. United Presbyterian Church in the United States, 464 N.E.2d 454 (N.Y. 1984).

178. Gibson v. Brewer, 952 S.W.2d 239 (Mo. 1997) (en banc) (court will not address the applicability, if any, of the Missouri constitution even though the U.S. Supreme Court has previously held that the Missouri provisions with regard to religion "are not only more explicit, but more restrictive"). *Id.* at 246; *accord,* Jaeggi, 682 S.W.2d at 467 ("Neither side claims that the neutral principles approach is inconsistent with any of the religious freedom provisions of the Constitution of Missouri").

179. Bishop and Diocese of Colorado v. Mote, 716 P.2d 85, 91, n. 5 (Colo. 1986) (en banc), *cert. denied,* 479 U.S. 826 (1986). *See also* Kleppinger v. Anglican Catholic Church, Inc., 715 A.2d 1033 (N.J. Super. Ct. Ch. Div. 1998) (neutral principles under the establishment clauses of both the federal and state constitutions prevail where no inquiry is being made into church doctrine, but courts must abstain if decision necessitates determination on ecclesiastical matters). *Id.* at 1037.

180. 67 Cal. App.3d 506 (Cal. Ct. App. 1977).

181. *Id.* at 510.

182. *Id.* at 511, n. 3.

183. Barr v. United Methodist Church, 90 Cal. App. 3d 259, 261–62 (Cal. Ct. App.1979). For a critique of the *Barr* case, *see* Mark E. Chopko, "Derivative Liability," in this volume.

184. *Barr,* 90 Cal. App. 3d at 275.

primarily on federal First Amendment precedent to reach this holding, the court never indicated whether the state constitution provided the religious institution with different protection.[185] By calling a ministry of care for the elderly a secular activity, the court thus permitted neutral principles to apply, and required the church to litigate.[186]

Although very few courts explain why litigants do not seek more expansive religious liberty protections under state constitutions, most recognize that in property disputes the First Amendment divests jurisdiction if the parties allege ecclesiastical issues or require doctrinal interpretation to reach a resolution. In one Minnesota case, *Basich v. Board of Pensions, Evangelical Lutheran Church in America*, 540 N.W.2d 82 (Ct. of App. Mn. 1995), the court first found that the First Amendment deprived it of jurisdiction to determine whether the Board of Pensions had violated its fiduciary duty to pastors and lay people by adding a moral and social responsibility screen to the board's investment decisions. The defendant pension board also raised a second ground precluding court review of its decision, pleading that the Minnesota constitution's freedom of conscience clause provided greater protection against court intrusion into the dispute.[187] After first holding that the necessity of investigating Lutheran doctrinal principles deprived it of jurisdiction, the court then recognized that Minnesota's freedom of conscience clause "affords greater protection against government action than the federal constitution."[188] Significantly, while *Hershberger* might be read as an individual conscience case, *Basich* demonstrates that at least in the view of the Minnesota court, this religious liberty right can also be claimed by religious institutions.

The silence of so many courts with respect to state constitutional claims suggests that once a court invokes the neutral principles test, then no religious dispute exists and the protections of the religious liberty clauses do not apply. In addition, many state courts have developed similar common law precedents involving neutral principles, thus avoiding the need to turn to state constitutions. Moreover, because neutral principles arose out of a common law decision of the Supreme Court, many states have already developed a similar common law.[189] Therefore, at least with regard to neutral principles cases, state constitutional provisions rarely provide any approaches to institutional religious liberty that are distinct from the law as developed by the Supreme Court.

The uncertainty of federal law

During the last decade, not only have Supreme Court decisions muddied the water, but the dueling between Congress and the Court following the *Smith* decision has also led to greater confusion for state supreme courts and lower federal courts. With the rel-

---

185. *Id.* at 273.

186. *Id.* at 274. The court did note that neither the federal nor the state court had ever permitted organizations "under the cloak of religion" to commit fraud or avoid lawful obligations that arise from their secular activities "because the satisfaction of those obligations may, in some tangential fashion, discourage religious activities." *Id.* at 275.

187. *Basich*, 540 N.W.2d at 87.

188. *Id.*

189. *See* H. Reese Hansen, "Religious Organizations and the Law of Trusts," Patty Gerstenblith, "Associational Structures of Religious Organizations," and Thomas C. Berg, "Religious Structures Under the Federal Constitution," in this volume.

atively rapid changes in law from the *Smith* decision in 1990, the enactment of RFRA in 1993,[190] and the *Boerne*[191] decision in 1997, states relying on federal analysis have often decided cases under their state constitutions without full development of the federal law. The frequent federal changes foster uncertainty, which states replicate when they choose federal law to guide their state analysis. For example, in *State of Vermont v. De-LaBruere*,[192] parents sought a religious exemption from state truancy laws to permit their children to be educated at home. The Vermont Supreme Court held that the state's compelling interest in education outweighed the parents' rights, and also that the state had provided the least restrictive means by offering the parents more than one educational option. The court refused to extend the state constitution's protections beyond those already provided by the federal Constitution, noting that other states with constitutional language similar to Vermont's had previously interpreted such language only as broadly as that in the federal Constitution. Although the court noted that the Vermont constitution contained major textual differences with the First Amendment, both Vermont precedent and the historical development of the Vermont constitution led the court to conclude that the state's protections were no more extensive than those in the First Amendment.[193] Angela Carmella correctly critiqued this lockstep analysis as an abdication of Vermont's responsibility to interpret its own constitution.[194]

When RFRA was passed, Vermont simply followed the federal lead without further analysis of RFRA's constitutionality or of whether Vermont should continue to follow the federal lead in a particular child custody case.[195] In this case, the court first analyzed the father's claim under the First Amendment.[196] Recognizing that RFRA had recently been passed, the court concluded itself bound to it in its own analysis of the Free Exercise Clause of the federal Constitution, while specifically noting that it would express no opinion as to RFRA's constitutionality.[197] Although it found the father's religious beliefs

---

190. 42 U.S.C. Sec. 2000bb(1)(a), (b). Congress sought in effect to repeal the *Smith* decision and restore the compelling interest test of *Sherbert*.

191. City of Boerne v. Flores, 521 U.S. 507 (1997). *See* Thomas C. Berg's discussion of *Boerne* in "Religious Structures Under the Federal Constitution," in this volume; *see also* Angela Carmella's discussion of further developments under RLUIPA in this volume.

192. 577 A.2d 254 (Vt. 1990).

193. Vt. Const., ch. I., art. 3 contains language very different from that of the First Amendment, stating:

> That all men have a natural and unalienable right, to worship Almighty God, according to the dictates of their own consciences and understandings, as in their opinion shall be regulated by the word of God; and that no man ought to, or of right can be compelled to attend any religious worship, or erect or support any place of worship, or maintain any minister, contrary to the dictates of his conscience, nor can any man be justly deprived or abridged of any civil right as a citizen, on account of his religious sentiments, or peculiar mode of religious worship; and that no authority can, or ought to be vested in, or assumed by, any power whatever, that shall in any case interfere with, or in any manner control the rights of conscience, in the free exercise of religious worship.

See also Mefford v. White, 770 N.E.2d 1251 (Ill. App. Ct. 2002) (even though federal and Illinois constitution had different language, state would still follow federal jurisprudence). *Id.* at 7.

194. Carmella, *supra* note 3, at 316–17 citing *DeLaBruere* to demonstrate that the unfortunate result of such analysis "automatically amends state constitutions and their interpretations" whenever the Supreme Court makes a change in the law.

195. Hunt v. Hunt, 648 A.2d 843 (Vt. 1994).

196. *Id.*

197. *Id.* at 850, n.4.

sincere, the compelling state interest in parental support of children and the lack of any other means of imposing such support absent a court order led the court to hold that the support order did not violate the First Amendment.[198]

The court then proceeded to its analysis of the state constitution, suggesting that it might afford greater protection than the First Amendment.[199] Rather than truly examining the question of how the *DeLaBruere* holding may have been affected by RFRA, the court simply accepted RFRA's strict scrutiny as the new state standard. The court concluded that it possessed "no principled basis to say that the Vermont constitution offers greater protection for a free exercise claim such as defendant's than the strict scrutiny standard at issue."[200] Although two other states relied on by *DeLaBruere* court had found that the shifting sands of federal law warranted their charting of state tests for religious liberty different from the federal test,[201] the court simply adopted the RFRA strict scrutiny standard without any discussion of whether the Vermont constitution also offered one. It also failed to provide an independent analysis of the state's constitutional protection, especially as it might exist if RFRA were later to be held unconstitutional in application to the states. RFRA, therefore, clouded the court's understandings of the distinct role of state constitutional adjudication.[202]

State law

Proponents of the role of state constitutions in defining such liberty interests as religion often claim that proximity to the local or state community enables the law to respond to actual community interests better than the federal government can, especially given the relative ease of amending state constitutions as compared to the difficulty of amending the federal Constitution.[203] Alan Tarr points out that as state constitutions developed over time, they responded to specific problems within the states, and thus became more likely to contain concrete language to address those problems.[204]

---

198. *Id.* at 851.

199. *Id.* at 852.

200. *Id.*

201. *Id.* Maine and Minnesota both departed from the federal lockstep analysis. Maine, however, simply refused to decide whether *Smith* eliminated the *Sherbert* test. *See* Rupert v. City of Portland, 605 A.2d 63, 66 (Me. 1992), which thus applies *Smith* in its federal analysis and the *Sherbert* test in its state analysis. In Minnesota, the court applied a higher standard in *Hershberger*, 462 N.W.2d at 396.

202. *See* Crane, *supra* note 2, at 270, stating that "…the passage of RFRA deterred some state courts from considering the meaning of their own free exercise clause equivalents in light of Smith."

203. Emily Fowler Hartigan, Law and Mystery: Calling the Letter to Life Through the Spirit of the Law of State Constitutions, 6 J.L. & Religion 225 (1988).

204. Tarr, *supra* note 2, at 94. *See also* Kotterman v. Killian, 972 P.2d 606, 625 (Ariz. 1999) (en banc) (emphasizing the difference between the approach to religion taken by the framers of the Arizona constitution, who had been living under the influence of Spain and Mexico, and that taken by the framers of the Washington constitution, who had been influenced by trans-Pacific immigration); Board of Educ. v. Bakalis, 299 N.E.2d 737, 745 (Ill. 1973) (stressing that the framers of the 1970 Illinois constitution feared making any changes in the language of the religious liberty clauses because the depth of emotion on the issue in Illinois would probably have led to an erroneous judicial interpretation of their actions, thus causing the drafters to retain the 1870 language).

While the interplay between constitutional amendment and new legislation might lead to more specific clauses, it might also hinder development of a distinct state constitutional jurisprudence.[205] The turmoil of the *Boerne* litigation and the unconstitutionality of RFRA as applied to the states encouraged many legislatures to enact state religious freedom acts[206] which typically restore the strict scrutiny tests much as Congress attempted to do through federal legislation.[207] As Tarr and others have pointed out, local politics plays a greater role in state court adjudications than in federal cases. Efforts to pass state RFRAs may have made courts and litigants reluctant to resolve issues by carving out distinctive state constitutional protection.[208] The effort to gain legislative support of religious freedom has many causes, but it certainly reveals that notwithstanding

---

205. *See* Crane, *supra* note 2, at 268.

206. Alabama adopted a constitutional amendment. Alabama, Ala. Const. amend. 622, §V which provides, in part:

> SECTION V. (a) Government shall not burden a person's freedom of religion even if the burden results from a rule of general applicability, except as provided in subsection (b).
> (b) Government may burden a person's freedom of religion only if it demonstrates that application of the burden to the person:
> (1) Is in furtherance of a compelling governmental interest; and
> (2) Is the least restrictive means of furthering that compelling governmental interest.

Several states have enacted state legislation: Arizona, Ariz. Rev. Stat. Ann. §§41–1493.01 (West Supp. 1999); Connecticut, Conn. Gen. Stat. Ann. §52-571b (West Supp. 2000); Florida, Fla. Stat. Ann. ch. 761.01–.05 (Harrison Supp.1999); Idaho, Idaho Code §73-402 (Lexis Supp. 2000); Illinois, 775 Ill. Comp. Stat. Ann. 35/1-99 (West Supp. 2000); New Mexico, N.M. Stat. Ann. §§28-22-1 to -5 (Michie 2000); Oklahoma, 2000 Okla. Sess. Law Serv. 272 (West); Rhode Island, R.I. Gen. Laws §§42-80.1-1 to -4 (1998); South Carolina, S.C. Code Ann. §§1-3210 to -60 (Law. Co-op. Supp.1999); Texas, Tex. Civ. Prac. & Rem. Code Ann. §§110.001–.012 (Vernon Supp. 2000). The Illinois amendment reads, in part:

> Sec. 15. Free exercise of religion protected. Government may not substantially burden a person's exercise of religion, even if the burden results from a rule of general applicability, unless it demonstrates that application of the burden to the person (i) is in furtherance of a compelling governmental interest and (ii) is the least restrictive means of furthering that compelling governmental interest. §775 ILCS 35/15.

See also W. Cole Durham, State RFRAs and the Scope of Free Exercise Protection, 32 U.C. Davis L. Rev. 665 (1999); Eugene Volokh, A Common-Law Model for Religious Exemptions, 46 UCLA L. Rev. 1465 (1999).

207. The early litigation under these provisions has frequently involved organizations facing zoning regulations. In one Illinois case, the legislature had passed its version of RFRA after the case had been tried but before a decision had been reached. The parties submitted briefs on the new law, but no new record evidence was submitted to meet the new tests. The court held that even under the new law's strict scrutiny test, the city had a compelling interest in its zoning regulation, thus requiring the court to deny the church's request for a zoning variance. City of Chicago Heights v. Living Word Outreach Full Gospel Church and Ministry, 707 N.E.2d 53 (1999), *rev'd on other grounds,* 749 N.E.2d 916, 932 (Ill. 2001) (therefore leaving no need to address the state RFRA issue). In a subsequent Illinois case, *Vineyard Christian Fellowship v. Evanston,* 250 F.Supp.2d 961 (N.D. Ill. 2003), although the court held that the zoning decision had violated the federal and state constitutions, it further held that the Vineyard had failed to demonstrate a substantial burden on its exercise of religion, and therefore did not need to address whether the city had violated the state RFRA. *Id.* at 993–4. In a Florida case, the court acknowledged its new state RFRA but betrayed a misunderstanding of what the legislature had intended to protect subsequent to the *Smith* decision, stating that the Florida RFRA was "obviously designed to protect" the First Amendment Free Exercise Clause, and then citing cases that did not comport with the new test of the statute. First Baptist Church of Perrine v. Miami Dade Cty., 768 So. 2d 1114, 1117 (Fla. Dist. Ct. App. 2000).

208. *See, e.g.,* Jesuit College Preparatory School v. Judy, 231 F.Supp.2d 520 (N.D. Tex 2002) (plaintiffs unsuccessfully claimed that state violated Texas RFRA by excluding private religious school from state-run athletic program, but did not make any state constitutional claim).

textual and historical differences, most state courts have failed to set forth independent grounds for religious institutional autonomy.

The funding of religious institutions under state constitutions

State and federal interest in education

The control of education and inculcation of values in children has been a major battleground in the states over the last two centuries, and it remains both a local and a national concern. Thus, state law and litigation respond to federal law and jurisprudence as well as to state-specific issues and laws, providing an experiment with religious participation in education.

Many of the issues raised by Berg in his chapter on religiously affiliated education had roots in state court contests prior to Supreme Court decisions.[209] Bible reading,[210] textbook provision,[211] and home schooling issues[212] all have worked their way through the state courts. Most recently, the Supreme Court has upheld Washington's refusal to provide scholarships to individuals pursuing a degree in theology.[213] Decisions involving transportation for students attending parochial schools demonstrate how arguments

---

209. *See* Thomas C. Berg, "Religiously Affiliated Education," in this volume; *see also* School Dist. of Abington Twnshp. v. Schempp, 374 U.S. 203 (1963). While recognizing that state constitutions provided the legal context for the debate on funding of religious education in the United States in the nineteenth century, former Justice Brennan observed that "Particularly relevant for our purposes are the decisions of the state courts on questions of religion in the public schools. Those decisions, while not, of course, authoritative in this Court, serve nevertheless to define the problem before us and to guide our inquiry." *Id.* at 274–75 (Brennan, J., concurring). In *Lemon v. Kurtzman*, Justice Brennan similarly cited state constitutional amendments and state court decisions prohibiting public aid to religious schools, concluding that "thus, for more than a century, the consensus enforced by legislatures and courts with substantial consistency, has been that public subsidy of sectarian schools constitutes an impermissible involvement of secular with religious institutions." 403 U.S. 602, 646–49 (1971) (Brennan, J., concurring).

210. *See, e.g.*, Kaplan v. Indep. Sch. Dist., 214 N.W. 18 (Minn. 1927) (holding that no constitutional right is infringed by requiring teachers to read extracts from the Bible); *id.* at 22. (Stone, J., Concurring) ("Liberty of conscience, whatever else it may mean, does not include license to remain wholly ignorant"). For other cases, see Zollman, *supra* note 2, at 32; Friesen, *supra* note 14, at 200–209.

211. *Compare, e.g.*, Chance v. Mississippi State Textbook and Purchasing Bd., 200 So. 706, 710 (Miss. 1941) ("The state which allows the pupil to subscribe to any religious creed should not, because of his exercise of this right, proscribe him from benefits common to all") and Borden v. Louisiana State Bd. of Educ., 123 So. 655, 660 (La. 1929) (the school children and the state are the beneficiaries of the aid, not the religious schools), *with* Gaffney v. State Dept. of Ed, 220 N.W.2d 550, 555 (Neb. 1974), stating that "By the phraseology and diction of this provision, it is our conclusion that the framers of our constitution intended to more positively enunciate the separation between church and state than the framers of the U.S. Constitution." Furthermore, the *Gaffney* court noted, "It is clear to us the fact that the benefit of the secular textbooks goes originally to the student rather than directly to the school is a mere conduit and does not have the cleansing effect of removing the identity of the ultimate benefit to the school as being public funds." *Id.* at 557. *See also* People v. Howlett, 305 N.E.2d 129 (Ill. 1973).

212. *See, e.g.*, People of the State of Michigan v. DeJonge, 501 N.W.2d 127 (Mich. 1993) (teacher certification requirement is unconstitutional in cases of families whose religious beliefs ban the use of certified instructors).

213. Locke v. Davey, 540 U.S. 712 (2004).

eventually presented at the federal level were first articulated, refined and rebutted at the state level. Many state courts found the text of no-aid provisions conclusive and prohibited any type of financial aid for transportation.[214] Many others, however, adopted child benefit theory to find it constitutional. In Connecticut, the court approved transportation assistance to protect children from the hazards of walking on dangerous highways, noting that "the state is under a duty to ignore the child's creed, but not its need."[215] Similarly, one Massachusetts court drew the line between the state anti-aid amendments and a "public safety measure" that benefited the students.[216] Kentucky's supreme court has held its state constitution to be more restrictive of such funding than its federal counterpart, yet it upheld a transportation subsidy against a challenge under both constitutions, finding that it benefited children, rather than their religious school, by highlighting public safety concerns.[217] Those states adopting lockstep analysis have looked to federal law for exceptions to state constitutional bars to funds being used for religious purposes.[218] In New Jersey, the experiment came full circle as the state relied on *Everson* in ratifying a new state constitutional provision that embraced the meaning of the federal Establishment Clause.[219]

Vouchers and tax credits

Currently, public debate and litigation have focused on the control of public education institutions and the concomitant wrestling over the funding of sectarian schools, involving such issues as vouchers, scholarships, and tax credits. As the Florida court in *Holmes v. Bush* signaled, litigators will focus on state constitutional provisions in the next challenge against public funding, thus attracting attention from those who believe such funding diminishes public as well as religious organizations.[220] Although the ninth

---

214. *See* footnote 32 and text; *See also* Judd v. Board of Educ., 15 N.E.2d 576 (N.Y. 1938) (holding that New York transportation statute violated the no-aid provisions of the New York state constitution, art. 9, Sec. 1). Epeldi v. Engelking, 488 P.2d 860 (Idaho 1971) (although it was clear after the Supreme Court's decision in *Everson* that aid for transportation had passed First Amendment test, the Idaho constitution's explicit terms rejected child benefit theory and the secular purpose test and forced the court to focus on whether the aid itself was directed to any particular church or helped "support or sustain any church affiliated school"). *Id.* at 865–66. *See also* Spears v. Hardin, 449 P.2d 130 (Haw. 1968) (language of Hawaii constitution clearly revealed intent of framers to reject child benefit theory and instead emphasized need to support public school in a democratic state). *Id.* at 134–35; Board of Educ. v. Antone, 384 P.2d 911 (Okla. 1963) (finding Oklahoma state constitution to prohibit any aid, indirect or direct, and rejecting arguments that transportation funding for parochial pupils simply served the general welfare of the community).

215. Snyder v. Newton, 161 A.2d 770, 777 (Conn. 1960) (holding statute constitutional as it applied to the religious freedom clauses of the Connecticut constitution, but unconstitutional as applying to any monies coming out of a school fund).

216. Attorney General v. School Comm. of Essex, 439 N.E.2d 770, 775 (Mass. 1982). *See also* Bowker v. Baker, 167 P.2d 256, 263 (Cal. Ct. App. 1946) (balancing state's police power to protect the safety of children against state's constitutional prohibitions against funding of religious schools).

217. Neal v. Fiscal Court, Jefferson Cty., 986 S.W.2d 907, 912–13 (Ky. 1999).

218. Board of Educ. v. Bakalis, 299 N.E.2d 737 (Ill. 1973).

219. Fox v. Board of Educ., 226 A.2d 471, 478 (N.J. Super. Ct. Law Div. 1967): "[P]erusal of constitutional debates...reflects a clear intent to incorporate the principles of *Everson* into the fundamental law of our state so as to empower the Legislature to provide for the transportation of school children to public and nonpublic schools, and to prevent a possible judicial construction to the contrary in the future."

220. 2002 WL 1809079 (Fla. Cir. Ct. Aug. 5, 2002) (holding that Supreme Court decision in *Zelman v. Simmons-Harris* decided federal Establishment Clause challenge, but further holding Florida voucher statute to be unconstitutional under Florida state constitution); *Id.* at 3; *see also* Zelman v.

circuit in *Davey v. Locke*[221] had appeared to diminish the potential barrier state constitutions placed in the way of public funding, the Supreme Court reversal reveals, at least in funding of clergy training, that state constitutions may continue to have an impact on these funding issues. State legislative and judicial contests have become a critical national laboratory for addressing funding possibilities, and the ensuing debate reveals the ultimate weakness of state constitutional law as a source of autonomy for religious organizations in the United States.

Text, history, and tradition have led to a variety of outcomes in state court litigation concerning no-aid provisions. The different histories include the early dovetailing of church and school in the New England colonies, subsequent exemptions for conscientious objectors to paying taxes for religious schools,[222] nativist discrimination against Catholics and immigrants,[223] federal requirements for statehood,[224] and a general tendency of state legislators and state constitutional conventions to mimic provisions in the constitutions of other states.[225] Differences in individual state histories have also led to different means of educating children. In states with large rural areas, economies of scale have precluded some towns from providing secondary education. Some of these states have enacted provisions granting parents financial assistance to send their children to private schools.[226] Others have refused to divert aid to private schools, citing a strong commitment to public schools as the means of furthering republican principles and representative government.[227] In some states with large urban poor populations, however, the perceived public education crisis calls for funding reform.[228] The current federal trend toward government neutrality and private choice in education also raises the fairness issue when religious institutions are denied access to government funds.[229]

Responding to all these different needs highlights how states can experiment to invent distinctive yet constitutional ways to improve public education and permit sectarian and private education to flourish. In Milwaukee, Wisconsin, for example, up to fif-

---

Simmons-Harris, 122 S.Ct. 2460 (2002); Mitchell v. Helms, 120 S. Ct. 2530 (2000); Agostini v. Felton, 521 U.S. 203 (1997); *see also* Thomas C. Berg, "Religiously Affiliated Education" and appendix; Ira C. Lupu, The Increasingly Antagonistic Case Against School Vouchers, 13 Notre Dame J.L. Ethics & Pub. Pol'y 375 (1999); *but see* Steven Green, Private School Vouchers and the Confusion Over "Overt Aid," 10 Geo. Mason U. Civ. Rts. L.J. 47, 49 (1999–2000), which notes that even with the developments of federal law, state constitutional decisions still result in uncertainty.

221. 299 F.3d 748 (9th Cir. 2002), *rev'd*, 540 U.S. 712 (2004).

222. *See* footnotes 76–78, *supra*; Chittenden Town Sch. Dist. v. Dept. of Educ., 738 A.2d 539 (Vt. 1999), *cert. denied, sub nom.* Andrews v. Vt. Dept. of Educ., 528 U.S. 1066 (1999); Snyder v. Newton, 161 A.2d 770, 775–76 (Conn. 1960).

223. *See* text at footnotes 97–108, *supra*.

224. *Id. See also* text at footnote 107–108, *supra*.

225. *See* Linde, First Things First, *supra* note 3, at 381; Lutz, *supra* note 49; Kotterman v. Killian, 972 P.2d 606 (Ariz. 1999) (en banc), *cert. denied*, 528 U.S. 921 (1999).

226. *Chittenden*, 738 A.2d at 539.

227. *See* Spears, 449 P.2d at 135. *See also In re* Opinion of the Justices, 102 N.E. 464 (Mass. 1913) (constitution adopted no-aid prohibition based on a deep-seated conviction to preserve the public school system); *see also Malyon*, 935 P.2d at 1279, finding that "the driving concern of the state constitutional convention was religious influence in, and control over, public education," leading to a distinctly different approach to religion and government and calling for a "stern separation of church and the public education clause."

228. *See* Jackson v. Benson, 578 N.W.2d 602, 608–09 (Wis. 1998); Simmons-Harris v. Goff, 711 N.E.2d 203, 211 (Ohio 1999).

229. *See* Thomas C. Berg, "Religiously Affiliated Education" and appendix, in this volume; Zelman v. Simmons-Harris, 122 S. Ct. 2460 (2002); Mitchell v. Helms, 120 S. Ct. 2530 (2000); *see also* Lupu, *supra* note 220.

teen percent of public school students are eligible for state aid to attend private schools, which comes in the form of payments to the student's parents or guardians with no restrictions regarding which private school to attend.[230] Ohio has provided a scholarship program in which parents receive a check for the private school, but only religious schools have applied for the program.[231] Maine, on the other hand, prohibits any religious school from accessing its tuition assistance program, even in rural towns that have no public schools.[232] Arizona provides parents with a $500 tax credit.[233] A Vermont statute authorized school districts to pay tuition to nonpublic schools selected by parents where towns provided no public secondary school.[234] In Illinois, the legislature provides a tax credit up to $500 for any qualified educational expense incurred by a student in any public or nonpublic school that meets certain minimum requirements.[235]

Each of these legislative responses has attempted to balance First Amendment concerns with the requirements of state constitutional provisions. Although federal law has been characterized as banning direct aid to religious schools,[236] new developments in that law now emphasize private choice in a way that might indirectly benefit those schools.[237] State provisions have been interpreted to ban direct aid, but some now argue that their text, which is often ambiguous, can permit tax credits,[238] insubstantial aid, or aid financed through private choice.[239]

At first glance, those states adopting lockstep analysis or holding their religious liberty clauses coextensive with federal law would suggest little distinction from their federal counterpart. For example, one Illinois court upheld a $500 tax credit, available to all parents regardless of their children's choice of public or private school, under what an Illinois court called persuasive federal analysis.[240] Ironically, the court's decision to follow the federal lead on this issue betrays a weakness of state jurisprudence that will continue to foster some uncertainty about the exact meaning of the state constitutional provisions. First, the court reserved the right to analyze the state constitution as an independent document, but then it held that for purposes of religious liberty protection, it would follow in lockstep with the federal lead.[241] Second, when Illinois adopted a new constitution in 1970, the constitutional convention reviewed several proposals to change the religious liberty language, including one that mirrored the language of the federal First Amendment. The committee responsible for dealing with the issue ultimately decided to make no change from the 1870 language, confessing a fear that any

---

230. Jackson v. Benson, 578 N.W.2d 602, 608–09 (Wis. 1998).
231. *Simmons-Harris*, 711 N.E.2d at 211.
232. Bagley v. Raymond Sch. Dept., 728 A.2d 127 (Me. 1999).
233. *Kotterman*, 972 P.2d 606.
234. *Chittenden*, 738 A.2d at 548.
235. Toney v. Bower, 744 N.E.2d 351 (Ill. App. Ct. 2001).
236. *See* Carmella, *supra* note 2, at 95.
237. *See* Thomas C. Berg, "Religiously Affiliated Education," in this volume; Zelman v. Simmons-Harris, 122 S. Ct. 2460 (2002); Mitchell v. Helms, 120 S. Ct. at 2552.
238. *Toney*, 744 N.E.2d at 363.
239. *See, e.g.,* Commonwealth v. School Comm. of Springfield, 417 N.E.2d 408 (Mass. 1981) (test for state constitutionality includes whether aid is substantial) *Id.* at 416. *See also* Minn. Fed. of Teachers v. Mammenga, 500 N.W. 2d 136 (Minn. Ct. App. 1993), where the court held that even though the free exercise equivalent of the Minnesota constitution provided a higher protection than the federal law, the Establishment Clause equivalent argument was not persuasive, and that indirect and incidental aid even to a "pervasively sectarian" university was therefore constitutional. *Id.* at 138.
240. *Toney*, 744 N.E.2d at 360; *accord*, Griffith v. Bower, 747 N.E.2d 423 (Ill. App. Ct. 2001).
241. *Toney*, 744 N.E.2d at 359–60.

change could encourage erroneous interpretations by the courts and greater uncertainty about the balance between the state and religion. Instead, the committee and the convention decided that the 1870 language was sufficient because it followed federal Establishment Clause law.[242] Thirty years later, litigants still challenge whether this doctrine means that the convention chose to mirror Establishment Clause law as it was at the time of its adoption in 1870, as it was in 1970, or as it has since been viewed with every change in federal interpretation. In *Toney v. Bower,* the court held that Illinois would continue to follow this lockstep doctrine even as federal law shifted.[243] Given the many transformations and multiple tests developed by the U.S. Supreme Court over the last half century, especially with regard to public funding of religious education, the *Toney* holding suggests that Illinois will frequently need to respond with adjustments in its interpretations of the relevant laws. *Toney*'s clarification reveals a court abdicating its responsibility to independently interpret its own state constitution.[244]

Even when purporting to engage in dual analysis, some courts find federal analysis powerfully persuasive in interpreting state clauses. The Wisconsin Supreme Court has held that although its state constitutional language is more terse and explicit than the Establishment Clause, both documents share the same purpose. Therefore according to the court, the two are coextensive.[245] The court analyzed the funding plan under both the Establishment Clause and the state constitution. Under the Establishment Clause, the court found that the Milwaukee plan was facially similar "in all significant aspects" to the Washington state educational plan upheld in *Witters,* pointing out that in that case, the U.S. Supreme Court did not find it unconstitutional to provide neutral aid to students who might pursue education in a religious institution.[246] Surprisingly, when it proceeded to examine the Wisconsin constitution, the Wisconsin Supreme Court never acknowledged that on remand, its sister state court had interpreted the Washington constitution more strictly than it had the federal Constitution in denying aid to Larry Witters. Instead, the Wisconsin court held that the Milwaukee aid plan violated neither the "benefits clause" nor the "compelled support clause" of Article I, section 18 of the Wisconsin constitution.[247]

---

242. *See* 1970 Illinois Constitutional Convention, Report of the Education Committee; *see also* Board of Educ. v. Bakalis, 299 N.E.2d 737, 744–45 (Ill. 1973).

243. *Toney,* 744 N.E.2d at 360. *See also* Virginia College Building Authority v. Lynn, 538 S.E.2d 682, 691 (Va. 2000) (recognizing that "the Establishment Clause landscape is ever changing" but continues to be informed by United States Supreme Court Establishment Clause Jurisprudence in construction of state constitutions).

244. *See, e.g.,* Carmella, *supra* note 2, at 316.

245. Jackson v. Benson, 578 N.W.2d 602, 621 (Wis. 1998). *But compare* Holmes v. Bush, 2002 WL 1809079, at *2 n.5 (Fla. Dist. Ct. Aug. 5, 2002).

246. *Id.* at 615, n. 11.

247. *Id.* at 620. Wis. Const. art. I, Sec. 18 provides that:
The right of every person to worship Almighty God according to the dictates of conscience shall never be infringed; nor shall any person be compelled to attend, erect or support any place of worship, or to maintain any ministry, without consent; nor shall any control of or interference with, the rights of conscience be permitted, or any preference be given by law to any religious establishments or modes of worship; nor shall any money be drawn from the treasury for the benefit of religious societies, or religious or theological seminaries.

In *Witters,* the Washington court construed its constitution's Article I, section 11, which provides in part that "no public money or property shall be appropriated for or applied to any religious worship, exercise or instruction, or the support of any religious establishment"—language that, although not identical, is similar to Wisconsin's benefits clause. *Witters,* 771 P.2d at 1121.

Similarly, the Ohio Supreme Court reserved the right to examine its state constitution independently, thus leaving open the possibility of a distinct jurisprudence. Nonetheless, it held the federal *Lemon* three-part test both "logical and reasonable" as the interpretive tool in evaluating the Ohio religious funding provision. It held that a public scholarship program for Ohio children attending religious schools did not violate that provision, but it nonetheless rejected the plan as a violation of another Ohio constitutional clause requiring all legislative acts to be limited to one subject. The U.S. Supreme Court, in *Zelman v. Simmons-Harris*, upheld the plan under the Establishment Clause after noting that the Ohio legislature had repaired the procedural defect.[248]

Differing results in Vermont and Arizona suggest some of the possibilities of state constitutional jurisprudence on school funding issues. Vermont's jurisprudence highlights a particular state approach to these funding issues while simultaneously portending that state law may not be significantly different from federal law.[249] Vermont's state legislature permitted school districts to offer financial support to parents sending their children to private schools instead of requiring costly high school buildings in sparsely populated areas where they were not required. In a 1994 decision, the Vermont Supreme Court had held this educational plan constitutional under the First Amendment,[250] but subsequently in *Chittenden* it held the same plan unconstitutional under the Vermont constitution's equivalent provisions.[251] Holding that it had an obligation to interpret its own "fundamental charter" as a "free standing document," the court also looked to the state's history of experimenting with religious education and public funding. Although early on the state had taxed its citizens for religious education, it also had granted exemptions for those whose religious beliefs forbade them from supporting the classrooms of other denominations. With the growth of new religions and the recognition of the rights of nonreligious citizens, the exemptions no longer worked—so Vermont had amended its constitution to read in part that no one "ought to, or of right can be compelled to attend any religious worship, or erect or support any place of worship, or maintain any minister contrary to the dictates of conscience."[252] The Vermont court stressed that this all had occurred prior to the anti-Catholic rhetoric and Blaine amendments that other states adopted.[253] Vermont's commitment to republican government had led it to combine strict protection of free exercise with a bar to any funds or support for religious education.[254] The court also stressed, however, that the act suffered from a lack of legislative safeguards against commingling of funds for religious use, and suggested that a legislative fix could alter this provision to allow such indirect funding of religious education.[255]

---

248. *Zelman*, 122 S. Ct. at 2465. *Simmons-Harris*, 711 N.E.2d at 216. Coextensivity does not automatically lead to funding of religious education under a plan that would otherwise deny funds for private religious education; the Maine Supreme Court resolved its funding issue without even looking to the Maine constitution, noting that the federal and state rights were "coextensive." Bagley v. Raymond Sch. Dist., 728 A.2d 127, 132 (Me. 1999).

249. *Chittenden*, 738 A.2d 539.

250. Campbell v. Manchester Bd. of Sch. Directors, 641 A.2d 352 (Vt. 1994).

251. *Chittenden*, 738 A.2d at 546. *See also* Asociacion de Maestros de Puerto Rico v. Torres, 1994 WL 780744 at 9 (P.R. Nov. 30, 1994) (Puerto Rico also read its constitutional language more strictly than its federal counterpart, invalidating a legislative incentive of $1,500 that had been intended to encourage transfers of students from one school to another, including private religious schools).

252. Vt. Const., ch. I, art. 3. *Chittenden*, 738 A.2d at 553–4.

253. *Chittenden*, 738 A.2d at 558.

254. *Id*. at 552.

255. *Id*. at 562–63. The court stressed that its greatest concern was the commingling of funds between educational goals and religious goals. *See also* Opinion of the Justices (Choice in Educ.),

In contrast, after reviewing the ratification history of the Arizona state constitution, the *Kotterman* court refused to speculate whether the constitution's drafters had intended a more "stringent prohibition against aid than had their federal counterparts."[256] Indeed, despite constitutional language stating that "no public money or property shall be appropriated for or applied to any religious worship, exercise, or instruction, or to the support of any religious establishment,"[257] the court held that the $500 tax credit was neither public money nor a tax, thus upholding the legislation.[258] The court found no evidence that the citizens of Arizona had ever "intended to divorce completely any hint of religion from all conceivably state-related functions, nor would such a goal be realistically attainable in today's world."[259]

While upholding a tax credit under textual analysis, the *Kotterman* court recognized, in dicta, the impact of the *Blaine*-type amendments in Arizona and many of the western states.[260] Although the court acknowledged that these amendments were grounded in religious bigotry, it found no historical evidence that such sentiments had found their way into the Arizona constitution.[261] Instead, the delegates to Arizona's 1919 constitutional convention had borrowed language from other states such as Washington, Oregon, Texas, and Oklahoma.[262] *Kotterman* illuminates how even when constitutional texts are similar, distinctive state histories and cultures infuse them with different meanings. The *Kotterman* court then distinguished cases in Washington that relied on similar provisions that had held public funding of religious schools unconstitutional.[263] In contrast, a Massachusetts court pointed to that state's particular history prior to the *Blaine* controversies, yet still found that its constitution's drafters had attempted to avoid religious divisiveness by adopting text that precluded public funding of any religious institution.[264] These cases reveal how peoples with different heritages and approaches to religious liberty can define institutional autonomy differently. When taken seriously, these questions can add to the investigation of appropriate balance between religious institutional autonomy and government regulation.

---

616 A.2d 478, 480 (N.H. 1992) (holding a reimbursement plan unconstitutional under the New Hampshire constitution because "no safeguards exist to prevent the application of public funds to sectarian uses"). *Id.* at 480.

256. *Kotterman*, 972 P.2d at 624.

257. *Id.* at 617, *citing* Ariz. Const. art. II, sec. 12.

258. *Id.* at 625. *But see* Opinion of the Justices to the Senate, 514 N.E.2d 353 (Mass. 1987) (tax deduction is a "practical equivalent of direct governmental grant" and thus unconstitutional under the Massachusetts constitution). *Id.* at 355.

259. *Kotterman*, 972 P.2d at 623.

260. *Id.* at 624–5.

261. *Id.*

262. *Id.*

263. *Id.* at 624–5. *Kotterman* also reveals the ongoing difficulty of apprehending original meaning. The majority opinion details an understanding of the history and culture of Arizona considerably different from that in the dissenting opinion. The majority claims that it cannot speculate on the meager history of ratification. *Id.* at 624. The dissent strenuously details Arizona's history in arguing that the state's provision in Article II, section 12 that "no public money...shall be applied to any religious worship, exercise, or instruction or to the support of any religious establishment" contains a stringent proscription on educational aid (Feldman, J., dissenting, at 631).

264. Commonwealth v. School Comm. of Springfield, 417 N.E.2d 408, 418 (Mass. 1981). Alleged *Blaine*-type bias in the adoption of state constitutional language, citizens sought a referendum to change Massachusetts' no-aid provision. The state attorney general refused to place the initiative on the ballot. Citizens then filed a federal lawsuit. Andrea Estes, Federal Court Asked to Support Ballot on School Vouchers, Boston Herald, May 4, 2000, available in 2000 WL 4324163, *cited in* Church & State, June 2000.

Notwithstanding distinctive textual provisions, the structure of particular educational ministries has not been a significant issue in state constitutional law. For example, a footnote in *Jackson* minimized an argument regarding the structure issue, concluding that the lower court had improperly raised the question of whether religious schools were necessarily seminaries and thus subject to the constitutional ban on funds.[265] The supreme court stated that the lower court would instead have been correct to question the indirect benefit the schools received from student enrollment. By linking its state analysis to Establishment Clause jurisprudence, the *Jackson* court held that this plan did not violate the state constitution. In *Chittenden,* the court refused to distinguish between religious education and religious worship — the latter subject to a ban on public funding — and thus banned funds for both.[266]

The particularity of state language may also mitigate the need to distinguish one type of ministry from another. In *Witters,* for example, the Washington court noted that its constitution specifically prohibited funding for "worship, exercise, or instruction."[267] On the other hand, the specificity of anti-aid language forces some courts to find religious activities secular, and thus eligible for public funds.[268] But the reality remains that despite this history, state constitutions have not provided many distinctive approaches to determining the constitutionality of public funding of religious education.

The nation's experiment

Notwithstanding the uniqueness of state constitutional texts, national jurisprudence and experience still heavily influence state adjudication. The national experiment may reveal the overwhelming influence of factors that militate against a distinct state jurisprudence. As revolutionary and imaginative as republican political theory was in influencing state constitutional development during the colonial period and the early years of the republic, that theory had lost much of its force by the time the Federalists had triumphed and the Constitution was adopted.[269] Moreover, some suggest that rights embedded in the Constitution are so fundamental that they must not be subject to diverse interpretations in the various states.[270] With the U.S. Supreme Court's incorporation doctrine, federal law took on an increased significance — especially during the years when the activist Warren court was perceived to be actually fleshing out new con-

---

265. The court addressed the structure issue at the heart of this book, noting that when the 1848 constitution was adopted, the word "seminaries" was "synonymous with academies or schools.... Sectarian private schools, therefore, constitute 'religious seminaries' within the meaning of art. I, § 18." *Jackson v. Benson,* 578 N.W.2d at 621 (citations omitted).

266. *Chittenden,* 738 A.2d at 562. *See also Virginia College,* 538 S.E.2d at 689 (theological education held as preparing students in a vocation associated with ordination as opposed to preparing them for secular vocation).

267. *Witters,* 771 P.2d at 1121.

268. *Compare Malyon,* 935 P.2d 1272. *See, e.g.,* Saucier v. Employment Security Dept. of the State of Washington, 954 P.2d 285, 288 (Wash. Ct. App. 1998); Needham Pastoral Counseling Ctr. v. Needham, 557 N.E.2d 43, 47 (Mass. App. Ct. 1990); *see also* Frederick Mark Gedicks, The Rhetoric of Church and State: A Critical Analysis of Religion Clause Jurisprudence 75–80 (1995), *citing* Mark V. Tushnet, Of Church and State and the Supreme Court: Kurland Revisited, 1989 Sup. Ct. Rev. 373, 399; *see also* Curry, *supra* note 40, at 92 suggesting that religious institutions should have a choice in accepting aid and increased government regulation for secular work.

269. *See* Lutz, *supra* note 49, at 171–72; Wood, *supra* note 58, at 229–30.

270. For the power of the federal Constitution, *see, e.g.,* Williams, *supra* note 126, at 165.

stitutional rights.[271] Moreover, the increasing influence of federal educational policy, regulations, and funding assistance fuels the perception that the federal government can sway the ideological and cultural battles that occur in the schools. Other practical reasons drive federal understandings of state constitutional rights. The cost of litigation in state courts encourages litigants to seek resolution at the federal level, thereby transforming local contests into potential platforms for national adjudication.[272] Similarly, national religious denominations may seek to protect their institutional rights and limit the expense and unpredictability of litigating under the multiple standards of various states by instead seeking federal legal action.[273]

Another new trend also tends to favor national interpretations of these local issues. As Robert Wuthnow reports, among the fastest growing elements of religion in the United States are national organizations that are independent of denominations but tied to issues or causes that might find favor with a specific denomination or faith tradition.[274] Moreover, national advocacy organizations have spearheaded research and litigation to influence national policy.[275] Although these recent education funding cases all involve specific state laws, many of the litigants and *amici* represent nongovernmental agencies with national membership.[276] Certainly, all have their right to persuade the courts, and all contribute to the experimentation with ways to fund education for the nation's children. Yet the increased national focus on these state cases must somehow gradually diminish the particularity of state responses to religious liberty. These na-

271. *See id.* at 165, noting that many jurists and practitioners came of age when the Supreme Court was recognizing new rights, thereby adding a powerful federal impetus for change of both federal and state law.

272. *See, e.g.,* Douglas Laycock, Summary and Synthesis: The Crisis in Religious Liberty, 60 Geo. Wash. L. Rev. 841, 854 (1992). The Ohio voucher litigation discussed in the text at footnote 248 reveals some of these problems of multiple court proceedings and federal resolution of issues. The dispute was also litigated in federal court. Simmons-Harris v. Zelman, 234 F.3d 945 (6th Cir. 2001), *rev'd* Zelman v. Simmons-Harris, 122 S.Ct. 2460 (2002). Thomas C. Berg discusses the Supreme Court decision in his appendix to his chapter "Religiously Affiliated Education" in this volume. Because the state court had dismissed the case based on a violation of the Ohio constitution's one-subject rule, that decision could not bar federal litigation on the Establishment Clause. *Simmons-Harris,* 234 F.3d at 961.

273. *Id.* at 854.

274. Robert Wuthnow, The Restructuring of American Religion, Society and Faith Since World War II (1988) 101–108.

275. *See* Martha Minow, Partners, Not Rivals?: Redrawing the Lines Between Public and Private, Non-Profit and Profit, and Secular and Religious, 80 B.U. L. Rev. 1061, 1077 (2000). *See also* Wuthnow, *supra* note 274, at 114 ("special interests have arisen for the express purpose of combating, restraining, or promoting certain types of governmental action").

276. The Wisconsin suit finds groups such as People for the American Way, Christian Legal Society, American Jewish Congress, Family Research Institute, Americans United for Separation of Church and State, Maine School Choice Coalition, and Arkansas Policy Foundation listed as parties or *amici. Jackson v. Benson,* 578 N.W.2d at 605–606. In Arizona, the Institute for Justice, Washington DC, People for the American Way, and Americans United for Separation of Church and State, among others, participated in that suit. *Kotterman,* 972 P.2d at 609. Similarly, in Vermont the National Committee for Public Education & Religious Liberty filed an amicus brief while the Institute for Justice represented the school district that wanted to fund the religious schools. *Chittenden,* 738 A.2d at 541. In Ohio, the state issue was contested by such groups as the Rutherford Institute, the Beckett Fund for Religious Liberty, the National Jewish Commission on Law and Public Affairs, Agudath Harabonim of the United States and Canada, the Institute for Public Affairs, the Union of Orthodox Jewish Congregations of America, the North Carolina Education Reform Foundation, and the National Committee for Public Education & Religious Liberty. *Simmons-Harris,* 711 N.E.2d at 206. *See also* Virginia College Building Authority v. Lynn, 538 S.E.2d 682, 684 (Va. 2000).

tional legal forces, federalism and national advocacy, may be at work furthering the weakening of distinctive state protections.

Other factors, however, suggest the need to continue exploring religious liberty issues in this national experiment. With changes and developments in the ongoing struggle between Congress and the Supreme Court to define religious liberty, federal uncertainty certainly fails to provide a strong benchmark worthy of emulation throughout the land. Litigants may waive potential state constitutional protection if they fail to raise the appropriate state constitutional issues, especially if state text and history suggest room for an independent law.[277]

The particular way in which state constitutions tend to address the issue of state funding raises a more important question with regard to the freedom of religious institutions to educate youth. Critical to any ultimate understanding of the autonomy of religious institutions is the question of freedom itself. The question Robin Lovin asked with regard to individual human freedom—whether "the nature of human freedom has to come prior to the question of the legal status of religious freedom"—is one worth asking with regard to institutional autonomy as well.[278] Definitions of freedom conflict with each other in state constitutional litigation over funding issues. The classic republican understanding of funding led to early state clauses banning all aid to religious institutions and related educational ministries. The drafters of state constitutions sought to combine strict protection of a wide variety of religious activities with a high wall of separation preventing taxes or public funds from aiding any religious institutions.[279] Experiments with funding religious schools in the New England colonies and later in the states, complete with exemptions for those who did not want their tax monies supporting worship, led to this high level of free exercise protection balanced with prohibitions against public funding. In the contemporary environment, however, few religious institutions seeking to support education would perceive their freedom to be enhanced by the prohibition of funding.[280] Nonetheless, arguments that such prohibitions on funding derive simply from *Blaine*-type amendments miss this complex, three-hundred-year history of colonial and state constitutions.[281] Only by developing new understandings of religious freedom in light of that history will state constitutions provide a clear path to greater autonomy.

For example, this republican theory grew out of the particular challenge of emphasizing individual freedom while simultaneously anticipating that individuals would form voluntary associations to further their personal and communal goals. These associations provide a place for individuals to differentiate themselves from the greater society in order to pursue their own development.[282] Religious voluntary associations,

---

277. *See, e.g.*, Swanson v. Guthrie Indep. Sch. Dist. No. I-L, 135 F.3d 694 (10th Cir. 1998) (finding the raising of the issue of stricter state constitutional protection at the appeals level to be confusing and inadequate, thus causing the court to refuse to address the issue). *See also* Laycock, *supra* note 272, at 854 (it may be malpractice not to raise a state constitutional issue in a religious case).

278. Robin Lovin, What Kind of Freedom Does Religion Need?, 42 DePaul L. Rev. 311, 316 (1992). *See also* Ira C. Lupu and Robert Tuttle, The Distinctive Place of Religious Entities in Our Constitutional Order, 47 Vill. L. Rev. 37 (2002).

279. *See, e.g.*, Locke v. Davey, 540 U.S. at 723. Society of Separationists v. Whitehead, 870 P.2d 916, 934 (Utah 1993). *Accord*, *Chittenden*, 738 A.2d at 552.

280. *See, e.g.*, Jackson v. Benson, 578 N.W.2d 602, 605–606 (Wis. 1998).

281. In *Locke v. Davey*, anti-Catholic animus based on *Blaine*-type amendments was raised, but the Court failed to find in the record before it sufficient evidence to "establish a credible connection between the Blaine Amendment and... the relevant [state] constitutional provision." *Id.* at 723, n.7.

282. James Luther Adams, The Voluntary Principle in the Forming of American Religion, *in* Voluntary Associations, Socio-Cultural Analyses and Theological Interpretations, ed. J. Ronald

moreover, frequently welcome the power of the transcendent to further this freedom.[283] As discussed above, development of state constitutional theory has often recognized the transcendent element of religion in society.[284] Scholars such as John Courtney Murray have argued the critical importance of religious liberty not only for individuals but for the institutions that forge conscience and give expression to faith.[285] These religious communities provide the alternative voice not expressed in the culture at large.[286] Trends in federal jurisprudence noted elsewhere in this book treat religious institutions similarly to other not-for-profit organizations.[287] Sociological trends suggest similar cultural forces at work.[288] A federal jurisprudence that limits the questions of religious freedom to neutrality may show little concern for small minority religious institutions. All these forces, moreover, ignore the transcendent aspect of many religious institutions.

Without a distinctive state jurisprudence, religious freedom may lose much of its vitality. The roots of state constitutional law embody, at the very least, a recognition of the transcendence and sovereignty of God that stands in contrast to contemporary trends toward neutrality. One must recognize Marshall's concerns about religious interference in civil life, but also agree with him that the distinctive religious voice needs to be heard in civil discourse.[289] Although it remains difficult to articulate, it cannot be ignored.[290] A full development of the protections embedded in state constitutions suggests greater potential for institutional protection than has been developed to date.[291]

Moreover, national denominations may not reflect all of the issues faced by their constituents or congregations in a large part of national religious life. More than half of

---

Engel 173 (1986) stating that "freedom of association, viewed as a social function in the open society, represents a dynamic institutional force for social change or for resistance to it. As such, the voluntary association brings about differentiation in the community, as a separation of powers." *Id.* at 173. *See also* Stephen Warner, *supra* note 13, at 71 (the "congregation is one of the few places in our society where the oppressed can predictably find encouragement").

283. As W. Cole Durham, Jr., and Elizabeth A. Sewell note in their chapter, "Definition of Religion," in this volume, protecting religious freedom requires protecting more than only those religions that recognize transcendence in worship and belief. Nonetheless, transcendence as a part of many religious traditions cannot be ignored in understanding and protecting religious liberty in the United States. *See also* Carl S. Dudley & David Roozen, A Report on Religion in the United States Today (March 2001) http://fact.hartsem.edu/executive_summary.htm.

284. *See* text at footnotes 35–38, *supra*.

285. John Courtney Murray, We Hold These Truths: Catholic Reflections on the American Proposition (1960); Robin Lovin, Freedom and Religion: A Late-Century Appreciation of the Work of John Courtney Murray, *in* John Courtney Murray & The Growth of Tradition 177 (1997).

286. Lovin, *supra* note 285, at 178, 181. *See also* Adams, *supra* note 282, at 173.

287. *See* Thomas C. Berg, "Religious Structures Under the Federal Constitution," Thomas C. Berg, "Religiously Affiliated Education," Angela C. Carmella, "Land Use Regulation of Churches," and Rhys H. Williams & John P.N. Massad, "Religious Diversity, Civil Law, and Institutional Isomorphism," in this volume. *See* Lupu and Tuttle, *supra* note 278.

288. *See* Stephen Warner, *supra* note 13, at 74. This is not new. James Luther Adams has noted that historically, small sects have become larger institutions, ultimately becoming denominations and losing some of the energy and freedom associated with smaller sects. Adams, *supra* note 282, at 182. *See also* Wuthnow, *supra* note 274, at 85–87.

289. *See* William P. Marshall, "Constitutional Coherence and the Legal Structure of American Churches," in this volume.

290. *See* John Noonan, Religious Liberty at the Stake, 84 Va. L. Rev. 459, 460 (1998); Lovin, *supra* note 285, at 178, 181; Carl E. Esbeck, "The American System of Church-State Relations," in Gerhard Robbers, ed., Church Autonomy: A Comparative Survey 174 (2001); Hartigan, *supra* note 203, at 261, *citing* Walter Lippman that "the law and the republic were in desperate need of reconnection with the Ultimate." *Compare* Smith, *supra* note 35.

291. *See* Carmella, *supra* note 2, at 314. *But see* Conkle, *supra* note 3, at 118, n. 120.

the congregations in this land have less than one hundred members.[292] Stephen Warner worries that local congregations face legal and practical pressures that may harm their futures more than those of national denominations.[293] States amend their constitutions more frequently than the federal Constitution, thus permitting swifter response to minority religions. Admittedly, this might lead to greater restrictions, but the very process of state constitutional amendment and law enactment, combined with the intent to encourage voluntary institutions in accordance with republican theory, may increase the potential for greater congregational autonomy.[294] The proximity of state constitutions to the local community, which enables interpretation of state constitutions in response to specific problems within the state, also invites alternative approaches[295] to pluralism and changed circumstances of life.

Conclusion

However great the potential for a distinctive state constitutional jurisprudence in the arena of religious liberty may once have seemed, the current results surely belittle those dreams. The proponents of new federalism had hoped that increased attention to state constitutions would result in expanded judicial interpretations of religious liberty, but for the most part those hopes have been undercut. By reconciling apparent differences and seeking narrow theories that resolve incongruities, law requires litigants to present courts with theories that harmonize. Moreover, the success of particular theories in court provides the tools that lawyers employ to succeed in the next argument. State constitutional drafters have already demonstrated a remarkable ability to share language, experiences, and jurisprudence.[296] This mimesis further undermines the distinctiveness of state constitutional language. Federalism, with its emphasis on Supreme Court decisions, the nationalizing consequences of the Fourteenth Amendment, and a core constitutional jurisprudence, also tends to promote a common nationwide understanding.[297] To some extent, the states serve as laboratories that give the Supreme Court data to use in discerning the impact of constitutional holdings.[298] With the growth of national denominations and national advocacy groups, these forces only accelerate.[299]

This book considers the need for a particular jurisprudence that recognizes the self-understanding of religious institutions. Given the uncertainty of federal developments, state constitutions offer a non-federal option to the debate over possibilities that exist under the First Amendment. Religious institutions seeking distinctive autonomy for self-

---

292. *See* Dudley, *supra* note 283, at 8.

293. Warner, *supra* note 13, at 58.

294. *See* footnotes 201–202 and text regarding the state RFRA enactments. *See also* Carmella, *supra* note 2, at 314.

295. *See* Tarr, *supra* note 2, at 76.

296. *See* Linde, First Things First, *supra* note 3, at 381.

297. *Id.* at 382, 392; Williams, *supra* note 126, at 165.

298. *See, e.g,* School Dist. of Abington Twnshp. v. Schempp, 374 U.S. 203 (1963).

299. Certainly national denominations following the call of their sacred traditions and doctrine deserve full religious liberty. There are advantages to operating religious institutions in fifty states under a standard federal law of religious liberty. But should they not also recognize the potential loss that could result from homogenizing and standardizing one law of religious liberty in all fifty states?

governance continue to investigate religious liberty under state constitutions. At the very least, state constitutional experimentation may provide an alternative debate on neutrality and private choice, on government funding and institutional freedom, and on state support for goals that converge with the aims of religious institutions to worship in community, to educate and train their leadership, and to further the ministries that feed the hungry, clothe the naked, house the homeless, and pastor to the imprisoned.

Section II

Legal Structuring of Religious Institutions

W. Cole Durham, Jr.

The chapters in this section explore the fundamental legal structures available to religious institutions in the American setting. They address unincorporated associations, trusts, corporations of various types, and resolution of disputes regarding property held by religious communities through such structures. Further, in the increasingly complex setting of the modern welfare state, the final chapter examines the complex impact modern laws and regulations have on organizational decisions that religious institutions must make in structuring their affairs, particularly where state funding is involved.

These chapters constitute the essential starting point for analysis of the fundamental questions that gave rise to this volume in the first place. Are the *legal* structures available to religious communities sufficiently flexible to facilitate full and free expression of the religious freedom of individuals and religious communities, including providing a satisfactory fit for the varying *religious* structures that characterize diverse religious communities?[1] Are the laws that establish the various types of legal entities, and that govern access to various types of entity status, sufficiently supple to accommodate the increasingly diverse range of religious institutions and beliefs that are found in contemporary America? Are there features of the various legal structures which create unnecessary constraints on religious life? Are laws based on unwitting assumptions about the nature of religious beliefs and ecclesiology that benefit some to the detriment of others? None of these questions can be addressed without an accurate picture of the standard organizational forms the law provides and the nature of the regulatory environment in which religious communities find themselves.

It is important to note at the outset that in fundamental respects, these questions are different from those which typically arise in constitutional settings where the issue is whether the state may restrict free exercise or affirmatively support the establishment of religion. One is dealing here with the broad intermediate region where the aim is not to control or determine action but to provide the necessary mechanisms or facilities for religious communities to carry out their affairs.[2] Like the law of contracts, it is

---

1. *See* Rhys H. Williams and John P.N. Massad, "Religious Diversity, Civil Law, and Institutional Isomorphism," in this volume, text accompanying notes 2–3, for further discussion of the legal structures/religious structures distinction.

2. In a chapter on "The Variety of Laws," H.L.A. Hart notes the basic distinction between laws constituting orders backed by coercive sanctions and "[l]egal rules defining the ways in which valid contracts or wills or marriages are made." The latter "provide individuals with *facilities* for realizing

an area in which the relevant body of law is not aimed essentially at controlling or sub-sidizing individual or group action, but at simply providing the legal mechanisms people can use to structure their own affairs. Certain aspects of this body of law may be designed to prevent abuses of religious freedom, but fundamentally it is designed to facilitate rather than to impede the religious activity that is chosen by religious individuals and communities.

With that in mind, it is not enough to ask whether the available structures avoid causing infringements of religious freedom under current constitutional tests. The question of whether legal structures are sufficiently flexible to accommodate the full range of religious expression is motivated by concern for religious freedom, but it is not exhausted by the question of whether those structures can pass constitutional muster. Constitutional norms set minimum standards; the law of religious associations should ideally be more accommodating, more facilitative, and less bureaucratic. In the hierarchy of state norms, the law of religious associations is naturally thought of as a kind of "sub-constitutional law," or as second-order "implementing norms" that "revolve in constitutional orbits."[3] It is perhaps better to think of it as a body of law built on constitutional foundations and designed to give human beings the legal tools and materials they need to engage freely in the architecture of the life of the spirit.

In fact, the legal mechanisms described in this section are well designed for facilitating religious freedom. We have come to take institutions such as trusts and religious corporations for granted, and indeed tend to think of these devices as part of the mundane mechanics or religious life—a kind of legal infrastructure lacking the richness of religious life and the glamour of the pursuit of religious freedom through constitutional adjudication. But in fact the mechanisms themselves and the administrative and judicial practices in which they are embedded are part of common law and constitutional traditions that have proven themselves integral to the protection of religious autonomy.

As can be demonstrated by a contrast with religious association law in Europe, the legal evolution in the United States could have taken a very different turn. Traditions that used the antecedents of modern religious association law to control or privilege religious communities hung on much longer in Europe than in this country. Needless to say, such laws had a particularly restrictive tenor in countries subject to communist rule. Simple statutory features, such as requiring identification of what we would call the "incorporators," could be used to mark individuals for discrimination or persecution. Bureaucratic obstruction at the stage of seeking legal-entity status gave the state powerful controls over religious groups and over whether their religions could be practiced. Following what are now long-standing patterns of religious freedom in western

---

their wishes, by conferring legal powers on them to create, by certain specified procedures and subject to certain conditions, structures of rights and duties within the coercive framework of the law." H.L.A. Hart, The Concept of Law 27 (1961) (emphasis original). Hart characterizes this facilitative power as "one of the great contributions of law to social life...." *Id.* at 28.

3. The reference here is to Ira C. Lupu, Statutes Revolving in Constitutional Law Orbits, 79 Va. L. Rev. 1 (1993). Lupu used the phrase to designate a more specialized class of statutes, but particularly since laws in many countries include rules governing access to legal entity status in laws implementing constitutional norms on religious freedom, the reference seems apt. For examples of such laws, *see generally* W. Cole Durham, Jr. and Silvio Ferrari, eds., Laws on Religion and the State in Post-Communist Europe (Leuven: Peeters Publishers, 2004).

Europe,[4] religious association law in former socialist bloc countries has undergone a major transformation in a positive direction since the collapse of communism in the early 1990s. But even now, the older "control mentality" dies hard. In the post-socialist world, religious association law too often continues to be understood as a mechanism for asserting state influence in religious life,[5] for obstructing "new entrants" in the religious environment,[6] for entrenching existing religious traditions and privileges,[7] and in general for asserting a stronger measure of state control with respect to religion.[8] Such

---

4. For a useful overview of the religious association laws of Western Europe, see Gerhard Robbers, ed., State and Church in the European Union (Baden-Baden: Nomos Verlagsgesellschaft, 1996).

5. For example, provisions in religious association law are sometimes taken as an invitation to engage in substantive review of the nature and organization of religious bodies with distinctive organizational characteristics. In general, the intensity and duration of review of proposed charters or statutes of new religious organizations (counterparts to articles of incorporation) reflects inappropriate assumptions about the legitimacy of intervention in religious affairs.

6. Whatever ostensible rationales may be given, obstruction of new entrants appears to be the primary motivation of lengthy presence-in-country requirements, such as the problematic fifteen-year rule in Russia, Law on Freedom of Conscience and on Religious Associations, Section 9 (1997), or excessive minimum-member requirements in a number of other countries. While most OSCE countries require fifteen or fewer members in order to register or incorporate a religious body, six now require substantially more. The highest requirement by far is Slovakia's requirement of twenty thousand. Registration of Churches and Religious Societies 192/1992 Act of the Slovak National Council dated 26 March, §2. Croatia recently adopted legislation setting the minimum-membership requirement at five hundred. Law on Legal Position of Religious Communities, July 4, 2002, art. 21. The Czech Republic now requires three hundred. Act No. 3/2002 of January 7, 2002 on the Freedom of Religious Expression and the Status of Churches and Religious Societies, section 10. Armenia requires two hundred. The Republic of Armenia Law on the Freedom of Conscience and on Religious Organization (17 June 1991), as amended 19 September 1997, art. 5(e). Hungary requires one hundred. Law on Freedom of Conscience and Religions as Well as Churches (Act No. IV of 1990), sec. 9. The Constitutional Court of the Former Yugoslav Republic of Macedonia recently struck down a legislative provision setting fifty adults as the minimum necessary for recognition of a religious association. Decision of the Macedonian Constitutional Court of Dec. 23–24, 1998. Similarly, the Constitutional Council in Kazakhstan has struck down a law including a minimum-member requirement of fifty. Constitutional Court of Kazakhstan, Decision of April 4, 2002. High minimum-member requirements of this type can be extremely problematic for smaller religious groups, particularly those that are organized on a congregational basis. In some areas, even well-established Protestant groups may have congregations of less than one hundred or even fifty members; the number of adults can be still less. High minimum-member requirements can prevent access to entity status, thereby substantially complicating practical challenges such as securing a place of worship.

7. Many countries afford a higher level of cooperation, often including financial support, to religious communities that have traditionally played a significant role in the country. A few examples are representative. Lithuanian law affords "traditional" religions favored treatment. Law on Religious Communities and Associations of the Republic of Latvia, Oct. 4, 1995, arts. 5–6. Particularly where Roman Catholicism has had a significant presence, countries often grant such heightened status through concordats or agreements with specified denominations. See Silvio Ferrari, The Emerging Pattern of Church and State in Western Europe: The Italian Model, 1995 B.Y.U. L. Rev. 421, 421. Austria has established a model that distinguishes "recognized churches," "confessional communities," and other religious groups. Federal Law Concerning the Legal Status of Religious Confessional Communities, January 9, 1998. Confessional communities can be promoted to the status of recognized churches after a wait of twenty years, provided they have a population of one one-thousandth of the total Austrian population. See id.; see generally Christopher J. Miner, Losing My Religion: Austria's New Religion Law in Light of International and European Standards of Religious Freedom, 1998 B.Y.U. L. Rev. 607.

8. See generally W. Cole Durham, Jr. & Lauren B. Homer, Russia's 1997 Law on Freedom of Conscience and Religious Associations: An Analytical Appraisal, 12 Emory Int'l L. Rev. 101 (1998);

vestiges of an older and more control-oriented approach to religion are inconsistent with contemporary European standards,[9] but they still tend to hang on in the crevices of legislation[10] and in unenlightened administrative practice.[11]

In contrast, as explored in greater depth by the chapters that follow, the common law tradition — particularly as it has evolved in the American context — has laid the foundation for a profound commitment to religious autonomy. The evolution of the law of trusts and religious corporations, coupled with the constitutional commitment to freedom of religion, have combined to energize a facilitative orientation toward religious entities in the United States.

The institution of the trust has played a significant role in this regard. Now taken for granted in the common law world, the trust is a unique institution that is essentially unknown in continental European legal systems, although many of its functions can be duplicated there using other legal devices.[12] As noted by Hansmann and Mattei, "[t]he Anglo-American concept of the trust, together with the equity jurisprudence of which it forms a part, are the fortuitous product of the peculiar historical path followed by English law."[13] Among its myriad uses has been the holding of religious property. This was made possible with the development of the idea of the charitable trust, which allowed trusts for a particular use or group, including religious uses or groups.[14]

One of the most significant contributions trust law has made to religious freedom may be that in effect it provided an early type of legal entity that could be created autonomously without securing state approval. That is, as a practical matter one of the most important features of a trust is that it "facilitates the partitioning of assets into

---

Silvio Ferrari and W. Cole Durham, Jr., eds., Church and State in Post-Communist Europe (Leuven: Peeters Publishers, 2004).

9. Interpreting the language of Article 11 of the European Convention (parallel to Article 22 in the ICCPR), the European Court of Human Rights has held that the right to association includes as an integral part the right to entity status, and that this applies to religious associations as well. See Freedom and Democracy Party (OZDEP) v. Turkey (No. 23885/94) (ECtHR, Decision of Dec. 8, 1999); United Communist Party of Turkey v. Turkey (ECtHR, Decision of 30 January 1998); Sidiropoulos & Others v. Greece (No. 26695/95) (ECtHR, Decision of 10 July 1998. That this reasoning extends to religious organizations is clear from several cases. See Canea Catholic Church v. Greece (No. 25528/94) 27 E.H.R.R. 521 (1999) (ECtHR, Dec. 16, 1997) (legal personality of Roman Catholic church protected); Hasan and Chaush v. Bulgaria (No. 30985/96) (ECtHR, Oct. 26, 2000) (interference with internal organization of Muslim community and managing of its affairs violates religious freedom, and decision on grounds of freedom of association was unnecessary because freedom-of-religion analysis was carried out in light of freedom-of-association requirements); Metropolitan Church of Bessarabia v. Moldova (No. 45701/99) (ECtHR, Dec. 13, 2001) (refusal to recognize Bessarabian Church constituted a violation of freedom of religion).

10. See generally Durham & Homer, supra note 8.

11. See generally Lauren B. Homer & Lawrence A. Uzzell, Federal and Provinvial Religious Freedom Laws in Russia: A Struggle For and Against Federalism and the Rule of Law, 12 Emory Int'l L. Rev. (1998) (noting a variety of problems emerging at local-level practice in Russia).

12. Technically, the trust emerged in equity rather than common law. There are canon law antecedents. See Helmholz, The Early Enforcement of Uses, 79 Col. L. Rev. 1503 (1979). Many of the key functions played by trusts can be arranged by contract or agency law. See Henry Hansmann & Hugo Mattei, Trust Law in the United States: A Basic Study of its Special Contribution, 46 Am. J. Comp. L. 133 (Supp. 1998) [hereinafter "Trust Law"]; Hansmann & Mattei, The Functions of Trust Law: A Comparative Legal and Economic Analysis, 73 NYU L. Rev. 434 (1998); John Langbein, The Contractarian Basis of the Law of Trusts, 105 Yale L.J. 625 (1995).

13. Hansmann & Mattei, Trust Law, supra note 12, at 134.

14. Paul G. Kauper and Stephen C. Ellis, Religious Corporations and the Law, 71 Mich. L. Rev. 1499, 1502 (1973).

bundles that can conveniently be pledged separately to different classes of creditors."[15] In effect, a trust functions as a legal entity with distinct legal personality that can be set up by private parties with no action of any kind by the state. A religious congregation could avoid the countless complexities that arise in attempting to hold property in an unincorporated association by conveying the property to one or more trustees, who can hold it for the benefit of the church or congregation. Similarly, the congregation could avoid the difficulties of trying to obtain a state charter, particularly from a sovereign espousing a different faith, by making use of the trust mechanism. In the religious arena, this has contributed to an expectation that private parties are free to set up autonomous entities for holding religious property and carrying out religious affairs. Of course, in the event of disagreements or other problems, parties have had to resort to courts to enforce their interests, but no formal state action has been required at the creation stage. This is in sharp contrast to European and early English treatment of religious associations.

The history of corporations or charters in the United States initially followed the English pattern, according to which a corporation could be established only with the express approval of the sovereign. In the colonial period, many church bodies were unable to secure the corporate privilege because this was reserved for the established church.[16] After the revolution, with the spirit of equalitarian democracy taking hold in the United States, the notion of a corporation as a grant of a special sovereign favor gradually led to the demise of this "special charter" conception of incorporation.[17] The old system of special charters and religious favoritism gave way to statutes that "granted corporate form to all bodies that could comply with certain minimal prerequisites."[18] If these requirements had been set very high, the simple trust mechanism could have been used in its stead. This no doubt contributed over time to the practice of making access to corporate status quite easy in general, and also contributed to the evolution toward simple, nondiscriminatory access to legal personality for religious bodies. The importance of these developments for religious freedom and autonomy can be fully appreciated only from the perspective of the contrasting experience in other countries, alluded to above, where acquisition of entity status is more difficult.

It is against this background that the chapters by Patricia B. Carlson on unincorporated associations and trusts and by Patty Gerstenblith on corporate structures must be understood. These chapters provide a comprehensive overview of the range of legal entities (and nonentities) that are available for religious communities to use in carrying out their affairs. They cover the types of entities that are available in various states, as well as the various factors that may affect a particular religious group's choice of entity.

One of the most significant findings of the empirical study analyzed in the earlier chapter by Rhys H. Williams and John P.N. Massad is that despite the broad range of legal mechanisms available, and despite the ever-growing diversity of religious communities in the United States, there is a strong convergence toward the use of religious corporations as the entity of choice among religious communities in this country. Eighty-seven percent of the religious organizations sampled use the religious corporation form.

---

15. Hansmann & Mattei, Trust Law, *supra* note 12, at 134.
16. Kauper & Ellis, *supra* note 14, at 1507.
17. *Id.* at 1509.
18. *Id.* at 1510.

A surprising eight percent are structured as unincorporated associations.[19] Only three percent indicated that they were organized as ordinary "not for profit" corporations. This would appear to reflect the fact that out of deference for religious freedom, laws that create separate status for "religious corporations" generally afford somewhat more favorable treatment for religious than for other public benefit corporations.[20] Only one percent of respondents indicated organization in each of the remaining categories: corporation sole, for-profit corporations, charitable or religious trusts, and other legal structures.[21]

Williams and Massad suggest that this convergence may reflect "institutional isomorphism"—a pattern of religious organizations succumbing to a conveniently available form. My own view is that legal evolution has resulted in the development of a *legal* structure that is sufficiently flexible that it in fact works for a very broad range of *religious* structures. Carlson's analysis of some of the limitations of the trust form helps explain the shift toward the religious corporation form. She notes that one of the major difficulties with the charitable trust is that it is difficult to change the purpose of the trust once it has been established.[22] If a religious corporation's purposes (as formally articulated in its articles of incorporation) are suitably broad, its board of directors or trustees can adapt its concrete objectives over time. This heightened autonomy, combined with greater insulation against personal liability, explains the much greater attractiveness of the corporate form. Adding in the advantages afforded to religious (as opposed to normal nonprofit) corporations (for example, lighter reporting responsibilities and various other advantages), the convergence on the religious corporation seems easy to understand—particularly for the national bodies surveyed in the Williams/Massad study. The religious corporation appears to be a functional legal structure equally available to all, and sufficiently flexible to house a variety of religious structures.

However one interprets the survey results, it is clear that what has emerged in the United States is a system that affords broad flexibility to religious groups in structuring their affairs. A variety of puzzles and dilemmas remain for religious groups, as is noted at various points throughout the chapters in this section. Where these result from insufficient flexibility of structure, the general preference for facilitating freedom of religion would appear to call for reforms allowing greater flexibility. In the post-*Smith*[23] environment, it is difficult to imagine judicially mandated adaptation of legislatively crafted religious association laws. By contrast, a leading German case has held that where a religious association law creates formal structural requirements inconsistent with the belief structure of a religious community, the statutory formalities should give way to accom-

---

19. It is so cumbersome to hold property in this form that it is surprising that such a high percentage indicated organization in this form. Conceivably, this could be an indication that respondents thought their religions themselves were unincorporated associations, though their property was held through various legal entities.

20. This approach is evident in the Revised Model Nonprofit Corporation Act. Subcommittee on the Model Nonprofit Corporation Law of the Business Law Section, American Bar Association, Michael C. Hone, Reporter, Revised Model Nonprofit Corporation Act (1987), Section 1.80 ("If religious doctrine governing the affairs of a religious corporation is inconsistent with the provisions of this Act on the same subject, the religious doctrine shall control to the extent required by the Constitution of the United States or the constitution of this state or both").

21. *See* Williams and Massad, *supra* note 1.

22. *See* Patricia B. Carlson, "Unincorporated Associations and Charitable Trusts," in this volume.

23. Employment Division v. Smith, 494 U.S. 872 (1990).

modate the autonomy of the religious community.[24] Given that the primary state interest in religious corporation laws is facilitating religious activity, such flexibility would seem to be appropriate, and even demanded by classical free exercise analysis.[25] Unfortunately, the *Smith* decision makes it far too easy to override autonomy concerns in those relatively rare situations in which religious groups cannot effectively use existing legal structures in a way that is consistent with their beliefs.

Turning from the chapters that deal primarily with the various types of structures available to religious organizations, we reach the chapters by H. Reese Hansen and Patty Gerstenblith dealing with questions about resolution of church property disputes. These chapters build on the analysis of types of structures available, adding additional insight into the nature of these structures. But they focus on the issue of religious autonomy in one of the most significant test settings: when conflict occurs within a religious community.

Crucial to the analysis of both the Hansen chapter and the second Gerstenblith chapter is one of the oldest and richest strands of case law on freedom of religion in the United States—namely, the cases dating back to *Watson v. Jones*[26] dealing with the sensitive issue of how the state should respond when there is a dispute within a religious community. At their core, these cases deal with what has typically been called the problem of religious autonomy in "internal affairs"—or more accurately, the autonomy of a religious community in carrying out its own affairs.[27] These cases were originally anchored in common law principles, but over time they have acquired constitutional rank.[28] Significantly, they have never been clearly affixed to either the nonestablishment or free exercise sides of our Religion Clause jurisprudence,[29] perhaps because of recognition that they belong more clearly to the intermediate realm between nonestablishment and free exercise where facilitation of religious autonomy is the focus.

The Hansen and Gerstenblith chapters in this section can be understood as a dialogue concerning rival approaches to understanding the state's role in the resolution of religious controversies, and their implications for state protection of religious autonomy. Both approaches underscore the significance of religious autonomy and of the state's abstention from involvement in religious disputes. Hansen in the last analysis argues for deference to realities of religious structure, even if these sometimes diverge from the

---

24. Bahá'i Case, BVerfGE 83, 341 (354–56) (1991).

25. If classical strict scrutiny were to be applied, it would be hard to imagine that the state has a compelling state interest in insisting woodenly on a particular formality in an incorporation law. If the alternative organizational structure used by the religious organization reflects sincere religious beliefs, it seems highly unlikely that some alternative approach to meeting the state's interests that takes into account the actual mode of organization cannot be found.

26. 80 U.S. (13 Wall.) 679 (1871).

27. The reference to "own affairs" or to "eigene Angelegenheiten" derives from a recognition in German constitutional theory that the domain of autonomy involved extends beyond strictly internal matters such as determining matters of membership, selecting religious personnel, dealing with matters of church discipline, setting boundaries for congregations, deciding how church resources should be expended, and so forth, to broader questions about determining mission, charitable activities, outreach, and the like, which may have "external" as well as internal impacts. For an excellent comparative study of the issues, see Gerhard Robbers, ed., Church Autonomy: A Comparative Survey (Frankfurt: Peter Lang, 2001).

28. For one of the leading analyses of these cases, see Dallin H. Oaks, Trust Doctrines in Church Controversies (1984).

29. Carl H. Esbeck, The Establishment Clause as a Structural Restraint on Governmental Power, 84 Iowa L. Rev. 1, 50 (1998).

ways a religious group has formulated its preferences on paper. Gerstenblith argues for a stricter "neutral principles" approach, which insists that courts should respect religious autonomy as framed in legal instruments accessible to courts using normal interpretive techniques. The latter approach has the advantage of insulating secular courts from intervening in religious affairs except on terms expressly specified by the religious groups themselves, and creates incentives for religious groups to be explicit in the requisite way. The former approach recognizes that, either through omission or through the sheer difficulty of predicting all religious stances in advance, there may be situations in which courts need to look beyond express formulations of religious autonomy to religious realities that a reasonably objective secular observer is capable of discerning.

Both the religious dispute cases analyzed by Hansen and Gerstenblith and the rival approaches they defend have tremendous significance for the remainder of this volume. Indeed, one of the challenges in the making of the entire book has been to avoid excessive repetition of the analysis of these cases, because they have such profound importance for issues of institutional autonomy faced in almost every other area of religious activity.

Significantly, this line of cases has not been overruled by *Smith.*[30] Indeed, the *Smith* Court cited key religious controversy cases in its summary of the basic axioms of Religion Clause law.[31] Significantly, some of the fundamental worries that apparently triggered the *Smith* decision do not arise in the context of religious autonomy. As Perry Dane has noted, "religious autonomy claims differ radically from the more purely 'retail' claims to religious exemptions."[32] In contrast to individualized claims for exemptions from general laws, protection of religious autonomy does not "court anarchy," lead to constitutional anomalies, or "permit every citizen to become a law unto himself."[33] This is because while claims of religious autonomy "might invoke rights that are special to religion as a category, [they] do not depend on the specific religious norms of a particular religion."[34] Thus, these decisions provide a solid constitutional anchor for the protection of religious autonomy — one which has not been undermined by either the express language or the rationale of *Smith.* They articulate a critical dimension of religious freedom anchored in the First Amendment but not exhausted by the lines of cases that have focused on either the "free exercise" or the "establishment" dimensions of the Religion Clause.

One potential problem for the vitality of the religious autonomy cases is a misguided blurring and confusion of the "neutral principles" approach articulated in *Jones v. Wolf*[35] — the leading Supreme Court case articulating the neutral principles approach in church autonomy cases — and in the *Smith* decision's determination that "neutral, generally applicable regulatory laws"[36] override religious freedom claims. In effect, courts construe the "neutral principles" doctrine articulated in *Jones* to justify resolution of re-

---

30. Lee Boothby, Religious Freedom in the United States Following *City of Boerne v. Flores*, 2 NEXUS 111, 117–18 (Fall 1997) (arguing that "*Smith* in no way encroaches upon the long line of church autonomy cases").

31. Employment Division v. Smith, 494 U.S. 872, 877 (1990) (government may not "lend its power to one or the other side in controversies over religious authority or dogma").

32. Perry Dane, The Varieties of Religious Autonomy, in Gerhard Robbers, ed., Church Autonomy: A Comparative Survey 117, 122 (2001).

33. *Id.* at 122 n. 19, *citing* Employment Division v. Smith, 494 U.S. 872, 888, 886, 879 (1990).

34. *Id.* at 122 n. 19.

35. 443 U.S. 595 (1979).

36. Employment Division v. Smith, 494 U.S. 872, 880 (1990).

ligious controversies in accordance with "neutral, generally applicable laws" or policies. The result is that religious autonomy concerns can be ignored whenever an ostensibly neutral or secular principle or policy seems relevant. This type of reading stands the "neutral principles" doctrine of *Jones* on its head. As originally formulated, the doctrine was designed to protect religious autonomy by assuring that secular courts would intervene in religious affairs only when the religious community itself had expressly stated, in terms accessible to a secular court, how a particular controversy should be resolved. As described in *Jones*, the neutral principles doctrine involves "settling a local church property dispute on the basis of the language of the deeds, the terms of the local church charters, the state statutes governing the holding of church property, and the provisions in the constitution of the general church concerning the ownership and control of church property."[37] The idea is to use standard "objective, well-established concepts of trust and property law familiar to lawyers and judges."[38] In the view of the *Jones* Court, "the neutral-principles analysis shares the peculiar genius of private-law systems in general — flexibility in ordering private rights and obligations *to reflect the intentions of the parties*."[39] The idea behind the neutral principles approach was not, as some subsequent courts have thought it to be, a blank check to authorize courts to invoke any "wholly secular legal rules whose application to religious parties does not entail theological or doctrinal evaluations."[40] In effect, the neutral principles doctrine was designed to protect *internal* express formulations of religious doctrine and polity, thereby *respecting* religious autonomy. The misguided application of the doctrine invokes *external* neutral standards to *override* religious autonomy. This inverted distortion of the doctrine profoundly weakens the protection the religious autonomy cases have long provided against government intrusion in religious affairs.[41] It is used by secular courts to take state power into protected domains in which the still-binding religious autonomy cases do not allow it to go.

The insistence of the autonomy cases on the independent constitutional value of religious autonomy points toward the challenge addressed at the end of this section: Carl H. Esbeck's chapter on problems posed for religious structure by the flood of regulatory norms associated with life in the modern welfare state, and his appendix dealing specifically with charitable choice issues. In both, he provides analysis of the difficult autonomy issues that arise once religious groups and affiliated entities seek various types of government assistance or seek to provide state-funded services. Esbeck's analysis is extensive — but because of the magnitude and complexity of the issues involved, it cannot be exhaustive. If the Hansen and Gerstenblith chapters work out the implications of religious autonomy for disputes arising in classic domains of private law, Esbeck identifies the types of challenges posed in the highly regulated world characteristic of states at the beginning of the twenty-first century.

After identifying the major changes in attitudes toward the role of the church and the state that have accompanied the shift to the welfare state, and after spelling out key parameters that affect the regulation and its impact on religious structures, Esbeck explores a series of types of legislative constraints that have become typical: reporting and

---

37. 443 U.S. at 603.

38. *Id.*

39. *Id.* (emphasis added).

40. *See, e.g.,* South Jersey Catholic Sch. Teachers Org. v. St. Teresa of the Infant Jesus Church Elem. Sch., 696 A.2d 709, 723 (N.J. 1997).

41. *See* Frederick Mark Gedicks, Towards a Defensible Free Exercise Doctrine, 68 Geo. Wash. L. Rev. 925, 943 (2000).

auditing requirements to make sure government funds are used appropriately; conditions imposed to assure appropriate separation of church and state institutions; conditions affecting church polity; structuring of curricular or other service offerings; conditions that further general public policies such as nondiscrimination, procedural fairness, and the like; and so on. For each type of regulatory structure, he provides a wealth of concrete examples of how regulatory reach can impair religious autonomy. The chapter will have particular relevance for those sorting out how (and whether) to structure their affairs to take advantage of increased opportunities for faith-based communities to have equal access to governmental largesse.

"Charitable choice" emerged as a hot issue after the original plans for a chapter on structural issues triggered by welfare state issues had crystallized. Moreover, the reinterpretation of the *Lemon*[42] test in *Agostini*[43] and *Helms*[44] that has helped clarify the permissibility of charitable choice legislation is of relatively recent provenance. Developments in this area will no doubt remain controversial for years to come, but Esbeck's analysis helps to describe the new contours that religious autonomy is likely to take on in the post-*Agostini* setting. In a world in which government often turns to private parties to carry out its mandates, a blanket rule excluding "faith-based organizations" would be discriminatory—and given the track record of such groups, it would often be counterproductive or at least inefficient. At the same time, religious groups should not be permitted to abuse the economic power that could accrue from participation in such programs. The challenge is to make certain that religious groups are not required to compromise their distinctive character in order to become eligible to be service providers in government programs routinely conducted through private partners. Autonomy in defining religious mission, in structuring programs, and in selecting personnel is vital if the new configuration of church and state in the twenty-first century undermines the distinctiveness that gives religious service providers their particular commitment and vitality.

Esbeck's chapter and charitable-choice appendix are a bridge to succeeding chapters of the book that deal with particularly important areas of state regulation and interaction with religion (taxation, employment, land use, and derivative liability) and special social service areas (education, health care, and other social services). It raises in all its concreteness the challenge of protecting autonomy in an increasingly complex social and regulatory setting.

Secularization theory predicted the withering away of religion in the increasingly complex and interdependent world created by the Industrial Revolution and compounded by each successive wave of technological advance. In fact, rising complexity and concomitant processes of secularization have not rung religion's death knell, but instead have challenged religion to find ways to adapt to the increasingly complex social and legal setting. If religion in all its diversity is to be able to meet this challenge with authenticity, then protecting religious autonomy is vital. The challenge will be to protect the values that have come down to us through our common law and constitutional heritage, as described in the first four chapters of this section, and to preserve them against the more complex challenges set forth in the Esbeck chapter and in many of the other chapters dealing with the regulatory morass of the modern state.

---

42. Lemon v. Kurtzman, 403 U.S. 602, 612–613 (1971).
43. Agostini v. Felton, 521 U.S. 203 (1997).
44. Mitchell v. Helms, 530 U.S. 793 (2000).

Associational Structures of Religious Organizations

Patty Gerstenblith

A legal structure is the organizational framework within which the law permits business to be conducted. Over the past three centuries, religious organizations in America have used various structures to gain legal recognition, status, and rights, particularly the right to acquire and to hold property. During the colonial era, the colonists borrowed extensively from English law in all areas, including their treatment of religious societies. Guided by the prevailing English method of the time, most of the colonies (and subsequently the states) provided legal status and certain rights to religious organizations, as to business corporations, by the granting of special charters.

The purpose of a special charter was to create a corporation for a particular purpose and to assure certain rights or powers. A special charter required an act of the sovereign or legislature. Just as the crown and the Parliament in England held the power to approve or deny the creation of a corporation, the states similarly continued to maintain the special charter system to which both ecclesiastical and lay corporations were subject. However, abuses inherent in the special charter system, including favoritism and obstruction of the work of legislatures because of the numerous demands for such charters, became apparent during the nineteenth century. States therefore gradually replaced the special charter system with general incorporation statutes. These general incorporation statutes included within their scope a variety of charitable and not-for-profit corporations including religious organizations.[1]

Despite the inherent differences in the natures of not-for-profit and business corporations, state statutes for not-for-profit corporations often mirror the state statutes for general for-profit business corporations. This similarity may lie in the fact that in the development of American statutory law, business corporations received more attention from legislatures, progressed more rapidly, and were of greater concern to the legal and business communities than not-for-profit corporations.[2] For example, the study and preparation of model acts for business corporations preceded the drafting of a model act for not-for-profit corporations, and the drafters of the Model Non-Profit Corpora-

---

1. Paul G. Kauper & Stephen C. Ellis, Religious Corporations and the Law, 71 Mich. L. Rev. 1499, 1507 (1973).
2. Louis P. Haller, The Model Non-Profit Corporation Act, 9 Baylor L. Rev. 309, 316 (1957).

tion Act clearly borrowed heavily from the previously published model and actual business corporation statutes.[3] A second reason for the apparent similarity may be that the same attorneys, coming from corporate business backgrounds, tend to draft both types of statutes.[4] This influence may be seen especially in those states which use a single act to govern both business and not-for-profit corporations, even though particular provisions may apply to only one type of corporation.[5]

State law is the primary source for the formation, structure, operation, legal rights and duties, nontax regulation, and dissolution of organizations.[6] Under the different state statutes,[7] the current legal structures available to religious organizations include the

---

3. The Conference of Commissioners on Uniform State Laws approved the Uniform Business Corporation Act in 1928 after nearly twenty years of study, while the Model Business Corporation Act was published in its initial form in 1946. *Id.* at 315. On the other hand, the original draft of the Model Non-Profit Corporation Act was not published until 1952 and was subsequently revised in 1957, 1964, and 1987. *Id.* at 320; Henry B. Hansmann, Reforming Nonprofit Corporation Law, 129 U. Pa. L. Rev. 497, 528 (1981).

4. Almost all members of the American Bar Association committees that draft or amend model not-for-profit corporation acts have been corporate business attorneys, although it is possible that, as the number of not-for-profit organizations expands, this may change. Howard L.Oleck, Nonprofit Corporations, Organizations, and Associations 61 (5th ed. 1988). The approach taken by these drafters may become skewed by their business backgrounds. Hansmann, *supra* note 3, at 528. Oleck criticizes the validity of such an approach by business lawyers. Instead, Oleck contends that the drafters should include "philosophers, anthropologists, biologists, statisticians and demographers, theologians, sociologists, economists, psychologists, and the like, plus a few lawyers to crystallize the principles enunciated by the committee into workable rules of law." Oleck, *supra*, at 61.

However, another commentator suggests a possible argument to support the business-oriented approach. Not-for-profit corporation acts which resemble business corporation acts will be easier to use and apply by lawyers who are already familiar with the procedures of the more widely used business corporation acts and with the case law that has developed construing them. Thus, any knowledge of or expertise in the business law area would conceivably help a lawyer work with and understand a similarly constructed not-for-profit corporation act. Haller, *supra* note 2, at 320.

5. For example, the not-for-profit corporation laws of Delaware, Kansas, and Oklahoma are embedded in each state's general corporation law. *See* Del. Code Ann. tit. 8, §101-398 (1996); Kan. Stat. Ann. §§17-6001 to 17-7405 (1996); Okla. Stat. Ann. tit. 18, §§1001-1155 (West 1997).

6. Two "levels" or sources of law—the federal government and the fifty state governments—regulate business, as well as nonbusiness organizations. As applied to not-for-profit organizations, including charitable organizations, this is significant because different aspects of formation, benefits or favorable treatment, and regulation arise variously from state or federal law. Perhaps the most characteristic feature of not-for-profit organizations is their tax-exempt status and, in the case of charitable organizations, the deductibility of donations for federal income tax purposes of the donor. These benefits arise from federal income tax law and are mirrored, with some variations, in comparable tax benefits at the state level—for example, exemption from state corporate income tax, property taxes and state sales tax. The federal Internal Revenue Service is the primary means of preventing abuses and restricting certain types of activities in which such organizations may engage—primarily political activity, such as campaigning and lobbying, and unrelated business activities. IRC §§501(c)(3), 170 (1997).

7. An organization which wishes to obtain various legal rights or privileges, such as federal tax-exempt status, would likely choose to receive a legal status under state law first. However, in the United States, unlike many other nations, it is not necessary for legal status to be acquired or for religious organizations to register in any form before they are able to operate. Many religious organizations in the United States have the status of an unincorporated association or charitable trust, for which no registration or incorporation is required. The purpose of the legal formalities is only to confer certain specific legal benefits on religious organizations and to facilitate the achieving of certain other benefits, such as tax-exempt status, although incorporation is by no means necessary to achieving tax-exempt status.

charitable trust, the unincorporated association, the corporation sole, religious corporations, and not-for-profit corporations. However, not all of these legal structure are available in every state. According to the 1994 Report on the Survey of Religious Organizations at the National Level, the surveyed organizations adopted each of these available structural forms in the following proportions: eight percent use the form of an unincorporated association; three percent use the general not-for-profit corporation; eighty-seven percent use the religious not-for-profit corporation form; and less than one percent each use the charitable or religious trust, a corporation sole, a for-profit corporation, or "some other type of legal structure."[8] It is likely that the eighty-seven percent that indicated use of the religious not-for-profit corporate form encompasses both those organizations using the specific religious corporation form and those using the not-for-profit corporation organized for religious purposes. These results are not necessarily indicative of the distribution of structural forms which would be found at the local level where, although the religious corporation form might still prevail, some of the other forms, particularly the unincorporated association, may appear more frequently.

The primary characteristic (and the one necessary to receive advantageous tax status) of not-for-profit organizations is the "nondistribution constraint."[9] This means that the members, officers, and directors of the organization do not receive any profit from the activities of the organization. A "not-for-profit" organization may, in fact, earn a profit; it simply cannot distribute that profit to its membership but must, instead, utilize that profit in furthering its not-for-profit purpose.[10] Most state statutes grant an exception to this nondistribution constraint so that reasonable compensation [can be paid] to members, directors and officers for services rendered.[11]

In addition to being characterized by the nondistribution constraint, most not-for-profit organizations may be categorized as falling into one of two groups—the *mutual benefit organizations* and the *public benefit organizations*. The latter is largely synonymous with the general category of charitable organizations; they receive significantly more advantageous tax treatment at the federal and generally also state level and usually have a religious, educational, or eleemosynary purpose.[12] Charitable organizations also have stricter regulation of their activities and dissolution processes, and some state laws define the category more narrowly than does federal tax law.[13] The mutual benefit cate-

---

8. Center for Church/State Studies, DePaul Univ. College of Law, 1994 Report on the Survey of Religious Organizations at the National Level, Q4 (unpublished survey, on file with the Center for Church/State Studies, DePaul University College of Law) [hereinafter Survey]. For a discussion of the Survey's method and findings, see Rhys H. Williams & John P.N. Massad, "Religious Diversity, Civil Law, and Institutional Isomorphism," in this volume.

9. Henry B. Hansmann, The Role of Nonprofit Enterprise, 89 Yale L.J. 835, 838 (1980).

10. State statute may define a not-for-profit corporation as "a corporation no part of the income or profit of which is distributable to its members, directors or officers." D.C. Code Ann. § 29-502 (1996); *see also* Mich. Comp. Laws Ann. § 450.2108(2) (West 1997) (defining a not-for-profit corporation as a corporation "incorporated to carry out any lawful purpose or purposes not involving pecuniary profit or gain for its directors, officers, shareholders, or members"). The nondistribution constraint is embodied in the Internal Revenue Code § 501(c)(3). IRC § 501(c)(3) (1997).

11. Christine Chute, Comment, Personal Liability for Directors of Nonprofit Corporations in Wyoming, 18 Land & Water L. Rev. 273, 276–77 (1983). Other forms of nonpecuniary benefits, particularly status and prestige, may inure to officers and directors of not-for-profit organizations and are generally considered permissible.

12. IRC § 501(c)(3) (1997).

13. *See* Utah Code Ann. § 16-6-63 (1997); Utah County v. Intermountain Health Care, Inc., 709 P.2d 265, 267 (Utah 1985) (holding that although a property owner is a nonprofit corporation, it is

gory may include social clubs and trade associations; they have fewer tax advantages but also less strict regulation, and some states permit the distribution of an organization's assets to its membership upon dissolution. Because virtually all religious organizations would fall into the category of public benefit or charitable not-for-profit organization, this chapter will focus exclusively on this not-for-profit form.[14]

This chapter will first present an explanation of the various associational structures made available to religious organizations under state law, including the unincorporated association, charitable trust, not-for-profit corporation, religious corporation, specific denominational corporation, and, finally, the corporation sole. While some of these structures are available to a wide variety of associations, some are limited to religious organizations and some are even further limited to particular religious denominations. At the conclusion of this section, the chapter considers whether a particular religious group can choose its structural form when the state makes more than one form available and whether a religious group can organize in a state which offers an advantageous structural form but then function in a different state. The second section considers some of the implications for free exercise claims which can be brought by religious organizations in light of these structural choices and recent developments in constitutional jurisprudence.

Structural Forms of Religious Organizations

Where the chapters in this book by Patricia B. Carlson and H. Reese Hansen examine the least formal of the organizational forms available to religious groups, namely, unincorporated associations and charitable trusts, this section will focus on the three forms of corporation available to religious organizations: the not-for-profit corporation, the religious corporation, and the corporation sole.

The not-for-profit corporation with religious purpose

Statutory scheme of not-for-profit corporation statutes

All states have enacted laws to provide for the incorporation of not-for-profit organizations. While all of these statutes share certain characteristics, other provisions vary from state to state. The common significant elements include the requirement of a purpose clause, a procedure to incorporate, an enumeration of general powers, a method

---

not exempt from property tax under state constitution requiring property to be used exclusively for religious or charitable purposes). Revised regulations, which ensured that the required "element of gift to the community" would be satisfied to qualify as a charitable purpose, were upheld. *See* Howell v. County Bd. *ex rel.* IHC Hosps., Inc., 881 P.2d 880, 884–85 (Utah 1994).

14. In tax code terminology, most religious organizations would qualify as §501(c)(3) organizations as long as they conform with the other requirements of §501(c)(3). The typologies used by state statutes vary considerably, however. In one prominent example, California uses a tripartite classification of mutual benefit, public benefit, and religious organizations, thus treating religious organizations as a distinct type of not-for-profit organization.

for merger and consolidation, and a provision for distribution of assets upon dissolution. Some of the characteristics of those elements which are distinctive of not-for-profit organizations and religious organizations in particular will be briefly considered.[15]

The purpose clause of a state statute determines the purposes for which an organization may be formed as a not-for-profit corporation. Throughout the states two types of statutory provisions prevail. The first type of statute specifically restricts the purposes for which not-for-profit corporations may be formed by enumerating a lengthy list of permissible purposes which generally includes a religious purpose.[16] The second type of purpose clause simply states that a not-for-profit corporation may be formed for any lawful purpose or purposes and does not include a detailed list of permissible ones.[17] The trend in state statutes seems to be toward adoption of the general purpose clause provisions, particularly as illustrated in the current Model Nonprofit Corporation Act.

The general powers granted to not-for-profit corporations are similar to those granted to business corporations,[18] with a few restrictions to ensure compliance with

---

15. The procedures for incorporation of religious organizations under the general not-for-profit corporation statutes do not raise any issues particular to religious organizations. State statutes generally require one or more individuals to act as incorporators who sign the articles of incorporation, which include basic information concerning the corporation—particularly, the purpose for which the corporation exists—and file them in the office of the secretary of state. Corporate existence usually becomes effective on the date of filing, after which the board may adopt bylaws (the regulations governing the internal affairs of the corporation), elect officers, and transact any other business.

16. For example, the Illinois statute restricts the permissible purposes for which a not-for-profit corporation may be organized to one or more of thirty listed acceptable purposes or similar purposes, including charitable, benevolent, eleemosynary, educational, civic, patriotic, political, religious, social, literary, athletic, scientific, research, agricultural, soil improvement, crop improvement, livestock or poultry improvement, trade and professional associations, and certain cooperative and condominium associations. 805 Ill. Comp. Stat. Ann. 105/103.5 (West 1997); *see, e.g.*, People *ex rel.* Padula v. Hughes, 16 N.E.2d 922 (Ill. App. Ct. 1938) (holding that incorporation under the not-for-profit corporation act permitted only for those associations which organize for one of the statutorily enumerated purposes). The states of Virginia and West Virginia form exceptions to this discussion in that they do not permit the incorporation of religious organizations; they will be considered later in a separate section.

17. The New Jersey Nonprofit Corporation Act provides an example of a non-restrictive purpose clause which nonetheless enumerates specific purposes by way of illustration, as follows:

A corporation may be organized under this act for any lawful purpose other than for pecuniary profit including, without being limited to, any one or more of the following purposes: charitable; benevolent; eleemosynary; educational; cemetery; civic; patriotic; political; religious; social; fraternal; literary; cultural; athletic; scientific; agricultural; horticultural; animal husbandry; volunteer fire company; ambulance, first aid or rescue; professional, commercial, industrial or trade association; and labor union and cooperative purposes.

N.J. Stat. Ann. § 15A:2-1 (West 1997).

The difference among states in permissible purposes is not particularly significant for religious organizations, because religion is generally considered a permissible purpose. However, the difference does represent a philosophical dispute as to whether not-for-profit organizations must merely conform to the nondistribution constraint or whether they must be further restricted to particular categories of purposes considered beneficial to society. This disagreement is epitomized in the work of Hansmann and Oleck. *See, e.g.* Oleck, *supra* note 4, at 57–100 (advocating restricting not-for-profit organizations to specific categories); Hansmann, *supra* note 3, at 509–37 (arguing that not-for-profit organizations can carry out any legal purpose so long as they follow the nondistribution constraint).

18. Such powers typically include the right to perpetual succession, the ability to own and deal with real and personal property, the right to sue and be sued, the right to borrow and lend money,

the nondistribution constraint.[19] Some states specifically limit a not-for-profit corporation's ability to merge or consolidate with for-profit corporations; generally, domestic not-for-profit corporations may merge or consolidate with both domestic and foreign corporations with similar purposes.[20]

When a not-for-profit corporation undergoes either voluntary or involuntary dissolution, its assets must be dealt with differently than those of a for-profit corporation. In general, assets must first be used to pay creditors. Second, the not-for-profit corporation must return to donors those contributions which were received and held on the condition that they would be returned upon dissolution of the corporation. Third, remaining assets must be transferred to another corporation engaged in substantially similar activities if they were received and held by the corporation subject to limitations permitting their use only for a particular purpose, such as a charitable, religious, eleemosynary, benevolent, or other similar purpose. Finally, in the case of mutual benefit organizations, assets are to be distributed to members or other persons as required by the articles of incorporation or bylaws. Thus, the assets of a dissolving corporation are typically distributed, in order, to creditors, to contributors who have conditioned their gifts, to another corporation with similar purposes, and to members or other persons when not inconsistent with statutory restrictions.

Most gifts to a not-for-profit corporation with a religious purpose would be interpreted as conditioned on use for similar purpose, and therefore, upon dissolution of such a corporation, the assets would be given to a corporation with a similar mission. A determination of similarity of mission would be most easily resolved in cases of religious organizations by turning to an organization belonging to the same religious denomination. In cases of schism within a denomination or when one faction accuses another of departure from the denomination's doctrine, it would seem to pose a very difficult task, and perhaps one that would be unconstitutional, for a court to make a determination of similarity.

Incorporation under the general not-for-profit corporation statutes that require incorporation as a specific type

At least six states and the Revised Model Nonprofit Corporation Act of 1987 (RMNCA)[21] employ statutory schemes which require an organization to incorporate as

---

the right to enter into contracts, the ability to indemnify its officers and directors and the ability to enact bylaws. *See, e.g.*, Vt. Stat. Ann. tit. 11B, § 3.02 (1997); *see also* Pilgrim Evangelical Lutheran Church of Unaltered Augsburgh Confession v. Lutheran Church-Missouri Synod Found., 661 S.W. 2d 833 (Mo. Ct. App. 1983) (finding that no distinction exists between the powers of a not-for-profit and a for-profit corporation).

19. The most typical distinctions concern the restrictions on the ability to compensate officers and directors, which is generally limited to a "reasonable" amount, and restrictions on the ability to make loans to officers and directors.

20. *See, e.g.*, N.J. Stat. Ann. §§ 15A:10-1, -2, -7 (West 1997).

21. The New York Not-for-Profit Corporation Law of 1970 was the final result of a 17-year revision of the state's corporation statutes. N.Y. Not-For-Profit Corp. Law §§ 101–1515 (Consol. 1997). California's current Nonprofit Corporation Law took effect in 1980. Cal. Corp. Code §§ 5000–10841 (Deering 1996). The RMNCA was adopted in 1987, Revised Model NonProfit Corp. Act (1987), and the Tennessee Nonprofit Corporation Act became law on January 1, 1988. Wyoming, Arkansas and Florida have more recently adopted the Revised Model Nonprofit Corporation Act. Much of the following discussion is based on Hansmann, *supra* note 3, at 528–37, and Harry G. Henn & Jeffery H. Boyd, Statutory Trends in the Law of Nonprofit Organizations: California, Here We Come!, 66 Cornell L. Rev. 1103 (1981).

a specific type of not-for-profit corporation (by designating a specific category of purpose) under the general not-for-profit corporation statute. This then contrasts with most states which use either a restrictive or nonrestrictive purpose clause. The purpose of this statutory scheme is to provide a single regulatory framework for all not-for-profit corporations, while also permitting differences in the treatment of the various types of corporations.

The New York Not-for-Profit Corporation Law (N-PCL)[22] establishes a single supporting statute not only for the different types of not-for-profit corporations which can incorporate under the general statute but also for those organizations which can incorporate under entirely distinct statutes.[23] Organizations incorporated under the Type B category of not-for-profit corporations, which is equivalent to the public benefit organizations, are subjected to greater judicial supervision than are mutual benefit organizations.[24]

The California Nonprofit Corporation Law[25] divides not-for-profit corporations into three separate classifications—public benefit, mutual benefit, and religious corporations—and provides a separate set of provisions to regulate each classification.[26] As with the New York scheme, the purpose of these three categories is to allow different degrees of regulation of the different types of corporations: while the public benefit category is subjected to the most extensive regulation, the religious corporation category receives the least regulation. This varying degree of regulation can be seen in the

---

22. N.Y. Not-For-Profit Corp. Law §§ 101–1515 (Consol. 1997).

23. For example, a religious organization can choose to incorporate as either a Type B corporation under the general statute, which category includes charitable, educational, religious, scientific, literary, cultural and prevention of cruelty to children and animals organizations, or under the specific Religious Corporations statute, in which case it is subjected to the provisions of the N-PCL as a Type D corporation and the N-PCL is used as a default provision for any elements which are lacking under the Religious Corporations Act. N.Y. Relig. Corp. Law § 2-b (Consol. 1997); N.Y. Not-For-Profit Corp. Law § 201(c) cmt. (Consol. 1997).

24. The classification scheme is designed to allow variation in the degree of regulation of the different classes of not-for-profit corporations, with the amount of regulation determined by the purpose for each classification. *See* Hansmann, *supra* note 3, at 531; Henn & Boyd, *supra* note 21, at 1116. For example, state attorney general approval is required for the incorporation of a Type B organization. N.Y. Not-For-Profit Corp. Law § 404(a) (Consol. 1997). Type B and C corporations are subject to inspection visits by the justices of the Supreme Court or their appointees, and the court may require the corporation to make an inventory and accounting when a member or creditor of the corporation claims that the corporation or its directors, officers or agents has engaged in some impermissible activity such as misappropriation of funds or property. *Id.* at § 114. Judicial approval is also required for a variety of transactions, including the sale, lease, exchange, or disposal of all or substantially all of the corporations assets (*id.* § 510(a)(3)), merger or consolidation (*id.* § 907(a)), and a plan for distribution of assets upon dissolution of the corporation (*id.* § 1002(d)).

25. Cal. Corp. Code §§ 5000–10841 (Deering 1996).

26. *Id.* §§ 5110–6910 (public benefit corporations); §§ 7110–8910 (mutual benefit corporations); §§ 9110–9690 (religious corporations) (Deering 1996). The California statute takes a distinctly different approach than that of New York in that the three categories of not-for-profit corporations are each provided a complete and distinct regulatory scheme, while the New York statute attempts to integrate the provisions through default mechanisms, thereby avoiding repetition. The California scheme has been discussed in William T. Fryer, III & David R. Haglund, New California Nonprofit Corporation Law: A Unique Approach, 7 Pepp. L. Rev. 1, 10–11 (1979); Henn & Boyd, *supra* note 21, at 1133–34; Michael C. Hone, California's New Nonprofit Corporation Law—An Introduction and Conceptual Background, 13 U.S.F.L. Rev. 733, 736–37 (1979). Hansmann has criticized this trend in both the New York and California approaches to create multiple categories of not-for-profit corporations in that they add ambiguity and reflect "fundamental confusion concerning the proper role and structure for nonprofit organizations." Hansmann, *supra* note 3, at 538.

supervisory role of the state attorney general and the disclosure requirements imposed upon the different types of corporations.[27]

The RMNCA[28] is similar to the California scheme in that it divides all not-for-profit corporations into public benefit, mutual benefit, and religious corporations, but it does not provide three separate sets of provisions for each of these not-for-profit categories. However, it does follow the California pattern in establishing a tripartite regime of regulation with the public benefit corporations receiving the most regulation, the religious corporations receiving the least, and mutual benefit corporations occupying an intermediate position.[29] Tennessee also follows a similar pattern but recognizes only two categories: mutual and public benefit corporations. It thus permits religious corporations to organize as either,[30] but, regardless of their choice, it subjects them to the least amount of regulation.[31]

Corporate structures designed only for religious organizations

Some states permit the incorporation of religious organizations in forms other than the not-for-profit corporation. The various statutory schemes that pertain only to reli-

---

27. For example, while public benefit corporations are subject to examination at all times by the attorney general, only those assets held subject to a charitable trust by mutual benefit corporations are subject to such supervision. However, the attorney general has the most limited role in terms of supervising religious corporations, presumably to avoid raising First Amendment problems. Cal. Corp. Code §§ 7140–42; §§ 8510–19, and § 9230 (Deering 1996). *See also* Hone, *supra* note 26, at 743–44. Similarly, the disclosure requirements vary in degree according to the type of not-for-profit corporation. Public benefit corporations have the most extensive statutory requirements for record keeping and reporting; religious corporations have the least, and the mutual benefit corporations have an intermediate standard and are treated selectively according to size. Cal. Corp. Code §§ 6310–24, § 9510-14; §§ 8310–24.

28. Revised Model Nonprofit Corp. Act (1987).

29. *Id.* §§ 1.70, 3.04(c), 6.30(f), 7.03(a)(3), 8.31(b)(2), 8.55(d), 11.02(b), 12.02(g), 14.03. In fact, the RMNCA specifically states that

> [i]f religious doctrine governing the affairs of a religious corporation is inconsistent with the provisions of this Act on the same subject, the religious doctrine shall control to the extent required by the Constitution of the United States or the constitution of this state or both.

Id. § 1.80. In the light of the Supreme Court's decision in *Employment Division, Department of Human Resources v. Smith*, 494 U.S. 872 (1990), it seems unlikely that a court would find a constitutionally compelled deference to a religion's doctrine. However, Justice Scalia did seem to approve of legislatively enacted exemptions from government regulation, so that a state statute that incorporated a requirement of deference to religious doctrine should be permissible.

30. Tenn. Code Ann. § 48-51-201(31) (1997).

31. Sample statutory restrictions placed on public benefit corporations include: purchase of memberships prohibited, *id.* § 48-56-303; notice to the attorney general of derivative suits, *id.* § 48-56-401(g); attorney general initiation of a court-ordered meeting, *id.* § 48-57-103(a)(1); limitations on mergers, *id.* §§ 48-61-102, -106; notice to the attorney general for the sale of assets other than in the regular course of activities, *id.* § 48-62-102(g); restrictions on voluntary dissolution, *id.* § 48-64-103. On the other hand, religious corporations are specifically exempted from several statutory provisions, including those dealing with transfers of memberships, *id.* § 48-56-202; resignation and termination of memberships, *id.* § 48-56-302; notice to attorney general of removal of directors by judicial proceeding, *id.* § 48-58-110(d); the general prohibition of loans to or guarantees for directors and officers, *id.* § 48-58-303; and provision for receivership or custodianship in judicial dissolution, *id.* § 48-64-303. The Tennessee statute also exempts religious corporations from provisions which are inconsistent with religious doctrine, but only to the extent required by the federal and state constitutions. *Id.* § 48-67-102(b).

gious corporations include general religious corporation laws, special statutes for particular denominations, and corporation sole acts.

General religious corporation laws

Twelve states have statutes restricted to the incorporation of religious organizations,[32] while eight additional states have distinct incorporation statutes which encompass particular types of benevolent, educational, and charitable associations, along with religious organizations.[33] Most of these statutes follow a pattern similar to the general not-for-profit corporation statutes discussed previously, except that several of them do not include complete sets of provisions for handling all corporate matters. In general, however, these statutes grant authority and provide procedures for the incorporation of any church or religious organization.[34] Within this they delineate the powers granted to such a corporation, including the rights to acquire, hold, and dispose of real and personal property, to borrow money, to have perpetual succession, to sue and be sued, and to adopt bylaws for their governance.[35] The statutes may, however, be incomplete in that only a few of them specify the ability to merge and consolidate with similar corporations,[36] and even fewer

---

32. Connecticut, Conn. Gen. Stat. Ann. § 33-264a (West 1997); Delaware, Del. Code Ann. tit. 27, § 101 (1996); Illinois, 805 Ill. Comp. Stat. Ann. 110/35 (West 1997); Maine, Me. Rev. Stat. Ann. tit. 13, § 2861 (West 1996); Maryland, Md. Code Ann., Corps & Ass'ns § 5-301 (1997); Massachusetts, Mass. Gen. Laws Ann. ch. 67, § 22 (West 1997); Michigan, Mich. Comp. Laws Ann. § 450.159 (West 1997); Minnesota, Minn. Stat. Ann. § 315.01 (West 1997); New Jersey, N.J. Stat. Ann. § 16:1-2 (West 1997); New York, N.Y. Relig. Corp. Law § 2 (Consol. 1997); Wisconsin, Wis. Stat. Ann. § 187.01 (West 1995–96); and Wyoming, Wyo. Stat. Ann. § 17-8-103 (Michie 1997).

33. Alabama ("Churches, Public Societies and Graveyard Owners"), Ala. Code § 10-4-20 (1996); Colorado ("Religious, Educational, and Benevolent Societies"), Colo. Rev. Stat. § 7-50-101 (1997); District of Columbia ("Charitable, Educational, and Religious Associations"), D.C. Code Ann. § 29-1001 (1996); Kansas ("Religious, Charitable and Other Organizations"), Kan. Stat. Ann. § 17-1701 (1996); Missouri ("Religious and Charitable Associations"), Mo. Ann. Stat. § 352.010 (West 1996); Ohio ("Religious and Benevolent Organizations"), Ohio Rev. Code Ann. § 1715.01 (Anderson 1997); Oklahoma ("Religious, Charitable and Educational Corporations"), Okla. Stat. tit. 18, § 543 (1997); and Wyoming ("Charitable, Educational, Religious and Other Societies"), Wyo. Stat. Ann. § 17-7-101 (Michie 1997).

34. In its Religious Corporations Law, New York attempts to distinguish a religious corporation from an incorporated church. "A 'Religious Corporations Law corporation' is a corporation created for religious purposes...." On the other hand, an incorporated church "is a religious corporation created to enable its members to meet for divine worship or other religious observances." N.Y. Relig. Corp. Law § 2 (Consol. 1997). Some states require that the religious organization consist of a certain number of persons before a corporation may be formed. See, e.g., Connecticut, Conn. Gen. Stat. Ann. § 33-261a (West 1997) (three members); Delaware, Del. Code Ann. tit. 27, § 101 (1996) (fifteen individuals required); District of Columbia, D.C. Code Ann. § 29-1001 (1996) (three members); Massachusetts, Mass. Gen. Laws Ann. ch. 67, § 21 (West 1997) (ten members required); Oklahoma, Okla. Stat. tit. 18, § 562 (1986) (three members). Some states also set a minimum and/or maximum number of trustees (or members of the governing board) of the religious corporation. See, e.g., Michigan, Mich. Comp. Laws Ann. § 450.159 (West 1997) (Church Trustee Corporations must have a minimum of three and a maximum of nine trustees); Minnesota, Minn. Stat. Ann. § 315.01(2) (West 1997) (maximum of fifteen trustees).

35. The list of specific powers may be brief, see, e.g., Minnesota, Minn. Stat. Ann. § 315.09 (West 1997), or lengthy, see, e.g., New Jersey, N.J. Stat. Ann. § 16:1-4 (West 1997).

36. Minnesota, Minn. Stat. Ann. § 315.365 (West 1997) (merger of religious corporations); Missouri, Mo. Ann. Stat. §§ 352.140–352.170 (West 1996) (benevolent corporations may be merged); New Jersey, N.J. Stat. Ann. §§ 16:1-20 to -21 (West 1997) (consolidation procedure and effect); New

have specific provisions for the dissolution and subsequent distribution of assets of religious corporations.[37]

Denominational statutes

Fifteen states[38] include special statutory provisions for particular religious denominations[39] which thus enable religious groups that belong to one of these denominations to match their religious precepts and legal requirements far more closely than would be possible in the absence of such an accommodation. Several reasons have been advanced to explain the existence of the special statutes for particular denominations. First, these statutes may be viewed as a continuation of the special charter system, in which the state, following the older English model, authorized legal status to particular individual churches through a charter grant.[40] Second, these special incorporation statutes may be an extension of the earlier established status of particular churches.[41] Third, the modern exis-

York, N.Y. Relig. Corp. Law § 13 (Consol. 1997) (consolidation of incorporated churches); Ohio, Ohio Rev. Code Ann. § 1715.08, -21 (Anderson 1997) (consolidation of churches having same form of faith and consolidation with corporation created by representative body); Wisconsin, Wis. Stat. Ann. § 187.14 (West 1995–96) (consolidation of church corporations or congregations).

37. *See, e.g.*, Colorado, Colo. Rev. Stat. § 7-50-114 (1997); Connecticut, Conn. Gen. Stat. Ann. §§ 33-264e and 33-264f (West 1997); Missouri, Mo. Ann. Stat. §§ 352.180–.240 (West 1996); New York, N.Y. Relig. Corp. Law § 18 (Consol. 1997). Two states specifically provide for dissolution of a religious society, one by the superior body in which the assets will vest if the society dissolves (Minn. Stat. Ann. §§ 315.37, .38 (West 1997)), and the other upon petition by the governing body if it is a separately incorporated ecclesiastical body (N.Y. Relig. Corp. Law § 18 (Consol. 1997)). Upon dissolution and after payment of debts, the assets of the religious corporation may revert to those persons who gave or contributed the assets (D.C. Code Ann. § 29-911 (1996)), or they may belong to a superior ecclesiastical body or to another organization with similar purposes (Conn. Gen. Stat. Ann. § 33-264e), or they may be distributed according to the constitution of the church. *See* German Evangelical Lutheran St. Johannes Church v. Metropolitan New York Synod of the Lutheran Church in America, 366 N.Y.S.2d 214 (N.Y. App. Div. 1975). The distribution plan must often be approved by a court. *See, e.g.*, Mo. Ann. Stat. § 352.210(3); N.Y. Relig. Corp. Law § 18.

38. One state, Nevada, repealed its statute.

39. Much of the following discussion is based on Kauper & Ellis, *supra* note 1, at 1533–38. *See infra* notes 44–48 for the specific denominations included in each of these states' statutes.

40. Kauper & Ellis, *supra* note 1, at 1533.

41. *Id.* In 1775, nine of the thirteen colonies had established churches. Connecticut, Massachusetts, and New Hampshire had established the Congregational Church; Georgia (in 1758), Maryland (in 1702), New York's lower counties (in 1693), North Carolina (in 1711), South Carolina (in 1706), and Virginia (in 1609) had established the Anglican Church. R.L. Cord, Separation of Church and State 3–4 (1982). Established churches were generally known as territorial parishes, which were public corporations, and any person who resided within the territorial boundaries of the designated parish had to be a member of that parish. Carl Zollmann, Classes of American Religious Corporations, 13 Mich. L. Rev. 566, 566–68 (1915). These religious establishments by the state governments were not prohibited by the federal Constitution until the application of the First Amendment Religion Clauses to the state governments through incorporation by the Fourteenth Amendment in *Cantwell v. Connecticut*, 310 U.S. 296 (1940) (Free Exercise Clause), and *Everson v. Board of Educ.*, 330 U.S. 1 (1947) (Establishment Clause). However, established churches had been gradually eliminated between 1776 and 1833. The Congregational Church was disestablished in Connecticut in 1818, in New Hampshire in 1819, and in Massachusetts in 1833. North Carolina and New York disestablished the Anglican Church during the Revolutionary War, but disestablishment in Virginia did not occur until 1786. Disagreement exists as to when disestablishment occurred in Georgia, Maryland, and South Carolina, although it probably happened between 1776 and 1789. Cord, *supra*, at 4.

This explanation is partially supported by the fact that most such statutory schemes are found in the older states, particularly among the original colonies, including Connecticut, Delaware, Maine, Maryland, Massachusetts, New Hampshire, New Jersey, New York, and Vermont. Kauper & Ellis, *supra* note 1, at 1534. However, other historical factors may account for the existence of some par-

tence of these statutes may represent an unwillingness on the part of legislatures to disrupt any organizations which had formed under earlier statutes.[42] Finally, special provisions for particular denominations may be viewed as necessary because general religious incorporation statutes may not provide a suitable mechanism for some denominations.[43]

The states vary considerably in the number of denominations included in their special statutes. Illinois, Louisiana, Minnesota, and New Hampshire name only one denomination in their special statutory provisions for particular denominations,[44] while New York provides for more than thirty-five different denominations.[45] However, most states specify no more than seven denominations.[46] Similarly, the states differ in which denominations they include. For example, only two states provide for the Universalist Church,[47] and only three states include Lutheran churches of various kinds.[48] The four

---

ticular denominational statutes. For example, the enactment of statutes pertaining to the various Eastern Orthodox churches seems to have occurred during the middle of the twentieth century following the spread of Communism in Central and Eastern Europe and the Soviet Union.

42. Kauper & Ellis, *supra* note 1, at 1533 (noting that "any attempt to impair corporate privilege and powers under earlier statutes might be held invalid as an impairment of the obligation of contracts").

43. William J. Boyer, Jr., Property Rights of Religious Institutions in Wisconsin, 36 Marq. L. Rev. 329 (1953) (explaining that the Wisconsin legislature was aware that "certain religious bodies could not readily comply with the uniformity required by the statutes concerning religious corporations without drastically altering their government"); *see also* Wis. Stat. Ann. § 187.01 (West 1995–96).

44. 85 Ill. Comp. Stat. Ann. 110/50 (West 1997) (Eastern Orthodox Church); La. Rev. Stat. Ann. §§ 12:481–.483 (West 1997) (Orthodox Church); Minn. Stat. Ann. §§ 315.17–.19 (West 1997) (Protestant Episcopal Church); N. H. Rev. Stat. Ann. § 292:15-:17 (1996) (Orthodox Church).

45. All the following citations refer to N.Y. Relig. Corp. Law (Consol. 1997): art. 3 (Protestant Episcopal Parishes or Churches); art. 3A (Apostolic Episcopal Parishes or Churches); art. 3B (Parishes or Churches of the Holy Orthodox Church in America); art. 3C (Parishes or Churches of the American Patriarchal Orthodox Church); art. 4 (Presbyterian Churches); art. 5 (Roman Catholic Churches); art. 5A (Christian Orthodox Catholic Churches of the Eastern Confession); art. 5B (Ruthenian Greek Catholic Churches); art. 5C (Churches of the Orthodox Church of America); art. 6 (Reformed Dutch, Reformed Presbyterian, and Lutheran Churches); art. 7 (Baptist Churches); art. 8 (Churches of the United Church of Christ, Congregational Christian and Independent Churches); art. 8A (Churches of the Ukrainian Orthodox Churches of America); art. 8B (Churches of the Holy Ukrainian Autocephalic Orthodox Church in Exile); art. 9 (Free Churches); art. 9A (Churches of Christ, Scientist); art. 10 (Other Denominations, including § 202 (United Society of Shakers), § 201a (Religious Society of Friends), § 206 (Christian Church (Disciples of Christ) or Church of Christ (Disciples)), § 207 (Jewish Congregations), § 210 (Independent Associated Spiritualist), and § 211 (Spiritualist Science Mother Church, Inc.)); art. 11 (Union Church); art. 11A (Free Methodist Churches); art. 13 (Spiritualist Churches); art. 14 (Churches of the Nazarene); art. 15 (Orthodox Greek Catholic (Eastern Orthodox Churches)); art. 16 (Spiritualist Churches Connected with the National Spiritualist Association); art. 17 (Methodist Churches); art. 18 (churches of the Byelorussian Autocephalic Orthodox Church in America); art. 19 (Unitarian and Universalist Societies); art. 20 (Assemblies of God Churches); art. 21 (Coptic Orthodox Churches).

46. *See, e.g.,* Delaware, Del. Code Ann. tit. 27, §§ 114–118 (1996) (two denominations); Kansas, Kan. Stat. Ann. §§ 17-1711-13c, 17-1716a-16c, 17-1732-33, 17-1753-55 (1996); Maine, ME. Rev. Stat. Ann. tit. 13, § 2982 (West 1997); Maryland, Md. Code Ann., Corps. & Ass'ns §§ 5-314 to -336 (1997) (three denominations); Massachusetts, Mass. Gen. Laws Ann. ch. 67, §§ 39–55 (West 1997) (four denominations); Vermont, Vt. Stat. Ann. tit. 27, §§ 781–944 (1997) (seven denominations); Wisconsin, Wis. Stat. Ann. §§ 187.01–.24 (1995–95) (six denominations). Michigan, however, includes fifteen denominations. Mich. Stat. Ann. §§ 21.1691–.2021 (Law. Co-op. 1997).

47. New York, N.Y. Relig. Corp. Law §§ 400–414 (Consol. 1997) (Unitarian and Universalist Societies); Vermont, Vt. Stat. Ann. tit. 27, §§ 941–944 (1997) (Universalist Church).

48. Connecticut, Conn. Gen. Stat. Ann. §§ 33–277 to 278 and §§ 33-278a–278b (West 1997) (Augustana Evangelical Lutheran Church and Lutheran Church in America, respectively); New Jer-

most common denominations written into the various statutes are, in order, the Protestant Episcopal church, Methodist churches, the Roman Catholic church, and the Eastern Orthodox church.[49]

Corporation sole
Introduction

The third and least common form of corporate structure available to religious organizations is the corporation sole. This corporate form exists in only twenty-six states and the territory of Guam and is usually available only to religious organizations. The corporation sole has been described as the practical equivalent to the modern one-person corporation[50] in which an office is incorporated and the individual holding the office at a given time has the corporate privileges.[51] Upon the death of the officeholder, his or her successor becomes the corporation, thus granting perpetuity to the individual in his or her capacity as an officeholder. In the religious context a corporation sole involves the incorporation of the bishop or other presiding church officer for the purposes of administering and managing the affairs, property and temporalities of the church.[52] The principal purpose of a corporation sole is to insure that a religious organization maintains ownership of its property. When the individual holding the office dies, church property passes to this officeholder's successor for the benefit of the religious group, rather than passing to the officeholder's heirs.[53]

The corporation sole is a particularly useful organizational form for hierarchical religions because it enables the organization's legal structure to mirror its internal theological structure. For example, in a hierarchical church the bishop often has control over church property according to the internal church polity and structure. By incorporating as a corporation sole, the bishop also has legal authority to deal with church property. Because hierarchical churches generally invest church officials with power and authority, they can easily identify which offices to incorporate as corporations sole.[54]

Under English common law two types of corporations sole were possible: civil and ecclesiastical. The ecclesiastical corporation sole is the older form, dating to the mid-fifteenth century, while the civil corporation sole developed one hundred fifty years later

---

sey, N.J. Stat. Ann. §§ 16:5-1 to 16:5-27 (West 1997) (Evangelical Lutheran Church); New York, N.Y. Relig. Corp. Law §§ 110–116 (Consol. 1997) (Reformed Dutch, Reformed Presbyterian and Lutheran Churches).

49. Kauper & Ellis, *supra* note 1, at 1535.

50. Oleck, *supra* note 4, at 20.

51. Kauper & Ellis, *supra* note 1, at 1540. Blackstone defined a corporation sole as "one person only and his successors, in some particular station, who are incorporated by law, in order to give them some legal capacities and advantages, particularly that of perpetuity, which in their natural persons they could not have had." 1 William Blackstone, Commentaries *469.

52. *See, e.g.*, Cal. Corp. Code § 10002-5 (Deering 1996).

53. *See, e.g.*, County of San Luis Obispo v. Ashurst, 194 Cal. Rptr. 5, 6–8, (Cal. Ct. App. 1983) (stating that "[t]he creditors of the corporation sole may not look to the assets of the individual holding office, nor may the creditors of the individual look to the assets held by the corporation sole"). Berry v. Society of Saint Pius X, 81 Cal. Rptr. 2d 574, 581 (Cal. Ct. App. 1999) (citing County of San Luis Obispo that "One principal purpose of the corporation sole is to insure the continuation of ownership of property dedicated to the benefit of a religious organization…").

54. Kauper & Ellis, *supra* note 1, at 1540.

when the English monarch was deemed to be a corporation sole.[55] It developed as a product of early property law principles which did not permit the devise of real property to a church in fee simple absolute, a form of complete ownership. A conveyance to the religious leader (usually a parson or minister) personally thus ran the risk that the property might descend to the leader's heirs or be subject to personal debts or encumbrances.[56] By making the parson and his successors a corporation, the church preserved the parsonage property for the benefit of the church; because the present officeholder, his predecessor and his successor were deemed by law to be one and the same person, any property given to one was considered the property of the successor. As it developed in the New England colonies, the corporation sole functioned as a municipal corporation, and alienation of property required the consent of the parish.[57]

While the earliest corporations sole came into existence as a product of the common law, after the Reformation in England, a corporate charter was required for their formation.[58] While the special charter system was used for corporations sole, as for other corporations, during the nineteenth century, this system was gradually replaced by general corporation statutes. In the case of the corporation sole, however, considerable resistance arose over the enactment of such legislation because the corporation sole was viewed as hierarchical and antidemocratic. However, at the urging of primarily the Roman Catholic church,[59] many states did enact either special legislation permitting the church to incorporate as a corporation sole or a general incorporation statute permitting corporations sole.[60] Today, as has been said, slightly more than half of the states (twenty-six) permit some form of the corporation sole, and it continues to be a useful structural form of organization for many religious groups.

Of this rough half of the Union twelve states and the territory of Guam have statutes which explicitly permit religious groups to organize as a corporation sole.[61] These twelve states share similar statutory patterns, although they vary on specific provisions. An additional three states have statutes which appear to permit some form of the corporation sole, either allowing a form of organization similar to the corporation sole but not explicitly described as such, or limiting the corporation sole form to certain reli-

---

55. Blackstone, *supra* note 51, at *469; Frederic W. Maitland, The Corporation Sole, 16 L.Q. Rev. 335, 337 (1900).

56. Blackstone, *supra* note 51, at *469.

57. Kauper & Ellis, *supra* note 1, at 1504–07.

58. Earlier churches which had operated as a corporation sole before the charter requirement became prevalent were permitted to continue as corporations under the fiction of a "lost grant." Kauper & Ellis, *supra* note 1, at 1504. The Episcopal Church also enjoyed the status of a common law corporation sole in those states where it was established, although this status was lost as the result of the disestablishment process. *See* Terret v. Taylor, 13 U.S. (9 Cranch) 43, 46 (1815) (noting that the minister of a church was seized of the freehold of church property while he held office and was capable of transmitting that property to his successor in the form of a corporation sole).

59. While opposition to the corporation sole was probably based on anti-Roman Catholic sentiment, the Roman Catholic church favored this corporate form because it most closely mirrored the theological and doctrinal polity of the church and, in particular, it assured that church property would be controlled by the church hierarchy.

60. James B. O'Hara, The Modern Corporation Sole, 93 Dick. L. Rev. 23, 31 (1988).

61. *See* Ala. Code §§ 10-4-1 to -7 (1996); Alaska Stat. §§ 10.40.010–.150 (Michie 1997); Ariz. Rev. Stat. Ann. §§ 10-1851 to 1857 (West 1997); Cal. Corp. Code §§ 10000–10015 (Deering 1996); Colo. Rev. Stat. §§ 7-52-101 to -106 (1997); Guam Code Ann. § 10102 (1996); Haw. Rev. Stat. §§ 419-1 to -9 (1997); Mont. Code Ann. §§ 35-3-101 to -209 (1996); Nev. Rev. Stat. §§ 84.010–.150 (1997); Or. Rev. Stat. § 65-067 (1996); Utah Code Ann. §§ 16-7-1 to -14 (1997); Wash. Rev. Code Ann. §§ 24.12.010–.060 (1997); Wyo. Stat. Ann. §§ 17-8-101 to -117 (Michie 1997).

gions.[62] Moreover, nine states either have passed special legislative acts granting certain religious groups (or certain bodies within a particular religion) the authority to incorporate as a corporation sole or had a corporation sole statute at one time that has since been repealed. The case law in these states describes some religious organizations as corporations sole, but no current statute allows newly organized religious groups to incorporate as such.[63] Finally, two states recognize the common law corporation sole.[64]

Functioning of a corporation sole

With only one exception[65] all states that permit the formation of a corporation sole limit its use to religious organizations. In some cases the statutes further limit the per-

---

62. The North Carolina statute is the most similar to the typical corporation sole statute. It allows a duly appointed bishop, minister, or other ecclesiastical officer many of the same powers as a corporation sole, including the power to acquire, hold, or sell church property whenever the laws of the church permit it. In addition, in the event of the transfer, removal, resignation or death of the officer, such property vests in the duly elected successor to the office. However, the statute does not specifically refer to such an office as a corporation sole. N.C. Gen. Stat. §61-5 (1997). New Hampshire appears to allow the minister of a church or religious society to act as a corporation sole only in reference to parsonage lands and with the limitation that unless the minister has the consent of the parish, no conveyance made by the minister is valid for longer than the minister continues to hold office. N.H. Rev. Stat. Ann. §§306:6–8 (1996).

The Idaho Nonprofit Corporations Act appears to allow a form of organization similar in operation to a corporation sole. According to the statute, corporations sole created under the prior statute will be deemed single director, nonmembership corporations. Idaho Code §30-304 (1997). Thus, it may follow that a church or religious society incorporating under Idaho's current law could organize as a single director, nonmembership corporation which would then be very similar in operation to the corporation sole. *Id.* at §§30-308, 30-315, 30-318(e). By extension, one might further posit that any not-for-profit corporation organizing in Idaho might attain similar advantages by choosing to incorporate as a single director, nonmembership corporation.

Finally, the Michigan statute permits only Roman Catholic bishops and Protestant Episcopal bishops to form corporations sole. The statute grants a Roman Catholic bishop a full set of corporate powers but only grants a Protestant Episcopal bishop authority to deal with property. Mich. Comp. Laws Ann. §§458.1–2; 458.271–273 (West 1997).

63. District of Columbia, *see, e.g.,* Dietrich v. District of Columbia Bd. of Zoning Adjustments, 293 A.2d 470 (D.C. 1972) (Archbishop of Washington described as a corporation sole); Illinois, *see, e.g.,* Fintak v. Catholic Bishop, 366 N.E.2d 480 (Ill. App. 1977) (Catholic Bishop of Chicago described as a corporation sole); Kentucky, *see, e.g.,* Roland v. Catholic Archdiocese, 301 S.W.2d 574 (Ky. 1957) (Roman Catholic Bishop of Louisville described as a corporation sole); Maine, *see, e.g.,* Parent v. Roman Catholic Bishop, 436 A.2d 888 (Me. 1981) (Roman Catholic Bishop of Portland described as a corporation sole); Maryland, *see, e.g.,* Smith v. Maryland Casualty Co., 229 A.2d 120 (Md. 1967) (Archbishop of Baltimore described as a corporation sole); Massachusetts, *see, e.g.,* Director of the Div. of Employment Sec. v. Roman Catholic Bishop, 420 N.E.2d 322 (Mass. 1981) (Roman Catholic bishop of the diocese of Springfield described as a corporation sole); New Hampshire, *see, e.g.,* Opinion of the Justices, 345 A.2d 412 (N.H. 1975) (Roman Catholic Bishop of Manchester described as a corporation sole); New Mexico, *see, e.g.,* Moya v. Catholic Archdiocese, 587 P.2d 425 (N.M. 1978), *rev'd on other grounds,* 755 P.2d 583 (1988) (Catholic Archdiocese of New Mexico described as a corporation sole); South Carolina, *see, e.g.,* Decker v. Bishop of Charleston, 147 S.E.2d 264 (S.C. 1966) (Bishop of Charleston described as a corporation sole created by legislative act). Although not permitting incorporation of a new corporation sole, the South Carolina Nonprofit Corporations Act provides for the amendment of the charter of a corporation sole. S.C. Code Ann. §33-31-140 (Law. Co-op. 1997).

64. Arkansas, *see, e.g.,* City of Little Rock v. Linn, 432 S.W.2d 455 (Ark. 1968); Florida, *see, e.g.,* Reid v. Barry, 112 So. 846 (Fla. 1927).

65. Arizona permits the formation of a corporation sole for the purpose of acquiring, holding and disposing of the property of scientific research institutions maintained solely for pure research without expectation of pecuniary gain or profit. Ariz. Rev. Stat. §10-1851 (1997).

missible purposes of a corporation sole to the management of a religious group's property for such objectives as the benefit of the religion itself, works of charity, and public worship.[66] In general, the presiding officer of any church or religious society is authorized by statute to form a corporation sole if this format conforms with the rules and canons of the religious entity and if title to the property is vested in that person.[67] The process of incorporation,[68] the powers granted by statute to the corporation sole,[69] and the methods of dissolution[70] are usually comparable to those delineated for general not-for-profit corporations.[71]

Perhaps the most distinctive area of functioning for a corporation sole is the manner in which it provides for vacancy in and succession to the corporation sole office. In general, upon the officeholder's death, resignation, or removal, his or her successor is vested with the title of all property held by the previous officeholder, with the same power and authority over the property and subject to the same legal liabilities and obligations with reference to the property.[72] Some statutes also deal with the particular problems of interim vacancy in the office[73] and situations where an individual who was

---

66. For example, the Utah statute states: "Corporations sole may be formed for acquiring, holding or disposing of church or religious society property for the benefit of religion, for works of charity and for public worship..." Utah Code Ann. § 16-7-1 (1997); *see also* Alaska Stat. § 10.40.010 (1997); Ariz. Rev. Stat. § 10-1851 (1997); Nev. Rev. Stat. § 84.010 (1997); Wyo. Stat. Ann. § 17-8-109 (Michie 1997).

Other statutes state the permissible purposes more broadly; for example, the Hawaii statute which allows a corporation sole to organize for the purposes of "administering and managing the affairs, property, and temporalities or the church." Haw. Rev. Stat. § 419-1 (1997); *see also* Cal. Corp. Code § 10002 (Deering 1996).

67. For example, the Nevada statute provides that:

An archbishop, bishop, president, trustee in trust, president of stake, president of congregation, overseer, presiding elder, district superintendent, other presiding officer or clergyman of a church or religious society or denomination, who has been chosen, elected or appointed in conformity with the constitution, canons, rites, regulations or discipline of the church or religious society or denomination, and in whom is vested the legal title to property held for...the church or religious society or denomination, may make and subscribe written articles of incorporation.

Nev. Rev. Stat. § 84.020 (1997); *see also* Cal. Corp. Code § 10002 (Deering 1996) (specifying the "bishop, chief priest, presiding elder, or other presiding officer"); Or. Rev. Stat. § 65-067 (1996) (specifying "any individual").

68. *See, e.g.,* Mont. Code Ann. § 35-3-202 (1996). A few statutes present variations. For example, Alaska requires the articles of incorporation to state the estimated value of property owned by the corporation at the time of executing the articles of incorporation, Alaska Stat. § 10.40.040(3) (Michie 1997), and California requires a statement as the method for filling a vacancy in the incorporated office according to the rules, regulations or constitution of the religious group, Cal. Corp. Code § 10003(d) (Deering 1996).

69. *See, e.g.,* Ala. Code § 10-4-4 (1996). The corporation sole may be explicitly exempted from any general requirement that the membership of the religious group must consent to property transfers. Utah Code Ann. § 16-7-7 (1997).

70. *See, e.g.,* Ala. Code § 10-4-7 (1996); Alaska Stat. § 10.40.150 (Michie 1997); Cal. Corp. Code § 10012-10015 (Deering 1996); Haw. Rev. Stat. § 419-8 (1997); Utah Code Ann. § 16-7-12 (1997).

71. Oregon, for example, explicitly places the corporation sole under its general not-for-profit corporation statute, as a form of religious corporation, and subjects it to the same statutory treatment, differing only in that the corporation sole is managed by a single director without a board of directors. Or. Rev. Stat. § 65-067 (1996).

72. *See, e.g.,* Ariz. Rev. Stat. Ann. § 10-1856 (1997).

73. The incorporated office holder may appoint an administrator to act in case of temporary vacancy or, in the absence of such an administrator, the superior ecclesiastical authority to whom the office holder is subject may appoint an administrator. The administrator must file an application for a certificate of administratorship with the secretary of state. *See, e.g.,* Ala. Code § 10-4-6 (1996);

never formally incorporated as a corporation sole but who, at the time of death, resignation, or removal was holding title to trust property for the use or benefit of a religious group.[74]

Case law that deals with particular issues involving the corporation sole is scarce. Most of the cases that do mention it merely describe the office involved as a corporation sole but do not treat it differently than other legal structures.[75] Occasionally, judicial opinions speak of the corporation sole with deference.[76] One area where courts have wavered involves the question of whether the corporation sole bears liability as the principal for the actions of the officeholder, as its agent. While a corporation sole seems to bear liability on an agency theory when the matter involved is business-related (as would any other corporation), at least one court has held that the corporation sole does not bear liability when the agency issue involves an ecclesiastical, rather than a business, matter.[77]

The main advantage of the corporation sole is the ability of the legal structure to mirror the doctrinal structure of a religious group in terms of property ownership, au-

---

Colo. Rev. Stat. § 7-52-104 (1997). On the other hand, Montana permits the superior ecclesiastical authority to appoint a board of advisors to exercise the powers of the corporation or to further delegate the executive and administrative functions of the corporation to an elected administrator. Mont. Code Ann. § 35-3-208 (1996).

74. These statutes specifically provide that such property shall be deemed to be in abeyance until the vacancy is filled and shall then vest immediately in the successor without any further required act or deed so as to prevent either a reversion of the property to the donor or a vesting of the property in the heirs of the deceased office holder. *See, e.g.,* Alaska Stat. § 10.40.120 (Michie 1997); Ariz. Rev. Stat. Ann. § 10-1857 (West 1997); Colo. Rev. Stat. § 7-52-105 (1997); Utah Code Ann. § 16-7-10 (1997); Wyo. Stat. Ann. § 17-8-117 (Michie 1997). These provisions allow religious groups which have not met the formal statutory requirements for incorporation as a corporation sole to enjoy the most important advantage of this organizational form in that succession to church property is thus permitted.

75. *See, e.g.,* Property Associates, Inc. v. Archbishop of Guam, No. 93-00003A, 1993 WL 470277 (D. Guam Oct. 12, 1993) (describing archbishop as corporation sole in dispute involving termination of a lease); St. Gregory's Church v. O'Connor, 477 P.2d 540 (Ariz. Ct. App. 1970) (Bishop of the Roman Catholic Church of the Diocese of Tucson described as a corporation sole in a negligence suit); Larson v. Archdiocese of Denver, 631 P.2d 1163 (Colo. Ct. App. 1981) (Archdiocese of Denver described as a corporation sole in a negligence action); Corporation of the President of the Church of Jesus Christ of Latter-day Saints v. Wallace, 590 P.2d 343 (Utah 1979) (church president described as a corporation sole in case involving issuance of a restraining order due to disruptive conduct of the defendant).

76. *See, e.g.,* Hurley v. Werly, 203 So. 2d 530, 534 (Fla. Dist. Ct. App. 1967) (reversing a lower court decision which decreed specific performance of a real estate contract against the bishop of the Diocese of St. Augustine because the bishop had failed to appear at a deposition and stating that because the corporation sole has protective attributes, the lower court should have "in deference to his privileged legal status, proceeded more cautiously than precipitately").

77. The Alabama Supreme Court refused to hold a corporation sole liable for the actions of a priest in damaging an abortion clinic and found that the Bishop's relationship with the priest was ecclesiastical in nature. The court relied on the fact that according to Alabama's corporation sole statute, a corporation sole's functions related to conducting business, not to ecclesiastical duties, and thus no liability could be created on the part of the corporation sole unless a business activity were involved. Wood v. Benedictine Soc'y, 530 So. 2d 801, 805 (Ala. 1988). A California appellate court, on the other hand, held a corporation sole liable on an agency theory in a wrongful death action based on a car accident in which a priest was involved, without addressing the question of whether the underlying matter was ecclesiastical or business-related. The court concluded that there was agency liability because the bishop had the right to control the priest's activities within its jurisdiction and the priest was acting within the scope of the agency when the accident occurred. Stevens v. Roman Catholic Bishop, 123 Cal. Rptr. 171, 178 (Cal. Ct. App. 1975).

thority and control. As has been suggested, the corporation sole is an especially attractive option for religious groups with hierarchical polity. Because it insures that the religious group's property will pass to the successor of the corporation sole upon his or her death, many view it as a secure method of owning property, one that in particular prevents members or trustees from using their property ownership to pressure the religious group on doctrinal issues. In addition, it is more secure than fee simple ownership by the officeholder, which risks the passing of religiously held property to an officer's heirs or creditors.

Yet these advantages may also be counted as disadvantages. For while the vesting of assets, extensive powers, and complete authority in one person[78] may reflect a religious group's doctrinal structure, it may also lead to confusion between personal and religious assets, difficulty in government monitoring, and lack of accountability or proper controls. Unlimited authority by one who is not legally subject to the will of a group's membership or other directors does risk abuses. However, while the corporation sole may have great legal autonomy, a church organization may nevertheless have safeguards to prevent abuses.[79] In light of these advantages and disadvantages, the corporation sole form still clearly offers significant advantages to religious groups that find the form the most appropriate for their theological principles.

States that prohibit incorporation of religious organizations

The constitutions of two states, Virginia and West Virginia, bar the granting of a charter of incorporation to any church or religious denomination.[80] The reasons for this anomalous treatment of religious organizations seem to lie in the strong historical tradition of Virginia, one that dates to the revolutionary period. Indeed, such a constitu-

---

78. *See, e.g.*, Estate of Zabriskie, 158 Cal. Rptr. 154, 157 (Cal. Ct. App. 1979) (stating that "[t]he will and judgment alone of the presiding officer regulate his acts, like any other individual acting in his own right").

79. O'Hara, *supra* note 60, at 30–31 (stating that in the Roman Catholic Church, approval of a board of consultors is now required on major property decisions). In a recent decision, *Berry v. Society of Saint Pius X*, 81 Cal. Rptr. 2d 574 (Cal. Ct. App. 1999), the California court presented something of a paradox. In deciding the issue of whether the previous pastor, who was the officer of a corporation sole, could amend the bylaw pertaining to appointment of a successor, the court held that the amendment was invalid because the method of amendment failed to comply with the statutory provision requiring that the amendment be "duly authorized by the religious organization governed by the corporation." Although rejecting the argument that the corporation sole and the religious corporation were identical, the court explicitly refused to identify the "religious organization."

80. Va. Const. art. IV, § 14, and W. Va. Const. art. VI, § 47. The constitution of South Carolina expressly prohibits special laws, but not general laws, relating to the incorporation of religious institutions as well as a variety of other charitable and not-for-profit corporations and business corporations. S.C. Code Ann. § 33-31-10 (Law. Co-op. 1996). It is not unusual for state constitutions to address matters of concern to religious groups, but these are typically restricted to provisions regarding the free exercise of religion, prohibitions against aid to religious groups, tax exemptions to religious institutions, and protection of civil rights regardless of religious beliefs. Individual state constitutional provisions regarding religion are examined in Chester J. Antieau, et al., Religion under the State Constitutions (1965); Kauper & Ellis, *supra* note 1, at 1528; Linda S. Wendtland, Note, Beyond the Establishment Clause: Enforcing Separation of Church and State Through State Constitutional Provisions, 71 Va. L. Rev. 625 (1985).

tional ban reflects the beliefs of Virginians Thomas Jefferson and James Madison[81] on matters of church/state separationism and religious liberty. Some have also suggested that these prohibitions are the descendants of English mortmain statutes.[82]

The constitutional ban was intended to prevent the potential favoritism created by the granting of special corporate charters to religious organizations,[83] rather than to preclude all incorporation of religious organizations. In any case, the Virginia Nonstock Corporation Act now permits an entity to incorporate under it for any lawful purpose,[84] mentioning elsewhere that religious purposes are among those permitted. It appears that sev-

---

81. The development of Virginia's church/state relationship began in 1609 with the establishment of the Anglican Church (later the Episcopal Church), Cord, *supra* note 41, at 4. A disestablishment movement had begun by 1784, led by Thomas Jefferson and James Madison, *id.* at 121. In 1784, the General Assessment Bill was introduced into the Virginia legislature and was intended to raise funds to support "Teachers of the Christian Religion" through compulsory public payments. Richard E. Morgan, The Supreme Court and Religion 18–19 (1972); Robert S. Alley, The Supreme Court on Church and State 10 (1988). Madison's well-known pamphlet, "A Memorial and Remonstrance Against Religious Assessments," was authored to oppose the assessment. In the 1785 session of the General Assembly, the legislature defeated the assessment bill, and in 1786, it passed Jefferson's Bill for Establishing Religious Freedom, which remains in the Virginia code today. Va. Code Ann. § 57-1, 2 (Michie 1997). *See also* Morgan, *supra*, at 19–24; Alley, *supra*, at 12–15; Gerard v. Bradley, Church-State Relationships in America 37, 149–50; Cord, *supra* note 41, at 4–47.

82. *See, e.g.*, Osnes v. Morris, 298 S.E.2d 803, 805 (W. Va. 1982) (Stating that "this constitutional provision [restricting the ability of churches and religious denominations to own real estate] is the legitimate progeny of the English statutes of mortmain which played a central role in the law of property in England" and describing the purpose of mortmain acts "to repress the alarming influence of ecclesiastical corporations, which had, even as early as the Norman conquest, monopolized so much of the land in England, that the Abbot of St. Albans told the conqueror that the reason why he had subjugated the country by the single victory at Hastings was because the land, which was the maintenance of martial men, was given and converted to pious employments and for the maintenance of holy votaries.") (quoting from *Lathrop v. Commercial Bank*, 38 Ky. (8 Dana) 114 (1839) and also citing to *Goetz v. Old National Bank of Martinsburg*, 84 S.E.2d 759, 768 (W. Va. 1954).

83. The Virginia Constitution states, "The General Assembly shall not grant a charter of incorporation to any church or religious denomination.…" Va. Const. art. 4 § 14, para. 20. Thus, by its literal terms, the constitution only prohibits legislatively-created religious corporations but does not seem to prohibit religious corporations created by some other method, as is now the case under the Virginia Nonstock Corporation, which is a general incorporation statute. *See* A.E. Dick Howard, 1 Commentaries on the Constitution of Virginia 545–46 (1974) (arguing that these provisions represent a "safeguard against an establishment of religion, since the legislature will not be in a position, by chartering some churches but not others, to give preferment to any denomination or religion").

84. Both Virginia and West Virginia not-for-profit corporation statutes allow not-for-profit corporations to be organized broadly for "any lawful purpose or purposes." Va. Code Ann. § 13.1-825 (1997); W. Va. Code § 31-1-17 (1994) (listing examples of lawful purposes as including, but not limited, to: charitable, benevolent, eleemosynary, educational, civic, patriotic, social, fraternal, literary, cultural, athletic, scientific, agricultural, horticultural, animal husbandry, and professional, commercial or industrial or trade association). Although such a broad statement of permissible purpose would seem to include incorporation of churches or religious denominations, both states have provisions within their state constitutions prohibiting the incorporation of churches or religious denominations. Va. Const. art 4, § 14, para. 20 ("[T]he General Assembly shall not grant a charter of incorporation to any church or religious denomination, but may secure title to church property to an extent to be limited by law"); W. Va. Const. § 47 (stating, "[n]o charter of incorporation shall be granted to any church or religious denomination. Provisions may be made by general laws for securing the title to church property, and for the sale and transfer thereof, so that it shall be held, used, or transferred for the purposes of such church, or religious denomination"). In West Virginia, this constitutional prohibition is specifically included within the previously mentioned "purposes of incorporation" section of the West Virginia code. W. Va. Code § 31-1-7(c); *see also* Lunsford, Withrow & Co. v. Wren, 63 S.E. 308 (W. Va. 1908) (noting the constitutional prohibition on the granting of

eral organizations with religious purposes but which are not *per se* churches or other specific denominational organizations do in fact incorporate pursuant to these provisions. In addition, it seems some denominational groups (such as individual churches, synagogues, and mosques) incorporate funds for the purpose of holding financial assets, while not themselves incorporating.[85] Whether this is the result of a perceived constitutional ban or merely the continuation of a tradition is difficult to determine.

Added to these apparent or real obstacles to incorporation, the Virginia statutes limit the amount of real and personal property which a religious denomination may own.[86]

---

articles of incorporation to a church and a church's incompetency to sue or be sued or to enter into contracts).

85. In both Virginia and West Virginia, churches and other denominational groups are able to become involved in not-for-profit incorporation. For example, for purposes of incorporation in West Virginia, a "religious-oriented" organization will not be deemed a "church or religious denomination" if it will have no "ecclesiastical control" of persons engaged in religious worship and will not prescribe the forms of such worship. *See* Op. Att'y Gen. 252 (1957) (permitting a group whose stated purpose was to "win people to Christ" through evangelism and missionary work to incorporate because each individual was free to select the church or denomination of his choice). Auxiliary or para-church organizations have been incorporated with the purpose of maintaining or operating child care centers, retirement homes, education funds, fellowship funds, and preservation funds, even when such groups have an explicit denominational affiliation. Religious groups seem to follow the method of incorporating a fund for the purpose of owning property which is then used to support the activities of the group, but without the group itself formally incorporating. *See, e.g.*, Westminster-Canterbury of Hampton Roads, Inc., 385 S.E.2d 561, 562 (Va. 1989) (describing corporation organized by the Episcopal Diocese and the Presbyterian Church to own and operate a housing and health-care facility as a nonstock corporation "organized exclusively for charitable, religious, educational, and scientific purposes"); St. John's Protestant Episcopal Church Endowment Fund, Inc. v. Vestry of St. John's Protestant Episcopal Church, 377 S.E.2d 375, 376 (Va. 1989) (describing the fund as incorporated in order "to acquire and establish in perpetuity a fund...and to appropriate the income therefrom...to the preservation, insurance and improvements of the real and [personal] property [of the church] and also to its religious, charitable and benevolent uses"); St. Paul A.M.E. Church House Corp. v. Buckeye Union Ins., 379 F. Supp. 562, 563 (S.D.W. Va. 1974) (stating purpose of church housing corporation was to "build a number of low-cost public apartment house units for rental"); Application of Virginia United Methodist Homes, Inc., No. SEC940121, 1994 WL 725338 (Va. Corporation Commission Nov. 18, 1994) (describing Virginia United Methodist Homes, Inc. as incorporated under the Nonstock Corporation Act in an application to be exempt from securities registration requirements); Application of Southeastern District-LCMS Church Extension Fund, Inc., No. SEC940035, 1994 WL 258467 (Va. Corporation Commission Apr. 28, 1994) (describing religiously-affiliated fund as incorporated exclusively for "religious, educational, charitable and benevolent purposes" under the Nonstock Corporation Act in an application for exemption from securities registration requirements); Application of the Christian Broadcasting Network, Inc., No. SEC930080, 1993 WL 359564 (Va. Corporation Commission Aug. 9, 1993) (describing religiously-affiliated network as incorporated under the Nonstock Corporation Act with a "religious, educational, and charitable purpose" in an application for exemption from securities registration requirements). Op. Att'y Gen., June 23, 1969 (permitting a West Virginia Christian recreational center, which was nondenominational and nonsectarian, and where no specific church was represented, to incorporate).

86. Specific statutes permit religious groups to own property. *See* Va. Code Ann. § 57-7.1 (Michie 1997); W. Va. Code § 35-1-1 (1997). However, in Virginia, the trustees may not hold property for religious purposes which exceeds 15 acres of land in a city of town, or 250 acres outside of a city or town and within the same county. The local government may permit the holding of up to 50 acres within a town or city under certain circumstances. The trustees may not hold personal property which exceeds $10 million in worth. Va. Code Ann. § 57-12 (Michie 1997). In West Virginia, the statute has been amended to permit trustees to hold 10 acres of land within a city, town or village and 60 acres outside of a city, town or village. There is no limitation placed on the amount of personal property which may be owned. W. Va. Code § 35-1-8 (1997); W.Va. H.B. 2569, 72nd Legislature (1995). These limits are not, however, applicable only to religious groups.

Despite the prohibition's origin, to the extent the prohibition is retained it appears outdated in light of the prevailing trend toward incorporating religious organizations under general incorporation statutes. Furthermore, limitations or obstacles to incorporating or owning property that are not generally applicable to all charitable or not-for-profit organizations raise serious questions of constitutionality under the Free Exercise Clause.

The element of choice

The myriad of variations in structural form available to religious organizations in the different states raises two key practical questions for every such group. First, what are the available structural options in the state where the group is based, and what are the particular burdens or advantages that attend each option? Second, can a religious organization that functions primarily in one state incorporate in another state merely to benefit from a legal structure that closely mirrors the group's religious polity? Finally, both these questions lead to a provocative corollary issue which will be addressed in the next section: Can a state's exclusion of a legal form which best mirrors the theology of a particular religion be a violation of the group's right to free exercise?

Choice of structural forms within a state

In every state except West Virginia, a religious organization has the option of incorporating as a not-for-profit or nonstock corporation. In states whose statutes make no provision for specific forms of religious corporations, this may be the only choice. However, as has been discussed, most states offer more than one statutory model. With such a great variation of statutory incorporation forms available—not only among the different states but even within the same state—a religious organization needs to evaluate its choices carefully when considering the type of legal structure to adopt. Some of these variations and choices will now be considered.

A few states require religious organizations to incorporate under a religious corporation or religious societies statute. Although these states have a not-for-profit corporation act, they stipulate that special provisions pertaining to religious corporations govern the formation of these corporations.[87] Yet most states with more than one type of incorporation statute do not specify whether a religious organization may choose under which statute to incorporate; in the absence of a specific prohibition, the ability to choose can only be assumed.[88]

Yet another variant on incorporation is offered by those states that add to their more general statutory models the specific denominational statutes. Many of these states per-

---

87. *See* Del. Code Ann. tit. 27, § 101 (1996); Md. Code Ann., Corps & Ass'ns § 5-302 (1996); N.H. Rev. Stat. Ann. § 306.4 (1996); N.C. Gen. Stat. § 55-A-3(A)(2) (1997); Ohio Rev. Code Ann. § 1702.03 (Anderson 1997).

88. Many of the statutes specifically mention that a religious society may incorporate under them. *See, e.g.,* Colo. Rev. Stat. §§ 7-20-104, 7-40-106, 7-50-101, 7-51-101 (1997); D.C. Code Ann. §§ 29-504, -1001 (1996); 805 Ill. Comp. Stat. Ann. 105/103.05, 110/35 (West 1997); Kan. Stat. Ann. §§ 17-1701, 17-6001(b) (1996); Minn. Stat. Ann. §§ 315.01, 315.05 (West 1996); Mo. Ann. Stat. §§ 355.025, 352.010 (West 1966); Okla. Stat. Ann. tit. 18, §§ 562, 1002(A) (West 1996). A Missouri statute specifically states that the right of a religious group to organize as it wishes is not affected by the statute. Mo. Ann. Stat. § 355.500 (West 1996).

mit a religious group to incorporate under whichever statute it chooses,[89] but a few
states limit the choices available to particular denominations.[90] Those statutes which
limit the choices available to specific religious groups, especially those which mandate
that a group incorporate under a particular denominational provision, are probably not
viewed by adherents of that denomination as an infringement on the free exercise of
their religion. In fact, the existence of the denominational statutes may be the product
of a lobbying effort by the denomination itself and may thus raise the question of a
preference granted to particular religious groups. In fact, it might be argued that any
situation in which the state acts as more than a "rubber stamp" to the religious organization's choice of corporate form raises a possible problem of "excessive entanglement."
Moreover, those states that do not have denominational provisions or that limit such
provisions to a select group of denominations are implicitly limiting the choices of
those groups that do not have the benefit of such provisions. The limited presence of
the corporation sole as a structural choice further suggests limitations on a religious
group's ability to choose the legal form best suited to its religious polity.

Foreign corporations

It is also necessary to consider an extension of the question about organizational
choice: can a religious group that has been formed in one state function in a different
state? Following the model of the business corporation statutes, many states provide in
their general not-for-profit or religious corporation statute for the operation of foreign
corporations within their state borders.[91] Given such a provision, can a religious organi-

---

89. *See, e.g.,* Mass. Gen. Laws Ann. ch. 67, §§ 23, 40, 44 (West 1997) (permitting a religious
group to incorporate under the religious society provisions or under the denominational statutes for
Methodist, Episcopal, and Roman Catholic churches); Mich. Comp. Laws Ann. §§ 450.159,
450.178, 458.262 and 458.428 (West 1997) (allowing a choice to religious groups as to whether to
incorporate under trustee corporation provisions, ecclesiastical corporation provisions, not-for-
profit corporation provisions, or specific denominational statutes); N.J. Stat. Ann. §§ 15A:2-1(b);
16:2-12, 16:5-1, 16:3-1, 16:10A-2, 16:11-1, 16:12-1, 16:13-1, 16:10A-2, 16:11-1, 16:12-1, 16:13-1,
16:15-1, 16:16-1, 16:17-3 (West 1997) (allowing religious groups to incorporate as either a not-for-
profit corporation or under one of ten specific denominational statutes); Me. Rev. Stat. Ann. tit. 13,
§§ 901, 2861, 3021, 2982, 2986 (West 1996) (granting a choice to religious groups).

90. *See, e.g.,* Conn. Gen. Stat. Ann. §§ 33-264a, 33-268, 33-279 (West 1997) (generally permitting a choice whether to organize under the Religious Corporation and Societies provision, the specially chartered corporations provision, or the specific denominational provisions, but prohibiting
formation as a nonstock corporation); Wis. Stat. Ann. §§ 181.03, 187.01, 187.19, 181.76(3) (West
1995–96) (generally permitting a choice whether to incorporate as a nonstock corporation or under
religious societies statutes but excluding Roman Catholic churches from the religious society provisions). One may speculate as to the constitutionality of any statute that, on its face, dictates different
treatment for specific denominations. *See* Church of Lukumi Babalu Aye, Inc. v. Hialeah, 508 U.S.
520 (1993). It would seem that specific denominational statutes could only pass constitutional
muster if sufficient options were made available through the total statutory scheme so that, in effect,
no denominations were excluded.

91. Most states seem to permit foreign not-for-profit corporations to perform the same activities
as domestic corporations. In some cases, the foreign corporation may be required to register or obtain a certificate from the secretary of state (*see, e.g.,* Wash. Rev. Code § 24.03.305 (1997)), while in
other states there are no requirements (*see, e.g.,* Wis. Stat. § 181.66 (1995–96)). Most statutes limit
the foreign corporation to acting in ways permitted to similar domestic corporations, and some
specifically state that "nothing contained in this chapter shall be construed to regulate the organization or the internal affairs of a foreign corporation." *Id.* § 181.66(1). It would seem to be possible for
a particular corporation to organize in a state which permits corporations sole and to then conduct
activities in a state which does not but which has such a specific provision.

zation that desires to operate in one state, the statutes of which do not expressly provide for the structural model that the organization prefers, incorporate in a different state that does offer the preferred structure? An analogy is provided by the practice of for-profit corporations incorporating in Delaware because of its favorable corporation statute and judicial interpretations, regardless of where these corporations conduct their primary business. Could a religious organization in West Virginia incorporate in a different state, as a way of circumventing West Virginia's restrictions on incorporation for religious organizations? Could a religious organization incorporate in a state that provides for a particular corporate form, such as a denominational form or corporation sole, and then operate and conduct business in a state that does not specifically permit this type of incorporation? While virtually no case law addresses this subject, many state statutes would seem to permit this arrangement. Whether this would create collateral issues or complications, such as in property ownership by a foreign entity, is not clear in current law.

Another question is whether a state that does not recognize the corporation sole would consider corporations sole incorporated outside of the home state (by organizations wishing to take advantage of this form) to be contrary to its public policy. In addition to the availability of particular corporate structures, religious organizations need to consider their respective pros and cons. For example, some states grant exemptions from certain regulations to religious corporations. Perhaps the most common example is the exemption from registration requirements imposed on other types of not-for-profit corporations.[92] A more interesting question arises in those states that exempt volunteer directors and officers of not-for-profit corporations from liability for simple negligence.[93] Such protection would today be considered highly desirable and would thus provide a significant incentive to incorporate in such a state.

The Relationship of Institutional Structure to the First Amendment

This discussion of the legal structures available to religious organizations leads to the crux of a dilemma which must be confronted — the relationship between legal structure and the Religion Clauses of the First Amendment.[94] A religious organization need not

---

92. While the considerable majority of states that impose particular requirements under Solicitation Acts exempt religious organizations from those requirements, four states do not. *See* Cal. Corp. Code §§ 17510–17510.7 (Deering 1996); La. Rev. Stat. Ann. §§ 51:1901–1909 (West 1997); Me. Rev. Stat. Ann. tit. 9, §§ 5001–5016 (West 1996); Pa. Stat. Ann. tit. 10, § 152.3 (1996) (exempting religious institutions which comply with IRC § 501(c)(3) and which are supported primarily by government grants and funds solicited from their own membership). A state's ability to regulate solicitation would be restricted to its own jurisdiction but would subject foreign corporations to the same requirements as domestic corporations.

93. *See, e.g.*, 805 Ill. Comp. Stat. Ann. 105/108.70 (West 1995) (exempting uncompensated officers and directors from liability except for willful and wanton conduct).

94. The First Amendment states: "Congress shall make no law respecting an Establishment of religion or prohibiting the free exercise thereof." U.S. Const. amend. I. The Supreme Court has generally treated this provision as embodying two distinct clauses and two distinct values pertaining to the status of religion and its relationship to the government. However, their interpretation and interconnectedness are complex and produce little agreement. *See, e.g.*, Mary Ann Glendon and Raul F. Yanes, Structural Free Exercise, 90 Mich. L. Rev. 477 (1991).

adopt formally any legal structure in order to carry out its religious mission or even to attain favorable tax status, and yet if it wishes to attain various other advantages, then it must squeeze itself into the mold of one of the legal forms that a particular state makes available, regardless of how well or how poorly the particular mold may fit its theology. Many religious organizations now take those advantages for granted; in fact, they often regard them as necessary to the carrying out of their religious mission. If one views state corporation statutes as primarily facilitating the attainment of certain legal advantages, then perhaps there is no requirement that the state provide the most flexibility or optimal choices to any particular religious organization. On the other hand, if the statutes are viewed as primarily regulatory and therefore imposing a burden on religious organizations, then there could seem to be a requirement of equality of treatment of different denominations so as to avoid a problem of endorsement. As a result, the extent to which the available forms fit the theologies of particular religious groups may implicate the concerns of the Free Exercise Clause.

Still, some of those who work (both as practitioners and as legal theoreticians) in the field of not-for-profit and charitable organizations question whether the creation of special exemptions from otherwise generally applicable regulations for religious groups in their organizational form violates the Establishment Clause. In sum, the question posed is whether religious organizations, as institutions rather than as aggregates of individuals, should be held accountable to government and society by the same standards as other charitable organizations or whether the First Amendment should largely exempt them from such accountability.

The question of the accountability and responsibility of religious organizations under the law is a complex and intriguing one that illustrates well the conflict between an individual-oriented and an institution-oriented constitutional jurisprudence of civil liberties. The extent to which laws can require or prohibit conduct that contradicts religious mandate is central to the functioning of relationships among religious institutions, individuals, society, and government. Indeed, it brings out a fundamental conflict between two deeply rooted values—the desire to protect freedom of religion and the desire to hold all equally accountable under the law.

Despite the fact that religious belief is exempt from governmental interference under the Free Exercise Clause,[95] individuals and religious organizations are, at least to some extent, accountable to society for their conduct and activities under governmental regulation.[96] Proponents for an expansive approach to religious free exercise have asserted the need for a "constitutionally compelled" or a "judicially created" exemption from such regulation when the regulation unduly burdens the free exercise of religion.[97]

---

95. The freedom of belief, whether grounded in what would be generally recognized as a religious belief or in a more secular conscientious belief, has been given absolute protection under both the Free Exercise Clause and the Free Speech Clause. *See, e.g.,* School Dist. v. Schempp, 374 U.S. 203, 231 (1963) (Brennan, J., concurring).

96. *See, e.g.,* Sherbert v. Verner, 374 U.S. 398, 403 (1963); Cantwell v. Connecticut, 310 U.S. 296, 303–04 (1940); Intercommunity Ctr. for Justice and Peace v. INS, 910 F.2d 42, 44 (2d Cir. 1990) ("[T]hese clauses have been interpreted as providing full protection for religious beliefs but only limited protection for overt acts prompted by those beliefs"). For criticisms of this belief/action dichotomy in First Amendment jurisprudence, *see, e.g.,* Shelley K. Wessels, Note, The Collision of Religious Exercise and Governmental Nondiscrimination Policies, 41 Stan. L. Rev. 1201, 1207–08 (1989).

97. The argument for such an exemption is essentially that the attempt to impose governmental regulation in conflict with religious mandate creates a violation of the rights guaranteed by the Free Exercise Clause. For a strong presentation in support of a broad interpretation of accommodation

Throughout modern constitutional jurisprudence until 1990, the boundaries of such accountability were determined by requiring a compelling state interest to justify the burden imposed on the free exercise of religion.[98] Through the application of this test, the Supreme Court produced a bewildering patchwork of permissible and impermissible forms of governmental regulation.[99]

Against this inconsistent patchwork, the Supreme Court in 1990, under the leadership of Justice Scalia, changed fundamentally the evaluation of claims to exemption from governmental regulation based on the right to religious free exercise. In 1990 in *Employment Division, Department of Human Resources v. Smith*,[100] the Supreme Court disclaimed the applicability of the compelling government interest test for evaluating laws that make no distinctions based on religion. According to *Smith*, facially neutral governmental regulation which nonetheless had a disproportionate impact on particular religious practices would be evaluated under the lowest level of judicial scrutiny, which requires only that the government have a legitimate interest in the regulation and that the regulation be rationally related to that interest. Because regulations rarely target particular religious practices,[101] *Smith* seemed to imply the almost total elimination of the constitutionally compelled exemption of individuals from otherwise valid, generally applicable governmental regulation. The application of *Smith* thus seemed to usher in a new era of regulation for religious organizations: they would be shielded from such reg-

---

and exemptions for religious interests, *see* Michael W. McConnell, Accommodation of Religion: An Update and a Response to the Critics, 60 Geo. Wash. L. Rev. 685 (1992).

98. The extent of this accountability was premised on a three-part test which evaluated: (1) the extent of the governmental interference with sincerely held religious belief; (2) the existence of a compelling state interest to justify the burden imposed on the free exercise of religion, and (3) the extent to which an exemption from the regulation would impede the objectives which the government sought to advance through the regulation. *See, e.g.,* Wisconsin v. Yoder, 406 U.S. 205 (1972); Sherbert v. Verner, 374 U.S. 398, 403 (1963). This formulation is substantially similar to the "compelling government interest" test used to evaluate the legitimacy of governmental interference with other fundamental freedoms, particularly freedom of speech. *See, e.g.,* Burson v. Freeman, 504 U.S. 191 (1992); Sable Communications v. FCC, 492 U.S. 115, 126 (1989).

99. For example, parents could direct their children's education, *see* Wisconsin v. Yoder, 406 U.S. 205 (1972) (mandating exemption for members of Old Order Amish religious groups from state statute requiring school attendance until age 16), and individuals could not be denied unemployment compensation when their jobs required them to work on their religiously-mandated day of rest or employment demands conflicted in other ways with their religious beliefs, *see* Hobbie v. Unemployment Appeals Comm'n., 480 U.S. 136 (1987) (denial of unemployment benefits because of refusal to work on Sabbath); Thomas v. Review Bd. of Indiana Employment Sec. Div., 450 U.S. 707 (1981) (denial of unemployment benefits to applicant whose religion forbade manufacture of weapons); Sherbert v. Verner, 374 U.S. 398 (1963) (denial of unemployment benefits because of refusal to work on Sabbath). On the other hand, individuals could be required to comply with various government regulations, including social security laws. *See* Bowen v. Roy, 476 U.S. 693 (1986) (federal statute requiring states to use social security numbers in administering welfare programs did not violate Native American Indians' religious rights); they could be required to keep their businesses closed on a state-mandated day of rest, *see* Braunfeld v. Brown, 366 U.S. 599 (1961); Gallagher v. Crown Kosher Super Mkt., Inc., 366 U.S. 617 (1961); and the government could construct a road and permit timber-harvesting in a sacred area, *see* Lyng v. Northwest Indian Cemetery Protective Ass'n, 485 U.S. 439 (1988).

100. 494 U.S. 872 (1990). Arguably, the Supreme Court had already abandoned the compelling government interest test in, for example, *Lyng*, 485 U.S. 439, and *Bowen*, 476 U.S. 693.

101. In *Church of Lukumi Babalu Aye, Inc. v. Hialeah*, 508 U.S. 520 (1993), the Supreme Court held that an ordinance which prohibited the killing of animals only in connection with sacrifice and ritual purpose was unconstitutional because it was motivated by antireligious animus and thus violated the Free Exercise Clause.

ulation only when it was motivated by an animus against particular religious practices or when it created a denominational preference.

Congress enacted the Religious Freedom Restoration Act (RFRA) in 1993 in an effort to restore heightened pre-*Smith* scrutiny, but RFRA was declared unconstitutional in 1997.[102] However, between 1990 and 1993, lower court decisions gave an indication of free exercise jurisprudential developments in a *Smith* world. In light of the invalidation of RFRA this period may suggest future religion clause jurisprudence in the lower courts.

After *Smith* the analysis of religion clause jurisprudence shifted significantly.[103] Because the Free Exercise Clause had been virtually eliminated as an avenue of relief, the Establishment Clause was used to invalidate governmental regulation when it conflicted with religious beliefs. Historically,[104] the Establishment Clause was used primarily to evaluate situations in which the government created a potential endorsement or support of a particular religious viewpoint, as in the cases of public religious symbols,[105] prayer in public schools, and other forms of government-sponsored prayer,[106] or conferred a benefit on religious institutions, such as public aid to parochial schools.[107]

---

102. City of Boerne v. Flores, 521 U.S. 507 (1997).

103. In addition to the effects of *Smith* on Religion Clause jurisprudence within the United States, *Smith* had also raised some question on the status of freedom of religion in the United States under international law.

104. The Establishment Clause was, in fact, originally intended to prevent the federal government from interfering with the state religious establishments which existed at the end of the eighteenth century and into the first half of the nineteenth. *See* Kauper & Ellis, *supra* note 1, at 1557–64. Thus, unlike many of the other rights guaranteed by the Bill of Rights, the Establishment Clause was not intended to give general protection to individuals or even religious institutions, but rather to protect state-government sponsored religious activity from interference by the federal government. The process of incorporation for the Establishment Clause, which occurred in *Everson v. Board of Educ.*, 330 U.S.1 (1947), and which applied this restriction to the state governments, thus required a bigger leap than the incorporation of the other fundamental freedoms and, although generally accepted today, is considerably more controversial from an historical perspective. *See* School Dist. v. Schempp, 374 U.S. 203, 254–58 (1963) (Brennan, J., concurring); Glendon & Yanes, *supra* note 94, at 480–92 (criticizing incorporation of the Establishment Clause and the reasoning in *Everson*). Carl H. Esbeck, Myths, Miscues, and Misconceptions: No-Aid Separationism and the Establishment Clause, 13 Notre Dame J. L. Ethics & Pub. Pol'y 285, n. 55 (1999) (describing the purpose of the Establishment Clause as "to limit the government including any decisions by the government to improperly ally with religion"); Douglas Laycock, Towards a General Theory of the Religion Clauses: The Case of Church Labor Relations and the Right to Church Autonomy, 81 Columbia L. Rev. 1373, 1384–85 (1981) (arguing that government support for religion is the essential concern of the Establishment Clause).

105. *See, e.g.,* Lynch v. Donnelly, 465 U.S. 668 (1984); County of Allegheny v. American Civil Liberties Union Greater Pittsburgh Chapter, 492 U.S. 573 (1989).

106. The subject of religious activity in public schools has been considered by the Supreme Court in several cases. *See* Lee v. Weisman, 505 U.S. 577 (1992) (prohibiting state-sponsored "non-denomination" prayer at public school graduation); Edwards v. Aguillard, 482 U.S. 578 (1987) (striking down statute mandating balanced treatment for evolution science and creation science); Wallace v. Jaffree, 472 U.S. 38 (1985) (silent prayer or meditation in schools); Stone v. Graham, 449 U.S. 39 (1980) (holding that requiring the posting of Ten Commandments in classrooms violated the Establishment Clause); Epperson v. Arkansas, 393 U.S. 97 (1968) (striking down statute which prohibited teaching of evolution in public schools); School Dist. v. Schempp, 374 U.S. 203 (1963) (holding that state-sponsored daily prayer, even if denominationally neutral and voluntary, violated the Establishment Clause because such prayer served to advance religion); Engel v. Vitale, 370 U.S. 421 (1962).

107. The Court has considered various forms of government aid to parochial schools. *See* Board of Educ. of Kiryas Joel Village Sch. Dist. v. Grumet, 512 U.S. 687 (1994) (holding unconstitutional creation of a school district for the exclusive purpose of providing special education to

However, during the period after *Smith* and before RFRA, the excessive entanglement prong of the Supreme Court's test for evaluating government activity under the Establishment Clause[108] became the primary vehicle for challenges to governmental regulation of religious organizations. Although not part of a free exercise analysis, the test for excessive entanglement was used to strike down governmental regulation which would otherwise have been permissible under the *Smith* test. Thus what was intended as a method to evaluate the granting of a governmental benefit to religious organizations became the test for evaluating the imposition of burdens on religious activity,[109] even though the test for "establishment" does not address the question of accountability and responsibility under societal norms, as expressed in legislative enactments.

The use of the Establishment Clause to resolve what had traditionally been thought of as free exercise claims resulted in two further changes in judicial analysis of such issues. The first of these was that only institutions, and no longer individuals, were able to obtain exemptions from government regulation. Establishment Clause analysis as it came to be utilized in court decisions emphasizes almost exclusively the relationship between government and religious institutions, not the relationship between government and individuals who are carrying out their religious obligations.[110] The result is an iron-

---

the children of a Satmar Hasidic community insulated from the surrounding non-Hasidic communities). Aguilar v. Felton, 473 U.S. 402 (1985) (striking down federal funding for salaries of public school employees assigned to provide remedial services to low-income children in parochial schools); School Dist. v. Ball, 473 U.S. 373 (1985) (holding that public funding of full-time parochial school teachers to teach secular subjects held unconstitutional); Lemon v. Kurtzman, 403 U.S. 602 (1971) (salary supplements for parochial school teachers); *see also* Zobrest v. Catalina Foothills School Dist., 509 U.S. 1 (1993) (permitting reimbursement for expenses for deaf child attending parochial school); Bowen v. Kendrick, 487 U.S. 589 (1988) (upholding federal grants program to public and private social service agencies, including religious agencies); Mueller v. Allen, 463 U.S. 388 (1983) (upholding a Minnesota tax deduction for parochial school expenses); Everson v. Board of Educ., 330 U.S. 1 (1947) (upholding publicly funded transportation to parochial school). The requiring of equal access to public school and university facilities for religious organizations has been approved in *Rosenberger v. Rector and Visitors of the Univ. of Virginia*, 515 U.S. 819 (1995), *Lamb's Chapel v. Center Moriches Union Free Sch. Dist.*, 508 U.S. 384 (1993); *Board of Educ. of Westside Community Schools v. Mergens*, 496 U.S. 226 (1990); and *Widmar v. Vincent*, 454 U.S. 263 (1981). The Supreme Court has also held that federal funding of educational programs where remedial services were delivered to the students' schools, including religious schools, did not violate the Establishment Clause. *See* Agostini v. Felton, 521 U.S. 203 (1997).

108. The Supreme Court enunciated a three-part test in *Lemon v. Kurtzman*, 403 U.S. 602 (1971), to determine when a government action constitutes an impermissible "establishment" of religion: (1) whether the statute or other government action has a secular purpose; (2) whether its principal or primary effect neither advances nor inhibits religion; and (3) whether the government action creates an excessive entanglement between government and religion. *Id.* at 612–13. Although the viability of the *Lemon* test has been hotly debated, it was specifically reaffirmed in *Lee v. Weisman*, 505 U.S. 577 (1992). The test for excessive entanglement has itself been split into three factors: (1) the character and purpose of the institution involved; (2) the nature of the regulation's intrusion into religious affairs; and (3) the resulting relationship between the government and the religious authority. However, in *Agostini v. Fenton*, 521 U.S. 203 (1997), Justice O'Connor recently suggested that "excessive entanglement" be considered as part of the "effect" prong.

109. For discussions of the use of excessive entanglement to gain exemption from government regulation before the *Smith* decision, see Ira Lupu, Free Exercise Exemption and Religious Institutions: The Case of Employment Discrimination, 67 B.U. L. Rev. 391, 409–11 (1987), and William P. Marshall & Douglas C. Blomgren, Regulating Religious Organizations under the Establishment Clause, 47 Ohio St. L.J. 293 (1986).

110. Even before enactment of RFRA, some commentators had suggested that the right of religious free exercise belongs only to individuals and not to institutions at all. *See, e.g.,* Lupu, *supra*

ically reversed dichotomy of protection for individuals and institutions under *Smith:* institutions are granted free exercise rights, though they be won through the guise of an excessive entanglement challenge, while individuals are largely denied any right to free exercise based on religious beliefs.

The second result of the *Smith* decision was the abandonment of the courts' role in protecting minority rights. The fundamental freedoms contained in the Bill of Rights are generally phrased as negative rights,[111] preventing the government, through the legislature or by any other means, from interfering with these rights. It has been the role of the judiciary, through its interpretation of the Constitution, to strike down legislative enactments that interfere with these rights. While the legislature and to a large extent the executive branches are repositories of majoritarian power, the judiciary represents a countermajoritarian factor and provides the only protection for the minority's right to these fundamental freedoms.[112]

In his *Smith* decision Justice Scalia largely eliminated the courts as protectors of these minoritarian rights but reiterated that the legislature was still free to create legislative exemptions from such regulation for specific religious practices.[113] Thus religious groups with large numbers of adherents or with greater amounts of political influence would be able to win protection of their free exercise rights through legislatively created exemptions. On the other hand, smaller groups and individuals who did not possess equivalent political power would be largely unable to achieve either legislatively created or judicially created exemptions.

The effects of these two changes may be demonstrated by some lower court decisions between 1990 and 1993. In accord with the dictates of *Smith*, these courts refused to entertain free exercise challenges to the imposition of facially neutral government regulations. For example, in *Black v. Snyder*, a 1991 Minnesota appellate decision, the court rejected a church's claim to be exempted under the Free Exercise Clause from the state's human rights statute when the associate pastor brought claims of employment discrimination, defamation, breach of contract, and retaliatory discharge against her

---

note 109, at 419–31; School Dist. v. Schempp, 374 U.S. 203, 223 (1963) (characterizing the purpose of the Free Exercise Clause as "to secure religious liberty in the individual"). For criticisms of this view, see Glendon & Yanes, *supra* note 94, at 495–96. The idea that the Free Exercise Clause protects only individuals and not institutions makes an appealing basis for arguments in favor of increased accountability of religious organizations because it eliminates a category of free exercise challenges to governmental regulation. However, it is difficult to ignore that at times individuals who belong to a group may only be able to fulfill their religious obligations through an organizational structure. Nonetheless, this is not a reason to grant free exercise rights exclusively to religious organizations while effectively denying them on an individual, minoritarian basis, as seems to be the dictate of the *Smith* decision. This tension between the rights of individuals and the rights of institutions becomes even more significant when viewed against the earlier discussion of institutional structures available to religious groups and the concomitant rights and responsibilities which these structures impose upon the religious group.

111. The concept of the "negative" Constitution is more typically used to describe the fact that, with only a few exceptions, the government is required only to refrain from interfering with individuals and not to provide specific benefits or protections. *See, e.g.*, Susan Bandes, The Negative Constitution: A Critique, 88 Mich. L. Rev. 2271, 2273–78 (1990).

112. *See* Charles M. Freeland, The Political Process as Final Solution, 68 Ind. L.J. 525, 526–27 (1993).

113. *Smith*, 494 U.S. at 890. For a critique of reliance on a majoritarian democratic political process to protect fundamental rights, particularly in the context of *Smith*, see Freeland, *supra* note 112, at 560–62.

church and the senior pastor.[114] The court dismissed her claims against the church based on the entanglement prong of the Establishment Clause but allowed her suit based on sexual harassment against the senior pastor to continue, justifying it because it related to conduct during the employment relationship rather than to the plaintiff's pastoral qualifications or church doctrine. The church was thus protected, while the pastor was not. Thus although not part of a free exercise analysis, the excessive entanglement test could be used to exempt religious organizations from governmental regulation that would otherwise be considered permissible under the *Smith* formulation of free exercise analysis.

The preceding discussion of the various associational structures available to religious organizations and the 1994 Report on the Survey of Religious Organizations at the National Level demonstrate the tensions that religious organizations face in choosing amongst available legal structures and their attendant advantages. One approach suggested by this discussion and survey is that the more a religious organization chooses the advantages offered to other forms of not-for-profit organizations, the more it should be regulated like these other organizations. One might then argue that those burdens that fall more heavily on the religious organization in its institutional form should be analyzed differently than those burdens that fall directly on individuals.

For example, one might wish to set up a continuum of types of governmental regulations determined by their relative impact directly on individuals and their relative impact directly on religious institutions. While not all types of regulations would be easily classified, a few examples might demonstrate the application of such a continuum. At one end of the continuum, one could examine some types of landmark and historic preservation ordinances that arguably burden only institutions (most typically the corporate or associational owners of the buildings) and not individuals, except in their roles as members of the institutions.[115] In such cases, religious organizations should be regulated in the same way as secular not-for-profit organizations.

At the other end of the continuum would fall religious practices which are undertaken largely by individuals separated from the institutional structure adopted by a religious group. The best example here is the factual basis of *Smith*, in which the smoking of peyote, although sometimes engaged in within a group context, bears no relation to the formal structure or corporate aspects of the religious group.[116] Here, because the individuals were not taking advantage of any structured benefits, they should receive the benefit of free exercise protection. A middle ground, and perhaps the thorniest issue, is represented by controversies involving the application of antidiscrimination laws to reli-

---

114. Black v. Snyder, 471 N.W.2d 715, 719 (Minn. Ct. App. 1991). In *NLRB v. Hanna Boys Center*, 940 F.2d 1295 (9th Cir. 1991), the Ninth Circuit relied in part on *Smith* in denying a religiously affiliated youth center's claim to be exempt from NLRB jurisdiction under the Free Exercise Clause.

115. *See, e.g.*, Rector, Wardens and Members of the Vestry of St. Bartholomew's Church v. City of New York, 914 F.2d 348, 353–56 (2d Cir. 1990) (holding that application of Landmark Law to prevent a church from building an office tower did not violate the Free Exercise Clause because it does not hinder the church's religious and charitable mission). For examples in the labor context, see *Tony and Susan Alamo Found. v. Secretary of Labor*, 471 U.S. 290 (1985) (application of Fair Labor Standards Act to religious organizations); *See also* King's Garden, Inc. v. FCC, 498 F.2d 51 (D.C. Cir. 1974) (application of FCC rules to religious organization).

116. One might also note the decision in *Society of Jesus v. Boston Landmarks Comm'n*, 564 N.E.2d 571, 572–73 (Mass. 1990), which, although involving a landmark ordinance, directly affected the method of worship because the ordinance applied to the internal arrangement of furniture within the church.

gious organizations and, in particular, to clergy.[117] In these situations, although the actor seems to be an institution or corporation, the institution may in fact be acting merely as an aggregate of individuals rather than exclusively in its institutional capacity.

This summary of the current law in the United States concludes with a few observations and suggestions for future thought. First, the limited availability of structural forms for religious groups with different theological polities may place an undue or excessive burden on the free exercise of religion, which falls unevenly on religions with different polities. This inequality should prompt states to make available a wider array of structural forms and, in particular, to permit religious organizations to adopt the corporation sole form when they so wish.

An expansion of available structural forms, however, leads to the second question of whether religious organizations should be held to the same standards of accountability as other types of charitable, not-for-profit organizations. While they clearly should not and cannot be subjected to more regulation, are there circumstances, particularly those which involve compelling or significant government interests, such as protection of children and eradication of employment discrimination, in which religious organizations should be held to the same standards as other charitable and not-for-profit organizations? Such a standard of accountability based on equality norms should, in turn, be tempered by considerations of whether the burden of government regulation falls primarily on individuals, who may require greater protection from government regulation, or on institutions. Thus in evaluating the burdens imposed on religious organizations as part of a free exercise analysis, the standard or level of scrutiny should depend on whether the burdens fall more on the institutional than on the individual aspects of religious free exercise.

---

117. *See, e.g.,* McClure v. Salvation Army, 460 F.2d 553, 560–61 (5th Cir. 1972); EEOC v. Southwestern Baptist Theological Seminary, 651 F.2d 277, 282–83 (5th Cir. 1981); Assemany v. Archdiocese of Detroit, 434 N.W.2d 233 (Mich. Ct. App. 1988); Alicea v. New Brunswick Theological Seminary, 608 A.2d 218 (N.J. 1992); Scharon v. St. Luke's Episcopal Presbyterian Hosp., 929 F.2d 360, 362–63 (8th Cir. 1991); Rayburn v. General Conference of Seventh-Day Adventists, 772 F.2d 1164, 1168–71 (4th Cir 1985); Young v. Northern Ill. Conference of United Methodist Church, 21 F.3d 184 (7th Cir. 1994). *See also* Jane Rutherford, Equality as the Primary Constitutional Value: The Case for Applying Employment Discrimination Laws to Religion, 81 Cornell L. Rev. 1049 (1996).

Unincorporated Associations and Charitable Trusts

Patricia B. Carlson

The prior chapter by Patty Gerstenblith discusses the fact that many religious organizations incorporate and discusses the advantages and disadvantages of the corporate form for religious entities. However, not all religious organizations form corporations; a few are charitable or religious trusts and some are unincorporated associations. This chapter will discuss these noncorporate forms, the reasons why some religious organizations use them, and the problems that can result. It will also suggest some changes in the law that could make it possible for these forms to better serve religious organizations.

Charitable Trusts

Description of charitable trusts

As explained in the chapter on charitable trusts, there are express and implied trusts. In an express trust there must be a clear intent to create a trust for charitable purposes. This is usually done through a written document that states the purposes for which the funds in the trust may be spent and establishes the procedures by which those funds may be disbursed. In addition to express trusts, there are resulting trusts, in which a court infers an intention to establish a trust, and constructive trusts, which courts impose to remedy injustices. There are also implied trusts, in which a court assumes that one body is holding property in trust for another.

Any trust must have a beneficiary, which is an entity or group of persons who are to receive benefits from the trust. It is interesting to note that an unincorporated association, including an unincorporated religious association, may be the beneficiary of a trust.[1]

---

1. *See* 15 Am. Jur. 2d Charities §116 (1973); Barnhart v. Bowers, 57 P.2d 60 (Kan. 1936); *In re* Matter of Anderson's Estate, 571 P.2d 880 (Okla. Ct. App. 1977).

Use of charitable trusts by religious organizations

Historically, religious organizations could only use charitable trusts for the repair of churches.[2] The rationale for this restriction was that since monarchs could declare some beliefs to be truly religious and others only superstitions, trusts established to support a particular religion might eventually be seen as only supporting superstitions. This would allow the land in the trust to be confiscated by the crown.[3] In the seventeenth century, however, courts began allowing trusts to be used for more broadly religious purposes. For example, in 1639 a court held that a charitable trust could be established to support a minister.[4] Nowadays most states allow charitable trusts to benefit churches.[5]

Only a few religious organizations are organized as charitable or religious trusts. According to the 1994 Report on the Survey of Religious Organizations at the National Level, a survey of national-level offices of religious organizations, only one percent of the organizations surveyed reported that they were organized as charitable or religious trusts.

Reasons why religious organizations use charitable trusts

While few religions are organized as charitable trusts, religious organizations do use charitable trusts in a variety of ways, sometimes in response to government action. For example, as discussed in H. Reese Hansen's chapter in this book on the law of trusts, after the *Jones v. Wolf*[6] decision both the United Presbyterian Church in the United States of America and the Protestant Episcopal Church in the United States of America amended their constitutions to provide that the local churches hold their property in trust for the national church.

In addition, many religious groups that are either corporations or unincorporated associations use trusts to perform some of their functions. For example, Catholic religious orders often use charitable trusts to hold assets for the retirement needs of their members. Other religious organizations have also established trusts to perform such functions as church restoration.

Courts also often impose trusts upon assets held by religious organizations. For example, in *In re Estate of Muhammad*,[7] there was a bank account entitled "The Honorable Elijah Muhammad's Poor Fund Account" which had been opened by Elijah Muhammad,

---

2. *See* Statute of Charitable Uses, 43 Eliz. I, ch.4 (1601) *quoted in* John W. Whitehead, Tax Exemption and Churches: A Historical and Constitutional Analysis, 22 Cumb. L. Rev. 521, 532 (1991–1992).

3. *See* Whitehead, *supra* note 2, at 532 (citing John Witte, Jr., Tax Exemption of Church Property: Historical Anomaly or Valid Constitutional Practice?, 64 S. Cal. L. Rev. 363, 376 n.49 (1991) quoting G. Duke, Law of Charitable Uses 131–132 (R.W. Bridgman ed., 1805)).

4. *See* 4A Austin Wakeman Scott, The Law of Trusts § 371 (4th ed. 1989) (citing Pember v. Inhabitants of Knighton, *noted in* Duke, Law of Charitable Uses 82 (1639)).

5. *See* Evelyn Brody, Charitable Endowments and the Democratization of Dynasty, 39 Ariz. L. Rev. 873, 909 (1997).

6. 443 U.S. 595 (1979).

7. 520 N.E.2d 795 (Ill. App. Ct. 1987).

the leader of the Nation of Islam religious group. When Muhammad died, both the religious group and Muhammad's children claimed this account. Looking at all the facts, the court imposed a constructive trust on the funds, having found that they were intended to benefit the Nation of Islam and not the children of Muhammad.

Issues involved in the use of charitable trusts by religious organizations

There are several ways in which the laws impinge upon religious organizations that use charitable trusts to try to achieve their goals. The law dictates whether those goals qualify as charitable and whether the organization's methods are acceptable. Another potential problem is that under the laws, it is hard to change the purposes of a charitable trust once it has been established. An examination of the ways in which religious orders use charitable trusts to protect their retirement assets shows that this structure is not an ideal vehicle for reaching these goals.

Purpose of the charitable trust

One of the major characteristics of the charitable-trust form is that its funds may only be used for the dedicated purpose. If the trustee tries to release those funds for other purposes, the attorney general of the state usually may intervene.

Although the purpose of the trust must in fact be charitable, the term "charitable" is subject to no single definition in all instances.[8] This means that the government, either through statute or case law, may dictate what is or is not a proper charitable purpose for a trust. This does leave open the possibility that the state may decide that the advancement of certain religions or religious practices is not charitable. As discussed above, from at least the 1600s courts have held that trusts may promote religion. At first, however, the courts did not allow trusts that furthered religions other than the one established by the state. For example, in 1754 in *Da Costa v. De Pas*, an English court held that a trust to establish an assembly for reading the Jewish law and providing instruction about Judaism was illegal.[9] As recently as 1923, another court in England held that the establishment of a college to train spiritual mediums did not qualify as a charitable purpose.[10]

It appears that courts in the United States have been more lenient in upholding the advancement of many different forms of religion.[11] For example, trusts for Christian Science,[12] the Roman Catholic religion,[13] and a Buddhist temple[14] have all been upheld. Trusts for more esoteric beliefs have also been allowed; for example, in *Jones v. Watford* the testator left money "in trust for the purchase of books upon the philosophy of spiritualism; not sectarian, or of any creed, church, or dogma, but of free, liberal bearing.

---

8. *See* 4A Austin W. Scott, The Law of Trusts § 368.
9. *See id.* § 371 (citing 1 Amb. 228 (1754)).
10. *See id.* § 370.4 (citing *In re* Hummeltenberg, [1923] 1 Ch. 237).
11. *See id.*
12. *See* Chase v. Dickey, 99 N.E. 410 (Mass. 1912); Maguire v. Loyd, 67 S.E.2d 885 (Va. 1951).
13. *See In re* Estate of Freshour, 345 P.2d 689 (Kan. 1959).
14. *See* Kopsombut-Myint Buddhist Ctr. v. State Bd. of Equalization, 728 S.W.2d 327 (Tenn. Ct. App. 1986).

Said books to be placed by my executors where they can be free to all who desire to think for themselves, and who are seeking for the truth from the true and living God; for I believe in one God, one church, and one country."[15] In raising the issue about whether this was a charitable purpose, the court then discussed an English case, *Thornton v. Howe,* in which there was a bequest for the publishing of the "sacred writings of Joanne Southcote,"[16] which were also about spiritualism. The judge in the English case had held that the bequest was charitable, although he disagreed with it.[17] Likewise, the court in *Jones v. Watford* agreed that the bequest in that case was charitable and, therefore valid. It concluded by stating that "No charge has been made against the bequest because of any alleged tendency to immorality or irreligion, nor, in view of the principles expounded in the above-cited cases...does there seem to be any room for such an objection."[18]

However, there is at least one case in which a United States court held that a trust was not charitable, apparently on the grounds that the court did not subscribe to the philosophical or theological beliefs behind the trust. In this case, called *In re Carpenter's Estate,* the testator, who was a believer in the "cults of theosophy and occultism,"[19] left money for a trust to pay "such highly evolved individuals, with much occult knowledge, who are ceaselessly working for the advancement of the Race and the allevia[tion] of the suffering of Humanity."[20] This wording was typical of how believers in theosophy described certain of their members. However, although the court recognized that theosophy and occultism had been taught for centuries in India and Tibet, it also noted that several courts had held that theosophy was a school of philosophy and not a religion. Then the court decided that inasmuch as the gift in this case was not to theosophy as such but to unspecified individuals who possessed much occult knowledge, it could not identify proper recipients of the gift. It reasoned that "[h]owever sincere the believers of the cults of mysticism or theosophy or occultism in its higher sense, may be, the great body of opinion among sound thinking men and women rejects belief in the existence of occult powers in individuals in a continuing form of manifestation."[21] Therefore, the court concluded that no charitable trust was created in this case because any such trust would be for a class of individuals "impossible of ascertainment or identification by any logical test."[22] It appears that the court vetoed this charitable religious trust because it was unwilling to allow believers in theosophy to specify which individual adherents were to be beneficiaries of the trust. If the trust had been framed in language more familiar to the court—such as if it had said that it was for the benefit of "ministers" of theosophy—then the trust probably would have been sustained.

This example illustrates how there is always a danger that a court will void a trust if the purpose of the trust is to benefit beliefs, religious or otherwise, that the court finds illogical. Therefore, if religions that are new or esoteric use charitable trusts, there is a risk, albeit small, that a court uncomfortable with the religious beliefs might not uphold the trust. In order to protect the variety of forms that religious beliefs take, the courts must be willing to give religious organizations great latitude in describing their own charitable and religious purposes.

---

15. Jones v. Watford, 50 A. 180 (N.J. Ch. 1901), *modified,* 53 A. 397 (N.J. 1902).
16. *Id.* at 182.
17. *See id.*
18. *Id.*
19. 297 N.Y.S. 649, 653 (Sur. Ct. 1937).
20. *Id.* at 652.
21. *Id.* at 654.
22. *Id.* at 658.

Methods of advancing religion

It appears that courts do allow charitable trusts to perform many different tasks to advance religion. These include "the erection or maintenance of a church; the erection of a memorial window in a church; the care of a graveyard attached to a church; the payment of or augmentation of the salary of a minister; the payment of the salary of an organist or of a choir; the preaching of sermons; the distribution of religious literature; the promotion of the work of home and foreign missions."[23] In fact, the "great weight of authority in the United States" now holds that it is permissible to have a charitable trust for the saying of masses.[24]

Of course this is no guarantee that courts will always uphold all methods of advancing religion. For example, in certain states a trust to buy peyote for religious purposes might not be upheld.[25] Again, freedom of religion dictates that religious organizations be allowed to use many different means to meet their goals.

Change of charitable purpose

Another major problem with a religious organization's use of a charitable trust is that it can be hard to change the purpose of the trust. As mentioned above, if the trust tries to deviate from its stated charitable purposes, the trustee and the state attorney general are required to stop such deviation. Usually the purpose of a trust may be changed only if it becomes impossible for it to fulfill its original purpose. Religious organizations may find that this feature creates problems because they may not be able to change the uses of their trust assets even though their religious beliefs have changed. For example, if a charitable trust states that it is for the promotion of the belief in a particular saint and then the church ceases to venerate that saint, the church may not be free to allow the trust assets to be used to promote the veneration of a different saint.

Even more important, the religious group may not be able to use the trust assets for new ministries even though people's needs have changed. For example, many religious orders that used to concentrate on service in parochial schools have since expanded into other activities, such as operating shelters for abused women and lobbying against the death penalty. If such an order has originally established a charitable trust to promote its educational mission, it probably will not be able to use those assets for its new ministries. Similarly, if a religious group establishes a trust to operate an orphanage, it might be difficult to use those funds for assisting foster children. In fact, other groups still performing the old ministries might be able to claim the assets of the original charitable trust.

This problem can be alleviated by wording the charitable purpose clause broadly enough to allow some flexibility in how the funds can be spent. Another alternative is to designate a trust advisor with the power to modify the terms of the trust. But courts also must be cognizant that religious beliefs and ministries are not static.

---

23. 4A Scott, *supra* note 4, § 371.1.
24. *Id.* § 371.5.
25. *See* Employment Div. v. Smith, 494 U.S. 872 (1990) (holding that state could deny unemployment compensation to employees who used peyote at a religious ceremony because such use violated the state controlled substance laws).

Charitable trusts to protect retirement assets of religious orders

One major specific example of how religious organizations are using charitable trusts today is the funding of retirement needs of members of Roman Catholic religious orders.[26] As their members diminish in number and increase in average age, religious orders find that they can no longer use current income to fund the needs of their retired members. Moreover, as law suits against religious orders increase, so does the danger that these orders will have to use assets intended for retirement to pay legal liabilities.

Therefore, many religious orders are looking for ways to protect their retirement assets. Although most Americans use some type of tax-qualified plan for this purpose, such plans do not perfectly fit the way in which religious orders operate. Tax-qualified church plans may only be established to cover "employees" of a church or of a convention or association of churches.[27] Members of a religious order are not ordinarily regarded as employees of the order. The Internal Revenue Code does expand the definition of employee to include "a duly ordained, commissioned, or licensed minister of a church in the exercise of his ministry, regardless of the source of his compensation,"[28] thus enabling religious orders to use a tax-qualified church plan to cover members who are ordained priests. However, some ambiguity exists concerning whether women religious qualify as "duly ordained, commissioned or licensed ministers," and whether a religious order may use a tax-qualified plan to cover them.

Another problem with tax-qualified plans for religious orders is that the Internal Revenue Code only allows defined-benefit plans to pay the lesser of a dollar amount indexed for increases in the cost of living[29] or one hundred percent of the participant's average compensation for his three high years.[30] It is unclear what "compensation" a member of a religious order has. The Internal Revenue Service has stated that for the purpose of determining the amount of allowable defined contribution, compensation only includes amounts includable as gross income.[31] Members of religious orders often only receive small stipends for their services. Moreover, if they are working for Catholic institutions, their income is not includable as gross income.[32] Therefore, if they are working for a Catholic institution, they arguably have no compensation and therefore are entitled to no benefits from a defined-benefit plan.

However, the IRS has implied that members of a religious order who have no taxable compensation may still receive benefits from a tax-qualified church plan. In Rev. Rul 83-126,[33] the IRS dealt with a member of a religious order who had taken a vow of poverty and was receiving retirement benefits under a tax-qualified plan. The IRS ignored the issue of whether the member had ever been paid any "compensation" that would entitle her to receive retirement benefits. Instead, it simply stated that if the member had earned the income while acting as an agent of the religious order and had

---

26. *See* Peter E. Campbell, Charitable Trusts Reviewed, 68 Legal Bull. 13 (1997).

27. *See* IRC § 414(e) (2004).

28. *Id.* § 414(e)(3)(B)(i).

29. The dollar limitation is $160,000 for years beginning in 2002. *See* 2003 U.S. Master Tax Guide (CCH) ¶ 2127.

30. *See* IRC § 415(b)(1)(B) (2004).

31. *See* Tech. Adv. Mem. 84-16-003 (Dec. 19, 1983).

32. *See* Rev. Rul. 77-290, 1977-2 C.B. 26.

33. Rev. Rul. 83-126, 1983-2 C.B. 24.

remitted that income to the order, then the member did not have to pay income tax for the retirement benefits.

Another problem with a tax-qualified church plan is the requirement that at some point in time, benefits must "vest." This means that at some specific point, members must acquire the right to receive benefits. Members of religious orders are divided on the issue of whether this "vesting" violates their vow of poverty. Some believe that they should never "own" their retirement benefits, while others argue that such payments are permissible since they are analogous to situations in which members earn income and remit it to the order.[34]

More troublesome is the fact that once a member's benefits vest, he or she is entitled to continue receiving the benefits even if he or she leaves the order. Canon law does provide that a religious order give departing members some assistance. However, having to pay the entire defined amount to a departing member whose benefits have vested may trouble some religious orders. In fact, it could even be seen as giving members some incentive to depart once their benefits have vested.

Because of these problems with tax-qualified plans, many religious orders are using charitable trusts to protect their retirement assets. As discussed above, the assets of a charitable trust may only be used for its stated purposes. Therefore, such a trust established by an order for the retirement needs of its members may not be used for other purposes.

However, one problem with using charitable trusts to fund retirement needs is that it is unclear whether retirement needs qualify as a charitable purpose. In his book *The Law of Trusts*, Austin Scott has stated that sometimes a trust for the religious benefit of a specific group of persons does not qualify as a charitable trust.[35] As examples he offers two English cases: *Cocks v. Manners*, in which the court held that promotion of the spiritual welfare of a group of nuns was not a charitable purpose and *Gilmour v. Coats*, in which the court held that a charitable trust could not be established for the purposes of a convent belonging to the Carmelites, a cloistered, contemplative Catholic religious order. He also finds that a trust to provide medical assistance to named persons is not charitable.[36]

Another problem is that the law normally does not prevent the assets of a charitable trust from being used to pay the liabilities of the person who donated or granted the assets to the trust if the trust assets may be used to otherwise benefit the grantor.[37] Thus, there is a danger that if a court finds that a religious order has simply put money in the charitable trust for its own benefit, then it may allow those assets to be used to pay the order's general liabilities. In addition, as discussed above, it is difficult to change the purposes for which charitable trust assets may be used. Therefore, when a religious order uses such a charitable trust to fund its retirement needs, it may not take out excess funds for other purposes, even if the trust is overfunded.

To circumvent all these various restrictions, many religious organizations resort to the use of a purpose clause that defines the purpose of the trust as something broader than

---

34. *See* Daniel J. Ward, Charitable Trusts, Tax-Qualified Church Plans and Canon Law, 68 Legal Bull. 25 (1997).

35. *See* 4A Scott, *supra* note 4 § 371.6.

36. *See id.* § 372.2.

37. *See* Joan Edmonds Brophy & Daniel W. Luther, Protecting Retirement Assets, 68 Legal Bull. 3, 5 (1997).

simply covering retirement needs.[38] It might state, for example, that the trust is for charitable purposes including but not limited to providing for infirm and aged members of the order. However, such a broadly worded purpose clause can have disadvantages of its own, such as allowing the possibility that the assets may not be used for retirement purposes at all. Weighing the advantages and disadvantages of a broad purpose clause, at least one commentator, Brother Peter Campbell, believes it better to establish a charitable trust just to fund the retirement of the members of the religious order, and discounts the danger that this will make the assets available to cover all the order's liabilities.[39]

As shown, neither tax-qualified church plans nor charitable trusts are perfect ways to protect the retirement assets of members of religious orders; both solutions present their own technical problems. For example, a tax-qualified plan bases the provision of benefits on the amount of monetary compensation the beneficiary normally receives, which can be a problem since some members of religious orders may receive no compensation at all. In the case of a charitable trust, a religious order may have to distance itself from control over the trust in order to ensure that its assets really will be protected from the order's liabilities. Even more important, both of these solutions may conflict with the beliefs and values of a religious order. For example, the tax-qualified plan requires that benefits vest, which can conflict with the vows of poverty taken by members of a religious order who consequently should have no property rights.

Some recent state legislation arguably would make charitable trusts more useful for religious orders.[40] In 1998 Alaska and Delaware enacted statutes that would help protect the assets in a charitable trust from the creditors of the grantor of the trust.[41] Under both of these laws, creditors are only allow to bring a cause of action until the later of four years after the transfer is made or one year after the creditor could reasonably have discovered the transfer.[42] In addition, a person who becomes a creditor subsequent to the transfer may only bring an action within four years after the transfer is made.

For religious orders there is still the problem that both statutes exclude from this protection those charitable trusts in which the income or principal of the trust may be distributed to the grantor. For example, Alaska provides that the protection does not apply if the "trust requires that all or a part of the trust's income or principal, or both, must be distributed to the settlor."[43] Therefore, in Alaska a creditor might argue that an order's charitable trust must still pay the order's liabilities because, by distributing money to individual members of the order, the trust is really distributing money to the order itself.

Delaware appears to provide more protection to the trust. Its statute states that charitable trusts are safe from the grantor's creditors even if the grantor has the potential to receive income or principal from the trust as long as this potential is either in the sole discretion of a qualified trustee or is pursuant to an ascertainable standard contained in the trust instrument.[44] Therefore it appears that if the charitable trust has a qualified trustee, who may not

---

38. *See id.*

39. *See* Peter E. Campbell, More on Charitable Trusts, 68 Legal Bull. 17, 21 (1997).

40. *See* John T. Bannen, New Trust Laws May Help Protect Retirement Assets, In Brief Apr. 1998, at 1.

41. *See* Alaska Stat. § 34.40.110 (2004); Del. Code Ann. tit. 12, §§ 3570–3576 (2004).

42. *See* Alaska Stat. § 34.40.110; Del. Code Ann. tit. 12, § 3572. Delaware limits this protection by stating that it does not apply to anyone who suffers death, personal injury or property damage before the transfer. *See* Del. Code Ann. tit. 12, § 3573(3).

43. Alaska Stat. § 34.40.110(b)(3).

44. *See* Del. Code Ann. tit. 12, §§ 3570(9), 3572.

be the grantor, then the trust is protected from the grantor's creditor. This means that if a religious order, as grantor, is willing to relinquish control of its retirement trust to another entity, then the trust would be protected from the creditors of the order. Also, the assets of the trust are protected if the trustee may only distribute them to the members pursuant to an ascertainable standard. Of course, most charitable retirement trusts of religious orders currently have fairly loose standards regarding when members of the order may receive benefits. This is to comply with the vow of poverty by assuring that members do not "own" assets in the charitable trust and may not force the order to pay them benefits.

Since these statutes are relatively new, it is still unclear whether they wilsocharitable trusts from judgments against the grantor entered by courts in the grantor's state.[45] Thus, the issue is whether Alaska and Delaware would refuse to allow the assets of a religious order's charitable trust to be used to satisfy judgments entered against the order in the state where the order is located.

It can be seen that even with the new statutes, neither tax-qualified plans nor charitable trusts adequately allow religious orders to protect their retirement assets. Either the existing structures need to be changed or a new structure must be developed. In the meantime, it appears to be easier for courts to understand and deal with structures and alternatives that are similar to those used in the secular world. Therefore, since the secular world uses tax-qualified plans to protect its retirement needs, it probably makes sense for religious orders to do the same.

Unincorporated Associations

Description of unincorporated associations

An unincorporated association is a group of people who have joined together for "purpose of promoting common enterprise or prosecuting common objective."[46] Usually an unincorporated association has a document, such as articles of association or a constitution,[47] that generally describes its purpose and how it will be governed. In many ways this document is similar to a corporation's articles of incorporation, but an unincorporated association does not file its papers with the secretary of state. Many unincorporated associations also have a separate set of bylaws that describes more specifically how the entity operates.

Use of the unincorporated association form by religious organizations

It was once most common for nonprofit organizations to be organized as unincorporated associations.[48] In fact, in 1916 Sydney Wrightington asserted that "religious orga-

---

45. *See* Bannen, *supra* note 40, at 4.
46. Black's Law Dictionary 1373 (5th ed. 1979).
47. For sample Articles of Association, see William W. Bassett, Religious Organizations and the Law app. B (1997); Howard L. Oleck & Martha E. Stewart, Nonprofit Corporations, Organizations & Associations §63 (6th ed. 1994).
48. *See* Oleck & Stewart, *supra* note 47, §1.

nizations are usually unincorporated."[49] In more recent years, however, the unincorporated association form has been losing ground to the corporate form.[50] This is confirmed by The 1994 Report on the Survey of Religious Organizations at the National Level, which shows that only eight percent or one in thirteen of the religious organizations responding to the survey reported being organized as unincorporated associations. Although this number may be skewed by the survey's underrepresentation of storefront and house churches, it is nonetheless clear that the percentage of religious groups organized as unincorporated associations is relatively small.

Reasons why religious organizations use the unincorporated association form

At least one commentator has noted that groups usually begin by coming together in an informal structure and then gradually become more sophisticated and "corporate."[51] This is confirmed by the survey which noted an apparent trend among religious organizations to become corporations. There are, however, many reasons why a new church might choose to be an unincorporated association. One reason is that this form enables the church to avoid the complexities of filing articles of incorporation with a state government. Another reason is that the church or a portion of the church may historically have been unincorporated. For example, Roman Catholic religious orders are unincorporated associations. Although many form corporations to hold their assets, the orders themselves remain unincorporated and are governed by their constitutions, not by articles of incorporation or bylaws of a civil corporation.

A third reason why some religious organizations may opt for the unincorporated association form is that the state may not allow them to incorporate. As mentioned in Patty Gerstenblith's chapter in this book, "Associational Structures of Religious Organizations," the constitutions of Virginia and West Virginia bar the incorporation of any church or religious denomination. These two states do, however, permit churches to incorporate for religiously oriented purposes. Therefore, while a church itself may not incorporate, it can organize a separate corporation to hold its assets.

Fourth, it appears that the unincorporated association form has appealed to churches that want to avoid government interference. Courts have tended not to interfere in the internal affairs of unincorporated associations unless property rights were involved. Courts have also followed the decisions of tribunals established by these associations, in which disputes are usually settled by majority rule.[52] This has made the unincorporated association form particularly attractive to congregational churches.

Finally, some religious groups might like the anonymity inherent in the unincorporated-association form, which does not require a group to file articles of incorporation or annual reports with the state. A religious group that holds unusual beliefs or that fears government interference may want to avoid contact with the state as much as possible, and therefore be naturally inclined to organize itself as an unincorporated association.[53]

---

49. Sydney R. Wrightington, The Law of Unincorporated Associations §61 (1916).
50. *See* Oleck & Stewart, *supra* note 47, §47.
51. *Id.*
52. *See* Wrightington, *supra* note 49, §61.
53. *See* Note, Cox v. Thee Evergreen Church: Liability Issues of the Unincorporated Association, Is It Time for the Legislature to Step In? 46 Baylor L. Rev. 231, 234 (1994).

Issues involved in the use of unincorporated associations by religious organizations

Variance in laws

Historically, unincorporated associations have not been treated as distinct legal entities as corporations are. Instead, they are usually considered to be groups of people. This has a number of implications that make it very difficult for a religious organization to use this form.

This problem is exacerbated by the fact that the laws governing such entities are "few, vague and inadequate to spell out a system of organization and operation."[54] Some states have no statutory provisions about unincorporated associations, while others have provisions scattered throughout their various laws that alter the established common law rules. A few states have adopted the Uniform Unincorporated Nonprofit Association Act promulgated by the National Conference of Commissioners on Uniform State Laws in 1992.[55]

Holding title to property
Usually may not hold title

Because an unincorporated association is usually not treated as a distinct legal entity, it normally may not own property. This is particularly true for holding title to real property.[56] For example, in *Trustees of Philadelphia Baptist Ass'n v. Hart's Executors*, the United States Supreme Court held that although the testator left property to a Baptist Association that met in Philadelphia, this "association…not being incorporated, is incapable of taking this bequest."[57]

Ways to hold title

As a result of this general rule, unincorporated religious organizations have used a number of devices to hold property. Some have entrusted property titles to chosen members of the organization, some have appointed trustees, and others have formed corporations to hold title to property.

Members hold title

Jeffery v. Ehrhardt is an example of a court holding that all members of an unincorporated association together own the association's property.[58] In this case, property was conveyed to the "Protestant Episcopal Church in St. Paul in Radcliffeboro, its successors and assigns," which was an unincorporated church. The South Carolina Supreme Court held that the deed conveyed title to the "members organized as the Church, an unincor-

---

54. Oleck & Stewart, *supra* note 47, §1.

55. *See* Larry E. Ribstein, Unincorporated Business Entities §14.02 (1996).

56. *See*, Trustees of Philadelphia Baptist Ass'n v. Hart's Executors, 17 U.S. 1 (1819); Johnson v. Sweeney's Lane Church of God, Inc., 116 So. 2d 899 (Ala.1959); *In re* Anderson's Estate, 571 P.2d 880 (Okla. Ct. App. 1977).

57. *Philadelphia Baptist Ass'n*, 17 U.S. at 28.

58. *See* Jeffery v. Ehrhardt, 43 S.E.2d 483 (S.C. 1947).

porated religious association or society, and is now vested in the present members."[59] While this result could be good for congregational churches, it probably would not be good for hierarchical churches. This is because in a congregational church, the desires of the majority of the members do control the church. However, under the polity of an hierarchical church, the hierarchy—most likely the minister or his superior—should "own" the property and be able to convey title to it. The *Jeffery* court acknowledged that early English ecclesiastical law did vest legal title to church property in the minister and his successor, but it did not adopt the rule here. The rule of early English ecclesiastical law would be consistent with the polity of an unincorporated hierarchical religious association, while the rule adopted in *Jeffery* would not.

Trustees hold title

Some churches use trustees to hold property, either because a state statute requires that title of property for unincorporated religious organizations vests in trustees, or because the church itself simply chooses to do so. For example, Florida vests title to property of an unincorporated church in its trustees, directing that every conveyance of real property to "named or unnamed trustees of a named unincorporated church...vests title to the real property in the trustees of the named unincorporated church."[60] In other situations, churches themselves have adopted organizational documents that specifically name trustees to hold title to the property. For example, in *Humphries v. Wiley*, the Colored Methodist Episcopal Church had adopted a book of regulations, called a "discipline," under which each local church was supposed to elect a board of trustees "for holding church property."[61] Under the "discipline," the trustees could only sell with the consent of the members of the local church. In this case the court found that because the members had not consented to the transfer of real property held by the trustees of the church, the transfer was invalid.

However, one problem with transferring land to trustees for use by an unincorporated church is that a court might find that the transfer is invalid because the beneficiary of the trust—that is, the unincorporated church—was not identified specifically enough. This was the result in *Salem Church of United Brethren in Christ v. Numsen*,[62] in which a grantor had given land to several trustees for the construction of a church to be used primarily by the Methodist Episcopal Church South. The court held that no trust was created because the deed was too vague and did not name a specific beneficiary and thus was void. In addition, even though an unincorporated religious society known as Hookstown Methodist Episcopal Church South had been occupying the land for over seventy years, it could not obtain title to the real property by adverse possession because as an unincorporated association it was unable to hold title.

Formation of corporation

Often, unincorporated religious associations have been forced to form a corporation in order to hold title to their property. It is interesting to note that in *Trustees of the General Assembly of the Presbyterian Church in the United States v. Guthrie*,[63] the

---

59. *Id.* at 485.
60. Fla. Stat. Ann. §692.101 (West 1994).
61. Humphries v. Wiley, 76 S.W.2d 793, 795 (Tex. Civ. App. 1934, writ dism'd).
62. 59 A.2d 757 (Md. 1948).
63. 10 S.E. 318 (Va. 1889).

Supreme Court of Appeals of Virginia states that although the Virginia Constitution forbids the incorporation of a church or religious denomination, a North Carolina corporation created to hold the property of the church was not itself a church, thus making it permissible for the corporation to receive a bequest.

Nuances in federal and state statutes

This is further complicated by the fact that various states have adopted different statutes to deal with the issue of how an unincorporated association, and sometimes specifically an unincorporated religious association, may hold title to property. Therefore, an unincorporated religious organization must be aware of the very different laws of each of the states in which it operates. The following examples illustrate some of the ways in which specific states have dealt with this issue.

California

Pursuant to statute, California allows an unincorporated association to own the property it needs for its purposes indefinitely. In addition, it may own property that is not needed for its purposes for up to ten years.[64] For religious associations, an obvious problem of this statute is that it requires a court to determine the purposes of the religious group. This probably would not be an issue when a group defines its aims as those usually considered church or religious purposes, such as owning a church or temple building or operating a religious school. However, it could become an issue if the religious group described its purposes as something more specific, such as spreading the gospel. A court could then decide that operating a soup kitchen was not spreading the gospel, and that the religious group could therefore only hold property for this use for ten years.

Connecticut

Connecticut allows unincorporated religious societies to take bequests of personal property. In *New York East Annual Conference of Methodist Church v. Seymour*, the Supreme Court of Errors in Connecticut stated that "the fact that the Bald Hill Methodist Episcopal Church was unincorporated did not impair its right and power to receive a bequest of personal property for religious or charitable purposes."[65] The court reached this result by relying on one Connecticut statute that allows three or more persons uniting for public worship to form a voluntary association,[66] and on another that allows bequests "for the maintenance of the ministry of the gospel."[67]

Illinois

Illinois has a statute that allows an unincorporated lodge to own real property if it is chartered by its grand lodge.[68] But there is no similar provision allowing an unincorpo-

---

64. *See* Cal. Corp. Code § 20001 (West 2004).
65. New York E. Annual Conf. of Methodist Church v. Seymour, 199 A.2d 701, 703 (Conn. 1964).
66. *See* Conn. Gen. Stat. Ann. § 33-264a (West 2004).
67. Conn. Gen. Stat. Ann. § 47-2 (West 2004).
68. *See* 765 Ill. Comp. Stat. 115/1 (West 2004).

rated religious organization to own real property, nor is it clear why the legislature discriminated in this way.

Massachusetts

Massachusetts has a statute that treats certain officers of unincorporated religious associations who are residents of Massachusetts as corporations for property purposes. Specifically, "deacons, wardens or similar officers of churches or religious societies, and the trustees of the United Methodist churches, appointed according to the disciplines and usages thereof, shall, if residents of the commonwealth, be deemed bodies corporate for the purposes of taking and holding...real or personal property."[69] Based upon this statute, the New York Surrogate's Court in *In re Wagners' Will*[70] has allowed an unincorporated Methodist Episcopal Church located in Massachusetts to take a bequest of personal property given to it by a New York testator. It is unclear how a religious association without deacons or similar officers would be able to hold title to property. It fact, it seems unfair for Massachusetts to make specific provisions for certain types of unincorporated religious associations and not for others.

Minnesota

Minnesota also has a statute that applies only to unincorporated religious associations connected with certain specific denominations.[71] It provides that a religious association may create a board of trustees to control its property, and adds that "Each trustee must be a member in good standing of some Protestant Evangelical church."[72] Presumably this statute does not apply to Catholic, Jewish, Buddhist, or other religious associations that do not hold Protestant Evangelical beliefs.

New York

New York has an even greater variety of laws dealing with specific unincorporated religious denominations. For instance, property devised to an unincorporated parish or religious society "under the jurisdiction of or in communion with the Protestant Episcopal Church" is held by the diocesan corporation.[73] Similarly, property bequeathed to an unincorporated Methodist church is held by the incorporated annual conference for the benefit of that church.[74] New York also has a statute that specifically allows a society or meeting of Shakers or the Religious Society of Friends to hold title to property, whether or not the society or meeting is incorporated.[75]

Courts in New York have adopted a rule that if an unincorporated religious group receives a bequest that is not saved by one of the above-referenced statutes, then the parent corporation of the group will be allowed to have the bequest for the group's benefit. Thus in *First Methodist Church v. Putnam*, the New York court held that a bequest made

---

69. Mass. Gen. Laws Ann. ch. 68, § 1 (West 2004).
70. 148 N.Y.S.2d 110 (Sur. Ct. 1955).
71. *See* Minn. Stat. Ann. §315.46 (West 2004).
72. *Id.*
73. N.Y. Relig. Corp. Law §48 (McKinney 2004).
74. *See id* §334.
75. *See id.* §202.

to an unincorporated ladies' aid society should go to the incorporated church that was the parent corporation of the society.[76]

In addition, New York has a statute that allows unincorporated associations to take bequests of property if they incorporate within three years after the will is probated.[77] In this way the government is probably encouraging unincorporated associations, including religious associations, to incorporate.

The advantage of New York's plethora of laws dealing with different specific denominations and religious organizations is that various laws can be tailored to the polities of various religious groups. For instance, a statute can give property belonging to unincorporated hierarchical religious associations to a corporation that is the next step up on that church's hierarchy. Alternatively, for such nonhierarchical groups as the Quakers, a statute can allow the local congregation or meeting to hold title to property. The disadvantage appears, however, if the polity of a religious organization changes. For example, if a congregational denomination decided to become hierarchical, it might want an entity in the hierarchy to hold title instead of the local congregation. However, it is doubtful whether the state would be sufficiently cognizant of the changes in a religious group's polity to amend specific statutes to reflect those changes.

Since it is impossible for state law to deal separately with every different religious group, New York has general provisions to deal with those organizations that are not covered by particular statutes. For example, since the idea that the parent corporation of an unincorporated group is entitled to its property only makes sense for churches with a hierarchical structure, it is good that New York states that unincorporated associations that incorporate within three years after a will is probated may receive bequests. This allows the religious association itself to determine which entity will own the property and how that entity will relate to the larger church.

Tennessee

Tennessee has a statute allowing unincorporated religious associations to own real estate "for purposes of public worship, or for a parsonage, or for a burial ground."[78] Based on that statute, Tennessee courts have reasoned that unincorporated religious organizations may also take bequests of money to be used for repairs and equipment.[79] They may not take bequests of personal property to be used simply as investments. This rule may have made sense in earlier times when religious groups were smaller and needed few assets. As they grow larger, however, they do much more than hold religious worship services and operate cemeteries and, therefore, need investments to enable them to carry out their expanded ministries. The state needs to make provisions for all of the charitable work that religious groups do.

Puerto Rico

Another example of one unincorporated religious group obtaining more favorable treatment than another is found in the case of *Ponce v. Roman Catholic Apostolic Church*

---

76. *See* First Methodist Church v. Putnam, 72 N.Y.S.2d 70 (Sup. Ct. 1947).

77. *See* N.Y. Est. Powers & Trusts Law § 3-1.3 (McKinney 2004).

78. Tenn. Code Ann. § 66-2-201 (West 2004).

79. *See* Sales v. Southern Trust Co., 185 S.W.2d 623 (Tenn. 1945); *In re* Kirby's Will, 240 N.Y.S.2d 214 (Sur. Ct. 1963).

in Porto Rico.[80] There the United States Supreme Court recognized that the Roman Catholic church, whether it was incorporated or not, was entitled to hold title to property in Puerto Rico. The Court reasoned that at the time the United States annexed Puerto Rico from Spain, certain treaties between the papacy and Spain recognized the right of the Catholic church to own property.[81] However, it is unclear whether other unincorporated religious bodies without this history would also have the right to own property.

Assets on dissolution

One issue that arises for unincorporated religious associations that hold property is that of where their assets go on dissolution of the association. Under federal tax law, any organization, including an unincorporated association, that is exempt from taxation under section 501(c)(3) of the Internal Revenue Code must upon dissolution give its assets to another 501(c)(3) organization.[82] Some state statutes provide guidance as to which organization should receive the assets of a dissolving corporation—for example, in Illinois, assets of a dissolving not-for-profit corporation are to go to an organization "engaged in activities substantially similar to those of the dissolving corporation"[83]— but there is usually little guidance on how to distribute the assets of an unincorporated association.

One exception to this rule is Minnesota, which currently has a statute that specifies that if an unincorporated religious society "under the control or supervision of a superior body" ceases to exist, then its property goes to the "next higher governing or supervisory corporate body of the same denomination."[84] This provision works well for hierarchical churches but might not work as well for congregational churches.

Adjudication of property disputes

Unincorporated religious associations that own property are also often faced with the problem of what happens to that property when factions develop within the association. At least one state, Louisiana, presumes that the property is owned by the majority of members of the association.[85] However, that state also allows this presumption to be overcome "by the showing of a contrary intention within the constitution, charter, by-laws, rules, or regulations under which the association is organized or governed."[86] Thus, when an unincorporated church acknowledged that it was regulated by the rules of its hierarchical parent church, which dictated that the property of its unincorporated associations was held in trust for the main body of the church, the court gave the property to the parent church.[87]

There is at least one other case in which a court used neutral principles of law to determine ownership of property by an unincorporated religious association. In *Skelton v. Word Chapel, Inc.*,[88] the founders of a religious association had a falling out with some

---

80. 210 U.S. 296 (1908).
81. *See id.* at 309.
82. *See* Rev. Proc. 82-2, 1982-1 C.B. 367.
83. 805 Ill. Comp. Stat. 105/112.16(c) (West 2004).
84. Minn. Stat. Ann. §315.37 (West 2004).
85. *See* La. Rev. Stat. Ann. §9:1051 (West 2004).
86. Bethany Indep. Church v. Stewart, 645 So. 2d 715, 720 (La. Ct. App. 1994).
87. *See id.*
88. 637 P.2d 753 (Ariz. Ct. App. 1981).

new members and decided to eject them. From the association's articles of association and bylaws, the court concluded that the association was congregational in nature, and therefore that its property was controlled not by its original founders, but by a numerical majority of its members.

It appears that the use of neutral principles to decide factional property disputes in unincorporated religious associations may be more difficult than it is for similar disputes in corporations. Since an unincorporated religious organization may not have many written documents governing it, it may be hard for a court to determine whether control of the association's property rightly belongs to the majority of the association members, to particular members holding certain religious beliefs, or to the church hierarchy.

Ability to enter into contracts

A corollary to the issue of whether an unincorporated association may hold title to property is whether it may enter into contracts in its own name. The common-law rule is that it may not, and that its members who do sign contracts may be individually liable.[89] Thus, in *Thurmond v. Cedar Spring Baptist Church*[90] the Georgia Supreme Court held that members of an unincorporated church were liable on its contract as joint promissors. This rule has been modified in many states to allow the trustees of an unincorporated association to contract for it. In *Lunsford and Withrow & Co. v. Wren*, the Supreme Court of Appeals of West Virginia noted that although an unincorporated church could not contract, its trustees could.[91]

Merger

Merger is another area where unincorporated associations, including unincorporated religious associations, are at a disadvantage. This is because there is no general rule on whether they may merge with other entities. Because of this lack of law, at least one court has held that an unincorporated religious association may not merge with an incorporated church. In *Trinity Pentecostal Church v. Terry*[92] the court held that under Missouri law, entities must be incorporated in order to merge.

Capacity to sue and be sued

Another major problem for unincorporated religious associations is that historically such an entity could neither sue nor be sued in its own name.[93] Instead, some or all of its members had to sue or be sued. Thus, in *Wimmer v. Saint John the Apostle Parish*,[94] the United States District Court for the District of Kansas stated that in Kansas, the unincorporated religious association could not be sued in its own name, and that instead the suit had to be brought against a member of the association as its representative. Moreover, in *Libhart v. Copeland*,[95] the Court of Appeals of Texas noted that although

---

89. *See* Richard B. Couser, Ministry and the American Legal System 280 (1993).
90. 36 S.E. 221 (Ga. 1900).
91. *See* Lunsford and Withrow & Co. v. Wren, 63 S.E. 308 (W. Va. 1908).
92. 660 S.W.2d 449 (Mo. Ct. App. 1983).
93. *See* 66 Am. Jur. 2d Religious Societies §76 (1973).
94. No. 88-1645-K, 1989 WL 145443 (D. Kan. Dec. 1, 1989).
95. 949 S.W.2d 783 (Tex. App. 1997, no writ).

Texas now allowed an unincorporated association to sue in its own name, suits could also still be brought on its behalf by its full membership or by individual members acting as representatives of the full membership.

In addition to Texas, many other states have adopted statutes allowing unincorporated associations to sue and be sued in their own names. These include, but are not limited to, Alabama, Illinois, North Carolina, and Ohio.[96] Other states have adopted statutes allowing certain officers of unincorporated associations to sue on behalf of the entity. In New York, for example, the president or the treasurer of such an association may bring or defend an action on its behalf,[97] and if the association has no president or treasurer, then another officer in an equivalent position may bring or defend the action.[98]

Members' liability for acts of the unincorporated association

Another problem with unincorporated associations is that all members of an association may be held liable for its acts. This is particularly true if the members actually participated in those acts by ratifying them or by serving as officers or directors. For example, as recently as 1991 in *Hutchins v. Grace Tabernacle United Pentecostal Church*,[99] the Court of Appeals of Texas discussed the fact that although the church could now be sued in its own name, it could not be liable on its contracts because it was an unincorporated association. Instead the members of the church could be liable for the rent due pursuant to its lease. Such liability would exist if the members had assented to or ratified the lease, or if the lease had been made by agents or employees of the church acting within the scope of their authority.[100]

Again, some states have changed this rule by statute so that only the association is responsible for judgments against it.[101] Of course, an unincorporated religious organization may not know whether its state has adopted such a statute. Also, if the association functions in more than one state, its members may have protection in one state and not in another.

Whether members may sue the unincorporated association

The common law rule is that a member of an unincorporated association may not sue the association.[102] The rationale is that the members of an unincorporated association are engaged in a joint enterprise. "Thus, the negligence of one member, acting in furtherance of the enterprise, is imputable to all. Allowing such a member to sue the association or another member, as a part of the association, would be tantamount to al-

---

96. *See* Ala. Code §10-3B-8 (2004); 735 Ill. Comp. Stat. 5/2-209.1 (West 2004); N.C. Gen. Stat. §1-69.1 (2004); Ohio Rev. Code Ann. §1745.01 (West 2004).

97. *See* N.Y. Gen. Ass'ns §12 (McKinney 2004).

98. *See* Cadman Mem'l Congregational Soc'y v. Kenyon, 116 N.E.2d 481 (N.Y. 1953), (allowing the General Council of the Congregational Christian Churches of the United States to be sued in the name of its Moderator and Presiding Officer).

99. 804 S.W.2d 598 (Tex. App. 1991, no writ).

100. *See id.* at 599.

101. *See* Ohio Rev. Code Ann. §1745.02 (West 2004).

102. *See* Oleck & Stewart, *supra* note 47, §53; *see also* Cox v. Thee Evergreen Church, 836 S.W.2d 167, 175 (Tex. 1992) (Gonzalez, J., dissenting); Hanson v. Saint Luke's United Methodist Church, 704 N.E.2d 1020, 1022 (Ind. 1998) (discussing the common law rule).

lowing that person to sue himself."[103] Courts have found this rationale particularly persuasive when the member was actively involved in the wrongdoing, such as being a director of the association and being present at the meeting where the association's negligence allegedly occurred.[104]

However, the trend has been to move away from this common law rule and to allow members to sue unincorporated associations. Some jurisdictions have made an exception to this common law rule when the unincorporated association is large and the members do not control the activities of the association. For example, in *Marshall v. International Longshoremen's and Warehousemen's Union, Local 6, Dist. 1*,[105] the California Supreme Court found that an unincorporated labor union had been recognized as a separate legal entity for many purposes and that the rank and file individual did not conduct the business of the organization. Therefore, the court allowed a member of a union "to sue the union for negligent acts which he neither anticipated in nor authorized."[106]

Similarly, in *Williamson v. Wallace*,[107] the Court of Appeals of North Carolina stated that perhaps a member of a hierarchical unincorporated religious association might be able to sue the association. In that case, the court did not allow a member of an unincorporated Baptist church to sue the church because the governing body of the church was its entire congregation, including the member. However, the court did note that "Other questions might arise had defendant church been…one having a more hierarchical structure."[108] In such a church, the member would not have control over the operation of the church, and therefore, the member might be able to sue such a church.

Several courts have recently gone even farther and allowed all suits against unincorporated associations, including unincorporated religious associations. For instance, the the New Jersey Superior Court[109] and the Ohio Supreme Court[110] have held that members of an unincorporated association may sue it for torts. The supreme courts of Indiana,[111] South Carolina,[112] and Texas[113] have specifically extended the right to sue to members of all unincorporated religious associations.

The rationale for many of these decisions is that state statutes now treat unincorporated associations more like legal entities. For example, in *Buteas v. Raritan Lodge No.*

---

103. Boehm v. Cody Country Chamber of Commerce, 748 P.2d 704 (Wyo. 1987). Pennsylvania, Rhode Island, Vermont, Washington and Wisconsin are other jurisdictions that have applied the common law rule. *See* De Villars v. Hessler, 70 A.2d 333 (Pa. 1950); Aetna Casualty and Surety Co. v. Curley, 585 A.2d 640 (R.I. 1991); Duplis v. Rutland Aerie, No. 1001, Fraternal Order of Eagles, 111 A.2d 727 (Vt. 1955); Carr v. Northern Pac. Beneficial Ass'n, 221 P. 979 (Wash. 1924); Hromek v. Gemeinde, 298 N.W. 587 (Wis. 1941).

104. *See* Zehner v. Wilkinson Mem'l United Methodist Church, 581 A.2d 1388 (Pa. Super. Ct. 1990).

105. 371 P.2d 987 (Cal. 1962).

106. 57 Cal.2d at 787.

107. 224 S.E.2d 253 (N.C. Ct. App. 1976).

108. *Id.* at 254.

109. *See* Buteas v. Raritan Lodge No. 61 F. & A.M., 591 A.2d 623 (N.J. Super. Ct. App. Div. 1991).

110. *See* Tanner v. Columbus Lodge No. 11, Loyal Order of Moose, 337 N.E.2d 625 (Ohio 1975).

111. *See* Hanson, 704 N.E.2d at 1027.

112. *See* Crocker v. Barr, 409 S.E.2d 368 (S.C. 1991).

113. *See* Cox v. Thee Evergreen Church, 836 S.W.2d 167 (Tex. 1992).

61 F. & A.M.,[114] the court noted that New Jersey had adopted a statute[115] allowing unincorporated associations to be sued in their own names. The statute had also made the property of an association available for judgments and insulated the individual members of the association from liability. Therefore, the court reasoned that since this statute made unincorporated associations liable to nonmembers, they also ought to be liable to members. Similarly in *Crocker v. Barr*, the South Carolina Supreme Court found that a statute that capped any recovery against a charitable organization "clearly contemplates liability actions against unincorporated associations, including churches."[116] Therefore, the court reasoned, unincorporated religious associations should be liable for injuries that they do to their members.

This trend is also based upon the fact that the failure to allow such suits results in injustice and is against public policy. As the New Jersey Superior Court said in *Buteas*, not allowing members to sue unincorporated associations "serves no useful purpose, results in injustice, and does not advance public policy."[117] Also, in *Crocker*, the court reasoned that failure to allow volunteer members to sue an unincorporated church "chills the very volunteerinsm that unincorporated associations require."[118] In fact, the court in *Hanson*, specifically stated that even when the legislature has not overturned the common law rule prohibiting members of unincorporated associations from suing the association, there are many other policy reasons to reach this result, including the following:

> (1) it is inherently unfair to require an injured member, who is one of a number of equally faultless members, to bear a loss incurred as a result of the association's activities; (2) there is no reason to limit the availability of the insurance that associations can, and presumably often do, obtain to avoid unexpected liabilities of the members as a result of exposure to third party claims; and (3) contribution is available to avoid unjust allocation of any loss as among the members.[119]

Therefore, public policy has also dictated that members be allowed to sue unincorporated associations.

At least one jurist has expressed a concern that allowing such suits might have negative consequences for churches. The dissent in *Cox* asserted that concerns over liability would cause churches to discontinue a wide range of beneficial services that they render to their members.[120] Nonetheless, allowing members to sue unincorporated churches appears to be the wave of the future.

Recommendations

Churches should usually incorporate

Given all of the legal uncertainty concerning unincorporated associations, churches are usually best served if they incorporate. It is interesting to note that most commentators

---

114. 591 A.2d at 628.
115. *See* N.J. Stat. Ann. § 2A:64-1 to -6 (West 2004).
116. *Crocker*, 409 S.E.2d at 371.
117. *Buteas*, 591 A.2d at 628.
118. *Crocker*, 409 S.E.2d at 371.
119. *Hanson*, 704 N.E.2d at 1025.
120. *See Cox*, 836 S.W.2d at 179 (Gonzalez, J., dissenting).

make this recommendation. For example, Howard Oleck recognizes that local religious societies may not want the formality of incorporating, but states that all organizations should use the corporate form whenever possible[121] and that if they nonetheless prefer to remain unincorporated they should adopt formal articles of association in order to avoid misunderstandings and personal liability for the members.[122] Richard Couser also poses the question of whether churches should incorporate, and concludes that in almost all cases they should.[123] The only exceptions he gives are for states that either do not allow religious organizations to incorporate or have statutes that provide unincorporated religious associations the advantages of incorporation without the disadvantages.

Of course, some religious organizations will always remain unincorporated associations. The majority will probably do so not for any principled reason but because they are newly formed and do not want to use their limited resources to incorporate. Others might remain unincorporated because that appears to make it easier for the local religious body to retain total control over its property at the local level. For example, in *Coles v. Wilburn*,[124] the main church required its local churches to incorporate and to create express trusts by deed to the main church. One local church did not do so. In the ensuing conflict over control of the local church's property, the court held that because the local church had never incorporated and deeded its property as required by the church rules, it retained ownership of the property.

States should adopt the Uniform Unincorporated Nonprofit Association Act

In 1996 the National Conference of Commissioners on Uniform State Laws adopted the Uniform Unincorporated Nonprofit Association Act ("UUNA Act"). As of August 11, 1999, at least eight states had adopted most, if not all, of this act. These states are Alabama, Arkansas, Colorado, Delaware, Idaho, Texas, West Virginia, Wisconsin, and Wyoming.[125]

How the UUNA Act benefits religious organizations

One advantage of the UUNA Act is that it treats all unincorporated associations equally, without giving those that are not churches advantages over those that are. Nor does it favor one particular religious group over another. More importantly, it gives unincorporated associations a number of rights that corporations have. First, it allows an unincorporated association to own real and personal property in its own name[126] and to be a legatee or beneficiary of a trust or contract.[127] It is interesting that this even allows for property in a state that has adopted the UUNA Act to be owned by an unincorporated association based in a state that has not.

---

121. *See* Oleck & Stewart, *supra* note 47, §62.

122. *See id.* at §50.

123. *See* Couser, *supra* note 89, at 180.

124. 245 S.E.2d 273 (Ga. 1978).

125. *See* Ala. Code §§ 10-3B-1 to -18 (2004); Ark. Code Ann. §§ 4-28-501 to -517 (2004); Colo. Rev. Stat. Ann. §§ 7-30-101 to -119 (West 2004); Del. Code Ann. tit. 6, §§ 1901–1916 (2004); Idaho Code §§ 53-701 to -717; Tex. Rev. Civ. Stat. Ann. art. 1396-70.01 (West 2004); W. Va. Code §§ 36-11-1 to -17 (2004); Wis. Stat. Ann. §§ 184.01–.15 (West 2004); Thomas L. Frenn, 1997 Wisconsin Act 140 Defines Unincorporated Nonprofit Association, Limits Liability, 71 Wis. Law. 9 (1998); Wyo. Stat. Ann. §§ 17-22-101 to -115 (2004).

126. *See* Uniform Uninc. Nonprofit Ass'n Act § 3 (1996) [hereinafter UNNA Act].

127. *See id.* § 4.

In addition, one of the biggest advantages to the UUNA Act is that it limits the liability of members, directors and officers of unincorporated associations.[128] As noted above, under common law directors, officers, and sometimes even members were often held liable for the contracts or torts of an unincorporated association. The UUNA Act specifies that a person is not liable for the contracts and torts of an association just because the person is a member of the association or is able to participate in its management. Neither are members liable for judgments and orders against the association.[129] Section 6 of the act also allows a member to sue an unincorporated association and the association to sue the member. As shown by the *Cox v. Thee Evergreen Church*[130] case, this follows the trend of the law.

The UUNA Act also allows an unincorporated association to sue and be sued in its own name.[131] As set out above, many states have already adopted statutes giving unincorporated associations the rights ordinarily associated only with corporations, but the advantage of the UUNA Act is that it puts them all in one place. These rights are particularly beneficial to many new religions or new religious groups that might begin very informally—for example, by meeting in someone's home—and may not have the ability or desire to obtain legal advice and become incorporated.

This act may also be useful to religions that, because of their beliefs, prefer little or no government involvement. It grants unincorporated associations many of the benefits of incorporation, such as the ability to own property, without requiring them to file annual reports and other written statements with the state as most corporations are required to do. For example, it allows, but does not require, unincorporated associations to file statements of authority regarding real property[132] and statements appointing a registered agent authorized to receive service of process.[133] Therefore, if an unincorporated religious association wishes to remain anonymous and have no contact with the state, it may do so.

Problems that the UUNA Act poses for religious groups

Definition of unincorporated association

However, the UUNA Act does create some problems for religious organizations. For example, they may find its definition of "nonprofit association" problematical. The act defines this term as "an unincorporated organization...consisting of [two] or more members joined by mutual consent for a common, nonprofit purpose."[134] However, independent church groups might want to come together without forming a nonprofit association.

For example, in *Barr v. United Methodist Church*,[135] residents of retirement homes argued that they could sue the United Methodist Church under the California statute allowing suits against unincorporated associations. The trial court found that "The United Methodist Church is no more than a 'spiritual confederation' and is not a jural

---

128. *See id.* § 6.
129. *See id.* § 8.
130. 836 S.W.2d 167 (Tex. 1992).
131. *See* UUNA Act, *supra* note 122, § 7.
132. *See id.* § 5.
133. *See id.* § 10.
134. *See id.* § 1.
135. 153 Cal. Rptr. 322 (Ct. App. 1979).

entity or unincorporated association subject to suit under Code of Civil Procedure 388."[136] On appeal, the United Methodist Church argued that the trial court's decision should be upheld because the United Methodist Church was "merely a loose connectional system and not a jural entity."[137] The Court of Appeal of California reversed, holding that the United Methodist Church was an unincorporated association that could be sued. The Court of Appeal based its decision on the fact that the United Methodist Church functioned more like "a single entity than completely autonomous and independent units."[138] As evidence, the court noted that the "Council of Bishops is equivalent to the board of directors" of the United Methodist Church and that the United Methodist Church exercised control over the local churches — for example, by selecting local pastors.[139] Unincorporated religious organizations like the United Methodist Church will find no comfort in the UUNA Act's loose definition of "nonprofit association," because under the provisions of this act they will be treated as legal entities, rather than as separate independent units.

To mitigate this problem, the UUNA Act could carve out a category of religious organizations that come together only to perform religious functions and do not otherwise operate as unified entities. For example, instead of covering all groups that come together "for a common, nonprofit purpose," the UUNA Act could state that it does not cover persons who come together for religious purposes unless these persons also perform secular functions, such as hold title to property. In this way, persons could decide to meet and be governed by common religious doctrines without thereby creating an unincorporated association.

Narrow definition of member

Another problem with the UUNA Act is its definition of *member*. It states that a member is "a person who, under the rules or practices of a nonprofit association, may participate in the selection of persons authorized to manage the affairs of the nonprofit association or in the development of policy of the nonprofit association."[140] This definition helps religious organizations because it uses the term *person,* thereby permitting corporations and other legal entities to be members of an unincorporated association. Thus, churches that are members of a national or regional unincorporated conference are members of that association under this definition.

Depending on a religious organization's polity, however, this definition may exclude people who consider themselves to be members of the religious organization and whom the organization also considers to be members. This is because a person who is a member of an unincorporated religious association may or may not be able to select the people who will manage its affairs, and may or may not be able to participate in the development of its policy. If the organization has a hierarchical polity, then the members might not select the members of the hierarchy. For example, members of an unincorporated Catholic church would neither select leaders for the church nor develop its policy; instead, the church hierarchy consisting of the pope and bishops would perform those functions. Also, if the religious organization is governed by one person, such as its

---

136. *Id.* at 324.
137. *Id.*
138. *Id.* at 329.
139. *Id.*
140. UUNA Act, *supra* note 122, § 1.

founder, then the members may not be able to select the management or determine policy. An unincorporated Unification Church might be one example of this type of religious group.

The Comment to section 1 of the UUNA Act states that its definition of member was designed to cover only those who have the ability to select management and develop policy because those are the only people whom the common law would hold responsible for acts of the unincorporated association. Also, section 6 of the act specifies that a person is not liable for the acts of the unincorporated association merely because he or she is a member or is considered by the association to be one.

However, there is still some ambiguity about whether people who are considered to be members of an unincorporated association, but who do not meet the UUNA Act's definition of member, can be liable for something that the association does. This is because section 8 of the act only states that "members" are not liable for judgments against the association. It does not explicitly state that those who are considered by the association to be members, but who do not meet the UUNA Act's definition of member, are also not liable for judgments.

To deal with this problem, Idaho has added that a person considered to be a member is also not liable for the judgments against the association.[141] Colorado goes further by actually changing the definition of member to include someone "who is considered to be a member by such person and the nonprofit association."[142] Given the fact that there are many variations of common law principles for unincorporated associations, it makes sense to allow the unincorporated association, particularly if it is a religious group, to specify which people it considers to be its members. In this way, all those who consider themselves members of an unincorporated religious group can have the protection against liability provided by the statute.

Numerical membership requirements

There is also the issue that the UUNA Act requires that an unincorporated nonprofit association have at least two members.[143] The Texas and Wisconsin versions change this to require at least three members.[144] However, since the UUNA Act defines member to include only those who may participate in selecting management and developing policy, it is possible that if the individuals belonging to an unincorporated association neither pick managers nor develop policy, then the association might have no "members" at all.

More likely would be an unincorporated religious association with just one member. For example, when the association begins, the founder may be the only one who belongs, or at least the only one who meets the definition of member because he is the only one who can select management and develop policy. On the other hand, an unincorporated religious association that is dying may get down to just one member. For example, Catholic religious orders are usually unincorporated associations, and if an order is unable to attract any new members it may eventually have only one. In all of these scenarios, the unincorporated religious association no longer meets the definition

141. *See* Idaho Code § 53-708 (2004).
142. Colo. Rev. Stat. Ann. § 7-30-101 (West 2004).
143. *See* UUNA Act, *supra* note 122, § 1 (2).
144. *See* Tex. Rev. Civ. Stat. Ann. art. 1396-70.01, § 2 (2) (West 2004); Wis. Stat. Ann. § 184.01(2) (West 2004).

of "nonprofit association" found in the UUNA Act, and therefore no longer enjoys the powers and the protections that the act provides.

Requirement of address for association

Section 5(c)(3) of the UUNA Act allows an unincorporated association to file a statement of authority that includes its address in order to transfer real property. However, as the Comment notes, this subsection may create problems for small ad hoc associations that might simply meet in someone's home. Since this is the manner in which many religious organizations start, the UUNA Act should develop a solution to this problem.

Transfer of assets of inactive unincorporated association

Section 9 of the UUNA Act provides that if an unincorporated association is inactive for "[three] years, or for a longer or shorter period specified in a document of the association, a person in possession or control of the personal property of the nonprofit association may transfer custody of the property" either to a person specified in a document of the association or, if no such person is specified, to an organization "pursuing broadly similar purposes." To avoid problems with religious groups, the UUNA Act should be amended to specify that if the inactive association is part of a hierarchical church, then its assets should go to the next level of the same denomination. If the inactive association is part of a congregational church, then its assets should go to another church of the same denomination. This section should be inapplicable to active religious associations that decide to change their affiliation.

Texas provision on records

In adopting the UUNA Act, Texas added a provision that requires all nonprofit associations to keep correct records of account for at least three years and to make these available to their members. It also allows the attorney general to inspect these records "to determine if a violation of any law of this state has occurred."[145] This gives the state, and particularly the attorney general, too much power over unincorporated religious associations.

Responsibility of nonprofit association

The UUNA Act allows nonprofit associations to sue and be sued. It states that "A nonprofit association is a legal entity separate from its members for the purposes of determining and enforcing rights, duties, and liabilities in contract and tort."[146] However, the UUNA Act does not provide any guidance as to when a nonprofit association is liable for the acts of its members. If a member commits a tort, is the association liable?

If a religious association believes that it can be sued for all actions of its members, then it may try to control its members' actions. For example, in *Barr v. The United Methodist Church*, the Court of Appeal of California found that the United Methodist Church was an unincorporated association that could be sued by residents of fourteen retirement homes operated by Pacific Homes, a corporation that described itself as "an agency of the United

---

145. Tex. Rev. Civ. Stat. Ann. art. 1396-70.01, §11.
146. UUNA Act, *supra* note 122, §6 (a).

Methodist Church Southern California Arizona Conference."[147] Although the Court of Appeal did not reach the issue of whether the United Methodist Church was liable for the actions of Pacific Homes, commentators have argued that allowing religious associations like the unincorporated United Methodist Church to be sued for actions of their "members" will force them to police their members' activities.[148] If being subject to such suits causes religious associations to try to control their members more, that will conflict with the religious polity of those that are presbyterian or congregational, rather than hierarchical, and whose polity dictates that they have independent subunits or members.[149]

To avoid this result, the UUNA Act should specify when nonprofit associations are liable. Normally, corporations are not liable for the acts of their shareholders or of their parent, subsidiary or affiliated corporations.[150] Liability only occurs when a court finds a reason to "pierce the corporate veil" and hold the corporation liable for actions of these other entities. Therefore, the UUNA Act should also specify that nonprofit associations are normally not liable for the acts of their members. Religious nonprofit associations should not be liable for entities that are affiliated with them or sponsored by them; a plaintiff should have to show that the association actually participated in the wrongdoing of its affiliate and that there is good reason to pierce the barrier between them.

Conclusion

A religious organization may find that a charitable trust helps it further a limited purpose of the organization. However, a charitable trust does not operate well as the general form of the religious organization. Moreover, there are problems with the current use of this form to hold the retirement assets of members of Catholic religious orders.

The old rules governing unincorporated associations make that form also undesirable for most religious organizations. Moreover, the current upheaval in the rules for such associations makes it very difficult to know how they will be treated. However, the UUNA Act certainly solves many of the old problems of the unincorporated association form and provides a great deal of protection to these associations, even though it still leaves many issues unresolved.

---

147. Barr v. United Methodist Church, 153 Cal. Rptr. 322, 331 (Ct. App. 1979).

148. *See* Note, Imposing Corporate Forms on Unincorporated Denominations: Balancing Secular Accountability with Religious Free Exercise, 55 S. Cal. L. Rev. 155, 180 (1981).

149. *See id.* at 182.

150. *See* Bright v. Roadway Servs., Inc., 846 F. Supp. 693, 700 (N.D. Ill. 1994); 1 William Meade Fletcher, et al., Fletcher Cyclopedia of the Law of Private Corporations §43.10, at 758 (perm. ed. rev. vol. 1990).

Religious Organizations and the Law of Trusts

H. Reese Hansen

Simply defined, charitable trust doctrine requires that goods donated for a particular charitable purpose be used for that purpose. While the doctrine may be readily defined, its application is often significantly more problematic. Because churches and other religious institutions, unlike commercial organizations, are frequent recipients of donations for charitable purposes,[1] charitable trust doctrine adds a complexity to church decisions and operations that typically is not present in the commercial context.

In particular, when disputes concerning the disposition or use of property arise either within a church organization or between the church and a donor or his heirs, the court may employ charitable trust principles to resolve the issue. Application of charitable trust doctrine may differ, however, depending upon the structure of a church's organization, the language of or circumstances surrounding the donation itself, and applicable state statutes regarding incorporation, solicitation of donations, etc. This is especially true since Supreme Court decisions in 1969[2] and 1979[3] overturned long-standing state court precedents that permitted judicial resolution of internal church property disputes by consideration of church doctrine.[4] Prior to these decisions,

---

1. A 1994 survey conducted by the DePaul University Center for Church/State Studies indicates that nine in ten religious organizations depend primarily on member donations or dues to bring in funds. DePaul University, 1994 Survey of American Religions at the National Level, Public release Document 3.

2. Presbyterian Church in the United States v. Mary Elizabeth Blue Hull Memorial Presbyterian Church, 393 U.S. 440 (1969).

3. Jones v. Wolf, 443 U.S. 595 (1979).

4. *See, e.g.*, Morgan, The Significance of Church Organizational Structure in Litigation and Government Action, 16 Val. U. L. Rev. 147, 148–51 (1981); and Ellman, Driven from the Tribunal: Judicial Resolution of Internal Church Disputes, 69 Cal. L. Rev. 1378, 1386 (1981), for a detailed analysis of the historical development of jurisprudence on this subject and of these early decisions. Watson v. Jones, 80 U.S. (13 Wall.) 679 (1871), is the Supreme Court's first attempt at applying a methodology to resolve internal religious disputes. The case involved a dispute over the issue of slavery within a local church that belonged to the Presbyterian Church in the United States. The Supreme Court established three principles that have dominated subsequent jurisprudence in resolving internal religious disputes. The first principle confirmed that civil courts have the authority to settle internal church disputes and are required to do so. The second principle was the rejection of the "departure from doctrine" approach, which held that when a church group split into factions, the court was required to award the disputed property to the faction that remained most loyal to the precepts followed at the time the property was donated. The third principle that the Court estab-

courts had frequently relied on a distinct legal doctrine developed especially for religious property disputes, the implied trust doctrine, to reach relatively consistent results. Application of the implied trust doctrine required, however, that a court consider the relative fidelity of rival church factions to ecclesiastical doctrine. In the 1969 case *Presbyterian Church in the United States v. Mary Elizabeth Blue Hull Memorial Presbyterian Church*,[5] the Supreme Court held that judicial involvement in property disputes among factions of church members implicates both the Establishment and Free Exercise clauses of the First Amendment. The Court prohibited courts from examining church doctrine to resolve conflicting claims, and indicated that "neutral principles of law" could be employed in resolving such conflicts.[6] The Court did not require, however, that a neutral principles approach be used, nor did it delineate precisely what it meant by "neutral principles" or the parameters of their application. Consequently, although at least thirty states have purportedly followed the Court's ruling,[7] the neutral principles approach has been sustained on the basis of a variety of

---

lished became known as the "polity approach." This methodology was based on the internal structure, or polity, of the particular denomination—either a congregational polity or a hierarchical polity. The court concluded that when a dispute occurs within a congregational church, property rights must be adjudicated in accordance with the ordinary principles that govern voluntary associations. In the hierarchical church polity, the court decided that the civil court must defer to decisions of the highest church judicatory in resolving internal disputes involving questions of faith, discipline, custom, or belief.

5. 393 U.S. 440 (1969).

6. *See* Presbyterian Church in the United States v. Mary Elizabeth Blue Hull Memorial Presbyterian Church, 393 U.S. 440, 449 (1969) (instructing courts to rely on those neutral principles of law used in resolving all property disputes in settling church disputes involving property); *see also* Arlin M. Adams & William R. Hanlon, Jones v. Wolf: Church Autonomy and the Religion Clauses of the First Amendment, 128 U. Pa. L. Rev. 1291, 1295 (1980) (citing dicta in *Jones v. Wolf* declaring use of neutral principles as consistent with First Amendment requirements).

7. Trinity Presbyterian Church of Montgomery v. Tankersley, 374 So. 2d 861 (Ala. 1979); Skelton v. The Word Chapel, Inc., 637 P.2d 753 (Ariz. Ct. App. 1981); Vukovich v. Radulovich, 286 Cal. Rptr. 547, 554 (Cal. Ct. App. 1991); Bishop and Diocese of Colorado v. Mote, 716 P.2d 85, 102 (Colo. 1986); Trinity-St. Michael's Parish, Inc. v. Episcopal Church in the Diocese of Connecticut, 620 A.2d 1280 (Conn. 1993) *(Jones* and *Watson* approaches "complement one another"); The Conference of African Union First Colored Methodist Protestant Church v. St. Thomas A.U.M.P. Church of Glasgow, No. 319, 1996, 1997 Del. Lexis (Del. 1997); Williams v. Mount Jezreel Baptist Church, 589 A.2d 901 (D.C. 1991); Grace Evangelical Lutheran Church v. Lutheran Church-Missouri Synod, 454 N.E.2d 1038 (Ill. App. Ct. 1983); Grutka v. Clifford, 445 N.E.2d 1015 (Ind. Ct. App. 1983); Fonken v. Community Church of Kamrar, 339 N.W.2d 810 (Iowa 1983) (can use either *Watson* or neutral principles approach); Fluker Community Church v. Hitchens, 419 So. 2d 445 (La. 1982) (though the neutral principles approach has not been expressly adopted, it has been much used in Louisiana); Attorney General v. First United Baptist Church of Lee, 601 A.2d 96 (Me. 1992); Maryland & Virginia Eldership v. Church of God at Sharpsburg, Inc. 241 A.2d 691 (Md. 1968), *vacated*, 393 U.S. 528, *reaff'd*, 254 A.2d 162 (1969) (Supreme Court approved neutral principles approach followed by Maryland at that time); Fortin v. Roman Catholic Bishop of Worcester, 625 N.E.2d 1352 (Mass. 1994); Bennison v. Sharp, 329 N.W.2d 466 (Mich. Ct. App. 1982) (can use either neutral principles or *Watson* approach); Piletich v. Deretich, 328 N.W.2d 696 (Minn. 1982); Reorganized Church of Jesus Christ of Latter-day Saints v. Thomas, 758 S.W.2d 726 (Mo. Ct. App. 1988); Reardon v. Lemoyne, 454 A.2d 428 (N.H. 1982); Elmora Hebrew Ctr. v. Fishman, 593 A.2d 725 (N.J. 1991); Atkins v. Walker, 200 S.E.2d 641 (N.C. 1973); Poesnecker v. Ricchio, 631 A.2d 1097 (Pa. 1993) *appeal denied*, 647 A.2d 905 (1994); Foss v. Dykstra, 319 N.W.2d 499 (S.D. 1982) (courts may use only neutral principles approach); Church of God in Christ, Inc. v. Middle City Church of God in Christ, 774 S.W.2d 950 (Tenn. Ct. App. 1989); Libhart v. Copeland, 949 S.W.2d 783 (Tex. App. 1997); Reid v. Gholson, 327 S.E.2d 107 (Va. 1985); Sacred Heart Sch. Bd. v. Labor & Industry Review Comm'n, 460 N.W.2d 430 (Wis. Ct. App. 1990).

legal theories and, as expected, interpreted to produce seemingly different results in various federal and state courts since *Hull* and *Jones v. Wolf*[8] were decided in 1969 and 1979 respectively.

In many jurisdictions, courts have applied various presumptions in settling internal church property disputes. These presumptions affect various churches differently depending on each church's internal structure.[9] That is, if the court determines that a church is governed hierarchically[10] with authority for the local congregation residing in a national or international body, it often defers to the decisions of the higher church authority to determine property disputes. If, on the other hand, church polity is deemed congregational[11] and the local church body is relatively autonomous, the local congregation frequently prevails over the national or international church. In congregational churches, majority vote of the congregation typically prevails over the minority in intracongregational disputes.[12] Although since *Hull* and *Jones* courts can no longer overtly examine church doctrine, the present approaches in resolving church property disputes generally require judicial investigation into forms of ecclesiastical government and relationships. Such inquiries may themselves violate principles governing separation of church and state.[13] Further, the inquiry as to whether a church's organizational structure is hierarchical or congregational entails an oversimplification. Although most churches fit into one of those two categories, a hierarchical/congregational analysis fails to reflect the complexity of the organizational structures of American churches.[14]

Different "neutral principles" may be implicated when a religious body is legally structured as a corporation rather than as a trust. Moreover, regardless of the church's legal structure, state statutes may regulate donations given in trust.[15] The result of these complexities is a body of law which is in transition without a clear indication of its heading.[16] This uncertainty complicates many important decisions of religious organizations.

---

8. 443 U.S. 595 (1979).

9. The DePaul survey asked religious organizations whether their internal structure was hierarchical, congregational, presbyterial, connectional, along a continuum of types, or of some other structural form. *See* DePaul University, *supra* note 1.

10. Approximately 21.5% of the religious organizations responding to the survey indicated that their organizational structure was hierarchical. *Id.*

11. Nearly 40% of the religious organizations responding to the survey indicated that their organizational structure was congregational. *Id.*

12. *See, e.g.*, Bouldin v. Alexander, 82 U.S. (15 Wall.) 131 (1872); Brunnenmeyer v. Buhre, 32 Ill. 183 (1863); Smith v. Pedigo, 33 N.E. 777 (Ind. 1893); First Constitutional Presbyterian Church v. Congregational Soc'y, 23 Iowa 567 (1867); McBride v. Porter, 17 Iowa 203 (1864); American Primitive Soc'y v. Pilling, 24 N.J.L. 653 (1855); App v. Selingsgrove Lutheran Congregation, 6 Pa. 201 (1847); Holiman v. Dovers, 366 S.W.2d 197 (Ark. 1963).

13. *See* Dallin H. Oaks, Trust Doctrines in Church Controversies 42 (1984).

14. For instance, the DePaul study reveals that when entities were asked what type of organizational structure they employed, nearly 40% indicated a structure other than hierarchical or congregational. *See* DePaul University, *supra* note 1.

15. Statutes may also regulate accumulations. *Compare, e.g.*, Wis. Stat. Ann. §701.21 (West 2001) and 765 Ill. Comp. Stat. Ann. 315/1 (West 2000); N.Y. Est. Powers & Trusts §§8-1.1; 8-1.6; 9-2.1.

16. Compare Maryland and Virginia Eldership of the Churches of God v. Church of God at Sharpsburg, Inc., 396 U.S. 367, 368–70 (1970) (per curiam) (Brennan, J., concurring); and Presbyterian Church in the United States v. Mary Elizabeth Blue Hull Memorial Presbyterian Church, 393 U.S. 440, 449 (1969) (describing "neutral principles of law" to be applied in church disputes) with Serbian Eastern Orthodox Diocese for the United States and Canada v. Milivojevich (majority holding that a dispute involving the replacement of a bishop within the Serbian Eastern Orthodox Church was primarily a doctrinal dispute, and that the dispute over the control of property was

This chapter begins with brief overviews of both trust law and traditional forms of church polity. It then sketches the history of the implied trust doctrine (the theory most frequently applied to church property disputes during the century before *Hull*), and a discussion of the Supreme Court decisions in *Hull* and *Jones*. Next, it reviews the various ways in which state and federal courts have applied *Hull* and *Jones*, considering the impact of each approach upon church decision-making.[17] The chapter concludes by suggesting church actions that could facilitate resolution of property disputes, and by recommending a more uniform interpretation and application of the neutral principles theory.

Overview of Charitable Trust Law

In internal disputes involving church property, obviously a vital step in resolution is the determination of where title to the property is vested.[18] In its simplest form, title is vested in the grantee named in the deeds or other relevant documents, but frequently these conveyances are complicated and include provisions for the divestiture of the property under certain circumstances.[19] Such divestiture clauses often take the form of a trust.[20]

Trusts may be generally categorized as express (private or charitable), resulting, or constructive,[21] and courts must consider which of these categories the language of the pertinent documents or circumstances establishes. While all trusts require a trustee or legal titleholder, a beneficiary or equitable titleholder, and trust property,[22] each type of trust has its own distinguishing features.

---

merely a secondary issue; therefore, the court held that since the dispute was primarily doctrinal, it must defer to hierarchical authorities).

17. For an excellent analysis of these developments, see Patty Gerstenblith, Civil Court Resolution of Property Disputes Among Religious Organizations, 39 Am. U. L. Rev. 513 (1990). The author of this chapter wishes to express particular indebtedness to Professor Gerstenblith's work; while disagreeing with some of her conclusions, he has relied heavily on her research, which has been influential throughout this chapter.

18. The DePaul study revealed that of those religious organizations reporting that activities, meetings, or services were held in one facility owned, leased, or rented by the organization, two in five reported that these locations were owned and title held by the local group as a not-for-profit corporation. One-third reported that these locations are owned and title held by the local group as a religious corporation. One-fourth of the religious organizations reported that these locations were owned and title held in the name of the trustee(s) for the use of the local group. DePaul University, *supra* note 1. Additionally, the study indicated that more than 50% of the religious organizations surveyed had local units that owned property used for other than religious purposes. *See id*. Likewise, the survey disclosed that approximately 53% of the religious organizations reporting owned property "in the form of land, buildings, or facilities other than those used for religious services or meetings at the national level." *Id*.

19. For instance, those religious organizations that reported having clauses in property deeds which upon dissolution of the local unit revert ownership of the property to the national organization are more likely to have a hierarchical or congregational structure. *Id*. Interestingly, nearly 60% of the religious organizations responded that they do not use reverter clauses in property deeds. *Id*.

20. Other forms of these provisions include the possibility of reverter, right of entry clauses, or executory interests.

21. *See* Richard R. Powell, Powell on Real Property 40 ¶ 500 (Michael Allen Wolf ed., Matthew Bender, 2001).

22. Restatement (Second) of Trusts § 2 cmt. h, 3 (1959). *See also* Gurley v. Lindsley, 459 F.2d 268, 276 (5th Cir. 1972), *mandate withdrawn*, 466 F.2d 498 (1972); Yardley v. Yardley, 484 N.E.2d 873, 882 (Ill. App. 1985) (judicial outline of trust requirements).

Express trusts

Express trusts are distinguished by the requirement of some judicially recognizable manifestation or expression of intent by the grantor to create a trust relationship.[23] Inquiry into the grantor's intent insures that the grantor meant to impose fiduciary duties upon the trustee[24] rather than to transfer the property as an unencumbered gift. Thus, for example, through the use of an express trust a local church entity could be named trustee of property for the benefit of the hierarchical church. If the local congregation leaves the denomination, title to the property would vest according to the provisions of the trust.[25]

Proving a trust may be difficult, however, without a clear manifestation of the settlor's intent. Although there is no general rule defining sufficient proof of intention to create a trust, unclear or incomplete language may be viewed as merely precatory.[26]

Express charitable trusts must, in addition to having a clear expression of intention to create a trust, have a valid charitable purpose.[27] In some cases it may be difficult to determine how particularized the donor's charitable purpose was. It may be unclear, for example, whether the donor had a general (e.g., "for religious purposes") or specific (e.g., "for maintenance of the church organ") charitable intent. Likewise it may be unclear who the donor intended to be beneficiaries in the event of a church schism, or whether there are any privately enforceable duties on the trustees.

Resulting and constructive trusts

Resolving property disputes becomes even more complex when the deeds and other documents do not contain express trust provisions.[28] Trust law distinguishes between two types of trusts that may be imposed in the absence of a settlor's expressed intention to create a trust. A resulting trust is based upon an "inferred or presumed intent of the [settlor],"[29] while a constructive trust does not consider the grantor's intent at all, but is used by a court to redress wrongdoing.[30]

Typically, a resulting trust arises when evidence indicates that the settler did not intend to grant the titleholder the entire interest in the property.[31] Such trusts are found only in three specific circumstances: (1) when the express trust fails entirely or (2) fails to dispose of the entire trust res, or (3) when a purchaser of property directs that title

---

23. Restatement (Second) of Trusts § 4 (1959).

24. Austin W. Scott & William F. Fratcher, The Law of Trusts § 24, at 250 (4th ed. 1987).

25. *See generally* G. Bogert, Trusts § 149 (6th ed. 1987).

26. *See* 1 Scott, Trusts, 4th ed. §§ 25.1, 25.2 (suggesting that trusts are less likely to be found today when language is unclear).

27. *See* Agudas Chasidei Chabad of United States v. Gourary, 650 F. Supp. 1463, 1474 (E.D.N.Y.), *aff'd*, 833 F.2d 431 (2d Cir. 1987).

28. According to the DePaul study, those responding indicated that where property was owned at the local level, it was held either in corporate form or "in the name of the trustee(s) for use of the local group." DePaul University, *supra* note 1. As a result, resolution of property disputes will not generally hinge on or be remedied by the use of a resulting or constructive trust.

29. Bogert, *supra* note 25, §§ 1, 71.

30. *See* Restatement (Second) of Trusts § 1, cmt. e (1959).

31. *Id.*

be put in the name of another individual.[32] In these situations a resulting trust in favor of the settlor may be found.[33] A constructive trust is imposed by a court as a remedy for unjust enrichment where transfer of property was induced by fraud, under duress or undue influence, or through a breach of fiduciary duty.[34] Most church property disputes do not involve either incomplete or failed trusts or fraudulent inducement, and generally neither resulting nor constructive trusts are appropriate remedies in such disputes.

Although courts usually agree that resulting and constructive trusts are seldom appropriate remedies in church property disputes,[35] many courts use the term "implied trust"[36] to describe a trust assumed by the court in the absence of express trust provisions.[37] Not derived directly from trust principles, the "implied trust" arose from a legal fiction.[38] In *First Presbyterian Church v. United Presbyterian Church in the United States*,[39] the court identified three kinds of "implied trusts" in church property disputes: (1) a trust benefiting all the members of the local congregation; (2) a trust benefiting only those members of the local congregation who remain loyal to the original doctrinal tenets; and (3) a trust benefiting the hierarchical church.[40]

Application of this implied trust theory originally involved examination of church doctrine. Even though the Supreme Court has declared such investigation a violation of First Amendment protections,[41] a number of state courts continue to employ a form of implied trust doctrine either by showing deference to the decisions of the church's hierarchy or by presuming that the hierarchical structure of the church indicates the implied intent of the local congregation to hold the property in trust for the general church. Thus, while the departure-from-doctrine approach of older cases is now moribund, churches must still be aware of the potential impact of implied trust theory on property disputes.

Church Polity

In addition to trust law, church structure, or polity, also can affect resolution of a church property dispute. Stated very broadly, courts have tended to identify three types of church governance based upon the degree of local autonomy: hierarchical or episcopal, presbyterial, and congregational.[42]

---

32. Also called a "purchase money resulting trust."

33. Restatement (Second) of Trusts ch. 12 at 323 (1959).

34. V. Scott, *supra* note 24, § 404.2.

35. *But see* Reorganized Church of Jesus Christ of Latter-day Saints v. Thomas, 758 S.W.2d 726, 732–33 (Mo. Ct. App. 1988).

36. Hereafter, the term "implied trust" will refer to the trusts developed by courts for use in resolving church property disputes in structuring property arrangements.

37. The Colorado Supreme Court in *Bishop & Diocese of Colorado v. Mote*, 716 P.2d 85 (Colo. 1986), described a trust not created by express language but implied from the circumstances of the gift and the conduct of the parties as an "implied express trust."

38. *See infra*, Historical Treatment of Internal Religious Disputes.

39. 464 N.E.2d 454 (N.Y. 1984).

40. *Id.* at 462.

41. Presbyterian Church in the United States v. Mary Elizabeth Blue Hull Memorial Presbyterian Church, 393 U.S. 440 (1969).

42. The Encyclopedia of Religion Church: Church Polity 473–80 (1987). Some commentators distinguish only between congregational and hierarchical structures. The DePaul study revealed that

In the hierarchical[43] or episcopal form of church government local congregations have very restricted autonomy.[44] Generally these churches are governed by a national or international presiding authority that appoints leaders over specific geographical areas. Authority over individual congregations is delegated by the presiding organization.

The presbyterial[45] form of church governance is also hierarchical, but while authority in presbyterial churches is usually vested in a single individual at each level, administrative bodies govern presbyterial churches.[46] Local congregations are governed by a representative body rather than by the congregation as a whole, and the body governing the local entities in a geographical area is usually composed of members from the local governing boards.

Congregationally[47] organized churches are characterized by independent local congregations which are typically very democratic.[48] Each local church chooses its own leaders by majority vote (usually of the congregation as a whole) and determines the terms that bind it internally and to other congregations.

In reality, however, the varieties of church polity are better represented as a continuum,[49] and it is frequently difficult to classify a religious organization as strictly congregational or hierarchical. This uncertainty adds complexity to any prediction of judicial decisions.

Historical Treatment of Internal Religious Disputes

The role of the courts in resolving internal religious disputes is at once mandated and circumscribed by the First Amendment. An inherent tension between the Establishment and Free Exercise clauses of the amendment requires courts to remain neutral toward religion while accommodating religious groups.[50] While the United States zeal-

---

over 60% of the religious organizations surveyed have a congregational or hierarchical structure. *See* DePaul University, *supra* note 1. The other responding organizations indicated that their organizational structure was presbyterial, connectional, along a continuum of types, or of some other structural form. *See id.*

43. *See* DePaul University, *supra* note 1.

44. Examples of episcopally governed religious bodies include the Roman Catholic Church, Anglican Church, and Orthodox Church.

45. Of the religious organizations responding to the DePaul study, approximately 9% indicated that their organizational structure is presbyterial. *See* DePaul University, *supra* note 1.

46. Examples of presbyterially governed churches include the Presbyterian Church, Evangelical Church, and Reformed Church of America.

47. A Congregational structure was the most common type of organizational structure among the respondents to the DePaul study. Nearly 40% indicated that their organizational structure was congregational. *See* DePaul University, *supra* note 1.

48. Examples of congregational churches include the Baptist, Congregational, Quaker, and Unitarian.

49. Adams & Hanlon, *supra* note 6, at 1292 & n.6. Approximately 17% of the religious organizations responding to the DePaul study answered that their organizational structure is either along a continuum of types or of some structural form other than hierarchical, congregational, presbyterial, or connectional. *See* DePaul University, *supra* note 1.

50. *See, e.g.,* Everson v. Board of Educ., 330 U.S. 1, 8–16 (1947) (discussing historical development of First Amendment and tension between the two clauses); Zorach v. Clauson, 343 U.S. 306, 314 (1952) (describing narrow government path between establishment and free exercise).

ously advocates separation of church and state, and its judicial system has always asserted that it cannot involve itself in theological disputes, the courts have been unable to completely avoid decisions that bear on religious doctrines when adjudicating property disputes between competing church factions. Indeed, it is ironic that attempts to prevent judicial involvement in church affairs led to the widespread use of the implied trust doctrine that was later discredited in the *Hull* and *Jones* decisions.

The English court system developed the legal fiction of the implied trust as a means of settling property disputes among competing religious factions. Under this doctrine, as developed in *Craigdallie v. Aikman*,[51] in the absence of evidence of an express trust provision the court assumed that property was held in "implied trust" by and for the benefit of individuals or groups that adhered to the same religious standards and beliefs as the donors did.[52] This analysis required the English Court of Chancery and the attorney general to rule on church doctrine. Because this kind of analysis presented a potential violation of the separation of church and state, early American cases rejected the implied trust doctrine.[53]

In 1846, the Vermont Supreme Court rejected the doctrine noting that it depended on judicial consideration of church doctrines, a practice that "could not...be tolerated in this country."[54] Thus, in *Smith v. Nelson*,[55] when a dispute arose as to which minister was entitled to the annual interest from a devise to the "trustee"[56] of a religious society, the court held that the devise was an unencumbered gift to the congregation and not an implied trust. The minister selected by the congregation was to receive the interest.[57]

Similarly, in *Robertson v. Bullions*,[58] one church faction sought an equitable order removing the trustees of the incorporated religious society and requiring an accounting of church property. The court outlined two positions available to it: (1) that the board held the church property as trustees for the members of the congregation or (2) that the religious society was a corporation and held the property free of any trust relationship. The court refused to adopt the former position, noting that it would "devolve upon the courts of equity the administration of the entire property of religious corporations throughout the state,"[59] with resultant state involvement in religious doctrine. Dallin H. Oaks has observed that

> As the leading case expounding what might be called "the corporate autonomy" model, *Robertson v. Bullions* stands for the proposition that, in the absence of some specific express trust provision to the contrary, religious charitable corporations do not hold their property in trust for the support of a particular doctrine, denomination, or membership. Corporate officials, typi-

---

51. 4 Eng. Rep. 435 (1820).

52. *Id.* at 439.

53. For an excellent and lucid discussion of the theoretical basis for the implied trust doctrine and its complete unsuitability as an American legal device, see generally Oaks, *supra* note 13.

54. Smith v. Nelson, 18 Vt. 511 (1846).

55. *Id.*

56. *Id.* at 214.

57. *Id.* at 225–26.

58. 11 N.Y. 243 (1854).

59. *Id.* at 247. *See also* Kauper & Ellis, Religious Corporations and the Law, 71 Mich. L. Rev. 1500, 1511–13 (1973) (discussing the importance of this decision to American religious corporation law).

cally the trustees or deacons elected by the congregation, have complete control over the corporation's property, without the limitation of trust obligations and without regard to religious doctrines, affiliations, or practices.[60]

Finally, in the United States Supreme Court's first intrachurch property case, *Watson v. Jones*,[61] the Court declined to use the implied trust doctrine:

> [T]he local congregation is itself but a member of a much larger and more important religious organization, and is under its government and control, and is bound by its orders and judgments.
>
> ... [T]he legal tribunals must accept such decisions as final, and as binding on them, in their application to the case before them.[62]

The Court's holding in *Watson* "rejected the English doctrine of implied trust by deferring to the decisions of church judicatory bodies."[63] *Watson* involved a local church that was part of a hierarchical organization, so deference to the higher authority was readily available to the Court. But dicta in the opinion dealt with disputes involving churches with other polities. The Court noted, for example, that when a self-governing congregational or independent society holds property without any specific trust attached, other than that it be "for the use of that congregation as a religious society,"[64] ownership rights are determined by "the ordinary principles which govern voluntary associations."[65]

Although this dictum was in agreement with many state court decisions of the time,[66] the implied trust doctrine had already been embraced by at least four state supreme courts[67] and momentum favoring its adoption by other states continued in spite of Supreme Court disapproval.[68] During the century following *Watson*, an increasing number of courts relied on the implied trust doctrine to resolve disputes involving a variety of church polities.[69]

As mentioned previously, in its earliest applications the implied trust doctrine actually supported the courts' deference to decisions of hierarchical church organizations, thus reducing the need to inquire into religious doctrines and making adoption of the implied trust attractive to state judiciaries. Courts came to realize, however, that such reliance resulted in decisions that invariably favored established doctrines; there was need for some flexibility regarding change. To accommodate this need, later decisions invoked the implied trust theory only in situations in which deviations from fundamental doctrines were deemed "substantial" departures.[70] Unfortunately, "[t]his plunged the

---

60. Oaks, *supra* note 13, at 36–37.

61. 80 U.S. (13 Wall.) 679 (1871).

62. *Id.* at 726–27.

63. Oaks, *supra* note 13, at 38.

64. 80 U.S. (13 Wall.) at 725.

65. *Id.*

66. Oaks, *supra* note 13, at 39, and text accompanying n.104.

67. *Id.* n.105.

68. *See, e.g.*, Baker v. Ducker, 21 P. 764 (Cal. 1889); Apostolic Holiness Union v. Knudson, 123 P. 473 (Idaho 1912); Christian Church v. Church of Christ, 76 N.E. 703 (Ill. 1906); Lindstrom v. Tell, 154 N.W. 969 (Minn. 1915); Mt. Helm Baptist Church v. Jones, 30 So. 714 (Miss. 1901); Peace v. First Christian Church, 48 S.W. 534 (Tex. Civ. App. 1898); Marien v. Evangelical Creed Congregation, 113 N.W. 66 (Wis. 1907).

69. Oaks, *supra* note 13, at 41 & n.113.

70. *Id.* n.114.

courts even deeper into religious doctrines, since the application of this modification required the courts not only to define doctrine but also to evaluate its significance in the overall theology and practice."[71]

Almost a century elapsed before the Supreme Court again addressed the issue of the implied trust. In 1969 it considered a property dispute arising from the withdrawal of two local churches from the Presbyterian Church in the United States. The withdrawals were precipitated by doctrinal changes introduced by the general church.[72] In this case, the Court specifically rejected the departure-from-doctrine element of the implied trust theory[73] and instructed lower courts to employ traditional civil law principles, without reference to religious doctrine, to settle church property disputes.[74] The Court stated:

> [T]here are neutral principles of law, developed for use in all property disputes, which can be applied without "establishing" churches to which property is awarded.... [T]he Amendment therefore commands civil courts to decide church property disputes without resolving underlying controversies over religious doctrine. Hence, States, religious organizations, and individuals must structure relationships involving church property so as not to require the civil courts to resolve ecclesiastical questions.[75]

A state court decision indirectly approved by the Supreme Court, *Maryland and Virginia Eldership of the Churches of God v. Church of God at Sharpsburg, Inc.,*[76] further developed the neutral principles analysis. The Maryland Court of Appeals recognized two distinct governing forms within the same denomination.[77] The court found that while the religion's governing bodies were organized in a presbyterial or synodial polity, a congregational polity applied to the use and control of the local congregation's property.[78] After examining the state statute regarding the holding of property by church trustees, the deeds of the property in dispute, and the constitution of the Maryland and Virginia Eldership,[79] the court concluded that title to the local church's property did not vest in the hierarchy upon the withdrawal of the local church from the hierarchy.[80] Rather, despite evidence of a hierarchical church structure, the court held that the language of pertinent documents indicated that property was to be controlled by the local congregation.

Although the Supreme Court dismissed the appeal of *Sharpsburg* in a per curiam decision, the justices were not unanimously agreed as to the legal theory behind the deci-

---

71. *Id.* at 41.

72. Presbyterian Church in the United States v. Mary Elizabeth Blue Hull Memorial Presbyterian Church, 393 U.S. 440, 442 (1969).

73. *Id.* at 450.

74. *Id.* at 449.

75. *Id.*

76. 241 A.2d 691 (Md. 1968), *vacated and remanded,* 393 U.S. 528 (1969), 254 A.2d 162 (1969), *appeal dismissed,* 396 U.S. 367, 367–68 (1970) (per curiam) (dismissing appeal because the Maryland court had not inquired into religious doctrine in resolving dispute).

77. Maryland and Virginia Eldership of the Churches of God v. Church of God at Sharpsburg, Inc., 241 A.2d 691, 700–01 (Md. 1968).

78. *Id.* at 700–01.

79. *Id.* at 693–96.

80. *Id.* at 703.

sion. Indeed, Oaks suggests that the justices followed three different approaches in their opinions and that an awareness of these legal theories is necessary to understanding subsequent application of neutral principles by the Court.[81] These theories include what Oaks defines as the strict deference approach,[82] the strict neutral principles approach,[83] and the nondeterminationist approach.[84]

Strict deference theory defers to decisions made by the church polity itself even if a neutral principles approach would dictate a different conclusion. The reasoning of this approach is that it allows full free exercise and does no harm to church members since they chose their church structure themselves.[85]

The second theory, strict neutral principles, emphasizes that the Establishment Clause requirement of judicial neutrality among churches does not demand "blind deference" to church tribunal decisions. Rather, the court should examine a controversy in light of neutral legal principles.[86] Advocates of strict neutrality argue that religious organizations should be treated the same as any other voluntary association.[87]

In a concurring opinion in *Sharpsburg,* Justice Brennan outlined the "nondeterminationist approach" for resolving disputes.[88] Under nondeterminationist theory, courts could resolve disputes using deference, neutral principles of common law, or by reliance on special statutes, so long as the judiciary is not required to resolve doctrinal questions or extensively examine internal religious structure.[89]

These different approaches not only shaped the Supreme Court decisions following *Hull,* but, as will be discussed in the next section, have animated numerous state court holdings as well.

While *Hull* and *Sharpsburg* seemed to be advocating a strict neutral principles approach, in the Court's next decision, *Serbian Eastern Orthodox Diocese for the United States of America and Canada v. Milivojevich,*[90] a majority of justices supported a deference approach.[91] The Court characterized the dispute regarding the replacement of a bishop as primarily doctrinal, and ruled that the property dispute was only a secondary issue.[92] The Court held that it must defer to the hierarchical authorities on the doctrinal issue,[93] and it specifically rejected any court review that required the judiciary to determine "whether the decisions of the highest ecclesiastical tribunal of a hierarchical church complied with church laws and regulations."[94]

---

81. Oaks, *supra* note 13, at 117.
82. *Id.* at 120–21.
83. *Id.* at 118–20.
84. *Id.* at 117–18.
85. *See* Jones v. Wolf, 443 U.S. 595, 612–13 (1979) (Powell, J., dissenting).
86. Serbian Orthodox Diocese for the United States of America and Canada v. Milivojevich, 426 U.S. 696, 726–34 (1976) (Rehnquist, J., dissenting).
87. *Id.* at 728–29 (Rehnquist, J., dissenting).
88. Maryland and Virginia Eldership of the Churches of God v. Church of God at Sharpsburg, Inc., 396 U.S. 367 (1970) (per curiam) (Brennan, J., concurring).
89. Oaks, *supra* note 13, at 118.
90. 426 U.S. 696 (1976).
91. *Id.* at 697.
92. *Id.* at 709.
93. *Id.*
94. *Id.* at 712–18.

The most recent Supreme Court holding in this area is the 1979 case *Jones v. Wolf*,[95] which sustained the permissibility of the neutral principles approach.[96] The Court concluded that reliance on secular, objective, traditional rules of trust and property law provided the flexibility needed to determine rights and obligations in accordance with party expectations.[97]

The *Jones* opinion outlined a two-step approach for resolving property disputes among religious organizations.[98] The first issue to be determined is the vesting of property title.[99] The Court recommended a neutral examination of the wording of both the property deeds and the corporate charter of the religious group to determine where the title is vested and whether it is impressed with a condition or trust in favor of the general church.[100] A general church constitution could provide for an express trust in its favor,[101] and the Court reiterated the obligation of civil courts to enforce the parties' intent when it is manifest in a legal agreement or document.[102]

If the court finds that the title is vested in the local church, it must then determine who controls the local congregation or entity.[103] In *Jones* the Court allowed the use of a presumption that the majority faction controls the local church,[104] but it provided that upon a showing that control is to be determined in some other way, the presumption could be rebutted.[105] Evidence of provisions in the corporate charter of the local church, the constitution of the general church, or state statutes requiring a local congregation to remain affiliated with the general church could also support rebuttal of the presumption of majority control.[106]

Although the Court in *Jones* approved the neutral principles approach with its two-step analysis, it did not require its application, and left state courts free to adopt either compulsory deference (based on an examination of polity) or neutral principles.[107] As a result, considerable diversity has developed among the states' approaches to resolving church property disputes.

State Court Decisions After *Hull* and *Jones*

State court adoption of neutral principles has occurred chiefly, but not exclusively, in the decade following *Jones*. In fact, some state courts purported to embrace the doctrine of neutral principles soon after *Hull* and *Sharpsburg*—even holding that neutral analy-

---

95. 443 U.S. 595 (1979).
96. *See id.* at 602–03.
97. *Id.* at 603–04.
98. *Id.* at 602–06.
99. *Id.* at 606.
100. *Id.*
101. *Id.*
102. *Id.*
103. *Id.* at 606–10.
104. *Id.* at 607.
105. *Id.* at 607–08.
106. *Id.*
107. *Id.* at 607–09.

sis indicated that an implied trust had been created.[108] (Other courts applying neutral principles found no evidence of implied trusts.)[109]

Since *Hull* and *Jones*, state court decisions have tended to divide into three theoretical positions, two of which are roughly analogous to the strict deference and strict neutral principles positions of the Supreme Court. The third approach purports to follow neutral principles, but invariably interprets the documents examined as imposing either an express or implied trust in favor of the church hierarchy on the disputed property.

State courts also frequently follow a two-step analysis analogous to that followed by the Supreme Court. That is, they consider first where the title is vested, and whether it is impressed with restrictions, conditions, or trusts. If there is evidence of a trust, the beneficiary is ascertained. Next, if the court decides that the local entity holds the property in fee simple, it then determines who controls this local titleholder.

Sometimes, however, courts focus first on church polity. If they conclude that the denominational hierarchy controls the local congregation, they may not determine the vesting of the title at all,[110] deeming further investigation unnecessary since decisions of the hierarchy will control in the dispute.

Strict deference

State courts in Florida, Nevada, New Jersey, West Virginia, Michigan, and Texas have followed strict deference to denominational hierarchy in cases concerning ownership and control of property, but they use two distinct legal theories to justify such deference. Some cases reason that deference to a hierarchy's determination of the proper leadership of a local church entity is necessary because such decisions involve questions of doctrine, faith, and governance, and that to make such determinations would embroil the court in the "departure-from-doctrine" analysis expressly prohibited by *Hull*.[111] Other courts consider these disputes to involve primarily a determination of

---

108. *See, e.g.*, Carnes v. Smith, 222 S.E.2d 322, 327–28 (Ga. 1976) (holding that deed created implied trust in favor of general church); United Methodist Church v. St. Louis Crossing Indep. Methodist Church, 276 N.E.2d 916, 923–25 (Ind. Ct. App. 1971) (finding that neutral principles analysis of local hierarchical documents evidenced implied trust in favor of hierarchy); Calvary Presbyterian Church v. Presbytery of Baltimore of the United Presbyterian Church in the United States, 386 A.2d 357, 363–65 (Md. App. 1978) (finding an implied trust in favor of the hierarchy based on deed and Maryland statute); Fairmount Presbyterian Church v. Presbytery of Holston of the Presbyterian Church of the United States, 531 S.W.2d 301, 304–06 (Tenn. Ct. App. 1975) (holding that under neutral principles analysis, charter of local church created an implied trust in favor of the denominational hierarchy).

109. *See, e.g.*, Coles v. Wilburn, 245 S.E.2d 273,274 (Ga. 1978) (per curiam) (no evidence of implied trust in hierarchical church); Presbyterian Church in the United States v. Eastern Heights Presbyterian Church, 167 S.E.2d 658, 659 (Ga. 1969) (neutral principles analysis indicates no implied trust in favor of hierarchical church); Serbian Orthodox Church Congregation of St. Demetrius v. Kelemen, 256 N.E.2d 212, 215–17 (Ohio 1970) (no trust in denominational hierarchy when charter and law of local church examined by neutral principles).

110. *See, e.g.*, Crumbley v. Solomon, 254 S.E.2d 330, 333 (Ga. 1979) (per curiam); United Methodist Church v. St. Louis Crossing Indep. Methodist Church, 276 N.E.2d 916, 925 (Ind. Ct. App. 1971) (awarding property to general church upon finding that local church was not independent).

111. Townsend v. Teagle, 467 So. 2d 772, 775 (Fla. Dist. Ct. App. 1985); Mills v. Baldwin, 362 So. 2d 2, 6–7 (Fla. 1978), *vacated and remanded*, 443 U.S. 914 (1979), *reinstated*, 377 So. 2d 971 (Fla. 1979); Tea v. Protestant Episcopal Church in the Diocese of Nevada, 610 P.2d 182, 184 (Nev.

property rights and thus to be secular in nature.[112] Nevertheless, these courts cite *Jones* as allowing use of the deferential approach in secular disputes.[113] The legal reasoning is that the church's hierarchical structure either creates an implied trust in favor of the hierarchy or grants control of property disposition to the hierarchy.[114]

Regardless of which legal theory is used, courts adopting the strict deference approach[115] first make a determination that the church structure is hierarchical.[116] This decision is sometimes a matter of law.[117] Determination of hierarchical structure has been considered dispositive of the result in some cases.[118] Thus, for hierarchically structured churches, control of the titleholder, rather than property ownership, is at issue.

1980); Protestant Episcopal Church in the Diocese of New Jersey v. Graves, 417 A.2d 19, 24, (N.J. 1981); Diocese of Newark v. Burns, 417 A.2d 31, 34 (N.J. 1980); Church of God v. Noel, 318 S.E.2d 920, 923–24 (W. Va. 1984).

112. *See, e.g.*, Calvary Presbyterian Church v. Presbytery of United Presbyterian Church, 384 N.W.2d 92, 93 (Mich. Ct. App. 1986); Episcopal Church in the Diocese of New Jersey v. Graves, 391 A.2d 563, 567 (N.J. Super. Ct. Ch. Div. 1978), *aff'd*, 901 A.2d 548 (N.J. Super Ct. App. Div. 1979) (per curiam), *aff'd*, 417 A.2d 19 (N.J. 1980).

113. *See, e.g.*, Calvary Presbyterian Church v. Presbytery of United Presbyterian Church, 384 N.W.2d 92, 94 (Mich. Ct. App. 1986) (deference to hierarchy appropriate although issue is property, not doctrine); Tea v. Protestant Episcopal Church in the Diocese of Nevada, 610 P.2d 182, 184 (Nev. 1980) (deferral to church hierarchy appropriate in absence of state statutes or internal regulations granting local congregation right to withdraw from hierarchy and retain property); Episcopal Church in the Diocese of New Jersey v. Graves, 391 A.2d 563, 567 (N.J. Super. Ct. Ch. Div. 1978), *aff'd*, 401 A.2d 548 (N.J. Super Ct. App. Div. 1979) (per curiam), *aff'd*, 417 A.2d 19 (N.J. 1980) (holding that issue was entirely matter for church hierarchy).

114. *See Calvary*, 384 N.W.2d at 95–96 (hierarchical structure creates an implied trust in favor of the general church); *Graves*, 391 A.2d at 576–77 (church property impressed with implied trust); *Tea*, 610 P.2d at 184 (church's structure and state statute creates trust in favor of denominational hierarchy).

115. There are apparently at least seven states which follow the strict deference approach. *See, e.g.*, Mills v. Baldwin, 362 So. 2d 2 (Fla. 1978), *vacated and remanded*, 443 U.S. 914 (1979), *reinstated*, 377 So. 2d 971 (Fla. 1979); Townsend v. Teagle, 467 So. 2d 772 (Fla. Dist. Ct. App.), *review denied*, 479 So. 2d 118 (Fla. 1985); Kendysh v. Holy Spirit Byelorussian Autocephalic Orthodox Church, 683 F. Supp. 1501 (E.D. Mich. 1987), *aff'd*, 850 F.2d 692 (6th Cir. 1988); Calvary Presbyterian Church v. Presbytery of Lake Huron of the United Presbyterian Church in the United States, 384 N.W.2d 92 (Mich. Ct. App. 1986); Bennison v. Sharp, 329 N.W.2d 466 (Mich. Ct. App. 1982); Tea v. Protestant Episcopal Church in the Diocese of Nevada, 610 P.2d 182 (Nev. 1980); Protestant Episcopal Church in the Diocese of New Jersey v. Graves, 391 A.2d 563 (N.J. Super. Ct. Ch. Div. 1978), *aff'd*, 401 A.2d 548 (N.J. Super. Ct. App. Div. 1979) (per curiam), *aff'd*, 417 A.2d 19 (N.J. 1980); Diocese of Newark v. Burns, 417 A.2d 31 (N.J. 1980); Schismatic and Purported Casa Linda Presbyterian Church v. Grace Union Presbytery, Inc. 710 S.W.2d 700 (Tex. App. 1986).

116. *See, e.g.*, Bennison v. Sharp, 329 N.W.2d 466, 472 (Mich. Ct. App. 1982) (must first determine church polity before ruling on property issue); Organization for Preserving the Constitution of Zion Lutheran Church of Auburn v. Mason, 743 P.2d 848, 851 (Wash. Ct. App. 1987) (determination of church structure required as basis for evaluating holding of lower court); Church of God v. Noel, 318 S.E.2d 920, 923 (W. Va. 1984) (determining structure is prerequisite to ruling).

117. *See* Protestant Episcopal Church in the Diocese of New Jersey v. Graves, 391 A.2d 563, 575 (relying on *Sharpsburg* analysis to conclude that hierarchical polity is matter of law) (N.J. Super. Ct. Ch. Div. 1978), *aff'd*, 401 A.2d 548 (N.J. Super. Ct. App. Div. 1979) (per curiam), *aff'd*, 417 A.2d 19 (N.J. 1980).

118. *See, e.g.*, African Methodist Episcopal Zion Church v. Union Chapel African Methodist Episcopal Zion Church, 308 S.E.2d 73, 87 (N.C. Ct. App. 1983) (determination of hierarchical structure dispositive of result); Southside Tabernacle v. Pentecostal Church of God, Pacific Northwest Dist., Inc., 650 P.2d 231, 237 (Wash. Ct. App. 1982) (remanded for court to determine extent of hierarchical control over local church); Organization for Preserving the Constitution of Zion Lutheran Church of Auburn v. Mason, 743 P.2d 848, 852 (Wash. Ct. App. 1987) (determination of hierarchical structure to be made instead of applying neutral principles doctrines).

In cases involving a schism within a local religious entity, the court ascertains the titleholder by determining which faction was intended as the original grantee of the property.[119] To decide in which faction title is vested, however, the court defers to the denominational hierarchy's determination of the "true" leadership of the local congregation. This can be particularly problematic for congregationally organized churches, since courts that follow a deferential approach may regard the existence of a national organization as evidence of hierarchical structure even if the local church does not consider itself subject to the national body.[120] Property and trust law are, then, not directly relevant to resolution of the dispute because the decision of the hierarchy will invariably be deferred to. Dissenters, according to these courts, are free to practice their religion, but they must sacrifice the property of the local entity to do so.[121]

Strict neutral principles

Courts in Alabama, California, Georgia, Illinois, Kentucky, Minnesota, New York, Ohio, Pennsylvania, and South Dakota apply a strict neutral principles approach which relies on the legal rules developed in trust, property, and corporate law when resolving church property disputes.[122] Unlike the strict deference approach, strict neutral principles theory employs no special rules when dealing with intrareligious disputes rather than secular issues.

These courts follow the same two-step approach outlined by the Supreme Court, focusing first on a determination of where the title to the disputed property is vested. The court examines the deed itself to ascertain the express grantee,[123] then considers whether there are conditions, express trusts, reverter clauses, or other restrictions on

---

119. *See, e.g.*, Bennison v. Sharp, 329 N.W.2d 466 (Mich. Ct. App. 1982); *Mason*, 743 P.2d 848 (Wash. Ct. App. 1987); Church of God v. Noel, 318 S.E.2d 920 (W. Va. 1984).

120. For a detailed discussion of this problem, see Giovan Harbour Venable, Courts Examine Congregationalism, 41 Stan. L. Rev. 719 (1989).

121. Mills v. Baldwin, 362 So. 2d 2, 6–7 (Fla. 1978), *vacated and remanded*, 443 U.S. 914 (1979), *reinstated*, 367 So. 2d 971 (Fla. 1979); Tea v. Protestant Episcopal Church in the Diocese of Nevada, 610 P.2d 182, 184 (Nev. 1980).

122. *See, e.g.*, Trinity Presbyterian Church v. Tankersley, 374 So. 2d 861, (Ala. 1979); Protestant Episcopal Church in the Diocese of Los Angeles v. Barker, 115 Cal. App. 3d 599 (Cal. Ct. App. 1981); First Evangelical Methodist Church v. Clinton, 360 S.E.2d 584 (Ga. 1987); York v. First Presbyterian Church, 474 N.E.2d 716 (Ill. App. Ct. 1984); Bjorkman v. Protestant Episcopal Church in the United States for the Diocese of Lexington, 759 S.W.2d 583 (Ky. 1988); Piletich v. Deretich, 328 N.W.2d 696 (Minn. 1982); Presbytery of Elijah Parish Lovejoy v. Jaeggi, 682 S.W.2d 465 (Mo. 1984) (en banc); First Presbyterian Church v. Presbyterian Church in the United States, 464 N.E.2d 454 (N.Y. 1984); Christensen v. Roumfort, 485 N.E.2d 270 (Ohio Ct. App. 1984); Presbytery of Beaver-Butler of the United Presbyterian Church in the United States v. Middlesex Presbyterian Church, 489 A.2d 1317 (Pa. 1985); Presbytery of Donegal v. Calhoun, 513 A.2d 531 (Pa. Commw. Ct. 1986); Presbytery of Donegal v. Wheatley, 513 A.2d 538 (Pa. Commw. Ct. 1986); Mikilak v. Orthodox Church in Am., 513 A.2d 541 (Pa. Commw. Ct. 1986), *appeal denied*, 528 A.2d 958 (Pa. 1987); Board of Bishops of the Church of the Living God v. Milner, 513 A.2d 1131 (Pa. Commw. Ct. 1986); Foss v. Dykstra, 319 N.W.2d 499 (S.D. 1982), *aff'd on rehearing*, 342 N.W.2d 220 (1983).

123. The DePaul study revealed that where property is used for religious purposes at the local level, title is generally held in one of four ways: "title is held in the name of the trustee(s) for the use of the local group, title is held by local group as a not-for-profit corporation, title is held by local group as a religious corporation, [and] title is held by a regional/national body with which the local group is affiliated." DePaul University, *supra* note 1. The most prevalent form of ownership found title being held by the local group as a not-for-profit or religious corporation. *See id.*

the title.[124] In the absence of restrictions, title is vested in fee simple in the grantee named in the deed.[125] In *First Evangelical Methodist Church v. Clinton*,[126] for example, the deed for the disputed church building stated that it was a conveyance to the trustees of the local church, affiliated with the specific denomination, and that "said connection is to be maintained in the use of the property...."[127] Interpreting this phrase as an express restriction, the Georgia Supreme Court awarded the church building to the hierarchical organization. The parsonage, however, was conveyed by separate deed that did not mention the denominational affiliation,[128] and the court determined that title to this property vested in the local church.[129]

Without a clear showing that the grantor intended to create a trust, courts adhering to the neutral principles approach will not impose a trust on a property and will generally refuse to find an implied trust.[130] In instances in which an express charitable trust has been created, the court next determines whether the general church or the local congregation is the beneficiary.[131]

The second step of the analysis is the determination of who controls the titleholder. Generally, the grantee is an incorporated religious or not-for-profit corporation and thus is governed by its articles of incorporation and bylaws and by state statutes. But the titleholder can also be an unincorporated association or a trust. If the titleholder is a corporation, the court examines the controlling documents and statutes to determine whether the disputed action[132] conforms with relevant requirements.[133]

Some courts view the incorporated ecclesiastical body as consisting of two separate entities: the religious organization, which remains affiliated with the general church;

---

124. *See* First Presbyterian Church v. Presbyterian Church in the United States, 464 N.E.2d 454, 461 (N.Y. 1984) (property deed contains no restrictions, forfeiture, or reverter clauses). The DePaul study disclosed that where title to property is held at the national level, deeds to the property contain reverter clauses only 40% of the time. *See* DePaul University, *supra* note 1.

125. *See* Protestant Episcopal Church in the Diocese of Los Angeles v. Barker, 115 Cal. App. 3d 599, 605 (Cal. Ct. App. 1981) (owner of legal title is presumed to hold full beneficial interest in the property); First Presbyterian Church v. Presbyterian Church in the United States, 464 N.E.2d 454, 461 (N.Y. 1984) (property deed contains no restrictions, forfeiture, or reverter clauses).

126. 360 S.E.2d 584, 585 (Ga. 1987).

127. *Id.*

128. *Id.*

129. *Id.*

130. *See* Presbytery of Beaver-Butler of the United Presbyterian Church in the United States v. Middlesex Presbyterian Church, 489 A.2d 1317, 1324 (Pa. 1985) (standard of intent required to impose a trust is "clear and unambiguous language or conduct"); *See also* Presbytery of Riverside v. Community Church of Palm Springs, 89 Cal. App. 3d 910, 931 (Cal. Ct. App. 1979) (existence of trust is a question of fact to be determined by intent of parties; intent to be established by use of objective criteria); First Presbyterian Church v. Presbyterian Church in the United States, 464 N.E.2d 454, 462 (N.Y. 1984) ("sufficient manifestation of intent" necessary to create trust); Christensen v. Roumfort, 485 N.E.2d 270, 273 (Ohio Ct. App. 1984) (considering parties' objective intent); Mikilak v. Orthodox Church in America, 513 A.2d 541, 545–46 (Pa. Commw. Ct. 1986) (trust created only when intent of local church to do so shown by unambiguous language or clear conduct).

131. Protestant Episcopal Church in the Diocese of Los Angeles v. Barker, 115 Cal. Ct. App. 3d 599, 621 (Cal. Ct. App. 1981) (employing neutral principles that would apply to any organization having both local and national operations).

132. Disputed actions could include changes in name, affiliation, or members of the governing body, or transfers of property.

133. *See* Foss v. Dykstra, 342 N.W.2d 220, 225–26 (S.D. 1983) (documents examined to determine that church was governed by majority representation); Piletich v. Deretich, 328 N.W.2d 696, 700 (Minn. 1982) (local charter and bylaws give local church authority to determine membership).

and the secular corporate entity, which exists under state law and must comply only with state, not ecclesiastical, law in its actions.[134] While a court will defer to the general church's determination of doctrinal loyalty and affiliation,[135] it will usually refuse to grant the hierarchy secular authority and control.[136] In some cases, courts have construed the authority of churches quite narrowly. For example, in *Presbytery of Donegal v. Wheatley*,[137] property deeds stipulated that the property would belong to the congregation provided it adhered to the doctrinal system "agreeable to" the Synod of New York and Philadelphia.[138] The general church argued that the issue was therefore doctrinal, and that the court should defer to the decision of the ecclesiastical hierarchy.[139] The court held that though a doctrinal issue existed, after the disaffiliation of the local church from the general church the session of the local congregation became the highest church judicatory to which the local church was subject.[140] Consequently, the court deferred to the local session's decision that local church doctrine was "agreeable" to the Synod.[141]

Following this analysis, the hierarchy may determine the membership of a particular church as consisting only of those persons loyal to the hierarchy or its doctrine, but the court could still decide that the dissenting faction is the legal successor to the secular corporation that controls the disputed property.[142]

Courts that apply the strict neutral principles approach either expressly or impliedly follow the presumption of *Jones v. Wolf* that the local corporate entity is controlled by majority rule.[143] This presumption was criticized in *Bishop & Diocese of Colorado v. Mote*,[144] but it may not present significant problems where state incorporation law or the constitution or bylaws of the local organization providing for some other method of corporate control can be used to rebut the presumption.[145] Indeed, the Supreme Court has explained:

> Most importantly, any rule of majority representation can always be overcome, under the neutral-principles approach, either by providing, in the corporate charter or the constitution of the general church, that the identity of the local church is to be established in some other way, or by providing that the church property is held in trust for the general church and those who remain loyal to it. Indeed, the State may adopt any method of overcoming the majoritarian

---

134. *See* Trinity Presbyterian Church v. Tankersley, 374 So. 2d 861, 866 (Ala. 1979) (corporate entity of incorporated church subject to civil corporate and property law).

135. York v. First Presbyterian Church, 474 N.E.2d 716, 722 (Ill. App. Ct. 1984) (hierarchy permitted to replace local church's session, but not to decide secular issues); First Presbyterian Church v. Presbyterian Church in the United States, 464 N.E.2d 454, 461–62 (N.Y. 1984) (if general church had appointed a competing session, court might not have been permitted to resolve conflict).

136. Trinity Presbyterian Church v. Tankersley, 374 So. 2d 861, 866 (Ala. 1979) (corporate entity of incorporated church subject to secular, not ecclesiastical, law).

137. 513 A.2d 538 (Pa. Commw. Ct. 1986).

138. *Id.* at 539–40.

139. *Id.*

140. *Id.*

141. *Id.*

142. *See* Foss v. Dykstra, 342 N.W.2d 220, 225 (S.D. 1983) (to grant control of property to loyal group on grounds that it is the "true" church would require inquiry into religious doctrine).

143. *See, e.g.*, Piletich v. Deretich, 328 N.W.2d 696, 702 (Minn. 1982) (presumption of majority rule overcome only by explicit provisions calling for alternate resolution).

144. 716 P.2d 85, 99–100 (Colo. 1986).

145. *See Piletich*, 328 N.W.2d at 702; *Foss*, 342 N.W.2d at 225–26.

presumption, so long as the use of that method does not impair free exercise rights or entangle the civil courts in matters of religious controversy.[146]

No clear guidelines outline what evidence would be sufficient to rebut the majority presumption, however.

Although the neutral principles approach permits analysis of secular documents because actual church ownership of property does not implicate religious freedom issues, this does not insure uniformity of interpretation. For example, courts read differently provisions regarding property distribution following the dissolution of the local congregation, replacement of the governing board, or encumbrances on the property.[147] In *Presbytery of Donegal v. Calhoun*[148] the court held that a transfer of property differed from a sale or encumbrance,[149] and in several cases courts have distinguished between disaffiliation and dissolution.[150] Courts have held that if a local congregation separates from the general church, it may no longer be subject to the regulations of the denominational hierarchy.[151] Because of these definitional distinctions, denominational hierarchies may be less certain of their right to control property in the event of a schism despite provisions to that effect in their bylaws.

This does not mean, however, that all decisions based on strict neutral principles analysis will favor the local congregation over the hierarchical church. If, for example, the grantee of the title is a representative of the church hierarchy and there is no contradictory evidence of a clear intent to establish a trust in favor of the local church, the court will decide in favor of the hierarchy.[152]

In other cases, courts will not decide the dispute at all. For instance, in *Atterberry v. Smith*,[153] although the parties viewed their dispute as secular, the court held that determining matters such as the highest church judicatory, the powers of the local pastor, and the form of church governance implicate both doctrinal and civil concerns.[154] While the court will adjudicate control of the corporate entity, if it characterizes the

---

146. Jones v. Wolf, 443 U.S. 595, 607–08 (1979).

147. *Compare* Bishop & Diocese of Colorado v. Mote, 716 P.2d 85, 105–07, 110 (Colo. 1986) (holding that restrictive language in general church's constitution created an implied trust) with Presbytery of Beaver-Butler of the United Presbyterian Church in the United States v. Middlesex Presbyterian Church, 489 A.2d 1317, 1325 (Pa. Commw. Ct. 1985) (general church's governing by-laws relate to spiritual matters and are not applicable to settlement of property disputes) and Bjorkman v. Protestant Episcopal Church in the United States, 759 S.W.2d 583, 586–87 (Ky. 1988) ("exclusively ecclesiastical" relationship between general and local church and so hierarchical law governing property has no legal effect).

148. 513 A.2d 531 (Pa. Commw. Ct. 1986).

149. *Id.* at 534–36.

150. *See, e.g.*, Presbytery of Riverside v. Community Church of Palm Springs, 89 Cal. App. 3d 910, 930 (Cal. Ct. App. 1979); York v. First Presbyterian Church, 474 N.E.2d 716, 721 (Ill. App. Ct. 1984); First Presbyterian Church v. Presbyterian Church in the United States, 464 N.E.2d 454, 461(N.Y. 1984); Christensen v. Roumfort, 485 N.E.2d 270, 273 (Ohio Ct. App. 1984).

151. *See* Presbytery of Elijah Parish Lovejoy v. Jaeggi, 682 S.W.2d 465, 474 (Mo. 1984); Foss v. Dykstra, 342 N.W.2d 220, 224–25 (S.D. 1983).

152. *See, e.g.*, Paradise Hills Church, Inc. v. International Church of the Foursquare Gospel, 467 F. Supp. 357, 362–64 (D. Ariz. 1979) (no indication that local church was beneficiary); Harris v. Apostolic Overcoming Holy Church of God, Inc., 457 So. 2d 385, 387 (Ala. 1984) (title vested in trustee of general church, so local church has no claim); Reorganized Church of Jesus Christ of Latter-day Saints v. Thomas, 758 S.W.2d 726, 730–31 (Mo. Ct. App. 1988) (general church is beneficiary of property held in express trust by regional church corporation).

153. 522 A.2d 683 (Pa. Commw. Ct. 1987).

154. *Id.* at 686–87 (concluding that it was a doctrinal concern and thus applying the rule of deference).

issue as one of control of the religious organization, it may refuse to enter the dispute.[155] Similarly, courts have refused to adjudicate claims in which members of the local congregation seek not to leave the general church, but to force the hierarchy to accommodate their wishes.[156] The court will allow individuals to leave the hierarchical church, but it will not permit them to interfere with the denominational hierarchy's own free exercise of religion.

Combined deference and neutral principles

Courts in Colorado, Connecticut, Indiana, Iowa,[157] Louisiana, Maryland, and Virginia have adopted an approach to church property disputes that seems to be an awkward melange of both deferential and neutral principles theories. These courts seem not to choose this mixed approach intentionally. Rather, they explicitly adopt the neutral principles concept,[158] but continue to show deference to denominational hierarchy decisions.[159] For example, despite a clear showing that title is vested in the local congregation, the court may grant control of the property to the general church based on two major lines of legal reasoning—intent and consent.

Intent

First, the court determines whether the title is impressed with an implied or express trust, or with some other restriction that prevents the local entity from owning the

---

155. *Id.*

156. *See generally* Save Immaculata/Dunblane, Inc. v. Immaculata Preparatory Sch., Inc., 514 A.2d 1152 (D.C. Ct. App. 1986) (school property not in trust for parents of students attending parochial school); Galich v. Catholic Bishop, 394 N.E.2d 572, 574–75 (Ill. App. Ct. 1979) (refusing relief to members suing to prevent closing of parish church); Grutka v. Clifford, 445 N.E.2d 1015 (Ind. Ct. App. 1983) (refusing relief to members objecting to bishop's transfer of church cemetery); Parent v. Roman Catholic Bishop, 436 A.2d 888 (Me. 1981) (court will not review ecclesiastical authority to close parish church); Streumph v. McAuliffe, 661 S.W.2d 559 (Mo. Ct. App. 1983) (no injunction will issue to prevent bishop from altering interior of church).

157. Uses both deference and neutral principles approaches.

158. *See, e.g.*, Bishop and Diocese of Colorado v. Mote, 668 P.2d 948, 952–53 (Colo. Ct. App. 1983) (analyzing church polity despite adoption of neutral principles), *rev'd on other grounds*, 716 P.2d 85 (Colo. 1986); New York Annual Conf. of the United Methodist Church v. Fisher, 438 A.2d 62, 68 (Conn. 1980) (deference to be shown within context of neutral principles); Hinkle Creek Friends Church v. Western Yearly Meeting of Friends Church, 469 N.E.2d 40, 43 (Ind. Ct. App. 1984) (neutral principles demands that documents be examined for evidence of trust in favor of general church); Emberry Community Church v. Bloomington Dist. Missionary and Church Extension Soc'y, Inc., 482 N.E.2d 288, 293 (Ind. Ct. App. 1985) (possible to find implied trust if church polity is hierarchical even using neutral principles); Fonken v. Community Church, 339 N.W.2d 810, 816 (Iowa 1983) (both neutral principles and deference approaches used); Fluker Community Church v. Hitchens, 405 So. 2d 1223, 1225 (La. Ct. App. 1981) (neutral principles applies to nondoctrinal issues such as property disputes), *vacated and dismissed on other grounds*, 419 So. 2d 445 (La. 1982); Presbytery of Baltimore of the United Presbyterian Church v. Babcock Mem'l Presbyterian Church, 449 A.2d 1190, 1192 (Md. 1982) (property ownership decided by neutral principles), *aff'd*, 464 A.2d 1008 (Md. 1983); Green v. Lewis, 272 S.E.2d 181, 184 (Va. 1980) (property issue decided by neutral principles).

159. *See, e.g.*, *Hinkle Creek*, 469 N.E.2d at 44–45 (deferring to hierarchy's authority); *Hitchens*, 419 So. 2d at 448 (hierarchy power supersedes majority decision of local church); *Babcock Memorial*, 449 A.2d at 1194–95 (finding intent in local charter to make local congregation subject to decisions of general church).

property in fee simple.[160] The court may find that the intent to create a trust for the benefit of the national church arises from the wishes of the grantor or from provisions and documents of either the national or local church entity. As evidence of this intent, the court relies on references to the denomination or beliefs in the deeds or in the charter, bylaws, or articles of incorporation of the local church; on state incorporation statutes that require affiliation with the denomination; or on provisions in the constitution or charter of the hierarchical church. Because a careful examination of church doctrine is prohibited by *Hull* and *Jones*, courts following this mixed approach often find even the mention of the general denomination in church documents sufficient to indicate an intention by the local congregation to be subject to hierarchical control.

The deeds, incorporation documents, or bylaws of the local congregation may contain restrictions that the court will interpret as creating an implied trust in favor of the national entity. If, for example, there is express mention of a particular denomination in the deed, the court can find that the grantor intended to create a trust with the denomination as beneficiary.[161] This conclusion is reached by reasoning that the mention of the denomination evidences the intent of the donor to grant beneficial ownership to the denominational church.[162] While this line of legal reasoning is much like the implied trust theory, it does not depend on the departure-from-doctrine analysis, but relies instead on the assumption that the mention of the denomination indicates that the grantor intended to create a trust in favor of it.

The same conclusion is often reached when the documents of the national church contain language that can be construed as restricting the holding and use of property. The canon or bylaws of the hierarchical church may specifically mandate that all local church property is held in trust[163] for the national church,[164] or they may restrict the ability of the local entity to encumber or alienate the property without approval of the hierarchy.[165] Other national church constitutions provide for local church property to pass to the hierarchical church if the local entity is dissolved.[166]

Regardless of the kind of provision, courts applying a mixed deference and neutral principles approach view the clauses as restricting any conveyance of the property at all. In *Bishop and Diocese of Colorado v. Mote*,[167] for example, the local church reincorpo-

---

160. This examination of intent is somewhat analogous to the first step of the analysis followed by the deference and neutral principles approaches, i.e., determination of where title is vested.

161. *See* Fluker Community Church v. Hitchens, 405 So. 2d 1223, 1226 (La. Ct. App. 1981) (deed conveyed land to the local chapel as a member of the general church).

162. *See Hitchens*, 419 So. 2d at 448 (deed's mention of general church indicates grantor's intent that land remain with denomination).

163. It is unclear how the court can use national church documents as evidence of intention by the local congregation to create a trust since trust intent must be found in the grantor. In these instances the national church, which is the beneficiary or grantee, evidences the intent to create the trust. The language in the documents is probably viewed as a legal limitation on the holding of property by the local church rather than as a trust.

164. *See* African Methodist Episcopal Zion Church in Am., Inc. v. Zion Hill Methodist Church, Inc., 534 So. 2d 224 (Ala. 1988).

165. *See* Babcock Memorial Presbyterian Church v. Presbytery of Baltimore of the United Presbyterian Church in the United States, 464 A.2d 1008, 1017 (Md. 1983); Bishop and the Diocese of Colorado v. Mote, 716 P.2d 85, 107 (Colo. 1986).

166. *See Mote*, 716 P.2d at 107; Hinkle Creek Friends Church v. Western Yearly Meeting of Friends Church, 469 N.E.2d 40, 45 (Ind. Ct. App. 1984) (property vests in hierarchy when congregation discontinued); Fonken v. Community Church, 339 N.W.2d 810, 815 (Iowa 1983); Fluker Community Church v. Hitchens, 419 So. 2d 445, 448, (La. 1982).

167. 716 P.2d 85 (Colo. 1986).

rated as a different entity and then transferred local church property to the new entity. The hierarchical church's constitution contained an express restriction on alienation, and the court held that the withdrawal of the local church from the hierarchy was effectively a revocation of the charter, thereby triggering provisions which required that local property revert to the general church.[168] Even in the absence of such express provisions, some courts have maintained that a local church has implied its consent to general church control of a property if it has previously sought hierarchical approval or permission before encumbering the property.[169] Any history of subordination by the local church to hierarchical authority may be viewed as implying its intent to be subject to national control.

Consent

The second line of reasoning courts use in following this mixed approach is that regardless of where title is actually vested, the documents of a local church or its membership in a hierarchical organization indicate that the local entity has impliedly consented to control of its property[170] by the general church.[171] Thus, these courts will generally conclude that those loyal to the general church (as determined by the hierarchical authority) control the property whether they represent a majority or a minority of the local membership.[172] This position is similar to that of the deferential courts, and is unlike that of the strict neutral principles adherents.

The Supreme Court held in *Jones v. Wolf*[173] that a presumption of majority control of the local congregation was consistent with the neutral principles approach so long as the presumption could be rebutted upon a showing of contrary evidence.[174] Courts employing the mixed approach purport to apply neutral principles, but frequently rely either on provisions in local church documents or on state statutes requiring affiliation with a denomination's national church to find control of a local denomination vested in other than the majority.[175] For instance, local church bylaws may require the local entity

---

168. *Id.* at 108–09.

169. *See* Ohio Southeast Conference of Evangelical United Brethren Church v. Kruger, 243 N.E.2d 781, 786 (Ohio Ct. App. 1968) (local church had sought approval before remodeling property); Green v. Lewis, 272 S.E.2d 181, 186 (Va. 1980) (the "name, customs, and policies" showed that the property was subject to the hierarchical church).

170. This is somewhat analogous to the second step of the analysis used in the strict deference and neutral principles approaches. That is, after determination of the vesting of title, the court determines who controls the titleholder.

171. *See Green*, 272 S.E.2d at 186 (membership in hierarchy evidences implied consent).

172. *Hitchens*, 419 So. 2d at 448; *Fonken*, 339 N.W.2d at 816–18.

173. 443 U.S. 595 (1979).

174. Jones v. Wolf, 443 U.S. 595, 607–08 (1979).

175. *See* Protestant Episcopal Church in the Diocese of Los Angeles v. Barker, 115 Cal. App. 3d 599, 625–26 (1981) (relying on a California statute). Note, however, that the general church was granted the property of only one of the four local churches involved in this case. The statute was held to be inapplicable to one church because the local entity was not expressly identified as subordinate to the general church, and because the statute was enacted after the incorporation of the other two churches. *Id.* at 625–6. A similar situation arose in *Babcock Memorial Presbyterian Church v. Presbytery of Baltimore of the United Presbyterian Church of the United Presbyterian Church*, 449 A.2d 1190 (1982), *aff'd*, 464 A.2d 1008 (1983). While the trial court relied on a Maryland statute, the Maryland Court of Appeals held that the statute was inapplicable since it was enacted after the church was incorporated. *Babcock*, 464 A.2d at 1011 n.1. A statute enacted subsequent to incorporation may be controlling if the local church reincorporates or modifies its incorporation documents

to maintain allegiance to the denomination.[176] Similarly, the church's documents may give the hierarchy the right to replace the local governing body,[177] and when the local entity considers disaffiliation the general church can appoint new directors loyal to the hierarchical church.[178] In such cases, the court will defer to the hierarchy's decision, based not on polity as with the strict deference approach, but on the language of the documents.[179] Regardless of the reasoning, however, the result in these cases is identical to that reached in states that adopt the strict deference approach.

Impact of Different Approaches
on Church Decisions

All of the above approaches purport to be impartial and neutral and to safeguard both the Free Exercise and Establishment clauses of the Constitution. Clearly, though, the extremely diverse legal results that flow from the deference, strict neutral principles, and hybrid approaches are problematic in church decision making. More specifically, religious bodies must consider the impact that their denominational polity, their choice of legal structure, the language of wills or trusts conveying assets to the church, and relevant state statutes will have on the outcome of potential property disputes.

Although it may be impractical for churches to dissolve and reorganize themselves in order to make the outcome of property disputes more predictable, religious organizations may be able to achieve the same result by redrafting documents to clarify their ecclesiastical and legal structures. Following *Jones*, for example, both the United Presbyterian Church in the United States of America and the Protestant Episcopal Church in the United States of America amended their constitutions in an attempt to create express trust provisions.[180] The validity of these amendments has not been litigated, but if they establish judicially recognized trusts, they may reduce or eliminate litigation because courts usually prefer to defer to a church authority or policy in intrachurch disputes, thus avoiding potential violations of the Establishment or Free Exercise clauses.[181]

It is equally possible, however, that a court may find that amendments made after the affiliation of the local congregation cannot be applied to a local body.[182] Further, courts may determine that these trust provisions do not reflect the intent of the local congregation.[183] Rather, in these cases the national church, which is the beneficiary

---

after enactment of the statute. First Presbyterian Church of Schenectady v. United Presbyterian Church in the United States, 464 N.E.2d 454, 461 (N.Y. 1984).

176. *See* Fonken v. Community Church of Kamrar, 339 N.W.2d 810, 816–18 (Iowa 1983).

177. *Id.* at 815.

178. *Id.* at 816.

179. *Compare* Draskovich v. Pasalich, 280 N.E.2d 69, 81(Ind. Ct. App. 1972) (deference because of church polity) with *Fonken* 339 N.W.2d at 815–16 (legal document grants right to replace governing body).

180. William G. Ross, The Need for an Exclusive and Uniform Application of "Neutral Principles" in the Adjudication of Church Property Disputes, 32 St. Louis U. L.J. 263, 303 (1987).

181. *Id.* at 313–15.

182. *See* Protestant Episcopal Church in the Diocese of Los Angeles v. Barker, 115 Cal. App. 3d 599, 623–24 (1981).

183. *See* York v. First Presbyterian Church of Anna, 474 N.E.2d 716, 721 (Ill. App. Ct. 1984) (lack of mutual understanding of amendments between United Presbyterian Church and local con-

rather than the settlor, establishes and determines the terms of the trust. Local congregations desiring affiliation with the national organization may be required to accept the property arrangements of the national church. Trust provisions in the documents of the hierarchical church may not, therefore, truly reflect an intention of the local congregation to limit its control of its property.

The Continuing Relevance of Church Polity Analysis

Because the Supreme Court has thus far left to the states the right to determine which of the three major approaches to resolving church property disputes they wish to follow, lower courts will continue to be forced to wrestle with the difficult choice of which approach to prefer. In her chapter "Civil Court Resolution of Property Disputes Among Religious Organizations," Patty Gerstenblith contends that a strict neutrality approach is preferable on general policy grounds, and is also better attuned to underlying constitutional principles. In her view, the strict neutral principles approach is more likely to afford equal treatment to rival religious parties in an internal property dispute. Gerstenblith believes that the Supreme Court's rejection of the departure-from-doctrine methodology, if pressed to its logical conclusion, requires that subtle forms of privileging of hierarchical religious bodies involved in implying trusts or contracts are tantamount to veiled violations of the rejected doctrine. Cases in the hybrid category are essentially incoherent, because they give lip service to the neutral principles ideal but immediately go on to compromise it. Presumably, insistence on a strict neutral principles approach will create incentives for legal groups to be more cautious in drafting legal instruments to reflect their intended ecclesiastical structures, and this in the long run will make it easier for courts to resolve property disputes using secular legal techniques.

While there is much that is commendable about encouraging religious organizations to do all they can to be as clear as possible in drafting the legal instruments that govern their affairs, and while there is every reason to think that courts will follow express and clear indications of intent, it seems shortsighted to insist too rigidly on the strict neutral principles approach. The fundamental concern under the Religion Clauses is to protect the religious freedom of religious communities and to assure the impartiality of the state in resolving disputes that appropriately come within its jurisdiction. This objective is not always best furthered by wooden interpretation of relevant legal instruments.

In a perfect world, all such instruments would be drafted by lawyers who perfectly understand the internal structures, beliefs, and practices of the relevant religious communities, who translate that understanding into clear and unambiguous legal documents, and who provide for all the contingencies that can occur as religious communities continue to evolve, grow, decline, or divide. Needless to say, none of these assumptions is realistic. Moreover, the assumptions are least realistic at the level of local congregations whose rights Gerstenblith seems most concerned to protect. Hierarchical churches with centralized administrations are most likely to have the resources to retain

---

gregation; Presbytery of Elijah Parish Lovejoy v. Jaeggi, 682 S.W.2d 465, 474 (Mo. 1984) (amendment not binding on faction of church because adopted subsequent to schism).

legal counsel that possesses the level of expertise needed to take full advantage of the strict neutral principles approach. Religious communities with congregational structures, or local religious bodies in general, are more likely to rely on pro bono or non-specialized help that may not adequately understand all the potential issues. Indeed, they may not even seek legal counsel and may leave some aspects of their property ownership either inadequately or altogether undocumented. The result is that the legal documents may be inconsistent with normal practice and understanding within the religious community. Wooden application of neutral principles doctrine in such settings is not compatible with constitutional protection of freedom of religion. It imposes insensitive and legalistic readings of legal documents, thereby sacrificing respect for genuine, if imperfectly articulated, principles of religious ordering in order to further a misguided notion of neutrality. The problem is compounded where, as is very typically the case, the inadequacy of the documents reflects evolution or change within religious communities.

Part of the continuing appeal of the deference and hybrid approaches is precisely that they take into account the recognition that formal documents are too often inadequate when it comes to reflecting the spiritual and organizational realities and expectations within a belief tradition. The very existence of the hybrid approach, with its tendency to acknowledge the neutral principles ideal while accommodating the practical realities of ecclesiastical polity, is evidence that common sense and sound judicial judgment recognizes the importance of both remaining neutral and respecting the distinctive choices of religious communities.

Each of the three major approaches to resolution of church property disputes ultimately requires some examination of church structure to determine which group or organization is the authorized representative of the church. While this inquiry might seem straightforward, it poses a number of potential problems. First, the relationship between a local church and its regional, national, or international organization is often unclear. In hierarchically organized churches, local congregations are subject to the authority of the general church, while in congregational religions the larger organization is subject to the will of the local entity.[184] There is danger that without an understanding of the philosophy and doctrine of a particular religion, the mere presence of some regional or national organization may be seen as evidence of traditional hierarchical structure.[185] There may be some risk that jurisdictions which have adopted either the strict deference or the mixed neutral principles and deference approaches will be more likely to presume the existence of another legitimate authority to which they can defer. But it is just as likely and just as problematic that a strict neutral principles jurisdiction will overlook authentic religious realities.

Similarly, courts adopting a strict neutral principles approach generally employ a presumption of majority control in the absence of clear hierarchical authority—a practice that may be as suspect as the deferential presumption, and that disadvantages hierarchical churches since courts are less inclined to defer to their decisions.

Any investigation into polity that depends on consideration of church doctrine is, of course, expressly prohibited by *Hull* and *Jones*. In fact, any judicial inquiry into the internal relationships between local congregations and national churches has the potential to violate separation of church and state because choice of religious polity may be a

---

184. *See generally* Venable, *supra* note 120.
185. *See* Cadman Memorial Congregational Soc'y v. Kenyon, 116 N.E.2d 481 (N.Y. 1953); Venable, *supra* note 120, at 728 & n.47.

doctrinal matter.[186] Further, determination of polity, once made, is not reliably predictive of judicial outcome. Even though courts exhibit a clear inclination to defer to the decisions of a church hierarchy, in *Serbian Orthodox Diocese v. Milivojevich*[187] the Supreme Court upheld the ruling of the hierarchical church while in *Jones v. Wolf*[188] the Court majority rejected deference to the church tribunal. Both decisions purportedly relied on a neutral analysis of legal documents. Examination of deeds and documents may arguably result in more fair resolutions of disputes, but the strict neutral principles approach may also be too flexible to result in consistent outcomes.

Rejecting such considerations, Gerstenblith advances a variety of reasons for favoring the strict neutral principles approach. The fundamental concern is suspicion of unequal treatment of the rivals in a religious dispute. Without application of a strict neutral principles approach, she contends, courts will subtly privilege one party to a dispute. Moreover, she claims, by indulging presumptions favorable to hierarchical church bodies, courts afford preferences to religious groups that are not available to normal nonprofit organizations. The difficulty is that the version of neutral principles that she defends operates equally to create somewhat less obvious presumptions running in favor of local congregations. By preventing judges from drawing inferences that reasonable minds could plausibly draw, her approach makes it impossible to reach decisions that may constitute a more apt resolution of a dispute in light of religious realities that would be evident to any fair-minded arbiter. In general, if the applicable legal documents leave no ambiguity, courts clearly should follow them. But all too often in genuine disputes, the difficulty is precisely that the documentation is ambiguous, fails to cover the dispute in question, or seems flagrantly inconsistent with normal practice in the community. Examination of the facts and drawing relevant inferences in such cases is typically necessary if sensible results are to be achieved.

An excessively rigid interpretation of the neutral principles doctrine misunderstands its fundamental thrust. In effect, such an interpretation demands that courts follow all and only the express and clear legal documents that parties have executed to govern particular property ownership issues. In Gerstenblith's view, for example, only the strictest showing of actual intent, consent, acquiescence, or estoppel should suffice to justify recognition of trusts or implied contracts in favor of centralized religious bodies. Implied trusts or contracts are suspect because they may rely on presumptions that are tantamount to departure-from-doctrine analysis.

But this line of reasoning goes much too far. The idea behind the neutral principles doctrine is that while judges are not competent to intrude themselves into matters of doctrine and ecclesiastical polity, they are competent to apply standard legal doctrines and interpretive techniques. In describing the neutral principles doctrine, the Supreme Court has never suggested that courts applying it are restricted to using those aspects of normal judicial craft relevant to interpretation of express language, or that they must use analysis stripped of all the doctrines of implied trusts and implied contracts. On the contrary, courts are simply not allowed to engage in second-guessing of doctrinal analysis—including analysis of doctrines of ecclesiastical polity—in applying the broad set of doctrines and interpretive techniques that judges normally use when faced with ambiguous or insufficient language. Not every recognition of an implied trust or contract entangles courts in impermissible analysis

---

186. *See generally* Venable, *supra* note 120.
187. 426 U.S. 696 (1976).
188. 493 U.S. 595 (1979).

of religious doctrine. Common sense allows them to take into account generally known features of ecclesiastical polity that do not involve intrusive analysis of religious doctrine.

It is important to remember that the Supreme Court has recognized the validity of both deference and neutral principles approaches.[189] The Court has thus not drawn the conclusion that Gerstenblith recommends, namely that only a strict neutral principles approach is consistent with the First Amendment. Even if one concludes that a neutral principles approach is to be preferred, sound application of this approach does not require rigorous exclusion of implied trusts or contracts. In many cases, courts will better respect and protect the autonomy of religious communities if they take into account aspects of ecclesiastical polity that can be discerned using normal and neutral interpretive techniques. This is much less likely to impose harshly on religious communities for inadequacies in the legal documentation of their temporal affairs.

Given some of the residual uncertainties about how courts will resolve property disputes in particular jurisdictions, churches—especially those organized congregationally—would do well to carefully draft documents that explicitly define the form of their governance and the relationships between local and national entities. Authority to speak for the church and to acquire, own, manage, and dispose of property and funds should be expressly stated. Churches must consider whether in the event of an intracongregational dispute they would prefer a plan for distribution of assets other than the majority control that the courts will most likely adopt. If a percentage or minority-loyal-to-doctrine distribution is desired, it should be specifically outlined.[190] Likewise, hierarchically organized religions must assure that control of property is specifically outlined in organizational documents and not left to presumption. By describing its polity in detail, a church involved in a property dispute can better prevent possible judicial misinterpretation of its structure.

Legal Structure

Churches may be structured on either a corporate or a trust model, and while most organize as religious corporations,[191] charitable trust concepts have important applications to the corporate model as well.

---

189. *Milivojevich*, 426 U.S. 696 (1976); *Jones*, 493 U.S. 595 (1979).

190. Note, also, that if a church desires a loyal-to-doctrine distribution, it must designate some authority to make the determination of doctrinal fidelity because courts are forbidden to consider church doctrine in their decisions. Justice Brennan maintains that reverter clauses premised on an analysis of departure from doctrine are unenforceable. *See* Maryland & Virginia Eldership of the Church of God v. Church of God at Sharpsburg, Inc., 396 U.S. 367, 370 (1970) (per curiam) (Brennan, J., concurring).

191. The survey conducted by the DePaul University Center for Church/State Studies indicates that 87% of the religious organizations that responded reported a legal structure that was "Religious-Not-for-Profit Corporation." DePaul University, *supra* note 1. The other legal structures religious organizations reported included an unincorporated association (8%) and a not-for-profit corporation (3%). *Id.* Other legal structures only nominally used included a charitable or religious trust, a corporation sole, and a for-profit corporation. *Id.*

Considerations in choosing a legal structure

The initial decision a religious organization must consider concerns the legal structure it will use as an operating vehicle. As previously mentioned, the most common structure used by religions is the nonprofit corporation. However, the corporate model is not the only available structure. The code for a section 501(c)(3) organization—which allows tax exemption for the entity as well as deductions for donors—permits an entity to be organized as a corporation, trust, or unincorporated association.[192] The only limitation is that the entity may not choose to operate as a partnership or as an individual.[193]

After their initial inquiry concerning the availability of legal structures, the organizers should determine which structure most satisfies their needs by considering certain non-tax factors[194] including but not limited to "the speed with which one needs to establish the organization, concerns with limited liability, the sophistication and goals of the organizers, financial resources, and the type and scale of activities to be conducted."[195] Other considerations include "the capacity to own property, capacity to contract, capacity to sue and to be sued, continuity of existence, management, and liabilities to third persons."[196]

Corporate model

Historically, charitable corporations have been subject to less judicial enforcement and supervision than have charitable trusts.[197] Incorporation also offers such advantages as limited liability, organizational continuity, and administrative convenience.[198] In the

---

192. *See* IRC § 501(c)(3). Although trusts are not specifically mentioned in this section as an eligible legal structure, it is well settled that a trust may be so used. *See* Paul E. Treusch, Tax-Exempt Charitable Organizations 34 & n.9 (1988) (citing G.C.M. 15778, XIV-2 C.B. 118 (1935) which accepted the decision of *Fifth Union Trust Co. v. Comm'r*, 56 F.2d 767 (6th Cir. 1932) that a trust may be used as a legal structure for a tax exempt organization).

193. *See* Treusch, *supra* note 192, at 33. Professor Treusch notes that if the partnership is classified as an association taxable as a corporation, then it would be an appropriate legal structure. *See id.*

194. Generally, a charitable organization must also consider tax factors including but not limited to "the appropriate type of federal tax exemption, the organization's classification as a public charity or private foundation, the forms of organization permitted under the Internal Revenue Code, and the consequences of each type." James J. Fishman & Stephen Schwarz, Nonprofit Organizations Cases and Materials 61 (1995). However, since most religious organizations prefer to operate as section 501(c)(3) organizations because of the ability for donors to deduct their contributions and because of the federal filing exemptions for churches, I will assume that the tax factors weigh equally in favor of using the trust or corporate model. For an interesting look at an analysis of the tax factors as it relates to charitable organizations in general, see Treusch, *supra* note 192, at 36–45.

195. Fishman & Schwarz, *supra* note 194, at 61.

196. Harry G. Henn & Michael George Pfeifer, Nonprofit Groups: Factors Influencing Choice of Form, 11 Wake Forest L. Rev. 181, 187 (1975).

197. Oaks, *supra* note 13, at 61–64.

198. Daniel L. Kurtz, Board Liability: Guide for Non-Profit Directors 4 (1988). However, a trust model also offers the benefits of administrative convenience and continuity of existence. Additionally, even the limited liability offered to a corporation can be available to the trustees of a trust if state law allows the trustee to be a limited liability company.

United States prior to the twentieth century, the two most common religious corporate models were the trustee corporation and the corporation sole. In a trustee corporation the trustees comprise the corporate body and possess the powers and duties of the corporation, while in the corporation sole all corporate powers and duties are vested in a single person.[199] During the twentieth century, many states began to deal with religious corporations under general nonprofit corporation statutes. Currently, most states incorporate religious entities under a membership corporation model.[200] This model resembles the business corporation in that its members are roughly analogous to shareholders and theoretically hold the same power.[201] While the membership model can usually accommodate a congregational polity (which is more likely to be governed by a body analogous to a board of directors and to have a congregation that functions with power similar to that held by shareholders), it is less well suited to a hierarchical structure.[202]

Thus, while there may be advantages to organizing on a corporate rather than on a trust model, a church must be certain that the corporate structure harmonizes with its ecclesiastical polity. Since at present most states do not offer alternative corporate models that effectively accommodate noncongregational religious structures, episcopal and presbyterial churches are at some disadvantage when incorporating.[203]

Churches that adopt a corporate legal structure must also contend with a growing concern about regulation of religious nonprofit corporations. While nonreligious nonprofit corporations are subject to a variety of regulatory mechanisms,[204] religious corporations have generally been significantly less scrutinized, presumably because of constitutional considerations and because of the nature of the corporate legal structure.[205] Unlike a charitable trust, the enforcement of which requires involvement of the attorney general,[206] a charitable corporation contains self-regulating enforcement mechanisms.[207] It is formed by a public act in accordance with state law, and is subject to specific statutory laws of governance.[208] Generally this structure requires a specific number of directors or trustees "who can serve as a check on one another."[209] Furthermore, corporate legislation requires annual or more frequent reporting to the state.[210]

---

199. James J. Fishman, The Development of Nonprofit Corporation Law and an Agenda for Reform, 34 Emory L.J. 617, 624–37 (1985).

200. *Id.* at 635–37 & nn.199–203.

201. *Id.* at 654–55.

202. Claude D. Morgan, The Significance of Church Organizational Structure in Litigation and Government Action, 16 Val. U. L. Rev. 145, 149 (1981).

203. *Id.* at 152–53. In addition, noncongregational religious structures could consider the more flexible trust model for their legal structure. *See infra.*

204. Many commentators consider all nonprofit corporations to be underregulated, and a number of proposals for reform have been tendered. *See generally* James J. Fishman, The Development of Nonprofit Corporation Law and an Agenda for Reform, 34 Emory L.J. 617 (1985); Henry B. Hansmann, The Evolving Law of Nonprofit Organizations: Do Current Trends Make Good Policy?, 39 Case W. Res. L. Rev. 807 (1988–89); Henry B. Hansmann, Reforming Nonprofit Corporation Law, 129 U. Pa. L. Rev. 497 (1981); Daniel D. Tobergte, Comment, Regulating the Nonprofit Corporation, 16 N. Ky. L. Rev. 325 (1988); Erin M. Ryan, The Crumbling Wall Between Church and State: Attorney General Supervision of Religious Corporations in California, 9 Hastings Const. L.Q. 691 (1982).

205. *See* Dallin H. Oaks, Trust Doctrines in Church Controversies, 1981 BYU L. Rev. 805, 850 (1981).

206. *See infra* notes 225–29 and accompanying text.

207. *See id.*

208. *See id.*

209. *See id.*

210. *See id.*

Nevertheless, some well-publicized abuses in certain religious ministries—as well as recent tendencies in cases,[211] treatises,[212] and statutes[213] to subsume churches under the general heading of nonprofit corporations—have opened the way for churches to be regulated more like secular organizations. These developments make it more difficult for them to rely on continued limitations on external supervision. Although they may have a very defensible constitutional case against most state regulation,[214] they cannot rely solely on that limitation to shield them from increased legislative and judicial control. Rather, they should reinforce the prevailing view of religious organizations as largely self-regulatory by expressly providing for increased internal regulation, thus circumventing perceived needs for external control. In particular, in nonreligious nonprofit corporations, internal regulation is achieved by such means as giving corporate members the right to access corporate records, the right to challenge corporate decisions, and the standing to initiate such a challenge. Although some of these provisions may be contrary to church doctrine, religious bodies should consider whether these or similar rights may be adapted in a way that complies with doctrinal requirements but provides increased internal regulation. For example, a religious corporation might suggest reservation of an express visitorial power in some body outside the corporation to monitor use of donated property. Similarly, development of antagonistic interests within the managerial structure of the corporation could provide sufficient initiative and standing for private enforcement of responsibilities and duties.

Ironically, churches may be able to limit external interference by drafting incorporation documents with an eye toward the civil remedy of quo warranto. Any corporation, charitable or otherwise, is able to exercise only those powers conferred upon it by its charter. To prohibit a corporation from exceeding or misusing its charter powers, an action or writ of quo warranto[215] may be initiated by the attorney general.[216] The more explicitly the duties and responsibilities of corporate officers are outlined, the more readily they may be enforced without judicial inquiry into or interpretation of doctrinal matters. Churches, therefore, may choose to delineate in corporate documents how the powers of the corporation and its directors are to be defined, limited, and regulated; the characteristics, qualifications, rights, obligations, and limitations of the members; how assets are to be disposed of upon dissolution or schism; who is to have access to corporate books and records; or how the corporate officers are to be replaced.[217]

Religious corporations might also consider naming specific positions of power (particularly in fiscal matters) and describing how and by whom this power may be checked. Such provisions will likely be deferred to if accompanied by evidence that this checking authority is real and effective. The methods will probably need to be at least somewhat autonomous from the church hierarchy since, for instance, it would be of little use to

---

211. *See, e.g.*, Gospel Tabernacle Body of Christ Church v. Peace Publishers & Co., 506 P.2d 1135 (Kan. 1973).

212. *See, e.g.*, H. Oleck, Non-Profit Corporations § 348 (3d ed. 1974).

213. *See, e.g.*, Mich. Comp. Laws Ann. § 450.2123 (West 1990).

214. *See generally* Oaks, *supra* note 13.

215. S. Thompson, Commentaries the Law of Corporations, §§ 5780–5811 (3d ed. White 1927); W. Fletcher, Cyclopedia of the Law of Private Corporations, § 2332 (rev. perm. ed. 1975); Comment, Quo Warranto in Pennsylvania: Old Standards and New Developments, 80 Dick. L. Rev. 218, 237–44 (1975).

216. S. Thompson, *supra* note 215, § 5792; National Association of Attorneys General, Common Law Powers of Attorneys General 1 39–41 (rev. ed. 1977).

217. Revised Model Nonprofit Corp. Act (Am. Bar Ass'n 1987) (superseding the Model Nonprofit Corp. Act (1952)) § 2.02 & official cmt.

make the minister of a local congregation responsible for checking the power of his superior in a hierarchical organization. Similarly, there must be some incentive to enforce this checking power so that overseer provisions will be effective.

Because the membership corporate model may not be entirely suitable for churches with a hierarchical polity, such an organization may need to adopt a civil corporate hierarchy analogous to its religious hierarchy, or to expressly provide for accommodation of its ecclesiastical structure in the corporate bylaws.[218] For example, a church could establish a corporate parent/subsidiary relationship between the national and local entities. By making the local congregation a subordinate corporate subsidiary of the parent religious corporation, the church can use neutral legal principles to produce deference to hierarchical decisions. This can be accomplished either by explicitly subordinating the subsidiary organization or by vesting all voting power in the parent corporation. Likewise, the corporate bylaws could provide that the rights to elect directors for the subsidiary, amend its bylaws, control its property, or merge or dissolve it rest with the parent corporation. Alternatively, the corporate charter could expressly limit the power of the subsidiary.[219] Regardless of the method chosen, if the parent corporation effectively controls the subsidiary, a reviewing court could use objective criteria to defer to hierarchical decisions.

The corporation sole is an alternative legal structure available to all, but attractive only to hierarchical churches. Following this model, subordinate churches deed property to the corporation sole, centralizing control in the ecclesiastical officer. Should the corporation sole be dissolved, its assets would revert to the organization that controlled it, rather than to the subordinate organization.[220]

Not all of these recommendations will be applicable in any given situation, but churches may find that by explicitly outlining and strengthening their own internal organization and accountability they may be able to avoid external regulation.

Trust model

Some of the attractions to using the trust model include: "ease and swiftness of formation, administration with fewer formalities than the corporate form, fewer housekeeping requirements, perpetual or indefinite period of existence, and the possibility of continuing control by the grantor."[221] In general, a trust is a more informal device than a corporation.[222] Unlike a corporation, a trust is not required to obtain a state charter[223]

---

218. *See* Comment: Structuring California Church Corporations to Allow Judicial Identification of Charitable Trustees in Church Property Disputes, 16 U.S.F. L. Rev. 463, 485–88 and notes (Spring 1982).

219. *Id.* at 488.

220. *Id.* at 489.

221. Fishman & Schwarz, *supra* note 194, at 63.

222. *See* Treusch, *supra* note 192, at 45.

223. *See id.* The fact that a trust does not require a state charter may be significant for a religious organization which attempts to limit state intrusion into its operation. However, unless the trust instrument is properly drafted, there may be a greater level of court involvement in a trust than in a corporation. For instance, Treusch notes:

> Corporate management is generally elected annually by the shareholders or members, whereas the trust management is generally not removable except by a court for misconduct unless otherwise provided in the trust instrument. Nor may trust management resign, as may corporate directors, without court permission in the absence of a provision

or produce annual reports. It merely requires the intent of the grantor to create a trust and trust property. Unlike a private trust, a charitable trust does not require identifiable beneficiaries.[224] The grantor must only specifically describe the charitable purpose of the trust.[225]

The disadvantages to using a trust must also be considered. For instance, "a trustee's fiduciary duties of management and the manner of their enforcement are more strictly defined than those for corporate managers."[226] The trustees also are personally liable for contracts entered into in administering the trust, unless the contracts stipulate otherwise.[227] Furthermore, the trustees will be personally liable for torts committed by themselves as well as for those committed by their agents acting within the scope of their employment.[228]

As noted earlier, most churches have organized on the corporate model because traditionally, charitable corporations were subject to less judicial supervision than were charitable trusts.[229] At common law, state attorneys general are responsible for the enforcement of charitable trusts. Private trusts have identifiable beneficiaries to whom the trustee owes a fiduciary duty. Therefore the beneficiaries, or ones suing on their behalf, are the proper parties to bring suit against the trustee to enforce a private trust.[230] On the contrary, in the case of charitable trusts the public at large, an indefinite and shifting class, is deemed to be the beneficiary. Accordingly, the attorney general as representative of the public has been deemed the appropriate party to enforce a charitable trust.[231] Bogert explains:

> Since the Attorney General is the governmental officer whose duties include the protection of the rights of the people of the state in general, it is natural that he has been chosen as the protector, supervisor, and enforcer of charitable trusts, both in England and in the several states, either because of a specific delegation of that power to him by statute, or by reason of a general statement of his duties or because of judicial decisions.[232]

In addition, because the class of beneficiaries is large and shifting, were the enforcement of charitable trusts not limited to the attorney general, the trust would be faced with unreasonable and vexatious litigation.[233] Even so, there may be instances in which the attorney general is not the proper party to enforce a charitable trust.[234]

---

in the trust.
Id. at 46.

224. Fishman & Schwarz, *supra* note 194, at 64.

225. *Id.*

226. *See* Treusch, *supra* note 192, at 45–46.

227. *See* Henn & Pfeifer, *supra* note 196, at 204. However, the trustee has a right of indemnification from the trust for contracts properly entered into on behalf of the trust. *See id.* at 205. Furthermore, if state law allows, the grantor could appoint a limited-liability company as trustee and avoid the personal liability issue.

228. *See id.* & n.124.

229. *See supra* notes 204–10 and accompanying text.

230. *See* 4A Scott, *supra* note 24, §391.

231. *See* G. Bogert, The Law of Trusts and Trustees §411 (2d. ed. 1977). Similarly, the Restatement provides: "A suit can be maintained for the enforcement of a charitable trust by the attorney general or other public officer, or by a co-trustee, or by a person who has a special interest in the enforcement of a charitable trust...." Restatement (Second) of Trusts §391 (1959).

232. Bogert, *supra* note 231.

233. *Id.*

234. *See* Attorney General v. Clark, 45 N.E. 183 (Mass. 1896) (holding that the Twelfth Baptist Church, and not the attorney general, was the proper party to enforce rights in donations made for the benefit of the church and held by defendant bank because the church was "a definite body capa-

Although the common law provides the attorney general with the power to "enforce" charitable trusts, the extent of such power is vague and ambiguous. The courts have divided the attorney general's common law power to enforce charitable trusts into what Oaks classifies as three main categories: the powers to establish and defend,[235] to responsively represent,[236] and to correct breaches of charitable trusts.[237] The attorney general's common law power for the first two categories is well established.[238] However, the judicial opinions concerning the attorney general's power to bring suit against the trustee for breach of trust is extremely sparse. Additionally, Oaks notes that the case law "dealing with this subject are dicta on the facts of the case or represent statements with at least partial reliance on statutory rather than common law authority."[239]

Twenty-nine states have buttressed the common law by granting enforcement power to their attorneys general. New Hampshire was the first to do so,[240] followed by California, Ohio, Rhode Island, and South Carolina.

In 1951, the National Association of Attorneys General requested that the National Conference of Commissioners on Uniform State Laws draft a uniform act to require trustees and others to report to the attorney general the existence and administration of property held for charitable purposes.[241] The Uniform Supervision of Trustees for Charitable Purposes Act, which was drafted and approved by the American Bar Association in 1954, has been adopted in only four states.[242] Twelve other states have enacted similar provisions,[243] and nine more have adopted statutes providing for attorney gen-

---

ble of enforcing whatever rights it may have in the fund or controversy"); *see also* Bogert, *supra* note 231, at 414; Oaks, *supra* note 205, at 849.

235. *See* Oaks, *supra* note 205, at 844. This power places responsibility on the attorney general to defend valid charitable trusts against attack and attempts to terminate them by the donor's heirs. *See id.*

236. *See id.* at 845. Oaks explains responsive representation as
> where the attorney general performs a relatively routine representative role, most often at the initiative of the trustees and usually not adverse to them... [such as] cases in which the attorney general participates in litigation proposing an alteration of the charitable activity by cy pres,... substituting trustees or construing the meaning of the trust instrument.

Id.

237. *See id.* In cases of breach of trust, the attorney general brings suit against the trustees for personal use of trust assets, not conforming with the trust's charitable purpose, or failure to meet their standard of care in investment and administrative matters. *See id.*

238. *See id.* at 844–45 & n. 142 (authorities in support of common law power to establish and defend charitable trusts); 143–145 (authorities in support of common law power to responsively represent charitable trusts).

239. *See id.* at 845–46.

240. 1943 N.H. Laws ch. 181.

241. Uniform Supervision of Trustees for Charitable Purposes Act, Commissioners' Prefatory Note (1985).

242. Cal. Gov't Code §§ 12580–12597 (West 1992); Ill. Rev. Stat., ch. 55, para. 1 to 19 (West 1993); Mich. Comp. Laws §§ 14.251–.266 (West 1994); Or. Rev. Stat. §§ 128.610–.750 (1993).

243. Ga. Code Ann. §§ 53-12-110 to -116 (1997); Md. Code Ann., Est. & Trusts §§ 14-301 to -308 (1991); Mass. Gen. Laws Ann. ch 12, § 8-8K (West 1996); Minn. Stat. Ann. §§ 501B.33–.45 (West 1990); N.H. Rev. Stat. Ann. §§ 7:19–7:32a (1988 & Supp. 1997); N.M. Stat. Ann. §§ 57-22-1 to 57-22-9 (Michie 1994); N.Y. Est. Powers & Trust Law §§ 8-1.l to .7 (McKinney 1992); N.C. Gen. Stat. §§ 36A-47 to -54 (Michie 1993); Ohio Rev. Code Ann. §§ 109.23–.33 (Anderson 1994); R.I. Gen. Laws §§ 18-9-1 to -17 (1996); S.C. Code Ann. §§ 62-7-501 to -507 (Law Co-op 1987); Wash. Rev. Code Ann. §§ 11.110.010–.900 (West 1987).

eral enforcement of charitable trusts.[244] However, the law made concessions to religious trusts similar to those afforded to religious corporations, and religious trusts have been universally exempted from these comprehensive supervisory statues.[245] Furthermore, lack of staffing and of interest in monitoring charitable organizations "makes the attorney general oversight more theoretical than real."[246] For instance, most states' attorney general offices have not even one full-time attorney devoted to supervision of charitable organizations.[247] Nevertheless, in the absence of a clear Supreme Court ruling denying civil courts enforcement power over religious trusts, churches cannot want to rely solely on the current hands-off policy of most attorneys general in deciding church trust matters.[248]

In general, the concerns and recommendations outlined for religious corporations are applicable also to charitable trusts. Specifically, churches should create an express and effective infrastructure with sufficient checks and balances to eliminate the need for external controls. For instance, the rationale behind attorney general enforcement of charitable trusts is that as the public is the beneficiary of the trust, no individual has standing to enforce trust provisions. A religious organization, by using multiple trustees, could structure the trust to create enforceable duties among the trustees themselves, effectively protecting interests without civil court involvement. Likewise, provisions for altering the objects of the trust, rules applicable upon dissolution, and liabilities of the directors should be explicitly delineated in trust documents.

As mentioned earlier, at least two denominations amended their constitutions after *Jones* to create express trust provisions in favor of the national organization. These amendments have not been litigated and their validity is not certain. In particular, there may be some question as to whether the provisions reflect the intent of the local church. Requiring local congregations to include express trust provisions in favor of the denomination could eliminate the problem of local intent while still allowing the national body to control the property in a dispute.

---

244. Conn. Gen. Stat Ann. § 3-125 (West 1988); Idaho Code § 67-1401 (1995); Me. Rev. Stat. Ann. tit. 5, § 194 (West 1989); Mont. Code Ann. § 72-33-503 (1997); Neb. Rev. Stat. § 21-614 (1997); Nev. Rev. Stat. § 165.230 (1995); N.D. Cent. Code § 59-04-02 (1995); S.D. Codified Laws Ann. § 55-9-5 (Michie 1997); Wis. Stat. Ann. § 701.10(3) (West 1981).

245. Cal. Gov't. Code § 12583; Ga. Code Ann. § 53-12-116(j); Haw. Rev. Stat. § 467B-11 (1993); Mass. Gen. Laws Ann. ch. 12 § 8F; Mich. Comp. Laws Ann. § 14.253; Minn. Stat. Ann. § 501B.36; N.H. Rev. Stat. Ann. § 7:19; N.M. Stat. Ann. §§ 57-22-4; N.Y. Est. Powers & Trust Law §§ 8-1.4(b); Or. Rev. Stat. §§ 128.640 (1997); R.I. Gen. Laws § 18-9-15; S.C. Code Ann. § 62-7-505; Wash. Rev. Code Ann. § 11.110.020. In Ohio, the attorney general has exempted religious organizations by regulation. Ohio Rev. Code Ann. § 109.26; Ohio Admin. Code § 109:1-1-02 (B) (3) (Page 1993).

246. Fishman & Schwarz, *supra* note 194, at 247. Scott notes:

> Both in England and in the United States the attorney general is charged with many duties that have nothing to do with the enforcement of charitable trusts. The result has been that, in the absence of statutory changes in the law, the enforcement of charitable trusts is bound to be more or less sporadic.

VI. A. Scott *supra* note 24, § 391.

247. *See id.*

248. California has permitted attorney general involvement in the supervision and regulation of churches. *See* People v. Worldwide Church of God, No. C 267 607 (L.A. Super. Ct., filed Jan. 2,1979), *mandamus denied*, Worldwide Church of God v. Superior Court, No. 31091 (Cal. March 22, 1979) (dismissed from L.A. Super. Ct., Oct. 16, 1980); Yonger v. Faith Ctr., Inc., Civ. No. 56574 (Cal. Ct. App. Aug 29, 1980). For a discussion of criticism of these cases, see Oaks, *supra* note 13, at 79–98.

Language of Conveyances of Property

Regardless of a religious body's choice of legal structure, the language of the documents conveying property to the organization will determine which principles of law apply to the management of those particular assets. That is, if donations are deemed to have been given in trust, the church will be subject to charitable trust law, but if the donation is viewed as an unencumbered gift, trust law will not be applicable.

If a donation is given explicitly as an unqualified gift, a religious corporation controls disposition of the assets subject only to restrictions imposed upon it by its own charter or by contractual agreements attached to the gift. Similarly, if a settlor states expressly that his donation is given in trust, a trust will be enforced.

A general trust statement is not, however, sufficient. Rather, provisions of the trust should be expressly outlined. For example, a donor to a religious organization should consider whether his charitable intent is to benefit the organization generally or only some limited purpose of the church. Especially if the intent is more particularized, the donor must consider what he would wish done with his gift if the purpose he seeks to benefit later becomes impossible or impracticable. A provision governing application of cy pres might outline possible alternative purposes or delineate which body or individuals have authority to alter the purpose of the donation and under what circumstances. The donor might, alternatively, insert a reverter clause in the event that the donation ceases to be used for the designated purpose. Similarly, donors sometimes contribute to building funds or other purposes under the presupposition that their contribution will be matched or augmented. If these supplementary funds are not forthcoming, or if there is a diminution in the trust res sufficient to render it inadequate for its stated purpose, express provisions for disposing of the property can prevent court involvement. Churches that accept donations with express trust provisions must consider whether the beneficiaries are adequately identified according to applicable state statutes.

Since much litigation arises when there is uncertainty about whether particular property was given in trust or as an unencumbered gift, potential disputes may be avoided by clearly drafting documents that specify the terms of the donation. When possible, churches should request that property be donated outright as a gift to the religious organization.

State Statutory Considerations

While it is beyond the scope of this chapter to enumerate the various state statutes that could influence judicial decisions in church property disputes, they must be considered in many aspects of church legal organization. For example, some states have denominational incorporation statutes requiring that the incorporating congregation continue affiliation with a denomination. In *Protestant Episcopal Church in the Diocese of Los Angeles et al. v. Barker et al.*,[249] the court relied on a California incorporation statute which required that property revert to the national organization when the charter of a

---

249. 115 Cal. App. 3d 599, 624–25 (1981).

subordinate body was revoked.[250] Local churches can alter their incorporation documents to avoid this result, and in some states they may be able to reincorporate under a nondenominational statute.[251]

Similarly, state statutes may restrict solicitation of donations. At least thirty-seven states regulate charitable solicitations in some way.[252] First Amendment considerations may make many of these regulations inapplicable to religious organizations,[253] but provisions regulating time, place, and manner of solicitation have generally been upheld.[254]

Uniform Application of Neutral Principles

Courts attempting to apply a neutral principles analysis to resolution of church property disputes have relied on a variety of legal theories, which has resulted in inconsistent holdings. To achieve more predictability and fairness in judicial outcomes and to preserve First Amendment rights, courts and legislatures should require churches to express intentions rather than rely on presumptions of intent.

Specifically, courts must insist on an explicit expression of intention to create a trust before imposing a trust on church property. All vestiges of the implied trust doctrine should be eliminated and courts should return to the reasoning of *Smith v. Nelson*[255] and *Robertson v. Bullion*,[256] holding that in the absence of language creating an express

---

250. *Id.* at 624–25.

251. Presbytery of Donegal v. Calhoun, 513 A.2d 531, 536–37 (Pa. Commw. Ct. 1986).

252. Ala. Code §§13A-9-70 to 13A-9-76 (1994); Ariz. Rev. Stat. Ann. §§44-6551 to 44-6561 (West 1994); Ark. Code Ann. §§4-28-401 to 4-28-410 (1996); Cal. Business and Professional Code §§17510 to 17510.95; Cal. Penal Code §532d; Cal. Welfare & Institutions Code §§148 to 148.9; Conn. Gen. Stat. Ann. §§21a-175 to 21a-190(l) (1994) ; Fla. Stat. Ann. §§496.401 to 496.424 (West 1997 & Supp. 1998); Ga. Code Ann. §§43-17-2 to 43-17-23 (1994 & Supp. 1997); Haw. Rev. Stat. §467B-1 to B-13 (1993 & Supp. 1997); Ill. Comp. Stat. Ann. 460/0.01 to 460/21 (West 1992 & Supp. 1997); Iowa Code Ann. §13.c1 to 13.c8 (West 1995); Kan. Stat. Ann. §§17-1761 to 17-1771 (1995); Ky. Rev. Stat. Ann. §367.652 (1996); La. Rev. Stat. Ann. §§1901 to 1909.1 (West 1987 & Supp. 1998); Me. Rev. Stat. Ann. tit. 9 §§5001 to 5016 (West 1997); Md. Code Ann., Bus. Reg. §6-501 to 6-509 (1992 & Supp. 1997); Mass. Gen. Laws Ann. C.68, §§18-35 (1988 & Supp. 1997); Mich. Comp. Laws Ann. §§14.301 to 14.327 and 400.271 to 400.293 (1994); Minn. Stat. Ann. §§309.50–309.61 (West 1996 & Supp. 1998); Miss. Code Ann. §§79-11-501 to 79-11-529 (1996 & Supp. 1997); Mo. Ann. Stat. §§407.450 to 407.478 (1990 & Supp. 1998); N.J. Stat. Ann. §§45:17A-18 to 45:17A-40 (West Supp. 1995); N.M. Stat. Ann. §§57-22-1 to 57-22-11 (Michie 1995); N.Y. Exec. Law §§171-a to 177 (McKinney 1993 & Supp. 1998); N.C. Gen. Stat. §§131F-1 to 131F-32 (1997); N.D. Cent. Code §§50-22-02 to 50-22-04 (Supp. 1997); Ohio Rev. Code Ann. §§1716.01–1716.99 (Anderson 1992); Okl. Stat. Ann. §§552.1 to 552.18 (West 1986 & Supp. 1998); Or. Rev. Stat. §§128.201 to 128.898 (1997); Pa. Stat. Ann. tit. 10 §§162.1–162.24 (West Supp. 1997); R.I. Gen. Laws §§5-53-1 to 5-53-14 (1995); S.C. Code Ann. §§33-56-10 to 33-56-200 (Law Co-op Supp. 1997); Tenn. Code Ann. §§48-101-501 to 48.101-521 (1995 & Supp. 1997); Utah Code Ann. §§13-22-1 to 13-22-21 (1996 & Supp. 1998); Va. Code Ann. §§57-48 to 57-69 (Michie 1995 & Supp. 1997); Wash. Rev. Code Ann. §19.09.010 to 19.09.915 (West 1989); W. Va. Code §§29-19-1 to 29-19-16 (1992 & Supp. 1997); Wis. Stat. Ann. §440.41 to 440.48 (Supp. 1997).

253. *See, e.g.*, Cantwell v. Connecticut, 310 U.S. 296 (1940) (conditioning grant of solicitation license on determination by state authority of religious use held unconstitutional).

254. *Id.*

255. 18 Vt. 511 (1846).

256. 11 N.Y. 243, 247 (1854).

trust, donations to churches should be viewed as unencumbered gifts. A high standard of intent should be required to impose a trust upon religious property.[257]

Similarly, legislatures must require more information from churches incorporating under state statutes. In particular, incorporation documents should require religious organizations to outline how various potential property disputes are to be resolved. Incorporation applications may ask, for example, for an outline of responsibilities within the organization, a designation of where title to property is vested, and a determination of a property distribution plan upon dissolution. Such requirements would create "neutral" law on which a court could rely in resolving church property disputes while being able to defer to church preferences.

In resolving church property disputes, courts must rely on the express language of church and state documents rather than blindly deferring to decisions of denominational hierarchies. Likewise, they must clearly delineate types of evidence that can be used to rebut presumptions of majority control.

Conclusion

Because there is no single understanding of the neutral principles doctrine, the impact of charitable trust law on church property disputes is uncertain. Until a more defined application is developed, churches should try to avoid judicial involvement in disputes. Although there is no certain way to prevent litigation, careful drafting of pertinent documents and increased efforts to provide for internal resolution of property disputes may prevent some lawsuits while providing legal authority to which a court can defer if litigation does occur. Similarly, courts should avoid undue involvement in church affairs by relying on clear expressions of intention before imposing trusts on church property.

---

257. *See generally* Oaks, *supra* note 13.

Civil Court Resolution
of Property Disputes among
Religious Organizations

Patty Gerstenblith

Most jurisprudence concerning the Religion Clauses of the First Amendment directly addresses the relationship between a governmental activity and a religious activity. This relationship generally is examined either from the perspective of a governmental benefit or exemption granted to religious groups or individuals on the basis of their religion,[1] or from that of a governmental burden placed on religious groups or individuals in the exercise of their religion.[2] The first of these perspectives implicates the prohibition against the establishment of religion, while the second implicates the right to free exercise of religion.[3] In both categories of cases, however, the government's action or inac-

---

1. *See, e.g.,* Board of Educ. of the Westside Community Schools v. Mergens, 496 U.S. 226 (1990) (upholding Equal Access Act allowing student religious groups access to public school facilities). Comm. for Pub. Educ. & Religious Liberty v. Regan, 444 U.S. 646, 662 (1980) (upholding statute appropriating public funds to reimburse private schools for state-mandated testing and services); Walz v. Tax Comm'n, 397 U.S. 664, 680 (1970) (approving state tax exemption for real or personal property used exclusively for religious educational or charitable purposes); Zorach v. Clauson, 343 U.S. 306, 314–15 (1952) (allowing release-time program in which children were excused from class to attend off-campus religious instruction); McCollum v. Board of Educ., 333 U.S. 203, 212 (1948) (striking down public school release-time program for religious instruction held on public school property); Everson v. Board of Educ., 330 U.S. 1, 18 (1947) (permitting public funding of transportation for both parochial and public schools).

2. *See, e.g.,* Employment Div., Dep't of Human Resources v. Smith, 494 U.S. 872, 890 (1990) (permitting state to deny unemployment benefits to Indians dismissed from employment because of ceremonial drug use). Thomas v. Review Bd., 450 U.S. 707, 720 (1981) (holding that denial of un-employment compensation to factory worker who was forced to quit because of religious faith violated Free Exercise Clause); Wisconsin v. Yoder, 406 U.S. 205, 234–36 (1972) (finding that Free Exercise Clause forbids states from compelling Amish parents to send their children to secondary school); Sherbert v. Verner, 374 U.S. 398, 410 (1963) (declaring that Seventh-Day Adventist was en-titled to unemployment compensation after quitting job because of religious beliefs); Braunfeld v. Brown, 366 U.S. 599, 603 (1961) (upholding application of Sunday-closing law to Orthodox Jews); Reynolds v. United States, 98 U.S. 145, 168 (1878) (holding that Mormon practice of polygamy is not protected under Free Exercise Clause).

3. *See* U.S. Const. amend. I (forbidding Congress from making any law "...respecting an estab-lishment of religion, or prohibiting free exercise thereof..."); *See also* L. Tribe, American Constitu-tional Law § 14-2, at 1155–57 (2d ed. 1988) (discussing dichotomy of and relationship between First Amendment Religion Clauses).

tion is directly at issue.[4] Courts have, therefore, developed a unique set of legal principles in the context of First Amendment jurisprudence to resolve these disputes with special consideration for the impact of governmental action on religion in light of First Amendment values.[5]

Different jurisprudential concerns are implicated when the government is not a primary actor but is involved only because of its judicial role as arbiter of private disputes. These concerns arise when the judicial system is asked to resolve a conflict between two competing religious factions.[6] Although one could argue that courts should refrain from entering such disputes,[7] a strong policy favoring dispute settlement and the protection of civil interests mandates civil court intervention in this area.[8] Such intervention, however, is restricted to the resolution of civil issues because courts are prohibited from resolving purely ecclesiastical and doctrinal issues.[9] Once policy concerns dictate civil court jurisdiction, then courts must determine which principles to use. Courts have recognized such jurisdiction in the realm of property disputes, which provide a para-

---

4. *See* L. Tribe, *supra* note 3, § 14-1, at 1154 (noting that core ideal to religious autonomy would place religion beyond reach of government intervention); *see also* School Dist. v. Schempp, 374 U.S. 203, 305 (1963) (Goldberg, J., concurring) (noting that fundamental principles underlying Religion Clauses are that government neither participate in nor require religious practices).

5. On the Establishment Clause side, these principles were enunciated in *Lemon v. Kurtzman*, 403 U.S. 602, 612–13 (1970) (establishing three-prong Establishment Clause test in which government must show: (1) that action taken has secular legislative purpose; (2) that primary effect neither advances nor inhibits religion; and (3) that such action does not foster excessive government entanglement with religion). This test has been adapted and made more flexible in *Agostini* and *Helms*. Agostini v. Felton, 521 U.S. 203 (1997); Mitchell v. Helms, 530 U.S. 793 (2000). On the free exercise side, the classic principles were articulated in *Sherbert v. Verner*, 374 U.S. 398, 403–07 (1963) and *Wisconsin v. Yoder*, 406 U.S. 205 (1972) (establishing test for free exercise violation requiring government to demonstrate compelling state interest after claimant illustrates burden on free exercise of religion). However, the strength of these free exercise protections was substantially curtailed as a result of *Employment Div., Dep't of Human Resources v. Smith*, 494 U.S. 872 (1990), which held that neutral and general laws will normally override religious freedom protections. These frameworks have continually been reformed and expanded. *See* L. Tribe, *supra* note 3, §§ 14-12, 14-13, at 1242, 1251 (describing present formulations of tests for Free Exercise and Establishment Clause violations).

6. *See* Presbyterian Church in the United States v. Mary Elizabeth Blue Hull Memorial Presbyterian Church, 393 U.S. 440, 445 (1969) (holding state interest legitimate in resolving property disputes where parties are religious factions and indicating civil courts as appropriate forum). Some disputes which arise in the context of a schismatic disagreement between religious groups may also pose the question of the constitutionality of granting a specific benefit in which case the government is no longer acting solely as an arbiter. *See* United Christian Scientists v. Christian Science Bd. of Directors, First Church of Christ, Scientist, 829 F.2d 1152, 1171 (D.C. Cir. 1987) (holding that grant of extended copyright for religious materials to one religious group violated Establishment Clause).

7. *See* United States v. Ballard, 322 U.S. 78, 87 (1944) (stating that one's religious belief is no concern of the state, and that religious doctrines should not be subject to trial by jury).

8. *See* Ellman, Driven from the Tribunal: Judicial Resolution of Internal Church Disputes, 69 Cal. L. Rev. 1378, 1382-83, 1410-12 (1981) (positing that judicial restraint from adjudication of such disputes may burden religious groups by denying them benefit of secular rules).

9. *See* Serbian Eastern Orthodox Diocese for the United States and Canada v. Milivojevich, 426 U.S. 696, 697 (1976) (deciding that adjudication of primarily religious controversies by civil courts is violation of First Amendment). *See generally* Young & Tigges, Into the Religious Thicket: Constitutional Limits on Civil Court Jurisdiction over Ecclesiastical Disputes, 47 Ohio St. L.J. 475 (1986) (discussing distinctions in judicial approach between ecclesiastical and property disputes).

digm for determining the types of principles that courts should use to adjudicate all internal religious disputes that implicate civil interests.[10]

A growing body of literature has advocated the uniform and mandatory application of "neutral principles" of law to resolve these disputes.[11] This chapter seeks to deepen analysis of this neutral principles approach and of the overriding policy it should effectuate.[12] The chapter will contend that when faced with an internal religious dispute, a court should adopt the same legal principles that are used to resolve equivalent nonreligious disputes instead of applying a special set of legal doctrines. Although unique legal principles developed in the context of First Amendment jurisprudence may be required to evaluate the impact of governmental activity on religious concerns, they should not be needed for resolving internal religious disputes. In such disputes, the most important value to maintain is equality of treatment between religious factions, without which courts risk establishing one religious faction at the expense of the free exercise rights of the other. Courts must recognize the need for such equality and must maintain it through the application of a truly neutral set of legal principles.[13]

---

10. *See, e.g.,* Jones v. Wolf, 443 U.S. 595, 599 (1979) (citing Presbyterian Church in the United States v. Mary Elizabeth Blue Hull Memorial Presbyterian Church, 393 U.S. 440, 449 (1969) (deciding that neutral principles of law can be applied to resolve internal religious property disputes without violating Establishment Clause)); Presbytery of Riverside v. Community Church, 89 Cal. App. 3d 910, 925 (1979) (acknowledging Supreme Court decisions permitting civil court resolution of internal religious property disputes); Protestant Episcopal Church v. Graves, 417 A.2d 19, 22 (N.J. 1980) (recognizing that civil courts can resolve property disputes among religious groups although subject to some limitations); *cert. denied sub nom.* Moore v. Protestant Episcopal Church, 449 U.S. 1131 (1981).

11. *See* Adams & Hanlon, Jones v. Wolf: Church Autonomy and the Religion Clauses of the First Amendment, 128 U. Pa. L. Rev. 1291, 1332-39 (1980) (examining tensions inherent in judicial scrutiny of property disputes between religious factions in context of First Amendment Religion Clauses); Ross, The Need for an Exclusive and Uniform Application of "Neutral Principles" in the Adjudication of Church Property Disputes, 32 St. Louis U. L.J. 263, 305-16 (1987) (examining reluctance of lower courts to forego deference approach for adoption of neutral principle doctrine in deciding civil disputes between religious factions). Other commentators are critical of the Jones v. Wolf adoption of neutral principles. *See, e.g.,* John E. Fennelly, Property Disputes and Religious Schisms: Who Is the Church? 9 St. Thomas L. Rev. 319 (1997).

12. *See* Ellman, *supra* note 8, at 1402-21 (representing an attempt to explore the implications of neutral principles analysis exception by attempting to define the "contract principle" developed in Watson v. Jones, 80 U.S. (13 Wall.) 679 (1871), to achieve a consistent resolution of all internal religious disputes); *see also infra* notes 177-98 and accompanying text (considering application of "contract principle").

Ross has also advocated the adoption of a neutral principles approach. Ross, *supra* note 11, at 305-16. His discussion, however, is flawed because he analyzes recent cases based on the denomination involved rather than on the court's approach. *Id.* at 280-304. Furthermore, Ross's variant of neutral principles would still lead to inconsistent results in that it does not depend on strictly neutral legal principles developed in other areas of the law.

13. *See* Jones v. Wolf, 443 U.S. 595, 603 (1979) (holding neutral principles approach consistent with constitutional principles); *see also* Adams & Hanlon, *supra* note 11, at 1297 (suggesting that Constitution mandates neutral principles approach to adjudicating religious property disputes); Ross, *supra* note 11, at 265 (arguing for neutral principles over polity approach).

Commentators and students of First Amendment jurisprudence have used the term "neutrality" in various contexts and with differing definitions. *See, e.g.,* P. Kurland, Religion and the Law 18 (1962) (concluding that neutrality theory prevents governmental actions based on religious classifications); Marshall, Solving the Free Exercise Dilemma: Free Exercise as Expression, 67 Minn. L. Rev. 545, 547 (1983) (arguing that free exercise claims to religion-based exemption should be resolved in same manner as claims based on Free Speech Clause); McConnell & Posner, An Economic Ap-

The first part of this chapter will highlight aspects of the judicial application and inter-pretation of the First Amendment in the context of internal religious disputes that support the neutral principles approach. The second part will show how legal concepts from trust, property, and other areas of the law should be applied in order to accomplish a truly neutral approach to the resolution of such disputes. Only through the application of such concepts can courts effectuate the values of both First Amendment Religion Clauses.

Historical and Constitutional Framework

Defining how far the courts may go in resolving internal religious disputes without vi-olating the First Amendment is difficult due to uncertainty regarding the scope of the First Amendment itself.[14] A survey of court decisions regarding property disputes among religious organizations further depicts the uncertainty of the First Amendment's scope.[15] Courts have employed various methods to handle the inherent tension between the Es-tablishment and Free Exercise clauses.[16] Although the clauses do not allow government to discriminate among religions,[17] the deference that courts have afforded certain religious

---

proach to Issues of Religious Freedom, 56 U. Chi. L. Rev. 1, 1 (1989) (defining neutral or equal treatment of religious and nonreligious institutions and activities using economic efficiency analy-sis). This chapter intends the term "neutral principles" to indicate those relevant legal principles de-veloped in analogous contexts of property, trust, contract, and corporate law that are utilized to re-solve disputes among nonreligious individuals and institutions. As such, this definition approximates that proposed by Ellman, *supra* note 8, at 1383.

14. *See* Nutting, Is the First Amendment Obsolete?, 30 Geo. Wash. L. Rev. 167, 167 (1961) (de-scribing First Amendment as collection of contradictions). In attempting to evaluate First Amend-ment jurisprudence, this commentator wrote:

> The one thing that can be asserted about the first amendment with complete confidence is that it does not mean what it says. It means more than it says. It means less than it says. Depending on the circumstances it may, at different times, mean either more or less than it says. It speaks, through the Supreme Court, not with the clear voice of unanimity but with the uncertain tones of doubt and division.

15. *See infra* notes 47–118 and accompanying text (discussing Supreme Court and lower court treatment of such property disputes).

16. *See, e.g.,* Walz v. Tax Comm'n, 397 U.S. 664, 680 (1970) (differentiating between tax exemp-tions given to religious groups and subsidies for purposes of Establishment Clause analysis); Zorach v. Clauson, 343 U.S. 306, 314 (1952) (requiring government neutrality toward religion while allow-ing accommodation of religious groups); Everson v. Board of Educ., 330 U.S. 1, 8–16 (1947) (dis-cussing tension between Establishment Clause and Free Exercise Clause in context of historical de-velopment).

17. *See Everson,* 330 U.S. at 15 (interpreting Establishment Clause as precluding passage of laws to aid or to prefer one religion over another); Laycock, Toward a General Theory of the Religion Clauses: The Case of Church Labor Relations and the Right to Church Autonomy, 81 Colum. L. Rev. 1373, 1414 (1981) (stating general agreement on meaning of Religion Clauses that government cannot discriminate among churches); *see also* Jimmy Swaggart Ministries v. Board of Equalization, 493 U.S. 378 (1990) (upholding imposition of sales tax on religious materials where state was not required to determine content of materials to be taxed); Hernandez v. Commissioner, 109 S. Ct. 2136, 2146–48 (1989) (outlining analytical framework for claim of denominational preference); Texas Monthly, Inc. v. Bullock, 109 S. Ct. 890, 896 (1989) (stating that Constitution prohibits gov-ernment endorsement of one particular set of religious beliefs); Larson v. Valente, 456 U.S. 228, 244 (1982) (stating Establishment Clause prohibits preference of one denomination over another); Adams & Hanlon, *supra* note 11, at 1337 (noting that First Amendment requires equality of treat-ment for all religious groups); Casad, The Establishment Clause and the Ecumenical Movement, 62

groups in the name of free exercise appears to subordinate the requirements of the Establishment Clause.[18] The two clauses, however, are "correlative and coextensive ideas,"[19] and "[w]e should not be less strict to keep strong and untarnished the one side of the shield of religious freedom than we have been of the other."[20] Courts, thus, should afford each clause equal consideration in resolving church property disputes.[21]

In 1969, the Supreme Court in *Presbyterian Church in the United States v. Mary Elizabeth Blue Hull Memorial Presbyterian Church*[22] first acknowledged that judicial intervention in property disputes among religious organizations implicates both the Establishment Clause and the Free Exercise Clause. The introduction of the concept of "neutral principles of law" to deal with these disputes can be understood as an effort to respond to values emanating from both clauses.[23] An underlying tension is created by the juxtaposition of the Free Exercise Clause, which may require that the government

Mich. L. Rev. 419, 432 (1964) (recognizing that Religion Clauses mandate equal treatment of all denominations).

18. *See* Watson v. Jones, 80 U.S. (13 Wall.) 679, 723–26 (1872) (permitting court deference to certain religious groups with hierarchical organizations). In *Watson*, the Court applied a contractual approach by distinguishing three categories of property-related disputes. *Id.* at 722. These included (1) disputes over property subject to express trusts, (2) disputes involving strictly independent congregations, and (3) disputes involving hierarchical churches in which religious congregations hold the property subordinate to a general church's highest tribunal. *Id.* Only property disputes that fell in the first and second categories were resolved according to ordinary principles governing other voluntary organizations. *Id.* at 723–26. If the dispute involved a hierarchical religious organization, deference was given to that organization's highest tribunal's resolution of the dispute. *Id.* at 726–35; *see infra* notes 62–5 and accompanying text (discussing Supreme Court's criticism of "departure from doctrine" approach to resolving church property disputes).

19. Everson v. Board of Educ., 330 U.S. 1, 40 (1947) (Rutledge, J., dissenting) (citing IX The Writings of James Madison 484–87 (G. Hunt ed. 1910). *But see* Walz v. Tax Comm'n, 397 U.S. 664, 673 (1970) (stating that parameters of government's ability to accommodate religion are not parallel to nonintervention mandated by Free Exercise Clause).

20. Everson, 330 U.S. at 40 (Rutledge, J., dissenting); *See* Texas Monthly, Inc. v. Bullock, 109 S. Ct. 890, 899–902 (1989) (discussing whether state-granted exemption of religious organizations which is not required by Free Exercise Clause constitutes violation of Establishment Clause); Corporation of the Presiding Bishop v. Amos, 483 U.S. 327, 338 (1987) (upholding exemption from Title VII granted to religious organizations which, although not required by Free Exercise Clause, would prevent potential violation of religious liberty); United Christian Scientists v. Christian Science Bd. of Directors, First Church of Christ, Scientist, 829 F.2d 1152, 1166 n.67 (D.C. Cir. 1987) (holding that government promotion of free exercise values through grant of special benefits to religious denomination is subject to Establishment Clause scrutiny when no governmental constraint on religious practice mandates such intervention); Cummins v. Parker Seal Co., 516 F.2d 544, 557 (6th Cir. 1975) (Celebrezze, J., dissenting) (noting that "[t]he Free Exercise Clause provides a shield against government interference with religion, but it does not offer a sword to cut through the strictures of the Establishment Clause"), *vacated on other grounds*, 443 U.S. 903 (1977).

Although the above point has been argued frequently, the Supreme Court has yet to support it in a majority holding. *See* Dayton Christian Schools, Inc. v. Ohio Civil Rights Comm'n, 766 F.2d 932, 954 n.41 (6th Cir. 1985) (asserting that exceptions granted in pursuit of free exercise values have been overwhelmingly allowed despite Establishment Clause concerns) (citing Wisconsin v. Yoder, 406 U.S. 205, 220–21 (1972); Sherbert v. Verner, 374 U.S. 398, 409 (1963); School Dist. of Abington Township v. Schempp, 374 U.S. 203, 295 (1963), *rev'd on other grounds*, 477 U.S. 619, 622 (1986).

21. Laycock, *supra* note 17, at 1379.

22. 393 U.S. 440 (1969).

23. *See* Presbyterian Church in the United States v. Mary Elizabeth Blue Hull Memorial Presbyterian Church, 393 U.S. 440, 449 (1969) (endorsing courts' reliance on neutral principles of law developed for use in all property disputes as means of settling disputes involving church property); *see also* Adams & Hanlon, *supra* note 11, at 1295 (citing dicta in Jones v. Wolf justifying use of neutral principles to decide property disputes for all religious groups as consistent with First Amendment);

provide a certain amount of support to religion, and the Establishment Clause, which places certain limits on that support.[24] Justice Rehnquist's dissent in *Serbian Eastern Orthodox Diocese v. Milivojevich*[25] also noted the inherent conflict between the two clauses and recognized that allowing civil courts to validate ecclesiastical decisions of certain religious organizations, while furthering free exercise values, would exacerbate Establishment Clause problems.[26] Furthermore, Laurence Tribe has described this tension in terms of a conflict between furthering religious values by "governmental disentanglement from decisions of a religious organization" and compromising religious independence when such disentanglement results in uncontrolled "domination by oppressive religious authorities."[27]

A significant function of the Establishment Clause is to prevent the development of structural relationships between religious organizations and government which are vulnerable to abuse.[28] Consequently, both the probable effect on religious groups and the intent of legislatures are considered when testing the validity of regulations that affect religious organizations.[29] The Supreme Court's holdings, which grant hierarchical religious organizations greater deference in property disputes than their congregational counterparts,[30] would seem to create a structural relationship violative of the Establishment Clause.[31] Such a relationship may cause a corruption of religious liberty that results when an individual is placed at the mercy of the unchecked discretion of a hierarchical religious organization.[32]

The way to ensure that neither the Establishment Clause nor the Free Exercise Clause is compromised by judicial intervention in religious property disputes is for the courts to treat such disputes in the same manner as they treat disputes among other voluntary associations.[33] For example, in *Watson v. Jones*,[34] the Supreme Court drew parallels between religious organizations and other voluntary associations, noting that for each, the

---

Ellman, *supra* note 8, at 264 (citing Court's statements in *Jones v. Wolf* regarding neutral principles doctrine as consistent with First Amendment for deciding church property disputes).

24. Mansfield, The Religion Clauses of the First Amendment and the Philosophy of the Constitution, 72 Cal. L. Rev. 847, 849 (1984).

25. 426 U.S. 696 (1976).

26. Serbian Eastern Orthodox Diocese for the United States and Canada v. Milivojevich, 426 U.S. 696, 734 (1976) (Rehnquist, J., dissenting).

27. L. Tribe, *supra* note 3, § 14-11, at 1242.

28. Oaks, Trust Doctrines in Church Controversies, 1981 BYU L. Rev. 805, 891.

29. *Id.* For example, an Alabama statute that permitted 65 percent of a congregation, regardless of internal governance structure, to withdraw from the parent church and also retain control of the local church property was held to violate the Establishment Clause because it impermissibly intruded on traditional practices and favored one religious faction over another. Northside Bible Church v. Goodson, 387 F.2d 534, 538 (5th Cir. 1967).

30. *See infra* notes 68–73 and accompanying text (addressing dispute resolution methodology based on internal church structure). Watson v. Jones, 80 U.S. (13 Wall.) 679, 722, 725 (1871).

31. Mark Ellman, who argues that church disputes should be adjudicated under basic contract law principles, suggests that deference to decisions of religious hierarchies should not extend beyond the authority granted or agreed to by the individual members. Ellman, *supra* note 8, at 1404. According to Ellman, this contractual approach will ensure religious freedom mandated by the First Amendment because it simply implements the parties' intentions. *Id.*

32. C. Zollman, American Civil Church Law 205 (1917).

33. *See infra* notes 91–198 and accompanying text (discussing application of trust and property law to settlement of religious disputes).

34. 80 U.S. (13 Wall.) 679 (1871).

rights in property or contract are equally deserving of the protection and restraints available under the law.[35] Granting a hierarchical religious organization immunity from judicial dispute resolution, as the rule of compulsory deference requires,[36] denies members of religious groups the same protection of law that members of other voluntary associations receive.[37] Not only does this impair individuals' contractual and property interests and violate their free exercise rights, it also unconstitutionally favors hierarchical religious groups by bestowing on them greater authority than is granted to religious organizations with different polities.[38] In the words of one scholar:

> It would be simple indeed to deal with all of these conflicts with a policy of non-involvement.... But courts serve neither the church nor its members by placing their affairs in a special law-free zone. Law-free is also lawless, and the consequence is that neither the faithful, nor the church or those with which it deals, can rely on the other parties playing by the rules, for there are then no enforceable rules.... The solution most of the time is to honor internal church agreements just as a court would honor the internal agreements of a secular organization.[39]

The fulfillment of *both* Religion Clauses of the First Amendment thus requires that courts not only treat religious organizations like other voluntary associations in the resolution of their internal disputes but also apply truly neutral principles of law in doing so.

As the overview of case law provided in this volume by H. Reese Hansen makes clear, and as I have explained elsewhere at greater length,[40] there is now a division of authority among the states on how secular courts should deal with intrareligious disputes. Some courts continue to follow a compulsory deference model, always deferring to centralized or hierarchical authorities when a hierarchical church is involved.[41] Others follow a

---

35. Watson v. Jones, 80 U.S. (13 Wall.) 679, 714 (1871).

36. *See id.* at 726–35 (explicating "compulsory deference" approach to resolving interreligious disputes).

37. *See* Ellman, *supra* note 8, at 1382–83; Adams & Hanlon, *supra* note 11, at 1337.

38. *See* Casad, *supra* note 17, at 432 (asserting that courts' refusal to consider controversies over contract or property merely because one party is a religious group violates equal protection and First Amendment rights). In an intrachurch dispute, the state should enforce contracts made by its citizens regardless of the contract's religious character. Zollman, *supra* note 32, at 206. The principle of religious freedom requires courts to recognize both the legal rights of a religious organization and the legal rights of its members. *Id.*

39. Ellman, *supra* note 8, at 8.

40. *See* H. Reese Hansen, "Religious Organizations and the Law of Trusts," in this volume. Patty Gerstenblith, Civil Court Resolution of Property Disputes among Religious Organizations, 29 Am. U. L. Rev. 513; 521–50 (1990).

41. *See, e.g.,* Kendysh v. Holy Spirit Byelorussian Autocephalic Orthodox Church, 683 F. Supp. 1501, 1510 (E.D. Mich. 1987) (relying on analysis that avoids intruding into ecclesiastical decisions), *aff'd*, 850 F.2d 692 (6th Cir. 1988); Mills v. Baldwin, 362 So. 2d 2, 17 (Fla. 1978) (stating issue as one based on hierarchy, not property), *vacated and remanded*, 443 U.S. 914 (1979), *reinstated*, 377 So. 2d 971 (Fla. 1979); Townsend v. Teagle, 467 So. 2d 772, 775–76 (Fla. Dist. Ct. App. 1985) (holding that courts are precluded from rendering decision effectively judging authority of church hierarchy), *review denied*, 479 So. 2d 118 (Fla. 1985); Calvary Presbyterian Church v. Presbytery of Lake Huron of the United Presbyterian Church in the United States, 384 N.W.2d 92, 94 (Mich. Ct. App. 1986) (rejecting neutral principles and finding implied trust in favor of hierarchical denomination when church members have agreed to resolve disputes within hierarchical structure); Bennison v. Sharp, 329 N.W. 2d 466, 471 (Mich. App. Ct. 1982) (holding that court will defer to hierarchy's identification of faction representing congregation when denomination's polity is easily ascertained and deference reflects relationship among parties); Tea v. Protestant Episcopal Church in the Diocese of Nevada, 610 P.2d 182, 184 (Nev. 1980) (deferring to hierarchy's identification of "true" local congregation when local congre-

strict neutral principles approach.[42] Still others hold hybrid positions that reflect a mix

---

gation has voluntarily submitted to denomination's internal organization); Protestant Episcopal Church in the Diocese of New Jersey v. Graves, 391 A.2d 563, 574–75 (N.J. Super. Ct. Ch. Div. 1978) (characterizing dispute as primarily doctrinal and requiring deference when hierarchical denomination is involved), *aff'd*, 401 A.2d 548 (N.J. Super. Ct. App. Div. 1979) (per curiam), *aff'd*, 83 N.J. 572, 417 A.2d 19 (1980), *cert. denied sub nom.* Moore v. Protestant Episcopal Church, 449 U.S. 1131 (1981); Diocese of Newark v. Burns, 417 A.2d 31, 33–34 (N.J. 1980) (requiring deference to hierarchical determination of true church); Schismatic and Purported Casa Linda Presbyterian Church v. Grace Union Presbytery, Inc., 710 S.W. 2d 700, 707 (Tex. Ct. App. 1986) (deferring to hierarchy's identification of loyal faction as "true and lawful" church which is entitled to property); Organization for Preserving the Constitution of Zion Lutheran Church v. Mason, 743 P.2d 848, 851 (Wash. Ct. App. 1987) (holding that if church is found to have hierarchical polity then deference to hierarchy's resolution would be required); Church of God v. Noel, 318 S.E.2d 920, 923 (W. Va. 1984) (holding that in hierarchical church property is held in trust for general church and hierarchy can determine identity of proper leaders of local church). At least one state court has applied both the deference and neutral principles approaches, achieving the same result under both methods. *See* Fonken v. Community Church, 339 N.W.2d 810, 816–19 (Iowa 1983) (finding implied trust in hierarchical church under both methods).

42. *See, e.g.*, Haney's Chapel United Methodist Church v. The United Methodist Church, 1998 Ala. LEXIS 115 (Ala. 1998) (examining language of donor's deed conveying property to local church); Trinity Presbyterian Church v. Tankersley, 374 So. 2d 861, 866 (Ala. 1979) (finding loyal faction estopped to assert dominion over church property for failure to follow proper church procedures for challenging adverse ruling); Protestant Episcopal Church in the Diocese of Los Angeles v. Barker, 115 Cal. App. 3d 599, 613–14 (1981) (determining that no express trust exists under neutral principles of law to preclude local churches from keeping property except where reversion to *Diocese* is specifically mentioned); First Evangelical Methodist Church v. Clinton, 360 S.W.2d 584, 585 (Ga. 1987) (examining express provisions of conveyance instruments); Apostolic New Life Church of Elgin v. Bernardo Dominquez, et al., 686 N.E.2d 1187 (Ill. App. Ct. 1997) (holding that neutral principles analysis applies regardless of church polity); York v. First Presbyterian Church, 474 N.E.2d 716, 720–21 (Ill. App. Ct. 1984) (maintaining that general church had no right to local church property because amendment creating express trust to benefit general church was passed after property was conveyed to not-for-profit organization), cert. denied, 474 U.S. 865 (1985); Bjorkman v. Protestant Episcopal Church in the United States of the Diocese of Lexington, 759 S.W.2d 583, 586 (Ky. 1988) (concluding that no express or constructive trust exists in favor of general church because local church independently acquired and maintained property); Piletich v. Deretich, 328 N.W.2d 696, 700 (Minn. 1982) (characterizing action as matter of property ownership and membership qualification); Presbytery of Elijah Parish Lovejoy v. Jaeggi, 682 S.W.2d 465, 473 (Mo. 1984) (en banc) (holding that under application of neutral principles, property belongs to local church because no express or implied trust in favor of national church exists under Constitution and that national church failed to invoke dissolution procedures); Church of God Pentecostal, Inc. v. Freewill Pentecostal Church of God, Inc., 1998 Miss. LEXIS 269 (1998) (adopting neutral principles and finding no documents or intent by which local church's property would have been transferred to denomination); First Presbyterian Church v. United Presbyterian Church in the United States, 464 N.E.2d 454, 459–60 (N.Y. 1984) (holding that mere fact of local congregation's association with general denominational body does not create implied trust in favor of general church); Christensen v. Roumfort, 485 N.E.2d 270, 272 (Ohio Ct. App. 1984) (holding that local church is entitled to property under deed which contained no reversionary interest in favor of general church); St. Cyprian's Chapel, Inc. v. Fraternity of the Apostles of Jesus and Mary, No. 83-6030 (E.D. Pa. Sept. 16, 1985) (1985 Westlaw 2877, DCTU Database) (awarding property to general church when criteria for establishing constructive trust under neutral principles of law are satisfied), *aff'd*, 800 F.2d 1138 (3rd. Cir. 1986); Presbytery of Beaver-Butler of the United Presbyterian Church in the United States v. Middlesex Presbyterian Church, 489 A.2d 1317, 1324–25 (Pa. 1985) (holding that no trust language existed in favor of UPCUSA in denomination's documents); Presbytery of Donegal v. Calhoun, 513 A.2d 531, 537 (Pa. Commw. Ct. 1986) (construing local church charter calling for forfeiture of property to denomination as means to ensure local church obedience rather than creation of trust); Presbytery of Donegal v. Wheatley, 513 A.2d 538, 540 (Pa. Commw. Ct. 1986) (holding general church not beneficiary of trust stated in property deed); Mikilak v. Orthodox Church in Am., 513 A.2d 541, 545 (Pa. Commw. Ct. 1986) (stating that under neutral principles approach, hierarchical body failed to show congregation's intent to create trust in favor of hierarchy), *appeal denied*, 528 A.2d 958 (1987); Board of Bishops of the Church of the Living God v. Milner, 513

of the first two.[43] Typically the hybrid approaches express commitment to neutral principles but in fact continue to defer to the decisions of the hierarchy, at least to some extent.[44] In contrast to Hansen's more sympathetic view toward deferentialist approaches, this chapter supports the view that courts should apply truly neutral legal principles.

Discussions of relevant case law elsewhere underscore the complexity of the issues involved[45] and obviate the need to go into full detail here. For these reasons, this discus-

---

A.2d 1131, 1133 (Pa. Commw. Ct. 1986) (awarding property to local church because property was deeded to church as not-for-profit organization without any reference to national denomination); Foss v. Dykstra, 319 N.W.2d 499 (S.D. 1982), *aff'd on rehearing*, 342 N.W.2d 220, 220 (1983) (holding that neither local church's deed nor corporate charter nor national church's Book of Order created trust over local church's property in favor of national church). The Colorado Court of Appeals had adopted this approach in *Dickey v. Snodgrass*, but was overruled in *Bishop & Diocese of Colorado v. Mote*. Bishop & Diocese of Colorado v. Mote, 716 P.2d 85, 96 (Colo. 1986); Dickey v. Snodgrass, 673 P.2d 51, 52 (Colo. Ct. App. 1983). Other courts had adopted this approach prior to *Jones*.

43. *See, e.g.*, Bishop and Diocese of Colorado v. Mote, 668 P.2d 948, 952–53 (Colo. Ct. App. 1983) (adopting neutral principles in property dispute, then analyzing polity), *rev'd on other grounds*, 716 P.2d 85 (Colo. 1986); New York Annual Conference of the United Methodist Church v. Fisher, 438 A.2d 62, 68 (Conn. 1980) (holding that deference must be applied with neutral principles); Conference of African Union First Colored Methodist Protestant Church v. St. Thomas A.U.M.P. Church of Glasgow, 1997 Del. LEXIS 273 (1997) (affirming lower courts' adoption of neutral principles); Trustees of the Peninsula-Delaware Annual Conference of the United Methodist Church, Inc. v. East Lake Methodist Episcopal Church, Inc., 1998 Del. Ch. LEXIS 23 (1998) (adopting neutral principles but relying on implied trust doctrine); Hinkle Creek Friends Church v. Western Yearly Meeting of Friends Church, 469 N.E. 2d 40, 43 (Ind. Ct. App. 1984) (holding that neutral principles require examination of church documents and state laws for language setting up trust to benefit general church); Emberry Community Church v. Bloomington Dist. Missionary and Church Extension Soc'y, Inc., 482 N.E.2d 288, 293 (Ind. Ct. App. 1985) (stating that implied trust can be found under neutral principles if church is hierarchical); Fonken v. Community Church, 339 N.W.2d 810 (Iowa 1983) (using both neutral principles and deference approaches); Fluker Community Church v. Hitchens, 405 So. 2d 1223, 1225 (La. Ct. App. 1981) (finding property matters governed by neutral principles analysis because they do not involve issues of doctrine), *vacated and dismissed on other grounds*, 419 So. 2d 445 (La. 1982); Presbytery of Baltimore of the United Presbyterian Church v. Babcock Memorial Presbyterian Church, 449 A.2d 1190, 1192–93 (using neutral principles analysis to decide property ownership), *aff'd*, 464 A.2d 1008 (Md. 1983); Green v. Lewis, 272 S.E.2d 181, 184 (Va. 1980) (deciding property issue by examining neutral principles).

Some courts had adopted this hybrid approach during the decade between *Hull* and *Jones*. *See, e.g.*, Crumbley v. Solomon, 254 S.E.2d 330, 332–34 (Ga. 1979) (determining that general church rules dictate in favor of hierarchy); Carnes v. Smith, 222 S.E.2d 322, 327–28 (Ga. 1976) (applying implied trust in favor of hierarchy); United Methodist Church v. St. Louis Crossing Indep. Methodist Church, 276 N.E.2d 916, 923–25 (Ind. Ct. App. 1972) (finding numerous indications of trust in favor of general church); Calvary Presbyterian Church v. Presbytery of Baltimore of the United Presbyterian Church in the United States, 386 A.2d 357, 363–65 (Md. 1978) (implying trust based on Maryland statute and deed). Some decisions are not easily classified because they are indeterminate in their result or utilize alternative basis for their holding. *See* Aglikin v. Kovacheff, 516 N.E.2d 704, 709 (Ill. App. Ct. 1987) (remanding for determination of diocesan authority to dismiss local church's governing board and evaluation of local church agreement to subordinate to diocese), *appeal denied*, 522 N.E.2d 1240 (Ill. 1988); St. Cyprian's Chapel, Inc. v. Fraternity of the Apostles of Jesus and Mary, No. 83-6030 (E.D. Pa. Sept. 16, 1985) (1985 Westlaw 2877, DCTU Database) (holding that both express and constructive trusts in favor of general church are justified under neutral principles analysis).

44. *See, e.g., Hinkle Creek*, 469 N.E.2d at 44–45 (deferring to hierarchy's power to reduce local organization's status); *Hitchens*, 419 So. 2d at 448 (holding that church hierarchy's power overcame local church majority decision to retain property); *Babcock Memorial*, 449 A.2d at 1194–95 (finding that intent of local charter binds local church to general church decisions).

45. *See, e.g.*, H. Reese Hansen, "Religious Organizations and the Law of Trusts," in this volume (discussion of case law dealing with church property disputes at Supreme Court and state level); Gerstenblith, *supra* note 40, at 521–50 (same).

sion will focus on those aspects of the case law that lay the foundations or otherwise set the background for a neutralist approach.

The question of the proper methodology by which to resolve internal religious disputes has long been a source of judicial contention and reaches back into English legal history.[46] American jurisprudence on the subject traces its origins to *Watson v Jones*,[47] which the Supreme Court decided in 1871 in exercise of its diversity jurisdiction.[48] Because the First Amendment had not yet been applied to state governments and the case did not raise a federal question, the source of the substantive law upon which the Court relied was not entirely clear.[49] Nonetheless, this decision is often cited as having a "clear constitutional ring," and both federal and state courts followed its principles for nearly a century.[50]

Watson involved a dispute within a local church that belonged to the Presbyterian Church in the United States.[51] The dispute had split the congregation into pro-slavery and antislavery factions.[52] Although the latter faction represented a majority of the membership, the former had control of the "session," the local church's governing body.[53] The issue facing the Supreme Court could have been framed in two different ways: who were the properly elected members of the session, or which of the two factions represented the "true" church and therefore had the right to control its property?[54] The Court chose to adjudicate the latter issue, primarily in order to distinguish this case from an earlier proceeding involving the same dispute which the Kentucky state courts had resolved in favor of the pro-slavery faction.[55] In order to avoid a *res judicata* defense, the Supreme Court thus characterized the controversy as a property dispute.[56]

In its opinion, the Court established three important principles that have dominated all subsequent jurisprudence on the resolution of internal religious disputes.[57] The first principle confirmed that civil courts have the authority to settle internal church disputes and are required to do so.[58] Specifically, the Court stated that courts of equity had an obligation to ensure that property was not illegally diverted from its

---

46. For a more detailed discussion of the historical development of the jurisprudence on this subject and of these early decisions, see Ross, *supra* note 11, at 265–80; Adams & Hanlon, *supra* note 11, at 1297–1301; Ellman, *supra* note 8, at 1385–1400; Morgan, The Significance of Church Organizational Structure in Litigation and Government Action, 16 Val. U. L. Rev. 147, 148–51 (1981); Young & Tigges, *supra* note 9, at 476–82.

47. 80 U.S. (13 Wall.) 679 (1871).

48. Watson v. Jones, 80 U.S. (13 Wall.) 679 (1871).

49. *See* Adams & Hanlon, *supra* note 11, at 1293 n.10 (recognizing that *Watson* was decided prior to *Erie R. Co. v. Tompkins*, 304 U.S. 64 (1938), and that Religion Clauses had not yet been applied to states).

50. *See* Presbyterian Church in the United States v. Mary Elizabeth Blue Hull Memorial Presbyterian Church, 393 U.S. 440, 445–46 (1969) (citing to principles established in Watson nearly one hundred years earlier).

51. *Watson*, 80 U.S. (13 Wall.) at 681.

52. *Id.* at 690–91.

53. *Id.* at 693–94.

54. *Id.* at 717–18.

55. *Id.* at 721–22.

56. *Id.* at 714–22; 66 Ky. (3 Bush) 635 (1868); Avery v. Watson, 65 Ky. (2 Bush) 332 (1867).

57. Ellman, *supra* note 8, at 1386.

58. Watson v. Jones, 80 U.S. (13 Wall.) 679, 714–15 (1871).

rightful owner.[59] Furthermore, the Court noted that the doctrine applied equally to ecclesiastical disputes.[60]

The second principle that the Court established was the rejection of the "departure-from-doctrine" approach to the resolution of such disputes.[61] This approach had developed in English courts primarily in response to cases involving the Scottish Presbyterian and Free Churches, and it had been used by the Kentucky Court of Appeals in resolving the earlier *Watson* dispute.[62] The "departure-from-doctrine" approach held that when a church group split into factions, the court was required to award disputed property to the faction that remained most loyal to the religious precepts followed by the church at the time the property had been donated.[63] This approach was based on the theory that any gift of property was impressed with an implied trust that required the donee to use the property for the purposes which the donor originally intended.[64] The Court rejected this approach because it infringed upon the individual's right to free exercise of religion and seemed inappropriate in a nation that valued freedom of religious thought and belief.[65]

The third principle that the Court established in *Watson* became known as the "polity approach" to intrareligious dispute resolution.[66] This methodology was based on the internal structure, or polity, of the particular denomination to which the church involved in the dispute belonged.[67] The Court recognized two types of polities: congregational and hierarchical.[68] In a congregational church polity, each local church independently governs its own affairs.[69] The Court concluded that when a dispute occurs within a congregational church, property rights must be adjudicated in accordance with "... the ordinary principles which govern voluntary associations."[70] As a re-

---

59. *Id.* at 723.

60. *Id.* From the context, it is unclear whether the Court made this statement merely as an assertion of its authority to settle the dispute or whether it intended it as a principle that would settle the dispute itself. *See id.* at 714 (acknowledging rights of organizations as well as individual citizens to seek justice in judicial forum).

61. *Id.* at 729.

62. *Id.* at 728, 732.

63. *Id.* at 705.

64. *Id.*

65. *Id.* at 727–29. Application of this approach required the Court to examine carefully the doctrine and beliefs of the church and caused the Court to favor the previously accepted doctrines of the church over more recent doctrines. *See supra* note 63.

66. Casad, *infra* note 17, at 436.

67. *See id.* at 436–42 (discussing "polity approach" for resolving church property disputes).

68. Watson v. Jones, 80 U.S. (13 Wall.) 679, 722 (1871). The Supreme Court actually divided property disputes into three types: those involving each of the two structural forms discussed and those involving property which, under the express terms of a donor's deed or will, is devoted to the teaching and support of a specific religious doctrine. *Id.* For this third type of dispute the structural form and the decision of either a hierarchy or a majority of a congregational church are irrelevant, because the Court is required to enforce the express terms of such a trust. *Id.* at 723–24.

There is some disagreement as to how church polities should be classified. Hierarchical polities may be subdivided into an episcopal form, in which authority emanates from the top of the structure and descends, and a presbyterial form, in which authority originates at the bottom among the local churches and then is carried through successively higher levels of church bodies and tribunals. Adams & Hanlon, *supra* note 11, at 1292 & n.6. Some commentators have criticized the attempt to categorize church polities, preferring to view them as being on a continuum with sometimes subtle variations among different denominations. *Id.* Finally, some courts have also taken the position that a denomination may have one polity for some purposes and a different one for other purposes.

69. *Watson*, 80 U.S. (13 Wall.) at 722.

70. *Id.* at 725.

sult, the governing structure of the individual entity resolves any disputes, whether that depends on the majority rule of the membership or the decision of an elected board of officers.[71] In contrast, in the hierarchical church polity a general church organization with a system of superior tribunals controls the local church.[72] The Court decided that the highest church judicatory must resolve internal disputes, and that the civil court must defer to such church decisions when they involve questions of discipline, faith, custom, or belief.[73]

Nonetheless, the Court, in finally resolving the *Watson* dispute, did not have to rely upon this typology.[74] The highest church tribunal and a majority of the congregational members both supported the antislavery position.[75] The civil courts, therefore, were required to enforce this coalition.[76]

The *Watson* case thus set the framework within which subsequent church property dispute cases would unfold. First, it recognized the legitimacy of civil court involvment in the resolution of such disputes. At the same time, by criticizing the "departure from doctrine" approach, it signaled the importance for courts to maintain neutrality. Finally, it drew attention to the significance of ecclesiastical polity. To some extent the second and third of these principles are in tension, because the second appears to call for an approach that is neutral toward religious differences, while the third acknowledges the importance of taking these very differences into account. The question of the proper methodological approach to church property disputes turns on how this tension should be resolved. The contention of this chapter is that greater weight should be given to assuring a neutral judicial posture, by applying a strict version of the neutral principles approach. This avoids the need to second-guess religious communities on matters of their religious beliefs, avoids the apparent privileging of hierarchical churches that would be implicit in a "compulsory deference" approach, and affords equal treatment both among differing religious communities and between religious and other types of nonprofit organizations. Moreover, the strict neutral principles approach is consistent

---

71. *Id.*

72. *Id.* at 722.

73. *Id.* at 726–29. In support of this deference approach, the Court referred to such factors as the superior expertise of the ecclesiastical tribunals in the interpretation of church documents and teachings and in the examination of church doctrine, customs, and laws. *Id.* at 728–29. Furthermore, the Court felt that it would be a violation of freedom of religion for a civil court to become involved in such an inquiry. *Id.* Finally, the Court stated that freedom of religion required that the individual be allowed to submit to a hierarchical church with an established system of tribunals and, in so doing, impliedly consent to be bound by the decisions of such tribunals. *Id.* If a secular court were permitted to reverse the decisions of a church tribunal, the state would subvert the hierarchy and thus undermine the individual's ability to worship freely within such a church structure. *Id.*

74. *Id.* at 734–35.

75. *Id.* The Court found that because the dissident faction was no longer part of the church organization, it had no right to the disputed property. *Id.*

76. *Id.* A dispute involving a similar fact pattern was resolved by the Supreme Court a few years later. In *Bouldin v. Alexander*, 82 U.S. (15 Wall.) 131 (1872), a small minority of a Baptist congregation belonging to the general Baptist Church of the United States, which was considered to have a congregational rather than hierarchical polity, attempted to exclude the majority from the church building. *Id.* at 135. The Court framed the issue as being based on the legal ownership of the church property, not on the identity of the proper church officers. *Id.* at 137. Nevertheless, the Court decided the case on the basis of the irregularity of the meeting at which the former trustees were retired and the new trustees elected. *Id.* at 140. The Court also noted that the Philadelphia Baptist Association had heard the dispute and decided that the original trustees had been improperly removed. *Id.* at 136. Thus, as in *Watson*, the Court avoided having to choose between the decision of an ecclesiastical tribunal and that of a majority of the local church membership. *Id.* at 137.

with achieving an appropriate reconciliation of the competing demands of the Establishment and Free Exercise clauses.

Neutral Principles of Law

Courts attempt to derive the neutral legal principles relevant to the resolution of disputes among religious groups from several areas of law, the most significant of which is trust and property law.[77] In addition, courts may rely on contract law when examining a contractual basis for the relationship between the local entity and the national religious organization.[78] Finally, courts may examine corporate law as established in the not-for-profit corporate statutes and particular state religious or denominational corporate statutes.[79] These relevant bodies of law are described in greater detail elsewhere in this volume.[80] In this chapter, the aim is not so much to describe these legal domains as to show how they can and should be used to provide a neutral vantage point for resolving church property disputes.

Trust and property law

Formal title

Each of the three major approaches to resolving church property disputes appears to start with a two-step analysis similar to that employed by the Supreme Court in *Jones v. Wolf*.[81] The first step involves determination of the title to the property. Specifically, a court must determine where the title to the disputed property is vested, whether the original conveyance created any restrictions, conditions, or trusts, and, in the case of a trust, who is the beneficiary. The second step is a determination of who controls the local church if the court finds that title to the property is vested in it.[82] This, of course, is relevant only if the court determines that the local entity possesses title in fee simple absolute. Some courts, however, do not bother to determine the state of the title if they conclude that the national denomination controls the local entity.[83] Indeed, in deferentialist jurisdictions, the court first determines whether the polity of the denomination

---

77. *See infra* notes 91–176 and accompanying text (analyzing cases and techniques for employing uniform principles of trust and property law to resolve such disputes).

78. *See infra* notes 177–198 and accompanying text (discussing use of contractual basis for resolving internal religious property disputes).

79. *See infra* notes 177–198 and accompanying text (noting effects of state corporate law on resolving such property issues).

80. *See, e.g.*, H. Reese Hansen, "Religious Organizations and the Law of Trusts," and Patty Gerstenblith, "Associational Structures of Religious Organizations," in this volume.

81. Jones v. Wolf, 443 U.S. 595, 606–610 (1979).

82. *Id.* at 606–10.

83. *See* Crumbley v. Solomon, 254 S.E.2d 330, 333 (Ga. 1979) (per curiam) (relying on church hierarchy's disciplinary rule to find in favor of general church); United Methodist Church v. St. Louis Crossing Indep. Methodist Church, 276 N.E.2d 916, 925 (Ind. Ct. App. 1971) (holding trial court's determination that local church was independent erroneous and awarding property to general church).

involved is hierarchical[84] and sometimes accepts it as a matter of law.[85] As in the *Serbian Eastern Orthodox* case,[86] the court focuses primarily on the issue of control of the title-holder rather than on legal ownership of the disputed property.[87] Courts identify the local entity or the "true" church to whom the property was originally granted in order to decide the question of control of the titleholder.[88] To determine identity, they defer to the hierarchy's recognition of the proper leadership of the local church, reasoning that such decisions involve questions of doctrine, faith, custom, or governance.[89] After *Watson* discouraged and *Hull* later prohibited application of the departure-from-doctrine theory, courts felt compelled to defer to the religious hierarchy's determination of which competing faction represented the "true" church.[90]

---

84. *See, e.g.,* Bennison v. Sharp, 329 N.W.2d 466, 472 (Mich. Ct. App. 1982) (establishing hierarchical structure of church as prerequisite to ruling on property law issue); Organization for Preserving the Constitution of Zion Lutheran Church v. Mason, 743 P.2d 848, 851 (Wash. Ct. App. 1987) (requiring determination of hierarchical church structure as matter of law as basis to evaluate lower court holding); Church of God v. Noel, 318 S.E. 2d 920, 923 (W. Va. 1984) (relying on documents to determine structure of church as requisite to deciding issue). Some decisions from states relying on the compulsory deference approach resulted in a remand for a factual determination of polity because this was viewed as dispositive of the result. *See, e.g.,* African Methodist Episcopal Zion Church v. Union Chapel African Methodist Episcopal Zion Church, 308 S.E.2d 73, 87 (N.C. Ct. App. 1983) (holding hierarchical relationship to be dispositive of result); Southside Tabernacle v. Pentecostal Church of God, Pacific Northwest District, Inc., 650 P.2d 231, 237 (Wash. Ct. App. 1982) (directing court to determine extent to which local church is subject to higher central authority); Organization for Preserving the Constitution of Zion Lutheran Church of Auburn v. Mason, 743 P.2d 848, 852 (Wash. Ct. App. 1987) (directing determination of hierarchical structure in lieu of applying neutral principles doctrine).

85. *See* Protestant Episcopal Church v. Graves, 391 A.2d 563, 575 (applying *Sharpsburg* analysis to determine that hierarchical structure constitutes a matter of law) (N.J. Super. Ct. Ch. Div. 1978), *aff'd*, 401 A.2d 548 (N.J. Super. Ct. App. Div. 1979) (per curiam), *aff'd*, 417 A.2d 19 (N.J. 1980).

86. 426 U.S. 696, 697–710 (1976).

87. *See, e.g., Bennison*, 329 N.W.2d at 472–74 (discussing hierarchical structure of church and distinguishing neutral principles approach focus on property law); *Mason*, 743 P.2d at 851 (distinguishing between property law focus of neutral principles and determination of hierarchical control in deference approach); *Noel*, 318 S.E.2d at 922–23 (holding that decisive issue in case is structure of church, not validity or provisions of deeds).

88. *See, e.g., Bennison*, 329 N.W.2d 474–75 (discussing control over local entity by hierarchy as determining entity that keeps property); *Mason*, 743 P.2d at 851 (holding that control over local church decides its identity and, hence, property issue); *Noel*, 318 S.E.2d at 924 (stating that control of local entity determines property issue).

89. Parish of the Advent v. The Protestant Episcopal Diocese of Massachusetts, 688 N.E.2d 923 (Mass. 1997) (characterizing dispute as to which individuals were members of a parish as being religious in nature so that court should defer to hierarchy's determination); Townsend v. Teagle, 467 So. 2d 772, 775 (Fla. Dist. Ct. App. 1985); Mills v. Baldwin, 362 So. 2d 2, 6–7 (Fla. 1978), *vacated and remanded*, 443 U.S. 914 (1979), *reinstated*, 377 So. 2d 971 (Fla. 1979); *Bennison*, 329 N.W.2d at 473, 475 (relying also on notion that use of deference comes closest to reflecting relationship between parties); Tea v. Protestant Episcopal Church in Diocese of Nevada, 610 P.2d 182, 184 (Nev. 1980); Protestant Episcopal Church in the Diocese of New Jersey v. Graves, 417 A.2d 19, 24 (N.J. 1980); Diocese of Newark v. Burns, 417 A.2d 31, 34 (N.J. 1980); Schismatic & Purported Casa Linda Presbyterian Church v. Grace Union Presbytery, Inc., 710 S.W. 2d 700, 706–07 (Tex. Ct. App. 1986); Church of God v. Noel, 318 S.E. 2d 920, 923–24 (W. Va. 1984).

90. In *Presbyterian Church in the United States v. Mary Elizabeth Blue Hull Memorial Presbyterian Church*, 393 U.S. 440 (1960), the Court rejected, as a matter of constitutional mandate, the departure-from-doctrine element of the implied trust theory that had been considered in *Watson*. The Court reaffirmed civil court jurisdiction over church property disputes and appeared to urge lower courts to settle such disputes by reference to traditional civil law principles without examining religious doctrine or resolving ecclesiastical conflicts. On remand, the Georgia Supreme Court held that it could not apply the implied trust theory without the departure-from-doctrine element and

The inquiry into the vesting of title to the disputed property must begin with the formal title doctrine. Under this doctrine, title is vested in the entity named as grantee in the deed to the disputed property. The deed, however, may contain other provisions calling for divestiture of the property title under certain circumstances. For example, a possibility of reverter or a right-of-entry clause could accomplish such a result. In this case, the property returns to the grantor upon the occurrence of a particular event or the breach of a particular condition.[91] The use of an executory interest would permit the property, upon breach of the condition, to vest in a third party such as the national organization or its representative. This result could be achieved through the creation of an express trust, providing that the local entity is the trustee of the property which is to be used exclusively for the benefit of the general denominational church. In such a case, if the local entity withdraws from the denomination, then title to the property vests in the beneficiary in accordance with the terms of the express trust.[92] Examination of a deed to determine the designated grantee and the presence of an express condition or express trust involves application of accepted principles of property and trust law.

The analysis becomes considerably more complex when the property deeds do not include any express trust provisions or conditions. Courts under these circumstances have engaged in considerable analysis to determine whether some other form of trust is present that would justify the court's divestment of the named titleholder and vesting of the property in the national church organization.[93] This analysis justifies examination of the various facets of trust law to determine whether these courts are applying truly neutral principles or are in fact engaging in deference under the guise of a neutral principles analysis.[94] Trusts come in several varieties: express trusts, either private or charitable, and implied trusts, either resulting or constructive.[95] Each type must be examined separately to determine how neutral principles doctrine applies in these different contexts.

---

therefore vested title in the local churches. *See* Presbyterian Church in the United States v. Eastern Heights Presbyterian Church, 167 S.E. 2d 658 (Ga. 1969).

91. Under the "formal title" doctrine, civil courts can determine ownership by studying deeds, reverter clauses, and general state corporation laws. Maryland and Virginia Eldership of the Churches of God v. Church of God at Sharpsburg, Inc., 396 U.S. 367, 370 (1970) (Brennan, J., concurring). General principles of property law may not be relied upon if their application requires civil courts to resolve doctrinal issues. *Id.* at 368. For example, Justice Brennan supported limiting the enforceability of a condition or restriction when such provisions depend on a determination of departure-from-doctrine. *Id.* at 370. Justice Harlan, however, explicitly stated that if a deed or will is expressly conditioned on a religious organization's use of the property, and if the condition is not satisfied, then the gift should lapse and the property should be returned to the donor. Presbyterian Church in the United States v. Mary Elizabeth Blue Hull Memorial Presbyterian Church. 393 U.S. 440, 452 (1969) (Harlan, J., concurring).

92. *See generally* G. Bogert, Trusts § 149 (6th ed. 1987) (stating that upon termination of trust, trustee will have large part in distribution of trust property); Bjorkman v. Protestant Episcopal Church in the United States, 759 S.W.2d 583, 586 (Ky. 1988) (stating that without reversionary clause, deed could not be interpreted as creating express trust).

93. *See* Bishop and Diocese of Colorado v. Mote, 716 P.2d 85, 103–04 (Colo. 1986) (discussing various types of trusts including express, implied, resulting, constructive, and express implied-in-fact trusts).

94. Because courts apparently do not engage in the creation of implied restrictions or conditions that result in forfeiture of the property to the national organization, it is not necessary to explore this area of property law in greater detail.

95. *See* 4 R. Powell, The Law of Real Property ¶ 500 (Rohan ed. 1989) (providing general discussion of several types of trusts). In the context of these religious disputes, the type of trust at issue is that of a charitable trust. *See* P. Haskell, Preface to Wills, Trusts and Administration 236 (1987) (defining charitable trust as one whose purpose may include advancement of religion). Regardless

Express trusts

An express trust is defined as a fiduciary relationship with respect to property "which arises as a result of a manifestation of an intention to create it" and which subjects the legal titleholder to equitable duties to deal with the property for the benefit of another person.[96] A trust requires three elements: the trustee, who holds legal title; the beneficiary, who holds equitable title; and the trust property, which must be specific and identifiable.[97] In addition, the settlor is the individual who creates the trust and may also be the trustee or the beneficiary.[98] The distinguishing element of an express trust is the requirement of manifestation or external expression of intent, in a judicially recognizable form, to create a trust relationship by written words or conduct.[99] Each of the foregoing features of express trusts is routinely analyzed by courts in secular contexts, and neutral principles methodology assumes that the same type of analysis can be used in resolving internal church disputes.

Courts often fail to distinguish between property donated by an individual, who is then the settlor of the trust, and property purchased by a local church with funds raised exclusively from within its membership.[100] Property donated by an individual to a religious organization is generally held by the latter as a charitable trust, and the donor may impose various restrictions on use of the property, designate the beneficiaries, and provide for the trust's termination.[101] In the case of donated property, the court must

---

of whether the trust is private or charitable, the same criteria are applicable in determining the existence of a trust and the identities of the trustees and beneficiaries. *Id.* at 237. In *Agudas Chasidei Chabad of United States v. Gourary*, 650 F. Supp. 1463 (E.D.N.Y.), *aff'd*, 833 F.2d 431 (2d Cir. 1987), the court described the requirements for creation of a charitable trust as follows:

> To create a charitable trust, the settlor must (1) describe with definiteness a charitable purpose, (2) name the group of beneficiaries, either definite or indefinite, and (3) either deliver the trust property to the trustee with an intent expressed clearly and unequivocally by words or actions to create a trust or declare through clear and unequivocal words or acts that he holds the property in trust.

Id. at 1474.

96. Restatement (Second) of Trusts § 2 (1959). The purpose of the inquiry into the settlor's intent is to insure that the settlor clearly demonstrated an intent to impose upon a trustee "equitable duties to deal with the property for the benefit of another person." 1 Austin Wakemann Scott, The Law of Trusts § 24, at 250 (4th ed. 1987). Furthermore, the duties imposed on the trustee must be sufficiently ascertainable that a court of equity could enforce them. Gurley v. Lindsley, 459 F.2d 268, 276 (5th Cir. 1972).

97. *Mitchell*, 463 U.S. at 225.

98. *See* Restatement (Second) of Trusts §§ 2 comment h, 3 (1959) (detailing elements of effective trust). For judicial statements of the requirements of a trust, see Gurley v. Lindsley, 459 F.2d 268, 276 (5th Cir. 1972) and Yardley v. Yardley, 484 N.E.2d 873, 882 (Ill. App. Ct. 1985).

99. Restatement (Second) of Trusts § 4 (1959); *See id.,* § I comment (asserting that no trust is established unless settlor indicates intention to do so). The intent must be to create a trust in the present and not at some future time. *Id.* § 26; 1 Scott on Trusts, *supra* note 96, § 26.

100. If a local church receives financial assistance in purchasing its property from other churches within the denomination or directly from the parent organization, then the court would be justified in imposing a resulting trust on the property for the benefit of the denomination. *See infra* notes 104–5 and accompanying text (discussing concept and definition of resulting trust). Courts have consistently refused to impose a resulting trust on property paid for by the local church but held in the name of a regional or national body of the denomination. *See* Reorganized Church of Jesus Christ of Latter-day Saints v. Thomas, 758 S.W. 2d 726, 733 (Mo. Ct. App. 1988) (holding that monetary gifts to local church to purchase property did not establish resulting trust).

101. Trustees owe a duty of loyalty to carry out the terms imposed by the donor of a charitable trust. *See* St. Joseph's Hosp. v. Bennett, 22 N.E.2d 305, 311 (N.Y. 1939) (providing that funds donated to hospital for endowment and maintenance purposes could not be used for mortgage payments). Because the public is considered to be the beneficiary of a charitable trust, standing to en-

determine the intended beneficiaries if the settlor has failed to do so clearly.[102] If the titleholder simply purchased the property, however, then there is no reason to presume that the form of property ownership is that of a trust, unless the titleholder is not empowered by state law to hold real property. Accordingly, if the donor fails to express a restriction or if the local church simply purchases property and takes title in its own name, then there is no expression, either complete or incomplete, of intent as required under trust law from which to imply the existence of a trust.[103] Failure to recognize this distinction can result in the imposition of a trust for the benefit of a central church even though the property in question was in fact purchased by the local congregation. Courts applying the neutral principles approach should be careful not to presume the presence of a trust relationship where none in fact exists.

Implied trusts

An express trust must be distinguished from both types of implied trusts. The first type of implied trust, the resulting trust, arises when circumstances indicate that the settlor did not intend the titleholder to take the entire interest in the property.[104] Generally, only three circumstances may lead to the creation of a resulting trust: when an express trust fails entirely, when an express trust fails to dispose of the entire trust *res*, and when the purchaser of property directs the seller to put title in the name of another individual.[105] Unlike a resulting or express trust, a constructive trust arises contrary to the

---

force the terms of a charitable trust is restricted to the state attorney general under both common law and state statute even though it is the grantor's heirs or devisees who benefit from a failure of the trust. *See* People *ex rel* Scott v. George F. Harding Museum, 374 N.E.2d 756, 760 (Ill. App. Ct. 1978) (relying on statutory basis for attorney general's standing to enforce trust terms); Estate of Prumer, 136 A.2d 107, 109 (Pa. 1957) (setting forth common law limitation on standing).

If the terms of the trust can no longer be executed, the trustees must request a court to apply the doctrine of cy pres or "equitable approximation" to modify the purposes for which the trust property can be used. G. Bogert, Handbook of the Law of Trusts § 147, at 523 (1973). Before a court applies cy pres, it must determine whether there has been a change in circumstances, that the donor failed to anticipate and which threatens to defeat the trust's purpose. *Id.* at 524. The court must also determine whether the donor had a general charitable intent and how best to achieve the donor's intended purpose. *Id.* at 527; *See* Davison v. Duke Univ., 194 S.E.2d 761, 777 (N.C. 1973) (permitting changes in investment policies of Duke Endowment in response to changes in tax code). If, however, the court finds that the donor lacked a general charitable intent, then the trust will fail and the trust property will either pass to an alternative beneficiary named in the original trust instrument or else revert to the original donor's estate. *See* Evans v. Abney, 396 U.S. 435, 447 (1970) (causing trust of park land to fail when city decided to integrate park, contrary to donor's express intent that park remain segregated).

In considering charitable trust doctrine, the California appellate court in Protestant Episcopal Church in the Diocese of Los Angeles v. Barker, 115 Cal. App. 3d 599 (1981), did not consider a change in affiliation comparable to the types of changes desired in other charitable trust cases, such as a change from not-for-profit to for-profit or proprietary status. *Id.* at 619.

102. *See* P. Haskell, Preface to the Law of Trusts ch. 9 § 1, 142 (1975) (stating that court of equity determines when trust assets should be applied).

103. *See* Restatement (Second) of Trusts § 23 (1959) (requiring manifestation of settlor's intent to create trust).

104. V.A. Scott, *supra* note 96, § 404, Restatement (Second) of Trusts § 1 comment e (1959).

105. Restatement (Second) of Trusts ch. 12 at 323 (1959). The third type of resulting trust, termed a "purchase money resulting trust," is relevant to church property disputes where, for example, a local entity provides the purchase price but title is taken in the name of a regional or statewide representative of the national religious organization. *See* P. Haskell, Preface to the Law of Trusts 143 (1975); Reorganized Church of Jesus Christ of Latter-day Saints v. Thomas, 758 S.W.2d 726, 733 (Mo. Ct. App. 1988) (rejecting argument of purchase money resulting trust and stressing

intent of the settlor.[106] Courts impose constructive trusts in exercise of their equity jurisdiction as a remedy for unjust enrichment.[107]

Courts that consider the imposition of an implied trust in the context of church property disputes agree that neither the resulting trust nor the constructive trust is an appropriate remedy.[108] Nevertheless, in the absence of written language creating an express trust, these courts have used the term "implied trust" without attempting to define it.[109] Only one court has attempted to devise a term for a trust that neither fits into one of the categories of implied trusts nor contains specific language in its documents creating an express trust. In *Bishop & Diocese of Colorado v. Mote*,[110] the Colorado

---

extraordinary burden of proof necessary to establish such trust); *see also* Fonken v. Community Church of Kamrar, 339 N.W.2d 810, 825 (Iowa 1983) (Schultz, J., dissenting) (describing creation of resulting trust under state law). *See generally* Price v. State, 398 N.E.2d 365, 370 n.2 (Ill. App. Ct. 1979) (offering background material on basis for resulting trusts); Williams v. Teachers Insur. & Annuity Assoc., 304 N.E.2d 656, 660 (Ill. App. Ct. 1973) (refusing to impose resulting trust on insurance policy proceeds); Zelickman v. Bell Fed. Sav. & Loan Assoc., 301 N.E.2d 47, 53 (Ill. App. Ct. 1973) (providing general definition of resulting trusts).

106. *See* Restatement (Second) of Trusts § 1, comment e (1959) (noting that constructive trusts do not effectuate intent but redress wrongdoing).

107. 5 Scott on Trusts, *supra* note 96, § 404.2. The imposition of a constructive trust is employed as a remedy where transfer of property was made under fraud, duress, undue influence, mistake, or breach of a fiduciary duty. *Id.* In *Bjorkman v. Protestant Episcopal Church in the United States*, 759 S.W.2d 583 (Ky. 1988), the court described constructive trusts as an equitable remedy imposed to redress wrongful conduct by a titleholder who has deprived another party of beneficial ownership. *Id.* at 587. In *St. Cyprian's Chapel, Inc. v. Fraternity of the Apostles of Jesus and Mary*, No. 83-6030 (E.D. Pa. Sept. 16, 1985) (1985 Westlaw 2877, DCTU Database), the court imposed a constructive trust on local church property because the directors of the local church had misrepresented the legal status of the local church to the representatives of the general Church when they promised to change the composition of the board of directors. *Id.* at 18–21. The directors of the local church had abused their confidential relationship, and a constructive trust was imposed to avoid their unjust enrichment. *Id.*

108. *See* Bishop & Diocese of Colorado v. Mote, 716 P.2d 85, 103–04 n.14 (Colo. 1986) (discussing concept of implied trusts). Some courts, however, have recognized that constructive or resulting trusts would apply in certain situations. Reorganized Church of Jesus Christ of Latter-day Saints v. Thomas, 758 S.W.2d 726, 732–33 (Mo. Ct. App. 1988) (noting that resulting trust may be imposed where different party furnishes consideration for purchase); St. Cyprian's Chapel, No. 83-6030, at 18–21 (E.D. Pa. Sept. 16, 1985) (1985 Westlaw 2877, DCTU Database) (applying constructive trust where party engaged in fraud or misrepresentation and benefited from unjust enrichment).

109. Fonken v. Community Church of Kamrar, 339 N.W.2d 810, 818–19 (Iowa 1983). In First Presbyterian Church v. United Presbyterian Church in the United States, 464 N.E.2d 454 (N.Y. 1984), the court distinguished three types of implied trusts: (1) an implied trust for the benefit of the members of the congregation; (2) an implied trust for congregation members who adhere to the original tenets of the religion, which is similar to the impermissible departure-from-doctrine theory; and (3) an implied trust for the denominational church, which the court rejected because of insufficient evidence of intent. *Id.* at 462.

110. 716 P.2d 85 (Colo. 1986). Other courts have rejected the notion that an implied trust would be imposed when there was insufficient evidence to conclude that an express trust had been created. *See* Bjorkman v. Protestant Episcopal Church in the United States, 759 S.W.2d 583, 587 (Ky. 1988); Reorganized Church of Jesus Christ of Latter-day Saints v. Thomas, 758 S.W.2d 726, 732–33 (Mo. Ct. App. 1988) (limiting constructive trusts to situations of fraud or unjust enrichment and holding that record did not show evidence meeting this standard). In one decision, the California appellate court used the terms "express trust" and "implied-in-fact trust" interchangeably. *See* Presbytery of Riverside v. Community Church, 89 Cal. App. 3d 910, 929 (1979) (finding no trust "express" or "implied-in-fact"). In another decision, the court used the term "implied trust" to indicate the "departure-from-doctrine" theory and used the term "express trust" to indicate a trust whose existence is predicated on statements in state statutes and documents such as the constitution of the national

Supreme Court used the term "implied express trust" to describe an express trust that was not created by actual language but instead was implied by the conduct of the parties and by the circumstances surrounding donation of the gift.[111]

This use of the "implied trust" terminology may derive historically from the time when particular denominations—and in some jurisdictions, all religious organizations—were prohibited from incorporating and owning real property in their own right.[112] A conveyance to an individual, often the minister or priest, was sometimes construed to be a holding of that individual by virtue of his official status in an early form of the corporation sole.[113] At other times, such an arrangement was construed to constitute a trust with the religious leader holding the property for the benefit of the church or entire denomination.[114] This implied trust device was used in jurisdictions where incorporation was either prohibited or attainable only through special legislative grant.[115] The need for this device, however, has been eliminated because virtually every state now freely permits the incorporation of religious institutions as not-for-profit corporations, religious corporations, or corporations sole.[116]

Implied trust theory and its problematic connection to departure-from-doctrine theory

The problem for application of neutral principles posed by such implied trusts becomes clear when one realizes the latter's connection with departure-from-doctrine theory. Along with the development of the implied trust theory to permit churches to own

---

organization. *See* Protestant Episcopal Church in the Diocese of Los Angeles v. Barker, 115 Cal. App. 3d 599, 606 (describing implied trust theory as local church holding local church property for benefit of general church, and express trust theory as relying on statutes, title deeds, and articles to establish local church property ownership).

111. Bishop & Diocese of Colorado v. Mote, 716 P.2d 85, 103–04 n.14 (Colo. 1986); *cf.* 89 C.J.S. Trusts § 12 (1955) (defining "implied express trust" as express trust derived from construction of language used by settlor). According to C.J.S., an express trust can arise from the intention, express or implied, to create a trust. *Id.* § 11. In addition, a minority of writers and judges use the term "implied trust" in situations where the settlor intended to create a trust but did not clearly and unambiguously manifest this intent. G. Bogert & G. Bogert, The Law of Trusts and Trustees § 451, at 611–12 (1979). For lack of a better term, and to avoid confusion with the constructive and resulting trusts, this type of trust may be referred to as an "implied express trust" or as an "express trust implied in fact." *Mote*, 716 P.2d at 103–04 n.14; Sears v. First Fed. Sav. and Loan Assoc., 275 N.E.2d 300, 303 (Ill. App. Ct. 1971) (preferring use of term "express trust" to designate trust that arises from construction of language in document).

112. Kauper & Ellis, Religious Corporations and the Law, 71 Mich. L. Rev. 1499, 1505 (1973).

113. *Id.* at 1501, 1506.

114. *Id.* at 1501–02, 1511. Some jurisdictions replaced the trustee form of ownership of real property with the membership corporation form in which the members of the congregation could directly control the affairs of the incorporated congregation. *Id.* at 1511–13. This led the New York Court of Appeals to eliminate the implied trust doctrine entirely as applied to incorporated congregations and local churches. *See* Robertson v. Bullions, 11 N.Y. 243, 263–64 (1854) (holding that religious corporations could not make use of implied trust); Petty v. Tooker, 21 N.Y. 267, 275 n.3 (1860) (refusing to bind corporate property in trust). The legislature, however, subsequently overruled the court when it statutorily reinserted the implied trust doctrine. Kauper & Ellis, *supra* note 112, at 1513–14.

115. *See* Kauper & Ellis, *supra* note 112, at 1505–11 (describing emergence of trust principles to deal with legislative unwillingness to allow religions to incorporate).

116. *Id.* at 1527. Only two states, Virginia and West Virginia, statutorily or constitutionally prohibit the incorporation of religious institutions. *Id.* at 1529. Both states, however, expressly grant to religious associations a statutory ability to hold and deal with real property. *Id.* at 1529–33.

real property, courts in both England and the United States during the nineteenth century developed the departure-from-doctrine requirement to help guide decisions about who should benefit from a particular implied trust.[117] Under this theory, courts considered a denomination to be the beneficiary of a trust of property held by a religious institution only so long as the denomination did not depart in any fundamental manner from the doctrine of the church in existence at the time the gift was made.[118] This theory was based on the presumption that the donor of the property intended to impress such a restriction on the gift.[119] In case of a schism, the court awarded church property to the group which it determined had remained most faithful to the religion's original tenets.[120] The Supreme Court, however, disapproved the departure-from-doctrine element in *Watson v. Jones* and held it to be unconstitutional in *Hull*.[121]

Following the U.S. Supreme Court's decision in *Hull*, the Georgia Supreme Court held on remand that it could not employ the implied trust theory without the departure-from-doctrine element and thus adopted the neutral principles analysis.[122] Nevertheless, other courts have continued to apply the implied trust doctrine as an element of the polity-compulsory deference approach.[123] Without the requirement of loyalty to the original religious doctrine, however, the hierarchy remains the beneficiary of the implied trust, regardless of any doctrinal changes, and the faction loyal to the hierarchy retains control of the local entity and its property.[124] These courts often rely on the theory that the local entity has impliedly consented to the rules and regulations of the national organization and that these precepts create a trust for the benefit of the general church.[125] In short, implied trust doctrine continues to be applied even though departure-from-doctrine theory has been abrogated.

The use of an implied trust, however, only makes sense in combination with the departure-from-doctrine theory. In other words, the court is only justified in implying a trust on the assumption that the property donor intended that the purposes for which the property is used remain immutable. Given that the departure-from-doctrine ele-

---

117. *Id.* at 1511–12.

118. *Id.* at 1511; Watson v. Jones, 80 U.S. (13 Wall.) 679, 705, 727–29, 732. *See supra* notes 61–65 and accompanying text (describing Supreme Court rejection of departure-from-doctrine approach).

119. *See supra* note 62 and accompanying text. Watson v. Jones, 80 U.S. (13 Wall.) 679, 728, 732 (1871) (explaining basis of departure-from-doctrine approach to resolving church property disputes).

120. *See supra* note 61 and accompanying text. *Id.* at 729.

121. Presbyterian Church in the United States v. Mary Elizabeth Blue Hull Memorial Presbyterian Church, 393 U.S. 440, 450–52 (1969); Watson v. Jones, 80 U.S. (13 Wall.) 679, 732–35 (1871).

122. *See* Presbyterian Church in the United States v. Eastern Heights Presbyterian Church, 167 S.E.2d 658 (Ga. 1969) (recognizing that once "departure-from-doctrine" element is abandoned, entire implied trust theory cannot be applied to impose trust on local church property for benefit of general church).

123. *See* Calvary Presbyterian Church v. Presbytery of Lake Huron of the United Presbyterian Church in the United States, 384 N.W.2d 92, 95–96 (Mich. Ct. App. 1986) (holding that denomination's permission for church to sell house did not estop denomination to assert implied trust on present real estate); Protestant Episcopal Church in the Diocese of New Jersey v. Graves, 391 A.2d 563, 577 (N.J. Super Ct. Ch. Div. 1978) (holding local church to be part of hierarchical organization and that its property is held in implied trust for general church).

124. *See Graves*, 391 A.2d at 576–77 (holding that plaintiffs could withdraw from diocese, but property had to remain under diocesan control).

125. *See Calvary Presbyterian Church*, 384 N.W.2d at 95–96 (1986) (observing that decision to be bound by authority of hierarchy must have taken into account that members of local church may at times disagree with hierarchy).

ment is inapplicable because of its unconstitutionality, the courts must also refrain from indulging in other presumptions concerning the donor's intent.[126] There is no reason to assume that a donor wished to devote the property in perpetuity to the purposes of the hierarchy rather than to the purposes of the individual church, because both the hierarchy and the individual church are free to change their interpretations and practice of religious doctrine.[127] A court, therefore, must rely exclusively on the express intent of the donor in naming the grantee in a deed and in specifying any restrictions to be placed on the future use of the property. The use of presumptions to favor the hierarchy over the local church or to favor one faction in a schism over another is nothing less than the establishment of one religious group at the expense of another's free exercise rights.[128]

Implied trusts and residual presumptions

More significantly, those courts that apply the "hybrid" approach to resolve church property disputes, although claiming to adopt neutral principles, actually use the implied trust theory.[129] While employing the language of neutral principles and examining church documents and state statutes, these courts are nonetheless applying a concept that is entirely unique to church-related cases.[130] This usage does not accord with legal principles from any other recognized branch of the law.[131] Instead, the courts base their opinions on presumptions of implied intent and implied consent without any inquiry into the actual intent of the presumed settlor.[132] As indicated earlier, this doctrine of implied trust does not fit within the definitions found in other areas of trust law.[133] Courts

---

126. *See* Protestant Episcopal Church in the Diocese of Los Angeles v. Barker, 115 Cal. App. 3d 599, 618 (noting that it is as difficult and unconstitutional to attempt to identify "true" church to which property has been dedicated as it is to identify "true" doctrine to which property is to be dedicated). In *Barker*, the court stated that application of the implied trust doctrine

> would lead us back to the thicket of ecclesiastical controversy, for a court would be required to deduce and infer the nature of the general church and its implied authority over the property of its affiliated congregations... [This theory] forces the court to determine the true implied beneficiaries of the church entities involved. If the civil courts cannot properly determine which competing group is the bearer of the true faith, they cannot determine for whose benefit title to church property is impliedly held in trust.

Id. Other courts that recognize that the property is held in the form of a charitable trust have grappled with the question of whether the trust is for the benefit of the local church or for the denomination in general. *See* Crumbley v. Solomon, 254 S.E.2d 330, 333 (Ga. 1979) (finding that intent of grantor was uncertain and therefore unenforceable).

127. *See* Presbytery of Riverside v. Community Church, 89 Cal. App. 3d 910, 929 (rejecting inquiry into doctrinal issues).

128. *See supra* notes 117–21 and accompanying text (discussing rejection of departure-from-doctrine presumptions).

129. *See supra* notes 43–46 and accompanying text; *see also* Gerstenblith, *supra* note 40, at 536–542.

130. *See supra* notes 43–46 and accompanying text (discussing methods by which courts interpret various church documents and state statutes to derive presumptions regarding settlor's intent and trusts created); *see also* Gerstenblith, *supra* note 129, at 536–542.

131. *See supra* notes 95–127 and accompanying text (illustrating neutral principles of trust law and problems created by applying implied trusts to resolve church property disputes).

132. *See supra* notes 43–6 and accompanying text (describing how courts construe church documents and state statutes to arrive at presumptions of settlor's intent); *see also* Gerstenblith, *supra* note 40, at 536–542.

133. *See supra* notes 95–111 and accompanying text (examining principles of trust law and defining common usage of express and implied trust).

using both the hybrid and deference approaches have failed to apply the standards for finding intent applicable to other types of trusts to the doctrine of implied trust. Instead, they have displayed a special predisposition toward evidence favoring hierarchic litigants.[134] Application of neutral principles would not allow this type of privileging.

Implied trusts and consent

In place of a finding of actual intent to create a trust in favor of the hierarchy, courts have relied primarily on the concept of implied consent to the hierarchy's rules.[135] Some courts have extended even this notion by finding intent to create a trust even where the hierarchy's rules do not explicitly require forfeiture of property upon disaffiliation.[136] In such cases, courts rely on various factors such as participation in conferences, acceptance of hierarchically-appointed clergy, use of educational materials and liturgy, use of a particular name, and payment of dues to the national church to conclude that the local church is a part of the hierarchical organization.[137] These courts conclude that once the local church has become a member of the national church and has accepted the benefits of affiliation, then the local church must recognize its obligations and responsibilities and cannot unilaterally renege on them.[138] None of these factors, however, proves intent on the part of the local church or the property donor.

If a court adopts the neutral principles analysis for the resolution of these disputes, it must be willing to apply the same standards of intent as are required in trust law for the imposition of an express trust.[139] The Colorado Supreme Court in *Bishop & Diocese of Colorado v. Mote* stated that although no specific words were necessary, the intent to create a trust had to be established by "[c]lear, explicit, definite, unequivocal and unambiguous language or conduct."[140] The courts that have refused to impose a trust, in favor of either a denominational organization or a local church entity, have used similar language.[141]

---

134. *See supra* notes 43–4 and accompanying text (indicating that courts using hybrid approach generally conclude that local entity and property is controlled by hierarchy); *see also* Gerstenblith, *supra* note 129, at 540–542.

135. *See supra* notes 123–5 and accompanying text (citing cases where courts have created implied trust based on local entities' implied consent to church rules).

136. *See* Lowe v. First Presbyterian Church, 308 N.E.2d 801, 807 (Ill. 1974) (ruling that local church was subordinate member of general church and had implicitly consented to its rules so that hierarchy's decision bound local church); Fairmount Presbyterian Church v. Presbytery of Holston, 531 S.W.2d 301, 306 (Tenn. Ct. App. 1975) (purporting to apply neutral principles but citing local church's corporate charter's purpose clause requiring adherence to denomination's standards).

137. *See* New York Annual Conference of the United Methodist Church v. Fisher, 438 A.2d 62, 70–71 (Conn. 1980) (evaluating several factors to determine whether local church was part of hierarchy); United Methodist Church v. St. Louis Crossing Indep. Methodist Church, 276 N.E.2d 916, 923 (Ind. Ct. App. 1971) (considering use of Sunday school literature, attendance of representatives at denominational conferences, and other evidence of parent/local church relationship and requiring local church's independence to be maintained in operational aspects such as polity, name, and finances).

138. *See Fisher*, 438 A.2d at 70–71 (holding that local church may not secede and take church property with it).

139. *See supra* notes 96–103 and accompanying text (detailing standards of intent required for imposition of express trust).

140. Bishop and Diocese of Colorado v. Mote, 716 P.2d 85, 100–01 (Colo. 1986) (citing Morgan v. Wright, 399 P.2d 788, 790–91 (1965).

141. *See, e.g.*, First Presbyterian Church v. United Presbyterian Church in the United States, 464 N.E.2d 454, 462 (looking at objective evidence to indicate creation of trust); Christensen v. Roum-

The courts that apply the "strict" neutral principles approach have recognized the need to adhere to general principles of trust law and have thus used a strict standard of intent.[142] These courts have refused to impose trusts on property held by local churches on the basis of either mere membership in a hierarchical church organization or statements in the documents of the national church which grant it control over some aspects of the corporate transactions of its constituent local members.[143] For example, the Pennsylvania courts have consistently recognized the right of a local church to change its corporate name and structure, to engage in property transactions, and to disaffiliate from a national organization as long as these actions are taken in conformance with the statutory and corporate requirements of the individual entity.[144] Furthermore, the Pennsylvania Supreme Court has characterized the claims of the hierarchy and its interpretation of its rules as self-serving and not indicative of the expectations and intent of its local churches.[145]

Courts choosing to impose a trust have reasoned that such a course gives expression to the parties' true intent and expectations.[146] Nevertheless, when both the United Pres-

---

fort, 485 N.E.2d 270, 273 (Ohio Ct. App. 1984) (stating that courts should examine evidence to determine objective intentions of parties); Presbytery of Beaver-Butler of the United Presbyterian Church in the United States v. Middlesex Presbyterian Church, 489 A.2d 1317, 1324 (stating that clear and unequivocal language or behavior must demonstrate intent of parties with primary focus on settlor's intent at time of creation of trust). In *Beaver-Butler*, the court relied on an earlier decision in a nonchurch context, in which the court stated:

> [L]ack of formality does not obviate the necessity for the appearance of all the elements of a complete trust. Every trust symptom must be present, regardless of informality surrounding the inception of the relationship or none exists. A trust must be created by clear and unambiguous language or conduct, it cannot arise from loose statements admitting possible inferences consistent with other relationships.

Beaver-Butler, 489 A.2d at 1324 (quoting Bair v. Snyder County State Bank, 171 A.2d 274, 275 (Pa. 1934)).

Similar statements are found among cases in which the dispute does not concern church property. *See* Gurley v. Lindsley, 459 F.2d 268 (5th Cir. 1972) (noting that trustee's duties must be specific enough so that court of equity can enforce them); Samuel v. Northern Trust Co., 340 N.E.2d 162, 166 (Ill. App. Ct. 1975) (requiring unambiguous acts or words to create trust). In addition, the "intent to create an express trust must be evidenced by all the parties to the transaction." *In re* Estate of Wilkening, 441 N.E.2d 158, 164 (Ill. App. Ct. 1982). Accordingly, the question of intent must focus primarily on the donor of the property, whether a third party or the local church entity, and not on the intent of the national organization.

142. *See supra* note 42 and accompanying text (describing methods that strict neutral principles courts use to establish intent of settlor); *see also* Gerstenblith, *supra* note 40, at 543–549.

143. *See* Bjorkman v. Protestant Episcopal Church in the United States, 759 S.W.2d, 583, 586 (Ky. 1988) (finding PECUSA's canons dictate moral behavior, not legal rights); Beaver-Butler, 489 A.2d at 1325 (determining that affiliation with national church and provisions in UPCUSA's Book of Order did not meet burden of unequivocable intent); Mikilak v. Orthodox Church in Am., 513 A.2d 541, 546 (Pa. Commw. Ct. 1986) (deciding no trust exists where national church statute fails to authorize trust clearly).

144. Presbytery of Donegal v. Calhoun, 513 A.2d 531, 536–37 (Pa. Commw. Ct. 1986) (determining that local church could disaffiliate because local church could modify its own corporate charter which required affiliation with hierarchy).

145. *Beaver-Butler*, 489 A.2d at 1325 (concluding that church rules represent desires of trustees, not intent of donor). It is a settled rule of trust law that neither the absence nor the presence of the word "trust" is dispositive in determining whether a trust has been created. 4 R. Powell, *supra* note 95 ¶ 506. If such usage of the word "trust" is not determinative of the settlor's intention, *a fortiori* it cannot be considered determinative when used only by the putative beneficiary. *Id.*

146. Bishop & Diocese of Colorado v. Mote, 716 P.2d 85, 109–10 (Colo. 1986) (creating trust in favor of diocese consistent with intent of all concerned that property remain with diocese).

byterian Church in the United States (UPCUSA) and the Protestant Episcopal Church in the United States (PECUSA) changed their national constitutions in response to the Supreme Court's decision in *Jones v. Wolf*, several local churches attempted to disaffiliate in order to preserve their property rights.[147] These attempts spawned the relatively large amount of litigation on this subject during the 1980s.[148] Some courts refused to view these amendments as an admission by the national churches that the property of a local church was not previously impressed with a trust.[149] Other courts, however, interpreted them as indicating that the local churches were not aware of such trust relationships within the hierarchical structures of their denominations.[150] The inconsistent interpretation of identical provisions in national church constitutions is not merely attributable to some courts' continued application of the deference approach.[151] Rather, such inconsistencies are also caused by the failure of those courts purporting to apply neutral principles to recognize the role of actual intent in the creation of trusts.[152]

In order to apply truly neutral principles, the courts must require a showing of actual intent, not merely presumed or implied intent. Actual intent is best demonstrated by statements of the party who is the settlor of the trust—either a donor of the property or the local entity that purchases the property.[153] Accordingly, acceptable evidence of intent should include only statements in the property deeds, whether they create a trust in favor of the national denomination or a restriction on use of the property, and statements in the articles of incorporation and bylaws of the local entity.[154] In addition, if the local entity *chooses* to incorporate under a state denominational statute requiring continued affiliation with the denomination, then that statute also controls.[155] This separately incorporated entity, however, may change its corporate documents or, if permit-

---

147. *See* Ross *supra* note 11, at 303 (addressing enactment of provisions by several national denominations in order to create express trusts).

148. *Compare* York v. First Presbyterian Church of Anna, 474 N.E.2d 716, 721 (Ill. App. Ct. 1984) (concluding that local church's reaction to UPCUSA's amendments illustrated absence of mutual understanding with regard to property rights within religious organization) *and* Presbytery of Elijah Parish Lovejoy v. Jaeggi, 682 S.W.2d 465, 474 (Mo. 1984) (finding that amendment adopted subsequent to schism was not binding on defecting faction) with Bishop & Diocese of Colorado v. Mote, 716 P.2d 85, 105–07 (Colo. 1986) (stating that 1979 amendments to PECUSA's canons merely affirmed prior custom and practice) *and* Fonken v. Community Church, 339 N.W.2d 810, 819 (Iowa 1983) (concluding that neither UPCUSA's prior failure to pass amendment nor its passage of such amendment in 1981 would affect court's decision to impose implied trust on disputed property) *and* Protestant Episcopal Church in the Diocese of New Jersey v. Graves, 417 A.2d 19, 24 (N.J. 1980) (stating that amendment reflects church custom).

149. Fonken v. Community Church of Kamrar, 339 N.W.2d 810, 819 (Iowa 1983) (stating that general church's passage of amendment would not affect court's imposition of trust).

150. Presbytery of Elijah Parish Lovejoy v. Jaeggi, 682 S.W.2d 465, 474 (Mo. 1984) (holding that subsequently adopted amendment has no effect on local church).

151. *See supra* note 41 and accompanying text; *see also* Gerstenblith, *supra* note 40, at 531–534.

152. *See supra* notes 44–5 and accompanying text; *see also* Gerstenblith, *supra* note 40, at 537–542.

153. *See supra* notes 96–99 and accompanying text (discussing importance of settlor's intent in determining existence of trust).

154. *See supra* notes 104–28 and accompanying text (discrediting use of implied trust theories where basis of ascertaining settlor's intent derives from documents of national church).

155. *See* Protestant Episcopal Church in the Diocese of Los Angeles v. Barker, 115 Cal. App. 3d 599, 624–25 (finding one local church bound by California statute that provided that property of subordinate body would revert to national organization upon revocation of charter by national organization).

ted by state statute, reincorporate under a different nondenominational statute, provided that these actions conform with statutory and corporate requirements.[156]

Interpretation of national church documents creates great difficulty for courts. Although the constitutions of national organizations such as UPCUSA and PECUSA had previously attempted to control the property dealings of local churches, courts requiring a strict standard of intent have held that these restrictions did not create an express trust.[157] The amendments to these constitutions enacted following *Jones v. Wolf*, however, do attempt to create express trusts through explicit provisions.[158] One commentator has asserted that these provisions will eliminate litigation because they are sufficiently clear in creating judicially cognizable express trusts.[159] Courts applying strict neutral principles and the accompanying high standard of intent, however, may determine that such provisions do not indicate the intent of a local church or of the settlor of the presumed trust.[160] Moreover, it must be emphasized that these declarations of trust are made by the putative beneficiary of the trust—the national organization—and not by the local entity.[161] Because the creation of a trust is determined by the intent of the *settlor*, and not by the intent of the beneficiary,[162] the amendments to the national church constitutions should provide little justification for construing a trust in the hierarchy's favor.[163]

---

156. Presbytery of Donegal v. Calhoun, 513 A.2d 531, 536–37 (Pa. Commw. Ct. 1986). An interesting parallel is provided in *Attorney General v. Hahnemann Hospital*, 494 N.E.2d 1011 (Mass. 1986). In this case, the court concluded that a hospital, which was a charitable corporation, could amend its corporate charter and bylaws and thereby change its purpose provided that this was done in conformance with statutory requirements. Attorney Gen. Hahnemann Hosp., 494 N.E.2d 1011, 1017–18 (Mass. 1986). Funds were required to be applied in conformance with express trust restrictions. *Id.* at 1026. Other assets of the hospital, however, were free of these restrictions. *Id.* at 1026. This case limited a charitable corporation's ability to change its corporate purpose, at least in the absence of judicial direction. *See id.* at 1020–21 (noting that limit only applied to specific and objective purpose clearly enunciated by donor of major trust fund).

157. *See supra* note 148 (citing cases where courts refused to interpret amendments as representing local church's intent).

158. *See* Ross, *supra* note 11, at 303 (outlining provisions enacted by various denominations attempting to create express trusts).

159. *See* Ross, *supra* note 11, at 313–15 (discussing development of neutral principles approach).

160. *See Barker*, 115 Cal. App. 3d at 623–24 (holding that amendments to diocesan documents made after affiliation of local entity are ineffective with respect to that entity).

161. *See* Ross, *supra* note 11, at 303 209 and accompanying text (examining declarations made by national church organization in attempt to impose express trusts on local church property). Because the trust envisioned by the national church constitutions is created at the time that the implied condition is broken, not when the property interest comes into existence, it is difficult to assign roles clearly on the basis of traditional trust terminology. *See* Crumbley v. Solomon, 254 S.E.2d 330, 336 n.2 (Ga. 1979) (per curiam) (Bowles, J., dissenting) (questioning whether title to local church property divests as soon as national church adopts express trust provision).

162. *See supra* notes 96–99 and accompanying text (establishing requirements for express trust creation); *Crumbley*, 254 S.E.2d at 336–37 (Bowles, J., dissenting) (emphasizing that neither trustee nor beneficiary acting alone can modify terms of trust). In *Crumbley*, Justice Bowles criticized the majority's imposition of an implied trust because it failed to "separate [the] actions, duties and responsibilities" of the settlor, trustees, and beneficiaries, "[a]lthough there is clear legal distinction and purpose in the[ir] significance and identity." *Id.* at 336 n.3 (Bowles, J., dissenting).

163. A far more effective way for national church organizations to retain control of property is to require the local entities to insert express trust provisions in their own property deeds. *See supra* notes 91–2 and accompanying text (explaining use of express provisions in deeds of local entities to create trusts in favor of denomination). This action, undertaken by the local entity alone, would ac-

Implied trusts and estoppel

Even if a court refuses to consider the trust provisions added to national church documents as evidence of the local entities' intent, the denominations may argue that the local churches' failure to withdraw from the denomination following the amendments' enactment will estop the local affiliates to deny their intent regarding the national organization's beneficial interest in the property.[164] The theory that property may be transferred by means of estoppel is based on the unfairness in "allowing a person to act in a manner inconsistent with his own prior conduct."[165] The principles of equitable estoppel apply to implied misrepresentations arising from silence when there is a duty to speak.[166]

The argument that the local church's silence provides sufficient manifestation of intent to create a trust contains several weaknesses. First, it is a settled principle of trust law that an express trust is created only when the settlor's intent is clear and unambiguous.[167] Silence is an inherently ambiguous form of manifestation.[168] In addition, for silence to be interpreted as a form of intent, the court must find that the silent party had specific knowledge of the trust provisions.[169] For example, in *African Methodist Episcopal Zion*

---

cord with the manifest expression of intent required to create a trust under generally accepted principles of trust law. *See* G. Bogert, *supra* note 92, §§ 9, 11 (1987) (describing requisite intent and manifestation required for trust to exist). If the local entity truly intends to bind itself to an express trust or forfeiture provision, then it should be willing to execute or amend its property deeds in a manner conforming with this intent. *See supra* notes 96, 99, and accompanying text (considering implications of settlor's intent to create trust); *cf.* Protestant Episcopal Church in the Diocese of Los Angeles v. Barker, 115 Cal. App. 3d 599, 622 (1981). In *Barker*, the court noted that some national churches do hold property directly in their own name or in that of some regional entity, such as a diocese. If, however, the denomination grants autonomy to its local churches to hold property in their own names, then the denomination must be willing to accept the possible loss of such property when the local church disaffiliates in exchange for the administrative convenience gained through freedom from property management responsibilities.

164. *See Crumbley*, 254 S.E.2d at 336–37 (Bowles, J., dissenting) (discussing application of estoppel theory). In *Crumbley*, the deed to the local church's property vested title in the trustees of the local church. *Id.* at 332. After twenty years of affiliation, the denominational association, which was found to be hierarchical although composed of Baptist congregations, changed its bylaws to impose a trust in its own favor upon the local church's property. *Id.* at 332. The majority upheld the trust by reasoning that the local church had not contested the bylaw for thirty years after its adoption and had accepted the benefits of membership in the association. *Id.* at 333.

The dissent read this as an estoppel argument and asserted that transfer by estoppel was invalid under Georgia law because of strict guidelines concerning the transferability of property. *Id.* at 336; *See also* Coles v. Wilburn, 245 S.E.2d 273 (Ga. 1978) (per curiam) (deciding that despite national church rules and fifty-year relationship between general and local church, implied trust theory does not apply to divest property from local entity).

165. 2A R. Powell, *supra* note 95, ¶ 275[4][b](iii). Estoppel that effects a transfer of property is most often based on a deed that one party has conveyed to another. *Id.* ¶ 927. Estoppel, however, is not permitted to fulfill the legal requisites of a conveyance where such requisites are absent. *Id.*

166. *See* 31 C.J.S. Estoppel § 59 (1964) (discussing general nature and components of estoppel). Equitable estoppel also includes quasi-estoppel that arises from the acceptance of benefits or from acquiescence in another's act. *Id.* § 107.

167. G. Bogert, *supra* note 92, § 11.

168. *See* Fonken v. Community Church of Kamrar, 339 N.W.2d 810, 824 (Iowa 1983) (Schultz, J., dissenting) (stating that court should not impose trust on local church property where local entity failed to express intent); *See also* Crumbley v. Solomon, 254 S.E.2d 330, 336 (Ga. 1979) (per curiam) (Bowles, J., dissenting) (noting that terms of trust cannot be modified without consent of all parties).

169. *See* G. Bogert, *supra* note 92, § 11 (describing intent factors for trust formation). It is clear that those churches that chose to disaffiliate before such amendments became effective had actual

Church in America, Inc. v. Zion Hill Methodist Church, Inc.,[170] the court undertook extensive fact finding as to knowledge and intent before it would find that the local church members were aware of provisions in the constitution of the national organization.[171]

Moreover, the national churches fail to meet the basic elements of an estoppel action. The party asserting estoppel must show that it was prejudiced from an action, belief, or reliance induced by the party it seeks to estop.[172] The national organization, however, is not damaged or prejudiced in the case of church property disputes. Although the organization may claim that it has relied to its detriment on the existence of an express trust in bestowing various benefits of membership on the local church, a court should not assume the existence of such benefits. Although local churches receive liturgy and accept religious leaders appointed by the national organization, most of them also pay considerable dues to the national organization.[173] Perhaps the single most important consideration is the source of the funds used to purchase the disputed property. Unless the national church organization or other affiliated entities provided significant assistance to the local church, detrimental reliance by or prejudice toward the national organization is difficult to establish.[174]

---

knowledge of the effect that these amendments would have on their property interests. In most of these cases, however, there was a preexisting doctrinal dispute between the local church and the parent organization which led the local church to realize that it might wish to disaffiliate at some time in the future. The attribution of the same knowledge, or the realization of the significance of these amendments, to those local churches which were not contemplating disaffiliation for other reasons is questionable. Whenever a doctrinal change occurs, some local churches will choose to disaffiliate in protest. *See* Protestant Episcopal Church in the Diocese of Los Angeles v. Barker, 115 Cal. App. 3d 599, 606 (noting that both Anglican and Episcopalian Churches were result of two prior schisms and that in both, seceding churches retained their property).

170. 534 So. 2d 224 (Ala. 1988).

171. African Methodist Episcopal Zion Church in Am., Inc. v. Zion Hill Methodist Church, Inc., 534 So. 2d 224, 225–27 (Ala. 1988).

Estoppel relating to real estate requires that the party seeking to estop the titleholder was unaware of the true state of the title and had no way to acquire such knowledge. Bennett v. Davis, 39 S.E.2d 3, 7 (Ga. 1946). When the hierarchy changes its rules, however, the local church is the party without knowledge, while the hierarchical organization is certainly aware of the change in rules and is generally aware of the state of the title of the local entity's property. *See* Ross, *supra* note 11, at 303–09 and accompanying text (discussing implementation of amendments to national church constitutions).

172. *See* 31 C.J.S. Estoppel § 87 (1964) (stating that silence will not lead to estoppel unless there was justifiable reliance giving rise to damages); G. Bogert & G. Bogert, *supra* note 111, § 143 (listing requirements for trust created by estoppel).

173. *Barker*, 115 Cal. App. 3d at 607–09 (determining that contributions from three local Episcopal churches to PECUSA or diocese totaled approximately $127,000, $161,000, and $51,000, respectively).

174. Adverse possession may provide an additional circumstance in which silence serves to divest a titleholder. 3 American Law of Property § 15.2 (A. Casner ed. 1952). It is unclear, however, whether the purpose of the doctrine is to "reward" the industry and investment of the adverse possessor or to "punish" the silence of the titleholder. Nonetheless, the doctrine establishes clarity of land titles and encourages productive use of the land, thereby serving significant societal goals. *See* Ellickson, Adverse Possession and Perpetuities Law: Two Dents in the Libertarian Model of Property Rights, 64 Wash U. L.Q. 723, 723–27 (1986); Epstein, Past and Future: The Temporal Dimension in the Law of Property, 64 Wash. U. L.Q. 667, 674–80 (1986).

Bogert refers to the possibility that a trust may be created through the application of adverse possession or estoppel when an individual acts like the trustee and therefore is regarded as a trustee rather than as the legal titleholder. G. Bogert, *supra* note 101, § 143. The imposition of a trust, however, depends on the representations of the trustee, not on the intent or conduct of the putative beneficiary. *Id.*

General problems with implied trusts

The implied trust theory not only violates several precepts of property and trust law but also has adverse consequences in the context of property law and real estate transactions. First, the use of implied trusts, which are not revealed by a search of the land records, serves to obfuscate land titles and will make real estate transactions more complex and costly.[175] Second, this theory may also discourage productive use of the land by the current titleholder because any investment in the property would be lost if the local entity chooses to disaffiliate.[176]

The most important considerations in the resolution of these disputes, however, do not involve questions of property transactions and land titles. Rather, in determining whether to use the implied trust theory, courts must focus on maintaining a balanced treatment of two competing religious groups. In some contexts, harmony between the two Religion Clauses of the First Amendment may require that religious groups be treated the same as other charitable organizations. This similarity of treatment is particularly important when a civil court is called upon to resolve a dispute between two religious groups. By engaging in presumptions, whether they concern implied intent or implied consent, the civil courts ignore neutral principles of law, thus favoring, and thereby establishing, one religious group at the expense of the free exercise rights of the other religious group.

Other sources of neutral legal principles

Contract and corporate law

Contract law and corporate law comprise the other primary sources of neutral legal principles that would be relevant to the resolution of internal disputes among religious organizations. Ellman, although apparently decrying the use of neutral principles of law, nonetheless advocated the adoption of the "contract principle."[177] According to this view, documents, such as the corporate papers of the local entity and the constitution and regulations of the parent organization, create a contract between the parent organization and the local entity.[178] Accordingly, when a dispute over the disposition of property arises, the court should then seek to enforce this contract.[179]

---

175. Johnson, Purpose and Scope of Recording Statutes, 47 Iowa L. Rev. 231, 231–33 (1962) (discussing nature and role of recording system for real property).

176. *See* Epstein, *supra* note 174, at 670 (discussing that certainty of land ownership encourages efficient and diligent use, reduction in transaction costs, and lower cost of development and sale).

177. Ellman, *supra* note 8, at 1385. Ellman contends that enforcing the agreements between the parties can achieve religiously neutral adjudication and avoid the imposition of external rules and policies. *Id.* at 1402. Ellman apparently equates the application of neutral principles of law with the substitution of legislatively and judicially created rules for the rules and agreements created by the parties. *Id.* at 1410, 1437–39. Both Ellman's "contract principle" and the use of neutral legal principles advocated in this chapter depend on the identification of intent of the parties, which should then be given effect through the court's resolution of the dispute. *See id.* at 1402–04 (noting that "contract principle" requires determining intent of parties); *supra* notes 96–99 and accompanying text (discussing intent requirement for express trusts). Application of the "contract principle" and of any other neutral legal principle should produce the same result in any particular case.

178. Ellman, *supra* note 8, at 1385.

179. *Id.*

Some courts have used a contract approach or at least have alluded to it in their choice of terminology.[180] In some of these decisions, the courts give the parent church an interest in the local's property based on the local church's implied consent to the rules of the parent organization.[181] Other courts have referred to the notion that the local entity's receipt of various benefits from the national organization makes the rules of the latter binding on the former, presumably through the mechanism of an implied contract.[182]

This discussion of a contractual basis for awarding the property of the local church to a parent religious organization upon the local's disaffiliation finds an interesting parallel in a series of decisions that confront the same issue in the context of labor unions.[183] Courts have analyzed the relationship between a union local and the national or international union in terms of their structural relationship, their relative dates of creation, and their need to remain loyal to the constitution and purposes of the union.[184] The contractual relationship between the local and the parent unions often

---

180. *See* Green v. Lewis, 272 S.E.2d 181, 186 (Va. 1980). For example, the Virginia statute prohibits the creation of express trusts and implied trusts for supercongregational churches. *Id.* at 186. The Virginia Supreme Court has therefore relied on a contractual theory according to which the hierarchy may have a contractual interest in the property held by the local church based on statements in the property deeds or other documents and on the local church's implied consent to the rules of the general church. *Id.* at 186. *See* Norfolk Presbytery v. Bollinger, 201 S.E.2d 752, 758 (Va. 1974) (commenting that courts should look to local church deed and general church constitution in order to determine ownership). Other courts have referred more generally to the use of contract principles without specifically relying on a contractual basis for their result. *See* Bishop and Diocese of Colorado v. Mote, 716 P.2d 85, 101 (Colo. 1986) (holding that principles of property, contracts, and corporations are basis for determination that general church has property interest); Avitzur v. Avitzur, 446 N.E.2d 136 (applying contract law as source of neutral legal principles to resolve dispute concerning interpretation of secular terms of ketubah, or traditional Jewish marriage contract); Maryland and Virginia Eldership of the Churches of God v. Church of God at Sharpsburg, Inc., 254 A.2d 162, 166–68 (Md. 1969) (examining express language in property deeds, charter, and constitution).

181. *See supra* note 136 (citing cases where courts found in favor of hierarchy based on implied consent theory).

182. *See supra* note 137 (citing cases where courts found for hierarchy based on benefits conferred to local church).

183. Note, Rights to Local Union Property After Secession, 58 Yale L.J. 1171, 1174 (1949) [hereinafter Note, *Rights*]. The relationship among unions has been viewed as based on a twofold contract—a contract between the local and the parent union and a contract between the local and the individual members. *Id.* at 1171. The contract is composed of the charters and constitutions of the parent and local unions and "impresses monies collected by the local with a trust for the benefit of all members, and is impliedly accepted by workers on joining the union." *Id.*; *See also* Note, The Legal Consequences of Labor Union Schisms, 62 Harv. L. Rev. 1413, 1414–16 (1950) [hereinafter Note, Legal Consequences] (addressing contract theory regarding forfeiture clauses in relation to awarding union property); M. Malin, Individual Rights Within the Union 4 (1988) (discussing that union bylaws were regarded as contracts between union, their members, and their locals). It seems to be generally accepted that these constitutional provisions favor the parent organization.

In *New Jersey Association for Children with Learning Disabilities v. Burlington County Association for Children with Learning Disabilities*, 415 A.2d 1196 (N.J. Super. Ct. App. Div. 1980), the court cited labor union cases in the context of a property dispute arising from the disaffiliation of the local chapter of a charitable corporation from its parent organization. *Id.* at 1197. The court also analyzed the relationship between a local chapter and the larger nonprofit corporation as a contract based on the bylaws of the parent organization. *Id.* at 1197. The court refused to award the local's assets to the parent organization because the latter's bylaw did not specifically require forfeiture upon the local's secession from the parent. *Id.* at 1197–98.

184. *See* Note, Rights, *supra* note 183, at 1177 (noting that courts have derived analytic model from dealings within benevolent associations); *see also* Harker v. McKissock, 76 A.2d 89, 91–92, 97 (N.J. Super. Ct. App. Div. 1950) (awarding property to seceding local based on structural relation-

forms the basis of such analysis.[185] When a local union votes to disaffiliate, unless the vote is unanimous,[186] the assets and property of the local typically are awarded to either the loyal minority or the parent union on the basis of their contractual relationship.[187]

One commentator has criticized the use of the contract theory in the context of labor union secessions because the constitutional provisions of parent organizations are not the product of a true negotiation or bargaining process.[188] The locals are at a considerable disadvantage: they may lack any effective choice and may not be aware of the consequences of a forfeiture provision.[189] Courts should enforce only those terms of the supposed contract that have been freely negotiated and thus reflect the true intent and understanding of both parties. This argument is especially persuasive when those terms have severe consequences for the smaller local entity, whose very existence may depend on retention of its property and other assets. As a result, some courts and commentators have suggested that the fair resolution of such disputes depends primarily on such

---

ship of unions and intended use of disputed funds), *aff'd*, 81 A.2d 480 (1951). It is interesting to note that *Harker* was authored by Justice William J. Brennan, who at the time sat as a judge of the New Jersey Superior Court. 76 A.2d at 90. The last factor involved in analyzing the relationship between the local and parent union, loyalty to the constitution of the respective organizations, is similar to the departure-from-doctrine analysis in the church property cases. *See* Watson v. Jones, 80 U.S. (13 Wall.) 679, 705, 727–29, 732 *supra* notes 61–65 and accompanying text (considering departure-from doctrine approach to resolving church property disputes); *see also* Note, Legal Consequences, *supra* note 183, at 1413 (discussing factors such as structural relationship and effect of labor union disaffiliation).

185. *See* Note, Legal Consequences, *supra* 183, at 1414–15 (discussing application of intra-union contracts).

186. International Bhd. of Pulp, Sulphite and Paper Mill Workers v. Delaney, 442 P.2d 250, 254–55 (Wash. 1968) (en banc).

187. *See, e.g.*, International Bhd. of Boilermakers v. Local Lodge D504, 866 F.2d 641, 646–47 (3d Cir. 1989) (awarding property of seceding local to international union based on provisions of international's constitution); International Bhd. of Boilermakers v. Local Lodge D405, 699 F. Supp. 749, 754–55 (D. Ariz. 1988) (resolving property dispute in favor of international union by applying constitutional provisions); International Bhd. of Boilermakers v. Local Lodge D474, 673 F. Supp. 199, 200–01, 205 (W.D. Tex. 1987) (deciding to award property of seceding local union to international union after analyzing international constitution). The Labor-Management Reporting and Disclosure Act of 1959 provides a statutory basis for permitting a parent union to impress a trusteeship on the assets of the local union when certain conditions have been met and when done for certain enumerated purposes. 29 U.S.C. §§ 461–464 (1982). *See generally* M. Malin, *supra* note 183, at 175–204 (discussing trusteeships as mechanism by which national union directs local body's affairs). The international union's desire to inhibit a disaffiliation by itself is not generally considered sufficient basis for the imposition of a trusteeship. *See Local D474*, 673 F. Supp. at 203–04 (finding that trusteeship was imposed to inhibit disaffiliation and to avoid other problems such as supervisory control of assets). Other courts have held, however, that disaffiliation itself is adequate justification for creation of such a trust because disaffiliation would impair the collective bargaining process. *See Local D474*, 673 F. Supp. at 203 (stating that in absence of contract, trusteeship can be imposed to preserve existing bargaining unit); *see also* M. Malin, *supra* note 183, at 185–88.

188. Note, Legal Consequences, *supra* note 183, at 1415–16.

189. *Id.* This commentator noted that when new unions are formed, the constitutions of existing unions are copied word for word. *Id.* at 1416. Furthermore, he explained that the newly affiliating union is rarely strong enough to bargain for changes in the parent's constitution and that union members are more interested in the provisions that affect day-to-day activities. *Id. See* Harker v. McKissock, 76 A.2d 89, 95–96 (N.J. Super. Ct. App. Div. 1950) (awarding disputed property to local union partly because forfeiture provisions of national union's constitution were not freely negotiated at time of affiliation), *aff'd*, 81 A.2d 480 (1951); International Bhd. of Pulp, Sulphite and Paper Mill Workers v. Delaney, 442 P.2d 250, 256 (Wash. 1968) (en banc) (refusing to require forfeiture of property because forfeiture provision was viewed as "exploitative or punitive measure").

considerations as the relative size of the majority and minority factions within the local union.[190]

Courts justify awarding a local union's property and other assets to its parent organization by emphasizing that fragmentation of unions and their corresponding assets weakens these organizations' relative bargaining position with respect to management.[191] Furthermore, state limitations on the ability of unincorporated associations to hold and manage real property preclude resolution in favor of the local unions, which generally are not incorporated.[192] One commentator has noted that the prevailing view allows an incorporated local union to secede without forfeiting its property to the parent union regardless of the organization dates or provisions in the parent's constitution.[193] This view is based on the belief that the local organization derives its powers from its state charter and that such powers cannot be surrendered to another body.[194]

This parallel to labor union disputes highlights two significant factors. First, when a local entity receives a state incorporation charter, which includes the ability to hold and manage property, this state-granted power supercedes externally imposed organizational regulations, which attempt to limit those powers.[195] Thus, in addition to the contract principle, another source of neutral legal principles is state incorporation law, which generally grants to not-for-profit and religious corporations the power to hold and to deal with property.[196] Although some state religious and denominational incorporation statutes may explicitly subject this power to the national organization's regulations, such a limitation should not otherwise be implied to restrict the state-granted authority.[197]

---

190. *See* Note, Legal Consequences, *supra* note 183, at 1419 (recommending that decision be based on balancing factors such as breaches of duty to union, relationship between local and international, purpose for collection of assets, and size of local union).

191. *See* International Bhd. of Boilermakers v. Local Lodge D474, 673 F. Supp. 199, 203 (W.D. Tex. 1987) (justifying imposition of trusteeship to avoid damaging collective bargaining process).

192. M. Malin, *supra* note 183, at 2–3. Courts generally use the factors discussed earlier to analyze the rights of local unions that are not separately incorporated. *See supra* note 183 and accompanying text (listing factors courts consider in determining contractual basis to award union property). *Compare*, Note, Legal Consequences, *supra* note 183, at 1414–15 (applying contract theory for intraunion disputes) *with* Note, Rights, *supra* note 183, at 1173 (discussing disposition of assets when dealing with unincorporated labor organizations). Funds raised by unincorporated locals for local purposes, however, are *not* impressed with a trust for the parent's purposes. *Id*. The court's consideration of all these factors, therefore, at least under analogy to the common law of unincorporated associations, supercedes the provisions of the constitutions of both the local and parent unions, even when the local is unincorporated. *Id. See* generally Kauper & Ellis, *supra* note 112, at 1505–07 (examining historical treatment of churches regarding incorporation and property ownership).

193. Note, Rights, *supra* note 183, at 1172–73.

194. *Id*. at 1173.

195. *Id*.

196. Del. Code Ann. tit. 27, § 102 (1974). To answer Ellman's criticism that imposition of legislative rules on religious organizations infringes on their free exercise rights, one should recall that most state incorporation statutes permit the bylaws of individual corporations to supercede statutory provisions, and in such situations, the bylaws should clearly be given precedence. *See supra* note 177 (setting out Ellman's "contract theory"). The local corporation, however, can modify the bylaws when it is done in conformance with statutory requirements. Del Code Ann. tit. 27, § 102 (1974). This prevents the implication of external rules and regulations into the local corporation's bylaws. If the rules of the national organization truly reflect the intent and desires of the local entities, then the latter will voluntarily and expressly incorporate such rules into their incorporation documents.

197. Fla. Stat. Ann. § 617.21 (1986); Idaho Code § 30-307 (1980). In order to vindicate both the Free Exercise and Establishment Clause interests of all religious groups, statutory schemes need to

This discussion of secession among labor unions also illustrates the effect of limiting a local union's ability to retain its property upon disaffiliation. The explicitly stated purpose of such limitation is to strengthen the national labor organization and increase its bargaining power.[198] In the context of church property disputes, the goal of favoring and strengthening the religious hierarchy is not legitimate because it would clearly violate the Establishment Clause of the First Amendment.

Most significantly, one must recognize that even in the union context, the contract principle contains limitations. A contract should be enforceable only when it is the product of an open negotiation process between two parties of equal bargaining power who have a true choice. In addition, the parties must fully comprehend or at least have the ability to determine the significance of negotiated terms and the implications of their choices. All of these factors should be used to determine whether the contractual relationship as expressed in the constitution and bylaws of the parent organization accurately reflects the intent and understanding of both parties to the contract. This discussion of the relationship between parent and local labor unions thus illustrates the relevance of the treatment of other voluntary and not-for-profit organizations to the treatment of religious organizations. In both situations, the application of principles derived from contract law and corporate law shows why the use of such neutral principles is the best method for effectuating the parties' intent.

Conclusion

The Supreme Court's decisions in the area of resolving church property disputes have left it to state courts to determine whether their respective jurisdictions will follow a "deference" model, a "strict neutrality" model, or something in between. Not surprisingly, this has resulted in an unsettled situation, with a variety of judicial methodologies being deployed depending on the jurisdiction. While recognizing that the Supreme Court has not pronounced a definitive answer, this chapter argues that the strict neutrality model should in fact be preferred. State neutrality toward religion is the underlying constitutional axiom, and it is difficult to see how use of a deferentialist approach can ultimately be squared with the underlying values of either the Establishment Clause or the Free Exercise Clause. The deferential approach and its weaker hybrid sisters inevitably tend toward privileging hierarchy, which runs counter to the non-privileging imperatives of the Establishment Clause. Allocating property to the privileged side of a

---

take two factors into account. First, those statutory schemes which include specific denominational statutes must offer a choice of whether to incorporate under the specific statute or under a more general not-for-profit or religious corporation statute. In addition, the individual corporations must also be permitted to reincorporate under an alternate statute as long as proper statutory procedures are followed. Second, state law should permit a variety of statutory models so that religions with different polities may select a statutory structure which accords with their practical management and operations.

198. *See supra* note 183 and accompanying text (explaining rationale for courts awarding property to national or international union); Note, Rights, *supra* note 183, at 1177–78 (arguing that secession of local unions undermines power of national bargaining unit and thereby obstructs goals of National Labor Relations Act). This commentator, however, notes that national labor relations policy is in fact best furthered by fostering the democratic rights of workers and not forcing discontented workers to remain with dissatisfactory leadership. *Id.* at 1178; *see also* Note, Legal Consequences, *supra* note 183, at 1418–19 (discussing new approaches to labor schisms).

dispute inevitably burdens free exercise, even if only in requiring the losing party to abandon its preferred place of worship and to find and finance a new meeting place.

By invalidating the departure-from-doctrine approach to church property disputes while allowing states broad discretion to resolve such disputes by implying trusts on other grounds, the Supreme Court has left too much room for state courts to diverge from a sound, neutral position. Far too often, this latitude is used to smuggle departure-from-doctrine analysis into decisions in the guise of merely applying standard "implied trust" analysis.

Judicially-created legal rules that permit enforcement of otherwise unenforceable restrictions on a local entity's retention of its property would have the effect of strengthening religious hierarchies and discouraging the formation of new schismatic religions. Although seeking a comparable result in nonreligious disputes is certainly permissible and may be desirable to effectuate other policies, such as national labor policy, achieving such a result among religious organizations appears to involve the privileging of hierarchy in ways that run counter to the Religion Clauses of the First Amendment. Only the use of truly neutral legal principles can guarantee the fairness, evenhandedness, and equality of treatment required of the courts in adjudicating disputes between competing religious groups. The intent and knowledge of both parties provide the touchstone for resolving such disputes. Courts should pay special attention to the intent of the group that is to suffer forfeiture of its real property and other assets when seeking to practice its religious faith as it sees fit. To determine true intent, courts must avoid presumptions and the use of implied intent because these can lead to the favoring of one religious group at the expense of the free exercise rights of another. The application of strictly neutral legal principles of contract, corporate, trust, and property law thus provides the only satisfactory means of honoring both First Amendment Religion Clauses in the resolution of such disputes among religious organizations.

Regulation of Religious Organizations via Governmental Financial Assistance

Carl H. Esbeck

How do governmental regulations that attend financial assistance to health care, social welfare, and educational providers affect the autonomy of religious organizations engaging in these activities? This chapter addresses the manner in which such regulations mandate, limit, or otherwise shape the way a religious organization ministers in its particular field of calling. Specifically, the concern is how program-eligibility requirements restrict the options by which a ministry may organize itself. Thus it inquires into whether church polity is at cross-purposes with such regulations. The study also explores the issue of regulations affecting religious control, particularly in human resource decisions of supervising and dismissal and in maintaining an organization's religious character, moral standards, and mission. Because such regulations broaden the scope of civil rights liability, this chapter discusses how that exposure may push religious organizations toward decisions about corporate structure that limit this liability.

What costs must a religious ministry pay in loss of autonomy and fidelity to doctrine when it participates in a program of governmental assistance? The topic is the flip side of a question that has been much litigated and is thereby far more familiar, namely: Do the requirements of the Establishment Clause prohibit religious organizations from participating in a governmental social welfare or educational program? This chapter assumes, *arguendo,* that no constitutional proscription exists on the nondiscriminatory flow of tax funds to independent religious schools and social welfare agencies. Presuming that religious groups are proper participants along with secular providers in the given program of aid, the focus here is on the regulatory strings that come attached to the governmental assistance.

The following hypotheticals illustrate some of these issues from the perspective of a religious provider and its interest in self-definition and autonomy. Although fictional, the cases are composites of restraints that have occurred.

Case one

Bethlehem Home, a maternity home for unwed teenagers, is a nonprofit charitable corporation. It was founded five years ago by the Interfaith Alliance, a voluntary association of Protestant churches whose members are interested in a positive, Bible-centered response to the pro-life/pro-choice debate. The municipal community services board awards a one-time, fifteen-thousand-dollar grant to upgrade the home's plumbing and meet fire code requirements. As a condition on all its community service grants, the city requires that a grantee's governing board be "representative of the community's diversity," and that a client's dismissal from a grantee's program for alleged rule infractions be safeguarded by a due process hearing. Because of the home's religious status, the board also appends a special requirement that a teenager's involvement in faith-based counseling, biblical studies, and church attendance be voluntary.

Case two

A state income tax code allows taxpayers with a dependent attending a primary or secondary school to deduct educational expenses not to exceed twenty-five-hundred dollars per year. However, the student must enroll in a school accredited by the state. Accreditation entails, *inter alia*, being organized as a nonprofit corporation that is not controlled by any other organization, group, or society. As a matter of polity and tradition, Roman Catholic parish schools are under diocesan governance and are not separately incorporated.

Case three

A federal program provides capital-improvement grants for the renovation of inner-city buildings to serve as quarters suitable for sheltering and feeding the homeless and steering individuals into vocational training. If derelict church property is the site of a grant, all icons, art, scripture, and other religious objects must be permanently removed from the walls, and the renovated space may not be used at any time for worship, confession, prayer, or other inherently religious activity.

Case four

The Tiny Tots Center is presently organizing as a for-profit corporation. The center will be near a low-income housing project where the need for quality, low-cost child care is acute. The brainchild of a local pastor, the center plans to keep its fees affordable by locating rent-free in the educational wing of the church and using volunteers from the congregation as part-time staff. Over three-quarters of the mothers are unmarried teens. The center aims to reach the mother and child holistically, stressing the spiritual dimension of life and character building. The United States Small Business Administration will authorize a loan only on condition that the center engage in no proselytizing, Bible stories, religious music, or similar activities, and that the center's advertising and other literature does not present it as church-related.

Case five

A state has an annual charity drive among its more than thirty-five thousand civil servants. Employees are encouraged to sign an annual pledge authorizing payroll deductions for the employee's favorite charity from an approved list. To make the list, every organization must sign a compliance agreement that commits it to nondiscrimination in its employment practices and in the clientele served. "Religion" and "sexual orientation" are among the prohibited bases of discrimination. Many Muslim, Orthodox Jewish, and conservative Christian charities are unable to sign the pledge due to their respective doctrines and thus cannot make the list.

Each of the foregoing constraints on ministry, especially in program design, the choice of organizational structure or governance, and in the hiring of personnel, are typical of what may be termed financial assistance regulation. As government increasingly implements its domestic social policies through cooperative arrangements with voluntary-sector providers, such regulations will be increasingly problematical for religious institutions.

Perspective and Parameters

For centuries, churches have engaged in education and the collection of alms as part of their self-understanding and their calling to meet the physical and mental needs of humanity, along with the spiritual. The earliest formal education in colonial America was instituted by religious societies. Indeed, this was true not only of grammar schools, but of the first colleges, which were founded as seminaries to train a learned clergy for the pulpits of America's churches.[1] From before the Republic's founding in the late eighteenth century, and through much of the nineteenth century, social welfare was dominated by voluntary, faith-based agencies.[2]

Following the Civil War, and accelerating during the first third of the twentieth century, government undertook a more direct and affirmative role in allocating society's goods and opportunities, profoundly affecting the structure of the social order. A few northeastern states continued to purchase services from religious charities, but this was atypical. The needs of the waves of immigrants coupled with the nation's industrialization and urbanization placed growing demands on government. The religious charities were simply overwhelmed by the widespread poverty.[3]

---

1. See David W. Beggs & R. Bruce McQuiff, Historical Background, in America's Schools and Churches: Partners in Conflict 37, 39–44 (1965); William Clayton Bower, Church and State in Education 23–28 (1944); Robert H. Bremner, U.S. Dep't of Treasury, Private Philanthropy and Public Needs: Historical Perspective, in Comm'n on Private Philanthropy and Public Needs, U.S. Dep't of Treasury, Research Papers: Vol. I History, Trends, and Current Magnitudes 89, 90–98 (1977); Nathan E. Cohen, Social Work in the American Tradition 19–39 (1958); Michael O'Neill, The Third America: The Emergence of the Nonprofit Sector in the United States 24–34, 53–59, 72–73, 98–101 (1989); Phillip R. Popple & Leslie Leighninger, Social Work, Social Welfare, and American Society 94–101 (2d ed. 1993); 1 Anson Phelps Stokes, Church and State in the United States 628–38, 680–85, 691–96 (1950).

2. See Samuel Mencher, Poor Law to Poverty Program: Economic Security Policy in Britain and the United States 147–53, 233 (1967); Marvin Olasky, The Tragedy of American Compassion 6–41, 217–20 (1992); O'Neill, supra note 1, at 98–104; Timothy L. Smith, Revivalism and Social Reform: American Protestantism On the Eve of the Civil War 149–77 (1980). Some religious agencies received funds from state and local governments, but private funds made up over half of the budget. The federal government provided no subsidies. See Steven Rathgeb Smith & Michael Lipsky, Nonprofits for Hire: The Welfare State in the Age of Contracting 47–48 (1993).

3. See Mencher, supra note 2, at 233–39, 405–06; O'Neill, supra note 1, at 103–04.

Gradually, many spheres of society once deemed voluntary, or at least nonstatist, progressively yielded to this governmentalization. Concomitantly, religious groups came to understand their task in the world differently, some seeing their role as supplementing the statist order, others as a corrective to it,[4] and still others as called to separate from the secular world. Many of these charities drifted from their moorings in fervent religion as society became more secular, as social work became more specialized and professionalized, and as the Progressive Era gave rise to settlement houses and the social gospel movement.[5] Thus changing theology contributed to the shift, as did prejudice against certain religions: for example, the suspicion directed at Catholicism's heavy investment in maintaining its own K–12 schools.[6]

The government responded to the Great Depression with the New Deal, thus effectively determining that government agencies rather than voluntary charities would have primary responsibility for meeting social welfare needs.[7] From the mid-1930s through the 1970s, intervention by the federal government increased because liberals supported, while conservatives acceded to, the popular desire to compensate for the vicissitudes of free-market capitalism. Even terminology changed: government-provided services came to be called "public," whereas the voluntary sector was now regarded as "private," "sectarian," "parochial," and "paternalistic." Religious ministries continued to work alongside, but remained largely uninvolved with, their government counterparts.

This reallocation of responsibility from independent to governmental entities paralleled the growing notion of state police power. Initially addressing only the health and moral concerns of the population, police power expanded into an authority to legislate on behalf of the "general welfare," which was expansively defined. A similar development took place at the federal level with the enlargement of congressional power pursuant to the interstate Commerce Clause. This evolution toward government-provided services also grew with the government's ability to raise the large sums of money required to pay for health care, educational, and social welfare programs through the taxation of an expanding economy.

Moreover, a profound shift in the popular understanding of the causes of poverty occurred during the middle third of the twentieth century. No longer was being poor regarded as a spiritual or moral failing. Rather, the causes of poverty were attributed to the business cycles of capitalism, inadequate employment opportunities, racism and other invidious discrimination, and substandard education.[8] As the older understanding gave way, the popular conception of society's appropriate response to poverty underwent a sea change: from "Christian charity" to "social insurance,"[9] and still later to "statutory entitlements."

Yet a third phase has unfolded: a plateauing of the aspirational goal of government as the principal provider of social services and a return to a model whereby social welfare is provided, *inter alia*, by the independent sector through purchase-of-service contracts

---

4. *See infra* text accompanying notes 180–83.

5. *See* Mencher, *supra* note 2, at 258–62.

6. *See* Cohen, *supra* note 1, at 43–79; Bernard J. Coughlin, Church and State in Social Welfare 15–43, 111–16 (1965); Religion and Social Work 1–194 (F. Ernest Johnson ed., 1956); Popple, *supra* note 1, at 101–03.

7. *See* Mencher, *supra* note 2, at 313–32, 403–07; Lester M. Salamon, America's Nonprofit Sector: A Primer 41–43 (1992).

8. *See* Mencher, *supra* note 2, at 144–47, 273–77, 325.

9. *Id.* at 381–403, 405–07.

with the government.[10] The period from 1965 through the 1970s saw a sharp rise in federal expenditures for social welfare services, including cooperative arrangements with nonprofit agencies in the independent sector.[11] This taxpayer subsidization of independent-sector organizations operates on a track parallel to the government's own social service agencies.

A host of considerations continue to fuel this transition to a two-track paradigm: (1) budgetary constraints on government; (2) discontent with the impersonalization, inefficiency,[12] and poor quality of government-delivered services; (3) growing concern that welfare eligibility criteria create dependency by discouraging work, job training, and birth control, while encouraging profligate living;[13] (4) a desire to take advantage of entrepreneurship, volunteerism, and other free-market virtues operative in the independent sector; (5) the neoconservative emphasis on individual empowerment, personal responsibility, and private initiative;[14] (6) a renewed appreciation for the moral and spiritual dimension of the causes of poverty, coupled with a growing acknowledgment that government is impotent to bring about the fundamental change in human nature that it takes to turn large numbers of people away from destructive behaviors;[15] and (7) the versatility of a differentiated welfare system available through pursuit of a two-track strategy (that is, certain people being successfully reached by the voluntary sector who have not responded to government-operated programs).[16]

Despite the existence of government social service agencies, religious people in great numbers are involved in aid to the poor and enjoy impressive effectiveness.[17] As many as

---

10. *See* Coughlin, *supra* note 6, at 117–26; Salamon, *supra* note 7, at 46–47, 51–52, 81–87; Popple, *supra* note 2, at 103–05.

11. *See* Salamon, *supra* note 7, at 44–45; Smith & Lipsky, *supra* note 1, at 53–57, 70–71.

12. *See* Stephen Moore, Privatization Lessons for Washington, Part II, in Improving Human Services, The Heritage Foundation Backgrounder 2 (1988) (study of 57 county agencies in California conducted in 1984 found that contracting out social services to private organizations generally improved the quality and effectiveness of care); John Hilke, Mackinac Ctr. for Pub. Policy and Reason Found., Cost Savings From Privatization: A Compilation of Study Findings 12 (undated) (studies reported in 1980 show savings of 20 to 60 percent from welfare privatization).

13. *See* Charles Murray, Losing Ground: American Social Policy, 1950–1980 (1984); Olasky, *supra* note 2; Michael Novak et al., The New Consensus on Family and Welfare: A Community of Self-Reliance (1987).

14. *See* Anna Kondratas, Welfare Policy: Is There Common Ground?, Hudson Briefing Paper (Hudson Inst., Indianapolis, Ind.), Aug. 1993; Novak, *supra* note 13, at 13–16.

15. *See* Novak, *supra* note 13, at 10–13, 107–10; Lawrence W. Reed, Welfare Reform: Have We Gone Far Enough?, Viewpoint On Public Issues (Mackinac Ctr., Midland, Mich.), 1995 ("Unlike private efforts that stress character-building, one-on-one mentoring and a spiritual dimension, the impersonal public dole does nothing to resolve the behavioral poverty that keeps millions in demoralizing dependency").

16. Social scientist and management expert Peter F. Drucker believes that "government has proved itself incompetent at solving social problems. . . . [T]he nonprofits have the potential to become America's social sector—equal in importance to the public sector of government and the private sector of business." Editorial, What Should We Do About the Poor?, First Things, Apr. 1992, at 6, 9. Drucker observes that nonprofit agencies in the independent sector "spend far less for results than governments spend for failure." What America needs, he says, is "a public policy that establishes the nonprofits as the country's first line of attack on its social problems." Andrew C. Little, The Future of Social Welfare May Be Just Down the Street, Viewpoint on Public Issues (Mackinac Ctr., Midland, Mich.), Sept. 7, 1992. *See generally* Peter F. Drucker, The Age of Social Transformation, Atlantic Monthly, Nov. 1994, at 53, 76, 77–80.

17. *See* Henry G. Cisneros, U.S. Dep't of Housing and Urban Dev., Higher Ground: Faith Communities and Community Building (1996); National Inst. on Drug Abuse Servs. Research Report, An Evaluation of the Teen Challenge Treatment Program (1977) (showing a material difference in

ninety million volunteers and nine hundred thousand nonprofit organizations, many of which are faith-based, presently provide social services, health care, and education.[18] Municipalities now contract over half of their human services funding to independent organizations.[19] Such contracting was encouraged by the Clinton administration's "reinventing government" effort, because nonprofits are more flexible and responsive to social problems and in order "to leverage public resources with private ones."[20]

The virtual reversal in roles played by church and state that occurred over the past two centuries in matters of education and social welfare, indeed in family life as well, has been summarized as follows:

> [T]he role played by government in the social life of America in the 1780s (and for almost a century and a half thereafter) was openly and strongly influenced and directed by religion, whereas in the 1980s that is much less true and in many respects not true at all, while the role played by religion in the social life of America in the 1980s is openly and strongly influenced and directed by government.

> To put this last point in strong terms, and perhaps with some exaggeration: whereas two centuries ago, in matters of social life that have a significant moral dimension, government was the handmaid of religion, today religion—in its social responsibilities, as contrasted with personal faith and collective worship—is the handmaid of government.[21]

Notwithstanding the continued maintenance of a "wall of separation" preventing many forms of direct aid to primary and secondary religious schools, government assistance to faith-based charities, hospitals, and colleges has never been disallowed by the Supreme Court.[22] Because of the Court's forbearance in these cases, this third phase, in which government helps to finance services provided by faith-based charities, has been emboldened and promises to expand.

With the past in perspective, it is helpful to chart the several parameters that bracket this chapter. A daunting welter of factors confronts anyone who sets out to systematize the government's financial assistance regulation of social welfare ministries and schools operated by religious organizations.

The first of these parameters is the nature of the organization that is the object of the government's program of aid and, hence, the object of regulation. Religious chari-

---

success rate for faith-based over secular drug treatment programs for youth); John J. DiIulio, Jr., Jeremiah's Call, 5 Prism 19 (1998) (summarizing early findings of social science studies); Olasky, *supra* note 2, at 204–06, 213–16, 222–30.

18. *See* Editorial, *supra* note 16, at 9.

19. *See* Moore, *supra* note 12, at 2. Some governments have become quite dependent on churches in the delivery of welfare services. For example, $1.754 billion of the Roman Catholic New York Archdiocese's operating budget of $2.1 billion is federal, state, and local government funds. These funds go to support a large network of foster-care agencies, day-care and mental-health centers, elderly and youth programs, and agencies reaching the homeless, AIDS victims, and drug addicts. *See* Church Services Public: Funds Help O'Connor to Help Others, Newsday, May 17, 1993, at 6.

20. Kondratas, *supra* note 14, at 9.

21. Harold J. Berman, The Challenge of the Modern State, *in* Articles of Faith, Articles of Peace: The Religious Liberty Clauses and the American Public Philosophy 40, 43 (J.D. Hunter & O. Guiness eds., 1990).

22. *See* Bowen v. Kendrick, 487 U.S. 589 (1988) (church-based teenage counseling centers); Roemer v. Board of Pub. Works, 426 U.S. 736 (1976) (religious college); Hunt v. McNair, 413 U.S. 734 (1973) (religious college); Tilton v. Richardson, 403 U.S. 672 (1971) (religious college); Bradfield v. Roberts, 175 U.S. 291 (1899) (religious hospital).

ties characterized by the clientele they serve comprise quite a long and differentiated list: everything from education to health care to legal services to financial counseling centers.[23]

A second parameter is the degree of connection between the religious school or social welfare agency and the central religious body. Some schools or agencies are at the very core of the central religious body. Others are parachurch groups, meaning that they are not *de jure* affiliated with any church or denomination, although they are explicitly and self-consciously Protestant, Jewish, etc.[24] Gauging the degree of this connection can be accomplished in many different ways. For example, any of the following might be considered: the extent to which religious creed guides decision making; the extent of religious content in the curriculum or program; the degree of control by a parent church; the extent to which the governing board is comprised of officers or members of a parent church; whether officers and staff are selected exclusively from members of a parent church; the extent of financial support by a parent church; the extent to which funding is supplied by contributors of the same faith; and the extent to which the clientele served are exclusively of the same faith. Quite apart from the degree of connectedness, the extent to which the social service provider has retained its religious fervor and distinctives is a parameter of interest to anyone posing the question of institutional autonomy.

The third of these parameters is the myriad of means by which the governmental assistance is delivered. Governmental benefits are delivered through the following mechanisms:[25] direct payments for a specified use; project grants such as training or research funds; high-risk loans, low-interest loans, and guarantees of loans from private lenders; insurance at favorable premiums; in-kind donations of goods such as used furniture or

---

23. A nonexhaustive list includes preschools and child day-care centers; temporary shelters for abused children; foster homes and adoption placement agencies; residential-care or group-care homes for abused or neglected children and adjudicated juvenile offenders; adolescent or teen counseling centers; crisis-pregnancy counseling centers; maternity homes for women with crisis pregnancies; temporary shelters for battered women; rehabilitation centers for alcoholics, drug abusers, and the unemployed; AIDS hospices; prison ministries, police and prison chaplaincies; halfway houses for adults convicted of crimes; storehouses of free or reduced-price food, used clothing, and household items; centers for free meals (soup kitchens) and temporary shelters for the homeless (rescue missions); low-income housing renovation programs; refugee aid and resettlement; disaster relief; clearinghouses for volunteers rendering home-based care to the disabled; long-term care facilities for the disabled, retarded, and mentally ill; long-term care facilities for the elderly (retirement, nursing, and invalid homes); elderly day-care centers; centers for vocational training or employment of the disabled; literacy and English-as-a-second-language programs; hospitals and community-health clinics; dispute resolution and legal-aid centers; draft counseling centers; financial-counseling centers; marital and family-counseling centers; recreational programs, summer camps and retreat centers for youth and adults; and support groups of every stripe for persons suffering from life's many vicissitudes. *Cf.* Religion and Social Work, *supra* note 6, at 19–25; Popple, *supra* note 1, at 105–08.

24. *Compare* Religion and Social Work, *supra* note 6, at 17–19 *with* Popple, *supra* note 1, at 105–08.

25. *See* Office of Mgmt. and Budget, Executive Office of President of U.S., Catalog of Federal Domestic Assistance XV–XVI (32nd ed. 1998). The catalog lists and defines fifteen types of federal assistance. As classified by the General Services Administration, federal benefits and services are provided through seven categories of financial assistance (grants, loans, insurance, donated property, etc.) and eight categories of nonfinancial assistance (training, counseling, supplying technical literature, investigation of complaints, etc.). *See* Douglas J. Besharov, Bottom-up Funding, *in* To Empower People: From State to Civil Society 124 (Michael Novak ed., 2d ed. 1996) (comparing the strengths and weaknesses that arise when funding comes directly and indirectly from government).

surplus food; free use of government property, facilities, or equipment; free assistance by government personnel to perform certain tasks; free instruction, consultation, or training by government personnel; reduced postal rates; low-interest bonds for capital improvements; educational vouchers and child-care certificates; student scholarships, grants, and fellowships; and tax credits, deductions, and Internal Revenue Code (IRC) section 501(c)(3) exempt status enabling receipt of tax-deductible contributions. The federal government has programs numbering in the thousands providing financial and nonfinancial assistance.[26] Religious institutions are presumptively eligible for many of these programs.

Yet a fourth parameter is whether governmental assistance goes directly to the religious institution or the program only indirectly aids a faith-related charity or school. Several governmental programs confer aid to needy individuals. In turn, these individuals are free to use the benefit at any qualifying institution, whether governmental or independent, nonsectarian or religious. Examples are found in: federal child-care certificates for low-income parents, federal tax credits for the child-care expenses of working parents, special-education services for students with disabilities, the G.I. Bill and federally guaranteed loans for postsecondary education students, and state income tax deductions for parents paying tuition to primary and secondary schools. These indirect forms of aid can carry with them financial assistance regulation of religious institutions. For example, guaranteed student loans are restricted to students enrolled at institutions of higher education that comply with nondiscrimination requirements in the provision of services to the institution-wide system.

A final parameter is the multiple levels of government that may be involved in a given program. Although many federal assistance programs provide their aid directly from the agency to the voluntary-sector charity, other programs are intergovernmental ventures between federal agencies and the states or between federal agencies and municipalities. These grants allocate money to states and municipalities in accord with a formula prescribed by statute for social welfare activities in an identified subject area of need (a block grant), as opposed to being confined to a site-specific project. In turn, the state or municipality has direct interaction with, and oversight of, the voluntary sector. In these programs it is common for state or local authorities to have frontline responsibility for the enforcement of federal minimum standards by the charitable or educational recipients. Further, these formula grants by the federal government routinely impose matching or cost-sharing requirements, levels of effort and earmarking limitations, and other mandates on participating state and local governments.[27]

The Various Types of Regulatory Restraints Imposed as a Condition of Governmental Assistance

Participation by the independent sector in programs of governmental assistance to health care, social welfare, and education is of course contingent on fiscal accountabil-

---

26. *See* Catalog of Federal Domestic Assistance, *supra* note 25, at *passim*.
27. *See* Office of Mgmt. and Budget, Executive Office of President of U.S., Compliance Supplement for Single Audits of State and Local Governments (1990).

ity. Governments meet this need for accountability by mandatory audits of providers, as well as by requiring providers to file informational forms and sign "assurance of compliance" certificates.

A charity's nonprofit, tax-exempt status under IRC section 501(c)(3) requires annual filing of informational Form 990. Although a church, a convention of churches, an interchurch organization, and their "integrated auxiliaries" are exempt from the filing requirement, most other religious organizations must file.[28]

The government understandably has an interest in insuring that tax funds are spent in accord with the purposes of a given assistance program. However, the rigor of the government's independent auditing requirements may take some religious organizations unawares, especially those groups that are small in overall budget, less formal in operational structure, not accustomed to operating in the public eye, or whose personnel supervision is not tightly controlled, such as ministries heavily dependent on volunteers. Moreover, the audits go beyond fiscal accounting (including matching and cost-sharing requirements) and require a certified auditor to inquire into compliance with, for example, applicable civil rights acts and prohibitions on partisan political activity.[29]

---

28. Pursuant to IRC § 6033(a)(2)(A)(i) (1988) and Treas. Reg. § 1.6033-2(g)(5)(i) (1988), the IRS once took the position that an organization is an "integrated auxiliary of a church" exempt from filing Form 990 if it is: (1) tax-exempt, (2) affiliated with a church, and (3) exclusively religious in its principal activity. Under Treas. Reg. § 1.6033-2(g)(5)(ii), "[a]n organization's principal activity will not be considered to be exclusively religious if that activity is educational, literary, charitable, or of another nature (other than religious) that would serve as a basis for exemption under § 501(c)(3)."

The courts rejected, as inconsistent with congressional intent, the IRS's view that religious charities cannot be "exclusively religious." *See* Tennessee Baptist Children's Homes, Inc. v. United States, 790 F.2d 534 (6th Cir. 1986) (holding that separately incorporated residential care home was integrated auxiliary of church and thus exempt from annual informational filing of Form 990); Lutheran Soc. Serv. v. United States, 758 F.2d 1283 (8th Cir. 1985) (church-affiliated charity can be "exclusively religious integrated auxiliary" exempt from annual filing of informational Form 990); Lutheran Children and Family Serv. v. United States, Civ. No. 83-5205, 1986 WL 7834 (E.D. Pa. July 10, 1986).

Negotiations between the IRS and several religious groups led to a mutually satisfactory formulation that is set out in Revenue Procedure 86-23, 1986-1 C.B. 564. The formulation does not require filing Form 990 if the ministry is affiliated with a church or convention or association of churches and meets an internal support requirement. On December 15, 1994, the IRS published proposed rules incorporating Rev. Proc. 86-23 into the regulations defining "integrated auxiliary" for purposes of determining what entities must file information returns. *See* Prop. Treas. Reg. EE-41–86, 59 Fed. Reg. 64,633 (1994). The proposal became final December 20, 1995. *See* Treas. Reg. §§ 1.508-1, 1.6033-2 (as amended in 1995). Under the final regulations, a church-affiliated organization that does not offer admissions, goods, services, or facilities for public sale would be exempt from filing. If the organization offers these items for public sale, then it would be exempt from filing only if 50 percent or less of its support comes from a combination of government sources, public contributions, and sale proceeds other than those from an unrelated trade or business.

Also exempt from filing Form 990 are (1) a school below the college level that is affiliated with a church or run by a religious order; (2) a mission society more than half of whose activities are conducted in or directed at persons in foreign countries and are sponsored by or affiliated with one or more churches or denominations; (3) exclusively religious activities of a religious order; (4) a religious or apostolic organization as described in IRC § 501(d) (1994); and (5) organizations whose annual gross receipts are less than $25,000.

29. For religious institutions, the requirements of an audit are set out in Office of Mgmt. and Budget, Executive Office of President of U.S., Circular A-133, Audits of Institutions of Higher Learning and Other Non-Profit Institutions (1990) [hereinafter OMB Circular A-133], *reprinted in* 55 Fed. Reg. 10,019–10,025 (Mar. 16, 1990), and Circular A-110, Uniform Administrative Requirements for Grants and Cooperative Agreements with Institutions of Higher Education, Hospitals and

Of principal interest in this chapter is not the fiscal accounting requirement for providers of governmental assistance, but the regulatory controls that implicate a church's polity, its hiring of personnel, and the content of its programming. The subparts that follow are organized by the various types of regulations affecting the structure and autonomy of religious organizations.

Conditions imposed because of the putative requirement to separate church and state

When federal or state legislation confers a subsidy, grant, or tax benefit on welfare agencies generally, including those operated by religious institutions, at times lawmakers have thought it incumbent to add safeguards specially addressing the matter of church/state relations. Some of these provisions stem from exaggerated or antiquated notions of the requirements of the Establishment Clause.[30] At the state and local levels, however, these provisions may properly reflect the more stringent requirements of some state constitutions.[31]

Conditions imposed by financial assistance regulations because of apparent requirements of church/state relations can be usefully organized around five types of textual provisions: (1) the requirement that the central religious body form a separate nonprofit corporation to receive and administer the aid; (2) prohibitions on funds being used for the purchase or improvement of sectarian-use real estate; (3) prohibitions on benefits being used to render services in a building where the facility itself has religious symbols and fixtures; (4) prohibitions on benefits being used to obtain training or education to enter a religious vocation; and (5) prohibitions on benefits being used for religious instruction, worship, prayer, or other inherently religious activity.

A tangle between the United States Department of Housing and Urban Development (HUD) and Congress generated one of the more revealing social service funding debates. The Emergency Shelter Grants Program (ESGP) was adopted by Congress in Oc-

---

Other Non-Profit Organizations (1976), *reprinted in* 41 Fed. Reg. 32,016–32,037 (July 30, 1976); I.R. Manual, Exempt Organizations Examination Guidelines Handbook, § 342 Colleges and Universities (1994) (especially § 342.(11) on Scholarships and Fellowships and § 342.(12) on Legislative and Political Expenses). For instructions to the independent auditor concerning compliance requirements beyond the financial, see Office of Mgmt. and Budget, Executive Office of President of U.S., Compliance Supplement for Audits of Institutions of Higher Learning and Other Non-Profit Institutions (1991) [hereinafter Compliance Supplement for Audits].

In order to keep the government "at arms length," the National Council of Churches insists that government auditors not enter upon ecclesiastical premises to perform audits. Rather, the council makes all books of account and supporting records pertinent to the grant program available at the offices of the council's legal counsel. *See* Marvin Braiterman & Dean M. Kelley, When Is Governmental Intervention Legitimate?, *in* Government Intervention in Religious Affairs 170, 186 (Dean M. Kelley ed., 1982).

30. The Supreme Court, for example, has never struck down aid to a church-affiliated college or social-welfare agency. *See supra* note 22.

31. *See* Linda S. Wendtland, Note, Beyond The Establishment Clause: Enforcing Separation Of Church And State Through State Constitutional Provisions, 71 Va. L. Rev. 625 (1985); F. William O'Brien, The Blaine Amendment 1875–1876, 41 U. Det. L.J. 137 (1963). Although now dated, a still useful work in the area of religion and state constitutions is Chester James Antieau et al., Religion Under the State Constitutions (1965).

tober 1986.[32] The 1986 ESGP authorized HUD to make grants to private nonprofit organizations to convert buildings into emergency shelters for the homeless and to pay certain social service expenses in connection with the operation of these shelters. In December 1986, HUD issued proposed regulations concerning the administration of the grants.[33] Buildings owned by churches and other "primarily religious organizations" were completely prohibited from receiving funds to renovate, rehabilitate, or convert their buildings for use as homeless shelters.[34]

In early 1987, Congress considered the Stewart B. McKinney Homeless Assistance Act, which was approved by the president in July of that year.[35] Subtitle B of the McKinney Act modified the ESGP of the prior year.[36] In considering the 1987 ESGP legislation, Congress sharply criticized HUD's proposed ban on grants to religious organizations.[37] The committee report in the House of Representatives indicated that HUD was to administer both the 1986 and 1987 ESGP in a manner permitting participation by religious organizations. The report stated that funds under the 1986 act should be made available to religious recipients under the following conditions:

- No person applying for funded services shall be discriminated against on the basis of religion.
- No religious instruction or counseling, and no religious worship will be provided in connection with the provision of secular nonreligious assistance.
- No sectarian or religious symbols may be used in the portion of the facility used to provide secular services unless such said symbols had been previously permanently affixed to the facility.
- All federal funds must be accounted for separately from all other funds of the institution so that the federal government will not have to monitor the general accounts of the religious organization.
- Any real property that is owned by a religious organization or an organization with religious affiliation and rehabilitated with federal funds must be dedicated solely to secular purposes.... If the property reverts to sectarian use, the grant amount must be repaid.[39]

In accord with this expression of congressional disapproval, HUD did issue final regulations in October 1987 that lifted the ban on grants to religious ministries.[40] But the final regulations also codified the foregoing conditions worked out in congressional committee.

HUD's restriction on capital-improvement grants being expended to improve only secular-use facilities is in line with Supreme Court cases on aid to faith-based colleges.[41]

---

32. The 1986 ESGP is found in Part C, Title V of HUD's appropriation for Fiscal Year 1987, Pub. L. No. 99-500 § 101(g), 100 Stat. 1783 (approved Oct. 18, 1986).

33. *See* Emergency Shelter and Grants Program, 51 Fed. Reg. 45,277 (1986).

34. *See id.* at 45,283.

35. *See* Stewart P. McKinney Homeless Assistance Act, Pub. L. No. 100-77 (codified at 42 U.S.C. §§ 11371–11378 (1994 & Supp. III 1997)).

36. The McKinney ESGP is codified at 42 U.S.C. §§ 11371–11378 (1994 & Supp. III 1997).

37. *See* Stewart P. McKinney Homeless Assistance Act, H.R. Rep. No. 100-10 (I), at 23–25 (1987), *reprinted in* 1987 U.S.C.C.A.N. 362, 369–71.

39. *Id.* at 25, *reprinted in* 1987 U.S.C.C.A.N., at 370.

40. *See* Emergency Shelter Grant Program, 52 Fed. Reg. 38,863 (1987) (presently codified at 24 C.F.R. pt. 576 (1999)). The constitutionality of public funding of religious shelters for the homeless was upheld in *Henry v. Life Haven, Inc.*, No. 329566, 1993 WL 182313 (Conn. Super. Ct. May 18, 1993).

41. *See* Roemer v. Board of Public Works, 426 U.S. 736 (1976) (upholding noncategorical state grants for religious colleges); Hunt v. McNair, 413 U.S. 734 (1973) (upholding issuance of state rev-

Still, it is questionable whether the other conditions are compelled by the Establishment Clause. Consider HUD's requirement that accounts of public and private funds be kept distinct. The apparent concern is administrative entanglement between church and state. In light of Supreme Court decisions summarily rejecting excessive administrative entanglement arguments,[42] HUD's rule exaggerates the Establishment Clause prohibition.

The regulation requiring religious symbols to be stripped from shelters, thereby creating a religion-free zone, is particularly offensive. HUD sought removal of the religious symbols to create the impression that the aid was being delivered by a secular agency. Such an impression is not only false but, especially where adults are involved, unnecessary if the aim is to prevent religious coercion by mere exposure to these symbols. The Establishment Clause should not be read as requiring desacralization as if religious distinctives were to be handled like toxic waste.[43]

The final regulations promulgated by HUD require religious organizations to create a separate nonprofit corporation for administration of the grants.[44] A separate corporate shell is a mere paper wall not capable of meeting the substantive concerns of the Establishment Clause. In addition to conflicting with the polity of some churches, the separate incorporation requirement increases administrative expense.[45]

---

enue bonds for construction of buildings at religious colleges); Tilton v. Richardson, 403 U.S. 672 (1971) (upholding federal construction grants for secular building at religious colleges, except for twenty-year limitation period concerning prohibition on use of buildings for religious purposes).

Examples of sectarian-use restrictions on building grants are common. The Hill-Burton Act, 42 U.S.C. §§ 291 to 291o-1 (1994), is a federal program designed to improve the standards of medical care in the United States by subsidizing the cost of hospital construction. Both public and private hospitals are eligible, including hospitals that are religiously affiliated. However, the construction of buildings is understood to be restricted to facilities that have a secular use. Coughlin, *supra* note 6, at 69–74.

The Child Care and Development Block Grant Program (CCDBG), 42 U.S.C. §§ 9858–9858q (1994 & Supp. III 1997), makes funds available to improve and expand child care. Capital-improvement grants are available to qualifying child-care providers, including centers that are church-based. However, in addition to not improving sectarian-use facilities (unless needed to meet minimum health and safety standards), a church-based center receiving capital-improvement grants must be fully state-licensed and not discriminate on the basis of religion in its enrollment. *See* 42 U.S.C. §§ 9858c(c)(2)(E), 9858d(b)(2), 9858k(a), 9858l (1994 & Supp. III 1997).

42. *See* Jimmy Swaggart Ministries v. Board of Equalization, 493 U.S. 378 (1990); Tony and Susan Alamo Found. v. Secretary of Labor, 471 U.S. 290 (1985).

43. The Supreme Court first faced the question of the constitutionality of public funding for church-affiliated colleges in *Tilton v. Richardson,* 403 U.S. 672 (1971). The Court upheld construction grants, but under a rationale suggesting that the colleges be largely secular in character. Following the decision in *Tilton,* the attorney for the four colleges reported having put them through a process of "secularization," including the removal of crucifixes from classroom walls. *See* Lynn R. Buzzard & Samuel Ericsson, The Battle For Religious Liberty 159 (1982).

In a case involving state funding of church-related foster homes, a civil rights claim resulted, *inter alia,* in a court order requiring stripping religious symbols at the homes. *See* Wilder v. Bernstein, 848 F.2d 1338 (2d Cir. 1988), *aff'g* 645 F. Supp. 1292 (S.D.N.Y. 1986). For a discussion of the *Wilder* case see *infra* text accompanying notes 76–84.

These two examples are not unlike the desacralizing of homeless shelters required by HUD. In a heartening development, the Child Care and Development Block Grant Program, 42 U.S.C. §§ 9858–9858q, permits church-based child-care centers to receive child-care certificates whether or not they display religious symbols. *See* 42 U.S.C. § 9858n(2) (Supp. III 1997). The CCDBG is discussed in the text accompanying notes 93–99.

44. *See* Emergency Shelter Grant Program, 52 Fed. Reg. 38,863, 38,870 (1987) (codified at 24 C.F.R. § 575.21(b)(2)(i) (1992)).

45. Similar to HUD's requirement that religious recipients form a nonprofit corporation to administer ESGP grants is a provision in the Iowa income tax code. In 1987, Iowa amended its tax

It is common for financial assistance regulations to prohibit the use of governmental benefits for obtaining religious education or training. This is illustrated by the American Schools and Hospitals Abroad Program (ASHA).[46] The program assists in the construction of schools and hospital centers for medical research sponsored by citizens but located outside the United States. ASHA is administered by the Agency for International Development (AID), which awards grants to sponsoring United States institutions or individuals. Funds are then transferred by the sponsor to the foreign school or hospital. Religiously affiliated schools and hospitals are eligible for grants, but AID's criteria explicitly require that the assistance not be used to train persons for religious pursuits.[47]

Similar conditions are found in state aid programs. For example, Minnesota permits high school juniors and seniors to enroll in college classes.[48] If a student wants the course credit to apply toward high school graduation requirements, the government will pay for the tuition, fees, textbooks, and transportation. The student may select any postsecondary institution, including church-related colleges, but enrollment must be

---

code to provide a deduction or credit for the tuition and textbook expenses of parents with students attending primary and secondary schools. *See* Iowa Code Ann. §§ 422.9, 422.12(2) (West Supp. 1999). Obviously, the benefit is most helpful to those with dependents attending parochial schools; however, the student must be enrolled at a school accredited by the state. *See* Iowa Code Ann. § 256.11 (West 1996). Accreditation requires that private schools be incorporated as nonprofits, including church-related schools. *See id.* The Iowa tax deduction is discussed in the text accompanying notes 63–69.

46. 22 U.S.C. § 2174(b) (1994). Similar illustrations are found in the Individuals with Disabilities Education Act (IDEA), 20 U.S.C. §§ 1400–1487 (Supp. III 1997), and the National Service Trust Program, 42 U.S.C. §§ 12571–12595 (1994).

IDEA concerns the provision of free, special-education services to primary and secondary education students through a federal-state cooperative funding program. Regulations promulgated under IDEA prohibit the use of funds to pay for religious worship, instruction, or proselytization. *See* 34 C.F.R. § 76.532 (1998); *see also* Thomas Guernsey & M. Grey Sweeney, The Church, the State, and the EHA: Educating the Handicapped in Light of the Establishment Clause, 73 Marq. L. Rev. 259 (1989). In *Zobrest v. Catalina Foothills Sch. Dist.,* 509 U.S. 1 (1993), the Supreme Court held that the Establishment Clause was not violated when IDEA funds were spent providing a sign-language interpreter to a deaf student attending a parochial high school.

The National Service Trust Program provides federal financial assistance, including college expenses, to young adults who volunteer their services to nonprofit organizations. Churches and other religious entities are expressly eligible as recipients of these volunteer services. *See* 42 U.S.C. § 12511(5) (1994). However, 42 U.S.C. § 12584(a)(4) of the program bars volunteer services "to give religious instruction; to conduct worship services; to provide instruction as part of a program that includes mandatory religious education or worship; to construct, operate, or maintain facilities devoted to religious instruction or worship; or to engage in any form of proselytization." *See* Timothy B. Shah, National Service: Will AmeriCorps Serve America? 37 (Crossroads Monograph Series in Faith and Public Policy, 1995) ("Because AmeriCorps directly funds organizations, not individual volunteers…religious charities would have two choices: either secularize to receive AmeriCorps money, or play David against Goliath in a struggle for scarce volunteers and resources. This means that religious organizations that have an integral religious identity will be effectively discouraged from participating"); *id.* at 39 ("Of the 57 organizations chosen so far to receive AmeriCorps grants, only four are religious—even though religious organizations are the source of roughly *half* of all charitable activities. Some religious organizations did not apply for AmeriCorps grants because they wanted to preserve their autonomy against government intrusion; others applied but were not accepted, perhaps because the [government] deemed them too religious").

47. *See* American Schools and Hospitals Abroad Program, 44 Fed. Reg. 67,543, 67,544 (1979) (also prohibiting use of grants for constructing buildings used for worship). The constitutionality of ASHA, as applied, has been questioned in *Lamont v. Woods,* 948 F.2d 825 (2d Cir. 1991), *aff'g* 748 F. Supp. 1043 (S.D.N.Y. 1990) (three-part *Lemon* test held applicable to claim challenging grant for twenty religiously affiliated schools).

48. *See* Post-Secondary Enrollment Options Act, Minn. Stat. Ann. § 124D.09 (West Supp. 1999).

"in nonsectarian courses."[49] In another Minnesota program authorities are authorized to issue tax-exempt bonds for the purpose of raising capital for postsecondary institutions, including faith-related colleges.[50] However, financial assistance may not be provided to "any facility used or to be used for sectarian instruction or as a place of religious worship nor any facility which is used or to be used primarily in connection with any part of the program of a school or department of divinity for any religious denomination."[51]

Such restrictions on governmental funding for religious education are consistent with Supreme Court cases striking down direct aid to faith-based schools that risk the transmission of religion[52] and cases disallowing funds for the purchase of religious materials.[53] However, the Court has held that the Establishment Clause is not violated by aid-to-education programs where the benefit goes to the individual student, who in turn exercises personal choice in taking the benefit to any school, whether government or independent, nonsectarian or religious.[54] The acceptance of such aid, albeit indirect, will still carry with it some regulation of religious schools.[55]

An example of regulations prohibiting grant monies from being used for religious instruction, worship, prayer, or other inherently religious activity is found in *Fordham University v. Brown.*[56] In *Forham University*, a federal district court upheld regulations of the National Telecommunications and Information Administration (NTIA), part of

---

49. *See* Minn. Stat. Ann. § 124D.09 (5), (10). The act's constitutionality was sustained in *Minnesota Federation of Teachers v. Nelson,* 740 F. Supp. 694 (D. Minn. 1990), and *Minnesota Fed'n of Teachers v. Mammenga,* 500 N.W.2d 136 (Minn. Ct. App. 1993).

50. *See* Minn. Stat. Ann. §§ 136A.25 to 136A.42 (West 1994 & Supp.1999).

51. Minn. Stat. Ann. § 136A.28 (3). The constitutionality of the act was upheld, as applied, in *Minnesota Higher Education Facilities Authority v. Hawk,* 232 N.W.2d 106 (Minn. 1975). Although church-related, the court found all of the colleges in question were "nonsectarian." None of the institutions discriminated on the basis of race, color, creed, or national origin, none required chapel attendance, none promulgated distinctive doctrines or tenets of a particular religious sect, and religious courses were taught according to the requirements of the discipline as opposed to a slant toward a particular faith.

52. *See, e.g.,* Committee for Public Educ. and Religious Liberty v. Regan, 444 U.S. 646 (1980); Lemon v. Kurtzman, 411 U.S. 192 (1973).

53. It is widely assumed that states supplying textbooks to primary and secondary schools must limit such aid to secular materials. *See, e.g.,* Wolman v. Walter, 433 U.S. 229 (1977); Board of Educ. of Cent. Sch. Dist. No. 1 v. Allen, 392 U.S. 236 (1968); Cochran v. Louisiana State Bd. of Educ., 281 U.S. 370 (1930). Accordingly, the statutes in several states provide for the loaning of textbooks to nonpublic schools but expressly limit the aid to materials that are nonsectarian. *See, e.g.,* S.D. Codified Laws § 13-34-23 (Michie 1991); 24 Pa. Cons. Stat. Ann. § 9-973(b) (West 1992).

54. *See* Zobrest v. Catalina Foothills Sch. Dist., 509 U.S. 1 (1993); Witters v. Washington Dep't of Servs. for Blind, 474 U.S. 481 (1986). Notwithstanding the inapplicability of the Establishment Clause, such indirect aid may be barred by state constitutions. *See, e.g.,* Witters v. Washington Comm'n for Blind, 771 P.2d 1119, 1121 (Wash. 1989) (prohibiting, under state constitution, the granting of vocational rehabilitation funds to a visually handicapped applicant to use at a religious college for course of study as pastor, missionary, or church youth director).

55. *See* Frank R. Kremerer, et al., Vouchers and Private School Autonomy, 21 J.L. & Educ. 601 (1992) (providing an account of autonomy issues that arose in the Milwaukee independent-school voucher program).

56. 856 F. Supp. 684 (D.D.C. 1994). See also *Church on the Rock v. City of Albuquerque,* 84 F.3d 1273 (10th Cir. 1996), concerning access to senior-citizen centers funded in part under the Older Americans Act. The act requires, as a condition of receiving federal funds, that the premises not be used for sectarian worship or teaching. A local church sought to show a religious film and distribute Bibles at the center. Municipal authorities refused the request citing, *inter alia,* fear of losing federal funding. The circuit court ordered the city to grant access to the centers as a matter of the church's right to free speech. Further, the court held that neither the Establishment Clause nor the congres-

the United States Department of Commerce, denying funding for university radio broadcast facilities because the station's programming included weekly Roman Catholic masses. Regulations written by NTIA prohibited grants for "essentially sectarian purposes."[57] The prohibitions denied all funding notwithstanding that masses were only a small part of a larger, secular programming schedule. Fordham challenged the regulations as violative of the Free Exercise and Establishment clauses, as well as the Equal Protection Clause. The regulations were upheld as a proper response to the requirement of the Establishment Clause that government not sponsor or endorse religion.[58] While the appeal filed by Fordham was pending, the case was settled.[59] NTIA agreed to no longer bar public radio stations from grants based on religious elements in programming. Henceforth, an eligibility determination would be based on whether any benefit to a sectarian program was merely "attenuated or incidental." Funding would be denied where the "essential thrust" of the station's program was religious.[60]

In late 1995 the Small Business Administration, also part of the Department of Commerce, reviewed and revised its regulations concerning loan applications from organizations promoting religious objectives. For some time the SBA had refused assistance to churches. Organizations that carried on some religious activities were denied loans. One litigated example is a for-profit child-care center that involved the children in prayer and the reading of Bible stories.[61] New regulations continue to deny assistance to businesses which "principally engage in teaching, instruction, counseling or indoctrinating religion or religious beliefs, whether the setting is religious or secular." However, businesses are not denied assistance "merely because they offer religious books, articles, or other products for sale or because they support or encourage moral and ethical values based upon religious beliefs."[62]

Conditions affecting polity, curriculum, self-definition and other issues of institutional autonomy

In 1987 Iowa modified its income tax code to permit taxpayers enrolling dependents in nongovernmental primary or secondary schools to claim a deduction for the cost of

---

sional restriction in the act were sufficient to justify overriding First Amendment expressional rights. *See id.* at 1280.

57. 15 C.F.R. § 2301.5(d)(2)(xvi) (1994). *See Fordham Univ.*, 856 F. Supp. at 691.

58. *See Forham Univ.*, 856 F. Supp. at 695–98. Similar regulations appear in municipal grants. *Compare* Ronald J. Sider & Heidi Rolland, Correcting the Welfare Tragedy: Toward a New Model for Church/State Partnership, *in* Welfare in America: Christian Perspectives on a Policy in Crisis 454, 473 n.69 (Stanley W. Carlson-Thies & James W. Skillen eds., 1996) (reporting on Circle Urban Ministries, a Christian emergency housing program, reaching a funding accommodation with the City of Chicago whereby Circle Urban does not require church attendance and does not use government funds to pay for its evangelistic activity, but evangelism still may hold a central place in the housing program), *with* Olasky, *supra* note 2, at 214–15 (reporting on City Team, a Christian substance-abuse ministry in San Jose, refusing an offer of funding to expand its program because the grant was conditioned on City Team dropping religious requirements for participants).

59. *See* Larry Witham, Radio Stations with Religious Content Cleared to Get Grants, Wash. Times, Dec. 21, 1995, at A5.

60. 60 Fed. Reg. 66,491 (Dec. 22, 1995); *see especially id.* at 66,494 & nn.35 & 37.

61. *See* Blocker v. Small Business Admin., 916 F. Supp. 37, 42 (D.D.C. 1996) (dismissing claim as moot as a result of change in SBA policy).

62. Proposed Rules, 60 Fed. Reg. 64,356, 64,360 (Dec. 15, 1995).

tuition and textbooks.[63] To qualify, the independent school must be accredited by the state.[64] The act defines "textbooks" and "tuition" for which the deduction applies as excluding expenses related to, or used in, "the teaching of religious tenets, doctrines, or worship," and activities or materials "the purpose of which is to inculcate those tenets, doctrines, or worship."[65] Although Iowa's Department of Revenue and Finance has the power to subpoena books, papers, and records of taxpayers and the independent school involved,[66] the primary interaction prescribed in the act is between the taxpayer and the state.[67]

The requirements for accreditation in Iowa that implicate the religious freedom of independent schools are as follows:

· Educational programs shall be taught from a multicultural, nonsexist approach.
· Global perspectives shall be incorporated into all levels of the educational program.[68]

The terms "multicultural approach" and "global perspectives" are not defined in the legislation or underlying regulations, nor is there reported case law on the question. If Iowa were to aggressively impose a doctrinaire perspective on faith-based schools through these ambiguous and controversial concepts,[69] costly litigation would be necessary to resist its overreaching into a matter of curricular freedom.

---

63. *See* Iowa Code Ann. §§ 422.9, 422.12 (West Supp. 1999). Non-itemizing taxpayers may claim a credit. *See* § 422.12(2).

64. *See* Iowa Code Ann. § 256.11 (West 1996).

65. Iowa Code Ann. § 422.12(2).

66. *See* Iowa Code Ann. § 17A.13 (West 1995).

67. The constitutionality of the tax benefit was upheld in *Luthens v. Bair,* 788 F. Supp. 1032 (S.D. Iowa 1992).

68. Iowa Code Ann. §§ 256.11. Although requiring education in sexually transmitted disease and drug abuse, the code accommodates the religious objections of parents:

   · The following areas shall be taught in grades one through six…health…. The health curriculum shall include the characteristics of communicable diseases including acquired immune deficiency syndrome.
   · The following shall be taught in grades seven and eight…health…. The health curriculum shall include the characteristics of sexually transmitted diseases including AIDS.
   · The minimum program to be offered for grades nine through twelve is:…
   (j) One unit of health education which shall include…substance abuse and nonuse… and prevention and control of disease, including sexually transmitted diseases and AIDS.
   —A pupil is not required to enroll in either physical education or health courses if the pupil's parent or guardian files a written statement with the school principal that the course conflicts with the pupil's religious belief.

Id. § 256.11(3), (4), (5), (6).

69. Multiculturalism and globalism are controversial largely because of confusion over their meaning. Does multiculturalism mean that schools should emphasize the particularity of each ethnic group represented in America? And does globalism mean instilling an appreciation for the interconnectedness of the world's peoples, economies, and environment? If so, then there is little problem. However, some proponents of multiculturalism are vehemently anti-Western. By seeking to suppress the contributions of Western society, they in essence argue that two wrongs make a right. Still other multiculturalists speak as if all cultural practices and worldviews are of equal value, thus implying relativism. This would be taking a good idea (e.g., the teaching in public schools of comparative religious knowledge and the virtue of religious tolerance) and mistaking it for something that is directly contrary to the tenets of many of the world's religions (i.e., the teaching that all religious faiths are equally valid in their truth claims). Likewise, when globalism is reduced to a syrupy,

Phillips University, located in Enid, Oklahoma, is associated historically with the Christian Church (Disciples of Christ). Due to a financial crisis, a plan was devised for the city to purchase the university and lease back the campus to the original owner, a nonprofit corporation. The funds came from a sales-tax increase narrowly approved by voters. The plan was challenged in court as violative of the state constitution, but was upheld because: (1) sufficient consideration was exchanged in the transaction and (2) the university was not a "sectarian institution" despite being under the influence of the church.[70]

The structural changes required of the university in order to participate in the plan were material: (1) the covenant between the Disciples of Christ and Phillips was replaced with a "statement of relationship" secular in tone; (2) the university's seminary was not included in the sale and lease-back, creating a real and permanent separation between the seminary and Phillips (as a result, officers and trustees of the university and the seminary were prohibited from serving on each other's boards);[71] (3) the university's trust fund was not to be used for a sectarian purpose or to repair or construct buildings used for religious purposes; and (4) Phillips was precluded from allocating funds for tuition discounts or scholarships for the children of Disciples of Christ ministers.[72]

Although the plan kept Phillips University financially afloat, a heavy price was paid in severed ties with both the seminary and the parent church. While obtaining governmental funds to maintain the university, the plan stripped the school of its Christian roots and close connection to the church, essentially creating another public university.[73]

To be eligible for educational grants and loans, college students are required by the United States Department of Education (ED) to be enrolled at an accredited institution

---

sentimentalist blurring of the profound philosophical differences between East and West (as in, "We're a small world after all!"), the schools are simply teaching students a falsehood.

70. Burkhardt v. City of Enid, 771 P.2d 608, 613 (Okla. 1989).

71. Restrictions on the makeup of an agency's governing board are particularly invasive of institutional autonomy. Another example of such a restriction is found in the McKinney 1987 ESPG administered by HUD. *See supra,* notes 35–45. To be an eligible grant recipient for the homeless shelter program, an organization (including religious agencies) must, *inter alia,* have a voluntary board. *See* 42 U.S.C. § 11371(5) (1994). Such a requirement, of course, could conflict with church polity and raises questions of institutional autonomy.

72. *See Burkhardt,* 771 P.2d at 613.

73. A similar process of secularization is reported to be taking place at Liberty University (LU), located in Lynchburg, Virginia. LU is associated with the Reverend Jerry Falwell and grew out of his evangelistic ministry, The Old Time Gospel Hour, and Thomas Road Baptist Church in Lynchburg.

In mid-1993, the Council of Higher Education in Virginia voted to allow LU students to receive state educational grants provided that LU implemented significant changes regarding religion. The grants would be in violation of church/state separation requirements in the state constitution if LU was "pervasively sectarian." Accordingly, university authorities agreed to change several practices to make LU sufficiently secular. Among the policy changes are elimination of LU's mandatory attendance at church services, discontinuing the requirement that students and faculty sign a statement of faith, ensuring academic freedom for faculty to disagree with LU's doctrinal positions, and stopping the practice of asking student applicants for a personal testimony or pastoral recommendation. *See* 7 Nat'l & Internat'l Religion Rep. 7 (June 14, 1993).

LU had an earlier run-in with Virginia's constitution in *Habel v. Industrial Development Authority,* 400 S.E.2d 516 (Va. 1991). In *Habel,* municipal authorities approved issuance of industrial development bonds to enable LU to consolidate debt and finance capital improvements. Local taxpayers challenged the bond issuance as violative of the Establishment Clause and similar provisions in the state constitution. The Virginia Supreme Court agreed, finding that LU was of a pervasively sectarian character.

of postsecondary education.[74] Accreditation is in the hands of a few private agencies. In 1988 one of these agencies, Middle States Association of Colleges and Schools, adopted a "diversity standard" requiring racial, ethnic, and gender balance on both the faculty and governing board. Pursuant to this standard, Westminster Theological Seminary in Philadelphia was threatened by Middle States with loss of accreditation and thereby loss of federal aid to its students. Associated with Reformed Christianity, Westminster was cited with not having a woman on its governing board, an exclusion the seminary said was required by its religious convictions.

In response to the diversity standard, the secretary of education in the Reagan administration expressed concern that ethnic and gender requirements might jeopardize academic freedom and diversity, and, in the case of religiously affiliated institutions, religious freedom as well. Accordingly, the secretary notified Middle States that it was being reviewed to determine whether its accrediting powers as recognized by ED should be curtailed. In mid-December of 1991, Middle States backed down and adopted a resolution, the sense of which is that diversity standards are not to be used as a mandatory condition for accreditation and no adverse actions are to be taken solely on the basis of such principles. In turn, no formal action was taken by ED against Middle States.[75] The lure of federal aid—albeit indirect aid to Westminster, because the benefit went directly to its students—caused three years of anxiety and a near crisis for the seminary. A less friendly federal administration might well have forced Westminster to litigate the First Amendment claims.

Protracted litigation in the State of New York resulted in a very real loss in operational autonomy for religiously affiliated foster-care agencies. For many years New York has provided public assistance to those placing children in voluntary-sector foster-care homes. The state constitution provides for religious matching in this child placement.[76] In *Wilder v. Sugarman* (*Wilder I*)[77] several plaintiffs challenged the religious-matching provisions as discriminatory on the bases of religion and race. Their challenge was based on the fact that in New York City the number of Protestant African-American children needing placement far exceeded the number of openings in Protestant foster agencies. That was not the case with Roman Catholic and Jewish children desiring placement in homes consonant with their religion. Consequently, a disproportionate number of Protestant African-American children had to go to state-operated shelters and training schools that were significantly less desirable. The district court in *Wilder I* considered only the issue of whether the religious-matching provision of the state constitution facially violated the Establishment Clause, holding that it did not.[78]

---

74. *See* 20 U.S.C. § 1099b (1994) (see § 1099b(k), a rule of special accommodation for religious institutions of higher education).

75. *See* Editorial, Wash. Post, Apr. 21, 1991, at B7; Editorial, Wash. Post, Apr. 27, 1991, at A18; Editorial, Wash. Post, June 24, 1991, at A11; News Article, Wash. Post, Oct. 31, 1991, at A19; Editorial, Wash. Post, Dec. 12, 1991, at A26; News Article, Wash. Post, Dec. 13, 1991, at A10; and News Article, Wash. Post, Dec. 14, 1991, at A10. For a discussion of the incident by legal counsel for the seminary, see William Bentley Ball, Intrusions upon the Sacred, 215–17, *in* In Search of a National Morality: A Manifesto for Evangelicals and Catholics (William Bentley Ball ed., 1992).

76. Article VII, § 32 of the New York State Constitution provides that a child "shall be committed or remanded or placed, when practicable, in an institution or agency operated by persons, or the custody of a person, of the same religious persuasion as the child."

77. Wilder v. Sugarman, 385 F. Supp. 1013 (S.D.N.Y. 1974) (Wilder I).

78. *See id.* at 1021–27.

In *Wilder v. Bernstein (Wilder II* and *Wilder III)*[79] taxpayer plaintiffs were found to have standing to sue. The plaintiffs were permitted to amend their complaint and the suit was certified as a class action. Several years of discovery and other trial preparation ensued. Shortly before trial, the plaintiffs and the defendant city entered into negotiations. In mid-1984 these parties arrived at a proposed stipulated settlement. The court then permitted several voluntary-sector child-care agencies to intervene and oppose the settlement. Following further proceedings and modification of the settlement, a final stipulation was reached and approved in *Wilder III.*

The stipulated judgment was essentially that children in need of placement would be assigned (with some exceptions) on a "first come, first served" basis without regard to the religion of the parents. Further, the agencies receiving the children would then be responsible for providing the opportunities for religious observance and training in accord with each child's faith.

If the child was of a religion other than that of the foster home, meeting his or her needs would often mean transporting the child for religious services, holy days, and other occasions to a house of worship of the child's faith or bringing a minister of that faith to the foster home.[80] As a result of the stipulated judgment, the state continued to rely principally on voluntary-sector agencies of religious affiliation to care for foster children, but the discretion of the religious agencies in selecting the children assigned to them was severely restricted.

Not all religious homes agreed to the stipulated judgment. The district court heard several objections by these homes and rejected them. The most serious objection, which addressed the financial and logistical difficulties just described, was articulated by the Roman Catholic and Jewish agencies.

A second objection by the religious homes to the stipulated judgment concerned children's access to contraception and abortion services. Under the judgment, the city would supply birth-control and abortion services. However, Roman Catholic agencies and others have serious doctrinal objections to the provision of such services. Nonetheless, the district court rebuffed these arguments.[81]

A third objection by the religious foster-home agencies divided the circuit court panel assigned to the appeal.[82] The stipulated judgment placed restrictions on the display of religious symbols in foster homes. This was to reduce any coercion or proselytizing of a foster child placed in a home of a religious persuasion different from the child's. Upholding the stipulated judgment, the panel majority construed it narrowly to reach only situations "where plaintiffs can demonstrate that a religious symbol or aggregation

---

79. Wilder v. Bernstein, 499 F. Supp. 980 (S.D.N.Y. 1980) (Wilder II); Wilder v. Bernstein, 645 F. Supp. 1292 (S.D.N.Y. 1986) (Wilder III), *aff'd,* 848 F.2d 1338 (2d Cir. 1988).

80. *See Wilder III,* 645 F. Supp. at 1326–27.

81. *See id.* at 1328. A similar conflict occurred in New York over providing contraception counseling services to AIDS patients lodged in Roman Catholic facilities. *See* Bruce Lambert, A Church-State Conflict Arises Over AIDS Care, N.Y. Times, Feb. 23, 1990, at B2. In a compromise, Roman Catholic officials agreed to provide patients with a sealed envelope containing addresses of agencies who could provide condoms and counseling services. This was believed to meet the state's regulation on providing adequate counseling while technically not forcing the church to provide contraception counseling. *See* Catharine Woodward, Agreement on AIDS Homes Archdiocese Won't Have to Promote Condoms, Newsday, July 28, 1990, at 7. A similar conflict with Roman Catholic doctrine was raised in *Arneth v. Gross,* 699 F. Supp. 450 (S.D.N.Y. 1988) (foster-care home), discussed *infra* notes 174–78 and accompanying text.

82. *See* Wilder v. Bernstein, 848 F.2d 1338 (2d Cir. 1988).

of symbols displayed in the common areas of a child-care agency has the effect of impermissibly chilling the Free Exercise Clause rights of children in the agency's care."[83]

As evidenced in the *Wilder* litigation, the acceptance of government funds can seriously curtail the institutional autonomy of a religious social ministry by causing it to desacralize its facilities and to act inconsistent with its doctrine on moral questions, as well as to lose control over who receives the ministry's services.[84]

Real estate owned by religious charities is typically exempt from property taxes. As a result of welfare subsidies, this tax exemption was nearly lost by a faith-based provider of housing for the homeless. The tax assessor reasoned that the ministry's properties were taxable because it received subsidies from the state which, argued the assessor, amounted to the government performing the charitable service. However, the appeals court ruled that the properties were tax-exempt because any subsidies the faith-based provider received from the state were actually rental payments. All rental payments (including subsidies received from the state) were used by the ministry's charitable, hence exempt, purposes. According to the appeals court, when an organization performs a service that the government would otherwise have to provide and does so at a lower cost, then a charitable tax exemption should apply.[85]

Conditions imposing public norms of fairness

Nondiscrimination requirements of civil rights legislation

Financial assistance regulations impose civil rights norms on a social welfare agency's employment practices, treatment of needy beneficiaries, or both. For religious organizations, the prohibited bases of discrimination that raise the greatest difficulties are religion and sexual orientation. Issues also arise when discrimination on the basis of disability is interpreted to embrace drug and alcohol addiction and when gender discrimination takes into account the availability of abortion services.

The most serious problem is a civil rights restriction on a ministry employing its own coreligionists, including limits on terms and conditions of employment that arise from the organization's tenets. The organization will struggle to retain its religious character under such a restriction, a consequence that Justice Brennan recognized in a concurring opinion:

> For many individuals, religious activity derives meaning in large measure from participation in a larger religious community. Such a community represents an

---

83. *Id.* at 1349. This narrowing construction, however, did not satisfy the dissent. Judge Cardamone thought the restriction on religious symbolism violated the Establishment Clause prohibition on excessive entanglement between state officials and religious agencies. *See id.* at 1350–52.

The adversaries finally brought a halt to the class action with a settlement of most disputed questions. The district court approved the settlement over the objections of just a few of the litigants. *See* Marisol A. *ex rel.* Forbes v. Giuliani, 185 F.R.D. 152 (S.D.N.Y 1999). Regretfully, the provisions of *Wilder III* that undermine religious autonomy are incorporated into the settlement. *See id.* at 166.

84. The dispute generated considerable legal commentary. *Wilder II*, 645 F. Supp. at 1297, lists some of the journal articles. Other publications include Nina Bernstein, The Last Children of Wilder: The Epic Struggle to Change Foster Care (2001); Martin Guggenheim, State-Supported Foster Care: The Interplay Between the Prohibition of Establishing Religion and the Free Exercise Rights of Parents and Children: Wilder v. Bernstein, 56 Brook. L. Rev. 603 (1990); Gregory A. Horowitz, Accommodation and Neutrality Under the Establishment Clause: The Foster Care Challenge, 98 Yale L.J. 617 (1989).

85. *See* Salt and Light Co. v. Mount Holly Township, 15 N.J. Tax 274, 291–92 (Tax Ct. 1995), *aff'd*, 16 N.J. Tax 40 (Super. Ct. App. Div. 1996).

ongoing tradition of shared beliefs, an organic entity not reducible to a mere aggregation of individuals. Determining that certain activities are in further-ance of an organization's religious mission, and that only those committed to that mission should conduct them, is thus a means by which a religious com-munity defines itself. Solicitude for a church's ability to do so reflects the idea that furtherance of the autonomy of religious organizations often furthers in-dividual religious freedom as well.

The authority to engage in this process of self-definition inevitably involves what we normally regard as infringement on free exercise rights, since a reli-gious organization is able to condition employment in certain activities on subscription to particular religious tenets. We are willing to countenance the imposition of such a condition because we deem it vital that, if certain activi-ties constitute part of a religious community's practice, then a religious organi-zation should be able to require that only members of its community perform those activities.[86]

An almost unlimited variety of mechanisms exists for imposing nondiscrimination requirements on schools and social welfare ministries receiving governmental assis-tance. Iowa's tuition-tax deduction for nonpublic school parents,[87] AID's requirements in the ASHA program for medical facilities and schools abroad,[88] and HUD's condition on grants for homeless shelters[89] all mandate nondiscrimination as to the students and clientele served. In the past the Federal Communications Commission (FCC) required that radio station licensees owned by religious organizations not discriminate in em-ployment on the basis of religion in jobs having no substantial connection with a sta-tion's program content. By administrative order, the FCC recently lifted this restriction for religious broadcasters so as to prevent governmental interference with religious af-fairs.[90] The 1993 National Service Trust Program requires that churches and other reli-gious entities not discriminate on the basis of religion concerning those volunteers par-ticipating in the program and receiving federally funded educational benefits in return for their service.[91]

---

86. Corporation of Presiding Bishop v. Amos, 483 U.S. 327, 342–43 (1987).

87. *See supra* notes 63–69 and accompanying text. The deduction is available only if the depen-dent is enrolled at a state-accredited, nonpublic school. Accreditation is conditioned on compliance with Iowa's civil rights act. *See* Iowa Code Ann. §§ 216–216.20 (West 1994 & Supp. 1999). Although a religious organization may discriminate on the basis of religion, the exemption obtains only if the position relates to a religious purpose of the institution. *See* Iowa Atty. Gen. Op. (Chiodo), February 23, 1978.

88. *See supra* notes 46–47 and accompanying text. AID's criteria require that an overseas school or hospital receiving a grant be open to all persons without discrimination.

89. *See supra* note 39 and accompanying text. Notwithstanding the ban on religious discrimina-tion as to clients served, Congress indicated that religious grant recipients could discriminate as to their employees to the extent permitted by § 702 of Title VII of the Civil Rights Act of 1964, as amended, 42 U.S.C. § 2000e-1 (1994). *See* H.R. Rep. No. 100-10(I), at 26 (1987), *reprinted in* 1987 U.S.C.C.A.N. 362, 371.

90. The administrative order reversing *King's Garden, Inc. v. FCC* is *In the Matter of Amending Section 1.80 of the Commission's Rules*, M.M. No. 96-16 (Feb. 5, 1998). The prior rule was litigated in *King's Garden, Inc. v. FCC*, 498 F.2d 51, 61 (D.C. Cir. 1974), holding religious station's First Amend-ment rights not violated by nondiscrimination regulations with respect to jobs having no religious dimension or connection with program content.

On December 1, 1998, the FCC published proposed rules revising the equal-employment regula-tions for religious broadcasters. 66 Fed. Reg. 66,104. The proposed rules limit the religious-hiring exemption to stations owned by, or closely affiliated with, a church. *Id.* at 66, 109.

91. *See* 42 U.S.C. § 12635(c) (1994).

Only recently have states begun to require nondiscrimination pledges from charities that raise funds through payroll programs directed at state employees.[92] Civil servants in most states are urged to sign payroll authorizations that allow deductions for a favorite charity appearing on an approved list. To make the list, a social welfare agency must sign an agreement not to discriminate on the bases of, *inter alia,* religion and sexual orientation. For religious agencies with doctrinal reasons for wanting to set behavioral standards for employees and volunteers, this presents an intractable problem.

One of the federal government's most recent forays into social services is the provision of major subsidies for child-care facilities. The Child Care and Development Block Grant (CCDBG) Act of 1990[93] provides for child-care certificates for low-income parents, as well as direct contract payments and capital-improvement grants to eligible facilities. Parents may elect to tender the certificate to a participating child-care facility of their choice, including a religiously affiliated agency.[94] Child-care facilities that accept certificates but not direct contract payments or grants are subject to far less regulation. In general, certificate-only facilities may discriminate on the basis of religion.[95]

The acceptance of capital-improvement grants and contracts under the CCDBG entails compliance with rules prohibiting discrimination on the basis of religion, both as to the children served by the facility and the employees working directly with the children.[96] Nonetheless, even in these facilities exceptions complicate the rule of nondiscrimination. Concerning employees, the facility may require compliance with religious teachings and rules forbidding use of drugs and alcohol.[97] With regard to children not

---

92. *See* Nonprofits, States Clash: States Add Sexual Orientation Provisions To Requirements, 8 World 12, 12 (1993). Wisconsin bans discrimination on the bases of religion, whereas Massachusetts and Pennsylvania require nondiscrimination agreements on the basis of religion and sexual orientation. In contrast, federal law has an exception for religious organizations discriminating in employment on a religious basis and makes no reference to homosexuality.

93. 42 U.S.C. §§ 9858–9858q (1994 & Supp. III 1997).

94. *See* 42 U.S.C. § 9858c(c)(2)(A) (1994 & Supp. III 1997).

95. Child-care certificates are fairly unrestricted should the parents choose to enroll their child in a religious facility. Section 9858n(2), which defines "child care certificate," states that "[n]othing... shall preclude the use of such certificates for sectarian child care services if freely chosen by the parent." 42 U.S.C. § 9858n(2) (Supp. III 1997). This is reinforced by § 9858k(a) which states: "[n]o financial assistance... pursuant to the choice of a parent under § 9858c(c)(2)(A)(i)(I)... or through any other grant or contract under the State plan, shall be expended for any sectarian purpose or activity, including sectarian worship or instruction." 42 U.S.C. § 9858k(a) (1994). That language is couched in the negative, but its failure to cross-reference a parent's free use of the child-care certificate in § 9858c(c)(2)(A)(i)(II) is intentional. *See also* 45 CFR § 98.30 (1998). In general, therefore, there is no limit in the CCDBG on the use to which a religious organization may put monies received from a parent tendering a certificate, including religious teaching or worship. *See* 45 C.F.R. § 98.30(c)(4). However, the CCDBG requires that religious organizations accepting government funding totaling more than 80 percent of their budget waive their right under § 702 of Title VII of the Civil Rights Act of 1964 to discriminate on the basis of religion in their employment practices. *See* 42 U.S.C. § 9858l(a)(4) (1994).

96. *See* 42 U.S.C. § 9858i (1994 & Supp. III 1997). The distinction between capital grants and child-care certificates is intentional, as HHS explains. *See* 56 Fed. Reg. 26,198 (1991). All child-care providers must comply with health and safety requirements. But providers receiving only child-care certificates need not comply with the religious nondiscrimination requirements, unless 80 percent or more of their operation budget is from government funding. *See* 45 C.F.R. §§ 98.46, 98.47 (1998). The distinction protects the religious autonomy of providers and allows parents the choice of a sectarian provider.

97. *See* 42 U.S.C. § 9858l(a)(1)(B) (1994).

funded by certificates, church-based facilities may favor families that regularly attend the church.[98]

Under the CCDBG, the acceptance of government aid paid directly through contracts or capital-improvement grants makes the provider a recipient of "federal financial assistance" under federal civil rights legislation, thereby invoking additional nondiscrimination requirements covering race, color, national origin, gender, visual impairment, age, and disability. However, if a church-operated child-care facility only receives child-care certificates, then presumably the facility is not covered by these additional civil rights acts.[99]

All religiously affiliated organizations that receive federal financial assistance are presumptively subject to four civil rights statutes that prohibit discrimination against the beneficiaries that the social ministry is seeking to help. "Federal financial assistance" is broadly defined and includes grants, loans, and in-kind transfers of goods or services, but does not include tax credits or tax exemptions.[100] The definition of a recipient of federal financial assistance does not, however, include the intended "ultimate beneficiary" of the aid program.[101] The four statutes are Title VI of the Civil Rights Act of 1964, as amended, which prohibits discrimination on the bases of race, color, and national origin;[102] the Age Discrimination Act of 1975, as amended, which prohibits discrimination

---

98. *See id.* 42 U.S.C. § 9858l(a)(2)(B).

99. *See* H.R. Rep. No. 101-964, at 924 (1990), *reprinted in* 1990 U.S.C.C.A.N. 2374, 2629 (stating the legislative intent that the determination of whether child-care certificates and capital-improvement grants are "federal financial assistance" under the four civil-rights statutes is to be made under those acts). However, § 658P(2) of the CCDBG, 42 U.S.C. § 9858n(2), states that for purposes of the CCDBG, "child care certificates shall not be considered to be grants or contracts." *See also* 45 C.F.R. § 98.30(c)(5). Elsewhere the regulations also differentiate between "child-care certificates" and "grants, contracts, or loans." Both are "services for which [federal] assistance is provided," but only "grants, contracts, or loans" are "assistance direct[] to child care providers" whereas "certificates" are "assistance to the parents" and "indirect[] assistance to providers." *See* 45 C.F.R. § 98.2(kk) (1991). Although the question is not entirely free of doubt, the better view is that a provider that receives only certificates is not a recipient of "federal financial assistance" as that term appears in the four federally assisted nondiscrimination acts. This is because in formulating the CCDBG, Congress was concerned that church-related providers retain their institutional autonomy.

100. *See, e.g.,* Paralyzed Veterans of America v. Civil Aeronautics Bd., 752 F.2d 694, 708–09 (D.C. Cir. 1985), *rev'd on other grounds,* 477 U.S. 597 (1986); Chaplin v. Consolidated Edison Co., 628 F. Supp. 143 (S.D.N.Y. 1986); Martin v. Delaware Law Sch. of Widener Univ., 625 F. Supp. 1288, 1302 n.13 (D. Del. 1985), *aff'd,* 884 F.2d 1384 (3d Cir. 1989); Bachman v. American Soc'y of Clinical Pathologists, 577 F. Supp. 1257, 1263–64 (D.N.J. 1983). *But see* McGlotten v. Connally, 338 F. Supp. 448 (D.D.C. 1972).

101. *See* section 7 of the Civil Rights Restoration Act of 1987 (reproduced in the statutory notes to Title IX, 20 U.S.C. § 1687 (1994)). Although not defined in the 1987 Act, "ultimate beneficiary" means the individual in need who is intended to be helped by the social-welfare program in question and who is protected from discrimination by these civil rights acts. *See* S. Rep. No. 100-64, at 17 (1987), *reprinted in* 1988 U.S.C.C.A.N. 3, 26. For example, the orphan, the widow, the single parent, the homeless, the hungry, and those in need of education, job training, or medical care would be ultimate beneficiaries. "Ultimate beneficiary" includes such classes as farmers receiving crop assistance checks and recipients of social security benefits, Medicaid and Medicare, welfare, and food stamps. *See id.*

By the same token, religious organizations or entities that receive monies from an "ultimate beneficiary" of general-purpose welfare assistance are not recipients of federal financial assistance. For example, a church-operated school that received in payment for tuition the money that came from a Social Security or AFDC check would not be considered a recipient of federal financial assistance. *See* Grove City College v. Bell, 465 U.S. 555, 565 n.13 (1984).

102. *See* 42 U.S.C. §§ 2000d to 2000d-7(1994). Section 2000d-3 states that the title does not pertain to employment discrimination. *See id.* § 2000d-3.

on the basis of age;[103] Section 504 of the Rehabilitation Act of 1973, as amended, which prohibits discrimination against otherwise qualified handicapped individuals,[104] including individuals with a contagious disease or infection such as HIV;[105] and finally, Title IX of the Educational Amendments of 1972, as amended, which prohibits discrimination on the bases of sex and visual impairment in educational institutions.[106]

These four statutes (hereinafter the "federally assisted nondiscrimination acts") were amended by the Civil Rights Restoration Act of 1987.[107] Called by some the "Grove City College Bill" (introduced, in part, to overturn the Supreme Court's decision in *Grove City College v. Bell*),[108] the Restoration Act broadened the coverage for all four of these nondiscrimination acts. The entire operations of a church-affiliated college or other postsecondary institution are now covered when only a single division within the institution receives aid. Also covered is an entire religious primary or secondary "school system" when only one school within the system receives aid. To be considered a school system, the relationship between individual schools must be more than incidental. For example, a group of schools under the direction of a Catholic diocese would be considered a school system. In contrast, "any group of schools whose only connection to one another is an umbrella advocacy or membership group or that are accredited by one central accrediting agency, would not constitute a school system."[109]

Additionally, concerning religious schools not part of a school system and religious social service agencies, the coverage of the four acts was extended by the following language:

> For the purposes of this [act], the term "program or activity" and the term "program" mean all of the operations of— ...
>
> (3)(A) an entire corporation, partnership, or other private organization, or an entire sole proprietorship—
>
> > (i) if assistance is extended to such corporation, partnership, private organization, or sole proprietorship as a whole; or (ii) which is principally engaged in the business of providing education, health care, housing, social services, or parks and recreation; or
>
> (B) the entire plant or other comparable, geographically separate facility to which Federal financial assistance is extended, in the case of any other corporation, partnership, private organization, or sole proprietorship...any part of which is extended Federal financial assistance.

As to each of the federally assisted nondiscrimination acts, subsection 3(A)(i) and (ii) added coverage over the "entire corporation, partnership, or other private orga-

---

103. *See* 42 U.S.C. §§ 6101–6107 (1994).

104. *See* 29 U.S.C. § 794 (1994). As discussed *infra* note 151, § 504 also covers employment discrimination. *See* Hunt v. St. Peter Sch., 963 F. Supp. 843 (W.D. Mo. 1997) (finding that § 504 was applicable to parochial school receiving federal funds through national school lunch program and national breakfast program).

105. *See* 29 U.S.C. § 706(8)(c) (1994).

106. *See* 20 U.S.C. §§ 1681–1686 (1994). The term "educational institutions" is defined broadly so as to include nearly all preschools, primary and secondary schools, colleges, universities, and vocational schools. *See* 20 U.S.C. § 1681(c). As discussed in note 151, Title IX also covers employment discrimination.

107. Civil Rights Restoration Act, Pub. L. No. 100-259, 102 Stat. 28 (1988).

108. 465 U.S. 555 (1984).

109. Civil Rights Restoration Act, S. Rep. No. 100-64, at 17 (1987), *reprinted in* 1988 U.S.C.C.A.N. 3, 19.

nization, or an entire sole proprietorship"—any part of which is provided financial assistance—if assistance is given to the entity "as a whole" or the entity is "principally engaged in the business of providing education, health care, housing, social services, or parks and recreation." In the case of entities not reached in their entirety by subsection 3(A)(i) or (ii), subsection 3(B) added coverage over separate "plants or other comparable, geographically separate" facilities any part of which receive assistance.

Accordingly, the nondiscrimination requirements may affect a religious school or social service ministry in three ways. First, pursuant to subsection 3(A)(i), if the federal assistance is to aid the organization as a whole, as distinct from a benefit for a limited purpose, the federally assisted nondiscrimination acts would cover the entire religious organization. The Senate committee report suggests, by way of example, that financial assistance to Chrysler Corporation for the purpose of preventing it from going bankrupt would be assistance to the corporation "as a whole," whereas a grant to a religious organization to enable it to assist refugees would not be assistance to the organization as a whole "if that is only one among a number of activities of the organization."[110]

A more likely means whereby a religious school or social ministry would be covered by the federally assisted nondiscrimination acts is under the "principally engaged" language of subsection 3(A)(ii). If a religious organization targets a single, or primarily a single, social problem or need (for example, a nonprofit corporation operating only a maternity home or only a children's residential-care home), then the entire corporation is covered. However, if a church merely engaged in health care or social services, the church would not be considered to be "principally engaged in the business" of health care or social services, even if the church were to conduct a number of such programs.[111]

If an organization involved in any of the above-mentioned activities is not already covered under subsection 3(A)(i) or (ii), coverage of separate plants or facilities under subsection 3(B) is possible. The plant or facility directly receiving the federal assistance is, of course, covered. Likewise, facilities "that are part of the same complex or that are proximate to each other in the same city" would be covered. However, "geographically separate" facilities are not covered. Hence, facilities situated in "different localities or regions" than the recipient of direct aid (for example, in different cities) are not covered by subsection 3(B).[112]

To illustrate the operation of subsections 3(A)(i), 3(A)(ii), and 3(B), assume that a large church operates a soup kitchen as one of its numerous outreach ministries. Assume that the kitchen comprises a tenth of the church budget and a fifth of all staff activity. Further assume that the outreach ministry receives federal aid in the form of surplus powdered milk and cheese from the United States Department of Agriculture.

Example A If the church operates the soup kitchen out of the church basement, under subsection 3(A)(i) neither the kitchen nor the church is covered. Likewise, under subsection 3(A)(ii) neither the kitchen nor the church is covered. This is because the church is not principally engaged in providing a social service. Under subsection 3(B) both the kitchen and the rest of the church are covered. The latter is true because the church is considered part of the "plant" of which the kitchen is a part.

---

110. *Id.*
111. *Id.*, at 20.
112. *Id.*

Example B Assume the same facts, except that the soup kitchen is located in a separate building on the same parcel of real estate as the church. Because the soup kitchen is not "geographically separate" from the church, the coverage is the same as in example A.

Example C Assume the same facts as in example B, except that the soup kitchen is located in a depressed part of the city's urban center, some twenty-five blocks from the church. Because the soup kitchen is now "geographically separate" from the church, the kitchen is covered under subsection 3(B) but the church is not.

Example D Assume the same facts as in example B, except that the church separately incorporates its soup kitchen ministry. Under subsection 3(A)(i), the kitchen is covered (it receives aid "as a whole") but the church is not. The church is not covered under subsection 3(A)(ii) either because it does not engage in social services. Finally, the church is not covered under subsection 3(B) by this rationale: although the church and kitchen are not "geographically separate," subsection 3(B) pertains only to coverage of "any other corporation" not addressed in 3(A)(i) or (ii). Subsections 3(A)(i) and (ii) address a single corporation, thus subsection 3(B) addresses the same entity but a corporation that happens not to be covered by 3(A)(i) or (ii).

Example E Assume the same facts as in example A, except that the church separately incorporates its soup kitchen ministry. Notwithstanding its being housed in the same building, the coverage is the same as in example D.

Accordingly, to keep the nondiscrimination regulations under these four federally assisted acts from reaching into the church *qua* church, a church should separately incorporate (if polity permits) its social service ministries. An alternative is to locate the social service ministry on a property a considerable distance from the main house of worship.

The 1987 Restoration Act has two accommodations for religious organizations. The act is "abortion-neutral," meaning that to deny abortion services is not discrimination on the basis of gender.[113] Additionally, Title IX exempts educational institutions "controlled by" a religious organization if compliance with the prohibition on gender discrimination "would not be consistent with the religious tenets of such organization."[114]

The "price" to a religious organization of coverage under these four civil rights acts is not only compliance with nondiscrimination requirements. Often the heavier costs lurk in the regulations that accompany the nondiscrimination mandates. These obligate reli-

---

113. There are two provisions that deal with abortion. The first pertains to Title IX only, whereas the latter pertains to all four of the federally assisted nondiscrimination acts. *See* 20 U.S.C. § 1688 (1994) and § 8 of Pub. L. No. 100-259, 102 Stat. at 31 (1988) (reproduced in the statutory notes to § 1688).

114. The exemption appears in two places, 20 U.S.C. §§ 1681(a)(3), 1687 (1994). Concerning colleges closely identified with, but not "controlled by," a denomination, the application of the exemption is ambiguous. Several hundred colleges and universities possess a clear religious mission, but only a few are actually "controlled by" a church. An amendment to resolve this ambiguity by modifying the language from "controlled by a religious organization" to "closely identified with the tenets of a religious organization" was defeated. *See* S. Rep. No. 100-64, at 17, *reprinted in* 1988 U.S.C.C.A.N., at 29.

Also unclear is whether a qualifying "tenet" must appear in a formal creedal statement of the affiliated church or if any sincere religious belief qualifies as a "tenet." The exemption apparently leaves the burden of proof on the educational institution to convince the Department of Education that there is a particular "tenet" at issue. Such a burden is problematic because it invites administrative scrutiny (and, in the event of litigation, judicial scrutiny) into matters of religious doctrine and a doctrine's centrality.

gious organizations to do the following: undertake a self-evaluation study, publicize the ministry's obligations to protected classes, file annual compliance reports, submit to compliance reviews, keep extensive records, submit to federal investigations looking into complaints, waive rights of confidentiality, and keep abreast of new regulations.[115]

It should be remembered that a religious organization, or part thereof, covered by the federally assisted nondiscrimination acts may still discriminate on the basis of religion. The four acts pertain only to discrimination on the bases of race, color, national origin, gender, visual impairment, age, and disability.[116]

Concerning the matter of racial discrimination in independent-sector education, the federal courts have upheld the utilization of tax-exempt status under IRC sections 170

---

115. *See* John H. Garvey, The "Program or Activity" Rule in Antidiscrimination Law: A Comment on S. 272, H.R. 700, And S. 431, 23 Harv. J. on Legis. 445, 474 (1986); Stephen L. Mikochik, Caesar's Coin: Federal Funds, Civil Rights, and Churches, 9 J.L. & Religion 193, 209 (1991).

116. Some have claimed that by receiving financial assistance, a religious organization loses its statutory religious exemptions from nondiscrimination legislation. Precedent and common sense are to the contrary. A federal district court in *Siegel v. Truett-McConnell College, Inc.,* 13 F. Supp. 2d 1335 (N.D. Ga. 1994), *aff'd,* 73 F.3d 1108 (11th Cir. 1995) (unpublished table decision), granted judgment to a Baptist college sued for employment discrimination. A recently signed faculty member's employment contract was rescinded for religious reasons. When the instructor brought suit under Title VII alleging religious discrimination, the college raised the religious-exemption defense in 42 U.S.C. § 2000e-2(e)(1). The instructor countered that the defense was unavailable because the college received substantial government funding. The district court granted summary judgment for the college. The court rejected the argument that the religious exemption was lost when the college elected to take government funds. *See* 13 F. Supp. 2d at 1343–45. The court went on to say that the religious exemption could not be waived because once granted by Congress no act by the college or the complainant could expand the scope of coverage under Title VII. *See id.* at 1345. *Accord* Hall v. Baptist Mem'l Health Care Corp., 215 F.3d 618 (6th Cir. 2000).

Another federal district court rejected the argument that a Seventh Day Adventist hospital lost its Title VII exemption because it received federal Medicare funding. *See* Young v. Shawnee Mission Med. Ctr., No. 88-2321-5, 1988 U.S. Dist. LEXIS 12248 (D. Kan. Oct. 21, 1988). For additional cases holding that a religious organization does not waive its religious rights when it accepts government funding, see *Saucier v. Employment Security Department,* 954 P.2d 285 (Wash. Ct. App. 1998) (Salvation Army's religious exemption from state unemployment compensation tax does not violate Establishment Clause merely because the employee's job in question funded through a government grant); *Seale v. Jasper Hospital District,* No. 09-95-231 CV, 1997 WL 606857 (Tex. App. Oct. 2, 1997, writ denied) (religious hospital does not waive right to refuse to perform sterilizations and abortions because it had building lease with the government).

In what can only be called a bizarre case with a questionable holding, in *Dodge v. Salvation Army,* 48 Empl. Prac. Dec. (CCH) ¶ 38,619 (S.D. Miss. 1989), a religious social service ministry dismissed an employee when it was discovered she was a member of the Wiccan religion and was making unauthorized use of the office photocopy machine to reproduce cultic materials. When the employee sued for religious discrimination, the Salvation Army invoked the religious exemption in Title VII. The employee countered that the exemption should not apply because her salary was directly paid for by a federal grant. The grant was awarded to the Salvation Army to hire an employee to do certain work that the federal government wanted done. The court agreed with the employee, holding that the Title VII exemption would be unconstitutional in this case. The court thought that allowing the exemption would have the effect of advancing religion where the job was entirely federally funded. The Supreme Court's prior decision holding that the Title VII exemption did not violate the Establishment Clause, *Corporation of Presiding Bishop v. Amos,* 483 U.S. 327 (1987), was distinguishable, the court thought, on the basis that in *Presiding Bishop* the job position in question was not federally funded. That *Presiding Bishop* is inapplicable on that basis is doubtful. In any case, the facts in *Dodge* are very different from normative financial assistance grants and contracts. Unlike *Dodge,* typical government funding is not a grant to hire certain employees to do a job that the government wants done. Typically funding is used to purchase a service via a contract or voucher. *Accord Siegel,* 13 F. Supp. 2d at 1343–44 (distinguishing *Dodge* on that basis).

and 501(c)(3) to disfavor organizations acting contrary to "public policy."[117] The Internal Revenue Service has promulgated guidelines for determining whether an independent nonprofit college, secondary school, primary school, or preschool (including one that is religious) is engaging in racial discrimination. When annually filing required Form 5578, each such school must certify that it has satisfied these guidelines directed at preventing racial discrimination.[118]

Mandated procedural due process for social welfare beneficiaries

It is not uncommon for government programs to require social welfare agencies to afford procedural due process rights to those receiving benefits. Notice to beneficiaries that they are being served by a religious ministry, albeit one receiving governmental aid, would seem to be the most rudimentary and reasonable due process of law. However, additional due process requirements can be complex and costly. Illustrative of such a regulation is the Safe Havens for Homeless Individuals Program[119] administered by HUD. The purpose of this program is to establish demonstration projects for testing the feasibility of providing low-cost housing for homeless persons who at the time are not receiving mental-health treatment or other services. Regarding a recipient-agency's decision to terminate services to a homeless person, the program provides:

> If an eligible person who resides in a safe haven or who receives low-demand services or referrals endangers the safety, welfare, or health of other residents, or repeatedly violates a condition of occupancy contained in the rules for the safe haven (as set forth in the application submitted under this subtitle), the recipient may terminate such residency or assistance in accordance with a formal process established by the rules for the safe haven, which may include a hearing.[120]

In many cases it is prudent to voluntarily extend public-sector norms of due process. However, prescribing a formal process means increased expense and loss of autonomy. Mandating due process also raises ambiguities concerning how much process is due before the government's regulations are satisfied. For example, questions arise as to whether a respondent has a right to appeal, to make a record, to confront adverse witnesses, and to be represented by legal counsel. Moreover, the regulations are not always clear as to whether the violation of an internal rule must be of a certain severity before services may be terminated. In the Safe Havens Program, for example, the above-quoted passage can be read as denying authority to terminate services in the event of a first-time rule violation, no matter how severe, so long as it did not endanger other residents.

Mandated disclosures of information to social welfare beneficiaries and/or the public

Because they are in the voluntary sector, religiously affiliated schools and welfare agencies have books, records, and other information that normally are private. Increas-

---

117. *See* Bob Jones Univ. v. United States, 461 U.S. 574 (1983).
118. *See* Rev. Proc. 72-54, 1972-2 C.B. 834; Rev. Proc. 75-50, 1975-2 C.B. 587.
119. 42 U.S.C. §§ 11391–11402 (1994).
120. *Id.* § 11396. Similar due process mandates in programs administered by HUD are found at 42 U.S.C. §§ 11386(j), 11403g (1994 & Supp. III 1997).

ingly, however, financial assistance regulations are requiring recipients to disclose information in their files to ultimate beneficiaries or to the public.

For example, a church-based child-care center that participates in the Head Start Program must open nearly all of its records to the public.[121] Moreover, the Child Care and Development Block Grant (CCDBG) program requires that each state maintain a public file of parental complaints against child-care providers.[122] The CCDBG also requires that participating providers permit unlimited parental access to their child during operational hours.[123] The Internal Revenue Service requires tax-exempt organizations other than private foundations to make their Forms 1023 and 990 available for public inspection.[124]

Just the reverse of the situations described in the prior paragraph is the Family Educational Rights and Privacy Act ("Buckley Amendment"). Adopted in November 1974, the Buckley Amendment requires schools and colleges receiving federal financial assistance to maintain, with certain exceptions, the privacy of most academic and disciplinary records of their students.[125]

Mandated employment benefits

When required by a federal grant program, all laborers and mechanics employed to work on federally financed construction projects must be paid wages not less than those established for the locality by the United States Secretary of Labor. This is required by the Davis-Bacon Act.[126] To illustrate, a faith-related college or social welfare agency receiving a federal capital-building grant is responsible for ensuring that the general contractor and subcontractors pay sufficiently high wages. An example of a federal grant program mandating conformity to Davis-Bacon is hospital construction financed with the help of the Hill-Burton Act.[127] In the required audit of the grant recipient, both the social welfare agency overseeing the grant and an independent auditor are to monitor for Davis-Bacon compliance.[128]

Conditions Restricting Lobbying and Partisan Political Activity

As a condition of receiving tax-exempt status pursuant to IRC sections 170 and 501(c)(3), the federal government imposes two restrictions on nonprofit charitable organizations, including religious schools and social ministries. First, it mandates a blanket prohibition on an organization's involvement in political campaigns for public office. Second, it requires that no substantial part of an organization's activities be

---

121. *See* 42 U.S.C. § 9839(a) (1994) (with the exception of confidential information such as matters pertaining to health or legal advice).

122. *See* 42 U.S.C. § 9858c(c)(2)(C) (Supp. III 1997).

123. *See id.* § 9858c(c)(2)(B).

124. *See supra* note 28 and accompanying text.

125. *See* 20 U.S.C. § 1232g (1994).

126. 40 U.S.C. §§ 276a to 276a-5 (1994).

127. 42 U.S.C. § 291e(a)(5) (1994).

128. *See* Compliance Supplement for Audits, *supra* note 29, at 2–3.

devoted to influencing legislation through lobbying or similar activity.[129] These political-activity restrictions have been found not to violate the First Amendment rights of freedom of speech and association.[130]

Until recently the only penalty the IRS could impose for a violation of these provisions was to revoke the nonprofit's exempt status. Since late 1995, the IRS has been able to impose excise taxes, force accelerated payments, or seek injunctions against violators. Moreover, nonprofit executives who approve unlawful political spending are subject to fines.[131]

The Lobbying Disclosure Act[132] imposes lobbying registration and reporting requirements. All nonprofit and for-profit organizations that spend twenty thousand dollars or more in a six-month period to lobby federal officials and that have at least one employee who spends twenty percent or more of his or her time in lobbying activities must disclose those activities. Excluded from the definition of lobbying are communications by a church, its integrated auxiliary, a convention or association of churches, or a religious order.[133] The required disclosures include lobbying expenditures, a list of legislation the group opposed or supported, and the members of Congress, congressional staff, and executive branch officials the organization contacted. Organizations must file reports every six months or face a fine. Nonprofits organized under section 501(c)(3) may comply with the filing requirement simply by submitting their Form 990 in lieu of the form prescribed by the act. Most religious nonprofits fall under this category. However, for those nonprofit groups organized under section 501(c)(4), the act prohibits them from receiving federal funds, including awards, grants, contracts, or loans.[134]

Conditions imposing public norms of health, safety, and employee training

It is not uncommon for government to offer funding as both an incentive and a means to raise health and safety standards in the social services provided by the voluntary sector. Indeed, on occasion, Congress has gone further by using its spending power in a coercive manner to meet such goals.

Missouri legislation concerning child-care centers took the financial-incentive approach to health and safety. Missouri exempts church-related child-care facilities from full licensure. However, the exemption does not apply if the "facility receives any state or federal funds for providing care for children."[135] Accordingly, by accepting govern-

---

129. *See generally* Lynn R. Buzzard & Sherra Robinson, I.R.S. Political Activity Restrictions on Churches and Charitable Ministries (1990); Richard Haight, Lobbying for the Public Good: Limitations on Legislative Activities by Section 501(c)(3) Organizations, 23 Gonz. L. Rev. 77 (1987); Wilfred R. Caron & Deirdre Dessingue, IRC § 501(c)(3): Practical and Constitutional Implications of "Political" Activity Restrictions, 2 J.L. & Pol. 169 (1985).

130. *See* Regan v. Taxation With Representation, 461 U.S. 540 (1983).

131. *See* Political Expenditures by Section 501(c)(3) Organizations, 60 Fed. Reg. 62,209 (1995) (to be codified at 26 C.F.R. pts. 1, 53, 301).

132. 2 U.S.C. §§ 1601–1612 (Supp. III 1997).

133. *See id.* § 1602(8)(B)(xviii).

134. *See id.* § 1611.

135. Mo. Ann. Stat. § 210.211 (1)(5), (2) (West 1996). Similarly, South Carolina exempts child-care facilities from licensure if they are church-related, provided that they do "not receive state or federal financial assistance for day care services." S.C. Code Ann. § 20-7-2700(b)(10) (West Supp. 1998).

ment money, religious facilities must acquiesce in full licensure and hence compliance with a panoply of health and safety requirements.

The Child Care and Development Block Grant (CCDBG)[136] program makes federal funds available through the states. Some funds are available for capital-improvement grants to raise the quality and availability of facilities.[137] Religious facilities are ineligible for capital-improvement monies except for minor remodeling "necessary to bring the facility into compliance with health and safety requirements."[138]

Three-quarters of the block-grant funds, however, are to be available for direct assistance to low-income families in need of child care — with no restrictions on the providers being religious. States are to distribute these latter funds in two basic ways: (1) by issuing an eligible child-care facility a direct grant or contract for the provision of child-care services to low-income families and (2) by providing parents with child-care certificates that are exchangeable for services at qualifying facilities.[139] Regardless of which of the two means is followed for distribution of the aid, states are required to ensure that child-care providers comply with applicable safety and health requirements imposed by state and local law. These requirements must ensure that providers implement regulations for: (1) the prevention and control of infectious diseases, including immunization; (2) building and physical premises safety; and (3) minimum health and safety training of personnel as appropriate to the provider setting.[140] Each state is to devise its own compliance plan, subject to submission to the United States Department of Health and Human Services.[141]

The Child and Adult Care Food Program[142] authorizes assistance to states that in turn help administer grants-in-aid, surplus agricultural commodities, and other programs providing nutritious food to child-care centers, after-school care centers, and adult-care centers. Nonprofit, tax-exempt centers operated by religious organizations are presumptively eligible to participate. However, any such center must be fully licensed by the state in which it is operating,[143] which means it must satisfy a plethora of minimum standards touching on health, safety, fire codes, staffing levels, and staff training. Unlike the CCDBG, the Child and Adult Care Food Program does not account for unlicensed centers in states that do not require full licensure of religious centers. Accordingly, the health, safety, and staff-training requirements for participating church-affiliated centers are the same as for secular programs.[144]

---

136. 42 U.S.C. §§ 9858–9858q (1994 & Supp. III 1997). For the CCDBG discussion, see *supra* notes 93–99 and accompanying text.

137. *See* 42 U.S.C. § 9858c(c)(3) (Supp. III 1997).

138. 42 U.S.C. § 9858d(b)(2) (1994); 45 C.F.R. § 98.54(b)(2) (1998).

139. To be a qualifying facility, the child-care center must be licensed or otherwise registered under state law. *See* 42 U.S.C. § 9858c(c)(2)(E) (Supp. III 1997).

140. *See* 42 U.S.C. § 9858c(c)(2)(F) (1994 & Supp. III 1997).

141. *See* 45 C.F.R. § 98.41 (1992). Regulations issued under the CCDBG acknowledge that some states exempt church-operated child-care centers from full licensure. These exemptions need not be eliminated in order to accomplish the forgoing health, safety, and training requirements. The example is given where current building and fire codes may be sufficient to cover the matter of premises safety. *See* 45 C.F.R. § 98.41(a)(2) (1992). The regulations warn states that overzealous health and safety regulation is not needlessly to drive out of the market certain caregivers, thereby limiting the range of available child care. *See* 45 C.F.R. § 98.41(b) (1992).

142. 42 U.S.C. §§ 1766, 1766a (1994 & Supp. III 1997). The implementing regulations are found at 7 C.F.R. pt. 226 (1999). The program is part of the National School Lunch Act, 42 U.S.C. §§ 1751–1769h (1994 & Supp. III 1997).

143. *See* 42 U.S.C. § 1766(a)(1), (d) (1994).

144. Similarly, the federal Head Start Program, 42 U.S.C. §§ 9831–9852 (1994 & Supp. III 1997), is presumptively available to child-care facilities operated by nonprofit, religious organizations. *See*

The Drug-Free Workplace Act is exemplar of congressional spending power used to coerce obedience. As a precondition to receiving a grant from a federal agency, the act requires recipients to certify that they will provide a drug-free workplace.[145] Certification means that the recipient will: (1) issue a policy notifying employees that drug abuse at work is prohibited and is subject to discipline; (2) establish a drug-awareness program for employees; (3) require employees involved in administration of the grant to tell their employer of a criminal drug conviction resulting from conduct at work; (4) notify the federal agency overseeing the grant of such a criminal conviction; and (5) as to said convicted employee, sanction the employee or require completion of an approved drug-abuse program. The act binds religious organizations by the same requirements as nonreligious grantees.

Remedies for Noncompliance

All federal programs of financial assistance to nonprofit institutions require an audit every two years, unless the organization receives less than twenty-five thousand dollars a year in total federal awards. Sanctions for continued failure or refusal to submit a proper audit include withholding part of the award, disallowing overhead costs, and suspending the award.[146]

Additional civil remedies for the violation of federal regulations are found in: (1) the congressional legislation authorizing the program in question; (2) the federally assisted nondiscrimination acts and their implementing regulations; and (3) the case law of the federal courts. These civil remedies, of course, are in addition to laws pertaining to fraud, embezzlement, and other crimes.

The congressional act that authorizes a social program or its underlying regulations typically provides for termination of an award because of a recipient's noncompliance with the act's provisions or regulations.[147] Occasionally legislation even provides for debarment, rendering the recipient ineligible for any grant from any federal agency for a specified period of years.[148] Pursuant to the Administrative Procedures Act,[149] the agency overseeing the federal program must give appropriate notice and a due process hearing to a recipient whose award is in jeopardy. An aggrieved recipient may seek review of a sanction in federal court, but concerning disputed facts the court is bound to the administrative findings.[150]

The federally assisted nondiscrimination acts provide additional remedies in the event that a recipient fails to comply with the requirements of nondiscrimination on the bases of race, color, national origin, gender, visual impairment, age, and disability. The

---

42 U.S.C. § 9836(a) (1994). By its terms the program does not differentiate between religious and nonreligious facilities. Personnel standards are set forth in 42 U.S.C. § 9839 (1994).

145. See 41 U.S.C. §§ 702–703 (1994 & Supp. III 1997).

146. See OMB Circular A-133, *supra* note 29, at 4, 7.

147. See, for example, the Health and Human Services Department's requirements (42 U.S.C. § 300s-1a (1994)) concerning loans, guarantees, and project grants for the development of health resources.

148. See, for example, 41 U.S.C. § 702(b) of the Drug-Free Workplace Act.

149. 5 U.S.C. §§ 551–559 (1994 & Supp. III 1997).

150. See 5 U.S.C. §§ 701–706 (1994).

available arsenal of remedies is threefold: first, a private cause of action; second, administrative proceedings to terminate the financial assistance; and third, a claim for breach of contract.

The Supreme Court has said that the federally assisted nondiscrimination acts provide an implied private cause of action for individuals personally aggrieved by acts of discrimination in federally assisted programs. In addition to injunctive relief terminating the federal aid, damages can be recovered if the discrimination was intentional.[151] At least one federal court has granted prospective injunctive relief to private litigants found to be the victims of discrimination, ordering that the discrimination cease.[152]

Following appropriate notice, a due process hearing, and attempts at voluntary compliance, the federal agency overseeing the social program is authorized to terminate the financial assistance.[153] Where administrative enforcement is lax and other remedies are inadequate, a private action may be attempted against the federal agency to compel more attentive and vigorous enforcement of the nondiscrimination requirements.[154]

Recipients of federal financial assistance are required to sign an assurance of compliance that they do not discriminate on the bases of race, color, national origin, gender, visual impairment, age, or disability.[155] The oversight agency may bring a breach-of-contract action based on the nondiscrimination pledge in the assurance. In this contract

---

151. Concerning Title VI of the Civil Rights Act of 1964, and its underlying regulations, see *Guardians Association v. Civil Service Commission*, 463 U.S. 582 (1983) (implied private cause of action to enjoin practices having discriminatory effect; and, if the discrimination was intentional, damages may be recovered as well). Title VI does not cover employment discrimination. *See* 42 U.S.C. § 2000d-3 (1994).

Concerning Title IX of the Educational Amendments of 1972, see *Cannon v. University of Chicago*, 441 U.S. 677 (1979) (finding implied private right of action for sex discrimination). Unlike Title VI, Title IX covers discrimination in employment. *See* North Haven Bd. of Educ. v. Bell, 456 U.S. 512 (1982). Sexual harassment is prohibited by Title IX. *See* Franklin v. Gwinnett County Pub. Schs., 503 U.S. 60 (1992).

Concerning § 504 of the Rehabilitation Act, in 1978 Congress added 29 U.S.C. § 794a(a)(2) (1994), which adopts for handicap discrimination the same remedial rights enjoyed by Title VI plaintiffs. Like Title IX, § 504 covers employment discrimination. *See* Consolidated Rail Corp. v. Darrone, 465 U.S. 624 (1984).

152. *See* Ireland v. Kansas Dist. of Wesleyan Church, No. 94-4077-DES, 1994 WL 413807 (D. Kan. July 1, 1994). A church-operated child-care center received federal financial assistance in the form of reimbursement for food it provides to the children. Plaintiffs were parents of a severely disabled child. The child-care center sought to dismiss the child because it could not provide the needed services. Huge financial investments in staff and facilities were required if the center was to meet the disabled child's needs. The parents secured a determination that the center was violating § 504 of the Rehabilitation Act of 1973 and an order enjoining dismissal of the child. The church did not raise any First Amendment defenses. *Cf.* Hunt v. St. Peter School, 963 F. Supp. 843 (W.D. Mo. 1997) (holding religious school subject to § 504 because school received Title I educational funds and participated in the federal school lunch program; however, policies of the school were found not to be discriminatory); Dupre v. Roman Catholic Church of Diocese of Houma-Thibodaux, No. Civ.A. 97-3716, 1999 WL 694081 (E.D. La. Sept. 2, 1999) (holding religious schools subject to § 504 because school received multiple forms of federal aid).

153. The Title VI administrative enforcement proceedings are set out at 42 U.S.C. § 2000d-2 (1994); the Age Discrimination Act's proceedings are set out at 42 U.S.C. §§ 6104–6105 (1994); Title IX proceedings are set out at 20 U.S.C. § 1683 (1994); and § 504 adopts by reference the proceedings under Title VI (*see* 29 U.S.C. § 794a(a)(2) (1994)).

154. *See* Adams v. Richardson, 480 F.2d 1159 (D.C. Cir. 1973) (en banc). The relief sought is called an "Adams Order." The order in *Adams* was not dissolved for eighteen years. *See* Women's Equity Action League v. Cavazos, 906 F.2d 742 (D.C. Cir. 1990).

155. *See* Grove City College v. Bell, 465 U.S. 555 (1984).

action the government may seek specific performance of the terms of the assurance,[156] and possibly a refund of the federal benefit that was paid to a social welfare provider found to have discriminated.[157]

Unlike the uniformity inherent in federal law, sanctions for noncompliance with state and municipal financial assistance regulations vary widely depending on the particular state or municipality concerned. Accordingly, it is not possible to catalog all of the available remedies in the event of noncompliance. At a minimum, state and local programs authorize the government agency overseeing the benefit to suspend that portion of the award not yet tendered to the voluntary-sector charity and to disqualify the offending charity from consideration for future award until the problem is rectified.

Special Constitutional Questions

Unconstitutional conditions:
When do financial assistance regulations violate the First Amendment freedoms of religious institutions?

As a general rule, the courts have held that neither the Free Exercise Clause nor the Establishment Clause is violated by financial assistance regulation of religious institutions, so long as other similarly situated secular organizations are subject to the same law.[158] However, where an unconstitutional condition occurs the courts will strike down the overreaching legislation. An unconstitutional condition occurs when, as a consequence of the exercise of First Amendment rights, the government exacts a "penalty."[159]

---

156. *See* United States v. Marion County Sch. Dist., 625 F.2d 607 (5th Cir. 1980) (permitted HEW to sue to enforce school district's Assurance of Compliance under Title VI); *see also* United States v. Baylor Univ. Med. Ctr., 736 F.2d 1039, 1050 (5th Cir. 1984) (although government may have action for common-law remedies, in § 504 proceedings Congress intended that benefits not be cutoff until passage of thirty-day grace period). In some cases a claim on the Assurance of Compliance need not be based on the theory of an implied breach of contract, but is provided for by statute. *See, e.g.,* 42 U.S.C. § 300s-6 (1994) (codifying HHS claim for enforcement of Assurances).

157. *See* Bell v. New Jersey, 461 U.S. 773 (1983) (holding that federal government may bring action under educational act for refund of misapplied monies).

158. *See* Jimmy Swaggart Ministries v. Board of Equalization, 493 U.S. 378 (1990); Tony and Susan Alamo Found. v. Secretary of Labor, 471 U.S. 290 (1985); *see also* Texas Monthly, Inc. v. Bullock, 489 U.S. 1, 14 n.4, 15 n.5, 16 n.6, 18 n.8 (1989) (plurality opinion). *But cf.* NLRB v. Catholic Bishop, 440 U.S. 490 (1979) (it would raise serious church/state conflicts if Congress regulated parochial schools the same as nonreligious schools).

These cases do not distinguish between core religious functions, such as worship, and the more ancillary activities of religious auxiliaries, such as schools and charities. Such a distinction, says the Supreme Court, only increases the judicial involvement in religion, especially questions of centrality. *But cf.* Bob Jones Univ. v. United States, 461 U.S. 574, 604 n.29 (1983); Corporation of Presiding Bishop v. Amos, 483 U.S. 327, 340–46 (1987) (Brennan, J., concurring in judgment).

159. Harris v. McRae, 448 U.S. 297, 317 n.19 (1980) (abortion funding; "penalty" is a waiver of rights as a condition on receipt of governmental funds when the condition is not germane to the government's program or its purposes). Following the recent decision in *Rust v. Sullivan*, 500 U.S. 173 (1991) (sustaining restrictions on federally funded family planning clinics by prohibiting abortion-related counseling, referrals, or advocacy by health care professionals, and by requiring funded clinics to maintain facilities, personnel, and records separate from clinics that provide abortion-related services), in a government-funded program the government may restrict a participant's free

Of primary interest here is when the penalty withholds benefits from a social program because of its refusal to comply with a financial assistance regulation that putatively interferes with its First Amendment rights.[160]

A penalty is imposed on free exercise rights when government promulgates, pursuant to a social welfare program, a financial assistance regulation that purposefully discriminates against particular beneficiaries of the program because of their religion.[161] However, absent purposeful discrimination, mere discriminatory effect or impact of such a regulation is not unconstitutional.[162]

Moreover, a penalty is imposed on free speech rights when government enforces a financial assistance regulation that fails to give speech of religious content the same access to public forums granted to speech of nonreligious content (for example, political, cultural, or educational expression).[163] Additionally, when regulating speech the government may not purposefully discriminate against a religious viewpoint.[164] Moving beyond speech *qua* speech to the implied freedom of belief, it is a penalty when government compels an individual, upon the threat of loss of governmental benefit or advantage, to profess (or renounce) a religious belief.[165]

---

speech in furtherance of reasonable governmental policies unrelated to suppression of the speech. In *Rust*, the Court rejected the argument that congressional spending power was being used to create an unconstitutional condition. The regulations placed a condition on the federally funded program, explained the Court, not a condition on the health-care professional:

> The Title X *grantee* can continue to perform abortions, provide abortion-related services, and engage in abortion advocacy; it simply is required to conduct those activities through programs that are separate and independent....
>
> ... [O]ur "unconstitutional conditions" cases involve situations in which the government has placed a condition on the *recipient* of the subsidy rather than on a particular program or service, thus effectively prohibiting the recipient from engaging in the protected conduct outside the scope of the federally funded program.

Id. at 196–97; *see also* Webster v. Reproductive Health Servs., 492 U.S. 490 (1989) (abortion funding); FCC v. League of Women Voters, 468 U.S. 364 (1984) (free press and funding); Regan v. Taxation With Representation, 461 U.S. 540 (1983) (tax-exempt status and free speech); Grove City College v. Bell, 465 U.S. 555, 575–76 (1984) (institutional autonomy of private college); Bob Jones Univ., 461 U.S. 574 (religious free exercise); Maher v. Roe, 432 U.S. 464 (1977) (abortion funding).

160. An unconstitutional "penalty" could arise in other circumstances. For example, should an educational funding program impose as a condition the waiver of rights under the Free Exercise Clause in matters quite unrelated to the program, that would be an unconstitutional condition. *See* Gay Rights Coalition v. Georgetown Univ., 536 A.2d 1, 30 n.23 (D.C. 1987).

161. *See* Church of Lukumi Babalu Aye, Inc. v. City of Hialeah, 508 U.S. 520 (1993); Fowler v. Rhode Island, 345 U.S. 67 (1953); *see also* McDaniel v. Paty, 435 U.S. 618 (1978). However, the government may nonetheless override the First Amendment claim and proceed upon a showing that compelling interests support the law and its aims are achieved by means that are the least restrictive on fundamental rights. *See* Bob Jones Univ., 461 U.S. 574; United States v. Lee, 455 U.S. 252 (1982); Gillette v. United States, 401 U.S. 437 (1971). Compliance with the requirements of the Establishment Clause is, of course, another type of compelling governmental interest. *See* Widmar v. Vincent, 454 U.S. 263, 271 (1981).

162. *See* Employment Div. v. Smith, 494 U.S. 872 (1990); Hernandez v. Commissioner, 490 U.S. 680 (1989).

163. *See Widmar*, 454 U.S. 263; Niemotko v. Maryland, 340 U.S. 268 (1951); *see also* Board of Educ. v. Mergens, 496 U.S. 226 (1990).

164. *See* Rosenberger v. Rector of Univ. of Va., 515 U.S. 819 (1995); Capitol Square Review and Advisory Bd. v. Pinette, 515 U.S. 753 (1995); Lamb's Chapel v. Center Moriches Union Free Sch. Dist., 508 U.S. 384 (1993).

165. *See McDaniel*, 435 U.S. 618; Wooley v. Maynard, 430 U.S. 705 (1977); Torcaso v. Watkins, 367 U.S. 488 (1961); West Virginia State Bd. of Educ. v. Barnette, 319 U.S. 624 (1943).

Finally, a penalty may not be exacted in a way that implicates the institutional autonomy of a religious organization as recognized by the Establishment Clause. Institutional autonomy indicates a sphere within which religious organizations can provide for the definition, development, and transmission of their beliefs and practices without governmental interdiction, and freely select, promote, discipline, and dismiss their clerics, officers, and members.[166] Moreover, institutional autonomy means that a religious organization is protected from regulations that generate detailed inquires into religious doctrine, civil-court resolution of disputes over doctrine,[167] and any civil determinations as to the centrality of a religious doctrine.[168]

Very few Supreme Court cases have involved the presence of an unconstitutional condition successfully pleaded by an individual religious claimant.[169] Indeed, not one such case has successfully been brought before the Court by a religious institution where the allegation addressed a regulation appended to a financial assistance program as a penalty violative of the First Amendment.[170]

---

166. *See* Serbian E. Orthodox Diocese v. Milivojevich, 426 U.S. 696 (1976); Gonzalez v. Roman Catholic Archbishop, 280 U.S. 1 (1929); *see also* Corporation of Presiding Bishop v. Amos, 483 U.S. 327, 340–46 (1987) (Brennan, J., concurring in judgment); NLRB v. Catholic Bishop, 440 U.S. 490 (1979).

167. *See Milivojevich*, 426 U.S. 696; Maryland & Va. Churches v. Sharpsburg Church, 396 U.S. 367 (1970); Presbyterian Church in United States v. Hull Mem'l Presbyterian Church, 393 U.S. 440 (1969); Kedroff v. St. Nicholas Cathedral, 344 U.S. 94 (1952); Bouldin v. Alexander, 82 U.S. (15 Wall.) 131 (1872); Watson v. Jones, 80 U.S. (13 Wall.) 679 (1872).

168. *See* Employment Div. v. Smith, 494 U.S. 872, 886–87 (1990); Thomas v. Review Bd., 450 U.S. 707, 715–16 (1981); *see also Widmar*, 454 U.S. at 269 n.6, 272 n.11.

169. There are four unemployment compensation cases. *See* Frazee v. Illinois Dep't of Employment Sec., 489 U.S. 829 (1989); Hobbie v. Unemployment Appeals Comm'n, 480 U.S. 136 (1987); *Thomas*, 450 U.S. 707; Sherbert v. Verner, 374 U.S. 398 (1963). In *McDaniel*, 435 U.S. 618, the Court struck down a law that candidates for public office cannot be clerics.
Although not based on the First Amendment, there are two other helpful cases in which the Court ruled in favor of individual liberty. In *Girouard v. United States*, 328 U.S. 61 (1946), the Court held that (as a matter of statutory construction) Congress had not required as a condition of naturalization the taking of an oath to bear arms. Plaintiff was a religious pacifist. Although not a First Amendment case, it is clear from the dicta that the Justices think religious freedom indicates this result. In *Cummings v. Missouri*, 71 U.S. (4 Wall.) 277 (1866), an individual was arrested for performing his duties as a Catholic priest contrary to the state constitution. Following the Civil War, the constitution was amended to require the taking of an oath denying certain past acts having to do with the war. Failure to take the oath disqualified an individual from assuming numerous offices, including clerical. The Court struck down the provision as an ex post facto law. The issue of religious liberty was not discussed.
There have been several unsuccessful cases brought by individual religious claimants where a benefit or public advantage was denied, albeit the claimant was being pressured to act contrary to sincere religious belief. *See* Hernandez v. Commissioner, 490 U.S. 680 (1989) (denying tax deduction for purchased religious services); Bowen v. Roy, 476 U.S. 693 (1986) (officials administering welfare benefits would not be enjoined from use of SSN that individual believed to be religiously harmful); Harris v. McRae, 448 U.S. 297 (1980) (free exercise claim by indigent that Medicaid cannot be denied for abortion sevices rejected on standing grounds); Johnson v. Robison, 415 U.S. 361 (1974) (upholding statute granting educational benefits to military draftees, but not to draftees who for religious reasons perform alternative civilian service); Hernandez v. Veterans' Admin., 415 U.S. 391 (1974) (same); *In re* Summers, 325 U.S. 561 (1945) (application to state bar refused to religious conscientious objector for inability to take oath to support state constitution due to clause on serving in militia); Hamilton v. Regents of Univ. of Cal., 293 U.S. 245 (1934) (denying enrollment at state university to individual who refused to take R.O.T.C. for religious reasons).

170. *Bob Jones University v. United States*, 461 U.S. 574 (1983), is such a case, but the religious organization lost. The case was lost, however, not because the elements of a free exercise claim were not shown, but because the government overrode the claim by showing a compelling govern-

Exempting religious institutions from regulation: Is it constitutional?

Significantly, government may, without violating the Establishment Clause, refrain from imposing regulatory burdens on religious organizations, even if it imposes the same burden upon secular groups who are otherwise similarly situated.[171] The rule makes common sense: when the government remains *passive* by deciding to "leave religion alone," it cannot thereby be viewed as having *acted* to establish religion. Moreover, enhancing the desired separation of church and state, reducing civic/religious conflicts, and minimizing church/state entanglement are all legitimate secular purposes for the decision to exempt religious groups from regulations newly imposed on others.[172]

Is a religious institution receiving governmental financial assistance a "state actor?"

If an otherwise private party such as a religious institution were considered a "state actor" for purposes of the Fourteenth Amendment, then compliance with the duties of the Equal Protection and Due Process clauses, as well as nearly all of the provisions of the Bill of Rights, would be the responsibility of that private party. Indeed, if this were the law, it would erase any meaningful distinction between the governmental and voluntary sectors. Fortunately, this has not been the path of the law. The pronouncements of the Supreme Court declare that an entity is not a state actor simply because it is licensed or pervasively regulated by a state, nor is there "state action" merely because the operating and capital costs of the private entity are heavily subsidized by governmental social programs.[173]

---

mental interest.

First Unitarian Church v. County of Los Angeles, 357 U.S. 545 (1958) (striking down loyalty oath requirement for obtaining property tax exemption), is an example of a victory for a religious organization. But the holding was based on procedural due process, expressly stating that it was not necessary to reach the religious liberty claim raised under the First Amendment.

171. *See* Corporation of Presiding Bishop v. Amos, 483 U.S. 327 (1987); Wisconsin v. Yoder, 406 U.S. 205, 234 n.22 (1972); Gillette v. United States, 401 U.S. 437 (1971); Walz v. Tax Comm'n, 397 U.S. 664 (1970); United States v. Seeger, 380 U.S. 163 (1965); The Selective Draft Law Cases, 245 U.S. 366 (1918); *cf.* Texas Monthly, Inc. v. Bullock, 489 U.S. 1, 16 n.6, 18 n.8 (1989) (plurality opinion).

172. The constitutionality of exemptions from regulation for religious groups was not securely established until the decision in *Presiding Bishop,* 483 U.S. 327 (1987). Since *Presiding Bishop,* lower courts have fallen in line and sustained such exemptions as consistent with the establishment clause. *See, e.g.,* Forest Hills Early Learning Ctr., Inc. v. Grace Baptist Church, 846 F.2d 260 (4th Cir. 1988) (upholding religious exemption in state legislation concerning the licensing of child-care facilities); Forte v. Coler, 725 F. Supp. 488 (M.D. Fla. 1989); Pre-School Owners Ass'n v. Department of Children and Family Servs., 518 N.E.2d 1018 (Ill.), *appeal dismissed,* 487 U.S. 1212 (1988) (same).

173. *See* Rendell-Baker v. Kohn, 457 U.S. 830 (1982) (not finding state action where 90 percent of private school's operating budget provided by tax funds); Blum v. Yaretsky, 457 U.S. 991 (1982) (state action not present where nursing homes are extensively regulated by the state); Jackson v. Metropolitan Edison Co., 419 U.S. 345 (1974) (no state action despite extensive state regulation); NCAA v. Tarkanian, 488 U.S. 179 (1988) (state university's compliance with rules and recommendations of voluntary athletic association upon threat of sanctions did not make athletic association a state actor). *Norwood v. Harrison,* 413 U.S. 455 (1973), is not to the contrary. *Norwood* held unconstitutional a program for loaning textbooks to private schools, including religious schools; however,

Notwithstanding these consistent pronouncements of the Supreme Court, a few lower courts persist in concluding that faith-based social ministries (as recipients of state funding) are indeed state actors that must comply with the First and Fourteenth Amendments. For example, in *Arneth v. Gross*[174] New York City had placed two teenage girls as foster children in the Mission of the Immaculate Virgin, an agency of the Roman Catholic church. The girls sued the Mission because it enforced an internal rule denying foster children contraception devices and prescriptions. The rule prevented their option of being sexually active while practicing birth control. The Mission sought to enforce its rule for reasons of Catholic doctrine.

The district court held that the Establishment Clause was implicated because the city's placement of children in a religious home must function in a manner that does not "impermissibly foster" religion.[175] The Mission, of course, not the city, was enforcing the rule on contraception. Nonetheless, the court reasoned that because the Mission was financed with substantial public funds, it was thereby "engaged in state action under the fourteenth amendment and thus controlled by the said establishment clause."[176]

This makes no sense. It is saying that the government is essentially operating a religious foster home, an absurdity. The very reason for the Mission's existence is fundamentally religious. If every act of the Mission is state action because of public funding, then the home cannot operate in any way other than to be devoid of religious teaching and practice—the Establishment Clause requires no less of any state actor. Accordingly, under the court's view, the foster home would have to be secular in all its operations. Indeed, the court presumed this was the case when it found that the operation of the foster home was a "secular branch of [the Mission's] work."[177] One might inquire what remains of the "religious" branch of the Mission's work if the caring for children is "secular."[178]

Perhaps the earliest series of cases that mistakenly conflates the receipt of governmental assistance by the independent sector with "state action" is the litigation over Hill-Burton funding for hospitals, including those that are church-related.[179] That line

---

the defendant was the Mississippi Textbook Purchasing Board, a state agency, and obviously a "state actor." *Norwood* does not stand for the proposition that a parochial school receiving state aid thereby becomes a "state actor" for purposes of the Fourteenth Amendment.

174. 699 F. Supp. 450 (S.D.N.Y. 1988).

175. *Id.* at 452. The plaintiffs might have prevailed for free exercise reasons. The argument would be that foster children should not be coerced into a religious practice that they do not share simply because they are placed by the city in a religious foster home; however, a free exercise right of the plaintiffs got no mention by the court.

176. *Id.* This "state action" holding is contrary to *Rendell-Baker*, 457 U.S. 830.

177. *Arneth*, 699 F. Supp. at 453. Following this interlocutory decision, the plaintiffs received the remedy requested when the Mission agreed to stop enforcement of the rule against contraceptives.

178. Although not involving financial assistance as the basis of finding "state action," *Scott v. Family Ministries*, 135 Cal. Rptr. 430 (Ct. App. 1976), evidences a similar confusion of what constitutes "state action" for purposes of the Fourteenth Amendment with action that constitutes impermissible advancement of religion under the Establishment Clause. In *Scott* a religious foster and adoptive home placement agency lost the freedom to place children exclusively with families who were active members of the same faith. Because the foster home was licensed by the state, the court said that the actions of the private agency were "state action in the context of the Establishment Clauses." *Id.* at 438. Thus, the court reasoned, if the state must be neutral in matters of religion, so must the licensed placement agency. Obviously the holding is contrary to *Blum*, 457 U.S. 991, and *Jackson*, 419 U.S. 345.

179. *See* Simkins v. Moses H. Cone Mem'l Hosp., 323 F.2d 959, 968 (4th Cir. 1963) (stating that an independent hospital receiving public funds, pursuant to an administrative plan whereby state and federal authorities cooperate in determining community hospital needs and in designating the hospitals to receive the grants, had in effect become "state actor").

of cases was rejected in other circuits and by Congress in the 1973 "Church Amendment" to the Hill-Burton Act.[180]

Directions and Challenges

There can be little doubt that the long-term direction is for government to assume an ever larger role in social welfare and education, both in the direct delivery of these services and in cooperative ventures with voluntary-sector agencies through programs of financial assistance. Moreover, the pursuit of this two-track delivery system does not hold much promise that the voluntary sector will be either autonomous, in the sense of operating independently of government, or private, in the sense of not being an instrument of governmental policy. That government will absorb ever larger portions of society's social space is a truism, however much it might be resisted by an array of religious organizations and conservative political groups. It seems that the complexities and problems of modern life drive a reluctant citizenry in the direction of more government being the answer of expediency and utility.

The challenge to religious freedom, which is enormous, is made more difficult because of sharp division among the religious. America's religious communities have long been at odds over whether it is wise to seek governmental assistance for their social welfare and educational agencies, the concern over loss of control being central to the debate. For heuristic purposes, the disputants can be arranged into roughly two camps. For the proponents of governmental aid, the function of the church in relation to the state may be analogized to a priestly role. The opponents see the prophetic stance as the church's ordained role. The priest counsels increased cooperation between government and ministries performing social welfare and education. The prophet assumes the posture of one outside the halls of power, warning against entangling alliances and loss of freedom as the inevitable consequence of a symbiotic relationship between church and state. Each claims that history, rightly understood, and the First Amendment, rightly construed, legitimates its view.

Those of the priestly model argue along the following lines:[181]

1. The democratic state is an agent for good. There is something pathological about a religious community that fears its own government, which, after all, is a creature of civil society.

2. Government exists to build on and encourage the voluntary impulse. In this way the state engenders a variety of voluntary-sector institutions and empowers the individual.

3. Avoiding a monolithic, state-monopolized structure to the delivery of services is desirable. Words such as diversity, enrichment, enliven, pluralistic, innovative, cre-

---

180. *See* Section 401(b) of the Health Program Extension Act of 1973, Pub. L. No. 93-45, 87 Stat. 91, 95 (1973) (codified, as amended, at 42 U.S.C. §300a-7 (1994)). The legislative and litigation history leading up to the Church Amendment is set out in *Taylor v. St. Vincent's Hospital,* 523 F.2d 75, 76–77 (9th Cir. 1975), and *Chrisman v. Sisters of St. Joseph of Peace,* 506 F.2d 308, 310–11 (9th Cir. 1974).

181. *See* Bernard J. Coughlin, Toward a Church-State Principle for Health and Welfare, 11 J. Church & St. 33, 42–46 (1969); Mark E. Chopko, Religious Access to Public Programs and Governmental Funding, 60 Geo. Wash. L. Rev. 645, 645–71 (1992).

ative, competitive, and free choice attractively package this sought-after, differentiated social order.

4. A natural, common-sense distinction divides the church, the "core" religious institution, and its voluntary agencies, which are about meeting temporal needs. Thus voluntary agencies such as social welfare and educational ministries may be funded by the government without violating the principle of disestablishment.

5. That government will engage in excessive regulation and control of religious institutions is unsubstantiated. Moreover, these unproven fears should not be elevated to a rule of law and embossed onto the Establishment Clause. In any case, it is prudent not to let the perfect get in the way of the good.

6. Only a religious ministry putatively interfered with by government can complain about intrusion into its autonomy. Permitting hyper-separationists to bring lawsuits challenging state aid to religion because the aid might lead to governmental interference with the church violates the legal doctrine of standing. Standing requires that persons filing lawsuits complain only of their own injuries, not harm to others. And, after all, the true goal of hyper-separationists is not to protect the church from governmental intrusion, but to prevent an equal flow of tax funds to religious ministries.

7. Through taxation and other powers the modern state controls most of the resources being diverted to charitable use. Thus the church must look to government for the resources to adequately finance social welfare and education. The church simply must adjust to modern realities or lose altogether these auxiliary agencies.

8. The courts have held that states already have the authority to regulate social welfare ministries as a matter of police power. Thus as a matter of juridical realism, participating in financial assistance programs does not increase government's net power to regulate religious social welfare ministries.

Those of the prophetic model argue along different lines:[182]

1. Religious ministries are motivated by unselfish love of neighbor, not to serve the aims of governmental policy. The church must be moved by the promptings of faith, not ends set by government. State aid means the ministry follows the money. Once charity becomes a response to state policy instead of volunteerism, spontaneity dulls and the fervor and allegiance of its workers wane. Both quality and efficiency suffer, two characteristics that are now strengths of the voluntary sector.

2. It is a myth that religious welfare and educational ministries take place within discrete and clearly defined boundaries easily segregated (like corporate subsidiaries) between the temporal and the sectarian. What others stigmatize as "proselytizing," is actually evangelism, a necessary ingredient of the religious motivation for ministry. The evangelistic component cannot be artificially severed from the social welfare ministry, nor may it be funded by the state without violating the disestablishment principle.

---

182. *See* A Shared Vision: Religious Liberty In The Twenty-First Century, 90 Liberty 18, 21 (1995); Peter L. Berger, The Serendipity of Liberties, *in* The Structure of Freedom: Correlations, Causes & Cautions 1, 16 (R.J. Neuhaus ed., 1991); Paul G. Kauper, Religion & the Constitution 81–84 (1964); Dean M. Kelley, Institute of Human Relations Public Funding of Social Services Related to Religious Bodies 1, 24–27 (1990); Franklin H. Littell, The Basis of Religious Liberty in Christian Belief, 6 J. Church & St. 132, 132–38 (1964); Marvin Olasky, The Corruption of Religious Charities, in To Empower People, *supra* note 25, at 94 (telling the story of the corruption by state regulation of a highly successful religious ministry to homeless men).

3. When religious groups enter into a cooperative venture with government, the relationship is unequal. Government inevitably dictates the terms of the cooperation. However intrusive, financial assistance regulations are nearly always upheld by the courts—deferring to the regulatory bodies with the unsympathetic quip, "Churches always have the option of turning down the money if they think the regulations are too intrusive." But pulling out of a governmental program is often not feasible because ministries have come to depend on the tax funds.

4. Taxpayer's funds are political monies. A recipient of political money cannot act to undermine the civil status quo. He who pays the piper calls the tune. Consequently, the recipient church soon finds itself posing a diminished prophetic challenge to the political standing order. It becomes tepid in its critical and countervailing witness to the ways of the world.

5. Government programs are conventional and ordinary. They use up considerable time and resources in bureaucratic administration. Why should the church empty itself doing that which can be done as easily by the state? To be truly innovative and visionary, the church must operate outside this straitjacket.

6. Religious groups are forever starting ministries that then drift from church control. Underfinanced, they look beyond the church for support. As ministries receive funding from the wider community, they evolve to meet the expectations of that community. Taking government funds only hastens and institutionalizes this drift.

7. The temporal contribution of religion is possible only if religion itself remains otherworldly, that is, defined by the task of explaining life's purpose and answering other ultimate questions. It is fundamental, and admittedly paradoxical, that the pull of religion and its ability to maintain a hold on its members often diminish in precisely the same degree that religious ministries themselves become worldly. If a religious group insists on being just another special-interest group in the sense of meeting this or that political agenda, it will lose its spiritual distinctives and, in a sense, become redundant and in want of new converts.

8. To be sure, the entire nation gains when religious ministries raise the moral character of the population, as well as serve the temporal needs of society for health care, charity, and education. Ultimately, however, the church does not exist to sustain the social and political order. The church must return to its primary mission and identity—not as a program for moral improvement or national salvation, but as a proclaimer of ultimate truths as each church understands them. When government uses religion as a mere tool to achieve the policies of state, the church is in danger of becoming a harlot to state aims. For the church to be pure, the church must be free.

Both models are held by parties that care deeply about religion and its embodiment as manifested in the church. And, of course, there are those who stand outside both these models and want no government aid to religion—not because they care about church autonomy but because they care about freedom from religion, or because they are from that quarter of liberal modernity that rejects any public role for religion.[183] Obviously, not all of these views can be accommodated. Religious organizations can be left free to define for themselves their destiny by pursuing either the priestly or prophetic path as each sees the light. This is the better view because it is the one of maximum religious freedom, which is also the central thrust of the First Amendment and

---

183. *See* Stephen L. Carter, The Culture of Disbelief: How American Law and Politics Trivialize Religious Devotion (1993).

the nation's better traditions. If this leaves frustrated those whose first concern is freedom from religion, so be it. If there must be losers, those unsympathetic to religious free exercise and church autonomy are appropriate candidates.

At bottom these visions of the priestly and the prophetic roles are the result of differences over theology, and thus reconciliation will be difficult. The common ground, however, on which both the priestly and prophetic models agree is that modern liberal democracy, including its notion of full religious freedom, is dependent on religion doing public good as both salt and light in the world. Religious faith gives meaning and direction to the citizenry and a fixed moral code, prompting them to good deeds, self-discipline, and unselfish service to neighbor, including support for the democratic state and its legal structures.

Appendix

Charitable Choice and the Critics[*]

Carl H. Esbeck

Charitable choice is now part of three federal social service programs. The provision first appeared in the Welfare Reform Act of 1996,[1] was incorporated two years later into the Community Services Block Grant Act of 1998,[2] and most recently was made part of the Substance Abuse and Mental Health Services Administration[3] signed by President Bill Clinton on October 17, 2000. In each of these programs, government funds are directly placed into the hands of private social service providers via grants and purchase of service contracts.

Charitable choice interweaves three fundamental principles, and each receives prominence in the legislation. First, the statute imposes on government the duty to not discriminate with regard to religion when it comes to the eligibility of providers to deliver social services under these programs.[4] Rather than examining the nature of the service provider, charitable choice focuses on the nature of the services and the means by which they are provided. The relevant question concerning provider eligibility is not "Who are you?" but "What can you do?"

---

[*] This chapter and appendix are current as of 2003. For updated information concerning President Bush's faith-based initiative see Carl H. Esbeck, Stanley W. Carlson-Thies & Ronald J. Sider, The Freedom of Faith-Based Organizations to Staff on a Religious Basis (Center for Public Justice Nov. 2004).

1. 42 U.S.C. § 604a (Supp. II 1996). Charitable choice appeared as § 104 of the Personal Responsibility and Work Opportunity Reconciliation Act of 1996, Pub. L. No. 104-193, 110 Stat. 2105, 2161 (1996). Section 604a applies to federal revenue streams: Temporary Assistance for Needy Families and Welfare to Work monies. Welfare to Work funds were made subject to PRWORA in the 1997 Balanced Budget Act.

2. 42 U.S.C. § 9920 (1998). Charitable choice appeared as § 679 of the Community Services Block Grant Act, which was Title II of the Coats' Human Services Reauthorization Act of 1998, Pub. L. No. 105-285, 112 Stat. 2702, 2749 (Oct. 27, 1998).

3. 42 U.S.C. § 300x-65 (Supp. 2000). SAMHSA concerns expenditures for substance abuse treatment and prevention. The charitable choice provision pertaining to SAMHSA appears as Title XXXIII, § 3305 of the Children's Health Act of 2000, Pub. L. No. 106-310, § 3305, 114 Stat. 1212 (Oct. 17, 2000).

Somewhat redundantly, SAMHSA expenditures were again made subject to a charitable choice provision in the Community Renewal Tax Relief Act of 2000, signed by President Clinton on December 21, 2000. This act was incorporated by reference in the Consolidated Appropriation Act of 2001, Pub. L. No. 106-554. It is codified at 42 U.S.C. § 290kk.

4. 42 U.S.C. § 604a(b) and (c).

Second, the statute imposes on government the duty to not intrude into the religious autonomy of faith-based providers. To each faith-based organization (FBO) that agrees to participate, charitable choice extends a guarantee that the organization "shall retain its independence from Federal, State, and local governments, including such organization's control over the definition, development, practice, and expression of its religious beliefs."[5] A private right of action to sue a government that tries to renege on that duty gives real teeth to the guarantee.[6] Additionally, there are prohibitions on specific types of governmental interference such as demands to strip religious symbols from the walls of FBOs and bans on regulations requiring FBOs to adjust their governing boards to reflect some ethnic or gender balance thought more politically correct.[7]

Third, the statute imposes on both government and participating FBOs the duty to not abridge certain rights of the ultimate beneficiaries of these programs. Charitable choice not only protects the rights of the religious conscience of beneficiaries, but also seeks to expand the number of providers from which the beneficiaries can choose to receive services, including the choice of a religious provider. Each of these federal social service programs has a secular purpose—namely, helping the poor and needy—and each seeks to achieve this object by providing resources in the most effective and efficient means available. Of course, the purpose of the program is not aid to the participating social service providers, whether secular or religious. Rather, the purpose is to benefit the poor and needy, who are the ultimate beneficiaries.

I will touch on these three principles below, and do so in reverse order.

I

In programs subject to charitable choice, when funding goes directly to the social service providers[8] the ultimate beneficiaries are empowered with a choice. Beneficiaries who want to receive services from an FBO may do so—assuming, that is, that an FBO has otherwise qualified for a grant or service contract.[9] On the other hand, if a beneficiary objects for religious reasons to receiving services from an FBO, then the state is required to provide equivalent services from an alternative provider.[10] This is the "choice" in charitable choice. The choice to receive services from an FBO is every bit an exercise of religious freedom as is the choice not to be served by a provider that one finds objectionable for reasons of religious conscience. There is much concern by civil libertarians about the latter choice, whereas the former is often overlooked. Charitable choice regards these choices as being of equal importance.

If a beneficiary selects an FBO that receives direct funding, the provider cannot discriminate against beneficiaries on account of religion or a refusal to actively participate

---

5. 42 U.S.C. § 604a(d)(1).

6. 42 U.S.C. § 604a(i).

7. 42 U.S.C. § 604a(d)(2).

8. Charitable choice contemplates both direct and indirect forms of aid. 42 U.S.C. § 604a(a)(1). Some statutory rights and duties pertain only to direct funding.

9. It may be that no FBOs successfully compete for a grant or service contract. Charitable choice is not a guarantee that aid will flow to FBOs. It guarantees only that FBOs will not be discriminated against with regard to religion.

10. 42 U.S.C. § 604a(e)(1).

in a religious practice.[11] Protection of the ultimate beneficiaries was bolstered by charitable choice provisions to the Substance Abuse and Mental Health Services Administration. Now they not only have the right of choice and protection from discrimination, but also must receive actual notice of these rights.[12]

II

If the availability of government money causes the undermining of the religious character of FBOs, then charitable choice will have failed. If it causes FBOs to become dependent on government, or if it silences their prophetic voice, then again charitable choice will have failed. Accordingly, charitable choice acts to safeguard the "religious character" of FBOs. Protecting their institutional autonomy enables them to succeed at what they do so well — namely, helping the poor and needy in a holistic way. This protection is also required in order to get reluctant FBOs to participate in government programs, something they are far less likely to do if they face invasive or compromising regulations.

One of the most important guarantees of institutional autonomy is the ability to select staff on a religious basis. FBOs can hardly be expected to sustain their religious vision without the freedom to employ individuals who observe the tenets and practices of the faith. This guarantee is central to each organization's ability to define its own mission according to the dictates of conscience. Accordingly, in addition to the broad guarantee of "independence" from government, charitable choice specifically provides that FBOs need neither alter their policies of "internal governance" formed as a matter of religious faith[13] nor lose their exemption from federal employment discrimination laws.[14] While it is essential that they be permitted to make employment decisions based on religious considerations, like all other providers FBOs must obey federal civil rights laws prohibiting discrimination on the bases of race, color, national origin, gender, age, and disability.[15]

As a general proposition FBOs must comply with existing state and local employment nondiscrimination laws which were enacted pursuant to each state's police power. Some states and municipalities also have nondiscrimination laws and procurement policies adopted pursuant to governmental spending power. When these spending power laws do not permit FBOs to select staff on the basis of faith commitments, they

---

11. 42 U.S.C. § 604a(g).

12. *See* 42 U.S.C. § 300x-65(e)(2). Of course, nothing in prior versions of charitable choice prevents states from giving actual notice of beneficiary rights. It would be prudent to provide notice of rights whether required by the legislation or not, but the absence of a requirement in older versions of the law hardly rises to the level of a constitutional concern.

13. 42 U.S.C. § 604a(d)(2)(A).

14. 42 U.S.C. § 604a(f).

15. *See* Title VI of the Civil Rights Act of 1964, 42 U.S.C. § 2000d et seq. (1994) (prohibiting discrimination on the bases of race, color, and national origin); Title IX of the Educational Amendments of 1972, 42 U.S.C. §§ 6101–6107 (1994) (prohibiting discrimination in educational institutions on the bases of sex and visual impairment); Section 504 of the Rehabilitation Act of 1973, 29 U.S.C. § 794 (1994) (prohibiting discrimination against otherwise qualified disabled individuals, including individuals with a contagious disease or an infection such as HIV); The Age Discrimination Act of 1975, 29 U.S.C. § 706(8)(c) (1994) (prohibiting discrimination on the basis of age).

are not enforceable against FBOs when acting pursuant to charitable choice revenue streams. This is because the federal statutory guarantees in charitable choice that promise to protect the "religious character" and "internal governance" of FBOs preempt contrary provisions in state and local laws.[16]

Occasionally the charge is made that charitable choice is just government-funded job discrimination. This charge is untrue. The purpose of the funding is not to create jobs, but to fund social services for the poor and needy. Whether or not the social service provider is an FBO with employment policies rooted in its religion is probably unknown to the government, and that is the way it ought to be. Of course, it is the FBO, not the government, that is selecting on the basis of religion in its staffing decisions, not the government. The discrimination, if there is any, is not "state action" in the sense of that term in the Fourteenth Amendment.[17] Moreover, the private act of selection by an FBO is not out of intolerance or malice. Rather, the FBO is acting positively—and understandably so—in accord with the dictates of its sincerely held religious convictions. If FBOs cannot operate in accord with their own sense of mission, they will be unable to sustain their impressive record of successfully helping the poor and needy.

A religious organization favoring the employment of those of like-minded faith is comparable to an environmental organization favoring employees devoted to environmentalism, a feminist organization hiring only those devoted to the cause of expanded opportunities for women, or a teacher's union hiring only those opposed to school vouchers. To bar a religious organization from hiring on a religious basis is to assail the very cause for which the organization was formed in the first place.

Section 702 of Title VII of the Civil Rights Act of 1964[18] permits religious organizations to make employment decisions based on religion.[19] Occasionally claims are made that the section 702 exemption is waived when an FBO becomes a provider of federally funded social services. The law is to the contrary. Indeed, charitable choice expressly states that the section 702 exemption is preserved.[20] Having just promised FBOs that they will not be "impair[ed]" in their "religious character" if they agree to provide social services, it would be wholly contradictory to then deem FBOs to have implicitly waived valuable autonomy rights. Waiver of rights is always disfavored in the law, and,

---

16. This is not unlike when claims of religious freedom override state laws protecting sexual orientation or martial status. *See, e.g.,* Altman v. Minn. Dept. of Corrections, 80 Fair Empl. Prac. Cas. (BNA) 1166 (D. Minn. 1999) (sexual orientation); Madsen v. Erwin, 481 N.E.2d 1160 (Mass. 1985) (sexual orientation); Walker v. First Presbyterian Church, 22 Fair Empl. Prac. Cas. (BNA) 762, 23 Empl. Prac. Dec. (CCH) ¶ 31,006 (Cal. Super. 1980) (sexual orientation); McCready v. Hoffius, 586 N.W.2d 723 (Mich. 1998), *vacated in part on other grounds,* 593 N.W.2d 545 (Mich. 1999), *summary judgment granted,* slip op. No. 94-69472 (Cir. Ct. for Jackson Cty., Mich., Dec. 6, 2000) (martial status); Attorney General v. Desilets, 636 N.E. 2d 233 (Mass. 1994) (martial status); Arriaga v. Loma Linda Univ., 10 Cal. App. 4th 1556, 13 Cal. Rptr.2d 619 (1992) (martial status); Cooper v. French, 460 N.W.2d 2 (Minn. 1990) (martial status).

17. *See* Blum v. Yaretsky, 457 U.S. 991 (1982) (holding that pervasive regulation and receipt of government funding at private nursing homes does not, without more, constitute state action); Rendell-Baker v. Kohn, 457 U.S. 830 (1982) (holding that private school heavily funded by state is not state actor); Flagg Brothers, Inc. v. Brooks, 436 U.S. 149, 164 (1978) (stating that mere acquiescence by the law in private actions of warehouse does not convert the acts into those of the state).

18. 42 U.S.C. § 2000e-1(a) (1994). Religious educational institutions are separately exempt under 42 U.S.C. § 2000e-2(e)(2) (1994).

19. The Title VII religious exemption was upheld in *Corporation of Presiding Bishops v. Amos,* 483 U.S. 327 (1987). *Amos* held that the exemption was not a preference violative of the Establishment Clause.

20. 42 U.S.C. § 604a(f).

as would be expected, the credible case law holds that the § 702 exemption is not lost when an FBO becomes a provider of publicly funded services.[21]

Occasionally the suggestion is made that, as federal taxpayers each of us has a personal right of conscience to not have our taxes paid to a religious organization via government programs such as charitable choice. The putative legal claim by such a taxpayer is that he or she has a right not to be coerced or otherwise "religiously offended" when general federal revenues end up going to a religious organization. The idea has a certain superficial appeal, but the law is to the contrary and for good reason.

The U.S. Supreme Court has refused to recognize a federal taxpayer claim of coercion or other personal religious harm. In *Tilton v. Richardson*,[22] plaintiffs claimed that payment of federal taxes, the monies of which were later appropriated to faith-based colleges and other institutions of higher education, caused them to suffer coercion in violation of the Free Exercise Clause. Finding no plausible evidence of compulsion relating to matters of faith, the Court held that a federal taxpayer's cause of action for religious coercion failed to state a claim under the Free Exercise Clause.[23] In *Valley Forge Christian College v. Americans United*,[24] plaintiffs challenged as violative of the Establishment Clause the transfer of government surplus property to a religious college. The Supreme Court rebuffed all asserted bases for standing to sue because the plaintiffs lacked the requisite personal "injury in fact." One of the rejected claims was that the plaintiffs had a "spiritual stake" in not having their government give property away to a religious organization or otherwise act in a manner contrary to no-establishment values. The high court rejected the plaintiffs' characterization of "injury" and held that a spiritual stake in having one's government comply with the Establishment Clause is not a constitutionally cognizable harm.[25]

As federal citizens we support with our taxes all manner of policies and programs with which we deeply disagree. Taxes pay the salaries of public officials whose policies we despise and oppose at every opportunity. None of these complaints give rise to constitutionally cognizable "injuries" to us as federal taxpayers. There is no reason why a

---

21. Hall v. Baptist Mem'l Health Care Corp., 215 F.3d 618, 625 (6th Cir. 2000) (dismissing religious discrimination claim filed by employee against religious organization because organization was exempt from Title VII and the receipt of substantial government funding did not bring about a waiver of the exemption); Siegel v. Truett-McConnell College, 13 F. Supp.2d 1335, 1343–45 (N.D. Ga. 1994), *aff'd*, 73 F.3d 1108 (11th Cir. 1995) (table) (dismissing religious discrimination claim filed by faculty member against religious college because college was exempt from Title VII and the receipt of substantial government funding did not bring about a waiver of the exemption); Young v. Shawnee Mission Medical Ctr., 1988 U.S. Dist. LEXIS 12248 (D. Kan. Oct. 21, 1988) (holding that religious hospital did not lose Title VII exemption merely because it received thousands of dollars in federal Medicare payments); *see* Arriaga v. Loma Linda Univ., 10 Cal.App.4th 1556, 13 Cal. Rptr.2d 619 (1992) (religious exemption in state employment nondiscrimination law was not lost merely because religious college received state funding); Saucier v. Employment Security Dept., 954 P.2d 285 (Wash. Ct. App. 1998) (Salvation Army's religious exemption from state unemployment compensation tax does not violate Establishment Clause merely because the job of the employee in question was funded by a government grant); Seale v. Jasper Hosp. Dist., 1997 WL 606857 (Tx. Ct. App. Oct. 2, 1997) (Catholic hospital does not waive its rights to refuse to perform sterilizations and abortions merely because it had a lease with the government on its building). The only case to the contrary is criticized by the court in *Siegel*, as well as limited to its facts. 13 F. Supp.2d at 1343–44 (discussing Dodge v. Salvation Army, 48 Empl. Prac. Dec. (CCH) ¶ 38619 (S.D. Miss. 1989)).

22. 403 U.S. 672 (1971).

23. *Id.* at 689.

24. 454 U.S. 464 (1982).

25. *Id.* at 486 n.22.

federal taxpayer alleging "religious coercion" or being "religiously offended" should, on the merits of the claim, be treated any differently.

III

Charitable choice requires that social service providers be selected without regard to religion. Because religion may not be taken into account in awarding a contract or grant, government need never face the problem of having to pick and choose among competing religious groups, nor of having to determine which groups are "genuinely" religious.

When discussing the restraints of the Establishment Clause on generally available programs of aid, this principle of equal treatment or nondiscrimination is termed "neutrality theory." A Supreme Court case that recently addressed the neutrality principle is *Mitchell v. Helms*.[26] The four-justice plurality, written by Justice Thomas and joined by the Chief Justice and Justices Scalia and Kennedy, embraced the neutrality principle.[27] In the sense of legal positivism, however, Justice O'Connor's opinion concurring in the judgment is controlling in the lower courts.[28]

From O'Connor's opinion, in combination with the plurality, it can be said that: (1) neutral, indirect aid to a religious organization does not violate the Establishment Clause,[29] and (2) neutral, direct aid to a religious organization does not, without more, violate the Establishment Clause.[30] Having indicated that program neutrality is an important factor but not sufficient in itself to determine the constitutionality of direct aid, O'Connor went on to say that: (a) *Meek v. Pittenger*[31] and *Wolman v. Walter*[32] should be

---

26. 530 U.S.793, 120 S. Ct. 2530 (2000) (plurality opinion).

27. Before proceeding under the assumption that Justice O'Connor's opinion is controlling, at least until the Supreme Court should again address this issue, it is well to extol the virtues of the plurality opinion. The plurality adopted the neutrality principle without any qualifications. Hence, the plurality is not only a bright-line rule of easy and sure application, but brings the constitutional theory of the Establishment Clause—heretofore in confusing disarray—in line with the Free Exercise Clause and the Free Speech Clauses. *See* Carl H. Esbeck, Myths, Miscues, and Misconceptions: No-Aid Separationism and the Establishment Clause, 13 Notre Dame J.L. Ethics & Pub. Pol'y 285, 300–02 (1999). In the plurality opinion, Justice Thomas said that failing to adhere to the neutrality principle "would raise serious questions under the Free Exercise Clause." *Mitchell*, 120 S. Ct. at 2555 n.19.

28. *Id.* at 2556 (O'Connor, J., concurring in the judgment). Justice Breyer joined Justice O'Connor's opinion.

29. *Id.* at 2558–59.

30. *Id.* at 2557.

31. *Id.* at 2556, 2563–66. *Meek v. Pittenger,* 421 U.S. 349 (1975) (plurality in part), had struck down loans to religious schools of maps, photos, films, projectors, recorders, and lab equipment, and also disallowed services for counseling, remedial and accelerated teaching, psychological, speech, and hearing therapy.

32. *Id.* at 2556, 2563–66. *Wolman v. Walter,* 433 U.S. 229 (1977) (plurality in part), had struck down use of public school personnel to provide guidance, remedial and therapeutic speech and hearing services away from the religious school campus, disallowed the loan of instructional materials to religious schools, and also disallowed transportation for field trips by religious school students.

overruled, (b) the Court should do away with presumptions of unconstitutionality, thus making the "pervasively sectarian" test no longer relevant to the Court's analysis, (c) proof of actual diversion of government aid to religious indoctrination would be violative of the Establishment Clause, and (d) while adequate safeguards to prevent diversion are called for, an intrusive and constant governmental monitoring of organizations is no longer required.

The issue in *Mitchell* concerned the scope of the Establishment Clause when evaluating a program of governmental assistance entailing direct aid to organizations, including religious organizations.[33] The federal program at issue entailed federal aid to K–12 schools, public and private, secular and religious, allocated on a per-student basis. The same principles apply, presumably, to social service or health care programs, albeit the Court has scrutinized direct aid to K–12 schools more closely than similar aid to social welfare and health care services.[34]

In cases involving programs of direct aid to K–12 schools, O'Connor started by announcing that she would follow the analysis used in *Agostini v. Felton*.[35] She began with the two-prong *Lemon* test: is there a secular purpose, and is the primary effect to advance religion? Plaintiffs did not contend that the program failed to have a secular purpose; thus she moved on to the second prong of *Lemon*.[36] Drawing on *Agostini*, O'Connor noted that the primary-effect prong is guided by three criteria. The first two inquiries are whether the aid is diverted to government indoctrination of religion and whether it is neutral with respect to religion. The third criterion is whether the program creates excessive administrative entanglement, now clearly only a factor under the primary-effect prong.[37] Alternatively, the same evidence sifted under the effect prong of *Lemon* can be examined pursuant to O'Connor's no-endorsement test.[38]

---

33. *Mitchell* does not speak—except in the most general way—to the scope of the Establishment Clause when it comes to other issues such as religious exemptions in regulatory or tax laws, issues of church autonomy, religious symbols on public property, or religious expression by government officials. In that regard, *Mitchell* continues the balkanization of doctrine, prescribing different Establishment Clause tests for different contests. This splintering of doctrine can be avoided because a comprehensive and integrated view of the Establishment Clause is possible. *See* Carl H. Esbeck, The Establishment Clause as a Structural Restraint on Governmental Power, 84 Iowa L. Rev. 1 (1998).

34. *See* Bowen v. Kendrick, 487 U.S. 589 (1989) (upholding, on its face, religiously neutral funding of teenage sexuality counseling centers); Bradfield v. Roberts, 175 U.S. 291 (1899) (upholding use of federal funds for construction at religious hospital).

35. *Mitchell*, 120 S. Ct. at 2556, 2560. *Agostini v. Felton*, 521 U.S. 203 (1997), upheld a neutral program whereby public school teachers go into religious schools to deliver remedial educational services.

36. *Mitchell*, 120 S. Ct. at 2560. Plaintiffs were wise not to argue that the program lacked a secular purpose. *See* Carl H. Esbeck, The Lemon Test: Should It Be Retained, Reformulated or Rejected?, 4 Notre Dame J.L. Ethics & Pub. Pol'y 513, 515–21 (1990) (collecting authorities holding that the secular-purpose prong of *Lemon* is easily satisfied when dealing with neutral programs of aid to education, health care, or social welfare).

37. In *Mitchell*, plaintiffs did not contend that the program created excessive administrative entanglement. 120 S. Ct. at 2560. For a survey of cases in which the Supreme Court sought to employ the excessive entanglement test, see Carl H. Esbeck, *supra* note 27, at 304–07 (1999).

The Supreme Court has long since abandoned "political divisiveness" as an aspect of entanglement analysis. *See* Carl H. Esbeck, A Restatement of the Supreme Court's Law of Religious Freedom: Coherence, Conflict, or Chaos?, 70 Notre Dame L. Rev. 581, 634–35 (1995) (collecting authorities).

38. *Mitchell*, 120 S. Ct. at 2560.

To summarize: when examining a government program of direct aid, the steps of an Establishment Clause analysis as outlined by O'Connor are as follows.

1. Does the program of aid have a secular purpose?

2. Does the program of aid have the primary effect of advancing religion? This effect inquiry is guided by three factors:

    a. Is the aid actually diverted to religious indoctrination?

    b. Does the program define the eligibility of participating organizations without regard to religion?

    c. Does the program create excessive administrative entanglement?

[Alt. 2.] The no-endorsement test asks whether an "objective observer" would feel civic alienation upon examining the program of aid.[39]

After reviewing the Court's application in *Agostini* of the above-outlined analysis, O'Connor then inquired into factors 2(a) and 2(b) on the facts as presented in *Mitchell*. Because the federal K–12 educational program was unquestionably neutral as to religion,[40] she spent most of her time on the diversion-to-indoctrination factor. O'Connor noted that the educational aid in question was meant to supplement rather than supplant monies from private sources, that the nature of the aid was such that it could not reach the coffers of a religious school, and that the use of the aid was statutorily restricted to "secular, neutral, and nonideological" purposes. On the point about nature of the aid, she noted that it consisted of materials and equipment rather than cash, and that the materials were loaned to the religious schools with government retaining title.[41]

O'Connor went on to reject as a criterion of unconstitutionality the capability of aid to be diverted to religious indoctrination, thus overruling *Meek* and *Wolman*.[42] In doing so, she rejected employing presumptions of unconstitutionality as the Court did in *Agostini*, and stated that she required proof that the government aid was actually diverted.[43] Because the "pervasively sectarian" test is a presumption of this sort—indeed, an irrebuttable presumption (that is, any direct aid to a K–12 parochial school is as-

---

39. Endorsement is unlikely unless a facially neutral program, when applied, singles out religion for favoritism. In *Mitchell*, O'Connor little utilized the alternative endorsement test. *See id.* at 2559. For criticism of the no-endorsement test for focusing on individual harm rather than on policing the line between church and state, see Esbeck, *supra* note 37, at 631. The endorsement test, if still used by courts facing claims under the Establishment Clause, is more suited to analyzing such issues as government display of religious symbols on public property.

40. Religious neutrality, explained O'Connor, ensures that an aid program does not provide a financial incentive for citizens intended to ultimately benefit from the aid "to undertake religious indoctrination." *Mitchell*, 120 S. Ct. at 2561 (quoting *Agostini*).

41. *Id.* at 2562. On at least one occasion the Supreme Court upheld direct cash payments to religious K–12 schools. *See* Committee for Public Educ. v. Regan, 444 U.S. 646 (1980). The payments were in reimbursement for state-required testing. Rejecting a rule that cash was never permitted, the *Regan* Court explained, "[w]e decline to embrace a formalistic dichotomy that bears so little relationship either to common sense or the realities of school finance. None of our cases requires us to invalidate these reimbursements simply because they involve [direct] payments in cash." *Id.* at 658. *See also Mitchell*, 120 S. Ct. at 2546 n.8 (noting that monetary assistance is not "*per se* bad").

42. 120 S. Ct. at 2562–68.

43. *Id.* at 2567.

sumed to advance sectarian or inherently religious objectives),[44] — O'Connor is best understood to have rendered the "pervasively sectarian" test no longer relevant.[45] Her opinion apparently requires that religious organizations monitor or "compartmentalize" program aid.[46] If the aid is utilized for secular educational functions, then there is no problem. If the aid flows into the entirety of an educational activity and some "religious indoctrination [is] taking place therein," then that indoctrination "would be directly attributable to the government."[47]

In the final part of her opinion, O'Connor explained why safeguards in the federal educational program at issue in *Mitchell* reassured her that the program, as applied, was not violative of the Establishment Clause. A program of aid need not be fail-safe, nor does every program require pervasive monitoring.[48] The statute limited aid to "secular, neutral, and nonideological" assistance, required that the aid supplement rather than supplant private-source funds, and expressly prohibited use of the aid for "religious worship or instruction."[49] State educational authorities required religious schools to sign assurances of compliance, with the above-quoted statutory spending prohibition made a term of the contract.[50] The state conducted monitoring visits, albeit infrequently, and did a random review of government-purchased library books for their religious content.[51] There was also monitoring of religious schools by local public school districts, including review of required project proposals submitted by the religious schools and annual program-review visits to each recipient school.[52] The monitoring did catch instances of actual diversion, albeit not a substantial number, and O'Connor was encouraged that when problems were detected they were corrected.[53]

---

44. *See id.* at 2561 (noting that *Agostini* rejected a presumption drawn from *Meek* and later *Aguilar*); *id.* at 2563–64 (quoting from *Meek* the "pervasively sectarian" rationale and noting it created an irrebutable presumption which O'Connor later rejects); *id.* at 2558, 2566–67 (reading out of *Bowen v. Kendrick* dependence on the "pervasively sectarian" test); *id.* at 2567 (requiring proof of actual diversion, thus rendering "pervasively sectarian" test irrelevant); *id.* at 2568 (rejecting presumption that teachers employed by religious schools cannot follow statutory requirement that aid be used only for secular purposes); and *id.* at 2570 (rejecting presumption of bad faith on the part of religious school officials).

45. While O'Connor did not join in the plurality's denunciation of the "pervasively sectarian" doctrine as bigoted, her opinion made plain that the doctrine has now lost all relevance. She did not, for example, take issue with plurality's condemnation of the doctrine as anti-Catholic, and in fact she explicitly joined in overruling the specific portions of *Meek* and *Hunt* that set forth the operative core of the "pervasively sectarian" concept. 120 S. Ct. at 2563.

Being a "pervasively sectarian" organization never totally disqualified a school from receiving direct state aid. For example, the Court repeatedly permitted school busing and secular textbooks. Other aid, such as reimbursement for mandatory testing, was occasionally upheld as well, but the line between permitted and prohibited forms of aid was unclear. Indeed, the permitting of textbooks but not wall maps, and the permitting of busing from home but not on field trips, let the Court in for considerable ridicule. This line drawing was unprincipled, and dispensing with the need to do so is yet another reason to welcome discarding of the "pervasively sectarian" test.

46. *Id.* at 2568.

47. *Id.* (explaining why her position in *Mitchell* is consistent with her position in *Grand Rapids Sch. Dist. v. Ball,* 473 U.S. 373 (1985)).

48. 120 S. Ct. at 2569.

49. *Id.*

50. *Id.*

51. *Id.*

52. *Id.* at 2569–70.

53. *Id.* at 2571–72.

The diversion-prevention factors of supplement/supplant, aid not reaching religious coffers, aid being given in kind rather than in cash, and statutory prohibitions on "worship or other ideological uses" are not talismanic. O'Connor expressly declined to elevate them to the level of constitutional requirements.[54] Rather, the factors are to be weighed in light of the overall nature of the government's program of aid.[55] In most programs application of the supplement/supplant factor makes little sense.[56]

Conclusion

Charitable choice is clearly responsive to many aspects of Justice O'Connor's opinion in *Mitchell*:

1. The legislation giving rise to the program of aid expressly prohibits diversion of the aid to "sectarian worship, instruction, or proselytization."[57]

2. Government-source funds may be kept in accounts separate from an FBO's private-source funds, and the government may audit the accounts with government funds at any time.[58]

3. The government requires regular audits by a certified public accountant. The results are to be submitted to the government, along with a plan of correction if any noncompliance is uncovered.[59]

---

54. *Id.* at 2572 ("[r]egardless of whether these factors are constitutional requirements...").

55. Cash payments, for example, are a mere factor to consider. This makes sense given O'Connor's concurring opinion in *Bowen v. Kendrick*, wherein she joined in approving cash grants to religious organizations, even in the particularly "sensitive" area of teenage sexual behavior, as long as there is no "use of public funds to promote religious doctrines." Bowen v. Kendrick, 487 U.S. 589, 623 (1988) (O'Connor, J., concurring). *See also* note 41, *supra.*

56. In *Committee for Public Education v. Regan*, 444 U.S. 646, 661–62 (1980), the Supreme Court upheld aid that "supplanted" expenses otherwise borne by religious schools for state-required testing. Even the dissent in *Mitchell* concedes that reconciliation between *Regan* and an absolute prohibition on aid that supplants rather than supplements "is not easily explained." 120 S. Ct. at 2588 n.17 (Souter, J., dissenting). *Regan* suggests that no "blanket rule" exists. *Id.* at 2544 n.7 (plurality). It would make no sense to elevate the supplement/supplant distinction to a principle of law. The Supreme Court's past practice is to trace the government funds to the point of expenditure, rejecting any analysis whereby government funds must be denied so as to "free up" private money which then might be diverted to religious indoctrination. Carl H. Esbeck, A Constitutional Case For Governmental Cooperation With Faith-Based Social Service Providers, 46 Emory L.J. 1, 17 (1997).

To get a fuller sense of what is important to O'Connor, one should also consider her multifactor analyses in her separate opinions in *Rosenberger v. Rector of the Univ. of Virginia*, 515 U.S. 819, 849–51 (1995), *Capitol Sq. Review & Adv. Bd. v. Pinette*, 515 U.S. 753, 776–83 (1995), and *Bowen v. Kendrick*, 487 U.S. 589, 622 (1989). O'Connor is prone to have a list of factors to examine in light of the totality of the circumstances. However, as her separate opinions demonstrate, the factors she deems relevant are heavily wedded to the particular program, policy, or practice under review. Accordingly, the factors she lists in *Mitchell* are not elevated to the level of constitutional requirements.

57. 42 U.S.C. § 604a(j).

58. 42 U.S.C. § 604a(h). For the Substance Abuse and Mental Health Services Administration the segregation of accounts is required. 42 U.S.C. § 300x-65(g)(2). This improves accountability with little loss of organizational autonomy.

59. Federal programs involving financial assistance to nonprofit institutions require annual audits by a certified public accountant when the nonprofit receives more than $500,000 a year in total federal awards. Executive Office of the President of the United States, Office of Management and Budget, Circular A-133, Audits of States, Local Governments, and Non-Profit Organizations (June

4. FBOs may self-monitor and, if need be, segregate aspects of their programs to ensure that the government-provided aid is spent only on program activities involving no religious indoctrination.[60]

Moreover, nothing in charitable choice prevents officials from implementing additional procurement regulations, such as requirements that all providers sign an assurance of compliance promising attention to essential statutory duties, thus making it a material breach of the contract if the provider's conduct does not measure up to the assurance. It is also common for procurement regulations to require self-audits, with the stipulation that any discrepancies uncovered must promptly be reported to the government along with a plan to correct the deficiency. These procurement policies would, of course, have to be equally applicable to secular providers, and none of the details of the procurement requirements may be intrusive of the "religious character" of FBOs. Charitable choice facially satisfies the parameters of O'Connor's *Mitchell* opinion, and for most FBOs it can be applied in accord with her requirements as well.

27, 2003). The independent audit is not just over financial expenditures, but also includes a review for program compliance.

60. O'Connor nowhere defined what she meant by "religious indoctrination." The Supreme Court has found that prayer, devotional Bible reading, veneration of the Ten Commandments, classes in confessional religion, and the biblical creation story taught as science are all inherently religious. Esbeck, *supra* note 27, at 307–08 (collecting cases).

Section III

Regulation of Religious Bodies

Edward McGlynn Gaffney, Jr.

In his Prologue to this book, James A. Serritella notes that perspective matters. One can see the Grand Canyon from the south rim, as most tourists do. But if one drives more than a hundred miles to come at the canyon from the north, the view is dramatically different. The viewer notices things previously overlooked. The same is true of a camera eye that can highlight either a sharp foreground with a blurred background or vice versa. That is what makes a rack focus shot — moving quickly from one focus to another — so dramatic in a film.

The commonplace that what we see is altered when we change our point of view applies with equal force to each of the themes explored in this section. Serritella observes, for example, that the full dimensions of the relationship between a priest and his church cannot be conveyed by the single commercial term "employee." Patrick J. Schiltz and Douglas Laycock show at great length the perils to a religious community if labor law and civil rights laws governing employment relations are applied without exception to churches, synagogues, and mosques. The easy case is that Jews must be free to hire an observant Jew to serve as a rabbi or cantor, not just a smart person who happens to know Hebrew or be a good baritone. Congress thought about these matters and decided, in Title VII of the Civil Rights Act of 1964, that religious communities should be exempt. In a case involving not-for-profit activities of a church, the Court sustained this same statutory arrangement unanimously against a challenge under the nonestablishment provision of the First Amendment Religion Clause. But there are harder cases in which the general public good of nondiscrimination in employment conflicts with practices of religious communities. Schiltz and Laycock explore the full range of cases, illustrating the difficulty of some of these decisions by their inability to reach agreement with one another about whether a particular case was rightly decided.

Serritella's observation applies with equal force to the places in which religious communities meet. As Angela C. Carmella demonstrates in her chapter on land use regulation, synagogues, churches, and mosques are not fully comprehended by identifying them as commercial real estate on a plat map in City Hall. Once again there are cases that should be easy, but the very fact that they were litigated at all shows that in the minds of some government attorneys there are no clear limits on their power to regulate. For example, no one would seriously maintain that a state legislature could ban attendance at Mass. But may a city keep worshipers from fulfilling their obligations of worship according to the dictates of conscience by declaring a church to be a historical landmark that may not be altered to accommodate a growing community? May a city go so far as to tell a church it may not change its architecture — the position of the altar or pulpit — to conform to the church's teaching about popular participation of the faithful in liturgical worship? May a planning commission keep all religious communities out of a new real estate development under a "generally applicable" norm that grants permits exclusively for residential use? Only a decent respect for the constitutional values of nonestablishment and free exercise can provide a sensible answer to questions such as these.

Perspective matters in the assignment of liability for contractual agreements or for tortious conduct when the defendant is a religious body. Mark E. Chopko brings years of experience as general counsel of the United States Conference of Catholic Bishops to bear on his chapter on derivative liability. Once again, the easy case is that religious communities can no longer claim charitable immunity as a constitutional prerogative. In fact, it was a group of Catholic nuns operating a hospital who forged the path to this result by insisting that their insurer pay for injuries sustained in a medical malpractice case. If we remember that it is not the government's business to tell religious communities how they should be governed, then the vast majority of the cases Chopko analyzes should be easy. As a practicing litigator for a large church who is aware of the difficulties encountered by his staff, by the diocesan attorneys throughout the country, and by his colleagues in many other faith communities, Chopko is all too painfully aware of the ingenious ways in which plaintiff injury lawyers are framing prayers for relief that insure access to the deepest pockets imaginable. Once again, the issue is not whether fair compensation should be given to a party who sustains an injury fairly attributable to an agent of a religious community. The issue is whether the community's religious integrity might be violated by ignoring its self-understanding of how it is to be governed. From the perspective of lawyers accustomed to thinking of corporations under the rubric of enterprise liability, it may seem proper to find a tie that binds a local parish or diocese to all members of that faith throughout the city, state, nation, or world. From the perspective of anyone familiar with canon law or analogous ways of describing theological commitments about how a community is governed, liability may not be measured in such global terms as ascending or descending liability.

Stephen J. Pope and Patricia B. Carlson provide fresh ethical and legal perspectives on one of the most difficult and painful problems affecting religious organizations today, the sexual misconduct with minors by some clergy. They canvass and critically evaluate religious liberty issues raised by this problem—issues that concern not only the religious organizations' responsibility for the misconduct of their clergy, but also the challenges presented to these organizations by the efforts of litigants, courts, and legislatures. These challenges and their ethical, legal, and constitutional dimensions are likely to be the subject of debate and discussion for some time to come. Pope and Carlson make an important contribution to that discussion. The thoughtful perspectives of some of our other authors are also reflected in these pages as well as in other forums.

Perspective also matters in the exercise of the most potent of all forms of regulation, taxation. As Chief Justice Marshall noted in *McCulloch v. Maryland,* "The power to tax is the power to destroy." He wrote these words to explain why a state could not tax an instrumentality of the federal government, the Second Bank of the United States. In my two chapters on the exemption of religious bodies from federal and state and local taxation, I suggest that Marshall's words might also apply to the taxation of the income or property of religious communities. I noted above that the cases in Carmella's chapter on land use regulation cannot be comprehended simply by thinking of the churches as commercial real estate. The same is true for tax purposes. In *Walz v. Tax Commission of the City of New York*—the classic case defending the practice of exempting houses of religious worship against a challenge under the Religion Clause—Chief Justice Burger noted that systematic taxation of the property owned by religious communities would entail greater entanglement of the government with religion—think of tax liens and foreclosure sales on churches—than does the system of exemption now practiced in all fifty states. The rationale the Court now seems comfortable with is that the enormous benefit that religious communities derive from exemption of income and property from taxation is provided on an evenhanded basis to all charitable organizations—schools, museums, and the like. This rationale has the added advantage of keeping the government from defining religious matters or attempting to control them. Unfortunately, this central theme of First Amendment law has been overlooked from time to time in regulations purporting to govern religious communities precisely because of their exempt status. In some instances these regulations may be annoying, but not overwhelmingly so. In other instances—such as the federal government's attempt to define a "church" or its component parts by whether it was at prayer or was engaged in the ministry of providing service to the world—Marshall's dictum needs to be modified: the power to exempt is the power to destroy. Finally, it is well for religious communities to be alert to the growing likelihood that states and local governments might seek income from religious communities. Moses, Jesus, and Muhammad did not promise their followers the best of all possible tax worlds. In their dialogue with taxing authorities, religious communities will probably be more successful if they persuade them that they provide enormous value to the local civic community, even if that value cannot easily be quantified by an accountant.

The thread running through all of these chapters is the central theme of the history that surrounds the adoption of the First Amendment and that was reinforced with the adoption of the Fourteenth Amendment. In the original debates on adoption of the Religion Clause, a unifying theme was that it was no part of the government's business to define religious matters or to attempt to control religious beliefs and practices. The state's regulation of faith can be overt—for example, a prohibition from reading the Bible—or it can be more subtle, as in a broader statute prohibiting anyone from teaching slaves to learn to read. As the Reconstruction Congress made plain, the second statute was not only a violation of equal protection of the laws, but also an assault on the free exercise of religion by the newly emancipated slaves. That is why the Fourteenth Amendment contains the critical three words "No State shall...," and that is why the same amendment conferred upon Congress the power to enforce the amendment by appropriate legislation. In the same era, the Reconstruction Congress placed limits on its own zeal to overcome racial segregation by exempting churches from civil rights legislation on the ground that Congress lacked authority to regulate them.

If it is not the government's business to define religious beliefs and practices, then what is its regulatory task? In the first place, it is to confine itself to adopting rules in good faith for a general public purpose. That is what is meant by the requirement that statutes have a legitimate secular purpose. Thus the term "secular purpose" should not imply hostility to religion but simply reflect a broad purpose within the scope of the powers granted to government by the people. In the second place, the government may and in many instances should acknowledge that a regulation that meets the secularity standard nonetheless creates an unintended burden on the exercise of religious beliefs and practices that the legislature did not focus upon when it created the general regulatory framework. As I argue in the final chapter of this volume, in circumstances such as these it is appropriate and sometimes necessary for the government to accommodate the needs of religious communities by crafting exemptions from generally applicable norms in order to enable the free exercise of religion to thrive in this country.

Exemption of Religious Organizations from Federal Taxation

Edward McGlynn Gaffney, Jr.

Americans place great value on their ability to join together in associations to pursue aims they cannot achieve either alone or under governmental control. From the time of Alexis de Tocqueville's famous visit in the 1830s, foreign observers have remarked upon the unusually prominent role that communal cooperation without governmental involvement plays in this country. For example, Tocqueville wrote in *Democracy in America*:

> Americans of all ages, all conditions, and all dispositions constantly form associations. They have not only commercial and manufacturing companies, in which all take part, but associations of a thousand other kinds, religious, moral, serious, futile, general or restricted, enormous or diminutive. The Americans make associations to give entertainments, to found seminaries, to build inns, to construct churches, to diffuse books, to send missionaries to the antipodes; in this manner they found hospitals, prisons and schools. If it is proposed to inculcate some truth or to foster some feeling by the encouragement of a great example, they form a society. Wherever at the head of some new undertaking you see the government in France, or a man of rank in England, in the United States you will be sure to find an association.[1]

Among the associations Tocqueville observed were political parties, commercial corporations, and "intellectual and moral associations," including Christian churches[2] and other religious communities. Indeed, he noted:

> Religion in America takes no direct part in the government of society, but it must nevertheless be regarded as the foremost of the political institutions of that country; for if it does not impart a taste for freedom, it facilitates the use of free institutions. Indeed, it is in this same point of view that the inhabitants of the United States themselves look upon religious belief. I do not know whether all the Americans have a sincere faith in their religion, for who can search the human heart? But I am certain that they hold it to be indispensable

---

1. Alexis de Tocqueville, 2 Democracy in America 106 (1985).
2. Throughout this chapter, the term "church" will be used to refer to all religious groups.

to the maintenance of republican institutions. This opinion is not peculiar to a class of citizens or to a party; but it belongs to the whole nation, and to every rank of society.[3]

As Tocqueville correctly noted about his native France, the social good is promoted in other countries primarily through governmental initiatives. But in America the role of the government in the economy swings back and forth like a pendulum. For example, the New Deal of the 1930s represented the zenith of governmental intervention in the economy through a host of welfare-benefit programs designed to respond to massive unemployment in the Great Depression. Nearly six decades later, President Clinton signed legislation that he said would dismantle "welfare as we know it."[4] Even at the peak of governmental involvement in the economy, however, America has retained a healthy regard for what is known variously as the voluntary sector, the private sector, or the "third sector" (third after the sectors of government and business).[5]

One of the most significant ways in which America expresses its respect for the voluntary sector is by leaving it alone—or more specifically, by refraining from taxing it. Thus when Congress wrote the first modern income tax statutes, the Revenue Act of 1894 and the Revenue Act of 1913, only "net income" was to be taxed. It intentionally excluded all nonprofit organizations, which have no "net income" precisely because they are not organized for the purpose of making a profit on their activities. Senator Cordell Hull, principal author of the 1913 act, resisted explicit categories of exemption because the law was designed to impose explicit categories of *taxation*, and all not listed would be exempt: "Of course any kind of society or corporation that is not doing business for profit and not acquiring profit would not come within the meaning of the taxing clause.... I see no occasion whatever for undertaking to particularize...."[6]

Americans pride themselves on being "taxpayers"—a fact that seems curious in many other cultures—or at least we insist on the point when we expect to receive some benefit from the government or to be relieved of a burden that the government might impose. For this very reason, it is important at the outset of this chapter to recall that nonprofit organizations are *not taxpayers* for a variety of good reasons grounded in our commitment to the value of associational freedom. As Chief Justice Burger wrote in the leading case on tax exemption for religious property:

> [The State] has not singled out one particular church or religious group or even churches as such; rather, it has granted exemption to all houses of religious worship within a broad class of property owned by nonprofit, quasi-public corporations which include hospitals, libraries, playgrounds, scientific, professional, historical, and patriotic groups. The State has an affirmative policy that considers these groups as beneficial and stabilizing influences in community life and finds this classification useful, desirable, and in the public interest.[7]

---

3. Tocqueville, *supra* note 1, at 305–6.

4. *See, e.g.,* 42 U.S.C. §601 (increasing "the flexibility of the States" in operating welfare programs and in ending "the dependence of needy parents on welfare benefits").

5. *See, e.g.,* Commission on Private Philanthropy and Public Needs, Giving in America: Toward a Stronger Voluntary Sector 31 (1975); Dean M. Kelley, Why Churches Should Not Pay Taxes 25–36 (1977); and Bruce R. Hopkins, The Law of Tax-Exempt Organizations 8–16, 25 (6th ed. 1992).

6. 50 Cong. Rec. 1306 (1913).

7. Walz v. Tax Comm'n of the City of New York, 397 U.S. 664, 673 (1970). This case is discussed in "Exemption of Religious Communities from State and Local Taxation," the next chapter in this volume.

Although all nonprofit organizations enjoy the benefit of exemption from taxation, this chapter and the one that follows both focus on one particular kind of nonprofit organization: the religious group. These two chapters explore three questions of considerable importance for these communities. First, where did we get the tradition of not taxing churches? Second, if churches are not generally taxed, should their tax-exempt status form a sufficient predicate for governmental regulation of religion? Third, does either exemption or regulation of churches depend upon their organizational form or structure? This chapter examines these issues as they arise in federal taxation, and the next explores them with respect to state and local taxation.[8]

Exemption of Religion from Taxation in History

Since the dawn of recorded history, taxation has been the most constant and pervasive form of governmental control both of individuals and of groups. For this very reason, the ways in which various societies have refrained from collecting revenue from some persons or groups serve as telling indicators of how these societies understand themselves. Practices of exemption from taxation are constitutional in the sense that they reflect core beliefs of society; they embody what the Canadian theologian Bernard Lonergan called "constitutive meaning."[9] Thus, to ask whether churches should be taxed at all is to ask a normative question.

The U.S. federal government and all fifty states maintain a system of general exemption of religion from the payment of most forms of taxation. This widespread American practice is not a recent invention; on the contrary, it is rooted deeply in the principle of religious freedom, a value at the very core of the American constitutional order. This value is, in turn, deeply imbedded within traditions and practices that long antedate the Republic. One purpose of this chapter is to describe these traditions, to narrate the central themes of these historical practices, in broad outline. In this way I hope to relate materials from the past to the current question of exempting churches from the payment of taxes. Because the practice has recently come under attack,[10] it is important to understand the principal rationales offered throughout history for the practice.

---

8. Since many of the foundational concepts in this chapter obviously apply to state taxation as well, they will not be repeated in the next chapter in this volume. There will, however, be cross-references where warranted.

9. *See* Bernard J.F. Lonergan, Method in Theology 78, 178, 362 (1972).

10. *See, e.g.,* John Witte, Tax Exemption of Church Property: Historical Anomaly or Valid Constitutional Practice? 64 S. Cal. L. Rev. 363 (1991). Witte traces the practice of tax exemption of church property to its roots in the common law and in the equity tradition that favored such exemptions on account of both the "religious uses" and the "charitable uses" to which church properties were devoted." *Id*. at 408. He proposes "a via media between the wholesale eradication of such exemptions proposed by opponents and the blanket endorsements of exemptions proffered by proponents." His alternative is "to remove tax exemptions for church property that are based on religious [internal, cultic, sacerdotal] uses but to retain those that are based on charitable, external, cultural, social uses to which they are devoted." *Id*. Witte published a revised version of this article in Religion and the American Constitutional Experiment: Essential Rights and Liberties, 185–215 (2000). Earlier attacks on tax exemption of churches were not as subtle or nuanced as Witte's. *See, e.g.,* Martin A. Larson and C. Stanley Lowell, The Religious Empire: The Growth and Danger of Tax-Exempt Property in the United States (1976); Martin A. Larson and C. Stanley Lowell, The

The ancient world

In the modern American context, the issue of tax exemption for religion is bifurcated into two questions, each with conflicting answers. Is tax exemption a benefit that amounts to a constitutionally impermissible establishment of religion?[11] And is it grounded in the free exercise of religion?[12] In the ancient world, the question of tax exemption for religion focused primarily on whether the state could demand financial tribute from believers even when doing so placed them in conflict with a religious obligation. Answers to this question varied over time, and the theme is rich and complex, involving what we would now characterize both as establishment and free exercise concerns.

Two legal systems in the ancient world—biblical law and Roman law—had a profound influence on the development of legal systems in Europe which in turn most directly influenced the practice of tax exemption for religious communities in America. Since these two legal systems held sway long after the destruction of Jerusalem by the Roman army in the year 70 and the fall of Rome to Alaric, king of the Visigoths, in 410, a few examples from these two legal systems can help to illustrate the origins of this theme in the ancient world.

The Hebrew Bible on tribute and taxation

The Hebrew Bible includes traditions providing for support of religious institutions such as the priesthood through offerings of the first fruits of agricultural harvests (Exod. 23:29; Deut. 26:2–10) and of tithes (Lev. 27:30; Num. 18:21–32; Deut. 14:22–29). Wars and threats of war are associated with the payment of tribute money to the more powerful nation. For example, King David occupied the city of Jerusalem around 1000 B.C.E. and supported the administration of the city by means of tribute collected from the surrounding peoples of Moab, Aram, and Hamath (2 Sam. 8). His son, King Solomon, initiated vast public-works projects, including the construction of the Temple and a lavish royal palace, which were supported by the creation of a new internal taxation system (I Kings 4:7–19, 22–23, 27–28), by forced labor, and by military conscription (I Kings 5:13–14). These innovations are identified in one narrative as the basis for a tax revolt that led to the division of the northern kingdom of Israel from the southern kingdom of Judah after the death of Solomon (1 Sam. 8:11–17; 1 Kings 12). A century later, both Israel and Judah were forced to pay one-time tribute money to hold off foreign attack (1 Kings 15:19; 20:3–7; 2 Kings 12:18; 15:19–20; 16:8; 18:14–16). One-time payments soon became annual payments (2 Kings 17:4; 2 Kings 24:1,17–18),

Churches: Their Riches, Revenues, and Immunities: An Analysis of Tax-Exempt Property (1969); D.B. Robertson, Should Churches Be Taxed? (1968).

11. *Contrast, e.g.*, Walz v. Tax Commission of the City of New York, 397 U.S. 664 (1970) (exemption of houses of worship from ad valorem property tax does not violate the Establishment Clause), *with* Texas Monthly, Inc. v. Bullock, 489 U.S. 1 (1989) (exemption of distribution of religious literature from sales and use tax violates the Establishment Clause), discussed in "Exemption of Religious Communities from State and Local Taxation," the next chapter in this volume.

12. *Contrast, e.g.*, Murdock v. Pennsylvania, 319 U.S. 105 (1943) (imposition of tax on door-to-door sale of religious literature by Jehovah's Witnesses violates Free Exercise Clause) *with* Jimmy Swaggart Ministries v. California Bd. of Equalization, 493 U.S. 378 (1990) (imposition of sales and use tax on distribution of religious literature by television evangelists does not violate the Free Exercise Clause), discussed in "Exemption of Religious Communities from State and Local Taxation," the next chapter in this volume.

and regular payment of tribute led eventually to complete absorption by the dominant state. The ten northern tribes—the kingdom of Israel—fell to the Assyrian empire in the eighth century B.C.E. The southern kingdom of Judah fell to the Babylonians, who destroyed Jerusalem—including the Temple of Solomon—and took the Judeans into captivity in Babylon in the early sixth century.

In 538 B.C.E., Cyrus the Persian let the exiles return to Judea to rebuild Jerusalem, and the Persians allowed the Jews considerable freedom to observe their distinctive religious practices. The Hellenists who defeated the Persians in the fourth century B.C.E. also granted considerable latitude to the Jews. This policy prevailed until the second century B.C.E., when the struggle between two Hellenistic dynasties, the Ptolemies and the Seleucids, over control of Israel led to increased taxation of Jews by their Hellenistic overlords. The power to tax soon led to the power to destroy. Antiochus IV Epiphanes (176–163 B.C.E.), a strong devotee of Greek culture who was committed to a systematic program of Hellenization, encouraged and then demanded that the Jews conform to pagan practices (1 Macc. 1:10–15). Far from exempting Jews from laws of general applicability, he desecrated their Jerusalem Temple (1 Macc. 1:19–24; 2 Macc. 5:15–16) by erecting within its sacred precincts the "abomination of desolation" (Dan. 11:31), a statue of the Olympian deity Zeus (1 Macc. 1:54). Far from exempting Jews from having to pay taxes to support pagan religion, he raided the treasury of the Temple and confiscated the funds used for its support. This direct assault on Jewish worship was coupled with a program of enforced assimilation that presented the gravest threat to Jewish religious freedom, and was followed by a threat of total annihilation, which sparked the successful rebellion of the Maccabees. Thus tax systems, both internal and external, are remembered negatively in the Hebrew Bible as a source of corruption and oppression.

The first written account of the exemption of religion from a tax system is found in the Book of Genesis. Within the saga of the ancestors, the Joseph story (Gen. 37–48) sets the stage for the central event of Israelite history, the exodus, by locating the descendants of Jacob-Israel in Egypt. The pattern of liberation from slavery is central to this narrative, in which Jacob's sons are surprised to learn that the royal official with whom they must deal is none other than their brother Joseph, whom they had sold into slavery but who rescues them in their time of dire need. Through his remarkable ability to interpret dreams, Joseph rises to prominence in the court of the pharaoh, where he is made grand vizier of Egypt with responsibility for developing a policy that will enable Egypt to survive a long period of famine. Joseph designs a series of radical reforms that would make the New Deal seem paltry by comparison. First, he stores abundant agricultural supplies in granaries as reserves for the hard times to come (Gen. 41:46–49). When famine hits, he appropriates all the people's money for the pharaoh in exchange for grain (Gen. 41:53–57; 47: 13–14). Next he takes the people's cattle in exchange for food (47:15–17). When the Egyptians finally offer themselves and their land to the pharaoh in order to survive, the concentration of power is completed; the people become state slaves in a feudal land-tenure system (47: 18–25) in which one-fifth of the land and its fruits is set aside for the pharaoh. The land of the priests, however, is exempted from this general plan (Gen. 47:22, 26)—a detail that reflects the ancient practice of exempting temples and temple personnel from various forms of internal taxation.[13]

---

13. According to Deut. 18:1, the Levitical priests did not hold land. Hence, this form of exemption did not arise—at least not during the period described in this book.

This system of exemption of the Egyptian priesthood lasted until the first century B.C.E., when according to one estimate the priests owned a third of the land, paid no taxes, and in socio-economic status were second only to the king.[14] Their accumulation of such vast wealth invited a struggle. Queen Cleopatra VII looted the temples after her lover Mark Anthony lost the battle of Actium in 31 B.C.E.; the Roman victors who pursued her then seized these assets as part of the spoils of battle,[15] thus setting a precedent for Roman looting of the treasury of the Jerusalem Temple a century later.

Roman law: tax exemption and taxation of the Jews

Roman law could be invoked both for exempting Jews from taxation and for taxing them in a way that directly violated their religious beliefs. The most significant events relating to tax exemption in the Second Temple period occurred during the Jewish struggle for survival under Antiochus Epiphanes described above. Escaping annihilation by the Hellenists, the Jews led by Judas Maccabee turned for protection to the newly emergent power of imperial Rome. This overture led to one of the most important examples of religious exemption in the ancient world. Eager to expand into Syria, the Romans entered into a pact of friendship with the Jews, to whom they granted special "privileges and immunities."[16] Roman emperors issued a series of "official edicts and letters to Greek cities in the East instructing them to permit resident Jews to observe their traditional religion."[17] The single most important "privilege" extended to Jews was the freedom to form religious associations (*collegia*) throughout the empire. This enabled Jews to travel throughout the Mediterranean world without abandoning their religious practices. The establishment of synagogues in virtually every province of the empire proved critical for the survival of Judaism in the diaspora communities outside of Judah. In addition to conferring this special "privilege" on Jews, Roman law also granted them a crucial "immunity" or exemption from many external acts of the Roman cult and from all public activities on the Jewish Sabbath. Jews were only required to offer prayers for the emperor, which did not conflict with any of their religious duties. Before the Christian era began, Judaism was recognized as the "only *religio licita* in the empire save the imperial cult itself."[18]

The practice of tax exemption must be examined against the background of these generous privileges and immunities. As noted above, the Romans exacted a general revenue or poll tax. It was a modest tax of one denarius (a day's wage) per year, and no one was exempted from it. But the Romans did grant the Jews an exemption from payment of the special tax designed to support the temples in Rome. This exemption lasted until the First Jewish War of rebellion against Roman rule (66–73 C.E.), which was triggered by the raiding of the Temple treasury by the Roman procurator Florus

---

14. *See* Robert M. Grant, Early Christianity and Society: Seven Studies 57 (1977).

15. *Id.*; the Egyptian priests continuously sought exemption from the Roman poll tax; *id.* at 57–60.

16. This phrase made its way into the United States Constitution, Art. IV, § 1, and Amend. XIV, § 1.

17. Peter Garnsey & Richard Saller, The Roman Empire: Economy, Society and Culture 169–70 (1987).

18. Edward H. Flannery, The Anguish of the Jews: Twenty-three Centuries of Anti-Semitism (2d ed., 1985) 16.

(64–66 C.E.). At the climax of this war, the Roman army destroyed the city of Jerusalem, including the Temple, toward the end of August in 70 C.E. Aware of the Jewish practice of sending a half-shekel annually to Jerusalem to support the Temple,[19] the Romans began to collect the same sum—a half-shekel—from Jews throughout the empire as a *fiscus judaicus* or "Jewish tax" to finance the temple of Jupiter Capitoline in Rome. With the imposition of this tax, the Romans implicated Jews in the support of pagan deities—a violation of the first and most basic command of Judaism, "You shall have no other gods to set against me" (Deut. 5:7). Thus, Roman law provides an example both of the accommodation of biblical faith through the exemption of Jews from taxation targeted for pagan worship, and of the imposition of a special tax imposed only upon Jews implicating them directly in the support of the imperial cult.

New Testament teaching on tax compliance

In the first text in the New Testament dealing with taxation, the Apostle Paul urged the Christians in Rome: "Pay each what you owe him—the tax to whom you owe the tax, the tribute to whom you owe the tribute, fear to whom you owe fear, honor to whom you owe honor" (Rom. 13:6–7). This support for a general duty of tax compliance is, moreover, harmonious with two texts within the Gospels, written much later.

The first passage, known as Caesar's coin, is found in all three of the Synoptic Gospels (Mark 12:13–17, Luke 20–26, and Matt. 22: 15–22). In all three versions of the story, adversaries of Jesus attempt to trip him up with a question about the payment of general revenue to the emperor. If Jesus were to teach that the tribute should be paid, he would fall out of favor with the Zealots opposed to Roman rule. If he were to deny the payment of tribute, he could be denounced to the Romans as an enemy of the emperor. Calling for his adversaries to produce a tribute coin, Jesus answered their question with another question about the image of Caesar on the coin. His reply—"What are Caesar's give back to Caesar and what are God's to God"—seems neutral on the surface, but the emphasis in this saying and in the life of Jesus is on giving to God what is God's.[20]

The second passage, the story of the coin in the fish's mouth (Matt. 17:24–27), is unique to the Gospel according to Matthew and is generally thought to have been written a decade or so after the destruction of Jerusalem referred to above. Several details in the story have led commentators to conclude that if the story describes an event in the life of Jesus, it has been modified to teach Jewish Christians after the destruction of the

---

19. In a Gospel narrative (Mt. 17:24–27) Jesus upheld the obligation of Jews to pay this tax in support of the Temple in Jerusalem. *See* David Daube, Responsibilities of Master and Disciples in the Gospels, 19 New Testament Studies 13 (1972); and J. Duncan M. Derrett, Law in the New Testament 247–65 (1970).

20. *See* Derrett, *supra* note 19, at 313–38. According to Luke 23:2, the opponents of Jesus twist his teaching into a flat command to refuse payment of taxes to Caesar, making this a principal charge against him before Pilate. The Lucan version of the coin tribute story may thus have an apologetic purpose, to explain to Roman authorities in the late first century that Christians were taxpayers. *See* Derrett, Luke's Perspective on Tribute to Caesar, in Political Issues in Luke-Acts 38–48 (Richard Cassidy et al. eds., 1983). Since Luke's Gospel stresses a social pattern of care for the needy, the Lucan version of this story may also ground the belief that "the only areas in which Caesar can expect allegiance are those in which his patterns are in conformity with God's desired patterns." Richard Cassidy, Jesus, Politics, and Society 58 (1978).

Jerusalem temple to pay the *fiscus judaicus*, even if it goes to the Temple of Jupiter on the Capitol in Rome.[21]

Roman law and religious exemptions for Christians

As noted above, Roman law provided important exemptions for Jews both from taxation in support of pagan temples and from participation in the imperial religion. Throughout the first three centuries of Christianity, however, Christians enjoyed no similar exemption from generally applicable laws about participation in Roman religion, including emperor worship.[22] On the other hand, there was no specific law targeting Christians in any particular way. Occasionally, as the laws governing participation in the religion of the empire were enforced with greater rigor, Christians would be subjected to sporadic persecution. The administrative reforms under the emperor Diocletian (284–305 C.E.) — doubling the number of provinces in the empire and overhauling the imperial army to guard the frontiers — entailed new forms of taxation based on agriculture, and the Christian church enjoyed no exemption from payment. Indeed, far from enjoying any special privileges, the church was subjected to special burdens.

With the sweeping administrative reforms of Diocletian came a revival of paganism and an intensification of the imperial cult. In 295 Diocletian attempted to purge the army of Christians. In 303 he mounted an intense and violent persecution of Christians, ordering the destruction of all Christian churches and books, because of the deliberate separation of the Christian community from Roman mores. The culmination of this persecution was an edict in 304 prescribing death for Christians for refusing to offer pagan sacrifice.[23]

After the death of Diocletian in 305 came the gradual unfolding of a major historical shift that continues to have profound ramifications to this day. The first phase of this shift centered on the *toleration* of Christianity under Roman law. In 311 Diocletian's successor, Galerius, issued an Edict of Toleration for Christians.[24] On October 28, 312, Constantine won supreme power in the West by his victory at the Milvian bridge on the Tiber, and was convinced that his victory was due to divine inspiration under the sign of the cross of Christ.[25] In 313 Constantine met in Milan with his co-emperor in the East, Licinius, and both agreed to a document known as the Edict of Milan.[26] Through a series of measures throughout his long reign (312–35), Constantine promoted the tol-

---

21. *See, e.g.*, Hugh Montefiore, Jesus and the Temple Tax, 11 New Testament Studies 60–71 (1964–65); and see Benedict Viviano, The Gospel according to Matthew, in New Jerome Biblical Commentary 661 (Raymond Brown et al. eds., 1990).

22. *See, e.g.*, Donald L. Jones, Roman Imperial Cult, in 5 The Anchor Bible Dictionary 806–9 (1992); Robert M. Grant, Emperor-worship in 2 Interpreter's Dictionary of the Bible 98–99 (1962); L. R. Taylor, The Divinity of the Roman Emperors (1931); Kenneth Scott, The Imperial Cult Under the Flavians (1975).

23. *See, e.g.*, Michael Grant, History of Rome 300–24 (1978); Karl Baus, From the Apostolic Community to Constantine 396–404 (1965).

24. Eusebius, The History of the Church from Christ to Constantine (hereafter Ecclesiastical History) (John Louth, ed., 1985) at 8.16.9.

25. *See* Eusebius, The Life of the Blessed Emperor Constantine 1, 27–32 (1845).

26. The Edict of Milan was not technically an imperial edict but it had broad impact, instructing provincial officials throughout the empire that Christians within their jurisdiction were to be tolerated as practicing a *religio licita* and that the churches should receive back property that had been confiscated. The Edict of Milan made sense politically as Christians became more numerous, but Lactantius, a third-century Latin writer, saw a deeper meaning in this document. He noted that since toleration is rooted in religious choice as a distinctively human activity, coercion about mat-

eration of Christianity as a *religio licita*.[27] He sought the doctrinal unity of Christians as a means of cementing the political unity of the empire. When Constantine became sole emperor of East and West in 325, he convened the first ecumenical or general council of the church and even presided over it in person when it assembled in Nicaea. Under Constantine, Christians confronted a new phenomenon: an emperor who was actively pro-Christian and who, for the first time in the Christian period, exempted the church from the payment of local taxes.[28]

The second phase of this historical shift gradually resulted in the *establishment* of Christianity as the official, preferred religion of the empire. During the brief reign of Julian (361–63) the emperor interrupted imperial support for the church and returned to the policy of general toleration of all religions, including pagans and Jews. The next period, especially during the reign of the emperor Theodosius (379–395), solidified the position of Christianity as the officially preferred or established religion, at least within the ruling class. A measure in 355 providing that a bishop could be sued only before another bishop[29] is an incipient form of clerical immunity from the jurisdiction of imperial courts. A decree in 412 extended the same immunity to all clerics, who could be accused only before a bishop.[30] Bishops and other clerics were also granted exemptions from public service.[31] These decrees may be viewed as ancient precedents establishing the principle that religious communities are entitled to deference from civil authorities regarding the structural form of their organization, which in this case was episcopal or hierarchical. Contemporary American constitutional law refers to this privilege or immunity as the protection of "church autonomy."[32] Roman law may thus be seen to adumbrate what we now call protection for the free exercise of religion. So emboldened was the church in this period that a leading bishop, Saint Ambrose of Milan, excommunicated Theodosius for ordering a massacre in Thessalonica in retaliation for an unrelated riot. Ambrose refused to allow the emperor to participate in the prayer life of the Christian community until he had formally repented of his crime.[33]

---

ters of the heart makes no sense. Lactantius, The Deaths of the Persecutors, 44; 7 Patrologia Latina col. 261 (J.P. Minge, ed.).

27. As one historian notes, "The policy of Constantine was one of toleration. He did not make Christianity the sole religion of the state. That was to follow under later Emperors. He continued to support both paganism and Christianity.... To the end of his days he bore the title of *pontifex maximus* as chief priest of the pagan state cult. The subservient Roman Senate followed the long-established custom and classed him among the gods. He did not persecute the old [pagan] faiths." Kenneth Scott LaTourette, A History of Christianity 92 (1953). On the other hand, Constantine did use his office to promote the end of the Donatist schism in Africa; Eusebius, Ecclesiastical History, *supra* note 24, at 10.5.11–20. He used bishops such as Eusebius as counselors of state. In 318 he gave legal force to the bishops' decisions in civil cases; The Theodosian Code, 1.27.1. (1952). He recognized the legitimacy of leaving legacies to the church; *id.* at 16.2.4. He also declared Sunday a holiday in the courts; *id.* at 2.8.1. For a discussion of the Roman law materials in the text accompanying notes 27–38 below, see John T. Noonan, Jr., & Edward McGlynn Gaffney, Jr., Religious Freedom: History, Cases, and Other Materials on the Interaction of Religion and Government 36–41 (2001); this book is a reworking of materials originally edited by Judge Noonan under the title, The Believers and the Powers that Are (1986).

28. Michael Grant, *supra* note 23, at 311.

29. Theodosian Code, *supra* note 27, at 16.2.12.

30. *Id.* at 16.2.41.

31. *Id.* at 16.2.1–3.

32. *See* Douglas Laycock, Towards a General Theory of the Religious Clauses: The Case of Church Labor Relations and the Right to Church Autonomy, 81 Colum. L. Rev. 1373 (1981).

33. Ambrose, St., in The Oxford Dictionary of the Christian Church 40 (F.L. Cross & E.A. Livingstone, eds., 2d ed., 1973).

Soon, however, the emphasis in imperial decrees began to create what we now refer to as the problem of an established religion. For example, in 380 a decree of Valentinian, Theodosius, and Arcadius announced the emperors' will that all the people they ruled should "practice that religion which the divine Apostle Peter transmitted to the Romans.... We command that those persons who follow this rule shall embrace the name of Catholic Christians. The rest, however, whom We adjudge demented and insane, shall sustain the infamy of heretical dogmas, their meeting places shall not receive the name of churches, and they shall be smitten first by divine vengeance and secondly by the retribution of Our own initiative, which we shall assume in accordance with the divine judgment."[34] Some forms of imperial protection of the church came at the very high cost of departure from the message of Jesus on nonviolence. For example, illegal entry into a Christian church was to be capitally punished.[35] Similarly, the prayer of Jesus for the unity of his disciples (John 17) was badly distorted as a proof text supporting the resort to imperial force to coerce both heretical Christians[36] and pagans[37] to abandon their beliefs in post-Theodosian establishment of Christianity. It was in this climate that a variety of tax exemptions for the church became codified in Roman law.[38]

The church historian Karl Baus notes irony in the fact that the establishment of the Christian church during this period not only burdened nonmembers of the church but also threatened the freedom of the church itself. "It must have been a temptation for many bishops especially in the East, after being oppressed for so long, to sun themselves

---

34. Theodosian Code, *supra* note 27, at 16.1.2.

35. *Id.* at 16.2.31.

36. In the effort to build a Christian society, both civil and religious leaders placed great value on doctrinal unity within the church. *See* Oliver O'Donovan, The Desire of Nations: Rediscovering the Roots of Political Theology (1996). The empire actively intervened in doctrinal disputes with decrees favoring those who confessed that the Father, Son, and Holy Spirit were "of the same glory," Theodosian Code, *supra* note 27, at 16.1.3; and it intervened in the internal discipline of the church, prohibiting priests to have unrelated women in their homes, *id.* 16.2.44. All privileges were denied "heretics and schismatics," *id.* 16.5.1. Indeed, imperial law forbade "all heresies," *id.* 16.5.5. Extensive legislation was enacted against the Manichees, depriving them of the right to bequeath or to inherit, *id.* 16.5.7. Apollinarians, Arians, Donatists, Eunomians, Macedonians, Montanists, Phrygians, and Priscillianists were all subjected to penalties as heretics, *id.* 16.5.12, 25, 34, and 38–39.

37. Under Constantine and other Christian emperors in the first half of the fourth century, pagans continued to hold high office. By midcentury the tide had begun to turn against pagans. An edict under the emperors Constantius and Constans sought to "eradicate completely all superstitions" but allowed pagan temples outside of Rome to remain untouched so that plays, circus performances, contests, and other "long established amusements" could continue to be performed. Theodosian Code, *supra* note 27, at 16.10.3. In 356 Constantius ordered that any persons proven to devote their attention to pagan "sacrifices or to worship images" would be subject to capital punishment, *id.* 16.10.6. By 392 Theodosius prohibited not only public worship through pagan sacrifices "to senseless images in any place at all or in any city," but also forbade the observance of ancient pagan religion in the home, including burning lights or placing incense before statutes of the deities or suspending wreaths for them, *id.* 16.10.12. Three years later the emperors Arcadius and Honorius directed the provincial governors to enforce the decrees prohibiting access to any pagan shrine or temple throughout the empire, *id.* 16.10.13. They revoked the privileges of the "civil priests" or ministers of the ancient pagan religion, *id.* 16.10.14. And finally in 399 they ordered pagan temples "in the country districts" to be torn down so that "the material basis for all superstition [would] be destroyed." *id.* 16.10.16. By the dawn of the fifth century, after decades of preferential treatment of Christians, no one could doubt that Christians played the major part in governing the empire. "God does not reject the powerful, because He is powerful," Jerome mistranslated Job 36:5—a significant mistranslation that, as part of the Latin Vulgate, was to assure Christian officeholders and reflect their belief that God was with them in the exercise of governmental power.

38. Theodosian Code, *supra* note 27, at 16.2.8, 10 and 36.

in the imperial favour and so lose their freedom. More dangerous was the tendency, deriving from the emperor's view, not to consider the Church as a partner *sui generis*, but to make her serviceable to the interests of the State and so to stifle her independence and necessary freedom in the realm of internal church affairs."[39]

Problems that emerged under Roman law may still linger on today, especially if they are not clearly identified. One way of identifying the dangers of the tax-exemption scheme enjoyed by the church under Roman law is to classify them, somewhat anachronistically, under the rubrics familiar to American constitutional law, established religion and free exercise of religion. Thus Roman law established Christianity as the official religion of the state and inhibited the free exercise of religion not only by non-Christians (such as Jews) but even by Christians whose orthodoxy ("correct belief") was suspicious in the eyes of church authorities (such as the heretics mentioned in the Theodosian Code).[40] Latent within the exemption of religion from taxation, moreover, is the possibility that the cost of this benefit for the church may be too high. Whenever the state assumes that it may exact from the church anything like total compliance to its decrees, the coin tribute story may be invoked for the proposition that the church must protect its freedom, reserving ultimate obedience for God alone. Centuries would intervene before a constitution would expressly prohibit the government from establishing a religion or from inhibiting its free exercise. Judge Noonan writes: "Free exercise—let us as Americans assert it—is an American invention. How foolish it would be to let a false modesty, a fear of chauvinism, obscure the originality."[41]

The Middle Ages: Complicated relationships between church and state

Long after the fall of the Roman empire in the fifth century to barbarian tribes such as the Vandals and the Goths, Roman law continued to have a powerful influence on Western civilization. Owing perhaps in part to this influence, a similar phenomenon of establishment of religion and violation of its free exercise occurred in England. The English experience had a direct impact on the history of the American colonies. Only after centuries of complicated interaction between church and state during the early and high Middle Ages, and only after the Reformation had shattered the unity of the church in the West, would there emerge a fully articulated theory of exemption of religion from taxation. There are some English antecedents for tax exemption of religious bodies—principally the exemption of charities, which include monasteries, hospices, and schools operated by religious communities. But English legal history is not a fruitful ground in which to search for anything like a solid precedent for our current arrangements on tax exemption. Nonetheless, it is important to explore the complexities of the relationship between church and state in medieval England as the necessary prologue to the later practice of tax exemption of religious bodies in America.

It is necessary at the outset to reject some historical falsehoods. It is not correct, for example, to claim that the church in England was generally exempt from the payment

---

39. Baus, *supra* note 23, at 432.
40. Theodosian Code, *supra* note 27.
41. John T. Noonan, Jr., The Lustre of Our Country: The American Experience of Religious Freedom 2 (1998).

of taxes to the crown throughout the medieval period. On the contrary, the bishops were expected to levy a large tribute for the crown when they gathered in their assembly or Convocation, just as the laity was expected to support the crown through Parliamentary subsidies.[42] Even the mechanisms relied upon by the local parish church for eliciting financial support from the people, such as tithes (donation of a tenth part of the harvest to the local church) and glebe lands (territory set apart for the support of the local church), were deemed a grant from kings and other lay magnates.[43]

Neither is it correct to describe the church as an autonomous body with separate jurisdiction or with power to govern itself as an independent sovereign. This view of church autonomy was asserted in the canon law, but not in the law of England as determined by its lay representatives acting in the House of Commons. Church autonomy eventually emerged as a central principle of American constitutional law,[44] but it is not descriptive of actual practice in the medieval period. On the contrary, these centuries are marked by seemingly continuous struggle between church leaders and laymen interested in the expansion of their respective influence and power.

To put a complicated matter simply, there was considerable overlap in the ways in which ecclesiastical and royal authority related to one another in medieval England.[45] To put it another way, there was no sharp distinction between church and state as we currently use those terms. The principal distinction was between clerics or spiritual rulers (such as bishops and abbots) and laypersons or secular rulers (such as kings, earls, barons, and other nobles), all of whom were members of the same church. Even this distinction was muddled. Church leaders were also secular magnates who wielded considerable power, and for this very reason the crown became keenly interested in the issue of who would wield such power.[46] The sheriff was empowered to enforce judgments of the church courts, which exercised jurisdiction over important aspects of human life, such as family law, that we now assume to be within the control of the secular authorities. Because ordained clerics (from which we derive the term "clerks") were literate, they served the crown as the bureaucrats who carried out the administration of the king's laws. The king rewarded faithful service by these clerks by awarding benefices of the church, such as the revenues of a parish priest, or even of a bishop or

---

42. *See, e.g.*, Robert E. Rodes, Jr., Ecclesiastical Administration in Medieval England (1977); and Robert E. Rodes, Jr., Lay Authority and Reformation in the English Church: Edward I to the Civil War 8–11 (1983).

43. As far as the church was concerned, the practice of tithing had scriptural warrant; *see, e.g.*, Num. 18:21, 24, 26; Deut. 12:17; 14:22, 23–28; 26:12; 2 Chron. 31:5–6; Neh. 10:38; 13:12; Mal. 3:10; Sir. 35:11. As far as the crown was concerned, the ability of the church to have this portion of the land of England dedicated to church use in this way was purely royal grace; the crown was obligated to support the church, but could have chosen other ways of doing so. In this sense the church was said to be "founded" (i.e., funded) by the king and lay magnates. Rodes, Lay Authority and the Reformation, *supra* note 42, at 2.

44. *See* Laycock, *supra* note 32; and see discussion of *Watson v. Jones* below in text accompanying notes 166–70, and discussion of church autonomy in Patrick J. Schiltz and Douglas Laycock, "Employment in Religious Organizations," in this volume.

45. For an account of these relationships, see, e.g., Robert E. Rodes, Lay Authority and Reformation, *supra* note 42, at 1–66.

46. "Before the canonical election process was formalized in the early thirteenth century, the king often played an active personal part in [the process of their selection], convening the electors, or even exercising some discretion over who was to participate." *Id.* at 4.

an abbot.[47] On the other hand, the church insisted upon the jurisdiction to try the clergy for crimes.[48]

Thus the relationships between the church and the crown were anything but tidy and were most emphatically not divided by any metaphorical "wall of separation."[49] That phrase is usually understood in the American constitutional context to describe the value of nonestablishment of religion. In the Middle Ages, however, it had a much different resonance, as used in a papal letter to describe the desire of the papacy to limit the participation of lay princes in the selection of bishops.[50]

The struggles between the church and the crown over the extent of their respective "rights and privileges" were complicated and continuous. These were conflicts not over abstract matters of political theory, but over intensely practical issues with important ramifications for tax policy. I focus now on two of these issues—the freedom of the church to select its leaders, and its freedom to discipline its clergy—as illustrations of the broader conflict that eventually brought about the practice of tax exemption.

As in the case of the ancient priests of Egypt, bishops and abbots of medieval monasteries came to control vast possessions and to enjoy popular influence that invited greater attention by the crown. As noted above, in many parts of Europe the lay authority extended its influence over society by involving itself in the selection of religious

---

47. *Id.* at 5.

48. This claim had its origins in Roman law. For example, an imperial decree issued in 384 holds that clerics may not be haled before a public court in ecclesiastical cases; Sirmondian Constitutions, Title 3, in The Theodosian Code, *supra* note 27, at 478. Another decree issued in 425 prohibits clerics from litigating in secular courts; Sirmondian Constitutions, Title 6, *id.* at 479–80.

49. Everson v. Board of Education, 330 U.S. 1, 16 (1947), *citing* Reynolds v. United States, 98 U.S. 145, 164 (1878). This metaphor is taken from a letter from Thomas Jefferson to the Baptist Association of Danbury, Connecticut dated January 1, 1802. Jefferson: Writings 510 (Merrill D. Peterson, ed., 1984). Jefferson had received a communication from these Baptists in October of 1801. His chief political advisors on New England were his postmaster general, Gideon Granger, and his attorney general, Levy Lincoln. He shared a draft of a reply with both of them. The draft expressed the view that since Congress was inhibited by the Constitution from enacting legislation "respecting religion" [*sic*], and the executive was authorized only to execute their acts, he had refrained from prescribing "even occasional performances of devotion," such as the proclamations of thanksgiving or fasting that his predecessors had done. *See* George Washington's Proclamation of a National Day of Thanksgiving, October 3, 1789, and John Adams's Proclamation of Day of Humiliation, Fasting, and Prayer, March 23, 1798, reprinted in Noonan & Gaffney, *supra* note 27, at 202–4. On December 31, 1801, Granger wrote to Jefferson urging him to send the letter as drafted. Jefferson wrote to Lincoln on January 1, 1802, and received a reply from Lincoln on the same day, cautioning against the language about thanksgivings since this might give uneasiness "even to Republicans" in the eastern states, where they had long been accustomed to proclamations of thanksgiving by their governors. Jefferson followed the advice of his attorney general and sent the letter to the Danbury Baptists that day, deleting the reference to thanksgiving days. This letter is reprinted in Noonan & Gaffney, *supra* note 27, at 205–6. *See* Dumas Malone, Jefferson the President: First Term, 1801–1805 109 (1970).

50. In early Christianity, liturgical worship emphasized the communal dimension of the people gathered to hear the scriptures and to celebrate the sacrament of the Eucharist. A leader presided over this prayer, but priests were not exalted over laypersons, all of whom were viewed as part of the holy people (in Greek, *laos*) of God. Situated in the power struggles of the medieval period, the term "layperson" or "laity" came to have a negative connotation: not priestly, not clerical. With the sacralization of the priesthood, priests were regarded as members of a different and "higher order." The Protestant reformers, principally Martin Luther and John Calvin, challenged these views both by regarding the clergy as ministers approved by the community and by placing emphasis in their teaching on the priesthood of all believers.

leaders, even to the extent of arranging that their own candidate be chosen for these church offices. This practice, which resulted in the "bestowal of ecclesiastical offices on entirely unqualified persons,"[51] met strong opposition from papal reformers, notably Pope Gregory VII (1073–85)[52] and Pope Paschal II (1099–1118).[53]

The practice of "lay investiture"—whereby a prince gave to a bishop the emblems of church office, a ring and a crozier (a staff indicating spiritual authority)—was condemned at the First Lateran Council in 1123.[54] Implicated in this symbolic gesture was a deeper political reality, but the formal resolution of this conflict had little practical impact on the continuing practice of lay involvement in the appointment of religious leaders. Sometimes the papal reformers claimed jurisdiction not only over spiritual matters, such as episcopal appointments, but also over temporal matters such as whether a prince was fit to govern. These exaggerated claims of papal authority over the secular order were ultimately unsuccessful and it would be centuries before the church would eventually prevail on the issue of its freedom to appoint its own leaders without the interference of lay princes.

However one regards these conflicts, there is no denying that the pope was an international figure with whom princes had to reckon. As early as the pontificate of Gregory I (590–604), the church had established a curia or court in Rome. By the time of Urban II (1088–99), the papal bureaucracy rivaled the organizational structure of the Holy Roman Empire. The pope thus sat as acknowledged head of a judicial and administrative system that extended to every corner of Europe from Ireland to Hungary. By maintaining its independent ability to promulgate laws governing all Christians in the West, the church began to wield a political power it had previously lacked. More importantly, it began to shape the legal culture of Europe through a jurisprudence that was grounded in the interpretation and application of its canons rather than on Frankish or Saxon local tribal customs, including the common law of England.[55]

---

51. Gregory VII, in Cross and Livingstone, *supra* note 33, at 584.

52. Shortly after his election in 1073 as Pope Gregory VII, Hildebrand issued a decree against greedy (simoniacal) clergy. In 1075 he forbade the practice of lay investiture. The Holy Roman Emperor Henry IV resisted the decree on the continent, and William the Conqueror resisted it in England. William escaped excommunication by complying zealously with other Gregorian reforms, but Henry was excommunicated, in part because he had ordered the pope deposed. In 1076 Gregory replied by issuing a decree known as *Dictatus papae* ("Pronouncements of the Pope"), which claimed not only that the pope has the power to transfer a bishop from one diocese to another under pressure of pastoral need, but also that he has the power to depose emperors. He then deposed Henry and freed his subjects of their allegiance to the emperor. The standoff between pope and emperor came to a dramatic halt a year later, with the emperor kneeling penitentially in the snow at Canossa and promising submission before being absolved. In 1080 the pope again excommunicated the emperor for failing to live up to the promises made in Canossa. The emperor again deposed Gregory, named a rival candidate or antipope, and occupied Rome after a two-year siege. The pope died in exile in Salerno in 1085. Gregory VII, St., in The Oxford Dictionary of the Christian Church 584–85 (Cross & Livingstone, eds., 1973); for a study of the impact of the Gregorian reform on the development of Western legal science, *see* Harold J. Berman, Law and Revolution: The Formation of the Western Legal Tradition 85–119 (1983).

53. For an account of the clash between Paschal II and Emperor Henry V, see Paschal II, in Cross and Livingstone, *supra* note 33, at 1020.

54. Gerd Tellenbach, Church, State, and Christian Society at the Time of the Investiture Contest (1940); Gerd Tellenbach, Libertas: Kirche und Weltordnung im Zeitalter des Investiturstreites (1996); Gerd Tellenbach, the Church in Western Europe from the Tenth to the Early Twelfth Century (1993); Karl Schmid, ed., Reich und Kirche vor dem Investiturstreit: Vorträge beim wissenschaftlichen Kolloquium aus Anlass des achtzigsten Geburtstags von Gerd Tellenbach (1985); Gerd Tellenbach, Die bischöflich passauischen Eigenklöster und ihre Vogteien (1928).

55. *See, e.g.,* Berman, *supra* note 52, at 199–224.

Perhaps the sharpest example of a conflict over church autonomy in English history is the twelfth-century confrontation between Henry II and Thomas Becket, Archbishop of Canterbury.[56] Thomas had served as the king's chancellor but, to the king's chagrin, resigned the post when at the king's urging the monks of Christ Church, Canterbury, chose Thomas as their archbishop in 1162. Henry is best known for his desire to create an efficient court system. The expanding jurisdiction of the royal courts led to conflict with the barons, who had previously dominated the administration of justice. In 1164 Henry won a major concession from Thomas and the other bishops, who agreed to observe the Constitutions of Clarendon, ceding to royal courts the power to punish clerics convicted of a crime by a church court.[57] But almost instantly, Thomas repented his surrender of the church's immunity from the crown's jurisdiction over the discipline of the clergy, and wrote to Pope Alexander III (1159–1181) asking to be absolved from his oath to the king.[58] Henry retaliated by summoning Thomas to answer in the royal courts a charge against him by one of his tenants. When Thomas failed to appear, he was fined for contempt of the king's court, and the king went on to have his barons try Thomas for not accounting for all the funds he had received as chancellor. In October 1164 he was found guilty.[59] The king thought he would prevail over Thomas by holding him accountable in courts where the king set the rules, but in Thomas's view this practice violated a bishop's immunity from civil suit, which was a tradition grounded in Roman law. Thomas appealed to the pope to overturn the verdicts. The other bishops filed a separate appeal with the pope, asking him to condemn Thomas or at least to let his case be tried by a papal legate in England.[60]

For the next six years the only litigation that went on was in the canonical system with the pope as supreme judge acting in person or by legates. Thomas issued excommunications against various bishops, clerics, and royal officials, but not against the king himself.[61] After a long exile from his see while the appeals before the pope were pending, Thomas returned to England in 1170. When he renewed an excommunication of three bishops, he roused again the wrath of Henry, who was heard to ask at court, "Who will rid me of this priest?" On the afternoon of December 29, 1170, four of Henry's knights burst into Canterbury Cathedral and murdered the archbishop.[62] The pope imposed

---

56. This account of the Becket controversy is drawn from Noonan & Gaffney, *supra* note 27, at 67–74; *see also* David Knowles, Thomas Becket (1971).

57. The Constitutions of Clarendon, in Cross & Livingstone, *supra* note 33, at 294–5: *See also*, Berman, *supra* note 52, at 255–69.

58. Knowles, *supra* note 56, at 92–93.

59. *Id.* at 94, 98.

60. *Id.* at 97–98, 104.

61. Gratian, Concordia discordantium canonum (Harmony of the Unharmonious Canons) 17.4.29.

62. Noonan notes that to see this controversy as church versus state is an anachronism. The church was divided. As noted above, some bishops sided with the king, and the pope was indecisive. On the state side of the controversy, the king was not a modern bureaucracy ideologically hostile to the church's claims. Henry was responding at least in part to what he saw as pride and disloyalty in Becket. That the bishops were divided was important to the king politically, for he could say in good conscience that he was not attacking the church when learned churchmen were on his side. But from the viewpoint of the universal church, Thomas died for his defense of its claims. Two years and two months after his death, he was proclaimed a saint, canonized by Alexander III himself. During the next six hundred years the church was often to be in conflict with Christian monarchs who had their own ideas as to how to limit the jurisdiction of the church. For popes or bishops involved in any of these encounters Thomas was an exemplar of adherence to principle and resistance to royal pretensions. By his life and by his death he had an impact on European views of the relation of bishop to prince. Noonan & Gaffney, *supra* note 27 above, at 74.

discipline on the king for the "murder in the cathedral" and for centuries afterwards pilgrims such as those described in Chaucer's *Canterbury Tales* flocked to the grave of Becket at Canterbury, not to the final resting place of the king. One consequence of the Becket controversy that would endure for centuries was that lay courts were deprived of most jurisdiction over clerics in criminal cases. This modest acknowledgment of the church's jurisdiction would in time become the basis for a fuller understanding of church autonomy. Before this was to happen, however, the momentous events of the Reformation would dramatically change the way in which church and state were thought to relate to each other.

The English Reformation: Supremacy of the crown and establishment of the church

The most obvious political consequence of the sixteenth-century Reformation is that it shattered the unity of the Western church. The Reformation in England proceeded on a very different path from the one blazed by the two principal continental reformers, Martin Luther and John Calvin, who attacked the papacy as an institution and called for a thoroughgoing reform of the church. To simplify a complicated story, the Reformation in England basically left the structure of the church intact but replaced the pope with the crown as supreme leader of the church. This major shift in the theory and practice of church law in England occurred during the long reign of the second Tudor monarch, Henry VIII (1509–47). When the pope refused to grant the king's request for an annulment of his marriage to Catherine of Aragon, Henry had the "Reformation Parliament" of 1532 enact statutes forbidding the payment of funds to support the papacy.[63] Henry then imposed upon the Convocation of the Clergy a severe criminal penalty on a trumped-up charge. Then, in a manner reminiscent of conquering emperors punishing ancient Israel, he exacted a huge sum of money from the bishops as tribute to the crown under the pretext of securing a royal pardon for their alleged misdeeds.[64] Within two years the Reformation in England took a more radical turn. In 1534 the king was declared "supreme head of the church in England"[65] and the church, in effect, became an arm of the crown.

Under that premise, it was a small step for Henry to seek and gain from a compliant Parliament statutes in 1536 and 1539 allowing the crown to dissolve the monasteries.[66] Given the wide acceptance of the principle of Parliamentary sovereignty, these enactments are not generally regarded as "unconstitutional" as they would be in a system like

---

63. Annates, the first year's revenue from a church benefice such as a diocese or headship of a monastery, were paid to the Roman curia. *See, e.g.*, W.E. Lunt, Papal Revenues in the Middle Ages 1:93–99; 2:315–72 (1934). In 1532 Parliament conditionally restrained the payment of annates; in exchange for papal documents sought by the crown, Henry refused the royal assent to the statute. Two years later, however, Parliament transferred annates to the crown, Restraint of Annates, 25 Hen. VIII, c. 20 (1534); and it forbade the ecclesiastical practice of sending a small head tax to the pope, Act Forbidding the Payment of Peter's Pence, 25 Hen. VIII, c. 21 (1534).

64. *See, e.g.*, David Harrison, Tudor England (1953).

65. Act of Supremacy, 26 Hen. VIII, c. 1 (1534).

66. Act for the Dissolution of Smaller Monasteries, 27 Henry VIII, c. 28 (1536); Act for the Dissolution of the Greater Monasteries, 31 Henry VIII, c. 13 (1539).

ours with judicial review. But one leading commentator on the Tudor period has described this confiscation of church property for the private good of the crown (and, more venally, of the king's toadies)[67] as a violation of the unwritten constitution of England.[68] In any event, the dissolution of the monasteries had devastating consequences for charity, the arts, and learning generally.[69]

As on the continent, the Reformation in England represented an assault on the universal authority of the pope, but in several respects the English Reformation left intact the arrangements that had governed the relationship between church and state throughout the Middle Ages. The most significant difference was that in the pre-Reformation period nearly everyone in England had belonged to the same religious community, while after the Reformation this was no longer the case. With the shattering of church unity, the twin problems of establishment and violation of free exercise became acute, at least for nonmembers of the Church of England. By the close of the long reign of Henry's daughter, Elizabeth I (1558–1603), Parliament had woven a web of statutory preferences for the Anglican church, with severe penalties for nonconformity. This pattern of special benefits and burdens would come to define precisely what we now refer to as an "established church." The "privileges and immunities" extended to the Christian church either by Roman law during the late fourth and early fifth centuries or by royal decrees after William I in England were now limited to the local Anglican diocese and parish, and were not extended evenhandedly to outsiders. This inequality led to the realization that tax exemption was a serious issue needing major rethinking—work that was to take place primarily in the American colonies. A decade before the Reformation in England, people took for granted a variety of mechanisms for supporting the church because there was consensus on what was meant by the term "church." Once this consensus was challenged and eventually destroyed, Recusant Catholics and dissenting

---

67. *See, e.g.,* David Knowles, Bare Ruined Choirs: The Dissolution of the English Monasteries (1976); David Knowles & R. Neville Hadcock, Medieval Religious Houses, England and Wales (1973); David Knowles, 3 The Religious Orders in England: The Tudor Age (1959); George William Otway Woodward, The Dissolution of the Monasteries (1966); Joyce A. Youings, The Dissolution of the Monasteries (1971). One writer of the period notes: "Overall the destruction of the monasteries unleashed a degree of greed far greater than any the corrupt monks had ever displayed. It embittered many among the devout without consolidating the loyalty of any segment of the population." Carolly Erickson, Bloody Mary: The Remarkable Life of Mary Tudor 174–75 (1978).

68. G.R. Elton, Studies in Tudor and Stuart Politics and Government (1974); *see also* Elton, Reformation and Renewal: Thomas Cromwell and the Commonweal (1973); Elton, Policy and Police: The Enforcement of the Reformation in the Age of Thomas Cromwell (1972). "Spasmodic attempts at reform [of the English monasteries] had met with little success and various small suppressions had taken place." Cross & Livingstone, supra note 33, at 411. Perhaps this is what one legal historian had in mind when he casually suggested that there was "mediaeval precedent for the confiscation of monastic property." Theodore Plucknett, A Concise History of the Common Law 41 (1965). For example, Henry VII had responded to situations in which a small monastery had decayed to virtual abandonment, but that was not a precedent for the wholesale expropriation of church property by his son, Henry VIII.

69. However much the monasteries were in need of reform, the royal "remedy" was deeply harmful to the spiritual and intellectual life of the country. The libraries at the monasteries were destroyed, along with the chapels where the people had gathered to pray. "The incidental losses to charity, art, and learning were considerable, many precious MSS. and church furnishings perishing through destruction and decay." Cross and Livingstone, *supra* note 33, at 411. *See also* Maria Renata Daily, The Effect on Feminine Education in England of the Dissolution of the Monasteries under Henry VIII (1934); Benjamin Kirkman Gray, A History of English Philanthropy from the Dissolution of the Monasteries to the Taking of the First Census (1905).

Protestants found it offensive to be required to pay taxes for the support of a religious community—"the Church of England as by law established"[70]—with which they disagreed deeply on various doctrinal grounds. One of the markers of religious establishment is coercive taxation imposed upon nonmembers of the church. This pattern of discriminatory tax benefits and tax burdens in England was to last until well into the nineteenth century.[71]

The first two Stuart monarchs, James I (1603–25) and Charles I (1625–49), asserted novel claims of royal power to impose taxes without the authority of Parliament. The bloody civil war that ensued led to the firm establishment in British constitutional law of the principle of parliamentary control over the power to tax and spend. After the Restoration of the monarchy under Charles II (1660–85), the clergy no longer insisted on its prerogative of taxing itself in Convocation as its means of providing subsidies to the crown, but instead subjected itself to parliamentary enactments on taxation.[72] Hence all tax exertions and exemptions, whether respecting the church or even the crown itself,[73] are now viewed as parliamentary prerogatives. Although both the church and the crown may be viewed as "autonomous" within their own spheres in the unwritten English constitution, they enjoy that status by legislative grace.

Colonial America: Local religious establishments

In modern American constitutional theory, the government may neither establish a religion not inhibit its free exercise. These constitutional goals are not polar opposites in tension with one another, as the Supreme Court[74] and many modern American commentators imagine,[75] but are complementary aspects of freedom.[76] A close examination of the history of colonial America helps to clarify this conclusion.

The disparate treatment of dissenting Protestants—religious communities who were not part of the official state religion, the Church of England—was one of the factors that

---

70. The phrase "established church" derives not from an Act of Parliament, but from canon 10, one of the religious rules for excommunicating Catholics and dissident Protestants from the Church of England, which is described in canon 10 as "by law established." These canons were formulated and promulgated by the Archbishop of Canterbury, Richard Bancroft, and were adopted by the Convocation in 1604. See J.V. Bullard, ed., Constitutions and Canons Ecclesiastical, 1604 (1934); and Robert E. Rodes, Jr., Law and Modernization in the Church of England: Charles II to the Welfare State 85 (1991). Rodes notes that "[b]y the late eighteenth century, it was widely accepted that it was one thing to set up a church and an entirely different thing to 'establish' it." Id. at 318. In an influential treatise, Alliance between Church and State (1736) the Anglican Bishop, William Warburton, wrote that churches are "set up" by anyone who cares to. Rodes summarizes Warburton's views as follows: "Then, if the civil magistrate, looking at the churches on the market, finds one that commands the allegiance of most of the people, he may choose to make an alliance with it for mutual benefit. An established church is one with which such an alliance has been negotiated; a Dissenting church is any other." Id.

71. See, e.g., Rodes, Jr., supra note 70, at 96–112.

72. Id.

73. To avoid the possibility of legislation that would have imposed a tax upon the wealth of the crown, Elizabeth II recently made a voluntary contribution to the state.

74. See, e.g., Walz v. Tax Commission, 397 U.S. at 668–9.

75. See, e.g., Suzanna Sherry, Lee v. Weisman: Paradox Redux, 1992 Sup. Ct. Rev. 123.

76. The Williamsburg Charter, a bicentennial document celebrating religious freedom, states that the First Amendment provisions on religion are "mutually reinforcing provisions [that] act as a double guarantee of religious liberty." The Williamsburg Charter, 8 J.L. & Relig. 5, 6 (1980).

impelled people to leave England during the Tudor and Stuart periods and go to the colonies in search of religious freedom. Some colonists were happy to extend the protection of religious freedom to all within their territory. The most notable practitioners of this policy were William Penn in Pennsylvania, Roger Williams in Rhode Island, and the Calverts in Maryland. Elsewhere in the American colonies religion appeared in the guise of established state churches, generally Congregationalist in New England and Anglican in the middle and southern colonies,[77] which led ironically to the very practice of religious preferences for members of the official church and penalties on nonconformity that had prompted many of the colonists to flee England in the first place.

Details varied from colony to colony, but religious establishments in America shared the following general characteristics:

> [a] state church officially recognized and protected by the sovereign; a state church whose members alone were eligible to vote, to hold public office, and to practice a profession; a state church which compelled religious orthodoxy under penalty of fine and imprisonment; a state church willing to expel dissenters from the commonwealth; *a state church financed by all members of the community*; a state church which alone could freely hold public worship and evangelize; a state church which alone could perform valid marriages [and] burials.[78]

By the same token, the movement for disestablishment embraced the following objectives:

> [a]n equal opportunity to hold public office and exercise political rights, regardless of religious beliefs; *an end to taxes for the support of a particular religious faith to which the taxpayer did not subscribe;* termination of laws requiring dissenters to attend services of the dominant faith; equal economic opportunities for dissenters and an end to advantages and preferences possessed by the members of the dominant faith; an end not only to "exclusive establishments," such as Anglican or Congregationalist, but also to "multiple establishments," such as Protestantism; toleration and equal opportunity to practice a faith, so long as it did not jeopardize the equal rights of others or imperil the common good.[79]

As the phrases italicized above suggest, the question of whether religion should be taxed provided a critical means of taking the constitutional measure of a society. It is not surprising that scant documentary evidence exists that in colonies with established

---

77. After the Glorious Revolution led to the rejection of the last Stuart king, James II, because he was a Catholic, the Protestant majority in Maryland seized the government in 1689 and limited the practice of religious toleration exclusively to Protestants. *See* Thomas J. Curry, The First Freedoms: Church and State in America to the Passage of the First Amendment 47 (1986). These events were entirely consistent with the narrow view of permissible toleration advanced by John Locke in his 1688 Letter Concerning Toleration, which expressly excluded Catholics, Muslims, and atheists from religious toleration.

78. *See* Chester James Antieau et al., Freedom From Federal Establishment: Formation and Early History of the First Amendment Religion Clauses 1–2 (1964) (emphasis added); each of these characteristics of an established church through coercive taxation is discussed *id.* at 20–24. For a more careful appraisal of the history of religious establishment in America, see Curry, supra note 77, at 105–33.

79. Antieau, *supra* note 78, at 31; the struggle to be free from taxes to support a particular religion to which a taxpayer did not subscribe is discussed *id.* at 31–41; *see also* Curry, *supra* note 77, at 137–48 (discussing Virginia) 168, 171, 181–88 (discussing Massachusetts and Connecticut).

state religions, churches were ever exempted from payments to the government. This is because in those colonies there was no adequate distinction between the church and the state. "The properties of the state church were in effect public property and 'could not but be exempt from taxation.'"[80] Even in the context of official establishments, however, there is evidence of tax exemption of religion. For example, throughout the eighteenth century Connecticut provided that:

> all lands, tenements and hereditaments, and other estates that either had been given or hereafter to be given and granted by the General Assembly, colony, or by any town, village or particular person or persons for the maintenance of the ministry of the gospel...shall be exempted out of the general list of estates, and free from the payment of rates.[81]

Taxation in support of religion tended also to reflect a bias in favor of the established church. For example, in the New England colonies, the inhabitants paid taxes to support the local "teacher of Christian religion," irrespective of whether they were members of the same church as that pastor. The sentence "Taxation without representation is tyranny" resonates as a slogan of the American revolution, which is commonly viewed as a tax rebellion against the imposition of duties by a Parliament in which the colonists had neither voice nor vote. Before Tom Paine used the slogan in his famous pamphlet *Common Sense*, however, the same basic idea had been voiced repeatedly by the famous preacher, Isaac Backus, to describe Baptist protest against the imposition of local taxes in New England to support the Congregational establishment. Thus in a long pamphlet entitled *An Appeal to the Public for Religious Liberty, Against the Oppressions of the Present Day*, Backus explained in 1773 why he would no longer submit certificates (which were themselves taxed at a moderate rate) seeking exemption for Baptists from payment of taxes for the support of a Congregational minister: "You do not deny the right of the British Parliament to impose taxes within her own realm; only complain that she extends her taxing power beyond her proper limits. And have we not as good right to say you do the *same thing*?.... Can three thousand miles possibly fix such limits to taxing power as the difference between civil and sacred matters has already done?"[82] In the following year Backus drafted a long letter explaining the same matter as follows: "The reasons why the leaders of our society [Baptists] did not conform to that law, were not any disregard to civil government, to which in its proper place we trust that we are as good subjects as you are, but because upon close examination of the case they were convinced that for civil rulers to assume a *power to impose taxes for religious worship* is *contrary* to the word of God, contrary to the charter of this province, and *to the very nature of true liberty and equity among mankind*."[83] Four years later, Backus wrote in a pamphlet entitled *Government and Liberty Described; and Ecclesiastical Tyranny Exposed*: "I need not inform you that all America are in arms against being taxed where they are not

---

80. Antieau, *supra* note 78, at 73, *citing* Carl Zollman, American Civil Church Law 239 (1917).

81. *Id*. at 73, *citing* 66 Conn. L. Rev., 1702.

82. William G. McLoughlin, ed., Isaac Backus on Church, State, and Calvinism: Pamphlets, 1754–1789 338 (1968) ("Pamphlets"). In the same pamphlet, Backus again drew a parallel between the injustice of American submission to the British taxing power and "our [Baptist] greatest difficulty at present...submitting to a taxing power in ecclesiastical affairs." *Id*. at 340.

83. William G. McLoughlin, ed., II The Diary of Isaac Backus 899 (1979) (emphasis added); for the definitive study of the Baptist protest against the established religion in New England, see William G. McLoughlin, New England Dissent, 1630–1833: The Baptists and the Separation of Church and State (1971).

represented. But it is not more certain that we are not represented in the British Parliament than it is, that our *civil* rulers are not our representatives in *religious* affairs."[84]

The American Republic:
The emergence of the free exercise principle

As Thomas Curry notes, coerced public support for a particular religion was viewed in colonial America as an "establishment of religion," but the practice was opposed "primarily as a violation of free exercise of religion."[85] Thinking of "establishment" and "free exercise" as precise and distinct categories in tension with one another is a modern invention. The terms "nonestablishment" and "free exercise of religion" were not mutually opposed, but were used almost interchangeably in America at the time of the framing of the First Amendment. According to Curry, "[t]o examine the two [religion] clauses . . . as a carefully worded analysis of Church-State relations would be to overburden them. Similarly, to see the two clauses as separate, balanced, competing, or carefully worded prohibitions designed to meet different eventualities would be to read into the minds of the actors far more than is there."[86]

The principal drafter of the First Amendment, James Madison, most assuredly did not think of disestablishment and free exercise as competing values. For Madison, the point of the amendment was to secure basic freedoms—of religion, speech, press, peaceable assembly, and petition for redress of grievance. As to religious freedom, Madison had clarified at the Virginia Convention to prepare a Declaration of Rights in May of 1776 which stated that mere toleration was not enough; something more—free exercise—was required.[87] There is something distinctively American about the resolution of the problem of an established religion through the promotion of free exercise of religion. In the Madisonian scheme of protecting religious freedom, any official preference or establishment of a religion was also to be avoided, at least at the federal level. But the purpose or teleological goal of nonestablishment was to guarantee free exercise of religion.[88]

Although the terms "establishment" and "free exercise" certainly had overlapping meanings, it is fair to say that in sixteenth-century Europe and seventeenth-century

---

84. William G. McLoughlin, ed., *supra* note 82, at 357 (emphasis in original). Backus also wrote: "Our real grievances are that we, as well as our fathers, have from time to time been *taxed on religious accounts where we were not represented*. . . . Is not all America now appealing to Heaven against the injustice of being taxed where we are not represented, and against being judged by men who are interested in getting away our money? And will heaven approve of your doing the same thing to your fellow servants? No, surely. We have no desire of representing this government as the worst of any who have imposed religious taxes; we fully believe the contrary. Yet, as we are persuaded that an entire freedom from being taxed by civil rulers to religious worship is not a mere favor from any man or men in the world but a right and property granted us from God, who commands us to stand fast in it, we have not only the same reason to refuse an acknowledgment of such a taxing power here, as America has the abovesaid power, but also, according to our present light, we should wrong our consciences in allowing that power to men, which we believe belongs only to God" (emphasis added).

85. Curry, *supra* note 77, at 192.

86. *Id.* at 216.

87. *See* Noonan & Gaffney, *supra* note 27, at 162–3; *see also* Noonan, *supra* note 41, at 2, 4, 46–47, 69.

88. For a discussion of the textual unity of the nonestablishment principle and the free exercise principle, *see* Noonan, *supra* note 41, at 357; John T. Noonan, Jr., The End of Free Exercise?, 42 De-

America the establishment of a state religion had the effect of both *advancing* that religion through benefits available to it and not to others,[89] and *inhibiting* that same religion by encouraging its complacency and rendering it inoffensive.[90] In this setting, moreover, the "primary and principal effect" of the state establishment of religion was the savage inhibition of other religions outside the communion of "the Church of England...by law established"[91] in Tudor and Stuart England.[92] It is this understanding of "inhibition" to which Justice O'Connor refers in her elaboration of an "endorsement" test, according to which official preference for an established religion sends "a message to nonadherents that they are outsiders, not full members of the political community" and are in this way treated as second-class citizens.[93]

However the correlated concepts of disestablishment and free exercise were understood in the early republic, it seems clear that strong supporters of disestablishment in Virginia, such as Thomas Jefferson and James Madison, did not equate religious tax exemption with an establishment of religion. As Justice Brennan noted in his concurring opinion in *Walz*, Jefferson was president when tax exemption was first given to churches in Washington, and Madison sat in the Virginia General Assembly that voted exemptions for churches in Virginia.[94] Further evidence of the practice includes the following examples. In 1781 Massachusetts exempted ministers of the Gospel from a poll tax.[95] In 1786 Rhode Island exempted ministers from an excise tax on carriages, and in 1789 it exempted all real estate granted or purchased for religious uses.[96] In 1787 South Carolina exempted ministers from a Charleston tax on professions,[97] and in 1788 South Carolina exempted from taxation "lands whereon any churches or other buildings for divine worship, or free schools, are erected."[98]

Paul L. Rev. 567 (1992); *see also* Richard John Neuhaus, Contending for the Future: Overcoming the Pfefferian Inversion, 8 J.L. & Relig. 115 (1990).

89. *See, e.g.*, Antieau, *supra* note 78, at 1–29 (describing general characteristics of establishments in colonial America).

90. The phenomenon of secularization provides one explanation of the decline of religious belief and practice in European establishments such as the Church of England and the Lutheran Church in Sweden. The very fact of their status as established churches may also explain the decline in the number of their adherents.

91. The phrase comes not from an Act of Parliament but from Canon 10, one of the religious rules for excommunicating Catholics and dissident Protestants from the Church of England. These canons were formulated and promulgated by the Archbishop of Canterbury, Richard Bancroft, in 1604. *See* J.V. Bullard, ed., Constitutions and Canons Ecclesiastical, 1604 (1934); and Rodes, *supra* note 70, at 84.

92. *See, e.g.*, Act against Jesuits and Seminary Priests, 27 Eliz. I c. 2 (1585); Act against Seditious Sectaries, 35 Eliz. I c 1 (1593); Act against Popish Recusants, 35 Eliz. I c. 2 (1593); Act concerning Jesuits and Seminary Priests, 1 & 2 James I c. 4 (1604); Act of Uniformity, 14 Chas. II c. 4 (1662); The Five Mile Act, 17 Chas. II c. 2 (1664); The Conventicle Act, 22 Chas. II c. 1 (1670); Test Act, 25 Chas. II c. 2 (1673); and The Second Test Act, 30 Chas. II c. 1 (1678).

93. *See* Lynch v. Donnelly, 465 U.S. 668, 688 (1984) (O'Connor, J., concurring). A majority of the Court adopted this approach in *County of Allegheny v. ACLU*, 492 U.S. 573 (1989).

94. *See, e.g.*, *Walz*, at 684–85 (Brennan, J., concurring), *citing* E. Swem and J. Williams, A Register of the General Assembly of Virginia, 1776–1918, 53 (1918); Journal of the House of Delegates of the Commonwealth of Virginia 94, 98 (1799–1800).

95. Acts and Resolves of 1781, c. 16.

96. Edward Field, History of Rhode Island I: 553, III: 238, 232 (1902).

97. South Carolina Acts of Assembly (1788) P.L. 435

98. State Gazette of South Carolina, Apr. 12, 1788.

Several amicus briefs in *Walz* offered extensive discussion of the history supporting the practice of religious tax exemption.[99] In his opinion for the Court, Chief Justice Burger noted the impressive historical pedigree of the practice, describing it as "a national heritage with roots in the Revolution itself." Burger concluded: "[A]n unbroken practice of according the exemption to churches, openly and by affirmative state action, not covertly or by state inaction, is not something to be lightly cast aside."[100] Describing the practice as "unbroken" subjected Burger to scholarly criticism.[101] But even if the practice of religious tax exemption was not in fact "unbroken," and even if some of its earlier manifestations emerged in the context of an established religion, it is important to recall that the granting of exempt status on an evenhanded basis to all religious communities is the achievement of the distinctively Madisonian contribution to constitutional jurisprudence, the emphasis on free exercise of religion.

Tax exemption as a statutory privilege with deep constitutional roots

However confused the current constitutional doctrine on religious freedom has become in modern jurisprudence, in the founding period the exemption of religious organizations from taxation was motivated by the desire to safeguard free exercise.[102] Thus, Chief Justice Burger noted in *Walz* that the Court, "reflecting more than a century of our history and uninterrupted practice, accepted without discussion the proposition that federal or state grants of tax exemption to churches were not a violation of the *Religion Clauses* of the First Amendment."[103] Although this statement appeared on its face to invoke concerns about both establishment and free exercise, the rationale elaborated by Burger focused almost exclusively on establishment, thus portraying the granting of tax-exempt status not as a matter of constitutional necessity, but as something within the scope of permissible legislation. Recent developments relating to exemption of religion from taxation under state law have reemphasized the

---

99. *See, e.g.*, Brief Amicus Curiae of United States Catholic Conference; and see Chester James Antieau, Phillip Mark Carroll, and Thomas Carroll Burke, Religion under the State Constitutions 120–72 (1965).

100. 397 U.S. 664, 678 (1970).

101. For a powerful critique of Chief Justice Burger's use of history in *Walz*, see John Witte, *supra* note 10, at 367. For Witte, "The Court's historical argument depends too heavily upon questionable assertions of fact and selective presentation of evidence. The Court asserts that tax exemptions of church property have been adopted by common consent for more than two centuries. But a strong vein of criticism has long accompanied the practice in America. The Court asserts that such exemptions have not 'led to' an establishment of religion. But historically these exemptions were among the privileges of established religions, while dissenting religions were taxed; the issue is whether such exemptions have shed the chrysalis of establishment. The Court adduces numerous examples of earlier tax laws that exempt church property. But it ignores the variety of theories that supported these laws. The Court asserts that such exemption laws 'historically reflect the concern of [their] authors' to avoid the 'dangers of hostility to religion inherent in the imposition of property taxes.' But little evidence from congressional and constitutional debates on tax exemption supports this assertion" (footnotes omitted).

102. *See, e.g.*, Curry, *supra* note 77, at 192; *see also* William G. McLoughlin, *supra* note 83.

103. *Walz*, 397 U.S. at 680.

dependence of religious organizations upon the legislatures rather than upon the courts for the "grace" of tax exemption.[104]

This view of exemption is consonant with legislative control over the power to tax and spend—a theme central to English and American jurisprudence since the early period of the Stuart monarchy. But the history of religious tax exemption sketched above underscores a tradition deeply rooted in the customs and traditions of the American people,[105] with roots going back to the Middle Ages and even to the ancient world.[106] In the face of this history, this practice reflects what Lonergan calls "constitutive meaning," and is constitutional at least in this sense. To quote Burger's opinion in *Walz* again:

> The legislative purpose of the property tax exemption is neither the advancement nor the inhibition of religion; it is neither sponsorship nor hostility. New York, in common with the other States, has determined that certain entities that exist in a harmonious relationship to the community at large, and that foster its "moral or mental improvement," should not be inhibited in their activities by property taxation or the hazard of loss of those properties for nonpayment of taxes.... Grants of exemption historically reflect the concern of authors of constitutions and statutes as to the latent dangers inherent in the imposition of property taxes; exemption constitutes a reasonable and balanced attempt to guard against those dangers.[107]

The history sketched above suggests that as a normative matter, our society has generally given a negative answer to the question of whether churches should be taxed either by the federal government or by the states. I turn now to explore more closely the exemption of religious organizations from federal taxation.

General Statutory Principles Governing Exemption of Religious Organizations

Section 501(c)(3) of the Internal Revenue Code (IRC) provides that several kinds of organizations, including religious organizations, are exempt from payment of federal-income taxation if they meet various tests set forth in the statute. Four other provisions

---

104. *See, e.g.*, Texas Monthly, Inc. v. Bullock, 489 U.S. 1 (1989), and Jimmy Swaggart Ministries v. California Bd. of Equalization, 493 U.S. 378 (1990), discussed in "Exemption of Religious Communities from State and Local Taxation," the next chapter in this volume.

105. For the view that courts have "no basis for proscribing as unconstitutional practices that do not violate any explicit text of the Constitution and that have been regarded as constitutional ever since the framing," *see* Board of County Comm'rs, Waubausee County v. Umbehr, 518 U.S. 668 (1996) (Scalia, J., dissenting); Kiryas Joel Village Sch. Dist. v. Grumet, 512 U.S. 687, 752 (1994) (Scalia, J., dissenting) (Establishment Clause should not be used to "repeal our Nation's tradition of religious toleration"); Rutan v. Republican Party of Ill., 497 U.S. 62, 95 (1990) (Scalia, J., dissenting) ("when a practice not expressly prohibited by the text of the Bill of Rights bears the endorsement of a long tradition of open, widespread, and unchallenged use that dates back to the beginning of the Republic, we have no proper basis for striking it down"); Burnham v. Superior Court of Cal., County of Marin, 495 U.S. 604 (1990) (plurality opinion of Scalia, J.). *And see* Antonin J. Scalia, A Matter of Interpretation: Federal Courts and the Law (1997).

106. *See* James J. McGovern, The Exemption Provisions of Subchapter F, 29 Tax Law. 523, 527 (1976) (the "history of mankind reflects that our early legislators were not setting precedent by exempting religious or charitable organizations").

107. *Walz*, 397 U.S. at 672–73.

of the tax code refer to religious organizations under the rubric "church" or "association of churches." Section 170(b)(1)(A)(i) lists churches first in its catalog of organizations contributions to which are deductible from taxable income. Section 508(c)(1)(A) gives churches a mandatory exception from the presumption of being a "private foundation," and section 6033(a)(2)(A) gives them a mandatory exception from the requirement that most exempt organizations must file annual informational returns (Form 990) with the Internal Revenue Service (IRS). Section 7605(c) limits the IRS in auditing or examining religious organizations.

IRC section 501(c)(3) states that a charitable entity must be both "organized and operated" exclusively for exempt purposes, and this language has given rise to two distinct tests, the organizational test and the operational test, both of which a church must pass in order to qualify as an exempt organization.[108]

The organizational test

The organizational test requires that a religious organization must be expressly limited to a religious purpose.[109] This test can be described as a "paper requirement," which simply means that the IRS only looks at a "creating document" (such as the organization's corporate charter, articles of association, or trust instrument) to determine whether the requirement is met.[110] The written instrument creating the organization must specify that the entity is organized exclusively for one or more tax-exempt charitable purposes.[111] There is no magic formula for meeting the organizational test. For example, the articles of incorporation may specify that the organization is formed "for religious or charitable purposes within the meaning of section 501(c)(3) of the Internal Revenue Code."[112] In at least one instance a court suggested that it would be "myopic" to consider only the articles of incorporation, and found that appropriate language in the bylaws satisfied the organizational test.[113]

To restate this test negatively, the originating document may not expressly empower the organization to engage substantially in activities that in themselves are broader than or not in furtherance of an exempt purpose.[114] In other words, the written instrument creating a religious organization may not authorize it to carry on substantial nonexempt activities.[115] The statute expressly prohibits two specific activities that I discuss

---

108. Reg. § 1.501(c)(3)-1(a); Levy Family Tribe Found. v. Commissioner, 69 T.C. 615, 618 (1978).

109. *See* Reg. § 1.501(c)(3)-1(d).

110. "[T]he organizational test cannot be met by reference to any document that is not the creating document. In the case of a corporation, the bylaws cannot remedy a defect in the corporate charter. A charter can be amended only in accordance with state law, which generally requires filing of the amendments with the chartering authority. In the case of a trust, operating rules cannot substitute for the trust indenture. In the case of an unincorporated association, the test must be met by the basic creating document and the amendments thereto, whatever that instrument may be called. Subsidiary documents that are not amendments to the creating document may not be called on." Colorado State Chiropractic Soc'y v. Commissioner, 93 T.C. 487 (1989).

111. Int. Rev. Reg. § 1.501(c)(3)-1(b)(2).

112. Reg. § 1.501(c)(3)-1(b)(1)(ii).

113. IRS Exempt Organizations Handbook (IBM 7751) § 332(2).

114. Reg. § 1.501(c)(3)-1(b)(1)(i).

115. Rev. Rul. 69-279, 1969-1 C. B. 152; Rev. Rul. 69-256, 1969-1 C.B. 151. Int. Rev. Reg. § 1.501(c)(3)-1(b)(iii). *See also* Interneighborhood Housing Corp. v. Commissioner, 45 T. C. M. 115 (1982); Santa Cruz Building Assoc. v. United States, 411 F. Supp. 871 (E.D. Mo. 1976).

below: (1) devoting more than an insubstantial part of its activities to lobbying or attempting to influence legislation; and (2) any kind of electioneering, i.e., participating in (including the publishing or distributing of statements) any political campaign, either on behalf of or in opposition to any candidate for public office. For now, it suffices to note that the originating documents of a religious organization may not authorize either of these purposes.

Even when a particular organization has actually operated to further an exempt purpose, it will still fail to qualify as exempt if its originating documents can reasonably be construed to permit activities broader than the specified charitable purposes. For this reason Bruce Hopkins, a highly regarded practitioner in the field of exempt organization law, counsels: "An organization wishing to qualify as a charitable entity should not provide in its articles of organization that it has all of the powers accorded under the particular state's nonprofit corporation act, since those powers are likely to be broader than those allowable under federal tax law."[116] A church will fail the organizational test if it is organized for both exempt and nonexempt purposes.[117]

Another aspect of the organizational test is the requirement that the assets of a church must be dedicated to an exempt purpose. Thus the founding papers must attend to the distribution of a church's assets to an exempt purpose in the event of its dissolution.[118] A church does not meet this aspect of the organizational test if its founding documents provide that upon dissolution its assets would be distributed to its founders or members.[119] The more common practice in such situations is for the assets to be transferred to another religious organization, but occasionally the organizational test is instead met by stipulating that assets be transferred toward charitable purposes, whether or not the recipient actually meets the definition of a charitable organization.[120] The trust law of most states includes the doctrine of cy pres, according to which a court may distribute the assets of a charitable trust to another organization to be used in a manner consistent with the religious or charitable purposes of the dissolved organization.[121] In states that have not adopted the cy pres doctrine, the organizing document must contain an express provision like the following: "Upon the dissolution of [this organization], assets shall be distributed for one or more exempt purposes within the meaning of section 501(c)(3) of the Internal Rev-

---

116. Hopkins, *supra* note 5, at 110, *citing* IRS General Counsel Memorandum 39633.

117. Rev. Rul. 69-256, *supra*, n. 8; Rev. Rul. 69-279, *supra*, n. 8.

118. In *Universal Church of Scientific Truth, Inc. v. United States*, 74-1 U.S.T.C. ¶9360 (N.D. Ala. 1973), however, the court ruled that the absence of a provision for dissolution of a religious organization's assets would not, without more, suffice to render the church ineligible for exempt status.

119. Int. Rev. Reg. § 1.501(c)(3)-1(b)(4). *See, e.g.*, Chief Steward of the Ecumenical Temples and the Worldwide Peace Movement and His Successors v. Commissioner, 49 T.C.M. 640 (1985); Bethel Conservative Mennonite Church v. Commissioner, 746 F.2d 388 (7th Cir. 1984); Church of Nature in Man v. Commissioner, 49 T.C.M. 1393 (1985); Stephenson v. Commissioner, 79 T.C. 995 (1982); Truth Tabernacle v. Commissioner, 41 T.C.M. 1405 (1981); Calvin K. of Oaknoll v. Commissioner, 69 T.C. 770 (1978), *aff'd*, 603 F.2d 211 (2d Cir. 1979); General Conference of the Free Church of America v. Commissioner, 71 T.C. 920 (1979).

120. IRS General Counsel Memorandum 37126, clarifying IRS General Counsel Memorandum 33207. Moreover, the absence of a dissolution clause has been held to not be fatal to IRC § 501(c)(3) status, in

121. For a general discussion of the religious or charitable trust, see William W. Bassett, Religious Organizations and the Law, ¶3:43 to 3:70 (1997, Supp. 2000); for a more particular discussion of the cy pres doctrine, see, e.g., Revised Model Nonprofit Corporation Act, § 14.06(a)(6); and *In re* Los Angeles County Pioneer Soc'y, 257 P. 2d 1 (1953).

enue Code, or corresponding section of any future Federal tax code, or shall be distributed to the Federal government, or to a state or local government, for a public purpose."[122]

In summary, federal tax regulations require the creating document of a charitable organization to (1) limit its purposes to those exempt from taxation, (2) not expressly empower it to engage substantially in nonexempt activities, and (3) provide that upon dissolution its assets will be distributed for one or more exempt purposes.

Hopkins suggests that the articles of organization or bylaws of a charitable organization might contain provisions such as the following:

> No part of the net earnings, gains or assets of the corporation [or organization] shall inure to the benefit of or be distributable to its directors [or trustees], officers, other private individuals, or organizations organized and operated for a profit (except that the corporation [or organization] shall be authorized and empowered to pay reasonable compensation for services rendered and to make payments and distributions in furtherance of the purposes as hereinabove stated). No substantial part of the activities of the corporation [or organization] shall be the carrying on of propaganda or otherwise attempting to influence legislation, and the corporation [or organization] shall be empowered to make the election authorized under section 501(h) of the Internal Revenue Code of 1986. The corporation [or organization] shall not participate in or intervene in (including the publishing or distribution of statements) any political campaign on behalf of or in opposition to any candidate for public office. Notwithstanding any other provision herein, the corporation [or organization] shall not carry on any activities not permitted to be carried on—

> (a) by an organization exempt from federal income taxation under section 501(a) of the Internal Revenue Code of 1986 as an organization described in section 501(c)(3) of such Code, or

> (b) by an organization, contributions to which are deductible under sections 170(c)(2), 2055(a)(2), or 2522(a)(2) of the Internal Revenue Code of 1986.

> References herein to sections of the Internal Revenue Code of 1986 are to provisions of such Code as those provisions are now enacted or to corresponding provisions of any future United States revenue law.[123]

Hopkins writes that in order to satisfy the organizational requirement, an organization *must* have in its articles of organization provisions substantially equivalent to the following:

> The corporation [or organization] is organized and operated exclusively for [charitable, educational, etc.] purposes within the meaning of section 501(c)(3) of the Internal Revenue Code of 1986.

> In the event of dissolution or final liquidation of the corporation [or organizations], the board of directors [or trustees] shall, after paying or making provision for the payment of all the lawful debts and liabilities of the corporation [or organization], distribute all the assets of the corporation [or organization] to one or more of the following categories of recipients as the board of directors [or trustees] of the corporation [or organization] shall determine:

---

122. *Id.* § 3.05.
123. Hopkins, *supra* note 5, at 113.

(a) a nonprofit organization or organization which may have been created to succeed the corporation [or organization], as long as such organization or each of such organizations shall then qualify as a governmental unit under section 170(c) of the Internal Revenue Code of 1986 or as an organization exempt from federal income taxation under section 501(a) of such Code as an organization described in section 501(c)(3) of such Code; and/or

(b) a nonprofit organization or organizations having similar aims and objects as the corporation [or organization] and which may be selected as an appropriate recipient of such assets, as long as such organization or each of such organizations shall then qualify as a governmental unit under section 170(c) of the Internal Revenue Code of 1986 or as an organization exempt from federal income taxation under section 501(a) of such Code as an organization described in section 501(c)(3) of such Code.[124]

Hopkins notes that some courts have adopted a sensible rule of construction respecting charitable exemptions that resolves ambiguities in favor of the definition of an exempt organization and that refuses to exalt form over substance.[125] Nevertheless, Hopkins concludes that "prudence dictates compliance with the organizational test whenever possible. There are many barriers to tax-exempt status and the organizational test is one of the easiest to clear.... Even if doing battle with the IRS over the tax-exempt status of an organization appears inevitable, presumably the struggle can be joined over matters of greater substance."[126]

The operational test

The IRS regulations also specify that a church must be operated as an exempt organization. The focus of the operational test is on the ongoing activities of a church, but the church will be deemed to fail this test if its originating documents—let alone its activities—permit private inurement by its founders.[127] Sometimes the technical distinction between the organizational and operational tests can become blurred, as when a court views the organizational test in light of how a religious organization actually operates.[128]

The First Amendment requires the government to acknowledge the hierarchical control of a church as a legitimate form of church polity.[129] Thus the Court of Claims has recognized that the control of a church by its founder does not by itself constitute a fail-

---

124. *Id.* at 113–14.

125. Hopkins, *supra* note 5, at 116, *citing* Samuel Friedland Found. v. United States, 144 F. Supp. 74, 84 (D.N.J. 1956); Peoples Translation Service/Newsfront Int'l v. Commissioner, 79 T. C. 42, 48 (1979).

126. Hopkins, *supra* note 5, at 117.

127. Reg. §§ 1.501(c)(3)-1(c)(2), 1.501(a)-1(c). *See, e.g.,* Athenagoras I Christian Union of the World, Inc. v. Commissioner, 55 T.C.M. 781 (1988); Levy Family Tribe Found. v. Commissioner, 69 T.C. 615 (1978). For an extended discussion of private inurement, see Hopkins, *supra* note 5, at 264–99.

128. *See, e.g.,* Passaic United Hebrew Burial Assoc. v. United States, 216 F. Supp. 500 (D.N.J. 1963).

129. *See* discussion of *Watson v. Jones* below in text accompanying notes 166–70 below; and *see* discussion of church autonomy in Schiltz and Laycock, *supra* note 44; *see also* God Alone is Lord of the Conscience: A Policy Statement Adopted by the 200th General Assembly (1988) (Louisville: Office of the General Assembly, The Presbyterian Church (U.S.A.), 1989), *reprinted in* 8 J. Law & Relig. 331, at 337–43.

ure to meet the operational test.[130] In another case, however, the tax court reached the remarkable conclusion that a church's organizational structure disqualified it from exempt status because an individual's control of church operations was not checked by any other governing body.[131]

The tax court has construed the operational test to deny exempt status to a religious organization involved in commercial enterprises that compete with other businesses. In *Living Faith, Inc. v. Commissioner*,[132] the tax court adopted the position that "[c]ompetition with commercial firms is strong evidence of a substantial nonexempt commercial purpose."[133] Following this standard, the court denied exempt status to an organization associated with the Seventh Day Adventist Church that operated vegetarian restaurants and health food stores in furtherance of the church's teachings on dietary requirements, finding that the organization's "activity was conducted as a business and was in direct competition with other restaurants and health food stores." This conclusion seems excessive, since religious organizations are not exempt from the payment of tax on income unrelated to its exempt purposes.[134] It is doubtful that the court would have reached a similar conclusion with respect to rabbinical councils that pass on the kosher slaughter of animals. Indeed, in the seminal case that established that the source of income and not its goal properly determines whether it should be exempt from taxation, the government did not seek to revoke the exempt status of a teaching order known as the Christian Brothers that operated a well-known winery in the Napa Valley, but simply insisted that the brothers had to pay tax on income derived from operation of the winery.[135] Similarly, in the late 1970s, Trappist monasteries that sustained themselves in part by the sale of jams and jellies or liturgical vestments managed to avoid the severe penalty of loss of exempt status because they were able to reach a mutually satisfactory understanding with the Internal Revenue Service.

The most significant aspect of the operational test is that an exempt organization may not engage in activities that characterize it as an "action organization."[136] This term

---

130. *See* The Church of the Visible Intelligence That Governs the Universe v. United States, 83-2 U.S.T.C. ¶ 9726 (Cl. Ct. 1983).

131. Chief Steward of the Ecumenical Temples and the Worldwide Peace Movement and His Successors v. Commissioner, 49 T.C.M. 640 (1985).

132. Living Faith, Inc. v. Commissioner, 60 T.C.M. 710, 713 (1990).

133. *Id.* at 713. The commerciality doctrine is related to the principle that a religious organization is not exempt from payment of tax on business income unrelated to its exempt purpose. *See* note 134 *infra*.

134. As Dean Kelley noted, "Until 1969, churches were unique among entities exempt under section 501(c)(3)of the Internal Revenue Code in not having to pay corporate income tax on 'unrelated business income'.... But in 1969, the National Council of Churches and the U.S. Catholic Conference jointly asked the House Ways and Means Committee to *close* that loophole, and it was closed by the Tax Reform Act of 1969 (with a five-year period of grace for existing church-owned businesses to be phased out, which expired on January 1, 1976).... It is not often that great institutions ask Congress to end the tax advantages from which they ostensibly benefit.... The churches did not want a tax advantage they did not think was right, and they voluntarily took action to eliminate it." Dean Kelley, *supra* note 5, at 17–18. For an extended discussion of the rules governing the taxation of unrelated income, the definition of unrelated trade or business, exceptions to unrelated income taxation, and unrelated debt-financed income, *see* Bruce Hopkins, *supra* note 5, at 827–975; and Joseph M. Galloway, The Unrelated Business Income Tax (1982).

135. *See* De La Salle Institute v. United States of America, 195 F. Supp. 891 (N.D. Calif. 1961) (schools and novitiate operated by nonprofit corporation composed of nonclerical members of religious order were not 'churches,' and corporation's income from winery was taxable as unrelated business income, even though schools and novitiate maintained chapels and canon law viewed teaching as church function).

136. Reg. § 1.501(c)(3)-1(b)(3).

refers to an organization that is involved in politics either through the devotion of a substantial part of its activities to attempts to influence legislation or though the direct or indirect participation or intervention in any political campaign on behalf of or in opposition to any candidate for public office. The restraints on lobbying and the prohibition of political activities are discussed below.

Specific Provisions in the Internal Revenue Code Relating to Religious Organizations

Federal employment taxes

A separate chapter of this book explores the regulation of employees of churches. This question is most closely analogous to the medieval controversies over the independence of the church in the selection and discipline of the clergy. As has been noted above, these controversies affected not only the general theory of church autonomy but also the more particular matter of whether the church should be taxed. The reader should refer to the other chapter for a detailed analysis of the impact of civil-rights laws on the employment practices of churches, and here focus briefly on the impact of federal employment taxes—primarily social security and unemployment tax—on those same churches.

The Social Security Act was one of the most significant pieces of New Deal legislation.[137] It provides a system of old-age and unemployment benefits that are supported by various taxes, including those collected under the Federal Insurance Contributions Act (FICA) and the Federal Unemployment Tax Act (FUTA). The FICA tax is paid in part by employees through withholding,[138] and in part by employers through an excise tax.[139] The FUTA tax is an excise tax imposed only on employers.[140] Both taxes are based on the amount of wages paid to employees, and the recordkeeping and transmittal of funds are obligations of the employer. Only the FICA tax is collected from self-employed individuals. Both taxes allow some legislative exceptions for religion.

The original Social Security legislation provided an exemption from FICA taxes for service performed in the employment of a religious organization. In 1983 Congress removed this exemption, extending Social Security coverage to all employees of churches except individual members of the clergy who met specific requirements as self-employed persons.[141] The statute survived a constitutional challenge brought in *Bethel Baptist Church v. United States*,[142] when the court rejected the argument that the 1983

---

137. 26 U.S.C. §§ 3101–3126; Titles II & VIII were sustained in *Helvering v. Davis*, 301 U.S. 619 (1937) (exclusively federal aspect of Social Security pension program permissible exercise of taxing and spending power); Title IX was sustained in *Steward Machine Co. v. Davis*, 301 U.S. 548 (1937) (federal assistance to state in administration of their unemployment compensation laws permissible exercise of taxing and spending power).
138. 26 U.S.C. § 3101.
139. 26 U.S.C. § 3111.
140. 26 U.S.C. § 3301.
141. 26 U.S.C. § 1401.
142. 822 F. 2d 1334 (3d Cir. 1987).

amendment violated the free exercise principle.[143] The court also rejected the claim that demanding compliance with statutory reporting requirements constituted excessive entanglement with religion in violation of the nonestablishment principle.[144] Although a sound argument can be made for treating clergy like employees of any other organization for Social Security purposes,[145] the court also rejected the claim that the provisions governing the self-employment income of ministers violated equal protection unless extended to all employees of religious organizations.[146]

Congress later restored the original exemption from FICA taxes, but only for service performed in the employ of "a church, a convention or association of churches, or an elementary school which is controlled, operated, or principally supported by a church, a convention or association of churches."[147] By filing Form 8274, a church can permanently exempt itself from the payment of Social Security tax by stating that it is opposed to this tax for religious reasons.[148] Employees of such a church are not themselves exempt from the payment of Social Security taxes, and are subject to the self-employment tax.[149]

FUTA also exempts from federal unemployment tax service performed in the employment of churches or of organizations controlled by churches.[150] In most instances—Oregon is an exception—this service is also exempted under parallel state unemployment tax schemes.[151] This issue has been of particular concern to teachers in church-operated schools. After repeated efforts by the Department of Labor to collect federal unemployment tax from religious schools, the Supreme Court clarified in *St. Martin Evangelical Lutheran Church v. South Dakota*[152] that employees working in such schools are "in the employ of . . . a church" for purposes of the statutory exemption. Although the schools at issue in *St. Martin* were unincorporated elementary and secondary schools, that fact should not be considered dispositive—even though the Court declined to rule on that precise point in a case involving religious elementary and secondary schools that were separately incorporated but controlled by a church.[153]

In *United States v. Lee*[154] the Court ruled that it could not allow any religious exemption beyond that expressly mandated by the Congress. As noted above, the tax code has special provisions dealing with self-employed persons. FICA specifically exempts from Social Security taxes self-employed members of religious groups, such as the Amish, with beliefs opposing the Social Security system.[155] The Court ruled that this statutory

---

143. 822 F.2d at 1338–39. The court resolved the free exercise claim primarily in the light of *United States v. Lee*, discussed in text accompanying notes 154–61 below.

144. *Id.* at 1340.

145. *See, e.g.*, God Alone is Lord of the Conscience, *supra* note 129, in 8 J. L. & Rel. 331, at 366–67 (urging that the value of clergy housing should be determined by the same provisions that apply to employees of other organizations).

146. 822 F. 2d. at 1341–42. The court offered three secular reasons for the distinction drawn in the tax code: avoidance of a church/state problem, assurance that the general rule would not be swallowed up by a host of exemptions, and avoidance of unnecessary taxation.

147. 26 U.S.C. §3121(w)(3).

148. IRS Gen. Counsel Memorandum 39,782 (Feb. 17, 1989).

149. 26 U.S.C. §3121(b)(8)(B).

150. IRC §3309(b).

151. IR-92-57 (May 4, 1992).

152. 451 U.S. 772 (1981).

153. Grace Brethren Church v. United States, 457 U.S. 393 (1982).

154. 455 U.S. 252 (1982).

155. 26 U.S.C. § 1402(g).

exemption is available only to self-employed individuals and does not apply to Amish employers or their employees.[156] Edwin Lee, an Amish farmer, was thus exempt from paying Social Security taxes on his own wages but was required to pay these taxes for other members of the Amish community who assisted him at his farm and carpentry shop. He sued for a refund of taxes, claiming that imposition of Social Security taxes violated his free exercise rights and those of his Amish employees. Relying in part on another case involving the Amish, *Wisconsin v. Yoder*,[157] decided a decade earlier, the district court held that statutes requiring an employer to pay Social Security and unemployment insurance taxes were unconstitutional as applied to Amish employers.[158]

Chief Justice Burger had written the opinion of the Supreme Court in *Yoder*, noting the Amish history of "three centuries as an identifiable religious sect and a long history as a successful and self-sufficient segment of American society…the interrelationship of belief with their mode of life, the vital role that belief and daily conduct play in the continued survival of Old Order Amish communities and their religious organization, and the hazards presented by the State's enforcement of a statute generally valid as to others."[159] None of this had changed in the decade since *Yoder*. The religious duty at issue in that case had been that of Amish parents to provide for their children's education in keeping them away from secular influences. The religious duty at issue in *Lee*, on the other hand, was the responsibility of the Amish community to care for its own aged members.

The Court rejected the Amish claim in *Lee*. Burger again wrote the opinion of the Court, agreeing at the outset that since payment of taxes or receipt of benefits violated Amish religious beliefs, to compel the Amish to participate in the Social Security system interfered with their free exercise rights. But the Court found that the government has a compelling interest in the uniform application of the tax code—an assertion belied by the very statutory exemption that the Court cited. Burger wrote that religious belief in conflict with payment of taxes afforded no basis for resisting "tax imposed on employers to support the social security system, which must be applied uniformly to all, except as Congress provides explicitly otherwise."[160]

In light of the facts in *Lee*, the Court's decision seems needlessly crabbed and ungenerous in construing the free exercise provision. The free exercise claim in *Lee*, moreover, was stronger than in *Bethel Baptist*. In *Lee*, the Amish had to pay a tax for a system from which they would never derive any benefit. If the fiscal stability of the Social Security system is in jeopardy, that problem cannot be blamed on the Amish because as a matter of conscience they have neither sought nor received any benefit from that program. In *Bethel Baptist*, on the other hand, it had been clear that both the clergy and other employees of the church would receive Social Security benefits when they retired. Since the Social Security tax for the clergy and other employees of the Baptist church was to be paid from the same source—the free-will offerings of the church members—it is difficult to see how the church's free exercise would be burdened by the method of payment called for in the statute.

Although the provisions in the tax code maintain some dubious distinctions (that is, between self-employed clergy and clergy employed by the church), they at least do not

---

156. 455 U.S. at 256.
157. 406 U.S. 205 (1972).
158. 497 F.Supp. 180 (W.D. Pa. 1980).
159. 406 U.S. at 235.
160. 455 U.S. at 261.

discriminate overtly for or against a particular religious community because of the community's beliefs or organizational structure. Hence, the courts have allowed these provisions to survive. This result—affirming the decisions of the political branches—is perhaps unsurprising since the principal point of the English Civil War was to restore parliamentary control over the power of the purse, which in our constitution is expressly granted to the Congress.[161]

The same result might even obtain in the case of a challenge to another tax-code provision much more difficult to justify than the exemption for church employees—namely, a provision that allows ministers of the gospel to exclude from taxable income a housing allowance or the value of the free use of a parsonage provided to them.[162] This exclusion applies to ordained persons who are educators, administrators, and other church functionaries, as well as to retired clergy.[163] Another section of the code permits employees of other organizations to exclude the value of housing furnished to them for the convenience of their employer at the place of employment,[164] but the clergy deduction applies whether or not the minister has any equity in the parsonage. If the value of clergy housing is to be determined by the same criteria that apply to employees of secular organizations, the pattern discussed above suggests that Congress rather than the courts will have to attend to this apparent imbalance of tax equities.[165]

Audit procedures

There are powerful reasons why the federal government has refrained from taxing the income that religious organizations derive from voluntary contributions by their members. Occasionally religious organizations have asserted, either on nonestablishment or free exercise grounds, a complete immunity from any summons or other compulsory process that would enable the government to probe the legitimacy of a tax issue. But this argument proves too much, and the courts have uniformly rejected the claim that any supervision or auditing of church records by the IRS constitutes impermissibly excessive entanglement between government and religion.[166] On the other hand, IRS

---

161. U.S. Const. Art. I, §8.

162. IRC §107 provides: "In the case of a minister of the gospel, gross income does not include—(1) the rental value of a home furnished to him as part of his compensation; or (2) the rental allowance paid to him as part of his compensation, to the extent used by him to rent or provide a home."

163. *See generally* Treas. Reg. §1.107-1(a). Rev. Rul. 63-156, 1963-2CB 79 permits the allowance to be paid to a retired minister in recognition of past services. A later ruling clarified that it may not be paid as a retirement to the minister's spouse. Rev. Rul. 72-249, 1972-1 CB 36.

164. IRC §162 includes among deduction for business expenses: "rentals or other payments required to be made as a condition to the continued use or possession, for purposes of the trade or business, of property to which the taxpayer has not taken or is not taking title or in which he has no equity."

165. *See, e.g.,* Kirk v. C. I. R., 425 F.2d 492 (1970) (where challenge to §107 was instituted in Tax Court by petition for redetermination of deficiency determined by Commissioner of Internal Revenue and plaintiff would not be entitled to the exclusion in any event, the courts could not consider constitutional challenge).

166. *See, e.g.,* United States v. Church of Reflection, Inc., 692 F. 2d 629 (9th Cir. 1982) (IRS summons for production of books of account and corporate minute books of a church to determine its eligibility for tax-exempt status is not excessive entanglement with religion); and United States v. Grayson County State Bank and First Pentecostal Church, 656 F. 2d 1070 (5th Cir. 1981) (IRS may enforce administrative summons issued to secure access to bank records pertaining to a church, as

agents have sometimes been ham-handed in carrying out such delicate tasks as exploring whether an organization qualifies for exemption, or is carrying on an unrelated business, or is otherwise subject to taxation. After conducting hearings into this matter, Congress struck an intelligent balance in the Church Audit Procedure Act,[167] which governs a "church tax inquiry" by the IRS.[168] This law does not excuse an organization from investigation merely because it describes itself as religious, but it does caution the government, for example, to limit the examination of a church to those records necessary to determine its qualification for exempt status or its liability for taxes. The government is also limited in the number of examinations it may conduct.[169] The Church Audit Procedure Act is neutral on its face, and does not allow the government to treat religious communities differently according to their different organizational forms.

Exemption as a Predicate for Governmental Regulation

The second large issue explored in this chapter is the regulation[170] of religious bodies as a direct result of their tax-exempt status. Specifically, I explore the two restraints im-

---

to which taxpayer, the minister of the church, had signature privileges or trustee assignment, and statute restricting examination by IRS of "the books of account of a church" was not applicable); *see also* South Ridge Baptist Church v. Industrial Comm'n of Ohio, 911 F. 2d 1203, 1210 (6th Cir. 1990) (state agency may require church to maintain records of payroll and wage expenditures and may inspect these church records without excessive entanglement in religion since audits and investigations do not seek information about the religious beliefs of the clergy or congregation and the bureau does not seek to interfere with the workings of the church or the school).

167. IRC §7611.

168. Treas. Reg. §301.7611-1; 1992 EO Technical CPE.

169. *See, e.g.*, Frances R. Hill and Barbara L. Kirschten, Federal and State Taxation of Exempt Organizations, ¶4.06[7], 4-51 to 4-53 (1994); and Bassett, *supra* note 121, at §10:38.

170. The term "regulation" refers to all forms of administrative rules. Tax rules descend through decreasing ranks or stages. The legislation itself—the Internal Revenue Code—obviously enjoys the broadest authority, and can be changed only by court order or legislative amendment or repeal. Next come the internal revenue regulations, which are issued under the authority of the secretary of the treasury, and the revenue procedures, which may be promulgated by the Commissioner of Internal Revenue. Then come revenue rulings. Finally there are private letter rulings, which are letters from the national office of the IRS to its district director stating an opinion on how a tax matter should be resolved. With the deletion of the identification of the taxpayer or exempt organization, a private-letter ruling may be "discovered" under the Freedom of Information Act but may not be cited as a precedent, IRC §6110(j)(3), and is subject to change as the National Office sees fit.

When all is said and done about this hierarchy of regulations, however, a rule looks and feels like a rule to a taxpayer or a regulated exempt organization no matter what the rule's status within the pecking order of the IRS. The technical way of saying this is that administrative regulations have the same force of law as acts of Congress. United States *ex rel.* Accardi v. Shaughnessy, 347 U.S. 363 (1957). The chief difference among the graduated forms of rules is an inverse proportion between flexibility and the level of governmental power involved in the issuance of the rule in the first instance. Thus when the IRS came to agree that its rules about an "integrated auxiliary of a church"— discussed below—were no longer defensible, it could not change that rule even though it wanted to do so, because the offending rule had been issued in the form of a revenue regulation by the secretary of the treasury. Since hundreds of formal regulations were already in the hopper awaiting the secretary's attention, the best the IRS could do under the circumstances was to offer to religious organizations a new revenue procedure, which it is within the authority of the Commissioner of Internal Revenue to promulgate, coupled with a promise to initiate the complicated process of changing

posed on political activity by churches: limits on attempts to influence legislation, and a complete ban on electioneering. I also explore the duty of church-related schools to conform to public policy against racial discrimination, and I differentiate that duty from the freedom of religious communities to decide for themselves whether women should be ordained as ministers.

The danger and the necessity of governmental definition of religion

Before turning to each of these specific issues, I address the potential danger of governmental attempts to define religion while acknowledging a general need for such attempts. The principal danger is that governments may violate religious freedom by stating criteria as though one size fits all religious communities. Such an insensitivity to diversity would offend against the very pluralism that the First Amendment is meant to protect. To guard against this evil, a line of cases that began with *Watson v. Jones*[171] has clarified a principle of nonentanglement by the government in ecclesiastical matters.[172] In *Watson*, Justice Miller stated: "The structure of our government has, for the preservation of civil liberty, rescued the temporal institutions from religious interference. On the other hand, it has secured religious liberty from the invasion of civil authority."[173] Now acknowledged as constitutional in stature,[174] this principle has been reinforced in subsequent decisions of the Court limiting the authority of secular courts to probe too deeply into the affairs of religious communities[175] or to take over decisions that are better left to the communities themselves.

The difficult task of administering tax laws fairly creates a need for substantively neutral criteria about religion. The government has additional reason for vigilance in this area because, to put the matter bluntly, some religious organizations have abused their exempt status—sometimes in a manner that seems plainly fraudulent. In other instances, individuals have tried to take advantage of the tax-exempt status afforded to religious groups in a manner that violates the prohibition against private inurement. For example, disclosures in the late 1980s that celebrated televangelists had diverted contri-

---

the regulation itself. *See* News Release, IRS Announces that Church-Affiliated Organizations Need Not File Forms *990*, IRS 86-63 (May 6, 1986). The regulation promised in 1986, Rev. Proc. 86-23, 1986-1, CB 564, was finally promulgated a decade later, Rev. Proc. 96-10, 1996-1 C.B. 577, 1996-2 IRB 17.

171. 80 U.S. (13 Wall.) 679 (1872).

172. *See* the discussion of excessive entanglement of the government in religion in Thomas C. Berg, "Religiously Affiliated Education," in this volume.

173. *Id.* at 730.

174. *Watson* was a federal case because of the diversity of citizenship of parties to the case, some of whom lived in Kentucky and some of whom lived in Ohio. It was decided before the Religion Clause was deemed to be incorporated against the states through the Due Process Clause of the Fourteenth Amendment; *see, e.g.,* Cantwell v. Connecticut, 310 U.S. 296 (1940), and Everson v. Bd. of Educ., 330 U.S. 1 (1947). In *Presbyterian Church in the United States v. Mary Elizabeth Blue Hull Memorial Presbyterian Church*, 393 U.S. 440 (1969), the Court clarified that the principle announced in *Watson* is now binding on the states as a matter of constitutional law, not as a matter of "federal common law."

175. The Court has expressly clarified that the free exercise of religion extends not only to individuals but also to religious communities. *See, e.g.,* Kedroff v. St. Nicholas Cathedral, 344 U.S. 94 (1952); Kreshik v. St. Nicholas Cathedral, 363 U.S. 190 (1960), discussed in Noonan, *supra* note 41, at 197–99. *And see* Serbian Eastern Orthodox Diocese for the United States and Canada v. Milivojevich, 426 U.S. 696 (1976).

butions to their own private benefit charged the atmosphere within which the delicate task of defining religion must be undertaken. The most celebrated case involving excessive compensation of religious leaders was that of Jim and Tammy Faye Bakker, founders of a ministry in Fort Mill, South Carolina known as PTL (an abbreviation for "Praise the Lord" or "People That Love"). Jim Bakker received nearly $3 million in total compensation during the fiscal year before the audit of Heritage Village Church and Missionary Fellowship that led to the revocation of PTL's exempt status. The government declined to prosecute Tammy Faye Bakker, but indicted and gained a criminal conviction of Jim Bakker for mail fraud, wire fraud, and criminal conspiracy.[176]

Although the Bakkers' luxuriant lifestyle[177] is by no means typical of religious ministers, their case undoubtedly led many to conclude that the government should "do something" to protect the public in all such circumstances. On the one hand, free exercise of religion does not require the IRS to avoid regulating flagrant abuse merely because the violator is a member of the clergy. On the other hand, in our constitutional order it is not normally the job of the government to save the people from false prophets, because doing so would involve it at least implicitly in the task of announcing religious "truth."[178] We, the people, must do that for ourselves. Even so, most would concede the need for some line to be drawn between legitimate religious autonomy and such violations of the tax code as illicit appropriation of charitable contributions to a religious body for personal use. Thus, although the salaries a church pays its ministers should normally be of no concern to the government, governmental inquiry may occasionally be warranted by the prohibition of personal benefit from contributions to an exempt organization.[179] This issue was at the heart of the government's successful, if highly controversial, prosecution of the Reverend Sun Myung Moon.[180]

---

176. United States v. Bakker, 925 F. 2d 728 (4th Cir. 1991).

177. "The Internal Revenue Service has questioned scores of luxury items charged by PTL founders to the ministry they founded ranging from a $592,000 oceanfront condominium in Palm Beach, Fla., to an $800 Gucci briefcase.... Such purchases are among $1.3 million worth of items charged by the Bakkers to PTL between 1981 and 1983 and which IRS auditors have questioned as possible personal expenses in the course of their continuing audit into the finances of the tax-exempt organization." "IRS Questions $1.3 Million in Purchases Bakkers Charged to PTL," Los Angeles Times, (May 17, 1987), I-17, cols. 1–2. The story omits several details from the IRS audit, such as the Bakkers' four other luxury homes in addition to the Palm Beach condominium, regular and unitemized cash advances in round amounts ($5,000), and the excess of charity for man's best friend reflected in a air-conditioned dog house! *See* Wendell Bird, Religious Organizations, in Frances R. Hill and Barbara Kirschten, Federal and State Taxation of Exempt Organizations ¶4.05[2], p. 4–37, note 229 (1994).

178. In *Gonzalez v. Roman Catholic Archbishop of Manila*, 280 U.S. 1 (1929), Justice Brandeis suggested that the civil courts might give "marginal" review to decisions of church authorities to ascertain whether the church had been involved in fraud. Similarly, the Court suggested that it was legitimate for the government to probe the sincerity, but not the truth, of religious claims, in *United States v. Ballard*, 322 U.S. 78, 86–87 (1944). For a thoughtful discussion of the *Ballard* case, see Noonan, *supra* note 41, at 141–76. In one of his "ten commandments" on religious freedom, Noonan writes: "You shall mark that government when it seeks to adjudicate the truth of a religion falls afoul of the First Amendment and when it attempts to adjudicate the sincerity of a believer enters on an enterprise beset by hazards." *Id.* at 357.

179. IRC § 501(c)(3) provides in part that an organization is exempt from taxation if it is organized and operated in such a manner that "no part...of [its] net earnings...inures to the benefit of any private shareholder or individual." For further clarification of the private inurement rule, *see* Hopkins, *supra* note 5, at 264–99.

180. United States v. Moon, 718 F.2d 1210 (2d Cir. 1983). Scores of religious bodies of wide diversity, few of whom agreed with the theological tenets of the Unification Church, filed briefs amicus curiae urging the Supreme Court to review this case.

Curiously, the government has not always been as successful or even as zealous in prosecuting tax fraud cases involving religion. After losing a tax case in 1974 against the Universal Life Church,[181] which issues a certificate of ordination to anyone who sends $25 to the founding "pastor," Kirby Hensley,[182] the government took a seemingly casual approach for several years to the problem of mail-order ministry before finally cracking down on the phenomenon in the 1980s.[183] The government's casual attitude may have stemmed from the difficulty that IRS officials have acknowledged to be inherent in any governmental attempt to define religion.[184] Even so, the IRS elaborated fourteen criteria for determining whether an organization is a church for tax purposes. These guidelines require such an organization to have:

---

181. United States v. Universal Life Church, 372 F. Supp. 770 (W.D. Cal. 1974). In this case the trial judge wrote: "Neither this Court, nor any branch of this Government, will consider the merits or fallacies of a religion. Nor will the Court compare the beliefs, dogmas, and practices of a newly organized religion with those of an older, more established religion. Nor will the Court praise or condemn a religion, however excellent or fanatical or preposterous it may seem. Were the Court to do so, it would impinge upon the guarantees of the First Amendment." *Id.* at 776. Although the court expressly relied upon *United States v. Ballard*, 322 U.S. 78, 86–87 (1944) for this view, it did not explore the very issue which the Supreme Court in *Ballard* had sent back to the trial court, viz., the sincerity of the beliefs as opposed to their truth or falsity. It is puzzling why the government did not choose to litigate this issue vigorously in *Universal Life Church*. In a more recent case before the Tax Court, a judge took a much less benign view of the use of religion in a situation where a taxpayer had "literally bathed himself" in personal benefits: "[O]ur tolerance for taxpayers who establish churches solely for tax avoidance purposes is reaching a breaking point. Not only do these taxpayers use the pretext of a church to avoid paying their fair share of taxes, even where their brazen schemes are uncovered many of them resort to the courts in a shameless attempt to vindicate themselves." Miedaner v. Commissioner, 81 T.C. 272, 282 (1983).

182. Hensley has stated publicly that the principal purpose of the Universal Life Church is to avoid the payment of taxes by his mail-order "ministers." He hopes thereby to eventually force the elimination of the tax-exempt status of all religious organizations. *See* Charles Whelan, Church in the Internal Revenue Code: The Definitional Problem, 45 Fordham L. Rev. 885 (1977).

183. In 1978 the State of New York revoked the sales tax exemption enjoyed by the Universal Life Church. In 1984 the IRS revoked the federal exempt status of the Universal Life Church. The tougher judicial attitude reflected in the *Miedaner* case, *supra* note 181, is paralleled in the IRS Training Manual, which now contains a section focused expressly on the problem of "Mail Order Ministries." IR Manual § 7(10)75. This approach to mail-order ministry is reflected in increased audits of such ministries by the IRS, which estimates, for example, that nearly one thousand "ministers" of the mail-order Church of Universal Harmony owe the government over $5 million in back taxes. Tougher enforcement policies have resulted in stiffer sentences of offenders. For example, a federal judge in Los Angeles sentenced Louis Pugliani, a mail-order minister in the Universal Life Church, to nine years in prison and imposed a fine of $95,000 after he was found guilty on nineteen counts of preparing false tax returns. (RNS, Aug. 4, 1982). A federal judge in Sacramento, California, sentenced William Richardson, another mail-order pastor in the Universal Life Church, to nine years in prison for preparing false tax returns. (RNS, Nov. 30, 1983). A federal judge in Fort Worth, Texas, sentenced the "pope" of the mail-order Basic Bible Church, Jerome Daly, to sixteen years in prison and imposed a fine of $100,000 on him after Daly and seven other pilots with Braniff Airlines were convicted in a scheme of defrauding the government and filing false tax returns. In sentencing the defendants, the judge noted: "None of you were [sic] prosecuted for your religious beliefs. You were prosecuted for the use of religion to avoid individual taxes and to defraud the government." (RNS, May 4, 1983). For a sociological study of mail-order religion, see Anson D. Shupe, Disembodied Access and Technological Constraints on Organizational Development: A Study of Mail-Order Religion, 15 J. for Scientific Study of Relig. 177 (1976); for a popular discussion of this problem, see Tim Ponder, Ring Around the Clerical Collar, Liberty (Sept.–Oct. 1982), 6–9.

184. *See, e.g.*, Difficult Problems in Tax Administration: 14 Religion and Race, Address of Jerome Kurtz, Commissioner of IRS, at Practicing Law Institute Seventh Biennial Conference on Tax Planning for Foundations, Tax-Exempt Status and Charitable Contributions, Jan. 9, 1977, reproduced in BNA, Daily Executive Report (Jan. 11, 1977) at J.8.

(1) a distinct legal existence; (2) a recognized creed and form of worship; (3) a definite and distinct ecclesiastical government; (4) a formal code of doctrine and discipline; (5) a distinct religious history; (6) a membership not associated with any other church or denomination; (7) an organization of ordained ministers; (8) ordained ministers selected after completing prescribed studies; (9) a literature of its own; (10) established places of worship; (11) regular congregations; (12) regular religious services; (13) Sunday schools for religious instruction of the young; and (14) schools for the preparation of its ministers.[185]

These criteria illustrate the dilemma of governmental efforts to define religion. Without any effort to distinguish among religious claimants, the government would seem unable to effectively enforce the tax code against those who would cloak themselves in religiosity solely in order to evade their fair share of the tax burden. On the other hand, these so-called "criteria" are really only loose guidelines. In any given application, one or more of the fourteen elements may be missing from an organization without yielding the conclusion that it is not "religious." Otherwise, the government would answer the third question posed by this chapter in a hollow, mechanical, and unconstitutional way, preferring some kinds of churches over others by virtue of how they are organized or structured. For example, loosely structured religious societies, such as the Society of Friends (also known as the Quakers) or the Christian Scientists, undoubtedly enjoy the protection of the First Amendment Religion Clause.[186] Although the IRS criteria have been criticized on this score by scholars,[187] they nonetheless have been adopted by the courts with only slight recognition of the difficulties they pose.[188] I conclude that the deepest structures of religious communities are rarely affected by the federal tax laws.

Although the government must be free to define religion for the purpose of applying tax policies neutrally and evenhandedly to all religious organizations, it has, in my view, overstepped its proper role in at least three specific instances discussed below. First I explore the regulation of political activities by religious organizations—including not only efforts to communicate moral convictions on matters of public concern to elected officials (lobbying activities), but also efforts to persuade voters of the correctness of certain moral convictions on these same matters (electioneering activities). Then I explore the requirement that religious organizations conform to "public policy," focusing particularly on the distinct issues of racial and gender discrimination. Finally, I look at how awkward attempts by the government to define religion, for the purpose of a tax-code provision relating to annual filing requirements, have undervalued the social ministry of religious organizations. This chapter explores both the necessity and the danger of governmental attempts to define religion by focusing on the legislative, administrative, and judicial involvement in unraveling the meaning of an "integrated auxiliary of a church."

---

185. As cited in *Lutheran Social Services of Minnesota v. United States*, 758 F. 2d 1283, 1286–1287 (8th Cir. 1985), discussed *infra*.

186. *See, e.g.*, Feldstein v. Christian Science Monitor, 555 F. Supp. 974 (D. Mass. 1983).

187. *See* Whelan, *supra* note 182, at 925–926; and Worthing, "Religion" Under the First Amendment, 7 Pepp. L. Rev. 313, 344–345 (1980).

188. *See, e.g.*, *Lutheran Social Services*, 758 F.2d at 1287 (ruling that in light of the IRS criteria, Lutheran Social Services of Minnesota is not a church), and American Guidance Found., Inc. v. United States, 490 F.Supp. 304, 306 (D.D.C. 1980) (acknowledging that some of the IRS criteria are "relatively minor," but ruling that the foundation failed to meet the "central" and "minimal" standards of a church: organized ministry serving an established congregation with regular religious services and religious education for its young and dissemination of a doctrinal code).

Political activity

In the discussion of the organizational test above, I mentioned that the definition of an exempt organization in the tax code prohibits an organization from devoting more than an insubstantial part of its activities to lobbying activity, and from engaging in any kind of electioneering or political campaign. I explore each of these restraints upon the political activity of religious and other exempt organizations.[189] One consequence of these provisions is that contributions made to an organization held to be violating them may not be deducted from a donor's taxable income.[190]

Limitation on substantial attempts to influence legislation

The tax code denies exempt status to any organization that spends a "substantial part of [its] activities in carrying on propaganda, or otherwise attempting, to influence legislation."[191] When added to the tax code in 1934, this provision did not target religious organizations at all, but sought to deny exempt status to "sham" organizations that were really a "front" for lobbying on behalf of wealthy donors' private interests.[192]

One difficulty with the regulation's use of the word "substantial" is vagueness. How much is too much? Neither the statute nor the Treasury regulations offer a clear answer to this obvious question. One case allowed exempt status to an organization that spent approximately five percent of its budget to attempt to influence legislation.[193] Another case revoked the exempt status of an organization for spending approximately twenty percent of its budget on lobbying efforts.[194] The case law discloses only that five percent is not substantial while twenty percent is.

Exempt status may be revoked, moreover, without any attention to the percentage of an organization's budget spent on lobbying activities. In the leading case applying this provision to religious organization, the court sustained the IRS revocation of exempt status from the Christian Echoes National Ministry on the ground that a radio evangelist named Billy James Hargis spoke frequently about political events in Washington and freely voiced his views on pending legislation.[195] According to the court, the "activities of Christian Echoes in influencing or attempting to influence legislation were not incidental, but were substantial and continuous."[196]

---

189. For a discussion of the history of these two provisions in the tax code, and an argument that the provisions are unconstitutional, see Edward McGlynn Gaffney, Jr., On Not Rendering to Caesar: The Unconstitutionality of Tax Regulation of Activities of Religious Organizations Relating to Politics, 40 DePaul L. Rev. 1 (1990); *see also* Gerald Stephen Endler, The Possible First Amendment Argument Against the Denial or Revocation of Section 501(c)(3) Tax-Exempt Status, 7 Geo. Mason L. Rev. 305 (1984).

190. IRC § 170(c)(2)(D).

191. IRC §501(c)(3). For a discussion of this limitation, see Hopkins, *supra* note 5, at 300–26.

192. For example, Senator Pat Harrison, floor manager for the bill, remarked: "I may say to the Senate that the attention of the Senate Committee was called to the fact that there are certain organizations which are receiving contributions in order to influence legislation and carry on propaganda. The committee thought there ought to be an amendment that would stop that, so that is why we have put this amendment in the bill." 78 Cong. Rec. 5959 (1934).

193. Seasongood v. Commissioner, 227 F.2d 907 (6th Cir. 1955).

194. Haswell v. United States, 500 F. 2d 1133 (Ct. Cl. 1974).

195. Christian Echoes Nat'l Ministry, Inc. v. United States, 470 F. 2d 849 (10th Cir. 1972).

196. *Id.* at 856.

The net result is that this provision of section 501(c)(3) may have a serious chilling effect on the exercise of protected political speech. It may also have differing effects on religious organizations not because of their formal organizational structure, but because of their different convictions about how to translate religious concerns into comments about the practical order of worldly politics.[197] As one prominent commentator on church/state relations wrote:

> The undefined word 'substantial' thus stands as an enigmatic threat to any public charity contemplating action on any legislative issue, and often has the 'chilling effect' of persuading it that the only really safe course is to refrain from such activity entirely. It serves to muzzle, immobilize, or emasculate public charities with respect to affecting public policy, even though their charitable purposes may be fully effectuated only by obtaining changes in public policy and, more importantly, the public dialogue may be impoverished without their free participation.[198]

Ban on political activity or electioneering

In 1954 Senator Lyndon B. Johnson added another provision to the tax code, denying exempt status to any organization that "participate[s] in, or intervene[s] in (including the publishing or distribution of statements), any political campaign on behalf of any candidate for public office."[199] Once again, the amendment was originally targeted not at religious organizations but at a charitable foundation in Texas that had provided funds to someone who had had the temerity to challenge Johnson in the Democratic primary.[200] This provision came into the law without hearings either in the House or the Senate. It was accepted by an unrecorded voice vote in the Senate, and then acceded to in the Conference Committee without discussion.[201] That committee understandably had more pressing concerns given the major revision of the Internal Revenue Code that occurred in 1954.

Johnson's provision has been more problematic for religious organizations than the restrictions on lobbying activities. As with the restriction on lobbying, the ban on electioneering came into the law without any focus on religious organizations, indeed without much congressional deliberation at all. Unlike the limitation on "substantial" lob-

---

197. For example, in 1988 the General Assembly of the Presbyterian Church USA stated: "Since the time of Calvin, Reformed Protestants have felt called to share their vision of God's intended order for the human community, and Presbyterians have recognized and acted on the responsibility to seek social justice and peace and to promote the biblical values of freedom and liberty as well as corporate responsibility within the political order.... In 'attempting to influence legislation' churches speak to the moral aspects of political issues. Such witness flows directly from fundamental faith and is integral to its free exercise. It is essential to the church's identity and mission, and to the moral authority of its pronouncements, that it speak as 'church' through its religious structures and leaders." God Alone is Lord of the Conscience, *supra* note 129, in 8 J.L. & Rel. 331, at 335. *See also* Legislative Activity By Certain Types of Exempt Organizations, Hearings Before the House Ways and Means Committee, 92d Cong., 2d Sess. 99 (1972) (statement by National Jewish Community Relations Advisory Council, whose mandate "requires those who adhere to the principles of Judaism to let their views be heard in support of justice for all"). *And see* Thomas C. Berg, Church-State Relations and the Social Ethics of Reinhold Niebuhr, 73 N.C. L. Rev. 1567 (1995).

198. Kelley, *supra* note 5, at 72.

199. IRC §501(c)(3). For a discussion of this limitation, see Bruce Hopkins, *supra* note 5, at 327–51.

200. 100 Cong. Rec. 9604 (1954).

201. *See* H. Report No. 2543, 83d Cong., 2d Sess. (1954).

bying activities, which creates problems because the IRS has never adequately defined the meaning of "substantial," the ban on electioneering is absolute. Thus in the case discussed above, the *Christian Echoes* court found no difficulty finding that "[i]n addition to influencing legislation, Christian Echoes intervened in political campaigns" because although Pastor Hargis generally did not formally endorse specific candidates for office, his ministry used "its publications and broadcasts to attack candidates and incumbents who were considered too liberal."[202]

Sometimes, however, the definition of electioneering lacks clarity. To resolve ambiguity of this sort, the IRS has issued regulations with remarkable regularity—corresponding rather precisely to the congressional election seasons—proscribing with greater particularity the kind of information that an exempt organization may publish and distribute. For example, in 1978 the IRS issued a revenue ruling that bans voter-education efforts by exempt organizations that compile and publish voting records of all members of Congress, if the votes reported are not on a wide range of topics but are limited to selected issues of interest to the organization, or if there is even an implied indication of the organization's approval or disapproval of the voting records, or if there is so much as an editorial comment offered by the organization.[203] Two years later the IRS issued another ruling that allows the publication of congressional voting records on selected issues with an indication of whether those votes correspond to the organization's views.[204] What might seem like progress is modified by the criteria the IRS announced it would consider to conclude whether an exempt organization had engaged in prohibited electioneering activity:

> (1) the voting records of all incumbents will be presented, (2) candidates for reelection will not be identified, (3) no comment will be made on an individual's overall qualifications for public office, (4) no statements expressly or impliedly endorsing or rejecting any incumbent as a candidate for public office will be offered, (5) no comparison of incumbents with other candidates will be made, (6) the organization will point out the inherent limitations of judging the qualifications of an incumbent on the basis of certain selected votes, by stating the need to consider such unrecorded matters as performance on subcommittees and constituent service, (7) the organization will not widely distribute its compilation of incumbents' voting records, (8) the publication will be distributed to the organization's normal readership (who number only a few thousand nationwide), and (9) no attempt will be made to target the publication toward particular areas in which elections are occurring nor to time the publication to coincide with an election campaign.[205]

These criteria not only favor incumbency but also needlessly shrink the protection of the First Amendment to the point of being feeble and ineffective. In neither case are they the sort of responsibilities normally associated with the tax-collecting function of the IRS. As noted above, these regulations are neutral on their face, but they obviously have a very

---

202. 470 F. 2d at 856. The court noted that Christian Echoes "attacked President Kennedy in 1961 and urged its followers to elect conservatives like Senator Strom Thurmond and Congressmen Bruce Alger and Page Belcher. It urged followers to defeat Senator Fulbright and attacked President Johnson and Senator Hubert Humphrey. The annual convention endorsed Senator Barry Goldwater. These attempts to elect or defeat certain political leaders reflected Christian Echoes' objective to change the composition of the federal government." *Id.*

203. Rev. Rul. 78-248; 1978-1 C.B. 154.

204. Rev. Rul. 80-282.

205. *Id.*

different impact on a church seriously concerned with public witness to the surrounding political culture than they would have on a more quietist religious organization.[206]

Two religious organizations that differ considerably from one another illustrate the difficulties a church can encounter under the absolute ban on electioneering. First, a group of plaintiffs known as the Abortion Rights Mobilization sued the secretary of the treasury, seeking an order requiring the IRS to revoke the tax-exempt status of the Catholic church because of various public pronouncements church officials had made relating to abortion. The district court ruled that the plaintiffs had standing in their capacities as voters and members of the clergy, on the ground that by failing to revoke the church's exempt status, the IRS had allegedly "denigrated" the plaintiffs' religious beliefs and "frustrated" their ministry by giving "tacit government endorsement of the Roman Catholic Church view of abortion."[207] The district court subsequently held the church in civil contempt and fined it $100,000 a day for its refusal to hand over massive amounts of sensitive internal documents to outsiders.[208] The Supreme Court ruled unanimously that the church was at least entitled to challenge the jurisdiction of the district court.[209] On remand, the court of appeals reversed the district court on the standing issue and dismissed the case for lack of jurisdiction. The Supreme Court denied review.[210] The litigation lasted over a decade and was very costly for the church, but it at least illustrated that virtually all religious organizations—including groups that strongly disagree with the Catholic church on abortion—were united in repudiating the use of the courts by private litigants to attack a church's exempt status in this way.[211]

---

206. *See, e.g.*, J. Richard Niebuhr, Christ and Culture (1975). For example, one prominent commentator has written that the purpose of the law is "to prevent harm, resolve conflicts, and create means of cooperation. Its premise, from which it derives its perceived legitimacy and therefore its authority, is that it strives to anticipate and give expression to what a people believes to be its collective destiny or ultimate meaning within a moral universe." Richard John Neuhaus, The Naked Public Square 253 (1983). Neuhaus argues that a democracy that cherishes its commitment to pluralism would welcome religion as one of the guiding influences of the political discourse within which the law takes shape: "[T]he public square cannot and does not remain naked. When particularist religious values and the institutions that bear them are excluded, the inescapable need to make public moral judgments will result in an elite construction of a normative morality from sources and principles not democratically recognized by the society. The truly naked public square is at best a transitional phenomenon. It is a vacuum begging to be filled. When the democratically affirmed institutions that generate and transmit values are excluded, the vacuum will be filled by the agent left in control of the public square, the state. In this manner, a perverse notion of the disestablishment of religion leads to the establishment of the state as church." *Id.* at 86.

207. Abortion Rights Mobilization, Inc. v. Regan, 544 F. Supp. 471 (S.D.N.Y. 1982) (standing as voters to challenge exempt status of church); Abortion Rights Mobilization, Inc. v. Regan, 552 F. Supp. 364 (S.D.N.Y. 1982) (denying petition of federal defendants for interlocutory appeal on standing of plaintiffs); Abortion Rights Mobilization, Inc. v. Regan, 603 F. Supp. 970 (S.D.N.Y. 1985) (denying church's motion for dismissal of suit for lack of standing by plaintiffs, but dismissing church as party defendant); *In re* Baker 788 F. 2d 3 (2d Cir. 1986) (denying petition of secretary of treasury for interlocutory appeal).

208. Abortion Rights Mobilization, Inc. v. Baker, 110 F.R.D. 337 (S.D.N.Y. 1986) (holding church in contempt for failure to comply with discovery order); *In re* United States Catholic Conference, 824 F. 2d 156 (2d Cir. 1987) (denying church's appeal on ground that it was a witness, not a party, in the suit).

209. United States Catholic Conf. v. Abortion Rights Mobilization, Inc., 487 U.S. 72 (1988).

210. *In re* United States Catholic Conf., 885 F. 2d 1020 (2d Cir. 1989).

211. The following religious organizations filed a joint brief amicus curiae supporting the United States Catholic Conference: National Council of Churches of Christ in the U.S.A., James E. Andrews and Stated Clerk of the General Assembly of the Presbyterian Church (U.S.A.), the Baptist Joint Committee on Public Affairs, the Catholic League for Religious and Civil Rights, the Lutheran

Although this case lodges authority for enforcement of section 501(c)(3) exclusively within the IRS, that does not guarantee that enforcement will be evenhanded. For example, the IRS concluded that Jimmy Swaggart Ministries (JSM) had jeopardized its exempt status when its leading pastor, Jimmy Swaggart, endorsed Pat Robertson's candidacy for the 1988 Republican presidential nomination.[212] The conduct by JSM[213] left no doubt that the organization had violated the plain meaning of the statute's prohibition. But the IRS settled the case, announcing that "[a]s a condition of its continued exempt status, JSM has agreed to refrain in future years from certain political activities."[214] Perhaps the settling of the case in this manner reflects an awareness that the IRS had neither applied the same standard when the Reverend Martin Luther King, Jr., had famously endorsed John F. Kennedy's presidential candidacy in 1960, nor sanctioned any of the Baptist churches that prominently supported the Reverend Jesse Jackson's presidential candidacy in 1984. Once again, the lack of uniformity in the government's enforcement of the electioneering ban is not related to the formal organizational structure of religious organizations, but it does call into question the neutrality of the IRS.

Conformity to public policy

Racial discrimination

In a series of cases after the rejection of racial segregation in *Brown v. Board of Education*,[215] the courts struggled with the question of whether the government could fund private academies that maintained a policy of racial exclusion. In the first case after *Brown* involving this issue, the Supreme Court viewed the simultaneous closing of the public elementary schools and generous funding of racially discriminatory private academies as a manifest attempt to avoid the logic of the *Brown* decision.[216] On the view that exemption from taxation is the functional equivalent of funding, the NAACP Education Fund then sought to revoke the exempt status of elementary schools in Mississippi that

Church-Missouri Synod, the National Association of Evangelicals, the Synagogue Council of America, and the Worldwide Church of God.

212. In a news release dated December 17, 1991, the IRS stated that its examination of the ministry "disclosed that on the afternoon of September 8, 1988, Jimmy Swaggart met with Pat Robertson to discuss Robertson's candidacy for the Republican nomination for president of the United States. On the evening of September 10, 1988, Jimmy Swaggart spoke at a regularly scheduled Wednesday night service of JSM's Family Worship Center, members and adherents of JSM were present. Members of the press were also in attendance. Jimmy Swaggart stated at the service that Pat Robertson would most probably announce his candidacy for President and that he, Jimmy Swaggart, would support him."

213. In the October 6, 1988, issue of the Evangelist, the official magazine of JSM, an endorsement of Pat Robertson's candidacy for president appeared in Jimmy Swaggart's column "From Me to You." The column stated that "we are supporting Pat Robertson for the office of President of the United States" and that "we are going to support him prayerfully and put forth every effort we can muster in his behalf." IRS News Release, Dec. 17, 1991.

214. *Id.* JSM explicitly agreed that Swaggart's endorsement of Robertson "constituted prohibited political campaign intervention within the meaning of § 501(c)(3) of the Code...." JSM also agreed to "changes in its organization's structure including the creation of an 'Audit and Compliance Committee' composed of members of an expanded board of trustees, to ensure that no further political campaign intervention activities will occur. Under no circumstances will any of JSM's resources, including financial resources, personnel or facilities, be utilized to participate or intervene in a political campaign." *Id.*

215. 347 U.S. 483 (1954).

216. Green v. County Sch. Bd. of New Kent County, 391 U.S. 430 (1968).

practiced racial discrimination.[217] Because this litigation did not involve religious schools, it did not present an opportunity for adjudication of a free exercise claim. That opportunity came in *Bob Jones University v. United States.*[218]

In an earlier phase of its litigation with the government, the university abandoned the racially discriminatory admissions policy that had made it literally unique among institutions of higher education in the United States.[219] The university, however, continued to prohibit interracial dating or marriage, and the Court construed this policy as affecting the university's admissions policy.[220] The Court held that the enforcement of this policy on the basis of religious doctrine disqualified the university as a tax-exempt organization under section 501(c)(3) of the tax code, and that contributions to the school were not deductible as charitable contributions under section 170 of the code.[221]

If Chief Justice Burger had justified this position simply on the ground that government support of any sort for Jim Crow is unconstitutional, his opinion for the Court would have had stronger support. But Burger made it a central feature of his opinion that "entitlement to tax exemption depends on meeting certain common-law standards of charity—namely, that an institution seeking tax-exempt status must serve a public purpose and not be contrary to established public policy."[222] Burger expanded on this theme as follows:

> Charitable exemptions are justified on the basis that the exempt entity confers a public benefit—a benefit which the society or the community may not itself choose or be able to provide, or which supplements and advances the work of public institutions already supported by tax revenues. History buttresses logic to make clear that, to warrant exemption under § 501(c)(3), an institution must fall within a category specified in that section and must demonstrably serve and be in harmony with the public interest. The institution's purpose must not be so at odds with the common community conscience as to undermine any public benefit that might otherwise be conferred.[223]

This suggestion that a religious organization might lose its exempt status by failing to conform with some "public policy" announced by the IRS or by failing to "serve and be in harmony with the public interest" caused great concern both on and off the Court.

---

217. In Green v. Kennedy, 309 F.Supp. 1127 (D.D.C.), *appeal dismissed sub nom.* Cannon v. Green, 398 U.S. 956 (1970), a three-judge court issued a preliminary injunction prohibiting the IRS from according tax-exempt status to private schools in Mississippi that discriminated as to admissions on the basis of race. Six months later the IRS concluded that it could "no longer legally justify allowing tax-exempt status [under § 501(c)(3)] to private schools which practice racial discrimination" nor allow contributions to such schools to be deductible under §170. IRS News Release (7/10/70). On June 30, 1971, the *Green* court issued its opinion on the merits, approving the IRS' amended construction of the tax code. Green v. Connally, 330 F.Supp. 1150 (D.D.C.), *aff'd sub nom.* Coit v. Green, 404 U.S. 997 (1971) (per curiam). The silence of Congress after this litigation was viewed by the Court in *Bob Jones* as "an unusually strong case of legislative acquiescence in and ratification by implication of the [IRS'] 1970 and 1971 rulings" 461 U.S. at 599; *see also* at 608 (Powell, J., concurring in part and concurring in the judgment).

218. 461 U.S. 574 (1983).

219. *See* Douglas Laycock, Tax Exemptions for Racially Discriminatory Religious Schools, 60 Tex. L. Rev. 259 (1982); and Karla W. Simon, The Tax-Exempt Status of Racially Discriminatory Schools, 36 Tax L. Rev. (1981).

220. 461 U.S. at 577.

221. *Id.* at 577–78.

222. *Id.* at 586.

223. *Id.* at 591–92.

Justice Powell tried to urge the chief justice to delete this material from the opinion he had drafted.[224] When Burger declined to do so, Powell prepared a concurring opinion that challenged Burger's insistence that the tax-exempt status of an organization could be revoked if an organization does not provide a clear "public benefit" as defined by the Court.[225] Noting that more than 106,000 organizations filed section 501(c)(3) returns in 1981, Powell found it "impossible to believe that all or even most of those organizations could prove that they 'demonstrably serve and [are] in harmony with the public interest' or that they are 'beneficial and stabilizing influences in community life.'"[226] He added:

> Even more troubling to me is the element of conformity that appears to inform the Court's analysis. The Court asserts that an exempt organization must "demonstrably serve and be in harmony with the public interest," must have a purpose that comports with "the common community conscience," and must not act in a manner "affirmatively at odds with [the] declared position of the whole government." Taken together, these passages suggest that the primary function of a tax-exempt organization is to act on behalf of the Government in carrying out governmentally approved policies. In my opinion, such a view of § 501(c)(3) ignores the important role played by tax exemptions in encouraging diverse, indeed often sharply conflicting, activities and viewpoints.[227]

Similarly, leading commentators criticized the Burger opinion for subordinating the free exercise claim to a mere "public policy" determination by the IRS.[228] *Bob Jones* thus set in motion a vague standard about exempt status that has considerable potential for mischief if given an expanded application beyond the issue of racial discrimination.

Gender discrimination

Within a decade of the decision in *Bob Jones* case a leading feminist, Mary Becker, urged reliance on the case for an "exceedingly moderate" change in the tax laws: the revocation of exempt status from religious "institutions subordinating women and denying women full religious freedom."[229] Becker acknowledged that "religion has often empowered women and has responded to and reflected the beliefs and values of women, who are, in general, more religious than men."[230] But, she claimed, it is also true that "religion perpetuates and reinforces women's subordination, and religious freedom impedes reform...[and] women's effective political participation."[231] Viewing exemptions

---

224. Memorandum of Justice Powell to Chief Justice Burger, Papers of Justice Marshall, Library of Congress.

225. 461 U.S. at 608 (Powell, J., concurring in part and concurring in the judgment).

226. *Id.* at 609.

227. *Id.* at 609.

228. *See, e.g.,* Robert M. Cover, Foreword: The Supreme Court: Nomos and Narrative, 97 Harv. L. Rev. 4, 67 (1983); Mayer G. Freed & Daniel D. Polsby, Race, Religion, and Public Policy: Bob Jones University v. United States, 1983 Sup. Ct. Rev. 1; and Thomas C. Berg, What Hath Congress Wrought? An Interpretive Guide to the Religious Freedom Restoration Act, 39 Vill. L. Rev. 1, 10, 36, 43 (1994).

229. Mary E. Becker, The Politics of Women's Wrongs and the Bill of "Rights": A Bicentennial Perspective, 59 U. Chi. L. Rev. 453, 486 (1992); *see also* Jane Vandeventer Goldman, Taxing Sex Discrimination: Revoking Tax Benefits of Organizations Which Discriminate on the Basis of Sex, Ariz. St. L. J. 1976: 641; this student note does not address the free exercise issue that would arise if the rationale of *Bob Jones* were to be applied to a church that does not ordain women.

230. *Id.* at 459.

231. *Id.*

from income and property taxes and awards of government contracts as "substantial government subsidies of religion...[that] perpetuat[e] the subordination of women,"[232] Becker urged that "courts could redefine, or legislatures amend, the Religion Clauses of the First Amendment to prohibit government subsidies to religions that close the ministry to women."[233]

The major flaw in Becker's argument is that it overlooks the tradition of church autonomy over its own ministry that, as noted above, traces its pedigree back to the medieval period. Whether or not church autonomy should continue to serve as a rationale for exemption of churches from taxation, there is little doubt that free exercise of religion includes the ability of a religious community to determine for itself the issue of who may exercise ministry within it.[234] However, this counterargument does not diminish the government's duty to refrain from sex discrimination without an exceedingly strong justification,[235] and that is precisely because of the great distinction the First Amendment draws between religious communities and the government—a distinction that cannot be overcome by characterizing grants of tax exemption as state action.[236]

Becker also opposed tax subsidies given to religions that "mobilize opposition to feminist issues" and that are denied to "women's political organizations."[237] Implicitly at least, Becker urged that an aggrieved plaintiff has standing to argue that in failing to revoke the church's exempt status, the IRS would be denigrating the plaintiff's religious beliefs by giving tacit government endorsement of the subordination of women. As noted above, this is precisely the view of standing that the courts rejected in the *Abortion Rights Mobilization* case,[238] decided five years before Becker published her article.

Governmental definition of social ministry of a religious organization

A 1988 policy statement adopted by the Presbyterian Church (U.S.A.) succinctly expressed the church's perspective on the problem of governmental definition of religion:

> When the state grants exemption from taxes to religious organizations, the basic definition of what constitutes religious activity must be made by those organizations. With increasing frequency, taxing jurisdictions seek to collect taxes from religious organizations on particular property or activity in the face

---

232. *Id.*

233. *Id.* at 457. Becker explicitly noted that Mormons, Roman Catholics, and Orthodox Jews do not allow the ordination of women; *id.* at 460.

234. *See, e.g.*, Schiltz and Laycock, supra note 44.

235. *See, e.g.*, Craig v. Boren, 429 U.S. 190 (1976) ("classifications by gender must serve important governmental objectives and must be substantially related to the achievement of those objectives").

236. *Id.* at 485.

237. *Id.* at 479.

238. Abortion Rights Mobilization, Inc. v. Regan, 544 F. Supp. 471 (S.D.N.Y. 1982) (standing as voters to challenge exempt status of church); Abortion Rights Mobilization, Inc. v. Regan, 552 F. Supp. 364 (S.D.N.Y. 1982) (denying petition of federal defendants for interlocutory appeal on standing of plaintiffs); Abortion Rights Mobilization, Inc. v. Regan, 603 F. Supp. 970 (S.D.N.Y. 1985) (denying church's motion for dismissal of suit for lack of standing by plaintiffs, but dismissing church as party defendant); *In re* Baker 788 F.2d 3 (2d Cir. 1986) (denying petition of Sec. of Treasury for interlocutory appeal).

of statutory provisions exempting "churches, conventions, or councils of churches and their integrated auxiliaries" from tax liability. In such instances, the justification is most often that the property or activity is not sufficiently "religious" to qualify, although wholly owned, operated, controlled, and defined by the religious organization as a part of its life and work. We urge Presbyterians, when dealing with such situations, to recognize that the issue is not "whether the church should pay taxes." The issue is: "Who defines the church's nature and ministry?"… Presbyterians must resist any attempt by taxing authorities to define some of the properties and activities wholly controlled and defined by the church as nonreligious.…

We concede that some properties and operations of religious organizations may be subjected to taxation by legislative act; but we will resist all efforts to do so by administrative determination, in the face of statutes that exempt churches from taxation, that some properties or activities wholly controlled and operated by the church as part of its mission are "nonreligious."[239]

If the main problem for religious organizations is the improper classification of their ministries as "nonreligious," the solution must lie in coming to terms with that problem. For more than a decade this was considerably difficult, because of an unfortunate and prolonged conflict between the IRS and various religious communities over the meaning of an obscure provision in the tax code exempting an "integrated auxiliary of a church" from reporting requirements.[240] Part of the difficulty is that the term "integrated auxiliary" was not grounded in the historical experiences of American churches. The term does not resonate richly in the ecclesiological vocabulary of any of the major American religious bodies, with the single exception of the Mormons. In short, most Americans' understanding of "integrated auxiliaries" would have increased if the IRS had caught one—perhaps in Utah—and put it in a cage so they could observe it firsthand and get some inkling of what the government had in mind when it invented the phrase in 1969.

The failure of theology and church history to shed light on the term might be less discouraging if the term were one rich with legal meaning in the practical experience either of politicians or of IRS officials. But it seems clear from the legislation's history that with the possible exception of Senator Wallace Bennett, a Mormon from Utah who originally suggested the term "auxiliary" in 1969, members of Congress had no clear meaning of the term in mind. Although much can be said for ignoring legislative history and focusing only on the meaning of statutes,[241] legislative history should be useful at least to establish the basic contours of statutory language.

---

239. God Alone is Lord of the Conscience, *supra* note 129, 8 J.L. & Rel. 331, at 365–66, 367–68.

240. For an extensive discussion of the IRS regulations on this topic, see Edward McGlynn Gaffney, Governmental Definition of Religion: The Rise and Fall of the IRS Regulations on an "Integrated Auxiliary of a Church," 25 Val. U. L. Rev. 203 (1991); and George J. Bain, The Unfortunate Church-State Dispute over the I.R.C. Section 6033 "Exclusively Religious" Activity Test, 23 New Eng. L. Rev. 1 (1988).

241. Lawyers and judges frequently invoke the history surrounding the passage of legislation to illustrate what the enactment means. Justice Scalia, however, has repeatedly criticized this approach on the view that "[i]t is the law that governs, not the intent of the lawgiver." Antonin Scalia, *supra* note 105 above; see also Scalia, Judicial Deference to Administrative Interpretations of Law, 1989 Duke L.J. 511. According to Scalia, the judicial function is not to discern legislative intent, but to give effect to the text that was actually enacted. For example, he wrote for the Court: "The best evidence of [the] purpose [of a statute] is the statutory text adopted by both Houses of Congress and submitted to the President. Where that contains a phrase that is unambiguous—that has a clearly accepted meaning in both legislative and judicial practice—we do not permit it to be expanded or

With no guidance from Congress, the IRS issued regulations that only made matters worse by first insisting that the activity of an integrated auxiliary had to be "exclusively religious," and then relying on a clumsy, unworkable definition of the church and its mission.[242] According to the new IRS guidelines, an organization would be deemed an "integrated auxiliary" of a church only if it did what the government thought people normally do in a church: worship God by reading the Bible, singing hymns, listening to sermons, saying prayers, and so forth. Once the church's "service" was over, its organizations that engaged in service to the world were not "integrated auxiliaries" as defined by the IRS.

Lutherans and Baptists decided to challenge these regulations, not because they believed the burden imposed on their schools and social ministries was all that severe,[243] but because they viewed the regulations as a classic instance of inappropriate governmental intervention in religious affairs. As in the *Abortion Rights Mobilization* case, religious communities were required to spend considerable time, energy, and financial resources resisting a misguided regulation that was premised on the exempt status of these communities. The churches prevailed in the litigation; two federal appellate courts and a district court found the Treasury regulations narrower than the statute allowed.[244]

Once again, the regulations were not aimed at any particular religious organization, but did mischief nonetheless. The IRS officials in five successive administrations (those of Presidents Nixon, Ford, Carter, Reagan, and Bush) demonstrated not only that they did not know with much clarity what an integrated auxiliary is, but that they little appreciated the delicacy of their own task or the fragility of the religious liberties at issue. The executive branch repeatedly claimed it had been following congressional guidance

---

contracted by the statements of individual legislators or committees during the course of the enactment process. See United States v. Ron Pair Enterprises, Inc., 489 U.S. 235, 241 (1989) ("[W]here, as here, the statute's language is plain, 'the sole function of the court is to enforce it according to its terms'")." West Virginia University Hospitals, Inc. v. Casey, 499 U.S. 83, 98–99 (1991). Where the Court has strayed from this direction, Scalia has written separately. For example, he wrote: "The Court begins its analysis with the observation: 'The statutory command...is unambiguous, unequivocal, and unlimited.' In my view, discussion of that point is where the remainder of the analysis should have ended. Instead, however, the Court feels compelled to demonstrate that its holding is consonant with legislative history, including some dating back to 1917—a full quarter century before the provision at issue was enacted. That is not merely a waste of research time and ink; it is a false and disruptive lesson in the law.... The greatest defect of legislative history is its illegitimacy. We are governed by laws, not by the intentions of legislators." Conroy v. Ansikoff, 507 U.S. 511, 518–19 (1993) (Scalia, J., concurring in the judgment). See also Puerto Rico Dept. of Consumer Affairs v. Isla Petroleum Corp., 485 U.S. 495, 500–01 (1988); United Savings Association of Texas v. Timbers of Inwood Forest Associates, Ltd., 484 U.S. 365, 371, 377–81 (1988); INS v. Luz Marina Cardoza-Fonseca, 480 U.S. 421, 452–53 (1987) (Scalia, J., concurring in the judgment); Green v. Bock Laundry Co., 490 U.S. 504, 527–30 (1989) (Scalia, J., concurring in the judgment). Whatever one makes of the approach commended by Scalia, which the Court has sometimes adopted and sometimes ignored, it is uncontroversial that the president only signs acts of Congress. Thus, committee reports (which are frequently drafted by staff counsel or by lobbyists for various interest groups, and are rarely read by members of Congress) and floor debates (which are sparsely attended by members of Congress, who typically attend to other business such as hearings or meetings with lobbyists and constituents and appear on the floor only when summoned for a critical vote) are obviously not enacted into law in any formal sense.

242. Treas. Reg. §1-6033-2(g).

243. Compliance is achieved by annual filing of an informational return (Form 990).

244. *See* Lutheran Social Services v. United States, 758 F. 2d 1283 (8th Cir. 1985); Tennessee Baptist Children's Homes, Inc., v. United States, 790 F. 2d 534 (6th Cir. 1986); and Lutheran Children & Family Services of Eastern Pennsylvania v. United States, 58 AFTR 2d 86-5662, 86-2 USTC 9593 (E.D. Pa. 1986).

on this matter, and it held that position until the judiciary had ruled otherwise in three cases.[245]

Conclusion: Consequences of the Nondiscrimination Principle for the Structures of Religious Organizations

In light of the principles set forth above, I can now conclude that neither the particular organizational form nor the scope or object of a particular religious ministry should affect whether it is regarded as a tax-exempt organization. If anything is clear from the decade-long dispute over the term "integrated auxiliary of a church," it is that the particular form or object of a ministry should be beyond the competence of the government to control. Similarly, the structural connection between a ministry and an organized church should not affect its status as an exempt organization.

No matter how the government may define the term "church" for tax purposes, it may not distribute benefits or impose burdens in a discriminatory way. For example, religious organizations that do not easily fall within the technical definition of a "church" and that are known loosely as "parachurches" are entitled to treatment under the tax code equal to that accorded to mainstream church ministries.[246] The cases discussed above sometimes illustrate the difficulty of obtaining evenhanded application of substantively neutral principles. But they do not undercut the validity of the principle deeply imbedded in the Religion Clause that all forms of religious ministries are entitled to equal treatment under the law,[247] including the tax code.

This conclusion is buttressed by several decisions not directly related to taxation and exemption of churches. In the leading case dealing with nondiscrimination among religious organizations, the Court ruled that a Minnesota charitable solicitation statute violated both establishment and free exercise principles by granting a de facto preference to older, more established churches. In *Larson v. Valente*,[248] Justice Brennan wrote: "The clearest command of the Establishment Clause is that one religious denomination cannot be officially preferred over another.... Free exercise...can be guaranteed only when legislators—and voters—are required to accord to their own religions the very same

---

245. In 1986 the government finally agreed to issue a new Treasury regulation that would not follow the "exclusively religious" activity test imbedded in its earlier regulation. Rev. Proc. 86-23, 1986-20 IRB 17.

246. In the same term in which *Frazee* was decided, the Court refused in *Hernandez v. Commissioner of Internal Revenue*, 490 U.S. 680 (1989) to allow payments for the religious practice of auditing in the Church of Scientology to be deducted as a charitable contribution in the same way that it has allowed fixed payments to other religions to be deducted. Justice White did not repudiate *Larson*, but distinguished it in *Hernandez* on the ground that "the line which IRC §170 draws between deductible and nondeductible payments to statutorily qualified organizations does not differentiate among sects." *Id.* at 695. Justice O'Connor, joined by Justice Scalia, dissented in *Hernandez*, on the view that the IRS's application of the quid pro quo standard in this case discriminated against the Church of Scientology as surely as the rigged rules on charitable solicitation discriminated against the Unification Church in *Larson*. *Id.* at 713.

247. *See, e.g.,* Michael J. Paulsen, Religion, Equality, and the Constitution: An Equal Protection Approach to Establishment Clause Adjudication, 61 Notre Dame L. Rev. 311 (1986).

248. 456 U.S. 228 (1982).

treatment given to small, new, or unpopular denominations."[249] Seven years later the Court expressly held that to deny unemployment compensation benefits to a person on the grounds that his refusal to work was not based on the tenets or dogma of an established religious community was a violation of the Free Exercise Clause.[250] More recently the Court adopted the nondiscrimination principle as an effective guard against the violation of nonestablishment principles in public funding of religious education.[251] Under these rulings as well as those discussed throughout this chapter, equal treatment of all religious organizations is the norm.

In this chapter I have suggested that the exemption of religious organizations from taxation is a statutory privilege with roots deep in our history, especially when our history is traced back further into the ancient and medieval world. It is constitutional in the sense that respect for the independence of religious communities from the state is a fundamental statement of the constitutive meaning or self understanding of American society reflected in the long-standing customs and traditions of our people. Although the legislative power to tax and spend theoretically includes the prerogative to change this ancient custom, there are no clear signs on the horizon that Congress will remove the federal income-tax exemption currently enjoyed by religious and other not-for-profit organizations.

---

249. *Id.* at 245.
250. Frazee v. Illinois Dep't of Employment Security, 489 U.S. 829 (1989).
251. Agostini v. Felton, 521 U.S. 203 (1997); *see also* Mitchell v. Helms, 530 U.S. 793 (2000).

Exemption of Religious Communities from State and Local Taxation

Edward McGlynn Gaffney, Jr.

As James A. Serritella notes in the Prologue to this volume, perspective matters. Serritella urges, for example, that the full dimensions of the relationship between a priest and his church cannot be conveyed by the single commercial term "employee." An analogous point must also be made about property used by religious communities and about the literature they distribute. No matter how religious communities are structured — congregationally or hierarchically — they all need space in which to gather periodically to nurture their communal self-understanding. These communities also need to think about the transmission of their message, or they will die out within a single generation. The spatial accommodations of a community — a synagogue, a church, a mosque — are not fully comprehended by identifying them as commercial real estate on a plat map in City Hall. Nor is the distribution of Torah, the Gospel, the Qu'ran, or of tracts on these scriptures fully explained by comparing it to a transaction at a commercial bookstore.

But what should the government do about the "property" of a religious community used for worship as it understands the term? What should it do about the community's "sales" of religious messages? To answer this question, one must first ask a descriptive question: what has the government done in the past? Then comes a question for understanding: why did this happen? Answers to these questions may guide us in the search for sensible solutions to the normative questions, whether undertaken by city councils, school boards, and state legislatures or pursued in litigation before state and federal courts.

The preceding chapter in this book, which discusses exemption of religious organizations from federal taxation, offers an account of the intellectual history of exemption of religion from taxation. It traces the roots of this idea in the ancient world, focusing on the concepts of tribute and taxation in the Hebrew Bible, on the teaching of the New Testament on tax compliance, and on provisions of Roman law exempting Jews and Christians from taxation, known under the label of "privileges and immunities." It also explores the complicated, often enmeshed, relationship between church and state in medieval England, and the supremacy of the crown and establishment of the Church of England as a result of the English Reformation. It discusses the phenomenon of local religious establishments in all but two of the American colonies, Pennsylvania and

Rhode Island. One prominent feature of these establishments was that nonmembers of the officially preferred state religion were required to provide financial support for a religious community whose beliefs they did not share. Only the established religions—Congregational in New England and Anglican in the southern colonies—were generally exempt from payment of taxes on their church's property. Finally, the earlier chapter offers an account of the revolutionary American insight that repudiated the establishment of religion so as to promote what James Madison termed "the full and free exercise of religion."[1]

This chapter does not repeat any of the historical material discussed in the preceding chapter. The first part analyzes the United States Supreme Court's use of history as a tool for explanation of its decision to sustain the practice of tax exemption in the leading decision on tax exemption, *Walz v. Tax Commission of the City of New York*.[2]

The next section of this chapter discusses the principal cases in the Court relating to the exemption of religious communities from payment of state and local taxes. In 1943 local authorities relied upon a facially neutral tax as the means of driving unwanted itinerant evangelists, the Jehovah's Witnesses, from their towns. According to the towns engaged in this hostility,[3] the fact that the Witnesses sought contributions for their two publications—*Salvation* and *Creation*—made them traveling salesmen upon whom the cities had jurisdiction to impose a license tax. Not so, said the Court in *Murdock v. Pennsylvania*[4] and seven other consolidated cases that conferred a constitutional immunity from such taxation on itinerant evangelists. A year later, in *Follett v. Town of McCormick, S.C.*,[5] the Court extended the principle of *Murdock* to the taxation of nonitinerant preachers in their own hometowns.

In the *Walz* case, mentioned above, the Court sustained the immunity of religious communities from payment of ad valorem property tax, at least where the state law confers this benefit upon religious communities along with other nonreligious nonprofit organizations. In 1989 in *Texas Monthly, Inc. v. Bullock*,[6] a plurality of three justices ruled that a statute conferring tax immunity on the distribution of religious literature without conferring a similar benefit on the distribution of nonreligious literature

---

1. In May of 1776, James Madison revised the text of the provision on religion in George Mason's draft of the of the Virginia Declaration of Rights. Madison removed the Lockean term "toleration" and replaced it with the following language: "That religion or the duty which we owe to our Creator, and the manner of discharging it, being under the direction of reason and conviction only, not of violence or compulsion; all men are equally entitled to the *full and free exercise* of it according to the dictates of Conscience; and therefore that no man or class of men ought, on account of religion to be invested with peculiar emoluments or privileges, nor subjected to any penalties or disabilities unless under &c...." [The remainder of Mason's text reads: "under Colour of Religion, any Man disturb the Peace, the Happiness, or Safety of Society, or of Individuals. And that is the mutual Duty of all, to practice Christian Forbearance, Love and Charity towards Each other."] William T. Hutchinson and William M. E. Rachal, eds., 1 The Papers of James Madison 174 (1962) [hereafter Madison Papers] (emphasis added). The texts of Mason's proposal and Madison's revision are reprinted in John T. Noonan, Jr., and Edward McGlynn Gaffney, Jr., Religious Freedom: History, Cases, and Other Materials on the Interaction of Religion and Government 162–63 (2001); for a discussion of this event, see John T. Noonan, Jr., The Lustre of Our Country: The American Experience of Religious Freedom 67–70 (1998).

2. 397 U.S. 664 (1970).

3. *See* Edward McGlynn Gaffney, Jr., Hostility to Religion America Style, 42 DePaul L. Rev. 263 (1992).

4. 319 U.S. 105 (1943).

5. 321 U.S. 573 (1944).

6. 489 U.S. 1 (1989).

violates the nonestablishment principle. In the following year the Court ruled in *Jimmy Swaggart Ministries v. California State Board of Equalization*[7] that a state is not compelled by the free exercise principle to confer tax immunity on the distribution of religious literature.

Exemption of religious communities from state and local taxation is by no means a uniform practice among all states. The federal Constitution allows a variety of practices to thrive in the laboratory of the states. The next section of this chapter suggests a way of thinking about these practices that is grounded both in state constitutional law and in several overlapping categories used to characterize basic principles in federal constitutional law governing religion: substantive neutrality, nondiscrimination or nonendorsement, and nonentanglement. This part of the chapter describes the role of state and local officials as interpreters of the constitutions of their states as well as of the federal Constitution.

The practice of religious tax exemption is coming increasingly under fire. The chapter concludes with the suggestion that civic communities and religious communities need to seek common ground if they are to thrive in this environment.

The Court's Use of History: A Case Study

The principal use of legal history by the Supreme Court in connection with the subject of this chapter was in *Walz v. Tax Commission of the City of New York*,[8] which sustained exemption of property used exclusively for religious worship from the payment of ad valorem property tax. As I conclude below, this result is defensible, but not on the historical grounds offered by the Court. Several amicus briefs in *Walz* offered extensive discussion of the history supporting the practice of religious tax exemption.[9] Relying heavily on these briefs, the justices allowed "law-office history" to enter into the United States Reports.

In his opinion for the Court in *Walz*, Chief Justice Burger articulated four interrelated historical claims in support of religious tax exemption. First, he wrote, the practice is grounded in an "unbroken" history that "covers our entire national existence and indeed predates it."[10] Second, "Few concepts are more deeply embedded in the fabric of our national life, beginning with pre-Revolutionary colonial times, than for the government to exercise at the very least this kind of benevolent neutrality toward churches and religious exercise generally so long as none was favored over others and none suffered interference."[11] Third, state legislatures universally have granted these exemptions for more than two centuries.[12] Fourth, the exemptions did not lead to an established religion but "operated affirmatively to help guarantee the free exercise of all forms of religious belief."[13] Cit-

---

7. 493 U.S. 378 (1990).
8. 397 U.S. 664 (1970).
9. *See, e.g.,* Brief Amicus Curiae of State of New York and thirty-seven other states; Brief Amicus Curiae of United States Catholic Conference; and see Chester James Antieau, Phillip Mark Carroll, and Thomas Carroll Burke, Religion under the State Constitutions 120–72 (1965).
10. 397 U.S. at 678.
11. *Id.* at 676–77.
12. *Id.* at 676.
13. *Id.* at 678.

ing Holmes's maxim that "a page of history is worth a volume of logic,"[14] Burger concluded that to disinter a practice so "deeply embedded" in our culture and so widely accepted by "common consent" requires a case more compelling than the bald assertion of Frederick Walz, unsupported by any historical evidence at all.[15]

In a similar vein, Justice Brennan offered historical evidence in support of his conclusion that religious communities may constitutionally be relieved of the burden of property taxation. Invoking the same maxim from Holmes,[16] Brennan wrote:

> The existence from the beginning of the Nation's life of a practice, such as tax exemptions for religious organizations, is not conclusive of its constitutionality. But such practice is a fact of considerable import in the interpretation of abstract constitutional language.... The more longstanding and widely accepted a practice, the greater its impact upon constitutional interpretation. History is particularly compelling in the present case because of the undeviating acceptance given religious tax exemptions from our earliest days as a Nation. Rarely if ever has the Court considered the constitutionality of a practice for which the historical support is so overwhelming.[17]

The tax commission's brief noted that Virginia enacted a tax exemption statute in 1800, just a year after it repealed various laws relating to the establishment of the Anglican Church in Virginia.[18] Brennan adopted this argument, arguing that strong supporters of disestablishment in Virginia, such as Thomas Jefferson and James Madison, did not equate religious tax exemption with an establishment of religion. As Brennan noted, Jefferson was president when tax exemption was first given to Washington churches, and Madison sat in the Virginia General Assembly that voted exemptions for churches in Virginia.[19] Brennan also cited evidence of the practice of religious tax exemption in the early republic. In 1781, he noted, Massachusetts exempted ministers of the Gospel from a poll tax.[20] In 1786 Rhode Island exempted ministers from an excise tax on carriages; and in 1789 it exempted all real estate granted or purchased for religious uses.[21] In 1787 South Carolina exempted ministers from a Charleston tax on professions,[22] and in 1788 it exempted from taxation "lands whereon any churches or other buildings for divine worship, or free schools, are erected."[23] Not all of the historical fragments were close fits to the problem at hand, but the general picture, thought Brennan, was that it was permissible to include religious communities among other charitable organizations whose property the government refrains from taxing.

---

14. *Id.* at 675–76, *citing* New York Trust Co. v. Eisner, 256 U.S. 345, 349 (1921).

15. *Id.* at 675.

16. *Id.* at 681 (Brennan, J., concurring); *id.* at 678, citing Holmes's opinion in *Jackman v. Rosenbaum*, 260 U.S. 22, 31 (1922): "If a thing has been practised for two hundred years by common consent, it will need a strong case for the Fourteenth Amendment to affect it."

17. 397 U.S. at 681 (Brennan, J., concurring).

18. Appellee's Brief at 15, *citing* 2 Virginia Statutes at Large 149 (disestablishment) and 200 (tax exemption).

19. *Id.* at 684–85 (Brennan, J., concurring), *citing* E. Swem & J. Williams, A Register of the General Assembly of Virginia, 1776–1918, 53 (1918); Journal of the House of Delegates of the Commonwealth of Virginia 94, 98 (1799–1800).

20. Acts and Resolves of 1781, c. 16.

21. *See* Edward Field, History of Rhode Island I:553, III: 238, 232 (1902).

22. South Carolina Acts of Assembly (1788) P.L. 435.

23. State Gazette of South Carolina, Apr. 12, 1788.

Justice Harlan agreed with the general thrust of Burger's opinion, but added in a separate concurring opinion a few sentences that became the basis for the political divisiveness test in nonestablishment cases. Harlan wrote:

> What is at stake as a matter of policy is preventing that kind and degree of government involvement in religious life that, as history teaches us, is apt to lead to strife and frequently strain a political system to the breaking point.... [G]overnmental involvement, while neutral, may be so direct or in such degree as to engender a risk of politicizing religion.... [H]istory cautions that political fragmentation on sectarian lines must be guarded against. Although the very fact of neutrality may limit the intensity of involvement, government participation in certain programs, whose very nature is apt to entangle the state in details of administration and planning, may escalate to the point of inviting undue fragmentation.[24]

Justice Douglas wrote in dissent that the serious problem of the case was that exemption gave to believers organized in church groups an economic benefit—echoing Justice Robert's dissent in *Follett*, discussed below, Douglas called it a "subsidy"—that nonbelievers, whether organized or not, do not enjoy.[25] Douglas fingered a serious problem with religious tax exemption: "If history be our guide, then tax exemption of church property in this country is indeed highly suspect, as it arose in the early days when the church was an agency of the state."[26] The main historical texts that Douglas relied on— appending them to his opinion as Justice Rutledge had done in his dissent in *Everson*— were Patrick Henry's proposal of a general assessment to pay for a "teacher of Christian religion" (a pastor) in each town of the Commonwealth of Virginia, and Madison's "Memorial and Remonstrance" against Henry's proposal.[27]

Each of these judicial opinions merits further comment. Chief Justice Burger noted the impressive historical pedigree of the practice of religious tax immunity, describing it as "a national heritage with roots in the Revolution itself." He concluded: "an unbroken practice of according the exemption to churches, openly and by affirmative state action, not covertly or by state inaction, is not something to be lightly cast aside."[28] Describing the practice as "unbroken" subjected Burger to sharp scholarly criticism. For example, in a leading article on the history of religious tax exemption, Professor John Witte wrote:

> The Court's historical argument depends too heavily upon questionable assertions of fact and selective presentation of evidence. The Court asserts that tax exemptions of church property have been adopted by common consent for more than two centuries. But a strong vein of criticism has long accompanied the practice in America. The Court asserts that such exemptions have not "led

---

24. 397 U.S. 664, 694–95 (Harlan, J., concurring).

25. *Id.* at 700 (Douglas, J., dissenting).

26. *Id.* at 703 (Douglas, J., dissenting).

27. Henry's proposal met with immediate and very strong opposition. Madison's Memorial gained 1,552 signatures. Another anonymous petition, asserting the General Assessment to be against "the Spirit of the Gospel," obtained 4,899. For the text of this petition and Madison's Memorial, see Noonan and Gaffney, Religious Freedom, *supra* note 1, at 173–79. In all, 10,929 persons indicated opposition to the measure, which died in the November 1785 session of the Virginia assembly. Madison provided the political leadership. The evangelicals, especially the Baptists, provided the decisive numbers. Thomas E. Buckley, S.J., Church and State in Revolutionary Virginia, 1776–1787 175 (1977).

28. 397 U.S. 664, 678 (1970).

to" an establishment of religion. But historically these exemptions were among the privileges of established religions, while dissenting religions were taxed; the issue is whether such exemptions have shed the chrysalis of establishment. The Court adduces numerous examples of earlier tax laws that exempt church property. But it ignores the variety of theories that supported these laws. The Court asserts that such exemption laws "historically reflect the concern of [their] authors" to avoid the "dangers of hostility to religion inherent in the imposition of property taxes." But little evidence from congressional and constitutional debates on tax exemption supports this assertion.[29]

Burger was right to conclude that it would be foolhardy for the federal judiciary to invalidate the decision of all fifty states to refrain from imposing property tax on a variety of nonprofit entities, including religious communities. But the defense of this conclusion must also be "more compelling" than the historical argument he offered in the opinion of the Court. As Witte's careful historical research on this matter demonstrates, Burger was wrong on all four points mentioned above. The history of the practice is not "unbroken" or "embedded in the fabric of our national life," nor has it been "universally granted" by legislatures for more than two centuries—and most critically, the practice did not avoid an establishment of religion, but was in some instances predicated upon it.

Justice Brennan's concurring opinion offered persuasive historical evidence in support of his conclusion. Regrettably, however, he inflated it into a justification for "undeviating acceptance."[30] Although he concluded that the New York practice was permissible, his exaggeration of the historical evidence does not lead one to the conclusion that the line drawn between the permissible and the impermissible is "one which accords with history and faithfully reflects the understanding of the Founding Fathers," or one "which the Court has consistently sought to mark in its decisions expounding the religious guarantees of the First Amendment."[31]

Justice Harlan's concurring opinion featured the claim that the First Amendment was intended to avoid political clashes between contending religious voices, a proposition for which there is no historical warrant. Harlan purported to articulate a general principle grounded in our historical experience, but offered no historical evidence in its support. A year later, in *Lemon v. Kurtzman*,[32] Chief Justice Burger elevated Harlan's anxiety in *Walz* into a full-blown test of constitutionality.

The political divisiveness test has had a checkered career on the Supreme Court. Chief Justice Burger, the author of the test, later acknowledged that the Court had never relied upon it as the basis for invalidating any state practice, but was unwilling to abandon it as a criterion of constitutionality.[33] Justices Brennan, Douglas, and Marshall became fond of the test. For example, they relied upon it in dissent to explain why they would not allow states to loan secular textbooks to children attending religious schools.[34] Justice Powell reflected the ambiguity of the Court about the test. In *Wolman*

---

29. *See* John Witte, Tax Exemption of Religious Property: Historical Anomaly or Valid Constitutional Practice?, 62 S.C. L. Rev. 363, 367 (1991); *see also* Witte, Modern Disestablishment Law, in Religion and the American Constitutional Experiment: Essential Rights and Liberties, 149–84 (2000).

30. 397 U.S. at 681 (Brennan, J. concurring).

31. *Id.* at 680 (Brennan, J. concurring).

32. 403 U.S. 602 (1971).

33. Lynch v. Donnelly, 465 U.S. 668 (1984).

34. Meek v. Pittenger, 421 U.S. 349, 373 (1975) (Brennan, J. dissenting). Brennan expressed the view that the textbook loan program approved in *Meek* was invalid because it rested on *Board of Ed-*

v. Walter, he wrote: "The risk of significant religious or denominational control over our democratic processes—or even of deep political division along religious lines—is remote, and when viewed against the positive contributions of sectarian schools, any such risk seems entirely tolerable in light of the continuing oversight of the Court."[35] Yet Powell managed to resurrect the political divisiveness test in *Aguilar v. Felton*: "[The] risk of entanglement is compounded by the additional risk of political divisiveness stemming from the aid to religion at issue here.... There remains a considerable risk of continuing political strife over the propriety of direct aid to religious schools and the proper allocation of limited governmental resources. In states such as New York that have large and varied sectarian populations, one can be assured that politics will enter into any state decision to aid parochial schools...."[36] Despite the unreliability of the historical evidence adduced in support of this test, the Court has never managed to drive a stake though its heart. Thus even when the Court reversed *Aguilar* in *Agostini v. Felton*, Justice O'Connor enabled the test to see the light of one more day, despite the fact that she and every other justice in the majority had been critical of it in the past. In short, the concern about political divisiveness expressed by Harlan in *Walz* did not yield a principle, much less one well grounded in history.[37]

Tax exemptions should not be granted or withheld simply because people might become divided politically along religious lines. If the history of the United States demonstrates anything, it is that people have indeed been divided politically along religious lines.[38] Two of the commandments with which Judge Noonan concluded his recent book speak powerfully to this point:

> You shall observe that the free exercise of religion generated the moral energy and the bitter passions that produced the Civil War and led to the liberation of the millions held in bondage.... You shall recognize that the free exercise of religion can be divisive and dangerous to established institutions and customary ways as well as beneficent for believers and empowering for the forgotten, and that the price of our constitutional liberty is acceptance of this precarious condition.[39]

---

ucation v. Allen, 392 U.S. 236 (1968), which had been decided before the Court's adoption of the political divisiveness test in *Lemon*. The Court overruled *Meek* in *Mitchell v. Helms*, 120 S.Ct. 2530, 2539 (2000).

35. Wolman v. Walter, 433 U.S. 229, 263 (1977) (Powell, J., concurring in part, concurring in judgment in part, and dissenting in part).

36. 473 U.S. 402, 416 (1985) (Powell, J. concurring).

37. *See* Edward McGlynn Gaffney, Political Divisiveness Along Religious Lines: The Entanglement of the Court in Sloppy History and Bad Public Policy, 24 St. Louis U. L.J. 205 (1980). For example, far from thinking that the First Amendment enabled Congress to repress religious speech it deemed divisive, James Madison came to the First Congress because of partisan support pledged by Baptists in Orange County, Virginia. Far from entertaining a bias against religious rights, Madison wrote: "In a free government, the security for civil rights must be the same as for religious rights." James Madison, Federalist No. 51; *see also* Federalist No. 10 in Jacob E. Cooke, ed., The Federalist 351 (1961). In Madison's view, the pluralism of contending religious voices is not a threat to the republic, but a safeguard against the tyranny of a religious majority "by comprehending in the society so many separate descriptions of citizens, as will render an unjust combination of a majority of the whole, very improbable, if not impracticable." *Id.*

38. *See* Michael J. Perry, Morality, Politics, and Law: A Bicentennial Essay (1968); Edward McGlynn Gaffney, Jr., Politics Without Brackets on Religious Convictions: Michael Perry and Bruce Ackerman on Neutrality, 64 Tul. L. Rev. 1143 (1990); Dean M. Kelley, The Intermeddling Manifesto, or the Role of Religious Bodies in Affecting Public Policy in the United States, 8 J.L. & Relig. 85 (1990); Kelley, The Rationale for Involvement of Religion in the Body Politic, in James E. Wood, Jr., and Derek Davis, eds., The Role of Religion in the Making of Public Policy 159–89 (1991).

39. Noonan, The Lustre of Our Country, *supra* note 1, at 357–58.

Justice Douglas took more seriously the evidence that links tax exemption to the privileges or immunities of an established church. But like the other justices who wrote in *Walz*, he did not follow up on this insight or offer a satisfactory account of the historical data. He took the easy way out, citing the assessment controversy of 1785 Virginia as though it clinched the argument against tax exemption for religious communities today. Years later, Justices Thomas and Souter clashed over whether the same frequently invoked assessment controversy resolved the current practice of allowing religious speech on a state campus to be included within a program funded by student activity fees. Souter relied on the historic debate between Henry and Madison in 1785 for the conclusion that "government must actively discriminate against religion."[40] Thomas criticized Souter for missing the focus of Henry's proposed assessment that had sparked the controversy:

> The assessment was to be imposed for the support of clergy in the performance of their function of teaching religion. Thus, the Bill Establishing a Provision for Teachers of the Christian Religion provided for the collection of a specific tax, the proceeds of which were to be appropriated "by the Vestries, Elders, or Directors of each religious society…to a provision for a Minister or Teacher of the Gospel of their denomination, or the providing places of divine worship, and to none other use whatsoever."[41]

Every justice who wrote in *Walz* made an effort to employ history. Regrettably, however, they all made historical errors that weakened their opinions. No one on the Court has tried again to offer a plausible explanation of why the practice of religious tax immunity is, on balance and considering the alternatives in the light of our history, a good or a bad idea. For all their fine talk about the importance of history as a tool for comprehending the meaning of the Religion Clause in general, and for assessing the practice of religious tax exemption in particular, the justices have not served us well. They are hopelessly divided over what the Religion Clause means. And in the only tax case in which they tried to practice what they preach about history, their sermons fell flat. None of the opinions in *Walz* succeed as sound historical arguments.

As has been noted above, Witte's careful research on state law demonstrates that the history of this matter is far richer and more complex than the historical explanations offered by the Court in *Walz*. In his groundbreaking 1991 article, Witte traced the practice of tax exemption of church property to its roots in the common law and in the equity tradition that favored such exemptions on account of the "religious uses" and "charitable uses" to which church properties were devoted.[42] All who struggle to find a sensible solution to the issue of religious tax exemption are deeply in debt to Witte. I take issue not with his historical work, but with the general policy recommendations in his conclusion. He proposed "to remove tax exemptions for church property that are based on religious [internal, cultic, sacerdotal] uses but to retain those that are based on charitable, external, cultural, social uses to which they are devoted." He characterized this proposal as "a via media between the wholesale eradication of such exemptions proposed by opponents and the blanket endorsements of exemptions proffered by proponents."[43] There is something to be said for attempts to identify a "via media." After all,

---

40. Rosenberger v. Rector and Visitors of the Univ. of Virginia, 515 U.S. 819, 853 (1995) (Souter, J., dissenting).

41. *Id.* at 852 (Thomas J., concurring).

42. Witte, Tax Exemption of Religious Property, *supra* note 29, at 408.

43. *Id.*

the via media is where Aristotle said that virtue lies.[44] But Witte's earlier proposal did not really occupy the middle ground; it opened up the very real possibility of routine violation of the central meaning of the Religion Clause by conceding to government the power of defining a religious use of property.

If Witte's proposed distinction between religious and charitable uses were accepted as a normative understanding of the First Amendment, moreover, it would undermine federalism. The state constitutions of thirty-seven states provide for religious immunity from state taxation. The resurgence of concern for the rights reserved to the states or to the people through the Tenth Amendment is a good reason not to invalidate all of these state constitutional provisions through an nationwide injunction issued by a federal court.

More importantly, Witte's proposal would violate the fundamental consensus on religious freedom in America embedded in the overlapping categories of substantive neutrality, nondiscrimination, and nonentanglement of the government in religion. The practice of conferring tax immunity on religious organizations along with other nonprofit organizations is substantively neutral in that it neither encourages nor discourages religious belief, practice, or observance. The government may decide to tax some aspects of all nonprofit organizations, but it can neither exempt nor tax religious communities exclusively among nonprofit organizations without discriminating for or against religion. The government may not entangle itself excessively in religious matters. It may define a secular category, as in setting out the qualifications for a nonprofit organization, but it may not define what counts for religious experience or what a religious use is. I will offer more extensive comments below in support of the conclusion that the government has no business telling religious communities which of their "uses" will qualify them for such an important benefit as exemption from taxation.

Not all religious uses can be redefined as charitable ones. Even if they could, the important thing to focus on is who does the defining, the religious community or the government. What the First Amendment prohibits is excessive entanglement by the government in religious matters, which are not within the scope of its power to control. The previous chapter on exemption from federal taxation detailed the recent conflict between religious communities and federal tax authorities over the definition of an "integrated auxiliary of a church."[45] It was a bureaucratic nightmare that does not need to be repeated state by state. In addition, Witte's earlier proposal assumed that the government has power to define religious uses, if only for purposes of abolishing them or melding them into acceptable charitable ones. As will become clear below, that assumption is ungrounded in the history that surrounds the twin values of nonestablishment and free exercise.

This view is articulated most clearly by Thomas Curry, who understands the First Amendment to be a self-denying ordinance that restrains government, a mandate that

---

44. In the Nicomachaean Ethics, Book II, chapter 6, 1106a, Aristotle describes equality as "a sort of mean between excess and deficiency." When speaking of the virtue of character in section 1106b, he again defines the category of the middle or mean as that which distinguishes excess and deficiency. The key to virtue is to have feelings and actions "at the right time, about the right things, towards the right people, for the right end, and in the right way." Thus, the virtue of courage lies between cowardice (too much fear) and foolish recklessness (not enough fear). Roger Crisp, ed., Aristotle: Nichomachean Ethics 30 (2000); see also D.S. Hutchinson, Ethics, in Jonathan Barnes, ed., The Cambridge Comparison to Aristotle 321 (1995).

45. See Edward McGlynn Gaffney, Governmental Definition of Religion: The Rise and Fall of the IRS Regulations on an "Integrated Auxiliary of a Church," 25 Val. U. L. Rev. 203, 222 (1991).

the state will exercise no power in religious questions.[46] According to Curry, a law would violate the Religion Clause if it required government to exercise power or make decisions in religious matters. Such a law is beyond the realm of government power, which is confined to the secular. Applying this insight to the issue of religious tax exemption, secular government may define the category of nonprofit organizations, as New York did broadly in the statute at issue in *Walz*. It may also tax all nonprofit organizations, as California purports to do in the sales and use tax law at issue in *Jimmy Swaggart Ministries*.[47] But it may not single out religious communities to confer on them a benefit not available to other nonprofit organizations, as in the sales tax statute at issue in *Texas Monthly*. Nor may it single out religious communities for exclusion from a broad-based benefit available to all other nonprofit organizations. Still less may it exclude an unpopular minority religious community from a benefit because of hostile or discriminatory animus.[48] Both of the last two statutes would be unconstitutional in Curry's proposal, because both involve the government impermissibly in defining religion.

Witte recently published a thoughtful collection of essays that includes a revised version of his 1991 article on tax exemption.[49] In the chapter that immediately precedes it, he tries to map modern disestablishment law for his reader,[50] treating the nonestablishment themes discussed by the Court and commentators under the following categories: separationism (which he labels "the dominant principle"),[51] accommodationism, neutrality, endorsement, coercion, and equal treatment. I am less confident than Witte that the Court is capable of sharpening these approaches when it announces a "formal test" like neutrality.[52] But even on Witte's own terms, it is difficult to defend his earlier proposal under any of the six categories mentioned above.

Whatever one makes of the intellectual history of the exemption of religious communities from taxation that I offered in the previous chapter, or of Witte's more focused exploration of the case law on state and local taxes, the practice of religious tax exemption cannot be justified merely by saying that some form of exemption has been around for millennia. On the contrary, rationales for the practice that predate the American Revolution cannot readily be transferred to our own contemporary situation, principally because justifications that were appropriate in the Roman empire, in the Middle Ages, in Reformation England, or in colonial America may not be normative at all in our constitutional order. Like any other governmental practice, tax exemption for religious communities must cohere with the twin constitutional values of nonestablishment and free exercise. Rationales that are connected inherently with establishment no longer have any validity. Only those rationales that have, in Witte's phrase, "shed the

---

46. *See* Thomas J. Curry, Farewell to Christendom: The Future of Church and State in America (2001).

47. For skepticism about uniformity of enforcement of the federal tax code, see *Hernandez v. Commissioner*, 490 U.S. 680, 703 (1989) (O'Connor, J., dissenting).

48. *See* Church of Lukumi Babalu Aye v. City of Hialeah, 508 U.S. 520, 532 (1993); Larson v. Valente, 456 U.S. 228, 244–45 (1982).

49. *See* Witte, Religion and the American Constitutional Experiment, *supra* note 29, 149–84.

50. *Id.* at 149–84.

51. *See* the discussion of instrumental causality and teleological purpose in text accompanying note 107 below. Nonestablishment is the principal means through which we achieve the goal of free exercise of religion. Witte had written earlier that the Religion Clause rests on a variety of "interlocking and interdependent" principles, none of which can be regarded as secondary. John Witte, Jr., The Essential Rights and Liberties of Religion in the American Constitutional Experiment, 71 Notre Dame L. Rev. 371, 376, 394–402 (1996).

52. Witte, Modern Disestablishment Law, *supra* note 29, at 157.

chrysalis of establishment"[53] can plausibly support the exemption of religious organizations from various forms of state and local taxation. This does not mean that the mere invocation of either term—nonestablishment or free exercise—suffices either to validate or invalidate the practice now recognized in the constitutions of thirty-seven states[54] and in statutes of all the others. Instead, serious constitutional analysis is needed.

The Relationship of Nonestablishment and Free Exercise

In the 1940s the Court ruled in *Murdock* and *Follett* that states may not use the taxing power as a pretext for penalizing unpopular Jehovah's Witnesses. No one imagined that a mandatory accommodation under the free exercise principle would later be deemed to violate the nonestablishment principle. Nearly thirty years later, after ignoring several challenges to religious immunity from property taxes, the Court held in *Walz* that a state does not violate the nonestablishment provision if it exempts a church from paying taxes on the property it uses for "exclusively religious" purposes. On the other hand, the free exercise provision does not require this exemption, which is a matter of legislative grace. That religious tax immunity would be deemed permissible but not mandatory is a conclusion that could be viewed as a sign of self-restraint on the part of the federal judiciary vis-à-vis the states. But the Court achieved that result by bifurcating the provisions on religion as though one provision commanded one result and the other provision required the opposite.

Consider what the Court did in the area of sales and use tax. In *Texas Monthly v. Bullock*[55] the Court held that the nonestablishment provision prohibits the states from providing an exemption for the distribution of religious literature that is not combined with similar exemption of a broader class of beneficiaries among charitable organizations. Perhaps on the view that *Murdock* and *Follett* still had some vitality, two of the concurring justices expressly left open the possibility that the free exercise provision might require a different conclusion. The logic of this view is that the Free Exercise and Establishment clauses are in conflict with one another. Within a year the Court unanimously held in *Jimmy Swaggart Ministries v. California State Board of Equalization*[56] that a state did not violate the Free Exercise Clause by refusing to grant an exemption for the distribution of religious literature by an unpopular out-of-state evangelist. *Jimmy Swaggart Ministries* had at least the virtue of clarifying that the free exercise provision does not require something that the nonestablishment provision prohibits. But Justice O'Connor's opinion in the case showed little regard for the experience that Justice Holmes described as "the life of the law."[57]

I discuss below a thread of meaning running through these five cases. For now, I would like to focus on the fact that all four opinions in *Walz*, and all of the other four Supreme

---

53. *Id.* at 367.
54. *See* appendix, "State Constitutions Containing Provisions for Tax Exemption of Charitable Organizations, Including Religious Bodies," following this chapter.
55. 489 U.S. 1 (1989).
56. 493 U.S. 378 (1990).
57. Oliver Wendell Holmes, Jr., The Common Law 1 (1890).

Court cases on religious tax immunity—*Murdock, Follett, Texas Monthly*, and *Jimmy Swaggart Ministries*—share in common a view that the two provisions of the Religion Clause, nonestablishment and free exercise, are not only distinct but almost mutually exclusive. In this view, the two provisions on religion in the First Amendment are viewed as separate "clauses" pulling in opposite directions in some grand tug-of-war. Positing such a conflict within the Religion Clause is about as plausible as believing that the Free Press Clause was intended both to foster greater dissemination of opinions and to repress any thought the government finds offensive. In the final chapter of this volume I discuss an alternative approach, that nonestablishment of religion is related to free exercise as means to end, and that these two ways of describing religious freedom are harmonious, not conflictual.

The commonplace—and in my view, mistaken—bifurcation of the Religion Clause into two separate competing clauses has deeply affected the Court's jurisprudence on religious exemption from state and local taxation. The following discussion of the principal cases dealing with this issue is an attempt to situate each case in its immediate historical context as well as within the broader history of the Religion Clause.

The Supreme Court on Religious Exemption from State and Local Taxation: *Murdock v. Pennsylvania* (1943) and *Follett v. McCormick* (1943)

The Court's first two cases on religious exemption from state and local taxation were decided in 1943 and 1944. It helps to understand these cases by situating them in the context of two important turns in constitutional interpretation, the Court's 1937 retreat from its posture of invalidating the New Deal, and its 1943 retreat from its decision three years earlier in the first flag salute case.

The Court's decision to back off of its opposition to the New Deal represented a huge shift. For decades it had been imposing its own conservative laissez-faire economic philosophy on a variety of regulatory schemes, state and federal. For example, in *Lochner v. New York*[58] it invalidated state legislation meant to regulate working hours in the baking industry. In cases like this, the Court dramatically expanded its power by inventing a new tool of judicial review, substantive due process. Under this approach it could invalidate a state law on the view that the substance of the law itself, not the procedure by which it had been passed or was being administered, violated the Due Process Clause of the Fourteenth Amendment.[59] In a single decision, the Court called into question hundreds of labor laws enacted by states throughout the country. During World War I it invalidated federal legislation regulating the sale in interstate commerce of items manufactured with child labor, calling it a violation of powers "always existing and carefully reserved to the States in the Tenth Amendment."[60] "Carefully reserved," that is, until the state legislation reached the Court, where it was struck down. Congress immediately re-

---

58. 198 U.S. 45 (1905).
59. "No State shall…deprive any person of life, liberty or property without due process of law." U.S. Const., Am. XIV.
60. Hammer v. Dagenhart, 247 U.S. 251 (1918).

sponded with a new child labor law putting a "punitive" tax on products manufactured by children. The Court invalidated this legislation too, ruling that this exercise of the taxing power also violated the Tenth Amendment.[61] Not even the global economic crisis of the Great Depression kept the Court from invalidating FDR's New Deal.[62] After receiving a broad mandate in 1936,[63] President Roosevelt initiated a plan to expand the Court by appointing a new justice for each one already over seventy years of age. Whether or not the Court was influenced by the president's Court-packing scheme, which the justices emphatically opposed, a bare majority of the Court suddenly announced in 1937 that it would no longer impose its conservative views of economics.[64] Thereafter, it would be broadly permissive of economic regulation both by Congress and by state legislatures. A year later, the Court suggested in a famous footnote that it would vigorously exercise "more exacting judicial scrutiny" in cases involving "statutes directed at particular religions…[or reflecting] prejudice against discrete and insular minorities."[65]

One such unpopular minority group that lacked political power was the Jehovah's Witnesses. The Witnesses saturated communities—usually on Sundays, their day off from work—with their tracts, ignoring local restrictions as infringements of their duty to carry out a divine command. In 1937 the Court, invoking the prohibition of polygamy in the Mormon cases,[66] unanimously dismissed for want of federal jurisdiction a case involving religiously motivated distributors of literature.[67] In the following year, the year of the famous footnote referred to above, by a vote of 8–0 the Court invalidated a municipal ordinance on the ground that it unconstitutionally abridged the Witnesses' freedoms of speech and the press.[68] These freedoms were characterized by Chief Justice Hughes as "among the fundamental personal rights" protected by the Fourteenth Amendment, while the Court still left a purely religious right without protection. In 1939 the Court, 8–1, struck down four more municipal ordinances as abridgements of the speech and press freedoms.[69] Not, however, until 1940 did the Supreme Court address affirmatively the claim of free exercise of religion.

Without mentioning the 1937 case that had unanimously decided that there is no free exercise right to public dissemination of religious literature, the Court in effect overruled it in 1940, invalidating the conviction of Jesse Cantwell, a Jehovah's Witness, for disturbing the peace as he went about his task of public proselytization.[70] The Court used the tool it had devised during the period of economic conservatism, substantive due process, to bind all the states through the Fourteenth Amendment to observe the requirements of the First Amendment's free exercise provision.

Cantwell was not an omen that the Witnesses would always enjoy special favor before judges. Within weeks, the Court ruled in the first flag salute case, *Gobitis*,[71] that a state

---

61. *See* Bailey v. Drexel Furniture Co., 259 U.S. 20 (1922).

62. *See, e.g.,* Carter v. Carter Coal Co., 298 U.S. 238 (1936).

63. Carrying every state except Vermont and Maine, Roosevelt received 523 of the 531 votes in the electoral college, and 60.8 percent of the popular vote.

64. *See* West Coast Hotel Co. v. Parrish, 300 U.S. 379 (1937).

65. United States v. Carolene Products Co., 304 U.S. 144, 152 n. 4 (1938); *see* John Hart Ely, Democracy and Distrust (1980).

66. *See* Reynolds v. United States, 98 U.S. 145 (1879).

67. *See* Coleman v. City of Griffin, 302 U.S. 636 (1937).

68. *See* Lovell v. City of Griffin, 303 U.S. 444 (1938).

69. *See* Schneider v. Irvington, 308 U.S. 147 (1939).

70. *See* Cantwell v. Connecticut, 310 U.S. 296 (1940).

71. Minersville Sch. Dist. v. Gobitis, 310 U.S. 586 (1940).

could expel children from school because their beliefs as Witnesses made it impossible for them to salute the flag without breaking what they saw as God's command to refrain from the worship of graven images.[72]

Although the Court was nearly unanimous in *Gobitis* (only Justice Stone dissented), the opinion was repudiated roundly in many journals of opinion. The *New Republic*, which Justice Frankfurter had helped found, said the Court had come "dangerously close" to being the victim of war hysteria. *Christian Century*, a liberal Protestant magazine, said, "Courts that will not protect even Jehovah's Witnesses will not long protect anybody." *America*, a Jesuit journal, said that the Court had permitted destruction of "one of the most precious rights under the Federal and our State Constitutions." The *Harvard Educational Review* said the decision subordinated the civil liberties of minorities to "the will of the majority." Of the thirty-nine law reviews that discussed the decision, thirty-one were critical. Few decisions of the Court in modern times have met with such across-the-board intellectual rejection.[73]

The Witnesses were already unpopular before *Gobitis*. They had been victims of several incidents of mob violence in Texas. The decision unleashed a fury against the Witnesses that made a mockery of the patriotism upon which it purported to rest. Witnesses were attacked in Maine (beatings, burning of the Kingdom Hall in Kennebunk), West Virginia (forced drinking of castor oil), Wyoming (tarring and feathering), Nebraska (castration), Arkansas (shooting), Illinois, Indiana, Maryland, Mississippi, and Oregon (mob attacks). Forty percent of the incidents occurred within two states, Oklahoma and Texas. Small towns, not tolerant of outsiders, were the usual sites.[74]

Gobitis had, moreover, a precise parallel in the tax field. Local authorities sought to protect their communities against unwanted proselytization by the pesty Witnesses, but they could not exactly bar the city gates against them. Looking to the Court's new willingness to allow economic regulation, state and local authorities seized upon "the fact that the religious literature is distributed with a solicitation of funds."[75] This, they contended, took the Witnesses' activities out of the protection of the First Amendment and into the realm of the commercial. Thus they chose to harass the Witnesses by means of a generally applicable, facially neutral occupation tax,[76] imagining that the device would be beyond judicial review.

The first reply they got from the Court was comforting to the authorities. In *Jones v. Opelika*,[77] Justice Reed wrote:

> When proponents of religious or social theories use the *ordinary commercial methods of sales* of articles to raise propaganda funds, it is a natural and proper exercise of the power of the state to charge reasonable fees for the privilege of canvassing. Careful as we may and should be to protect the freedoms safeguarded by the Bill of Rights, it is difficult to see in such enactments a shadow of prohibition of the exercise of religion or of abridgement of the freedom of

---

72. Exod. 20:4–5; Deut. 5:8–9. *See* David R. Manwaring, Render unto Caesar: The Flag-Salute Controversy (1962).
73. Manwaring, *supra* note 72, at 149–57.
74. *Id.* at 163–73.
75. Murdock v. Pennsylvania, 319 U.S. 105, 110 (1943).
76. *Id.* at 115.
77. 316 U.S. 584 (1942).

speech or the press. It is prohibition and unjustifiable abridgement which is interdicted, not taxation.[78]

This is a precise example of what James Serritella means in the Prologue to this volume by the problem of mischaracterization of religious activity as though it could be fully comprehended in commercial terms. Whatever one makes of itinerant evangelists—they have been unpopular since colonial times[79]—it is impossible to encompass either their self-understanding of their vocation or their contribution to American life by calling them traveling salesmen or by imposing a tax on the exercise of their faith.

Not only did Justices Black, Douglas, and Murphy dissent on the tax matter before them in *Jones*, they signaled to the Witnesses that the time was ripe for reconsideration of the flag salute case: "Since we joined in the opinion in the *Gobitis* case, we think this is an appropriate occasion to state that we now believe that it was also wrongly decided...."[80] As noted above, Justice Stone had dissented in *Gobitis*. There were four votes for hearing a new flag salute case. Only one more vote was needed to reverse it.

The ink was barely dry on *Jones* when the case of Robert Murdock and seven other proselytizing Witnesses reached the Court. The conference of the justices disclosed a switch of at least one vote in *Jones,* for in a highly unusual move the Court on February 15, 1943, not only granted certiorari in eight tax cases consolidated with *Murdock v. Pennsylvania* but also restored *Jones v. Opelika* to its docket for reargument. Arguments on the cases lasted two full days. Hayden Covington, the general counsel for the Witnesses, argued that their activity in distributing literature containing sermons on the Bible was their way of preaching the Gospel and worshiping God.[81]

Writing for the Court in *Murdock*, Justice Douglas described the imposition of the tax on the Witnesses as a "new device for the suppression of religious minorities."[82] He described the history of the practice at issue:

> The hand distribution of religious tracts is an age-old form of missionary evangelism—as old as the history of printing presses. It has been a potent force in various religious movements down through the years. This form of evangelism is utilized today on a large scale by various religious sects whose colporteurs carry the Gospel to thousands upon thousands of homes and seek through personal visitations to win adherents to their faith. It is more than preaching; it is more than distribution of religious literature. It is a combination of both. Its purpose is as evangelical as the revival meeting. This form of religious activity occupies the same high estate under the First Amendment as do worship in the churches and preaching from the pulpits. It has the same claim to protection as the more orthodox and conventional exercises of religion.[83]

Douglas added that "spreading one's religious beliefs or preaching the Gospel through distribution of religious literature and through personal visitations is an age-

---

78. *Id.* at 597 (emphasis added).

79. *See, e.g.*, Sydney E. Ahlstrom, A Religious History of the American People 285 (1972). In the colonial period, itinerant evangelists were mocked as arrogant, fanatical, intolerant, uneducated, and mercenary. See the string of adjectives employed in *Murdock* to describe the Witnesses: "provocative, abusive, and ill-mannered...unpopular, annoying, or distasteful." 319 U.S. 105, 115–16 (1943); *see id.* at 166–82 (Jackson, J., dissenting).

80. Jones v. Opelika, 316 U.S. at 623–624 (Black, J., dissenting).

81. Murdock v. Pennsylvania, 319 U.S. 105 (1943).

82. *Id.* at 115.

83. *Id.* at 108–09.

old type of evangelism with as high a claim to constitutional protection as the more orthodox types."[84] He addressed the issue of characterization stressed by Serritella in the Prologue to this volume, and concluded that a charge for the cost of dissemination of religious faith does not make it a taxable event:

> [T]he mere fact that the religious literature is 'sold' by itinerant preachers rather than 'donated' does not transform evangelism into a commercial enterprise. If it did, then the passing of the collection plate in church would make the church service a commercial project. The constitutional rights of those spreading their religious beliefs through the spoken and printed word are not to be gauged by standards governing retailers or wholesalers of books. The right to use the press for expressing one's views is not to be measured by the protection afforded commercial handbills.... It is plain that a religious organization needs funds to remain a going concern. But an itinerant evangelist however misguided or intolerant he may be, does not become a mere book agent by selling the Bible or religious tracts to help defray his expenses or to sustain him. Freedom of speech, freedom of the press, freedom of religion are available to all, not merely to those who can pay their own way. As we have said, the problem of drawing the line between a purely commercial activity and a religious one will at times be difficult. On this record it plainly cannot be said that petitioners were engaged in a commercial rather than a religious venture. It is a distortion of the facts of record to describe their activities as the occupation of selling books and pamphlets.[85]

Finally, Douglas referred in passing to the particular form of taxation—an occupational tax—at issue in *Murdock*, but broadly condemned the taxation of distribution of religious literature as an attempt to control or suppress the unfettered enjoyment of a fundamental constitutional right:

> It is one thing to impose a tax on the income or property of a preacher. It is quite another thing to exact a tax from him for the privilege of delivering a sermon. The tax imposed by the City of Jeannette is a flat license tax, the payment of which is a condition of the exercise of these constitutional privileges. The power to tax the exercise of a privilege is the power to control or suppress its enjoyment. Those who can tax the exercise of this religious practice can make its exercise so costly as to deprive it of the resources necessary for its maintenance. Those who can tax the privilege of engaging in this form of missionary evangelism can close its doors to all those who do not have a full purse. Spreading religious beliefs in this ancient and honorable manner would thus be denied the needy. Those who can deprive religious groups of their colporteurs can take from them a part of the vital power of the press which has survived from the Reformation.[86]

In 1943 no less than in 1940, devotion to the flag was important as a symbol of the unity of the nation, especially after the nation entered World War II. This very context, however, led the justices to reconsider its decision about requiring children to salute the flag. The imagery of a flag evoked not only the heroism of Marines at Iwo Jima, but also the massed banners at Nuremberg rallies that symbolized complete loyalty to a totalitarian regime with which we were locked in mortal combat. In this setting the claim of the

---

84. *Id.* at 110.
85. *Id.* at 111.
86. *Id.* at 112 (citations omitted).

Witnesses to be free from coercion to worship a graven image took on a profoundly different meaning. Within weeks of *Murdock*—on Flag Day, June 14—the Court reversed the first flag salute case on facts virtually identical to those in *Gobitis*. Justice Jackson wrote in *West Virginia State Board of Education v. Barnette*: "[I]f there is any fixed star in our constitutional constellation, it is that no official, high or petty, can prescribe what shall be orthodox in politics, nationalism, religion, or other matters of opinion or force citizens to confess by word or act their faith therein."[87] Assessed against this historical background, *Murdock* and *Barnette* were potent signals of a new constitutional order. *Murdock* reminded Americans that the Constitution does not require that the relations between church and state be the same as the relations between commerce and state.[88] *Barnette* reminded Americans that their violence against the Witnesses was profoundly—that is, constitutionally—un-American.

A year later, the Court heard a criminal case from the town of McCormick, South Carolina, which had imposed a fine on Lester Follett, a Witness, for refusing to pay a fee as a "book agent." Again Hayden Covington argued that the ordinance could not be applied to the sort of activity at issue in the case because it "unduly burdens the exercise of freedom to worship God as His minister."[89] Unlike the itinerant evangelists in the *Murdock* set of cases, Follett lived in the town. The South Carolina Supreme Court seized on the distinction between the itinerant Murdock and the domiciliary Follett, ruling that *Murdock* was applicable only to itinerants. The U.S. Supreme Court found this to be a distinction without a difference. Again, Justice Douglas wrote for the Court, reiterating the central holding in *Murdock* that taxing the distribution of religious literature is an unconstitutional attempt to control or suppress the exercise of a fundamental right:

> A preacher has no less a claim to that privilege when he is not an itinerant. We referred to the itinerant nature of the activity in the *Murdock* case merely in emphasis of the prohibitive character of the license tax as so applied. Its unconstitutionality was not dependent on that circumstance. The exaction of a tax as a condition to the exercise of the great liberties guaranteed by the First Amendment is as obnoxious as the imposition of a censorship or a previous restraint. For, to repeat, "the power to tax the exercise of a privilege is the power to control or suppress its enjoyment."[90]

Douglas also pointed out in *Follett* that taxing the distribution of religious literature would create greater hardships for small, struggling religious communities:

> Freedom of religion is not merely reserved for those with a long purse. Preachers of the more orthodox faiths are not engaged in commercial undertakings because they are dependent on their calling for a living. Whether needy or affluent, they avail themselves of the constitutional privilege of a "free exercise" of their religion when they enter the pulpit to proclaim their faith. The priest or preacher is as fully protected in his function as the parishioners are in their worship. A flat license tax on that constitutional privilege would be as odious as the early "taxes on knowledge" which the framers of the First Amendment sought to outlaw.[91]

---

87. 319 U.S. 624, 642 (1943).

88. As Justice Murphy put it: "The constitutional rights of those spreading their religious beliefs through the spoken and printed word are not to be gauged by standards governing retailers or wholesalers of books." 319 U.S. at 111.

89. 321 U.S. 573 (1944).

90. *Id.* at 577.

91. *Id.* at 576–77.

Dissenting in *Follett,* Justice Roberts hit on the same distinction that the lower Court had:

> [A] citizen of the community, earning his living in the community by a religious activity, claims immunity from contributing to the cost of the government under which he lives. The record shows appellant "testified that he obtained his living from the money received from those with whom he placed books, that he had no other source of income." Unless the phrase "free exercise," embodied in the First Amendment, means that government must render service free to those who earn their living in a religious calling, no reason is apparent why the appellant, like every other earner in the community, should not contribute his share of the community's common burden of expense.[92]

Roberts was the first to characterize exemption from payment of state and local taxes as a subsidy: "In effect the decision grants not free exercise of religion, in the sense that such exercise shall not be hindered or limited, but, on the other hand, requires that the exercise of religion be *subsidized.* Trinity Church, owning great property in New York City, devotes the income to religious ends. Must it, therefore, be exempt from paying its fair share of the cost of government's protection of its property?"[93] He also foresaw the difficulty of giving greater protection to those who claim benefits deriving from the Religion Clause than to those who claim benefits deriving from other First Amendment provisions: "We cannot ignore what this decision involves. If the First Amendment grants immunity from taxation to the exercise of religion it must equally grant a similar exemption to those who speak and to the press."[94]

After *Murdock* and *Follett,* the states acquiesced in a "hands-off" policy toward itinerant evangelists, generally imposing on them only those burdens that were strictly related to their actual impact on the communities in which they preached. For the most part, this meant that their religious activities were not taxed even though they partly consisted of the distribution of Bibles, tracts, and other literature for payment. Most states passed specific exemptions in their tax codes; others achieved the same result at the administrative level.[95]

In *Murdock* and *Follett* the Court was content to rest its decision on its reading of the free exercise provision, but the results are also harmonious with the requirements of the nonestablishment provision. For example, one of the more perplexing features of the established order in colonial Virginia was the use of licensure as a means of repressing speech of dissident and unpopular minorities.[96] The state practices at issue in *Murdock*

---

92. *Id.* at 581 (Roberts, J., dissenting).

93. *Id.* (Roberts, J., dissenting) (emphasis supplied). Dean Kelley supplies the empirical answer to Justice Roberts's rhetorical question: "Most church-owned businesses or investment properties used for purposes unrelated to the exempt purpose of the church pay property taxes like any other businesses. Trinity Parish in New York City, for instance, does indeed own a great deal of extremely valuable real estate on Manhattan Island. It also pays property taxes to the City of New York on all of it that is not actually used for religious purposes (that is, for chapels, cemeteries, schools). Most other jurisdictions also tax church-owned property that is not developed or not used for distinctly religious purposes." Dean M. Kelley, Why Churches Should Not Pay Taxes 17 (1977).

94. *Id.* at 581–82 (Roberts, J., dissenting).

95. *See* Jimmy Swaggart Ministries v. Board of Equalization of California, 493 U.S. 378 (1990), Brief for the Appellant, at 13.

96. *See* Thomas J. Curry, The First Freedoms: Church and State in America to the Passage of the First Amendment (1987) 69–70 (New York), 99 (Virginia), 118 (Connecticut), 171 (Massachusetts); Sanford H. Cobb, The Rise of Religious Liberty in America: A History (1902, reprint ed. 1968), at 126 (North Carolina), 174, 202–03 (Massachusetts), 273 (Connecticut), 317–18, 334–35, 344, 349–53 (New York), 390–94.

and *Follett* differed from established religion in the late colonial experience only in that burdensome taxation was added to licensure.

In 1742 James Davenport, a fiery preacher from Connecticut, was arrested for violating Virginia's law against itinerant preaching, tried by the colonial legislature, adjudged mentally disturbed, and deported under guard to Long Island.[97] In 1768 a Virginia prosecutor charged a group of zealous Baptist ministers in these words: "May it please your worship, these men are great disturbers of the peace: they cannot meet a man upon the road, but they must ram a text of scripture down his throat."[98] Another incident in colonial history had profound constitutional consequences; in May of 1774 James Madison witnessed "5 or 6 well meaning men in close Gaol for publishing their religious Sentiments which in the main are very orthodox."[99] These Separate Baptists had been imprisoned in Culpepper County for their refusal to seek a license to preach the word of God. This experience provided the spark for Madison's insight that linked nonestablishment with the "full and free exercise of religion."[100] With the end of establishment and the adoption of free exercise provisions in the various state constitutions, the right to proclaim the Gospel in unconventional, unsettling, and unpopular ways became recognized as one of the most fundamental elements of religious freedom. To end an established order in which the government decided who was fit to preach was to acknowledge the natural liberty to be free in religious concerns. In short, nonestablishment exists for the sake of free exercise.

Neither *Murdock* nor *Follett* yielded opinions grounded in both nonestablishment and free exercise concerns. Instead, court litigators and commentators began classifying or characterizing claims as having arisen under one provision or the other of the Religion Clause. After years of this way of thinking with inconsistent and incoherent results, the view emerged that the First Amendment contains competing provisions on religion, one favoring it (free exercise) and one opposed to it (nonestablishment). The Court would not address the issue of religious exemption from state and local sales taxes for another forty-five years. When it did so in *Texas Monthly* and *Jimmy Swaggart Ministries*, the theory implicit in *Murdock* and *Follett* had become fully explicit. State accommodation of transmission of religious literature was held to violate the nonestablishment provision in *Texas Monthly* because the statute did not expressly provide for similar benefits for nonreligious claims about transcendence. And in *Jimmy Swaggart Ministries* itinerant evangelists were held to have no free exercise claim to an immunity from the imposition of sales and use tax on the noncommercial distribution of religious materials to their fellow religious adherents for the purpose of advancing their religious doctrine.

Walz v. Tax Commission of the City of New York (1970)

I have already described above the use of history in the *Walz* case. In this section I analyze the legal arguments employed by the justices who wrote in the case. Since Jus-

---

97. *See* Ahlstrom, *supra* note 79, at 183–87.

98. Cobb, *supra* note 96, at 113.

99. James Madison to William Bradford, Jan. 24, 1774, 1 Madison Papers, *supra* note 1, at 105–06; *reprinted in* Noonan and Gaffney, Religious Freedom, *supra* note 1, at 159.

100. James Madison, 1 The Writings of James Madison 174 (1962), *as cited in* Noonan and Gaffney, *supra* note 1, at 163.

tice Douglas wrote the opinion of the Court in *Murdock* and *Follett*, I begin with his dissent in *Walz*.

As noted above, Justice Roberts expressed the view in dissent in *Follett* that exemption from payment of property tax amounts to a massive subsidy. The example he offered—commercial real estate in Manhattan owned by Trinity Church—was not a very telling one. As pointed out in the previous chapter, the two principal religious groups in the country—the National Council of Churches of Christ in the U.S.A. and the United States Catholic Conference—forged broad national consensus on the view that like any other nonprofit organization, religious communities should be required to pay tax on all business income that is unrelated to their exempt purposes. This would include rents or other profits from commercial real estate. Long before this issue was resolved in favor of taxing religious communities at the federal level, most states had already worked out similar formulas in the charters they granted to religious communities or in their general statutes governing religious tax exemption. With near unanimity, state law limits the definition of exempt property of religious communities to that which is used exclusively for religious purposes.

When the facts in *Follett* are explored more carefully, Roberts's argument proves thin because the correct answer to his hypothetical question is that religious communities such as Trinity Church do pay taxes on commercial real estate. Justice Douglas did not devote much time or energy rebutting Roberts's claim. Instead, he merely asserted that exemption "does not mean that religious undertakings must be subsidized. The exemption from a license tax of a preacher who preaches or a parishioner who listens does not mean that either is free from all financial burdens of government, including taxes on income or property."[101]

Twenty-seven years later, when Douglas was dissenting in *Walz*, he made subsidization of churches the linchpin of his argument that exemption is impermissible. In his dissent in *Walz*, he never alluded to the fact that he had casually rebuffed the concern about subsidization voiced by the dissent in *Follett*. What had caused Douglas to see things differently? Perhaps it was the decision in *Board of Education v. Allen*,[102] in which the Court sustained a state program of loaning textbooks on secular subjects, such as mathematics or chemistry, to students attending religious schools. There are three clues in Douglas's dissent in *Walz* that religious schools were the real focus of his concern. First, he expressed great alarm at the amount of federal funds appropriated for religious education as part of the Johnson administration's War on Poverty, and which would come to be litigated in *Aguilar, Agostini,* and *Mitchell v. Helms*.[103] Second, he cited in a footnote part of the oral argument in *Illinois ex rel. McCollum v. Board of Education* that characterized property tax exemption as a permissible subsidy if given "to religious faiths, equally."[104] Third, Douglas appended two documents to his dissent: Patrick Henry's bill for establishing a fund for a teacher of Christian religion in each town in

---

101. *Follett*, 321 U.S. at 577–78.

102. 392 U.S. 236 (1968). Chief Justice Burger cited *Allen* in *Walz*, 399 U.S. at 672.

103. Aguilar v. Felton, 473 U.S. 402 (1985) (provision of remedial reading and mathematics classes by public school teachers on premises of religious schools held impermissible because of potentially excessive entanglement of government with religion); Agostini v. Felton, 521 U.S. 203 (1997) (reversing *Aguilar* on identical facts); Mitchell v. Helms, 530 U.S. 793, 120 S.Ct. 2530, 2539 (2000) (provision of books, maps, and computers to eligible children attending religious as well as public schools permissible; reversing *Meek* and *Wolman* as "anomalies" in the case law); see discussion of these cases in Thomas C. Berg, "Religiously Affiliated Education," in this volume.

104. 333 U.S. 203 (1948).

Virginia, and James Madison's eloquent protest against Henry's proposed general assessment, which was defeated in 1785. On their face these documents have little to do with property tax exemption, but everything to do with the advancement of religious education. Justice Rutledge had also appended them to his dissent in the leading case on public funding of children attending religious schools, *Everson v. Board of Education*.[105]

The Walz Court relied on *Everson* to support its conclusion about provision of fire and police services to nonprofit organizations. Citing *Torcaso v. Watkins*[106] as more apposite than *Everson*, Douglas agreed with Justice Harlan that a tax exemption program restricted to religious believers would be impermissible. Harlan was content to make the observation that the New York statute probably extends to "groups whose avowed tenets may be antitheological, atheistic, or agnostic." Douglas did not, however, find any evidence in the record supporting Harlan's surmise.[107]

Finally, Douglas was unimpressed with the historical claim of long support for the policy made by Chief Justice Burger and Justice Brennan, because "it arose in the early days when the church was an agency of the state."[108]

Burger replied to Douglas's concern dismissively. First, he denied that exemption had yielded an established church: "If tax exemption can be seen as this first step toward 'establishment' of religion, as Mr. Justice Douglas fears, the second step has been long in coming."[109] Second, he assured his colleague, "Any move that realistically 'establishes' a church or tends to do so can be dealt with 'while the Court sits.'"[110]

Burger was confident that the Court could keep the practice of tax exemption from fostering attributes similar to those of an established religion. He sought to achieve this in part by adopting Harlan's proposal that an important indication that a practice tends toward establishment is that it tends to entangle the government excessively in religious matters. This criterion has been criticized both by other justices and by commentators, but it remains an important one that the Court still employs in cases dealing with public funding of children attending religious schools.[111]

In *Walz*, Burger thought of entanglement as an aspect of the possible effect of a policy or practice. The judicial function, he wrote, would be to ensure that "the end result—the effect—is not an excessive government entanglement with religion."[112] In the following year Burger would make this criterion an independent component of his three-part test in *Lemon v. Kurtzman*.[113] When cast in terms of excessiveness,

---

105. 330 U.S. 1 (1947).

106. 367 U.S. 488 (1961) (invalidating state prohibition against atheists serving in public office).

107. *Walz*, 399 U.S. at 700 (Douglas, J., dissenting).

108. *Id.* at 703 (Douglas, J., dissenting).

109. *Id.* at 678 (Douglas, J., dissenting).

110. *Id.*, *citing* Panhandle Oil Co. v. Mississippi *ex rel.* Knox, 277 U.S. 218, 223 (1928) (Holmes, J, dissenting).

111. *See, e.g.,* Mitchell v. Helms, 530 U.S. 793 (2000); Agostini v. Felton, 521 U.S. 203, 212 (1997).

112. *Walz*, 399 U.S. at 674.

113. "Every analysis in this area must begin with consideration of the cumulative criteria developed by the Court over many years. Three such tests may be gleaned from our cases. First, the statute must have a secular legislative purpose; second, its principal or primary effect must be one that neither advances nor inhibits religion; finally, the statute must not foster 'an excessive government entanglement with religion.'" Lemon v. Kurtzman, 403 U.S. 602, 613 (1971). In *Lemon* the Court relied primarily on the newly defined entanglement test to conclude that both state programs under review—a Rhode Island program offering salary supplements to teachers of secular subjects in religious schools, and a Pennsylvania program offering to purchase the services of teachers of sec-

the test was "inescapably one of degree." Specifically, Burger noted: "Either course, taxation of churches or exemption, occasions some degree of involvement with religion. Elimination of exemption would tend to expand the involvement of government by giving rise to tax valuation of church property, tax liens, tax foreclosures, and the direct confrontations and conflicts that follow in the train of those legal processes."[114]

In *Lemon*, Burger wrote that the kinds of entanglement the Court deemed to be prohibited were those that were "enduring." For example, in the programs under review in that case, inquiry had to be made about whether a subsidized teacher was limiting her instruction to nonreligious subjects. To discover the answer to that question meant that

> comprehensive, discriminating, and continuing state surveillance will inevitably be required to ensure that these restrictions are obeyed and the First Amendment otherwise respected. Unlike a book, a teacher cannot be inspected once so as to determine the extent and intent of his or her personal beliefs and subjective acceptance of the limitations imposed by the First Amendment. These prophylactic contacts will involve excessive and enduring entanglement between state and church.[115]

In tax cases, presumably this inquiry would require analysis of the determinations that must be made and the procedural interactions involved. I will return to this point in the discussion of *Jimmy Swaggart Ministries* below.

For Burger, another indicator of the permissibility of tax exemption is that the beneficiary class is broad.[116] It is not religious communities alone that enjoy this tax benefit, but all nonprofit charitable organizations. In the language of the New York statute under review in *Walz*, the exemption extended to "Real property owned by a corporation or association organized exclusively for the moral or mental improvement of men and women, or for religious, bible, tract, charitable, benevolent, missionary, hospital, infirmary, educational, public playground, scientific, literary, bar association, medical society, library, patriotic, historical or cemetery purposes...and used exclusively for carrying out thereupon one or more of such purposes."[117] Burger wrote: "if as in *Everson* buses can be provided to carry and policemen to protect church school pupils, we fail to see how a broader range of police and fire protection given equally to all churches, along with nonprofit hospitals, art galleries, and libraries receiving the same tax exemption, is different for purposes of the Religion Clauses."[118]

---

ular subjects in religious schools—were impermissible. *See* discussion in Thomas C. Berg, "Religiously Affiliated Education," in this volume.

114. *Walz*, 399 U.S. at 674.

115. *Lemon*, 403 U.S. at 619.

116. *See also* Rosenberger v. Rector and Visitors of the Univ. of Virginia, 515 U.S. 819 (1995); Lamb's Chapel v. Ctr. Moriches Union Free Sch. Dist., 508 U.S. 384 (1993); Witters v. Washington Dept. of Services for the Blind, 474 U.S. 481 (1986); Mueller v. Allen, 463 U.S. 388 (1983); Widmar v. Vincent, 454 U.S. 263 (1981).

117. New York Real Property Tax Law, McKinney's Consol.Laws, c. 50, §420, subd. 1; *see also* N.Y. Const. Art. 16, §1, which provides in relevant part: "Exemptions from taxation may be granted only by general laws. Exemptions may be altered or repealed except those exempting real or personal property used exclusively for religious, educational or charitable purposes as defined by law and owned by any corporation or association organized or conducted exclusively for one or more of such purposes and not operating for profit." As cited in *Walz*, 397 U.S. at 666–67.

118. *Walz*, 399 U.S. at 671.

All of the other three justices who wrote in *Walz* also stressed this fact.[119] For example, in his separate concurring opinion Justice Brennan wrote:

> The very breadth of this scheme of exemptions negates any suggestion that the State intends to single out religious organizations for special preference. The scheme is not designed to inject any religious activity into a nonreligious context, as was the case with school prayers. No particular activity of a religious organization—for example, the propagation of its beliefs—is specially promoted by the exemptions. They merely facilitate the existence of a broad range of private, non-profit organizations, among them religious groups, by leaving each free to come into existence, then to flourish or wither, without being burdened by real property taxes.[120]

Brennan took this fact in a different direction, justifying the inclusion of religious communities among the other nonprofit entities for two reasons that he thought would meet the requirement of secularity of a statute's purpose. First, religious communities, "among a range of other private, nonprofit organizations contribute to the well-being of the community in a variety of *nonreligious* ways, and thereby bear burdens that would otherwise either have to be met by general taxation, or be left undone, to the detriment of the community."[121] Second, inclusion of religious communities among nonprofit organizations reflected well the pluralism of American society: "Government may properly include religious institutions among the variety of private, nonprofit groups that receive tax exemptions, for each group contributes to the diversity of association, viewpoint, and enterprise essential to a vigorous, pluralistic society."[122]

Brennan's justification for the practice of religious tax exemption—linking it to secular benefit—contains the kernel of a good idea. The secularity requirement can be understood to mean that legislation must have a broad general purpose, not one that favors a particular religious community or tradition, or even one that favors religious ideas over nonreligious ones. For example, the Williamsburg Charter, a bicentennial document celebrating religious freedom, put it this way:

> [A] right for one is a right for another and a responsibility for all. A right for a Protestant is a right for an Orthodox is a right for a Catholic is a right for a Jew is a right for a Humanist is a right for a Mormon is a right for a Muslim is a right for a Buddhist—and for the followers of any other faith within the wide bounds of the republic. That rights are universal and responsibilities mutual is both the premise and the promise of democratic pluralism. The First Amendment, in this sense, is the epitome of public justice and serves as the golden rule for civic life. Rights are best guarded and responsibilities best exercised when each person and group guards for all others those rights they wish guarded for themselves.[123]

Brennan wrote powerfully about nondiscrimination in *Larson v. Valente*: "The clearest command of the Establishment Clause is that one religious denomination cannot be

---

119. *Id.* at 689 (Brennan, J. concurring); at 697 (Harlan, J. concurring; at 707 (Douglas, J. dissenting).

120. *Id.* at 689 (Brennan, J. concurring).

121. *Id.* at 689 (Brennan, J. concurring) (emphasis added), *citing* 1938 N.Y. Constitutional Convention, Report of the Committee on Taxation, Doc. No. 2, p. 2.

122. *Id.* at 689 (Brennan, J. concurring), *citing* Washington Ethical Society v. District of Columbia, 249 F.2d 127, 129 (D.C. Cir. 1957).

123. The Williamsburg Charter, 8 J.L. & Relig. 1, 18 (1990).

officially preferred over another.... Free exercise...can be guaranteed only when legisla-tors—and voters—are required to accord to their own religions the very same treat-ment given to small, new, or unpopular denominations."[124] Similarly, nondiscrimina-tion has emerged as a strong principle in cases dealing with public assistance to various secular aspects of education in religious schools (which is not the same thing as reli-gious education).[125] For example, Justice O'Connor wrote in *Agostini v. Felton* that aid is not likely to advance religion if it "is allocated on the basis of neutral, secular criteria that neither favor nor disfavor religion, and is made available to both religious and sec-ular beneficiaries on a nondiscriminatory basis."[126]

Neither Brennan nor many constitutional commentators have expressly connected the secularity requirement with nondiscrimination. Unless this link is forged, Brennan's approach could lead in the direction of governmental definition of religion and quan-tification of its "good works" according to some secular calculus of utility. Whether for this reason or another, the *Walz* Court chose not to adopt Brennan's suggestion that ex-emption was permissible to the degree that a religious community engages in tasks of which the government approves. In other words, far from guarding against the danger of an established religion, Brennan's approach could lead in the direction of established religion and the denial of free exercise. How a particular religious community defines itself and how it comprehends its mission to include service to the world are theological questions that have divided religious communities sharply. They are, in short, issues at the heart of free exercise of religion,[127] and may be seen as being beyond the ken of gov-ernment.[128] The exempt status of a religious organization cannot be made to stand or fall upon its proof of "good deeds" in a measure satisfactory to a tax official. Thus the Court rightly rejected any specific quid pro quo between tax exemption and perfor-mance of social service. As Burger put it:

> We find it unnecessary to justify the tax exemption on the social welfare ser-vices or 'good works' that some churches perform for parishioners and others—family counselling, aid to the elderly and the infirm, and to children. Churches vary substantially in the scope of such services; programs expand or contract according to resources and need. As public-sponsored programs en-large, private aid from the church sector may diminish. The extent of social services may vary, depending on whether the church serves an urban or rural, a rich or poor constituency. To give emphasis to so variable an aspect of the work of religious bodies would introduce an element of governmental evalua-tion and standards as to the worth of particular social welfare programs, thus producing a kind of continuing day-to-day relationship which the policy of neutrality seeks to minimize. Hence, the use of a social welfare yardstick as a significant element to qualify for tax exemption could conceivably give rise to confrontations that could escalate to constitutional dimensions.[129]

---

124. 456 U.S. 228, 244–45 (1982) (charitable solicitation statute invalid because of disparate treatment of older mainstream religious communities and new religious movements).

125. *See* Berg, *supra* note 103.

126. Agostini v. Felton, 521 U.S. 203, 231 (1997); *see also* Mitchell v. Helms, 530 U.S. 793 (2000).

127. *See, e.g.,* Douglas Laycock, Towards a General Theory of the Religion Clauses: The Case of Church Labor Relations and the Right to Church Autonomy, 81 Colum. L. Rev. 1373 (1981).

128. *See, e.g.,* Carl H. Esbeck, The Establishment Clause as a Structural Restraint on Govern-mental Power, 84 Iowa L. Rev. 1 (1998); *see also* Esbeck, Establishment Clause Limits on Govern-mental Interference with Religious Organizations, 41 Wash. & Lee L. Rev. 347 (1984).

129. 397 U.S. at 674.

There is an admirable flexibility in this part of Burger's opinion, one that respects important differences in the ways in which religious communities define themselves. This concern that communities and intermediate groups be able to set the conditions for their own development was absent in Burger's opinion for the Court in *Bob Jones University v. United States*,[130] requiring the revocation of exempt status of a church-related university for maintaining a policy of student discipline that forbade interracial dating or marriage. As suggested in the previous chapter, this result could have been justified solely on the ground that tax policy may not be used to advance racial discrimination.[131] Missing an opportunity to realize when less would have been more, Burger created in *Bob Jones University* two more "tests" described with such looseness that they easily could be given much broader effect than necessary. Burger wrote that a religious organization might lose its exempt status by failing to conform with some "public policy" announced by the Internal Revenue Service, or by failing to "serve and be in harmony with the public interest."[132]

Witte took issue with these views. As in his historical work on state law, he offers a more nuanced appreciation of the origin of "social benefit" theories of tax exemption in attempts to justify the exemption on properties devoted to "religious uses."[133]

> [R]eligious uses of property dispense a sufficiently unique form of social benefits and discharge a sufficiently large number of state burdens to warrant their inclusion as a separate category of tax exemption.... The social tasks discharged by one religious property might far outweigh the amount of tax that could have been collected from the property; for other religious properties this might be not be true. But, on the whole, society is better off, the state is more efficiently run, and religious bodies are more free to exercise their ministries if their properties are exempt from taxation.[134]

Interesting as I find Witte's explanation of the origins of this idea, I do not think the Court was wrong to reject the formulation of the idea that Brennan put forth in his concurring opinion in *Walz*. Attempts by the government to define religious uses tend to violate both the nonestablishment principle, by overstepping the limits of governmental power, and the free exercise principle, either by crude intrusion upon religious convictions or by more subtle if unintended encouragement of them. A much more satisfactory justification of tax exemption is that it enables all nonprofit organizations, whether religious or nonreligious, to assist in noncommercial ways to address societal issues in public life.

Another important issue in *Walz* was whether exemptions should be characterized as subsidies. Stanley Surrey, who served as assistant secretary of the treasury in the Kennedy administration, devised the budget planning device known as tax expenditures.[135] By defining all revenue losses occurring through exemptions, deductions, and credits, this enabled

---

130. 461 U.S. 574 (1983).

131. *See* Edward McGlynn Gaffney, "Exemption of Religious Organizations from Federal Taxation," in this volume.

132. *Id.* at 591–92; for criticism of the Burger opinion in *Bob Jones University*, see Robert M. Cover, The Supreme Court, 1982 Term—Foreword: Nomos and Narrative, 97 Harv. L. Rev. 4, 26 (1983); Mayer G. Freed and Daniel D. Polsby, Race, Religion, and Public Policy: *Bob Jones University v. United States*, 1983 Sup. Ct. Rev. 1; Richard A. Epstein, The Supreme Court, 1987 Term—Foreword: Unconstitutional Conditions, State Power, and the Limits of Consent, 102 Harv. L. Rev. 4, 95–96 (1988).

133. Witte, Tax Exemption of Religious Property, *supra* note 29, at 211–12.

134. *Id.* at 212.

135. *See, e.g.*, Stanley Surrey, Pathways to Tax Reform: The Concept of Tax Expenditures (1973).

both Congress and the Executive to make better informed policy decisions. On the other hand, Boris Bittker argued that it is not proper to include the income of nonprofit organizations within a tax expenditure budget.[136]

I offer two reasons—one historical, the other theoretical—in favor of Bittker's view. First, Congress has never defined "income" to include contributions to charitable or nonprofit organizations. For example, Senator Cordell Hull—principal author of the Revenue Act of 1913, the first income tax law enacted after the ratification of the Sixteenth Amendment—resisted explicit categories of exemption because the law was designed to impose explicit categories of *taxation* and assumed that all not listed would be exempt. Hull stated on the floor of the Senate: "Of course any kind of society or corporation that is not doing business for profit and not acquiring profit would not come within the meaning of the taxing clause.... I see no occasion whatever for undertaking to particularize...."[137] Second, the limit of the utility of applying Surrey's device to religious organizations is discovered in the nonestablishment principle, which prohibits expenditures of public funds to advance religion. Since this is so, why encumber the budgetary planning process with details that are, in the end, irrelevant to the construction of a budget?

Constitutional scholars are also divided about how to characterize exemptions. For example, Donald Giannella distinguished tax exemptions and subsidies as follows: "In the case of direct subsidy, the state forcibly diverts the income of both believers and nonbelievers to churches. In the case of an exemption, the state merely refrains from diverting to its own uses income independently generated by the churches through voluntary contributions."[138] I offer two reasons, one historical and the other theoretical, in support of Giannella. First, exemption has become a standard practice in all fifty states and the territories, in no small part because of the impracticality of any alternative policy. The issue of characterization raises its head again. Is a physical structure that houses a religious community at prayer to be comprehended as though it were commercial real estate? If so, how should its value be assessed? It is hard enough to determine the fair market value of a parcel of land with its improvements, whether it is residential or commercial real estate. How is a tax assessor to determine the fair market value of a building like St. Patrick's Cathedral? By its potential value if the land were sold to a developer willing to level the church structure and put up yet another high-rise building on Fifth Avenue?

To posit such hypothetical questions is to understand why we have reached an accord in America that they should not be raised in real life. To predicate an actual tax evaluation on such a speculative basis would itself violate common sense. There might be a willing buyer, such as Donald Trump, but at the moment there is not a willing seller. The people of the Archdiocese of New York wish to continue to use this site as "sacred space," dedicated—as the New York statute reads—to "exclusive use for religious worship." How shall religious worship be defined? Only the religious community can answer that question. When the government tries to do so, as it did in the protracted con-

---

136. *See* Boris I. Bittker, Churches, Taxes, and the Constitution, 78 Yale L.J. 1285 1304–10 (1969); Boris I. Bittker and George K. Radhert, The Exemption of Nonprofit Organizations from Federal Income Taxation, 81 Yale L.J. 299 (1976).

137. 50 Cong. Rec. 1306 (1913).

138. Donald Giannella, Religious Liberty, Nonestablishment, and Doctrinal Development, pt. II, 81 Harv. L. Rev. 513, 553 (1968); *see also* Paul Freund, Public Aid to Parochial Schools, 82 Harv. L. Rev. 1680, 1687 n. 16 (1969) ("the symbolism of tax exemption is significant as a manifestation that organized religion is not expected to support the state; by the same token the state is not expected to support the church"); *see also* Herb Titus, No Taxation or Subsidation: Two Indispensable Principles of Religion, 22 Cumb. L. Rev. 505 (1992).

flict over the definition of an integrated auxiliary of a church, it passes beyond its competence and jurisdiction into the prerogative of the religious community. Second, at a more abstract level, the very formulation of Surrey's clever device—tax expenditure—conjoins two distinct powers, taxing and spending, as though they were one. If a legislature enacts a tax exemption provision that is neutral and nondiscriminatory, the judiciary should normally defer to that decision without redefining it as though it were an affirmative act of legislation appropriating funds for an illicit purpose.

The *Walz* Court was also divided over whether exemptions constitute an impermissible subsidy. I noted above that Justice Douglas dissented in *Walz* on the ground that the property tax at issue was a subsidy. None of the other justices agreed. Analyzing this issue in terms of the entanglement concern, Chief Justice Burger wrote:

> Granting tax exemptions to churches necessarily operates to afford an indirect economic benefit and also gives rise to some, but yet a lesser, involvement than taxing them. In analyzing either alternative the questions are whether the involvement is excessive, and whether it is a continuing one calling for official and continuing surveillance leading to an impermissible degree of entanglement. Obviously a direct money subsidy would be a relationship pregnant with involvement and, as with most governmental grant programs, could encompass sustained and detailed administrative relationships for enforcement of statutory or administrative standards, but that is not this case.[139]

In his concurring opinion Justice Brennan cited Giannella and Bittker favorably, and he acknowledged that "[g]eneral subsidies of religious activities would...constitute impermissible state involvement with religion." But he concluded that "tax exemptions and general subsidies...are qualitatively different."[140]

> Though both provide economic assistance, they do so in fundamentally different ways. A subsidy involves the direct transfer of public monies to the subsidized enterprise and uses resources exacted from taxpayers as a whole. An exemption, on the other hand, involves no such transfer. It assists the exempted enterprise only passively, by relieving a privately funded venture of the burden of paying taxes. Tax exemptions, accordingly, constitute mere passive state involvement with religion and not the affirmative involvement characteristic of outright governmental subsidy.[141]

In an important footnote, Brennan amplified on the subsidy theme by stating expressly that "fire and police protection received by houses of religious worship are no more than incidental benefits accorded all persons or institutions within a State's boundaries, along with many other exempt organizations" and also by noting that the record did not contain any "arguable quantitative correlation between the payment of an ad valorem property tax and the receipt of these municipal benefits."[142]

Justice Harlan proposed that tax exemption is permissible under the circumstances of a statute like the one before the Court in *Walz* that "created a general class so broad that it would be difficult to conclude that religious organizations cannot properly be included in it."[143] Harlan supposed, for example, that the property tax exemption in New

---

139. 397 U.S. at 674–75.
140. *Id.* at 689 (Brennan, J., concurring).
141. *Id.* at 690–91 (Brennan, J., concurring).
142. *Id.* at 691, n. 10 (Brennan, J., concurring).
143. *Id.* at 697 (Harlan, J., concurring).

York extends to "groups whose avowed tenets may be antitheological, atheistic, or agnostic."[144] Although Douglas objected to the speculative character of Harlan's musing on this point, he agreed that any tax exemption scheme that preferred religious believers over nonbelievers was unconstitutional.

Harlan could agree with Douglas that one could think of an exemption as a subsidy in the loosest or broadest sense of the term—that is, a benefit. But he urged several distinctions between an outright grant (a subsidy, strictly speaking) and a governmental decision to refrain from collecting revenue from a person or a corporation. In the majority opinion, Burger also drew sharp contrasts between an exemption and a subsidy. A subsidy, he explained, would require continuous inspection and surveillance to ensure that the funds were being spent in accordance with the requirements of the federal statute and the Constitution.

Eight justices in *Walz* determined that the property tax exemption was not an impermissible subsidy. On this matter the justices are as susceptible to a change of mind or heart as any of us. For example, Douglas was quite certain in *Follett* that exemption was not a subsidy, and just as certain in *Walz* that it was. Brennan was certain in *Walz* that it was not a subsidy; as we shall see, he no longer held that view when he wrote the plurality opinion in *Texas Monthly*.[145]

The Thurgood Marshall Papers in the Library of Congress disclose that upon receipt of the chief justice's first draft in the *Walz* case, a prescient law clerk with the initials "tog" wrote a short memorandum expressing the view that the Burger draft contained

> serious substantive problems. First, there are hints that property taxation might violate free exercise—hints I wouldn't go along with. Second, and more serious, the opinion apparently holds (see last paragraph) that *all* exemptions for religions are ok. I would merely uphold a church tax exemption fitted into a broader exemption for non-profit organizations of all kinds, as set out in the NY statute (see footnote 1). If New York stripped down to what is provided in the state constitution, exemptions only for churches, I would find the most serious establishment clause dangers.[146]

It would be nearly twenty years after *Walz* that the Court would come to adopt this view in *Texas Monthly* and *Jimmy Swaggart Ministries*.

Texas Monthly v. Bullock (1989) and *Jimmy Swaggart Ministries* (1990)

In 1989 the Court ruled in *Texas Monthly, Inc. v. Bullock*[147] that the nonestablishment principle required the invalidity of a statute that conferred tax immunity on the distribution of religious literature without conferring a similar benefit on the distribu-

---

144. *Id.* Douglas objected that there was no support for this in the record. *Id.* at 700 (Douglas, J. dissenting).

145. *Texas Monthly*, 489 U.S. at 899 (sales tax exemption was invalid because it was a "subsidy exclusively to religious organizations").

146. Signed: tog; dated 2/16/70. Collections of the Manuscript Division, Library of Congress, Box 60, Folder 9.

147. 489 U.S. 1 (1989).

tion of nonreligious literature.[148] In the following year the Court ruled in *Jimmy Swaggart Ministries v. California State Board of Equalization*[149] that the free exercise principle does not require a state to confer tax immunity on the distribution of religious literature at all. Read together, these two cases not only express the current state of federal constitutional law on the subject, but also offer important clues about the kinds of public reasons that may be more persuasive than others in the increasingly difficult climate in which state and local government must function. This section of this chapter describes the Court's legal reasoning in these two cases, and discusses broad principles that can guide conversation about religious tax immunity between representatives of the people in state and local government and leaders of religious communities in the years ahead.

The interval between *Walz* and *Texas Monthly* was nearly three decades, during which several new developments influenced a change of attitude on critical issues before the Court. First, during the 1970s several factors—taxpayer revolts protesting high property tax bills, unfunded federal mandates, public-sector collective bargaining, high inflation, and high unemployment—combined to make it increasingly difficult for state and local government to make ends meet. Budget cuts are always possible, but not very feasible when the services on the chopping block are truly essential (for example, fire fighters, police officers, teachers). Under these circumstances it is understandable that state and local officials would explore all possibilities, including cutting back on exemptions or removing them altogether. Second, Surrey's influential volume appeared three years after *Walz*; Congress and several state legislatures soon incorporated its principal recommendations into their regular budget planning. Third, courts absorbed the new discourse about tax basis. For example, in *Regan v. Taxation with Representation of Washington*, Justice Rehnquist characterized exemptions as follows: "Both tax exemptions and tax-deductibility are a form of *subsidy* that is administered through the tax system. A tax exemption has much the same effect as a *cash grant* to the organization of the amount of tax it would have to pay on its income. Deductible contributions are similar to cash grants of the amount of a portion of the individual's contributions."[150] Fourth, leading constitutional commentators familiar with economic analysis incorporated this mode of thinking into their work, referring to both tax exemptions and direct cash appropriations as subsidies.[151]

Against this background it is not surprising that six years after the Rehnquist opinion referred to above, Brennan in *Texas Monthly* described exemption as "state sponsorship of religious belief"[152] and equated it with a "*subsidy* exclusively to religious organizations that is not required by the Free Exercise Clause and that either burdens nonbeneficiaries markedly or cannot reasonably be seen as removing a sig-

---

148. *See* Tex. Tax Code Ann. § 151.312 (1982).

149. 493 U.S. 378 (1990).

150. Regan v. Taxation With Representation of Washington, 461 U.S. 540, 544 (1983).

151. *See, e.g.*, Michael W. McConnell and Richard A. Posner, An Economic Approach to Issues of Religious Freedom, 56 U. Chi. L. Rev. 1 (1989). Without citing Surrey or discussing the tax expenditure theory, the authors analyze in economic terms a variety of issues decided under the Religion Clause, such as exemption of religious property from taxation, *id.* at 12–13, and public support for religious education, *id.* at 14–32; in a manner closely resembling what Laycock calls "substantive neutrality," they offer economic arguments to the effect that government should minimize incentives for or against religious practices, *id.* at 37–38.

152. *Texas Monthly,* 489 U.S. at 15.

nificant state-imposed deterrent to the free exercise of religion."[153] Brennan described the result in *Mueller v. Allen*[154] as follows: "we upheld a state income tax deduction for the cost of tuition, transportation, and nonreligious textbooks paid by a taxpayer for the benefit of a dependent. To be sure, the deduction aided parochial schools and parents whose children attended them, as well as nonsectarian private schools and their pupils' parents. We did not conclude, however, that this *subsidy* deprived the law of an overriding secular purpose or effect."[155] He described the property tax exemption in *Walz* as one that accorded "sizable tax savings [to] religious groups."[156]

Turning to the exemption from sales tax on the distribution of religious literature at issue in *Texas Monthly*, Brennan wrote:

> Every tax exemption constitutes a *subsidy* that affects nonqualifying taxpayers, forcing them to become "indirect and vicarious donors" [citing *Bob Jones University v. United States* and *Regan v. Taxation with Representation of Wash.*]. Insofar as that *subsidy* is conferred upon a wide array of nonsectarian groups as well as religious organizations in pursuit of some legitimate secular end, the fact that religious groups benefit incidentally does not deprive the *subsidy* of the secular purpose and primary effect mandated by the Establishment Clause. However, when government directs a *subsidy* exclusively to religious organizations that is not required by the Free Exercise Clause and that either burdens nonbeneficiaries markedly or cannot reasonably be seen as removing a significant state-imposed deterrent to the free exercise of religion, as Texas has done, it "provide[s] unjustifiable awards of assistance to religious organizations" and cannot but "conve[y] a message of endorsement" to slighted members of the community. This is particularly true where, as here, the *subsidy* is targeted at writings that promulgate the teachings of religious faiths.[157]

Having reached this conclusion, Brennan reduced the vitality of the two precedents from the 1940s discussed above, *Murdock* and *Follett*, which were limited to their precise facts. "To the extent that language in those opinions is inconsistent with our decision here, based on the evolution in our thinking about the Religion Clauses over the last 45 years, we disavow it."[158]

Disavow *Murdock*—a decision the Witnesses had barely won, at enormous cost and against great odds—on the basis of the Court's evolution in thinking about the Religion Clause(s)? Not all evolution is progress. The intervening half century had seen an increasing complexity in state and local sales and use tax, which had been invented in the 1930s as a flat tax (one percent) to pay for unemployment insurance during the Great Depression. It slowly "evolved," to use Brennan's term, into the most complicated and burdensome form of taxation ever devised.[159] *Texas Monthly* was not a collection case by the government against a religious community asserting a viola-

---

153. *Id.* (emphasis added).
154. 463 U.S. 388 (1983).
155. *Id.* at 10–11 (emphasis added).
156. *Id.* at 11.
157. *Id.* at 14–15 (emphasis added).
158. *Id.* at 21.
159. *See* description of state and local sales and use tax in text accompanying note 185, *infra*.

tion of its free exercise. Like *Walz*, it was a case brought by a taxpayer claiming that its tax liability was greater than it would have been without a statute that violated the nonestablishment provision. In a case in which the government was the only party defending religious freedom, it was unsurprising that the Court concluded as it did. Under the rationale of *Texas Monthly*, the Witnesses could be subjected to sales tax for "selling" their religious treatises as though they were engaged in a commercial transaction.

In *Murdock* the Court had ruled that it would be as impermissible to impose on itinerant evangelists an occupational license tax as it would be to impose a tax on delivering a sermon. In *Texas Monthly* the Brennan plurality of three justices required full compliance with the most complicated form of taxation ever devised: sales and use tax. The language about taxing a sermon disappeared. In its stead was discourse borrowed from the state's brief about how neutral and nondiscriminatory the Texas Tax Code is. The focus was on the form of the tax rather than on the effect that a narrowing construction of *Murdock* would have on the ministry of the evangelists like the Witnesses.

The result in *Texas Monthly* was not driven by a shift in tax theory that turned exemptions into subsidies, but by a statute that on its face offered to religious believers an economic benefit that was apparently unavailable to nonbelievers. The Court did not hear from any religious community in this case. None was a party or intervenor, and none filed a brief amicus curiae, even at the Supreme Court level. No religious community objected to a serious matter of church/state law being pursued by a commercial enterprise with dubious standing.[160] Perhaps the leaders of religious communities and their counsel assumed that *Texas Monthly* would simply follow *Walz*. Or perhaps they assumed that it was not proper for litigators or courts to expand tax categories, which it is normally the prerogative of legislatures to determine. In any event, no one in the *Texas Monthly* litigation presented a plausible construction of the statute that would have saved it by including others in a broader beneficiary class. The very fact that a court would not write a broader tax statute in order to save it from constitutional infirmity is, of course, no reason for the legislature not to amend the statute to bring it into compliance with constitutional requirements. Thus a legislature may create exemptions from sales and use tax that benefit all viewpoints *on religious matters*, those of believers and of nonbelievers.[161]

Construed to encourage religious belief and practice, the Texas statute violated the principle of substantive neutrality, which Douglas Laycock has described as the requirement that the government "minimize the extent to which it either encourages or discourages religious belief or disbelief, practice or nonpractice, observance or nonobservance."[162] Seen as a measure that was not evenhanded in religious matters, the statute

---

160. *See, e.g.*, Valley Forge Christian College v. Americans United for Separation of Church and State, 454 U.S. 464 (1982). The State of Texas argued the standing issue perfunctorily. Brief of Appellees, 7–10. Justice Brennan did likewise, citing but not discussing *Valley Forge* and concluding summarily: "Texas cannot strip appellant of standing by changing the law after taking its money." *Texas Monthly*, 489 U.S. at 7–8.

161. *See* Michael W. McConnell, The Problem of Singling Out Religion, 50 DePaul L. Rev. 1 (2000).

162. Douglas Laycock, Formal, Substantive, and Disaggregated Neutrality Toward Religion, 39 DePaul L. Rev. 993, 1001 (1990).

violated the closely related principle of nondiscrimination, which has been advanced as an aspect of both nonestablishment[163] and free exercise.[164]

The most important lesson that religious leaders must learn from *Texas Monthly* is that they probably will not—and in any event should not—prevail if the government singles out religious communities to confer upon them special privileges or immunities that are not available to other nonprofit organizations. Brennan focused on the fact that the Texas statute exempted from taxation the sales of "periodicals published or distributed by religious faith and consisting wholly of writings promulgating the teaching of the faith" and held that a statute that narrow in scope lacked sufficient breadth for compliance with the nonestablishment provision.[165]

The principal case that Brennan relied on for this conclusion was *Walz*, in which the state had "not singled out one particular church or religious group or even churches as such; rather, it has granted exemption to all houses of religious worship within a broad class of property owned by nonprofit, quasi-public corporations which include hospitals, libraries, playgrounds, scientific, professional, historical, and patriotic groups."[166] By contrast, wrote Brennan, the Texas statute "put an imprimatur on one religion, or on religion as such."[167] Alluding to Justice O'Connor's endorsement test, Brennan also wrote that government "may not place its prestige, coercive authority, or resources behind a single religious faith or behind religious belief in general, compelling nonadherents to support the practices or proselytizing of favored religious organizations and conveying the message that those who do not contribute gladly are less than full members of the community."[168]

Only two other justices, Stevens and Marshall, joined in Brennan's plurality opinion. O'Connor was not lured by Brennan's citation of her contribution to nonestablishment jurisprudence. Instead, she joined Justice Blackmun's opinion concurring in the judgment, which expressed the view that it is

> difficult to reconcile in this case the Free Exercise and Establishment Clause values. The Free Exercise Clause suggests that a special exemption for religious

---

163. *See, e.g.,* Agostini v. Felton, 521 U.S. 203, 231 (1997); *see also* Mitchell v. Helms, 530 U.S. 793 (2000) (aid is not likely to advance religion if it "is allocated on the basis of neutral, secular criteria that neither favor nor disfavor religion, and is made available to both religious and secular beneficiaries on a nondiscriminatory basis"); Larson v. Valente, 456 U.S. 228, 244–45 (1982) ("The clearest command of the Establishment Clause is that one religious denomination cannot be officially preferred over another"); *see* generally Michael A. Paulsen, Religion, Equality, and the Constitution: An Equal Protection Approach to Establishment Clause Adjudication, 61 Notre Dame L. Rev. 311 (1986).

164. *See, e.g.,* Church of Lukumi Babalu Aye v. City of Hialeah, 508 U.S. 520, 532 (1993) ("At a minimum, the protections of the Free Exercise Clause pertain if the law at issue discriminates against some or all religious beliefs."); Employment Division v. Smith, 494 U.S. 872, 877 (1990) (government may not "impose special disabilities on the basis of religious views or religious status"); *Jimmy Swaggart Ministries*, 493 U.S. at 390 (violation of free exercise to "single out" religious activity "for special and burdensome treatment"); Hobbie v. Unemployment Appeals Comm'n, 480 U.S. 136, 148 (1987) (Stevens, J., concurring) (the Free Exercise Clause "protect[s] religious observers against unequal treatment").

165. *Texas Monthly*, 489 U.S. at 14.

166. *Id.* at 12, *citing Walz*, 397 U.S., at 673.

167. *Id.* at 9, *citing* Gillette v. United States, 401 U.S. 437, 450 (1971).

168. *Id.* at 9, *citing* Lynch v. Donnelly, 465 U.S. 668, 688 (1984) (O'Connor, J., concurring); Justice Brennan also cited his dissent in *Lynch*, 465 U.S. at 701 (Brennan, J., dissenting) (the nonestablishment provision was designed to prevent "religious chauvinism" that tells "minority religious groups, as well as…those who may reject all religion,…that their views are not similarly worthy of public recognition nor entitled to public support").

books is required. The Establishment Clause suggests that a special exemption for religious books is forbidden. This tension between mandated and prohibited religious exemptions is well recognized. Of course, identifying the problem does not resolve it.[169]

Of course, identifying the wrong problem—how to "reconcile" two "conflicting" provisions—will not resolve *that* problem, but we might make progress if we were to question whether the two provisions really are or ought to be viewed as being in tension or competition with one another, as some theorists imagine. Some of the tension could be eased by appreciating nonestablishment as a way of allowing, in Madison's phrase, "full and free exercise of religion."

Blackmun's opinion remains a classic expression of the view that the Religion Clause contains two provisions in combat with one another. Thus he could criticize both Brennan's opinion, for resolving the tension by "subordinat[ing] the Free Exercise value, even, it seems to me, at the expense of longstanding precedents...*Follett* and *Murdock* to the extent inconsistent with the newfound proposition that a State generally may tax the sale of a Bible by a church," and Scalia's dissent for "subordinat[ing] the Establishment Clause value...running afoul of the previously settled notion that government may not favor religious belief over disbelief."[170] Blackmun almost succeeded in overcoming the conflict he saw in the Religion Clause when he expressed the desire to decide *Texas Monthly* without sacrificing either the free exercise value or the nonestablishment value. In deciding the case, however, he concurred in the judgment and left for another day the question of what to do with a case squarely presenting a free exercise claim.[171] Although in the end Blackmun could not tear himself away from the conflict model, he did write perceptively in *Texas Monthly* a formula for a win/win solution in which both religious communities and nonbelievers would be treated in a substantively neutral, nondiscriminatory, nonentangling way:

> It is possible for a State to write a tax-exemption statute consistent with both values: for example, a state statute might exempt the sale not only of religious literature distributed by a religious organization but also of philosophical literature distributed by nonreligious organizations devoted to such matters of conscience as life and death, good and evil, being and nonbeing, right and wrong.[172]

Scalia, joined by Rehnquist and Kennedy, filed a strong dissent that began: "As a judicial demolition project, today's decision is impressive."[173] Scalia observed that the formalistic distinction drawn by Brennan between one kind of tax or another makes little sense in constitutional analysis, which normally rests at a different order of generalization than the specific form of tax at issue. Thus he expanded the inquiry to "sales taxes on items other than publications and to other types of taxes such as property, income, amusement, and motor vehicle taxes—all of which are likewise affected by today's holding." He noted that all of the states that have sales and use tax[174] "provide exemp-

---

169. *Id.* at 27, *citing Walz*, 397 U.S. at 668–69.

170. *Id.* at 27 (citations omitted).

171. *Id.* at 27, 28.

172. *Id.* at 27–28.

173. *Id.* at 29 (Scalia, J., dissenting) (a third of the states that have sales and use tax had statutes similar to that at issue in *Texas Monthly*).

174. Only Alaska, Delaware, Montana, New Hampshire, and Oregon do not have state sales taxes.

tions for religious groups without analogous exemptions for other types of nonprofit institutions."[175]

One curious thing about the Brennan and Scalia opinions is that the justices "fundamentally disagreed on almost every issue in the case, but they both claimed to be neutral. Both of them used the word 'neutrality,' but neither of them defined it."[176] What the Brennan, Blackmun, and Scalia opinions in *Texas Monthly* share in common is the view of the Religion Clause as containing two conflicting provisions that are difficult to reconcile. Scalia used the Scylla and Charybdis metaphor referred to above, accusing Brennan of "completely block[ing] off the already narrow channel" between these two dangers "by saying that what is not required cannot be allowed."[177] Blackmun's concurring opinion set up the question that the Court answered unanimously in *Jimmy Swaggart Ministries*.[178]

Assume for the moment that the starting point in the discussion about the Religion Clause is that it contains two conflicting provisions. Assume further that the Court has ruled correctly in *Texas Monthly* that the nonestablishment provision prohibits a statute exempting only the transmission of religious ideas. As a matter of formal logic, the Court's effort in *Jimmy Swaggart Ministries* is an account of how and why to relieve the tension supposed to exist between the two provisions. At least the Court did not come to the conclusion that the free exercise principle required what the nonestablishment principle prohibited. But at a different level of analysis, the Court's opinion seems inattentive to what Holmes cherished more dearly: experience, not logic.[179] In particular, the Court needlessly diminished the historic significance of the decisions in *Murdock* and *Follett*. Contrary to the briefing of the American Civil Liberties Union,[180] which O'Connor repeated in her opinion, the appellant in *Jimmy Swaggart Ministries*[181] did not rely "almost exclusively" upon *Murdock* and *Follett*. For example, the brief addressed the history of discrimination against itinerant evangelists such as Jimmy Swaggart, the lack of nexus between the out-of-state evangelist and the taxing authority, and the myriad ways in which the government became entangled in the life of the religious community by enforcing the tax at issue.[182]

The deepest flaw in the Court's unanimous opinion in *Jimmy Swaggart Ministries* is that it treated the case as though it were simple and straightforward. On procedural grounds[183] it disposed of the most troubling dimension of the case, reliance on the presence of an itinerant evangelist to conduct occasional crusades in California as the basis

---

175. 489 U.S. at 29 (Scalia, J., dissenting).

176. Laycock, *supra* note 162, at 994.

177. 489 U.S. at 42 (Scalia, J., dissenting).

178. I served as one of the counsel in the litigation on behalf of Jimmy Swaggart Ministries in the Supreme Court.

179. *See* Holmes, *supra* note 57, at 1.

180. *Jimmy Swaggart Ministries*, Brief Amicus Curiae of the American Civil Liberties Union in Support of Appellee 6: "Swaggart Ministries bases virtually its entire argument on *Murdock*...."

181. *Jimmy Swaggart Ministries*, 493 U.S. at 385: "Appellant relies almost exclusively on our decisions in *Murdock* and *Follett*, for the proposition that a State may not impose a sales or use tax on the evangelical distribution of religious material by a religious organization."

182. *Jimmy Swaggart Ministries*, Brief for Appellant, at 11–12 (history of hostility to itinerant evangelists); 16–21 (lack of nexus between taxing state and occasional noncommercial meetings in state; 35–45 (excessive government entanglement in religious matters).

183. The Court declined to hear the Commerce Clause challenge to California's jurisdiction to impose use tax on the ground that the claim was barred procedurally by the failure of the ministries to raise this claim in the tax refund process. *Jimmy Swaggart Ministries*, 493 U.S. at 377–79.

for claiming a never-ending nexus between the taxing jurisdiction and the evangelist. In this case the corporate headquarters of the ministry is located in Baton Rouge, Louisiana, and the ministry had no employees in California. Although commercial retailers such as L.L. Bean of Maine do not collect state use tax for items sold on-line[184] to residents of California, the Court declined to hear the challenge to requiring a Louisiana-based religious ministry to collect and transmit use tax from all members of its religious community in California who receive Bibles, religious tracts, tape recordings of sermons, and the like by mail from Louisiana.

As noted above, state sales and use tax is complex—in some respects more burdensome than compliance with the convoluted income tax. There are more than seven thousand taxing jurisdictions in the country, and their rates of taxation vary significantly. Almost all require sellers to obtain a license or permit. Many states charge a flat fee for the license. All states conduct audits to determine accuracy of filings. All states enforce various provisions of their sales and use tax laws with both civil and criminal penalties (including fines and imprisonment). Some states impose the primary tax on the seller, and some on the buyer; this designation is important in determining deductibility for state income tax purposes. Some states prohibit sellers from absorbing the sales tax, insisting that it must be passed on to the buyer; others allow sellers to include the tax in the selling price or to "reimburse" after adding the tax to the selling price. Still other states do not require sellers to pass sales tax on to the buyer, but do require them to collect use tax from out-of-state buyers. Some states permit sellers to absorb the sales or use tax, but prohibit them from advertising their willingness to do so or, even more precisely, the fact that the tax is not considered an element of the price. There is no uniform tax filing day for state sales and use tax; some states require monthly filings (on varying days of the month); others, bimonthly, quarterly, semiannually, or annually.[185]

It would be a stretch to imagine that the government would disclose these facts to the Court. The brief for the State of Texas did not do so in *Texas Monthly*. Neither did the briefs filed in *Jimmy Swaggart Ministries* by the State Board of Equalization (a marvelous name for a taxing authority) or by its principal amicus, the ACLU, which was content to describe the tax at issue simply as "neutral" and "nondiscriminatory."[186] In support of its position, the ACLU cited *United States v. Lee*: "When followers of a particular sect enter into *commercial activity* as a matter of choice, the limits they accept on their own conduct as a matter of conscience and faith are not to be superimposed on the statutory schemes which are binding on others in that activity."[187] Just so. The Amish carpenters in the *Lee* case were like Jimmy Swaggart in that neither would make a claim on the public treasury—unless one maintains that immunity from taxation is the same thing as receiving a grant. The Amish are prohibited by conscience from taking government assistance. Jimmy Swaggart and other evangelistic ministries are prohibited by the nonestablishment principle from receiving government assistance. There is an important distinction between these cases. The Amish did not claim that they not were engaged in commercial activity. Jimmy Swaggart, by contrast, argued that conducting

---

184. The amount retrieved from noncommercial transactions conducted by nonprofit organizations is small by comparison to the enormous amount of lost sales tax revenue from admittedly commercial transactions conducted on the Internet.

185. *See Jimmy Swaggart Ministries*, Appellant's Brief, Tables 2, 3, and 4, App. A-4 to A-34.

186. *Jimmy Swaggart Ministries*, Brief Amicus Curiae of the American Civil Liberties Union in Support of Appellee.

187. *Id.* at 15, *citing* United States v. Lee, 455 U.S. 252, 261 (1982) (emphasis added).

evangelistic crusades in California could not properly be understood as "commercial activity." If it is, then so was the activity of the ACLU when it filed its amicus brief, which—unwittingly perhaps—undermined its classic position on the fragility of civil liberties by echoing the claim made by the city in *Murdock*: that its tax on the Witnesses was a legitimate levy on *commercial* activity.[188]

Once again, Serritella's point about characterization turns out to be critical. If religious ministry can be called "commercial," then it should be subject to taxation at the same corporate rate that applies to General Motors or Microsoft.[189] But that is a big "if" that the ACLU should ponder carefully, for if it is correct to characterize the noncommercial activity of a religious community in this way, what will be left to guard the ACLU, the Sierra Club, or the NAACP from taxation on their noncommercial exempt activities? The common ground between the ACLU and scholars like myself is that the relevant principles are substantive neutrality,[190] nondiscrimination,[191] and nonentanglement.[192] Because we have differing perceptions of the facts of this case, we disagree in some respects on the application of those principles to this record. But I agree in principle with Blackmun's statement of the neutrality problem in *Texas Monthly*, cited approvingly in the ACLU brief in *Jimmy Swaggart Ministries*:

> [B]y confining the tax exemption exclusively to the sale of religious publications, Texas engaged in preferential support for the communication of religious messages. Although some forms of accommodating religion are constitutionally permissible, this one surely is not. A statutory preference for the dissemination of religious ideas offends our most basic understanding of what the Establishment Clause is all about and hence is constitutionally intolerable.[193]

Turning to nonentanglement, O'Connor acknowledged that "the present controversy has featured on-site inspections of appellant's evangelistic crusades, lengthy on-site audits, examinations of appellant's books and records, threats of criminal prosecution, and layers of administrative and judicial proceedings,"[194] but she summarily dismissed the claim that the record contained far more reliable empirical evi-

---

188. *Murdock*, 319 U.S. at 110.

189. For the view that religious communities should have "the same rights in the public sphere as General Motors, no more and no less," see Issac Kramnick & R. Laurence Moore, The Godless Constitution: The Case Against Religious Correctness 15 (1996), discussed in McConnell, *supra* note 161, at 8–10.

190. *Jimmy Swaggart Ministries*, Brief Amicus Curiae of the American Civil Liberties Union in Support of Appellee 5: "Fashioning an exemption for sales made by religious organizations, while all other sales of tangible goods in California are taxed, including those sold by nonreligious charitable and educational organizations, would create an exclusive class of tax beneficiaries based solely on religion."

191. *Id.* at 23, n. 6 (relying on the opinion of the lower court for the proposition that there was no "question of selective prosecution of state laws at issue." If the ACLU litigated as vigorously on behalf of plaintiffs claiming violations of free exercise as it does on behalf of those claiming that their tax dollars are being "spent" when a religious ministry is left in the same position as the ACLU and other exempt organizations, it would become more familiar with patterns of discrimination in this area that are as troubling as those with which is it abundantly familiar in the area of racial and gender-based classifications. *See, e.g.,* Brief Amicus Curiae on Behalf of the National Council of Churches of Christ in the U.S.A. 11.

192. *Id.* at 24–27.

193. *Jimmy Swaggart Ministries*, Brief Amicus Curiae of the American Civil Liberties Union in Support of Appellee 19–20, *citing Texas Monthly*, 489 U.S. at 28 (Blackmun, J., concurring in the judgment).

194. *Jimmy Swaggart Ministries*, 493 U.S. at 392.

dence of *actual* governmental entanglement with religion than did the records in cases involving aid to some secular aspects of education in religious schools. In those cases, the Court invalidated the aid on the basis of a *potential* for excessive entanglement.[195]

A summary of the five cases in which the Court has dealt with religious exemption from state and local taxation might focus on the way in which the two provisions of the Religion Clause are conceived. Later in this book, I argue for a harmonious relationship between these provisions. But it is apparent that the Court has committed itself to the view that there are two Religion Clauses and that these provisions are in tension, sometimes severe, with one another. In *Murdock* and *Follett* the Court felt expansive about the free exercise principle but overlooked the way in which the nonestablishment principle supports the same result. The tension theory had not yet been generated; it was to come in *Everson*.

In *Walz* the Court held that a state does not violate the nonestablishment provision if it exempts a religious community from paying taxes on property used exclusively for religious purposes—at least as long as other nonprofit organizations enjoy a similar benefit. Burger wrote in *Walz* that "federal or state grants of tax exemption to churches were not a violation of the Religion Clauses of the First Amendment."[196] Although this statement appeared on its face to invoke both nonestablishment and free exercise concerns, Burger's rationale focused exclusively on nonestablishment, leaving the granting of tax-exempt status not as a matter of constitutional necessity, but as something within the scope of permissible legislation. The *Walz* Court, moreover, gave full voice to the tension theory, with abundant metaphors—such as walking a tightrope or avoiding a collision—to illustrate its understanding that the two provisions in the Religion Clause were not easy to reconcile.

When the Court returned to the issue of religious tax immunity in *Texas Monthly v. Bullock*,[197] it held that the nonestablishment principle prohibits the states from providing an exemption for the distribution of religious literature that is not balanced with an exemption of a broader class of beneficiaries among charitable organizations. Two of the concurring justices expressly left open the possibility that the free exercise principle might require a different conclusion. According to the logic of the Court, the Religion Clause is not unitary but has two competing clauses, different in scope and meaning. Within a year, the Court unanimously held in *Jimmy Swaggart Ministries*[198] that a state did not violate the Free Exercise Clause by refusing to grant an exemption for the distribution of religious literature by an unpopular out-of-state evangelist.

At one level, the result was progress. It at least relieved the "tension" that supposedly resulted from one provision being able to command what the other provision explicitly prohibits. But it did so at enormous cost, not only by placing a limiting construction on *Murdock* and *Follett* that was far stricter than state lawmakers had understood in the intervening half century, but also by severely devaluing the free exercise principle in general. Less than three months later, the Court announced in *Employment Division v.*

---

195. *Contrast Jimmy Swaggart Ministries*, Brief for the Appellant 35–45 (evidence of actual entanglement in the record), *with* Aguilar v. Felton, 473 U.S. 402, 410, 413 (1985) (mere suspicion or fear about possibility of entanglement suffices to terminate program of remedial instruction for educationally and economically disadvantaged children).

196. *Walz*, 397 U.S. at 680.

197. 489 U.S. 1 (1989).

198. 493 U.S. 378 (1990).

Smith[199] that states do not need to show that burdens placed on religious exercise by laws of general applicability are justified by a compelling governmental interest or that the state has no less restrictive means of effectuating its interest.

If one posits a severe version of the conflict between the two provisions of the Religion Clause, then the outcome in *Jimmy Swaggart Ministries* seems preordained as an exercise in formal logic. But the hypothesis of "tension" between conflicting provisions is itself unnecessary. The remedy advanced by the Court in *Employment Division v. Smith* is like treating a headache with a lobotomy instead of taking an aspirin.[200] Justice Holmes once described experience rather than logic as "the life of the law."[201] *Employment Division v. Smith* reflected a logic of sorts, but it did not attend to the broad experience of the American people favoring free exercise of religion.[202]

Leaders of religious communities can learn important lessons from this litigation. From *Murdock* and *Follett* they can learn that the Court may be more sympathetic and generous to religious concerns that arise from a community perceived to be suffering persecution at the hands of an intolerant majority, rather than from televangelists who appear to be suffering only from too much success. From *Walz* they can learn that arguments from history can be helpful but should not be exaggerated; it is enough that facts that shed light on constitutional interpretation be argued soberly and convincingly. From *Texas Monthly* they can learn that they should not expect the government to do an effective job of voicing their concerns, and that religious and nonreligious groups merit equal protection of the law, including the tax law. From *Jimmy Swaggart Ministries* religious leaders can learn the need for a theory of the Religion Clause better than the common conception of it as having two competing provisions, and they should not be surprised that the Court will diminish the value of precedents like *Murdock* and *Follett* in attempts to overcome the logical absurdity that one provision commands what

---

199. 494 U.S. 872 (1990).

200. *See* Douglas Laycock, The Supreme Court's Assault on Free Exercise, and the Amicus Brief that Was Never Filed, 8 J.L. & Religion 99, 102 (1990) (*Smith* was "inconsistent with the original intent, inconsistent with the constitutional text, inconsistent with doctrine under other constitutional clauses, and inconsistent with precedent"); Ira C. Lupu, *Employment Division v. Smith* and the Decline of Supreme Court-Centrism, 1993 BYU L. Rev. 259, 260 (Smith "substantively wrong and institutionally irresponsible"); Roald Mykkeltvedt, *Employment Division v. Smith*: Creating Anxiety by Relieving Tension, 58 Tenn. L. Rev. 603, 621 (1991).

201. Holmes, *supra* note 57, at 1.

202. *See* John T. Noonan, Jr., Religious Liberty at the Stake, 84 Va. L. Rev. 459 (1998). Justice Scalia was criticized for using history selectively, even disingenuously. For example, he cited the first flag-salute case without mentioning that the second flag-salute case had overruled it. This is a bit like relying on *Plessy v. Ferguson* without mentioning *Brown v. Bd. of Education*. *See* Douglas Laycock, The Remnants of Free Exercise, 1990 Sup. Ct. Rev. 1. Scalia salvaged *Murdock* and *Follett* in *Smith* as follows: "The only decisions in which we have held that the First Amendment bars application of a neutral, generally applicable law to religiously motivated action have involved not the Free Exercise Clause alone, but the Free Exercise Clause in conjunction with other constitutional protections, such as freedom of speech and of the press." Gordon calls this the "Hamburger Helper theory" of the Religion Clause: religion has no independent constitutional substance but is helpful in stretching a meal. James D. Gordon III, Free Exercise on the Mountaintop, 79 Cal. L. Rev. 91, 114–15 (1991) (*Smith* "'depublished' the Free Exercise Clause"). McConnell now takes a more positive view of this approach: "*Smith* left intact the requirement of strict scrutiny for laws burdening religious exercise...where the burden to religious exercise is combined with a burden to some other constitutional right.... [This] category, if generously interpreted, could prove to be a substantial exception to the *Smith* rule.... [A]ny creative lawyer should be able to properly allege a burden...on another constitutional right, such as property, speech, privacy, or association, in addition to the free exercise claim." McConnell, *supra* note 161, at 3–4.

the other forbids. From all these cases, religious leaders can learn that it is their responsibility to offer persuasive reasons that are factually reliable and that make sense to public policy makers.

Political and Constitutional Rationales for Religious Tax Exemption

This section of the chapter offers reasons that might prove useful for those who will have to bear the brunt of the litigation that presumably will continue over the constitutionality of measures designed to preserve the religious exemption from state and local taxes. This exemption appears to be more vulnerable at the state and local level than at the federal level. No matter where a conflict over tax exemption arises, religious leaders should not appear to engage in special pleading. Instead, arguments in support of exemption of religious communities from taxation will be stronger if they are offered in language that is accessible to public policy makers and that appeals to the general public. As it turns out, there is a close parallel between sound constitutional reasoning and viable political claims about these matters. The principal themes are substantive neutrality, nondiscrimination, and nonentanglement. State and local officials should be helped to discover these values in their state constitutions as well as in the federal Constitution they all swear to uphold.

Religious Tax Immunity and the Principle of Substantive Neutrality

The government may define a secular benefit such as exempt status, but it must do so in a manner that preserves its neutrality on ideological perspectives. The Court has often justified its decisions in Religion Clause cases by referring to the results as being harmonious with neutrality.[203] But what does neutrality mean? The term is not self-defining. As Justice Harlan observed, neutrality is "a coat of many colors."[204] For this reason, Steven Smith remains doubtful that it represents a serious principle in understanding issues arising under the Religion Clause. Thus he writes that the "multiple meanings [of neutrality] provide ample opportunity for equivocation and obfuscation, deliberate or accidental."[205]

It is precisely because of such multiple meanings that Laycock undertook the task of offering greater definitional clarity in his seminal article on this matter.[206] He noted that "[t]hose who think neutrality is meaningless have a point. We can agree on the principle of neutrality without having agreed on anything at all."[207] But he was unwilling to

---

203. *See, e.g, Walz,* 397 U.S. at 669–70; Tilton v. Richardson, 403 U.S. 672, 687–68 (1971); Committee for Public Educ. and Religious Liberty v. Nyquist, 413 U.S. 756, 792–93 (1973); School Dist. of Abington Township v. Schempp, 374 U.S. 203, 222 (1963).

204. Board of Educ. v. Allen, 392 U.S. 236, 249 (1968) (Harlan, J., concurring).

205. Steven D. Smith, Foreordained Failure: The Quest for a Constitutional Principle of Religious Freedom 78 (1995).

206. *See* Laycock, *supra* note 162.

207. *Id.* at 994.

give up on the possibility that neutrality could function as a principle—indeed, one that truly evokes the American experience of, and yearning for, religious freedom.

In a dialogue with Carl H. Esbeck, Laycock recently clarified the connection between neutrality and the theme of separationism. Esbeck had contrasted the two categories, preferring neutrality because he understood it to be "centered on the unleashing of personal liberty to the end that, with minimal governmental interference, individuals make their own religious choices."[208] Laycock agreed with that understanding of neutrality, but thought it misguided to contrast it with separationism.

> To frame the universe of possibilities in this way is to make the Court's doctrine seem more hostile than it is to Professor Esbeck's substantive position. It concedes the rhetorical benefits of the separationist label to those who do indeed believe that separation requires discrimination against religion; it suggests that neutrality requires repudiation of the separation of church and state. Neither the Court nor the American people are likely to accept such a repudiation, nor should they. Separation has important benefits that neither Professor Esbeck nor I are willing to abandon.
>
> The central meaning of separation is to separate the authority of the church from the authority of the state, so that "no religion can invoke government's coercive power and no government can coerce any religious act or belief." This separation is essential to the religious liberty of the numerically dominant faith, if any, and to the religious liberty of dissenters and nonbelievers.[209]

This chapter has referred to neutrality not in the weaker sense of formal neutrality,[210] illustrated for example in cases like *Aguilar v. Felton*[211] and *Employment Division v. Smith*,[212] but in the stronger sense of substantive neutrality, which Laycock defined to mean the requirement that the government "minimize the extent to which it either encourages or discourages religious belief or disbelief, practice or non-practice, observance or nonobservance."[213] Laycock acknowledges that "substantive neutrality is harder to apply than formal neutrality. It requires judgments about the relative significance of various encouragements and discouragements to religion."[214] For example, under this stronger sense of neutrality, the government would have to exempt Jews from laws of general applicability, such as prohibition of the sale or consumption of alcohol during the Prohibition era.[215]

---

208. Carl H. Esbeck, A Constitutional Case for Governmental Cooperation with Faith-Based Social Service Providers, 46 Emory L.J. 1, 4–5 (1997).

209. *See* Douglas Laycock, The Underlying Unity of Separation and Neutrality, 46 Emory L.J. 43, 48 (1997).

210. *See* Laycock, *supra* note 162, at 999–1001; *see also* Daniel O. Conkle, The Path of American Religious Liberty: From the Original Theology to Formal Neutrality and an Uncertain Future, 75 Ind. L.J. 1 (2000).

211. 473 U.S. 402 (1985).

212. 494 U.S. 872 (1990) McConnell has observed: "Adoption of the formal neutrality standard of *Smith* does not mean that religious liberty in the United States is at an end—though it does mean that the federal courts will cease to play a large role in enforcing it." McConnell, *supra* note 161, at 741–42. I return to this point at the end of this chapter.

213. Laycock, *supra* note 162, at 1001.

214. *Id.* at 1004.

215. *Id.* at 1003. Smith remains skeptical about the utility of Laycock's contribution; *see* Smith, *supra* note 205, at 81 (challenging the neutrality of Laycock's version of neutrality and suggesting that Laycock adopts as "constitutional orthodoxy a set of controversial beliefs about the nature and value of religion, the proper function of government, and human psychology"; *id.* at 97 (no neutral

To apply Laycock's understanding of substantive neutrality to the issue of religious tax immunity, the government may tilt neither toward religion (by defining favorably the religious uses it deems socially useful) nor against it (by denying it a secular benefit, such as tax exemption, that it makes available to comparable nonreligious groups). This approach avoids the violation of the nonestablishment principle inherent in most government attempts to define acceptable religious practices. It also fosters the free exercise of religion by allowing its convictions to be put into practice without governmental interference or inhibition.

Although Laycock's contribution is helpful, the context within which discussion of the neutrality of religious tax immunity will occur in coming decades is one in which the discourse of tax expenditure theory—with its assumption that an exemption is a subsidy—has become dominant. For example, in *Rosenberger v. Rector and Visitors of the University of Virginia*,[216] Justice Thomas wrote in a concurring opinion:

> A tax exemption in many cases is economically and functionally *indistinguishable from a direct monetary subsidy*. In one instance, the government relieves religious entities (along with others) of a generally applicable tax; in the other, it relieves religious entities (along with others) of some or all of the burden of that tax by returning it in the form of a *cash subsidy*. Whether the benefit is provided at the front or back end of the taxation process, the financial aid to religious groups is undeniable. The analysis under the Establishment Clause must also be the same....[217]

As noted above, moreover, state legislators who decide most of these issues have become accustomed to tax expenditure budgets, and to using the tax structure to achieve policy goals that may not be achievable through straightforward appropriations, for reasons as mundane as the membership on different legislative committees. It will, accordingly, require considerable effort to persuade state and local officials that immunity from sales and use tax liability is not truly a "subsidy," or at least not an impermissible one. But the argument is worth making; further discussion of the characterization of exemptions as subsidies is needed.

Tax exemptions targeted solely to religious communities might well be unconstitutional if the effect were to subsidize these communities by providing valuable public benefits at the expense of secular taxpayers, and if the tax presented no plausible dangers to the free exercise of religion. In other words, tax immunity would constitute a true subsidy only if the exempt entity received valuable public services but was not required to pay for them. That might well justify a tax that is reasonably calculated to defray the costs of benefits bestowed on the religious body. But a general revenue tax, such

---

vantage point permits theorist or judge to transcend competing positions; hence a theory of religious freedom is as illusory as the ideal of neutrality it seeks to embody); *but see* Berg, *supra* note 98.

216. 515 U.S. 819, 859 (1995) (Thomas, J., concurring).

217. *Id.* at 859–60 (emphasis added). Noting that "a government can appropriate money to a particular person or group by using a special, narrowly directed tax deduction or exclusion, instead of by using its ordinary direct spending mechanisms," Thomas referred to how a "large body of literature about tax expenditures accepts the basic concept that special exemptions from tax function as *subsidies*. The current debate focuses on whether particular items are correctly identified as tax expenditures and whether incentive provisions are more efficient when structured as tax expenditures rather than direct spending programs." *Id.* at 861, n.5, *citing* Bernard Wolfman, Tax Expenditures: From Idea to Ideology, Book Review of Stanley S. Surrey and Paul N. McDaniels, Tax Expenditures (1985), 99 Harv. L. Rev. 491, 491–492 (1985).

as a sales tax, is surely not one calculated to deal with the so-called free rider problem.[218] Still less can such a claim be made of the use tax, especially as applied to religious organizations that are not based in the taxing jurisdiction and that make only brief and occasional forays into the state. Under these circumstances the sales and use tax has no relation whatsoever to the level of benefits bestowed by the state on a religious body.

The Court has observed, moreover, that "there is no constitutional requirement that the benefits received from a taxing authority *by an ordinary commercial taxpayer*...must equal the amount of its tax obligation."[219] Ordinary commercial taxpayers ordinarily can protect themselves through the political process. But when taxes are imposed directly on the dissemination of religious doctrine, there must be a closer fit between taxes extracted and benefits conferred, lest the realm of religious action be reserved to those who "have a full purse."[220] As Justice Murphy observed:

> Respondents [the tax authorities] do not show that the instant activities of Jehovah's Witnesses create special problems causing a drain on the municipal coffers, or that these taxes are commensurate with any expenses entailed by the presence of the Witnesses. In the absence of such a showing, I think *no tax whatever can be levied on petitioners' activities in distributing their literature or disseminating their ideas.* If the guaranties of freedom of speech and freedom of the press are to be preserved, *municipalities should not be free to raise general revenue by taxes on the circulation of information and opinion in non-commercial causes*; other sources can be found, the taxation of which will not choke off ideas.[221]

Jimmy Swaggart Ministries was a case not about subsidies from California to a religious ministry, but about whether California could exact revenue from the ministry. At least under these circumstances, it is curious to call immunity a subsidy. It seems right to give Laycock the last word on this theme. He argued succinctly in *Jimmy Swaggart Ministries*:

> The constitutionally required neutrality is achieved by equal tax exemptions for all literature about religion, both pro and con. It is not achieved by equally burdening all exercises of religion. The argument that any exemption is prima facie an establishment leads to the absurd conclusion that churches should generally be taxed and regulated to the same extent as business corporations. But that would leave nothing of the free exercise clause. The exercise of religion is not free when it is taxed. The free exercise clause requires tax immunity, and nothing in the establishment clause forbids it.[222]

---

218. Dean Kelley wrote: "Lacking an adequate rationale for tax exemption, church leaders have often tended to accept the characterizations of their critics that they are somehow 'free-loading' on the community. Some, in a paroxysm of sentimental self-flagellation, have called their followers to repentance for conduct in which under a more sensible and realistic rationale there need be no sense of guilt." Dean M. Kelley, Why Churches Should Not Pay Taxes 16 (1977).

219. Cotton Petroleum Corp. v. New Mexico, 490 U.S. 163, 190 (1989) (emphasis added), *citing* Keystone Bituminous Coal Ass'n. v. DeBenedictis, 480 U.S. 470, 491, n. 21 (1987).

220. *Murdock,* 319 U.S. at 112.

221. Jones v. Opelika, 316 U.S. at 620 (Murphy, J., dissenting) (emphasis added), adopted by the Court in *Murdock,* 319 U.S. at 104.

222. *Jimmy Swaggart Ministries,* Brief Amicus Curiae of National Council of Churches of Christ in the U.S.A., at 10; *see also* McConnell, *supra* note 161, at 8: "The problem (if there is a problem) is not that religious people or institutions are favored over atheists, but rather, that religious exercise, whether engaged in by Catholics, atheists, or anyone else, is protected, while worthy nonreligious activity by the same parties does not receive protection." McConnell argues that singling religion out is required by the text of the Constitution and by the history of its interpretation: "The only constitutional regime that would not 'single out' religion would be one that deconstitutionalized the issue

The Exemption of Religion and Other Charitable Organizations and the Principle of Nondiscrimination against Religion

Closely related to the theme of substantive neutrality is the theme of nondiscrimination that the Court has clarified in several cases over the past decade. Discrimination against a particular religious community violates free exercise by imposing a needless burden upon the exercise of religious convictions. The Court has expressly — sometimes unanimously — taught that the free exercise provision prohibits the government from denying generally available benefits to otherwise eligible recipients on account of their religious exercise. For example, in *Jimmy Swaggart Ministries* Justice O'Connor wrote that to "single out" religious activity "for special and burdensome treatment" would violate the Free Exercise Clause.[223] In the Santeria case Justice Kennedy wrote: "At a minimum, the protections of the Free Exercise Clause pertain if the law at issue discriminates against some or all religious beliefs."[224] In the Native American peyote case, Justice Scalia wrote that government may not "impose special disabilities on the basis of religious views or religious status."[225] It has also taught that access to facilities may not be denied because of the religious nature of the speech that will ensue.[226]

Discrimination on the basis of religion is equally prohibited under the nonestablishment principle.[227] For example, in *Larson v. Valente* state regulation of charitable solicitation appeared on the surface to be formally neutral, but the context of the adoption of the statute as well as its actual implementation both pointed to discriminatory enforcement aimed at unpopular new religious movements. Justice Brennan wrote: "The clearest command of the Establishment Clause is that one religious denomination cannot be officially preferred over another."[228]

Nondiscrimination is at the heart of O'Connor's reformulation of the nonestablishment principle as one that prohibits government endorsement of a particular religion.[229] Perhaps that is what led her to dissent from the Court's holding in *Hernandez v. Commissioner of Internal Revenue*[230] that payments for the religious practice of auditing in the Church of Scientology could not be deducted as a charitable contribution in the same way that fixed payments to other religions were allowed to be deducted. Justice White distinguished *Larson* in *Hernandez* on the formalistic ground that "the line which

---

of religion, leaving issues regarding the extent of regulation, subsidy, and control of religious activities to the discretion of the political branches." *Id.* at 11.

223. *Jimmy Swaggart Ministries*, 493 U.S. at 390; *see also* Hobbie v. Unemployment Appeals Comm'n, 480 U.S. 136, 148 (1987) (Stevens, J., concurring) (the Free Exercise Clause "protect[s] religious observers against unequal treatment").

224. Church of Lukumi Babalu Aye v. City of Hialeah, 508 U.S. 520, 532 (1993).

225. Employment Division v. Smith, 494 U.S. 872, 877 (1990).

226. *See, e.g.,* Rosenberger v. Rector and Visitors of the Univ. of Virginia, 515 U.S. 819, 830 (1995); Lamb's Chapel v. Center Moriches Union Free Sch. Dist., 508 U.S. 384 (1993); Widmar v. Vincent, 454 U.S. 263 (1981).

227. *See generally* Michael A. Paulsen, Religion, Equality, and the Constitution: An Equal Protection Approach to Establishment Clause Adjudication, 61 Notre Dame L. Rev. 311 (1986).

228. 456 U.S. 228, 244–45 (1982).

229. *See* Lynch v. Donnelly, 465 U.S. 668, 688 (1984) (O'Connor, J., concurring); County of Allegheny v. ACLU, Greater Pittsburgh Chapter, 492 U.S. 573 (1989).

230. 490 U.S. 680 (1989).

IRC §170 draws between deductible and nondeductible payments to statutorily qualified organizations does not differentiate among sects."[231] Joined by Scalia, not ordinarily a supporter of O'Connor's endorsement test, O'Connor expressed the view that the IRS's application of the quid pro quo standard in this case discriminated against the Church of Scientology as surely as the rigged rules on charitable solicitation discriminated against the Unification Church in *Larson*.[232] It was O'Connor who forged the clearest expression of this principle in the context of aid to some aspects of education in religious schools. She wrote in *Agostini* that such aid would not have the impermissible effect of advancing religion if "allocated on the basis of neutral, secular criteria that neither favor nor disfavor religion, and...made available to both religious and secular beneficiaries on a nondiscriminatory basis."[233]

The results in *Texas Monthly* and *Jimmy Swaggart Ministries* may have been predictable. Certainly the result in *Jimmy Swaggart Ministries* was predictable after *Texas Monthly*. But both cases needlessly weakened the general principle, announced in *Murdock*, of tax immunity for noncommercial distribution of religious literature. The Court in *Texas Monthly* and *Jimmy Swaggart Ministries* has made it difficult if not impossible to ensure that the taxing power is exerted uniformly or without discrimination when sales and use taxes are applied to all "sales" of religious materials by religious bodies to their adherents. The promise that such abuse of the tax law will not occur "while this Court sits" is an empty one. After *Texas Monthly* and *Jimmy Swaggart Ministries*, religious communities will have a much harder time securing a practicable judicial remedy for the abuse of discriminatory administration of the tax laws. It is no comfort that "uniform administration of the tax laws" was the very rationale used by the Court as a governmental interest sufficiently compelling to defeat the claim that collection of social security tax from the Amish violated their free exercise of religion.[234]

One of the most disturbing features of the state taxing power struck down in *Murdock* and upheld in *Jimmy Swaggart Ministries* is the way in which it could be deployed against unpopular itinerants with no political base in the community. Once again, it is appropriate to let Laycock have the last word on this theme. He shrewdly observed in the amicus brief he filed in *Jimmy Swaggart Ministries*:

> Small and unpopular religions, the religions of minorities, are subject to disproportionate enforcement.... *Murdock* targeted the Jehovah's Witnesses; *Hernandez* targeted the Scientologists; the *ISKCON* case in California targeted the Hare Krishna; and this case targeted Jimmy Swaggart Ministries. It is no accident that each of these religious groups has been the victim of widespread public hostility. *Walz* and *Texas Monthly* are not exceptions; those were not tax collections suits, but abstract litigation in which no religious organization was represented. As is so often true, the assault on civil liberties begins with the marginal groups in our society. This assault may eventually reach mainstream groups as well, but enforcement will never be even-handed.[235]

---

231. *Id.* at 695.

232. *Id.* at 710–13 (O'Connor, J., dissenting).

233. Agostini v. Felton, 521 U.S. 203, 231 (1997).

234. *See* United States v. Lee, 455 U.S. 252, 257 (1982) (government's "compelling" interest in *uniform* collection of social security taxes outweighed burden on Amish taxpayers, whose religion forbids both payment and receipt of social security benefits).

235. *Jimmy Swaggart Ministries,* Brief Amicus Curiae of National Council of Churches of Christ in the U.S.A., at 11. Laycock was not quite correct about *Walz*, which did not involve a religious community as a party but did engage all major religious communities within Judaism and Chris-

The Distinction between Religious and Charitable Uses and the Principle of Nonentanglement of Government with Religion

A third theme central to the understanding of both provisions of the Religion Clause requires the government to set limits on its authority to avoid excessive entanglement with religious communities. The classic illustration of this theme occurred in a post-Civil War decision which held that secular tribunals lacked both competence and jurisdiction to decide internal issues of church governance. In *Watson v. Jones*, the Court ruled that courts had no business second-guessing the decision of the highest adjudicatory in a hierarchical church.[236]

As the term "excessive" indicates, this test is susceptible to various interpretations of how much contact is too much. For example, in *Walz* the Court expressly relied upon nonentanglement as a reason for sustaining property tax exemption for religious communities, on the view that exemption had a lower probability of entanglement than taxation.[237] In *Jimmy Swaggart Ministries* the Court made light of the evidence of entanglement and sustained a statute that imposed sales and use tax liability on a religious community for distribution of religious literature to its members.[238]

Some contacts between governmental agencies and religious communities have been regarded as "routine and factual."[239] Others have been deemed so "comprehensive, discriminating, and continuing"[240] as to require the invalidation of state legislation providing financial assistance to teachers of secular subjects in religious schools. Still other contacts have been deemed potentially so invasive that legislative immunity conferred upon religious communities was upheld by the Court.[241] On other occasions, the Court has deemed it necessary to construe federal legislation to require an affirmative showing of congressional intent to include religious communities within the scope of a broad regulatory scheme.[242]

The degree of entanglement can be analyzed in terms of the nature of both the *determinations* that must be made and the *procedural interactions* that are involved. The deci-

---

tianity as amici. Laycock's client in *Jimmy Swaggart Ministries*, the NCC, was represented in an amicus brief, as were the Synagogue Council of America and the United States Catholic Conference. Otherwise, his comment was right on the mark.

236. Watson v. Jones, 80 U.S. 666, 677 (1872); *see* Presbyterian Church v. Hull Memorial Presbyterian Church, 393 U.S. 440, 449 (1969) (hazards accompany excessive government involvement in or oversight of religious matters); Serbian Eastern Orthodox Diocese v. Milivojevich, 426 U.S. 696, 709 (1976) ("substantial danger that the State will become entangled in essentially religious controversies"). *See* the discussion of this line of cases in Patrick J. Schiltz and Douglas Laycock, "Employment in Religious Organizations," in this volume; and Laycock, *supra* note 202, at 43–44 (noting that the internal church dispute cases survive *Employment Division v. Smith*).

237. *Walz*, 397 U.S. at 674–75.

238. *Jimmy Swaggart Ministries*, 493 U.S. at 393–96.

239. *See* Tony and Susan Alamo Found. v. Secretary of Labor, 471 U.S. 290, 305–06 (1985) (reporting requirements in wage and hour laws); Hernandez v. Comm'r, 490 U.S. 680, 693–93 (1989) (tax laws).

240. *See* Lemon v. Kurtzman, 403 U.S. 602, 619 (1971).

241. *See* Corporation of Presiding Bishop v. Amos, 483 U.S. 327, 336 (1987); *see* Douglas Laycock, Towards a General Theory of the Religion Clauses: The Case of Church Labor Relations and the Right to Church Autonomy, 81 Colum. L. Rev. 1373 (1981).

242. *See* NLRB v. Catholic Bishop, 440 U.S. 490, 501–04 (1979).

sion on whether a community's property or "sales" are immune from taxation entails both general and specific determinations. Examples of a general determination would include whether the organization is religious, whether it in fact uses a particular space for religious purposes, or whether the items it "sells" are religious. As long as the government does not engage in close definition of what is and is not religious, determinations of this sort have been approved or even required by the Court in the context of many governmental programs.[243] The distinction between "religious" and other organizations is made regularly by state and federal tax authorities, since their treatment for purposes of property, gift, inheritance, and income tax, as well as in regard to filing and audit requirements, hinges on the distinction. Another determination that might also be made for purposes of immunity is whether the property used or the materials "sold" have a religious purpose, such as worship or spreading religious doctrine. Such determinations may be necessary and have been approved and even required by the Court.[244] General determinations of this sort about property and sales and use taxes do not make distinctions any more problematic than line-drawing of a similar nature in other contexts.

On the other hand, if the government were to engage in specific definitions of what it means by religious worship or religious literature, it would be interfering with the freedom of religious communities to define themselves according to their own self-understandings. At least it would be violating the principle of substantive neutrality by encouraging a religious community to conform to the governmental definition in order to qualify for the benefit of tax immunity.

Sales and use taxation on the distribution of religious literature could require numerous difficult and intrusive examinations of a religious community's operations. For example, how is the state to determine the "price" of a religious tape or pamphlet when it is sometimes offered free, sometimes sent in thanks for an unspecified donation (or a donation far in excess of its cost), and offered for different "prices" at different times? Will state agents monitor a ministry's religious broadcasts to listen to the "terms of sale" at different times? Will they attend the religious services at which these things are announced? Will they read newsletters published by the ministry? Will they interrogate church officials responsible for setting price or determining when materials should be given away? Will they attempt to set a "market value" on religious materials whose value to the "purchasers" is spiritual? Or will they attempt to determine "costs" of "production?" And if so, how will they "value" and allocate volunteer time, "overhead expenses" devoted to worship, prayer, or spiritual counseling, or the cost of "publicity," i.e., evangelism? Once again, Serritella's point about characterization is at the core of determinations such as these, all of which are beyond the ken and therefore the reach of the government.

---

243. *See* Bowen v. Kendrick, 487 U.S. 589 (1988) (under Adolescent Family Life Act, Secretary of Health and Human Services must determine whether potential grantees are "pervasively sectarian"); Hunt v. McNair, 413 U.S. 734, 743 (1973) (under programs to aid higher education, state officials must determine whether potential beneficiaries are pervasively sectarian); Hobbie v. Unemployment Appeals Comm'n, 480 U.S. 136 (1987) (state unemployment compensation commission must determine whether worker's reasons for discharge were "religious").

244. *See Kendrick,* 487 U.S. 589 (secretary of health and human services must determine whether materials used in the program "have an explicitly religious content or are designed to inculcate the views of a particular religious faith"); *Lemon,* 403 U.S. at 617 (review of textbooks for religious content is required, though review of a teacher's conduct would be excessively entangling); Board of Educ. v. Allen, 392 U.S. 236 (1968) (state must examine textbooks to determine whether they have religious content).

As the Court noted in *Walz*, the procedural interactions needed for recognition of immunity are also far less entangling than those needed for imposition of tax. The Court has recognized that "one-time, single purpose" interactions between church and state pose less serious entanglement problems than do "continuing financial relationships or dependencies,…annual audits, and…government analysis of an institution's expenditures."[245] The immunity determination can be made once and, unless circumstances change, need not be made again. When a determination of tax immunity has been made, there will be no further contacts between religious and governmental authorities—no forms to file, no questions to answer, no audits to endure, no criminal prosecutions to be threatened. But as the record in *Jimmy Swaggart Ministries* and in a parallel proceeding against the Hare Krishnas in California illustrate, the administration of the tax would involve repeated monitoring, investigation, on-site audits, and negotiations.

As noted above, there are more than seven thousand taxing jurisdictions in the United States that impose property and sales and use tax. If sales and use tax were imposed on the distribution of religious literature, a religious community that distributes it nationwide would be required to engage in virtually continuous compliance efforts, since there is no uniform tax filing day for state sales and use tax; some states require monthly filings (on varying days of the month); others, bi-monthly, quarterly, semiannually, or annually.[246]

State and Local Legislators as Interpreters of Constitutions

As Witte has demonstrated, the paths that have led us to the current practice of state and local tax exemption of charitable organizations, including religious communities, are complex. But these paths converge in a common fact: thirty-seven states embed this practice in their constitutions in one way or another, and all maintain it in some way by statute. In short, it is rooted deeply in the customs and traditions of the American people.[247] In light of this history, the practice reflects what Bernard Lonergan calls "constitutive meaning"[248] and is constitutional at least in this sense. To quote Burger's opinion in *Walz* again:

---

245. Tilton v. Richardson, 403 U.S. 672, 688 (1971); Roemer v. Bd. of Public Works, 426 U.S. 736, 763 (1976) (plurality); *see Kendrick,* 108 S. Ct. at 2596 (Blackmun, J., dissenting).

246. *See Jimmy Swaggart Ministries,* Appellant's Brief, Tables 2, 3, and 4, App. A-4 to A-34.

247. For the view that courts have "no basis for proscribing as unconstitutional practices that do not violate any explicit text of the Constitution and that have been regarded as constitutional ever since the framing," *see* Board of County Commissioners, Waubaunsee County v. Umbehr, 518 U.S. 668, 116 S. Ct. 2361, 2362 (1996) (Scalia, J., dissenting); United States v. Virginia, 518 U.S. 515, 567–70 (Scalia, J. dissenting); Kiryas Joel Village Sch. Dist. v. Grumet, 512 U.S. 687, 752 (1994) (Scalia, J., dissenting) (nonestablishment provision should not be used to "repeal our Nation's tradition of religious toleration"); Rutan v. Republican Party of Ill., 497 U.S. 62, 95 (1990) (Scalia, J., dissenting) ("when a practice not expressly prohibited by the text of the Bill of Rights bears the endorsement of a long tradition of open, widespread, and unchallenged use that dates back to the beginning of the Republic, we have no proper basis for striking it down"); Burnham v. Superior Court of Cal., County of Marin, 495 U.S. 604 (1990) (plurality opinion of Scalia, J.). *And see* Antonin J. Scalia, A Matter of Interpretation: Federal Courts and the Law (1997).

248. Bernard J.F. Lonergan, Method in Theology 78 (1972) (social institutions and human cultures, including law, have meanings as intrinsic components).

The legislative purpose of the property tax exemption is neither the advancement nor the inhibition of religion; it is neither sponsorship nor hostility. New York, in common with the other States, has determined that certain entities that exist in a harmonious relationship to the community at large, and that foster its "moral or mental improvement," should not be inhibited in their activities by property taxation or the hazard of loss of those properties for non-payment of taxes.... Grants of exemption historically reflect the concern of authors of constitutions and statutes as to the latent dangers inherent in the imposition of property taxes; exemption constitutes a reasonable and balanced attempt to guard against those dangers.[249]

Much of the analysis in this chapter, indeed throughout the entire book, has been based on a close reading of cases decided in the Supreme Court of the United States. That has its place in any serious work of constitutional interpretation. Even when writing critically of the Court's work, scholars make an implicit commitment both to the independence of the judiciary as a separate branch of government and to the preeminent role of the Court in authoritative construction of the meaning of the federal Constitution. Thus in an article that was deeply critical of the Court's decision in *Employment Division v. Smith*,[250] James Gordon correctly observed: "The right to practice one's religion should not be reduced to a question of political influence, completely subject to the whims of transient and shifting majorities."[251] Gordon was referring to shifting majorities in the political process, or to the classical problem of the tyranny of the majority addressed by James Madison in *Federalist* No. 10.[252] In our current situation, however, it may be irresponsible for leaders of religious communities to place excessive confidence in the Court as the instrument of government that will protect religious liberty vigorously in the new century. It, too, is "completely subject to the whims of transient and shifting majorities."

Before *Smith* was decided, Gerald V. Bradley reminded us that "it is debatable whether the Supreme Court has contributed to or taken away from the present state of religious liberty—if indeed that describes the present state."[253] Bradley's comment is provocative in the best sense of the term. It requires rethinking of the traditional assumption that religious and other civil liberties are secure "while the Court sits," as Burger wrote in *Walz*, citing Holmes.[254] No matter what you think of the results in the cases discussed above, or of the constitutional principles sketched above, it would be improper to conclude this chapter in a way that suggests that the Court has had the last word on exemption of religious communities from state and local taxation. I turn now to explore the role of state and local officials in constitutional interpretation.

The constitutions of the several states and of the United States are no less binding upon state legislators and local administrative officials than they are on federal and state judges. All state and local officials take the same oath of office—to uphold the Consti-

---

249. *Walz,* 397 U.S. at 672–73.

250. 494 U.S. 872 (1990).

251. James D. Gordon III, Free Exercise on the Mountaintop, 79 Cal. L. Rev. 91, 110 (1991).

252. Federalist No. 10 (Madison) The Federalist Papers 129–30 (1961) ("measures are too often decided, not according to the rules of justice and the rights of the minor party, but by the superior force of an interested and overbearing majority").

253. Gerard V. Bradley, The No Religious Test Clause and the Constitution of Religious Liberty: A Machine That Has Gone of Itself, 37 Case W. Res. L. Rev. 674, 734 (1987).

254. *Walz,* 397 U.S. at 678, *citing* Panhandle Oil Co. v. Mississippi ex rel. Knox, 277 U.S. 218, 223 (1928) (Holmes, J, dissenting).

tution—that federal and state judges do. All of these state and local officials must comply with the requirements not only of the federal Constitution but also of their state constitutions. I offer here but one example of how tax immunity for religious communities along with other nonprofit organizations has been expressly provided for in a state charter just as clearly committed to nonestablishment as is the First Amendment of the U.S. Constitution, or perhaps even more so. Article IX, § 10 of the Arizona constitution provides: "No tax shall be laid or appropriation of public money made in aid of any church, or private or sectarian school, or any public service corporation." Article IX, § 2 provides: "There shall be exempt from taxation all federal, state, county and municipal property. Property of educational, charitable and religious associations or institutions not used or held for profit may be exempt from taxation by law. Public debts, as evidenced by the bonds of Arizona, its counties, municipalities or other subdivisions, shall also be exempt from taxation. All household goods owned by the user thereof and used solely for noncommercial purposes shall be exempt from taxation, and such person entitled to such exemption shall not be required to take any affirmative action to receive the benefit of such exemption." Because of the importance of the state constitutions, the text of the relevant provisions on religious tax immunity is included as an appendix to this chapter.[255] Because of the complexity of the task of construing each of these state charters carefully, the reader is referred to the chapter on state constitutional law in this book.[256]

It is important to focus on the role of state and local officials in their constitutional tasks. Imagine that a state government were to devise an income tax with rates inversely proportional to ability to pay—that is, one that would fall most heavily on the poor. That would be disturbingly inequitable, contrary to the central thrust of Progressivism, the early twentieth-century movement that lent its name to a tax structure that imposes higher marginal rates on persons with higher incomes and confers immunity from income tax on those below an economic line that enables only bare survival. Would we say that such an antiprogressive tax is unconstitutional? Perhaps, but what court would declare it so? A federal court? The courts of a state?

Probably the correct answer is no court. Judges could adduce several reasons for refraining from nullifying the tax scheme just described. Even though it contains serious inequities, judges would undoubtedly not set it aside as a violation of equal protection. If a judge were to invent a "rational basis" for a scheme that seemed irrational as that described above, what that judge would really be saying is that the rationality of the scheme would better be left to the political branches to resolve. Although the worst form of unequal treatment is to pretend there is no difference between persons who are not equally situated, in our constitutional order judges are not empowered to intervene in the economy to impose a distribution of wealth they deem wiser than the arrangements devised by the people's representatives.

Separation of powers is another way of describing the basis for this prediction of what state courts would in fact do.[257] This constitutional doctrine allocates to the legis-

---

255. The relevant provisions of these state constitutions on religious tax immunity are set forth in the appendix following this chapter.

256. *See* Craig B. Mousin, "State Constitutions and Religious Liberty," in this volume; *see also* Daniel A. Crane, Beyond RFRA: Free Exercise of Religion Comes of Age in the State Courts, 10 St. Thomas L. Rev. 235 (1998).

257. According to Oliver Wendell Holmes, "[A] legal duty so called is nothing but a prediction that if a man does or omits certain things he will be made to suffer in this or that way by judgment of the court—and so of a legal right...The prophecies of what the courts will do in fact, and noth-

lature, not the judiciary, the power to tax and spend—an allocation deeply rooted in American constitutionalism, which in turn is grounded in British constitutionalism. The older source, British constitutionalism, repudiated in the seventeenth century the claim asserted by the early Stuarts, James I and Charles I, that they had inherent sovereign power to levy taxes. In the case of Charles I, Parliament made its point stick by trying and executing the king for treason. The principle that the crown may not impose taxes without the approval of Parliament was won in regicide and in a bloody civil war between Parliament and Stuart monarchs who asserted the crown's power to impose taxes as a matter of royal prerogative.

The American Revolution was premised on the people's right to alter or abolish a government that was acting unconstitutionally, imposing upon the Americans an "alien constitution." Thus, from the resolution of the Stamp Act Congress in 1765, through pamphlets such as Tom Paine's *Common Sense* in January of 1776, to the Declaration of Independence, the increasingly clear assertion of independence was premised on the conviction that taxation without representation was tyranny. This constitutional move did not repudiate British constitutionalism; it strengthened and deepened it. To justify the Glorious Revolution that ended the Stuart dynasty in 1689, John Locke had written in his *Second Treatise on Government* that Parliamentary sovereignty meant a monarch acting unconstitutionally could be deposed. What the American Revolution added to existing constitutional theory was popular sovereignty: the idea that the people have the right to alter or abolish a government acting unconstitutionally. This principle was secured constitutionally by reserving all revenue bills to the representatives of the people.[258]

For historical reasons such as these, judges might indeed be reluctant to nullify the hypothetical tax scheme described above that imposes significantly greater burdens on poor people than on the wealthy. Alas, the scheme is far too actual in many states. We call it not a tax but a lottery. But names do not always describe reality accurately, let alone fully. So if a governmental revenue-collection device walks and quacks like a tax, it must be or at least resemble a tax.[259]

The point of this characterization of state lotteries is not to persuade the reader of their evil but to illustrate a central conclusion: that the judiciary may be the wrong place to turn for help on matters of religious tax exemption. If some think of lotteries as governmentally induced gambling, then the debate on that subject must take place among the people—not in the language of the tax code, but in plainly accessible terms. A broad public discussion of the equities of lotteries and a rigorously honest disclosure of what happens to the revenues they collect would be a good thing for American democracy, even if state lotteries went on apace. Similarly, it would be a good thing for

---

ing more pretentious, are what I mean by the law." Sheldon M. Novick, ed., The Collected Works of Justice Holmes 391, 393 (1995).

258. U.S. Const. Art. I §8 provides: "The Congress shall have the power to lay and collect Taxes...to pay the Debts and provide for the common Defence and general Welfare of the United States."

259. The counterargument is that taxes are involuntary and playing the lottery is voluntary. This claim is flawed in two respects. First, it understates the misleading advertising by the government about the possibility of instant wealth. Second, it overstates the power of desperately poor people to allocate their scarce resources wisely. The predominant players of state lotteries are not like wealthy people playing the stock market and allocating risk judiciously according to the time when they will need to draw down income from their investments. They are typically misinformed and gullible people parting with money they cannot afford to lose, but willing to chance it because the government has induced them to do so.

the country if religious communities offered sound public reasons not for their receiving special privileges or benefits denied to others, but for their receiving, neutrally and evenhandedly, the same secular benefits accorded to other groups that also pursue the common good.

We will have to get used to seeing increasing attention given to the issue of religious tax exemption. If arguments in favor of taxing religious communities take a vicious turn or indulge in half-truths, that is no excuse for religious communities to reply in kind. On the contrary, especially when religious communities are misunderstood or mischaracterized by ideological adversaries, it will be important for them to remain serenely focused on the central issues — substantive neutrality, nondiscrimination, and nonentanglement — and to avoid becoming defensive about irrelevant red herrings.

Recent events suggest both that there is growing opposition to religious tax exemption and that religious communities may preserve their exempt status if they argue persuasively for their inclusion within tax benefits accorded to other charitable organizations. Three examples from the 1990s illustrate this point. The Benedictine Sisters in Erie County, Pennsylvania, managed to avert the imposition of massive taxes on hospitals they operated on a not-for-profit basis by demonstrating to the public and to local authorities the superlative quality of the health care they were providing to the community. Voters in Colorado rejected by a margin of more than 2–1 a proposed amendment to their state constitution that would have eliminated the tax-exempt status of all religious communities and many other kinds of nonprofit organizations. Religious leaders in Berkeley, California, successfully negotiated an agreement with the members of the local city council in which religious communities were exempted from a proposed tax on their revenues characterized as if they were derived from attendance at a play, movie, or concert.

These examples of satisfactory conclusions achieved outside of court mean not that there is no role for sound constitutional arguments on this issue, but simply that religious communities will have to get used to making their claims to their fellow citizens, to state and city governments, and to members of school boards and water districts. The constitutional arguments will be more or less the same — neutrality, nondiscrimination, and nonentanglement — as those used in litigation on this issue. But they may be greatly improved by being made not in lawyers' briefs submitted to courts, but in plain English in the court of public opinion and within well-designed ads in popular periodicals or on radio or television. As Bradley has noted, "we need to think about religious liberty free of the mental constraints that implicit commitments to judicial enforcement impose."[260]

Conclusion: Religious Communities and Other Mediating Structures in American Society

This project of the DePaul Center for Church/State Studies has taken the view that light will be shed on legal issues facing religious communities when law functions not in

---

260. Gerard V. Bradley, Protecting Religious Liberty: Judicial and Legislative Responsibilities, 42 DePaul L. Rev. 253, 260 (1992).

splendid isolation from other disciplines but in conjunction with social science research, theology, and history. In this interdisciplinary spirit I end this chapter with a few thoughts from scholars from disciplines other than the law.

In 1977 a leading sociologist, Peter L. Berger, and a prominent theologian, Richard John Neuhaus, wrote an important little volume on the host of intermediate institutions and associations that Americans have created to fill the huge gap between the vastness of the government and the loneliness of the isolated individual.[261] The enrichment of the American experience in this way was apparent to one of our most observant foreign visitors, Alexis de Tocqueville. Everywhere he turned, Tocqueville discovered that Americans had invented structures to mediate between the individual and the state. He coined a phrase—freedom of association—not found in our Constitution but expressive of a central theme in American life: "the most natural privilege of man, next to the right of acting for himself, is that of combining his exertions with his fellow creatures and of acting in common with them.... [The] right of association [is]...almost as inalienable in its nature as the right of personal liberty."[262]

These collectivities include above all the family,[263] then neighborhood associations, political parties, social clubs, professional associations, fraternities and sororities, schools and universities, labor unions and corporations, civil liberties groups, civil rights organizations—and yes, synagogues, mosques, and churches. Among all of these mediating structures, religious communities have played dynamic roles in shaping the republic.

Witte encapsulates the work of one of America's consummate historians, Martin E. Marty, summarizing several studies exploring the constructive role of religion in America:

> Religions deal uniquely with the deepest elements of individual and social life. Religions catalyze social, intellectual, and material exchange among citizens. Religions trigger economic, charitable, and educational impulses in citizens. Religions provide healthy checks and counterpoints to social and individual excess. Religions diffuse social and political crises and absolutisms by relativizing everyday life and its institutions. Religions provide prophecy, criticism, and exemplars for society. Religions force others to examine their presuppositions. Religions are unique repositories of tradition, wisdom, and perspective. Religions counsel against apathy. Religions are practiced and durable. Religions provide stamina and leadership, especially in times of individual and social crisis. Religions contribute to the theory and practice of the common good. Religions represent the unrepresented. Religions teach stewardship and preservation. Religions provide fresh starts for the desperate. Religion exalts the dignity and freedom of the individual.[264]

---

261. *See* Peter L. Berger and Richard John Neuhaus, To Empower People: The Role of Mediating Structures in Public Policy (1977); and Peter L. Berger and Richard John Neuhaus, To Empower People: From State to Civil Society (2d ed. 1996).

262. Alexis de Tocqueville, Democracy in America 196 (1945); *see* United Transportation Union v. Michigan, 401 U.S. 576 (1971); NAACP v. Alabama, NAACP v. Button, 371 U.S. 415 (1963); *see also* Rena Raggi, An Independent Right to Freedom of Association, 12 Harv. C.R.-C.L. L. Rev. 1 (1977); Mark De Wolfe Howe, Foreword: Political Theory and the Nature of Liberty, 67 Harv. L. Rev. 91 (1953); *but see* Roberts v. U.S. Jaycees, 468 U.S. 609 (1984).

263. *See* Robert Burt, The Constitution of the Family, 1979 Sup. Ct. Rev. 329.

264. John Witte, Religion and the American Constitutional Experiment: Essential Rights and Liberties 212 (2000). For the full discussion of the studies of religion in America, see Martin E. Marty, Politics, Religion, and the Common Good: Advancing a Distinctly American Conversation about Religion's Role in our Shared Life (2000).

A nonreligious reader need not smart at Witte's use of "unique" or "uniquely" in this passage. Note first that he uses the terms sparingly. He would be the first to acknowledge that many nonreligious groups also make their valuable, indeed their unique, contribution to public goods such as the dignity and freedom of the human person. Marty did not address the issue of tax immunity in his book, but he has offered powerful reasons to reject the antireligious mood that now prevails in some writing about tax exemption both on and off the Court.

Advocates and opponents of religious tax immunity can both claim to be arguing for religious freedom. Perhaps if both sides backed away from their advocacy roles long enough to contemplate that fact, they would also discover that religious freedom in America has long been a broad, all-encompassing terrain that offers both sides of the God question—believers and nonbelievers—room to breathe free.

In 1788 we, the people, ratified the U.S. Constitution in order to "form a more perfect union" than the weak confederation or league of states that had preceded it. Both the national government and the states need revenue to achieve the societal goals articulated in the preamble to our Constitution: "to...establish Justice, insure domestic Tranquility, provide for the common defence, promote the general Welfare, and secure the Blessings of Liberty to ourselves and our Posterity."[265] In fact, one of the principal reasons why the Constitution replaced the Articles of Confederation was the central government's inability to raise revenue to carry on essential attributes of governing. Very early in the life of our republic, however, we came to terms with immunities from state and local taxation. It was precisely a state tax levied upon an instrument of the national government, the Bank of the United States, that Chief Justice Marshall enjoined in *McCulloch v. Maryland*,[266] in which he described the power to tax as "the power to destroy."[267] The extension of the power of state and local taxation over religious communities may not be the power to destroy them. But Justice Douglas was right when he wrote in *Murdock* and repeated in *Follett*: "The power to tax the exercise of a privilege is the power to control or suppress its enjoyment."[268] That is why the privilege needs to be conjoined to the immunity.

Witte has demonstrated that the current practice of conferring immunity from state and local taxation upon religious communities was not, as the *Walz* Court led us to believe, "unbroken," "embedded in the fabric of our national life," "universally granted" by legislatures for more than two centuries, or even a successful avoidance of established religion. But the result in *Walz*—allowing states to confer tax immunity upon religious and nonreligious communities that engage in nonprofit, noncommercial activity to promote human well-being in a variety of ways—still has attractive arguments in its support.

The practice of declining to tax religious communities is no different from declining to tax labor unions or political parties that are bound by no particular religious ties. The government should neither dip into the collection plate at worship services nor take a slice of United Way contributions. If, in the pressing task of finding revenue, states and local governments become desperate enough to go after the churches, synagogues, and mosques, it is difficult to imagine what will keep them from also taking aim at other nonprofit entities within their jurisdiction.

---

265. U.S. Const., Preamble.
266. 17 U.S. 316 (1819).
267. *Id.* at 427.
268. *Murdock*, 319 U.S. at 112.

But who said that the government has jurisdiction over our minds and hearts? Thomas Jefferson challenged that way of thinking in his Bill for Establishing Religious Liberty:

> [*T*]*he opinions of men are not the object of civil government, nor under its jurisdiction,*...to suffer the civil magistrate to intrude his powers into the field of opinion and to restrain the profession or propagation of principles on supposition of their ill tendency is a dangerous fallacy, which at once destroys all religious liberty, because he being of course judge of that tendency will make his opinions the rule of judgment, and approve or condemn the sentiments of others only as they shall square with or differ from his own.[269]

Jefferson's colleague in the struggle for religious liberty in Virginia, James Madison, put it this way in his Memorial and Remonstrance:

> [I]f Religion be exempt from the authority of the Society at large, still less can it be subject to that of the Legislative Body. The latter are but the creatures and vicegerents of the former. Their jurisdiction is both derivative and limited: it is limited with regard to the coordinate departments, more necessarily is it limited with regard to the constituents. The preservation of a free Government requires not merely, that the metes and bounds which separate each department of power be invariably maintained; but more especially that neither of them be suffered to overleap the great Barrier which defends the rights of the people. The Rulers who are guilty of such an encroachment, exceed the commission from which they derive their authority, and are Tyrants. The People who submit to it are governed by laws made neither by themselves nor by an authority derived from them, and are slaves.[270]

Both Jefferson and Madison knew what they were talking about when they used the language of civil procedure to deny the power or jurisdiction of the government to intrude into the field of opinion. As Justice Brennan noted in his concurring opinion in *Walz*, moreover, though they were strong supporters of disestablishment in Virginia, Jefferson and Madison did not equate religious tax exemption with an establishment of religion. Jefferson was president when tax exemption was first given to churches in Washington, and Madison sat in the Virginia General Assembly that voted exemptions for churches in Virginia.[271]

Perhaps the vision of these two great Virginians will be abandoned in the twenty-first century. Yet the truths they perceived in Virginia are still relevant in our own age. To say this, of course, demands more reflection both about their times and about ours. One imagines that neither of them would want to have succeeding generations pay slight homage to them without taking them seriously as the challenging thinkers they were. In short, we are not bound to follow these two leaders simply because some graduate school committee selected them for inclusion within the American canon on religious freedom. That canon is now impressively broad enough that worry over excessive focus on Virginia is misplaced.[272]

---

269. Thomas Jefferson, A Bill for Establishing Religious Liberty (emphasis in original), *as cited in* Noonan and Gaffney, *supra* note 1, at 170.

270. James Madison, Memorial and Remonstrance ¶ 2, *as cited in* Noonan and Gaffney, *supra* note 1, at 174.

271. *Walz*, 397 U.S. at 684–85 (Brennan, J., concurring).

272. *See, e.g.*, discussion of William Penn in Arlin M. Adams and Charles Emmerich, A Nation Dedicated to Religious Liberty: The Constitutional Heritage of the Religion Clauses (1990); the treatment of the Baptists, notably Isaac Backus, discussed in previous chapter. *See, e.g.*, William G.

I have argued that the Madisonian and Jeffersonian insights that linked nonestablishment to free exercise of religion should not be abandoned lightly, especially not for the sake of mere expediency or for a secularist ideology that would jeopardize governmental neutrality, tend toward discriminatory application of tax laws to unpopular majorities, and enmesh government officials in matters of faith that they have no business defining or trying to probe or control. The attempt to split the two provisions into competing clauses, and worse yet, the inference that free exercise is therefore subservient to nonestablishment is an academic construct that fails to account for the incorrigibly religious character of American society.[273]

Walz endures as a precedent at the moment, but in the shifting sands of constitutional law, it too could pass. To avert that possibility, religious communities should make common cause with agnostics or atheists and with members of a wide variety of interest groups including the National Rifle Association and Handgun Control, the Sierra Club and Friends of the Earth, People for the American Way and the Institute for Justice, the National Organization for Women and Concerned Women of America.[274] In Madison's phrase, "it is proper to take alarm at the first experiment upon our liberties."[275] In short, all charitable groups that promote the human good in America deserve to be included in the broad range of communities and associations that are immune from state and local taxation.

McLaughlin, New England Dissent 1630–1833: The Baptists and Separation of Church and State (1971), and materials in Noonan and Gaffney, *supra* note 1.

273. *See* Richard John Neuhaus, ed., Unsecular America (1986); George H. Gallup and Robert Bezilla, The Religious Life of Young Americans: A Compendium of Surveys on the Spiritual Beliefs and Practices of Teenagers and Young Adults (1992); George H. Gallup and Robert Bezilla, The Role of the Bible in American Society: On the Occasion of the 50th Anniversary of National Bible Week (1990); George H. Gallup and Jim Castelli, The People's Religion: American Faith in the 90s (1990); James Davison Hunter, The Williamsburg Charter Survey: Methodology and Findings, 8 J.L. & Relig. 257 (1990); James Davison Hunter, Pluralism: Past and Present, 8 J.L. & Relig. 273 (1990); Edward McGlynn Gaffney, Jr., Religion and Public Life: Comments on the Williamsburg Charter Survey, 8 J.L. & Relig. 279 (1990); and Os Guinness, The Williamsburg Charter Survey: Bicentennial Reflections, 8 J.L. & Relig. 287 (1990).

274. *See* Bob Jones Univ. v. United States, 461 U.S. 574, 609 (1983) (Powell, J., concurring in part and concurring in the judgment) ("important role played by tax exemptions in encouraging diverse, indeed often sharply conflicting, activities and viewpoints").

275. Madison, Memorial and Remonstrance, ¶ 3, *as cited in* Noonan and Gaffney, *supra* note 1, at 174.

Appendix

State Constitutions Containing Provisions for Tax Exemption of Charitable Organizations, Including Religious Bodies

Edward McGlynn Gaffney, Jr.

There are no provisions expressly related to tax exemption for charitable organizations in the constitutions of the following eleven states: Connecticut, Kansas, Maine, Maryland, Massachusetts, Mississippi, Nebraska, Oregon, Rhode Island, Vermont, and Wisconsin. All these states provide for tax exemption of charitable organizations in their respective tax codes.

Alabama (1901)

Ala. Const., Art. I, § 3:

That no religion shall be established by law; that no preference shall be given by law to any religious sect, society, denomination, or mode of worship; that no one shall be compelled by law to attend any place of worship; nor to pay any tithes, taxes, or other rate for building or repairing any place of worship, or for maintaining any minister or ministry; that no religious test shall be required as a qualification to any office or public trust under this state; and that the civil rights, privileges, and capacities of any citizen shall not be in any manner affected by his religious principles.

Ala. Const., Art. IV, § 91:

The legislature shall not tax the property, real or personal, of the state, counties, or other municipal corporations, or cemeteries; nor lots in incorporated cities and towns, or within one mile of any city or town to the extent of one acre, nor lots one mile or more distant from such cities or towns to the extent of five acres, with the buildings thereon, when same are used exclusively for religious worship, for schools, or for purposes purely charitable.

Ala. Const., Art XI, § 217 as amended, Amend. 373:

The following property shall be exempt from all ad valorem taxation: the real and personal property of the state, counties, and municipalities and property denoted exclusively to religious, educational or charitable purposes....

Ala. Const., Art. XII, § 229 as amended, Amend. 27:

The Legislature shall, by general laws, provide for the payment to the state of Alabama of a business privilege tax by corporations organized under the laws of this state which shall be in proportion to the amount of capital stock; by strictly benevolent, educational or religious corporations...shall not be required to pay such a tax on their withdrawable or repurchasable shares....

Ala. Const., Art. XII, § 232 as amended, Amend. 473:

The legislature shall, by general law, provide for the payment to the state of Alabama of a business privilege tax by such corporation, but such business privilege tax shall be based on the actual amount of capital employed in this state. Strictly benevolent, educational, or religious corporations shall not be required to pay such a tax.

Alaska

Alaska Const., Art. IX, § 4:

Exemptions. The real and personal property of the State or its political subdivisions shall be exempt from taxation under conditions and exceptions which may be provided by law. All, or any portion of, property used exclusively for non-profit religious, charitable, cemetery, or educational purposes, as defined by law, shall be exempt from taxation. Other exemptions of like or different kind may be granted by general law. All valid existing exemptions shall be retained until otherwise provided by law.

Arizona (1912)

Ariz. Const., Art. IX, § 10:

No tax shall be laid or appropriation of public money made in aid of any church, or private or sectarian school, or any public service corporation.

Ariz. Const., Art. IX, § 2:

There shall be exempt from taxation all federal, state, county and municipal property. Property of educational, charitable and religious associations or institutions not used or held for profit may be exempt from taxation by law. Public debts, as evidenced by the bonds of Arizona, its counties, municipalities or other subdivisions, shall also be exempt from taxation. **All household goods owned by the user thereof and used solely for noncommercial purposes shall be exempt from** taxation, and such person entitled to such exemption shall not be required to take any affirmative action to receive the benefit of such exemption.

Arkansas (1874)

Ark. Const., Art. 16, § 5:

The following property shall be exempt from taxation: public property used exclusively for public purposes; churches used as such; cemeteries used exclusively as such; school buildings and apparatus; libraries and grounds used exclusively for school purposes; and buildings and grounds and materials used exclusively for public charity.

Ark. Const., Amend 32, § 1

Whenever in any county where there is located a public hospital owned by such county or by any municipal corporation therein, whether such hospital be operated by such county or municipal corporation or by a benevolent association as the agent or lessee of such county or municipal corporation, one hundred or more electors of such county shall file a petition with the county judge asking that an annual tax on real and personal property in such county be levied for the purpose of maintaining, operating and supporting such hospital and shall specify a rate of taxation not exceeding one mill on the dollar of the assessed value of real and personal property in the county.

California (1879)

Cal. Const., Art. XIII, § 2:

The Legislature may provide for property taxation, of all forms of tangible personal property, shares of capital stock, evidences of indebtedness, and any legal or equitable interest therein not exempt under any other provision of this article. The Legislature, two-thirds of the membership of each house concurring, may classify such personal property for differential taxation or for exemption. The tax on any interest in notes, debentures, or shares of capital stock, bonds, solvent credits, deeds of trust, or mortgages shall not exceed four-tenths of one percent of full value, and the tax per dollar of full value shall not be higher on personal property than on real property in the same taxing jurisdiction.

Cal. Const., Art. XIII, § 3:

The following are exempt from property taxation:...property used for libraries and museums that are free and open to the public and property used exclusively for public schools, community colleges, state colleges, and state universities. Buildings, land, equipment, and securities used exclusively for educational purposes by a nonprofit institution of higher education. Buildings, land on which they are situated, and equipment used exclusively for religious worship.

Cal. Const., Art. XIII, § 4:

The legislature may exempt from property taxation in whole or in part: Property used exclusively for religious, hospital, or charitable purposes and owned or held in trust by corporations or other entities (1) that are organized and operating for those purposes, (2) that are nonprofit, and (3) no part of whose net earnings inures to the benefit of any private shareholder or individual....

Real property not used for commercial purposes that is reasonably and necessarily required for parking vehicles of persons worshipping on land exempt by Section 3(f).

Colorado

Colo. Const., Art. X, § 5:

Property used for religious worship, schools and charitable purposes exempt. Property, real and personal, that is used solely and exclusively for religious worship, for schools or for strictly charitable purposes, also cemeteries not used or held for private or corporate profit, shall be exempt from taxation, unless otherwise provided by general law.

Connecticut

No relevant section.

Delaware (1897)

Del. Const., Art. X, § 3:

No portion of any fund now existing, or which may hereafter be appropriated, or raised by tax, for educational purposes, shall be appropriated to, or used by, or in aid of any sectarian, church or denominational school; provided, that all real or personal property used for school purposes, where the tuition is free, shall be exempt from taxation and assessment for public purposes.

Florida (1887)

Fla. Const., Art. VII, § 3

... Such portions of property as are used predominantly for educational, literary, scientific, religious or charitable purposes may be exempted by general law from taxation.

Georgia (1945)

Ga. Const., Art. VII, § 2, par. 4:

Any law which reduces or repeals exemptions granted to religious or burial grounds or institutions of purely public charity must be approved by two-thirds of the members elected to each branch of the General Assembly.

Hawaii

Hawaii Const., Art. VII, § 4:

No tax shall be levied or appropriation of public money or property made, nor shall the public credit be used, directly or indirectly, except for a public purpose. No grant shall be made except pursuant to standard provided by law.

Idaho

Idaho Const., Art. VII, § 4:

Public property exempt from taxation. The property of the United States, except when taxation thereof is authorized by the United States, the state, counties, towns, cities, villages, school districts, and other municipal corporations and public libraries shall be exempt from taxation; provided, however, that unimproved real property owned or held by the department of fish and game may be subject to a fee in lieu of taxes if the fees are authorized by statute but not to exceed the property tax for the property at the time of acquisition by the department of fish and game, unless the tax for that class of property shall have been increased.

Idaho Const., Art. XXI, § 19:

It is ordained by the state of Idaho that perfect toleration of religious sentiment shall be secured, and no inhabitant of said state shall ever be molested in person or property on account of his or her mode of religious worship. And the people of the state of Idaho do agree and declare that we forever disclaim all right and title to the unappropriated public lands lying within the boundaries thereof, and to all lands lying within said limits owned or held by any Indians or Indian tribes; and until the title thereto shall have been extinguished by the United States, the same shall be subject to the disposition of the United States, and said Indian lands shall remain under the absolute jurisdiction and control of the congress of the United States; that the lands belonging to citizens of the United States, residing without the said state of Idaho, shall never be taxed at a higher rate than the lands belonging to the residents thereof. That no taxes shall be imposed by the state on the lands or property therein belonging to, or which may hereafter be purchased by, the United States, or reserved for its use. And the debts and liabilities of this territory shall be assumed and paid by the state of Idaho. That this ordinance shall be irrevocable, without the consent of the United States and the people of the state of Idaho.

Illinois (1870)

Ill. Const., Art. IX, § 6:

The General Assembly by law may exempt from taxation only the property of the State, units of local government and school districts and property used exclusively for agricultural and horticultural societies, and for school, religious, cemetery and charitable purposes. The General Assembly by law may grant homestead exemptions or rent credits.

Indiana (1851)

Ind. Const., Art. 10, § 1:

The General Assembly shall provide, by law, for a uniform and equal rate of property assessment and taxation and shall prescribe regulations to secure a just valuation for taxation of all property, both real and personal. The General Assembly may exempt from property taxation any property in any of the following classes: (1) Property being used for municipal, education, literary, scientific, religious or charitable purpose....

Iowa

Iowa Const., Art. I, § 3:

The general assembly shall make no law respecting an establishment of religion, or prohibiting the free exercise thereof; nor shall any person be compelled to attend any place of worship, pay tithes, taxes, or other rates for building or repairing places of worship, or the maintenance of any minister, or ministry.

Kansas (1861)

No relevant section.

Kentucky (1891)

Ky. Const., § 170:

There shall be exempt from taxation public property used for public purposes; places of burial not held for private or corporate profit; real property owned and occupied by, and personal property both tangible and intangible owned by, institutions of religion; institutions of purely public charity, and institutions of education not used or employed for gain by any person or corporation, and the income of which is devoted solely to the cause of education, public libraries, their endowments, and the income of such property as is used exclusively for their maintenance....

Ky. Const., § 189:

No portion of any fund or tax now existing, or that may hereafter be raised or levied for educational purposes, shall be appropriated to, or used by, or in aid of, any church, sectarian or denominational school.

Louisiana (1921)

La. Const., Art. VII, § 21:

In addition to the homestead exemption provided for in Section 20 of this Article, the following property and no other shall be exempt from ad valorem taxation.... Property owned by a nonprofit corporation or association organized and operated exclusively for religious, dedicated places of burial, charitable, health, welfare, fraternal, or educational purposes, no part of the net earnings of which inure to the benefit of any private shareholder or member thereof and which is declared to be exempt from federal or state income tax....

None of the property listed in Paragraph (B) shall be exempt if owned, operated, leased, or used for commercial purposes unrelated to the exempt purposes of the corporation or association.

Maine

No relevant section.

Maryland

No relevant section.

Massachusetts

No relevant section.

Michigan

Mich. Const., Art. IX, § 4:

Property owned and occupied by nonprofit religious or educational organizations and used exclusively for religious or educational purposes, as defined by law, shall be exempt from real and personal property taxes.

Minnesota (1857)

Minn. Const., Art. X, § 1:

The power of taxation shall never be surrendered, suspended or contracted away. Taxes shall be uniform upon the same class of subjects, and shall be levied and collected for public purposes, but public burying grounds, public school houses, public hospitals, academies, colleges, universities, all seminaries of learning, all churches, church property, houses of worship, institutions of purely public charity, and public property used exclusively for any public purpose, shall be exempt from taxation except as provided in this section.... The legislature may authorize municipal corporations to levy and collect assessments for local improvements upon property benefited thereby without regard to cash valuation. The legislature by law may define or limit the property exempt under this section other than churches, houses of worship, and property solely used for educational purposes by academies, colleges, universities and seminaries of learning.

Mississippi

No relevant section.

Missouri (1945)

Mo. Const., Art. X, § 6:

All property, real and personal, of the state, counties and other political subdivisions, and nonprofit cemeteries, shall be exempt from taxation; all personal property held as industrial inventories, including raw materials, work in progress and finished work on hand, by manufacturers and refiners, and all personal property held as goods, wares, merchandise, stock in trade or inventory for resale by distributors, wholesalers, or retail merchants or establishments shall be exempt from taxation; and all property, real and personal, not held for private or corporate profit and used exclusively for religious worship, for schools and colleges, for purposes purely charitable, or for agricultural and horticultural societies may be exempted from taxation by general law....

Montana (1889)

Mont. Const., Art. VIII, § 5:

The legislature may exempt from taxation:... Institutions of purely public charity, hospitals and places of burial not used or held for private or corporate profit, places for actual religious worship, and property used exclusively for educational purposes.

Nebraska (1875)

No relevant section.

Nevada (1864)

Nev. Const., Art. 8, § 2:

All real property, and possessory rights to the same, as well as personal property in this State, belonging to the corporations now existing or hereafter created shall be subject to taxation, the same as property of individuals; provided, that the property of corporations formed for Municipal, Charitable, Religious, or Educational purposes may be exempted by law.

Nev. Const., Art. 10, § 1, par. 8:

The legislature may exempt by law property used for municipal, educational, literary, scientific or other charitable purposes, or to encourage the conservation of energy or the substitution of other sources for fossil sources of energy.

New Hampshire

N.H. Const., Pt. 1, Art. 12:

Every member of the community has a right to be protected by it, in the enjoyment of his life, liberty, and property; he is therefore bound to contribute his share in the expense of such protection, and to yield his personal service when necessary. But no part of a man's property shall be taken from him, or applied to public uses, without his own consent, or that of the representative body of the people. Nor are the inhabitants of this state controllable by any other laws than those to which they, or their representative body, have given their consent.

N.H. Const., Pt. 2, Art. 83:

Knowledge and learning, generally diffused through a community, being essential to the preservation of a free government; and spreading the opportunities and advantages of education through the various parts of the country, being highly conducive to promote this end; it shall be the duty of the legislators and magistrates, in all future periods of this government, to cherish the interest of literature and the sciences, and all seminaries and public schools, to encourage private and public institutions, rewards, and immunities for the promotion of agriculture, arts, sciences, commerce, trades, manufactures, and natural history of the country; to countenance and inculcate the principles of humanity and general benevolence, public and private charity, industry and economy, honesty and punctuality, sincerity, sobriety, and all social affections, and generous sentiments, among the people: Provided, nevertheless, that no money raised by taxation shall ever be granted or applied for the use of the schools or institutions of any religious sect or denomination.

New Jersey (1947)

N.J. Const., Art. VIII, § 1, par. 2:

Exemption from taxation may be granted only by general laws. Until otherwise provided by law all exemptions from taxation validly granted and now in existence shall be continued. Exemptions from taxation may be altered or repealed, except those exempting real and personal property used exclusively for religious, educational, charitable or cemetery purposes....

New Mexico (1913)

N.M. Const., Art. VIII, § 3:

The property of the United States, the state and all counties, towns, cities and school districts and other municipal corporations, public libraries, community ditches and all laterals thereof, all church property not used for commercial purposes, all property used for educational or charitable purposes, all cemeteries not used or held for private or corporate profit and all bonds of the state of New Mexico, and of the counties, municipalities and districts thereof shall be exempt from taxation. Provided, however, that any property required by public libraries, community ditches and all laterals thereof, property acquired by churches, property acquired and used for educational or charitable purposes, and property acquired by cemeteries not used or held for private or corporate profit, and property acquired by the Indian service, and property acquired by the United States government or by the state of New Mexico by outright purchase or trade, where such property was, prior to such transfer, subject to the lien of any tax or assessment for the principal or interest of any bonded indebtedness shall not be exempt from such lien, nor from the payment of such taxes or assessments. Exemptions of personal property from ad valorem taxation may be provided by law if approved by a three-fourths majority vote of all the members elected to each house of the legislature.

New York (1895)

N.Y. Const., Art. XVI, § 1:

The power of taxation shall never be surrendered, suspended or contracted away, except as to securities issued for public purposes pursuant to law. Any laws which delegate the taxing power shall specify the types of taxes which may be imposed thereunder and provide for their review. Exemptions from taxation may be granted only by general laws. Exemptions may be altered or repealed except those exempting real or personal property used exclusively for religious, educational or charitable purposes as defined by law and owned by any corporation or association organized or conducted exclusively for one or more of such purposes and not operating for profit.

North Carolina (1868)

N.C. Const., Art. V, § 2, par. (3):

Property belonging to the State, counties, and municipal corporations shall be exempt from taxation. The General Assembly shall exempt cemeteries and property held for educational, scientific, literary, cultural, charitable, or religious purposes....

North Dakota (1889)

N.D. Const., Art. 10, § 5:

...The legislative assembly may by law exempt any or all classes of personal property from taxation and within the meaning of this section, fixtures, buildings and improvements of every character, whatsoever, upon land shall be deemed personal property. The property of the United States, to the extent immunity from taxation has not been waived by an act of Congress, property of the state, county, and municipal corporations, to the extent immunity from taxation has not been waived by an act of the legislative assembly, and property used exclusively for schools, religious, cemetery, charitable or other public purposes shall be exempt from taxation. Except as restricted by this article, the legislative assembly may provide for raising revenue and fixing the situs of all property for the purpose of taxation. Provided that all taxes and exemptions in force when this amendment is adopted shall remain in force until otherwise provided by statute.

Ohio (1851)

Ohio Const., Art. XII, § 2:

...Without limiting the general power, subject to the provisions of Article I of this constitution, to determine the subjects and methods of taxation or exemptions therefrom, general laws may be passed to exempt burying grounds, public school houses, houses used exclusively for public worship, institutions used exclusively for charitable purposes, and public property used exclusively for any public purpose, but all such laws shall be subject to alteration or repeal; and the value of all property so exempted shall, from time to time, be ascertained and published as may be directed by law.

Oklahoma (1907)

Okla. Const., Art. X, § 6:

...all property used for free public libraries, free museums, public cemeteries, property used exclusively for nonprofit schools and colleges, and all property used exclusively for religious and charitable purposes, and all property of the United States except property for which a federal agency obtains title through foreclosure, voluntary or involuntary liquidation or bankruptcy unless the taxation of such property is prohibited by federal law; all property of this state, and of counties and of municipalities of this state; household goods of the heads of families, tools, implements, and livestock employed in the support of the family, not exceeding One Hundred Dollars ($ 100.00) in value, and all growing crops, shall be exempt from taxation: Provided, that all property not herein specified now exempt from taxation under the laws of the Territory of Oklahoma, shall be exempt from taxation until otherwise provided by law.

Oregon

No relevant section.

Pennsylvania (1874)

Pa. Const., Art. VIII, § 2(a):

The General Assembly may by law exempt from taxation:

Actual places of regularly stated religious worship;

Actual places of burial, when used or held by a person or organization deriving no private or corporate profit therefrom and no substantial part of whose activity consists of selling personal property in connection therewith;

That portion of public property which is actually and regularly used for public purposes;

That portion of the property owned and occupied by any branch, post or camp of honorably discharged servicemen or servicewomen which is actually and regularly used for benevolent, charitable or patriotic purposes; and

Institutions of purely public charity, but in the case of any real property tax exemptions only that portion of real property of such institution which is actually and regularly used for the purposes of the institution.

Rhode Island

No relevant section.

South Carolina (1895)

S.C. Const., Art. X, § 1:

The General Assembly shall provide by law for a uniform and equal rate of assessment and taxation, and shall prescribe regulations to secure a just valuation for taxation of all property, real, personal and possessory, except mines and mining claims, the products of which alone shall be taxed; and also excepting such property as may be exempted by law for municipal, educational, literary, scientific, religious or charitable purposes: Provided, however, That the General Assembly may impose a capitation tax upon such domestic animals as from their nature and habits are destructive of other property: And provided, further, That the General Assembly may provide for a graduated tax on incomes, and for a graduated license on occupations and business....

S.C. Const., Art. X, § 3:

There shall be exempt from ad valorem taxation:all property of the State, counties, municipalities, school districts and other political subdivisions, if the property is used exclusively for public purposes; all property of all schools, colleges and other institutions of learning and all charitable institutions in the nature of hospitals and institutions caring for the infirmed, the handicapped, the aged, children and indigent persons, except where the profits of such institutions are applied to private use; all property of all public libraries, churches, parsonages and burying grounds; all property of all charitable trusts and foundations used exclusively for charitable and public purposes....

S.C. Const., Art. X, § 4:

There shall be exempted from taxation all county, township and municipal property used exclusively for public purposes and not for revenue, and the property of all schools, colleges and institutions of learning, all charitable institutions in the nature of asylums for the infirm, deaf and dumb, blind, idiotic and indigent persons, except where the profits of such institutions are applied to private uses; all public libraries, churches, parsonages and burying grounds; but property of associations and societies, although connected with charitable objects, shall not be exempt from State, county or municipal taxation: Provided, That as to real estate this exemption shall not extend beyond the buildings and premises actually occupied by such schools, colleges, institutions of learning, asylums, libraries, churches, parsonages and burial grounds, although connected with charitable objects.

South Dakota (1889)

S.D. Const., Art. XI, § 6:

The Legislature shall, by general law, exempt from taxation, property used exclusively for agricultural and horticultural societies, for school, religious, cemetery and charitable purposes, property acquired and used exclusively for public highway purposes, and personal property to any amount not exceeding in value two hundred dollars for each individual liable to taxation.

Tennessee (1870)

Tenn. Const., Art. 2, § 28:

In accordance with the following provisions, all property real, personal or mixed shall be subject to taxation, but the Legislature may exempt such as may be held by the State, by Counties, Cities or Towns, and used exclusively for public or corporation purposes, and such as may be held and used for purposes purely religious, charitable, scientific, literary or educational....

Texas (1876)

Tex. Const., Art. VIII, § 2(a):

All occupation taxes shall be equal and uniform upon the same class of subjects within the limits of the authority levying the tax; but the legislature may, by general laws, exempt from taxation public property used for public purposes; actual places of religious worship, also any property owned by a church or by a strictly religious society for the exclusive use as a dwelling place for the ministry of such church or religious society, and which yields no revenue whatever to such church or religious society; provided that such exemption shall not extend to more property than is reasonably necessary for a dwelling place and in no event more than one acre of land; places of burial not held for private or corporate profit; all buildings used exclusively and reasonably necessary in conducting any association engaged in promoting the religious, educational and physical development of boys, girls, young men or young women operating under a State or National organization of like character; also the endowment funds of such institutions of learning and religion not used with a view to profit; and when the same are invested in bonds or mortgages, or in land or other property which has been and shall hereafter be bought in by such institutions under foreclosure sales made to satisfy or protect such bonds or mortgages, that such exemption of such land and property shall continue only for two years after the purchase of the same at such sale by such institutions and no longer, and institutions of purely public charity; and all laws exempting property from taxation other than the property mentioned in this Section shall be null and void.

Utah (1896)

Utah Const., Art. XIII, § 2(2):

The following are property tax exemptions: the property of the state, school districts, and public libraries; the property of counties, cities, towns, special districts, and all other political subdivisions of the state, except that to the extent and in the manner provided by the Legislature the property of a county, city, town, special district, or other political subdivision of the state located outside of its geographic boundaries as defined by law may be subject to the ad valorem property tax; property owned by a nonprofit entity which is used exclusively for religious, charitable, or educational purposes; places of burial not held or used for private or corporate benefit....

Vermont

No relevant section.

Virginia 1902

Va. Const., Art. X, § 6:

Except as otherwise provided in this Constitution, the following property and no other shall be exempt from taxation, State and local, including inheritance taxes:...Real estate and personal property owned and exclusively occupied or used by churches or religious bodies for religious worship or for the residences of their ministers.... Property owned by public libraries or by institutions of learning not conducted for profit, so long as such property is primarily used for literary, scientific, or educational purposes or purposes incidental thereto. This provision may also apply to leasehold interests in such property as may be provided by general law.... Property used by its owner for religious, charitable, patriotic, historical, benevolent, cultural, or public park and playground purposes, as may be provided by classification or designation by a three-fourths vote of the members elected to each house of the General Assembly and subject to such restrictions and conditions as may be prescribed.

Washington (1889)

Wash. Const., Art. VII, § 1 (Amend. 81):

Such property as the legislature may by general laws shall provide shall be exempt from taxation. Property of the United States and of the state, counties, school districts and other municipal corporations, and credits secured by property actually taxed in this state, not exceeding in value the value of such property, shall be exempt from taxation.

West Virginia

West Va. Const., Art. X, § 1:

...[P]roperty used for educational, literary, scientific, religious or charitable purposes, all cemeteries, public property, the personal property, including livestock, employed exclusively in agriculture as above defined and the products of agriculture as so defined while owned by the producers may by law be exempted from taxation....

Wisconsin (1848)

No relevant section.

Wyoming (1890)

Wyo. Const., Art. 15, § 12:

The property of the United States, the state, counties, cities, towns, school districts and municipal corporations, when used primarily for a governmental purpose, and public libraries, lots with the buildings thereon used exclusively for religious worship, church parsonages, church schools and public cemeteries, shall be exempt from taxation, and such other property as the legislature may by general law provide.

Employment in Religious Organizations

Patrick J. Schiltz and Douglas Laycock

Religious leaders play a critical role in the spiritual lives of Americans. They head the churches[1] to which most Americans belong.[2] They conduct worship services, perform sacraments, and direct the good works that are central to most major faiths. They teach the tenets of faith to children and adults. They provide support and guidance through life's triumphs and tragedies. And in some traditions, religious leaders are said to hold "the keys of the kingdom"[3] — the very means of achieving eternal salvation.

At its core, the free exercise of religion means the freedom to choose what to believe — a freedom so important that, unlike virtually all other freedoms, it has consistently been described as "absolute."[4] But the freedom to choose one's religious leaders is almost as important as the freedom to choose one's religious beliefs. Indeed, the two freedoms are largely inseparable. The free exercise of religion cannot exist in any meaningful way unless the faithful — individually and in community — are free to choose who will baptize their children, bury their parents, and help them discern God's will in all aspects of their daily lives.

Unfortunately, most employment decisions of religious organizations have received little constitutional protection. Decisions regarding those who are traditionally regarded as "ministers" — for example, the pastors who lead Methodist congregations or the rabbis who lead Jewish synagogues — have largely been protected. But decisions regarding others who play important roles in the lives of believers — parochial school teachers, faculty at sectarian colleges, church administrators, cantors, organists, and the like — have received so little constitutional protection that in many courts those decisions would literally be unaffected by the repeal of the First Amendment. And even the protection for ministers is now under attack.

---

1. By "church" or "religious organization" we mean not only Christian churches, and not only the traditional congregation, parish, synagogue, mosque, or temple, but also regional, national, and international religious organizations as well as religious schools, hospitals, social service agencies, and the like. Where judicial doctrine or other context requires, we distinguish the church as a place of worship, and church as a denomination or similar association of places of worship, from all other religious organizations.

2. Bureau of the Census, U.S. Dep't of Commerce, Statistical Abstract of the United States 70 tbl. 88 (116th ed. 1996).

3. Matt. 16:19.

4. Bob Jones Univ. v. United States, 461 U.S. 574, 603 (1983); Wisconsin v. Yoder, 406 U.S. 205, 219 (1972); Cantwell v. Connecticut, 310 U.S. 296, 303 (1940).

One goal of this chapter is to advise religious organizations about how they can reduce the risk that courts will interfere with their employment decisions. But first we
must discuss at some length the various approaches that courts have taken in deciding
when those employment decisions are constitutionally protected. For the most part, our
discussion will be descriptive. We view much of what we will describe as troubling and,
in some instances, indefensible. But because of space limitations, a detailed critique will
have to await another day.

Constitutional Protection of Religious Employment Decisions

Courts have taken four approaches in determining when employment decisions of
religious organizations are protected by the First Amendment.

First, some courts have explicitly invoked neither the Free Exercise Clause nor the
Establishment Clause, but instead the "*Watson* line of cases"—a series of Supreme
Court decisions beginning with *Watson v. Jones*.[5] Most of these cases do not specify a
constitutional clause, but they do protect religious autonomy. This line of cases has
evolved in complex and ambiguous ways; the later cases give significantly less protection
to religious autonomy than do the earlier ones. We will discuss the *Watson* line in detail,
because it is a rare religious employment decision that does not cite at least one case in
the line.

Second, some courts have looked to the Free Exercise Clause and, specifically, to the
understanding of the Clause expressed in *Sherbert v. Verner*.[6] Under the *Sherbert* interpretation, government may not burden religious exercise unless the burden is necessary
to further a compelling state interest.

Third, some courts have looked to the understanding of the Free Exercise Clause expressed in *Employment Division v. Smith*,[7] rather than the one expressed in *Sherbert*. According to *Smith*, government may burden religious exercise for any reason or no reason, as long as it acts pursuant to a "generally applicable law."

Finally, some courts have looked to the Establishment Clause. Although the Supreme
Court has used this clause only to invalidate governmental action that *benefits* religion,
some lower courts have relied upon its prohibition of entanglement between church
and state to protect churches from being *burdened*—such as through state regulation of
their employment decisions.

When we characterize courts as taking four approaches, we are being clearer than
the courts themselves have been. Many courts have used more than one of these approaches in a single case, while others have combined elements of two or three approaches—sometimes within the same sentence or paragraph—into an approach
unique to that court. Sometimes these combinations are theoretically coherent; often,
they are not.

---

5. 80 U.S. (13 Wall.) 679 (1871).
6. 374 U.S. 398 (1963).
7. 494 U.S. 872 (1990).

The *Watson* Line of Cases

Watson *and its progeny*

Like many churches during the Civil War, Walnut Street Presbyterian Church in Louisville, Kentucky, became deeply divided over the issue of slavery. A majority of the church's general membership was antislavery, but a majority of the elders and trustees was proslavery. Each group claimed to be the "true" church and to have the exclusive right to use and control the church's property. The General Assembly of the Presbyterian Church sided with the antislavery faction. Litigation ensued, and the matter ended up before the United States Supreme Court.

In *Watson v. Jones*,[8] the Court held that the decision of the General Assembly had to be enforced. *Watson* was a decision of federal common law, not constitutional law,[9] but, as the Court itself later recognized, it "radiate[d] ... a spirit of freedom for religious organizations, an independence from secular control or manipulation, in short, power to decide for themselves, free from state interference, matters of church government as well as those of faith and doctrine."[10] *Watson* said that although disputes within churches "should be regretted," courts when called upon to resolve those disputes "must perform their functions as in other cases."[11] In the case of a gift or bequest subject to an express trust for the support of a particular religious doctrine, a court's functions extended even to deciding whether the person holding the funds was still teaching that doctrine.[12]

What motivated the Court, then, was not a desire to protect the government from becoming entangled with religion—a concern sometimes identified with the Establishment Clause—but rather a desire to protect the freedom of believers to create churches, establish tribunals to resolve disputes within those churches, and have the decisions of those tribunals respected—concerns most naturally identified with the Free Exercise Clause. According to the Court, the Walnut Street Presbyterian Church had become "a member of a much larger and more important religious organization," had put itself "under [the] government and control" of that organization, and had agreed to be "bound by its orders and judgments."[13] To permit the local congregation to withdraw from the larger church or to ignore its orders and decisions would, in the Court's view, infringe religious liberty.

> The right to organize voluntary religious associations to assist in the expression and dissemination of any religious doctrine, and to create tribunals for the decision of controverted questions of faith within the association, and for the ecclesiastical government of all the individual members, congregations, and officers within the general association, is unquestioned. All who unite themselves to such a body do so with an implied consent to this government, and are bound to submit to it. But it would be a vain consent and would lead to the total subversion of such religious bodies, if any one aggrieved by one of their decisions could appeal to the secular courts and have them reversed. It is of the

---

8. 80 U.S. (13 Wall.) 679 (1871).

9. The Supreme Court did not hold that the First Amendment was applicable to the states until 1940. *See Cantwell*, 310 U.S. at 303.

10. Kedroff v. Saint Nicholas Cathedral, 344 U.S. 94, 116 (1952).

11. *Watson*, 80 U.S. at 713–14.

12. *See id.* at 723–27.

13. *Id.* at 726–27.

essence of these religious unions, and of their right to establish tribunals for the decision of questions arising among themselves, that those decisions should be binding in all cases of ecclesiastical cognizance, subject only to such appeals as the organism itself provides for.[14]

Of course, the power of church tribunals is not unlimited. They cannot try murder cases or tort cases or issue judgments that would bind secular courts.[15] But when a dispute is over "a matter which concerns theological controversy, church discipline, ecclesiastical government, or the conformity of the members of the church to the standard of morals required of them,"[16] and the church has established an internal means for deciding the dispute, then "legal tribunals must accept such decisions as final, and as binding on them, in their application to the case before them."[17]

Thus, according to *Watson*, the task of a court confronted with a dispute within a religious organization is narrow. The court can determine whether the dispute is "ecclesiastical," and it can identify the highest church body to have passed on the dispute. But then it must accept and enforce the decision of the church. It cannot review the decision of the highest church body, or consider arguments that that body has exceeded its own jurisdiction or authority.[18] To entertain such arguments would lead to regular appeals from religious to civil authorities, deprive individuals of the freedom to form meaningful religious communities, and "deprive these bodies of the right of construing their own church laws."[19]

Almost sixty years after *Watson*, the Supreme Court addressed a religious dispute of a different kind in *Gonzalez v. Roman Catholic Archbishop*.[20] Raul Gonzalez sought appointment to a Roman Catholic chaplaincy in the Philippines. The archbishop refused, on the ground that Gonzalez was ineligible for the chaplaincy under the code of canon law that had been adopted in 1917. Gonzalez sued and argued that his eligibility was governed not by the code of canon law adopted in 1917, but by the code in effect in 1820, the year the chaplaincy had been created under the terms of a will.

The Supreme Court enforced the decision of the archbishop. Its analysis was perfunctory: both parties adhered to a church that had invested the archbishop with authority to decide this matter, the archbishop had made a decision, the matter that he decided was ecclesiastical, and thus his decision had to be accepted. In the words of the Court:

> In the absence of fraud, collusion, or arbitrariness, the decisions of the proper church tribunals on matters purely ecclesiastical, although affecting civil rights, are accepted in litigation before the secular courts as conclusive, because the parties in interest made them so by contract or otherwise. Under like circumstances, effect is given in the courts to the determinations of the judicatory bodies established by clubs and civil associations.[21]

Gonzalez, like *Watson*, was not a constitutional decision, but one of federal common law. Nevertheless, both cases reflected the constitutional concern for religious liberty. And both cases emphasized the concern for church autonomy that lies at the heart of

---

14. *Id.* at 728–29.
15. *See id.* at 732–33.
16. *Id.* at 733.
17. *Watson*, 80 U.S. at 727.
18. *See id.* at 733.
19. *Id.*
20. 280 U.S. 1 (1929).
21. *Id.* at 16–17.

the Free Exercise Clause, rather than the concern about entanglement that, however illogically, is traditionally associated with the Establishment Clause.

In 1952 the Supreme Court finally resorted to the First Amendment to resolve an intrachurch dispute, in *Kedroff v. Saint Nicholas Cathedral*.[22] After the Bolshevik Revolution, a number of parishes that had belonged to the North American diocese of the Russian Orthodox Church declared their autonomy from the patriarch in Moscow, created an independent religious organization, and elected a bishop to head the new church. Numerous disputes erupted over who rightfully held various ecclesiastical offices and controlled various churches. The New York legislature attempted to resolve these disputes by enacting a law dictating, in essence, that all parishes in New York formerly controlled by the patriarch would henceforth be controlled by the new American church. Litigation ensued over who had the right to occupy and use Saint Nicholas Cathedral in New York City, the seat of the Russian Orthodox archbishop in North America. The outcome "depend[ed] upon whether...appointment...by the Patriarch or...election...[by] the American churches validly select[ed] the ruling hierarch for the American churches."[23]

The Supreme Court declared the New York statute unconstitutional. Just as the Walnut Street Presbyterian Church in *Watson* had been part "of a much larger and more important religious organization" and had put itself "under [the] government and control" of that organization,[24] so too the Russian Orthodox parishes in *Kedroff* were part of "an hierarchical church" and had put themselves under the control of a "governing body in Russia."[25] And just as *permitting* the Walnut Street Presbyterian Church to ignore the dictates of the Presbyterian General Assembly would have encroached upon religious liberty, so too would *compelling* the Russian Orthodox parishes to ignore the dictates of the patriarch:

> [The New York statute] undertook by its terms to transfer the control of the New York churches of the Russian Orthodox religion from the...Patriarch of Moscow.... Such a law violates the Fourteenth Amendment. It prohibits in this country the free exercise of religion. Legislation that regulates church administration, the operation of the churches, the appointment of clergy, by requiring conformity to church statutes "adopted at a general convention [of the dissident American parishes]..." prohibits the free exercise of religion.[26]

Like *Watson*, upon which it relied heavily, *Kedroff* "radiate[d]...a spirit of freedom for religious organizations."[27] The problem with the New York law, the Court said plainly, was that it "directly prohibits the free exercise of an ecclesiastical right, the Church's choice of its hierarchy."[28] Even in cases affecting the rights to real property, according to the Court, "the church rule controls" when a property right "follows as an incident from decisions of the church custom or law on ecclesiastical issues."[29] The Court explicitly and repeatedly rested its holding on the Free Exercise Clause—not on the Establishment Clause or on any concern about entanglement between church and state.

---

22. 344 U.S. 94 (1952).
23. *Id.* at 96–97.
24. *Watson*, 80 U.S. at 726–27.
25. *Kedroff*, 344 U.S. at 105.
26. *Id.* at 107–08.
27. *Id.* at 116.
28. *Id.* at 119.
29. *Id.* at 120–21.

Except for a reprise of *Kedroff*,[30] the Supreme Court did not again confront an internal religious dispute until 1969. The Court's involvement in such cases had been infrequent, but as we have described, its decisions had consistently deferred to church resolutions of internal church disputes. Those decisions had been explicitly grounded in the Court's desire to protect the liberty of individuals to form religious organizations and to resolve intrachurch disputes internally, and they contained sweeping language protecting churches from governmental interference in their internal affairs.

In four cases between 1969 and 1979, the Supreme Court changed its approach to intrachurch disputes. The conceptual basis of the change is still unclear; indeed, the authors of this chapter disagree to some extent about how to describe it. One of us (Schiltz) believes that the *Watson* line of cases is really two lines: the pre-1969 cases already described, whose overriding (but not exclusive) concern was with protecting the right of churches to conduct their affairs free from governmental interference, and the cases of 1969 and later, whose overriding (but not exclusive) concern was with protecting courts from having to interpret religious doctrine. The other author (Laycock) believes that all the cases in the *Watson* line are concerned with protecting churches, but that the scope of protection has shrunk from a general right of churches to create and control their own organizations, and thus necessarily to resolve their own disputes, to a much narrower right to resolve disputes over religious doctrine. We both agree that the emphasis has shifted to whether the courts can decide a church dispute without deciding a question of religious doctrine, and that this shift has been disastrous for the independence of churches.

In retrospect, the beginnings of the shift can be seen in *Presbyterian Church v. Mary Elizabeth Blue Hull Memorial Presbyterian Church*.[31] In *Hull Memorial*, as in *Watson* and *Kedroff*, a local church had attempted to separate from a presbyterial (hierarchical in *Kedroff*) religious organization and to maintain control of church property despite the separation.[32] In *Hull Memorial*, as in *Watson* and *Kedroff*, there was no doubt about the identity of higher religious authorities accepted by all sides before the dispute arose. And in *Hull Memorial*, as in *Watson* and *Kedroff*, the government had interfered in the church dispute in a manner that ignored the determinations of the higher authorities within the religious organization. The interference in *Hull Memorial* was only slightly less blatant than in *Kedroff*: The Georgia legislature, rather than specifying that one faction in a particular dispute was entitled to the denomination's property, instead provided generally that local churches seeking to separate from a denominational organization could take the church property with them if the denominational organization had "abandoned or departed from the tenets of faith and practice it held at the time the local churches affiliated with it."[33] *Hull Memorial* should have been an easy case after *Kedroff*: the Georgia statute should have been swiftly declared an unconstitutional infringement of religious liberty under the Free Exercise Clause.

---

30. In *Kreshik v. Saint Nicholas Cathedral*, 363 U.S. 190 (1960), the Court, in a brief *per curiam* opinion, held that New York could not do through its common law what *Kedroff* had forbidden it to do through its statutory law.

31. 393 U.S. 440 (1969).

32. Presbyterian polity is presbyterial; higher levels of authority in the denomination are constituted from below, by election of representatives and by the appointment of clergy by the lay leadership of local churches. In hierarchical polities, higher levels of authority are typically self-perpetuating or appointed from above. *See generally* Martin E. Marty and James A. Serritella, "Religious Polity," in this volume. The Supreme Court has disregarded this and similar distinctions, treating any denomination with an authority higher than the congregation as hierarchical.

33. *Hull Mem'l*, 393 U.S. at 441.

Justice Brennan, writing for the Court, did indeed invalidate the statute, but on grounds that failed to protect the religious organization. He quoted the language from earlier cases about the right of churches to establish their own tribunals and decide their own disputes, and about the necessity that those decisions be binding.[34] He even italicized some of that language. But when he finished reviewing the cases and began speaking in his own voice, and when he offered explicit instructions about what the Georgia courts could do on remand,[35] he did *not* say that Georgia must defer to the decision of the highest Presbyterian authority. He did not expressly rely on the Free Exercise Clause, but rather on "the First Amendment."[36] He said that "the Amendment...commands civil courts to decide church property disputes without resolving underlying controversies over religious doctrine," and that "States, religious organizations, and individuals must structure relationships involving church property so as not to require the civil courts to resolve ecclesiastical questions."[37]

Brennan did not announce any change in rule, nor did he repudiate the rule he had just quoted, but implicitly he left the Georgia courts a choice. Those courts could override the decisions of the relevant religious authorities if they could find a way to write the opinion without deciding a question of religious doctrine. On remand the Georgia court did just that, awarding the property to the local church on the basis that the deeds were in its name, and ignoring (in effect, nullifying) the denomination's authority to supervise the local church and its leadership.[38] The Supreme Court denied certiorari.[39] It is easy to cite *Hull Memorial* for the rule of deference to the highest religious authority; it quotes that rule repeatedly. But the end result was very different.

This doctrinal shift became more explicit in *Maryland and Virginia Eldership v. Church of God*.[40] This was another case of a state court awarding church property to the dissident leadership of local churches seeking to leave their denomination,[41] and it arrived at the Supreme Court while *Hull Memorial* was pending the first time. The Court vacated and remanded for consideration in light of *Hull Memorial*. The Maryland court again awarded the property to the local churches.[42]

The same day the Court denied the second petition for certiorari in *Hull Memorial*, it also dismissed a second appeal in *Church of God*. In a brief *per curiam* opinion, the Court recited the documents the Maryland court had considered in reaching its decision, including a statute that the denomination challenged as having effectively deprived it of its property. "*Since, however, the Maryland court's resolution of the dispute involved no inquiry into religious doctrine,*...the appeal is dismissed for want of a substantial federal question."[43] There was still no explanation, still no acknowledged shift in doctrine, still no repudiation of earlier cases. But the scope of protection had shrunk to a right to have the civil court not inquire into religious doctrine.

In a concurrence that has often been cited as authoritative, Brennan explained that in his view, "a State may adopt *any* one of various approaches for settling church property

---

34. *See id.* at 446–48.

35. *See id.* at 450.

36. *Id.* at 449–51.

37. *Id.* at 449.

38. *See* Presbyterian Church in United States v. Eastern Heights Presbyterian Church, 167 S.E.2d 658 (Ga. 1969).

39. *See* 396 U.S. 1041 (1970).

40. 396 U.S. 367 (1970).

41. *See* 241 A.2d 691 (Md. 1968), *vacated*, 393 U.S. 528 (1969).

42. *See* 254 A.2d 162 (Md. 1970), *appeal dismissed*, 396 U.S. 367 (1970).

43. 396 U.S. at 368 (emphasis added).

disputes so long as it involves no consideration of doctrinal matters."[44] He cited "the *Watson* approach"[45] as being one acceptable option, but with important new limitations. He explained that in his view, judicial deference to the decision of the highest religious authority would be possible only if there were no "substantial controversy" about the identity of that authority.[46] "[T]he *Watson* approach is consonant with the prohibitions of the First Amendment *only* if the appropriate church governing body can be determined without the resolution of doctrinal questions and without extensive inquiry into religious polity."[47] It was not clear how much inquiry into polity would be disqualifyingly "extensive," and hence not clear whether any obstreperous litigant would now be empowered to displace previously recognized religious leadership simply by disputing its authority.

Brennan also said, directly contrary to *Watson*,[48] that a court could not enforce a bequest of property to a church conditioned upon the church continuing to propagate a particular belief, because enforcement of such a condition would require "consideration of doctrine."[49] In other words, a person may bequeath a building to an organization on condition that it use the building to promote tourism or gun control or vegetarianism; but a person may not bequeath a building to a church on condition that it use the building to promote a particular religious belief. Brennan would thus transmogrify the *Watson* line of cases—a line animated by "a spirit of freedom for religious organizations"—into a line mandating discrimination *against* religious organizations.

Brennan's insistence that courts not interpret church doctrine next appeared in his opinion for the Court in *Serbian Eastern Orthodox Diocese v. Milivojevich*.[50] The Serbian Orthodox Church had become involved in a dispute with its American bishop, who eventually purported to withdraw his diocese from the church. In response, the church defrocked the bishop, divided his diocese into three new dioceses, and appointed three new bishops. Both sides sued, seeking, among other things, a declaration as to who was the true bishop or bishops. The Illinois Supreme Court ruled for the dissident bishop, largely on the ground that the church had failed to follow its own internal rules in defrocking him.

The federal Supreme Court reversed, holding that the Illinois court should have deferred to the decision of the church. Within its scope, *Serbian* is protective of religious freedom in the tradition of *Watson*, *Gonzalez*, and *Kedroff*. Brennan again quoted the rule of deference from *Watson* and *Gonzalez*,[51] and this time he restated it in his own words: "[C]ivil courts are bound to accept the decisions of the highest judicatories of a religious organization of hierarchical polity on matters of discipline, faith, internal organization, or ecclesiastical rule, custom, or law."[52]

In this respect, *Serbian* applied earlier cases in the *Watson* line; it required deference to the highest church authorities. The difficulty is in identifying the scope of that rule. The Court acknowledged no tension with *Hull Memorial* or *Church of God*, just as those cases had acknowledged no tension with *Watson*, *Gonzalez*, and *Kedroff*.

---

44. *Id.* at 368 (Brennan, J., concurring).
45. *Id.* at 370.
46. *Id.* at 369–70.
47. *Id.* at 370 (emphasis added).
48. *See* 80 U.S. at 723–24.
49. 396 U.S. at 369 n.2 (Brennan, J., concurring).
50. 426 U.S. 696 (1976).
51. *See id.* at 710–12.
52. *Id.* at 713; *see also id.* at 709, 724–25.

In retrospect, we believe the Court perceived the questions presented in *Serbian* to be religious questions: Who should be the bishop, did the church adhere to its own adjudicatory procedures, and even, how many dioceses?[53] The Court noted that the rule against deciding "controversies over religious doctrine...applies with equal force to church disputes over church polity and church administration."[54]

Control of church property was at stake, but that did not make this essentially a church property dispute. The Court correctly noted that certain named corporations would own the property in any event, and that the bishop would largely control those corporations, so that the dispute over property was derivative of the dispute over religious authority.[55] *Hull Memorial* had been subject to the same analysis, but the Court had not seen it that way. The property would belong to the Vineville Presbyterian Church in any event, and the dispute had been over who would control that church. The authoritative Presbyterian body had decided that question, rejecting the claim of one set of local church officials and validating the claim of another, much as the Serbian hierarchy had removed one bishop and appointed others. But the Court had treated *Hull Memorial* as primarily a dispute over property, and not just derivatively so. As a property dispute, the case seemed far more amenable to resolution by a civil court. The difference between *Hull Memorial* and *Serbian* lay partly in how the cases were presented.

The difference may also have depended on the polities of the two churches. In *Serbian*, "all parties agree[d] that the Serbian Orthodox Church is a hierarchical church, and that the sole power to appoint and remove Bishops of the Church resides in its highest ranking organs, the Holy Assembly and the Holy Synod."[56] The Presbyterian Church is presbyterial, a polity the Court has never understood. The Court divides all churches into hierarchical and congregational,[57] but presbyterial churches are neither. *Watson* treated Presbyterians as hierarchical and deferred to the highest church authority;[58] *Hull Memorial* let the local church put in issue whether it had submitted its property to denominational control.[59] Thus, in *Hull Memorial* one local faction was allowed to dispute whether denominational bodies were empowered to resolve conflicts arising out of schisms in local churches.

What if the defrocked bishop in *Serbian* had denied the authority of the church hierarchy? What if a local Catholic priest denies the authority of his bishop? If a litigant has the effrontery to dispute what everyone in a church knows, is the civil court unable to resolve that dispute and thus forced to turn to "neutral principles" instead of deferring to the highest church authority?

One of us (Laycock) believes that the Court did not intend for *Serbian* to be evaded so easily. The highest ecclesiastical authority to which a dispute has been carried is entitled to deference not only on the merits, but also on questions of procedure, allocations of authority within the church, and even its own jurisdiction.[60] What the Supreme

---

53. "[T]his case essentially involves not a church property dispute, but a religious dispute the resolution of which under our cases is for ecclesiastical and not civil tribunals." *Id.* at 709. For the dispute over the number of dioceses, see *id.* at 720–24.

54. *Serbian*, 426 U.S. at 710.

55. *See id.* at 709.

56. *Id.* at 715.

57. *See Watson*, 80 U.S. at 722–23. For further explanation of presbyterial polity, see *supra* note 32.

58. *See Watson*, 80 U.S. at 726–27.

59. Presbyterian Church in United States v. Eastern Heights Presbyterian Church, 167 S.E.2d 658 (Ga. 1969).

60. *See Serbian*, 426 U.S. at 713–14, 720.

Court forbids is for civil courts to "probe deeply," engage in "extensive inquiry," conduct a "detailed review," or conduct "a searching and therefore impermissible inquiry" into the allocation of religious authority.[61] The "highest ecclesiastical authority can be identified without the 'searching…inquiry' needed to identify the authority with responsibility for the particular issue, just as a foreigner could easily identify the Supreme Court of the United States as the highest court in the land without understanding the many rules that make lower courts the highest authority on particular issues."[62] But lower courts eager to evade *Serbian* have not always adhered to this limitation. Perhaps the most astonishing example is the Massachusetts court's conclusion that the Russian Orthodox Church is congregational with respect to property holding.[63] One of us (Schiltz) believes that such decisions are not really evasions of the rule announced in *Serbian*, but are rather the natural and perhaps even intended consequence of that rule.

The Supreme Court's last foray into an intrachurch dispute was *Jones v. Wolf*[64] in 1979, another Presbyterian case that was factually similar to *Watson*, *Hull Memorial*, and *Church of God*. A schism developed in a local congregation, the denominational authorities declared one of the two factions to be the true congregation, and litigation ensued. Justice Powell and three other justices wanted to resolve the case precisely as *Watson* had. After determining that the church had authority under its governing documents to resolve the dispute and that the church had done so, Powell would have required the state courts to defer to the church's decision.[65]

Justice Blackmun's opinion for the majority explicitly rejected Powell's "rule of compulsory deference,"[66] in part because such a rule might require courts to "examine the polity and administration of a church."[67] Instead, the Supreme Court described several approaches that lower courts could take in resolving church disputes. In *Hull Memorial* and *Church of God*, Brennan had mentioned "neutral principles of law" that could be brought to bear on intrachurch disputes without requiring courts to decide religious questions.[68] In a new elaboration of these "neutral principles" the Supreme Court said that courts *can* construe and enforce "religious documents, such as a church constitution," but that they must do so "in purely secular terms."[69]

The Court's statement of its rules embodies in a single opinion all the tensions inherent in the shift from *Watson* to *Hull Memorial* and back to *Serbian*. The Court said that the "[m]ost important" principle in resolving intrachurch disputes was to avoid "resolving church property disputes on the basis of religious doctrine and practice."[70] This principle had a "corollary," which the Court stated twice: that if the issue is one "of religious doctrine or polity," or if interpretation of church documents requires resolution of "a religious controversy," civil courts must defer to "the highest court of a hierarchical church organization," or to "the authoritative, ecclesiastical body."[71] Once again the

---

61. *Id.* at 709, 713, 723.

62. Douglas Laycock, Towards a General Theory of the Religion Clauses: The Case of Church Labor Relations and the Right to Church Autonomy, 81 Colum. L. Rev. 1381, 1413 (1981).

63. Primate of Russian Orthodox Church v. Russian Orthodox Church, 636 N.E.2d 211 (Mass. 1994).

64. 443 U.S. 595 (1979).

65. *See id.* at 618–21 (Powell, J., dissenting).

66. *Id.* at 605.

67. *Id.*

68. *Church of God*, 396 U.S. at 370 (Brennan, J., concurring); *Hull Mem'l*, 393 U.S. at 449.

69. *Jones*, 443 U.S. at 604.

70. *Id.* at 602.

71. *Id.* at 602, 604.

Court failed to explain what is a religious controversy and what is not. Its apparent guide was intuition, and its intuition was self-deceptive.

Although the Court twice reaffirmed that civil courts must defer to religious authorities for the resolution of religious controversies, it feared that identifying the highest church authority would require resolution of religious disputes. This reluctance to identify the highest church authority undermined the Court's commitment to defer when interpretation of church documents raised religious controversies; touting the avoidance of religious controversies as the advantage of neutral principles encouraged courts to interpret church documents in ways that raised no religious controversies and made secular language and secular rules dispositive.

The result was a powerful incentive to define church disputes in secular terms, to ignore any underlying religious disputes, and by ignoring them, to pretend not to have resolved them. Whether Presbyterian denominational bodies had authority to decide this dispute was a religious question, and the Georgia courts would acquire maximum authority to resolve that question if they ignored its existence. If a civil court acknowledged a religious controversy, it would have to defer to religious authorities. But if the court declared that no religious controversies existed, or that religious controversies were irrelevant to the outcome, the civil court could decide the case itself.

The Court denied that its rule placed any burden on free exercise of religion. Any religious organization could provide for any outcome it wanted in event of a dispute, including deference to religious authorities, by simply anticipating the dispute and specifying its preferred resolution in secular language in legally binding documents. "The burden involved in taking such steps will be minimal"[72]—almost certainly a sentence written by a law clerk with no experience of the real world. Churches could preserve their liberty under *Jones v. Wolf* if they had good legal representation, if they anticipated all the possible categories of disputes, if they could agree on solutions without provoking the very disputes they were trying to avoid, and if they were willing and able to write their rules in secular language instead of religious language. In the real world in which churches cannot foresee the future, are occupied with immediate issues to the exclusion of remote legal contingencies, have little money for lawyers, and often have little legal sophistication, many churches will not have documents drafted in secular terms that enable courts to resolve unanticipated disputes in accord with the church's own intentions. In insisting that its rule protected religious liberty as well as would the rule of deference to religious authorities, the Court ignored and misallocated "the substantial risk of inadvertence."[73]

In sum, the *Watson* line of cases really consists of two distinct parts. The first, which we will refer to as the "autonomy" part, consists of *Watson, Gonzalez, Kedroff*, and possibly *Serbian*. These cases are concerned with protecting people from government— giving people maximum freedom to organize themselves into religious communities, to control their own religious communities, and to decide in advance how disputes within those communities will be resolved.

The second part of the *Watson* line, which we will refer to as the "doctrine" part, consists of *Hull Memorial, Church of God, Jones v. Wolf*, and again possibly *Serbian*. These cases repeatedly stress the importance of avoiding any judicial examination of re-

---

72. *Id.* at 606.
73. Laycock, *supra* note 62, at 1404 (analyzing why the Court's rule will get more cases wrong than the rule of compulsory deference).

ligious doctrine or polity. Sometimes these cases seem to be concerned with protecting courts from the dangers of religious disputes. Other times they seem concerned with protecting churches from having their religious disputes decided by civil courts, but they reflect an extraordinarily narrow understanding of what that means. These cases demonstrate little understanding of religious liberty—so little, in fact, that they permit a court to refuse to defer to the decision of a religious tribunal even when the court could do so without in any way interpreting religious doctrine. Under these cases a court can decide, for any reason or no reason, to impose upon a religious organization a resolution of a dispute that is contrary to the decision of the tribunal that all parties recognized as authoritative before the dispute arose, so long as the court does not overtly decide a question of religious doctrine or polity.

Application of Watson *in religious employment cases*

The *Watson* line of cases is poorly suited for resolving religious employment disputes. For one thing, the cases are inconsistent, or at least in tension. Some are based on federal common law, some on the Free Exercise Clause, and some on vague allusions to the "First Amendment." More important, some say that churches enjoy sweeping protection from governmental interference, while others say that churches enjoy nothing more than protection from having their doctrines explicitly interpreted by civil courts.

The *Watson* line is also poorly suited for resolving religious employment disputes for another, more fundamental reason: all the cases involved disputes over interpretation of, or continued adherence to, standards that were internally derived—that is, found in the doctrines or governing documents of the religious organization. By contrast, in most employment disputes the government itself has made a policy choice and sought to impose it on a religious organization—by, for example, dictating that the organization may not make employment decisions on the basis of race or that its employees must be permitted to join unions. Different problems arise when the government is invited to referee an internal dispute within a religious organization—and to do so with reference to the organization's own internally derived standards—than when the government takes it upon itself to regulate religious organizations in pursuit of secular ends. Case law that appropriately safeguards religious liberty in one setting will not necessarily do so in the other.

This distinction has been lost on most courts. Both the *Watson* cases and the employment cases involve intrachurch disputes—disputes between factions or at least between one disgruntled church employee and the church leadership. The church typically applies internally derived standards to its employment decisions, and judicial review of those decisions is indeed secular resolution of an internal church dispute. But the government's insistence that the church should have applied statutory standards is also direct regulation and imposition of external standards. Which aspect of the case is more salient may depend on whether the church overtly resists the external standard, as in those churches that refuse to ordain women, or accepts the external standard and insists that it has made the employment decision for religious reasons that are consistent with it. Keeping these analytic strands distinct is not always easy even if one attends to the distinction, and many judges and lawyers have not attended to it. Whatever the reason, courts confronting religious employment disputes frequently look to the *Watson* line of cases for help. Not surprisingly, the resulting decisions are a disparate lot.

As one would expect, courts that apply the autonomy part of the *Watson* line usually give substantial protection to the employment decisions of religious organizations. Many of these opinions are short and perfunctory. They often quote passages from *Watson*, *Kedroff*, or *Serbian* and then summarily conclude that a particular employment dispute is unreviewable.[74] Like the *Watson* line itself, these opinions usually do not make clear whether they are based upon the Free Exercise Clause, the Establishment Clause, or both, nor do they identify the line dividing those matters touching religion that can be reviewed by courts from those that cannot. Rather, they simply conclude, with little explanation, that the particular employment dispute involves a matter of ecclesiastical concern and therefore is unreviewable.

Other cases relying on the autonomy part of the *Watson* line are quite explicit—even eloquent—in affirming the freedom of religious organizations to choose their own leaders. One of the most frequently cited of these cases is *McClure v. Salvation Army*,[75] which involved an employment discrimination claim under Title VII[76] brought against a religious organization by one of its ministers. The court recognized that "[t]he relationship between an organized church and its ministers is its lifeblood," and that "[t]he minister is the chief instrument by which the church seeks to fulfill its purpose."[77] After quoting at length from *Watson*, *Gonzalez*, and *Kedroff*, the court concluded:

> An application of the provisions of Title VII to the employment relationship...[between] a church and its minister...would...cause the State to intrude upon matters of church administration and government which have so many times before been proclaimed to be matters of a singular ecclesiastical concern. Control of strictly ecclesiastical matters could easily pass from the church to the State. The church would then be without the power to decide for itself, free from state interference, matters of church administration and government.[78]

Simpson v. Wells Lamont Corp.[79] was similarly protective of religious autonomy. A pastor and his wife sued his church for race discrimination and argued that because their claim would not require the court to interpret religious doctrine, the claim was not barred by the First Amendment. The opening lines of the court's opinion hit the nail on the head:

> This case involves the fundamental question of who will preach from the pulpit of a church, and who will occupy the church parsonage. The bare statement of the question should make obvious the lack of jurisdiction of a civil court. The

---

74. *See, e.g.*, Lewis v. Seventh Day Adventists Lake Region Conference, 978 F.2d 940 (6th Cir. 1992); Natal v. Christian and Missionary Alliance, 878 F.2d 1575 (1st Cir. 1989); Hutchinson v. Thomas, 789 F.2d 392 (6th Cir. 1986); Kaufmann v. Sheehan, 707 F.2d 355 (8th Cir. 1983); Yaggie v. Indiana-Ky. Synod Evangelical Lutheran Church, 860 F. Supp. 1194 (W.D. Ky. 1994), *aff'd*, 64 F.3d 664 (6th Cir. 1995); Farley v. Wisconsin Evangelical Lutheran Synod, 821 F. Supp. 1286 (D. Minn. 1993); Hafner v. Lutheran Church-Mo. Synod, 616 F. Supp. 735 (N.D. Ind. 1985); Pierce v. Iowa-Mo. Conference of Seventh-Day Adventists, 534 N.W.2d 425 (Iowa 1995); Gabriel v. Immanuel Evangelical Lutheran Church, 640 N.E.2d 681 (Ill. App. Ct. 1994); Williams v. Palmer, 532 N.E.2d 1061 (Ill. App. Ct. 1988); Downs v. Roman Catholic Archbishop, 683 A.2d 808 (Md. Ct. Spec. App. 1996); Tran v. Fiorenza, 934 S.W.2d 740 (Tex. App. 1996), no writ; Green v. United Pentecostal Church Int'l, 899 S.W.2d 28 (Tex. Ct. App. 1995), writ denied.

75. 460 F.2d 553 (5th Cir. 1972).

76. Civil Rights Act of 1964 tit. VII, 42 U.S.C. §§ 2000e to 2000e-17 (1994 & Supp. III 1997).

77. *McClure*, 460 F.2d at 558–59.

78. *Id.* at 560.

79. 494 F.2d 490 (5th Cir. 1974).

answer to that question must come from the church.... [A] congregation's determination as to who shall preach from the church pulpit is at the very heart
of the free exercise of religion, which plaintiffs would corrode with an overlay
of civil rights legislation.... [80]

The *Simpson* court did not get bogged down in whether it would have to interpret
church doctrine. It didn't care. Rather, it held that a church has a right under the First
Amendment to choose its own leader, and that not even the government's interest in
combating race discrimination can overcome that right.

These cases that apply the autonomy part of the *Watson* line protect religious employment decisions, but they have their limitations, the most important of which is that
they almost always involve claims brought against churches by ordained ministers.
These "ministerial exception" cases, as some courts refer to them,[81] are easily distinguished by courts that are hostile to religious autonomy. For example, courts have refused protection under the *Watson* line from employment claims brought by a director
of religious education of a Jewish synagogue,[82] a professor at a "pervasively sectarian"
Baptist college,[83] a Catholic parochial school teacher,[84] nuns teaching at a Catholic university,[85] ordained ministers on the support staff of a Baptist seminary,[86] an editorial
secretary at a Seventh-Day Adventist publishing house,[87] and even an ordained minister
seeking employment with a Methodist social service agency.[88] In all these cases, the
courts permitted the claims to go forward on the grounds that the claimants were "not
'ministers' of a 'church' entitled to *McClure*-type protection."[89] A few cases are more
protective of the relationship with employees who are not ministers but who perform
functions with readily apparent religious significance.[90]

Many other courts apply the doctrine part of the *Watson* line. In this view, the constitutional permissibility of an employment claim against a religious organization depends entirely on whether resolution of the claim would require judicial interpretation
of religious doctrine.[91] (Once again, most of these courts derive this principle from neither the Free Exercise Clause nor the Establishment Clause, but from general concerns
underlying the First Amendment.) The track record of religious organizations under
this approach is predictably mixed. Some courts dismiss employment claims on the

---

80. *Id.* at 492.

81. *See* EEOC v. Catholic Univ. of Am., 83 F.3d 455, 462 (D.C. Cir. 1996).

82. *See* Elbaz v. Congregation Beth Judea, Inc., 812 F. Supp. 802 (N.D. Ill. 1992).

83. *See* EEOC v. Mississippi College, 626 F.2d 477 (5th Cir. 1980).

84. *See* Gallo v. Salesian Soc'y, Inc., 676 A.2d 580 (N.J. Super. Ct. App. Div. 1996).

85. *See* Welter v. Seton Hall Univ., 608 A.2d 206 (N.J. 1992).

86. *See* EEOC v. Southwestern Baptist Theological Seminary, 651 F.2d 277 (5th Cir. 1981).

87. *See* EEOC v. Pacific Press Publ'g Ass'n, 676 F.2d 1272 (9th Cir. 1982).

88. *See* Shirkey v. Eastwind Community Dev. Corp., 941 F. Supp. 567 (D. Md. 1996), *modified*,
993 F. Supp. 370 (D. Md. 1998).

89. *Southwestern Baptist*, 651 F.2d at 285; *see also* Elbaz v. Congregation Beth Judea, Inc., 812 F.
Supp. 802, 807 (N.D. Ill. 1992) ("The 'application of Title VII's race and sex discrimination ban to
non-ministerial employees does not violate the First Amendment'") (citation omitted)).

90. *See* NLRB v. Catholic Bishop, 440 U.S. 490 (1979) (interpreting National Labor Relations
Act to avoid regulation of teachers in religious schools); Miller v. Catholic Diocese, 728 P.2d 794
(Mont. 1986) (dismissing wrongful discharge suit by parochial school teacher).

91. *See, e.g.,* Drevlow v. Lutheran Church, Mo. Synod, 991 F.2d 468 (8th Cir. 1993); Knuth v.
Lutheran Church, Mo. Synod, 643 F. Supp. 444 (D. Kan. 1986); McAdoo v. Diaz, 884 P.2d 1385
(Alaska 1994); Belin v. West, 864 S.W.2d 838 (Ark. 1993); Reardon v. Lemoyne, 454 A.2d 428 (N.H.
1982); Elmora Hebrew Ctr., Inc. v. Fishman, 593 A.2d 725 (N.J. 1991).

grounds that their adjudication would require interpretation of church doctrine,[92] while other courts find no constitutional bar to these claims because interpretation of doctrine is unnecessary.[93]

The most striking thing about the cases that apply the doctrine part of the *Watson* line is their detached, almost otherworldly nature. Like a dysfunctional family at the dinner table, they talk about everything but the real issues. Consider, for example, *Drevlow v. Lutheran Church, Missouri Synod*.[94] A pastor affiliated with the Lutheran Church-Missouri Synod tried without success to get a "call" (offer of a position as pastor) from a congregation. Upon investigation, he discovered that the personnel file that the synod had been circulating to prospective employers erroneously reported that his wife had previously been married. The pastor claimed that this made him effectively unemployable, and he sued the synod for defamation.

One would expect that a court adjudicating this claim would be concerned first and foremost about religious liberty. One would expect it to take a page from *New York Times Co. v. Sullivan*,[95] and to think hard about the extent to which applying defamation law to intrachurch communications might chill the ability of ecclesiastical superiors to discuss frankly the qualifications of prospective pastors with congregations. One would also expect the court to assess the importance of the government's interest in applying defamation law to this rather narrow category of communications, and to balance that interest against the burden on religious liberty.

One would be wrong. The Eighth Circuit did none of these things; in fact, it showed absolutely no concern about the possible consequences for religious autonomy of applying defamation law to intrachurch communications. Even more oddly, it appears that the synod's attorneys did not argue about religious liberty. They argued that the pastor's claim should be barred because to recover damages he would have to prove that but for the inaccurate information about his wife, he would have been hired by a congregation—and thus "any assessment of Drevlow's claim for loss of income would necessitate a forbidden inquiry into Drevlow's marketability as a pastor."[96] The Eighth Circuit's response to this argument was as odd as the argument itself. According to the court, employment decisions by churches are constitutionally protected only "where review by civil courts would require the courts to interpret and apply religious doctrine or ecclesiastical law."[97] No such interpretation or application would be required in this case, the Eighth Circuit said. True, for the district court to determine whether the erroneous information about the pastor's wife had prevented him from being employed, it would have to determine the religious beliefs of the congregations that declined to employ him. However, the Eighth Circuit said, "[w]hile the district court cannot constitu-

---

92. *See Drevlow*, 991 F.2d at 470–71 (with respect to non-defamation claims); Little v. Wuerl, 929 F.2d 944 (3d Cir. 1991); Scharon v. St. Luke's Episcopal Presbyterian Hosps., 929 F.2d 360 (8th Cir. 1991); Yaggie v. Indiana-Ky. Synod Evangelical Lutheran Church, 860 F. Supp. 1194 (W.D. Ky. 1994), *aff'd*, 64 F.3d 664 (6th Cir. 1995); *Knuth*, 643 F. Supp. 444; *Belin*, 864 S.W.2d at 841–42; United Methodist Church v. White, 571 A.2d 790 (D.C. 1990); Music v. United Methodist Church, 864 S.W.2d 286 (Ky. 1993); McElroy v. Guilfoyle, 589 A.2d 1082 (N.J. Super. Ct. Law Div. 1990).

93. *See Drevlow*, 991 F.2d at 471–72 (with respect to defamation claim); EEOC v. Pacific Press Publ'g Ass'n, 676 F.2d 1272 (9th Cir. 1982); *McAdoo*, 884 P.2d at 1390–91; Marshall v. Munro, 845 P.2d 424 (Alaska 1993).

94. 991 F.2d 468 (8th Cir. 1993).

95. 376 U.S. 254 (1964) (holding that First Amendment restricts defamation claims by public officials).

96. *Drevlow*, 991 F.2d at 471.

97. *Id.*

tionally decide the *validity* of these beliefs, the court may properly determine their *existence*."[98] The Eighth Circuit then remanded the case to the district court for trial of the defamation claim unless "further proceedings reveal that this matter cannot be resolved without interpreting religious procedures or beliefs."[99]

Under the obvious influence of the doctrine part of the *Watson* line, the Eighth Circuit managed to get just about everything wrong. First, it said absolutely nothing about the most important issue in the case: the impact on religious liberty of permitting a pastor to bring defamation actions against ecclesiastical superiors for inaccurate communications to congregations that have considered hiring the pastor. Second, the court did not even apply the doctrine part of the *Watson* line correctly. *Hull Memorial, Serbian,* and *Jones v. Wolf* clearly bar courts not just from assessing the *validity* of religious beliefs, but also from resolving internal disputes over a belief's existence, nuance, or detail. Under the departure-from-doctrine standard at issue in *Hull Memorial,* Georgia courts did not purport to determine whether the denominational teachings of the Presbyterian Church were valid, but only whether they had changed since the seceding local church had affiliated. The Illinois courts in *Serbian* did not purport to decide whether the procedural rules of the Serbian Orthodox Church were valid, but only whether the church had followed its own rules. Nowhere in any of those cases did the Supreme Court so much as hint at the distinction made by the Eighth Circuit. And finally, the Eighth Circuit remanded the case with incoherent instructions. The district court was told both that it may "properly determine the[] existence" of religious beliefs against pastors marrying divorced women, and that it may not "interpret[] religious beliefs." It is beyond us how a district court can determine whether a congregation holds a particular religious belief without interpreting the religious beliefs that congregation holds. The only thing that seems clear is that the district court, like the Eighth Circuit before it, will spend a lot of time on an issue that should not make much difference, and no time on an issue that should be critical.

Drevlow is troubling not only for its analysis, but also because it carves out an exception to "the ministerial exception." It is not the only such case.[100] Even the relationship between the church and its clergy is no longer fully protected from judicial interference.

The *Sherbert* Understanding of the Free Exercise Clause

A second approach taken by courts in religious employment cases is to look to the Free Exercise Clause—and, in particular, to its interpretation in *Sherbert v. Verner.*[101] In *Sherbert,* a Seventh Day Adventist was denied unemployment compensation benefits because she refused to accept available employment that would require her to work on Saturday (her Sabbath). The Supreme Court held that the state had burdened her free

---

98. *Id.* at 472 n.3 (emphasis added; citation omitted).

99. *Id.* at 472.

100. 100 *See also* Bollard v. California Province of the Society of Jesus, 196 F.3d 940 (9th Cir. 1999) (refusing to dismiss Title VII suit by novice priest); Hayden v. Schulte, 701 So. 2d 1354 (La. Ct. App. 1997) (refusing to dismiss defamation suit by priest against archbishop); Babcock v. New Orleans Baptist Theological Seminary, 554 So. 2d 90 (La. Ct. App. 1989) (ordering theology student reinstated into seminary).

101. 374 U.S. 398 (1963).

exercise of religion even though the burden was "only an indirect result of welfare legislation"[102] and not the result of direct discrimination against religion. The Court next inquired "whether some compelling state interest enforced in the eligibility provisions of the…statute justifies the substantial infringement of appellant's First Amendment right."[103] It stressed that "'[o]nly the gravest abuses, endangering paramount interests,'"[104] could justify burdening the claimant's exercise of religion. Moreover, even if such "grave abuses" existed, "it would plainly be incumbent upon [the state] to demonstrate that no alternative forms of regulation would combat such abuses without infringing First Amendment rights."[105] Finding no compelling state interest in denying benefits to the claimant, the Court held that her rights under the Free Exercise Clause had been violated.

For nearly thirty years, the Supreme Court applied the *Sherbert* test to free exercise claims in a variety of contexts. Some scholars have argued that the *Sherbert* doctrine "was more talk than substance."[106] The Supreme Court was indeed too willing to create exceptions to the doctrine, and lower courts were too willing to find that free exercise rights were not burdened and that governmental interests were compelling. But at least the Court was asking the right questions—the questions that, in our view, should be asked in religious employment cases: Has the free exercise of religion been burdened—and if so, exactly how? What state interest is furthered by that burden? How important is that state interest? Is there another way of furthering that interest that would put a lesser burden on free exercise rights?

In adjudicating religious employment disputes, courts frequently have resorted to the *Sherbert* test, even after it appeared to have been superseded by *Employment Division v. Smith*.[107] But with few exceptions[108] churches have fared poorly in these cases, as courts have continually underestimated the burden on churches and overestimated the importance of governmental interests.

---

102. *Id.* at 403.

103. *Id.* at 406.

104. *Id.* (citation omitted).

105. *Id.* at 407.

106. Michael W. McConnell, Free Exercise Revisionism and the Smith Decision, 57 U. Chi. L. Rev. 1109, 1109 (1990).

107. As noted, in *Smith* the Supreme Court effectively overruled *Sherbert* by holding that, except in unemployment-compensation cases (and subject to other exceptions of disputed scope), the Free Exercise Clause permits government to burden religion through generally applicable laws, even if the governmental interest being furthered is trivial, and even if that interest can be furthered as well or better without burdening religion. But for some reason many lower courts were slow to notice *Smith*, and they continued to apply the *Sherbert* test in analyzing free exercise questions, not even citing *Smith*, much less explaining why they were ignoring it. *See, e.g.*, South Ridge Baptist Church v. Industrial Comm'n, 911 F.2d 1203 (6th Cir. 1990); Shirkey v. Eastwind Community Dev. Corp., 941 F. Supp. 567 (D. Md. 1996), *modified*, 993 F. Supp. 370 (D. Md. 1998); Powell v. Stafford, 859 F. Supp. 1343 (D. Colo. 1994); St. John's Lutheran Church v. State Compensation Ins. Fund, 830 P.2d 1271 (Mont. 1992). Other courts have applied the *Sherbert* test under the directive of the Religious Freedom Restoration Act of 1993, 42 U.S.C. §§ 2000bb to 2000bb-4 (1994) (which was declared unconstitutional as applied to the states in *City of Boerne v. Flores*, 521 U.S. 507 (1997)). *See, e.g.*, Porth v. Roman Catholic Diocese, 532 N.W.2d 195 (Mich. Ct. App. 1995). Still other courts have applied *Sherbert* after expressly concluding that religious employment fell into one of *Smith*'s exceptions. *See* EEOC v. Catholic Univ., 83 F.3d 455, 467 (D.C. Cir. 1996) (hybrid right); *cf.* Douglas Laycock, The Remnants of Free Exercise, 1990 Sup. Ct. Rev. 1, 43–44 (internal church dispute).

108. *See, e.g.*, Rayburn v. General Conference of Seventh-Day Adventists, 772 F.2d 1164 (4th Cir. 1985); *Powell*, 859 F. Supp. 1343; O'Connor Hosp. v. Superior Court, 240 Cal. Rptr. 766 (Ct. App. 1987) (denied review and ordered not published, Dec. 23, 1987).

Underestimating the burden

It should be obvious that the free exercise of religion is burdened by governmental regulation of the employment decisions of religious organizations. As we noted at the beginning of this chapter, religious leaders play a critical role in the lives of individual believers, and an even more critical role in the lives of religious communities. One court put it well:

> The right to choose ministers without government restriction underlies the well-being of religious community, for perpetuation of a church's existence may depend upon those whom it selects to preach its values, teach its message, and interpret its doctrines both to its own membership and to the world at large.[109]

For these reasons, "introduction of government standards to the selection of spiritual leaders would significantly, and perniciously, rearrange the relationship between church and state"[110] and would impose an "extraordinary" burden upon religion.[111]

Most courts reject these assessments and have strained mightily to argue against them. Courts have argued, for example, that enforcement of an employment regulation against a church does not burden religion unless "compliance with the regulation [is] directly contrary to [the church's] religious beliefs."[112] In this view, when the regulations being enforced are generally consistent with the religious organization's beliefs, religion is not burdened.[113] Thus these courts profess not to understand how a church that supports the rights of workers to organize is burdened when it is forced to permit its workers to form unions and engage in collective action,[114] how a church whose beliefs do not mandate age discrimination is burdened by permitting its employees to sue for age discrimination,[115] or how a church that believes workers should be paid "a decorous and fair salary" is burdened when the government dictates the minimum wage that the church must pay to its employees.[116] It has apparently not occurred to these courts that even if the government and a church support the same general goal, they may have radically different understandings of how that goal should be achieved. Moreover, these courts are oblivious to the risk of judicial error and to the difficulties of mixed motive—to the risk that churches with religious reasons for dismissing or not hiring an

---

109. *Rayburn*, 772 F.2d at 1167–68 (citation omitted).

110. *Id.* at 1169.

111. *Id.* at 1168.

112. Catholic High Sch. Ass'n v. Culvert, 753 F.2d 1161, 1170 (2d Cir. 1985).

113. *See* Dole v. Shenandoah Baptist Church, 899 F.2d 1389, 1397 (4th Cir. 1990); EEOC v. Fremont Christian Sch., 781 F.2d 1362, 1368 (9th Cir. 1986); EEOC v. Pacific Press Publ'g Ass'n, 676 F.2d 1272, 1279 (9th Cir. 1982); EEOC v. Southwestern Baptist Theological Seminary, 651 F.2d 277, 286 (5th Cir. 1981); Shirkey v. Eastwind Community Dev. Corp., 941 F. Supp. 567, 578 & n.48 (D. Md. 1996), *modified*, 993 F. Supp. 370 (1998); EEOC v. Tree of Life Christian Schs., 751 F. Supp. 700, 711 (S.D. Ohio 1990); Russell v. Belmont College, 554 F. Supp. 667, 676 (M.D. Tenn. 1982); Black v. Snyder, 471 N.W.2d 715, 721 (Minn. Ct. App. 1991).

114. *See* NLRB v. Hanna Boys Ctr., 940 F.2d 1295, 1304, 1306 (9th Cir. 1991); *Catholic High Sch. Ass'n*, 753 F.2d at 1170; Tressler Lutheran Home for Children v. NLRB, 677 F.2d 302, 306 (3d Cir. 1982); NLRB v. World Evangelism, Inc., 656 F.2d 1349, 1354 (9th Cir. 1981); Hill-Murray Fed'n of Teachers v. Hill-Murray High Sch., 487 N.W.2d 857, 865 & n.3 (Minn. 1992).

115. *See* Geary v. Visitation of Blessed Virgin Mary Parish Sch., 7 F.3d 324, 328 (3d Cir. 1993).

116. Archbishop of Roman Catholic Apostolic Archdiocese v. Guardiola, 628 F. Supp. 1173, 1183 & n.7 (D.P.R. 1985).

employee will erroneously be held to have discriminated on some ground forbidden by secular law. They are also oblivious to the tendency of disappointed employees to assume that some such discrimination must have been afoot, so that entertaining these cases results in a substantial litigation burden and exposure to the risk of error in a large number of cases.

We do not have space to describe, much less analyze, the many excuses courts have used in arguing that enforcement of employment regulations against churches does not burden religion. But we would like to discuss just one of these excuses in detail so that we can convey some sense of the lengths to which courts will go.

Many courts contend that judicial review of a church's employment decision does not burden that church's exercise of religion if the decision was made for secular rather than religious reasons.[117] For example, in *Weissman v. Congregation Shaare Emeth*,[118] the court found no burden in permitting the administrator of a synagogue—an employee with some religious duties—to sue the synagogue for age discrimination. "Because...the Temple has asserted no religious grounds for [the administrator's] termination, his...claim does not pose a significant risk of infringement."[119] Similarly, in *Gallo v. Salesian Society, Inc.*,[120] the court held that permitting a parochial school teacher to sue for sex and age discrimination would not burden religion. Because the religious order that operated the school claimed to have fired the teacher "for budgetary reasons only," and not "on any religious grounds," the court concluded that "enforcing the prohibition against discrimination would have no impact on religious belief, doctrine, or practice."[121]

This creates multiple problems. One is the need to distinguish religious from secular reasons, and the corresponding tendencies to define religious reasons narrowly and to ignore religious reasons not squarely articulated as the central issue in the case. How can budgetary reasons not be religious? The church budget allocates resources devoted to religious uses; a decision to cut here instead of there is necessarily a decision that cutting here does the least harm to the church's overall mission. But courts easily ignore that implicit religious judgment, just as they ignore implicit religious disputes in the doctrine cases.

Second, if a church states an unmistakably religious reason for an employment action, may the court inquire into whether the stated reason is pretextual? The Supreme Court seems to be of two minds on this issue. In *NLRB v. Catholic Bishop*,[122] the Court

---

117. Other courts strongly reject this contention, recognizing that "the free exercise clause of the First Amendment protects the act of a decision rather than a motivation behind it." Rayburn v. General Conference of Seventh-Day Adventists, 772 F.2d 1164, 1169 (4th Cir. 1985); *see also* EEOC v. Catholic Univ., 83 F.3d 455, 465 (D.C. Cir. 1996); Young v. Northern Ill. Conference of United Methodist Church, 21 F.3d 184, 186 (7th Cir. 1994); Scharon v. St. Luke's Episcopal Presbyterian Hosps., 929 F.2d 360, 363 (8th Cir. 1991); Powell v. Stafford, 859 F. Supp. 1343, 1348 (D. Colo. 1994); Gabriel v. Immanuel Evangelical Lutheran Church, Inc., 640 N.E.2d 681, 684 (Ill. App. Ct. 1994); Assemany v. Archdiocese of Detroit, 434 N.W.2d 233, 237 (Mich. Ct. App. 1988).

118. 38 F.3d 1038 (8th Cir. 1994).

119. *Id.* at 1045.

120. 676 A.2d 580 (N.J. Super. Ct. App. Div. 1996).

121. *Id.* at 591. Other cases citing the "secular" reason for an employment action as a justification for permitting governmental interference with that action include Roxas v. Presentation College, 90 F.3d 310, 318 n.6 (8th Cir. 1996); Drevlow v. Lutheran Church, Missouri Synod, 991 F.2d 468, 472 (8th Cir. 1993); EEOC v. Mississippi College, 626 F.2d 477, 488 (5th Cir. 1980); Whitney v. Greater New York Corp. of Seventh-Day Adventists, 401 F. Supp. 1363, 1368 (S.D.N.Y. 1975); and Geraci v. Eckankar, 526 N.W.2d 391, 397 (Minn. Ct. App. 1995).

122. 440 U.S. 490 (1979).

"construed" the National Labor Relations Act (NLRA)[123] to not apply to teachers at parochial schools, in order to avoid the "significant risk that the First Amendment will be infringed" if the act were construed otherwise.[124] The Court pointed out that a parochial school might respond to an unfair-labor-practice charge by arguing that the challenged action was motivated by religious belief, and therefore:

> The resolution of such charges by the [National Labor Relations] Board, in many instances, will necessarily involve inquiry into the good faith of the position asserted by the clergy-administrators and its relationship to the school's religious mission. It is not only the conclusions that may be reached by the Board which may impinge on rights guaranteed by the Religion Clauses, but also the very process of inquiry leading to findings and conclusions.[125]

Thus, *Catholic Bishop* strongly suggests that pretext inquiry—that is, "inquiry into the good faith" of a religious explanation for an employment decision—is impermissible under the First Amendment.

A few years later, the Supreme Court seemed to hold precisely the opposite in *Ohio Civil Rights Commission v. Dayton Christian Schools*.[126] A teacher at a religious school had been fired, ostensibly for religious reasons. She filed sex-discrimination charges with the Ohio Civil Rights Commission, which commenced an administrative proceeding against the school. The school sought to have the proceeding enjoined on the grounds that "the very process of inquiry" into its reason for dismissing the teacher would violate the First Amendment. The Supreme Court disagreed.

> [H]owever [the school's] constitutional claim should be decided on the merits, the Commission violates no constitutional rights by merely investigating the circumstances of [the teacher's] discharge in this case, if only to ascertain whether the ascribed religious-based reason was in fact the reason for the discharge.[127]

The Court's analysis was perfunctory. Perhaps because its attention was focused on a question of federalism,[128] it neither explained nor even acknowledged the apparent inconsistency with *Catholic Bishop*.[129]

Like the Supreme Court, the lower courts are of two minds on the permissibility of pretext inquiries. Some courts, following *Catholic Bishop*, hold that such inquiries are

---

123. 29 U.S.C. §§ 151–169 (1994).

124. *Catholic Bishop*, 440 U.S. at 502.

125. *Id.*

126. 477 U.S. 619 (1986).

127. *Id.* at 628.

128. The case arose as a suit in federal court to enjoin pending proceedings before the state agency. The Court held the action barred by the abstention doctrine of *Younger v. Harris*, 401 U.S. 37 (1971). The church tried to escape the *Younger* doctrine by arguing that the mere pendency of the state proceeding was unconstitutional, and the statements quoted in text were designed to brush that objection aside.

129. The Court flip-flopped again in *Jimmy Swaggart Ministries v. Board of Equalization*, 493 U.S. 378, 396 (1990), when it explained that the most significant reason for its upholding the application of a general sales and use tax against sales of merchandise by a religious organization was that application of the tax "does not require the State to inquire into the religious content of the items sold *or the religious motivation for selling or purchasing the items*, because the materials are subject to the tax regardless of content or motive" (emphasis added). Of course, inquiring into "religious motivation" is precisely what pretext analysis requires.

forbidden.[130] Other courts, following *Dayton Christian Schools*, disagree.[131] If a church alleges that an employment action was taken for a religious reason, these courts do not hesitate to inquire into whether the church is telling the truth.

This creates a third problem. If pretext inquiry is to be done right, the court must (1) identify the action taken by the church; (2) require the church to state a reason for the action; (3) determine whether the stated reason is "religious"; and (4) if it is, determine whether this religious reason was the actual reason for the action. This last determination might include, among other things, considering whether the belief that allegedly motivated the church is reflected in a constitution, bylaw, creed, or other "official" document, whether the employment action is in fact consistent with the stated belief, and whether the church has acted inconsistently with the belief in the past.[132] All of this would seem to require a profoundly detailed examination of church doctrine, practice, and belief, in violation even of the doctrine part of the *Watson* line.

Courts that undertake pretext inquiries get around these problems in the only way they can: by stubbornly misrepresenting the law. All that the First Amendment prohibits, these courts insist, is judicial determination of the *validity* of a religious belief; the First Amendment presents no obstacle whatever to judicial determination of *what* a church believes or of whether that church belief actually motivated an employment ac-

---

130. *See, e.g.*, Young v. Northern Ill. Conference of United Methodist Church, 21 F.3d 184, 187 (7th Cir. 1994); Little v. Wuerl, 929 F.2d 944, 948 (3d Cir. 1991); Scharon v. St. Luke's Episcopal Presbyterian Hosps., 929 F.2d 360, 363 (8th Cir. 1991); Minker v. Baltimore Annual Conference of United Methodist Church, 894 F.2d 1354, 1360–61 (D.C. Cir. 1990) ("the first amendment forecloses any inquiry into the Church's assessment of Minker's suitability for a pastorship, even for the purpose of showing it to be pretextual"); Cochran v. St. Louis Preparatory Seminary, 717 F. Supp. 1413, 1416 (E.D. Mo. 1989); Singleton v. Christ the Servant Evangelical Lutheran Church, 541 N.W.2d 606, 611 (Minn. Ct. App. 1996); Black v. Snyder, 471 N.W.2d 715, 720 (Minn. Ct. App. 1991) ("Inquiry into a church's reasons for rejecting an individual for pastorship, even for the purpose of showing pretext, would cause excessive entanglement").

131. *See, e.g.*, Gargano v. Diocese of Rockville Centre, 80 F.3d 87, 90 (2d Cir. 1996); Geary v. Visitation of Blessed Virgin Mary Parish Sch., 7 F.3d 324, 329–31 (3d Cir. 1993); DeMarco v. Holy Cross High Sch., 4 F.3d 166, 170–71 (2d Cir. 1993); Lukaszewski v. Nazareth Hosp., 764 F. Supp. 57, 60 (E.D. Pa. 1991); Dolter v. Wahlert High Sch., 483 F. Supp. 266, 270 (N.D. Iowa 1980); Fellowship Tabernacle, Inc. v. Baker, 869 P.2d 578, 583 (Idaho Ct. App. 1994); Diocese of Galveston-Houston v. Stone, 892 S.W.2d 169, 176–77 (Tex. App. 1994), no writ.

132. "The pretext inquiry . . . normally focuses upon factual questions such as whether the asserted reason for the challenged action comports with the [church's] policies and rules, whether the rule applied to the [employee] has been applied uniformly, and whether the putative non-discriminatory purpose was stated only after the allegation of discrimination." *DeMarco*, 4 F.3d at 171. Several courts have suggested that if a church has not always acted consistently with the religious belief that purportedly justifies an employment decision, that inconsistent behavior gives reason to believe that the asserted justification is pretextual. *See, e.g.*, Boyd v. Harding Academy of Memphis, Inc., 88 F.3d 410 (6th Cir. 1996); Vigars v. Valley Christian Ctr., 805 F. Supp. 802 (N.D. Cal. 1992); *Dolter*, 483 F. Supp. at 271. Such inquiries may be unavoidable when a church or believer claims exemption on the basis of religious objections to the substantive content of a secular law. But they are readily avoidable when courts are in effect reviewing an internal decision of a religious organization; in that context, courts can and should defer to the religious resolution of any dispute over religious matters. The implicit judicial approach seems to be either to decide or avoid deciding questions of religious doctrine, depending on which will maximize government's power to regulate religion. Thus the Supreme Court has argued, erroneously in our view, that the avoidance of inquiries into religious doctrine is a reason to limit religious exemptions under the Free Exercise Clause. *Employment Division v. Smith*, 494 U.S. 872, 886–87 (1990). But in the church employment cases, the lower courts regularly inquire into religious doctrine as a step toward regulating church employment.

tion.[133] In other words, a court cannot determine whether adultery *is* a sin; but it can determine whether a particular church *believes* that adultery is a sin, as well as whether adultery was the real reason why the church fired an employee. But if courts could do all that, *Hull Memorial* would necessarily have approved Georgia's departure-from-doctrine standard in church schism cases. Georgia never purported to decide which faction's beliefs were true, but merely which faction's beliefs were the same as the church's original teaching.

Courts may go astonishingly far once they claim the power to decide the existence of religious reasons for personnel decisions. In their view, even adjudicating the claims of a parochial school teacher fired for "failure to fulfill the spiritual mission of" the school,[134] for "'not adequately prepar[ing]...children for the sacraments,'"[135] or for "'unchristian behavior'"[136] does not create excessive entanglement with religion. Courts argue that these justifications, although religious, involve "very specific, testable allegations"[137] or "easily isolated and defined" instances of religious misconduct[138] (such as "failure to begin...classes with prayer and failure to attend Mass with...students"[139]), and therefore adjudicating their truth would not involve excessive entanglement with religion.

Overestimating the governmental interest

To a court sympathetic to government regulation of religious employment decisions, every governmental interest seems compelling. The government's interest in combating race, sex,[140] and age[141] discrimination, even inside a religious organization, has repeatedly been deemed sufficiently compelling to justify burdening the free exercise of religion. Likewise, courts have viewed as compelling the government's interest in subjecting

---

133. *See, e.g.*, *Gargano*, 80 F.3d at 90; *Geary*, 7 F.3d at 330; *DeMarco*, 4 F.3d at 170–71; *Lukaszewski*, 764 F. Supp. at 60; *Dolter*, 483 F. Supp. at 270–71; *Fellowship Tabernacle*, 869 P.2d at 583.

134. *DeMarco*, 4 F.3d at 172.

135. *Gargano*, 80 F.3d at 90.

136. New York State Employment Relations Bd. v. Christ the King Regional High Sch., 682 N.E.2d 960, 966 (N.Y. 1997).

137. *Geary*, 7 F.3d at 331.

138. *DeMarco*, 4 F.3d at 172.

139. *Id.* at 168.

140. *See* EEOC v. Fremont Christian Sch., 781 F.2d 1362, 1368–69 (9th Cir. 1986); EEOC v. Pacific Press Publ'g Ass'n, 676 F.2d 1272, 1280 (9th Cir. 1982); EEOC v. Mississippi College, 626 F.2d 477, 488 (5th Cir. 1980); EEOC v. Tree of Life Christian Schs., 751 F. Supp. 700, 711 (S.D. Ohio 1990); McLeod v. Providence Christian Sch., 408 N.W.2d 146, 151 (Mich. Ct. App. 1987); Gallo v. Salesian Soc'y, Inc., 676 A.2d 580, 593–94 (N.J. Super. Ct. App. Div. 1996).

141. *See Gallo*, 676 A.2d at 593–94. Some courts disagree. *See, e.g.*, Minker v. Baltimore Annual Conference of United Methodist Church, 894 F.2d 1354, 1357 (D.C. Cir. 1990) (interest in barring age discrimination is "not sufficiently compelling" to overcome right of hierarchical church to decide where pastor would be assigned); Powell v. Stafford, 859 F. Supp. 1343, 1347 (D. Colo. 1994) ("although the government clearly has an interest in eradicating age discrimination, it is not compelling"). The *Powell* court might reconcile these cases on the ground that plaintiff in *Gallo* taught English and history whereas plaintiff in *Powell* taught theology and plaintiff in *Minker* was a minister.

parochial schools and other religious employers to the NLRA or state law equivalents.[142] This interest has variously been described as the government's interest in "minimizing economic disruptions caused by labor unrest,"[143] "'promot[ing] the peaceful settlement of industrial disputes,'"[144] and "preserv[ing]...industrial peace and a sound economic order"[145] — none of which seems to capture exactly why the government has a compelling need to regulate, say, the labor relations between a Catholic parish and its parochial school teachers. Other interests deemed compelling include the government's interest in "controlling the flow of aliens" into the United States,[146] in "protecting workers and their dependents against costs of workplace accidents,"[147] in "eradicating sexual harassment in the work place,"[148] and in forcing employers to pay a minimum wage.[149] Some of these holdings are more plausible than others, but most of them depend on the fallacious view that a church is an essentially economic organization and that religious employment is no different from commercial employment.

The *Smith* Understanding of the Free Exercise Clause

A third approach taken by courts in religious employment cases applies the Free Exercise Clause as interpreted in *Employment Division v. Smith*[150] rather than as interpreted in *Sherbert*. In *Smith*, the Supreme Court made *Sherbert* one of several exceptions to a new and very different rule. The Court held that government can apply "a 'valid and neutral law of general applicability'"[151] in ways that burden the exercise of religion, and that no matter how severe, the burden does not have to be justified by a compelling governmental interest — or for that matter, even by a trivial governmental interest. *Smith* understood the Free Exercise Clause to provide an "equality" right — a requirement of special justification for the *discriminatory* burdening of religious exercise — rather than a "substantive" right — a requirement of special justification for *any* burdening (or any substantial burdening) of religious exercise. Thus, under *Smith* the government cannot bar *only* religious organizations from discriminating on the basis of sex, but it can bar sex discrimination by *all* employers and enforce that prohibition

---

142. *See* NLRB v. Hanna Boys Ctr., 940 F.2d 1295, 1304, 1306 (9th Cir. 1991); Catholic High Sch. Ass'n v. Culvert, 753 F.2d 1161, 1171 (2d Cir. 1985); Hill-Murray Fed'n of Teachers v. Hill-Murray High Sch., 487 N.W.2d 857, 863 n.2 (Minn. 1992); South Jersey Catholic Sch. Teachers Org. v. St. Teresa of Infant Jesus Church Elementary Sch., 696 A.2d 709, 722–23 (N.J. 1997).

143. Universidad Cent. de Bayamon v. NLRB, 793 F.2d 383, 390 (1st Cir. 1985).

144. *Hanna Boys Ctr.*, 940 F.2d at 1306 (citation omitted).

145. *Catholic High Sch. Ass'n*, 753 F.2d at 1171.

146. Intercommunity Ctr. for Justice and Peace v. INS, 910 F.2d 42, 46 (2d Cir. 1990).

147. South Ridge Baptist Church v. Industrial Comm'n, 911 F.2d 1203, 1206 (6th Cir. 1990).

148. Black v. Snyder, 471 N.W.2d 715, 721 (Minn. Ct. App. 1991).

149. *See* Dole v. Shenandoah Baptist Church, 899 F.2d 1389, 1398 (4th Cir. 1990); Mitchell v. Pilgrim Holiness Church Corp., 210 F.2d 879, 884 (7th Cir. 1954); Archbishop of Roman Catholic Apostolic Archdiocese v. Guardiola, 628 F. Supp. 1173, 1183 (D.P.R. 1985).

150. 494 U.S. 872 (1990).

151. *Id.* at 879 (citation omitted).

against religious organizations—for example, in forcing the Roman Catholic Church to ordain women priests.[152]

The general rule in *Smith* leaves religious organizations virtually unprotected in employment litigation, and courts have had no difficulty recognizing that fact. Although most employment litigation plausibly falls into *Smith*'s exception for internal religious disputes,[153] courts have generally minimized all the *Smith* exceptions. Among those statutes already found by courts to be neutral and generally applicable, and thus to be fully enforceable against churches, are the NLRA[154] and state law equivalents,[155] Title VII[156] and state law equivalents,[157] the Age Discrimination in Employment Act (ADEA),[158] and the Immigration Reform and Control Act.[159] Likewise, most common law doctrines, such as those providing remedies for breach of contract or defamation, have been held generally applicable and thus have been fully enforced against churches under *Smith*.[160]

There seems little chance that future employment decisions of churches will receive much protection under the Free Exercise Clause. However, the situation is not entirely hopeless. To begin with, it is not yet clear just how broadly applicable a law must be before it will be considered "generally" applicable for *Smith* purposes. Few employment regulations apply to all employers; Title VII, for example, applies only to employers with fifteen or more employees,[161] which means that more than eighty percent of employers are excluded.[162] Many state laws have less dramatic exceptions. Thus, if "generally applicable" means "applicable to all or nearly all employers," many regulatory burdens on churches will remain subject to the compelling interest test even after *Smith*. But if "generally applicable" means "applicable to at least a few secular employers, in addition to religious employers," *Smith* will substantially eliminate Free Exercise protection for churches in employment litigation.[163]

---

152. Indeed, according to the EEOC, such a law is already in existence in Title VII, and "the Free Exercise Clause does not bar its application to ministers employed by religious organizations." EEOC v. Catholic Univ. of Am., 83 F.3d 455, 461–62 (D.C. Cir. 1996).

153. *See* Laycock, *supra* note 107, at 43–44.

154. *See* NLRB v. Hanna Boys Ctr., 940 F.2d 1295, 1304, 1305 (9th Cir. 1991).

155. *See* Hill-Murray Fed'n of Teachers v. Hill-Murray High Sch., 487 N.W.2d 857, 862–63 (Minn. 1992); South Jersey Catholic Sch. Teachers Org. v. St. Teresa of the Infant Jesus Church Elementary Sch., 696 A.2d 709, 721 (N.J. 1997); New York State Employment Relations Bd. v. Christ the King Regional High Sch., 682 N.E.2d 960, 963–64 (N.Y. 1997).

156. *See* Vigars v. Valley Christian Ctr., 805 F. Supp. 802, 809 (N.D. Cal. 1992).

157. *See* Porth v. Roman Catholic Diocese, 532 N.W.2d 195, 198–99 (Mich. Ct. App. 1995) (assuming the point without discussion); Black v. Snyder, 471 N.W.2d 715, 719 (Minn. Ct. App. 1991).

158. 29 U.S.C. §§ 621–634 (1994 & Supp. III 1997); *see* Stouch v. Brothers of Order of Hermits of St. Augustine, 836 F. Supp. 1134, 1144 (E.D. Pa. 1993); Lukaszewski v. Nazareth Hosp., 764 F. Supp. 57, 61 (E.D. Pa. 1991).

159. Pub. L. No. 99-603, 100 Stat. 3359 (codified as amended in scattered sections of 8 U.S.C.); *see* American Friends Serv. Comm. Corp. v. Thornburgh, 961 F.2d 1405, 1407–08 (9th Cir. 1991); Intercommunity Ctr. for Justice and Peace v. INS, 910 F.2d 42, 44 (2d Cir. 1990).

160. *Black*, 471 N.W.2d at 719.

161. *See* 42 U.S.C. § 2000e(b) (1994).

162. *See* U.S. Dept. of Commerce, Economics and Statistics Administration, Bureau of the Census, 1992 Enterprise Statistics: Company Summary, tbls. 2 and 9 (1992). These tables report data on 4,610,829 companies, of which 3,621,943 had nine or fewer employees, and 507,319 had ten to nineteen employees.

163. The early returns on this question do not look promising for churches. Title VII has been considered generally applicable, even though it does not apply to employers with fewer than fifteen workers, *see* Vigars v. Valley Christian Ctr., 805 F. Supp. 802, 809 (N.D. Cal. 1992); the ADEA has been considered generally applicable, even though it does not apply to employers with fewer than twenty employees, *see Lukaszewski*, 764 F. Supp. at 61 ("The ADEA is a neutral law of general ap-

In addition, Justice Scalia's opinion for the majority in *Smith* suggested several possible limitations on the reach of the decision. For example, Scalia referred to the *Watson* line of cases in a manner suggesting that those cases remain valid.[164] And as already noted, most employment disputes within churches do involve an internal church dispute, even if they also involve government regulation of the church. Scalia also suggested that in "hybrid" cases—that is, cases in which governmental action implicates *both* the Free Exercise Clause *and* another constitutional guarantee—application of the *Sherbert* test may be appropriate.[165] As with other exceptions, hybrid rights claims have had only limited success in employment cases[166] and perhaps slightly more success in other contexts.[167] It is far from clear what substance, if any, the Supreme Court will give

plicability to any employer with greater than twenty employees"); the Immigration Reform and Control Act has been considered generally applicable, even though it does not apply to household employees or to employees hired before November 1986, *see Intercommunity Ctr.*, 910 F.2d at 44; and state equivalents of the NLRA have been considered generally applicable, even though they exempt all public sector employers, *see* Hill-Murray Fed'n of Teachers v. Hill-Murray High Sch., 487 N.W.2d 857, 862–63 (Minn. 1992). For more helpful interpretations of the requirement of general applicability, see *Fraternal Order of Police v. City of Newark*, 170 F.3d 359 (3d Cir.) (rule forbidding police officers to wear beards, with exception for beards required by medical conditions, was not generally applicable law), *cert. denied*, 120 S. Ct. 56 (1999); *Keeler v. Mayor of Cumberland*, 940 F. Supp. 879, 883–87 (D. Md. 1996) (landmark ordinance with three secular exceptions was not generally applicable); *Rader v. Johnston*, 924 F. Supp. 1540, 1549–56 (D. Neb. 1996) (university rule requiring all freshmen to live in residence halls, with written and unwritten exceptions that exempted nearly one-third of freshmen, was not generally applicable law).

164. *See Smith*, 494 U.S. at 877.

165. *See id.* at 881–82.

166. *Compare* EEOC v. Catholic Univ. of Am., 83 F.3d 455, 467 (D.C. Cir. 1996) (finding a hybrid of Free Exercise and Establishment clause rights in response to discrimination claim by theology professor), *with* New York State Employment Relations Bd. v. Christ the King Regional High Sch., 682 N.E.2d 960, 964 (N.Y. 1997) (refusing to find hybrid right in response to collective bargaining at religious school); South Jersey Catholic Sch. Teachers Org. v. St. Teresa of Infant Jesus Church Elementary Sch., 696 A.2d 709, 721–22 (N.J. 1997) (finding that collective bargaining in Catholic school would not affect parents' right to educate their children, so that hybrid rights claim could not arise); *and Hill-Murray*, 487 N.W.2d at 863 (refusing to find hybrid of free exercise and parental rights in case about collective bargaining at religious school).

167. *Compare* Thomas v. Anchorage Equal Rights Comm'n, 165 F.3d 692, 703–09 (9th Cir. 1999) (finding hybrid Free Exercise and Takings clause right protecting religiously motivated behavior of landlord), *vacated and rehearing granted*, 192 F.3d 1208 (9th Cir. 1999) (en banc); Cornerstone Bible Church v. City of Hasting, 948 F.2d 464 (8th Cir. 1991) (remanding for consideration of hybrid free exercise and free speech right in church zoning case); People v. DeJonge, 501 N.W.2d 127, 134–35 (Mich. 1993) (finding hybrid of free exercise and parental rights to home school children without using certified teachers); State v. DeLaBruere, 577 A.2d 254, 261 n.8 (Vt. 1990) (finding hybrid of free exercise and parental rights overridden by compelling interest in monitoring education in religious schools); First United Methodist Church v. Hearing Examiner, 916 P.2d 374, 379 (Wash. 1996) (finding hybrid free exercise and free speech right in church landmarking case); *and* First Covenant Church v. City of Seattle, 840 P.2d 174, 181–82 (Wash. 1992) (finding hybrid free exercise and free speech right in church landmarking case); *with* Swanson v. Guthrie Indep. School Dist. No. I-L, 135 F.3d 694, 699–700 (10th Cir. 1998) (refusing to find hybrid of free exercise and parental rights to enroll home-schooled child for selected courses in public school); Brown v. Hot, Sexy and Safer Productions, Inc., 68 F.3d 525, 539 (1st Cir. 1995) (refusing to find hybrid of free exercise and parental rights to keep child out of bawdy school assembly with content offensive or embarrassing to many); Kissinger v. Board of Trustees, 5 F.3d 177, 180 (6th Cir. 1993) (rejecting the hybrid rights exception in principle as "completely illogical"); American Friends Serv. Comm. Corp. v. Thornburgh, 961 F.2d 1405, 1408 (9th Cir. 1991) (refusing to find hybrid free exercise and substantive due process right to employ aliens not authorized to work); *and* Health Servs. Div. v. Temple Baptist Church, 814 P.2d 130, 135–36 (N.M. Ct. App. 1991) (holding that church could not assert parents' claim to hybrid of free exercise and parental rights to control discipline of children).

to the *Smith* "exceptions," but attorneys representing churches in employment litigation have much opportunity to limit and distinguish *Smith*.

The Establishment Clause

In *Lemon v. Kurtzman*,[168] the Supreme Court held that governmental action violates the Establishment Clause if it has the primary effect of either "advancing or inhibiting religion" or if it fosters "'an excessive government entanglement with religion.'"[169] In *Agostini v. Felton*[170] the Court merged these two inquiries; an entanglement is excessive if, and apparently only if, it has the primary effect of advancing or inhibiting religion.[171]

Under these formulations, a burdensome regulation of church employment relations might be attacked as a law inhibiting religion, or as an entanglement that is excessive because it inhibits religion. These formulations sound more in free exercise than in disestablishment; they were introduced to the Establishment Clause by judicial misquotation and have persisted through judicial repetition.[172] But the lower courts sometimes,[173] and the Supreme Court occasionally,[174] have taken them literally, considering whether regulatory burdens on religious organizations violate the Establishment Clause. Many courts have either betrayed confusion about the matter, referring to how "excessive entanglement...burdens the free exercise of religion,"[175] or frankly admitted that they have difficulty separating Establishment Clause analysis from Free Exercise Clause analysis.[176]

---

168. 403 U.S. 602 (1971).

169. *Id.* at 612–13 (citation omitted).

170. 521 U.S. 203 (1997).

171. *See id.* at 232–33.

172. *See* Laycock, *supra* note 62, at 1380–81 (tracing the evolution of the Court's Establishment Clause test).

173. *See, e.g.*, NLRB v. Hanna Boys Ctr., 940 F.2d 1295, 1303 (9th Cir. 1991); EEOC v. Fremont Christian Sch., 781 F.2d 1362, 1369 (9th Cir. 1986); Rayburn v. General Conference of Seventh-Day Adventists, 772 F.2d 1164, 1170 & n.7 (4th Cir. 1985); EEOC v. Pacific Press Publ'g Ass'n, 676 F.2d 1272, 1282 (9th Cir. 1982); EEOC v. Southwestern Baptist Theological Seminary, 651 F.2d 277, 286 (5th Cir. 1981); EEOC v. Mississippi College, 626 F.2d 477, 486–87 (5th Cir. 1980); Powell v. Stafford, 859 F. Supp. 1343, 1348 (D. Colo. 1994); EEOC v. Tree of Life Christian Schs., 751 F. Supp. 700, 715 (S.D. Ohio 1990); Russell v. Belmont College, 554 F. Supp. 667, 678 (M.D. Tenn. 1982); Hill-Murray Fed'n of Teachers v. Hill-Murray High Sch., 487 N.W.2d 857, 864 (Minn. 1992).

174. *See* Jimmy Swaggart Ministries v. Board of Equalization, 493 U.S. 378, 392–97 (1990); Tony and Susan Alamo Found. v. Secretary of Labor, 471 U.S. 290, 305–06 (1985).

175. South Jersey Catholic Sch. Teachers Org. v. St. Teresa of Infant Jesus Church Elementary Sch., 696 A.2d 709, 715 (N.J. 1997); *see also* Shirkey v. Eastwind Community Dev. Corp., 941 F. Supp. 567, 578 (D. Md. 1996), *modified*, 993 F. Supp. 370 (D. Md. 1998) (finding no Establishment Clause violation because "there is no conflict between § 1981's prohibition with regard to race discrimination and any proffered religious doctrine of the Methodist Church").

176. *See, e.g.*, Catholic High Sch. Ass'n v. Culvert, 753 F.2d 1161, 1166 (2d Cir. 1985) ("[T]he claims under the Establishment Clause and the Free Exercise Clause involve the same considerations and are not easily divided and put into separate pigeon holes"); *Southwestern Baptist*, 651 F.2d at 285 n.5 ("The precise challenge presented by this case falls between the two religion clauses and between the tests used under them"); Van Osdol v. Vogt, 908 P.2d 1122, 1126 (Colo. 1996) ("Whether the courts should intrude into ecclesiastical decisions regarding choice of a minister is an issue that bridges both religion clauses of the First Amendment"); Gallo v. Salesian Soc'y, Inc., 676 A.2d 580, 594 (N.J. Super. Ct. App. Div. 1996) (finding "no analytic difference between the two religion clauses for purposes of this [religious employment] case").

With rare exceptions,[177] courts that analyze the constitutionality of governmental regulation under the Establishment Clause also do so under the Free Exercise Clause. Moreover, when both clauses are considered, courts almost never find a regulation constitutional under one clause but unconstitutional under the other. Whether the church wins[178] or loses,[179] the Establishment Clause analysis always goes the way of the Free Exercise Clause analysis.[180] For these reasons, a court's willingness to consider the constitutionality of a regulation under the Establishment Clause will likely not help a church in an employment case. It may produce a different set of explanations for why the church's decision is or is not constitutionally protected, but the ultimate outcome of the case will almost surely not be affected.

The most striking thing about the application of the Establishment Clause in religious employment cases is the broad array of excuses courts have used to find that the government is not excessively entangled with religion even when it is obvious that such entanglement does exist. We do not have space to describe all of these excuses, much less to evaluate them—but we want to list a few, for they give churches some hint as to how they might increase the chances that their employment decisions will enjoy constitutional protection. Discussion of these excuses may be organized in terms of "the factors [the Court has] use[d] to assess whether an entanglement is excessive. [These include] 'the character and purposes of the institutions that are benefited, the nature of the aid that the State provides, and the resulting relationship between the government and religious authority.'"[181] To apply these factors to labor regulation requires courts to reformulate them in terms of burdens instead of benefits.[182]

1. "The character and purposes of the institutions that are benefited [or burdened]." The first factor in the reformulated *Lemon* entanglement test looks at the nature of the institution that is burdened. Courts tend to rely on this factor when the employee does not work for a "church" (narrowly defined), but rather for a religious entity affiliated with a church, such as a school, hospital, nursing home, publishing house, or social

---

177. *See, e.g.,* Geary v. Visitation of Blessed Virgin Mary Parish Sch., 7 F.3d 324 (3d Cir. 1993); Denver Post of Nat'l Soc'y of Volunteers of Am. v. NLRB, 732 F.2d 769 (10th Cir. 1984); Himaka v. Buddhist Churches, 917 F. Supp. 698 (N.D. Cal. 1995); Singleton v. Christ the Servant Evangelical Lutheran Church, 541 N.W.2d 606 (Minn. Ct. App. 1996). *Denver VOA* has a subsequent history that is not easily summarized and not actually relevant to this chapter. The Tenth Circuit subsequently repudiated the legal rule that controlled the disposition of a different issue in *Denver VOA*. *Aramark Corp. v. NLRB,* 179 F.3d 872, 874 n.2, 877–78 & n.10 (10th Cir. en banc 1999). This change in legal rule would neither have changed the result in *Denver VOA* nor affected the analysis of the issues considered in this chapter.

178. *See, e.g.,* EEOC v. Catholic Univ. of Am., 83 F.3d 455 (D.C. Cir. 1996); Scharon v. St. Luke's Episcopal Presbyterian Hosps., 929 F.2d 360 (8th Cir. 1991); *Rayburn,* 772 F.2d 1164; *Powell,* 859 F. Supp. 1343; McCormick v. Hirsch, 460 F. Supp. 1337 (M.D. Pa. 1978); *Van Osdol,* 908 P.2d 1122.

179. *See, e.g.,* NLRB v. Hanna Boys Ctr., 940 F.2d 1295 (9th Cir. 1991); South Ridge Baptist Church v. Industrial Comm'n, 911 F.2d 1203 (6th Cir. 1990); EEOC v. Fremont Christian Sch., 781 F.2d 1362 (9th Cir. 1986); *Catholic High Sch. Ass'n,* 753 F.2d 1161; EEOC v. Pacific Press Publ'g Ass'n, 676 F.2d 1272 (9th Cir. 1982); *Shirkey,* 941 F. Supp. 567; Vigars v. Valley Christian Ctr., 805 F. Supp. 802 (N.D. Cal. 1992); Lukaszewski v. Nazareth Hosp., 764 F. Supp. 57 (E.D. Pa. 1991); EEOC v. Tree of Life Christian Schs., 751 F. Supp. 700 (S.D. Ohio 1990); Russell v. Belmont College, 554 F. Supp. 667 (M.D. Tenn. 1982); Hill-Murray Fed'n of Teachers v. Hill-Murray High Sch., 487 N.W.2d 857 (Minn. 1992); *Gallo,* 676 A.2d 580.

180. One exception of which we are aware is *Black v. Snyder,* 471 N.W.2d 715 (Minn. Ct. App. 1991).

181. *Agostini,* 521 U.S. at 232, quoting *Lemon,* 403 U.S. at 615.

182. For examples of such reformulation, see cases cited *supra* note 173.

service agency. Courts conclude that such an institution is secular—and therefore that governmental regulation of its employment decisions does not create excessive entanglement—when the institution's "primary purpose,"[183] "primary function,"[184] "primary activity,"[185] or "primary business"[186] is not religious.

Courts take an extraordinarily narrow view of what qualifies as "religious." Commercial activity does not qualify,[187] of course, but neither does health care,[188] charitable work,[189] education,[190] or anything else that does not directly involve worship or proselytizing. It makes no difference whether the organization was established by a church for religious reasons, whether its work is religiously motivated, or even whether its atmosphere is "religious"[191] or "pervasively sectarian."[192] Courts are always able to argue that a given organization is secular because it is less religious than some other organization. A commercial venture is less religious than a not-for-profit hospital, which is less religious than a sectarian college, which is less religious than a parochial school, which is less religious than a seminary, which is less religious than a church.[193]

A good example of how narrowly courts define "religion" for these purposes is a series of cases involving the National Society of the Volunteers of America (VOA). VOA is a religious organization founded over a century ago for the purpose of "perform[ing]

---

183. Volunteers of Am.-Minn.-Bar None Boys Ranch v. NLRB, 752 F.2d 345, 348 (8th Cir. 1985); Denver Post of Nat'l Soc'y of Volunteers of Am. v. NLRB, 732 F.2d 769, 772 (10th Cir. 1984), *subsequent history explained supra* note 177.

184. St. Elizabeth Hosp. v. NLRB, 715 F.2d 1193, 1196 (7th Cir. 1983); Tressler Lutheran Home for Children v. NLRB, 677 F.2d 302, 305 (3d Cir. 1982).

185. *St. Elizabeth Hosp.*, 715 F.2d at 1196.

186. NLRB v. Salvation Army Dorchester Day Care Ctr., 763 F.2d 1, 6 (1st Cir. 1985).

187. *See* NLRB v. World Evangelism, Inc., 656 F.2d 1349 (9th Cir. 1981); King's Garden, Inc. v. FCC, 498 F.2d 51, 57 (D.C. Cir. 1974).

188. *See St. Elizabeth Hosp.*, 715 F.2d at 1196 (hospital); *Tressler Lutheran Home*, 677 F.2d at 305 (nursing home).

189. *See* Volunteers of Am., Los Angeles v. NLRB, 777 F.2d 1386 (9th Cir. 1985) (alcoholism treatment facilities); *Salvation Army*, 763 F.2d 1 (day care center); Volunteers of Am.-Minn.-Bar None Boys Ranch v. NLRB, 752 F.2d 345 (8th Cir. 1985) (residential treatment center for children with emotional problems); Denver Post of Nat'l Soc'y of Volunteers of Am. v. NLRB, 732 F.2d 769 (10th Cir. 1984) (multiple programs and facilities), *subsequent history explained supra* note 177; NLRB v. St. Louis Christian Home, 663 F.2d 60 (8th Cir. 1981) (residential treatment center for abused children).

190. *See* Universidad Cent. de Bayamon v. NLRB, 793 F.2d 383 (1st Cir. 1985); EEOC v. Mississippi College, 626 F.2d 477 (5th Cir. 1980).

191. *St. Elizabeth Hosp.*, 715 F.2d at 1196; *Tressler Lutheran Home*, 677 F.2d at 305.

192. *Mississippi College*, 626 F.2d at 487.

193. *See, e.g., Universidad Cent. de Bayamon*, 793 F.2d at 386–88 (Catholic university is less religious than a parochial school); *Salvation Army*, 763 F.2d at 6 (day care center is less religious than a parochial school); *VOA-Minn.*, 752 F.2d at 348 (treatment facility for children is less religious than a parochial school); *Denver VOA*, 732 F.2d at 772 (shelters for runaways and battered women are less religious than parochial schools); *Tressler Lutheran Home*, 677 F.2d at 305 (nursing home is less religious than a parochial school); EEOC v. Pacific Press Publ'g Ass'n, 676 F.2d 1272, 1282 (9th Cir. 1982) (publishing house is less religious than a seminary); EEOC v. Southwestern Baptist Theological Seminary, 651 F.2d 277, 281 (5th Cir. 1981) (seminary is more religious than a college); *Mississippi College*, 626 F.2d at 485 (sectarian college is less religious than a church); Lukaszewski v. Nazareth Hosp., 764 F. Supp. 57, 60 (E.D. Pa. 1991) (hospital is less religious than a parochial school); *cf.* Rayburn v. General Conference of Seventh-Day Adventists, 772 F.2d 1164, 1170 (4th Cir. 1985) ("the dangers of entanglement were severe with respect to parochial schools.... They are all the more serious with respect to the church itself").

religious missionary activities; all other activities are secondary to that prime goal."[194] It does not believe in proselytizing new members; rather, it "seek[s] to bring people to a knowledge of God by providing humanitarian services to those in need."[195] VOA's hope is that its clients will "return to and...actively practice the faith of their choice."[196] In furtherance of its ministry, VOA operates a number of social outreach programs, including shelters for runaway teens and battered women and residential treatment facilities for children with emotional and developmental problems.

In the late 1970s and early 1980s, VOA employees began to join unions, and the NLRB ordered VOA to bargain with those unions. VOA resisted, arguing that the NLRB could not constitutionally interfere with the relationship between VOA and those working in its social ministries. The federal courts repeatedly sided with the NLRB,[197] finding that despite VOA's characterization of its own mission, its programs were actually secular and thus subject to government regulation. One of the major reasons cited by courts for this conclusion was the fact that VOA did not proselytize either its employees or its clients.[198] Courts simply could not understand how an organization could be "religious" without proselytizing— even though one of the central tenets of VOA is that it should *not* proselytize.

In determining whether a church-related organization is secular, courts consider many factors in addition to the organization's primary purpose or function. If the organization hires employees[199] or serves clients[200] without regard to religion, it is more likely to be deemed secular. The same is true if it has few or no ordained ministers on its staff or board of directors,[201] or if it does not proselytize its clients[202] or require them to attend worship services or religious education classes.[203] If the organization accepts governmental funding,[204] it will almost certainly be deemed secular. After all, courts ask,

---

194. *Denver VOA*, 732 F.2d at 772. There may have been reasons to reject VOA's claims other than the one discussed in text. Denver VOA strained credulity by arguing both that it was too religious to be regulated by the government, *id.* at 771–73, and that it was already so regulated by the government that it qualified for the government agency exemption to the NLRA, *id.* at 773–75. The court did not rely on the apparent inconsistency.

195. *VOA-Minn.*, 752 F.2d at 347.

196. *Id.*

197. *See, e.g.* Volunteers of Am., Los Angeles v. NLRB, 777 F.2d 1386 (9th Cir. 1985); *VOA-Minn.*, 752 F.2d 345; *Denver VOA*, 732 F.2d 769.

198. *See VOA-Los Angeles*, 777 F.2d at 1390; *VOA-Minn.*, 752 F.2d at 348; *Denver VOA*, 732 F.2d at 772.

199. *See* NLRB v. Hanna Boys Ctr., 940 F.2d 1295, 1304 (9th Cir. 1991); Universidad Cent. de Bayamon v. NLRB, 793 F.2d 383, 386 (1st Cir. 1985); *VOA-Los Angeles*, 777 F.2d at 1387; NLRB v. Salvation Army of Mass. Dorchester Day Care Ctr., 763 F.2d 1, 6 (1st Cir. 1985); *VOA-Minn.*, 752 F.2d at 348; *Denver VOA*, 732 F.2d at 772; Tressler Lutheran Home for Children v. NLRB, 677 F.2d 302, 303 (3d Cir. 1982); NLRB v. St. Louis Christian Home, 663 F.2d 60, 64 (8th Cir. 1981).

200. *See Hanna Boys Ctr.*, 940 F.2d at 1304; *Universidad Cent. de Bayamon*, 793 F.2d at 386; *Salvation Army*, 763 F.2d at 6; St. Elizabeth Hosp. v. NLRB, 715 F.2d 1193, 1196 (7th Cir. 1983); *Tressler Lutheran Home*, 677 F.2d at 303; *St. Louis Christian Home*, 663 F.2d at 64; NLRB v. World Evangelism, Inc., 656 F.2d 1349, 1353 (9th Cir. 1981).

201. *See Hanna Boys Ctr.*, 940 F.2d at 1304; *Salvation Army*, 763 F.2d at 6; *VOA-Minn.*, 752 F.2d at 348; *Tressler Lutheran Home*, 677 F.2d at 305.

202. *See VOA-Los Angeles*, 777 F.2d at 1390; *Salvation Army*, 763 F.2d at 6; *VOA-Minn.*, 752 F.2d at 348; *Denver VOA*, 732 F.2d at 772; *St. Louis Christian Home*, 663 F.2d at 64.

203. *See Universidad Cent. de Bayamon*, 793 F.2d at 386; *Salvation Army*, 763 F.2d at 6; *VOA-Minn.*, 752 F.2d at 348; *Denver VOA*, 732 F.2d at 772; *Tressler Lutheran Home*, 677 F.2d at 304; *St. Louis Christian Home*, 663 F.2d at 64.

204. *See VOA-Los Angeles*, 777 F.2d at 1387, 1390; *Denver VOA*, 732 F.2d at 772 n.2; *Tressler Lutheran Home*, 677 F.2d at 304; *St. Louis Christian Home*, 663 F.2d at 64.

how can an institution that is secular enough to receive governmental *benefits* be too religious to be subject to governmental *regulation?*[205] Of course, that logic has not stopped courts from permitting intrusive governmental regulation of the same parochial schools that are considered too religious to receive governmental funding.[206]

2. "The nature of the aid [or burden] that the State provides [or imposes]." The second factor in the reformulated *Lemon* entanglement test looks at the nature of the burden imposed on churches. This analysis has been almost indistinguishable from burden analysis under *Sherbert*, which we discussed earlier. Courts use the same excuses to argue that enforcement of employment regulations against churches does not burden religion. For example, governmental interference with the relationship between a church and a non-minister imposes a less substantial burden than governmental interference with the relationship between a church and a minister. Just as almost any institution can be made to seem less religious than a church, almost any employee can be made to seem less religious than a minister.[207] If a church fires or disciplines an employee for secular rather than religious reasons, the church is considered to be only minimally burdened by the resulting litigation because no inquiry into religious belief is necessary.[208] This raises all of the problems with pretext inquiry, discussed above, and has produced similar evasions.

3. "The resulting relationship between the government and the religious authority." The third factor in the reformulated *Lemon* entanglement test looks at actual entanglement—at the nature of the day-to-day contact between government and religion. The cases that dwell at length on this factor tend to fall into two categories. In the first category, courts hold that Title VII or the ADEA or their state equivalents may be applied against churches because this will not create the continuing and pervasive entanglement with religion that application of the NLRA would create. In the second category, courts hold that the NLRA or its state equivalents may be applied against churches because this will not create continuing and pervasive entanglement.

Courts say that enforcing Title VII or the ADEA against churches would not cause excessive entanglement because these statutes "present...a simple prohibition, not ongoing or pervasive supervision."[209] The Equal Employment Opportunity Commission

---

205. *See Universidad Cent. de Bayamon*, 793 F.2d at 387; *Denver VOA*, 732 F.2d at 772 n.2; *Tressler Lutheran Home*, 677 F.2d at 305–06.

206. *See, e.g.*, Gargano v. Diocese of Rockville Centre, 80 F.3d 87 (2d Cir. 1996); Geary v. Visitation of Blessed Virgin Mary Parish Sch., 7 F.3d 324 (3d Cir. 1993); DeMarco v. Holy Cross High Sch., 4 F.3d 166 (2d Cir. 1993); Catholic High Sch. Ass'n v. Culvert, 753 F.2d 1161 (2d Cir. 1985); Hill-Murray Fed'n of Teachers v. Hill-Murray High Sch., 487 N.W.2d 857 (Minn. 1992); South Jersey Catholic Sch. Teachers Org. v. St. Teresa of Infant Jesus Church Elementary Sch., 696 A.2d 709 (N.J. 1997); New York State Employment Relations Bd. v. Christ the King Regional High Sch., 682 N.E.2d 960 (N.Y. 1997).

207. *See* Weissman v. Congregation Shaare Emeth, 38 F.3d 1038, 1045 (8th Cir. 1994); *Geary*, 7 F.3d at 331; EEOC v. Fremont Christian Sch., 781 F.2d 1362, 1369–70 (9th Cir. 1986); EEOC v. Mississippi College, 626 F.2d 477, 485 (5th Cir. 1980).

208. *See Geary*, 7 F.3d at 328; Stouch v. Brothers of Order of Hermits of St. Augustine, 836 F. Supp. 1134, 1144 (E.D. Pa. 1993); Elbaz v. Congregation Beth Judea, Inc., 812 F. Supp. 802, 808 (N.D. Ill. 1992); Gallo v. Salesian Soc'y, Inc., 676 A.2d 580, 594–95 (N.J. Super. Ct. App. Div. 1996).

209. *Gallo*, 676 A.2d at 596; *see also Geary*, 7 F.3d at 328; *DeMarco*, 4 F.3d at 169–70; EEOC v. Pacific Press Publ'g Ass'n, 676 F.2d 1272, 1282 (9th Cir. 1982); Vigars v. Valley Christian Ctr., 805 F. Supp. 802, 809 (N.D. Cal. 1992); Lukaszewski v. Nazareth Hosp., 764 F. Supp. 57, 60 (E.D. Pa. 1991); Ninth & O St. Baptist Church v. EEOC, 616 F. Supp. 1231, 1233 (W.D. Ky. 1985), *aff'd*, 802 F.2d 459 (6th Cir. 1986); Dolter v. Wahlert High Sch., 483 F. Supp. 266, 270 (N.D. Iowa 1980); McLeod v. Providence Christian Sch., 408 N.W.2d 146, 152 (Mich. Ct. App. 1987). A few courts disagree. *See, e.g.*, EEOC v. Catholic Univ. of Am., 83 F.3d 455, 467 (D.C. Cir. 1996) (application of

(EEOC) cannot initiate actions under Title VII or the ADEA; rather, such actions must be filed by individual employees.[210] Moreover, the EEOC has no power to issue coercive orders; it must seek the intervention of a federal court, and at that point the court can protect the First Amendment rights of religious employers.[211] Finally, employees bringing Title VII or ADEA actions often seek only monetary damages, not the type of ongoing injunctive relief that might raise entanglement concerns.[212] For all these reasons, applying Title VII and the ADEA to religious employers would not create anything like the "continuous,"[213] "ongoing,"[214] "comprehensive,"[215] "pervasive,"[216] "extensive,"[217] and "expansive"[218] entanglement that would be created if the NLRA were applied to religious employers.

Reading these cases, one would assume that at least the application of the NLRA to religious employers would be forbidden. After all, if "continuous," "ongoing," "comprehensive," "pervasive," "extensive," and "expansive" entanglement does not violate the Establishment Clause, what does? Unfortunately, rulings against religious liberty are not marked by a high degree of consistency. When the question is whether the NLRA or state equivalents should be applied to religious employers, courts conveniently forget everything they have said about the NLRA in Title VII and ADEA cases.[219] Instead, they

---

Title VII to religious institution would create "impermissible entanglement"); Rayburn v. General Conference of Seventh-Day Adventists, 772 F.2d 1164, 1171 (4th Cir. 1985) (application of Title VII to religious organizations might result in "a protracted legal process pitting church and state as adversaries"); Powell v. Stafford, 859 F. Supp. 1343, 1348–49 (D. Colo. 1994) ("[T]he ADEA's application to the Archdiocese's hiring policy for its religious instructors is subject to continuing and comprehensive government surveillance").

210. *See Pacific Press*, 676 F.2d at 1282.

211. *See id.*; *Mississippi College*, 626 F.2d at 487–88; *Ninth & O*, 616 F. Supp. at 1233.

212. *See Pacific Press*, 676 F.2d at 1282; Congregation Kol Ami v. Chicago Comm'n on Human Relations, 649 N.E.2d 470, 473 (Ill. App. Ct. 1995); *McLeod*, 408 N.W.2d at 152.

213. *DeMarco*, 4 F.3d at 169–70 ("While the NLRB is 'continuously involved in the enforcement of collective bargaining agreements and resolution of labor disputes,' ADEA actions do not require extensive or continuous administrative or judicial intrusion into the functions of religious institutions." (citations omitted)); *Lukaszewski*, 764 F. Supp. at 60 ("Once a labor union has been certified, the NLRB is continuously involved in the enforcement of collective bargaining agreements and resolution of labor disputes.... The EEOC is not authorized to exercise such continued regulatory activity").

214. *Geary*, 7 F.3d at 328 (contrasting the "ongoing supervision" of the NLRB with the "limited inquiry" of the EEOC); *DeMarco*, 4 F.3d at 169 ("[There is] an important distinction between the ongoing government supervision of all aspects of employment required under labor relations statutes like the NLRA and the limited inquiry required in anti-discrimination disputes").

215. Weissman v. Congregation Shaare Emeth, 38 F.3d 1038, 1042 (8th Cir. 1994) (citing the distinction "between the application of a comprehensive regulatory statute like the NLRA and the comparatively minimal intrusions of the ADEA").

216. *Geary*, 7 F.3d at 328 (contrasting the "pervasive jurisdiction" authorized by the NLRA with the "simple prohibitions of the ADEA").

217. *DeMarco*, 4 F.3d at 170 (unlike application of the NLRA, application of the ADEA to churches does "not require extensive or continuous administrative or judicial intrusion").

218. Dolter v. Wahlert High Sch., 483 F. Supp. 266, 270 (N.D. Iowa 1980) ("The labor relations context...is clearly distinguishable since that context would entail Board scrutiny of the entire panoply of teacher employees' work obligations and responsibilities.... Such expansive scrutiny into the day-to-day administration of defendant's school would not in the least be required in this [Title VII] case").

219. *Compare* Catholic High Sch. Ass'n v. Culvert, 753 F.2d 1161, 1166–67 (2d Cir. 1985) (application of New York equivalent of NLRA to parochial schools does not create excessive entanglement because governmental supervision would be "neither comprehensive nor continuing"), *with DeMarco*, 4 F.3d at 169 (application of ADEA to parochial schools does not create excessive entangle-

find that subjecting religious employers to the strictures of the NLRA and to the jurisdiction of the NLRB (or to their state equivalents) will create little or no entanglement.

Courts first argue that permitting religious employees to unionize and forcing religious employers to bargain with unions will hardly intrude on religion at all. After all, courts say, "[i]t is a fundamental tenet of the regulation of collective bargaining that government brings private parties to the bargaining table and then leaves them alone to work through their problems. The government cannot compel the parties to agree on specific terms."[220] Moreover, the duty to bargain extends only to such "secular" subjects as wages, hours, and conditions of employment.[221] Of course, this argument conveniently ignores about ninety-five percent of labor law, including, most prominently, that it requires religious institutions to share control of their mission with a secular organization, constrains the employer's ability to hire, and more emphatically constrains its ability to assign, promote, or discharge the personnel responsible for the religious mission.[222] This argument also fits awkwardly with the contention of courts that government has a compelling interest in applying the NLRA to religious employers.[223] If the NLRA demands so little, how can the government have a compelling interest in applying it?

In explaining why the prosecution of unfair-labor-practice charges against churches does not excessively entangle government with religion, courts make a number of arguments. First, the NLRB cannot initiate action against an employer until it receives a complaint from an employee or union.[224] Second, the NLRB's investigative authority is limited to matters reasonably related to the charge filed.[225] Third, most of the labor disputes in which the board will intervene will involve secular subjects.[226] Fourth, NLRB orders are not self-enforcing. An employer can resist a board order and force the board to seek judicial enforcement; the court can then safeguard the First Amendment rights of the employer.[227] And finally, "the Board is required to be sensitive to and to accommodate the [employer's] religious concerns."[228]

---

ment because ADEA does not require the "ongoing government supervision of all aspects of employment required under labor relations statutes like the NLRA").

220. *Catholic High Sch. Ass'n*, 753 F.2d at 1167; *see also* Hill-Murray Fed'n of Teachers v. Hill-Murray High Sch., 487 N.W.2d 857, 864 (Minn. 1992); South Jersey Catholic Sch. Teachers Org. v. St. Teresa of Infant Jesus Church Elementary Sch., 696 A.2d 709, 718 (N.J. 1997); New York State Employment Relations Bd. v. Christ the King Regional High Sch., 682 N.E.2d 960, 965 (N.Y. 1997).

221. *See Catholic High Sch. Ass'n*, 753 F.2d at 1167; *Hill-Murray*, 487 N.W.2d at 866; *South Jersey Catholic Sch. Teachers*, 696 A.2d at 718.

222. *See, e.g.*, NLRB v. Catholic Bishop, 440 U.S. 490, 501–04 (1979) (holding that mandatory collective bargaining for parochial school teachers would raise serious First Amendment questions).

223. *See supra* note 142.

224. *See* NLRB v. Hanna Boys Ctr., 940 F.2d 1295, 1304 (9th Cir. 1991); Universidad Cent. de Bayamon v. NLRB, 793 F.2d 383, 388 (1st Cir. 1985); *Catholic High Sch. Ass'n*, 753 F.2d at 1167.

225. *See Universidad Cent. de Bayamon*, 793 F.2d at 388; *Catholic High Sch. Ass'n*, 753 F.2d at 1167.

226. *See Hanna Boys Ctr.*, 940 F.2d at 1306; *Universidad Cent. de Bayamon*, 793 F.2d at 389; *Catholic High Sch. Ass'n*, 753 F.2d at 1167.

227. *See Universidad Cent. de Bayamon*, 793 F.2d at 389; *Catholic High Sch. Ass'n*, 753 F.2d at 1167.

228. *Universidad Cent. de Bayamon*, 793 F.2d at 390. *But see* Catholic Bishop v. NLRB, 559 F.2d 1112, 1126 (7th Cir. 1977), *aff'd*, 440 U.S. 490 (1979) (NLRB's charging a Catholic bishop with an unfair labor practice for publicly reciting a prayer "does very little to establish the Board's sensitivity to the principles of the Religion Clauses").

Advice to Religious Organizations

As this chapter has sought to make clear, the law governing religious employment decisions is a mess. In any given case, a court may choose to apply one, some, or all of the four major approaches that we have described in this chapter, or a court may invent its own test by picking and choosing elements from more than one approach. Employment decisions made by churches (narrowly defined) about ministers (narrowly defined) for religious reasons (narrowly defined) will receive significant constitutional protection. Employment decisions made by secular institutions (broadly defined), about non-ministers (broadly defined), or for secular reasons (broadly defined) will receive little or no constitutional protection. But the sheer doctrinal confusion and the vague boundaries of existing categories mean that many religious employment decisions are "in play." If the church can explain to a court what is really at stake, the court still has doctrinal flexibility to decide either way. What should religious organizations do to maximize the chances that their employment decisions will receive constitutional protection?

First, religious organizations should act like religious organizations. A judge will understand that the church or synagogue is a religious organization when it is conducting worship services, but every other religious organization and activity will be made to seem less religious by comparison. Religiously affiliated schools, hospitals, social service agencies, and the like must decide whether they retain a serious and present religious commitment, or merely a religious history or affiliation that has lost most of its operational significance. Those that retain a serious religious commitment should adopt mission statements drafted in explicitly religious terms, and daily operations should reflect the mission statement. If possible, ordained ministers should be on the staffs or boards of directors of the organizations. An organization should take religion into account in hiring employees or (if consistent with its mission) in choosing clients; prospective employees should at least be *asked* about religion, and if the organization can do so consistently with its mission and beliefs, it should show preference to those who share its faith or are interested in converting to its faith. Even if the institution is unwilling to discriminate in this fashion, it should at least make certain that employees and clients are well aware of its religious nature. When an organization's employees testify "that they were not told of the [organization's] religious mission when they were hired... [and] remained unaware of that mission,"[229] one can hardly expect a court to be sympathetic to the organization's First Amendment arguments.

Religious organizations should make certain that departments or divisions that receive governmental funding or that are already subject to extensive governmental regulation do not secularize the entire organization by association. Churches should structure their affairs so that "nonchurch" is clearly separate from "church" and "arguably church." If, for example, a church operates a counseling center that receives substantial governmental funding, the center should be separately incorporated and its finances kept separate from the finances of the church. If the church makes the opposite choice, it should do so deliberately and understand the risk.

Second, a religious organization should think through the religious significance and religious responsibilities of each position in the organization. Again, a judge will under-

---

229. Denver Post of Nat'l Soc'y of Volunteers of Am. v. NLRB, 732 F.2d 769, 772 (10th Cir. 1984), *subsequent history explained supra* note 177; *see* Douglas Laycock, Academic Freedom, Religious Commitment, and Religious Integrity, 78 Marq. L. Rev. 297, 311 (1995) (reporting a professor who said, "This wasn't even a Catholic school when I was hired").

stand that the ordained minister or rabbi who leads the worship service has a religious job, but every other kind of position will be made to seem less religious by comparison. Employees of religious organizations should have job descriptions, and those job descriptions should be written as religiously as the facts permit. Job descriptions and job titles must make clear that employees perform a type of *ministry*. A church should hire a "pastoral assistant for worship space" rather than a "building administrator," a "music minister" rather than an "organist."

Employment contracts should be written with care. Like job descriptions, employment contracts should make clear that employees are being hired to perform a ministry, and they should use religious language in describing the standards that will be applied to employees. Employees should be subject to discipline for "unchristian" or "sinful" behavior, rather than "immoral" or "improper" behavior, or for "ineffective ministry" rather than "ineffective performance." It is extremely important that employment contracts be drafted so as not to waive the employer's First Amendment rights. "[R]eligious institutions are free to bargain away the right to unimpeded discretion in deciding which persons are most qualified to minister the religion."[230] If a church "burden[s] its activities voluntarily through contracts," such contracts will be "fully enforceable in civil court."[231] Churches can give up their rights explicitly or implicitly. A court has held that a Roman Catholic university waived its right to take action based on canon law against two nuns on its faculty because "the parties' employment contract did not incorporate an implied covenant to abide by Roman Catholic Canon Law."[232]

Religious organizations must be equally careful not to waive First Amendment rights through *conduct*. A Roman Catholic diocese that voluntarily enters into a collective bargaining relationship with a union purporting to represent its parochial school teachers will have trouble convincing a court that continuing to bargain with that same union will burden its religious liberty.[233] A church that voluntarily contributes to a state workers' compensation fund for several years will have trouble convincing a court that continuing to contribute to that fund will violate the First Amendment.[234] A church that voluntarily ends its religiously based policy of providing life and disability insurance only to heads of households will have trouble convincing a court that it has a constitutional right to provide health insurance only to heads of households.[235] And a church that does not fire *all* employees—male and female—who commit adultery will have trouble arguing that its decision to fire an unmarried female employee who became pregnant was based upon adultery rather than sex or pregnancy.[236]

---

230. Welter v. Seton Hall Univ., 608 A.2d 206, 214 (N.J. 1992).

231. Minker v. Baltimore Annual Conference of United Methodist Church, 894 F.2d 1354, 1359 (D.C. Cir. 1990); *see also* Alicea v. New Brunswick Theological Seminary, 608 A.2d 218, 223 (N.J. 1992); Gabriel v. Immanuel Evangelical Lutheran Church, Inc., 640 N.E.2d 681, 683 (Ill. App. Ct. 1994).

232. *Welter*, 608 A.2d at 216.

233. *See* South Jersey Catholic Sch. Teachers Org. v. St. Teresa of Infant Jesus Church Elementary Sch., 696 A.2d 709 (N.J. 1997).

234. *See* St. John's Lutheran Church v. State Compensation Ins. Fund, 830 P.2d 1271 (Mont. 1992).

235. *See* EEOC v. Fremont Christian Sch., 781 F.2d 1362 (9th Cir. 1986).

236. *See, e.g.,* Boyd v. Harding Academy of Memphis, Inc., 88 F.3d 410 (6th Cir. 1996); Vigars v. Valley Christian Ctr., 805 F. Supp. 802 (N.D. Cal. 1992); Dolter v. Wahlert High Sch., 483 F. Supp. 266 (N.D. Iowa 1980).

Third, religious organizations should ensure that the reasons given for employment actions are stated as religiously as the facts permit. Employees should be fired for "inability to submit to religious authority and lack of Christian humility," rather than "insubordination" or "bad attitude," or for "diversion of material resources from the Lord's work" rather than, or in addition to, "theft." The more strongly and specifically an employment decision is grounded in the doctrine and beliefs of the church, the more uncomfortable courts will be in second-guessing that decision.

Churches need to be very careful about how they describe the reasons for an employment action at the time the action is taken. Courts that are hostile to religious autonomy will nitpick statements made by churches. If an unmarried female teacher at a religious school is being fired for adultery, the school should not describe the reason for her firing as being "pregnant without benefit of marriage."[237] Churches must carefully choose the level of generality at which the reason for an employment action is stated. The more specifically the reason is stated, the less likely it is that there will be other employees who did the same thing yet did not suffer the same consequences. If an employee is told that he is being fired for "sinful" conduct, he will point to many other employees of the church who have sinned and not been fired, and argue that the reason given for his firing was pretextual. By contrast, if an employee is fired for "disrupting the ministry of the church by engaging in adulterous conduct with a married parishioner," it will be more difficult for the employee to find others who were similarly situated but differently treated.

Fourth, religious organizations should anticipate employment disputes. The governing documents of a church, as well as the employment contracts into which it enters, should require that all employment disputes—or at least all disagreements about church doctrine or standards underlying such disputes—be decided within the religious organization. And here the drafting style should change. Churches should describe the obligation of employees to resolve disputes internally in unambiguous *secular* terms. The initial and final decision maker should be identified unambiguously, and the finality of the internal decision should be stated unambiguously. Under both the autonomy and doctrine parts of the *Watson* line of cases, courts should defer to the secular terms of religious documents. So the commitment to internal resolution should be stated as secularly as possible, and the standards to be applied by that internal decision maker should be stated as religiously as possible.

Policies and documents drafted in the ways we suggest must be consistent with an underlying operational reality or they will not be credible. If religious references appear only in documents in the file cabinet and in response to litigation, courts will be justly skeptical of the organization's claims that its religious nature entitles it to a First Amendment defense. But when the organization's mission and operation are religious, legal protection requires that that religious reality be recorded in written policies and documents in terms that courts can recognize.

Jones v. Wolf said that one of the advantages of courts simply enforcing the secular terms of church documents is that any church can then provide, before a dispute arises, for its own preferred means of resolving property disputes.[238] Employment disputes are more complicated; employment regulation is imposed from outside the church, and employees generally cannot waive its protections.[239] But churches and their employees

---

237. *Vigars*, 805 F. Supp. at 804; *see also Boyd*, 88 F.3d at 414.
238. *See* Jones v. Wolf, 443 U.S. 595, 603–04 (1979).
239. *See* 29 U.S.C. §626(f) (1994) (expressly providing that employee cannot waive rights under Age Discrimination in Employment Act, except in settlement of claims that arose before the settle-

can agree, before any dispute arises, on the religious nature of the employment and on the internal means of resolving religious disputes arising in the course of the employment relationship. Such agreements do not guarantee that courts will protect the religious liberty interests of the church as employer, but they are an important step towards making it possible for courts to do so.

Finally, religious organizations should be certain to raise First Amendment defenses in litigation and to pursue those defenses competently and aggressively. By and large, churches do an awful job litigating constitutional issues in employment cases. In many such cases, churches fail even to mention the First Amendment. This failure is inexplicable. We cannot understand why attorneys would not vigorously argue the First Amendment in defending, for example, an action brought against a pontifical institution by a nun denied tenure by the Department of Canon Law,[240] an action brought against a Roman Catholic college by the priest who served as its chaplain,[241] or an action brought against an Episcopal diocese by a priest who was removed from two mission congregations for ineffective ministry.[242]

In our experience, even when First Amendment defenses are raised in religious employment litigation, they are often argued poorly. Quite frequently, churches are defended by attorneys hired by insurance companies for their low billing rates and their knowledge of tort law rather than for their knowledge of constitutional law, or they are defended by well-meaning church members with little or no experience litigating First Amendment issues. Too often, the briefs filed by these attorneys are little more than a mishmash of quotations of prior cases. As we hope this chapter has demonstrated, the law governing religious employment disputes is complex and confusing. It holds many dangers for churches, but also many opportunities. The dangers cannot be avoided, nor the opportunities pursued, without hard work and a thorough understanding of the Religion Clauses.

Most judges treat governmental regulation of *anything* as the norm; they are skeptical of *anyone's* claim for exemption. They will not be persuaded to extend constitutional protection in religious employment cases by a compilation of quotations. Rather, an attorney representing a church must explain—specifically, concretely, realistically—exactly how religious freedom will be burdened if parochial school teachers are permitted to unionize or pastors are permitted to sue their bishops for defamation. Too many attorneys have failed to do so.

In sum, there is good news and bad news to report regarding religious employment litigation. The bad news is that courts have extended far too little constitutional protection to the employment decisions of religious organizations. The good news is that reli-

---

ment agreement, and even then subject to multiple safeguards); NLRB v. Magnavox Co., 415 U.S. 322, 325 (1974) (holding that union may not waive any right necessary to protect employees' right to freely choose their collective bargaining representative); Alexander v. Gardner-Denver Co., 415 U.S. 36, 51–52 (1974) ("an employee's rights under Title VII are not susceptible of prospective waiver"); J.I. Case Co. v. NLRB, 321 U.S. 332, 337–38 (1944) ("Individual contracts, no matter what the circumstances that justify their execution or what their terms, may not be availed of to defeat or delay" employee rights under the National Labor Relations Act or a collective bargaining agreement); Brooklyn Sav. Bank v. O'Neil, 324 U.S. 697 (1945) (holding that employee cannot waive protections of Fair Labor Standards Act).

240. *See* EEOC v. Catholic Univ. of Am., 83 F.3d 455, 471 n.1 (D.C. Cir. 1996) (Henderson, J., concurring).

241. *See* Roxas v. Presentation College, 90 F.3d 310, 318 n.6 (8th Cir. 1996).

242. *See* McDonnell v. Episcopal Diocese, 381 S.E.2d 126, 127 (Ga. Ct. App. 1989).

gious organizations and their attorneys are partly responsible for the bad news, and thus may have it within their power to make things better. We hope that this chapter will help religious organizations structure their employment relationships to enhance the chances that their employment decisions will receive constitutional protection. We also hope that it will help their attorneys to argue more effectively for constitutional protection.

Land Use Regulation of Churches

Angela C. Carmella

The classical common law of property presupposes a limited state and focuses on conflicting ownership claims to a particular piece of property—precisely the topic of Patty Gerstenblith's chapter in this book, "Civil Court Resolution of Property Disputes Among Religious Organizations," in which she explores the dilemmas that arise when courts are asked to determine property rights disputed between church factions. With the rise of the affirmative, administrative state in the twentieth century, the field of property law has grown to include the areas of zoning and planning, historic preservation, urban renewal, environmental protection, and nondiscrimination in housing. These newer statutory and regulatory schemes—together referred to as *land use regulation*—pose a new set of questions involving the interaction of the state with the religious domain.

This volume defines the religious structure of a church as its self-understanding, mission, and polity—essentially the faith, acts, and organization that define each church. The use and ownership of land and buildings dedicated to religious purposes are vital to the ways in which churches structure their religious life. Property provides a physical reality through which the church manifests its religious structure. This chapter focuses on the multiple impacts of land use regulation on the ability of churches to define and carry out their missions: such regulation variously prohibits, restricts, channels, mandates, enables, discourages, and promotes the uses, appearance, and development of church property. Because of the connection between religious structure and property, land use regulation will be subject to some level of constitutional scrutiny. But how, when, and whether to accommodate religious land use appears to depend on whether equality or liberty is considered the paramount value in contemporary constitutional interpretation.[1] A constitutional jurisprudence placing a high value on equality[2] emphasizes parity among religious groups and between comparable religious and nonreligious activity. Thus, while such an emphasis seeks to protect religion from discriminatory treatment, it does not shield religion from burdens that result inadvertently from the enforcement of generally applicable, facially neutral laws. In contrast, a constitutional jurisprudence founded on liberty[3] emphasizes the uniqueness of religion and protects it without regard to comparable nonreligious conduct, typically by exempting

---

1. *See* Angela C. Carmella, Liberty and Equality: Paradigms for the Protection of Religious Property Use, 37 J. Church & St. 573–98 (1995).
2. *See* Employment Div. v. Smith, 494 U.S. 872 (1990).
3. *See* Sherbert v. Verner, 374 U.S. 398 (1963).

religious activity from burdensome legal requirements, even those that are neutral and generally applicable, when no overriding public interest exists. Said differently, under an equality rationale, religious exercise is treated like its secular counterparts; under a liberty rationale, it is treated differently from, and better than, those counterparts. Thus the overarching constitutional inquiry concerning land use regulation is whether protection of the free exercise of religion requires the exemption of church property use from regulations applicable to secular uses (or some other accommodation[4]), or whether it requires that church property use be treated like its secular counterpart.

That inquiry has expanded to include federal statutory protection. In 2000, Congress passed the Religious Land Use and Institutionalized Persons Act, which employs both liberty and equality rationales in a complementary fashion. The law embraces a liberty rationale when it sets out to protect religious land use from burdensome zoning and historic preservation regulations that lack compelling justification. It adopts an equality rationale when it sets a protective floor, preventing government discrimination towards and exclusion of religious land use. This may signal the beginning of a substantive commitment to what James A. Serritella, in his Prologue to this volume, calls a jurisprudence that respects a religious tradition's self-understanding.

Religious Structure and Property Use

Churches engage in a wide variety of religious activities. The 1994 Report on the Survey of Religious Organizations at the National Level, conducted by the Northwestern University Survey Laboratory and DePaul Law School's Center for Church/State Studies, shows that nearly all churches hold religious gatherings at least once a week;[5] additionally, two-thirds of religious organizations engage in social service or welfare activities;[6] more than eighty percent are involved in education;[7] nearly sixty percent provide recreation or social activities;[8] eighty-five percent are involved in communications;[9] one-third have retreat centers;[10] and forty percent have cemeteries.[11]

All this activity and more must take place at some physical location, typically land and buildings owned or leased by churches.[12] Given the primacy of weekly worship, it

---

4. Other accommodations might include presumptions regarding religious property use that result in fewer conditions or requirements, limits on governmental inquiry into church affairs, explicit restraints on the types of conditions that can be placed on development, or specific statutory protections for religious property use.

5. Ninety-four percent of the Survey respondents described their local units as holding meetings once a week or more. *See* Center for Church/State Studies, DePaul Univ. College of Law, The 1994 Report on the Survey of Religious Organizations at the National Level, MQ38 (unpublished survey on file with the Center for Church/State Studies, DePaul University College of Law) [hereinafter Survey].

6. *See id.* MQ48.

7. *See id.* MQ51.

8. *See id.* MQ57. Of those, 54% provide recreation centers, 80% have camp grounds. *See id.* MQ58(D), (G).

9. *See id.*, MQ54; 10% of those provide a TV station and 24% provide a radio station. *See id.* MQ55(J), (K).

10. *See id.* MQ60(H).

11. *See id.* MQ60(K).

12. For a detailed discussion of the use of homes for worship and other religious activities, see generally Mark W. Cordes, Where to Pray? Religious Zoning and the First Amendment, 35 U. Kan.

should come as no surprise that the main piece of church real estate is the house of worship.[13] In fact, the vast majority of houses of worship are owned, not rented, either by the local church group or by a regional or national body with which the local group is affiliated.[14]

Houses of worship are often used for multiple purposes, given the wide range of churches' educational, community, recreational and social service activities. These activities are commonly referred to as *accessory uses*, on the assumption that they are related or incidental to the worship use. But most churches, at both the national and local levels, also own nonworship buildings dedicated to religious uses.[15] Educational facilities and clergy housing are the most commonly held non-worship properties.[16]

In a very real sense, then, buildings and land used for religious purposes are essential to carrying out a church's religious mission and self-definition. But just as property can facilitate a church's worship and non-worship life, inadequate property can constrain it. A building in the wrong location can fail to serve its intended community. Moreover, a building that is too small, oddly configured, or incapable of adaptation can make it difficult or impossible to accommodate the church's pastoral goals and community ministries, or changes in them. If physical structure is not to constrict and distort religious structure, then movement and change must be normal aspects of church property use. Thus freedom to locate and relocate, to expand and renovate, and to adaptively reuse and rebuild ensures that buildings serve the faith, and not the other way around.

Property is not only used to directly accommodate religious structure; it is used indirectly as a commodity to support it financially. Nearly one in five national religious organizations reports that it invests in real estate in order to raise funds.[17]

Constitutional Approaches to Church Land Use Regulation

Prior to 1963 the general approach to protecting the free exercise of religion emphasized nondiscrimination among religious groups and equal treatment between compa-

---

L. Rev. 697, 752 (1987); Comment, Zoning Ordinances, Private Religious Conduct, and the Free Exercise of Religion, 76 Nw. U. L. Rev. 786 (1981).

13. Religious gatherings are held at a single permanent location, building, or facility for 96% of the respondents. *See* Survey, *supra* note 5, MQ39.

14. Of the 96% of churches that hold religious meetings at least once a week, 89% of the buildings are owned and 11% are leased. *See id.* MQ41. Home churches, synagogues, temples are not uncommon—some as temporary quarters and others as permanent places to worship. Note that with respect to rental space, public property that is available widely to the community may be rented for church use depending on the categories of uses generally permitted. *See* Lamb's Chapel v. Center Moriches Union Free Sch. Dist., 508 U.S. 384 (1993); Deeper Life Christian Fellowship, Inc. v. Board of Education, 852 F.2d 676 (2d Cir. 1988); Concerned Women for America, Inc. v. Lafayette County, 883 F.2d 32 (5th Cir. 1989).

15. These uses are often referred to as "accessory uses" when conducted in or near the house of worship. Fifty-three percent of the respondents reported that their national bodies own real property that is not used for worship purposes, *see* Survey, *supra* note 5, MQ10, and 54% of their local units do the same, *see id.* MQ42.

16. Forty-four percent of the organizations reported owning at least one educational facility, and nearly one-third reported owning clergy housing or other real estate. *See id.* MQ14.

17. *See id.* MQ30.

rable religious and secular activities. Exemptions or special accommodations for religion were typically understood as legislatively permissible but not constitutionally compelled. While the Supreme Court had not spoken to the merits of any church land use case, it nevertheless intimated that an equality approach would govern in that context as well. It said in 1950,

> We recently dismissed for want of substantiality an appeal in which a church group contended that its First Amendment rights were violated by a municipal zoning ordinance preventing the building of churches in certain residential areas.[18]

Presumably the Court thought religious organizations simply had to abide by zoning laws like everyone else.[19] In this period, then, legislative and judicial accommodations for church land use—and there were many—were not based on encouragement or mandate from the nation's high court. They were based instead on state court interpretations of substantive due process and free exercise and on a general respect for the beneficial role of churches in the community.

In 1963 the Supreme Court adopted a liberty rationale in *Sherbert v. Verner*[20] and decided that in some instances, courts should mandate accommodations where legislatures had failed to do so. The *Sherbert* test required that a religious claimant show that government action burdened its religious exercise. Even in the case of generally applicable, facially neutral laws where such a burden was inadvertent, the government was required to justify the burden by demonstrating some compelling interest and the lack of any less restrictive alternative means of furthering that interest. If the government failed to justify the burden with an overriding state interest, the court would protect the religious exercise, typically by exempting it from the law's reach. *Sherbert* recognized that burdens to religious practice could result even when government lacked discriminatory intent. Unfortunately, during the period of *Sherbert*'s prominence (1963–1990) the Supreme Court never adjudicated a land use issue, so we have no clear guidance from the high court on what the application of *Sherbert* would mean in this context.[21]

The 1990 Supreme Court decision in *Employment Division v. Smith*[22] rejected *Sherbert*'s liberty-oriented balancing test. Emphatically adopting an equality rationale, *Smith* held that the government must justify its burdens on religion only where it has been overtly discriminatory or where its discretionary application of law creates the potential for discrimination. Further, a liberty rationale would continue to prevail in areas where other constitutional rights, such as free speech, are implicated. With respect to laws that are general in application and neutral on their face, *Smith* declared that courts only have to make sure they are reasonably related to some proper legislative goal. For many

---

18. American Communications Ass'n v. Douds, 339 U.S. 382, 397–98 (1950). The Court was referring to Corporation of Presiding Bishop v. City of Porterville, 203 P.2d 823 (Cal. Ct. App.), *appeal dismissed*, 338 U.S. 805 (1949). In *Presiding Bishop* a California court found "no merit" in a church's argument that an ordinance excluding churches from residential areas restricted religious worship. The Supreme Court apparently agreed, as this quote from *Douds* suggests.

19. Assuming, of course, that those zoning laws were not based on antireligious discrimination.

20. 374 U.S. 398 (1963).

21. The most the Court said of "fire and zoning ordinances" is that they are examples of reasonable regulation in the religion context. Tony and Susan Alamo Found. v. Secretary of Labor, 471 U.S. 290 (1985).

22. 494 U.S. 872 (1990).

cases, then, *Smith* replaced *Sherbert's* strict scrutiny standard of judicial review with the much lower standard of rational basis.

In 1993 the Supreme Court reaffirmed *Smith* in *Church of Lukumi Babalu Aye v. City of Hialeah.*[23] In this case the city had passed four land use ordinances all aimed at suppressing the church's practice of ritual animal sacrifice. The Court held that because these laws targeted only religious practice and not analogous secular conduct, and were thus not genuinely neutral and general, they remained subject to a compelling governmental interest test that they could not pass, and therefore violated the Free Exercise Clause. Such intentional antireligious state action was unconstitutional, but inadvertent burdens on religion by way of general laws remained permissible.

After *Lukumi* we can thus assume that any land use ordinance that could be shown to be such an overt attempt to suppress a particular religion would fail even *Smith's* minimal standard of scrutiny. The difficulty in the land use setting, however, is that it is notoriously easy to mask intolerant motivation in neutral sounding language concerning the possible negative impacts the church's use might have on surrounding properties or on the municipal budget.[24] Reviewing courts are often reluctant or unable to pierce this veil of seeming neutrality, in no small part because courts are required to defer to the expertise of zoning boards. Thus even an equality-based rationale may not fully ensure nondiscrimination among religious groups and equal treatment between comparable religious and secular activities.

Shortly after *Lukumi* a federal statute was passed to protect free exercise in cases of unintentional burdens on religion resulting from general, neutral laws. The objective of the Religious Freedom Restoration Act (RFRA) was to restore the *Sherbert* strict scrutiny standard of review.[25] However, RFRA failed to pass constitutional muster when challenged in 1997 in *City of Boerne v. Flores.*[26] In that case, in which a historic preservation ordinance was challenged as violating RFRA, the court did not adjudicate on RFRA's merits, but focused instead on the question of congressional authority to pass it. In clear language the decision strongly reaffirmed *Smith's* equality rationale. The topic of land use laws comes up only in the case's dicta, where Justice Kennedy wrote:

> It is a reality of the modern regulatory state that numerous state laws, such as the zoning regulations at issue here, impose a substantial burden on a large class of individuals. When the exercise of religion has been burdened in an incidental way by a law of general application, it does not follow that the persons

---

23. 508 U.S. 520 (1993).

24. *See* discussion of zoning, *infra.*

25. Congress explicitly found that "laws 'neutral' toward religion may burden religious exercise as surely as laws intended to interfere with religious exercise," and that "governments should not substantially burden religious exercise without compelling justification." Religious Freedom Restoration Act of 1993 § 2(a)(2), (3), 42 U.S.C. § 2000bb(a)(2), (3) (1994). Free exercise of religion protected:

> (a) In General[.] Government shall not substantially burden a person's exercise of religion even if the burden results from a rule of general applicability, except as provided in subsection (b) of this section. (b) Exception[.] Government may substantially burden a person's exercise of religion only if it demonstrates that application of the burden to the person: (1) is in furtherance of a compelling governmental interest; and (2) is the least restrictive means of furthering that compelling governmental interest.

26. 521 U.S. 507 (1997).

affected have been burdened any more than other citizens, let alone burdened because of their religious beliefs.[27]

Kennedy's statement assumes that zoning and preservation laws are neutral and general. This is largely inaccurate because land use laws are shot through with exemptions and discretionary mechanisms. Zoning boards, planning boards, historic preservation boards, and architectural review boards craft highly individualized solutions to land use issues, by conditioning permits, retaining ongoing review, or exempting some applicants from the reach of certain provisions altogether, to name a few methods. This is entirely different from the application, say, of a general, neutral criminal law. Thus *Smith* and *Lukumi* may leave open strict scrutiny review in many land use cases, not because of discriminatory intent but simply because the state action is not the application of a general, neutral law.

If land use laws are deemed neutral and general, however, the Free Exercise Clause as the Court now interprets it offers limited aid to church land use: exemptions and accommodations can be built into land use laws, but will not be constitutionally compelled because, on the current Court's reading of the Constitution, churches deserve only to be treated as well as comparable secular (and other religious) uses. Of course, equal treatment offers a nondiscriminatory floor of protection that may be sufficient in some cases where churches seek only to be treated as well as their secular (and religious) counterparts. But limiting constitutional protection to equal treatment is at variance with long standing liberty-based practices in many states where church land use is treated different from, and better than, its secular counterpart.

Simply because the Supreme Court thinks that religion is best protected through the political process, one cannot assume that any legislative accommodation will be constitutional. In addition to the category of mandatory accommodation found under the Free Exercise Clause, we find two other categories: impermissible accommodations forbidden by the Establishment Clause and permissible accommodations, neither mandated nor forbidden, that fall "in between" the clauses. The Supreme Court has held, for instance, that a local zoning ordinance giving churches veto power over liquor licenses for restaurants within a five-hundred foot radius was an unconstitutional delegation of civil authority to a church, hence an establishment of religion.[28] Additionally, while religion-specific exemptions have been upheld,[29] a religion-specific *tax* exemption was held to violate the Establishment Clause because it was found to be unrelated to the promotion of free exercise and to place too great a burden on those who did not benefit from the exemption.[30] Unfortunately this analysis, which should be confined to the tax context, has been applied to religion-specific exemptions in the land use area. Nevertheless, the Court of Appeals for the Seventh Circuit found an ex-

---

27. *Id.* at 535. Note also that Justice Scalia, in a concurring opinion, wrote:
> The issue presented by *Smith* is, quite simply, whether the people, through their elected representatives, or rather this Court, shall control the outcome of those concrete cases. For example, shall it be the determination of this Court, or rather of the people, *whether...church construction will be exempt from zoning laws?...*It shall be the people.

Id. at 544 (Scalia, J., concurring) (emphasis added).

28. *See* Larkin v. Grendel's Den, Inc., 459 U.S. 116 (1982). On the other hand, a zoning provision that created a flat prohibition on the sale of liquor within five hundred feet of church, school, and residential use would be constitutional.

29. *See* Corporation of Presiding Bishop v. Amos, 483 U.S. 327 (1987).

30. *See* Texas Monthly, Inc. v. Bullock, 489 U.S. 1 (1989).

emption from zoning permit requirements for religious day care and nursery schools to be a "permissible accommodation" because it removed identifiable burdens to free exercise, enabled churches to define and carry out their missions, did not require nonbeneficiaries to subsidize religious activity, and effected a more complete separation of church and state.[31] Additionally, the Court of Appeals for the First Circuit upheld as a permissible accommodation a Massachusetts law that protects churches and schools from zoning regulations that restrict the use of land for religious or educational purposes.[32] Further, the Supreme Court of California has upheld the exemption of churches from historic preservation laws because it was found to have a secular purpose and to be designed to relieve churches from potential burdens on the free exercise of religion.[33]

Given the holdings of *Smith* and *Lukumi,* and Justice Kennedy's dicta in *Boerne,* the constitutional analysis appears to be confined to an equality rationale. Congress has stepped in, however, to create federal statutory protection for religious land use. Unlike RFRA, which attempted a sweeping restoration of the *Sherbert* strict-scrutiny standard of review for all burdens on religious exercise, the Religious Land Use and Institutionalized Persons Act of 2000[34] restores this scrutiny for only two categories of burdens: those associated with land use regulation, and those associated with the institutionalization of individuals. With respect to the first category, it is fair to say that nearly all local zoning and historic preservation regulations are subject to this statute's reach.

Under this federal statute, if an individual or church demonstrates a substantial burden caused by land use regulation, the government must show that the regulation is in furtherance of a compelling governmental interest and is the least restrictive means of furthering that interest.[35] This restoration of *Sherbert*'s standard of review is also coupled with further protections to ensure freedom from discrimination, exclusion, and unequal treatment.[36] It emphasizes the complementarity of the liberty and equality rationales, creating a floor of general protection together with an exemption mechanism to alleviate specific burdens. The statute also encourages governmental use of exemptions and other measures in order to eliminate specific burdens to religious exercise.

---

31. Cohen v. City of Des Plaines, 8 F.3d 484 (7th Cir. 1993).

32. Boyajian v. Gatzunis, 212 F.3d 1 (1st Cir. 2000); *cert. denied*, 2001 U.S. LEXIS 132 (2001).

33. East Bay Asian Local Development Corp. v. State of California, 13 P.3d 1122 (Cal. 2000).

34. 42 U.S.C. §2000cc (2001). A challenge to its constitutionality will be heard by the U.S. Supreme Court. *See* Cutter v. Wilkinson, 125 S. Ct. 308 (2004).

35. SEC. 2. Protection of Land Use as Religious Exercise
(a) Substantial Burdens.
(1) General rule.—No government shall impose or implement a land use regulation in a manner that imposes a substantial burden on the religious exercise of a person, including a religious assembly or institution, unless the government demonstrates that imposition of the burden on that person, assembly, or institution—
(A) is in furtherance of a compelling governmental interest; and
(B) is the least restrictive means of furthering that compelling governmental interest.

36. SEC. 2. Protection of Land Use as Religious Exercise
(b) Discrimination and Exclusion.
(1) Equal Terms.—No government shall impose or implement a land use regulation in a manner that treats a religious assembly or institution on less than equal terms with a nonreligious assembly or institution.
(2) Nondiscrimination.—No government shall impose or implement a land use regulation that discriminates against any assembly or institution on the basis of religion or religious denomination.
(3) Exclusion and limits.—No government shall impose or implement a land use regulation that
(A) totally excludes religious assemblies from a jurisdiction; or
(B) unreasonably limits religious assemblies, institutions, or structures within a jurisdiction.

Land Use Regulation of Churches

Zoning

Zoning and planning officials consider church property use (both worship and non-worship) to be regulable land use because it, like many other types of land use, is capable of generating one or more of the following secondary effects: noise, traffic, and on-street parking; burdens on public facilities and infrastructure; increased need for fire and police protection; overcrowding; deterioration of the tax base; lower property values of surrounding homes; loss of neighborhood character; architectural and aesthetic disharmony; and negative environmental impacts. Municipalities attempt to prevent or control these real or presumed secondary effects by categorizing and regulating church use and other religious uses: allowing them *as of right* in some zones, prohibiting them altogether in other zones, and considering them to be *conditional uses* in still others.[37] They are often categorized like other comparable secular activities with similar secondary effects (for example, theaters, meeting halls, educational, and other noncommercial uses). Because zoning regulations often prevent or restrict church plans for location and changes in use, conflicts between churches and municipal land use authorities have not been uncommon during the last fifty years.[38]

In addition to use control, zoning ordinances govern the configuration, height, dimensions, bulk, density, and placement of physical structures as these relate to lot size and shape.[39] As with use restrictions, the dimensional aspects of a particular church's proposal may be permitted as of right, forbidden, or conditionally permitted. Proposals to change existing buildings—most commonly by expansion, by demolition and rebuilding, or by adding new accessory uses such as soup kitchens—serve to accommodate larger membership and new ministries. These will often generate concerns about increased traffic and density on the part of municipal land use authorities.

Most of the conflicts involve the issues of church location and accessory uses, arising typically from the denial of a permit to locate worship or nonworship religious uses at a particular site. While zoning officials may claim only to be enforcing the ordinance to prevent negative impacts on the neighborhood or municipal budget, this may simply disguise religious intolerance (either on their own part or on the part of powerful pressure groups). The stated concerns about possible negative secondary effects could also be sincere. In either case, the decisions made by zoning officials result in significant pas-

---

37. Conditional uses are those likely to generate negative secondary effects within the surrounding neighborhood and are therefore permitted only if the proponent agrees to abide by specific conditions that mitigate those effects. Of course, nuisance actions and enforcement of parking, noise, and public health ordinances are also available to curtail unanticipated problems that seriously interfere with the use and enjoyment of nearby property.

38. More than four hundred zoning cases have been reported in this period, the vast majority of which occurred at the local (municipal or county) level. Note that numerous additional cases are unreported. The fact that the Survey was conducted at the national level may explain why so few problems were reported. Of the 16% of the national religious bodies involved in legal matters within the last five years, one-third said that a matter of zoning restrictions required an attorney's assistance. *See* Survey, *supra* note 5, Q17 E. For general information on the case law, see Robert M. Anderson, American Law of Zoning §§ 12.21–.31 (4th ed. 1996); 2 Zeigler & Rathkopf's The Law of Zoning and Planning §§ 20.01–.04 (1997).

39. Location and size of accessory buildings and signs are also regulated.

toral, theological, and economic burdens to churches: they influence the composition of church membership, the worship and fellowship experience, the ministries offered, and the community served. These burdens on the free exercise of religion occur in different degrees to different churches, but the most severe burdens appear to be concentrated among minority faiths with very small fractions of the total population. A recent study shows that

> while minority religions represent considerably less than 9% of the population, they are involved in over 49% of the cases involving the right to locate a church at a particular site, and in over 33% of the cases seeking approval of accessory uses of an existing church site (e.g., for sheltering or feeding the homeless). The disproportionate burden carried by minority religions becomes even more distressing if one takes into account cases involving non-denominational groups, or groups that cannot be classified on the basis of information in case reports. If these unclassified cases are counted, over 68% of reported location cases, and over 50% of accessory use cases, involve... [small] minority religions.[40]

Places of worship

For nearly fifty years the issue of locational freedom for churches has been adjudicated primarily in state courts. Increasingly during this period, however, church land use cases have been brought to federal court. Indeed, today federal zoning litigation on church issues appears to be nearly as common as its state counterpart. An enormous body of case law has resulted, and in summary a few generalizations can be made.[41] It is well settled, for instance, that a municipality cannot categorically exclude church use entirely from its borders. Church use must be permitted in some zone either as of right or as a conditional use requiring a special permit. In fact, the most common church zoning issue of the last fifty years has been whether a municipality can prohibit church use in an exclusively residential zone. Many jurisdictions say no, on the grounds that church buildings are constitutionally protected and deserve special regard—essentially a liberty rationale.[42] But many other jurisdictions say yes, finding that church buildings are no different from all other nonresidential uses that are clearly excluded—essentially an equality rationale. (It is important to note that church location cases have increas-

---

40. Brief of the Church of Jesus Christ of Latter-day Saints as Amicus Curiae in Support of Respondents, City of Boerne v. Flores, 521 U.S. 507 (1997) (No. 95-2074).

41. Commentary on these cases is abundant. *See generally* Cordes, *supra* note 12; Laurie Reynolds, Zoning the Church: The Police Power Versus the First Amendment, 64 B.U. L. Rev. 767 (1985); Terry Rice, Re-evaluating the Balance between Zoning Regulations and Religious and Educational Uses, 8 Pace L. Rev. 1 (1988); Note, The Future of Zoning Limitations Upon Religious Uses of Land: Due Process or Equal Protection? 22 Suffolk U. L. Rev. 1087 (1988); Kenneth Pearlman, Zoning and the Location of Religious Establishments, 31 Cath. Law. 341 (1987); Comment, Land Use Regulation and the Free Exercise Clause, 84 Colum. L. Rev. 1562 (1984); Note, Justice Douglas' Sanctuary: May Churches Be Excluded from Suburban Residential Areas? 45 Ohio St. L.J. 1017 (1984); Comment, Zoning Ordinances Affecting Churches: A Proposal for Expanded Free Exercise Protection, 132 U. Pa. L. Rev. 1131 (1984); Comment, Zoning the Church: Toward a Concept of Reasonableness, 12 Conn. L. Rev. 571 (1980); Recent Developments: Constitutional Law- Free Exercise Clause of the First Amendment Protects Houses of Worship from Zoning Ordinances, 44 Fordham L. Rev. 1245 (1976); James E. Curry, Public Regulation of Religious Use of Land: Analysis of 100 Court Cases (1964); and Note, Churches and Zoning, 70 Harv. L. Rev. 1428 (1957).

42. Blanket exclusions of churches from residential neighborhoods are held to infringe constitutional rights based either on freedom of worship and assembly or substantive due process.

ingly involved the prohibition of churches from zones other than residential; many churches try to locate in business, commercial and manufacturing districts.[43])

A liberty approach recognizes no secular analogue to the house of worship, while an equality approach treats a house of worship like any other building for assembly, like a meeting hall or theater. Thus if a church seeks to build a house of worship in an exclusively residential zone, a court applying a liberty rationale will permit the church to locate where other nonresidential uses would not be permitted. These courts consider church use to be fundamentally distinct from other uses and intimately connected to the church's free exercise. Moreover, they give potential negative "secondary effects" less weight and, in fact, often presume a positive contribution to the surrounding community and society at large.[44]

New York is one of the most protective jurisdictions with respect to religious property use, holding repeatedly that "greater flexibility is required in evaluating an application for a religious use than [in evaluating] an application for another use and [that] every effort to accommodate the religious use must be made."[45] In the zoning context, "churches and schools occupy a different status from mere commercial enterprises and, when the church enters the picture, different considerations apply.... [C]hurch and school and accessory uses are, in themselves, clearly in furtherance of the public morals and general welfare."[46]

In contrast, other jurisdictions, notably California and Florida, have adopted an equality rationale and find churches subject to the same restrictions as all comparable nonresidential uses. These courts are highly deferential to municipal decisions to exclude churches from residential zones, as long as alternative sites are (theoretically) available somewhere in the municipality. Neighborhood tranquility is of primary importance; the municipalities must protect citizens from the secondary effects of churches. Thus blanket exclusions of churches from residential zones implicate no fun-

---

43. Municipal planners like to exclude churches especially from business districts because they are thought to take up space without generating any revenue to the district.

44. Many state courts exempt churches from certain locational restrictions or at least provide a presumption in favor of church use that is rebuttable only by specific showings of harmful secondary effects. Under this view churches have an inherently beneficial quality that either (1) conclusively outweighs negative secondary effects such as traffic and noise that might disturb residential tranquility or (2) gives rise to a presumption in their favor that is rebuttable in specific circumstances. See, e.g., Church of Christ v. Metropolitan Bd. of Zoning Appeals, 371 N.E.2d 1331 (Ind. Ct. App. 1978); City of Minneapolis v. Church Universal and Triumphant, 339 N.W.2d 880, 890 (Minn. 1983); Ohio ex rel. Synod of Ohio v. Joseph, 39 N.E.2d 515 (Ohio 1942).

45. Genesis Assembly of God v. Davies, 617 N.Y.S.2d 202, 203 (App. Div. 1994); see also Young Israel v. Town of Hempstead Bd. of Zoning Appeals, 634 N.Y.S.2d 199, 200 (App. Div. 1995) (holding conditions on a variance designed to mitigate problems of traffic congestion arbitrary and capricious considering that none of the congregants attending synagogue services could drive on the sabbath).

46. Diocese of Rochester v. Planning Bd., 136 N.E.2d 827, 834, 836 (N.Y. 1956). Early New York cases took the most protective position in favor of religious property use. See, e.g., Community Synagogue v. Bates, 136 N.E.2d 488 (N.Y. 1956); Westchester Reform Temple v. Brown, 239 N.E.2d 891 (N.Y. 1968); Jewish Reconstructionist Synagogue v. Village of Roslyn Harbor, 342 N.E.2d 534 (N.Y. 1975); American Friends of Soc'y of St. Pius v. Schwab, 417 N.Y.S.2d 991 (App. Div. 1979). This position has been modified to reflect growing concerns of negative secondary effects. See Cornell Univ. v. Bagnardi, 503 N.E.2d 509 (N.Y. 1986), which holds that the presumption that religious or educational uses of property are always in furtherance of health, safety, and morals may be rebutted by a showing that the use actually has a net negative impact and that a reasonably drawn special permit may be used to set out mitigating conditions. The inherently beneficial nature of religious property use remains the presumption nonetheless.

damental rights, so long as alternative sites are available. Yet if other assembly uses or other noncommercial uses have been permitted in a given zone, an equality rationale will place church use within that larger category and will require that it be treated as well as these secular counterparts.

Dimensional regulations are subject to the same liberty/equality choice. New York state, for instance, treats dimensional restrictions as it treats locational controls: the liberty rationale prevails to allow church expansion and change where no "direct and immediate adverse effect upon the health, safety or welfare of the community"[47] has been demonstrated. For jurisdictions that employ an equality rationale, however, variances, special permits, and hardship exemptions are available only to the extent that they are for any property owner.

Federal courts, facing a growing number of cases concerning regulation of religious land use, have also had to confront the "liberty/equality" choice. Since the early 1980s nearly every court of appeals has decided a major land use case involving religious property. Six cases addressed the constitutionality of restrictions on the location of worship activity.[48] Another four decisions dealt with restrictions on nonworship religious activity.[49] One would think that during the *Sherbert* period (1963–1990), when a strict-scrutiny standard of judicial review was applied to cases involving the Free Exercise Clause, this liberty-oriented balancing test would have been applied in the land use context. Not so. Nearly all these appellate cases reflect an equality rationale, whether decided before or after *Smith*; they ignore the reality that property and religious exercise are inextricably linked and fail to acknowledge any social contribution of churches.

To sum up the federal law on religious land use, one can say that where overt discrimination is lacking, churches can be excluded from a zone as long as an "alternative location" is legally possible.[50] Alternative location does not mean that an identifiable comparable site exists; it means only that some zoning district in the municipality does not exclude the proposed religious uses. Even where a church was prevented from locat-

---

47. *Westchester Reform*, 239 N.E.2d at 895.

48. *See* Grosz v. City of Miami Beach, 721 F.2d 729 (11th Cir. 1983); Lakewood, Ohio Congregation of Jehovah's Witnesses v. City of Lakewood, 699 F.2d 303 (6th Cir. 1983); Messiah Baptist Church v. County of Jefferson, 859 F.2d 820 (10th Cir. 1988); Islamic Ctr. v. City of Starkville, 840 F.2d 293 (5th Cir. 1988); Christian Gospel Church, Inc. v. City of San Francisco, 896 F.2d 1221 (9th Cir. 1990); Cornerstone Bible Church v. City of Hastings, 948 F.2d 464 (8th Cir. 1991). These cases involve church exclusions from agricultural or commercial zones as well as exclusions from residential zones.

Use of an equal protection analysis also drives an equality rationale. In *Cornerstone Bible Church v. City of Hastings,* 948 F.2d 464, the court permitted the equal protection claim to proceed because the church showed that the ordinance prevented churches from locating in a commercial district but allowed similar noncommercial uses.

49. *See* Christ College, Inc. v. Board of Supervisors, 944 F.2d 901 (4th Cir. 1991), *reported in full in* No. 90-2406, 1991 U.S. App. LEXIS 21680 (4th Cir. Sept. 13, 1991) (school); Rector of St. Bartholomew's Church v. City of New York, 914 F.2d 348 (2d Cir. 1990) (services for the poor); First Assembly of God v. Collier County, 20 F.3d 419 (11th Cir.), *modified*, 27 F.3d 526 (11th Cir. 1994) (homeless shelter); *see also* Salvation Army v. Department of Community Affairs, 919 F.2d 183 (3d Cir. 1990) (state licensure of adult rehabilitation center as boarding house). *But cf.* Cohen v. City of Des Plaines, 8 F.3d 484 (7th Cir. 1993) (a constitutional challenge to an accommodation of religious accessory use).

50. This has also been the trend where churches are conditional uses. Courts consistently find that denial of a permit causes no burden to religion, but only a burden of expense and inconvenience resulting from necessary relocation. This is the case for denials of permits for worship use as well as for denials of permits for nonworship religious use.

ing its house of worship in ninety percent of the city's land area, the burden of moving to a theoretical site in the remaining ten percent of the city was considered only financial and aesthetic and not a burden on religious exercise.[51] One dissenting judge, however, rejecting such a relaxed standard, argued that

> [a]lthough other sites may be available, the first amendment demands that we know where, how many, how suitable, how convenient, and at what cost before we properly can judge the burden on exercise as compared to the burden on the state's legitimate interests.... It is not self-evident that an attempt to acquire and use an alternative site is always a trivial burden. Nor is it self-evident that a congregation's attendance pattern can be easily accommodated at an alternative site without substantial individual and collective burden.[52]

In federal jurisprudence this remains very much a dissenter's view.

Even in an era of the *Sherbert* liberty-oriented balancing test, the alternative location standard dramatically changed the notion of what constituted a burden on free exercise in the first place. The "alternative site" rule was developed because the courts simply did not make the connection between location and religious exercise. RFRA's purported restoration of *Sherbert* thus would not necessarily have changed the alternative site analysis.[53]

The Court of Appeals for the Second Circuit held in 1995 that a zoning ordinance designed to limit the number of home synagogues also served to make dwellings unavailable to Jews because of their religion in violation of both the Free Exercise Clause and the federal Fair Housing Act.[54] Because Orthodox Jewish communities have a high

---

51. *See Lakewood, Ohio Congregation,* 699 F.2d 303. An additional interpretive technique that tends to justify the use of the "alternative site" analysis is a requirement set out by some courts of appeals that the location or construction of a church must itself be integrally related to the religious tenets of the church. Without this showing, religious exercise is not even implicated. Yet the vast majority of religious communities could never make a showing that because of a religious tenet they must be situated in a particular location. *See id.*

52. *Messiah Baptist,* 859 F.2d at 830 (McKay, J., dissenting).

53. RFRA's explicit mandate to employ a liberty rationale seemed in some locational zoning cases to challenge the alternative site standard. Most dramatic was the Eleventh Circuit's "new" decision in *Grosz v. City of Miami Beach. See* Grosz v. City of Miami Beach, 82 F.3d 1005 (11th Cir. 1996). In its 1983 decision the court's Free Exercise Clause analysis gave Rabbi Grosz no protection for the use of his home as a synagogue in a zone in which houses of worship were forbidden. *See* Grosz v. City of Miami Beach, 721 F.2d 729 (11th Cir. 1983). The court employed an alternative site analysis: the rabbi could move to a zone that permitted houses of worship. However, the city chose not to enforce its ordinance until 1993, after RFRA's enactment. When Rabbi Grosz brought a RFRA claim to enjoin enforcement of the ordinance, the court held that collateral estoppel did not apply. On the other hand, one federal district court found that because a church could locate in sixty percent of the municipality, no substantial burden had been suffered (as required by RFRA). *See* International Church of Foursquare Gospel v. City of Chicago Heights, 955 F. Supp. 878 (N.D. Ill. 1996). For a general discussion, see Simon J. Santiago, Zoning and Religion: Will the Religious Freedom Restoration Act of 1993 Shift the Line Toward Religious Liberty? 45 Am. U. L. Rev. 199 (1995).

54. *See* LeBlanc-Sternberg v. Fletcher, 67 F.3d 412 (2d Cir. 1995). On remand Judge Goettel enjoined the municipality "from promoting religious discrimination; from denying equal opportunity to religion by use, interpretation, or enforcement of the zoning code in such a manner that it prevents home worship; from discriminating because of religion or interfering with the free exercise of religion in connection with housing; and from taking any action that limits the availability of housing on the basis of religion." LeBlanc-Sternberg v. Fletcher, 922 F. Supp. 959, 964–65 (S.D.N.Y.), *judgment entered,* 925 F. Supp. 160 (S.D.N.Y.), *aff'd,* 104 F.3d 355 (2d Cir. 1996). He also required the municipality to revise its zoning code "so that it will not be construed to prevent home worship, or to prevent persons from walking to and from religious services at such places of worship, or to prevent home worship services on any day in all residential zones." *Id.* at 965.

number of home synagogues to accommodate daily prayer meetings and no-car rules on the sabbath, the exclusion of houses of worship meant the exclusion of Jews. The decision rests on the fact of intentional discrimination and is therefore a clear manifestation of the equality principle; but its effect may actually be to invigorate the liberty rationale because a clear connection between the church members' religious rights and church location has been made.

Uses accessory to a place of worship

If worship use is permitted, accessory uses are usually permitted along with it, as long as they are normally related to or customarily incidental to a house of worship. As we have suggested,[55] the term "accessory use" typically encompasses counseling, education, and community service. In fact, the term has been broadly interpreted so that a wide variety of activities are considered to be accessory. A softball field and other recreational facilities, radio towers, a drug treatment center, a coffee house, and a homeless shelter have all been found "accessory" to church use.[56] Because the determination of what is customarily incidental or normally related to religious worship engages courts in defining religion, they generally find it prudent to defer liberally to church decisions on this issue. Justice Brennan said it best when he encouraged a broad freedom to a church to "[d]etermin[e] that certain activities are in furtherance of [its] religious mission [because that]...is...a means by which a religious community defines itself."[57]

However, not all courts follow this route. Some find other uses—particularly accessory uses like schools, soup kitchens, and counseling centers—to be less religious or not religious at all.[58] A recent federal appeals court found that a homeless shelter was not a customary use of the church building, and that the shelter could move to some other zone where it was a permitted use.[59] Thus courts do not always defer to the church's definition of what is customarily incidental to its worship use. One persistent issue is the definition of church schools and day-care centers. Courts are split, with many upholding restrictions on these uses and rejecting the "accessory use" characterization. These courts have agreed with zoning authorities that the negative impacts of these uses are more intense and need to be separately regulated.[60]

Prior to its demise, RFRA brought some impressive victories to churches on issues involving accessory uses. The federal district court in Washington, D.C., held in *Western Presbyterian Church v. Board of Zoning Adjustment* that once a church is permitted to locate in a neighborhood for worship and prayer, it also has the right to minister to the poor (in-

---

55. *See* section on Religious Structure and Property Use, *supra*.

56. *See* Corporation of Presiding Bishop v. Ashton, 448 P.2d 185 (Idaho 1968).

57. Corporation of Presiding Bishop v. Amos, 483 U.S. 327, 342 (1987) (Brennan, J., concurring).

58. For instance, a pastoral counseling center housed in a church and run by several denominations was considered a secular undertaking because modern psychological techniques were employed by the counselors. *See* Needham Pastoral Counseling Ctr., Inc. v. Board of Appeals, 557 N.E.2d 43 (Mass. App. Ct. 1990); *see also* Robert S. Walker, What Constitutes a Religious Use for Zoning Purposes, 27 Cath. Law. 129 (1982); Case Note, Introducing South Dakota to the Mire of "Religious Use" in Zoning: City of Rapid City v. Kahler, 29 S.D. L. Rev. 156 (1983); Angela C. Carmella, A Theological Critique of Free Exercise Jurisprudence, 60 Geo. Wash. L. Rev. 782 (1992). For some courts, any resemblance a use may have to a secular operation renders that use secular.

59. *See* First Assembly of God v. Collier County, 20 F.3d 419 (11th Cir.); *modified,* 27 F.3d 526 (11th Cir. 1994).

60. Cordes, *supra* note 12, at 739–47; Reynolds, *supra* note 41, at 810–14.

cluding running a feeding program), subject only to nuisance laws.[61] This court deferred to the church's understanding of its religious functions; a denial of a permit to engage in social programs was tantamount to interfering with prayer.[62] The federal district court in Colorado used the same reasoning (but under the First Amendment, not RFRA), to permit a church school to operate within a church building on the grounds that a restriction on educational uses would be analogous to restricting the ceremonial practices in the church.[63]

Also under RFRA, the provision of housing to the poor was recognized as an expression of religious belief in *Jesus Center v. Farmington Hills Zoning Board of Appeals*.[64] In both *Western Presbyterian* and *Jesus Center*, the municipalities argued that the churches had alternative locations in which to undertake their charitable services. Both courts rejected this because the charity was seen as an integral part of worship: once the house of worship was permitted to operate, accessory uses were permitted as well, even though those uses standing on their own would not have been allowed. In their relating of worship and accessory use, these cases produced an appropriate articulation of *Sherbert*'s liberty-oriented balancing test.

But courts applying RFRA did not always make the connection between the property and religious exercise. Just like the federal decisions in the church location cases, the court in *Daytona Rescue Mission, Inc. v. City of Daytona Beach* found the existence of an alternative site for an accessory use sufficient to satisfy the statute.[65] A church trying to establish a homeless shelter or food bank (precluded by the zoning ordinance from being defined as accessory uses) could simply run its charitable activities elsewhere, in a zone in which those activities were permitted.

Nonworship religious buildings

As part of a complex or alone, church property that is not a place of worship and not a permitted accessory use will fall under land use regulations governing the particular use category in question, such as schools, hospitals, colleges, administrative centers, office buildings, nursing homes, day-care centers, and low-income housing. Municipalities and courts will have to address the definitional issue: are these religious uses? And if they are religious, which approach—equality or liberty—comports with constitutional protection of the churches' free exercise?

---

61. *See* Western Presbyterian Church v. Board of Zoning Adjustment, 862 F. Supp. 538 (D.D.C. 1994). Note that the assumption appears to be that preventing nuisance is a compelling governmental interest. *See also* Stuart Circle Parish v. Board of Zoning Appeals, 946 F. Supp. 1225 (E.D. Va. 1996) (under RFRA, court issued a temporary restraining order against city enforcement of restrictions on feeding program, finding a likelihood of success on the merits); Shelley Ross Saxer, When Religion Becomes a Nuisance: Balancing Land Use and Religious Freedom When Activities of Religious Institutions Bring Outsiders into the Neighborhood, 84 Ky. L.J. 507 (1996).

62. "It must be noted that the concept of acts of charity as an essential part of religious worship is a central tenet of all major religions." *Id.* at 544.

63. *See* Alpine Christian Fellowship v. County Comm'rs, 870 F. Supp. 991, 995 (D. Colo. 1994).

64. 544 N.W.2d 698 (Mich. Ct. App. 1996). Interestingly, the court in *Jesus Center* did not feel constrained by the "customarily operated" standard of accessory uses. Finding a burden under RFRA, the court said, "[i]t is substantially burdensome to limit a church to activities and programs that are commonly practiced by other churches rather than allowing it to follow its faith even in unique and novel ways." *Id.* at 704–05.

65. *See* Daytona Rescue Mission, Inc. v. City of Daytona Beach, 885 F. Supp. 1554, 1560 (M.D. Fla. 1995).

Private land use restrictions

The government is not the only regulator of land use. Private restrictive covenants and defeasible estates often function just like zoning restrictions.[66] Church-owned land may be subject to some private restriction that curtails property use, much as a zoning provision would. For instance, a subdivision may be limited by restrictive covenant to single-family residences—which is equivalent in its effect to creating an exclusively residential zone. Since many states prevent zoning ordinances from banning churches from residential areas, the question arises whether courts should also prevent subdivisions from enforcing such private covenants that ban churches as nonresidential uses. The great weight of authority says no; private covenants that prohibit religious uses (in this indirect way) are enforceable. Because they do not invoke state action, these private agreements are not subject to constitutional scrutiny in the way that zoning is.[67] Churches must therefore check carefully for any deed restrictions before purchasing property, particularly a lot in a subdivision. Private covenants or defeasible estates that exclude whatever worship or nonworship use the church is proposing most likely will not be subject to constitutional challenge.

Private covenants are used not only to exclude religious use in these indirect ways but also to perpetuate religious use. The donor or seller of property to a church, or the church itself, can define and limit the use of the property by restrictions in the deed or other conveyancing instrument. In fact, the 1994 Survey shows that of those religious groups owning nonworship property at the national level, thirty percent hold deeds containing clauses that limit use or sale of the property.[68]

Historic preservation and architectural controls

Preservation ordinances

Municipalities restrict building design in two ways: through preservation of existing buildings considered historically or culturally valuable, and through architectural con-

---

66. The difference between controlling property use by way of a covenant versus controlling it by way of a defeasible estate is that a breach of a restriction in the form of a covenant is enforceable by damages or injunction, while the breach of a restriction in the form of a defeasible fee simple estate is enforceable by forfeiture of the property (either to the grantor or some named third party).

67. Of course any covenant that expressed antireligious discrimination—such as a covenant that prohibited the building or locating of a particular religion's place of worship, but permitted other places of worship—would be actionable under *Shelley v. Kraemer*, 334 U.S. 1 (1948), where judicial enforcement of a racially restrictive covenant was held to constitute state action. Furthermore, private restrictions based upon religion—for example, prohibiting sale to certain religious groups—are not enforceable because they violate the federal Fair Housing Act which prohibits discrimination in housing on the basis of religion. *See* Fair Housing Act §804(c), 42 U.S.C. §3604(c) (1994). The only case the author has found that has held single-family restrictions (which indirectly preclude churches) to constitute state action in violation of the Free Exercise Clause is *West Hill Baptist Church v. Abbate*, 261 N.E.2d 196 (Ohio Ct. C.P. 1969). *See also* Conrad v. Dunn, 154 Cal. Rptr. 726 (Ct. App. 1979); Note, Restrictive Covenants and Religious Uses: The Constitutional Interplay, 29 Syracuse L. Rev. 993 (1978).

68. *See* Survey, *supra* note 5, MQ12. And of those groups owning nonworship property, 13% said that if the national organization dissolved, property would revert to donors. *See id.* MQ16. This obviously refers to a restriction on the user, not on the particular type of use.

trols which prospectively govern new construction. (Unlike zoning codes which regulate area, bulk, and dimensions, these architectural controls typically mandate architectural style and often use boards of architects to review proposed designs.) While this section focuses exclusively on preservation mechanisms, the issues raised are also relevant to churches planning to build under architectural control laws.

A typical municipal preservation ordinance sets out general criteria of age and aesthetic quality, making all buildings that meet these criteria potential landmarks. Buildings are *landmarked* only after citizens or a landmarks commission petitions for a particular building or all buildings within a historic district to be designated. Preservation promotes aesthetics, economic revitalization, and neighborhood stability.[69]

Beautiful older church buildings are frequently landmarked, often at the request of the church itself.[70] But preservation gives rise to three main concerns regarding government interference in church design, use, and financial decision making. First, with respect to church design, preservation requires a church to make or maintain a particular architectural proclamation or message; second, with respect to use, preservation often prevents changes to buildings that would accommodate a new or expanded mission or larger membership; and finally, with respect to economics, preservation often diverts funds away from religious mission, causes diminution in value, or reduces the return on investment. The ultimate question is the degree to which churches should be accountable to the public for maintaining a historic landmark.

As in the field of zoning, courts have split along the equality and liberty line in the preservation area.[71] Still, it seems that the liberty rationale is more common when preservation interferes with the design and use of a place of worship: the special quality of the house of worship is recognized. The strict scrutiny applicable under a liberty rationale has been employed even after *Smith* either by interpreting the landmarks law as one not "generally applicable," or by interpreting a state's constitutional protections for

---

69. Similarly, architectural design review ordinances ensure visual harmony of areas regardless of historic merit. These ordinances cover new construction and changes to existing buildings. The issues raised in historic preservation of churches are equally applicable to architectural review.

70. For discussion of how landmark status can "enhance a church's ability to carry out its mission and protect itself from encroaching development," see Russell S. Bonds, Comment, First Covenant v. City of Seattle: The Washington Supreme Court Fortifies the Free Exercise Rights of Religious Landmarks Against Historic Preservation Restrictions, 27 Ga. L. Rev. 589, 615 (1993).

71. Commentary on these cases is abundant. *See* Angela C. Carmella, Houses of Worship and Religious Liberty: Constitutional Limits to Landmark Preservation and Architectural Review, 36 Vill. L. Rev. 401 (1991); Thomas Pak, Note, Free Exercise, Free Expression, and Landmark Preservation, 91 Colum. L. Rev. 1813 (1991); Alan C. Weinstein, The Myth of Ministry vs. Mortar: A Legal and Policy Analysis of Landmark Designation of Religious Institutions, 65 Temp. L. Rev. 91 (1992); Steven P. Eakman, Note, Fire and Brownstone: Historic Preservation of Religious Properties and the First Amendment, 33 B.C. L. Rev. 93 (1991); Ted L. Wills, Note, Religious Landmarks, Guidelines for Analysis: Free Exercise, Takings, and Least Restrictive Means, 53 Ohio St. L.J. 211 (1992); Richard F. Babcock & David A. Theriaque, Landmarks Preservation Ordinances: Are the Religion Clauses Violated by their Application to Religious Properties? 7 J. Land Use & Envtl. L. 165 (1992); Bonds, *supra* note 66, at 589; Dina A. Keever, Comment, Public Funds and the Historical Preservation of Churches: Preserving History or Advancing Religion? 21 Fla. St. U. L. Rev. 1327 (1994); Patty Gerstenblith, Architect as Artist: Artists' Rights and Historic Preservation, 12 Cardozo Arts & Ent. L.J. 431 (1994); Felipe M. Nunez & Eric Sidman, California's Statutory Exemption for Religious Properties from Landmark Ordinances: A Constitutional and Policy Analysis, 12 J.L. & Religion 271 (1995–1996).

religious liberty. Courts have repeatedly held that historic preservation does not reflect a compelling governmental interest.[72]

It is perhaps easiest to see that church interiors would receive protection from government interference. Indeed, one striking example is found in Massachusetts. A Catholic church renovation, undertaken to reflect changes in liturgy and theology ushered in by the Second Vatican Council, was halted by the Boston Landmarks Commission. After the commission put the design of a church sanctuary (and the altars in it) under its jurisdiction, the high court of Massachusetts, interpreting the state constitution, ordered an exemption of sanctuaries from landmark ordinances on the grounds that the "configuration of the church interior is so freighted with religious meaning that it must be considered part and parcel of the...worship."[73]

Although the Massachusetts court suggested that the interior would receive greater constitutional protection than the church's exterior, other courts have not made such a distinction. Washington's highest court, for example, held landmark designation of a Seattle church unconstitutional under state and federal free exercise provisions because, among other things, it burdened the architectural "proclamation" of religious belief inherent in the church's design.[74] Another factor in this case was a peculiar liturgy exemption, in which the church was permitted to make certain liturgically related changes without approval of the landmarks commission. Because the commission retained ultimate authority to decide what changes fell within this exemption, however, the provision was found to place religious decisions in the government's hands. The Seattle Landmarks Commission next landmarked a church but held the restrictions in abeyance until the building ceased to be used for "religious purposes."[75] The Washington Supreme Court was similarly concerned that determining when "religious purposes" ceased would involve the government in a religious decision, and thus struck down the designation.[76]

A Maryland district court has held that the Free Exercise Clause allows a church to demolish its buildings in order to "improve worship...[,] increase accessibility to worship and other religious services for the handicapped, elderly, and other parishioners, and to use its property as an expression of religious belief."[77] The court, citing the above

---

72. *See* Society of Jesus v. Boston Landmarks Comm'n, 564 N.E.2d 571 (Mass. 1990); First Covenant Church v. City of Seattle, 840 P.2d 174 (Wash. 1992); First United Methodist Church v. Hearing Examiner, 916 P.2d 374 (Wash. 1996); Munns v. Martin, 930 P.2d 318 (Wash. 1997); Keeler v. Mayor of Cumberland, 940 F. Supp. 879 (D. Md. 1996); 79 Op. Atty. Gen. (Md. 1994) (Op. No. 94-037), *reprinted in* 21 Md. Reg. 1600 (Sept. 16, 1994).

73. *Society of Jesus*, 564 N.E.2d at 573.

74. *First Covenant*, 840 P.2d 174.

75. *First United Methodist*, 916 P.2d 374.

76. *Id.* See also *Munns*, 930 P.2d 318, which held that a demolition permit ordinance that could potentially delay a construction project of a Catholic pastoral center (and involve religious and secular officials in negotiation) was an unconstitutional administrative burden on the free exercise of religion under the state constitution.

77. *Keeler*, 940 F. Supp. at 883. The church was denied permission to demolish a church and monastery which were part of a historic district and replace it with smaller facilities. In an earlier disposition, *Keeler v. Mayor of Cumberland*, 928 F. Supp. 591 (D. Md. 1996), the court granted the city's motion to dismiss on the RFRA count (on grounds that RFRA is unconstitutional), but denied the motion on all other constitutional claims.

Of particular interest is how the court accepted the church's evidence:

The city characterizes the church's evidentiary support as 'a number of self-serving affidavits...' The city seems to suggest that this Court should regard the affidavits with sus-

decisions, applied a liberty rationale, reasoning that strict scrutiny applies because preservation is not accomplished by way of generally applicable laws.

The *Boerne* dispute, wherein RFRA was held unconstitutional, arose from the landmarking of a Catholic church building, but the issue before the federal courts all the way up to the Supreme Court was only the question of RFRA's constitutionality, which the city had raised in defense against the church's RFRA claim. The church intended to demolish all but the facade of its house of worship to accommodate its rapidly growing parish; the designation would have prevented this action.[78] When preservation interferes with church use to the point that the needs of the congregation cannot be met or the mission cannot be accommodated, a direct conflict arises between a building's religious purposes and the public's desire to preserve beautiful architecture. While we have no statement from the Supreme Court on the merits of the case, dicta suggest that the Supreme Court would reject the analysis of the courts discussed above and would employ an equality rationale—treating a landmarked house of worship like any other landmarked building.[79] In so doing, it appears that the majority simply assumed that historic preservation was a generally applicable, facially neutral law.

In contrast to the liberty approach to design and use concerns, the economic concern raised by preservation ordinances is typically treated under an equality rationale. When it comes to money, most courts are unwilling to consider a financial burden to be a true burden on religion. Churches have to suffer these burdens of regulation just like any other property owner.

Obviously, preservation goals are thwarted when a church can itself alter or demolish the building or sell it free of restrictions to be altered or demolished by the new owner. But churches argue that the maintenance of old church buildings requires expenditures that force a diversion of limited funds, and that the maintenance itself is more expensive because repair and replacement often require original materials.[80] These "economic" concerns are inextricably connected to pastoral goals: having to spend scarce resources on custom-made windows and expensive roofing materials may force the closure of a soup kitchen because the costs directly restrict the number and size of pro-

---

picion, in part because they represent a subjective belief that there is a religious aspect to the Church's decision to demolish the Monastery. Under the circumstances of this case, however, this Court has no authority to disregard the affiants' declaration of their beliefs. After all, what is the First Amendment about if not about one's subjective beliefs? (This Court has yet to encounter any objective beliefs.)

Keeler, 940 F. Supp. at 883.

78. The city has suggested that if the church needs more space, it should simply build another house of worship elsewhere—borrowing the "alternative location" analysis from zoning.

79. *See* City of Boerne v. Flores, 521 U.S. 507, 535 (1997).

80. Of course all land use regulation could be said to require some "diversion" of funds. To ensure a safe building, it must be built to safety and building code specifications—and that may be more "expensive" than if inexpensive and unsafe materials were used. To get a conditional use permit to build a house of worship in a neighborhood, construction may be more expensive because the church may need to add a buffer zone of trees or a larger parking lot to minimize secondary effects like noise and traffic. But the increased expense of preservation is unrelated to increased building safety and unrelated to the mitigation of negative effects on the surrounding community. It is related instead to maintaining the aesthetic benefits of buildings that have long been part of the community.

grams a church can maintain. Particularly because of Establishment Clause constraints on direct public funding of church renovations, the economic burden typically falls entirely on the churches.[81] Churches also argue that preservation drastically reduces the fair market value of church property[82] or makes it less attractive for sale, and that they have the right to dispose of the property and use the funds to continue their religious mission.

The churches' economic arguments, often coupled with the argument that government has "taken" the church's property without just compensation, have generally been unsuccessful.[83] In one widely noted case, St. Bartholomew's Episcopal Church in New York City sought to demolish not the house of worship but an accessory building (a landmark) and replace it with a commercial office tower. Even though the church planned to expand its community ministries and fund religious programs throughout the city with the revenues it would earn from the forty-seven-story office building, the Court of Appeals for the Second Circuit found no free exercise violation (and no taking). It held that the landmark status of the accessory building did not interfere with the church's current level of ministries at the site: free exercise did not include the right to expand ministries or to make property lucrative, even if to fund religious programs.[84]

Still, the economic argument was successful in 1996 on free exercise grounds.[85] The Washington Supreme Court held that if Seattle's First United Methodist Church

> decides to sell its property in order to respond to the needs of its congregation, it has a right to do so without landmark restrictions creating administrative or financial burdens. The free exercise clause prevents government from engaging in landmark preservation when it has a coercive effect on religion. This protection does not cease if United Methodist sells its property... [The landmark law] severely burdens free exercise of religion because it impedes United Methodist from selling its property and using the proceeds to advance its religious mission.[86]

This analysis respects the autonomy of church decision making regarding the disposition of property. Decisions about sale, moving, and church closings are made in many different ways—by congregational vote, by the local bishop, or by a church at some higher level. In the Survey nearly three in five churches reported that the final decision to move to another location would be made by a majority agreement of local members; nearly one in five held that it would be made by the state, regional, or national religious

---

81. Some states that provide funds for the renovation of landmarked buildings also give monies to historic churches subject to certain restrictions. The constitutionality of such funding has not yet been challenged, but the Supreme Court has ruled in the religious school funding context that the state may not finance the maintenance of a church building. *See* Committee for Public Educ. And Religious Liberty v. Nyquist, 413 U.S. 756 (1973).

82. This argument was successful in *First Covenant Church v. City of Seattle*, 840 P.2d 174 (Wash. 1992).

83. *See* Society for Ethical Culture v. Spatt, 415 N.E.2d 922 (N.Y. 1980); Church of St. Paul and St. Andrew v. Barwick, 496 N.E.2d 183 (N.Y. 1986). But this argument proved successful in *Keeler v. Mayor of Cumberland*, 940 F. Supp. 879 (D. Md. 1996), where the ordinance was found to effect a regulatory taking.

84. *See* Rector of St. Bartholomew's Church v. City of New York, 914 F.2d 348 (2d Cir. 1990).

85. *See* First United Methodist Church v. Hearing Examiner, 916 P.2d 374 (Wash. 1996).

86. *Id.* at 381.

body.[87] Regulation that interferes with this decision making process can seriously inhibit the direction and self-definition of churches.

In addition to these decisions regarding the disposition of property, churches have enjoyed much independence in decision making regarding the purchase and use of church property and the use of church funds. This makes the issue of accountability to the public especially acute in the preservation area. Property and budgetary decisions are generally made in accordance with each church's internal organization. The vast majority of churches report that decisions about the general operating budgets of local churches are made either by majority vote or by a board of trustees.[88] The vast majority of local churches do not even have to submit budgets for approval of their regional or national bodies.[89] Three-fourths of the churches in the 1994 Survey reported that the final decision or authorization to purchase, build, or renovate local properties is made by agreement of a majority of local members.[90] With so much independence—often even from higher levels of the church—churches are rightly concerned with government requirements that could force different decisions on the disposition of their property or the redistribution of their funds.

Building codes

Generally, churches must comply with building and safety codes.[91] In fact, such regulations, unlike historic preservation laws, are often presumed to serve a compelling governmental interest that justifies burdens on religion. But churches are exempt from the federal Americans with Disabilities Act (ADA) which requires, among other things, the removal of architectural barriers from public accommodations.[92] Despite this exemption, local building, zoning, or preservation ordinances may contain provisions requiring wheelchair accessibility that cover religious buildings. One church in the Nantucket (Massachusetts) Historic District was denied a building permit to remodel the area around its altar because its plans did not include wheelchair access to that part of the sanctuary.[93]

---

87. Majority agreement of local members, 57%; state or regional religious body, 11%; national religious body, 8%. *See* Survey, *supra* note 5, MQ40.

More than half of the churches in the Survey whose local units own nonworship property reported that the final decision to sell such property is made by those local churches through majority vote or agreement of members, 53%. *See id.* MQ43. For those churches that own nonworship property at the national level, about 30% say the decision to sell is made at the national level. *See id.* MQ11.

88. *See id.* MQ44.

89. 93%. *See id.* MQ45.

90. *See id.* MQ47.

91. *See* Congregation Beth Yitzchok v. Town of Ramapo, 593 F. Supp. 655 (S.D.N.Y. 1984) (nursery school). *But see* City of Sumner v. First Baptist Church, 639 P.2d 1358 (Wash. 1982) (flexible application of building code to allow school to operate).

92. *See* Americans with Disabilities Act of 1990 § 307, 42 U.S.C. § 12187 (1994). The ADA public accommodations provisions do not apply to "religious organizations or entities controlled by religious organizations, including places of worship." *Id.*

93. *See* First Congregational Church v. Architectural Access Bd., Civ. No. 0009381 (Mass. Super. Ct. filed 1994).

Private preservation

Many churches are committed wholeheartedly to the preservation of their worship structures.[94] Indeed, many have requested or supported the landmark designation of their houses of worship. Others have done so using private mechanisms. The Catholic church that brought the RFRA action in *Boerne* has voluntarily preserved its original house of worship, built in the 1860s, near its current worship structure. Many churches are beginning to undertake sophisticated preservation efforts through wholly internal processes without governmental oversight. The Archdiocese of Santa Fe, as one example, has collected a group of preservation professionals, church members, and clergy to inventory and review all the houses of worship in its jurisdiction. The group undertook this project with a view to determining which churches needed repair or restoration and which were historically, theologically, and architecturally significant enough to warrant a commitment to preservation.[95]

Another way to ensure preservation is to create a preservation easement. The Unitarian community in Oak Park, Illinois, that owns Unity Temple—a Frank Lloyd Wright design—has granted a "facade easement" (interior and exterior) to the Landmarks Preservation Council of Illinois, a private, nonprofit preservation organization that now holds the right to enforce specific preservation requirements. A church could also set up a separately incorporated religious organization to hold such a preservation easement.

Environmental regulation

Environment and development

In addition to landmarking regulations, states often have comprehensive land use policies that direct municipalities to implement local zoning and planning schemes in ways that protect the environment. This connection is not surprising because development affects not only the built environment but the natural environment as well. Statutory exemptions from environmental regulations for religious use generally do not exist; and no court decision has expressed a liberty rationale when environmental protection

---

94. Organizations have emerged to provide technical assistance for restoration and preservation work. *See generally* Inspired, Quarterly Publication Devoted to the Preservation of Historic Religious Buildings (available from Philadelphia Historic Preservation Corporation); Common Bond (quarterly publication of the New York Landmark Conservancy for preservation of religious buildings). A series of "Sacred Trusts" conferences sponsored jointly by local preservation organizations and religious groups from various parts of the country offer programs on preservation and restoration techniques and fund-raising. Because these private organizations are closely linked to governmental preservation programs, however, certain forms of assistance may be available only on the condition that the church submit to landmark commission jurisdiction.

95. For examples of internal church commitment to preservation and creation of sophisticated internal preservation commissions, see Archdiocese of Santa Fe, Report of the Select Committee on the Preservation of New Mexico Historic Churches (1987); Architecture and Building Commission of the Roman Catholic Diocese of New York, Architecture and Building in the Diocese of Albany (1982); Bishops' Committee on the Liturgy, National Conference of Catholic Bishops, Environment and Art in Catholic Worship (1977).

is at stake, even where a liberty approach applies to the traditional zoning issues.[96] Churches are as fully subject to environmental regulation as any other user of property: the development laws apply to "land use and not to the particular institutional activity associated with that land use."[97]

Hazardous waste [98]

The federal Comprehensive Environmental Response, Compensation and Liability Act (CERCLA),[99] also known as the Superfund Law, creates strict liability for cleanup costs for owners of property that contains hazardous waste; whether one put the hazardous waste there or not is irrelevant. This liability affects all owners (and "operators") in the chain of title. Churches might acquire a dirty site (by purchase, devise, or gift) and then be liable for costs of cleanup.[100] It is therefore very important that prior to purchase, an environmental audit or assessment be ordered. A church should not purchase a dirty site unless the seller agrees to indemnify the church; but even in that case, an indemnification will have effect only between the parties to the contract. The church can still be held statutorily liable.

A very limited "innocent purchaser" defense exists for purchasers who conduct adequate site investigations that fail to uncover hazardous waste at the site and for those who inherit property.

Asbestos

Because of past widespread use of asbestos in insulation and other materials, the removal and containment of asbestos have become important goals of health and environmental regulation. School buildings, including parochial schools, are subject to the federal Asbestos Hazard Emergency Response Act of 1986, which requires the removal of asbestos. For other buildings state and local laws often require similar attention to asbestos, but removal is not yet a widespread mandate.[101] Whether for removal or containment, churches must inspect buildings, disclose the presence of any asbestos that is identified, prepare a management plan for dealing with the asbestos, and implement

---

96. *See* Southern New England Conference Ass'n of Seventh-Day Adventists v. Burlington, 490 N.E.2d 451, 452, 455 (Mass. App. Ct. 1986) (wetlands regulations are not covered by state law that prohibits local zoning laws from "regulat[ing] or restrict[ing]...the use of land or structures for religious...purposes" (quoting Mass. Gen. Laws ch. 40A, §3 (added 1975))).

97. *In re* Baptist Fellowship, 481 A.2d 1274 (Vt. 1984) (state development law).

98. This section and the following section on asbestos summarize materials of Joseph J. Giamboi, Stroock, Stroock & Lavin, presented at The 26th Meeting of the National Diocesan Attorneys 1990, sponsored by the United States Catholic Conference Office of General Counsel; Barry Kellman, Environmental Concerns for the Religious Institution (Feb. 1992) (unpublished manuscript, on file with the Center for Church/State Studies, DePaul University College of Law).

99. Comprehensive Environmental Response, Compensation, and Liability Act of 1980, 42 U.S.C. §§9601–9675 (1994 & Supp. III 1997). States often have their own hazardous waste laws, which create additional liability for owners and users of dirty sites.

100. CERCLA also permits liable parties to sue other responsible parties for their fair share of the cleanup costs.

101. Some litigation has arisen surrounding the question of recovery of removal costs, with churches as plaintiffs; *see* First United Methodist Church v. United States Gypsum Co., 882 F.2d 862 (4th Cir. 1989), and Borders v. United States Gypsum Co., 704 F. Supp. 615 (D. Md. 1989). As defendants, *see* Joy v. Louisiana Conference Ass'n of Seventh-day Adventists, No. 91-4025 Sec. M, 1992 U.S. Dist. LEXIS 9901 (E.D. La. July 1, 1992). But no arguments relating to the religious identity of the party or the religious use of the buildings were made.

the plan. Additionally, any construction work or rehabilitation of a building where asbestos is present needs Environmental Protection Agency approval.

Because asbestos management can be very expensive, some states provide assistance to lessen the economic burden. In Illinois, for instance, nonpublic schools can be reimbursed for up to half the costs of correcting asbestos problems. In New York a grant program provides monies.

Takings

Takings pursuant to eminent domain powers

The government's power to take private property—its "eminent domain" power—includes the power to take church-owned property. All takings must be justified by a public purpose, and the government must pay just compensation for the property. While such takings often occur as part of a larger urban revitalization plan, the government can single out an individual building—even a religious building—for taking. A Seventh-Day Adventist school in California was taken because the public school district needed a school building.[102] In response to this government action, the California legislature passed a law applicable to nonprofit properties (including religious ones) to require a greater showing of need before a taking of such property can occur.

Some courts have adopted a liberty-oriented balancing test, holding government agencies to a higher standard in the taking of church property than in the taking of other private property by requiring a showing of more than public use and just compensation. For instance, when the City of Denver proposed (as part of an urban renewal project) the taking and demolition of a church building that had special historical and religious significance to its congregation, the Colorado Supreme Court held that such action would burden free exercise. Denver was required to show that destruction of the building and forced relocation from the site was justified by a compelling interest "without a reasonable alternative means of accomplishment."[103] The Court of Appeals for the Second Circuit required a similar showing when the City of Yonkers tried to take two acres of a Catholic seminary's grounds.[104] Yet other courts do not hold officials to higher standards when taking church-owned property. Treating this property like other properties, such courts hold that it can be taken as long as the constitutional requirements of public use and just compensation are met, although takings that will deprive a congregation of a place to worship will typically be given greater scrutiny.[105]

Regulatory takings

As described above, the government can take property explicitly pursuant to its eminent domain powers. Yet it can also be charged by a court with having taken property

---

102. *See* Marilyn Thomsen, They Took Our School, 88 Liberty 19–22 (1993).

103. In the final analysis, the church's claim was outweighed by the government interest in a major downtown urban renewal project. *See* Pillar of Fire v. Denver Urban Renewal Auth., 509 P.2d 1250 (Colo. 1973), *appeal after remand*, 552 P.2d 23 (Colo. 1976); *see also* Order of Friars Minor of Province of Most Holy Name v. Denver Urban Renewal Auth., 527 P.2d 804 (Colo. 1974) (condemnation of church parking lot).

104. *See* Yonkers Racing Corp. v. City of Yonkers, 858 F.2d 855 (2d Cir. 1988).

105. Thomsen, *supra* note 101.

when its regulations deprive property owners of virtually all economic use of their land—or, in the nonprofit context, of the ability to carry on their charitable purposes. Zoning,[106] preservation,[107] environmental regulation,[108] and eminent domain actions can be challenged as effecting such a "regulatory" taking. These challenges are usually coupled with free exercise challenges, but one effect of this coupling has been to collapse the distinction between free exercise and takings by analyzing the free exercise issue with a takings test.[109]

Legal Structure and Property Use

In conclusion we pose the larger question of this volume here in the matter of religious land use regulation: Do civil corporate forms provide religious organizations with sufficient ability to implement their own religious self-understanding free of intrusion by the state? Asked another way, does legal structure protect religious structure? These questions return us to the overarching constitutional inquiry concerning the regulation and accommodation of religious land use, but incorporation adds another dimension to the question. Does the act of a church taking on a corporate form affect the constitutional analysis applicable to the church's religious structure (that is, does it give a church more or less protection than if it were not incorporated)? And does the act of a church taking on a corporate form shared by other entities predispose us toward an equality rationale in constitutional adjudication of land use issues?

The government provides by law a variety of incorporation options to enable churches to take on a legal structure. The corporate forms available to churches—religious corporations, nonprofit corporations, and corporations sole, among others—enable them to gain legal recognition, status, and rights, particularly the right to own, hold, and transfer property (and to enter into contracts like leases for the right to use property).[110] As the

---

106. *See* Ramona Convent of Holy Names v. City of Alhambra, 26 Cal. Rptr. 2d 140 (Ct. App. 1993) (where rezoning of convent's property to "open space" made it undevelopable, convent's inability to sell parcel did not constitute a taking or infringe free exercise of religion).

107. Finding a taking, see Galich v. Catholic Bishop, 394 N.E.2d 572 (Ill. App. Ct. 1979); Lutheran Church in America v. City of New York, 316 N.E.2d 305 (N.Y. 1974). Finding no taking, see Society for Ethical Culture v. Spatt, 415 N.E.2d 922 (N.Y. 1980); Church of St. Paul and St. Andrew v. Barwick, 496 N.E.2d 183 (N.Y. 1986); Rector of St. Bartholomew's Church v. City of New York, 914 F.2d 348 (2d Cir. 1990).

108. Flood protection, see First English Evangelical Lutheran Church v. County of Los Angeles, 482 U.S. 304 (1987), *after remand*, 258 Cal. Rptr. 893 (Ct. App. 1989) (compensation is due for the time before it is finally determined that a regulation constitutes a taking; on remand, court held that ordinance was not a taking).

109. *See, e.g., Ethical Culture*, 415 N.E.2d 922 (applying the takings test developed in *Trustees of Sailors' Snug Harbor v. Platt*, 288 N.Y.S.2d 314 (App. Div. 1968), to a free exercise claim); *St. Bartholomew's*, 914 F.2d 348. But see *Keeler v. Mayor of Cumberland*, 940 F. Supp. 879 (D. Md. 1996), where the analyses were kept separate.

110. The 1994 Report on the Survey of Religious Organizations at the National Level showed that 92% of respondents have taken on some corporate form, while 8% were unincorporated associations, which would normally not be able to hold title as an entity. *See* Survey, *supra* note 5, Q4. Nonetheless, "while most states still prohibit an [unincorporated] association from owning or transferring title to property in its own name, many states do permit an association to hold or transfer title to property in the name of 'trustees' acting on behalf of the association." Richard R. Hammar, Pastor, Church & Law 272 (2d ed. 1991).

1994 Survey demonstrates, the vast majority of churches take on one of these corporate forms. The act of obtaining entity status does not seem to be correlated with any particular internal polity, although some churches elect certain corporate forms over others because they better reflect ecclesiastical reality. For instance, religiously hierarchical churches tend to incorporate as corporations sole, in which the office of the bishop is considered to be the entity—he holds title to property, enters into contracts, sues, and gets sued.

On the one hand, courts have found that incorporation has no effect on our constitutional understanding of the religious structure:

> [A] church does not lose its ecclesiastical function, and the attributes of that function, when it incorporates. It does not, by incorporating, lose its right to be governed by its own particular form of ecclesiastical government. Incorporation operates merely to create a legal entity to hold and administer the properties of the church.[111]

On the other hand, courts may interpret incorporation as pulling churches fully within the law's reach on "temporal" matters:

> The law recognizes the distinction between the church as a religious group devoted to worship, preaching, missionary service, education and the promotion of social welfare, and the church *as a business corporation owning real estate and making contracts....* The former is a matter in which the state or the courts have no direct legal concern, while in the latter the activities of the church are *subject to the same laws as those in secular affairs.*[112]

Notice how this court has separated religious from temporal affairs without acknowledging any connection between religion and the property that provides the physical space for its exercise. Notice further how the court assumes that subjecting church property use and ownership to the same laws as secular ownership raises no constitutional issue. This indicates the choice of an equality rationale that treats churches like their secular corporate counterparts.

The notion that the act of incorporation constituted an implicit acceptance of government regulation was expressed in an early church land use decision, *Corporation of Presiding Bishop v. City of Porterville.*[113] The California court wrote:

> We find no merit in [the church's] contention that the application of the ordinance [banning churches in residential neighborhoods] to [it] results in an unwarranted restriction of religious worship. *The [church] is not a congregation, but holds [its] property as a corporation sole, the existence of which depends upon the laws of the State. Having such right from the State, the enjoyment of the property is subject to reasonable regulations.*[114]

Under such reasoning, a church that is an unincorporated association is treated as a group of religious people, possessing the combined constitutional rights of the individuals involved. But an incorporated church is treated like any other incorporated entity, making it subject to land use regulation under an equality rationale.

---

111. Providence Baptist Church v. Superior Court, 243 P.2d 112, 115 (Cal. Ct. App. 1952), *vacated,* 251 P.2d 10 (Cal. 1952), *quoted in* Hammar, *supra* note 105, at 276.

112. Gospel Tabernacle Body of Christ Church v. Peace Publishers & Co., 506 P.2d 1135, 1137 (Kan. 1973), *quoted in* Hammar, *supra* note 105, at 276 (emphasis added).

113. 203 P.2d 823 (Cal. Ct. App. 1949), *appeal dismissed,* 338 U.S. 805 (1949).

114. *Id.* at 825 (emphasis added).

Notwithstanding the incorporation/regulation connection in *Presiding Bishop*, the vast majority of land use cases do not mention the corporate structure or implications of that structure. With widespread incorporation and property ownership among churches, the relationship between corporate structure and land use regulation seems largely irrelevant to the courts. This is most likely attributable to the fact that land use regulation focuses on the use, dimensions, design, and secondary effects of buildings, and not the identity of the owner.[115] Putting property to a forbidden use will get the attention of local zoning officials, regardless of the identity or corporate form of the user.

Furthermore, the case law does not conclusively correlate a particular jurisdiction's use of the liberty or equality approaches and church corporate structure. While the few cases mentioned in this section suggest an equality rationale and could lead us to speculate that such an approach flows naturally from incorporation, contrary evidence abounds—far too many land use cases employ a liberty approach under state and federal constitutional interpretation, both before and after *Smith*. Thus, whether churches *should* be subject to land use regulations in the same way as other nonprofit corporations (the equality approach) or be treated instead in a class by themselves as religious entities (the liberty approach) is a constitutional issue quite independent of corporate form.[116]

Religious communities should be able to use their properties for what they are: extensions of their religious exercise and instruments of self-definition. Zoning, preservation, environmental protections, and eminent domain actions can seriously interfere with liturgical, pastoral, educational, community service, and economic goals. Whether the detriment suffered results from intentional discrimination, the simple enforcement of general laws, or the treatment of churches without regard to their particular religious needs, the harm is the same. An equality approach provides only a floor to ensure that land use laws are not applied in antireligious ways. The liberty approach is needed to protect the broad range of church goals. Church decision making regarding design and dimensions, location and uses, and economic resources deserves deference. Government should regulate only when specific secondary effects are produced by the church's land use, and then only in a narrowly tailored fashion.

---

115. *See* Hayes v. Fowler, 473 S.E.2d 442 (N.C. Ct. App. 1996) (refusing to look to the religious identity of the property owner in order to define "church use"; instead looking to way in which property was used).

116. *See also* Catherine Knight, Comment, Must God Regulate Religious Corporations? A Proposal for Reform of the Religious Corporation Provisions of the Revised Model Nonprofit Corporation Act, 42 Emory L.J. 721 (1993).

Derivative Liability

Mark E. Chopko

There is no longer any serious debate about whether religious organizations are held responsible for the consequences of their actions. The demise of charitable immunity generally and its limitation in virtually every jurisdiction means that these entities must pay attention to their legal relationships and conduct. Religious entities can be sued for their own debts and for their own negligence.[1] However, another concern is even more vexing for religious organizations: the potential to be held responsible for the conduct of a member, employee, or agent of the organization, or even another related group or its members, employees, or agents, including volunteers.

An important reason why litigants may seek some form of liability deriving from the actions of others turns on simple economics. It is relatively easy for a plaintiff to establish that a particular individual drove a vehicle negligently or made a poor business judgment or otherwise acted improperly. Indeed, it is sometimes easier to establish this layer of liability than to establish the same kind of direct liability on the part of an organization. If the organization can be forced to take responsibility for those actions committed by another as if it were its own, then the potential for financial recovery increases.[2]

Yet the body of law in this area shows that ultimate success may be problematic for a plaintiff. The subtleties of the law can be deceptive; liability depends on the nature of the conduct, its relationship to the community's mission, and the character of the organization's operations. The effort to find an organization liable in these kinds of situations is called, in some circles, *ascending liability*—or as in this chapter, *derivative liability,* which more accurately reflects the law and the litigation experience.[3] An

---

1. In most states, charitable immunity is no longer available to preclude recovery. In New Jersey, which preserves charitable immunity, the beneficiary of the charity may not maintain an action in tort for the negligence of the entity and its personnel. *But compare* Gray v. St. Cecilia's Sch., 526 A.2d 264 (N.J. Super. Ct. App. Div. 1987), *with* Brown v. St. Venantius Sch., 544 A.2d 842 (N.J. 1988) (illustrating limitations on immunity). In four states—Massachusetts, New Hampshire, South Carolina, and Texas—charities enjoy a limited immunity related to caps on recovery. *See* materials collected *infra* note 190. More states immunize volunteers and volunteer boards by statute. *See* Volunteer Protection Act of 1997, Pub. L. No. 105-19, 111 Stat. 218. The discussion here concerns not immunity, but the circumstances under which a religious entity can be found vicariously liable for the actions of another's agent or employee or related entity.

2. *See* Samuels v. Southern Baptist Hosp., 594 So. 2d 571, 574 (La.Ct. App. 1992).

3. "Derivative liability" is more than (and includes) *respondeat superior* liability. It may even include ostensibly direct negligence claims that could not be asserted but for the negligence or misconduct of another. Derivative liability encompasses efforts to follow links in a denominational chain to impose responsibility in a coordinate or superior entity, not just an "employing" entity. Several important works address in complete detail the important facets of this topic. *See* Edward

extremely complex bundle of law and policy, derivative liability refers to the potential institutional responsibility that rests on and is derived from the actions of others. Consider these examples from the cases:

A worshiper slips in a church, injures her leg, and sues for damages. The church is insured, it is undisputed that a condition in the church caused her to fall, and she certainly has injuries. Given the rather common injury and tort theory, recovery would seem to be fairly straightforward. The final answers, however, are sometimes elusive in this area of the law. Was the church organized as a hierarchical or a congregational community? Was the particular church incorporated or unincorporated? Was she a visitor to the church or a regular member? Answers to these questions are relevant in determining whether this woman receives compensation for her injuries.[4]

The superintendent of a senior citizen housing center owned by a religious community arranges for repairs to the center's boiler. The center refuses to honor the bill for services. The repair service, in turn, sues both the center and the religious community to recover the unpaid balance in dispute. Again, all other things being equal, recovery would seem obvious. But in this area of the law other factors may be determinative. Does separate incorporation of the center and the community protect the community from liability? Or, on the other hand, is there such a link between the housing center and the community that one can be seen as the alter ego of the other? Was the community leadership involved in the decision-making process for the repair? Was the center's employee who arranged for the repair the "agent" of the corresponding community?[5] Depending upon the answers to these questions, recovery may be allowed or denied.

A minor and her mother sue the regional director, the regional governing body, and a national churchwide mission board for damages arising out of the sexual molestation of the child while the family was stationed overseas in a church assignment. The perpetrator, a minister of that community, was also the victim's father. When asked for assistance, the regional mission director declined to intervene. Instead, he advised the victim to remain silent about this question until the family could be transferred back to the United States where professional help would be available. To the victim and her sister

---

M. Gaffney, Jr., & Philip C. Sorensen, Ascending Liability in Religious and Other Nonprofit Organizations (1984); *see also* Mark E. Chopko, Ascending Liability for the Actions of Others, 17 Am. J. Trial Advoc. 289 (1993). Others would tend to distinguish solely between vicarious and direct liability. "Derivative liability" as used here includes that distinction but also applies in settings beyond traditional tort theories.

Additional information on liabilities of religious organizations and liability theory can be found in Mark E. Chopko, Stating Claims Against Religious Institutions, 44 B.C. L. Rev. 1089 (2003). A thorough review of liability theory in various circumstances is in 2 William Bassett, Religious Organizations and the Law, chs. 7 (Fundamentals of Litigation) and 8 (Specific Causes of Action) (1997); Richard Hammar, Pastor, Church & Law, chs. 4 (Liabilities, Limitations, and Restrictions) and 12 (Church Legal Liability) (2d ed. 1991); *see also* Carl H. Esbeck, Tort Claims Against Churches and Ecclesiastical Officers, 89 W. Va. L. Rev. 1 (1986); David Frohlich, Note, Will Courts make Change for a Large Denomination?: Problems of Interpretation in an Agency Analysis in which a Religious Denomination Is Involved in an Ascending Liability Tort Case, 72 Iowa L. Rev. 1377 (1987). While commentators tend to review the law by liability theory, this chapter organizes the law by liability principles that cut across denominational lines and legal theories.

4. *See* Egerton v. R.E. Lee Mem'l Church, 395 F.2d 381 (4th Cir. 1968); Prentiss v. Evergreen Presbyterian Church, 644 So. 2d 475 (Ala. 1994); Davis v. Church of Jesus Christ of Latter-day Saints, 796 P.2d 181 (Mont. 1990), *overruled in part by* Richardson v. Corvallis Pub. Sch. Dist. No. 1, 950 P.2d 748 (Mont. 1997) (issue of natural versus artificial hazard).

5. *See* Crest Chimney Cleaning Co. v. Ahi Ezer Congregation, 310 N.Y.S.2d 217 (Civ. Ct. 1970), Ruffin v. Temple Church of God, 749 A.2d 719 (D.C. 2000).

the delay was devastating—both were abused. In the court of public opinion, questions about appropriate "links" and liability limitations seem less relevant than in the other examples: there is a vulnerable plaintiff alleging a volatile claim. The derivative liability question is whether the church bodies are liable for the failings of the director. Was he acting within the course and scope of his employment by the mission board when he offered his advice? Are the actions of the regional director attributable to the national churchwide mission board? In these times the plaintiff will sue everyone and let the defendants (and their insurers!) sort out the answers to these difficult liability questions.[6]

Definitions and Background

In its broadest sense derivative liability is the effort by injured parties to place legal responsibility in an organization for the damage or debt caused by its own employees or agents, or the action of a related but separate organization and/or its employees or agents. Religious communities involve clergy, staff, and volunteers and other members (or those of a related entity). The actions complained of can range from something as simple as failing to wipe a floor of spilled water or pay a bill to something as complex as failing to report child abuse or to assure against securities fraud.

Often the employing or corresponding institutional entity has greater assets than the individual who created the situation. In these circumstances derivative liability is an attempt to shift responsibility to a presumably more solvent entity for these damages or debts. For some, to deny recovery based on immunity or corporate distinctions may seem artificial, unfair, or outdated.[7] In this most basic sense derivative liability encompasses traditional tort policy concepts, both risk-spreading financial and social reform goals. Indeed, social reform and risk-spreading considerations are behind decisions in which one entity must answer for the actions of a related entity's minister, staff, or volunteer. This is more apparent in attempts to force liability on larger national or regional groups affiliated with smaller local groups. The courts presume that if a "superior" body, however defined or connected, can be forced to take responsibility for the local matter, harm to future plaintiffs might be precluded. Thus although this form of liability action has at its root the most basic litigation urge to find a solvent or insured defendant, it also includes an element of social purpose, an attempt to enforce some greater responsibility through the liability system and deter future harm. The dilemma confronting the legal system is how best and most justly to allocate responsibility among the parties, a dilemma explored below in the next section of this chapter.

---

6. *See* Foreign Mission Bd. v. Wade, 409 S.E.2d 144 (Va. 1991).

7. *But see* Plate v. St. Mary's Help of Christians Church, 520 N.W.2d 17 (Minn. Ct. App. 1994). In *Malloy v. Fong*, 232 P.2d 241 (Cal. 1951), the California Supreme Court abandoned charitable immunity, holding a regional Presbyterian Church board responsible for an accident caused by a minister and volunteer. The court, through Justice Traynor, found that nonprofit, even religious, entities should compensate the victims of negligence. Parts of Traynor's opinion reflect notions that charitable immunity and corporate insulation were both unfair if recovery were barred. *See also* McAtee v. St. Paul's Mission, 376 P.2d 823, 825 (Kan. 1962). In some cases, such as *Reid v. Lukens*, No. 56046 (Mich. Ct. App. Sept. 10, 1984) (per curiam), courts are unwilling to allow higher religious bodies to escape liability if the court believes compensation should fairly lie. In others, the doctrine almost resembles strict liability. *See* Doe v. Samaritan Counseling Ctr., 791 P.2d 344 (Alaska 1990).

In the last fifteen years, the novelty of the claims asserted against religious entities has been quite remarkable. And, precisely because religion is constitutionally protected, both those suing and those defending religious institutions have an obligation to determine whether a particular claim can constitutionally be asserted against a particular defendant. A departure from the principles outlined here would raise a serious question as to whether the claim is constitutionally permitted.

While derivative liability may be defended on the grounds just named, religious entities, like their secular counterparts, need the assurance that their "corporate" independence will be respected. Religious entities, to a greater extent than secular entities, rely on the exuberant goodwill and good-faith efforts of volunteers to make their operations run. Occasionally these entities seek to structure their operations as separate civil units to guard against the possibility that another unit (or the whole body) might be made vulnerable by the actions of an individual. Having chosen to plan operations in a particular way following the dictates of the civil law, religious entities should not have to fear that these corporate structures will be imploded or rewritten in litigation. A failure to respect civil corporate limits may be constitutionally suspect.[8]

When the individual actor who causes the damage or creates the debt is an agent or employee (for example, in general terms, a minister or volunteer) of a religious organization, an effort is inevitably made to pass the liability to the religious organization that in the broadest sense employs the individual. In that sense the liability may be shifted to the institutional body. There may also be an attempt to shift the liability to a coordinate or superior ecclesiastical entity. To that extent the term "ascending liability" (as used by commentators)[9] most plainly denotes a hierarchical form of religious organization.[10] Authority and power are presumed to descend through the various layers of an organization to the individual adherent. Obedience is seen as ascending through the organization with each individual adherent or intermediate group presumably acting at the behest of the next higher group in the organization.[11] Ultimately authority is thought to reside in a religious superior or entity at the top of the organizational ladder.

---

8. Such was the case in *Barr v. United Methodist Church*, 153 Cal. Rptr. 322 (Ct. App. 1979), when a California court asserted jurisdiction over the association of entities referred to as the "United Methodist Church" for the obligations created by separately incorporated but affiliated retirement homes. *See contra* N.H. v. Presbyterian Church, 998 P.2d 529 (Okla. 1999). In my view, failing to respect the polity of the denomination and how that polity has allocated the risk (involved in the case) is also beyond the constitutional competence of the secular courts. *See* Mark Chopko, Continuing the Lord's Work and Healing His People, 2004 BYU L. Rev. 1897. *See also* Carl H. Esbeck, The Establishment Clause as a Structural Restraint, 84 Iowa L. Rev. 1 (1998).

9. The term "ascending liability" appears in one reported decision, and that decision, *MacDonald v. Maxwell*, 655 N.E.2d 1249 (Ind. Ct. App. 1995), cites to Gaffney & Sorenson, *supra* note 3, and Chopko, *supra* note 3.

10. Religious entities tend to fall into two dominant types, "hierarchical" or "congregational." Congregational bodies are fairly autonomous, self-governing local entities. They select or elect ministers and conduct their own affairs with respect to doctrine and to worldly affairs with a high degree of independence. Hierarchical bodies are governed through "clerical" superiors, set in authority over others. A form of polity between the two is sometimes called "connectional" or "presbysterial." In that form, local congregations are autonomous, but are affiliated through regional or national groupings with a denominational identity. *See* 1 Bassett, *supra* note 3, § 3.3; Guinn v. Church of Christ, 775 P.2d 766, 771 n.18 (Okla. 1989) (citing other authorities).

11. Here one must distinguish direct liability from derivative liability. Plainly, a religious organization is directly responsible for its own debts and negligence. Derivative liability is the attempt to force a religious group to take responsibility for another person's or entity's conduct as if it were its own. *See supra* note 3.

Thus civil responsibility may follow ecclesial discipline as it moves through the various layers of the organization until it resides in *that entity which has both the juridical power and the civil duty to answer for the actions of individuals or organizations at a lower level.* This is certainly seen in litigation against hierarchical churches. In one case the plaintiff seeking damages for a personal injury sued the individual minister, the local church, the church school (where the injuries occurred), the separate organization that owned the school, the regional ecclesiastical authority, and the national and international bodies that were alleged to be responsible for the affairs of the religious organization.[12] In another case the international organization and those who governed it were alleged to be ultimately responsible for an injury suffered at a local level.[13] It was up to the defendants in those cases to sort out the various layers of civil responsibility.[14]

This principle is also seen in litigation targeting related religious corporate entities and ecclesiastical "coordinates" in congregational or connectional polities. Two of the examples which introduced this chapter concerned claims against not "superior" but "coordinate" religious organizations for the actions of separate civil (even secular-appearing) corporations. Responsibility may shift from one corporate entity to another even when they are in a more "horizontal" relationship than entities in a hierarchical polity. Indeed the litigation effort to shift responsibility from one level to another in a congregational body has all the trappings of litigation involving layers of a hierarchical body[15] and, for this reason, appears with cases in which liability "ascends" or "descends" under the heading "derivative liability."

This litigation effort to transfer responsibility is also seen in attempts to shift liability to the governing religious organization when its agents or employees act in concert with religious belief or doctrine. In some denominations ecclesial discipline is exercised by public criticism of the offending conduct from the pulpit. Not surprisingly, this form of discipline has resulted in defamation actions. The defendants in these cases are not just those who make pronouncements in the name of the religious group, but the group itself.[16] After all, those who minister are supposed to be acting in the name of and in complete accord with denominational doctrine. This too is a way in which liability may be seen to shift.

---

12. *See* Spann v. Thorne, No. J87-0114(b) (S.D. Miss. filed Mar. 1987). The literature abounds with other examples in other denominations. *E.g.*, Konkle v. Henson, 672 N.E.2d 450 (Ind. Ct. App. 1996); Houston v. Mile High Adventist Academy, 846 F. Supp. 1449 (D. Colo. 1994) (naming regional and national entities as codefendants in both cases).

13. *See* English v. Thorne, 676 F. Supp. 761 (S.D. Miss. 1987) (dismissing for lack of subject matter jurisdiction a claim that Vatican officials should answer for alleged abuse by a local priest); *see also* Package v. Holy See, No. 86-C-222 (N.H. Super. Ct. Nov. 30, 1988) (Vatican officials not responsible for hazard created by member of monastic community).

14. As noted in note 13, *English* was dismissed. The other case was settled (and voluntarily dismissed even though not all the defendants were involved in the settlement). Rewriting or ignoring ecclesial rules by a court raises constitutional questions.

15. *See* Crest Chimney Cleaning Co. v. Ahi Ezer Congregation, 310 N.Y.S.2d 217 (Civ. Ct. 1970).

16. In *Guinn v. Church of Christ*, 775 P.2d 766, 769 (Okla. 1989), discussed below, the parties stipulated that the church's liability was entirely dependent on the actions of individual ministers acting in accord with church discipline. *See also* Hadnot v. Shaw, 826 P.2d 978 (Okla. 1992). An attempt to punish a religious entity because of its doctrine, like an attempt to premise liability on an alleged religious duty, is constitutionally barred. *E.g.*, Williams v. Gleason, 26 S.W.3d 54 (Tx. Ct. App. 2000); Roman Catholic Bishop of San Diego v. Superior Court, 15 Cal. Rptr. 2d 399 (Cal. Ct. App. 1996).

Derivative liability as it is defined here is neither limiting nor limited.[17] It applies in diverse factual settings involving all forms of religious polity. Thus even though the principles discussed above are illustrated in religious denominations of every corporate stripe and are most easily illustrated in tort cases, the attempt to shift responsibility to another layer in a religious organization is seen in a wide range of cases, such as those involving the contracts or debts of an organization's agents or employees, the fraud or intentional misconduct (even crimes) committed by agents or employees, and, as illustrated immediately above, the actions of ministers in full accord with religious doctrine. Furthermore, although the doctrine is most easily illustrated by reference to incorporated religious bodies following the various ecclesial links in a civil corporate chain, it is also seen in efforts to hold unincorporated religious associations—for the most part congregational churches or synagogues—responsible for the conduct of a member, staff or cleric, or agent. Indeed changes in the statutory treatment of unincorporated associations presently make it easier for these entities to sue or be sued in their own name. Therefore it is now more possible for plaintiffs to have an institutional defendant statutorily able to take responsibility for the actions of individuals alleged to have acted in its name.[18]

Finally, by way of understanding the background of the problem which is discussed in this chapter, there is a certain temptation to think of liability shifting as a recent phenomenon. Indeed research confirms that most of the reported litigation against religious organizations has occurred in the last twenty years. However, the idea that larger, coordinate, or superior religious entities should be forced to take responsibility for the actions of their agents, employees, or coordinate/subordinate religious entities has more distant roots. All of the basic cases presented in today's environment have been litigated before.

In the area of tort law, for example, an effort was made in 1914 to hold the bishop of a Catholic diocese responsible for a priest's sexual assault upon a female parishioner. It was alleged that the bishop knew of the priest's unfitness for service and his immoral "proclivities." In rejecting the claim, the Supreme Judicial Court of Massachusetts found that the sexual assault committed by the priest was "entirely outside the scope of his alleged agency or of his duties: it was a crime committed of his own free will, the result of his own volition, for which no one but himself was responsible."[19] Similarly, other courts reviewing such cases have distinguished between ecclesiastical and civil responsibilities for liability purposes. While religious superiors certainly were found to have had ecclesiastical charge of the conduct of an organization's affairs, courts often found that these superiors had no direct control over their organizations' temporal affairs and thus could not be liable in damages.[20] The same results are seen in cases involving the contractual affairs of religious entities. For example, courts have rejected the idea that the pastor of a church is, in regard to the financial affairs of the church, the

---

17. There are even efforts to pierce the corporate veil to find adequate compensation in particular cases. *See* Edward M. Gaffney, Jr., National Inst. on Tort & Religion, Piercing the Veil of Religious Organizations (1990) (noting this form of litigation as example of derivative liability).

18. *See* Cox v. Thee Evergreen Church, 836 S.W.2d 167, 173 (Tex. 1992); Crocker v. Barr, 409 S.E.2d 368, 371 (S.C. 1991). Both cases note state statutory changes to allow litigation by or against unincorporated associations, among other things, to remove a bar to member lawsuits (known as the doctrine of imputed negligence).

19. *Compare* Carini v. Beaven, 106 N.E. 589, 589 (Mass. 1914), *with* Rita M. v. Roman Catholic Archbishop, 232 Cal. Rptr. 685 (Ct. App. 1986).

20. *Compare* Magnuson v. O'Dea, 135 P. 640 (Wash. 1913), *with* Nye v. Kemp, 646 N.E.2d 262 (Ohio Ct. App. 1994); White v. Blackburn, 787 P.2d 1315 (Utah Ct. App. 1990).

agent of his bishop, in the absence of express authority to engage in the transaction or the bishop's ratification.[21] Where there is such ratification, the church would be estopped to resist liability for the actions of its treasurer in making contracts.[22]

Perhaps the most significant aspect of this legal environment was the decision to hold religious corporations formed to conduct the temporal affairs of an entity responsible for the consequences of those actions. Such bodies could not as easily claim they were immune from liability for their debts on the grounds that they were charities.[23] In *Roman Catholic Archbishop v. Industrial Accident Commission*,[24] the Supreme Court of California held that the "Archbishop of San Francisco," a corporation sole, was responsible for the liabilities created by employment contracts of its pastors. In that case a worker hired by a pastor of a parish to do repair work in a church was injured. The worker claimed compensation against the "employer," the corporation sole archdiocese, not the parish or pastor. The archbishop claimed exemption from the law as a religious entity and distinguished the repair work on a church from employment—and lost. California allowed the formation of a corporation sole so that religious organizations could conduct civil business.[25] The temporal affairs of the religious community, including the maintenance and repair of property, were conducted under the auspices of this corporation. Having chosen to engage in such business through a civil entity, the religious organization could not claim exemption from the secular regulation that would accompany such a business and form.[26]

If one operates in the secular world, one assumes secular responsibilities (tempered however by the constitutional rights of religious institutions).[27] As more and more religious organizations choose a corporate civil form in which to conduct their missions, whether in a hierarchical polity[28] or in a congregational polity,[29] a church that sees fit to become incorporated is obliged to conduct its business activities in compliance with and under the supervision of those laws.[30]

---

21. *Compare* Leahy v. Williams, 6 N.E. 78 (Mass. 1886), *with* Eastern Renovating Corp. v. Roman Catholic Bishop, 554 F.2d 4 (1st Cir. 1977).

22. *Compare* Martin v. St. Aloysius Church, 95 A. 768 (R.I. 1915), *with* Crest Chimney Cleaning Co. v. Ali Ezer Congregation, 310 N.Y.S.2d 217 (Civ. Ct. 1970).

23. By contrast, at one time, charitable immunity provided a blanket exemption for religious and other charities from tort liability for negligence of agents. In some few states, vestiges of the doctrine remain. *See* Rupp v. Brookdale Baptist Church, 577 A.2d 188 (N.J. Super. Ct. App. Div. 1990); *see also* discussion *infra* note 190. *Cf. Malloy* and other cases cited *supra* note 7.

24. 230 P. 1 (Cal. 1924). Cf. EEOC v. Saint Francis Xavier School, 77 F. Supp.2d 71 (D.D.C. 1999) (parish, part of corporation sole, lacks legal capacity to be sued).

25. As explained elsewhere in this volume, a corporation sole is a creature of state statute, allowing a civil corporation to have only one (or a sole) member.

26. Having chosen to incorporate, and therefore obtain the benefits for civil incorporation, the corporation could not abandon the detriments, including liability for the actions of its agents. The court expressly rejected the idea that the pastor was not the agent of the corporation sole and that therefore the corporation was not the proper party defendant. The same result may be seen in tort litigation. *See* Macedonia Baptist Church v. Gibson, 833 S.W.2d 557, 559 (Tex. App. 1992, writ denied).

27. *See* Patty Gerstenblith, "Associational Structures of Religious Organizations," in this volume; *see also* Guinn v. Church of Christ, 775 P.2d at 776, 771 n.18 (Okla. 1989) (summarizes polities of different churches or denominations); Looney v. Community Bible Holiness Church, 405 S.E.2d 811, 812 (N.C. Ct. App. 1991).

28. *See Roman Catholic Archbishop*, 230 P. 1.

29. Bangor Spiritualist Church, Inc. v. Littlefield, 330 A.2d 793 (Me. 1975).

30. Unincorporated associations are not immune either, except in certain circumstances. *See infra* notes 37–39.

Principles Governing the Imposition of Responsibility

From the study of different church organization models, whether incorporated or unincorporated, hierarchical or congregational, and from the legal opinions governing liability, certain principles emerge from a divergent and complex body of law. Cutting across polities and corporate forms and governing the imposition of responsibility (in the broadest sense), these principles describe the circumstances under which liability may be shifted. Although the law does not always provide clarity, three general lines of inquiry appear. Liability will not be imposed without an affirmative finding that the defendant religious organization has exercised at least one of the following levels of responsibility over the matter being litigated.

These three principles for the imposition of responsibility are:

Statutory or Corporate Responsibility: the civil organizing or operational documents expressly place responsibility for the matter disputed in the superior or coordinate group;

Denominational Responsibility: the ecclesial discipline of the body expressly places responsibility in, or denies it to, a particular group within the body; and

Situational Responsibility: notwithstanding the above principles, a particular group has specifically involved itself in the underlying dispute or transaction giving rise to the litigation.

Whether liability is ultimately proven such that the organization must pay for the damage is a question which goes to the merits of a given case. Given the high incidence of settlement, merely the thought of allowing the lawsuit to proceed may cause an organization to make the prudential judgment to resolve a claim rather than either risk an adverse decision or expend its resources in a defense. Thus consideration of these principles under which a claim for derivative liability may be stated is very important for the ultimate resolution of a liability claim. Each of these areas will be dealt with in turn.

Statutory or corporate responsibility

Through its civil (as opposed to ecclesial) governing documents, articles of incorporation or bylaws, policy or personnel manuals, or similar documents, a targeted coordinate or superior body may be held to answer for claims if it has reserved to itself the authority over the matter in contention. Often this question is resolved under state statutory or common law. As was noted above, in *Roman Catholic Archbishop* a responsibility of the corporation sole was to hold real property of the religious body. In the opinion of the California Supreme Court, this responsibility included the necessary power to make arrangements for its maintenance and repair, such that the action of an individual pastor was attributable to the corporation. The corporation was estopped from denying its ultimate responsibility for such matters. The court viewed its holding as an unremarkable application of the California law authorizing religious corporations.[31]

---

31. *See Roman Catholic Archbishop*, 230 P. 1.

Conversely, where there is no legal basis to impute the matter in dispute to the power and authority of the corporation, the corporation may be dismissed from an action. For example, in an action which sought damages for a sexual assault, a corporation sole, organized under the laws of Rhode Island, was dismissed. Plaintiffs had contended that the bishop conducted all priestly supervision through the corporation sole and therefore the corporation sole (which also presumably held the assets) should be responsible for the control and direction of the negligent priest.[32] The bishop responded that under the 1900 legislation that allowed the creation of a corporation sole, the legislature provided that the corporation sole had no ability to control or supervise the functioning of the individual priests. Rather, as a creature of state law, the corporation sole had specifically limited powers relating to the purchase, holding, and conveyance of property for religious purposes. The court agreed.[33] Because of the separate and distinct concept of the corporation sole and the limitations that were found in both the governing documents and the state law, the court dismissed the corporation sole from this litigation.[34] Similarly, where the corporate powers limit the individual authority of agents and it can be shown that those who contract with individual agents are aware of the civil limitations of those with whom they deal, the corporate defendant may not be responsible.[35]

Although more easily illustrated by reference to large hierarchical religious bodies organized along corporate lines, the same result is seen in litigation involving single congregations. For example, in a case arising in congregational polity, a court rejected a writ of execution against real property held by a person, not as an individual, but in his capacity as "presiding apostle" of a church, a corporation sole. The appellate court indicated that the assets of the corporation sole are not the personal assets of its titular head, and therefore could not be used to satisfy personal debts.[36] Even in these polities the courts distinguish between personal/ecclesial and civil/corporate powers.

---

32. *See* Doe v. O'Connell, P.C., No. 86-0077, slip op. (R.I. 1990).

33. *See id.* at 3. To the same effect is *Plate v. St. Mary's Help of Christians Church*, 520 N.W.2d 17 (Minn. Ct. App. 1994). In that case, the court affirmed dismissal of a diocesan corporation from a wrongful death case holding that the action complained of was vested by corporate form in a separate entity, the local parish church. *See id.* at 20–21. In the secular world, related but separate entities rely on separate incorporation to limit liability, and courts do not look behind them except for compelling and narrowly restricted reasons. *E.g.*, Tatum v. Everhart, 954 F. Supp. 225 (D. Kan. 1997) (mere membership in United Way insufficient to create single employer for Title VII liability purposes). The same result should occur in the case of religious entities; Black v. Cardinal McCloskey Children and Family Services, No. 17865-96 (N.Y. Sup. Ct. May 11, 2000) (legally related but separate entity not liable for other's tort).

34. The court relied on cases from other jurisdictions reaching the same conclusion on the other facts in both the tort and the contract area. *See* Roman Catholic Archbishop v. Superior Court, 93 Cal. Rptr. 338, 341–42 (Ct. App. 1971) (contract for purchase of Saint Bernard dog with Swiss Abbey not enforceable against archbishop of San Francisco).

Wood v. Benedictine Soc'y, 530 So. 2d 801 (Ala. 1988), is to the same effect. In that case, the plaintiff was injured by a priest who trespassed upon an abortion clinic. She sued the priest, the bishop of the diocese, the abbot (as the religious superior of the priest), and the clerical order to which the priest belonged. The court indicated that the nature of control over the defendant exercised by the individual defendants was ecclesial and not civil. The powers of the corporate defendant indeed were related to business, not ecclesiastical duties. Citing the relevant provisions of the Alabama Code, section 10-4-4, the court found that none of the powers granted to a corporation sole included oversight of the actions of the individual priest such as to create a legal duty on the part of the corporation sole to be responsible for the behavior.

35. *See* Eastern Renovating Corp. v. Roman Catholic Bishop, 554 F.2d 4 (1st Cir. 1977); *see also* Apostolic Revival Tabernacle v. Charles J. Febel, Inc., 266 N.E.2d 545 (Ill. App. Ct. 1970).

36. *See* County of San Luis Obispo v. Ashurst, 194 Cal. Rptr. 5 (Ct. App. 1983); Mannix v. Purcel, 46 Ohio St. 102 (1888).

In unincorporated associations the courts distinguish between lawsuits brought by members and those brought by nonmembers. Suits involving claims of nonmembers proceed like any other litigation, in the absence of immunity statutes or doctrines. Yet when a member of an unincorporated church sues the church for injury arising out of the carelessness of some other member of the community, it is sometimes held that the member has no standing to recover. It is as if the member is suing himself.[37] However, in some states the statutes allowing an unincorporated association to sue and be sued in its own name are held to sever the responsibility of the association from that of its individual members and allow the maintenance of an action within certain limits, sometimes tied to insurance.[38] In these cases the association may be responsible even to its own members for such conduct, whether or not it is has ratified the conduct or the contract. Still, such rights of actions are circumscribed. Under such statutes the question is whether the actions are fairly attributable to the association such that the association should be held to respond to hazards or contracts created by individual members in the name of the association.[39] Thus the defense may increasingly be limited to smaller entities or particular factual circumstances.

Denominational responsibility

Denominational responsibility has as its starting point whether, in ecclesial documents or expressions of authority, the coordinate or superior body has reserved authority over the matter in dispute to itself. In other words, does the entity reserve to itself the authority to supervise or resolve the matter in dispute? Ecclesiastical control is not always identical to civil control, meaning that the control exercised by the related religious entity rests on the consent or adherence of the other person or entity to religious doctrine. Although the judicial development of this principle involves courts in the close scrutiny of discipline of the body itself, often this scrutiny is invited by the religious entity which has pleaded its governing ecclesial documents as a means to avoid ultimate responsibility for the matter in dispute.

Illustrating this principle is *Eckler v. General Council of Assemblies of God*.[40] In this case a Texas court of appeals ruled that regional and national church bodies were not liable to answer in tort for damages done by a teacher at a school operated by a local

---

37. This common law rule is the "doctrine of imputed negligence." In a lawsuit by an association member against the entity, the member is presumed to be suing himself (along with any other member). The negligence of one member is "imputed" to all. *See* Zehner v. Wilkinson Mem'l United Methodist Church, 581 A.2d 1388, 1389 (Pa. Super. Ct. 1990); Calvary Baptist Church v. Joseph, 522 N.E.2d 371 (Ind. 1988); *see also* Cox v. Thee Evergreen Church, 804 S.W.2d 190 (Tex. App. 1991), *rev'd*, 836 S.W.2d 167 (Tex. 1992). The Indiana Supreme Court has overruled the result in *Joseph* in *Hanson v. St. Luke's United Methodist Church*, 704 N.E.2d 1020 (Ind. 1998).

38. *See Cox*, 836 S.W.2d at 172; Crocker v. Barr, 409 S.E.2d 368 (S.C. 1991); Joseph v. Calvary Baptist Church, 500 N.E.2d 250 (Ind. Ct. App. 1986), *rev'd*, 522 N.E.2d 371 (Ind. 1988). The Indiana Supreme Court has implicitly adopted the rationale of the intermediate appellate court in overruling its opinion in *Joseph* and allowing unincorporated associations to be sued in their own names. *See Hanson*, 704 N.E.2d 1020.

39. Other states make a judicial exception for larger associations (such as unions, and one can imagine larger churches) whose identity is separate from the individual members in the eyes of the public. *E.g.*, Marshall v. International Longshoremen's and Warehousemen's Union, 371 P.2d 987 (Cal. 1962). *But see* White v. Cox, 95 Cal. Rptr. 259 (Ct. App. 1971) (announcing California rule allowing litigation).

40. 784 S.W.2d 935 (Tex. App. 1990, writ denied).

church affiliated with the denomination. No relationship existed between the local church and the denomination's General Council under the church's organizational structure sufficient to warrant the imposition of liability.[41] The constitution and bylaws of the denomination itself gave a District Council (an intermediate structure) the responsibility for the selection and endorsement of prospective ministers. Those documents also gave the authority to investigate, file charges, and conduct hearings on alleged allegations of misconduct to the District Council. The court held that "the constitution and bylaws...show the complete absence of supervisory control, which, in turn, negates a legal relationship, all as alleged in the motion."[42] Because each individual local church was self-governing, the General Council of the Assemblies of God had no civil duty, based on ecclesial right, to supervise or control their internal affairs. Even though the General Council would ordain and license ministers, their actual supervision would be in the hands of local churches or, at most, a District Council. Indeed, when a complaint is made about ministerial misconduct, the complaint is referred to the appropriate District Council rather than the General Council for investigation and disciplinary action.[43] Liability for failure to take disciplinary actions creating a risk of future misconduct would follow the denomination's decision to vest such responsibility in a particular entity, and not be spread throughout the denomination generally or its national institution.[44]

Conversely, where polities do place the denominational responsibility or supervision in the hands of a larger regional or other governing body, liability may attach to this body. For example, in *Olson v. Magnuson* the Evangelical Covenant Church of America, an Illinois corporation, was named as a defendant in a complaint for its alleged failure to supervise adequately one of its ministers serving at an affiliated church in Minnesota.[45] The national church body unsuccessfully moved to dismiss the case for lack of personal jurisdiction. On appeal the appellate court noted that the bylaws of the national church specifically provided for the formation of a "board of ministry" to supervise the conduct of, license, investigate, and discipline its ministers. Because the national church had held itself responsible for investigating claims of impropriety lodged against local church ministers and administering any discipline, the court found, from the church's own rules and regulations, that the national church body should be held to answer for the claimed misconduct.[46] Although particular constitutional considerations

---

41. By contrast, the parish in question in *Roman Catholic Archbishop v. Industrial Accident Comm'n*, 230 P.2d 1 (Cal. 1924) was part of the corporation sole. *See id.* at 8.

42. *Eckler*, 784 S.W.2d at 937; *see also* Doe v. Cunningham, 30 F.3d 879, 884 (7th Cir. 1994) (undisputed facts show clergy supervision vested in church body not named in litigation).

43. *See Eckler*, 784 S.W.2d at 938.

44. *See* Dewaard v. United Methodist Church, 793 So.2d 1038 (Fla. Dist. Ct. App. 2001) (regional body liable for supervision, local church dismissed); Evan F. v. Hughson United Methodist Church, 10 Cal. Rptr. 2d 748, 758 (Ct. App. 1992) (local body which possesses hiring authority liable for misconduct, not regional body).

45. *See* Olson v. Magnuson, 457 N.W.2d 394 (Minn. Ct. App. 1990). In one of six cases against the church for the misconduct of Rev. Magnuson, a jury returned a verdict in excess of $1 million, $200,000 against Magnuson and nearly $900,000 against the local church. The reports do not say what occurred with respect to the national body. *See* Nat'l L.J., June 14, 1993, at 6.

46. *See Olson*, 457 N.W.2d at 397. The court also concluded, however (in implicit accord with *Eckler*, 784 S.W.2d at 937) that mere membership in a national religious organization does not, by itself, confer jurisdiction over that national group to answer for a tort committed in a local church. *See id.*; *see also* Glover v. Boy Scouts of America, 923 P.2d 1383, 1387–88 (Utah 1996). Something more than a potential interest or authority must be shown. *See* Nye v. Kemp, 646 N.E.2d 262, 264–65 (Ohio Ct. App. 1994). Similarly, ecclesiastical supervisory authority can have civil law con-

need to be evaluated in these circumstances,[47] generally the religious entity itself has invited a court to consider its governing documents to avoid responsibility.

The best historical example of the assertion of denominational responsibility in the absence of some express statutory or corporate power is *Malloy v. Fong*.[48] In this case the California Supreme Court held a Presbyterian Church regional governing body in San Francisco responsible for the negligence of local clergy and volunteers in an auto accident in Los Angeles because of the ecclesiastical supervision directly exercised over particular churches. During a period of rapid growth in southern California, the Presbyterian Church regional body established a series of mission churches. The governing documents of the denomination suggested a higher degree of denominational supervision over a mission church than over an established congregation. In the name of the denomination, the regional body claimed additional power to supervise the activities of the mission church and those who administered it. The court found the church's status as a mission church attested "strongly to its embryonic character and indicate[d] that there was a close working relationship between the Church and the Presbytery."[49] The court easily reached a conclusion that denominational documents provided a basis for the assertion of responsibility on the regional body on the facts as presented. Its conclusion did not apply to a fully operational Presbyterian church, generally a separately incorporated entity with local autonomy.[50] Nonetheless, the court found that if (as here) the ecclesial authority assumed a higher degree of supervisory control, even for strictly religious reasons, the imposition of liability was fair. The religious regional body was more than just the title holder; it was intimately involved in the hiring, firing, and supervision of persons who caused the accident. It assumed the duty because of the ecclesial character of the community, not for some perceived inadequacy of personnel or to achieve some civil or secular advantage. Rejecting an argument for immunity,[51] the court could find no reason why the ordinary principles of *respondeat superior* (discussed below)[52] should not apply. Because of the close religious ties between the supervising and inferior religious organizations, liability was fairly imposed.

---

sequences when it is expressly reserved. In *Does v. CompCare, Inc.*, 763 P.2d 1237, 1241–44 (Wash. Ct. App. 1988), a Catholic bishop in Louisiana was held answerable to a claim for damages in Washington, because he continued to exercise ecclesial discipline over a suspended priest who was then in residence in Washington. The continued denominational relationship between the bishop and the priest provided sufficient links such that jurisdiction could be fairly asserted. *See also* Johnston v. United Presbyterian Church in United States, 431 N.E.2d 1275 (Ill. App. Ct. 1981).

47. The possibility of scrutiny of internal matters always raises the prospect of unconstitutional entanglement developed by the Supreme Court in *Serbian Eastern Orthodox Church v. Milivojewich*, 426 U.S. 696 (1976). It would also invite a court to scrutinize standards, policies, and actions (or the lack thereof) in violation of free exercise rights. *See* Hadnot v. Shaw, 826 P.2d 978, 987–88 (Okla. 1992) (free exercise also protects church autonomy in tort litigation). For this reason, courts usually determine polity-dependent questions if they can be answered without intrusion. *See* Werling v. Grace Evangelical Lutheran Church, 487 N.E.2d 990 (Ill. App. Ct. 1985). Courts routinely forbid litigation over internal religious matters, and bar the civil enforcement of religious duties. *See* Franco v. Church of Jesus Christ of Latter-day Saints, 21 P.3d 198 (Utah 2001); Phillips v. Marist Soc'y, 80 F.3d 274 (8th Cir. 1996).

48. 232 P.2d 241 (Cal. 1951).

49. *Id.* at 248. Its property was held in the name of the regional group which also hired, fired, and supervised ministers.

50. *See id.* at 248–49. "When" it might be ready to operate as a stand-alone Presbyterian church was, in a sense, a pastoral decision with civil law consequences, not vice versa. The court did not need to resolve the question in that case. In other situations, it would not have been unusual for it to defer to the religious bodies' assertions of authority.

51. *See id.* at 246–47.

52. *See infra* text accompanying note 64.

As is shown in *Malloy v. Fong*, the mere potential to exercise ecclesial discipline is not always sufficient to impose liability. The governing body must either assert or reserve authority over the particular matter in question. For example, to assert liability against a church for a deliberate personal injury committed by a minister, it is not enough that the church has exercised general ecclesial discipline or offered some general statements of concern. There must be some connection between the particular expression of ecclesial discipline and the particular matter in dispute.[53] The mere right to control conduct generally for ecclesiastical purposes does not make a religious body civilly responsible for all of the actions of any person related to it. As one court explained: "Mere potential for ecclesiastical control by the defendant over the actions of individual[s] by operation of ecclesiastical law was not sufficient to establish a civil relationship and therefore impute liability to the defendant."[54] Should ecclesiastical direction be manifest in the actions of the individual, there is little doubt under the principles established above that a higher ecclesial body would at least be held to answer in such a case in order to discern whether in fact it was negligent.

Situational responsibility

The third principle for the imposition of responsibility shows that liability may be asserted even in the absence of secular statutory or corporate responsibility over the matter in question, and in the absence of denominational authority to resolve the matter being litigated. The actual conduct of an organization can cause it to become involved situationally in the matter in review. For example, in *Eckler v. General Council of Assemblies of God*,[55] the court scrutinized the record to ascertain whether, notwithstanding the limitations in the governing documents, the General Council had involved itself in the situation sufficiently so as to be fairly subject to suit. In this case the court found no record that the General Council even knew that a complaint had been made against the local minister. The record also established, without dispute, that had the General Council become aware of such a complaint made against the local minister, the matter would have been referred to the District Council for resolution.[56] Thus the case implies

---

53. *See Olson*, 457 N.W.2d at 397. In *Wood v. Benedictine Soc'y*, 530 So. 2d 801 (Ala. 1988), for example, it was undisputed that the priest who entered the abortion clinic and committed the damage was religiously motivated and subject to ecclesial discipline. There had to be a connection between the trespass and religious action sanctioned by ecclesial superiors. *See* Nye v. Kemp, 646 N.E.2d 262, 265 (Ohio Ct. App. 1994). Absent some form of ecclesial "ratification," no liability is legitimate. *Cf.* House of God v. White, 792 So.2d 491 (Fla. Dist. Ct. App. 2001); Guinn v. Church of Christ, 775 P.2d 766 (Okla. 1989).

54. Package v. Holy See, No. 86-C-222 (N.H. Super. Ct. Nov. 30, 1988). In fact, the court found that notwithstanding ecclesiastical law, the religious body really had "little opportunity to control their actions so as to prevent harm to others." In that case, plaintiffs sued the international governing body for Catholics to compensate them for an automobile accident caused by the action of one individual monk. *Accord* N.H. v. Presbyterian Church, 998 P.2d 529 (Okla. 1999); M.L. v. Civil Air Patrol, 806 F. Supp. 845, 847 (E.D. Mo. 1992) (national entity not responsible for personnel decision at local level); *see* Plate v. St. Mary's Help of Christians Church, 520 N.W.2d 17 (Minn. Ct. App. 1994). *But see* Shirkey v. Eastwind Community Dev. Corp., 941 F. Supp. 567, 573–74 (D. Md. 1996) (Title VI claim stated against national religious entity that set the allegedly discriminatory standard being implemented by local agency).

55. 784 S.W.2d 935 (Tex. App. 1990, writ denied); *see* discussion *supra* notes 42–43.

56. *See id.* at 938; *see also* Doe v. New London Association of the United Church of Christ, 2001 WL 83883 (Conn. Super. Ct. 2001); Konkle v. Henson, 672 N.E.2d 450, 461 (Ind. Ct. App. 1996); Evan F. v. Hughson United Methodist Church, 10 Cal. Rptr. 2d 748 (Ct. App. 1992).

situational responsibility as a separate governing principle for the assertion of the derivative liability—courts specifically determine whether a coordinate or superior body has
so insinuated itself in an action that it can rightly be held in the given case as a defendant and therefore risk ultimate liability.

In contract cases the same principle applies. Courts determine whether the evidence
indicates that, notwithstanding separate corporate or ecclesial relationships, a religious
organization has so involved itself in operations of a related entity and the actions of its
employees that it should be estopped from denying its responsibility to pay debts created by "its" agent.[57] If the religious organization has delegated substantial authority to
an agent and in fact relied on the actions of the agent in the conduct of its affairs, it
cannot then deny responsibility based on some technical reading of its corporate documents. In unincorporated entities, members seeking relief against their own religious
body may avoid the operation of the bar to litigation on a showing that the particular
agent had the authority to enter into the transaction or that the association ratified the
conduct causing the injury.[58]

On the other hand, even where an organization has insinuated itself into a situation,
its liability is dependent on the liability of its agents. For example, where a religious organization has engaged itself in the placement of children for foster care and ultimate adoption, its liability for damages for injuries arising out of these placements derives from the
actions of the individuals with whom children were placed. In *LDS Social Service Corp. v.
Richins* the Georgia Court of Appeals held that the religious corporation was not liable, as
a matter of law, where no liability had been found in the actions of the foster parents who
had oversight of the child when the child was injured.[59] This principle should be understood as a rule of caution. When no statutory or denominational basis on which liability
may fairly shift otherwise exists, a court may nonetheless seek just results in particular
cases by scrutinizing the underlying transaction for actual involvement, not in the general
subject matter, but in the specific situation that is the subject of the complaint.

The above liability principles—statutory/corporate responsibility, denominational
responsibility, and situational responsibility—are not mutually exclusive. Each functions in the alternative, though an affirmative answer on any one level of inquiry can be
enough to hold a defendant in a case. As illustrated above, these principles cut across
denominational, corporate, organizational, and polity lines. Illustrations of how these
principles apply in given situations will be found in the next two sections.

Particular Areas of Organizational Liability

From a discussion of the principles that govern particular cases to a review of the cases
themselves, this section illustrates the differences apparent in denominational settings, especially differences between incorporated and unincorporated religious entities. The
analysis will consider first the responsibility of religious organizations for torts of individ-

---

57. *See* Crest Chimney Cleaning Co. v. Ahi Ezer Congregation, 310 N.Y.S.2d 217 (Civ. Ct. 1970).
58. *See* Flagg v. Nichols, 115 N.Y.S.2d 7 (Sup. Ct. 1952), *aff'd*, 120 N.Y.S.2d 917 (App. Div.
1953), *rev'd on other grounds*, 120 N.E.2d 513 (N.Y. 1954).
59. *See* LDS Soc. Serv. Corp. v. Richins, No. A 89 AO 382, slip op. (Ga. Ct. App. Apr. 28, 1989).
See also Osborne v. Payne, 31 S.W.3d 911 (Ky. 2000).

ual ministers, employees, or volunteers; next the contracts or indebtedness created by particular persons or related organizations; and then several other theories of liability, including actions undertaken in complete conformance to religious doctrine. One important note: here one must again distinguish between classes of claims. Plainly churches can be sued because of their *own* negligence or for their *own* contracts. This discussion does not concern such cases. Rather, it addresses *only* derivative or vicarious liability or instances where the conduct that causes an injury is being *attributed* to the organization.[60]

Torts[61]

Any form of personal injury claim is now generally actionable against an incorporated religious organization whether hierarchical or congregational in polity.[62] Although some limitations still apply when an unincorporated entity is involved *and* the plaintiff is a member of the organization, even these barriers are starting to fall.[63] The more common forms of injury claims filed against religious organizations are explained in this section. Under the doctrine of *respondeat superior* an employer or master is liable for the torts committed by employees or agents within the scope of their duties. For liability to shift (in those cases not involving direct negligence), the plaintiff must prove both aspects of a two-part test. The person who committed the tort must be found to be the agent, employee, or servant in a relationship with the religious organization. Even if a relationship can be established, without negligence in the actor,[64] no derivative organizational responsibility can be placed. Second, the activity in question must be determined to be within the scope of duties the person was to perform, or a foreseeable consequence of that person's normal activities in the task. As liability is asserted to higher or coordinate bodies, the principles articulated in the above section are employed. Torts are claimed for actions which are sometimes contrary to religious doctrine,[65] sometimes in accord with religious doctrine,[66] and sometimes on which religious doctrine has no bearing.[67]

Accident cases

Whether the cases involve vehicular mishaps,[68] injuries on church premises,[69] injuries to attendees at church functions,[70] or any other kind of accident, all cases involve the same set of principles. For liability to shift in these circumstances, one must find negli-

---

60. *See* J. v. Victory Tabernacle Baptist Church, 372 S.E.2d 391, 394 (Va. 1988); *see also supra* note 11.

61. A thorough review of tort law generally and its impact on religious communities is found in Esbeck, *supra* note 3.

62. *See* 2 Bassett, *supra* note 3, ch. 8; Hammar, *supra* note 3, ch. 12 § A. Of course, a few states allow limited charitable immunity. *See infra* note 190.

63. Perhaps the best example is the Texas Supreme Court's reversal of the intermediate court's dismissal (on imputed negligence grounds) in *Cox v. Thee Evergreen Church*, 804 S.W.2d 190 (Tex. App. 1991), *rev'd*, 836 S.W.2d 167 (Tex. 1992).

64. *See LDS Soc. Serv.*, No. A 89 AO 382, slip op. *Schieffer v. Catholic Archdiocese*, 508 N.W.2d 907, 913 (Neb. 1993), finds no "direct" negligence in a corporate defendant without negligence on the part of the individual cleric.

65. *See* Marco C. v. Catholic Bishop, No. 5 Civ. No. F3610 (Cal. Ct. App. Mar. 1985) (sexual assault).

66. *See* Paul v. Watchtower Bible & Tract Soc'y, 819 F.2d 875 (9th Cir. 1987) (shunning).

67. *See* Ambrosio v. Price, 495 F. Supp. 381 (D. Neb. 1979) (automobile accident).

68. *See id.*

69. *See* Bennett v. Gitzen, 484 P.2d 811 (Colo. Ct. App. 1971).

70. *See* Prentiss v. Evergreen Presbyterian Church, 644 So. 2d 475 (Ala. 1994).

gence on the part of some person "associated" with the religious group and then satisfy the two-part test—agency or employment and scope of duty.

Agent or employee

The question of who is an agent or employee of an organization is simple when the person who causes an accident is a staff member and the incident occurs within the confines of the religious enterprise. For example, a church may be liable for an accident caused by an employee or agent that it dispatched to purchase supplies in a church vehicle. Similarly, a church may be liable when its custodian fails to react to a hazardous condition in a building that results in harm to an individual.[71] These cases turn on a policy determination that the employer, even if it is a religious organization, has not only the opportunity but also the duty to insist that the allegedly hazardous conditions in question are properly and promptly addressed.[72]

The decision-making process can become more problematic in particular circumstances when volunteers are engaged in the actions that cause an injury.[73] In *Folwell v. Bernard*[74] a Florida appellate court rejected the imposition of liability on a parent church which did not exercise any control over the everyday secular affairs of a subordinate church. At the pastor's request, a vestryman was performing assigned, but certainly volunteer, gardening work for his church community. In so doing, he caused an injury to his own child, who was struck by a stone thrown by a lawn mower used in this task. The jury concluded that both the volunteer and the local church were agents of the Central Florida Diocese of the Episcopal Church, and the negligence of both the volunteer and the local church could thus be attributed to the Central Diocese. The jury returned a verdict in the amount of $676,000.[75] The court of appeals reversed, holding that the diocesan church, through its denominational documents and civil statutes, exercised neither the measure of dominance nor control over the local church to make tenable the assertion of an agency relationship.

The control between the diocese and the local church was ecclesial, not secular.[76] The temporal affairs including maintenance of property were, at best, in the hands of the local church, which alone would have to respond to the alleged negligence of one of its agents. There being no denominational responsibility, as discussed above, on which to find that the person involved was an agent or employee, the court then turned to a factual inquiry to determine whether the diocese had so insinuated itself in the conduct that the imposition of liability could be justified on these grounds. The court indicated a lack of evidence "from which a jury could conclude the diocese controlled or regu-

---

71. *See* Whetstone v. Dixon, 616 So. 2d 764 (La. Ct. App. 1993) (auto accident), Fleischer v. Hebrew Orthodox Congregation, 504 N.E.2d 320 (Ind. Ct. App. 1987) (hazardous condition).

72. *See* John R. v. Oakland Unified Sch. Dist., 769 P.2d 948, 955 (Cal. 1989).

73. *See* Cottam v. First Baptist Church, 756 F. Supp. 1433, 1438–39 (D. Colo. 1991) (no liability in church when volunteers act gratuitously and outside expected range of contemplated activity), *aff'd*, 962 F.2d 17 (10th Cir. 1992).

74. 477 So. 2d 1060 (Fla. Dist. Ct. App. 1985).

75. *See id.* at 1062.

76. *See id.* at 1063. In the same way, *Plate v. St. Mary's Help Christians Church*, 520 N.W.2d 17 (Minn. Ct. App. 1994), describes the level of ecclesial control over a local parish by a regional diocese and lodges the area of civil secular authority over cemetery maintenance in a parish. *See also* Nye v. Kemp, 646 N.E.2d 262, 264–65 (Ohio Ct. App. 1994). Attempts to rewrite or ignore ecclesial controls and relationships would be unconstitutional. Kedroff v. Saint Nicholas Church, 344 U.S. 94 (1952).

lated the church or [the volunteer] in the maintenance of its grounds or the manner in which the equipment used to maintain the ground was either operated or kept in repair."[77] The jury verdict was set aside.

In a series of cases involving automobile accidents caused by Catholic clergy, courts in three states reached different conclusions about whether a priest was an agent or employee and, if so, whether the scope of his responsibility included the situation during which the accident occurred. In each case the priest was visiting another member of the religious community. Although some "business" activities occurred, the business related more to pastoral visitation than the exercise of some sacramental or priestly duty. In each case the conduct was the result of private decisions made by the priest independent of the diocese.

In *Brillhart v. Scheier*[78] the Kansas Supreme Court ruled that when a parish priest conducts such activity within his own discretion and control, he becomes an independent contractor. Therefore, because he is not *then* an agent or employee of the diocese, his own negligence may not be imputed under *respondeat superior*. In this case the priest was involved in a social visit to another priest to discuss both business and personal matters. The Kansas Supreme Court restated the public policy basis for *respondeat superior*: If a person is conducting his business through others, he is bound to manage them so as to avoid injury to third parties. This rule is therefore "a rule of policy, a deliberate allocation of a risk."[79] Although the bishop of a diocese has substantial ecclesial control over the comings and goings of individual priests, the diocese's control does not include all day-to-day activities of a parish pastor, such as whom he might visit and when. In these circumstances the negligent driving of the parish priest was not attributed to the ecclesial superior. This result was also reached in the case of *Ambrosio v. Price*.[80] Again, because the diocese was not responsible for the social activities of a priest, neither could it be liable for an accident caused during a social visit.

Both cases reject the broader theory of "ecclesial" (or precisely, "canonical") agency which was used in *Stevens v. Roman Catholic Bishop*.[81] In that case, on the same basic facts as *Ambrosio* and *Brillhart*, the California court adopted a theory of agency in which every action of a priest is attributed to the bishop. The *Stevens* court relied on expert testimony on the scope of a bishop's ecclesial authority under church law.[82] It found that the breath of ecclesiastical control was such that all actions, including pastoral visi-

---

77. *Folwell*, 477 So. 2d at 1063. In *Doe v. Roman Catholic Church*, 615 So. 2d 410 (La. Ct. App. 1993), the court listed factors that could be evaluated to determine if a charity volunteer was acting gratuitously or was subject to sufficient direction to be considered an "agent" of a religious entity. "The right to control is a fact question, determined by the following questions: (1) the degree of contact between the charity and the volunteer, (2) the degree to which the charity orders the volunteer to perform certain actions, and (3) the structural hierarchy of the charity." *Id.* at 415 (sexual battery by youth ministry volunteer not committed by an "agent").

78. 758 P.2d 219, 224 (Kan. 1988).

79. W. Page Keeton et al., Prosser and Keeton on the Law of Torts § 69 (5th ed. 1984), *quoted in Brillhart*, 758 P.2d at 222; *see also* John R. v. Oakland Unified Sch. Dist., 769 P.2d 948 (Cal. 1989).

80. 495 F. Supp. 381 (D. Neb. 1979); *accord Nye*, 646 N.E.2d 262; Glover v. Boy Scouts of Am., 923 P.2d 1383, 1388–89 (Utah 1996).

81. 123 Cal. Rptr. 171 (Ct. App. 1975).

82. *See id.* 123 Cal. Rptr. at 174–77 (discussing testimony). John T. Noonan, now a judge on the U.S. Court of Appeals, and Roger Mahony, now cardinal archbishop of Los Angeles, were canonical experts for plaintiff and defendant respectively.

tation, of a priest should be attributed to his ecclesiastical superior. No other cases have reached this result; *Brillhart* and *Ambrosio* rejected it.[83]

Although it is somewhat easier to make the case for attribution of liability to ecclesiastical superiors in hierarchical incorporated churches, the same arguments are made against unincorporated churches and other polities. In *Cox v. Thee Evergreen Church*, and cases noted therein,[84] the courts allowed recovery even for the tortious conduct of a member or officer of an unincorporated association. The rise in insurance coverage and changes in state statutory law have made such a result no longer unforeseeable. In some states neither the legislatures nor the courts have changed the "doctrine of imputed negligence," a doctrine which prevents a member of a voluntary unincorporated association from maintaining an action in tort against that association for injuries sustained through the negligence of fellow members.[85] No recovery is possible. If the policy behind *respondeat superior* is to find some other entity which has benefited from the actions of the particular event to respond in damages for harm created by the event, it makes no sense to draw a line between members of an association and members of the general public. The ability to sue and be sued as an unincorporated association, however, may change the patterns on which different organizations depend to respond to this type of claim.[86]

Scope of duties or employment

In *Jeffrey Scott E. v. Central Baptist Church*[87] a California court described the "scope of duty" inquiry this way: "whether (1) the act performed was either required or incident to the person's duties; or (2) the employee's misconduct could be reasonably foreseen by the employer in any event."[88] In accident litigation it is sometimes easily determined whether the particular conduct occurred within the scope of a person's duties. For example, a slippery condition created by a custodian appears to be an accident caused by evident negligent performance of the job duties. Such liability determinations are not usually polity specific. However, in instances where the conduct has both a mixed business and personal character and where the control is not as narrowly exer-

---

83. Indeed, in *Ambrosio*, the district judge was sharply critical of the California court's decision on agency relations, stating flatly that Nebraska law did not extend so far. *See* 495 F. Supp. at 385; *see also* Edward Hotz, Diocesan Liability for Negligence of a Parish Priest, 26 Cath. Law. 228 (1981). More recent decisions in the same judicial district have *not* adopted this theory. *See* Marco C. v. Catholic Bishop, No. 5 Civ. No. F3610 (Cal. Ct. App. Mar. 1985).

84. *See* Cox v. Thee Evergreen Church, 836 S.W.2d 167, 172–73 (Tex. 1992); *see also supra* note 38.

85. *See supra* note 37; Zehner v. Wilkinson Mem'l United Methodist Church, 581 A.2d 1388 (Pa. Super. Ct. 1990). Where there is specific action particularly adverse to a member, however, the doctrine of imputed negligence will not apply. *See Cox*, 804 S.W.2d at 192, *rev'd on other grounds*, 836 S.W.2d 167 (Tex. 1992).

86. That was precisely the point of the Texas Supreme Court's reversal in *Cox* and the decision in *Crocker*. *But see* Joseph v. Calvary Baptist Church, 500 N.E.2d 250 (Ind. Ct. App. 1986), *vacated*, 522 N.E.2d 371 (Ind. 1988). This point is also discussed in text accompanying note 152. *See also* Hanson v. St. Luke's United Methodist Church, 704 N.E.2d 1020 (Ind. 1998).

87. 243 Cal. Rptr. 128 (Ct. App. 1988); *see* John R. v. Oakland Unified Sch. Dist., 769 P.2d 948 (Cal. 1989) (affirming the policy of accident prevention in the future, assurance of compensation, and spreading of risk behind respondeat superior).

88. *Jeffrey Scott E.*, 243 Cal. Rptr. at 130.

cised by religious authority, the issue of scope of duty or employment can sometimes be litigated.[89] The case of *Johnson v. Drake* illustrates this difference.[90]

In *Johnson* a bishop of the Church of Jesus Christ of Latter-day Saints was involved in an automobile accident on route to a youth conference to be held in Idaho. He was invited but not required to attend the youth conference and was not a scheduled presenter on the conference agenda. He could have taken bus transportation provided for the participants of the conference. However, in order to visit en route a sick member of his ward, he drove a family member's car to the proceedings. The controlling legal issue before the court was whether at the time of the accident the bishop was engaged in performing his volunteer service or merely traveling to the place where he would perform the service.[91] The plaintiffs had argued that at the time of the accident Bishop Drake was already performing his religious duties by traveling to assist the departure of the buses for the youth conference. Plaintiffs argued that he was therefore within the scope of his employment the entire time, including the time of the accident. The court rejected the plaintiffs' argument and found that where a member of a charitable organization voluntarily attends an organization meeting in another city and the organization has no right of control until the person arrives, then the member is not acting within the scope of his employment while travelling to and from the meeting. Thus the organization is not liable for the activities of the person en route.[92]

It would appear, for these purposes, the greater degree of supervision and control over the activities of the person and the closer the connection between the person and the organization, the more likely it is that the consequences of negligence will be asserted against the organization. These cases do illustrate the principle that some degree of statutory or ecclesial responsibility needs to be asserted before liability is imposed. If the accident occurs in circumstances closely connected to the religious enterprise, liability may follow because of the occurrence "within the scope of duties."

Sexual misconduct arising from unauthorized activities
Abuse of minors

A series of cases involving religious organizations deal with the attempts of plaintiffs to assert liability against a religious organization for the intentional sexual misconduct of a person who also serves in the name of the institution. Whether the alleged offender

---

89. "Scope of duty" questions dominate the litigation of intentional torts, discussed below.

90. *See* Johnson v. Drake, No. 89-C-490W (C.D. Utah Apr. 2, 1990), *aff'd*, 932 F.2d 975 (10th Cir. 1991).

91. Unlike the above cases which discuss the potential liability of the religious organizations for the actions of ordained clergy, the LDS church does not have an ordained clergy. Rather, the court in *Johnson* indicates that "Bishop Drake, as a lay officer of the church, was an unpaid volunteer for a charitable organization." There was no evidence in that case that he was required to attend the Youth Conference or that he would have been derelict in his duties had he not attended. He paid his own expenses for which he was not reimbursed. All of these facts indicated that, contrary to cases involving the clergy of other denominations, there was a lower ability to control the actions of the agent at the time of the incident and therefore a less distinct line between religious activity or employment and personal time. These factors distinguish litigation in this denomination from the accident cases involving Catholic clergy summarized above, at notes 78–83. *See also* Nye v. Kemp, 646 N.E.2d 262 (Ohio Ct. App. 1994).

92. *Johnson*, slip op. at 9–11.

served as a paid employee or a volunteer, ordained or nonordained, the defense is invariably the same: intentional torts are not a foreseeable incident of employment and, therefore, the religious organization should not be responsible.[93] Applying the two-step analysis for *respondeat superior,* regardless of whether the person is an agent or employee, courts generally have held that deliberate sexual misconduct (rape or sexual battery) is outside the foreseeable scope of expected duties of the employees, ministers, or volunteers.[94]

In *Jeffrey Scott E. v. Central Baptist Church*[95] the California Court of Appeals upheld a summary judgment that the church was not liable for sexual assaults by a Sunday school teacher. Certainly his assaults were not foreseeable incidents of his service, because they were a violation of the very things held sacred by the church.[96] The same conclusion was reached in cases involving other religious groups.[97] In trying to place responsibility on the Central Baptist Church, however, the plaintiff argued that the youth minister had developed a position of trust with respect to the abused child and that the trust relationship was directly related to his activities as a church member. Yet the law requires more than a relationship; it requires a legal duty and then foreseeability. The court found that the youth Sunday school teacher's acts of molestation were not foreseeable in light of the work that he was asked to perform.[98] Indeed, the Sunday school teacher had taken his victims away from the church grounds to avoid the potential of being discovered.[99]

Some courts seek to determine whether a particular person's misconduct was foreseeable. Although a general awareness may exist of this kind of misconduct, given the low incidence of deliberate sexual assaults on minors, such misconduct is not generally foreseeable for liability purposes.[100] If a church is aware of evidence warning of a

---

93. In *Doe v. Roman Catholic Church*, 615 So. 2d 410 (La. Ct. App. 1993) the diocese also contested liability on the grounds that the adult volunteer was not its servant or agent for vicarious liability purposes. *See id.* at 415. It prevailed.

94. *See, e.g.,* Evan F. v. Hughson United Methodist Church, 10 Cal. Rptr. 2d 748, 756 (Ct. App. 1992); Jones v. Trane, 591 N.Y.S.2d 927, 933 (Sup. Ct. 1992). Absent a special relationship or exceptional circumstances, a person (even a religious institute) has no duty to protect another from the criminal acts of a third person. *See* N.J. v. Greater Emanuel Temple Holiness Church, 611 So. 2d 1036, 1038 (Ala. 1992) (church-sponsored day care). Similarly, mere membership in a church, without more, does not trigger a fiduciary relationship. Doe v. Diocese of Dallas, 2001 WL 856963 (Tex. Ct. App. 2001); Hawkins v. Trinity Baptist Church, 30 S.W.3d 446 (Tex. Ct. App. 2000).

95. 243 Cal. Rptr. 128 (Ct. App. 1988).

96. *See id.* at 130.

97. *See* Konkle v. Henson, 672 N.E.2d 450 (Ind. Ct. App. 1996); Marco C. v. Catholic Bishop, No. 5 Civ. No. F3610 (Cal. Ct. App. Mar. 1985); Rita M. v. Roman Catholic Archbishop, 232 Cal. Rptr. 685 (Ct. App. 1986).

98. *See supra* note 87. The Restatement (Second) of Torts §317 (1965) indicates that even where an employee or agent acts outside the scope of his employment, the employer or master may still be liable if the person is acting on the premises of the master or employer and the premises upon which the servant has privilege to enter or is using the property of the employer or master and the master knows or has reason to know that he can control the activity of the servant or employee and has the opportunity to exercise that control. That rule was applied and illustrated in *Mt. Zion State Bank & Trust v. Central Ill. Conference of United Methodist Church,* 556 N.E.2d 1270 (Ill. App. Ct. 1990) (no liability in church).

99. *See Jeffrey Scott E.,* 243 Cal. Rptr. at 131–32; *Mt. Zion Bank,* 556 N.E.2d 1270; *see also* Doe v. Roman Catholic Church, 606 So. 2d 524 (La. 1992) (vacating and remanding lower court imposition of liability on religious entity for sexual assault by volunteer youth worker), *case dismissed,* 615 So. 2d 410 (La. Ct. App. 1993).

100. *See Marco C.,* No. 5 Civ. No. F3610; *see also Rita M.,* 232 Cal. Rptr. 685; Bender v. First Church of the Nazarene, 571 N.E.2d 475 (Ohio Ct. App. 1989) (same). The only aberration is a single trial court in Minnesota that based its foreseeability holding on newspaper accounts of the scope

propensity for such misconduct, then a *direct* action for negligence, not *respondeat superior,* may be involved.[101] Regardless of whether the polity is hierarchical or congregational, when a minor or other vulnerable person is the victim of a deliberate deviation from expected conduct by a member of the clergy or staff of a religious organization, vicarious liability is rarely if ever imposed.[102]

Counseling sessions

Sexual misconduct is not limited to involvement with minors or others who are unable to consent. Misconduct, as understood by religious organizations, can include any form of generic failure on the part of a person to remain chaste or celibate or similar conduct which the denomination regards as sinful. In cases involving sexual misconduct between adults, this form of sinful conduct is not necessarily actionable. Adults are presumed to consent to such activity. Thus though a religious organization might condemn it, such activity does not give rise to liability.[103] Even if the activity itself might ordinarily be criminalized, such as sodomy, a religious organization does not have to answer in tort for consensual activity between adults.[104]

---

of the problem generally which served, in the court's view, as a sufficient basis to require a hierarchical religious organization to answer whether there should be any liability on the merits. *See* J.D.W. v. Ruglovsky, No. PI 88-12887 (Hennepin Cty. Minn. Jan. 24, 1990).

101. *See* J. v. Victory Tabernacle Baptist Church, 372 S.E.2d 391 (Va. 1988). For example, if evidence shows that a person's conduct was brought to the attention of church authorities who refused to act, there may be an action for negligent supervision. *See also* Foreign Mission Bd. v. Wade, 409 S.E.2d 144 (Va. 1991); Hammar, *supra* note 3, ch. 12, at 618–24 (discussing preventive measures). For background on the definition of the torts involved and the response of religious institutions, see Mark E. Chopko, National Inst. on Tort and Religion, Sexual Misconduct of Clergy, An Institutional Perspective (1990); Mark E. Chopko, Restoring Faith & Trust, 19 Hum. Rts. Q. 22 (1992).

102. *See* Tichenor v. Roman Catholic Church, 869 F. Supp. 429, 434 (E.D. La. 1993), *aff'd*, 32 F.3d 953 (5th Cir. 1994); *see also* Dausch v. Rykse, 52 F.3d 1425 (7th Cir. 1994) (per curiam); *id.* at 1436 (Ripple, J., concurring). *Reid v. Lukens*, No. 56046, slip op. (Mich. Ct. App. Sept. 10, 1984), held both a regional synod and a district of a Lutheran Church, as distinguished from a congregation, liable for sexual assault. The ruling confuses claimants of direct and vicarious negligence torts. Although local churches retained hiring authority, the court found that failure to exercise this responsibility and investigate the background of a teacher before placing him on an employment list was enough to warrant the imposition of liability on these higher levels of the church. *Reid* is inconsistent with *Evan F. v. Hughson United Methodist Church* and the results reached *Eckler, Mt. Zion Bank, Marco C.,* and others. A decision of the Oregon Supreme Court further confuses the issue. *See* Fearing v. Bucher, 977 P.2d 1163 (Or. 1999). In that case, the court notes that sexual assault on a minor is never part of the scope of duty of a cleric. However, the court opens the door to pleading a cause of action in *respondeat superior* when the plaintiff states facts that, if true, show that the perpetrator was acting within the scope of his duty when he committed acts that led to those that caused the injury. In other words, the court may allow a claim for the deceit of a pastor that allowed him access to a minor if ministry to young adults is part of his official duties. It will be difficult to maintain the line between official acts and the abandonment of those acts. This rule is a departure from the rules that previously applied, and is contrary to other decisions. E.g., *Jeffrey Scott E.,* 243 Cal. Rptr. 128.

103. *See* Schieffer v. Catholic Archdiocese, 508 N.W.2d 907 (Neb. 1993); F.G. v. MacDonell, 696 A.2d 697, 704 (N.J. 1997); Bladen v. First Presbyterian Church, 857 P.2d 789 (Okla. 1993); Lund v. Caple, 675 P.2d 226 (Wash. 1984); Kohl v. Walmsley, No. 930375, slip op. at 8 (Mass. Sept. 1, 1994) (no *respondeat superior* liability). Some counselors suggest that in these settings, no adult woman really gives free consent. *See* Joy Jordan-Lake, Conduct Unbecoming a Preacher, Christianity Today, Feb. 10, 1992, at 26, 29.

104. *See* Carini v. Beaven, 106 N.E. 589 (Mass. 1914). This immunity also extends to alienation of affections, even when framed as "clergy malpractice." *See* Osbourne v. Payne, 31 S.W.3d 911 (Ky. 2000); *Dausch*, 52 F.3d at 1431–32; Greene v. Roy, 604 So. 2d 1359, 1362 (La. Ct. App. 1992).

Liability is sometimes imposed on religious organizations, again regardless of polity, for sexual battery occurring in adult counseling sessions. In these cases courts may regard such misconduct as a breach of fiduciary obligation to the counselee. If the pastor is acting as a professional counselor, the religious organization may be analogized to a professional group and liability may follow.[105]

However, vicarious liability of religious groups for such pastoral misconduct may not be presumed. In the context of pastoral counseling, *Destefano v. Grabrian*[106] found a cause of action for a breach of fiduciary duty in favor of both (former) marriage partners when one of them had been sexually involved with a member of the clergy. By contrast *Dausch v. Rykse*[107] did not shift liability for the breach of fiduciary obligation to the religious institution. To decide the issue of vicarious liability, the Supreme Court of Colorado focused on the nature of the conduct. The court applied the ordinary rule that sexual misconduct is outside the reasonable or foreseeable duties that a member of the clergy might undertake in the course of religious counseling and not protected against judicial scrutiny.[108] The Seventh Circuit protected a church from "spiritual" counseling liability, but one judge also opined that if a church counselor held himself out as a "secular" counselor, liability could follow on entirely secular terms.[109] This rule seems a restatement of the *Roman Catholic Archbishop* holding: if one operates in a civil, secular setting, one can expect secular consequences.[110]

---

105. *See* Doe v. Samaritan Counseling Ctr., 791 P.2d 344 (Alaska 1990). In this case the Alaska Supreme Court relaxed its *respondeat superior* rule to allow for attribution of liability for sexual misconduct by a pastoral counselor with a counselee. The center functioned as a Christian alternative to secular psychotherapy. Rejecting conventional *respondeat superior* theory as too restrictive, the Court held the employer responsible for all misconduct that arose out of the counseling sessions. It called its theory "enterprise liability" and declared it to be a fairer allocation of risk. Indeed, a criminal violation of a state therapeutic malpractice statute was sustained against a minister who engaged in sexual misconduct with a counselee. *See* Minnesota v. Dutton, 450 N.W.2d 189 (Minn. Ct. App. 1990).

106. 763 P.2d 275 (Colo. 1988).

107. *See Dausch*, 52 F.3d at 1429, 1438; *see also* Brown v. Pearson, 483 S.E.2d 477, 484–85 (S.C. Ct. App. 1997) (despite victims' allegations, absence of contact with national and regional church agencies supports finding that there is no fiduciary relationship; mere expectation of action is insufficient).

108. The fact that the cause of action arose in the context of religious counseling is not enough to shield the religious entity from review on constitutional grounds. As the Colorado Supreme Court said in *Grabian*, unless the entity is arguing conformance with religious doctrine between the conduct alleged and the religious context, no Free Exercise Clause right is implicated. *See Grabian*, 763 P.2d at 283–84; *see also* Sanders v. Casa View Baptist Church, 898 F. Supp. 1169, 1176 (N.D. Tex. 1995), *aff'd*, 134 F.3d 331 (5th Cir. 1998); Moses v. Diocese of Colo., 863 P.2d 310 (Colo. 1993). On the other hand, to allow broad inquiry into the hiring and supervision of clergy could involve a court in review of ecclesial decision making. For this reason, courts are reluctant to impose secular counseling standards and risk-management principles on religious entities. *See* Swanson v. Roman Catholic Bishop, 692 A.2d 441, 444–45 (Me. 1997) (ecclesial actions not analogous to secular actions); Gallas v. Greek Orthodox Archdiocese, 587 N.Y.S.2d 82, 86 (Sup. Ct. 1991) (distinguishing constitutionally prohibited inquiries from secular inquiries). *Compare* Schmidt v. Bishop, 779 F. Supp. 321, 328, 332 (S.D.N.Y. 1991) (constitutional barrier to negligent supervision), *with* Jones v. Trane, 591 N.Y.S.2d 927, 932 (Sup. Ct. 1992) (a broad constitutional ruling would expand immunities more than required).

109. *Dausch*, 52 F.3d at 1435 (Ripple, J., concurring). To this extent, secular agencies allowing religious conduct may find themselves liable for failing to assure the safety of those subject to religiously motivated conduct. *E.g.*, Zakhartchenko v. Weinberger, 605 N.Y.S.2d 205 (Sup. Ct. 1993).

110. *See supra* text accompanying notes 26–27. The rule is tempered by constitutional limitations on the authority of the state to dictate religiously motivated internal operations, e.g., the requirement of church membership for employees.

In *Grabrian*, even with a breach of fiduciary obligation found on the part of the priest,[111] the diocese was not held vicariously liable for this kind of misconduct. Rather, the court found that the plaintiffs had stated a direct claim for negligence against the diocese for its failure to adequately supervise this priest.[112] In evaluating the claim for purposes of vicarious liability, the court looked to the underlying nature of the conduct (deliberate misconduct), not to the nature of the claim (or even the court's own legal conclusion as to the viability of the claim) to ascertain whether liability could "shift" to the sponsoring religious organization.

Counseling that expresses religious doctrine

A more difficult liability problem occurs in cases arising out of religiously sanctioned counseling sessions. The most sensational claims involve situations in which a vulnerable or unstable young adult seeks religious counseling for severe personal problems and subsequently commits suicide. The grieving survivors blame the religious organization and ministers who provided the counseling. Such was the situation presented in *Nally v. Grace Community Church.*[113]

Whether liability would shift in those circumstances did not involve a question of corporate form or polity, the employment status of the individual, or even scope of duty. Rather, the actions of the ministers were pleaded to be precisely in accord with those of the employing religious organization. The difficulty the courts expressed with the case was how one would set a standard of care:

> Because of the differing theological views espoused by the myriad of religions in our state and practiced by church members, it would certainly be impractical, and quite possibly unconstitutional, to impose a duty of care on pastoral counselors. Such a duty would necessarily intertwined with the religious philosophy of the particular denomination or ecclesiastical teachings of the religious entity.

> We have previously refused to impose a duty when to do so would involve complex policy decisions, and we are unpersuaded by plaintiffs that we should depart from this policy in the present case.[114]

Whether the religion is being punished for being strange or unpopular is also another serious concern.[115] Thus the courts have not applied liability generally in circumstances where it is arguable that the complaint is really directed at the religious practice that is being counseled. Indeed, the California appellate courts were unwilling to go any further in *Nally* than urging ministers, through the threat of liability, to recognize their

---

111. *See Grabrian*, 763 P.2d. at 278–79. The plaintiffs in that case also presented some evidence of foreseeability as to the priest's predilections with respect to relations with women.

112. *Id.* at 287; *accord* Hammar, *supra* note 3, ch. 4 §K, at 191, 193; *see also* Byrd v. Faber, 565 N.E.2d 584 (Ohio 1991); Strock v. Pressnell, 527 N.E.2d 1235 (Ohio 1988); Erickson v. Christenson, 781 P.2d 383 (Or. Ct. App. 1989).

113. 763 P.2d 948 (Cal. 1988).

114. *Id.* at 960; *accord* Schmidt v. Bishop, 779 F. Supp. 321, 331–32 (S.D.N.Y. 1991); *see Dausch*, 52 F.3d at 1432 n.4 (collecting cases).

115. *Compare* Samuel Ericsson, Clergyman Malpractice: Ramifications of a New Theory, 16 Val. U. L. Rev. 163 (1981), *with* Ben Z. Bergman, Is the Cloth Unraveling? A First Look at Clergy Malpractice, 9 San Fern. V. L. Rev. 47 (1981). Many of these authorities for and against imposition of liability are summarized in Note, Nally v. Grace Community Church of the Valley, 11 Pace L. Rev. 137 (1990). *See also Schmidt*, 779 F. Supp. at 326–28.

own limitations and to refer individuals for appropriate psychiatric intervention.[116] Imposition of liability ultimately may turn on the presence or absence of objectively measured factors, such as the outrageousness of the behavior and the obviousness of the need for psychiatric intervention.

Discipline, defamation and other torts

In many instances consonance between religious belief and action (in this section, discipline) creates a potential for liability. Some religious organizations require formal discipline of errant members, for example, either verbal or written condemnation and withdrawal of fellowship. They believe that a public condemnation of sinful behavior is essential for the reform of the individual and an example to the religious community about the consequences of sin. In these cases the ministers and members of the congregation are acting fully in accord with the beliefs of the congregation. They are also acting, through such condemnations, according to the express directives of their religious superiors. There is no question that the person carrying out such formal discipline is acting in the name of the religious organization and that this person is conducting activities which are within the scope of what he or she is expected to do. The risk of liability extends directly to the church body, whether it is congregational or hierarchical, whether it is incorporated or unincorporated, simply by virtue of the actions taken against a member.

Whether liability is imposed in these cases seems to follow certain principles. The cases divide between those in which consequences occur solely within the fellowship of the organization (on the one hand) and those in which consequences are caused outside the organization in the larger community: either to the public at large, to other churches, or to a person who has been stripped of membership, excommunicated, or otherwise expelled from the community. Membership in the religious community occurs by consent. The consent can be freely given, as well as withdrawn.[117] Consent is an essential element of membership, to both the doctrines and disciplines of the community. If one dissents from the imposition of discipline or any matter of doctrine, one does not have the right to seek to reform the community through litigation.[118] As long as one remains a member of a particular community, he or she cannot recover for otherwise tortious conduct undertaken in the name of religious discipline.[119]

In *Guinn v. Church of Christ*[120] elders of a local church confronted an unmarried member about rumors that she had become sexually involved. She was warned that un-

---

116. In *Nally* the church itself was not opposed to psychiatric care. But even that referral requirement was reversed by the California Supreme Court. *See Nally*, 763 P.2d at 959. A case not presented in *Nally* is that of a minister who is excessively condemnatory. This situation straddles the distinction between "departure-from-doctrine" cases (like sexual battery) and counseling cases as an expression of religious mission. In such circumstances, if the counseling were otherwise sanctioned by the entity, the entity could be held to bear the risk of excessive conduct by its agent or employer. *Cf.* Molko v. Holy Spirit Ass'n, 762 P.2d 46, 59–60 (Cal. 1988) (majority distinguishes—apparently—between actionable conversions and nonactionable conversions almost as a warning to proselytizers).

117. *See* Watson v. Jones, 80 U.S. (13 Wall.) 679, 680 (1872) (on this basis, establishing a rule of deference to religious bodies on internal affairs).

118. *See* Struemph v. McAuliffe, 661 S.W.2d 559, 563–64 (Mo. Ct. App. 1983).

119. *See* Smith v. Calvery Christian Church, 614 N.W.2d 590 (Mich. 2000); Hadnot v. Shaw, 826 P.2d 978, 987 (Okla. 1992). *But see* House of God v. White, 792 So.2d 491 (Fla. Dist. Ct. App. 2001) (barring claims against church, but allowing personal claims against minister).

120. 775 P.2d 766 (Okla. 1989).

less she stopped her sinful conduct, she could be publicly branded a fornicator for vio-lating doctrine. She was subsequently denounced from the pulpit. Guinn sued the el-ders and the Collinsville Church for outrageous conduct and invasion of privacy.[121] The parties stipulated that the elders were, at all times, acting in accord with church doc-trine and were agents of the church corporation.[122] The Oklahoma Supreme Court is-sued a divided ruling. It ruled that Guinn could disassociate herself from the commu-nity, making the behavior of the religious organization after her withdrawal actionable. However, for the period of time in which she was a member of the community, by her voluntary membership she consented to the rules of the community, including disci-pline. Membership constituted an effective defense to liabilities alleged for that church's discipline.[123]

Even in cases involving the claims of former members for the consequences of disci-pline, courts have distinguished between discipline that causes serious harm in the gen-eral community and that which does not. In two leading cases members of religious groups were excommunicated for conduct contrary to church doctrine. Excommunica-tion required that the church community have nothing to do with the former member; this included a mandate that individual members neither speak nor socialize with the person, nor continue to do business with him.

In *Bear v. Reformed Mennonite Church* the Supreme Court of Pennsylvania ruled that shunning practices of the church might nonetheless constitute an excessive interference with paramount state concerns about the maintenance of marriage and family relation-ships and tortious interference with business.[124] In *Bear* the consequence of shunning meant that the former member's wife and family refused to associate with him, and his business was substantially undermined.[125] On the other hand, in *Paul v. Watchtower Bible and Tract Society*[126] the Ninth Circuit ruled that the Jehovah's Witnesses' practice of shunning was protected under the First Amendment. The court distinguished *Bear* by indicating that the conduct complained of in *Paul* was simply the refusal of private individuals, presumably for private reasons undertaken on account of religious belief, to speak or socialize with a former member. Consequences did not extend to the plain-tiff's marriage, family life, or business as they did in *Bear*. "No physical assault or bat-tery occurred. Intangible or emotional harms can not ordinarily serve as a basis for maintaining a tort cause of action against a church for its practices—or its members....

---

121. Ms. Guinn attempted to withdraw from the community and in fact communicated that fact to the elders. The Church of Christ of Collinsville nonetheless believes that one can never "leave" the church community. By contrast, Mr. Smith was dis-fellowed but still attended the church. Smith v. Calvery Christian Church, *supra*.

122. *See Guinn*, 775 P.2d at 771 n.3. The judgment that the jury rendered against the elders was therefore applied to the incorporated congregational church.

123. Accord *Hadnot*, 826 P.2d 978. The court recognized Free Exercise and Establishment clause limits to its ability to impose liability for discipline during a period of membership. Such a ruling would abridge constitutionally protected religious autonomy. *See* Gruenwald v. Bornfreund, 696 F. Supp. 838, 840 (E.D.N.Y. 1988) (court refuses to enjoin excommunication begun as punishment for member suing yeshiva under RICO). No such restraint applied for conduct after membership ceased or occurring outside of church doctrine. *See* First United Church, Inc. v. Udofia, 479 S.E.2d 146 (Ga. Ct. App. 1996). *But see* Dillavou v. Schaffner, No. C7-94-362, 1994 WL 373324 (Minn. Ct. App. July 19, 1994) (constitution or qualified privilege bars defamation action where expelled mem-ber seeks reinstatement).

124. *See* Bear v. Reformed Mennonite Church, 341 A.2d 105 (Pa. 1975).

125. Even if there is a religious right to shun, the protection of marriage and family interests and of business interests was sufficiently compelling to justify judicial interference. *See id.* at 107.

126. 819 F.2d 875 (9th Cir. 1987).

Offense to someone's sensibilities resulting from religious conduct is simply not actionable in tort."[127] In both *Paul* and *Bear* the church body accepted the responsibility for the conduct of its members pointing out that such actions were fully consistent with doctrine. Derivative liability was not so much contested as conceded. The only question was whether allowing a tort cause of action in those circumstances was consistent with the Constitution.

Finally, like the discipline cases discussed above, religiously sanctioned conduct designed to punish a former member (and intended to cause extreme duress) is actionable. For liability purposes the intention to create consequences for outsiders to the faith community is a critical factor. In *Wollersheim v. Church of Scientology* actions of ministers and members intended to implement the doctrine and directives of the religious institution and calculated to harm an individual were found actionable.[128] The individual had withdrawn from membership. Consistent with a doctrine known as "fair game," members set out to damage his business and otherwise punish him for his withdrawal of fellowship. Resistance to liability was predicated on adherence to church doctrine. A California court found no First Amendment protection for religious conduct that caused strong, adverse social consequences.[129] Moreover, in *Candy H. v. Redemption Ranch, Inc.* a federal district court allowed recovery against various Baptist churches whose practices were analogized to outright confinement.[130] When harm is caused to a person who protests the conduct and demands that it stop, invocation of religious doctrine will be insufficient to immunize the entity from liability.

Contracts and indebtedness

The law of derivative liability for contracts and indebtedness varies little from the two-part analysis employed in tort cases. Courts routinely ask whether the person who allegedly bound the religious organization was an agent or employee and, if so, whether the person was acting within the scope of his or her agency or employment. As with torts, there is very little real difference among polities or religious forms of organizations that would illustrate the different consequences for derivative liability that accompany

---

127. *Id.* at 883 (citations omitted); *see also Gruenwald*, 696 F. Supp. at 841. Courts also distinguish between claims against a church sounding in doctrinal concerns (barred) from claims against ministers (sometimes allowed). Sands v. Living Word Fellowship, 34 P.3d 955 (Alaska 2001).

128. *See* Wollersheim v. Church of Scientology, 260 Cal. Rptr. 331 (Ct. App. 1989), *vacated*, 499 U.S. 914 (1991) (vacated in light of *Pacific Mutual Life Insurance Co. v. Haslip*, 499 U.S. 1 (1991), on punitive damages). After remand, the California courts confirmed the constitutionality of their awards of damages. *See* Wollersheim v. Church of Scientology, 6 Cal Rptr. 2d 532 (Ct. App. 1992).

129. *See Wollersheim*, 260 Cal. Rptr. at 341. Following *Bear* and distinguishing *Paul*, even if there are protectable religious interests stated, the California court found there is a compelling interest preventing and compensating for the adverse consequences of the behavior. Again, the intention was to cause consequences to a nonmember, distinguishing this litigation from that which targeted *internal* religious practices or policies. *Cf.* Molko v. Holy Spirit Ass'n, 762 P.2d 46, 59–60 (Cal. 1988).

130. *See* Candy H. v. Redemption Ranch, Inc., 563 F. Supp. 505 (M.D. Ala. 1983). The rules were based on religious principles and enforced by strict corporal punishment, and included such things as the censoring of mail and telephone calls, a refusal of any outside contact, visits, or travel, and a prohibition against conversation with new members. In that case the court found a federal civil rights action (42 U.S.C. § 1985(3)) based on the claimed violation of a right to travel. It found that this right to freedom of movement was not outweighed any of the religious rights claimed in the organization. Litigation reformed the practices of the school.

differing polities. Differences appear to be related more to whether the entity is incorporated and whether the particular state has a statute which governs these relationships. Also characteristic of the reported decisions is the persistent argument of religious organizations that because they are charitable or religious entities, liability should not be imposed on them for the errant actions of an agent. Nonetheless, if the religious entity is functioning corporately "in the world," it will be measured by civic rules.[131] To determine such liability courts examine the actions of boards and committees, the denominational relationships implicated, and the facts of the particular transaction.

In *De LaSalle Institute v. United States* the owners of the Christian Brothers Winery disputed the taxability of income from that enterprise because it supported the religious activities of the community and its schools.[132] The Institute argued that the commercial winery corporation activities were integral to the religious activity. Therefore it asserted that the winery income became the income of the religious body and as such was exempt from taxation. The court denied an exemption. Because the Institute enjoyed the advantages of separate incorporation in its activities, giving it the freedom by which it conducted its business, it also "enjoyed" the disadvantages of separate incorporation.[133] Although certain powers were reserved to the religious community, the commercial activity generated taxable income because of its strict, secular, corporate separation. Because the Institute itself separately incorporated its activities for one kind of liability/business calculus, the court would not redraw the line to avoid another kind of liability.[134] The court relied on secular case law and contracts, and not on church law, to decide the disputed issues imputing liability for the taxes to the religious institute.[135]

Similarly, in *Benedictine Society v. National City Bank* a bank was allowed to recover against a religious society as guarantor of a loan to Catholic University of Peking, China. The archabbot of the religious community, as chancellor of the university, contracted for loans to support the university, an apostolic work of the community's abbey.[136] The court found that the religious order had expressly ratified that action. Having chosen to undertake secular commercial activities, the religious organization could not avoid those responsibilities by pleading that the actions of the community were mere ecclesial works.

Courts often look to the actions of the person or persons involved in a transaction and the knowledge of both parties in deciding whether to apply the debts created by one person to assets of the religious corporation. For example, in *Crest Chimney Cleaning Co. v. Ahi Ezer Congregation*[137] the court found that the synagogue contracted through an agent for maintenance and repair of its related properties. The congregation could

---

131. *E.g.*, Roman Catholic Archbishop v. Industrial Accident Comm'n, 230 P. 1 (Cal. 1924).

132. *See* De LaSalle Inst. v. United States, 195 F. Supp. 891 (N.D. Cal. 1961).

133. *Id*. at 901.

134. *See id*. at 903.

135. It has been held that the secular courts have the power "and perhaps the duty as well, to enforce secular contract rights, despite the fact that the contracting parties may base their rights on religious affiliations." Elmora Hebrew Ctr., Inc. v. Fishman, 593 A.2d 725 (N.J. 1991). In that case, the New Jersey Supreme Court enforced a secular contract between a religious congregation and a former rabbi to agree to submit their dispute to religious arbitration. The agents of the congregation essentially bound the congregation to a particular result which it could no longer avoid. *See* Straughter v. Holy Temple of Church of God and Christ, 150 So. 2d 124 (La. Ct. App. 1963) (action for salary, made payable on note ratified by trustees); Ruffin v. Temple Church of God, 749 A.2d 719 (D.C. 2000).

136. *See* Benedictine Soc'y v. National City Bank, 109 F.2d 679, 682 (3d Cir. 1940).

137. 310 N.Y.S.2d 217 (Civ. Ct. 1970); *see* Mathies Well & Pump Co. v. Plainview Jewish Ctr., 248 N.Y.S.2d 441 (Sup. Ct. 1964) (allowing a mechanic's lien for a repair).

not disassociate itself from the actions of its agent, arguing they had not been expressly authorized in particular cases. The congregation benefited directly from the contract. It was equitably estopped from denying its normal commercial practice and its liability for the debt.[138] On the other hand, when a secular party recognizes clear limitations on the contracting power of the religious agent, the commercial vendor is estopped from seeking recovery for debts it knows were created in excess of that authority.[139]

In unincorporated entities individual members can become liable for the debt of the organization. The association does not bind itself except in accord with the practices of that entity. Courts generally look for some evidence of ratification or approval by a governing board or authority before they will enforce a contract against the assets of an association. Absent ratification the member himself or herself may be answerable for the debt. In many states the unincorporated association does not have the "corporate" character to be held responsible for such contracts. On the other hand, equitable estoppel precludes even an unincorporated association from receiving the benefits of a particular arrangement and then refusing to answer for it. Such was the case in *Barr v. United Methodist Church*.[140]

In this case, which will be more completely explained later, the California court imputed liability for failed contractual arrangements made between individuals and religiously affiliated, but separately incorporated, retirement communities against the sponsoring unincorporated denomination. The court found that the denomination held itself out by a commonly understood name, The United Methodist Church, and could not avoid its liability under that name under California law. The opinion remains a singular example of how far courts can go to find responsible parties, even among unincorporated associations, in circumstances where it would simply be unfair, in the court's view, to allow for avoidance of liability.[141]

Undue influence, duress, and fraud

Undue influence, duress, and fraud is an area of law involving a specialized application of tort principle, trust principle, and public policy. It does not exhibit peculiarities along the lines of religious polity or corporate form. If a minister, an employee, or a volunteer is acting in the name of a religious community and is addressing matters on which that person is expected to speak, liability often shifts against the organization. The only question concerns the defenses that might be applied in a particular case. Undue influence is the generic term for efforts to recover gifts made to religious or

---

138. *See Crest Chimney*, 310 N.Y.S.2d at 225 (noting possible unjust advantage).

139. In *Eastern Renovating Corp. v. Roman Catholic Bishop*, 554 F.2d 4 (1st Cir. 1977), the corporation sole had signed written instruments with a contractor in which the contractor said he would not do any more renovation work in excess of $1,000 without the approval of the administrators of the corporation sole. Notwithstanding the agreement, the contractor undertook substantial renovation work, received partial payment, and then sued. The jury on special verdict found for the corporation sole that there had been no waiver of the express agreement resisting such contracts. The court looked at synodal statutes to preclude the contract in excess of $1,000 and found, as a fact, that the contractor had understood the limitations of the religious organization. *See id.* at 7.

140. 153 Cal. Rptr. 322 (Ct. App. 1979); *see Straughter*, 50 So. 2d 124.

141. The decision is critiqued below and remains constitutionally suspect insofar as it ignores the polity of the Methodist Church. Electronic research reveals that only nine cases even cite *Barr*, none for the religious proposition that so concerned commentators. Gaffney & Sorenson, *supra* note 3, note four cases that attempted to apply the decision. Only one ever resulted in an appellate decision, also discussed below.

other organizations. Recovery, when allowed, is based on a conclusion that the donor's ability to make a free gift was impaired by the active deceit or misconduct of those who sought the gift.[142] In cases involving religious organizations, a relationship of trust is presumed to exist between the agent of the religious organization and the donor. The dividing line between recovery and nonrecovery turns on whether the alleged misstatement is a matter of fact or faith.

In *Anderson v. Worldwide Church of God*[143] the court denied recovery of contributions allegedly made because of the representation that the world was coming to an end. The court found that the ministers throughout the church firmly believed this conclusion as an article of faith.[144] To allow the court to rescind a gift based on statements of faith would have involved the civil courts in litigating unverifiable matters of belief. In *United States v. Ballard* the Supreme Court held that courts are not to adjudicate the truth or falsity of religious doctrine.[145] Where recovery is allowed, the matters in contention are often overt facts that have been plainly misstated to cause a gift (or a larger gift) to be made. In *The Bible Speaks*, for example, while some claims involved matters of religious doctrine, others concerned overt facts which the court found were deliberately misstated by members of the religious organization.[146] Because the latter were verifiable by the court as misstated facts, recovery was permitted on these claims.

A variation on this theme occurs in cases seeking damages for duress or intentional infliction of emotional distress. Recovery is sought for emotional injuries alleged to have been received during conversion to a religion or on account of religious practices. Where recoveries have been allowed, like those in the undue influence cases immediately above, often some verifiable fact has been misrepresented.[147] Even when the cases reflect matters of religious doctrine, as discussed above under the discipline cases, recovery can occur in situations having severe consequences. When the damage is alleged to have been caused by those who minister in the name of the denomination and the religious group responds that the conduct is constitutionally protected, the courts are presented with a challenge: are they willing to extend liability for conduct that occurs either in the process of conversion to, or seeking membership in, the religious organization?[148] Some courts have extended liability in novel ways.

---

142. Substantive law in this area is summarized in *In re The Bible Speaks*, 869 F.2d 628, 641–42 (1st Cir. 1989).

143. 661 F. Supp. 1400 (D. Minn. 1987).

144. *See id.* at 1401. The court noted the frustration of the plaintiffs' attempts to find anyone who believed otherwise.

145. United States v. Ballard, 322 U.S. 78, 86–87 (1944); *see also* Rankin v. Howard, 527 F. Supp. 976 (D. Ariz. 1981) (courts may not determine what is a bona fide religion; First Amendment protects freedom to believe; the law knows no heresy).

146. *See The Bible Speaks*, 869 F.2d at 641, 645. In *Cantwell v. Connecticut*, 310 U.S. 296 (1940), the case in which the Supreme Court demanded that states protect federal free exercise rights, the Court distinguished protected belief from less protected action. *See id.* at 303–04. The Court singled out "fraud claims" as an area in which state action could be allowed. *Id.* at 306.

147. For example, the fraud alleged by claimants may be the identity of the religious group, Molko v. Holy Spirit Ass'n, 762 P.2d 46 (Cal. 1988), or the location of the member away from his or her own family, George v. International Soc'y of Krishna Consciousness, 262 Cal. Rptr. 217 (Ct. App. 1989), *vacated*, 499 U.S. 914 (1991), *aff'd in part and rev'd in part*, 4 Cal. Rptr. 2d 473 (Ct. App. 1992) (remanded for trial of a portion of a punitive damages award).

148. *Compare Molko*, 762 P.2d at 57–58 (allowing recovery for some aspects of emotional distress), *with* Murphy v. International Soc'y of Krishna Consciousness, 571 N.E.2d 340 (Mass. 1991) (barring litigation over any religious matter as unconstitutional).

In *George v. International Society of Krishna Consciousness* and *Molko v. Holy Spirit Ass'n,* California courts found the religious organizations responsible for the actions of their converters and ministers. In *Molko* the court found that church members deliberately concealed that they were recruiting the plaintiff for the Unification church. The Unification church argued that concealment was consistent with a doctrine called "heavenly deception," used by the church to protect it against a hostile secular world and to allow for the unconverted to hear the word of the church and make a decision based on its doctrine, not its reputation in the media.[149] In *George* the location of a minor was concealed from her parents. The court found that such deliberate misrepresentation triggered a series of events for which the organization could be liable.[150]

Liability Theory as an Engine of Social Change

Given the dominance of social policy arguments in the cases discussed above, it is not surprising that liability theory can be used as a means through which social change is either encouraged or regulated. To the extent that religious organizations can incur substantial liabilities for actions of their members or ministers—even when they are acting in complete accord with religious doctrine—litigation can change the organization, sometimes in ways that clash with the doctrine of the religious entity and raise serious constitutional claims. This is illustrated in both extraordinary and ordinary ways.

In *Cox v. Thee Evergreen Church* the Texas courts first allowed an unincorporated church to avoid tort liability for an accident suffered by a member under the doctrine of imputed negligence.[151] Before the appeals in this case were finally resolved, the church considered becoming and subsequently became incorporated. Here one is left to speculate why, after many years of operating as an unincorporated association, this church chose incorporation. The prospect that a judgment in favor of one member could be rendered against the assets of other individual members or against those who were responsible for the leadership of the organization could have been a motivating factor. The final judicial determination in the case, abandonment of the doctrine of imputed negligence, had the same effect as the church's incorporation: limiting liability to the entity but not the members in recognition of the unfairness of the old rule.[152] Indeed, in other cases, the courts have not hesitated to point out that such organizations have, at times, sought both the advantages of incorporation (the avoidance of responsibility on

---

149. *Molko*, 762 P.2d at 58. The court nonetheless imposed liability, *see id.* at 57–58, citing *Bear* and other cases. These cases involve not insincere remarks, but actions by agents of the church based on passionately held religious doctrine.

150. These actions included the intentional infliction of emotional distress for a parent's injuries resulting from concealment, libel for issuing a press release attacking the parents, and wrongful death of one parent whose heart ailment was exacerbated by the stress of searching for his daughter. *See George*, 262 Cal. Rptr. 217. The convert's claims were dismissed—she had participated in the conduct giving rise to her claim and was never forced against her will to remain in the Krishna community. To premise liability on religious practices would be barred by the First Amendment. *See id.* at 235–36.

151. That determination was later reversed. *See supra* note 37.

152. *See* Cox v. Thee Evergreen Church, 836 S.W.2d 167, 173 (Tex. 1992).

the part of individual members) and the advantages of unincorporation (lack of liability in the organization itself).[153]

A reverse of this trend toward consolidation into one corporation can be seen in corporate reorganizations triggered by the risk of liability. For example, church-related health care systems, once uniform and monolithic, have been reorganized and regionalized due to liability concerns.[154] Faced with the potential for crippling liability awards against large institutions, some religious entities have even considered protection of the bankruptcy laws as a means of allowing continued operations.[155] The concerns addressed by the consideration of a bankruptcy reorganization, namely, identifying and limiting liability exposure and allowing protection against enforced liquidation with its consequent impact on charitable and religious functions, are similarly resolved in a physical restructuring into new coordinate entitites, each assigned its proper function. Smaller corporate structures with circumscribed powers functioning within a larger ecclesial envelope might be sufficient to insulate an overall structure from the consequences of related entities, the larger from the actions of the smaller, or otherwise act as a shield against potential financial consequences to a whole system.[156] Liability considerations have directly affected the operations of religious organizations by changing their activities.[157] The difficulty arises when liability potentials begin to dictate a structure at odds with internal religious doctrine.

Change can also be caused through judicial "regulation." Plaintiffs and their attorneys are as creative in crafting new liability theories as defense lawyers are in resisting them. The attempted creation of a "clergy malpractice" tort to regulate ministerial conduct and to insinuate that conduct to his or her religious organization was such an effort. No supreme court has recognized this cause of action. As noted at some length, most courts distinguish between ecclesial control, which is largely not actionable, and civil control for purposes of determining agency. If adopted, clergy malpractice would have changed that equation, making civil courts, not the churches, judges of whether or

---

153. *See* Hutchins v. Grace Tabernacle United Pentecostal Church, 804 S.W.2d 598, 600 (Tex. App. 1991, no writ). As indicated above, however (*see supra* note 39), once a choice is made, the entity is bound to it.

154. *See* Frohlich, *supra* note 3, cites "ascending liability" concerns of the Southern Baptist Convention and others raising issues of corporate form.

155. The Archdiocese of Santa Fe, for example, struggled with liability for clerical misconduct as a lay religious corporation, even though the cases arose in specific local parishes. Some parishes were not affected, although the archdiocese is a corporation sole. The prospect of a large entity holding all of the assets of all of the local entities raised serious financial questions, leading ultimately to consideration of a bankruptcy proceeding. *See* Facing Costly Abuse Suits, Diocese Turns to Parishioners, N.Y. Times, Dec. 22, 1993, at A1. Such a proceeding raises serious constitutional concerns. In 2004, the bankruptcy filings by three Catholic dioceses meant that the serious corporate, financial, and constitutional issues are no longer hypothetical. In re Archdiocese of Portland in Oregon, No. 04-37154-ELP11 (filed 7/6/2004); In re Roman Catholic Church of the Diocese of Tucson, No. 4-04-04721-Jmm (filed 9/20/2004); In re Diocese of Spokane, No. 04-08822-PCW (Dec. 6, 2004).

156. *See* Plate v. St. Mary's Help of Christians Church, 520 N.W.2d 17 (Minn. Ct. App. 1994).

157. The litigation against the Redemption Ranch resulted in a reform of the practices of the school. *See* Candy H. v. Redemption Ranch, Inc., 563 F. Supp. 505, 511 (M.D. Ala. 1983). In particular cases courts will impose even punitive damages (as discussed below). On the other hand, courts could not predicate liability on some form of organization not adopted by the entity without violating constitutional principle. *See* Serbian E. Orthodox Church v. Milivojewich, 426 U.S. 696, 721–24 (1976). For a secular analogue, see *Glover v. Boy Scouts of America*, 923 P.2d 1383, 1388 (Utah 1996), in which the court refused to impose liability on the Boy Scouts based on a form of operational structure that BSA could have, but did not, embrace.

not a minister properly performs his or her ministry, and whether a church or congregation properly exercises its training and selection functions. Clergy malpractice would mean that the failure of ecclesiastical discipline in a particular instance could itself be the basis for liability against an organization.[158] The courts have uniformly rejected these claims.

Similarly, except when warranted by application of the three principles outlined herein, courts have resisted forcing entire congregations and denominations to answer for all misdeeds of their ministers. Courts have recognized the nonprofit character of the institutions in question and have been reluctant to treat them as if they were profit-making concerns for purposes of establishing liability.[159] Because vicarious liability is predicated on a policy to spread the risk and find financially responsible entities, the courts generally believe that the tort remedies now in existence are adequate to shift that risk in a fair manner.[160] Some courts have resisted the implication of clergy malpractice because of state policies against the non-legislative creation of new causes of action.[161] Others have done so because claims of clerical malpractice would stand on a different footing from malpractice alleged against other professions. Clergy practices do not involve monetary exchange or profit motive; and counseling is a service that is performed as part of a religious activity.[162] Finally, recognition of such a cause of action would impermissibly involve courts in setting internal standards for clergy training and religious supervision, contrary to constitutional provisions.[163]

By manipulating the standard of review, courts attempt to force change in either how religious entities operate or how they share risk of loss. The vast majority of courts limit risk of loss to foreseeable consequences of manageable actions rather than impose liability such that the line between negligence and strict liability is blurred.[164] In these cases religious/voluntary action generally bears no risk of liability for deliberate (even

---

158. "Clergy malpractice" means literally the failure of a member of the clergy to act as a reasonable cleric in given circumstances. The setting of a "reasonable cleric" standard necessarily involves the court in reviewing the polity and practices of a denomination. Selection and training of clergy are ultimate choices committed to religious, not civil, authority. *See* Lann v. Davis, 793 So.2d 463 (La.Ct. App. 2001); Dausch v. Rykse, 52 F.3d 1425, 1435 (7th Cir. 1994); Schmidt v. Bishop, 779 F. Supp. 321, 326 (S.D.N.Y. 1991) (collecting cases and other authority); *see also* 2 Bassett, *supra* note 3, §8:19 nn. 9–13; authorities cited *supra* notes 110 & 114. In one recent case, an intermediate appellate court allowed a litigant to state a "clergy malpractice" claim, but that determination was reversed on appeal. *See* F.G. v. MacDonell, 677 A.2d 258 (N.J. Super. Ct. App. Div. 1996), *aff'd in part and rev'd in part*, 696 A.2d 697 (N.J. 1997) (allowing, instead, a breach-of-fiduciary-duty claim against the alleged perpetrator, avoiding unconstitutional entanglement). The civil courts may not enforce religious duties. *See* Roman Catholic Bishop v. Superior Court, 50 Cal. Rptr. 2d 399, 406 (Ct. App. 1996) ("celibacy" is a religious, not a civil, duty).

159. *Nally v. Grace Community Church*, 763 P.2d 948 (Cal. 1988), the leading case in this area, specifically expressed this reservation. *Id.* at 960.

160. *See* Byrd v. Faber, 565 N.E.2d 584, 587 (Ohio 1991) (question is matter of legislative judgment). As the Ohio Supreme Court concluded, clergy malpractice does not address any aspect of the relationship between the religious organization and the adherent that is not already actionable under some other existing tort, whether a negligence or intentional tort.

161. *See Schmidt*, 779 F. Supp. at 327; Destefano v. Grabrian, 763 P.2d 275, 285 (Colo. 1988).

162. *See* White v. Blackburn, 787 P.2d 1315, 1318–19 (Utah Ct. App. 1990).

163. *See Schmidt*, 779 F.Supp. at 332. A constant theme in the case law is to recognize the constitutional implications of allowing such a claim either as clergy malpractice or as direct negligence for religious action. *See* Pritzlaff v. Archdiocese of Milwaukee, 533 N.W.2d 780 (Wis. 1995); Kohl v. Walmsley, No. 930375, slip op. at 8 (Mass. Sept. 1, 1994).

164. *Jeffrey Scott E. v. Central Baptist Church*, 243 Cal. Rptr. 128 (Ct. App. 1988), illustrates this concern, forcing some balance of risks including the social consequences of churches possibly being limited from social ministry or outreach by liability fears.

criminal) misconduct.[165] However, examples can be found where courts have departed from these ordinary principles of judicial review finding potential liability far beyond what the religious drafters of denominational statements[166] or organizer's works[167] envisioned. Such decisions have been criticized as both unfair and unwise.[168]

Change can also occur through the risk spreading when liability is attempted to be placed against an entire denomination. In *Barr v. United Methodist Church*[169] present and former residents of retirement homes brought a class action against a retirement home corporation (and various church regional bodies), naming the denomination as a defendant. The court held the denomination was an unincorporated association, answerable for the lawsuit in contract. The jurisdictional ruling by the court put at risk related United Methodist institutions and, indeed, every member of the community who would call himself or herself a "member" of this unincorporated association.[170] If every member of a denomination were now to be liable to answer for the misdeeds of coordinate or subordinate agencies or those who minister for them, the consequences to religious organizations would be disastrous. In a hierarchical community, which the court found the United Methodist polity to be, incentive to use specialized civil corporations and appropriate doctrinal changes to avoid that risk would greatly increase.[171] Some understanding of the case, the nature of the court's ruling, and subsequent litigation illustrates these points.

The litigation in *Barr* was commenced as a class action on behalf of two thousand residents of fourteen retirement homes operated in California, Hawaii, and Arizona by Pacific Homes Corporation. The complaint alleged that each member of the class had entered into a "continuing care agreement" with Pacific Homes, which had filed for relief under Chapter 11 of the federal laws on bankruptcy. The continuing care agreements provided that specific homes would furnish lifetime care, including medical, nursing, and convalescent care, accommodations, and food service. Many plaintiffs had prepaid their contracts and thus were entitled to life care at no additional cost. The complaint further alleged that the Southwest Annual Conference of the United Methodist Church (a California corporation), the General Council on Finance and Administration of the United Methodist Church (a Minnesota corporation), and the United Methodist Church (an unincorporated association) were jointly and severally responsible for the operation of the homes. The plaintiffs sought a judgment requiring the defendants to honor the contracts and operate the homes or to pay money damages. The potential liability exposure of the defendants in the case was, in a word, staggering.

---

165. Where an authority or custodian relationship gives rise to intentional misconduct, liability may attach. *See* Samuels v. Southern Baptist Hosp., 594 So. 2d 571 (La. Ct. App. 1992) (psychiatric aide sexual assault). That is not always the case with churches. *See* Evan F. v. Hughson United Methodist Church, 10 Cal. Rptr. 2d 748, 756 n.2 (Ct. App. 1992) (summarizing cases). Where courts take a more expansive view of the role or authority of these entities, occasionally even the judiciary corrects itself. *See* Doe v. Roman Catholic Church, 606 So. 2d 524 (La. 1992) (reversing lower court affirmation of judgment n.o.v. after jury dismissed institutional defendants as not vicariously liable).

166. *See, e.g.,* Martinelli v. Diocese of Bridgeport, 196 F.3d 409 (2d Cir. 1999) (parable of "good shepherd"); Reid v. Lukens No. 56046, slip op. (Mich. Ct. App. Sept. 10, 1984) (religious manual).

167. *See* Doe v. Samaritan Counselling Ctr., 791 P.2d 344 (Alaska 1990).

168. *E.g., id.* at 349–50 (Moore, J., dissenting).

169. 153 Cal. Rptr. 322 (Ct. App. 1979).

170. Whether this kind of liability is properly ascending or descending depends on one's ecclesiology. For liability purposes it is plainly "derivative" rather than "vicarious" as those terms are used here.

171. *See* Frohlich, *supra* note 3, at 1396–97 nn. 166–69, 174.

In holding the United Methodist Church responsible for a judgment as an unincorporated association, the court claimed to be resting its decision on neutral principles of civil law. The authority that the court consulted to establish its neutral legal principles for judicial review, however, was the Book of Discipline of the Church.[172] The court noted that, in 1967, the California legislature amended the Code of Civil Procedure to allow an unincorporated association "to sue or be sued either in the name which it had assumed or by which it was known."[173] If members of a group shared a common purpose and function under a common name, under circumstances where "fairness" required that the group be recognized, the organization by which they were known should be held responsible for actions in their name.[174] In concluding that the plaintiffs stated a claim against the United Methodist Church as an entity, the court echoed a familiar refrain:

> [The United Methodist Church], in fulfilling its commitment to society, has elected to involve itself in worldly activities by participating in many socially valuable projects. It has enjoyed the benefits, both economic and spiritual, of those projects. It has even, on occasion, filed suit for the protection of its interests. It must now, as part of its involvement in society, be amenable to suit.[175]

The practical effect of the litigation was to hold the association potentially responsible. Because no other constituent or coordinate member of the United Methodist Church, or any individual was named as a defendant, simply stating the claim and obtaining jurisdiction did not mean that ultimate liability would rest on the shoulders of any of these entities. Those questions would have to wait for another day.

Commentators have long criticized the results in *Barr* as contrary to the church's doctrine and to constitutional principles. Rather than allowing the religious organization the freedom to conduct its own affairs, the court was using ecclesiastical expressions to the secular detriment of the church.[176] The use of denominational expressions to determine the result for derivative liability is not itself remarkable. What is remarkable is that subsequent litigation involving other denominations such as the Presbyter-

---

172. *See Barr*, 153 Cal. Rptr. at 328, reviewing structure, relationships, and missions of elements of the church community. The court scrutinized the polity of the United Methodist Church, finding it hierarchical with 43,000 local churches and 114 Annual Conferences governed through the Book of Discipline. It described the various component elements of the United Methodist Church showing that each acted in concert with the other, functioning according to a common understanding of doctrine and purpose and desiring to be perceived in a uniform manner by the public. It even went so far as to call the Council of Bishops the equivalent of a Board of Directors. Among other things, the court even pointed to the fact that "the organization functioned under a group ruling issued by the Internal Revenue Service describing its General Conference on Financing and Administration as a central treasury and fiscal agent." It then found that there was a sufficient link between the Association and Pacific Homes through the constituent entities of Annual Conferences and the General Conference.

173. *Id.* at 326; *see also* White v. Cox, 95 Cal. Rptr. 259 (Ct. App. 1971).

174. *See Barr*, 153 Cal. Rptr. at 328: "The criteria applied to determine whether an unincorporated entity is an unincorporated association are no more complicated than (1) a group whose members share a common purpose, and (2) who function under a common name in circumstances where fairness requires the group be recognized as a legal entity. Fairness includes those situations where persons dealing with the association contend their legal rights have been violated."

175. *Id.* at 331. *Compare* Roman Catholic Archbishop v. Industrial Accident Comm'n, 230 P.1 (Cal. 1924), *with* De LaSalle Inst. v. United States, 195 F. Supp. 891 (N.D. Cal. 1961).

176. *See* Paul Karssen, Note, Imposing Corporate Forms on Unincorporated Denominations: Balancing Secular Accountability with Religious Free Exercise, 55 S. Cal. L. Rev. 155 (1981); Gaffney & Sorenson, *supra* note 3, at 42–48.

ian Church, the Assemblies of God, the Episcopal Church, and the Lutheran Church have all indicated the limits of the *Barr* rule.[177]

In *Eckler* the use of the name "Assembly of God" by a local church and its ecclesial relationship with the General Council of the denomination did not, by themselves, establish an agency relationship between the local church and the national body. The governing documents made plain that affiliation with the General Council did not destroy the local church's sovereignty.[178] Likewise, acting under a common book of prayer and discipline does not render a parent church liable for damages brought on by the actions of a local minister. In *Folwell* the substantial control by a parent church over dogma and discipline, the receipt of contributions, and even some modicum of control over finances did not demonstrate that the parent church was involved in or controlled the action of the local church giving rise to the litigation.[179] In *Hope Lutheran Church v. Chellew*[180] engagement of a number of Lutheran churches in organizing a retirement home as a joint agency or venture did not make each sponsoring church or their association of churches liable for return of down payments when the project failed. The project was a part of the churches' ministry, was targeted to Lutherans, used the name "Lutheran" in its sales literature, and called itself a "joint agency." The project was a separate corporation whose articles promised no financial responsibility to the sponsoring church.[181] "[O]nce incorporated, [the home] became a district and autonomous entity, one controlled by its board of directors."[182] Without even citing *Barr*, these cases reject its central premise. *Barr* represents an extreme view of the potential reach of derivative liability as a vehicle through which judges can spread risk and financial responsibility.

Finally, exemplary or punitive damages are often viewed as an instrument through which courts effect change. Such damages, of course, are allowed to make an example out of or punish an entity for a particularly reckless or wanton act.[183] It is expected that when such damages are imposed the body who receives them will reform its behavior and therefore correct the potential for such risks. In cases involving allegations of fraud or deceit, punitive damages have been imposed notwithstanding the alleged conformance between the conduct and church doctrine.[184] Because this result involves the

---

177. Perhaps this ruling is another unique California agency rule like *Stevens v. Roman Catholic Bishop*, 123 Cal. Rptr. 171 (Ct. App. 1975). *Barr*, 153 Cal. Rptr. at 377. Only nine cases even cite *Barr* (none concerns religious liability). A better statement of the general rule as related in this chapter is that liability must be based on more than a common name or adherence to common doctrine. *See* Roman Catholic Archbishop v. Superior Court, 93 Cal. Rptr. 338 (Ct. App. 1971) (no alter ego in common "catholic" name).

178. *See* Eckler v. General Council of Assemblies of God, 784 S.W.2d 935, 938 (Tex. App. 1990, writ denied). In a secular context, *Glover v. Boy Scouts of America*, 923 P.2d 1383, 1387–88 (Utah 1996), reaches the same conclusions, rejecting liability premised on similarity of dress, name, and even guidelines. The Supreme Court of Oklahoma in *N.H. v. Presbyterian Church*, 998 P.2d 529 (Okla. 1999), rejected an attempt to make the sexual misconduct of one Presbyterian minister the liability of all Presbyterians, a claim premised on the book of discipline of the denomination. The trial court dismissed the novel claim on constitutional grounds, but the Supreme Court dismissed on common law grounds, finding that there was no assertion of knowledge in the denominational governance.

179. *See* Folwell v. Bernard, 477 So. 2d 1060, 1062–63 (Fla. Dist. Ct. App. 1985).

180. 460 N.E.2d 1244 (Ind. Ct. App. 1984).

181. *See id.* at 1246; *see also* Olson v. Magnuson, 457 N.W.2d 394, 397 (Minn. Ct. App. 1990).

182. *Hope Lutheran Church*, 460 N.E.2d at 1248.

183. *See* Keeton et al., *supra* note 79, § 2, at 7.

184. In *Bredberg v. Long*, *George*, and *Wollersheim*, courts punished religious organizations for actions of those who minister in their names, fully consistent with religious doctrine. *See* Bredberg

courts in punishing religious organizations in these cases for the exercise of their beliefs, many commentators condemn it as constitutionally suspect.[185] Although this matter does not vary with either religious polity or corporate structure, it is technically derivative liability. The conformance between the actions of the minister and doctrine provides a basis by which essentially "vicarious" liability is presumed in the organization.

Defenses

Not surprisingly, the defenses which have been claimed reflect precisely the liability principles elucidated at the beginning of this article, with one addition. Because the principles discerned from the cases seem to affect the means by which liability is imposed, religious organizations must examine their governing statutory or corporate responsibilities, denominational relationships, and tendency to involve themselves in taking situational responsibilities.[186] This behavioral attitude sometimes tends to create exposures in organizations seeking to do good and avoid evil, the very same exposures avoided by their profit-making cousins.[187] In addition, they must look to the text and interpretation of state and federal constitutional rights to defend particular cases. Although such limits and protection are debated, where the actions complained of relate to religious doctrine or practices of the entity, constitutional defenses are important.[188]

---

v. Long, 778 F.2d 1285 (8th Cir. 1985) (malicious misconduct in inducing membership in, transfer of assets to, and control over religious community); George v. International Soc'y of Krishna Consciousness, 262 Cal. Rptr. 217 (Ct. App. 1989), *vacated*, 499 U.S. 914 (1991) (concealment of minor from parents); Wollersheim v. Church of Scientology, 260 Cal. Rptr. 331 (Ct. App. 1989), *vacated*, 499 U.S. 914 (1991) (punishment of former member perceived to be a threat to church), *opinion confirmed*, 6 Cal. Rptr. 2d 532 (Ct. App. 1992).

185. Imposition of punitive damages arguably involves the courts in punishing a church for exercise of beliefs, notwithstanding the cases cited immediately above. Punitive damages on account of internal practices, standards, and actions (or the lack thereof) should be constitutionally proscribed. *See* Lundman v. McKown, 530 N.W.2d 807 (Minn. Ct. App. 1995) (reversing award of punitive damages against a national church body on account of its doctrine on spiritual healing). The courts are naturally reluctant to allow this result, and distinguish permitted from unpermitted inquiry. *See* Molko v. Holy Spirit Ass'n, 762 P.2d 46, 59–60 (Cal. 1988). Because of this possibility, some states require (by statute) a showing of a *prima facie* case before punitive damages may be asserted against a religious entity. *See* Cal. Code Civ. Proc. § 425.14 (West Supp. 1999); Rowe v. Superior Court, 19 Cal. Rptr. 2d 625, 638 (Ct. App. 1993) (law designed to mitigate chilling effects on religion from punitive damages claims).

Moreover, when the actions do not conform to church doctrine, direct liability aside, there should be no basis on which to impute liability vicariously (either for compensatory or exemplary damages) against a religious organization. This is not to say that the organization may not have some liability for exemplary damages due to its own direct negligence. This would appear to turn more on the particular construction of state law and its public policy. *See* Mrozka v. Archdiocese of St. Paul, 482 N.W.2d 806 (Minn. Ct. App. 1992) (finding that no exceptions were possible absent some legislative directive).

186. *See* Frohlich, *supra* note 3, at 1396–97 nn. 166–69, 174.

187. *See* R. Hammar et al., Reducing the Risk of Child Sexual Abuse in Your Church, 19, 22 (1993) ("Churches tend to be trusting and unsuspecting institutions...").

188. *See* Pritzlaff v. Archdiocese of Milwaukee, 533 N.W.2d 780 (Wis. 1995); Murphy v. International Soc'y of Krishna Consciousness, 571 N.E.2d 340 (Mass. 1991). The United States Supreme Court in *Employment Div. v. Smith*, 494 U.S. 872 (1990), changed the standard of review under the Free Exercise Clause for facially neutral, generally applicable regulations. However, *Smith* did not abrogate the religious autonomy line of cases. *Id.* at 877. As also noted above, the Establishment

For a religious organization to be held liable, the first line of scrutiny can include statutory or corporate responsibilities. Liability may be premised on corporate authority based on the organizing documents or statutes governing the entity. Resisting the imposition of liability, many organizations use limitations either set forth in their organizing documents or in the civil statute allowing their incorporation. In short, the organization claims it is not empowered to act in the way that has been attributed to it. As noted above, some religious defendants have been successful in dismissing corporations sole when the action in question has concerned matters that go to ecclesial, and not civil, authority.[189] On the other hand, if the matter does concern an aspect of corporate action which is expressly authorized in the state law or the organizing documents, as seen in *Roman Catholic Archbishop*, liability may be attributed to the religious entity in question.[190] Where there are separate corporate entities that have no intercorporate operation and where one does not control or dominate the other, shifting or sharing responsibility should not be tenable. The existence of reserve powers between corporations or the allowance for some oversight of the matter in contention, as seen in *Barr*, may invite courts to speculate about the existence of a liability bridge (even despite constitutional objections). The result may very well turn on whether the control is only ecclesial of is in fact civil.[191] As illustrated by the *Benedictine Society* litigation,[192] separate organizations should be operated separately or liability may follow the links of the chain to determine the responsible party. The solution lies in careful drafting of the organic documents and clarity in expressing religious doctrine, and care in management and administration, as indicated below.

In an unincorporated association, state law may still offer immunity from member suits. For example, take the Pennsylvania court decision in the ordinary accident case of

---

Clause bars the exercise of jurisdiction over religious issues. *See* Brazauskas v. Diocese of Fort Wayne South Bend, 755 N.E.2d 201 (Ind. Ct. App. 2001) (constitution bars shifting tort liability from religious university to diocese on interpretation of church law). Tort litigation is inherently individualized adjudication, and courts have been reluctant to allow the targeting of religious belief in such cases. *E.g., Molko*, 762 P.2d 46; *George*, 262 Cal. Rptr. 217.

189. *See Doe v. O'Connell, P.C.*, No. 86-0077, slip op. (R.I. 1990) and cases cited *supra* notes 33–36. The converse is also true. In a copyright infringement case, a diocesan entity was alleged to be conspiring with parish entities to violate the copyright laws. *See* F.E.L. Publications, Ltd. v. Catholic Bishop, 754 F.2d 216 (7th Cir. 1985). The diocese claimed that the parishes were not all separate civil entities but rather a part of a corporation sole. Because no conspiracy was possible with only one legal person in the case, there could no violation of the copyright laws. The court agreed that the relationship charged by plaintiffs in that case was ecclesial and not civil.

190. *See supra* note 24. Of course there still are places that preserve some measure of charitable immunity, barring tort litigation against charities by their beneficiaries. *Compare* Rupp v. Brookdale Baptist Church, 577 A.2d 188 (N.J. Super. Ct. App. Div. 1990), *with* Williams v. First United Church of Christ, 318 N.E.2d 562 (Ohio Ct. App. 1973). Four states have capped the amount of potential recovery against charitable entities: South Carolina (S.C. Code Ann. §33-56-180 (Law Co-op. Supp. 1998)), Texas (Tex. Civ. Prac. & Rem. Code Ann. §84.006 (West 1997)), New Hampshire (N.H. Rev. Stat. Ann. §508:17(2) (1997)), and Massachusetts (Mass. Gen. Laws Ann. ch. 231, §85K (West Supp. 1999)). A useful discussion and references are found in 2 Bassett, *supra* note 3, §§7:10, :11. Except for these limited examples, liability claims may be asserted against religious organizations and other nonprofits. *See* Hammer, *supra* note 3, ch. 12, at 635–44 (discussing variations of immunity, litigation under state law, etc., and citing authorities). The availability of the liability cap was one factor considered in *Crocker v. Barr*, 409 S.E.2d 368 (S.C. 1991), in deciding to allow litigation against an unincorporated church.

191. *See* Malloy v. Fong, discussed *supra* notes 48–54. *Compare* Hope Lutheran Church v. Chellew, 460 N.E.2d 1244 (Ind. Ct. App. 1984), *with* Barr v. United Methodist Church, 153 Cal. Rptr. 322 (Ct. App. 1979).

192. *See* Benedictine Soc'y v. National City Bank, 109 F.2d 679 (3d Cir. 1940); *see also* Roman Catholic Archbishop v. Superior Court, 93 Cal. Rptr. 338 (Ct. App. 1971).

Zehner v. Wilkinson. The failure of a church board of directors to provide adequate lighting and other matters for the benefit of an unincorporated association was attributed to the individual member plaintiff, precluding her recovery.[193] Although the immunity will not apply against lawsuits brought by outsiders, it does provide a certain measure of comfort in litigation generated by those who are most often in contact with the entity.[194]

Denominational defenses are also employed by religious organizations who point to their limited authority as coordinate or superior entities in the universe of ecclesiastical matters. The division between ecclesial and civil authority and the limited nature of the civil effect, even of ecclesial powers, is illustrated by cases discussed above involving the Episcopal church (*Folwell*), the Presbyterian Church (*N.H.*), the Assemblies of God (*Eckler*), and Catholics (*Brillhart*). When authority is limited by the polity to particular matters or cases and those matters are not implicated in the litigation, a court can find little basis to allow the liability to shift to another unit or level.[195] To deny effect to religious organizations' own declarations on the limits and nature of their authority would directly impair the autonomy of religious organizations in managing their internal affairs, a protection guaranteed in constitutional law. In effect, a court would be reorganizing a religious institution.

Inviting scrutiny of a denomination's book of discipline or internal church law as a basis to limit liability is not, of course, without problems. As is illustrated in *Barr*, courts may be tempted to turn denominational policies offered to limit liability into expansive liability. Assuming proffered contrary testimony can survive a constitutional objection in limine, plaintiffs can find experts willing to testify that the interpretation offered by the church of its own rules or book of discipline is not in fact the best reading. In *Stevens v. Roman Catholic Bishop*, an automobile accident case, experts clashed over the scope of the individual priest's duties from the perspective of the Catholic church's canon law.[196] The court did not validate the opinion offered by the Catholic

---

193. The charitable benefit theory applied quite broadly—including, in one case, precluding a claim by a visitor who entered a chapel to view its unique stained glass. The court, applying Virginia law, found that the windows communicated a religious message to the "benefited" visitor. *See* Egerton v. R.E. Lee Mem'l Church, 395 F.2d 381 (4th Cir. 1968).

194. The Indiana Supreme Court in *Calvary Baptist Church v. Joseph*, 522 N.E.2d 371 (Ind. 1988), while preserving the doctrine of imputed negligence, expressed a willingness to entertain a judicial exception. The Indiana Supreme Court in *Hanson* overruled the applicability of the whole doctrine. *See* Hanson v. St. Luke's United Methodist Church, 704 N.E.2d 1020 (Ind. 1998). The courts have allowed such claims against unincorporated unions, "breaking the veil of incorporation" when the association becomes so large or structural that the individual member's control is minimal over the affairs of the entity. Such an approach did not apply in *Joseph* where the injured member, a deacon, was hurt during a volunteer project agreed to by a number of church members. *See Joseph*, 522 N.E.2d at 375. One can imagine that a larger entity with more separate identity and structure might not fare as well. *See also supra* note 39.

195. In *Kersh v. General Council of Assemblies of God*, 804 F.2d 546 (9th Cir. 1986), the plaintiff sued regional and national bodies in that denomination claiming securities fraud, for failure to supervise fund-raising at a local church. The plaintiff's success depended on his ability to show a conspiracy between a local church, which was accepting donation for a trust fund and a supervising entity, to pass along liability from the now-bankrupt church to the national body. Accepting the limited authority of the district council and General Council, the federal courts concluded that no "control" was shown as required under the securities law. On the other hand, where it was alleged that a congregational leader was using organizational bank accounts for the laundering of monies as part of a conspiracy to defraud a member, that member stated a case for violation of RICO. *See* Gruenwald v. Bornfreund, 668 F. Supp. 128 (E.D.N.Y. 1987).

196. *See* Stevens v. Roman Catholic Bishop, 123 Cal. Rptr. 171, 174–77 (Ct. App. 1975).

bishop's expert, who explained the supervision allowed under canon law. Instead, the court accepted the view offered by plaintiff's expert as consistent not only with canon law but California law. Those who evaluate such cases should take care to note that church law cannot be interpreted in the same way or by the same rules of construction as statutory law and that proposed interpretations may be unconstitutional.[197]

On the other hand, in *Kelly v. Lutheran Church in America* parents brought a personal injury action against various levels of a hierarchical church premised on operation of church law.[198] The property where the injury occurred belonged to a church which had merged into another congregation. The parents argued that under church law the property of the former corporation became property of the parent (regional and national) entities upon the local church's dissolution. The court acknowledged both the hierarchical structure of the religious entity and denominational rules under which the local congregation retained authority to control and maintain its own property. Upon merger (as opposed to the dissolution of the congregation) the assets, including the property merged into the surviving local body, did not cede to the parent body.[199] The plaintiff's denominational argument was rejected based on a counterargument offered by the religious organization.

The results in the above situations also illustrate the need for religious organizations not to involve themselves unnecessarily or uncritically in actions which could risk imposition of liability, regardless of the clarity of limits in their statutory or corporate documents or ecclesial rules that separate functions. A successful factual defense means that the plaintiff will not be able to show, even after discovery, that the charged entity has in fact been involved in the contested transaction.[200] Moreover, the plaintiff will not be able to show that the religious body continued to control the agent or otherwise ratified the agent's action.[201] Finally, for a more complex factual claim, the plaintiffs will not be able to demonstrate that the superior or coordinate religious body had knowledge of actions undertaken and the ability to have prevented the harm.[202] In such cases, notwithstanding the availability of other defenses, the religious entity will prevail because the plaintiffs simply will not be able to prove that the body, contrary to its doctrine or governing statutes, insinuated itself into the problem.

Indeed, the cases demonstrate that at the point where a religious entity severs relationships with an agent or employee, its liability ends. In *Schmidt v. Bishop* a woman filed a personal injury against a former Presbyterian minister and his former church and national body alleging sexual misconduct by the former minister during his service at the church. It appeared that the minister resigned his position as pastor, removing him-

---

197. *See* Brazauskas v. Diocese of Fort Wayne-South Bend, 755 N.E.2d 201 (Ind. Ct. App. 2001); Frohlich, *supra* note 3, at 1390 & nn. 129–30 (bewildering complexity of church or religious forms).

198. Kelly v. Lutheran Church in Am., 589 A.2d 1155 (Pa. Super. Ct. 1991).

199. *See id.* at 1158. In addition, there was no factual basis on which to apply liability. The title documents for the property at issue properly reflected the fact that the surviving religious body at the local level acquired title.

200. *See* Dunn v. Catholic Home Bureau for Dependent Children, 537 N.Y.S.2d 742 (Sup. Ct. 1989) (no showing contrary to director's affidavit that Catholic diocese exercised any supervisory authority over agency).

201. *See* Eastern Renovating Corp. v. Roman Catholic Bishop, 554 F.2d 4, 7 (1st Cir. 1977).

202. *See* N.H. v. Presbyterian Church, 998 P.2d 529 (Okla. 1999); Konkle v. Henson, 672 N.E.2d 450, 461 (Ind. Ct. App. 1996); Eckler v. General Council of Assemblies of God, 784 S.W.2d 935, 937–38 (Tex. App. 1990, writ denied).

self from the controlling supervision of the denomination. Although he continued to be listed as "pastor emeritus," he joined as a minister a different religious denomination. Rejecting the claim that the religious denomination should still be answerable for the crimes committed by its former minister, the court indicated that the religious denomination lacked the ability to supervise him. Having severed its relationships with its former minister, the religious body could no longer be responsible for the conduct of that person.[203] This kind of clarity is a lesson for all denominations and polities.

Finally, in addition to statutory, denominational, and factual defenses, constitutional defenses come to bear upon liability cases. Case law indicates that these are available in three areas: in barring church members to contest actions undertaken in furtherance of internal church practices,[204] in barring claims which target unverifiable religious beliefs expressed in the name of the denomination,[205] and in the unwillingness of courts to allow for a new cause of action that would result in greater judicial oversight of the conduct of the affairs of religious organizations, such as clergy malpractice.[206] The discussion above, however, warns of the possible limits of this defense wherever serious consequences are seemingly intended to third parties or to outsiders[207] or when the conduct has consequences that are particularly egregious when measured by secular standards.[208] In other cases courts are constitutionally denied the power to allow a secular standard to measure internal religious conduct, especially in the selection, training, and supervision of clergy or in the setting of (or failure to set) internal policy, but they are allowed to protect third parties against consequences of secular actions.

Conclusion

Derivative liability is an idea broader than holding hierarchical entities liable in tort for the actions of subordinates. Such liability may be seen in efforts to compel an organization to take responsibility for any dereliction of its agent, employee, or related entity. For religious groups, these efforts engage a court in reviewing the conduct of those who minister, in the broadest sense, for the group. Of course, religious groups, like

---

203. Schmidt v. Bishop, 779 F. Supp. 321, 331–32 (S.D.N.Y. 1991).

204. *See* Guinn v. Church of Christ, 775 P.2d 766 (Okla. 1989); Gruenwald v. Bornfreund, 696 F. Supp. 838 (E.D.N.Y. 1988). *But see Konkle*, 672 N.E.2d 450.

205. *See* Anderson v. Worldwide Church of God, 661 F. Supp. 1400 (D. Minn. 1987). Where claims relate not to conduct but to the beliefs held by church members and their expression of those beliefs, the First Amendment protects the church. *See* Eliason v. Church of Jesus Christ of Latter-day Saints, No. 81095 (D. Idaho Nov. 28, 1984).

206. Franco v. Church of Jesus Christ of Latter-day Saints, 21 P.2d 198 (Utah 2001); Pritzlaff v. Archdiocese of Milwaukee, 533 N.W.2d 780 (Wis. 1995). *See Schmidt*, 779 F. Supp. at 327. It is noted, however, that tort remedies are already available for the intentional harm and the direct negligence (failure of supervision) of the religious body. There is no need to make the counseling actionable itself. *See* Byrd v. Faber, 565 N.E.2d 584 (Ohio 1991). Such a result would also extend to claims that would make religious conduct actionable (e.g., failure to set adequate standards for clergy training). There are also constitutional limits on courts resetting the polity in accord with facts in a complaint. Chopko, Continuing the Lord's Work, *supra* note 8.

207. *Compare Guinn*, 775 P.2d 766, *with* Bear v. Reformed Mennonite Church, 341 A.2d 105 (Pa. 1975).

208. *See* Wollersheim v. Church of Scientology, 260 Cal. Rptr. 331 (Ct. App. 1989), *vacated*, 499 U.S. 914 (1991), *opinion confirmed*, 6 Cal. Rptr. 2d 532 (Ct. App. 1992).

other entities in this society, are liable for the direct consequences of their actions. Distinct from direct liability, however, derivative liability concerns only those cases in which the organization is asked to assume derivative (or sometimes precisely vicarious) responsibility for the actions of others. Such responsibility is found in cases without distinctions based on polity, organizational, or corporate lines.

This chapter began with a search for organizing principles in the diverse body of liability law. Liability has rested on three themes. First, if the civil statutory or corporate form of an entity vests it with the responsibility for the matter that gave rise to the litigation, liability may attach. A corporation formed to hold religious property, for example, may find itself liable for repair bills as an incident of its business. Second, if a denomination has reserved the power to decide the matter being litigated, liability may attach. Religious bodies that reserve the power to discipline clergy may find they must answer for the failure of discipline in particular cases. Third, if the group insinuated itself into a set of circumstances that gave rise to the matter being litigated, liability may attach.

Religious organizations struggling to understand their confrontations with the legal system might well pay attention to how their very structures, expressions of polity or discipline, or actions perhaps unwittingly commit them to liability. The risk is real and may very well encompass matters beyond the practical daily control of an organization and those who minister for it.

How the Legal System's Treatment of Clerical Sexual Misconduct with Minors Affects Religious Freedom

Stephen J. Pope and Patricia B. Carlson

In his chapter on derivative liability, Mark E. Chopko discusses the ways in which religious organizations can be held responsible under civil law for the conduct of others, such as their clergy or a related group, and how this affects religious liberty.[1] The plethora of recent claims of clerical sexual misconduct with minors has put a new focus on this topic. While abuse by Catholic priests has perhaps received the most media attention, the problem occurs in all religious denominations.[2] As one newspaper reported, "In the last decade, clergy sexual misconduct has been exposed in virtually every faith tradition. National studies have shown no differences in its frequency by denomination, religion, theology or institutional structure."[3]

Some fear that in trying to eradicate clerical sexual abuse, the legal system will ignore religious freedom. Others say that the problem needs to be solved at any cost.

This chapter will explore how the legal system's treatment of these claims, particularly its view of a church's polity and self-understanding, is affecting religious freedom. It deals with these issues not only from the legal point of view, but also from the ethical point of view. This is because churches obviously have a moral dimension and, as such, abhor clerical sexual abuse. Therefore, in approaching this problem, churches have to determine not only what they may be required or permitted to do legally, but also what they should morally and ethically do. Then they have to provide guidance to their attorneys and leadership to their members about the moral and ethical dimensions of the issue.

---

1. *See* Mark E. Chopko, "Derivative Liability," in this volume.

2. *See* Minister Sentenced for Sex Abuse: He Served Several Baptist Churches, Concord Monitor, Aug. 2, 2003, at http://www.cmonitor.com/stories/news/state2003/nh_rapesentence_2003.shtmil; Rabbi's Arrest on Sex Abuse Charges Divides Oklahoma City, World Religion News Service, May 3, 2002, at http://www.rockross.com/reference/clergy/clergy69.html; Buddhist Abbot Released on Bail for Sex Offenses, Taipei Times, July 30, 2000, at http://www.american-buddha.com/buddh.monk.htm.

3. Theresa Watanabe, Sex Abuse by Clerics—a Crisis of Many Faiths, Los Angeles Times, Mar. 25, 2002, at http://www.latimes.com/la-032502punish.story.

For the sake of clarity it bears mentioning that by "religious freedom" we refer to the two Religion Clauses of the First Amendment. The Establishment Clause provides that the government may not pass laws that establish a state religion, and the Free Exercise Clause requires that a citizen's right to practice his or her religion may not be interfered with by the state.[4] This chapter examines the ways in which responses of the courts and the government to the clerical sex abuse scandal are having an impact on both of these clauses.

Individual Liability of Clergy

There are a few instances in which people allege that acts involving sexual behaviors with minors are part of their religious beliefs. For instance, a religious organization founded by a person named Allen Harrod, who wrote his own interpretation of Mormon doctrine, allegedly believes that daughters should have sexual experiences when they reach seven years old and that he, Harrod, should rape and have oral sex with girls when they reach puberty.[5] Another example is David Koresh and his followers in the Branch Davidians, who believed on the basis of several scriptural passages that Koresh was the "lamb" and that as such, he had the only pure seed and was the only one who should have intercourse with his female followers, including those who were underage. One Koresh follower who met with him when she was fourteen and had intercourse with him when she was seventeen said it had been a very "spiritual" experience.[6]

Similarly, in *DeBose v. Bear Valley Church of Christ*,[7] a minister alleged that he massaged his young counselees only to facilitate their communication with God. The Colorado Court of Appeals found that the minister was entitled to a jury instruction such that if the jury agreed with the minister, his actions were protected by the First Amendment and the jury had to conclude that he had not engaged in outrageous conduct toward the minor. The Colorado Supreme Court reversed this holding on the basis that the minister's reliance on massage was based on his personal preference for massage as a relaxation technique and not on any "biblical, doctrinal, or spiritual basis, justification, or underpinning."[8]

For the most part, however, churches do not defend cases alleging clerical sexual misconduct with minors by stating that their religious beliefs mandate that their clergy abuse children. For example, in *Malicki v. Doe*[9] a minor and an adult sued the Archdiocese of Miami on the grounds that it had negligently supervised a priest who sexually assaulted them. In its March 14, 2002 decision, the Florida Supreme Court noted, "In this case, the Church Defendants do not claim that the underlying acts of its priest in committing sexual assault and battery was governed by sincerely held religious beliefs or practices."[10]

In fact, most religions explicitly condemn sexual abuse of minors. For example, rather than claiming freedom to engage in sexual abuse, the Catholic church explicitly

---

4. U.S. Const. amend. I.

5. *See* Mareva Brown and Denny Walsh, Texas Couple Held in Ritual Sex Abuse, Sacramento Bee, Aug. 28, 2003, at http://www.sacbee.com.

6. Dean M. Kelley, Waco: A Massacre and Its Aftermath, 53 First Things 22, 24 (May 1995).

7. 890 P.2d 214 (Colo. Ct. App. 1995), *rev'd*, 928 P.2d 1315 (Colo. 1997).

8. *Bear Valley*, 928 P.2d 1315, 1323 (Colo. 1997).

9. 814 So.2d 347 (Fla. 2002).

10. *Id.* at 360–361.

prohibits all forms of such abuse. Furthermore, it unequivocally forbids clergy to engage in sexual abuse of any kind. Special opprobrium is directed to the sexual abuse of minors. The 1983 revised Code of Canon Law, Canon 1395, par. 2 states: "If a cleric has otherwise committed an offense against the sixth commandment of the Decalogue with force or publicly or with a minor below the age of sixteen, the cleric is to be punished with just penalties, including dismissal from the clerical state if the case warrants it."[11]

Other denominations also condemn sex abuse. On May 3, 2002, the bishops of the United Methodist Church issued a statement that "There is little doubt that sexual abuse by clergy or representative lay ministers in church and society is troubling for our communities and congregations worldwide.... [T]hese acts damage the integrity of the church's witness. As members of the Council of Bishops of The United Methodist Church, we affirm our resolve to prevent and eradicate sexual abuse and misconduct in the church."[12] In about June 2003 the National Society for Hebrew Day Schools, which represents more than seven hundred Orthodox day schools, adopted policies designed to prevent sexual abuse of minors.[13] Buddhism's third precept, which is one of its major ethical principles, is abstention from sexual misconduct.[14] Thich Nhat Hanh, a Vietnamese Buddhist monk, has updated this precept to state, "I will do everything in my power to protect children from sexual abuse."[15]

Religious freedom refers to the right to practice the tenets of one's religious faith. Since most churches explicitly condemn sexually abusive behavior—even to the point of describing it as a "mortal sin" worthy of eternal damnation—one cannot claim that their ordained ministers ought to be legally immune from prosecution for such crimes on the grounds of religious freedom. Therefore, to punish them does not impinge upon religious freedom.

Moreover, even in cases where sexual abuse of minors is part of sincerely held religious beliefs, legislatures are free to prohibit it. The Free Exercise Clause of the First Amendment provides that "Congress shall make no law...prohibiting the free exercise [of religion]."[16] Although the freedoms to believe and to worship are absolute, the freedom to act is not.[17] As the United States Supreme Court stated in *Cantwell v. State of Connecticut,* the First Amendment "embraces two concepts,—freedom to believe and freedom to act. The first is absolute but, in the nature of things, the second cannot be. Conduct remains subject to regulation for the protection of society."[18]

---

11. *See also* the 1917 Code of Canon Law, Canon 2359, par. 2; *see also* the Code of the Eastern Churches from 1990, Canon 1435, par. 1.

12. M. Garlinda Burton, Bishops Speak out on Clergy Sexual Abuse, United Methodist News Service, May 3, 2002, at http://www.umns.umc.org/02/may/201.htm.

13. Julie Gruenbaum Fax, Schools Adopt Guide to Block Sex Abuse, The Jewish Journal of Greater Los Angeles, June 20, 2003, at http://www.jewishjournal.com/home/searchview.php?id=10717.

14. Paul D. Numrich, Case Study of Posting Five Precepts: A Buddhist Perspective on Ethics in Health Care, The Park Ridge Center for Health, Faith, and Ethics Bulletin, November/December 1999, at http://www.parkridgecenter.org/Page43.html.

15. Thich Nhat Hahn, For a Future to Be Possible; Commentaries on the Five Wonderful Precepts, 29 (1993), *quoted in* Rev. Leslie Heyboer, Things We Can't Talk About, Unitarian Universalist Northern Hills Fellowship Sermon Archive, Jan. 30, 1994, at http://www.uunhf.org/sunday/sermons/text/19940130/.

16. U.S. Const. amend. I.

17. *E.g.* NAACP v. Claiborne Hardware Co., 458 U.S. 886, 915 (1982); Brandenburg v. Ohio, 395 U.S. 444, 447 (1969).

18. 310 U.S. 296, 303–304 (1940).

Of course this does not mean there are no limits on the state's ability to regulate church conduct. As the Court stated in *Cantwell*, "In every case the power to regulate must be so exercised as not, in attaining a permissible end, unduly to infringe the protected freedom."[19] There the Court struck down a Connecticut statute that prohibited solicitation for religious or charitable causes without the approval of the secretary of the public welfare council. The Court found that "in light of the constitutional guarantees," the law was not "narrowly drawn to define and punish specific conduct as constituting a clear and present danger to a substantial interest of the State."[20] In that case, Newton Cantwell and his sons were just asking people to buy a religious book or contribute toward its publication. There was no evidence that their solicitation would cause a riot or otherwise immediately threaten public safety, peace, or order, so the Court struck down the statute. Moreover, as noted below, in 1990 the U.S. Supreme Court in *Employment Div., Dept. of Human Resources of Oregon v. Smith*[21] said that if a law is not neutral toward religion and if the government has no compelling interest in enforcing it, then the law is invalid. There the Court found that the prohibition against using peyote was a neutral law of general applicability, and so upheld it. Three years later, however, the Court struck down ordinances passed by a city in Florida that prohibited the ritual slaughter of animals because the ordinances were not neutral, but instead were targeted at the Santeria religion, and the city had no compelling interest in outlawing this religious practice.[22]

Even under these strict criteria, however, the First Amendment would allow the government to outlaw clerical sexual abuse of minors. Sexual abuse of minors presents a clear and present danger to society, and most if not all statutes outlawing it are neutral laws of general applicability. The state has a compelling interest in forbidding such conduct. Therefore, it can forbid clergy from sexually abusing minors.

Liability of a Church for Clergy Misconduct

While it is clear that clergy can and should be held civilly and criminally responsible for sexual misconduct, even if it is based on religious beliefs, there are different issues involved when one evaluates a church's responsibility for the acts of its clergy. The church itself did not abuse the child, nor did it request that the clergy perpetrator abuse the child. Instead, it is being held liable under other theories and, depending upon how the state holds it responsible, this may affect the church's exercise of its religious freedom.

Theories of liability

Three major causes of action have been brought to hold a church liable for clergy misconduct. As Chopko has discussed in his chapter on derivative liability in this volume, and in his recent article in the *Boston College Law Review*,[23] these are respondeat

---

19. *Id.* at 304.

20. *Id.* at 311.

21. 494 U.S. 872 (1990).

22. Church of the Lukumi Babalu Aye, Inc. v. City of Hialea, 508 U.S. 520 (1993).

23. Mark Chopko, Stating Claims Against Religious Institutions, 44 B.C.L. Rev. 1089, 1119 (July/Sept. 2003).

superior, breach of fiduciary duty, and negligent hiring or supervision of employees or other agents.

Respondeat superior

Under respondeat superior, a church is liable vicariously, regardless of its own fault, if the church's agents—its clergy—have caused the plaintiff's injury while acting within the scope of their employment and in furtherance of the church's business.[24] The overwhelming majority of jurisdictions hold that employers in general, and church entities in particular, cannot be vicariously liable for sexual abuse because sexual abuse, as a matter of law, is not within the scope of employment and not in furtherance of the "business" of the employer. As one court noted, "the majority of jurisdictions considering the issue of sexual contact between an ecclesiastic officer and a parishioner have held that the act is outside the scope of employment as a matter of law."[25]

A small minority of jurisdictions, however, have declined to follow the Restatement (Second) and do not require that the act itself be in furtherance of the employer's business. In these jurisdictions, a plaintiff is entitled to argue to a jury that under the totality of the circumstances, the sexual abuse was "foreseeable" (defined for these purposes

---

24. *See* Restatement (Second) of Agency.

25. N.H. v. Presbyterian Church (U.S.A.), 998 P.2d 592, 599 (Okla. 1999). The overwhelming majority of jurisdictions hold that there can be no vicarious liability for sexual abuse. *See* John R. Oakland Unified School Dist., 769 P.2d 948 (Cal. App.1989) *reh'g denied* (1989); Debbie Reynolds Prof. Rehearsal Studios v. Superior Court, 25 Cal. App. 4th 222, 227–228 (2d Dist. 1994); Rita M. v. Roman Catholic Archbishop of Los Angeles, 187 Cal. App. 3d 1453, 1461 (2d Dist. 1986), *review denied* (1987); Moses v. Diocese of Colorado, 863 P.2d 310 (Colo.), 329–331, *cert. denied*, 511 U.S. 1137(1994) (reversing jury verdict because sex with parishioner is outside the scope of employment "as a matter of law"); Nutt v. Norwich Roman Catholic Diocese, 921 F. Supp. 66, 71 (D. Conn. 1995) ("Sexually abusive conduct amounts to the abandonment of the Church's business. As a matter of law, therefore, the alleged sexual abuse, even if true, cannot be said to further the defendant's business and therefore is outside the scope of employment"); Iglesia Cristiana La Casa Del Señor, Inc. v. L.M., 783 So. 2d 353, 356–358 (Fla. App. 2001); Alpharetta First United Methodist Church v. Stewart, 472 S.E.2d 532, 535–536 (Ga. Ct. App. 1996) ("It is well settled under Georgia law that an employer is not responsible for the sexual misconduct of an employee"); Konkle v. Henson, 672 N.E.2d 450, 457 (Ind. App. 1996) (Minister's sex abuse was "not similar to his duties as a minister. [He] may have had access to [the victim] because of his position as pastor, but he was not engaging in authorized acts or serving the interests of his employer at the time he molested [the victim]"); Osborne v. Payne, 31 S.W.3d 911, 915 (Ky. 2000) (vicarious liability for priest's sexual activities "would in effect require the diocese to become an absolute insurer for the behavior of anyone who was in the priesthood and would result in strict liability on the part of the diocese...We must conclude that such an argument is absurd"); Tichenor v. Roman Catholic Church of the Archdiocese of New Orleans, 32 F.3d 953, 960 (5th Cir. 1994) (Applying Mississippi law, court holds that priest's "illicit sexual pursuits"...represent the paradigmatic pursuit of 'some purpose unrelated to his master's business.'") (citation omitted); H.R.B. v. J.C.G., 913 S.W.2d 92, 96 (Mo. App. 1995); Wilson v. Diocese of New York of the Episcopal Church, No. 96 Civ. 2400 (JGK), 1998 WL 82921, *5 (S.D. N.Y. Feb. 26, 1998) ("sexual misconduct by priests...[is] outside the scope of the priests' employment and [is] clearly not in furtherance of the Diocese's...business" even though assaults occurred on church property); Joshua S. v. Casey, 206 A.D.2d 839 (N.Y. App. Div. 1994) ("The alleged sexual assault was not within the scope of employment...and cannot be said to have been in furtherance of the employer's business") (citation omitted); N.H. v. Presbyterian Church (U.S.A.), 998 P.2d 592, 598–600 (Okla. 1999) ("the majority of jurisdictions considering the issue of sexual contact between an ecclesiastic officer and a parishioner have held that the act is outside the scope of employment as a matter of law. We agree") (footnote collecting cases omitted); C.J.C. v. Corp. of the Catholic Bishop of Yakima, 985 P.2d 262, 272, *as amended* (Wash. 1999); L.L.N. v. Clauder, 552 N.W.2d 879, 888 (Wis. Ct. App. 1996), *rev'd in part on other grounds*, 563 N.W.2d 434 (Wis. 1997).

as "possible") and therefore within the scope of employment because it occurred in the context of the clergy/parishioner relationship.[26]

Breach of fiduciary duty

Another claim that plaintiffs make is that churches are liable because they are in a fiduciary relationship to the plaintiffs and therefore must act in their best interests. Although, however, some courts have found such a fiduciary relationship between a priest and a parishioner, they rarely have found a fiduciary relationship between a larger church body, such as a diocese, and a parishioner.[27] It appears that the parishioner must have a unique relationship with the diocese, or the diocese must have assumed some duties toward the parishioner, for such a fiduciary relationship to occur.

For example, in *Moses v. Diocese of Colorado*,[28] where a fiduciary relationship was found, the adult plaintiff had a sexual relationship with an Episcopalian priest who was counseling her. When the bishop of the Episcopal Diocese of Colorado learned of the relationship, he scheduled a meeting with the plaintiff, during which he gave her absolution for the affair and told her not to talk to anyone about it. The Colorado Supreme Court affirmed the jury's finding that the bishop and the episcopal diocese had had a fiduciary relationship with the plaintiff because of the bishop's meeting with the plaintiff, and that they had breached their fiduciary duty because the bishop had not recommended counseling for the plaintiff and had "failed to assist her in understanding that she was not the only person responsible for her sexual relationship" with the priest.[29]

Similarly, in *Martinelli v. Bridgeport Roman Catholic Diocesan Corporation*[30] the U. S. Court of Appeals for the Second Circuit found that a jury could have determined that there was a fiduciary relationship between the Diocese of Bridgeport, Connecticut, and the plaintiff, who had been sexually abused as a minor by one of the priests of the diocese, because of the plaintiff's particular ties to the diocese and the "Diocese's knowledge and sponsorship of that relationship."[31] The court pointed to the fact that the plaintiff had attended a diocesan high school and had been taught by diocesan priests and that a monsignor, who was the guidance counselor at the high school, specifically knew that the priest perpetrator had been spending a considerable amount of time with the plaintiff. The court also noted that the diocese had encouraged the priest perpetrator to work with youth by putting him in charge of the diocese's Catholic Youth Organization, and also that the diocese must have known that the priest perpetrator was escorting boys on church field trips. Because of all these ties, the Second Circuit held that when the diocese learned that the priest perpetrator "had sexually molested boys, at least one of them unidentified, it owed the boys within the scope of its fiduciary obligations, including [the plaintiff], a duty to investigate and to warn possible past and future victims of the harm."[32] By failing to do so, the diocese kept the plaintiff from receiving the treatment he needed, and so exacerbated his injury.

---

26. *See, e.g.,* Fearing v. Bucher, 977 P.2d 1163 (Or. 1999); Fahrendorff v. North Homes, Inc., 597 N.W.2d 905 (Minn. 1999).
27. Doe v. Norwich Roman Catholic Diocesan Corporation, 268 F. Supp.2d 139, 149 (D. Conn. 2003).
28. 863 P.2d 310 (Colo. 1993), *cert. denied,* 511 U.S. 1137 (1994).
29. *Id.* at 323.
30. 196 F.3d 409 (2nd Cir. 1999).
31. *Id.* at 429.
32. *Id.* at 426.

In the 2003 case of *Doe v. Norwich Roman Catholic Diocesan Corporation*,[33] the U. S. District Court for the District of Connecticut refused to extend *Martinelli*. The court held that the fact that the plaintiff was a parishioner in one of the Norwich diocese's parishes was not enough to establish a fiduciary relationship between the plaintiff and the diocese. Therefore, there was no basis for a claim of breach of fiduciary duty.

Negligent hiring and supervision

The most common basis for suits based on clerical sexual misconduct is direct negligence by church entities in the hiring, placement, or supervision of clerical staff. Unlike vicarious liability, which imposes liability on an employer on the basis of the employment relationship alone without a showing of the employer's fault, negligence is based on an alleged breach of duty by the employer. Under the common law, a defendant will be liable for negligence when the plaintiff proves that (a) the defendant owed the plaintiff a legal duty, (b) the defendant breached its duty, and (c) the breach proximately caused the plaintiff injury, (d) resulting in recoverable damages.

In the context of a clergy misconduct case, the duty is typically found to be that of not placing a known child abuser in a position to abuse more children. This can also be phrased as a duty to supervise such a priest and/or to warn the congregation not to entrust its children to him.[34] The breach of duty would be a diocese's decision to assign, or leave in place, a priest about whom it knows or "should know" of a propensity to abuse children sexually.[35] Causation is established because there is a strong relationship between the diocese's actions (placing or retaining the priest) and the plaintiff's injury (the plaintiff only came in contact with the priest because the diocese held him out as a trustworthy minister). Damage is also easily established if the abuse is proved, since there is little doubt that sexual abuse causes serious damage to children, both at the time of the abuse and over the course of their lives. The current rule in the majority of states is that an individual diocese is liable if it "knew or should have known" of the

---

33. 268 F. Supp. 2d 139 (D. Conn. 2003). Note that the plaintiff then amended her complaint to allege that she was a member of certain church- or diocesan-sponsored activities, such as the Catholic Youth Organization and the church choir, and that she had consulted with the priest for spiritual and religious counseling. Based on these facts, the U.S. District Court for the District of Connecticut refused to dismiss the court in plaintiff's amended complaint that alleged breach of fiduciary duty. 309 F. Supp. 2d 247 (D.Conn. 2004).

34. Most of the cases deal with the duty to supervise, not the duty to warn. In *Miller v. Everett*, 576 So.2d 1162 (La. 1991), however, the plaintiffs did allege that pastor of church should have warned them that the church's youth minister, whom he was counseling, was abusing the plaintiffs' children. The court found that there was no duty to warn because the plaintiffs were not members of the pastor's church and the molestation was not connected to the youth minister's work for the church.

35. Negligence claims typically rely on the allegation that a diocese "knew or should have known" either of a priest's past incidents of child abuse or of his propensity to abuse children. In the clearest case, this allegation is based on the existence of previous complaints about the priest. Allegations that a diocese "should have known" of the danger because of a priest's suspicious but ambiguous conduct can present very subjective, fact-specific questions to a court, making early dismissal of the case quite difficult. Even more problematic are "notice" allegations based on the diocese's alleged knowledge that priests in general are sexually abusing minors, resulting in a duty to more aggressively supervise and screen clergy. These plaintiffs often seek to put a diocese's entire history of handling misconduct claims on trial.

priest's propensity to abuse minors, but negligently supervised or retained the priest, thus allowing him to injure others.[36]

Impact on religious freedom of respondeat superior, breach of fiduciary duty, and negligent hiring and supervision claims

Some attorneys have argued that the First Amendment prevents a church body from being held liable for sexual misconduct with minors.[37] For example, in 2003, L. Martin Nussbaum argued on behalf of the Archdiocese of Boston that "It is absolutely our position that when it comes to this bishop-priest relationship...the court can't get into the business of defining what a reasonably prudent bishop would do in that relationship."[38] In an earlier case, the priests who allegedly were negligent in their supervision of the Reverend John Geoghan, thereby allowing him to abuse children, argued that "their supervisory responsibilities and their responsibilities for training and retention of Geoghan are derived from ecumenical principles, precepts and law and thus under the First Amendment to the Constitution of the United States and under Art. II of the Declaration of Rights, a civil court has no power to inquire into them."[39]

Questions not yet decided

The question of whether courts are prohibited under the First Amendment from dealing with clergy sexual abuse has not yet been presented to the U. S. Supreme Court or to many other high courts.[40] Currently, both the courts and the commentators are divided on whether the First Amendment should bar such suits.[41]

---

36. *E.g.*, Moses v. Diocese of Colorado, 863 P.2d 310, 327–328 (Colo. 1993); Restatement (Second) of Agency § 213(b) (1958).

37. In *Kelly v. Marcantonio*, 187 F.3d 192, the First Circuit noted that "courts should not reach constitutional questions in advance of the necessity of deciding them." *Id.* at 197 (*quoting from* Parella v. Retirement Bd. of the Rhode Island Employees' Retirement System, 173 F.3d 46, 56 (1st Cir. 1999)). In that case, it first decided that the plaintiffs' claims were barred by the statute of limitations, and so did not decide whether the court lacked subject matter jurisdiction on the grounds that the First Amendment prevents a court from adjudicating clerical sexual misconduct cases. Thus, there are many cases in which courts do not have to reach the issue about whether these claims are barred by the First Amendment.

38. Kathleen Burge, Judge Rules Church Suits Can Proceed, Boston Globe, Feb. 20, 2003, at A1.

39. Leary v. Geoghan, 2000 WL 1473579 (Mass. Super. June 28, 2000) (footnotes omitted).

40. Malicki v. Doe, 814 So.2d 347, 357 (Fla. 2002). *See* Lisa J. Kelty, *Malicki v. Doe*: The Constitutionality of Negligent Hiring and Supervision Claims, 69 Brook L. Rev. 1121, 1122 fn. 6 (Spring 2004); Christopher L. Barbaruolo, *Malicki v. Doe*: Defining a Split of Authority Based on the State Tort Claims of Negligent Hiring and Supervision of Roman Catholic Clergy and the First Amendment Conflict, 32 Hofstra L. Rev. 423, 443 (Fall. 2003).

41. Christopher R. Farrel, Note: Ecclesiastical Abstention and the Crisis in the Catholic Church, 19 J.L. & Pol. 109, 143 (Winter 2003) ("the only conclusion consistent with the Supreme Court's prior First Amendment jurisprudence is that the ecclesiastical abstention doctrine prevents civil courts from entertaining any claims against church officials based on respondeat superior, negligence, or intentional failure to supervise); Brittany Reid, "If Gold Rust": The Clergy Child Abuse Scandal Demonstrates the Need for Limits to the Church Autonomy Doctrine, 72 Miss. L.J. 865, 884 (Winter 2002) ("In most negligent handling cases against churches, the state interest in preventing child abuse should outweigh the burden that is placed on the free exercise rights of the church"); John S. Brennan, The First Amendment is Not the 8th Sacrament: Exorcizing the Ecclesiastical Ab-

Some, but not absolute, deference to church decisions

It is true that the civil courts will respect the decisions of a church on ecclesiastical questions, such as church governance, and on religious questions, such as the interpretation of religious doctrine.[42] As noted above, however, although the principle of deference to church decisions on ecclesiastical matters is strong and well established, there have been exceptions. Before 1976 there was an exception for decisions procured by "fraud, collusion, or arbitrariness."[43] Since 1976, this exception has been narrowed to include only fraud and collusion while the arbitrariness component has been dropped. Moreover, since 1979[44] an alternative to the deference principle, referred to as the "neutral principles of law" approach, has been in place, at least in part because not all churches have well-established processes and clearly designated decision makers. According to this principle the courts will look to documents such as deeds and decide cases without any reference to church decisions. Subsequent decisions in the lower courts have extended this principle beyond the property questions to which it was originally addressed. Given these decisions and some commentaries, the principle is sometimes used almost as a slogan to eclipse the principle of deference to church decisions.

In 1990 a third principle was introduced into this mix, according to which religious organizations must observe neutral laws of general application. This principle was generated by the U. S. Supreme Court in *Employment Div., Dept. of Human Resources of Oregon v. Smith* to deal with practices, such as the use of prohibited drugs, which people attempted to justify because they were part of a bona fide religious observance.[45] However, if the law is not neutral or if the government has no compelling interest in enforcing it, then it is still invalid. Thus, in *Church of the Lukumi Babalu Aye, Inc. v. City of Hialeah*,[46] the U. S. Supreme Court invalidated a city ordinance relating to the ritual slaughter of animals on the grounds that it was not a neutral, generally applicable law and that the government did not have a compelling interest in enforcing it.

In short, the principle of deference to church decisions is not and never has been absolute. There are exceptions and alternative principles that can be used in difficult situations. It appears that sexual abuse of minors on the part of the clergy may well present such a situation.

---

stention Doctrine Defense from Legal and Equitable Claims for Sexual Abuse Based on Negligent Supervision or Hiring of Clergy, 5 T.M. Cooley J. Prac. & Clinical L. 243, 291 (2002) ("The tort is a neutral law of general applicability which may have the incidental effect of burdening a particular religious practice, and is thus constitutionally applied to churches. Even if the negligence action could be described as targeting religiously motivated conduct, there is hardly debate on the issue that protection of children and other vulnerable persons from sexual abuse is a 'compelling state interest'").

42. Serbian Eastern Orthodox Diocese v. Milivojevich, 426 U.S. 696, 720 (1976). Improper entanglement by courts in religious controversies occurs when the government becomes involved in the evaluation of religious practices or participates in an extensive investigation into church operations. *See* N.L.R.B. v. Catholic Bishop of Chicago, 440 U.S. 490, 502 (1979) (noting that the very process of inquiry into religious decisions violates the First Amendment); *Milivojevich,* 426 U.S. at 708–09. *See also*, Thomas C. Berg, "Religious Structures Under the Federal Constitution," H. Reese Hansen, "Religious Organizations and the Law of Trusts," Patty Gerstenblith, "Civil Court Resolution of Property Disputes Among Religious Organizations," in this volume.

43. Gonzalez v. Roman Catholic Archbishop, 280 U.S. 1, 16 (1929).

44. Jones v. Wolf, 443 U.S. 595 (1979).

45. 494 U.S. 872 (1990). *See also* Thomas Berg, "Religious Structures Under the Federal Constitution," in this volume.

46. 508 U.S. 520 (1993).

Claim that the financial burden of liability for misconduct impinges on a church's religious freedom

One of the broadest arguments made against holding a church liable for its clergy's misconduct has been advanced by legal scholar Patrick J. Schiltz.[47] Schiltz contends that using litigation to compensate victims of clerical sexual abuse threatens religious freedom because the costs of such litigation deprive the church of monetary resources it would otherwise be able to use for legitimate religious and even valuable social and educational purposes. Such litigation, Schiltz argues, has a detrimental effect on the church for a variety of reasons: it reduces the appeal of ministry to potential candidates, undercuts the trust and good relations between clergy and their parishioners, disturbs the trust and good relations between priests and their bishops, alters the nature of the hierarchy, and compromises the church's ability to function in public life. Schiltz's argument, note, is consequentialist rather than deontological. That is, he is not opposed to any and all litigation as opposed to religious freedom, but only to litigation that exacts such costs as to harm the church's ability to function effectively as a religious body in society. Since such high costs compromise the freedom of the church to operate, he argues, litigation that results in these costs constitutes an attack on religious freedom.

Schiltz's argument seems to include three propositions and a conclusion: (1) litigation over clerical sexual abuse has a negative impact on the church,[48] (2) this negative impact interferes with the church's ability to function *ad intra* and *ad extra*,[49] (3) this interference disturbs its freedom,[50] and (4) this disturbance constitutes a threat to its religious freedom.

Each of these claims, however, needs to be qualified. (1) Litigation over sexually abusive clergy has both negative and positive effects. It has a short-term negative economic impact on the church, and therefore on its ability to fulfill its mission of service to others. However, such litigation also brings serious benefits to the church to the extent that it makes it a more safe and just community. Judged ethically, litigation actually helps the church pursue its own ideals with regard to the needs of society's most vulnerable members, its children. In addition, since litigation promotes greater justice and accountability within the church, it also contributes to its long-term credibility.

(2) The negative impact of litigation does indeed interfere with the church's ability to pay for some of its ministries in the short term, because it forces the church to devote monetary resources to compensation and other costs associated with clerical sexual abuse. Yet this use of the church's resources is itself an expression of its mission — namely, the pursuit of justice and peace. It can also be argued, as has been mentioned already, that if credibility attracts adherents and reinforces loyalty, then short-term monetary loss can also be said to contribute to the church's long-term moral, and perhaps even economic, gain.

(3) The doctrine of religious liberty is, as is noted above, marked by two components: "non-establishment" and "free exercise." The first component bans the establishment of an official religion promoted by the state. The second forbids the state from in-

---

47. Patrick J. Schiltz, The Impact of Clergy Sexual Misconduct Litigation on Religious Liberty, 44 B.C.L. Rev. 949 (July/Sept. 2003) at http://www.bc.edu/schools/law/lawreviews/meta-elemtns/journals/bclawr/44_4/02_TXT.htm.

48. *Id.* at 964.

49. *Id.* at 965 to 972.

50. *Id.* at 973.

terfering with the beliefs of a religious community, and also limits its ability to interfere with religious practices. The infringement of religious liberty by the state disrupts the church's ability to function, but not every disturbance of the church's freedom constitutes a violation of religious liberty.

Schiltz's claim that compensatory damages undermine the church's religious freedom trades on an ambiguity in the phrase "religious freedom." Religious freedom can mean, very broadly, the *effective agency* of the church: that is, its power to enact its policies, *freedom to* implement its programs, and so on. It is in this sense that we say people with high incomes have more freedom than people with lower incomes. Applied to the church, the resources at its command give a wealthier parish or school more freedom of agency than a poorer parish or school. Religious freedom in the more precise sense, however, concerns the ability of individuals or communities to practice their faith without interference from the state. Religious freedom here means *freedom from* due and improper interference from the state in matters of worship, belief, and practice. It involves liberty, not empowerment, and in this sense is a purely negative form of immunity. Such interference is seen in countries where priests are forbidden to wear clerical garb in public, celebrate Mass, or establish seminaries. The claim that litigation attacks religious freedom confuses these two meanings of freedom. Just compensation to victims of crime is not a form of religious persecution.

(4) This distinction between broad and narrow senses of the phrase "religious freedom" allows that individuals who commit crimes are properly subjected to lawsuits to compensate for the harm they have done. Some priests have been guilty of sexually abusive acts and therefore are the proper objects of litigation. They are not being subjected to religious persecution by virtue of their religious identity or actions following from it, but for their criminal conduct.

The Catholic Church itself acknowledges this distinction when it insists that there are significant moral limits to the kind of acts that can be protected by the shield of religious freedom. The Second Vatican Council's *Dignitatis humanae* maintained: "Since civil society has the right to protect itself against possible abuses committed in the name of religious freedom the responsibility of providing such protection rests especially with the civil authority."[51] Civil authority must not regard all claims to religious freedom as absolute. The sphere of religious freedom must accord with the rights of citizens, public peace, and public order. It offers no justification for refusing to pursue the rights of litigants.

Schiltz objects to the fact that payment of compensation places an undue burden on innocent third parties in the church. Innocent members of the church are denied benefits that their church would otherwise have been able to afford, and are also forced to deal with other unfortunate consequences. Yet it is inappropriate to suggest that just compensation should not be pursued because of negative effects on third parties. It is simply a fact of social life that membership in communities exacts unchosen, unwanted, and undeserved costs on individual members. Citizens pay to clean up harbors and rivers polluted by prior generations, medically insured employees pay the costs of intensive medical treatment for smokers, and neighbors pay in various ways for crimes they have not committed. In these and many other cases, money that could have gone to good causes is taken from innocent third parties and used to pay for the harmful acts of

---

51. Dignitatis Humanae, Declaration on Religious Liberty, no. 7, in Vatican Council II: The Concilar and Post Conciliar Documents, ed. Austin Flannery, O.P., 1988 revised ed. (Northport, N.Y.: Costello Publishing Co., 1988), 805.

others. Responsible communities expend resources to meet their duties of justice despite the sacrifice entailed.[52]

Although it is important to justly compensate victims and arguably to deter religious organizations from negligently supervising their clergy, one item that has largely been ignored is the windfall that tort lawyers are receiving from these cases.[53] According to published sources, many lawyers are taking a contingent fee of forty percent, plus the actual costs they incur in processing these cases, even when the cases do not go to trial.[54] This means that after the contingency fees and costs are paid, the people who have been injured often receive only fifty percent or less of what the religious body is paying to help deal with the hurt that has been caused by clerical sexual misconduct. For example, according to a press account, when the Diocese of Louisville settled with 243 victims for $25.7 million, the lawyers received about $10,280,000 in fees and $158,000 in costs, leaving an average payment for each victim of about $63,000.[55] As one of the victims is quoted as saying about the attorney compensation, "That is a lot of money for one year's work."[56]

Yet contingency fees are not sacrosanct. The Model Rules of Professional Conduct prohibit them in criminal cases and in domestic relations matters.[57] As part of tort reform, Congress has also considered eliminating or abolishing contingency fees in other types of cases.[58] There appear to be many good reasons to eliminate them or sharply curtail them in tort cases against charitable, religious, or educational organizations. First, although the old laws on charitable immunity have largely disappeared, their stated purpose of protecting charitable assets would still seem to be relevant to an evaluation of excessive contingent fees. For example, when the Illinois Supreme Court held in 1905 that charities in Illinois were immune from suits based upon acts of their employees, it reasoned:

> The doctrine of respondeat superior does not extend to charitable institutions for the reasons, first, that if this liability were admitted the trust fund might be wholly destroyed and diverted from the purpose for which it was given, thus thwarting the donor's intent, as the result of negligence for which he was in nowise responsible; second, that, since the trustees cannot divert the funds by

---

52. *See, however*, Catherine Pierce Wells, Churches, Charities, and Corrective Justice: Making Churches Pay for the Sins of Their Clergy, 44 B.C.L. Rev. 1201 (July/Sept. 2003) at http://www. bc.edu/schools/law/lawreviews/meta-elemtns/journals/bclawr/44_4/02_TXT.htm. Wells argues that vicarious liability makes sense against commercial enterprises because otherwise the defendant business is allowed to impose some of its risks on others, thereby resulting in unjust enrichment to the business. In the charitable arena, however, there is no profit being made. Moreover, most people participate in some way in the activities of charities.

53. In his article, The Impact of Clergy Misconduct, Patrick J. Schiltz does state that "It is common for a clergy sexual misconduct case that results in, say, a $100,000 verdict or settlement to cost the defendants—pastor, congregation, and broader church—$200,000 or more in defense costs. The net result is that $300,000 is taken away from the ministries of the church in order to put about $250,000 into the pockets of lawyers and $50,000 into the pockets of victims." Schiltz, 44 B.C. L. Rev. at 965. In a footnote, Schiltz notes that the victim's attorneys often take between a third and fifty percent of the amount of settlement. *Id.* at 965, fn. 47. Such extreme results amply warrant a rule limiting the compensation of attorneys pursuing claims against charitable organizations.

54. David Schimke, "True Believer," City Pages, April 16, 2003, at www.citypages.com/databank/24/1167/article11177.asp.

55. Peter Smith, "Abuse Deals with Archdiocese Ok'd," The Courier Journal, Aug. 2, 2003.

56. *Id.*

57. Model Rules of Professional Conduct, Rule 1.5(d).

58. 141 Cong. Rec. H2651-03.

their direct act from the purposes for which they were donated, such funds cannot be indirectly diverted by the tortuous or negligent acts of the managers of the funds or their agents or employees.[59]

More importantly, there are many situations in which religious organizations could sustain a defense on statute of limitations or other grounds, thereby giving the victims nothing. Instead the religious organization decides to compensate the victims because of the organization's religious belief that the "moral" thing to do is to help those who may have been injured by church personnel, whether or not the church is legally obligated to do so. For example, in December 2004 the Milwaukee Archdiocese settled forty-seven sex abuse claims for amounts ranging from $20,000 to $50,000,[60] even though the Wisconsin Supreme Court has held that the First Amendment precludes it from deciding questions of a church's liability in cases of clerical sexual misconduct.[61]

In such cases, it seems that justice argues in favor of limiting the amount that the victim's attorney takes from the amount that the church provides the victim as compensation. When the churches are acting out of a "moral model" instead of the civil law model, the victims, not their attorneys, should benefit from the churches' payment. To enable religious organizations to put into practice their religious beliefs about compassion and justice, the legislatures should limit the amount of the settlement that the victim's attorney may receive to some reasonable percentage or reasonable hourly rate.

This is also in line with the current Internal Revenue Code. In order to be exempt under section 501(c)(3) of the code, organizations must be operated "exclusively for religious, charitable...or educational purposes."[62] In addition, no part of their net earnings may inure to the benefit of a private individual. The purpose of these requirements is to ensure that assets of a charitable or religious organization are used to benefit the general public instead of private individuals. Following this reasoning, the legislatures should ensure that charitable and religious assets are used for those purposes and not to pay victims' attorneys at amounts equal to, or more than, tens of thousands of dollars per hour worked.

Impact on religious freedom of respondeat superior and breach of fiduciary duty claims

As is discussed above, most courts do not hold churches liable for clergy misconduct under the theories of respondeat superior or breach of fiduciary duty.[63] To do so would probably impinge unnecessarily upon a church's religious freedom because both of these theories require a court to make a judgment about religion.

---

59. Parks v. Northwestern University, 75 N.E. 991, 993 (Ill. 1905). Charitable immunity was abolished in Illinois in 1965 in the case of *Darling v. Charleston Hospital*, 211 N.E.2d 253 (Ill. 1965), *cert. denied*, 383 U.S. 946 (1966). However, the court in *Darling* stated that its decision was only to be applied prospectively to allow charities the opportunity to purchase insurance to protect themselves from future losses.

60. "47 Claims of Clergy Sex-Abuse Resolved, Archdiocese Says," Chi. Trib., Dec. 21, 2004.

61. Pritzlaff v. Archdiocese of Milwaukee, 533 N.W.2d 780 (Wis. 1995), *cert. denied*, 516 U.S. 1116 (1996).

62. I.R.C. § 501(c)(3).

63. *See also*, Gaines v. Krawczyk, 2004 WL 2998752 (W.D. Pa. Nov. 18, 2004) (discussing breach of fiduciary duty).

Under the respondeat superior theory, the court is saying that because of some facet of the nature of the clergy, including their duties and responsibilities and the trust they engender, it is foreseeable to the church that its clergy person might abuse a child. Similarly, under the fiduciary duty theory, the court is evaluating the relationship between the church and its members and defining a special duty that the church owes its members. Usually that duty involves more than the fact that the victim was a member of the church. For example, in *Moses*[64] the court found that the bishop had assumed a special duty to take care of the victim by meeting with her, and that there was a special relationship because the plaintiff "was terrified about the loss of her salvation and feared having to meet with the Bishop." However, other cases have implied that a church owes a fiduciary duty whenever it has brought a person into contact with a clergy person whom it knows or should know is likely to harm the person.[65]

Thus, in both respondeat superior and fiduciary duty, a court is saying there is something special about clergy and religion that causes a church to be responsible under these theories for clerical sexual abuse. Yet, as Chopko has said, "To hear evidence about the character of a religious office, and then, based on those characteristics, to impose and enforce civil duties upon religious leaders by virtue of their position and role as religious leaders, clearly seems to be an unconstitutional exercise of governmental power."[66]

Impact on religious freedom of liability for negligent hiring

When courts discuss negligent hiring or retention of clergy, what they are really dealing with is the ordination or "calling" of someone to be a member of the clergy and to hold a religious position in the church. However, there is a strong First Amendment argument that churches should not be held liable for ordaining or retaining as clergy individuals who are pedophiles. It is a well-established principle that a church is free to use any criteria it wishes to select and retain its clergy.[67] Thus, in *Gonzalez v. Roman Catholic Archbishop*,[68] the U. S. Supreme Court held that only the church itself can say who is qualified to be a priest.

---

64. 863 P.2d at 318.

65. *See* C.J.C. v. Corp. of the Catholic Bishop of Yakima, 985 P.2d 262, 272, *as amended* (Wash. 1999).

66. Chopko, *supra* note 23, at 1124. *See also* Dausch v. Rykse, 52 F.3d 1425 (7th Cir. 1994) ("If a court were to recognize such a breach of fiduciary duty, it would be required to define a reasonable standard and to evaluate [the minister's] conduct against that standard, an inquiry…that is of doubtful validity under the Free Exercise Clause").

67. *See* Serbian Eastern Orthodox Diocese v. Milivojevich, 426 U.S. 696 (1976) (courts are not permitted to invade the internal governance of a hierarchical church); Kedroff v. St. Nicholas Cathedral of Russian Orthodox Church, 344 U.S. 94 (1952); Gonzalez v. Roman Catholic Archbishop, 280 U.S. 1 (1929) (only the church itself can say who is qualified to be a priest); Combs v. Central Texas Annual Conference of the United Methodist Church, 173 F.3d 343 (5th Cir. 1999) (applying "ministerial exception" to Title VII); McClure v. Salvation Army, 460 F.2d 553 (5th Cir. 1972) (recognizing "ministerial exception" to Title VII because government cannot interfere with the employment decision of a church regarding a minister); Starkman v. Evans, 18 F.Supp.2d 630 (E.D. La. 1998) (applying ministerial exception). *See also* Jacobs v. Mallard Creek Presbyterian Church, 214 F.2d 552 (W.D.N.C. 2002) (refusing to allow claims for procedural and "due process" violations in clergy removal); Hiles v. Episcopal Diocese of Massachusetts, 773 N.E. 2d 929, 934 (Mass. 2002) ("The assessment of an individual's fitness to serve as a priest is a particular ecclesiastical matter entitled to this constitutional protection").

68. 280 U.S. 1 (1929). *See also* Douglas Laycock and Patrick J. Schiltz, "Employment in Religious Organizations," in this volume.

Some courts have tried to get around this prohibition by analogizing the "hiring" of clergy to the hiring of any other employee. For example, in *Malicki*,[69] the plaintiffs alleged that the church negligently failed "to make inquiries into Malicki's background, qualifications, reputation, work history, and/or criminal history prior to employing him in the capacity of Associate Pastor."[70] The Florida Supreme Court held that there was no First Amendment bar to the plaintiff's bringing this claim of negligent hiring because the court was only looking at whether the employer should have known about the danger of sexual abuse when it hired the employee for this particular position.

However, churches do not "hire" their clergy. By using that language, the court is violating a church's own self-understanding. As discussed below, one could argue that a church negligently supervised its clergy person because it knew or should have known there was a danger to minors in putting that clergy person in a particular position, and because it did not take precautions to make sure the clergy person did not abuse anyone. But the state has no right under the First Amendment to state who can and cannot hold a particular position in the church organization. As the Fourth Circuit Court of Appeals held in *Rayburn v. General Conference of Seventh-Day Adventists*, "The role of an associate in pastoral care is so significant in the expression and realization of Seventh-day Adventist beliefs that state intervention in the appointment process would excessively inhibit religious liberty."[71]

Moreover, the religious laws of some churches make it very difficult to laicize or otherwise defrock a clergy person. For example, there are canon law requirements about disciplining and laicizing Catholic priests. These make it much more difficult for the Catholic Church to dismiss a priest than it is for a regular civil business to fire an employee.[72] Can a court hold a church liable for "negligent retention" if the church continues to say that a person is still a minister, even if the church has not put that person in a position where he or she can abuse children? Such a holding would obviously impinge upon a church's self-understanding and its religious freedom to name its own clergy. To prevent this, church leaders must help their attorneys educate courts on the church's own understanding and laws about ordination and priesthood, so that the courts do not punish it for continuing to call a person clergy as long as it properly supervises that person so that he or she cannot abuse children.

Liability for negligent supervision

Many First Amendment arguments have been raised as to why churches should not also be liable for negligent supervision of their clergy. One is that some churches believe in forgiveness and redemption and so believe that clergy can change. Another is that a negligent supervision claim requires a court to determine what is proper supervision.

---

69. 814 So.2d 347 (Fla. 2002).

70. 814 So.2d at 352.

71. 772 F.2d 1164, 1168 (4th Cir. 1985) (woman may not sue the church on the grounds that its refusal to appoint her to a pastoral position violated Title VII of the Civil Rights Act of 1964).

72. *See* Michael F. Aylward, Constitution, Crime, Clergy: First Amendment Implications of Sexual Abuse Claims, 70 Def. Couns. J. 196, 202 (April 2003); James T. O'Reilly and Joann M. Strasser, Clergy Sexual Misconduct: Confronting the Difficult Constitutional and Institutional Liability Issues, St. Thomas L. Rev. 31, 46 (Fall 1994).

Belief in forgiveness

Some have argued that certain churches should not be found liable for allowing their pedophile clergy to remain in ministry because of the churches' belief in forgiveness and redemption. For instance, in defending his clergy placement decisions, Cardinal Bernard Law said that "at the heart of our faith is a belief in the power of resurrection of new life, of starting over again."[73]

This argument from forgiveness, however, is flawed in two ways, First, it suggests too simplistically that granting forgiveness toward a perpetrator obviates justice for the perpetrator as well as for the victim. It is important, however, to distinguish justice in the ecclesial sphere from justice in the civil sphere. In fact forgiveness cannot be granted at the expense of justice. For example, under Roman Catholic theology, the church grants forgiveness when the guilty party engages in acts of confession, repentance, and penance in order to obtain reconciliation with the church and God. An important part of this process can involve repairing the damage done to innocent people, so even within the church, justice is not ignored. More importantly, religious forgiveness in a religious community is entirely consistent with pursuing in the civil order both compensatory justice for victims and retributive justice against the perpetrator. Civil law promotes and protects the public good, including the good of victims of crimes. Individuals can indeed change, but it would be hopelessly naive and even reckless to assume that since a person guilty of sexual abuse can change, he ought to be given a second chance and allowed to remain in ministry. Experience teaches, as the American bishops now acknowledge, that this opportunity has too often become a second chance to abuse more minors.[74] In fact, the present Norms on this issue insist that such priests be permanently removed from ministry.[75] Forgiveness does not negate the common good and the duties of justice, including the duty to protect innocent potential victims from future abuse.[76] For this reason the bishops of the United States have promised to remove alleged offenders from active ministry until they have been exonerated or, if proven guilty, to remove them from ministry permanently.[77]

In addition, some confusion has existed about the status of sexual abuse as sin or crime. Thomas Groome, a professor of theology and religious education at Boston College, said Cardinal Bernard Law's position on this matter relied on a "mistaken church perspective that they were dealing with sins, not crimes."[78] This observation points to a serious oversight in pastoral practice. As Professor Angela Carmella has noted, "[T]he public has grown increasingly aware of irresponsible decisions made by Catholic leader-

---

73. Wendy Davis, Priest Was Moved so He Could Start Afresh, Law Says, Boston Globe, March 14, 2003, at A1.

74. *See* Wilton Gregory, Presidential Address Opening Dallas Meeting, Origins NC Documentary Service 32 (June 27, 2002): 97.

75. *See* Charter for the Protection of Children and Young People, Revised, and Essential Norms for Diocesan/Eparchal Policies Dealing with Allegations of Sexual Abuse of Minors by Priests or Deacons, revised in Origins 32 (November 28, 2002): 409, 411-414 and 415-416, respectively.

76. On the relation between justice and forgiveness see Stephen J. Pope, The Convergence of Forgiveness and Justice: Lessons from El Salvador, Theological Studies 64 (December 2003): 812–835.

77. *See* United States Conference of Catholic Bishops, Charter for the Protection of Children and Young People Revised Edition, par. 5 and par. 14. *See also* United States Conference of Catholic Bishops, Essential Norms for Diocesan/Eparchial Policies Dealing with Allegations of Sexual Abuse of Minors by Priests or Deacons, 2002.

78. Davis, *supra* note 73, at A1.

ship regarding priests accused of sexual abuse of children and young people, particularly the practice of reassigning abusive priests who subsequently harmed other minors."[79]

However, the categories of sin and crime are not actually mutually exclusive. Though many acts that are considered "sins" by the church are not crimes in the civil order—for example, greed, most cases of lying, acts of pride, etc.—all crimes are considered objectively evil and therefore, if done with knowledge of this status, are also considered "sinful" by the church. There is, then, no reason why sinful acts of sexual abuse could not also have been recognized to be crimes, as they in fact now are.

Courts' ability to define proper supervision

The argument has also been raised that the First Amendment prohibits a court from finding that a church has "negligently" supervised its clergy because this requires the court to decide how it should supervise its clergy. A few courts have accepted this reasoning. For example, in *Pritzlaff v. Archdiocese of Milwaukee*, the Wisconsin Supreme Court held that the First Amendment precluded it from deciding a case in which the plaintiff was suing the Archdiocese of Milwaukee on the grounds that it had negligently supervised a priest and thus enabled him to use his position as a priest to coerce her, while she was an adult, into having a sexual relationship with him.[80] The court found that "Although state inquiry into the training and supervision of clergy is a closer issue than inquiry into hiring and retention practices because under some limited circumstances such questions might be able to be decided without determining questions of church law and policies, it is nonetheless prohibited by the First Amendment under most if not all circumstances."[81]

Similarly, in *Swanson v. The Roman Catholic Bishop of Portland*[82] a husband and wife sued the Diocese of Portland on the grounds that its negligent supervision had allowed a priest, who had given the couple marriage counseling, to have a sexual relationship with the wife. The Supreme Judicial Court of Maine concluded in 1991 that based "on the facts of this case, imposing a secular duty of supervision on the church and enforcing that duty through civil liability would restrict its freedom to interact with its clergy in the manner deemed proper by ecclesiastical authorities and would not serve a societal interest sufficient to overcome the religious freedom inhibited."[83]

The same result was reached in *Ayon v. Gourley*, which involved alleged sexual misconduct with a minor.[84] There the U. S. District Court for the District of Colorado dis-

---

79. Angela C. Carmella, The Protection of Children and Young People: Catholic and Constitutional Visions of Responsible Freedom, 44 B.C.L. Rev. 1031 (July/Sept. 2003) at http://www.bc.edu/schools/law/lawreviews/meta-elemtns/journals/bclawr/44_4/02_TXT.htm.

80. 533 N.W.2d 780 (Wis. 1995), *cert. denied*, 516 U.S. 1116 (1996). In November 2004, the Wisconsin Supreme Court agreed to hear a case pursuant to which it might reverse or limit the Pritzlaff decision. "47 Claims of Clergy Sex-Abuse Resolved, Archdiocese says," Chi. Trib., Dec. 21, 2004.

81. *Pritzlaff,* 533 N.W.2d at 791.

82. 692 A.2d 441, 445 (Me. 1997).

83. *See also* Schmidt v. Bishop, 779 F. Supp. 321 (S.D.N.Y. 1991) (dismissing a lawsuit against ecclesiastical authorities based on a pastor's initiation of sexual conduct during a counseling session).

84. 47 F. Supp. 2d 1246 (D. Col. 1998), *aff'd*, 185 F.3d 873 (Table), 1999 WL 516088 (10th Cir. (Colo.) 1999). *But also see* Ehrens v. Lutheran Church, 385 F.3d 232, 235 (2004) (expressly refusing to address the issue of whether the First Amendment prevents a court from finding that a church negligently retained or supervised a clergyman. The Second Circuit did note, however, that "the district court did not address our holding in Martinelli v. Bridgeport Roman Catholic Diocesan Corp., 196 F.3d 409 (2nd Cir. 1999), that the Free Exercise Clause 'does not prevent courts from deciding

missed the plaintiff's negligent hiring and supervision claims against the Archdiocese of Denver on the grounds that it would be a violation of the First Amendment for the court to examine the procedures that the archdiocese had in place regarding supervision. According to the court,

> consideration of the hiring policies of the Archdiocese Defendants would in-evitably require examination of church policy and doctrine. The choice of individuals to serve as ministers is one of the most fundamental rights belonging to a religious institution. It is one of the most important exercises of a church's freedom from government control....
>
> The Court finds that the result is the same for the negligent supervision and outrageous conduct claims.... The supervision model used by the Archdiocese Defendants is based on this unique relationship conceived by church doctrine.... While Plaintiff attempts to characterize this as a normal supervision claim, the reality is that practices of disciplinary actions, reprimand write-ups and grievance procedures are improbable in a church setting. Instead, like the hiring claim, the procedures that the Archdiocese Defendants have in place regarding supervision would have to be examined to determine whether they were reasonable and adequate. This would clearly be inappropriate governmental involvement and a burden on these Defendants' exercise of religion.[85]

However, the majority of courts, particularly in the more recent decisions, have not found the First Amendment to be a bar to clerical sexual misconduct claims based on negligent supervision. For example, in *Malicki v. Doe*,[86] a minor and an adult sued the Archdiocese of Miami on the grounds that it had negligently supervised a priest who sexually assaulted them. In its March 14, 2002 decision, the Florida Supreme Court held:

> The issue presented in this case is whether the First Amendment bars a third party tort action against a religious institution grounded on the alleged tortuous act by one of its clergy. We conclude that the First Amendment does not provide a shield behind which a church may avoid liability for harm caused to an adult and a child parishioner arising from the alleged sexual assault or battery of one of its clergy, and accordingly approve the Third District's decision. We thus join the majority of both state and federal jurisdictions that have found no First Amendment bar under similar circumstances.[87]
>
> [...]
>
> These courts conclude that there is no impermissible interpretation of religious doctrine because the courts are applying a neutral principle of generally applicable tort law. This is especially so where the religious institution does not allege that the conduct was undertaken in furtherance of a sincerely held religious belief.[88]

---

secular disputes involving religious institutions when and for the reason that they require reference to religious matters.' Id. at 431").
  85. *Ayon,* 47 F. Supp. 2d at 1250–1251.
  86. 814 So.2d 347 n. 2 (Fla. 2002).
  87. 814 So.2d at 350 (citations omitted).
  88. *Id.* at 358 (citations omitted).

The same reasoning has been made by courts in other cases. For example, in *Smith v. O'Connell*[89] the Diocese of Providence argued that the First Amendment prevents courts from adjudicating claims against church officials based on the church officials' failure to take appropriate action to prevent sexual assault by clergy. In that case, the court actually found that there was no conflict between tort law and church doctrine because the information presented to the court did not suggest that "canon law precludes hierarchical officials from taking appropriate action to *prevent* priests, who are known pedophiles, from sexually abusing children."[90] The court continued that even if there were a conflict between tort law and canon law, the court could, pursuant to the *Employment Div., Dept. of Human Resources of Oregon v. Smith* case,[91] still find the church liable because "the principles of tort law, at issue, are both neutral and generally applicable. It is not even alleged that they are directed at or were designed to suppress the religious practices of the Roman Catholic Church or that they selectively burden religiously-inspired conduct."[92]

For the legal system to respect a church's self-understanding and thereby promote religious freedom, what is probably needed is a more nuanced approach such as has been evidenced by some courts. For example, on February 19, 2003, Massachusetts Superior Court Judge Constance Sweeney ruled that under the First Amendment, alleged victims may not argue that a church wrongly ordained a priest or failed to laicize him.[93] However, Judge Sweeney did rule that the alleged victims could argue that a church was negligent in supervising a priest. This decision recognizes that a church's decision to ordain or laicize a person differs markedly from the decision of a secular employer to hire or fire an employee. Nonetheless, even while protecting that relationship, courts may punish churches whose negligence in supervising clergy permits the clergy to sexually abuse minors.

Another approach was taken by the Missouri Supreme Court in *Gibson v. Brewer*.[94] There the court held that the First Amendment prohibited it from deciding either questions of hiring clergy or questions of negligent supervision based upon what a church "should have known," because such questions would require inquiry into church doctrine. The court noted that "judicial inquiry into hiring, ordaining, and retaining clergy would result in an endorsement of religion, by approving one model for church hiring, ordination, and retention of clergy."[95] However, it would not violate the First Amendment for a court to hold the church liable if the church knew that harm was certain to result from its failure to supervise a priest. This is because "Religious conduct intended or certain to cause harm need not be tolerated by the First Amendment."[96]

---

89. 986 F. Supp. 73 (D.R.I. 1997).

90. *Id.* at 78.

91. 494 U.S. 872 (1990).

92. 986 F. Supp. at 80.

93. Burge, *supra* note 38, at A1.

94. 952 S.W.2d 239 (Mo. 1997).

95. *Id.* at 247.

96. *Id.* at 248. *See also* S.H.C. v. Lu, 54 P.3d 174 (Wash. App. 2002), *rev. den.* 69 P.3d 874 (Wash. 2003) (member of religious organization alleged that her religious leader sexually abused her and that religious order negligently supervised the leader. The religious tenets of the organization said that one should never criticize the religious leader. The Court of Appeals of Washington recognized that the First Amendment does not give churches absolute immunity to engage in tortious conduct. In this case, however, "the court would have to examine the religious doctrine of the [organization] to determine whether the [organization] was negligent in its 'supervision and retention' of [the religious leader]. That necessarily would involve the 'excessive entanglement that First Amendment jurisprudence forbids'").

Unlicensed mental health professionals

As a side note, in addition to the cases alleging clerical sexual abuse of minors, there are a number of cases that try to hold a church liable when one of its clergy members has sexual relations with an adult. Many of these cases rely upon state statutes governing unlicensed mental health professionals. For example, there is an Illinois statute that provides that a cause of action exists against an unlicensed mental health professional who engages in sexual contact with a patient.[97] Psychotherapy is defined as "the professional treatment, assessment, or counseling of a mental or emotional illness, symptom, or condition," but specifically excludes "counseling of a spiritual or religious nature, social work, or casual advice given by a friend or family member."[98] In addition, an employer of an unlicensed mental health professional is liable for failing to take action when the employer knows or has reason to know that the professional has engaged in sexual contact with the plaintiff or with any other patient or former patient.[99]

On their face, such statutes appear to implicate a church's self-understanding of whether its clergy are providing mental health counseling or just counseling of a spiritual or religious nature. However, at least one court has held that determining into which of these categories a particular communication falls does not "excessively entangle a court in religion."[100] The court reasoned that "Whether a communication is of a religious or spiritual nature is a question of fact frequently addressed by the courts in the context of the application of the clergy privilege."[101]

Review of records

An issue subsidiary to the question of whether churches can be held liable for negligently supervising their clergy is the extent to which church records are discoverable in such court proceedings. Some churches have argued either that their records are totally confidential[102] or that they should be available only to the parties in the litigation and not to the public in general.[103]

There are cases that have held that opening church documents to public review does violate the Free Exercise Clause. For example, in *Surinach v. Pesquera de Busquets*,[104] the First Circuit Court of Appeals held that the Inter-Diocesan Secretariat for Catholic Education of Puerto Rico and superintendents of Roman Catholic schools in a number of

---

97. 740 ILCS § 140/2.

98. 740 ILCS § 140/1.

99. 740 ILCS § 140/3.

100. Doe v. F.P., 667 N.W.2d 493, 499 (Minn. Ct. App. 2003), *relying on* Odenthal v. Minnesota Conference of Seventh-Day Adventists, 649 N.W.2d 426 (Minn. 2002).

101. *Id.*

102. For example, both the Archdiocese of Los Angeles and the Diocese of Cincinnati resisted turning over church records relating to clergy sex abuse cases to prosecutors. *See* William Lobdell and Richard Winton, Later Deadline for Priest Cases Sought, Los Angeles Times, March 13, 2003; Michael Paulsen and Michael Rezendes, Openness of Bishops Still at Issue, Boston Globe, June 17, 2003, at A1; Tracy Wilson and Richard Winton, Ventura County Seeks Clergy Sex Case Files, Los Angeles Times, November 1, 2002.

103. The Archdiocese of Boston, the Diocese of Cleveland, and the Diocese of Bridgeport, Connecticut, have all tried to keep such church records private. Paulsen and Rezendes, *supra* note 102.

104. 604 F.2d 73 (1st Cir. 1979).

Puerto Rican dioceses did not have to respond to a subpoena from the Puerto Rico Department of Consumer Affairs for documents pertaining to expenditures on Catholic schools. The court based its holding on the fact that the state had not shown that its interest in having these records justified the consequent infringement on the church's First Amendment freedoms.[105]

It is interesting to note, however, that when faced with cases involving alleged clergy sexual abuse of minors, the courts have required the churches to make their documents available. In *Hutchison v. Luddy*,[106] the Superior Court of Pennsylvania ordered the Diocese of Altoona-Johnston to produce records "contained in secret archive files as maintained by the diocese pursuant to Canons 489 and 490 of the Code of Canon Law."[107] The diocese had contended that the trial court's discovery in this sexual misconduct case violated Canon 490, which provides that "'[o]nly the bishop'...may possess the secret archive's key and that 'documents are not to be removed from the secret archive or safe.'"[108] The court found that the information in the secret archive was not covered by the priest/penitent privilege and that disclosure would not interfere with religious freedom because "there is not one iota of evidence that court ordered discovery will 'chill' the rights of appellants in the conduct of their religious affairs or inhibit their parishioners from engaging freely in the practice of their religious beliefs and activities."[109]

The Massachusetts courts have not only required the Archdiocese of Boston to turn over documents to the plaintiffs in sexual misconduct cases, but have also ordered that these church documents be released to the general public. On November 25, 2002, Judge Sweeney ordered that 11,000 documents dealing with the archdiocese's handling of priests accused of sexual misconduct be made public.[110] In addition, Sweeney granted the plaintiffs' lawyers the right to see the psychiatric records of a priest who had been accused of sexual abuse. Earlier, the Appeals Court of Massachusetts, in *Leary v. Geoghan*,[111] held that the archdiocese was not entitled to blanket protection from public filing for all discovery requests and responses, because that was "consistent with the well-established policy favoring the right of public access to the judicial records of civil proceedings." The court went on to note that the "defendants' position that they are constitutionally entitled to blanket protection is but another iteration of an argument which they unsuccessfully raised by motion to dismiss — that is, that they are constitutionally protected from legal proceedings which involve inquiry into religious doctrine, discipline, faith or internal church organization."[112] Therefore, at least for these courts, it appears that if the church is subject to suit on the grounds of negligent supervision of its clergy, then its actions dealing with that matter may not be confidential. Instead they may be discoverable by the attorneys representing the victims, and to some degree may also be available to the general public.

---

105. *Id.* at 80.

106. 606 A.2d 905 (Pa. Super. 1992).

107. *Id.* at 912.

108. *Id.* at 908.

109. *Id.* at 912.

110. Pam Belluck, Judge Denies Church's Bid to Seal Records on Priests, N.Y. Times, Nov. 26, 2002.

111. 2001 WL 1902391 (Mass. App. Ct. Dec. 21, 2001) (upholding Judge Sweeney's order allowing Globe Newspaper Company to intervene and ordering that all discovery responses be filed with the court unless a particular item is judicially determined to be privileged).

112. *Id.* The highest court in Massachusetts has also required a Catholic religious order to turn over the personnel file of a member of the order who was accused of sexual misconduct with a minor. Ken Maguire, SJC Forces Release of Accused Priest's Files, Boston Globe, May 13, 2004.

Although there does not appear to be a blanket exemption from production of church records, the courts apparently still honor the traditional privileges in determining whether the records relating to abuse are discoverable. For example, in *Corsie v. Campanalonga*[113] the Superior Court of New Jersey mandated an in camera inspection of certain documents to determine whether they were protected by the clergyman privilege.

One issue that apparently has not yet been decided is whether documents generated in purely religious proceedings are discoverable. At least one court has held that communications made by a person as part of a Catholic church proceeding to obtain sanctions for separate maintenance and divorce are protected by the priest/penitent privilege. In *Cimijotti v. Paulsen*,[114] the District Court for the Northern District of Iowa held that "a person must be free to say anything and everything to his Church, at least so long as it is said in a recognized and required proceeding of the religion and to a recognized official of the religion."[115] However, the court also recognized that in some instances the documents may have to be disclosed.

Similarly, in *Hadnot v. Shaw*[116] the Oklahoma Supreme Court held that the Free Exercise Clause prohibits "secular re-examination of merits and procedure in ecclesiastical judicature."[117] This decision was apparently based on the fact that the proceedings in question were undertaken to determine whether the plaintiffs could remain members of the church. Under the First Amendment, the court would have no jurisdiction over whether the church had properly expelled the plaintiffs from church membership. However, the court held that the plaintiffs might be able to discover "actionable post-expulsion facts or conduct that would lie outside the ecclesiastical privilege surrounding religious judicature and implementation."[118] Both *Cimijotti* and *Hadnot* leave open the question of whether a church proceeding may be discoverable not so that the court can examine the process used or the result obtained, but so that it may learn what the church knew or should have known at a particular time.

As discussed above, the courts have recognized that the issue of who may be ordained or laicized is a religious decision that may not be dictated by the courts. If certain documents are created solely to allow the church to decide whether to ordain or laicize a person, should those documents be open to discovery? What if these documents contain the opinions of canon lawyers or other church personnel on these issues? Will opening these records to the public infringe upon religious freedom? And if so, does the state have a compelling interest that overrides the church's right to free exercise? There are some strong First Amendment concerns here. For example, should non-church personnel be able to review the documents that a church relies upon in determining whether to ordain a person? Will a person be inhibited in presenting the information a church needs to determine whether to defrock a minister if he or she fears that the testimony will be discoverable in civil litigation, even if the litigation does not relate to the appropriateness of the ecclesiastical proceeding?

---

113. 721 A.2d 733 (N.J. super. 1998), *rev'd in part*, 734 A.2d 788 (1999). *See also* David T. v. Ball, No. CAL02-21862 (Md. Cir. Ct., Prince Georges County, Dec. 23, 2002) (holding that a priest's medical and psychiatric reports were privileged).
114. 230 F. Supp. 39 (N.D. Iowa 1964).
115. *Id.* at 41.
116. 826 P.2d 978 (Okla. 1992).
117. *Id.* at 989.
118. *Id.* at 990.

Mandating certain conduct

When a court finds that a church negligently has failed to supervise its clergy, it is finding that the church has failed to take some supervisory action it should have taken. An extension of this type of finding is the court's or government's mandating that a church adopt particular procedures in dealing with the issue of clergy sex abuse.[119] This occurred in December 2002 when, according to MSNBC News, "Attorney General Philip McLaughlin [of New Hampshire] announced an unprecedented settlement in which the Diocese of Manchester would avoid criminal prosecution by agreeing to submit to supervision of its handling of sexual-abuse complaints for the next five years."[120] Similarly, in June 2003 the Maricopa County Attorney's Office required the bishop of Phoenix, Arizona, to enter into an agreement on the handling of allegations of clergy sex abuse in order to avoid criminal prosecution.[121] The agreement required the diocese to hire an independent youth protection advocate who, together with an independent attorney, would coordinate sexual abuse policies for the diocese and report to the moderator of the curia.

These types of actions arguably infringe upon a church's ability to freely exercise its religion. Bishop Thomas O'Brien of Phoenix did say that his agreement with the state was only a delegation of authority, not a relinquishment of it.[122] Nonetheless, as Carolyn Warner, an associate professor of political science at Arizona State University who studies the church, has stated, "the immunity agreement could be perceived as diminishing the church's authority over its hierarchy and the priesthood."[123] This raises the question of whether the agreement sets a precedent that in order not to be found liable for negligent supervision, a church must adopt procedures similar to those dictated in Phoenix. In such a case, the government would be establishing which religious practices are good and which are not.

Another example of the state mandating certain actions is the recent agreement by the Archdiocese of Cincinnati to plead "no contest" to five misdemeanor counts for failing to report clerical sexual abuse. As part of that plea, the archdiocese agreed to pay a $10,000 fine and establish a $3 million fund to compensate victims.[124]

In addition to government mandates of appropriate practices, at least one commentator has argued that courts should provide equitable relief to claimants in certain circumstances.[125] The commentator offered the example of a priest who had successfully

---

119. The results in both Manchester, N.H., and Phoenix, Arizona, arose in the context of the state seeking to criminally prosecute bishops and their dioceses for their response to clerical sexual abuse. Baker argues that such conduct, while perhaps negligent, does not constitute criminal behavior and therefore the government should never have imposed these mandates of the dioceses. *See* John S. Baker, Jr., Prosecuting Dioceses and Bishops, 44 B.C.L. Rev. 1061, 1085 (July/ Sept. 2003) at http://www.bc.edu/schools/law/lawreviews/meta-elemtns/journals/bclawr/44_4/02_TXT.htm.

120. MSNBC News, "Smoking Gun" in Church Crisis, (Dec. 11, 2002).

121. Joseph A. Reaves, O'Brien Won't Surrender Power, Arizona Republic, June 4, 2003. This agreement ended in September 2004. Claudia I. Provencio, Agreement Between Diocese, County Attorney Completed, The Catholic Sun, Oct. 7, 2004, at http://www.catholicsun.org/archives/oct7.

122. Reaves, O'Brien Won't Surrender Power, Arizona Republic, June 4, 2003.

123. Joseph A. Reaves, Sides Will Try to Interpret O'Brien Deal, Arizona Republic, June 5, 2003.

124. Dennis O'Connor, Cincinnati Archdiocese Pleads "No Contest" on Failure to Report Abuse, NC Catholic Online, Nov. 21, 2003, at http:///www.nccatholic.org.

125. John S. Brennan, The First Amendment Is Not the 8th Sacrament: Exorcizing the Ecclesiastical Abstention Doctrine Defense From Legal and Equitable Claims for Sexual Abuse Based on Negligent Supervision or Hiring of Clergy, 5 T.M. Cooley J. Prac. & Clinical L. 243, 299 (2002).

used canon law to contest his removal from a parish. In such a situation, the courts could issue an injunction to force the church to remove the clergyman from a "situation creating an unreasonable risk of sexual abuse."[126] Injunctive relief of this kind raises larger First Amendment concerns because courts are impinging on church operations in such a direct fashion.

Taken individually, each of these actions might appear to have little impact on a church's polity or religious freedom. Taken as a whole, however, they show the state gradually encroaching more and more on a church's ability to govern itself.

Statutory reporting of child sexual abuse

Although the actions by the Maricopa County Attorney's Office and the attorney general of New Hampshire are somewhat unusual, several states are now requiring that clergy become mandatory reporters of child sexual abuse. For example, in 2003 Arkansas[127] and Vermont[128] amended their child abuse reporting laws to add clergy as mandated reporters, and Maine[129] added "a clergy member acquiring the information as a result of clerical professional work except for information received during confidential communications." This brings to twenty-one the number of states that designate clergy as mandated reporters.[130]

These statutes raise several issues involving a church's self-understanding. One is the question of who is a member of the clergy. Different states have different definitions of this.[131] For example, when Illinois added clergy to the list of mandated reporters, it defined a member of the clergy as "a clergyman or practitioner of any religious denomination accredited by the religious body to which he or she belongs."[132] This definition includes Catholic priests and deacons, but excludes nuns, sisters, and brothers. In contrast, Vermont defines member of the clergy as including "a priest, rabbi, clergy member, ordained or licensed minister, leader of any church or religious body, accredited Christian Science practitioner, person performing official duties on behalf of a church or religious body that are recognized as the duties of a priest, rabbi, clergy, nun, brother, ordained or licensed minister, leader of any church or religious body, or accredited Christian Science practitioner."[133] These examples do not take into account a church's own self-understanding about which people are included in the definition of clergy and which people receive confidential communications.[134]

A bigger issue for churches is whether their clergy may assert any type of privilege. Some states do recognize the priest/penitent privilege in their mandatory reporting statutes while others do not. For example, Illinois provides that a member of the clergy is not required to report confidential information he receives in his professional capac-

---

126. *Id.* at 293.
127. Ark. Code Ann. § 12-12-507 (b)(28).
128. Vt. Stat. Ann. tit. 33, §4913.
129. Me. Rev. Stat. Ann. tit. 22, §4011-A (27).
130. National Clearinghouse on Child Abuse and Neglect, Reporting Laws: Clergy as Mandated Reporters, (2003), published at nccanch.acf.hhs.gov/general/legal/statutes/readyref/clergymandated.cfm. About eighteen other states also require any person who suspects child abuse to report.
131. *See* W. Cole Durham, "Definition of Religion," in this volume.
132. 325 ILCS 5/3.
133. Vt. Stat. Ann. tit. 33, §4912.
134. *See* Martin E. Marty and James A. Serritella, "Religious Polity," in this volume.

ity or as a spiritual advisor, as long as the rules or practices of his religious denomination require him to keep that information confidential.[135] However, at least two states, New Hampshire and West Virginia, do not allow clergy to invoke the priest/penitent privilege in cases of child abuse.[136] Moreover, even in states that do recognize the priest/penitent privilege, there is still an issue of which communications a church believes should remain confidential versus which ones the state recognizes as confidential.

Derivative Liability

A more complicated question than whether a church should be liable for knowing its clergy might abuse minors and not acting to prevent the abuse is that of which part of a church should be liable. Originally the plaintiffs sued the local church if it had appointed the minister, or the local diocese if it had assigned the minister to the church.

Increasingly, however, plaintiffs' attorneys are suing not only the individual church or intermediate body, but also the larger church entity. For example, in *Rashedi v. General Board of Church of the Nazarene*[137] a parishioner, alleging that she had been seduced by her pastor, sued not only the church itself but also the General Board of the Church of the Nazarene and the Arizona/Southern Nevada District Church of the Nazarene. These lawsuits require courts to examine a church's polity and self-understanding. What is the interaction between the various segments of the church? Who has the power to appoint and remove a member of the clergy? Who is at fault if the minister has abused a minor?

Sometimes it is alleged that the local church or some intermediate body is an agent of a higher church entity so that the local church's negligence could be imputed to the higher entity pursuant to the vicarious liability principles explained above. At other times the plaintiffs allege that the higher church entity itself is directly liable for the misconduct because its actions have caused the abuse to occur.

Clergy as agent of a higher church body

Under an agency theory, plaintiffs are asserting that as a minister or other clergy person, the accused perpetrator is under the control of the highest church body and is therefore its agent. Alternatively the plaintiffs might assert that a local church is the agent of a higher level church body. In either case, the higher church body might be vicariously liable for the wrongful misconduct of the clergy person or the negligence of the local church.

An example of this type of pleading is found in the complaint filed on December 12, 2002 in the Court of Common Plea, Mahoning County, Ohio.[138] There the complaint alleges:

---

135. 325 ILCS 5/4. *See also* Seymour Moskowitz and Michael J. De Boer, When Silence Resounds: Clergy and the Requirement to Report Elder Abuse and Neglect, 49 DePaul L. Rev. 1, 61–62 (Fall 1999).

136. National Clearinghouse on Child Abuse and Neglect, *supra* note 130.

137. 54 P.3d 349 (Ariz. 2003).

138. John Doe 64 vs. Holy See, Case No. 02CV3902 (Ct. Common Pleas, Mahoning County, Ohio).

Defendant Holy See is the ecclesiastical, governmental, and administrative capital of the Roman Catholic Church. Defendant Holy See is the composite of the authority, jurisdiction, and sovereignty vested in the Pope and his delegated advisors to direct the worldwide Roman Catholic Church. Defendant Holy See has unqualified power over the Catholic Church including each and every individual and section of the church.... The Holy See engages in these activities through its agents, cardinals, bishops and clergy, including religious order priests, brothers and sisters.... It creates, appoints, assigns and re-assigns bishops, superiors of religious orders, and through the bishops and superiors of religious orders has the power to directly assign and remove individual clergy.

Similarly, in *John V. Doe vs. Holy See*[139] the complaint alleges that "At all times material, Defendant Holy See had the right to control its agents,... Defendant Archdiocese, Defendant [Religious] Order."

Such a contention requires the courts to examine church polity. This again raises the issue of whether doing so will violate the First Amendment.[140]

Once that obstacle is overcome, there is still the issue of whether the clergy or the local churches are simply agents of the higher church body. Certainly under a normal analysis most local churches are separately incorporated with no legal ties to the larger church entity. This is especially the case in congregational, connectional, and other nonhierarchical churches, in which the larger church entity cannot even select the local clergy.[141] For example, in *Stewart v. West Ohio Conference of the United Methodist Church*[142] the Court of Appeals of Ohio held that the West Ohio Conference of the United Methodist Church was not liable for negligently failing to supervise a local church pastor who had sexually abused an adult woman, because the pastor was not its employee. Even in Roman Catholicism, the most hierarchical of all churches, dioceses and archdioceses are separately incorporated. Therefore, since the general rule is that one corporation is not liable for the actions of another,[143] the higher church entity should not be liable for the actions of the local churches.

At least one court has held that the fact that an organization is hierarchical does not mean that the higher level is liable for the actions of the lower level. As the Court of Appeals of Texas stated in its August 28, 2003 decision in *Williams v. United Pentecostal Church International*, "We are aware of no authority and appellants cite none, whereby the larger organization was held vicariously liable under respondeat superior for the negligence of the local assembly on the basis of hierarchical organization."[144] Moreover, in that case the court held that even though the district organization did control certain

---

139. Case No. CV. 02430 BR (D. Ore.).

140. *See Rashedi*, 54 P.3d at 354–355 (holding that the court may examine the structure of the Church of the Nazarene to determine the roles of the various church entities. As the court stated, "Inquiry into the organizational structure would be to factually determine the roles the parties played in the licensing and hiring of an employee").

141. *See* Martin E. Marty and James A. Serritella, "Religious Polity," in this volume.

142. 2003 WL 21692670 (Ohio Ct. App. June 5, 2003).

143. *See, e.g.,* 1 W. Fletcher, Cyclopedia of the Law of Private Corporations §43.10, at 758 (perm. ed. rev. vol. 1990); Bright v. Roadway Servs., 846 F. Supp. 693, 700 (N.D. Ill. 1994); Chicago Florsheim Shoe Store Co. v. Cluett, Peabody & Co., 826 F.2d 725, 728–29 (7th Cir. 1987) ("[u]nder Illinois law, separate corporate existence is the rule to which piercing the corporate veil is a stringently applied exception" and the party seeking to pierce the veil "bears a heavy burden of establishing control and fraud").

144. 115 S.W.3d 612, 618 (Tex. Ct. App. 2003). *See also* Mark E. Chopko, "Derivative Liability," in this volume.

aspects of the local church and minister, it was not liable for the minister's sexual misconduct because it had no control over the local church's decision to hire the particular minister. Thus, even for a hierarchical organization, the only entity that should be liable for clerical sexual misconduct is the one that had actual supervisory control over the clergyperson who committed the abuse.

Higher church body directly negligent

Alternatively, some plaintiffs are alleging that a regional or national church body should be held liable because its acts were a proximate cause of the abuse. Under this scenario, the broader church body would be liable, not because the local church acted negligently and was its agent but because the broader church body itself was negligent. For example, if a national church body voluntarily assumed a duty to supervise local churches, it might be at risk if it were negligent in carrying out that duty. Similarly (subject to ability to obtain service on an international body[145] and, for a church body that is also a country, such as the Vatican, potential immunity as a foreign sovereign[146]), some plaintiffs even argue that international church bodies should be found liable if they actually require a local church to retain or reinstate a minister or clergy person who has a known propensity to abuse minors and subsequently does abuse a minor.

The Minnesota Court of Appeals decision in *Olson v. Magnuson*[147] is an example of a case in which the court implied that a national body could be liable because it had assumed certain duties in relation to clergy misconduct. In *Olson*, the plaintiff sued the Evangelical Covenant Church of America (ECC), which is the national body of the Evangelical Covenant Church, on the grounds that it had failed to adequately supervise one of its ministers who was serving in a Covenant church in Minnesota. The ECC moved to dismiss for lack of jurisdiction, arguing that the national denomination (headquartered in Illinois) was not involved in the local church's activities in Minnesota. The court held that Minnesota had jurisdiction because under the ECC's bylaws, the national body had assumed responsibility for "investigating claims of impropriety lodged against its local church ministers and administering discipline if deemed necessary."[148] This oversight was a "sufficient contact" to subject the ECC to the jurisdiction of Minnesota courts, and at least suggests exposure to claims based on the local church's handling of the misconduct issue.

---

145. There is at least one case in which a plaintiff has been able to accomplish service on the Holy See. *See* Notice of Suit (transmitted by the U.S. Department of State to secretariat of state of the Holy See on March 24, 2003) in John V. Doe v. Holy See, Case No. CV:02 430 BR (D. Ore.).

146. As a sovereign state, the Holy See is subject to the Foreign Sovereign Immunities Act, 28 U.S.C. § 1602, *et seq.* (the "FSIA"). Section 1604 of the FSIA provides that "a foreign state shall be immune from the jurisdiction of the courts of the United States and of the States except as provided in sections 1605 to 1607 of this chapter." One such exception is provided in Section 1605 (a) (5), which subjects foreign states to the jurisdiction of United States federal and state courts in certain personal injury cases. 28 U.S.C. § 1605 (a) (5). However, this exception is specifically made inapplicable to "any claim based upon the exercise or performance or the failure to exercise or perform a discretionary function regardless of whether the discretion be abused." 28 U.S.C. § 1605 (a) (5) (A). Thus, the Holy See will not be liable for its "discretionary functions." At least one court has dismissed claims against the Holy See for clergy sexual misconduct on the grounds that such claims are really no more than allegations that the Holy See abused its discretion in allegedly hiring, supervising, or retaining priests. English v. Thorpe, 676 F. Supp. 761, 762 (S.D. Miss. 1987).

147. 457 N.W.2d 394 (Minn. Ct. App. 1990).

148. 457 N.W.2d at 395.

Similarly, in *N.H. v. Presbyterian Church (U.S.A.)*, the plaintiff sued the national Presbyterian Church, which is an unincorporated association, for negligent hiring and supervision of a minister. The Oklahoma Supreme Court held that the national organization was not liable because it had no notice of the minister's propensities.[149] This decision implies that if there is authority to supervise ministers, notice to the broader church body might create a basis for liability for a minister's later acts of abuse.[150]

Plaintiffs are already making conclusory allegations that the Holy See controls the decisions that allow clergy misconduct to occur.[151] They are trying to prove that the Vatican has control over priests and that in the past it has required bishops to return alleged abusers to ministry.[152] For example, plaintiffs have recently been alleging that the Vatican orchestrated a conspiracy to require dioceses to keep information about clerical sex abusers confidential and to transfer such priests to other positions. In that connection, plaintiffs are pointing to a document issued in 1962 by the Holy See, *Crimen Sollicitationis* ("On the Manner of Proceeding in Cases of Solicitation"). According to one complaint, this document "mentions that church officials could transfer offending priests to different assignments.... At all points of the process of handling sex abuse cases dealing with a penitent, the matters are to be kept secret."[153] It should be noted, however, that this document pertains to one narrow concern, the specific sin of "solicitation" in association with the sacrament of confession, rather than the broader matter of the sexual abuse of minors. It has since been superceded by the 1983 Code of Canon Law and by subsequent teachings as well.[154] Moreover, the Vatican does not supervise the conduct of individual priests.

For Catholics, the fact that some clergy are not diocesan clergy, but instead belong to religious orders, also complicates the issue of which entity is liable when clergy sexual misconduct occurs. For example, one recent complaint alleges that an archdiocese is "responsible for the selection and assignment of clergy [and] supervision of clergy activities" and therefore is responsible when a clergy person abuses a child, even if that clergy person is a member of a religious order.[155]

---

149. 998 P.2d 592, 600 (Okla. 1999).

150. *See also Stewart*, 2003 WL 21692670 (noting that there was no negligence because the regional Methodist body did not have notice of the minister's conduct).

151. According to a 2002 report by Reuters, a coalition of abuse survivors, legal experts, and progressive Catholic groups are lobbying the United Nations to hold the Holy See accountable for violating the U.N. Convention on the Rights of the Child. *See* Shasta Darlington, Catholics Urge U.N. to Push Vatican on Sex Scandal, Reuters, October 8, 2002. It is also interesting to note that the Maricopa County attorney sent a letter to the Vatican asking it to order two priests who had been indicted for child sexual abuse to return to Phoenix for prosecution. Dennis Wagner, Romley's Letter to Vatican Sent Back, Arizona Republic, Aug. 6, 2003.

152. *See* Michael Rezendes, Arizona Abuse Case Names Bishop, 2 Priests, Boston Globe, August 20, 2002; Todd Lighty & Monica Davey, Archdiocese to Remove 8 Priests, 5 to Appeal, Chi. Trib., June 24, 2002, at 1; Jeff Coen & Sean D. Hamill, S. Side Pastor Vows Appeal if Removed; Priest Says He Will Take Case to Vatican, Chi. Trib., June 17, 2002, at 13.

153. John Doe v. Catholic Bishop of Chicago, Case. No. 03L 011B10 (Cir. Ct. of Cook County, Ill.).

154. The Instruction on the Manner of Proceeding in Cases of Solicitation is available at http://www.rcf.org/. *See* Cardinal George's statement on this Vatican document at http://www.archdiocese-chgo.org/cardinal/statement/stat_03/stat_080703.shtm.

155. John Doe 34A v. Salesians of Don Bosco, Case No. 01 L 1454 (Cir. Ct. of Cook County, Ill.). Moreover, in *Doe v. Cunningham*, 30 F.3d 879 (7th Cir. 1994), the Seventh Circuit affirmed the district court's grant of summary judgment to a Catholic religious order. The complaint claimed that the order was liable for the alleged adult misconduct of a priest who was a member of the order, but who was serving in a parish in the Archdiocese of Milwaukee. However, the order submitted affidavits saying that "once [the priest] was assigned to [the parish] he performed his duties under the direction and control of the Archbishop of Milwaukee and was accountable to the Archbishop." 30 F.3d at 881. Based on these

All of these types of cases involve a church's understanding of the relationship between its various church bodies. Under church doctrine, which body has the authority to set policy on misconduct issues? Which is responsible for enforcing that policy? If a national church body technically can overrule a decision of a local body, is it liable when it does not get involved in that decision?

As Martin E. Marty and James A. Serritella state in their chapter on religious polity, religious organizations need to work closely with their lawyers to ensure that the church's secular civil structure clearly reflects its polity with regard to responsibility and liability for church decisions. Then the lawyers need to articulate to the courts what the religious polity is and how the church's structure reflects it.[156]

Conspiracy and RICO

In addition to agency and vicarious liability, some lawsuits alleging sexual abuse of minors by clergy have included claims under the federal Racketeer Influenced and Corrupt Organizations Act (RICO)[157] in an apparent effort to extend liability from a particular local church to a group of churches. RICO is a federal statute that was enacted to assist law enforcement authorities in their fight against organized crime.[158] It prohibits any person who has received income from a pattern of racketeering activity from using that income in an enterprise engaged in interstate commerce.[159] Under the statute, "any person injured in his business or property by reason of a violation" of the RICO criminal provisions "shall recover threefold the damages he sustains and the cost of the suit, including a reasonable attorney's fee."[160]

The number of cases in which plaintiffs have tried, or are now trying, to use RICO to hold the broader church liable for sexual abuse by a clergy person appears to be diminishing.[161] Perhaps this is because none of these cases has been successful to date.[162]

---

undisputed facts, the court held that the order was not liable for the torts the priest committed in the parish. On the other hand, at least one plaintiff's attorney has dropped a diocese from a lawsuit when the alleged abuse occurred at an institution owned and operated by a religious order and the diocese did not manage the institution. William R. Levesque and Stephen Nohlgren, Judge Rules Against Suit Alleging Vatican Coverup, St. Petersburg Times, Nov. 27, 2002, at http://www.sptimes.com.

156. Martin E. Marty and James A. Serritella, "Religious Polity," in this volume.

157. 18 U.S.C. § 1962.

158. *See* Bryan Murray, Protesters, Extortion, and Coercion: Preventing RICO From Chilling First Amendment Freedoms, 75 Notre Dame L. Rev. 691, 696–702 (1999) (citing legislative history).

159. 18 U.S.C. § 1962(a).

160. *See* 18 U.S.C. § 1964(c).

161. For example, three such cases have been filed against the Archdiocese of Los Angeles. *See* (i) Cicchillo v. Archdiocese of Los Angeles, No. BC272370 (Superior Court of the State of Ca., L.A. County, Central District filed April 29, 2002); (ii) John B. Doe v. Archdiocese of Los Angeles, No. BC272371 (Superior Court of the State of Ca., L.A. County, Central District filed April 29, 2002); and (iii) John Doe 50 v. Archdiocese of Los Angeles, No. BC274215 (Superior Court of the State of Ca., L.A. County, Central District filed May 20, 2002). Two such cases have been filed against Bishop Anthony O'Connell and the Dioceses of Jefferson City, Knoxville, Palm Beach, and Kansas City, Missouri. See (i) John CC Doe v. Most Rev. Anthony J. O'Connell, No. CV302-147CC (Circuit Ct. of Marion Co., Mo. filed March 22, 2002), and (ii) John T. Doe v. Most Rev. Anthony J. O'Connell, No. 02CC-001538 (Circuit Ct. of St. Louis Co., Mo. filed April 18, 2002). Most of the claims in *John T. Doe* were dismissed in 2003 on statute of limitations grounds. The third lawsuit filed against Bishop O'Connell is pending in Marion County, Missouri and does not include RICO claims.

162. For example, a judge dismissed RICO charges against various Catholic entities in a 1995 New Jersey case and the plaintiffs dropped a RICO claim brought against the Catholic Diocese of Dallas in

In using RICO, plaintiffs accuse a church of conducting the enterprise through a "pattern of racketeering activity" in a number of ways. Most commonly, they borrow from the "fraudulent concealment" allegations on which they rely to toll the statutes of limitation. They claim that in conducting its business, the church has fraudulently concealed either the fact that the clergy person was a child abuser or the fact that it knew about the clergy person's past abuse. Mere fraud is not a RICO predicate act,[163] but federal mail fraud and wire fraud are.[164] Plaintiffs therefore allege that the church not only has "concealed" facts about the abusing clergy member, but also has somehow used the mails or wires in furtherance of the "fraud." This may be supported by allegations that the clergy member was transferred without warning the destination church of the prior allegations. Some plaintiffs allege that the predicate acts consist of obstruction of justice, obstruction of criminal investigations, and witness tampering, claiming that church officials have tried to conceal criminal conduct, remove clergy from jurisdictions to help them evade law enforcement, or prevent victims from reporting allegations to the police.

Plaintiffs are trying to hold all persons connected with the church liable, even if some of those persons have had nothing to do with attempts to move a particular priest or silence a particular victim.[165] That is essentially what the plaintiffs tried to do in *Scheidler v. National Organization of Women*, where they argued that the planners of protests should be held liable for the criminal acts of certain protesters, even though the organizers had not directed, or even known about, those acts.[166]

It is far from clear, however, that the law permits so broad an imposition of associational liability. For example, in *NAACP v. Claiborne Hardware Co.*,[167] the U. S. Supreme Court required proof of specific illegal intent of each defendant in an action brought to punish organizers of a civil rights boycott.

There are also a number of other strong defenses that a church can raise against these RICO claims.[168] One of the strongest and most direct arguments is that RICO is not applicable because to bring a civil RICO claim, a private party must have been "injured in his business or property." The federal courts have universally held that RICO does not apply to civil cases seeking recovery of expenses resulting from personal injury such as sex abuse.[169] This is true even though the personal injury might result in financial

---

1998. *See* Smith v. Estate of Kelly, 778 A.2d 1162, 1176 (N.J. Super. 2001); Lawrence Morahan, Use of Racketeer Statute to Sue Catholic Church Draws Fire, March 25, 2002, at www.Crosswalk.com.

163. Bajorat v. Columbia Breckenridge Dev. Corp., 944 F. Supp. 1371, 1379 (N.D. Ill. 1996).

164. 18 U.S.C. § 1961(1).

165. *See* 18 U.S.C. §§ 1962(c); 1962(d); (1961)(4).

166. 537 U.S. 393 (2003), reversing a finding of a RICO violation because the defendants had not committed the necessary predicate acts for RICO since they had not "obtain[ed]" property from the plaintiffs and so had not committed extortion under the Hobbs Act.

167. 458 U.S. 886 (1982).

168. Many experts state that RICO is not intended for prosecution of sex abuse claims. For example, G. Robert Blakey, one of the architects of the statute, states, "I know that law like the back of my hand.... Rape and sodomy are not in there." George Koelzer, a partner with Coudert Bros., agrees that "It's farfetched to think that Congress intended RICO to be used for prosecuting [sex abuse by clergy.]... This takes us back to the 1980s, when people used the statute for every rinky-dink case that came along." Jeffrey Anderson, Experts Doubt RICO Will Fit Clergy Scandal, Daily Journal, May 22, 2002, at http://www.kbla.com/active/clergy.pdf.

169. Allman v. Philip Morris, Inc., 865 F. Supp. 665, 667–668 (S.D. Cal. 1994). *See also* Blast v. Cohen Dunn & Sinclair, P.C., 59 F.3d 492, 495 (4th Cir. 1995); Oscar v. University Students Co-op Ass'n, 965 F.2d 783, 785–86 (9th Cir.), *cert. denied*, 506 U.S. 1020 (1992); Doe v. Roe, 958 F.2d 763, 770 (7th Cir. 1992); Grogan v. Platt, 835 F.2d 844, 847–48 (11th Cir. 1988), cert. denied, 488 U.S.

loss.[170] Although plaintiffs have creatively tried to turn their personal injury claims into injury to business or property claims by alleging that they have incurred costs or have been prevented from pursuing a profession, the courts have thus far refused to allow such claims to be brought under RICO.[171] Thus, a plaintiff in clergy sexual misconduct cases probably cannot state a legally cognizable claim under RICO because the sexual abuse has not caused an injury to "business or property."

But if plaintiffs are able to get around these defenses, the use of RICO raises some more fundamental First Amendment questions. One of the major ones is that of which church entity constitutes the enterprise and which constitutes the person. Under section 1962(c) of RICO (illegal conduct of an enterprise), the "person" and the "enterprise" generally cannot be identical.[172] However, it is unclear whether a plaintiff's description of a church will fit in with the church's own view of itself.

Moreover, at least one court has raised the issue of whether the First Amendment requires courts to interpret RICO in such a way that it does not apply to churches at all. In *Van Schaick v. Church of Scientology of California, Inc.*[173] a former member of the Church of Scientology sued five branches of the church and its founder and second-ranking person alleging, among other things, RICO violations. The U. S. District Court for the District of Massachusetts held that the plaintiff had failed to state a claim under RICO. The court went on to note:

> Although we dismiss plaintiff's RICO counts on the grounds stated above, we add that these counts would encounter further objection if the court should find Scientology entitled to protection as a religion. In order not to risk abridging rights which the First Amendment protects, courts generally interpret regulatory statutes narrowly to prevent their application to religious organiza-

---

981 (1988); Genty v. Resolution Trust Corp., 937 F.2d 899, 918 (3d Cir. 1991); Drake v. B.F. Goodrich Co., 782 F.2d 638, 644 (6th Cir. 1986).

170. *See* Grogan v. Platt, 835 F.2d 844, 847 (11th Cir. 1988). However, a number of courts have allowed RICO claims for financial losses resulting from personal injuries to survive motions to dismiss. *See, e.g.,* Guerrero v. Gates, 110 F. Supp. 2d 1287 (C.D. Cal. 2000); National Asbestos Workers Med. Fund v. Philip Morris, Inc., 74 F. Supp. 2d 221, 234 (E.D.N.Y. 1999). The First Circuit has also suggested in a footnote that physical harm or lost wages from racketeering might be recoverable under RICO. Libertad v. Welch, 53 F.3d 428, 437 n.4 (1st Cir. 1995), *vacated and remanded on other grounds,* 215 F.3d 206 (1st Cir. 2000).

171. Doe v. Roe, 958 F.2d 763 (7th Cir. 1992) (held that none of the plaintiff's losses from being sexually abused by her divorce attorney were property losses covered by RICO); Gaines v. Texas Tech University, 965 F. Supp. 886, 890 (N.D. Tex. 1997) (holding that "[p]ersonal injuries such as Gaines' knee injury, and their resulting pecuniary consequences, are not compensable under RICO").

172. *See* Bramon v. Boatman's First Natl. Bank of Okla., 153 F.3d 1144, 1146 (10th Cir. 1998); Jaguar Cars, Inc. v. Royal Oaks Motor Car Co., 46 F.3d 258, 268 (3d Cir. 1995); Riverwoods Chappaqua Corp. v. Marine Midland Bank, N.A., 130 F.3d 339, 343–344 (2d Cir. 1994); New Berkley Mining Corp. v. Int'l. Union UMWA, 18 F.3d 1161, 1163 (4th Cir. 1994); Davis v. Mutual Life Ins. Co., 6 F.3d 367, 377 (6th Cir. 1993), *cert. denied,* 510 U.S. 1193 (1994); Sever v. Alaska Pulp Corp., 978 F.2d 1529, 1534 (9th Cir. 1992); Miranda v. Ponce Fed. Bank, 948 F.2d 41, 44–45 (1st Cir. 1991); Yellow Bus Lines, Inc. v. Drivers, Chauffeurs & Helpers Local Union 639, 839 F.2d 782, 789–790 (D.C. Cir.), *cert. denied,* 488 U.S. 926 (1988), *vacated and remanded,* 492 U.S. 914 (1989), *on remand,* 883 F.2d 132, 139–41 (D.C. Cir. 1989); Ash v. Wallenmeyer, 879 F.2d 272, 275–76 (7th Cir. 1989); Atkinson v. Anadarko Bank & Trust Co., 808 F.2d 438, 439 (5th Cir.), *cert. denied,* 483 U.S. 1032 (1987); Bennett v. Berg, 685 F.2d 1053, 1061–62 (8th Cir. 1982), *aff'd in part, rev'd in part on other grounds en banc,* 710 F.2d 1361, 1365 (8th Cir. 1983), *cert. denied,* 464 U.S. 1008 (1983). *But see* United States v. Hartley, 678 F.2d 961, 986–90 (11th Cir. 1982), cert. denied, 459 U.S. 1178, 1183 (1983) (holding that the "person" and the "enterprise" may be the same entity).

173. 535 F. Supp. 1125 (D. Mass. 1982).

tions. At times, they will require "a clear expression of Congress' intent" before subjecting religious organizations to regulatory laws pertaining to other entities. *N.L.R.B. v. Catholic Bishop of Chicago*, 440 U.S. 490, 507. Even where clear proof of such intent exists, courts have sometimes construed statutes to exclude religious groups from coverage to avoid "an encroachment by the State into an area of religious freedom which it is forbidden to enter by the principles of the free exercise clause of the First Amendment." *McClure v. Salvation Army*, 460 F.2d 553, 560 (5 Cir. 1972), *cert. denied*, 409 U.S. 896 (1972).[174]

Therefore, there is at least some question whether RICO should apply to churches at all.

Bankruptcy

Churches have been expending large sums of money to deal with the many claims being made against them on account of clergy sexual misconduct.[175] Moreover, additional claimants continue to come forward. On October 1, 2003, a judge ruled that a class action lawsuit against the Diocese of Louisville could go forward.[176]

Paying for these settlements is causing financial difficulties for churches. On December 5, 2003, the Archdiocese of Boston announced its intention to sell some valuable property and twenty-eight acres of land to obtain funds for its $85 million settlement plan.[177] Earlier, in December 2002, the Boston Finance Council even authorized the cardinal to seek bankruptcy protection.[178] Faced with lawsuits alleging sex abuse of minors, in 2003 eleven temples of the International Society for Krishna Consciousness, also known as the Hare Krishnas, filed for Chapter 11 protection in West Virginia and California.[179]

On July 8, 2004, the Archdiocese of Portland filed for bankruptcy. It did so because it had already paid $53 million to settle more than 130 claims and was facing two lawsuits

---

174. Id. at 1138–39.

175. For example, in December 2004 the Archdiocese of Orange County, California settled with about eighty-seven claimants for $100 million. John Broder, "Clergy Abuse Suits Settled," Chi. Trib., Dec. 4, 2004. On October 16, 2003, the Diocese of Bridgeport said that it would pay $21 million to settle with forty claimants. Also in 2003, the Archdiocese of Boston paid $85 million to settle with 552 claimants. "Diocese Settles for $21 Million in Sex Scandal," Chi. Trib., October 17, 2003. *See also* Deborah Zabarenklo, "Sex Abuse Lawsuits Add to Catholic Churches Money Woes," Dec. 28, 2004, at http://news.yahoo.com; Jennifer Levitz, "Abuse Settlement: $13.5 Million," Providence Journal Company, Sept. 10, 2002, at A-01; Barbara Whitaker, "Jesuits to Pay $7.5 Million to 2 Men Who Contended Abuse," N.Y. Times, Sept. 6, 2002; Rachel Zoo, "Huge Church Sex Abuse Settlement May Bring Forward More Victims," Chicago Sun-Times, June 12, 2003, at 38.

176. "Class Action Status in Clergy Abuse Suit," Chi. Trib., October 2, 2003.

177. *See* Pam Belluck, "Archdiocese Agrees to Sell Mansion to Pay Abuse Claims," New York Times, December 6, 2003.

178. Thomas Farragher and Michael Rezendes, "Law Given Authority to Seek Ch. 11," Boston Globe, December 5, 2002 at http://www.boston.com/globe.

179. ISKCON Krishna Temples Seek Claimants in Chapter 11 Reorganization, April 29, 2003, at http://www.businesswire.com/cgi-bin/cb_headline.cgi?&story_file=bw.042903/231195664; Gurukuli Youth Abuse Claims Very Important Notice About JUNE 30, 2003 DEADLINE for filing claims re the Iskcon Chapter 11 Bankruptcy, at http://iskcon.krishna.org/Articles/2003/04/017.html; Hare Krishna Movement files for bankruptcy, Dallas Business Journal, Feb. 6, 2002, at http://dallas.bizjournals.com/dalla/stories/2002/02/04/daily25.html.

seeking about \$160 million in damages.[180] On September 20, 2004, the Diocese of Tucson also filed for bankruptcy. Two years prior to that, it had settled with sixteen claimants for \$10 million and was now facing twenty-two additional claims.[181] On December 6, 2004, the Diocese of Spokane also filed for bankruptcy stating that it had total assets of \$11 million but total liabilities of \$81 million, of which \$76 million was for sex abuse claims.[182] Given the broad powers the government can assert over a debtor, it appears that bankruptcy presents potential First Amendment problems. Under Chapter 11 a debtor must prepare a reorganization plan specifying how it will restructure its business and how creditors will be satisfied. The creditors then vote on the plan, which also must be approved by the court. From the time a bankruptcy proceeding is filed until the time a plan is confirmed, a church's financial activity is subject to the scrutiny of the court and input from the creditors, and significant actions (such as settling lawsuits) require court approval. All of this might require a church to reveal its entire operation to the court and its creditors. The entire process appears to excessively entangle the government in the church's affairs.

One issue that has already surfaced in the Catholic bankruptcy cases is whether the assets of the parishes belong to the dioceses and thus are included in the bankruptcy procedures. The Archdiocese of Portland is arguing that the assets of its parishes and schools should be excluded from the bankruptcy because under canon law—that is, church law—these assets belong to the parishes and schools and not to the archdiocese. The claimants, however, are arguing that because the parishes are all part of the archdiocesan civil corporation, all the assets should be available to satisfy their claims. It is not clear how the court will rule on this important point.[183]

Conclusion

The current sex abuse crisis involving clergy misconduct with minors has opened up, or at least put the focus on, a variety of new issues for churches. It is clear that members of the clergy are not to be shielded from criminal prosecution or civil lawsuits on grounds of religious freedom. There is a controversy over whether churches may be required to pay damages without an infringement on their religious freedom, but as of the end of 2004 only a minority of courts have accepted the position that religious freedom protects churches from ever paying damages. Courts cannot legitimately influence the selection of candidates for ministry, but they need not tolerate criminal behavior in religious quarters.

Under the First Amendment, the issue for the state and churches going forward will be how to prevent clerical sexual misconduct and compensate victims without violating a church's right to religious freedom and self-understanding as to its polities. In this context, the courts must respect the churches' views of their own polity. For instance, as the

---

180. Alan Coopersman, "Archdiocese of Portland, Ore., Declares Bankruptcy," Washington Post, July 7, 2004 at A01.

181. "Diocese of Tucson Becomes 2nd to File for Bankruptcy," N.Y. Times, Sept. 21, 2004 at http://www.nytimes.com.

182. Janet I. Tu, "Spokane Diocese Files for Bankruptcy," Seattle Times, Dec. 7, 2004 at http://seattletimes.nwsource.com.

183. Eli Sanders, "Catholics Puzzle Over a Bankruptcy Filing," N.Y. Times, July 8, 2004, at http://www.nytimes.com.

courts have recognized in the past, most churches do not "hire" their clergy. Instead the clergy are ordained or "called" or somehow selected by a higher power. Similarly, most churches do not view their clergy as unlicensed mental health providers. Churches, through their attorneys, would be wise to teach the courts not to try to fit churches and clergy into secular categories that do not apply.

In this vein, churches must be clear about who is responsible under their polity for supervising and disciplining clergy and they must ensure that courts respect this polity and only hold the appropriate parties responsible. Religious liberty permits churches to develop structures that reflect their historical interpretations of the Bible or other sacred texts. In some instances this will result in the local church being responsible for calling and supervising the clergy, and thus liable if it fails to supervise its clergy. In other churches, it will be the diocese that has this responsibility. Whatever the result, not every level of a church is responsible for clerical conduct, but only the level that actually has that duty under church polity. The state and courts should not rewrite church polity just to provide more "deep pockets" for plaintiffs or to make it easier for plaintiffs to be awarded damages.

Moreover, the state and courts should not place on churches standards higher than those to which other organizations are subject. The courts should not find a "special" relationship between a church and its members and then, based on the "uniqueness" of this relationship, hold the church responsible under respondeat superior or fiduciary duty.

Similarly, the state should not dictate how a church should deal with allegations of sexual abuse, as has been tried in Manchester and Phoenix. While the state can punish abuse that has occurred, it cannot give the churches a blueprint or mandate for how they should supervise and discipline their clergy in the future.

This does not necessarily mean that churches are always immune from liability for clerical sexual abuse. Instead, if a particular church entity is responsible for clergy conduct and has failed to supervise its clergy, then it may well be held responsible and be made to compensate victims for their abuse. This is particularly true if that church entity had actual knowledge that one of its clergy had a propensity to abuse minors, but then continued to allow him or her access to them. Moreover, if other professionals have to report child abuse, clergy can also be mandated reporters. Also, although courts do not have the authority to second-guess personnel decisions of churches, they should be able to review selected church records to ascertain whether the church had actual knowledge of clerical sexual abuse.

In treating churches like other organizations, however, the state and the court should respect a church's polity, especially when doing so does not greatly impinge upon the state's goal of preventing child abuse. For example, the discovery process for church records must be carefully tailored so as not to go beyond what the courts need, or unnecessarily chill free exercise. Similarly, while clergy can be required to report child sexual abuse, the government should not require such reports to be made when the knowledge is gained through a communication protected by the clergy member's privilege. One of the keystones of religious freedom is the ability to seek spiritual answers for one's problems by confiding in clergy. If people no longer consider such communications confidential, they will be deterred from seeking spiritual solutions to their problems. In return for the state's respecting the clergy privilege, churches should stay true to their self-understanding of that privilege and only use it to protect communications truly within its ambit. If both the churches and the state honor the privilege, it would probably not have an undue impact on the state's ability to prevent child sexual abuse.

Most importantly, the state should recognize that churches view clerical sexual abuse not only as a legal problem but also as a moral one. While churches are subject to legal consequences for such abuse, their moral concerns may well require them to go beyond what the law requires in order to deal with this issue in a moral way. Churches often want to prevent the problem, not just because there are financial penalties for allowing it to happen, but more importantly because such abuse violates their most deeply held ethical principles. Similarly, they sometimes seek to reach out to victims and compensate them, even when the law does not demand it, because of their basic belief in justice and fairness to those who have been injured by people holding positions of trust in the church.

One can see that there are many ways in which this broader concern is occurring today. Churches are acknowledging their responsibility not only to prevent this problem from reoccurring in the future, but also to make reparations for past abuse. This is illustrated by the many denominations that have recently adopted or amended their policies on dealing with clerical sexual misconduct. One example is the recent norms of the Catholic Church requiring that all church members comply with reporting laws and that any priest guilty of even one act of sexual abuse be permanently removed from ministry.

All things considered, three important principles shape reflection on our topic. One is that in this context religious freedom provides no shield from illegal behavior, including that of religious authorities. Second, the state, the churches, and their lawyers must be cognizant and vigilant about the fact that churches' religious liberty rights must also be protected. Third, both church and state should realize that there are moral complexities to this problem which go beyond the narrow legal issues involved in criminal responsibility and civil liability.

Section IV

Affiliated Ministries: Education, Social Services, Health Care[*]

Thomas C. Berg

Most religious communities do not engage only in worship and preaching; they seek to practice their faith in other aspects of life as well. Two of their most common such activities are educating the young and caring for people who are in need because of illness, poverty, or other misfortune. These three areas of ministry—education, health care, and social services—are high priorities for many religious bodies. But each area also implicates interests of government and the broader society, which are concerned with the education of children and the quality of care that sick or needy people receive. As a result, religiously affiliated entities in education, health care, and social services organize themselves and conduct their operations against a background of federal, state, and local regulation. The following three chapters survey the legal environment for religious organizations in these three crucial areas of ministry. The focus is on religious organizations' self-understanding of their role in society, and also on how the law facilitates, restricts, and otherwise affects that self-understanding.

As a general matter, there are some differences between educational, social service, and health care institutions according to the extent to which each category of institution engages in the direct, explicit transmission or application of religious values and doctrines. Because education seeks directly to transmit values to the young, government contact with religious schools—whether through common law liability, statutory or administrative regulation, or tax-supported financial assistance—has tended to raise the most sensitive questions concerning the special constitutional demands of religious autonomy and church/state separation. It is no accident that the largest number of

---

[*] The chapters in this section incorporate case law and other developments through the end of 2000. Since that time, there have been two major developments relevant to education and social service ministries, respectively. First the U.S. Supreme Court approved the inclusion of religious schools in elementary and secondary-school voucher programs under the Establishment Clause in *Zelman v. Simmons-Harris*, 536 U.S. 639 (2002). *Zelman* and its implications for constitutional analysis are discussed in detail in Thomas C. Berg, "Appendix: The Supreme Court's School Voucher Decision (*Zelman v. Simmons-Harris*)," in this volume. Second, there has been a great deal of discussion and debate concerning the federal "charitable choice" legislation, first passed in 1996, which allows religious social service providers to benefit from government assistance on roughly the same terms as other providers. Charitable choice is discussed in detail in Carl H. Esbeck, "Appendix: Charitable Choice and the Critics," in this volume.

Supreme Court decisions concerning the First Amendment's Religion Clauses have something to do with the relationship of religion and education.

On the other hand, religious hospitals are often regulated and supported by the government in much the same way as secular hospitals are, on the premise that medical treatment is largely the same no matter what the patient's faith. More than a century ago, the Supreme Court approved of federal funding to a Catholic hospital on the ground that the hospital was not a "religious corporation" but simply "a secular corporation being managed by people who hold to the doctrines of the Roman Catholic Church, but who nevertheless are managing the corporation according to the law under which it exists."[1] Much later, in a decision involving federal grants to social service entities to combat teenage pregnancy, five justices remarked that "[t]here is a very real and important difference between running a soup kitchen or a hospital, and counseling pregnant teenagers on how to make the difficult decisions facing them."[2]

But these generalizations about the three categories by no means hold in all cases. As the following chapters show, religious entities bring their distinctive values to social service and health care ministries as well. For example, Donald H. J. Hermann's chapter on health care enumerates how Roman Catholic ethical-religious directives (ERDs) are implicated by a number of procedures, from abortion to sterilization to termination of life-sustaining treatment.[3] The importance of religious distinctives in social services activity is recognized by the recent federal "charitable choice" statute, under which religious charities that contract with state and local governments to provide services are specifically permitted to retain religious symbols on their premises and engage in religion-based hiring.[4] Thus, government regulation in any area—education, social service, or health care—can affect the autonomy and self-definition of the religious entity.

Thomas C. Berg's chapter on religiously affiliated education sets out a framework for the kind of decisions that religiously-based ministries have to make: what legal form to adopt, how to treat personnel, how to treat clients or students, and whether to accept government aid.[5] The chapter also sets out models for how government can treat such entities: either favoring the government-run agency (for example, the public school or government social service provider), welcoming and supporting a wide range of institutions providing services (as, for example, with voucher or "charitable choice" programs), or trying to maintain strict "separation" between government and the religious entity (neither regulating it heavily nor providing it with aid). Berg shows how recent years have seen a shift from a separation model to an "equality" model: more and more, religious schools may be, and are being, both subsidized and regulated to the same extent as other schools. This trend toward equal treatment has culminated in the Court's recent approval of including religious schools in government voucher programs in *Zelman v. Simmons Harris*, a decision discussed at length in an appendix to the chapter on religiously affiliated education. This development has the advantage of treating religious schools as full contributors to educating American children, but it poses the danger that their distinctive values will be erased by the heavy hand of regulation. In particular in-

---

1. Bradfield v. Roberts, 175 U.S. 291, 298–99 (1899).
2. Bowen v. Kendrick, 487 U.S. 589, 641 (1988) (Blackmun, J., dissenting); *id.* at 623 (O'Connor, J., concurring).
3. Donald H.J. Hermann, "Religiously Affiliated Health Care Providers: Legal Structures and Transformations," in this volume.
4. Personal Responsibility and Work Opportunity Reconciliation Act of 1996, Pub. L. No. 104-93, §§ 104(d), (f), 42 U.S.C. §§ 604A(d), (f).
5. Thomas C. Berg, "Religiously Affiliated Education," in this volume.

stances, such as the federal unemployment-tax and religious-discrimination exemptions, legal protection of a religious school may depend, wrongly, on the formal legal structure that the school chooses.[6]

Finally, Hermann's chapter on health care emphasizes, as we have seen, how religious-ethical norms *do* affect decisions in religiously affiliated health care institutions—certainly not in all treatment situations, but in an important minority of them. Hermann sets this issue in the context of the most important current development in the health care field: the increasing integration of providers in response to economic pressures—including, in some cases, mergers between religious hospitals and their secular counterparts as well as the involvement of religious hospitals in ever-more-complex managed care plans. Hermann evaluates this trend in light of several legal considerations: antitrust limits, federal tax consequences, the mandates (for Roman Catholic hospitals) of canon law, and perhaps most importantly, the effects that follow when a hospital with distinctive restrictions on certain kinds of treatments (for example, abortion or sterilization) becomes legally integrated with another hospital that has no such restrictions. He concludes that religious hospitals and their sponsoring bodies face difficult questions about "the extent to which they are 'morally able to compromise' their philosophical positions in order to adapt to the evolving health care market."[7]

6. *Id.*
7. Hermann, *supra* note 3.

Religiously Affiliated Education[*]

Thomas C. Berg

Of all the activities in which religious groups in America engage, it has been education that has produced the most long-lasting and deeply felt conflicts with the state. When Roman Catholics first came to America in large numbers in the mid-1800s, their most severe clashes came with public school authorities, over the Protestant-style religious practices, from lay prayers to King James Bible readings, that permeated the schools.[1] In the last thirty-five years, both Amish parents and fundamentalist Baptist ministers have been jailed or threatened with jail for refusing to accept the state's dictates on how to educate the children in their communities. And most of the Supreme Court's case law on the Establishment Clause of the First Amendment has arisen out of disputes over either religious practices in the public schools or state funding for religiously affiliated private schools.

It is not surprising that education should be a primary flash point for conflicts between the values of religious groups and those of the state. As sociologist James Davison Hunter has described:

> The reason that the contemporary culture war extends to the realm of education is not difficult to divine. The education of the public at every level—from elementary school through college—is not a neutral process of imparting practical knowledge and technical skills. Above and beyond that, schools are the primary institutional means of reproducing community and national identity for succeeding generations of Americans.[2]

Because education is not "neutral," but is vital to "reproducing community and national identity," both the state and most religious groups naturally view the goals of education in terms of their own values. Those values are very different. To fundamentalist school officials in Hawaii, their "church and school are one and the same":[3] religion pervades

---

* This chapter incorporates case law and other developments through the end of 2000. Since that time, the major development has been that the U.S. Supreme Court approved the inclusion of religious schools in elementary and secondary-school voucher programs under the Establishment Clause, in *Zelman v. Simmons-Harris*, 536 U.S. 639 (2002). *Zelman* and its implications for constitutional analysis are discussed in detail in the appendix following this chapter.

1. *See, e.g.*, Charles L. Glenn, Jr., The Myth of the Common School (1988); Diane Ravitch, The Great School Wars (1974); Carl F. Kaestle, Pillars of the Republic: Common Schools and American Society, 1780–1860 (1983); Michael W. McConnell, Multiculturalism, Majoritarianism, and Education: What Does Our Constitutional Tradition Have to Say?, 1991 U. Chi. L. For. 132, 135–36.

2. James Davison Hunter, Culture Wars: The Struggle to Define America 198 (1991).

3. State *ex rel.* Minami v. Andrews, 651 P.2d 473, 475 (Haw. 1982).

education, and for the state to assert control over their teaching is to assert control over the core of their religion, tantamount to interfering with a sermon or a worship service. On the other side, state regulators assert the power to control aspects of religious school's offerings based on a variety of goals of the broader society. Particularly, they assert the need to make sure that children are prepared to be self-sufficient, productive citizens who are also aware of and can get along with fellow citizens of different backgrounds and beliefs.

Many of these conflicts involve the conscientious beliefs and mandates of the religious group: the state mandates behavior that for the school is religiously forbidden (for example, making certain teaching or leadership positions open to women as well as men), or forbids behavior that is religiously mandated (for example, the use of corporal punishment to discipline students). But as many observers have pointed out, the interest of religious organizations extends beyond situations where the organizations can point to a clear religious tenet that the state is forcing it to violate. Religious organizations have an important interest in maintaining their autonomy against government intervention, whether or not the government is forcing them to violate a specific tenet of their faith.[4] The Supreme Court, for example, found that Catholic schools had the right to be free from the federally imposed duty of bargaining with their teachers over employment terms, even though Catholic doctrine generally supports workers' right to unionize and bargain over employment conditions.[5] Included in the constitutionally guaranteed rights of religious freedom is the right of religious institutions "to decide for themselves, free from state interference, matters of church governance as well as those of faith and doctrine."[6]

This chapter discusses the effect of legal regulation on certain important structural and organizational choices that religious schools make. I first set the framework, describing some of the most important organizational decisions of religious schools as well as various models for legal approaches to religious education. Then I turn directly to the effect of legal rules on distinctive aspects of religious schools' decisionmaking. In the simplest terms, government action can either interfere with the school's operations (regulation) or assist those operation (financial subsidies). Sometimes government does both simultaneously, including regulatory conditions along with the financial aid that it offers.

Structural and Organizational Decisions of Religiously Affiliated Schools

This book concerns the effect of laws on the structure of religious organizations — specifically in this chapter, religiously affiliated schools. But it is important to define the term "structure," for it has several meanings. Religiously affiliated schools have several areas in which they typically must make decisions as to how to structure or organize their affairs.

---

4. *See, e.g.*, Douglas Laycock, Towards a General Theory of the Religion Clauses: The Case of Church Labor Relations and the Right of Church Autonomy, 81 Colum L. Rev. 1373 (1981).
5. *See* NLRB v. Catholic Bishop, 440 U.S. 490 (1979).
6. Kedroff v. St. Nicholas Cathedral, 344 U.S. 94, 116 (1952).

1. Formal legal structure: relationship to a religious body. In the narrowest sense, a religiously affiliated school must decide the formal, or *de jure*, legal structure it will adopt.[7] Many of these decisions concern the school's legal relation, if any, to a "church": that is, to a religious congregation, diocese, order, or denomination.[8] The leading survey of church-related colleges, for example, states that the formal legal relations between colleges and their sponsoring religious bodies are "varied and often complex," involving several potential forms of methods of legal control.[9] Will the school be a part of the church's legal structure, or will it be set up as a separate legal entity (and if it is a separate entity, will it adopt a corporate form)? Keeping the school formally within the church legal structure will increase the church's control over the school, but it may conversely subject the church to increased liability for the school's activities.[10]

If the school is separately organized, the question arises what, if any, formal control the church will exercise over the school. For example, will the church have the power to select all or a certain number of seats on the governing board of the school?[11] Or will the church maintain veto power over any of the school's decisions? Will the title to any of the real property used by the school remain vested in the church? By using some or all of these governance methods in varying degrees, churches can exercise different degrees of control over their affiliated schools. Of course, some religious schools, most commonly colleges and universities, have no association with any formal religious body but are still highly religious:[12] important examples include many evangelical Protestant Bible schools and institutes as well as evangelical liberal arts colleges such as Wheaton and Gordon.

If a school is a separate legal entity, it will have other decisions to make concerning the *de jure* form it will adopt. Will it be organized as a corporation or in some other form? If various corporate forms are available under state law, which form will it choose? Most separately organized religious schools utilize general nonprofit corporation laws. But in some states other corporate choices are available. Many states recog-

---

7. For discussion of the relationship between *de jure* legal structure and other organizational decisions that an institution must make, see Thomas C. Berg, "Religious Structure Under the Federal Constitution," in this volume; and also Carl H. Esbeck, Regulation of Religiously Based Social Services: The First Amendment Considerations, 19 Hastings Const. L. Q. 343, 347–48 (1992).

8. Elementary and secondary schools of a particular denomination will typically be tied to a particular congregation or diocese. Colleges and universities, on the other hand, will have ties to a particular religious order (in the case of many Catholic colleges), a state denomination or association (in the case of Baptist colleges), or the national denomination (in the case of Lutheran, Methodist, Presbyterian, and other Protestant colleges).

9. *See* Manning M. Pattillo, Jr. and Donald M. Mackenzie, Church-Sponsored Higher Education in the United States: Report of the Danforth Commission 52 (1966) (hereinafter Danforth Report); *see also* Philip Moots and Edward McGlynn Gaffney, Jr., Church and Campus: Legal Issues in Religiously Affiliated Higher Education 8 (1979) (discussing various forms of church control over school governance).

10. *See* Mark E. Chopko, "Derivative Liability," in this volume.

11. *See* Danforth Report, *supra* note 9, at 38 (describing this as a "widespread" method for a religious body to ensure control over an affiliated college). There can be a variety of arrangements concerning governing board selection. For example, the negotiations between Southern Baptist universities and the increasingly conservative leadership in state Southern Baptist conventions have often focused on the number of trustee board positions that will be independent and the number that will be elected by the convention. *See* Dictionary of Baptist in America 55, 127, 281 (Bill J. Leonard ed. 1994) (describing recent changes in trustee election at Baylor, Furman, and Wake Forest universities).

12. *See* Danforth Report, *supra* note 9, at 19 (discussing colleges "that cannot be classified technically as church related but do have a definite religious orientation").

nize a distinct "religious corporation" form;[13] choosing this form will strengthen the school's ability to exercise religious preferences in hiring without running afoul of civil rights laws, but it also increases the likelihood that the school will be barred from receiving certain forms of government financial assistance.[14] A school may also choose to organize primarily for educational purposes, and it may need to state this organizational choice in order to be eligible for certain programs of educational assistance.

A school's organizational decisions, however, extend not just to formal or *de jure* legal structure, but also to a number of other questions on which the law has an effect.

2. Curriculum and campus life. One crucial question, obviously, is the extent to which distinctively religious concepts will permeate the curriculum and other aspects of life in the school. Will religion classes or chapel services be required? Will other classes (in math, science, history, or literature) be taught with explicit reference to religious doctrines or values?

3. Relations with teachers and other employees. Religiously affiliated schools must assert policies concerning their employees—especially teachers, who play a "critical and unique role...in fulfilling the mission of a church-operated school."[15] In hiring teachers and other employees, will the school seek only those persons who belong to its sponsoring denomination or who will agree to specified doctrinal statements (or will it at least give some preference to those persons)? Once an employee is hired, what kind of standards will the school require the person to follow? To what extent will the school seek to control the content of instruction by teachers? What standards of personal behavior must employees follow? And what sorts of procedures are employees entitled to before being disciplined or fired for misconduct?

4. Student policies: admissions and discipline. The questions that arise for students are similar to those that arise for employees. What sorts of religious requirements or preferences will the school incorporate in admitting students? What standards of conduct must students follow, and what procedures will be followed before disciplining them?

The Supreme Court has summed up many of these factors in describing a profile of "pervasively sectarian" elementary and secondary schools. Schools that are pervasively religious

> (a) impose religious restrictions on admissions; (b) require attendance of pupils at religious activities; (c) require obedience by students to the doctrines and dogmas of a particular faith; (d) require pupils to attend instruction in the theology or doctrine of a particular faith; (e) are an integral part of the religious mission of the church sponsoring it; (f) have as a substantial purpose the inculcation of religious values; (g) impose religious restrictions on faculty appointments; and (h) impose religious restrictions on what or how the faculty may teach.[16]

The remainder of this chapter will discuss how these and other organizational decisions are affected by legal rules. As we will see, decisions on some of these matters also

---

13. *See* Patricia B. Carlson, "Unincorporated Associations and Charitable Trusts," in this volume.

14. *See* Ferdinand N. Dutile and Edward McGlynn Gaffney Jr., State and Campus: State Regulation of Religiously Affiliated Higher Education 5 (1984). Regarding the effects of this choice, see discussions of effect on religious employment preferences and on receipt of aid, *infra*.

15. *Catholic Bishop*, 440 U.S. at 501.

16. Comm. for Public Educ. and Religious Liberty v. Nyquist, 413 U.S. 756, 767–68 (1973).

affect the school's amenability to other actions by government, both regulation and aid. That is, structural and organizational decisions of religiously affiliated schools are affected by government actions, and the schools' decisions in turn affect what actions government can take toward the schools. To understand these reciprocal relations, it is necessary first to examine general legal approaches toward religiously affiliated schools.

Models for Legal Approaches to Religiously Affiliated Schools

Several different models can help in understanding the possibilities for legal treatment of religiously affiliated schools. The models differ on how they treat the two questions of regulating religious schools and providing financial assistance to them. Each model has had influence on both legislation and constitutional doctrine, but I will try to trace those which have been the most influential.

The common school model

One important model emphasizes the need for common, unitary schooling to give children have a chance to be exposed to other children of different races, ethnic groups, religious faiths, and ideological viewpoints. As one leader in the campaign to institute common state schools in the mid-nineteenth century said: "The children of this country, of whatever parentage, should be educated *together*— ...educated to be one harmonious people."[17] In the 1800s, the public school movement was designed to provide a "common denominator" education to children of various Protestant denominations, free from the theological controversies that divided the denominations. Today, obviously, the ideal of the common school seeks to encompass an even greater range of citizens and is more secular. Children of every religion and of no religion come together to be educated in secular learning and to be socialized into what it means to be an American, especially into the need for tolerance of others in the light of religious and cultural pluralism.[18]

The common school ideal privileges the state-operated school, the one institution where, it is claimed, students of all faiths can come together leaving the peculiarities of different beliefs behind. Perhaps the most dramatic judicial expression of this attitude was by Justice Frankfurter, who wrote that the public school is "a symbol of our secular unity," "designed to serve as perhaps the most powerful agency for promoting cohesion among a heterogeneous democratic people," and therefore "must keep scrupulously free from entanglement in the strife of sects."[19] The common school ideal may allow private schools (religious and secular) a right to operate. But it insists that, at least, govern-

---

17. *See* Glenn, *supra* note 1, at 223 (quoting W.S. Dutton).
18. For recent articulations and defenses of this model, see, e.g., James F. Dwyer, Religious Schools and Children's Rights (1998); Amy Gutmann, Democratic Education 1–70 (1987); Gutmann, Civic Education and Social Diversity, 105 Ethics 557 (1995); Suzanna Sherry, Responsible Republicanism: Educating for Citizenship, 62 U. Chi. L. Rev. 131 (1995).
19. McCollum v. Board of Educ., 333 U.S. 203, 216–17 (1948) (Frankfurter, J., concurring).

ment's resources and encouragement should be directed solely to schools that are publicly run and publicly accountable: in other words, there should be no state financial aid to private, especially religious, schools. Moreover, the preference for common schools suggests that private schools should be subject to substantial state regulation to ensure that their activities are consistent with general societal standards and values. In short, the common school model is hostile to the autonomy of religiously affiliated schools.

The common school model has had influence on the legal treatment of private and especially religious schools. Its greatest influence has been in the area of financial aid, where, as will be seen later, both federal and state constitutional doctrine have greatly restricted the kinds of government aid that may be provided to religious schools, at least at the elementary and secondary level.[20] The courts have also been willing to countenance substantial state regulation of private and religious schools. But the common school model does not explain all aspects of the law concerning religious schools. Those schools not only have a constitutional right to exist, they enjoy autonomy from state regulation in important areas. Moreover, at the college and university level, religious schools play a crucial role, educating hundreds of thousands of students and receiving millions of dollars in government aid, either directly from government agencies or indirectly through government grants and loans to students.

The problem with the common school model is that in attempting to be "common," the public schools run the great risk—perhaps unavoidable—of teaching not a common ideology, but a particular ideology that excludes many citizens. That was true in the mid-1800s, when what was seen as the common ideology was in fact a form of generic Protestantism. The state schools conducted prayers and Bible readings without the leadership or interpretation of clergy and read from the King James Bible, practices that were abhorrent to Catholics. When Catholic students refused to participate, they were punished; and when Catholic dioceses and parishes began forming their own schools in response, Protestants united to ensure that they would not receive any public financial support.[21]

In the late twentieth century, the problems faced by the common school are even greater. Because the range of religious faiths in America has expanded so greatly, almost any religious observance can be seen as partial and particular rather than common; this dynamic tends to drive the schools to teach no religious values whatsoever. Indeed, the Supreme Court has repeatedly held that for public elementary and secondary schools to promote any religious exercises or doctrines violates the "neutrality" required of the state by the First Amendment's Establishment Clause.[22] But a school that espouses no religious philosophy or ideas is not "neutral" to those who believe that religion is inseparable from the task of education and values inculcation (the latter of which schools inevitably must also do). Education is not a neutral process. Thus, critics of the common school model charge that it is decidedly non-neutral for the gov-

---

20. *See* section on The Effect of Legal Rules Concerning Government Financial Assistance to Religious Schools, *infra.*

21. *See* sources cited *supra* note 1.

22. *See, e.g.,* Engel v. Vitale, 370 U.S. 421 (1962) (government-sponsored prayers); Lee v. Weisman, 505 U.S. 577 (1992) (same); Doe v. Santa Fe Ind. Sch. Dist., 530 U.S.290 (2000); Abington School Dist. v. Schempp, 374 U.S. 203 (1963) (government-sponsored Bible readings); Epperson v. Arkansas, 393 U.S. 97 (1968) (government promotion of religious doctrine by prohibiting teaching of evolution); Edwards v. Aguillard, 482 U.S. 578 (1987) (government promotion of religious doctrine by requiring teaching of creation science); Stone v. Graham, 449 U.S. 39 (1980) (government-sponsored posting of Ten Commandments).

ernment to use funding to favor schools that must inevitably adopt or communicate some moral or social philosophy—multiculturalism, sexual traditionalism or sexual liberation, free-market economics or socialism—but are forbidden to communicate any religious philosophy.

The plurality of institutions model

An alternative view argues that true pluralism in education cannot be achieved by trying to teach the common denominator of material in a single institution, the public school. Real pluralism can be achieved only by permitting and encouraging education by a wide range of schools, including religiously affiliated ones. Society benefits from the diversity, and students and families who do not like one school can go to another. This view, not surprisingly, is held by many (though not all) religious communities. For these communities, religion cannot be separated from education; the attempt to do so in the public schools leads to the privileging of secular assumptions about learning and, implicitly if not explicitly, to an antireligious posture. In America, the view was first articulated by Roman Catholics who saw the neutrality of the nineteenth-century "common school" as a fraudulent cover for Protestant assumptions and sometimes explicit Protestant practices. Today the groups alienated from the state schools have expanded to include many conservative Protestants as well as Orthodox and some Conservative Jews.

Other proponents of the plurality of institutions model emphasize the importance of assigning social functions to the institutions of civil society rather than exclusively to the state. Some proponents, continuing in the wake of the observations of Alexis de Tocqueville, emphasize the importance of "mediating structures" between the individual and the state, voluntary activities through which citizens become involved in seeking the common good through voluntary activities.[23] Others emphasize the capacity of private institutions, including schools, to develop a moral framework for their members that makes their social efforts more effective.[24] For some commentators, such as Stephen Carter, the importance of these distinctive moral frameworks is precisely to serve as challenges or counterweights, where necessary, to the moral assertions of the state.[25] Finally, there are pedagogical reasons for encouraging a variety of educational systems: as frustration mounts with the failures of some public schools, even secular commentators look to competition and "choice" as a cure for what ails American education. As Justice Powell once put it, "parochial schools have provided an educational

---

23. *See, e.g.*, Peter Berger and Richard John Neuhaus, To Empower People: The Role of Mediating Structures in Public Policy (1977); Stephen V. Monsma, When Sacred and Secular Mix: Religious Nonprofit Organizations and Public Money 15–23 (1996); Thomas C. Berg, Civility, Politics, and Civil Society: Response to Anthony Kronman, 26 Cumb. L. Rev. 871, 873–76 (1996) (discussing Tocqueville's view of voluntary associations as a balancing force between individualism and authoritarianism).

24. *See, e.g.*, Anthony S. Bryk et al., Catholic Schools and the Common Good 301–02 (1993) (discussing philosophies of personalism and human dignity that help inspire efforts at Catholic schools); Michael W. McConnell, Political and Religious Disestablishment, 1986 B.Y.U. L. Rev. 405, 421–22 (discussing moral commitment of volunteer workers in religious institutions).

25. *See* Stephen L. Carter, The Constitution and the Religious University, 46 DePaul L. Rev. 479, 484–85 (1998). For general defenses of a plurality-of-schools model on grounds of parental rights and limiting state power, see, e.g., Stephen Arons, Compelling Belief: The Culture of American Schooling (1983); Stephen G. Gilles, On Educating Children: A Parentalist Manifesto, 63 U. Chi. L. Rev. 937 (1996).

alternative for millions of young Americans" and "often afford wholesome competition with our public schools."[26]

According to the plurality of institutions model, social policy should not only permit but encourage private schools to flourish: it should aim toward the decentralization of education. In other words, private schools should be free to pursue their own values and curricular emphases, subject only to minimal state regulation crucial to ensure a satisfactory education. On the question of government assistance, those who favor a "plurality of institutions" are of two minds. Some fear that the regulation that tends to accompany government aid will destroy the private school's independent vision. But many others argue that the state school should not be favored through the provision of free education while parents sending their children to private and religious schools have to pay tuition (a double payment, since they also pay taxes to support the public schools). In this view, the funding of public schools is an injustice that the government should correct by giving aid either directly to the private school or indirectly through vouchers or tax relief given to families.

The plurality of institutions model has also influenced America's legal treatment of religious schools, particularly by protecting them from some of the most intrusive forms of state regulation. In the 1920s, the Supreme Court struck down as unconstitutional state laws that, among other things, forbade parents to send their children to other than public schools. The decision, *Pierce v. Society of Sisters*, stated that

> [t]he fundamental theory of liberty upon which all governments in this Union repose excludes any general power of the state to standardize its children by forcing them to accept instruction from public teachers only. The child is not the mere creature of the state; those who nurture him and direct his destiny have the right, coupled with the high duty, to recognize and prepare him for additional obligations.[27]

Years later, the Court made clear that this "liberty of parents and guardians to direct the upbringing and control of their children"[28] rested on the Free Exercise Clause when the parents' chosen form of education was religious. *Wisconsin v. Yoder* held that the state could not force Amish parents to send their children to school after the age of fourteen because such a requirement was not necessary to serve governmental "interests of the highest order."[29] The decision to send children to religious schools has also been protected under state constitutions.[30]

But the plurality of institutions model also has been far from fully adopted in legislation and constitutional decisions. As already mentioned, government financial assistance has often favored the public schools, with private and religious schools and the families who use them being denied educational benefits: for many years, Supreme Court decisions held that the denial of assistance to religious education in particular was required by the Establishment Clause. Moreover, as will be seen shortly,[31] religious schools are subject to substantial state regulation; the law often fails to protect their autonomy vigorously. At the college and university level, religious schools enjoy more au-

---

26. Wolman v. Walter, 433 U.S. 229, 266 (1977) (Powell, J., concurring).
27. 268 U.S. 510, 535 (1925).
28. *Id.* at 534.
29. 406 U.S. 205, 215 (1972).
30. *See, e.g.,* State Board of Educ. v. Rudasill, 589 S.W.2d 877 (Ky. 1979) (striking down various state requirements including teacher certification).
31. *See* section on Government Regulation of Religious Schools, *infra*.

tonomy from regulation, receive substantial government funding indirectly through grants and loans to students, and generally play a bigger role in the provision of education to the population. But at the elementary and secondary level, they remain disfavored by the legal rules concerning government assistance.[32]

The separation of religion and state model

There is a third model, the "separation of religion and state" model, that until recently has been quite influential in explaining the legal approach to religiously affiliated schools. Under this general approach, government should stay out of the core religious activities of religious schools, neither regulating such activities nor giving them any financial assistance; but the "secular" aspects of religious schools' operations may be open both to regulation and to financial assistance. Insofar as the separation model frees religious schools from at least the most intrusive forms of state interference, it parallels the plurality of institutions model and its principle of school autonomy. But insofar as the separation model prevents religious schools from receiving all but limited forms of financial aid from the state, it parallels the common school model and its preference for secular schools.

As discussed above, the Free Exercise Clause was interpreted in *Wisconsin v. Yoder* to permit parents to challenge state interference with their right to choose an education for their children. *Yoder* and later cases did emphasize that the state may act to ensure educational quality in religious schools by regulation, as long as the regulation does not interfere with the core religious identity of the school.[33] Regulation of religiously affiliated schools may also be barred under the Establishment Clause because it creates "excessive entanglement" between state regulation and the religious activities of the school.[34] The Supreme Court applied this principle in *NLRB v. Catholic Bishop*[35] to bar federal Labor Board oversight over the terms and conditions of employment of lay teachers at parochial schools. Both of these protections, free exercise and nonestablishment, reflect the separation model by barring the government from involvement in central religious matters but allowing some regulation of the less religiously sensitive aspects of a school's operations. The third part of this chapter will expand on this balancing approach to the regulation of religious schools.

While "separation" thus recognizes the value of freeing private schools with religiously based values, it has also entailed that for the most part these schools may not receive government aid. In a series of cases in the 1970s and early 1980s, the Court held that religious elementary and secondary schools could not constitutionally receive government aid, and that certain religious colleges and universities could receive direct aid only because they were not pervasively religious and therefore the aid could be restricted to the wholly secular operations of the institutions. In short, a school could receive significant financial assistance only if it agreed to reduce the religiosity of its atmosphere—that is, to become more like a secular institution.

---

32. *See* Monsma, *supra* note 23, at 30-40, 131–42, for discussion of the differences in government policy toward college-level versus elementary and secondary-level schools.

33. *See Yoder*, 406 U.S. at 214; *see* cases cited in discussion of external social effects, *infra*.

34. *See* Lemon v. Kurtzman, 403 U.S. 602, 612–13 (1971).

35. 440 U.S. 490 (1979). More precisely, because of the potential for entanglement, the Court refused to allow Board oversight of the teacher/school relationship until Congress "clearly expressed" an intent to cover the relationship. *Id.* at 507.

Recent developments: equality between religion and nonreligion, deference to the political branches

For many years, the separation model—some constitutional limits on state regulation of religious schools, substantial constitutional limits on state financial assistance to them—was the most influential legal approach toward religious schools. In recent years, however, the Supreme Court has moved away from enforcing the separation model vigorously, both as to regulation and assistance, and under both the Free Exercise and the Establishment clauses. Instead, two other principles have become important in constitutional analysis. The first is a principle of equality: that religious institutions, including religious schools, should be treated no differently than comparable nonreligious institutions. The second is a principle of deference to the political branches: the current Court has more inclination, in its constitutional decisions, to allow legislatures and administrators to choose whether to regulate religious schools or exempt them from regulation, and whether to provide financial assistance to religious schools as with other schools or withhold such assistance.

In *Employment Division v. Smith*,[36] the Court significantly reduced special protection for religious conduct under the Free Exercise Clause. Under *Smith*, if a regulation applies to entities (for example, to public schools or secular private schools), it usually may also apply to religious entities (such as religious schools).[37] If this "equal treatment" rule were flatly applied, a state that required public schools to teach evolution, or give nondiscriminatory consideration to gay persons for teaching positions, could make the same demands on fundamentalist Christian schools as well. As these examples show, a vigorous application of the equality principle would greatly reduce the ability of religious schools to maintain a distinctive identity and viewpoint.

However, *Smith* mentioned two exceptions to its general rule that might preserve religious schools' autonomy even in the face of generally applicable laws. First, the Court recognized that religiously motivated conduct might take the form of speech or association protected under other provisions of the First Amendment.[38] The free speech guarantee might protect the school from having to teach evolution, and under *Boy Scouts of America v. Dale*[39] the freedom of expressive association would likely protect a school opposed to homosexual behavior from hiring a person who was open about his homosexual conduct.

Second, the Court indicated (in an effort to avoid directly overruling *Wisconsin v. Yoder*) that it would continue to apply strict scrutiny to "hybrid" claims that involved both religious tenets and the right of parents to control their children's education.[40] If this exception is taken seriously, it might preserve special protection for religiously affiliated schools in many situations. Unfortunately, however, some cases after *Smith* have not taken the "hybrid" right seriously, and instead have followed *Smith*'s general rule of deference to generally applicable state regulation. For example, the Minnesota Supreme

---

36. 494 U.S. 872 (1990).
37. *See id.* at 877 (holding that application of "neutral and generally applicable law" to religious conduct generally raises no free exercise issue).
38. *Id.* at 881–82.
39. 530 U.S. 640 (2000) (holding that the Boy Scouts' rights of expressive association were violated by state civil rights law applied to forbid them from expelling a scoutmaster who had publicly stated his homosexuality).
40. *Smith*, 494 U.S. at 881–2 (citing both *Yoder* and *Pierce*).

Court has held that only parents enjoy the right of educational freedom, that religious schools cannot assert the rights of the parents of their students, and thus that the schools have no free exercise objections to unionization of teachers under state labor laws.[41] On the same ground, the New Mexico Supreme Court refused to allow a religious day-care center to raise a free exercise challenge to intrusive state regulation.[42]

In rejecting the school's standing to assert rights of educational freedom, these courts passed over the obvious: respecting a religious school's autonomy is necessary to preserving the distinctive kind of education for which parents sent their children to the school. As Justice Brennan has recognized, believers " 'exercise their religion through religious organizations, and these organizations must be protected by the Free Exercise Clause.'... [F]urtherance of the autonomy of religious organizations often furthers individual religious freedom as well."[43] Nevertheless, in future cases involving constitutional challenges to educational regulations, attorneys for religious schools would be well advised to have parents join as original parties or as intervenors and raise the free exercise claims.[44]

Some other free exercise challenges have been barred by the Court's 1990 holding that there is no "constitutionally significant burden" on a religious group unless the law forces it to violate a specific religious tenet (command or prohibition).[45] Taken seriously, this rule means that a school has no free exercise objection to regulation that interferes with its operations—even drastically, even in highly religious elements of the school—if it cannot point to a tenet of conscience it is being forced to violate. For example, two courts have held that Catholic religious schools had no free exercise right to avoid being compelled to bargain with employees because Catholic doctrine does not condemn unionization and indeed generally supports it in the secular workplace.[46] Moreover, the current Court has also been reluctant to find that general regulation applicable to other entities creates excessive church/state entanglement, in violation of the Establishment Clause, when applied to a religious organization.[47] Other statutes such as

41. *See In re* Hill-Murray Fed'n of Teachers, 487 N.W.2d 857, 863 (Minn. 1992) (explaining only that "the rights of parents in the education of their children as outlined in *Yoder* are altogether different than the rights of a religiously affiliated" school over its teachers).

42. *See* State v. Temple Baptist Day Care Ctr., 814 P.2d 130, 136 (N.M. 1991). Therefore *Smith* applied and the church had no free exercise claim.

43. Corporation of Presiding Bishop v. Amos, 483 U.S. 327, 341–42 (1987) (Brennan, J., concurring) (quoting Laycock, *supra* note 4, at 1389).

44. There have been other negative judicial reactions to the educational rights hybrid exception, particularly in the Sixth Circuit. For example, in a decision rejecting a free exercise challenge to a public university curriculum requirement, that court stated that to give a government action greater free exercise scrutiny because of the presence of another constitutional right is "completely illogical" and therefore the court would not do so until the Supreme Court specifically directed. Kissinger v. Bd. of Trustees, Ohio State Univ., 5 F.3d 177, 180 (6th Cir. 1993). Earlier the Sixth Circuit held that a home-schooled student who transferred to public school and passed courses there could be required to pass standardized equivalency tests as well, on the ground that the additional test requirement did not interfere with his interest in religious home schooling, but only his interest in "minimizing the burdens of test-taking." Vandiver v. Hardin County Bd. of Educ., 925 F.2d 927, 933 (6th Cir. 1991). Plainly, however, the family was objecting that such a testing requirement would discourage them and others from pursuing religiously based home schooling in the first place.

45. *See* Jimmy Swaggart Ministries v. Bd. of Equalization, 493 U.S. 378, 391–92 (1990) (no "burden" from taxation when organization had no conscientious objection to paying taxes).

46. *See* Catholic High Sch. Ass'n. v. Culvert, 753 F.2d 1161, 1170 (2d Cir. 1985) (high schools bargaining with teachers); NLRB v. Hanna Boys Ctr., 940 F.2d 1295, 1305–06 (9th Cir. 1991) (residential boys' home and school bargaining with counselors and other employees).

47. *See Swaggart*, 493 U.S. at 392 (regulatory requirements under state sales tax laws); *Alamo Foundation*, 471 U.S. at 306 (regulatory requirements under minimum-wage laws).

antidiscrimination laws have likewise been held not to create excessive entanglement in the affairs of religious schools.[48]

The Court has also moved toward allowing government to treat religious schools equally in the provision of financial assistance. After the series of 1970s decisions barring direct state aid to religious elementary and secondary schools, a new line of decisions in the 1980s and 1990s permitted various forms of aid—tax breaks, in-kind assistance, and affirmative cash grants—to go to students or parents who could then use them at any school, public, secular private, or religious.[49] Such "indirect" forms of aid to religious schools were approved on the ground that the aid criteria treated all schools equally and left the choice of whether aid would flow to religion to the individual beneficiaries rather than to the state. More recent decisions have advanced the equal-treatment approach considerably further, approving even some forms of direct aid to schools that had been invalidated in earlier separationist decisions. The Court first approved a federal program supplying public school teachers to teach remedial education to low-income students in religious as well as secular schools,[50] and then another federal program supplying computers, software, multimedia tools, and other instructional materials to religious as well as secular schools.[51]

In short, the current Court's interpretations of the First Amendment embrace competing models of separation: equal treatment between religious and other institutions, and deference to whatever the political branches do. But that does not mean that the separation model is disappearing from the law in general. Several other sources of law together reflect the separation approach.

First, after *Smith*, Congress passed the Religious Freedom Restoration Act of 1993 (RFRA) to restore the "compelling interest" standard of *Wisconsin v. Yoder* for regulations that "substantially burden" religious exercise, including regulations that burden religiously affiliated schools.[52] Under RFRA, religious schools might once again use the separation principle to claim some autonomy from regulation. RFRA was struck down as applied to state and local laws—the most common of its applications—by the Supreme Court's decision in *City of Boerne v. Flores*,[53] and therefore religious schools can no longer use it to limit state educational regulations. But RFRA still may well be upheld as applied to federal laws,[54] which include most notably the many statutes regulating schools' relationships with their employees.[55]

Second, state constitutional provisions might still give special treatment to religious schools, both in blocking regulation and in restricting aid. Several state courts have rejected *Smith* and declared free exercise exemptions under state provisions.[56] At least one

---

48. *See, e.g.,* DeMarco v. Holy Cross High Sch., 4 F.3d 166, 169–70 (2d Cir. 1993) (age discrimination suit by parochial school teacher would not create excessive entanglement); section on employment relations and policies, *infra.*

49. *See* Mueller v. Allen, 463 U.S. 388 (1983); Witters v. Washington Dept. of Services, 474 U.S. 481 (1986); Zobrest v. Catalina Foothills Sch. Dist., 509 U.S. 1 (1993).

50. *See* Agostini v. Felton, 521 U.S. 203 (1997).

51. *See* Mitchell v. Helms, 530 U.S. 793 (2000).

52. 42 U.S.C. § 2000bb-1-7 (enacted Nov. 16, 1993).

53. 521 U.S. 507 (1997).

54. *See, e.g., In re* Young, 141 F.3d 854 (8th Cir. 1998) (so ruling).

55. *See, e.g.,* EEOC v. Catholic Univ. of America, 83 F.3d 455 (D.C. Cir. 1996) (applying RFRA to bar Title VII sex discrimination suit by canon law professor against religious university).

56. *See* Craig B. Mousin, "State Constitutions and Religious Liberty," in this volume; Angela C. Carmella, State Constitutional Protection of Religious Exercise: An Emerging Post-*Smith* Jurisprudence, 1993 B.Y.U. L. Rev. 275, 277–84.

state court decision gave special protection to religious school autonomy before *Smith*,[57] and another did so afterward (although that was reversed on further appeal).[58] State free exercise provisions are sometimes more emphatic than the federal Free Exercise Clause,[59] and some have more specific language protecting religious education.[60] Other states have restored the compelling interest standard by passing their own "mini-RFRA" statutes. On the other hand, many state constitutions are also stricter and more explicit in prohibiting aid to religious schools; thus some forms of nondiscriminatory aid permitted by the Rehnquist Court may be blocked by state courts.[61]

Finally, even if courts do not mandate distinctive protection or treatment for religious schools under the federal or state constitutions, the political branches are often convinced to write provisions in statutes or administrative rules that take account of the schools' religious freedom interests. *Employment Division v. Smith* itself specifically invited such exemptions;[62] and for the Court to uphold many such legislative exemptions would be consistent with *Smith*'s general posture of deference to the political branches. Statutory or administrative accommodation of religious schools is especially common in the area of teacher and curriculum certification[63] and under various labor and employment laws.[64] As will be seen, the availability of these "permissive" accommodations sometimes turns on the organizational decisions made by the religious entity seeking accommodation.

Government Regulation of Religious Schools

Having noted these general models and general legal principles, I now turn to discussing how legal regulation affects various aspects of the operation of religiously affiliated schools. In particular, this section is concerned with how legal rules affect the autonomy of religious schools.

---

57. *See* Kentucky Bd. of Educ. v. Rudasill, 589 S.W.2d 877 (Ky. 1979).

58. *See* Hill-Murray Federation of Teachers v. Hill-Murray High Sch., 471 N.W.2d 372, 376–77 (Minn. App. 1991) (exempting Catholic high school from required collective bargaining with teachers' organization), *rev'd*, 487 N.W.2d 857, 864–67 (Minn. 1992).

59. *See, e.g.*, State v. Hershberger, 462 N.W.2d 393 (Minn. 1990) (construing Minn. Const. art. I, §16, that no "control of or interference with the rights of conscience [shall] be permitted," to give greater protection than federal Free Exercise Clause).

60. *See, e.g.*, Ky. Const., Bill of Rights, §5 (providing that no one may "be compelled to send his child to any school to which he may be conscientiously opposed") (applied in *Rudasill*, 589 S.W.2d 877).

61. *See, e.g.*, Wash. Const., art. I, §8 ("[n]o public money or property shall be appropriated for or applied to any religious worship, exercise, or instruction, or the support of any religious establishment"); *id.* art. 9, §4 ("All schools maintained or supported wholly or in part by the public funds shall be forever free from sectarian control or influence"); S.D. Const., art. VI, §3 ("[n]o money or property of the state shall be given or appropriated for the benefit of any sectarian or religious society or institution"); *id.* §VIII, §16 ("No appropriation of lands, money or other property or credits to aid any sectarian school shall ever be made by the state,...and no sectarian instruction shall be allowed in any school or institution aided or supported by the state").

62. 494 U.S. at 890 (encouraging political branches to create "nondiscriminatory religious practice exemptions").

63. *See* section on curriculum and teacher certification, *infra*.

64. *See* section on employment relations and policies, *infra*.

In an important article defending religious organizations' constitutional right to autonomy, Douglas Laycock identified several factors affecting the analysis of such rights.[65] This framework is helpful in analyzing how courts and legislatures have balanced the government's regulatory interests against the autonomy interest of religious schools. First, Laycock argues, it matters whether the particular activity of the organization is primarily internal to the religious community or whether it has significant external effects on society, since in the former case the government's regulatory interests are minimal or nonexistent. Second, the religious intensity of the activity matters, for the greater this intensity, the greater is the organization's religious autonomy interest. Third, it matters what effect the regulation has on the organization's religious activity—both the nature of the effect and its magnitude. Finally, Laycock notes, some legal rules make it relevant how the organization is formally structured—for example, whether a religious school is directly owned by a church or is separately incorporated. As Laycock argues, such rules create improper preferences between religious groups based on their choice of formal structure;[66] and this volume on religious structures and the law will have a good deal to say about such rules.

I now turn to using these factors to analyze the effect of legal rules on religious schools in the major areas of operations identified above: curriculum and teaching, personnel and employment, and student admissions and discipline.

Curriculum and teacher certification

Certainly, at the center of the religious school's interest in self-definition is its ability to determine its classroom curriculum and other elements of the teaching that occurs on the the campus.

1. External social effects? Since the school's ability to determine what and how it will teach is so central to its self-definition, it could be argued that this matter is solely internal to the school and the government's regulatory power should be minimal. After all, families who send their children to a religious school volunteer to associate themselves with the school. Presumably they choose the curriculum and educational philosophy they prefer; perhaps the government should not override that choice.

The legislatures and courts, however, have refused to regard education at religious schools as a purely internal matter. The education of children has effects on those in the broader society who are not affiliated with the particular school. As the Supreme Court summarized in *Wisconsin v. Yoder*, the state has an interest in the matter because quality education "is necessary to prepare citizens to participate effectively and intelligently in our open political system" and "to be self-reliant and self-sufficient participants in society."[67] Therefore, the Court endorsed the state's power "to impose reasonable regulations for the control and duration of basic education."[68] Courts have also repeatedly rejected church schools' claim that they are completely exempt from state regulation because education "is an integral part of religion [and] . . . religious matters (including education) are subject to divine governance only."[69] And most every state in the Union provides that

---

65. Laycock, *supra* note 4, at 1403–14.
66. *Id.* at 1412–14.
67. 406 U.S. at 221.
68. *Id.* at 213.
69. *See* Windsor Park Baptist Church v. Arkansas Activities Ass'n., 658 F.2d 618, 620 (8th Cir. 1981) (rejecting the argument); State *ex rel.* Minami v. Andrews, 651 P.2d 473, 475 (Haw. 1982) (de-

if a child's compulsory education is to be received in a private school, the school must meet certain regulations concerning its basic curriculum, its hours and days of operation, the qualifications of its teachers, the safety of the premises, and so forth.

Yoder did refuse to rubber-stamp state assertions about the need for a particular educational regulation that interfered with the constitutionally protected interests in religious education. On the facts, the Court held that requiring Amish children to attend two years of school after age fourteen was not necessary to achieve the societal interest in having intelligent and self-reliant citizens. But *Yoder* added that "courts are not school boards or legislatures, and are ill-equipped to determine the 'necessity' of discrete aspects of a State's program of compulsory education."[70] And that qualification has proven crucial in later cases where religious schools have raised First Amendment challenges to state regulation of their teaching and curriculums. Courts overall have been extremely deferential to the state, accepting particular regulations as reasonable, sometimes when the need for them was questionable.

To the extent that religious schools have asserted a total freedom from any state regulation—for example, freedom from any duty to report their operations or what students are attending—the schools have uniformly failed in their challenges, and probably should fail. The states have an important interest "in receiving reliable information about where children are being educated and by whom."[71]

There have two more questionable and controversial kinds of regulation, however, that still have been upheld by courts. The first is state certification of teachers, which has been controversial at least when the requirements involve more than a basic education. For example, the Eighth Circuit upheld Iowa's requirement that teachers have either a bachelor's degree or some professional courses, as well as a "human relations" course that taught "understanding of the values, beliefs, life styles and attitudes of individuals and the diverse groups found in a pluralistic society"[72]—a requirement that the church school found objectionable because it suggested teachers would have to pass a course in tolerance of beliefs or actions that the church said was sinful. A second controversial subject has been direct state regulation of the curriculum to ensure that certain courses are taught.

In both of these categories—curriculum and teacher certification—schools have asserted that the state interest would be satisfied if the school's students were performing successfully on standardized tests, which would eliminate the need for direct regulation of the school's operations. But courts have regularly rejected the standardized-test alternative, deferring very broadly to the state. The Eighth Circuit in the Iowa case, for example, conceded that "there is a lack of empirical evidence concerning the relationship between certified teachers and a quality education."[73] But it upheld the teacher certification requirements, including the human relations course, on several grounds: Tests would "only look backward" and would not verify the continuing quality of the educa-

---

spite school's "assertion that the church and school are one and the same," state has compelling interest in quality of subjects taught).

70. 406 U.S. at 234–35.

71. *See* Fellowship Baptist Church v. Benton, 815 F.2d 485, 491 (8th Cir. 1987). *Accord Windsor Park Church*, 658 F.2d at 620; State *ex rel.* Douglas v. Bible Baptist Church of Lincoln, 353 N.W.2d 20, 21–22 (Neb. 1984); Attorney General v. Bailey, 436 N.E.2d 139 (Mass. 1982).

72. 815 F.2d at 492 (quoting Iowa Admin. Code § 670-13.18).

73. *Id.* at 494. It added that "there is a similar lack of empirical verification concerning plaintiffs' proposed alternative." *Id.* If, however, there is no evidence one way or the other, the "compelling interest" test should mean that the plaintiffs win.

tion, tests would determine only the students' objective knowledge and not other aspects of education, and teachers likewise needed to be capable of dealing with children in other ways besides simply imparting knowledge.[74] The decision allowed the state to act based on its distrust of the competence of schools that, it was conceded, were producing students with knowledge in the basic subject areas. Even more questionably, another federal court found that it was enough that it would be administratively easier for the state to check on certification requirements than to have it develop guidelines for evaluating standardized test results; administrative flexibility became a sufficient state interest.[75] The federal and state decisions upholding state regulation reflect the courts' increasing move toward deferring to legislatures and away from any special protection for religious education.[76]

But as courts have deferred to legislatures, the legislatures themselves have taken up the task of preserving the autonomy of religious schools. As Neal Devins has noted, in the early 1980s twenty-four states had certification requirements for teachers in private (including religious) schools, but by 1991 all but one of those states had repealed the requirement—and in that state (Michigan), enforcement was minimal.[77] In place of the certification requirements, the legislatures typically substituted performance on standardized tests and statements by parents that students were receiving instruction in core subjects.[78] Devins attributes the legislative resolution of the conflicts to several factors: the fact that religious schools are just as interested in children's welfare as the state is, the public distaste at the jailing of fundamentalist ministers who had refused to accept state regulation of their schools, and the growing power of the home schooling movement (which also secured legislative recognition of its legitimacy and its autonomy during this time period).[79]

2. Other factors: extent of religiosity, extent of state interference, and organizational structure of school. State educational regulation of religious schools curriculums has not been influenced much by the formal organizational structure of the schools. For example, as has already been mentioned, the courts and legislatures have been unwilling to reject regulation of a school entirely simply because the school is formally contained within the legal structure of its sponsoring church.[80] But some of the other factors identified by Laycock may have some influence on whether a particular aspect of the curriculum is regulated or not—especially the extent to which the regulation in question interferes with the school's distinctively religious operations.

---

74. *Id.*

75. *See* New Life Bapt. Church Acad. v. East Longmeadow, 885 F.2d 940, 947 (1st Cir. 1989) (Breyer, J.) (collecting numerous other decisions upholding state regulation of religious schools); North Valley Bapt. Church v. McMahon, 893 F.2d 1139 (9th Cir. 1990) (same with respect to religious day-care centers).

76. One major exception, where a court was willing to engage in stringent review of state education regulation, was in Kentucky—but primarily because, as noted above, that state has a stricter and more specific provision in its own constitution protecting religious education. *See Rudasill*, 589 S.W.2d 877 (striking down state regulations requiring that teachers at private schools be state-certified and that textbooks be taken only from a list approved by the state); *see* section on the plurality of institutions model, *supra*.

77. Neal Devins, Fundamentalist Christian Educators v. State: An Inevitable Compromise, 60 Geo. Wash. L. Rev. 818, 819, 832–33 (1992).

78. *Id.* at 826–32 (discussing legislation in North Carolina and Nebraska as examples).

79. *Id.* at 834–37. Between 1982 and 1992, thirty-four states adopted regulations permitting home schooling to satisfy compulsory education requirements as long as certain standards are met. *Id.* at 819.

80. *See* discussion of external social effects, *supra*.

For example, courts that have refused to exempt religious schools entirely from educational regulation have often emphasized that the bare assertion of state jurisdiction over the school does not in itself impose a serious burden on the school's religious self-definition. Thus, in the case concerning Iowa's state regulations, the court held that the burden on the school of having to report who attended there was "very minimal," "if one exists at all."[81] More questionably, the court also found that the requirement that teachers be certified and take a human relations course imposed no burden on the schools because it "d[id] not prevent teachers in plaintiff schools from teaching from a Biblical perspective," nor "prevent plaintiff schools from hiring only those teachers who meet their religious criteria."[82] But the repeal of teacher certification requirements by many states may have stemmed from their legislatures' belief that such requirements do constitute a significant interference with schools' autonomy in the crucial area of teaching.

In one extreme case, a court was willing to strike down state regulation of religious schools under the First Amendment on the ground that the regulation was simply too burdensome. In the mid-1970s, the Ohio Supreme Court invalidated that state's laws that required that private schools conform to public-school-board requirements in all activities, cooperate with the community, and follow pervasive state directions on the scheduling of the school day. The court found that the scheduling requirements were so strict as to crowd out religious instruction, and that the directives overall were "so pervasive and all-encompassing that total compliance...would effectively eradicate the distinction between public and non-public education."[83] But the Ohio case stands out both for the breadth of the state's regulations and for the court's willingness to strike it down.

Employment relations and policies

I now turn to the religiously affiliated school's interest in autonomy in the choice and supervision of its employees. Control over who will conduct the organization's activities is one of the most important forms of institutional autonomy for any religious organization, including schools.[84] But that interest runs up against a host of laws that regulate all aspects of the employment process. Title VII and other federal and state laws prohibit discrimination in hiring, firing, pay levels, or other decisions because of race, sex, religion, age, or other factors; the Fair Labor Standards Act sets minimum wage levels for all employees; the National Labor Relations Board and state agencies oversee bargaining concerning conditions of employment; and federal and state unemployment compensation laws require employers to contribute benefits for employees whose job has been terminated.

In employment cases, the line between the school's autonomy and the government's regulatory authority is set not only by court decisions under the Constitution, but also

---

81. *Fellowship Baptist Church*, 815 F.2d at 491. *Accord Minami*, 651 P.2d at 474–75 (no showing that licensing requirement alone burdened any religious beliefs).

82. *Fellowship Baptist Church*, 815 F.2d at 493; *see id.* at 495 (adding that "nothing in the certification statute or regulations requires agreement or acceptance of the beliefs or values of others").

83. State v. Whisner, 351 N.E.2d 750, 768 (Oh. 1976).

84. *See, e.g.*, Corporation of Presiding Bishop v. Amos, 483 U.S. 327, 342 (1987) (Brennan, J., concurring) ("Determining that certain activities are in furtherance of an organization's religious mission, and that only those committed to that mission should conduct them, is thus a means by which a religious community defines itself"); Laycock, *supra* note 4, at 1398 ("Deciding who will conduct the work of the church and how that work will be conducted is an essential part of the exercise of religion").

by a number of specific provisions in the relevant statutes. The labor laws are filled with various provisions concerning religious organizations, reflecting the legislature's concern to avoid interfering with the religious missions carried out by the organizations' employees.

1. External social effects? As with curriculum, there is a strong argument that regulation of a religious school's employment relations should be minimal because such relations are primarily an internal matter, limited to the school itself and those who choose to work for it. As Laycock has argued:

> The courts have recognized that modern collective bargaining [as one example of labor regulation] seriously conflicts with the fiduciary duty of employee to employer. They have responded by excluding from the NLRA a class of management personnel whose responsibilities make their fiduciary status particularly important.... [Analogously, the] free exercise clause includes the right to run large religious institutions.... Such institutions can only be run through employees. It follows...that the churches are entitled to insist on undivided loyalty from these employees.... Modern labor legislation may have deprived secular employers of the fiduciary duty once owed them by their rank and file employees, but to deprive the churches of that duty would be to interfere with an interest protected by the free exercise clause.[85]

The legislatures and courts, however, have not generally seen religious schools' employment relations as a solely internal matter. The statutes and the decisions interpreting them treat the subject as appropriate for regulation in order to protect both the employee (or prospective employee) and the broader society. For example, the Second Circuit upheld the application of state collective bargaining laws to Catholic school teachers on the ground of preserving "industrial peace and a sound economic order."[86] Such reasoning reflects a very weak conception of the autonomy of religious schools, for it is willing to countenance interference with their control over their employees based on no more than speculation about the effects that exemption would have on the broader society.

However, the statutes and constitutional decisions do preserve religious schools' control over their personnel in many situations, as for example in the exclusion of parochial school teachers from the federal collective bargaining laws. The patchwork of regulation and exemption depends on some of the other factors identified above, to which I now turn.

2. Nature of the regulated activity or position. In religious schools, there is one position where the school's interest in making its own decisions is particularly important: the teacher. As noted at the outset, the Supreme Court has repeatedly recognized "the critical and unique role" of the teacher in carrying out the religious school's mission.[87] Especially in elementary and secondary schools, the teacher is primarily responsible for transmitting the values of the school's religious community to the students. On this basis, the Court in *NLRB v. Catholic Bishop* excluded parochial school teachers from the coverage of the federal collective bargaining laws,[88] and earlier held that financial subsi-

---

85. *Id.* at 1408–09.
86. *Culvert*, 753 F.2d at 1171.
87. *Catholic Bishop*, 440 U.S. at 501.
88. *Id.* at 504.

dies given directly to parochial school teachers unconstitutionally advanced the central religious mission of the school.[89]

Given the crucial role that teachers play in carrying out a religious school's mission, the school clearly has a strong interest in requiring its teachers to adhere to its theological tenets and ethical standards. It might be argued, in fact, that the relationship between teacher and school is so important to the school's autonomy and religious identity that it should not be regulated at all. This argument analogizes teachers in religious schools to "ministers," who by administrative regulation or constitutional decision are excluded from the coverage of nearly all labor and employment statutes, from the minimum wage laws[90] to employment discrimination laws[91] to collective bargaining laws. Courts generally refuse to intervene in disputes between a church and its ministers, respecting both the church's free speech right to determine "whose voice speaks for [it]" and the Establishment Clause's prohibition on judicial determination of controversies over religious doctrine or authority.[92] And indeed, many schools do regard their teachers as "ministers."[93]

This argument has succeeded with respect to teachers who specifically teach theology or religion. They are analogized to ministers and are excluded not only from laws that prohibit discrimination based on religious belief, but from those that prohibit discrimination based on race, sex, or age as well. Although there is no specific ministerial exemption under Title VII, the courts have declared it under the First Amendment[94] and have applied to ordained faculty at theological seminaries,[95] to theology or canon law professors in universities,[96] and to lay theology teachers at religious high schools.[97]

However, the argument for a "ministerial" exemption has not succeeded with respect to lay teachers in the broad range of nontheological subjects. Courts are too solicitous of the government's asserted interests in protecting employees and "preserving industrial peace" to exclude all teachers from the coverage of employment laws. Non-theol-

---

89. Lemon v. Kurtzman, 403 U.S. 602, 618–19 (1971). The Court there quoted parochial school handbooks that stated that "[t]he prime factor for the success or the failure of the school is the spirit and personality, as well as the professional competency, of the teacher." *Id.* at 618.

90. *See, e.g.,* Dole v. Shenandoah Baptist Church, 899 F.2d 1389, 1396 (4th Cir. 1990) (noting exclusion of ministers from Fair Labor Standards Act, reflected in legislative history and Labor Department guidelines).

91. *See, e.g.,* McClure v. Salvation Army, 460 F.2d 553 (5th Cir. 1972) (clergywoman excluded from coverage of Title VII concerning sex discrimination); Rayburn v. General Conference of Seventh-Day Adventists, 772 F.2d 1164, 1169 (4th Cir. 1985) (same under statute and Free Exercise Clause); Minker v. Baltimore Annual Conf. of Methodist Church, 894 F.2d 1354, 1356–57 (D.C. Cir. 1990) (clergyman excluded from coverage under Age Discrimination in Employment Act); Scharon v. St. Luke's Episcopal Presbyterian Hosp., 929 F.2d 360 (8th Cir. 1991) (same). The "clergy exception" continues in force after *Employment Division v. Smith. See, e.g., Catholic University,* 83 F.3d at 461–63 (D.C. Cir. 1996); Combs v. Central Texas Annual Conf. of Methodist Church, 173 F.3d 343, 347–50 (5th Cir. 1999).

92. *Minker,* 894 F.2d at 1356. For further discussion, see Berg, *supra* note 7.

93. *See* note 3, *supra.*

94. *See* cases cited in note 91, *supra.*

95. *See* EEOC v. Southwestern Bapt. Theol. Seminary, 651 F.2d 277, 283 (5th Cir. 1981) (sex discrimination claim).

96. *See* EEOC v. Catholic Univ., 83 F.3d 455 (D.C. Cir. 1996) (sex discrimination suit by nun denied tenure in canon law department precluded by First Amendment and RFRA); Maguire v. Marquette Univ., 627 F. Supp. 1499, 1504–06 (E.D. Wis. 1986), *aff'd in part and vacated in part,* 814 F.2d 1213 (7th Cir. 1987).

97. *See* Powell v. Stafford, 859 F. Supp. 1343 (D. Colo. 1994) (age discrimination suit precluded by First Amendment and RFRA).

ogy teachers, therefore, have been held covered under the laws requiring payment of minimum wages, equal pay between the sexes, and nondiscrimination between the sexes in hiring.[98] As we will see, whether non-theology teachers are covered in particular instances has turned on other factors such as the degree to which the regulation interferes with the school/teacher relationship. It is also worth remarking that these past decisions have been willing to treat teachers like other employees for the purpose of regulating them, but the courts have treated the lay teacher as a highly religious position when it comes to government assistance to religious schools and have forbidden direct subsidization of the work of lay teachers.[99] This pattern reflects a troubling willingness to regulate religious schools while also denying them an equal share in educational benefits—a manifestation of a preference for the common, secular school.

The different treatment of theology versus non-theology teachers shows courts trying to distinguish between jobs with greater and lesser religious significance. Another example comes from the line of decisions about unionization of school employees. Although the Supreme Court in *Catholic Bishop* held that teachers were not covered by the federal collective bargaining statute, the Ninth Circuit in *NLRB v. Hanna Boys Center*[100] refused to extend that exemption to cooks, recreation assistants, maintenance workers, or even child-care workers at a school for orphaned boys. Some language in *Catholic Bishop* suggested that church-operated schools were entirely outside the Act,[101] but the Ninth Circuit rejected this institution-based analysis in favor of a job-related analysis: would oversight of the terms and employment of the particular job involve the Labor Board in religious questions? The court reiterated that teachers had a "unique" role in accomplishing the schools' mission,[102] and it found in contrast that the other positions—even, surprisingly enough, the child-care workers and counselors—were not sufficiently involved in the religious teaching of the children that resolution of these employees' grievances would "involve the Board in issues of theology."[103] Especially with respect to the counselors, the court read the autonomy rights recognized in *Catholic Bishop* in a very narrow and grudging fashion.[104]

However, there is one kind of personnel decision that the law almost always regards as recognizes as religiously significant: the decision to hire only members of the school's faith, or at least prefer members, as employees. Under several explicit provisions of Title VII, religious organizations, including religiously affiliated schools, may use religious preferences in employment without violating the statute's proscription against religious

---

98. *See Shenandoah Baptist Church*, 899 F.2d 1389 (minimum wage); EEOC v. Tree of Life Christian Schs., 751 F. Supp. 700, 705–07, 709–16 (S.D. Ohio 1990) (equal pay); EEOC v. Fremont Christian Schools, 609 F.Supp. 344, *aff'd*, 781 F.2d 1362 (9th Cir. 1986) (same); *Mississippi College*, 626 F.2d 477 (college may be subjected to Title VII inquiry to determine whether it is engaging in sex discrimination with respect to non-theology professors).

99. *See* section on the Effect of Legal Rules Concerning Governmental Financial Assistance Religious Schools, *infra* (discussing Lemon v. Kurtzman, 403 U.S. 602 (1971)).

100. 940 F.2d 1295 (9th Cir. 1991).

101. 440 U.S. at 504–05 (noting that "Congress simply gave no consideration to church-operated schools" and that there was no "affirmative intention that such schools be within the Board's jurisdiction").

102. 940 F.2d at 1301 (quoting *Catholic Bishop*, 440 U.S. at 501).

103. *Id.* at 1304.

104. The Labor Board had conceded that the counselors' duties included "teaching values[,] ethical principles, [and] religious observances." *Hanna Boys' Center*, 284 N.L.R.B. at 1083 (quoting Handbook part 1(D)). The Ninth Circuit did at least recognize that the institution was religious in purpose although it was not directly affiliated with the Catholic Church, did not require that employees or entrants be Catholic, and so forth. *Id.* at 1304.

discrimination. When the job in question involves religious teaching or authority—an administrator or a theology or religion teacher—such exemptions can hardly be questioned and surely are constitutionally required. But the Title VII exemptions, when they are applicable, protect a school's religious preferences for all of its employment decisions, even in jobs that do not have such obvious religious import.

Section 702 of Title VII protects "a religious corporation, association, educational institution, or society with respect to the employment of individuals of a particular religion" to carry out its activities.[105] Some states have a similar provision in their employment discrimination laws.[106] Even more directly relevant to schools, section 703(e)(2) of Title VII protects religious employment preferences by any educational institution that is, "in whole or substantial part, owned, supported, controlled, or managed by a particular religion or by a particular religious corporation, association, or society," or whose curriculum "is directed toward the propagation of a particular religion."[107]

The series of statutory exemptions for religious employment preferences reflects the constitutional magnitude of the organization's interest. As the Supreme Court recognized in upholding the constitutionality of the section 702 exemption, laws that compel religious organizations to employ members of other faiths create "significant governmental interference with the ability of religious organizations to define and carry out their religious missions."[108] Indeed, such laws deny to religious organizations a right of self-definition enjoyed by other ideological organizations: to tell a religious entity it must hire nonadherents is analogous to telling the Sierra Club it must hire people who do not believe in protecting the environment. The rule against religious discrimination therefore singles out religion as a concern and would trigger strict constitutional scrutiny if it applied to religious employers.[109] Moreover, the religious school's autonomy interest in religious hiring extends to all of its activities, not just supposedly "religious" ones; as the Supreme Court stated, "it is a significant burden on a religious organization to require it, on pain of substantial liability, to predict which of its activities a secular court will consider religious."[110] As the Third Circuit has summarized in *Little v. Wuerl*, applying the exemptions to protect the personnel decisions of a Catholic school:

> Congress intended the explicit exemptions to Title VII to enable religious organizations to create and maintain communities composed solely of individuals faithful to their doctrinal practices, whether or not every individual plays a di-

---

105. 42 U.S.C. § 2000e-1.

106. *See, e.g.*, Wisconsin Fair Employment Law, § 111. 337(2), Stats. (discussed in *Sacred Heart School Bd. v. Labor and Industry Review Comm.*, 460 N.W.2d 430 (Wis. App. 1990)).

107. 42 U.S.C. § 2000e-2(e)(2). Even under these exemptions, however, the government has power to initiate a proceeding to decide whether religious discrimination was the real basis for a school's action or just a pretext. *See, e.g.*, *Ohio Civil Rights Comm'n v. Dayton Christian Schs.*, 477 U.S. 619, 628 (1986); *Sacred Heart*, 460 N.W.2d at 432–33.

108. Corporation of Presiding Bishop v. Amos, 483 U.S. 327, 335 (1987).

109. *See Lukumi*, 508 U.S. at 532–33; *Smith*, 494 U.S. at 881–82 (retaining strictest constitutional scrutiny for laws that single out religiously motivated activity for prohibition).

110. *Amos*, 483 U.S. at 336. The Court upheld the constitutionality of the § 702 exemption as applied to a janitor (hardly an obviously religious position) at a nonprofit gymnasium owned by the Mormon church.

Other reasons for extending the exemption to all employees of a religious organization can be found in the legislative history of the section 703(e)(2) exemption for schools: a wide range of employees, not just those in "religious" jobs, might come into contact with students and influence them (110 Cong. Rec. at 2586) (Feb. 8, 1964) (Rep. Poff); *id.* at 2589 (Rep. Poage)); and religious bodies might hire their own members for varying positions as a form of charity (*id.* at 2588 (Rep. Roberts)).

rect role in the organization's religious activity. Against this background and with sensitivity to the constitutional concerns that would be raised by a contrary interpretation, [courts should] read the exemption[s] broadly.[111]

I will discuss shortly which kinds of schools qualify for these exemptions, and particularly whether a school's formal legal relation to a church or denomination affects its eligibility.[112]

A simple variation on the decision to hire only adherents is the decision to impose religious standards of conduct on employees, which should also be protected by the Title VII exemptions. In *Little v. Wuerl*, for example, a divorced teacher (a Protestant) working at a Catholic school remarried a Catholic but failed to obtain validation from the Church (and thus was committing bigamy in the Church's eyes). She was discharged for violating a provision in her employment contract (the "Cardinal's Clause") prohibiting any "public rejection of the [Church's] official teachings, doctrine or laws."[113] The Third Circuit acknowledged that this situation did not implicate the literal language of the religious-hiring exemption. But following its principle of reading the exemptions broadly, the court concluded that applying Title VII would require an unconstitutionally entangling determination "whether plaintiff has 'rejected' the [Church's teachings]" and whether her actions "make her unfit to advance th[e school's] mission. It is difficult to imagine an area of the employment relationship less fit for scrutiny by secular courts."[114] It should be noted that the school was wise to put an explicit requirement for teacher conduct in its employment contract; while courts should and will generally imply a duty to conform to the most obvious tenets of the faith, more specific requirements may have to be embodied in a contract in order to give fair notice.

Finally, protection for religion-conscious hiring should also encompass the school's decisions concerning academic freedom for faculty members in the classroom. A school has an important interest in ensuring that its classroom teaching is consistent with its sense of mission.[115] That mission may itself contain a substantial component of unrestricted academic inquiry, leading to a very broad policy on academic freedom; but at those points where a religious school draws the line, the law must not prevent it from doing so. Thus the Title VII exemptions should be, and have been, read to bar any lawsuit alleging that a religious school commits religious discrimination when it takes action against a faculty member based on the religious views he or she is propounding in class or in scholarship.[116] But even with this protection, religious schools might still be subjected to government sanctions for limiting teachers' academic freedom; some accrediting agencies (especially at the college and university level) require respect for academic freedom, and state regulations sometimes require accreditation by such agencies.

---

111. 929 F.2d 944, 951 (3d Cir. 1991).

112. *See infra* notes 144–149 and accompanying text.

113. *Little*, 929 F.2d at 945 (quoting contract).

114. *Id.* at 948–49. Similar principles apply under the Americans with Disabilities Act. See 42 U.S.C. § 12113(c) (providing that notwithstanding the prohibition on handicap discrimination, religious institutions may prefer individuals of particular religion and may require that all applicants and employees conform to religious tenets).

115. For discussion of the constitutional importance of the school's right to control the teaching in its classes, see Douglas Laycock and Susan E. Waelbroeck, Academic Freedom and the Free Exercise of Religion, 66 Tex. L. Rev. 1455 (1988); Michael W. McConnell, Academic Freedom in Religious Colleges and Universities, 53 L. & Contemp. Probs. 303 (Summer 1990).

116. *See, e.g.,* Killinger v. Samford Univ., 113 F.3d 196 (11th Cir. 1997) (dismissing Title VII religious discrimination alleging professor was denied ability to teach seminary class because of disagreement with his religious views).

If a school were sanctioned in such a situation, the action should be treated as state action and a violation of the school's First Amendment right to determine its message and mission.[117] A school may allow its teachers considerable leeway in teaching and writing, and if it has agreed to do so it may be held to that agreement. But courts should not find that the school has made such an agreement unless the terms are clear, for it amounts to a waiver of the constitutional right to control the school's message.[118] Moreover, many contract terms will involve religious terms and concepts, and courts generally must and do refrain from interpreting such terms or concepts; in such cases, they defer to the decision of the highest authority within the church.[119]

3. The nature of the regulatory interference. It is also important to consider the nature and extent of the burden that state regulation places on the school, and a number of cases concerning employment regulations have done so. At one end of the spectrum, the most severe burden results from a law that forces an institution to violate a tenet of the faith, by requiring conduct prohibited by the faith or forbidding conduct mandated by the faith. At the other end of the spectrum is a law that simply imposes a marginal increase in the cost of operating the institution, without affecting conscience or mission in any significant way. As already noted, the Court has ruled that the administrative or financial costs of a regulation alone raise no constitutional issue under the Free Exercise Clause. But sometimes courts have difficulty in identifying and categorizing the burden.

For example, a series of decisions have held that religious schools, in paying their lay teachers, may be subjected to the requirements of the Fair Labor Standards Act — requirements to pay minimum wages and to give equal pay to male and female employees performing comparable jobs. Several courts have held that the burden of the minimum-wage laws on religious schools is insignificant to the extent that it merely imposes a financial cost.[120] Some of these decisions ignored the fact that the particular schools — mostly conservative Protestant elementary and secondary schools — had a conscientious belief that married male teachers should be paid more than married female teachers, because the male biblically should be the head of the household and the chief wage-earner.[121] This line of "head of household" disputes, therefore, implicated the schools' tenets and not only their pocketbooks. Some courts sidestepped the issue, arguing that if the female teachers did not wish to receive the extra wages they could return the payments to the church voluntarily.[122] But the fact remains that the government intruded into the school-teacher relationship in an area where the schools had a significant doctrinal concern.

Employment discrimination laws likewise may or may not conflict with religious tenets. The courts view the burden on the institution as severe if the case involves hiring for a position of clear religious significance, or it involves hiring members of the particular faith, or if the institution has some doctrinal tenet against hiring employees of a certain protected class (for example, a doctrine that women should not be in positions

---

117. *See* McConnell, *supra* note 112.

118. *See* Laycock, *supra* note 112, at 1468–72.

119. *See* Serbian E. Orth. Diocese v. Milivojevich, 426 U.S. 696 (1976).

120. *See, e.g., Shenandoah Baptist Church,* 899 F.2d at 1394–99; *Tree of Life Schools,* 751 F. Supp. at 705–07, 709–16.

121. *Id.*

122. *Id.* The Supreme Court had made a similar suggestion with respect to a non-school organization in *Alamo Found. v. Sec'y of Labor,* 471 U.S. 290, 304 (1985) (stating that application of the FLSA did not burden church ministry because church workers who said they were volunteers could return the wages they would receive).

of teaching authority). Outside of these situations, however, the courts have tended to view the burden from antidiscrimination laws as insubstantial because it is not ongoing: the institution is simply forced to pay damages to a particular employee or at most reinstate her, with little likelihood of any continuing government oversight.[123]

By contrast, much more lively debate has ensued over the burdens imposed by the federal and state collective bargaining laws, which require employers to negotiate with employees over the terms and conditions of employment. As has already been mentioned, the Supreme Court in *Catholic Bishop* described the collective bargaining duty as a significant intrusion on the school's autonomy, at least with respect to teachers. Indeed, almost any area of a school's operations could be said to fall within the category of terms and conditions of employment for teachers.

As has already been noted, however, other courts have read *Catholic Bishop* narrowly, capitalizing on the fact that technically it represents only an interpretation of the federal labor law. For example, the Minnesota Supreme Court permitted its state's collective bargaining laws to be applied to the terms and conditions of teachers in parochial schools.[124] The court found no constitutionally significant burden on religious schools, or entanglement with them, as long as the negotiable "terms of employment" covered only secular matters such as hours and wages, and not "matters of religious doctrine and practice," which it said were already "intrinsically inherent matters of managerial policy and therefore nonnegotiable" under the statute.[125] The court further argued, in logic that simply rejected the reasoning of *Catholic Bishop*, that collective bargaining duty is relatively unobtrusive because it does not require a school to change its policies but merely "brings private parties to the bargaining table and then leaves them alone to work through their problems."[126] This seems overly optimistic; the union is able to bargain and push to affect the conduct of the school because it is backed by the threat of federal intervention if the school fails to bargain in "good faith." The intermediate appellate court had a more realistic view of the breadth of collective bargaining laws: "It is likely the BMS [the state labor board] will be asked to resolve disputes ranging from philosophical topics such as academic freedom, to practical topics such as teacher evaluation and termination."[127]

4. The effect of organizational structure. In several instances, regulation of the employment practices of a religious school is affected by the school's *de jure* organizational structure, especially its formal relationship (if any) to a religious body. But such differences in treatment based on organizational structure are troublesome, since a school's

---

123. *See, e.g.*, DeMarco v. Holy Cross High Sch., 4 F.3d 166, 169–70 (2d Cir. 1993) (age discrimination action by former lay teacher); Geary v. Visitation of Blessed Virgin Mary Parish Sch., 7 F.3d 324, 328 (3d Cir. 1993) (age discrimination suit); EEOC v. Mississippi College, 626 F.2d 477 (5th Cir. 1980) (sex discrimination claim by college professor). Of course, despite what these decisions indicate, reinstatement of a teacher is hardly a one-time matter.

124. *See* Hill-Murray Fed'n. of Teachers v. Hill-Murray Catholic Sch., 487 N.W.2d 857 (Minn. 1992).

125. *Id.* at 866 ("Hill-Murray retains the power to hire employees who meet their religious expectations, to require compliance with religious doctrine, and to remove any person who fails to follow the religious standards set forth"). The court added that religion and music teachers would be excluded from the bargaining unit.

126. *Id.* at 864 (quoting *Culvert*, 753 F.2d at 1167).

127. Hill-Murray Fed'n. of Teachers v. Hill-Murray Sch., 471 N.W.2d 372, 378 (Minn. App. 1991). The appellate court had noted that the school "has established grievance procedures, and bargains with its teachers in voluntary contract negotiations," measures that could fill the need for institutional peace. *Id.* at 377.

formal structure is not a reliable indicator of the strength of its religious identity or its interest in autonomy of operations. Courts should interpret these provisions so as to minimize such differential treatment based on organizational structure, treatment that impermissibly favors some forms of religious polity over others.

A serious instance of discrimination based on organizational structure is found in the exemptions from the federal unemployment tax. The Federal Unemployment Tax Act (FUTA),[128] a portion of the Social Security Act, generally requires employers to pay taxes, calculated according to the salaries and wages they pay to employees, to fund the provision of benefits to employees who become unemployed. However, the Act exempts an organization from paying taxes as "to service performed"

> in the employ of (A) a church or convention or association of churches; or (B) an organization which is operated primarily for religious purposes and which is operated, supervised, controlled, or principally supported by a church or convention or association of churches.[129]

The issues raised by this exemption are discussed generally elsewhere in this book;[130] the point here is to discuss their relevance to religiously affiliated schools. The exemption distinguishes between a school that is integrated into a church's legal structure and one that is separately incorporated. The former is exempt from FUTA under clause (A) without further inquiry, as the Supreme Court held in *St. Martin's Evangelical Lutheran Church v. South Dakota*.[131] But a school that is "separately incorporated" must meet the additional requirements of clause (B) in order to be exempt.[132] Thus, a school that is highly religious but is largely independent from the control or support of any church or group of churches would have to pay taxes, under the plain language of the exemption.

These distinctions, based on legal or other affiliation with a "church," discriminate on their face among religious entities and, if taken literally, are unconstitutional because there is no compelling reason for the distinction.[133] Different schools can be equally devoted to religion in their teaching and operations, even though one is "operated by church officials, another by persons separately appointed by a church congregation to conduct a school, and the third by persons independent of any organization describing itself as a church."[134] The FUTA exemption is thus an unconstitutional preference for some religious polities over others.[135]

In many FUTA cases involving schools, the schools are exempt anyway. Like the Lutheran school in *St. Martin's*, many elementary and secondary schools are legally part

---

128. 26 U.S.C. § 3301-3311.

129. 26 U.S.C. § 3309(b).

130. *See, e.g.,* Berg, *supra* note 7.

131. 451 U.S. 772, 782–83 & n. 12 (1981) (stating that "schools that have no legal identity separate from a church" are "uniformly...excluded from coverage by § 3309(b)(1)(A)").

132. *Id.* at 782–83 & n.12.

133. *See supra* section on Structural and Organizational Decisions of Religiously Affiliated Schools (discussing, e.g., *Larson v. Valente*, 456 U.S. 228 (1982)). *See also* Carl H. Esbeck, Establishment Clause Limits on Governmental Regulation of Religious Institutions, 41 Wash. & Lee. L. Rev. 347, 404 (1984) ("Statutory exemptions based on the distinction of whether a religious organization is church-affiliated or an independent, nondenominational ministry discriminate in a manner contrary to the Establishment Clause").

134. Salem College Academy v. Employment Div., 695 P.2d 25, 37 (Or. 1985).

135. *See* Christian Sch. Ass'n. v. Commwlth. Dept. of Labor, 423 A.2d 1340, 1347 (Pa. Commw. Ct. 1980) (striking down organizational distinction under Free Exercise Clause); *Salem Academy*, 695 P.2d at 40 (striking down distinction under state constitution).

of the sponsoring church or diocese.[136] When the church is separately incorporated, courts may still find that it is operated primarily for religious purposes.

However, the FUTA exemption still has serious unresolved problems. First, a court may fail to recognize the "religious purposes" of a separately incorporated denominational school. Maryland's highest court, for example, held that a Lutheran high school was not "operated primarily for religious purposes," even though there were mandatory chapel services and religion courses and the school sought to integrate Christian teaching into all courses.[137] The court held that the school failed to show that religion courses "'were devoted to deepening religious experiences in the particular faith rather than teaching a range of human religious experiences as an academic discipline'";[138] and that the school had failed to show that in other classes, "intellectual or academic freedom was overwhelmed by religious pressure."[139] The court simply ignored that if a high school with the same characteristics were legally incorporated into a Lutheran parish, it would have been exempt. And the court also failed to recognize that even a deeply religious school may respect academic freedom and the experiences of other faiths; the dismissive phrase "overwhelmed by religious pressure" speaks volumes about the court's pejorative view of the philosophy and activity of religious schools.

Second, the FUTA provision does not allow any exemption for a school that, however deeply religious, is unrelated to a "church or convention or association of churches." If that language is read literally, a truly independent religious school with no denominational ties may be excluded from protection even if religion pervades its curriculum and operations. That is almost certainly an unconstitutional discrimination against one religious polity or organizational form. It might be possible, however, to read the language "church or convention or association of churches" broadly, so that an organizationally independent school with a strong religious character would be deemed to be controlled or supported by a "church."[140]

The FUTA exemption thus exemplifies two potential dangers in the legal treatment of schools or other religious organizations. One danger is that a legal exemption may be conferred or withheld based on the formal organizational structure of the entity—a factor that, as I have just said, is not an accurate indicator of the strength of the organization's religious identity or its autonomy interest. The other danger is that courts may fail to recognize the religious identity of an institution if it does not confirm to a narrow idea of what is "religious." Professor Angela Carmella has shown how courts and administrative agencies often fail to give First Amendment protection to "acculturated" religious conduct—that is, to groups who act from deep religious motivation but

---

136. For examples of legally integrated Roman Catholic schools, see, e.g., Hickey v. Dept. of Employment Services, 448 A.2d 871 (D.C. App. 1982); Director of Employment Security v. Bishop of Springfield, 420 N.E.2d 322 (Mass. 1981); Begley v. Employment Security Comm., 274 S.E.2d 370 (N.C. 1981). For Lutheran schools, see, e.g., Grace Lutheran Church, 294 N.W.2d 767 (N.D. 1980).

137. Baltimore Lutheran High Sch. Ass'n. v. Employment Security Admin., 490 A.2d 701 (Md. 1985).

138. 490 A.2d at 705 (quotation omitted).

139. Id. at 707.

140. If a state legislature or court decides that the unemployment-tax exemption in FUTA is unconstitutionally discriminatory, it might refuse to extend the exemption to independent schools and instead eliminate the exemption for everyone. States lose their tax credit if they give less protection against unemployment than FUTA provides, but they are free under FUTA to give greater unemployment protection. Salem Academy, 695 P.2d at 29.

whose theology leads them to employ the same methods as secular institutions do.[141] To deny a religious school an exemption for which it is otherwise qualified, just because it gives its teachers academic freedom in the classroom, is a prime example of the kind of mistake against which Carmella warns. The school may have profound theological reasons for endorsing such freedom, and its action should not cause it to lose its religious autonomy in other areas.

These dangers of discrimination among organizations may arise in another employment context: the exemptions for religious organizations from Title VII's prohibition on religious preferences in employment. As is noted above, Congress was quite concerned to protect the ability of schools and other religious organizations to favor members of their own faith in employment, even for positions that did not have obvious religious importance. But there is a danger that the statutory exemptions available to religious schools, sections 702 and 703(e)(2), will be read too narrowly based on the formal structure or organizational affiliation of the school.

Section 702, which exempts religious employment preferences by "religious organizations," was upheld as constitutional in *Corporation of Presiding Bishop v. Amos*,[142] at least as applied to personnel in nonprofit religious organizations. Several justices left open the question of whether the Establishment Clause would bar the government from giving an exemption in the case of a for-profit organization.[143] But most if not all religiously affiliated schools are run as nonprofit entities.

The more important question is what features a school must have to qualify as "religious" under section 702. The exemption may automatically extend to schools that are legally part of their sponsoring church and to those formally organized as "religious corporations" under state law (although they may be subject to legal restrictions in other areas). Other schools, even though separately incorporated under general non-profit-corporation statutes, qualify because their activities are sufficiently suffused with religious teaching and activity. Thus a great many religiously affiliated schools—including, probably, most Catholic and evangelical Protestant elementary and secondary schools—qualify for the religious-entities exemption.

Questions have arisen, however, about other private schools with religious ties that are less obvious or perhaps no more than historical. In *EEOC v. Kamehameha Schools*,[144] for example, the Ninth Circuit denied exemption to a group of private schools that hired only Protestants as teachers. The court found that "the religious characteristics of the Schools consist of minimal, largely comparative religious studies, scheduled prayers and services, quotation of Bible services in a school publication, and the employment of nominally Protestant teachers for secular subjects." It concluded that the schools were not religious but were "essentially secular institution operating within an historical tradition that includes Protestantism."[145] Such reasoning again runs the risk of denying protection to schools that are deeply religious but whose practices are "acculturated" in Carmella's terms.

---

141. Angela C. Carmella, A Theological Critique of Free Exercise Jurisprudence, 60 Geo. Wash. L. Rev. 782 (1992).

142. 483 U.S. 327 (1987).

143. *See Amos*, 483 U.S. at 337; *id.* at 340 (Brennan, J., concurring in the judgment); *id.* at 346 (Blackmun, J., concurring in the judgment); *id.* at 348–49 (O'Connor, J., concurring in the judgment).

144. 990 F.2d 458 (9th Cir. 1993).

145. *Id.* at 463–64 (footnote omitted).

The question of how to treat acculturated schools is difficult, for courts must draw some line between religious and secular schools, and there is some danger that institutions that are really secular will try to assert a religious identity solely to avoid legal regulation. Perhaps the Kamehameha schools truly had discarded any significant religious character. But courts should be very cautious in reaching such a conclusion.[146] They have tended to read the religious-organizations exemption in too grudging a fashion.[147]

A broader exemption specifically for religious schools is found in section 703(e)(2), which protects educational institutions that are, "in whole or substantial part, owned, supported, controlled, or managed by a particular religion or by a particular religious corporation, association, or society."[148] This provision directly raises the matter of organizational relationships between a school and a religious body. The exemption should be read broadly, for the legislative history indicates that Congress intended to apply it to most religiously affiliated colleges.[149] Thus, courts must interpret the language flexibly, recognizing the variety of affiliations between schools and churches, or else the exemption will raise the danger identified above: it will unconstitutionally prefer those schools with a certain formal organizational structure and will exclude many others.

Two religious discrimination lawsuits brought in the mid-1990s against Southern Baptist colleges illustrate issues that can arise under the "religious organizations" exemption and the "owned, supported, controlled, or managed" standard, even though both suits were dismissed on summary judgment. In *Killinger v. Samford University*, a religion professor at Samford sued the university, claiming that he had been prevented from teaching classes at its divinity school because of theological disagreements with the school's dean.[150] In *Siegel v. Truett-McConnell College*, a Jewish sociology professor sued when the college decided not to renew his part-time contract because it had adopted a policy of hiring only professing Christians.[151]

---

146. *Kamehameha Schools* relied on an earlier Ninth Circuit decision, *E.E.O.C. v. Townley Engineering Co.*, 859 F.2d 610 (9th Cir. 1988), which held that a company that made mining equipment was not a religious corporation even though its owners were highly religious, it gave various forms of support to religion, and it held devotional services for employees. It is one thing to say that a for-profit business producing nonreligious merchandise is "secular." It is a large further step to dismiss a school's identity as nonreligious, since schools are nonprofit institutions—a crucial factor in *Amos*—and since religious values are so much more clearly intertwined with the activity of education.

147. *See, e.g., Kamehameha Schools*, 990 F.2d at 460 n.4; Fike v. United Methodist Children's Home, 547 F. Supp. 286, 290 n.3 (E.D. Va. 1982), *aff'd on other grounds*, 709 F.2d 284 (4th Cir. 1983) (both noting that § 702 has been interpreted narrowly).

148. 42 U.S.C. § 2000e-2(e)(2).

149. *See, e.g.*, 110 Cong. Rec. 2585 (Rep. Purcell, sponsor) ("The church-related school should never be called upon to defend itself for failure to hire an atheist or a member of a different faith"); *id.* at 2587 (Rep. Roush) (exemption "would touch almost every Member here because surely they have a denominational school in their district"); *id.* at 2588 (Rep. Poage) (exemption necessary to protect "hundreds of church-affiliated schools throughout the United States"). Indeed, one of the purposes of § 703(e)(2) was to extend protection for schools beyond that of the § 702 "religious corporation" exemption, which was thought insufficient because many religious schools "are chartered under the general corporation statutes as nonprofit institutions." *Id.* at 2585 (Rep. Purcell); accord *id.* at 2587 (Rep. Roush).

150. 113 F.3d 196 (11th Cir. 1997) (affirming summary judgment for defendant). Although I have worked for Samford, I am not a Southern Baptist and I played no role in the *Killinger* litigation. I advanced these arguments in a pro bono brief in the *Truett-McConnell* case (see next footnote) before Killinger's lawsuit was filed.

151. 73 F.3d 1108 (11th Cir. 1995) (per curiam, unpublished) (affirming summary judgment for college).

In both cases, the plaintiff asserted that the college was neither "religious" under section 702 nor "controlled" by the state Baptist convention under section 703(e)(2). Siegel argued that Truett-McConnell College was controlled by its trustee board rather than the convention—ignoring the fact that the convention elected and could remove the college's trustees, and the reality that a religious body must delegate authority to trustees to manage as complex an institution as a college.[152]

Killinger argued that Samford was not sufficiently "sectarian" to qualify under section 702 and that it fell outside section 703(e)(2) because its trustees had just declared themselves a self-perpetuating board, not removable by the Alabama Baptist Convention.[153] But the court of appeals found Samford exempt under section 702, noting that while it might be less "pervasively sectarian" than some other Southern Baptist colleges, the exemption did not require "some kind of rigid sectarianism."[154] The university showed its religious orientation in that it remained in several Baptist associations and received considerable financial support from the state Baptist convention, it required trustees to be Baptists, it required religion teachers to subscribe to a Baptist statement of faith, it required student attendance at chapel services, and so forth.[155] Compared to some other decisions, *Killinger* showed a hospitable attitude toward the religious-organizations exemption, correctly reasoning that a school need not fit a "rigid" sectarian mold, let alone be formally tied to a religious body, in order to be considered religious.

Although the court of appeals did not reach the issue, Samford also appeared to be religiously "controlled" under the even broader exemption in section 703(e)(2). The trustee board's declaration of independence from convention elections should not in itself defeat the exemption: all trustees still had to be Baptist, and the university still reported to the state convention on budgetary and other operational affairs. According to the leading studies of church-related colleges, there are numerous ways by which religious bodies control and influence their schools besides electing board members, and membership requirements for the board and church supervision of financial decisions are among the most common methods.[156] A school may have important reasons, including theological ones, for forgoing one particular kind of affiliation with a church body; courts should not favor one form of religious polity by accepting only one form of affiliation.

Moreover, Samford might have argued that even if it was not "controlled by...a particular religious association" (the Alabama Baptist Convention), it was still exempt under section 703(e)(2) because it was "controlled by a...particular religion" (the Baptist faith, given the general Baptist orientation that remained). In other words, the lan-

---

152. *See, e.g.*, James L. Sullivan, Baptist Polity as I See It 157 (1983) ("There is no practical way our Convention could operate its institutions except through trustees, unless it were willing to stay in constant session"); Edward V. Stanford, A Guide to Catholic College Administration 14 (1965) (because "the complexity of college operation has increased immeasurably,...each college needs and deserves its own functional board of trustees").

153. *Killinger*, 113 F.3d at 199. Eventually, Samford settled with the state Baptists and maintained some ties to them.

154. *Id.* at 198–99. As an example of such pervasive sectarianism, the court cited another Baptist college where nearly all faculty and students had been Baptist and every student had been required to take a Bible course. *Id.* at 198 (citing *EEOC v. Mississippi College*, 626 F.2d 477, 479 (5th Cir. 1980)).

155. *Id.* at 199.

156. Moots and Gaffney, *supra* note 9, at 8 (emphasizing these methods as well as ultimate control over assets); Danforth Report, *supra* note 9, at 52 (emphasizing these methods and adding that organizational relationships between colleges and religious bodies are "varied and often complex").

guage of the section extends to protect schools with a substantial relationship to a religious faith even if they have no affiliation with any denominational body. That result is proper, for as has already been mentioned, many independent or interdenominational colleges "cannot be classified technically as church-related but do have a definite religious orientation."[157] To exclude them from the exemption would plainly be an unconstitutional preference for one form of polity. The Title VII exemption is clearly broad enough to encompass the independent religious schools, while (as is noted above) the FUTA social security exemption must be stretched in order to protect them.

The plaintiffs in *Killinger* and *Siegel* also argued that the Baptist schools were not "substantially supported" by their respective conventions under section 703(e)(2) because each received a only a minority percentage of its annual revenue from the convention (Samford received about seven percent or $4 million, Truett-McConnell about ten percent or $600,000). But the courts correctly held the schools exempt under this prong too, finding that the support was large in absolute terms and quite important to the colleges at the margin; the support was therefore substantial because it was "neither illusory nor nominal."[158] Surveys confirm that most religious colleges, because of their large size and the steep costs of education, must rely primarily on tuition and fees[159] and only secondarily on denominational contributions.[160] But as a Methodist study has emphasized, "the amount provided by the church may make the difference between a balanced budget and a deficit or between the maintenance of educational quality and undesirable cutbacks forced by financial difficulties."[161] The courts have rightly read "substantial support" flexibly and realistically, to avoid excluding hundreds of religious colleges from the exemption's terms.

Student policies: Admissions and discipline

Religious schools also have important interests in determining what students will be admitted and how students must conduct themselves while in attendance. Admissions decisions, however, are potentially regulated by a variety of state and federal antidiscrimination laws. Racial discrimination in admissions is plainly prohibited by federal law,[162] and it is doubtful that a school can assert any constitutional right so to discriminate. In *Bob Jones University v. United States*,[163] the Supreme Court upheld the withdrawal of tax-

---

157. Danforth Report, *supra* note 9, at 19. See note 11, *supra*, and accompanying text (discussing independent evangelical Protestant Bible institutes and liberal arts colleges).

158. *Killinger*, 113 F.3d at 201 (quoting definition of "substantial" from Black's Law Dictionary 1428 (6th ed. 1990)).

159. *See* David W. Breneman, Liberal Arts Colleges: Thriving, Surviving, or Endangered? 82–84 (1994) (Tables 4-8 to 4-10).

160. In the mid-1960s, almost sixty percent of church-related colleges (473 of 817 surveyed) received ten percent or less of their general income through contributions from the denomination or order. Danforth Report, *supra* note 9, at 43 (Table 18). And recently, even among a class of "seriously religious" colleges, fifty-three percent received five percent or less of their funding from the religious body. Robert T. Sandin, Autonomy and Faith: Religious Preferences in Employment Decisions in Religiously Affiliated Higher Education 39 (1990) (Table 5).

161. National Commission on Methodist Higher Education, Toward 2000: Perspectives on the Environment for United Methodist and Independent Higher Education 49 (1976).

162. *See* 42 U.S.C. § 1981(prohibiting racial discrimination in the making of contracts); Runyon v. McCrary, 427 U.S. 190 (1976) (upholding § 1981 as applied to nonreligious school, reserving question of whether it could constitutionally bar school from discrimination based on religious tenets).

163. 461 U.S. 574 (1983).

exempt status from schools that practiced racial discrimination and segregation on the basis of religious tenets. Noting the nation's long, destructive history of racial segregation imposed or encouraged by government, the Court concluded there was a compelling interest in preventing government-supported racial discrimination that justified withdrawal of a tax exemption and overrode the schools' free exercise claims.[164] By treating tax exemption as a form of active support for discrimination, the court implied there might be less need to prohibit schools from discriminating on religious grounds; but in truth, it seems likely that the courts would find a compelling interest supporting an outright prohibition as well. Sex discrimination by religious schools, on the other hand, is given some protection under federal law. The provision of Title IX forbidding recipients of federal funds from discriminating based on sex contains an exemption for institutions that engage in such discrimination on the basis of religious tenets.[165] Under state antidiscrimination law, issues of discrimination in student admissions often turn on whether the institution is a place of "public accommodation."[166]

Religious schools are on the most solid ground in claiming the right to prefer students of the same faith in admissions. Although for some purposes the state may have an interest in ensuring that institutions serve all potential clients on a nondiscriminatory basis, the situation of religious schools admitting students is different: the school has a strong interest, if it decides, in ensuring that some or all of its students will be receptive to the message that the school promotes in its teaching. The policy identified by the Third Circuit of permitting religious institutions to "create and maintain communities composed solely of individuals faithful to their doctrinal practices"[167] applies to religious preferences in admissions as well. And under federal and most state laws, religious schools are permitted to prefer students of the same faith in admissions, either because there is no prohibition on religious admissions decisions in the first place (as is the case with federal law) or because religious schools are specifically excepted.[168] There is an important caveat, however: religious schools with such a policy may be disqualified from receiving direct government assistance. I will take up that matter in the fourth part of this chapter.

For similar reasons, a central aspect of a religious school's character may be the maintenance of standards of behavior for students. As Dutile and Gaffney have pointed out,

> [religious] colleges purport to teach more than purely academic theory. [They] legitimately claim to teach moral and religious lessons as well and therefore a student violating one of these moral or religious lessons may be deemed to have failed just as much as one who failed regular examinations.... Moreover, neither the nation nor the student has anything to fear from this arrangement. The nation gains a healthy diversity and the student gets no less than he bar-

---

164. *Id.* at 604.

165. 20 U.S.C. § 1687(c)(1).

166. In many states, private schools fall within the definition of "public accommodation" for purposes of race and sex discrimination. A counterexample, however, is *Roman Catholic Archdiocese v. Commonwealth*, 548 A.2d 328 (Pa. Commw. Ct. 1988), in which a Pennsylvania court held that parochial schools were not "places of public accommodation" under the Pennsylvania Human Relations Act. It thus upheld the Archdiocese's defense against state sex-discrimination laws that would have prohibited the Archdiocese's single-sex schools. The court held that although the schools accepted non-Catholic students from the general public, nevertheless their religious character made them "distinctly private" rather than public. *Id.* at 334, 450–51.

167. *Little*, 929 F.2d at 951.

168. *See* Dutile and Gaffney, *supra* note 14, at 23–24.

gained for since knowingly undertook the responsibility of adhering to the institution's rules.[169]

Private and religious schools also have the general legal authority to set and enforce such standards of student conduct. Students who have been expelled or otherwise disciplined for violating religious standards have sometimes sued religious colleges for violations of explicit or implicit contract terms or of alleged fiduciary duties. But in a leading case, *Carr v. St. John's University*,[170] the court rejected such claims and permitted a Catholic university to dismiss four students who participated in an off-campus civil marriage ceremony, a matter viewed as "seriously sinful" by the church. The court recognized two important points. The first was the essentially constitutional status of the college's interest in maintaining standards of conduct; the court said that this rested on "a fundamental American right" to "effectuate the religious principles in furtherance of which [the college is] maintained." The second was that the college's arrangements with its students should be construed to require that a student "not act subversively to the discipline of the college."[171] The court was willing both to imply such a term and to give force to an explicit provision in the school bulletin stating that "[i]n conformity with the ideals of Christian education and conduct, the University reserves the right to dismiss a student at any time on whatever grounds the University judges advisable." While a school might not be allowed to dismiss a student for entirely arbitrary reasons, it should be able to enforce, within broad limits, its understanding of what constitute "Christian ideals...of conduct." The same two principles, essentially, were recognized in *Lexington Theological Seminary v. Vance*,[172] which upheld a seminary's right to refuse to grant a degree to a student who was a practicing homosexual, when the seminary regarded such acts as sinful. The court first noted the "overriding importance" of a school having the legal right to maintain standards of conduct, and second noted that the school had set forth "reasonably clear standards concerning character" in its catalog.[173] A schools is well advised to set forth its clearest and most strongly felt standards of conduct in its official handbook, but also to include a clause reserving the right to make judgments that other sorts of behavior might violate the school's standards.

On the other hand, the procedures by which religious schools impose discipline on students may be subject to closer review by courts, who "are more expert at, and therefore more comfortable [with], dealing with procedure than with the substance of the institution's regulations."[174] In particular, courts will tend to hold a religious school to the procedural terms found in its publications to students. For example, in *Babcock v. New Orleans Theological Seminary*,[175] the court held that the seminary had failed to follow its prescribed procedures in expelling a ministerial student who had separated from his wife. By "outlining its divorce/separation policy and by describing its due process

---

169. *Id.* at 31–32.
170. 231 N.Y.S.2d 410(App. Div.), *aff'd*, 187 N.E.2d 18 (N.Y. 1962).
171. *Id.* at 412 (quoting N.Y. Educ. Law § 313).
172. 596 S.W.2d 11 (Ky. App. 1979).
173. *Id.* at 14, 12.
174. Dutile and Gaffney, *supra* note 14, at 29.
175. 554 So. 2d 90 (La. App. 1990). In a truly remarkable further ruling, the court ultimately ordered the seminary to issue Babcock a degree. The court said that issuing the degree did not, under Baptist congregational polity, certify him for a ministerial post in any congregation; this ruling unjustifiably second-guessed the seminary's understanding of what kind of endorsement it would be giving Babcock by conferring a degree. The sounder explanation for the unusual remedy was that the school had allowed Babcock to stay and take further classes and thereby arguably led him to believe he would receive a degree. *Id.* at 95–97.

procedures in the handbook, the Seminary has taken the issue of a student's dismissal out of the arena of a religious controversy and into the realm of a contract dispute." Moreover, the contract terms involving procedure were not religious or theological in nature and therefore could be reviewed by a court.[176]

Moreover, while schools have broad authority to set standards of conduct, one form of discipline used by some religious elementary schools—spanking, or corporal punishment—has conflicted with state regulations. Schools have raised First Amendment defenses to such regulations, on the ground that the Biblical statement "Withhold not the rod from the child"[177] mandates spanking as a form of discipline in some situations. But the courts have generally upheld the state's authority to forbid corporal punishment altogether. Some decisions hold that schools have no constitutional right whatsoever because parents alone have the right to spank and may not delegate it to the schools[178]—but as I have already argued, such reasoning overlooks the extent to which families in a religious community rely on institutions like schools to carry out conscientiously motivated activities like raising their children in the faith.[179] If the "compelling interest" test were to apply to the schools' claims, either under the constitution or under a state religious freedom statute, the state could certainly prohibit excessive or dangerous spanking, but it might not be able to outlaw spanking altogether.[180]

The Effect of Legal Rules Concerning Government Financial Assistance to Religious Schools

Finally, I turn to the effect of government financial assistance on the operations and autonomy of religiously affiliated schools. Government aid is an important factor because a good deal of it already flows to religious schools at the college and university level, and because more aid may be flowing at all levels in the future as the Supreme Court becomes increasingly willing to uphold such programs under the Establishment Clause.

Currently almost all religiously affiliated colleges receive government assistance, although mostly in the form of scholarships and loans to students who then use them for tuition, room, and board. Such forms of aid commonly constitute a large part of the payments made by students to the colleges.[181] Ironically, the aid amounts to the largest

---

176. *Id.* at 95.

177. Prov. 23:13–14.

178. *See, e.g., Temple Baptist Church*, 814 P.2d at 136; Cornhusker Christian Children's Home v. Dept. of Social Services, 416 N.W.2d 551, 562 (Neb. 1987); Johnson v. Dept. of Social Services, 123 Cal. App. 3d 878, 886, 177 Cal. Rptr. 49, 53 (1981).

179. *See supra* notes 40–44 and accompanying text.

180. Judges in child-abuse and custody cases have been able to make the distinction between reasonable and excessive punishment. *See, e.g.,* Dept. of Social Services v. Father and Mother, 366 S.E.2d 40 (S.C. App. 1988) (noting statute permitting reasonable corporal punishment but finding punishment by these parents excessive).

181. For example, in a 1978 survey of more than two hundred religiously affiliated colleges (excluding seminaries and bible colleges), only two had no students receiving federal or state financial assistance; student payments funded by government aid were a median of thirty percent of the colleges' budgets. Edward McGlynn Gaffney, Jr., and Philip Moots, Government and Campus: Federal Regulation of Religiously Affiliated Higher Education 13 (1982). *See also* Richard W. Solberg,

percentage of revenues at the most "sectarian," least assimilated, religious colleges, which might be expected to have less to do with government—perhaps because these institutions tend to have smaller endowments and less wealthy students.[182] Many religious colleges also receive aid directly from the federal and state governments, although these amounts are generally far less as a percentage of the schools' revenues.[183]

As Carl H. Esbeck's chapter in this book emphasizes, the receipt of government assistance can bring with it substantial government regulation that affects the mission or structure of the religious school.[184] That chapter examines such consequences in greater detail. In this chapter, I concentrate on some of the consequences for religiously affiliated schools. Following a model similar to Esbeck's, I divide the legal conditions on aid into two categories: those that restrict religious elements in recipient schools in order to preserve separation of church and state, and those that enforce civil rights norms of nondiscrimination and other conditions.

Conditions restricting the religious character of schools

A number of conditions on government assistance require that the activity being assisted be free of religious teaching or explicit religious elements, or even that some such elements be restricted in other parts of the institution receiving the assistance. Such conditions stem from a variety of sources: sometimes from the statutes and regulations authorizing the aid, sometimes from the documents by which government contracts with institutions receiving assistance, and sometimes from interpretations of the First Amendment's Establishment Clause or analogous state provisions. Whatever the source, the purpose of such conditions is generally to ensure that government does not directly aid religious teaching or become too enmeshed with the explicitly religious activities of religious institutions; in other words, the conditions rest on the model of strong separation between the state and religious activities.

As the separate chapter on government assistance shows, religious schools and educational activities receiving aid can be subject to a variety of restrictions on religious elements. Many federal and state programs giving aid to individuals provide that the aid may not be used for religious teaching, training, or worship.[185] Either by constitutional ruling or by statute, government grants to schools to construct or maintain buildings

---

Lutheran Higher Education 338 (1983) (forty percent of student costs at Lutheran colleges in 1981–82 came from government aid to students).

182. *See* Monsma, *supra* note 23, at 70–78.

183. In the 1978 survey, eighty-five percent of religious colleges responding received direct federal aid, although the median amount was only $130,000 (about one-sixth of the median amount of federal scholarships and loans). Only forty percent received direct aid from state governments, with a median amount of about $95,000. Gaffney and Moots, *supra* note 181, at 9–11.

184. *See* Carl H. Esbeck, "Regulation of Religious Organizations via Governmental Financial Assistance," in this volume.

185. *See, e.g.,* 44 Fed. Reg. No. 228 (Nov. 26, 1979) (not codified in C.F.R.) (Agency for International Development grants to colleges overseas may not be used "to train persons for religious pursuits"); 45 C.F.R §2520.30(a)(7) (participants in Americorps national-service program "may not engage in…religious instruction, conducting worship services, providing instruction as part of a program that includes mandatory religious instruction or worship," or "any form of religious proselytization"); Minn. Stat. Ann. §124D.09, Subd. 5 (permitting high school juniors and seniors to enroll at state expense in college courses, including at religious colleges, but only if courses are "nonsectarian").

exclude buildings used for religious activities.[186] Aid programs may require that religious symbols be removed from rooms of a school, either because the building is subsidized by government funds or because subsidized classes are occurring in the room. In a controversial ruling, a federal district court upheld the Commerce Department's refusal to provide funds to a radio station at Fordham University to build a transmission tower because the station broadcast a weekly Catholic mass as part of its programming.[187] State statutes subsidizing the grant or loan of textbooks to students or schools often require that the books be secular in nature, and the Establishment Clause may require the same.[188] And in at least one state, parents receive a tax deduction for tuition at a religious private school only if the school is separately incorporated from the church or religious denomination associated with it.[189]

In the past, many restrictions on religiously affiliated schools receiving aid have stemmed from the Supreme Court's interpretation of the Establishment Clause—although that is changing. Through the 1970s and 1980s, the Court's Establishment Clause rulings imposed a number of conditions that went beyond barring religious teaching in particular, discrete school programs receiving aid; instead, these decisions barred aid to nearly any program of a school when the school's overall character was significantly (or as the Court put it, "pervasively") religious. The framework for such results was erected in *Lemon v. Kurtzman*[190] and *Tilton v. Richardson*.[191] *Lemon* held that the state provision of salary supplements and other payments to teachers in parochial elementary and secondary schools violated the Establishment Clause. *Tilton* held that government grants for the construction and repair of buildings on religious college campuses did not violate the Establishment Clause as long as the buildings were not used for chapel services, theology classes, or other religious purposes. Although the two decisions reached opposite results, they followed the same analytical framework.

Both decisions rested on the premise that government could not give assistance that would be used in the religious activities of religious schools; that would be a unconstitutional advancement of religion. But the religious elementary and secondary schools in *Lemon* were "pervasively" religious; in such a school, as the Court later put it, it is "impossib[le to] separat[e] the secular education function from the sectarian" and thus "the state aid inevitably flows in part in support of the religious role of the schools."[192]

---

186. *See, e.g.,* Tilton v. Richardson, 403 U.S. 672 (1971) (holding that no college building funded by federal construction grants may be used for religious services); 44 Fed. Reg. No. 228, *supra* (AID grants to overseas colleges may not be used to "construct buildings intended for worship or religious instruction"); Esbeck, *supra* note 184 (reporting that religious colleges receiving aid after *Tilton* removed crucifixes from walls of their buildings).

187. Fordham Univ. v. Brown, 856 F. Supp. 684 (D.D.C. 1994). The court did not look at whether the overall programming of the station was sectarian, even though the governing regulation provided that the grant could not be used for "purposes the essential thrust of which are sectarian," 15 C.F.R. § 2301.22(d), which could easily be interpreted to require a determination of whether the station overall had the "essential thrust" of propagating religion. The court held that the religious, sacramental content of one program was enough to bar the grant. *Id.* at 705.

188. *See, e.g.,* Board of Educ. v. Allen, 392 U.S. 236 (1968) (upholding state loans of textbooks to parents on the condition that the books were secular); *see also* Minn. Stat. § 209.09 22 (upheld in *Mueller v. Allen*, 463 U.S. 388, 403 (1983)) (excluding from tax deductions the costs of textbooks "used in the teaching of religious tenets, doctrines, or worship, the purpose of which is to inculcate such tenets, doctrine, or worship").

189. Iowa Code Ann. § 422.12.

190. 403 U.S. 602 (1971).

191. 403 U.S. 672 (1971).

192. Wolman v. Walter, 433 U.S. 229, 250 (1977).

The government might try to ensure that the aid reached only "secular" classes or activities—as the statutes in *Lemon* in fact did—but policing that restriction would in turn create a "comprehensive" state surveillance of the religious content of various school activities, which itself would "excessively entangle" the state in religion and violate the Establishment Clause.[193] *Lemon* thus directly embodied the model of separation between the state and religious activity, both in forbidding state aid that would be used for religious teaching and in forbidding any significant surveillance to ensure that aid would not be so used.

By contrast, the religious colleges in *Tilton* were not "pervasively sectarian": Although they were formally tied to Catholic organizations, they commonly hired non-Catholic teachers and admitted non-Catholic students, they had no required chapel services and their required religion courses were taught in an objective rather than proselytizing manner, and they permitted their teachers academic freedom.[194] In short, the Court viewed the colleges as "institutions with admittedly religious functions but whose predominant higher education mission is to provide their students with a secular education."[195] Therefore there was "less likelihood than in primary and secondary schools" that any given subsidized activity would include religious teaching, and the state would be able, without "intensive surveillance," to channel aid to the secular aspects of the college's operations.[196] The building grant statute, modified to ensure that no chapel or other religious building would be subsidized, was upheld.

Later decisions solidified this approach, striking down most forms of aid to schools that the Court said were pervasively religious (mostly primary and secondary schools), but upholding aid limited to the secular functions of more secularized religious schools (primarily colleges and universities). In determining whether a school was pervasively religious, the Court looked to the same features that it had in *Tilton*: the presence of religious tests or preferences in the hiring of employees or the admission of students, religious symbols in school buildings, required attendance at religious services, required religion classes taught from the perspective of the faith, and religious instruction integrated into other subjects across the curriculum.[197] Of course these factors, which I have defined as structural or organizational policies in a broad sense, together constitute a large part of the school's definition of its religious identity. Thus, through the early 1980s federal constitutional case law generally placed significant limits on how strong a school's overall religious identity could be if it wished to receive direct government aid on the same terms as other schools.

To be sure, the Establishment Clause restrictions on aid did not turn primarily on a school's organizational decisions in the narrow sense of its formal legal structure. In that sense, they were unlike the Iowa provision that flatly states that parents may not deduct tuition at a religious school from their taxes unless the school is incorporated separately from a church. The Iowa provision makes formal legal structure the conclusive factor in determining whether a school may benefit from that form of aid. As I have argued above,[198] such an emphasis on formal legal relations creates a constitutionally

---

193. *Lemon*, 403 U.S. at 619–20.
194. *Tilton*, 403 U.S. at 687.
195. *Id.*
196. *Id.*
197. *See, e.g.,* Comm. for Public Educ. v. Nyquist, 413 U.S. 756, 767–68 (1973); Hunt v. McNair, 413 U.S. 734, 743–44 (1973); Roemer v. Board of Public Works, 426 U.S. 736, 752 n.18 (1976); Wolman v. Walter, 433 U.S. 229, 234 (1977); *see also* Helms v. Cody, 1990 WL 36124, at *3–4 (E.D. La. 1990) (striking down provision of textbooks to parochial schools on basis of same factors).
198. *See supra* notes 185–197 and accompanying text.

suspect distinction between institutions based on their legal polity. Just as the availability of an exemption from regulation should not depend solely on an institution's formal legal structure, neither should the availability of government aid. If the purpose of conditions on government aid is to ensure that taxpayers do not have to pay for religious teaching, any distinction between institutions should be based on the nature of their teaching rather than on a relatively arbitrary factor such as how they formally relate to a church. And indeed the Supreme Court in the *Lemon/Tilton* decisions looked to many factors to determine whether a school was pervasively religious; the school's formal structure was only one minor consideration.

Although the Court's decisions restricting aid did not disfavor schools based on formal polity structure, the decisions did disfavor schools that took their religious identity and commitment seriously. As Michael McConnell has put it, while the *Lemon* line of decisions "forbade any assistance to nonpublic schools" at the lower levels, the *Tilton* line of decisions at the college level "allowed assistance only upon conditions that undermined the [religious schools'] purpose for being."[199] An example of the secularizing effects of the Court's educational aid decisions is found in the tale of Liberty University's quest for state financing in Virginia. After being denied tax-exempt state bonds for construction,[200] the university (whose chancellor is the Reverend Jerry Falwell) later sought to make its students eligible for state educational grants. The university reportedly, at the behest of the state, relaxed a number of its policies concerning its religious identity, eliminating the previous requirement that students attend chapel services and allowing faculty more room to take positions at variance with the school's doctrinal beliefs. Liberty succeeded with its later request for state grants, but arguably at the cost of compromising its religious mission.[201]

It hardly seems an answer, however, to say that secularizing pressure can be avoided by denying direct government aid to all religiously affiliated colleges. That still leaves the government in the position of funding secular public and private schools, which creates pressure on parents to forgo their choice of a religiously informed education. Either way, by denying aid, the law placed pressure on religious colleges and the families wishing to use them: the school either had to forgo the state aid being given to its secular competitors, or it had to give up policies like preferring members of the faith in hiring or admissions, requiring chapel attendance and theology courses, and so forth.

In recent years, the Court has been more sympathetic to the pressure that the selective denial of funding can place on religious schools. It has begun to uphold programs that provide assistance to religious schools or their students on the same terms as to other schools, public and private. In the area of aid given directly to religious schools, the trend toward upholding equal aid is exemplified by two recent decisions. The first, *Agostini v. Felton*,[202] approved the provision of public school teachers to teach remedial education to low-income students in religious as well as secular private and public schools. The Court treated it as a significant factor that the assistance was provided

---

199. Michael W. McConnell, Religious Freedom at a Crossroads, 59 U. Chi. L. Rev. 115, 133 (1992).

200. Habel v. Industrial Development Authority, 400 S.E.2d 516 (Va. 1991).

201. *See* 7 Nat'l. & Internat'l. Religion Rept. 7 (June 14, 1993). It might be argued in return that the model of separation of church and state would free religious schools from regulation as well as disqualify them from receiving aid. But as we saw above, the courts have been willing to allow substantial regulation of even elementary and secondary religious schools. The overall pattern through the 1980s reflected less a commitment to separation than a preference for secular schools.

202. 521 U.S. 203 (1997).

equally to all schools;[203] and *Agostini* is also significant in that the Court was willing to overrule previous decisions that had struck down this form of aid under the strict separation model.[204]

However, *Agostini* also relied heavily on the fact that the particular form of aid would not be likely to involve religious activity, since the teaching in question was carried out by public school employees.[205] The Court has also recently said once again that "direct money payments to sectarian institutions" are suspect under the Establishment Clause.[206] These statements suggested that the Court would still demand that religion be segregated from any school activity that is directly subsidized, and in effect that the school redefine its religious identity and operations in order to receive direct aid. The Fourth Circuit recently reaffirmed that even after *Agostini*, colleges may not receive direct, unrestricted grant assistance from the state if they are pervasively sectarian under the factors set forth in the 1970s Supreme Court decisions.[207]

The Supreme Court, however, took the equal-aid approach one important step further in *Mitchell v. Helms*,[208] which upheld a federal program that paid for the provision of computers, software, multimedia tools, and other instructional equipment and materials directly to public and private schools including religious schools. The taxpayers challenging aid to religious schools argued that the provision of materials in *Mitchell* was impermissible because they would go to religious-school teachers and thus could easily be used for indoctrination, unlike the remedial classes taught by public-school teachers in *Agostini*. A majority of the Court rejected this argument, albeit in two different opinions without a majority.

Justice Thomas, writing for four justices, held that it was enough that (1) the instructional equipment and materials were provided equally to all schools "based on the private choices of the parents of schoolchildren," because each school was allocated the aid based on its number of students; and that (2) the equipment and materials did not themselves have "an impermissible [religious] content" (even if they could be used for religious purposes).[209] Justice O'Connor, providing the crucial fifth vote, approved the aid on narrower grounds: because it was provided directly to the religious school, it was permissible only because it was provided equally and also did not "result...in government [religious] indoctrination"—meaning, among other things, that it was not likely to be "diverted to religious instruction."[210] In other words, the four justices led by Thomas would approve programs of neutrally-allocated aid if the aid did not have a religious content on its face, even if it could be used for ("diverted to") religious purposes. For example, the state could not pay for Bibles at religious schools, but it could pay for computers (which are facially nonreligious) even if they were used to run Bible-study software.[211] O'Connor would require in addition that the computer not be used for the Bible software.

In addition to its approval of the specific form of aid, *Mitchell* is important because it appears to undermine the validity of the category of "pervasively sectarian"

203. *Id.* at 231.

204. *See* Aguilar v. Felton, 473 U.S. 402 (1985); Grand Rapids Sch. Dist. v. Ball, 473 U.S. 373 (1985).

205. *Agostini,* 521 U.S. 203, at 227–228, 232–234

206. *See* Rosenberger v. Rectors of Univ. of Virginia, 515 U.S. 819, 842 (1995).

207. *See* Columbia Union College v. Clarke, 159 F.3d 151 (4th Cir. 1998).

208. 530 U.S. 793 (2000).

209. *Id.* at 2552 (plurality opinion of Thomas, J.).

210. *Id.* at 2562 (O'Connor, J., concurring in the judgment).

211. *Id.* at 2548 (Thomas, J.) ("The issue is not divertability of aid but rather whether the aid itself has an impermissible content").

schools that had been held ineligible to receive even relatively limited forms of aid. Thomas's opinion explicitly attacked the "pervasively sectarian" concept, arguing, as has been suggested above, that it wrongly shows "special hostility for those who take their religion seriously" and was born out of the bigoted opposition to Catholics and Catholic schools in the late 1800s. He also argued that the inquiry into the degree of sectarianism wrongly requires courts to "troll...through a person's or institution's religious beliefs."[212] O'Connor did not explicitly attack the "pervasively sectarian" doctrine, but one part of her opinion dismissed it implicitly.[213] The Court's apparent rejection of the concept is a step forward for religious autonomy; the "pervasively sectarian" doctrine was particularly objectionable in that it required religious schools to secularize a wide range of their activities simply to receive aid in some part of the activities.

The other promising recent development for religious schools' autonomy has been the Court's increasing willingness to uphold programs of educational assistance to students and parents who may then choose to use it at any school, religious, secular private, or public—with no proviso that the school must remove religious elements from its programs in order to make the aid permissible. The leading decisions here are *Mueller v. Allen*,[214] which upheld tax deductions for the cost of tuition and supplies at any qualified school, including religious ones, and *Witters v. Dept. of Services for the Blind*,[215] which upheld the provision of a general vocational rehabilitation grant, usable at any qualified school, to a student who studying for the Protestant ministry at a pervasively religious Bible college. In these decisions, the Court has ruled based on the principle—also evident from *Agostini* and *Mitchell*—that educational benefits provided neutrally to individuals for use at any school do not unconstitutionally advance religion because the choice to use them at a religious school is made by the individual without any incentive from the state to favor religious over other schools.[216]

Significantly, the decisions approving equal "indirect aid" do not forbid the school receiving assistance from being pervasively sectarian, nor do they require schools to take steps to cordon off religion from subsidized activities. The elementary schools in *Mueller*, the Catholic high school in *Zobrest v. Catalina Foothills School District*, and the Bible college in *Witters* were all schools pervaded with religious mission and activity. The Court in effect says that because the provision of the assistance is attributable to the individuals' choice, it does not matter how religious the school is. This difference means that the indirect aid decisions do not create incentives for schools to compromise their religious identity—as the direct aid decisions did before *Mitchell v. Helms*.

These principles, and their recent reaffirmation by the Court, are what has made it possible for religious colleges and universities to receive massive financial assistance from federal and state governments through grants and loans to students that are then paid over the school. As noted above, almost every religious college in the nation re-

---

212. *Id.* at 2551–52.
213. *See id.* at 2558–60 (O'Connor, J.) (indicating approval for neutral "private choice" programs channeling aid through parents without regard to whether they use it at pervasively religious schools).
214. 463 U.S. 388 (1983).
215. 474 U.S. 481 (1986).
216. *See Witters*, 474 U.S. at 487–88; *Mueller*, 463 U.S. at 398–99; Zobrest v. Catalina Foothills Sch. Dist., 509 U.S. 1, 9–11 (1993) (upholding provision of sign-language interpreter to deaf student attending pervasively sectarian Catholic high school).

ceives substantial indirect government aid through students, and the most highly religious colleges tend to rely on that aid the most.[217]

The next major step, however, was to extend the principle of student and parental choice to the elementary and secondary level, through what are commonly called "school voucher" programs. As of 2001, the Court had not faced such a case on the merits, but in 2002 it finally confronted and resolved the issue in favor of school vouchers' constitutionality in *Zelman v. Simmons-Harris*,[218] which is discussed at length in an appendix to this chapter.

The Court's relaxation of Establishment Clause doctrine, however, will not by itself mean the end of legal conditions that require a school to remove religious elements from its programs as the price of receiving government assistance. As I have pointed out above, many programs of aid themselves contain such conditions, either in the governing statutes or regulations or in the particular documents memorializing the relationship between the government and the institution. Also, educational assistance by a state or local government that is permissible under the federal Constitution may still be unconstitutional under stricter state constitutional provisions.[219]

The more restrictive state constitutional provisions vary in terms but all have roots in the nineteenth-century opposition to the creation of Catholic parochial schools, which opponents labeled as "sectarian" institutions that would make it impossible to assimilate and "Americanize" the increasing numbers of immigrants coming from poorer parts of Europe. The separationist rationale behind such provisions is thus intertwined with, although to some extent distinct from, an anti-Catholic and nativist animus—the same animus to which Justice Thomas referred in his opinion in *Mitchell v. Helms*.[220] The stricter state provisions generally contain one or more of three different requirements, in order of increasing strictness.[221]

The first set of provisions mandate that no public money may be appropriated for applied to religious sects, worship, or instruction, and that no one may be compelled to support worship. For example, the Vermont Supreme Court held that allowing a student to use state full-tuition benefits at a religious high school, among other schools, when the student's own (rural) district did not have a high school violated the state's constitutional provision against compelled support of worship.[222] Such a provision in theory is the narrowest of the three, for it allows state money to be provided to nonreligious uses but still disapproves of unrestricted tuition benefits or vouchers. Under a broader second set of provisions, the state may not maintain, aid, or support "sectarian" schools—thus prohibiting aid not only to their religious functions but to any of

---

217. *See supra* notes 181–184 and accompanying text.

218. 122 S. Ct. 2460 (2002).

219. *See, e.g.*, Witters v. State Comm'n. for the Blind, 771 P.2d 1119 (Wash. 1989) (striking down provision of rehabilitation assistance to student in Bible college, even though Supreme Court had just upheld the aid under the Establishment Clause); Elbe v. Yankton Indep. Sch. Dist., 372 N.W.2d 113 (S.D. 1985) (striking down loans of secular textbooks to students in pervasively sectarian schools under state constitution, even though Supreme Court had upheld them under Establishment Clause in *Board of Education v. Allen*).

220. 530 U.S. 793 (2000).

221. *See* Linda S. Wendtland, Note, Beyond the Establishment Clause: Enforcing Separation of Church and State Through State Constitutional Provisions, 71 Va. L. Rev. 625, 631–34 (1985).

222. *See* Chittenden Town Sch. Dist. v. Vermont Dept. of Educ., 738 A.2d 539 (Vt. 1999), *cert. denied sub nom.*, Andrews v. Vermont Dept. of Educ., 528 U.S. 1066 (1999). (applying Vt. Const. ch. 1, art. 3).

their functions, and requiring schools to secularize their operations across the board in order to receive aid. For example, Maine's statute governing the provision of tuition benefits to students whose rural district lacks a high school—the same situation as in Vermont—requires that any school participating in the program be "nonsectarian."[223]

Finally, some state rules forbid or significantly restrict the provision of aid not oly to religious schools, but to private schools in general. For example, some state constitutions require that any school that receives public money must be under state control; a Florida court struck down the state's voucher program for students in failing public schools on the basis of the state constitutional provision making a "high-quality system of free public schools…the paramount duty of the state."[224]

State provisions that bar aid to all private schools may impose a burden on religious schools by disfavoring them in comparison to public schools, but they do not create an incentive for the school to secularize, since even a secular private school cannot receive aid. In contrast, under the first and second kinds of provisions above, a school does have an incentive to become more secular, if not completely secular, in its operations—which clearly has implications for the school's autonomy and mission.

To be sure, some state courts have interpreted their constitutions not to require the exclusion of significantly religious schools from voucher-type programs. Such a program for Cleveland passed review under two Ohio state provisions.[225] For example, both the Ohio and Wisconsin supreme courts held that pilot-type voucher programs did not compel the support of worship because the choice to use funds at religious schools was the individual's rather than the state's, and the beneficiaries were children, not the religious schools.[226] For the same reason, the Wisconsin court held that the program there did not violate the state provision prohibiting the drawing of state money for the benefit of religious seminaries;[227] the Ohio court also held that because the program's funding there was limited, it did not interfere with the state's duty to maintain a "thorough and efficient system of common schools."[228] Nevertheless, in much of the nation state constitutions and rules remain a legal barrier to the full inclusion of religious schools and their students in programs of educational aid.

As Establishment Clause restrictions have receded and state rules have become the main restrictions on equal aid to religious schools, it has become plausible to assert that such restrictions on equal aid not only are not required by the First Amendment, but actually violate it. The religious families and schools that challenge their exclusion rely on the *Smith/Lukumi* rule that the Free Exercise Clause prohibits singling out religion for disabilities,[229] and by the *Rosenberger* rule that the Free Speech Clause prohibits withholding benefits because of religious viewpoint. But if the increasing strength of these arguments reflects the increasing primacy of equality over separation, the remaining vitality of separationism still shows in the fact that these arguments have not succeeded in the context of full-fledged tuition vouchers.

---

223. *See Strout*, 178 F.3d at 59; *Bagley*, 728 A.2d at 130 (both quoting 20-A.M.R.S.A. § 2951(2)).

224. *See* Sue Ann Pressly and Kenneth J. Cooper, School Voucher Plan Struck Down; Florida to Appeal Judge's Ruling, Wash. Post, March 15, 2000, at Section A1 (2000 WL 2291129).

225. *See* Simmons-Harris v. Goff, 711 N.E.2d 203 (Ohio 1999).

226. *Goff*, 711 N.E.2d at 211–12; *Jackson*, 578 N.W.2d 602. The Ohio court did invalidate that program on an unrelated ground, later cured by the legislature.

227. *Id.*

228. *Goff*, 711 N.E.2d at 211–12.

229. *See supra* notes 36–37 and accompanying text.

Courts of appeal have held that the withholding of more limited benefits because of religion presumptively violates the First Amendment. The Eighth Circuit ruled that the denial of special education services violates free exercise, free speech, and equal protection,[230] and the Sixth Circuit ruled that the army's restrictions on any religious activity by day-care providers offered to military personnel violated free exercise and free speech.[231] But claims to equal access in tuition vouchers have failed so far. Such a restructuring of the basic rules of funding—to hold that religious schools must be eligible for vouchers if any private schools are—will have to wait until the courts are even more committed to the models of equality and "plurality of institutions" in education than they are now, and until the separationist approach has receded even further.

For now, it is worth noting that the courts have made highly questionable arguments in defending the constitutionality of excluding schools from benefit programs because they are religious. Decisions from Maine and Vermont held, for instance, that the plaintiffs had not shown that their religious tenets required them to send their children to religious schools.[232] But a discrimination like that against religious families also exists against the schools themselves, which operate on religious tenets. Moreover, flat-out discrimination against religion would seem to be unconstitutional even on matters not required by religious tenets. For example, a church need not have a bus, but a doubled license fee for church buses over other buses would certainly be unconstitutional. For similar reasons, it is very weak to claim, as courts have, that the denial of benefits merely makes it more expensive to attend religious school, but does not prevent such attendance.[233] Discrimination is objectionable in itself because it throws the state's weight against religious choice, and in any event the denial of benefits often makes private education impossible for low-income families. Least defensible of all is the argument that denial of benefits reflects no "animus" against religion.[234] History shows that aid restrictions often did stem originally from anti-Catholic animus, and in any event, all-out discrimination against religion is objectionable even without a showing of such animus.[235]

Thus, the arguments in defense of excluding religious schools from educational benefits programs are weak. Nevertheless, courts have not yet held that excluding religious schools from full-fledged voucher programs is an unconstitutional discrimination. For the foreseeable future, then, these schools will still have to consider the possibility that taking government assistance will require them to remove religious elements from their programs.

Other conditions on government educational assistance

As Esbeck notes, government aid programs may include a wide variety of other conditions besides those requiring a subsidized religious institution to remove religious ele-

---

230. *See* Peter v. Wedl, 155 F.3d 992 (8th Cir. 1998).
231. *See* Hartmann v. Stone, 68 F.3d 973 (6th Cir. 1995).
232. *See Strout,* 178 F.3d at 65; *Bagley,* 728 A.2d at 134; *Chittenden,* 738 A.2d at 539.
233. *See Strout,* 178 F.3d at 65; *Bagley,* 728 A.2d at 134–35.
234. *Strout,* 178 F.3d at 65.
235. Other recent decisions rejecting the claim that denial of equal benefits burdens religious freedom include Niewenhuis v. Delavan-Darien Sch. Dist., 996 F. Supp. 855 (E.D. Wis. 1998) (no burden under Free Exercise Clause); Goodall v. Stafford County Sch. Bd., 60 F.3d 168 (4th Cir. 1995) (no burden under RFRA).

ments from its activities. Aid programs at all levels typically require recipient institutions to refrain from discrimination on the basis of race, sex, age, or handicap in serving clients or in hiring employees. Such provisions in federal law apply quite broadly to the programs of religious colleges and universities, since under the Civil Rights Restoration Act of 1987, the receipt of federal aid through grants or loans to students means that a school is subject to the nondiscrimination requirements in all of its activities.[236] However, federal law contains an exemption from the restriction on sex discrimination for educational institutions whose religious tenets require treating the sexes differently;[237] and the general federal funding provisions do not require that institutions receiving assistance refrain from discrimination on the basis of religion.[238] But the conditions on government assistance may effectively incorporate the conditions imposed by accrediting agencies, since some funding statutes require that the recipient institution be accredited by a recognized agency.

Programs of assistance to educational institutions may also include a number of other conditions—for example, requiring a recipient school to meet certain standards of performance, keep designated records, teach certain subjects, and, of course, comply with all general educational and safety regulations that already apply to private schools. It is not clear to what extent increased government assistance to private schools, if it happens, will increase the scope of regulation to which the schools are subject. On the one hand, there will likely be pressure to hold accountable those schools that receive government funds. On the other hand, the movement for greater assistance to private schools is often fueled by a deregulatory, antibureaucratic attitude. California's 1994 ballot initiative to create a "school choice" program for elementary and secondary schools is instructive, even though it failed. The California initiative provided that private schools receiving vouchers "shall be accorded maximum flexibility to educate their students and shall be free from unnecessary, burdensome, or onerous regulation," and that new state or local regulations beyond those already in existence would have to pass stringent procedural requirements to be enacted.[239] It also accorded the private school freedom to "establish a code of conduct and discipline and enforce it with sanctions, including dismissal."[240] It did require that recipient schools choose and administer tests

---

236. Civil Rights Restoration Act of 1987, Pub. L. No. 100-557, 100th Cong., 2d Sess. (1988) (defining a covered "program or activity" to include "all of the operations of...an entire [organization] principally engaged in the business of providing [among other things] education"). The act reversed the result in *Grove City College v. Bell*, 465 U.S. 55 (1984), which had interpreted the previous statutory language to mean that the receipt of federal grants and loans by a college's student-aid office would not trigger coverage of all of the college's programs.

237. 20 U.S.C. § 1681(a)(3). As Esbeck notes, this exemption is limited to educational institutions "controlled by" a religious organization. Esbeck, *supra* note 184. It thus raises questions identical to those raised by the exemption for religious discrimination in employment in § 703(e)(2) of Title VII; and it should similarly be interpreted broadly to include a school with significant religious characteristics, even if the college is not formally tied to a church or denomination. *See* section on Employment Relations and Policies, *supra*.

238. Some other state and federal funding programs do forbid at least some kinds of religious discrimination by recipients. *See* Esbeck, *supra* note 184 (discussing Iowa tuition tax deduction and U.S. Agency for International Development's program of grants to medical schools abroad).

239. Proposition 174, *supra* note 220, § (b)(4). A state regulation would have to receive a three-quarters vote of the legislature, and a local regulation concerning health and safety or land use would have to receive a two-thirds vote of the governmental body and a majority vote of the qualified electors in the jurisdiction. Moreover, in any court challenge the regulatory body would be subject to stringent burdens of justifying the regulation. *Id.*

240. *Id.*at 66 (§ (b)(6)).

reflecting national standards for the purpose of measuring individual academic improvement.[241] The scholarship-redeeming school would have to meet the general standards applicable to California private schools, and in addition not discriminate on the basis of race, ethnicity, color, or national origin, and not "teach...hatred of any person based on race, ethnicity, color, national origin, religion, or gender."[242]

Conclusion

Religiously affiliated education is often at the heart of a religious community's identity, since it is often the main way that the faith is passed on to succeeding generations. Government has a necessary and inevitable role in regulating religious schools to ensure that students are being educated. But the regulation should be careful and pinpointed, and government should, as much as possible, respect and avoid interfering with the ability of such schools to define their religious message, identity, and mission.

---

241. *Id.* at 64 (§ (a)(6)).
242. *Id.* at 65 (§§ (b)(1), (b)(2)).

Appendix

The Supreme Court's Voucher Decision (*Zelman v. Simmons-Harris*)[*]

Thomas C. Berg

In June 2002, the Supreme Court decided a long-standing crucial question concerning government aid to religious affiliated schools, ruling that the inclusion of religious schools in a program of elementary- and secondary-school vouchers is consistent with the Establishment Clause. *Zelman v. Simmons-Harris*[1] upheld, by a 5–4 vote, an Ohio program under which students in the failing Cleveland public school system could receive a voucher of $2,250 for use at any participating private school within Cleveland or at a public school in any participating adjacent public school district. *Zelman* largely settles the permissibility of voucher programs under the Establishment Clause, but it raises new constitutional questions—some of which the Court has addressed more recently.

Zelman and Vouchers under the Establishment Clause

Zelman held that the Ohio program for Cleveland students was "a program of true private choice," one "in which government aid reaches religious schools only as a result of the genuine and independent choices of private individuals."[2] Such a program, the Court said, does not violate the Establishment Clause prohibition on government "advancing religion," because the decision to use the funds at a religious school "is reasonably attributable to the individual recipient, not to the government, whose role ends

* Portions of this appendix overlap with a joint statement of several law professors on *Zelman v. Simmons-Harris*, sponsored by the Pew Forum on Religion and Public Life (*see* http://www.pewforum.org). I wish to thank the Pew Forum and its executive director, Melissa Rogers, for inviting to me to contribute to drafting that statement. I also wish to thank Ms. Rogers and the other participants in the statement—Alan Brownstein, Erwin Chemerinsky, John Garvey, Douglas Laycock, Ira Lupu, William Marshall, and Robert Tuttle—for stimulating and cooperative discussion. It is important to emphasize that many portions of this appendix differ from the joint statement, and therefore the appendix reflects solely my view and not those of the other statement participants.

1. 122 S. Ct. 2460 (2002).
2. *Id.* at 2467, 2465.

with the disbursement of benefits."[3] The Court indicated three features that made the program one of true private choice.

First, the Court emphasized that the Ohio program was "neutral in all respects toward religion."[4] Both the class of beneficiaries—children in Cleveland public schools—and the class of eligible institutions were "defined without reference to religion." Both secular and religious private schools within Cleveland were eligible, as were adjacent public school districts (even though none actually chose to participate). There were no terms more favorable for religious schools than for other schools—indeed, several terms gave more favorable treatment to public schools than to private schools. Adjacent public schools participating would receive from the state not only the voucher amount, but also the state's ordinary per-pupil contribution. Beyond the voucher program, parents could choose community schools—Cleveland's term for charter schools—or magnet schools in the Cleveland public system and still receive free tuition.[5]

Neutrality in this sense—the same facial terms for both religious and secular recipients—should be fairly easy for a voucher program to satisfy. Neutrality is related to parental choice, in the Court's view, because "where the aid is made available on the basis of neutral, secular criteria," then it generally does not "'create [any] financial incentives for parents to choose a sectarian school.'" As noted above, the Ohio program actually gave less money to private schools, including religious schools, than the state gave to various public alternatives. *Zelman* used this to bolster the conclusion that the program did not skew incentives toward religion, but it added that "such features of the program are not necessary to its constitutionality."[6] It appears that while the state may provide less money per student to religious schools than to others, it may also provide an equal amount.

Second, although the point is not at issue in *Zelman*, it is worth emphasizing that the majority's approval extends only to programs in which aid reaches schools because of the "independent choices of private individuals"—as opposed to "programs that provide aid directly [from the government] to religious schools."[7] In referring to this distinction, *Zelman* cites *Mitchell v. Helms*,[8] where the Court upheld the provision of materials and equipment to religious schools—but where Justice O'Connor's concurrence, providing the crucial fifth vote, said that even formally neutral direct aid is constitutional only if it is restricted to secular uses.[9] Vouchers for private-school tuition typically contain no such restriction on use, and therefore to be constitutional they must channel aid through some mechanism of individual choice—for example, the Cleveland arrangement under which parents choosing a private school endorsed their state check over to the school. Nor will it suffice, at least at present, for the state to allocate direct aid to private schools based on a per-student formula. O'Connor in *Mitchell* rejected the argument that such a mechanism mirrors parental choice—in part, she said, because under the formula parents who chose a private school would not have the option of declining the aid attributable to their child.[10]

---

3. *Id.* at 2467.
4. *Id.*
5. *Id.* at 2468.
6. *Id.*
7. *Id.* at 2465.
8. 530 U.S. 793, 120 S. Ct. 2530 (2000).
9. *Id.* at 841–44 (O'Connor, J., concurring in the judgment).
10. *Id.* at 842.

Third and finally, *Zelman* emphasizes that the Ohio program "provide[d] genuine opportunities for Cleveland parents to select secular educational options"—that it "permits [them] to exercise genuine choice among options public and private, secular and religious."[11] The majority found genuine secular options in the nonreligious private schools, the community (i.e., charter) and magnet public schools, the adjacent suburban public schools that were eligible to accept voucher students (even though none had chosen to do so), and the tuition aid in the regular Cleveland public schools. The Court's analysis suggests several points about how to determine whether choice and options are genuine.

First, the actual percentage of aid that ends up at religious institutions usually will be irrelevant to whether other options are deemed genuine. Although in one year eighty-two percent of the participating schools were religious and ninety-six percent of the voucher aid was used at religious schools, the Court noted that eighty-one percent of private schools throughout Ohio were religious, independent of the program; and it added that basing a standard of constitutionality on the actual percentages of aid used could not provide "certainty" or "principled standards," since the statistics would vary from year to year and from location to location.[12] Second, and importantly, the universe of relevant options includes schools outside the voucher program itself—including, potentially, the regular public schools. The question of whether the state "is coercing parents into sending their children to religious schools," the Court said, "must be answered by evaluating *all* options Ohio provides Cleveland schoolchildren."[13] Thus the universe of relevant options included the community and magnet schools and even the supplemental tutoring offered in regular Cleveland public schools, since all of these options were available to parents—thus dropping the percentage of children in "nontraditional" schools who chose religious schools to less than twenty percent.[14] Finally, the Court is not likely to be highly demanding in evaluating the quality of secular educational options. The majority appears to place the burden of proof on those challenging the genuineness of the options, finding "no evidence that the program fails to provide [secular] opportunities."[15] It would be surprising, indeed, if the Court wished to open the door to close judicial evaluation of the quality of varying schools.

These principles suggest that most formally neutral voucher plans will probably be held to offer genuine choice and thus satisfy the Establishment Clause. Consider first plans for failing public schools like Cleveland's—currently the most politically attractive situation for vouchers. Since such systems are usually in large cities, there will usually be options such as charter or magnet schools, which *Zelman* declares to be relevant choices. The *Zelman* majority even indicates that the regular public schools with additional tutorial assistance count as a option.

Outside the context of a failing public system, vouchers face greater political resistance, but not necessarily greater Establishment Clause barriers. Imagine, most dramatically, that a state offers all parents a choice between free public schools and a voucher for private schools. Many areas of the state will not offer community or magnet schools, but in many or most areas the regular public schools will be adequate—unlike in the case of the failing public system—and therefore should count as a genuine option, al-

---

11. *Zelman*, 122 S. Ct. at 2469, 2473.
12. *Id.* at 2469–71.
13. *Id.* at 2469 (emphasis in original).
14. *Id.* at 2469, 2471.
15. *Id.* at 2469.

most always dwarfing private-school enrollment. There is some uncertainty because of *Zelman*'s treatment of *Committee for Public Education v. Nyquist*,[16] the leading precedent against voucher programs, which had struck down a tuition grant of $50 to $100 to parents of private school students, most of them in religious schools. Despite the similarity in the two programs, *Zelman* distinguished rather than overruled *Nyquist*, reasoning that the *Nyquist* program, unlike Ohio's, did not itself include any public schools, and that its purpose was to " 'offe[r]...an incentive to parents to send their children to sectarian schools.' "[17] These distinctions might be used to challenge a statewide voucher program that simply covered private schools as an alternative to traditional public schools; such a program, viewed in isolation, might be seen as primarily aiding religious schools rather than low-income parents as the Ohio program did. But it is doubtful whether the distinctions will survive, because they are at odds with the general thrust of *Zelman*—that courts must consider "*all* [genuine] options Ohio provides Cleveland schoolchildren," including those outside the specific program, such as the charter, magnet, and even (if they are adequate) regular public schools.

Questions Remaining After *Zelman*

State constitutional restrictions

Although voucher programs that include religious schools will now survive most Establishment Clause challenges, that eliminates only one source of basic challenges to their constitutionality. As was noted in the text,[18] a large number of states have constitutional provisions that restrict aid to religious organizations more explicitly—and perhaps more broadly—than does the Establishment Clause.

The state restrictions fall into several categories, with differing implications for school vouchers.[19] At the most restrictive, a few state provisions say that government funds may not be used for any private school—or, in the language of some provisions, that all schools supported by public funds must be under the "exclusive control" of public authorities. Such language, if applied to vouchers, would exclude secular as well as religious private schools. A second large category of provisions prohibits the expenditure of public funds "in aid of," or to "support or benefit," any "sectarian" school or school controlled by a "religious denomination." In all the variations, these provisions restrict aid to religious, but not to secular, private schools. The phrases in these provisions tend to be strict in forbidding aid, but they can leave room for argument about the permissibility of voucher programs. For example, courts occasionally have held that voucher-type programs are permissible because they "aid" or "support" students rather than religious schools.[20] In a third category are provisions that forbid the "compelled

---

16. 413 U.S. 756 (1973).

17. *Zelman*, 122 S. Ct. at 2472 (brackets and ellipses in original) (quoting *Nyquist*, 413 U.S. at 786).

18. *See* Thomas C. Berg, "Religiously Affiliated Education," in this volume.

19. For a fuller discussion of the provisions, see *id.*; *see also* Toby J. Heytens, Note, *School Choice and State Constitutions*, 86 Va. L. Rev. 117 (2000).

20. *See, e.g.*, Jackson v. Benson, 578 N.W.2d 602, 621 (Wis. 1998) (finding that voucher payments satisfied state provision because they were primarily "for the benefit" of students, not religious schools).

support of [religious] worship or instruction," or forbid state money to be "appropriated for or applied to religious worship or instruction." Such phrasing appears to forbid only aid to the religious teaching in a school, allowing the state to support the separable secular education component—if the court finds that there is any such component.[21] Again, a court here might argue that the "compelled support" is for education, not for instruction or worship.

If a state constitutional provision excludes religious schools from a voucher program, it may be challenged under the Free Exercise or Equal Protection clauses on the ground that discriminatory exclusion of religion is not merely not constitutionally required, but forbidden. The Supreme Court cast a shadow over such challenges recently in *Locke v. Davey*,[22] but it did not eliminate them. *Davey* held that Washington state did not infringe on free exercise or free speech when it excluded students majoring in "devotionally" oriented theology from state-funded scholarships open to college students. The majority first argued broadly that denying scholarships imposed at most a "mil[d]" burden on students because it did not involve criminal or civil sanctions. But much of the opinion focused on the fact that Davey was training for the ministry and that states have a "historic and substantial interest" in denying funds to support clergy. The majority said that clergy instruction was a "distinct category" from general education, that the Washington program included sectarian-college students majoring in subjects other than theology, that objections to tax support for clergy dated back to the Founding era, and that the Washington provision did not derive from the 1875 Blaine Amendment with its anti-Catholic roots.[23] None of these latter arguments justifies excluding religious elementary or secondary schools, which *do* offer general education in a variety of subjects, from voucher programs. Opposition to such funding dates to the nineteenth-century anti-Catholic campaigns and the Blaine Amendment, not to the Founding. Properly read, *Davey* preserves constitutional challenges to voucher exclusions.

Regulations accompanying vouchers

Assuming that the inclusion of religious schools in a voucher plan survives both federal and state constitutional challenges, the next round of litigation is likely to center on the regulation of schools that accompanies the receipt of voucher funds. The Cleveland plan in *Zelman* forbade participating schools to discriminate on the basis of race, ethnicity, or religion or to teach unlawful behavior or "hatred of any person or group" based on race, ethnicity, or religion.[24] Justice Souter's dissent argued that these conditions on religious schools' autonomy were a reason to invalidate the program,[25] but the majority ignored the point. Thus it appears after *Zelman* that regulations imposing on religious schools' autonomy can no longer serve as the basis for a taxpayer to raise an Establishment Clause challenge to voucher aid, as they did during the 1970s and early 1980s.[26] Rather, the two emerging categories of constitutional questions concerning regulation appear to be: (1) If the state imposes conditions on vouchers that would impact the autonomy of a participating religious school, may the school (or a parent who

---

21. Chittenden Town School Dist. v. Vermont Dept. of Educ., 738 A.2d 539.
22. 540 U.S. 712 (2004).
23. *Id.* at 72–23.
24. *Zelman*, 122 S. Ct. at 2463 (quotation omitted).
25. *Zelman*, 122 S. Ct. at 2499–2500 (Souter, J., dissenting).
26. *See, e.g., Lemon*, 403 U.S. at 619–20.

wishes to use a voucher at the school) challenge the condition as constitutionally forbidden? (2) If the state exempts religious schools from conditions on vouchers, is the
exemption constitutionally forbidden?

On the first question, an objecting school might argue that a condition on what a
school may teach is a form of viewpoint discrimination in the distribution of state
voucher benefits, and that under the doctrine of "unconstitutional conditions" the
state may not require an organization to give up constitutional rights—in particular,
First Amendment rights of expression, association, and religious exercise—as the
price of participating in a state benefit program. In response, the state will likely
point to recent Supreme Court decisions that give the government substantial power
to place conditions on persons or organizations that it subsidizes. For example, *Rust
v. Sullivan*[27] permitted the government, under a program funding family planning, to
prohibit projects receiving funds from discussing abortion, on the ground that the
government could choose the policy it favored without having to fund the alternative.
The state will likely analogize a voucher program to *Rust*, arguing that it is promoting
its favored educational policy and may set conditions accordingly. The objecting
school or individual will likely reply by analogizing vouchers to the funding program
in *Rosenberger v. Univ. of Virginia*,[28] which held that it was unconstitutional to exclude
an organization, because of its viewpoint, from a benefit available to a wide range of
organizations expressing a wide range of viewpoints. However, the Court in *Locke v.
Davey* distinguished educational aid programs from the "limited public forum" for
publications in *Rosenberger*. The *Davey* Court held that state-funded college scholarships were designed "to assist students from low- and middle-income families with
the cost of postsecondary education, not to 'encourage a diversity of views from private speakers,'" and thus *Rosenberger*'s requirement of viewpoint neutrality did not
apply.[29] This holding seems likely to bar many free-speech challenges to conditions on
voucher eligibility—although the Court has also said that conditions on government
funds may not "aim at the suppression of dangerous ideas."[30]

If a religious school is at all able to challenge conditions on voucher benefits, it will be
more likely to succeed in asserting rights that are shared by other, secular private schools.
For example, a religious school, like other participating schools, might be able to assert
the First Amendment associational right, recognized in *Boy Scouts of America v. Dale*,[31] to
refuse to accept leaders or members whose presence would "impair the ability of the
group to express those views, and only those views, that it intends to express." By contrast, religious schools or parents will face greater hurdles in asserting constitutional
rights not shared by secular private schools. This is partly because the Free Exercise
Clause, as interpreted by the Court in *Employment Division v. Smith*,[32] generally does not
give a religious claimant a right, even against direct regulation, if the regulation is "neutral and generally applicable." The *Smith* rule might not apply if a school or parent raises
what *Smith* calls a "hybrid" claim—the combination of religious exercise and parental
control over education is *Smith*'s prime example of such a hybrid[33]—or if a state consti-

---

27. 500 U.S. 173 (1991).
28. 515 U.S. 819 (1995).
29. Davey, 540 U.S. at 720 n.3 (quotation omitted).
30. Nat'l Endow. for the Arts v. Finley, 524 U.S. 569, 587 (1998) (quotation omitted).
31. 530 U.S. 640, 648 (2000) (holding that Boy Scouts could refuse to retain openly gay scoutmaster).
32. 494 U.S. 872, 877 (1990).
33. *Id.* at 881.

tutional provision or statute protects free exercise rights even against generally applicable laws.[34] But these arguments all have limits even against direct regulation, and will be even more uncertain against conditions accompanying voucher programs.

Moreover, religious schools asserting rights to exemption not shared by secular private schools will face the argument that such rights not only are not constitutionally protected, but are actually unconstitutional because they would prefer or "advance" religion in violation of the Establishment Clause. Such exemptions are not formally neutral in their terms between religious and secular schools—and as noted above, neutrality of terms is one of three main features to which *Zelman* pointed in upholding the Cleveland voucher plan.[35] Opponents will also likely rely on Supreme Court decisions striking down certain statutory exemptions for religious practice as unconstitutional "endorsement" or promotion of religion,[36] and will argue that religious exemptions are even more unacceptable in the context of a funding program. Defenders of religious exemptions will likely respond that the Court, even as it has struck down some statutory exemptions, has permitted others as long as the exemptions remove a significant government burden from religious exercise and do not impose a disproportionate burden on others.[37] Defenders will argue that some religious exemptions in funding schemes do meet this test.[38] These defenders will have to convince courts that the overriding criterion of *Zelman* is not the formal neutrality of a program's terms, but rather whether the program skews the choices of individuals toward religious schools. Then they will have to show that a particular religious exemption does not so skew the choices. Whether or not that argument succeeds, a religious exemption from voucher conditions will face a greater risk of invalidation than will an exemption that also extends to secular private schools.

There is one particular form of exemption whose nature is disputed: an exemption for religious schools from conditions forbidding schools to use religious preferences in hiring. Such an exemption may appear on its face as favoritism for religious schools over other schools. But as was argued in the preceding chapter,[39] it can be defended as giving religious schools the same right as other schools to require ideological commitment from their employees. This argument may help explain why the Court unanimously upheld such an exemption in *Corporation of Presiding Bishop v. Amos*[40]—albeit in the context of direct regulation rather than in conditions accompanying government funding.

---

34. Several state courts have interpreted their constitutions to reject *Smith* and require the state to show a "compelling" interest in burdening religion even through a generally applicable law. Also, several other state legislatures have rejected the *Smith* rule through "religious freedom restoration acts." For a summary, see, for example, Symposium, Restoring Religious Freedom in the States, 32 U.C. Davis L. Rev. 531 (winter 1999).

35. *See* notes 4–6 and accompanying text above.

36. *See* Estate of Thornton v. Caldor, 472 U.S. 703 (1985); Texas Monthly v. Bullock, 489 U.S. 1 (1989) (plurality opinion of Brennan, J.).

37. *See* Corporation of Presiding Bishop v. Amos, 483 U.S. 327 (1987); *Texas Monthly*, 489 U.S. at 15, 18 n. 8.

38. *See, e.g.,* Children's Healthcare Is a Legal Duty v. Min de Parle, 212 F.3d 1084 (8th Cir. 2000) (upholding provision allowing "religious nonmedical health care institutions" to receive Medicaid funds for nursing services without being subject to all regulations governing hospitals).

39. *See* Berg, *supra* note 18.

40. 483 U.S. 327.

Religiously Affiliated Health Care Providers: Legal Structures and Transformations

Donald H.J. Hermann

Throughout the history of the United States, various religious groups have been involved in a broad range of health care activities. Religiously affiliated health care providers combine the objectives of for-profit health care institutions in delivering medical services in an economically efficient manner with those of nonprofit organizations that are concerned with the medical needs of the specific community being served. To this combination, the religiously affiliated health care provider adds the particular goals and mission of its own sponsoring religious group, such as charity care or provision of medical services to those who are financially indigent. While the vast majority of these religiously affiliated institutions serve the public at large without any restrictions on medical service based on religious belief, some sectarian health care entities make their services contingent upon their comporting with the teachings of the supporting religious institution.[1] Nevertheless, there is a general consensus among these organizations that their mission includes the assurance that all necessary services are provided, that all needy populations are provided with care, and that a refuge is provided for all those in need of care.[2] The objectives of universal access and provision of charity care in community-owned nonprofit hospitals have reflected Dr. Albert Schweitzer's formulation of the ideal care-giving tenet of religiously affiliated health care providers: "Here, at whatever hour you come, you will find light and help and human kindness."[3]

Today, all health care institutions face many economic pressures. Medicare and Medicaid payments comprise more than fifty percent of the income of many hospitals in the United States. In the past few years, particularly after passage of the Balanced Budget Act, Medicare and Medicaid payments to the hospitals have been greatly reduced. Commercial payers, as well as the Medicare and Medicaid Programs, have placed a number of controls and limitations on inpatient hospital visits and have encouraged the use of

---

1. For an excellent and thorough discussion of the evolution and impact of religiously affiliated hospitals in the past and current markets, see Kathleen M. Boozang, Deciding the Fate of Religious Hospitals in the Emerging Health Care Market, 31 Hous. L. Rev. 1429, 1475 (1995).

2. *See* Volunteer Trustees Foundation for Research and Education, When Your Community Hospital Goes Up for Sale, http://www.healthonline.com [hereinafter Volunteer Trustees].

3. *Id.* (citing the inscription of Dr. Albert Schweitzer's lamp at his jungle clinic in Laberene).

office procedures and ambulatory surgery centers to reduce the number and length of such visits. At the same time there have been many technological advances which require hospitals to invest large sums of money in equipment and the development of employee-intensive procedures to provide the best care to patients. Finally, there is strong competition for managed care contracts. With all of these economic pressures, many institutional health care providers have sought mergers and integration in order to create efficiency by combining certain services, thus avoiding duplication of programs. The resulting entities can create new services at one campus instead of two, further reduce costs through the consolidation of administrative staff, provide a greater range of services, and attract managed care contracts.

Governing Structure

Until the middle of the twentieth century, most religiously affiliated health care facilities were not separately incorporated. Instead, they were part of the organizational structure of the sponsoring religious group, which often included the provision of charitable care as part of its stated purpose. In more recent years, however, various legal developments have produced a need for separate corporate structures for religiously affiliated health care organizations, which are usually created by articles of incorporation or a corporate charter that must comply with state laws governing corporations. The charter states the purposes of the organization, establishes the requirements for membership (or shareholder status), and sets out the constitution of the board. This charter also provides authority for adoption of bylaws, rules, and regulations. Federal law, particularly the Internal Revenue Code and Medicare/Medicaid statues, has had an important influence in the establishment of separate legal initiatives to be administered in compliance with the requirements of the tax law and reimbursement law. Third-party reimbursement has created a need to establish which expenses can be included in the reimbursable cost basis; creating a separate entity simplifies this process. Another important factor leading to the establishment of separate entities to provide health care services was state certificate-of-need laws which required proposed health care organizations to provide extensive financial disclosure, since many sponsoring organizations did not want to provide full access to their institution's financial records. Perhaps another early important factor leading to separate incorporation of religiously affiliated health care providers has been medical malpractice, which has created the need to isolate assets of the sponsoring group, the necessity of qualifying for malpractice insurance, and a desire to establish adequate risk-management monitoring.

Management of the health care organizations is usually overseen by a board of directors or trustees, many of which are either self-perpetuating or elected by the membership with requirements for members set out in the charter. Some religious sponsors have sought to maintain a level of control over the health care provider by establishing interlocking boards of directors between the provider and the sponsoring religious body or church. Another method of maintaining control uses the category of "membership" in the affiliate's corporate charter. In this process, control over the affiliate is ultimately held by a group designated "the members," constituted of individuals who usually belong to and represent the sponsoring religious organization. In some cases, the religious order sponsoring the health care entity is the sole corporate member. Control through use of powers reserved to the members facilitates significant ultimate decisional authority over matters involving fiduciary responsibility, including sale of corporate assets. Under this arrangement the members have the authority to appoint and remove board members, amend the health care provider's mission, and approve the purchase or sale of major assets. The members also select a board of directors to oversee the administrative responsibilities of the provider organization, and to develop and implement rules to promote the values of the sponsoring group. This board is usually composed of civic, business, and religious leaders along with physicians, ethicists, lawyers, and lay members of the community; often there is an effort to select individuals for board membership who represent the social makeup of the group receiving services from the provider. The board's authority to govern the health care entity is established by the documents creating the entity and by the general principles of corporate law. The board has ultimate responsibility for the effective operations of the organization and most often appoints a chief executive officer and other high-level members of the management team who take responsibility for day-to-day management.

The board of directors acts as the governing body of the health care provider, and may ultimately approve or deny any specific proposed treatment protocol. Depending on the sponsoring religious organization, the hospital may or may not provide treatments that some members of the general community may deem essential for quality patient care: for example, abortion, sterilizations, or withholding of treatment at the patient's request. It is in provision of such medical services that there is most often a potential clash of policy when different religiously affiliated hospitals consider merging, or when a religiously affiliated provider becomes associated with a for-profit entity or with another nonprofit institution that lacks any religious affiliation.

Religiously affiliated health care providers are most often not-for-profit (rather than for-profit or governmental) and private (rather than public), and are often organized as charitable entities in order to qualify for special tax treatment. The law has developed high standards for such charitable enterprises requiring scrupulous compliance with fiduciary standards. However, in some states directors are exculpated from ordinary negligence.

Changes in the Health Care Environment

Recent developments in the health care industry, as well as changes in demographics and in the expressed needs of various social communities, have had a marked effect on the structure of health care institutions. These developments also have changed the way in which health care services are delivered and paid for. The central role that third-party payers have assumed in the provision of health care has compelled all health care providers, both institutions and associated physicians, to streamline services in order to cut costs and remain competitive.

Religiously affiliated hospitals must constantly seek "to adapt to the ever-changing needs of their communities and [to conditions in] the health care market," while struggling to maintain and continue promoting their unique religious identities.[4] This means

---

4. Boozang, *supra* note 1, at 1433.

that health care institutions have had to cope with demands for reform along with the necessity of reducing overhead and controlling costs. This in turn has led to a large number of closings[5] and mergers[6] among religiously affiliated hospitals and nursing homes.[7] While these changes have resulted in limitations on patient choice of providers,[8] some commentators maintain that many of these changes have "increased efficiency"[9] and eliminated costly duplication of services.[10]

This chapter examines the legal implications of religiously affiliated hospitals joining forces with other institutions whether religiously affiliated or not, whether non-profit or not. The discussion begins with an overview of developments in the health care system in the United States, and then examines the response of religiously affiliated providers to the changing health care arena, including the various institutional arrangements used to establish cooperative arrangements with other providers. The discussion then focuses on a legal overview emphasizing the tax and antitrust implications of these arrangements. Next, a review is provided of recent federal and state legislation including model legislation and guidelines proposed by grassroots and professional organizations. Finally, the chapter identifies conflicts that have arisen as a result of ethical and moral views embedded in the policies of religiously affiliated hospitals, particularly in such areas as reproductive health, the right to refuse treatment or to have treatment withdrawn, physician-assisted suicide, and organ donation and transplantation.

As the influence of managed care limits patient choice of health care providers, patients may also be faced with new restrictions on services available, or on the sites where they may be obtained. This is often a result of participation in managed care and of institutional integration of health care organizations, and it requires policy makers and federal and state legislators to give attention to developing arrangements that balance the religious convictions of the provider with the treatment expectations present in the secular society regarding the delivery of health care services.[11]

---

5. *See id.* (citing Nanette Byrnes, Anatomy of a Merger, Fin. World, July 5, 1994, at 20, 20–21, noting that "over the past ten years, the cost pressures of managed care, coupled with chronic over-bedding, have caused an estimated 500 out of 5,800 U.S. hospitals to close. In big cities such as New York and San Francisco, consultants estimate, at least another 20% of current capacity will be wiped out within five years").

6. *See id.* (citing Byrnes, *supra* note 5, at 20–21; Jay Greene & Sandy Lutz, Systems Post 4th Straight Year of Income Growth, Mod. Healthcare, May 23, 1994, at 37).

7. *See id.* at 1435 (citing John Burns, Existing Nursing Homes Propel Strong Revenues, Mod. Healthcare, May 23, 1994, at 69, 72–73; John Burns, Sun Healthcare to Buy Mediplex Group in Deal Worth About $320 Million, Mod. Healthcare, Jan. 10, 1994, at 3).

8. *See id.* at 1433; *id.* n.9 ("This limitation on choice is especially true when mergers occur between the only two hospitals in a community"). *See generally* David Burda, Agencies Near Decisions on Two Hospital Mergers, Mod. Healthcare, Jan. 17, 1994, at 17, 17 (discussing the Federal Trade Commission and U.S. Department of Justice's concerns regarding the frequency of two-hospital mergers and the likelihood these mergers violate federal antitrust laws).

9. Boozang *supra* note 1, at 1433.

10. *See id.* (citing Byrnes, *supra* note 5, at 21).

11. *See id.* at 1475.

Evolution of the Health Care System

To understand the institutional arrangements that make up the health care system in the United States, one must study their evolution.[12] During the eighteenth and into the nineteenth century, almshouses, the predecessors to our hospital system, cared for the sick, homeless, and poor until their deaths.[13] Many of them were established by local governments, while others were run as charity institutions by religious institutions. As the need for such treatment centers became greater, the concept of hospitals providing care to the physically and/or mentally ill began to emerge.[14] While these new hospitals received substantial financial support from governmental agencies and religious organizations, wealthy people were largely treated by physicians in their homes or at physicians' clinics.[15]

By the late nineteenth century, hospitals developed into more than simply quarantine and treatment areas for the poor. The availability of anesthesia and asepsis motivated privately-treated patients to seek treatment in hospitals and physicians' clinics rather than in their own homes.[16] Despite new medical innovations and changing treatments, health care continued to be delivered in two very different ways according to one commentator who reports that: "Larger voluntary hospitals, typically supported by philanthropic contributions, served the poorer population, and small, physician-owned, proprietary hospitals generally catered to self-paying wealthier individuals."[17] By the early twentieth century, physicians and social reformers recognized the need for establishing hospitals adequate to meet the needs of their communities.[18] Even with the strong public interest in health care, the number of hospitals was divided between physician-owned or proprietary and charitable or voluntary hospitals.[19] Both types of facilities existed in most regions of the country.[20] The metropolitan cities of the eastern and midwestern United States often had a small number of municipal hospitals, a few small ethnic and religious hospitals, and some larger nongovernmental, non-sectarian hospitals operated by voluntary boards of trustees and largely supported by philanthropy.[21] Generally, municipal hospitals provided care to the nonpaying poor while vol-

---

12. For an informative historical overview of the health care system, see Nina J. Crimm, Evolutionary Forces: Changes in For-Profit and Not-For-Profit Health Care Delivery Structures; A Regeneration of Tax Exemption Standards, 37 B.C. L. Rev. 1, 9 (1995).

13. See id. at 10 (citing Stanley Joel Reiser, Medicine and the Reign of Technology 152 (1978); Paul Starr, The Social Transformation of American Medicine 149–152 (1982); Robert S. Bromberg, The Charitable Hospital, 20 Cath. U. L. Rev. 237, 239 (1970)).

14. See id.

15. See id. (citing Starr, supra note 13, at 145–79). By the mid-nineteenth century, most of the care provided in patients' homes or physicians' clinics was similar, if not identical, to the treatment provided in the hospital setting.

16. See id. (citing Charles E. Rosenberg, The Care of Strangers 116–65 (1987)).

17. Id. (citing Rosenberg, supra note 16, at 116; Bromberg, supra note 13, at 249; Henry Hansmann, The Evolving Law of Nonprofit Organizations: Do Current Trends Make Good Policy?, 39 Case W. Res. L. Rev. 807, 813 (1988–1989)).

18. See Crimm, supra note 12, at 10, 11.

19. See id. (citing Rosenberg, supra note 16, at 5).

20. See id. at 11.

21. See id. at 11–12 (citing Starr, supra note 13, at 170–72, 219; Rosemary Stevens, In Sickness and In Wealth: American Hospitals in the Twentieth Century 20 (1989)).

untary hospitals, often aligned with medical schools, provided acute care to low-income subsidized patients.[22] The newly developed western states typically provided health care through small proprietary hospitals.[23]

While the institutional structure of the health care sector remained mixed and subject to change, the importance of quality medical care became a vitally important concern. By the 1930s, the number of voluntary nonprofit hospitals began to grow while the number of proprietary hospitals declined.[24] In the mid-1940s, even more proprietary hospitals closed or were converted into nonprofit institutions.[25] After World War II and until the mid-1960s, non-government voluntary hospitals accounted for fifty-eight percent of all general acute-care hospitals, while proprietary hospitals accounted for only twenty-four percent.[26] The rapid expansion of not-for-profit voluntary institutions over the span of three decades can be attributed, at least in part, to the 1946 enactment of the Hospital Survey and Construction Act, also known as the Hill-Burton Act.[27] This legislation provided federal funds to subsidize the cost of constructing nonprofit and public acute-care general hospitals, health clinics, and nursing homes throughout the nation.[28]

Influence of Insurance and Reimbursement

The availability of health insurance was another influence on the growth in the number of voluntary hospitals,[29] and it caused an acceleration in demand for health care.[30] Competing with nonprofit Blue Cross and Blue Shield plans, private commercial insur-

---

22. *See id.* at 12 (citing Starr, *supra* note 13, at 112–23).

23. *See id.*; Crimm, *supra* note 12, at 12 n.34 ("In large part, proprietary hospitals were found in frontier communities because there were few funds to create not-for-profit hospitals, and a strong philanthropic tradition had not had time to develop"). *See* Starr, *supra* note 13, at 170–71; Bruce Steinwald & Duncan Neuhauser, The Role of the Proprietary Hospital, 35 Law & Contemp. Probs. 817, 820 (1970). It has been reported that the increased number of proprietary hospitals during the 1920s and 1930s may have been the result of physicians seeking hospital privileges, "who were excluded from the medical staffs of not-for-profit hospitals for professional, ethnic, religious, or other reasons." Starr, *supra* note 13, at 165; Douglas M. Mancino, Income Tax Exemption of the Contemporary Nonprofit Hospital, 32 St. Louis U. L.J. 1015, 1024 (1988).

24. *See* Crimm, *supra* note 12, at 12.

25. *See id.* (citing Starr, *supra* note 13, at 219).

26. *See id.* (citing *see* Starr, *supra* note 13, at 219).

27. *See id.*

28. *See id.*; *id.* at 14 nn. 47–48 (citing Ch. 958, 60 Stat. 1040 (1946) and noting that "[t]he express purpose of the Hill-Burton Act was to assist the states in modernizing health care facilities after World War II by furnishing 'adequate hospital, clinic or similar services to all their people'").

29. *See* Crimm, *supra* note 12 at 15.

30. *See id.* (discussing the explanations of Steven Golub, The Role of Medicare Reimbursement in Contemporary Hospital Finance, 11 Am. J.L. & Med. 501, 504 (1986) and quoting: "World War II...indirectly promoted the popularity of health insurance as an employee benefit, since wartime wages and price controls did not apply to fringe benefits. Hence, between 1940 and 1950, the number of people covered by hospitalization insurance increased from 12 million to 77 million. During the 1940s, as health insurance coverage increased in availability and scope, there was a concomitant rise in the development and use of new medical technology. As a result, both the demand for and cost of health care services accelerated").

ers began offering lower-priced plans to consumers.[31] The establishment of Medicare and Medicaid was critical to expanding the number of persons able to access health care providers.

Constant changes in the health care system have affected the manner in which religiously affiliated hospitals provide medical services.[32] During the last two decades of the twentieth century, the growth of hospitals aided by a system of reimbursement for actual costs ultimately became a national concern as health care costs spiraled upward. By the 1980s, managed care and the development of reimbursement schedules based on diagnosis represented efforts to contain health care costs. For example, the explosion of managed care in the 1990s has resulted from pressure to increase access to health care services while decreasing costs. Additionally, many nonprofit hospitals, including religiously affiliated hospitals, have been confronted with financial hardship,[33] and with the continuing existence of a significant low-income and indigent population in the United States, the need for charity care that generates little or no revenue has increased. Moreover, many health care providers have maintained that reimbursement levels under Medicaid and other state public aid programs have failed to cover the full cost of providing patient services. A major effect of managed care has been to reduce the actual level of reimbursement. Consequently, many nonprofit health care providers have argued that they have been left "with little choice but to merge with other not-for-profits or sell their assets to bigger for-profit [entities]."[34] These mergers and sales have resulted in some religiously affiliated providers becoming involved with institutions that deliver health care services that contravene their ethical, moral, or religious principles.[35] While current law does not require religious hospitals to provide any type of care contradicting their own religion-based policies and protocols, some commentators contend that the "extensive federal and state regulation of health care delivery coupled with increased government financing will compel religiously affiliated providers to provide care that is inconsistent with their sectarian principles."[36]

Tax Status

A primary reason for the corporate structural form of most religiously affiliated health care providers has been the objective of achieving tax-exempt status. Historically,

---

31. *See id.*; *id.* at 15 n.51 ("Since inception, Blue Cross and Blue Shield, not-for-profit organizations, had offered private insurance with premiums based on the average of the actuarial medical experiences of all employee groups of different companies in an area ('community rating'). Entry of for-profit private commercial insurers into the marketplace profoundly affected the private health insurance industry. These for-profit private insurers offered health insurance at lower premiums than available through Blue Cross and Blue Shield. They based their premiums on the use of medical care in the community [('experience rating')], which provided a broader base to spread their risk of loss, and hence enabled lower premiums to be offered. By the 1960s, Blue Cross and Blue Shield virtually abandoned community rating for experience rating based on smaller health insurance pools"). *See* Starr, *supra* note 13, at 295–310.

32. *See* Crimm, *supra* note 12, at 1430.

33. *See* Sougata Mukherjee, Hospital Conversions Draws Congressional Query, Inside Washington, Jan. 19, 1998, http://www.amcity.com/report/011998/report1.html.

34. *Id.*

35. *See* Boozang, *supra* note 1, at 1430.

36. *Id.*

religiously sponsored medical facilities were exempted from federal tax by virtue of their identification with the sponsoring religious group. For example, on March 25, 1946, an Internal Revenue Service ruling established federal tax exemption for agencies and instrumentalities including all educational, charitable, and religious institutions operated, supervised, or controlled by or in connection with the Roman Catholic Church in the United States.

Today, however, many religiously affiliated health care organizations are separately incorporated and operated as tax-exempt charities under section 501(c)(3) of the Internal Revenue Code, that requires tax-exempt entities be organized and operated for charitable purposes. In the past, to be considered a charity a health care organization had to provide free care to the indigent. Over time, though, the Internal Revenue Service came to accept the view that providing health care to the public constitutes tax-exempt charitable activity regardless of whether any of it is free. This revised requirement has since been formulated as a community-benefit standard, according to which a health care provider qualifies for the section 501(c)(3) tax exemption if it provides a community benefit and meets the other requirements established by the Internal Revenue Code. A rule against private inurement requires that there be no distribution of profits to private persons.

This discussion will focus on religiously affiliated hospitals. The tax treatment of other health care entities, such as nursing homes and family practice plans that are governed by other rulings and regulations, is beyond the scope of this chapter. The IRS applies one of two tests to determine whether a hospital qualifies as charitable: (1) whether the institution is, to the extent possible, providing free care to those unable to pay; or (2) whether the hospital serves a community purpose by, for example, making emergency-room care available to all members of the community or providing care to anyone able to pay.[37]

Charitable Trust Status

Prior to the separate incorporation of religiously affiliated health care organizations, hospitals most often were created as trusts for charitable purposes. This form can impose significant legal restraints on changes in organizational form or use of trust assets. For example, in California the state attorney general must approve of the disposition or use of funds from hospital sales or mergers where a trust is involved. However, with the increasing separate incorporations of health care entities, trust issues in relation to hospital governance have largely have been eliminated. Directors of not-for-profit corporations (whether called trustees or not) are not held to the same degree of fiduciary duty as a traditional trustee.

The aspect of charitable trust law that most often comes to bear on the operation of health care providers is the manner in which the organization holds property. Trust property is acquired under terms that provide for safeguarding the principal and using the income for a stated purpose set forth in the trust itself, with the requirement of return or transfer upon certain stated events.

---

37. *See* Rev. Rul. 69-545, 1969-2 C.B. 117. *See also* Internal Revenue Service Audit Guidelines for Hospitals, Manual Transmittal—(10) 69-38 for Exempt Organization Examination Guidelines Handbook (Mar. 27, 1992).

An action brought by the attorney general of California in 1977 against a Los Angeles hospital illustrates a strict approach to charitable trust status.[38] The hospital was incorporated in 1927 under the sponsorship of a Catholic religious order of nuns. In 1971, the hospital's board of directors approved a lease to a proprietary entity and intended to use the lease proceeds to establish and operate clinics in Los Angeles that would provide aid, advice, and free medical care to the poor and indigent. The board also intended to pay an agreed-upon sum to the religious order for the value of past services. However, the court held that the hospital's articles of incorporation and its representations to the public precluded it from abandoning its operation of a hospital in favor of operating clinics. The court reasoned that the issue was whether a specific purpose is authorized by the articles of incorporation, and not whether a new or different purpose is equal to or better than the original purpose. Perhaps most significantly, the court ruled that the board's payment to the religious order was a diversion of charitable assets.

A case more typical of the approach of courts to the issue of the application of charitable trust doctrine to hospitals is provided by a New Jersey case that held that a hospital originally incorporated to operate within the city limits was not a charitable trust in the strict sense.[39] Instead, the court denominated the hospital to be a charitable corporation governed by the corporation law and held that since its relocation to another municipality had been authorized by the corporate charter and deemed by the board relocation to be in the hospital's best interest, the change was lawful.

Religiously Affiliated Hospitals' Response to the Changing Health Care Market

With the current movement of the health care industry in America toward managed care and increased integration, it is clear that the types of services provided by religiously affiliated hospitals will be affected. Each provider is compelled to deal with the necessary changes in delivering and financing its services, as well as with the ethical, moral, and religious principles that underlie a provider's own purposes. While the 1980s were marked by a high number of mergers between sectarian health care providers, the 1990s witnessed an increasing incidence of mergers between religiously affiliated providers and nonreligious organizations.[40] These mergers are often prompted by the need for health care institutions to establish greater financial security and acquire greater technological capacity so that they can deliver appropriate medical services.[41] Although mergers between any health care institutions inevitably require compromises on the manner in which they will deliver services, mergers between religious and secular entities are often more challenging since some services that the secular provider intends to offer may be strictly prohibited by the religious beliefs represented by the other entity.

---

38. *See* Queen of Angels Hosp. v. Younger, 136 Cal. Rptr. 36 (Ct. App. 1977).

39. *See* City of Paterson v. Paterson Gen. Hosp., 250 A.2d 427 (N.J. Super. Ct. App. Div. 1969).

40. Boozang, *supra* note 1 (citing Howard J. Anderson, Catholic Hospitals Join Forces With Non-Catholic Competitors, Hospitals, Oct. 20, 1990, at 44; Bruce Jaspen, Church Puts Faith in System Mergers, Mod. Healthcare, June 6, 1994, at 32).

41. *See id.*

An important aspect of health care delivery in the United States that has become firmly established in the last two decades is the recognition of patient autonomy in decision making. This has particular significance in the determination of religion's role in the operation of managed care. After two decades in which patients or their families have successfully obtained the right to have treatment withdrawn over the objections of the provider (or the state),[42] several state courts have imposed relatively stringent requirements on protocols regarding treatment discontinuation.[43] On the other hand, some physicians are now challenging family requests to continue treatment deemed by the physicians to be futile or inappropriate.[44] These developments create special problems for religiously affiliated institutions, particularly for sectarian facilities that have joined or been integrated with secular providers.

Combinations and Transformations

Sponsoring institutions and religious bodies have expressed varied responses about the results of the combination of two or more nonprofit entities.[45] Some religious leaders, while encouraging cooperation and affiliation among the health care providers sponsored by their faith, have discouraged or prohibited them from becoming associated with, sold to, or affiliated with those sponsored by other religious sects or for-profit organizations.[46]

Others have encouraged their affiliated health care institutions to become part of new groupings, so long as that does not violate their religiously based policies and protocols. In other cases, those who control or oversee the operation of health care providers appear ready to tolerate practices originally banned in the former nonprofit institution. Nevertheless, it seems that some practices may simply be beyond the possibility of acceptance. Thus it appears no matter which direction the religious leaders choose to pursue, in some cases, particularly those involving Roman Catholic-affiliated providers, the accepted policies "can result in the complete elimination of certain services, such as sterilizations, in the community."[47]

---

42. *See id.* at 1437 (citing Brophy v. New England Sinai Hosp., Inc., 497 N.E.2d 626, 639–40 (Mass. 1986) (granting the patient's wife the authority to order the discontinuation of her husband's nutrition and hydration over the objections of both the hospital and physicians); *In re* Quinlan, 355 A.2d 647, 671–72 (N.J. 1976) (giving the adult patient's father the authority to consent to the withdrawal of a respirator over the objections of the hospital, physicians, local county prosecutor, and the state attorney general).

43. *See id.* (citing Cruzan v. Director, Mo. Dep't of Health, 497 U.S. 261 (1990)).

44. *See id.* (citing *In re* Baby K., 832 F. Supp. 1022 (E.D. Va. 1993) (denying a hospital's request to discontinue further treatment on an encephalic baby); In re Wanglie, No. PX-91-283 (Minn. Dist. Ct., Prob. Div. June 28, 1991) (denying patient's physician's request to remove patient's husband as her conservator because he insisted on continuing the ventilator treatment for his wife)).

45. *See id.* at 1435.

46. Cardinal Joseph Bernadin, Making the Case for Not-for-Profit Health Care, St. Louis: The Catholic Health Association of the United States (1995) at 16. "Healthcare is fundamentally different from most other goods and services. It is about the most human and intimate needs of people, their families, and communities. It is because of this critical difference that each of us should work to preserve the predominantly not-for-profit character of our healthcare delivery in Chicago and throughout the country."

47. Boozang, *supra* note 1, at 1435. *See id.* at 1435 n.24 (discussing Catholic health providers' awareness of some communities' concerns about Catholic health providers declining to provide certain female healthcare services. In order to determine both the risks and benefits of joint ventures

The process of combining forces

Health care delivery systems are consistently changing in structure and altering the relationships among providers. Similar change is occurring in the nature and availability of the services they provide, and the effects are starting to be felt.[48] For example, the availability of care for the uninsured and indigent is decreasing each year. There were 3,349 nonprofit hospitals in 1985, 3,191 in 1990, and 3,092 in 1995.[49] On the other hand, for-profit hospitals have steadily increased in number after an initial drop in the early 1980s.[50]

When a not-for-profit entity is transformed into a for-profit entity, it is often the result of a conversion: a transaction constituting the sale or restructuring of all or substantially all assets of a nonprofit organization into a for-profit company. These conversions generally occur by one of two methods: a joint venture or a sale of assets.

A joint venture occurs when the not-for-profit health care provider, for example a hospital, sells a share of its assets to the for-profit company for a portion of the total value of the assets of the seller. After the sale, the not-for-profit entity retains a certain level of control over the hospital that forms a part of the buying enterprise, while the for-profit investors realize a predetermined amount of the profits earned by the integrated entity. The control the not-for-profit seller retains generally takes the form of a seat on the board of directors of the for-profit entity. Although the board seat appears to provide a secure right to exercise authority over the activities of the institution, this control can be illusory since its effective voting power may in fact be limited.

The other manner in which a not-for-profit entity may convert into a for-profit company is through the sale of all of its assets — often in the form of an outright sale with the proceeds directed to a foundation to continue the charitable purpose of the nonprofit entity, most often through activities related to health care. Due to nonprofit enti-

---

involving a Catholic healthcare entity, the Catholic Health Association performed a study. The results of which follows:

> One of the difficulties Catholic providers face in attempting to be accountable to the community on its own terms is in the area of reproductive health. That is, what some perceive as a community need, or at least what the community expects in family planning services, Catholics are not authorized by the Church to provide. From the perspective of a community where the Catholic facility is the only provider, the facility is often seen as limiting access to needed services. Accountability to the community comes into direct conflict with accountability to the Church if the venture provides reproductive services.
>
> . . .
>
> When the joint venture has resulted in a new entity under Catholic sponsorship, with the condition that no contraceptive or sterilization services are offered, physicians are constrained from offering these services within the joint venture's framework. In some communities it may be virtually impossible to refer their patients elsewhere. These physicians and the women whom they treat in such communities see the Catholic prohibition as an unjust limitation of access.

Catholic Health Ass'n, Physician-Hospital Joint Ventures: Ethical Issues 11–12 (1991)).

48. *See* Marla Rothouse, Change in Nonprofit Entities, Issue Brief, May 1, 1998, http://www.hpts.org.

49. *See id.*

50. *See id.* "In 1985, there were 805 for-profit hospitals. By 1990 that number had dropped to 749. In 1994, there were 719 for-profit hospitals in existence, and by December 1995 that number had increased to 752." *Id.* (citing Hospital Statistics, 1996/1997 Edition Chicago: American Hospital Association, 1997).

ties' tax-exempt status under the Internal Revenue Code, and because of issues raised in certain cases because of a state's trust law, states' attorneys general and other designated regulating bodies have become involved in closely monitoring such sales. The tax status of nonprofit organizations and the tax implications of conversion transactions are discussed later in this chapter.

The results of combining forces

The formation of alliances by hospitals and hospital systems with each other and with other organizations results in new structures and combinations that have certain advantages and disadvantages. Advocates of these conversions claim advantages including efficiency, cost reduction, enhancement of choice and access to health care, and the resuscitation of distressed entities.[51] Opponents argue the "misplaced focus on profits, harm to patients from inappropriate cost cutting, and the increasing danger of harmful anticompetitive conditions."[52]

Proponents of such transactions often argue that the new alliances between nonprofit hospitals and for-profit companies will instill greater efficiency and create stronger bargaining power.[53] One commentator has argued: "By merging and becoming larger, medical corporations can reduce costs through economies of scale afforded by their larger size. They can also better meet operating costs, accumulate capital with which to purchase equipment, attract patients, and negotiate more effectively with third party payers."[54]

Large hospitals often do experience greater power in negotiating with managed care organizations,[55] not simply because they are larger, but because they can deliver services in more locations. This allows the health care provider to decrease costs while maintaining or even increasing access to care. Proponents of these transactions also maintain that combining different types of medical institutions will enable the resulting system to provide a wider range of services.[56] Proponents also argue that these new health systems will be able to thrive in the managed care market because their consolidation reduces administrative costs and increases efficiency by pooling resources.

Opponents of these transactions believe that in these large medical centers or integrated systems, the primary institutional concern becomes maintaining financial viability and profit rather than meeting the medical needs of patients. They maintain that

---

51. *See* Nancy L. Sander, Health Care Alliances: Good Medicine for an Ailing Health Care Industry, or Antitrust Illnesses to Fence In?, 27 U. Tol. L. Rev. 687, 713 (1996).

52. *Id.* at 717.

53. *See id.* at 713 (citing Medpartner/Mulliken Agree to Merge, PR Newswire, Aug. 15, 1995).

54. *Id.* at 713. *See id.* at 713 n.231 (citing Henry A. Holguin, New Health Care Antitrust Manual a Useful Resource Tool: Health Care Antitrust: A Manual for Changing Provider Organizations, Corp. Legal Times, May 1995, at 31 ("Through these mergers, joint ventures and networks, health care providers hope to reduce excess capacity, align economic incentives and gain control over the allocation of health care resources while maintaining or improving quality")); Paul T. Schnell et al., Mergers and Acquisitions in Health Care Industry, N.Y. L.J., June 26, 1995, at 7.

55. *See id.* at 714.

56. *See* Sander, *supra* note 51 at 714 (discussing Columbia/HCA's 1995 annual report which stated that "an expectant mother ready to enter the hospital, a senior adult [visiting] a rehabilitation center following surgery, or an employer [helping] a chemically dependent employee—can be assured that quality care will be delivered throughout the Columbia network of employees and volunteers").

hospitals, which for decades have been the cornerstones of the not-for-profit industry, now are converted into for-profit entities and become primarily concerned with pleasing shareholders.[57] These critics argue, therefore, that proper concern needs to be directed at such problems as: (1) "cream skimming" of more profitable patients while dumping uninsured patients on nonprofit hospitals; (2) access to free care by the uninsured and the indigent; (3) accountability to local health needs by companies with out-of-state headquarters; (4) the effects on the community when for-profit companies decide to close hospitals; and (5) the effect that for-profits will have on the state's nonprofit hospitals and insurers.[58]

Another concern is that traditional cost-cutting measures of managed care entities will result in misdiagnoses and the denial of access to medically necessary care.[59] By seeking to save money instead of lives, opponents argue, physicians and other health care providers are forced into making medical decisions without the necessary diagnostic information, which will result in lower quality patient care, more severe illnesses, and even patient deaths.

One commentator has put the case against the integration of not-for-profit religiously affiliated health care providers with managed care systems and for-profit enterprises as follows: "Saving money at the cost of saving lives" may be part of a larger anti-competitive situation. The consolidation of several health care providers often occurs to further the entities' "own interests in profitability," and this type of "coordinated inter-action...harms consumers."[60] As a result, these institutional transactions increasingly provoke government antitrust scrutiny.[61]

Antitrust concerns

While a thorough consideration of the implications of these mergers in an antitrust analysis is beyond the scope of this discussion, it is important to understand the government's interests and intent in prohibiting anticompetitive conduct in the health care market. It is under "a very narrow body of federal antitrust law[s]"[62] that the government may challenge the anticompetitive aspects of existing and proposed mergers. The Sherman Act,[63] the Clayton Act and its amendments,[64] the Federal Trade Commission Act,[65] and the Hart-Scott-Rodino Antitrust Improvements Act[66] provide the government with the authority to preserve the "competitive vitality" of the hospital-care industry.[67] To prevent an anticompetitive outcome, the government can disallow a pro-

---

57. *See id.* (citing Sandy Lutz, The Question: Who's in Columbia/HCA's Sights?, Mod. Health-care, Jan. 2, 1995, at 36).

58. *See id.* at 717 (citing Alex Pham, Harshbarger Seeks Power to Regulate For-Profit Health Care, Boston Globe, Nov. 8, 1995, at 50).

59. *See id.* at 717–18.

60. *Id.* at 719.

61. Michael D. Belsley, The Vatican Merger Defense: Should Two Catholic Hospitals Seeking to Merge be Considered a Single Entity for Purposes of Antitrust Merger Analysis?, 90 Nw. U. L. Rev. 720, 729 (1996).

62. *Id.* at 730.

63. 15 U.S.C. §§ 1–7 (1994).

64. 15 U.S.C. §§ 12, 13, 14–19, 20, 21, 22–27 (1994).

65. 15 U.S.C. §§ 41–77 (1994 & Supp. IV 1998).

66. 15 U.S.C. §§ 15c to 15h, 18a, 66 (1994).

67. Belsley *supra* note 61, at 744.

posed merger or force the entities involved to restructure the merger to maintain a level of competition in the relevant market.

When health care institutions seek to merge, they often attempt to establish that the merger will benefit consumers by lowering prices for health services.[68] Critics, however, maintain that any such benefit is realized only by those patients who obtain health care services from managed-care organizations or from coalitions that have enhanced their bargaining positions as a result of enhanced power.[69]

Tax Concerns

Not-for-profit institutions are granted tax-exempt status under section 501(c)(3) of the Internal Revenue Code by maintaining their charitable purposes.[70] A primary requirement is the prohibition on private inurement. In no case can earnings of the tax-exempt entity be paid out to private persons as dividend, profit sharing, or in any other disguised form of profit. Moreover, section 501(c)(3) classification subjects not-for-profit entities to aspects of the charitable trust laws.[71] These laws, in effect in many states, require that before a nonprofit sells its assets it must file an application with the appropriate court to change its fundamental purpose in order to become a for-profit entity.[72] Should a nonprofit proceed with conversion without adhering to the established procedural requirements, the state court may prohibit the transaction altogether through an injunction while holding the board of directors liable for breach of their fiduciary duty.[73] Although an individual does not have standing to challenge the sale of the nonprofit's assets, states' attorneys general, as representatives of the public's interests, are automatically made a party to any suit relating to conversions.[74]

The Internal Revenue Code and other federal laws require that all proceeds from the sale of a nonprofit hospital must be used for a charitable purpose.[75] Many states follow the doctrine of *cy pres*, a common law theory requiring that the proceeds of the sale of a nonprofit entity be used for a purpose as close as possible to the original charitable purpose of the organization.[76] This doctrine allows states to protect funds donated to charitable institutions from being diverted from their charitable purpose, and assures donors that these funds will continue to serve the purpose they originally intended.[77]

---

68. *See* William M. Stelwagon, Note, Does a Healthy Patient Need a Cure? A Response to Health Care Industry Proposals to Reform Analysis of Horizontal Hospital Mergers, 69 St. John's L. Rev. 553, 575 (1995).

69. *See id.*

70. *See* Rothouse, *supra* note 48.

71. *See id.*

72. *See id.*

73. *See id.* (citing Robert A. Boisture & Douglas N. Varley for Volunteer Trustees Foundation for Research and Education, State Attorneys General's Legal Authority To Police The Sale Of Nonprofit Hospitals and HMOs, Washington D.C., Sept. 19, 1995).

74. *See id.*; Hospital Conversion Spur States to Examine Community Benefit Issues, Health Care Pol'y Rep. (BNA) 666, 667 (Apr. 20, 1998) [hereinafter "BNA"].

75. *See* Rothouse, *supra* note 48; Volunteer Trustees, *supra* note 2.

76. *See* Volunteer Trustees, *supra* note 2; BNA, *supra* note 74, at 667.

77. *See* Volunteer Trustees, *supra* note 2.

If the nonprofit hospital seeks to maintain its charitable status after transferring all of its assets in a merger with a for-profit company, the contractual arrangement of the two parties must grant the not-for-profit entity the ability to pursue its exempt purpose and act "only incidentally for the benefit of for-profit partners."[78] For the newly integrated entity, formed by the integration of the not-for-profit and for-profit entities, to remain a 501(c)(3) organization, the nonprofit entity involved must maintain voting control over the integrated entity and its board must maintain specifically enumerated powers over program changes, disposition of assets, and any management agreement.[79]

On the other hand, if the board of the not-for-profit component of the new entity simply shares power with the board of the for-profit enterprise, the charitable purpose may be thwarted and the tax-exempt status lost. For example, if the nonprofit and for-profit components making up the new entity simply share voting control, the nonprofit component may lack the voting power to initiate community-oriented programs without the agreement of at least one governing board member appointed by the for-profit entity.[80] Further, without the nonprofit component maintaining voting control, a simple majority of the new entity's board may vote, without the possibility of effective opposition, to pursue activities resulting in a benefit to private interests. Such an arrangement cannot claim to be effectively devoted to the exclusive pursuit of exempt purposes and, therefore, cannot claim tax-exempt status.

State and Federal Legislative Overview

The large number of not-for-profit health care providers seeking court approval to either join or become for-profit entities has resulted in a similarly large number of state court proceedings. In an effort to facilitate an orderly basis for transformation or integration, many states have enacted legislation establishing procedures for converting not-for-profit entities.[81]

In December 1997, the United States General Accounting Office (GAO) reported on the effect of fourteen nonprofit hospital conversions in six states including Alabama, California, Louisiana, South Carolina, Tennessee, and Virginia.[82] In discussing the similarities among the conversions, the report noted that the net proceeds of twelve of the transactions went directly to charitable foundations, and that community response to

---

78. Catholic Health Association, Public Policy, http://www.chausa.org.

79. *See id.*

80. *See* Rothouse, *supra* note 48. Within two legislative sessions, the number of states introducing such legislation more than doubled from fifteen states in 1996 to thirty-five states and the District of Columbia in 1997. In 1997, of the thirty-five states that introduced such legislation, "50 measures moved from their chamber of introduction and 35 measures were enacted." *See id.* The 1998 legislative session may have had fewer states initiating legislation on the conversion issue, but more than thirty-two states were involved in what amounted to the introduction of eighty-five bills. The states introducing legislation were: Alabama, Arizona, California, Colorado, Florida, Georgia, Hawaii, Idaho, Indiana, Iowa, Kansas, Kentucky, Massachusetts, Maryland, Michigan, Minnesota, Missouri, Nebraska, New Hampshire, New Jersey, New Mexico, New York, Ohio, Oklahoma, Pennsylvania, Rhode Island, South Carolina, Tennessee, Vermont, Virginia, Washington, and Wisconsin. *See id.*

81. *See id.*

82. U.S. General Accounting Office, Not-For-Profit Hospitals: Conversion Issues Prompt Increased State Oversight, GAO/HEHS-98-24 (Dec. 1997).

proposed use of the proceeds was obtained through public hearings in six of the four-teen conversions.[83] The GAO report also included information about measures taken to grant attorneys general "the authority to oversee the transactions in a majority of the conversions...[and] the role[s] of the Internal Revenue Service (IRS), the Federal Trade Commission and the Department of Justice."[84]

In 1998, the IRS issued a ruling relating to transactions involving not-for-profit hospitals and for-profit entities.[85] The ruling focused on two examples of such transactions and established the basis on which a transaction may be designed to allow a nonprofit hospital to maintain its 501(c)(3) tax-exempt status.[86] According to the IRS guidelines, when a nonprofit hospital enters into a venture with a for-profit entity it must maintain control over the new venture, which in turn must give priority to the health needs of the community rather than to maximizing profits. A process prioritizing community needs can be established in the governing documents of the venture. The underlying as-sumption is that if the governing documents do not specifically oblige the health care provider to serve "charitable purposes or otherwise provide its services to the commu-nity as a whole," the provider then would be able to turn away patients and stop provid-ing health care services to the community.[87]

Legislation adopted by state and federal governments has focused on certain key is-sues, namely: (1) ensuring that patients, particularly those with limited resources or without insurance, still have access to nonprofit hospitals after their integration with for-profit entities; (2) disclosing the terms of sale of nonprofit hospitals to for-profit en-tities in order to determine any potential conflicts of interest and ensure that the com-munities' needs for patient care will continue to be met; (3) determining how to estab-lish the value of the nonprofit hospital before it is converted into a for-profit hospital; and (4) avoiding any conflicts of interest with the nonprofit hospital's board of directors and those in control of the acquiring entity both during and after the conversion.[88]

Since a nonprofit hospital's primary purpose is to serve its community, the issue of maintaining access to health care is an important concern confronting any nonprofit hospital that contemplates conversion into a for-profit entity or integration with a for-profit institution or system. Nonprofit hospitals are often the only places where people who otherwise could not afford medical attention can go to obtain needed health care. To ensure that communities do not lose such important facilities, nonprofit hospitals considering integration with for-profit entities increasingly are being required to assure communities of their intent to use the proceeds from any sale for the community's ben-efit, or to guarantee that health care services will continue to be available to needy pa-tients. Thus, in any conversion process, a religiously affiliated nonprofit health care provider will be required to ensure that the converted entity will maintain access to charity care for that population of needy patients that it has served in the past.

---

83. *See id.*

84. Internal Revenue Service, Rev. Rul. 98-15, 1998-12, 6, March 4, 1998. *See also* Deanna Bel-land, Charity's Tax Status in Doubt, Mod. Healthcare, May 11, 1998, at 4.

85. Internal Revenue Service, Rev. Ruling 98-12, 6, March 4, 1998. (Rev.-Rul. 98 FED ¶ 46, 321, Exempt Organizations: Hospitals: Exempt Status: Partnership's with for-profit corporation: Exempt purpose) *See* Belland, *supra* note 84, at 4.

86. *See* note 80, *supra*.

87. Marla Rothouse, Change in Nonprofit Entities, Issue Brief, May 1, 1998, at http://www.hpts.org citing Internal Revenue Service Ruling 98-15, 1998-12, 6, March 4, 1998.

88. *See* Rothouse, *supra* note 87, discussing National Association of Attorneys General, Pro-posed Model Healthcare Conversion Guidelines, March 2, 1998.

While transactions involving two for-profit entities are subject to securities regulation and other reporting requirements, not all the details of nonprofit conversions are made available to the public. By the time the community is made aware of a conversion, it is often too late for it to protect itself from any potential conflicts of interest or limitations on access to medical care. Increasingly there is concern that individuals responsible for monitoring religiously affiliated nonprofit institutions may fail to exercise proper oversight, or that they may even become involved in conflicts of interest when offered the prospect of purchase by or integration with a powerful and financially successful for-profit entity. Although the IRS is vigilant on the issue of private inurement, the lack of public reporting makes it almost impossible for the community to monitor whether officers or directors of nonprofit hospitals have been compensated for recommending a sale, and it is difficult to ensure that charitable assets are not being wasted or undervalued.[89] While the reasons for secrecy are unclear, many for-profit entities involved in these conversion transactions admit that full disclosure of the terms of the sale would likely impede competitiveness.[90]

Since the terms of nonprofit hospital conversions are often kept secret, determining the accurate fair-market value of the nonprofit hospital's charitable assets can be a difficult task. Upon conversion of a nonprofit hospital, the full and fair value of the hospital should be obtained from the purchasing entity with the proceeds being used in a charitable enterprise with a similar purpose.[91] Value can be determined by examining either the current or the projected value of the hospital. Current valuation of a hospital, however, often results in undervaluation because many of the hospital's greatest assets (education, teaching, research, intensive-care units, neonatal units, etc.) do not necessarily produce a profit, but these are much-needed activities in the community.[92] Likewise, basing valuation on a hospital's potential to earn money can also underestimate its actual value to the community, which is often much higher than its estimated monetary worth. While directors of nonprofit healthcare providers are held to strict responsibility on the basis of their fiduciary duty, matters involving transactions that can be viewed as corporate decisions are subject to the less demanding business judgment rule.

The nonprofit hospital's value to the community is also difficult to determine because the evaluation primarily will consider the hospital as a for-profit entity and give little consideration to the specialty units and other community-focused programs that usually do not earn a profit. Because projected valuations can vary widely, independent experts should be required to provide "valuation reports" which the nonprofit's board of directors should review thoroughly.

The board of directors of a religiously affiliated not-for-profit hospital must also avoid any conflicts of interest involving a conversion to or integration with a for-profit entity. A potential conflict arises when such directors are offered financial payments or future employment contracts by the for-profit entity as incentives for recommending that the transaction take place.[93] Both federal and state laws prohibit any person from profiting from the operation or sale of a nonprofit hospital. These laws are necessarily broad in scope to allow both federal and state governments the authority to enforce the directors' fiduciary duty to both nonprofit and for-profit hospitals. This duty is predi-

---

89. *See id.*
90. *See id.*
91. *See* Rothouse, *supra* note 48.
92. *See id.*
93. *See id.*

cated on the notion that the directors of an organization caring for the community must act in the best interest of that organization.[94] In reviewing challenges to director's acquiesence in these transactions, courts generally adhere to the "business judgement rule," which grants the directors of both nonprofit and for-profit health care facilities the authority to make decisions on behalf of the facility, assuming they inform themselves of the implications of such decisions and believe in good faith that they are in the facility's best interests.

The business judgment rule does not, however, grant directors unbridled power to act on behalf of the health care entity. Rather, this rule requires them to act as any "ordinarily prudent person" would in a comparable situation. Thus, when considering a transaction like a sale, conversion, or integration, directors must follow certain procedures including (1) determining that the officers or advisers on whom they rely for information about the transaction do not have any conflict of interest that might color their judgment, (2) determining the value of the assets to be sold, and (3) duly considering ramifications of the transaction including any *cy pres* implications.[95]

Proposed legislation and guidelines

With an increasing trend toward hospital conversions in recent years, many grassroots, public interest, and governmental organizations have drafted model legislation and guidelines to provide a basis for public and governmental scrutiny. The Volunteer Trustees, Families USA, the American Hospital Association (AHA), and the American Medical Association have all published model legislation or guidelines addressing the issue of hospital conversions.[96] Also, the National Association of Attorneys General has promulgated a draft of model legislation on the subject of health care conversions and integration.[97]

The Volunteer Trustees established guidelines for use by state regulators monitoring nonprofit hospital sales to or joint ventures with for-profit enterprises.[98] These guidelines involving application of charitable trust law doctrines focus on three objectives toward which state regulators should aim, including: safeguarding the value of charitable assets, safeguarding the community from loss of essential health care services, and ensuring that the proceeds of the sale are used for appropriate charitable purposes.[99]

In 1997, the AHA, a professional organization, published guidelines relating to actions that hospitals should take when considering or undergoing a conversion.[100] Although these guidelines are not mandatory for members, the AHA strongly recom-

---

94. *See id.*
95. *See id.* Should a *cy pres* proceeding be required, the "directors of a nonprofit hospital would also have to establish that '(a) it has become impossible, or at least impracticable, to accomplish the stated purpose of the hospital, and (b) the proposed alternative use of the charitable assets comes as close as present circumstances permit to fulfilling the original intent of the donor.'" *Id.* (citing Volunteer Trustees, *supra* note 2, at 5–7, 11–13).
96. *See* Rothouse, *supra* note 48.
97. *See id.;* BNA, *supra* note 74, at 667.
98. *See* Rothouse, *supra* note 48.
99. *See id.* (citing Volunteer Trustees Found. for Research and Educ. Proposed Guidelines for State Regulators' Oversight of Sale and Joint Venture Transactions in Which the Assets of Nonprofit Hospitals or HMOs are Transferred to For-Profit Enterprises (1995)).
100. *See* Rothouse, *supra* note 48.

mends that all hospitals follow them when altering any aspect of their nonprofit status. Specifically, the guidelines recommend (1) responsibility for care of the underserved in the community, and maintenance of essential community services; (2) identification of options available to the organization and awareness of any legal or operational limitations; (3) protection of charitable assets; (4) identification of conflicts of interest; (5) prevention of any private inurement or personal financial gain by employees or trustees of any not-for-profit entity involved in the transaction; and (6) education of constituencies, including medical staff, employees and the community, about the proposed changes.[101]

The National Association of Attorneys Generals' (NAAG) proposed model legislation focuses on making conversion transactions subject to public view, thus providing an opportunity for comment and criticism.[102] This proposed legislation focuses on (1) stringent requirements regarding notification to the state's attorney general about proposed conversions; (2) need for the court or attorney general to approve the conversion; (3) requirement that financial and other aspects of the conversion meet the standards set by state public records laws; (4) inclusion of public hearings, outside experts, community assessments, penalties and remedies; and (5) provision of adequate access to care.[103]

The Special Case of Integration Involving a Roman Catholic-Sponsored Hospital

Many of the entities in the United States which are referred to as "Catholic hospitals" are organized in the following manner: A religious congregation formed under the auspices of and recognized by the Roman Catholic church sets up a tax-exempt corporation. Often the exemption is obtained by registration in the Official Catholic Directory (this procedure is recognized by the IRS for the establishment of exemption for Catholic hospitals and some other specific Catholic health care corporations). This tax-exempt corporation may either hold title to real estate, the Medicare/Medicaid provider numbers, and the State Board of Health Licenses of Hospitals, or it may be the member of several separate tax-exempt organizations holding the title to the real estate license and provider numbers of each individual hospital. In either case, it is evident that the control of the property relates back directly to the religious order ("Religious Institute") that is under the direction of the Roman Catholic church.

Under canon law, when a "juridic person" (this would include the religious orders that control hospital property) seeks to make an alienation of property of value more than $3 million, approval of the Holy See is required. Alienation is defined as: "[E]ither the conveyance to another party or the encumbrance or placing in jeopardy of any interest in stable patrimony [immovable goods or fixed capital]."[104] While the definition is

---

101. *See id.* (citing Press Release from American Hospital Association, AHA Board Approves Guidelines for Shifts in Hospital Ownership, July 29, 1997).

102. *See id.*; BNA, *supra* note 74, at 667.

103. *Id.* (discussing National Association of Attorneys General, Proposed Model Healthcare Conversion Guidelines, Mar. 31, 1998).

104. Adam J. Maidia & Nicolas P. Cafardi, Church Property, Church Finances, and Church Related Corporations: A Canon Law Handbook, 302 (The Catholic Health Ass'n, St. Louis, Mo., 1984).

not familiar in civil law, it clearly covers the transfer of assets of a hospital held by Catholic organizations for religious and charitable purposes.

It is important to understand that canonists have stated that for a public juridic person to receive property from a church-affiliated entity without alienation occurring, the transferring entity should maintain certain reserved powers. The major reserve powers recognized by canonists are usually considered to include the powers (1) to establish or change the philosophy and mission of the work; (2) to change the corporate documents and by-laws; (3) to adopt "and remove" the board of directors, and the CEO; (4) to lease, sell, or encumber corporate real estate; (5) to contract debts; and (6) to establish subsidiary corporations, as well as possibly (7) to approve capital or operating budgets, or both; (8) to appoint the auditor; (9) to be involved in mergers, closures, etc., affecting the property or the work; and (10) to engage in activities that would entail risk of losing "Catholic identity."[105]

So long as these reserve powers are retained by the newly constituted entity, no alienation is considered to have taken place. The mission of the newly constituted health care provider is understood to remain under the direction or control of the sponsoring religious institute or order. This would not be the case with a simple merger between a Catholic facility and a non-Catholic one. The Catholic cosponsoring organization would maintain a proportionate dollar value of its interest in the resulting entity (that is, if it contributes fifty percent to the merger it would have fifty percent of control and the right to show such value on its accounting and bond documents). It would no longer, in this canon law view, be the sole possessor of the reserved powers. Therefore, there would be an alienation of the property.

In order to understand the dynamics that come into play in obtaining church approval of the merger of a Catholic sponsored hospital with a non-Catholic hospital, it is important to understand the procedure that needs to be followed. When a Catholic sponsor makes a request to the Holy See for permission to alienate property, it must submit the following documents:

(1) explanation of the just cause (Canon 1293, Section 1);

(2) written evaluation (Canon 1293, Section 1);

(3) notation as to how other precautions of particular law have been observed (Canon 1293, Section 2);

(4) consent of intermediate bodies and counsel, often in the form of minutes of the meeting;

(5) statement regarding divisible goods (Canon 1292, Section 3);

(6) offer to purchase, if possible (Canon 1293, Section 1);

(7) statement of what is to be done with the proceeds (Canon 1294, Section 2);

(8) sometimes, a statement regarding observance of the formalities of secular law (Canon 1296); and

(9) if the request is from a religious institute, a letter from the diocese bishop stating that he has no opposition to the proposed transfer.

When the property to be alienated—that is, the assets of the hospital or the hospitals—is located in more than one diocese, a statement of "no opposition" is required from each diocese involved. At that time the bishop or bishops can request an opinion from a canon lawyer that the alienation would be appropriate under canon law.

---

105. Francis G. Morrisey, CHA Canon Law Forum: Mergers and Joint Ventures, April 8, 1998.

Specifics to consider when seeking approval of alienation of property in order to merge a Catholic-sponsored hospital facility with a non-Catholic-sponsored facility

While the sponsor of a Catholic facility must be concerned about preservation of its mission and may face some difficulties in working with a non-Catholic facility, there are often strong economic circumstances leading to consideration of these mergers. In fact, in some circumstances the economic survival of the Catholic facility may be at stake. Often both institutions are tax-exempt corporations with a similar mission to provide health care to all persons, including Medicare/Medicaid recipients as well as the indigent. However, while the Catholic facility may be strongly committed to strict observance of the Ethical and Religious Directives ERDs promulgated by the National Council of Bishops, the secular institution may be equally committed to providing some services not be permitted by the ERDs. This discussion will use the provision of sterilization procedures as an example of such a service.

For many health care providers, sterilization by tubal ligation or vasectomy is simply an accepted form of care for individuals who desire to avoid pregnancy. The Roman Catholic church in the United States has been aware of this issue for more than twenty years as shown in the following two pronouncements:

National Conference of Catholic Bishops, "Sterilization in Catholic Hospitals," March 13, 1975

With regard to the administration of Catholic hospitals:

(1) The following is absolutely forbidden: cooperation, officially approved or admitted, in actions which of themselves (that is of their own nature and condition) have a contraceptive purpose, the impeding of the natural effects of the deliberate sexual acts of the person sterilized. For the official approval of direct sterilization and, all the more so, its administration and execution according to hospital regulations are something of its nature—that is, intrinsically—objectively evil. Nothing can justify a Catholic hospital cooperating in it. Any such cooperation would accord ill with the mission confided to such an institution and would be contrary to the essential proclamation and defense of the moral order.

(2) The traditional teaching on material cooperation, with its appropriate distinctions between necessary and freely given cooperation, proximate and remote cooperation, remains valid, to be applied very prudently when the case demands it.

(3) When applying the principle of material cooperation, as the case warrants it, scandal and the danger of creating misunderstanding must be carefully avoided with the help of suitable explanation of what is going on.

This sacred congregation hopes that the criteria outline in this document will meet the expectations of this episcopate, so that having removed the doubts of the faithful, they may more easily perform their pastoral duty.[106]

---

106. National Conference of Catholic Bishops, Sterilization in Catholic Hospitals, Mar. 13, 1975.

National Conference of Catholic Bishops, "Commentary on: Reply of the Sacred Congregation for the Doctrine of Faith on Sterilization in Catholic Hospitals," September 15, 1997

(1) As it was stated in the Roman document, the Catholic hospital can in no way approve the performance of any sterilization procedure that is directly contraceptive. Such contraceptive procedures include sterilizations performed as a means of preventing future pregnancy that one fears might aggravate a serious cardiac, renal, circulatory, or other disorder.

(2) The Catholic health facility has the moral responsibility (and this is legally recognized) to decide what medical procedures it will provide services for. Ordinarily, then, there will be no need or reason to provide services for objectively immoral procedures. Material cooperation will be justified only in situations where the hospital because of some kind of duress or pressure cannot reasonably exercise the autonomy it has (i.e., when it will do more harm than good).

(3) In judging the morality of cooperation, a clear distinction should be made between the reason for the sterilization and the reason for the cooperation. If the hospital cooperates because of the reason for the sterilization, e.g., because it is done for medical reasons, the cooperation can hardly be considered material. In other words, the hospital can hardly maintain under these circumstances that it does not approve sterilization done for medical reasons, and this would make cooperation formal. If the cooperation is to remain material, the reason for the cooperation must be something over and above the reason for the sterilization itself. Since, as mentioned above (#2), the hospital has authority over its own decisions, this should not happen with any frequency.

(4) As was stated in the Roman document, the Catholic health facility must take every precaution to avoid creating misunderstanding or causing scandal to its staff, patients, or general public by offering a proper explanation when necessary. It should be made clear that the hospital disapproves of direct sterilization and that material cooperation in no way implies approval.

Direct sterilization is a grave evil. The allowance of material cooperation in extraordinary cases is based on the danger of an even more serious evil, e.g., the closing of the hospital could be under certain circumstances a more serious evil.[107]

Each of these commentaries contains a general statement exemplifying the standards that are used in analyzing whether the proposed integration of a Catholic and non-Catholic facility creates a permissible or impermissible cooperation with a forbidden practice. In recent years, canonists have examined potential mergers between Catholic-sponsored hospitals and non-Catholic-sponsored hospitals which have engaged in activities prohibited by the ERDs. Canonists have used the standards set forth by the National Conference of Catholic Bishops to examine the nature of the cooperation between Catholic and non-Catholic facilities to determine whether the Catholic facility's intention creates a "formal" or "implicit formal" cooperation, both of which would be prohibited. Formal cooperation exists when the Catholic institution intends the wrongdoing (that is, it agrees with the activity). Implicit formal co-

---

107. National Conference of Catholic Bishops, Commentary On: Reply of the Sacred Congregation for the Doctrine of the Faith on Sterilization in Catholic Hospitals, Sept. 15, 1997.

operation exists when it denies agreement with the intention yet offers no other opposition to the prohibited activity.[108] If the canonist concludes that the latter is not the case, then he or she must seek to determine whether the Catholic facility is engaging in "immediate material" cooperation—that is, pursuing the same action as the wrongdoer even if for a different reason, as is permitted only if the facility is acting under duress.[109] If the action is not one of "immediate material" cooperation, then the canonist may seek to determine whether it is "mediate material" cooperation—that is, the facility is doing something clearly distinguishable from the wrongdoing, such as serving food to patients in a health care facility without awareness that forbidden procedures are being performed there. The canonist will also seek to determine whether the cooperation is proximate to the activity or merely remote, and whether it is contingent or necessary to another purpose, as in a Catholic facility engaging in a merger as the only means of continuing its existence in an area that would otherwise be deprived of a Catholic institution. In applying all of these standards, the canonist must next determine the level of scandal, or awareness of the forbidden practice, that would be created by the facility's cooperation leading others to believe the practice is permissible, and possibly becoming involved in such conduct themselves.

While not all canon lawyers will reach the same conclusions in their analysis of a specific proposed merger of a Catholic hospital with a non-Catholic hospital, many canonists view such a merger as occurring as a result of duress or necessity when the intention of the Catholic institution is to preserve a Catholic community presence that would not otherwise be possible, so long as the Catholic provider does not formally cooperate in actions that are impermissible under the ERDs. In such an arrangement, the Catholic hospital sees to it that such activities are "carved out of the transaction."

In examining "carve outs," it must be determined whether the Catholic facility is participating in (1) governance (that is, controlling and supervising the operation), in (2) management (by supplying the personnel that are providing the service), and in (3) deriving revenue from the service.[110]

A "carve out" occurs when prohibited services are provided not within the integrated facilities, but in a newly established facility operated by the non-Catholic partner. For example, in a "carve out," sterilizations would be performed not in the merged facilities by the merged entity, but rather, outside of the merged facilities or in an area immediately adjacent to them which would be under the complete control of the non-Catholic facility's parent and separate from the operation of the merged company. The non-Catholic parent would supply and control all personnel, separately bill for all such services, and obtain all revenue resulting from provision of the service.

Even in such a proposed "carve out," it is necessary for the canonists to determine whether or not the activity of the Catholic facility would create scandal. In the "carve out" described above, one could state that the Catholics examining the merger would not be prone to consider the Catholic-sponsored health care provider as having sanctioned or approved the sterilization procedures because they would be performed exclusively in an adjacent area that does not bear the name of the Catholic facility, and because anyone receiving such services would be billed by the parent of the non-Catholic facility rather than by the newly merged entity.

---

108. *See* Rev. Dennis Bordour, CHA Canon Law Forum, Apr. 8–9, 1999.
109. *Id.*
110. *See id.*

General Discussion of Differences about Permissible Treatments among Religiously Affiliated Hospitals

Missions and values

Most religiously affiliated hospitals seek to be multifaceted institutions serving the objectives of their sponsoring organizations and the needs of their communities. The mission statements of these institutions often stress the importance of providing disease management and prevention, continuing patient and physician education, encouraging applied and clinical research, and improving the communities in which they serve. Although some also express a commitment to further the teachings of the particular sponsoring religious organization, most are limited to advocating the promotion of patients' spiritual well-being.

With the growth of managed care, most mission statements of health care organizations now include phraseology relating to providing treatment in the "most efficient, cost-effective manner possible."[111] Though some statements do not include this language explicitly, the interest in allocating resources fairly and efficiently is clearly implied.[112] The mission statements of most religiously-affiliated health care institutions usually include such language, and in fact only show their differences in reference to their commitments to a sponsoring religious organization.[113] These latter statements require adherence and implementation by the medical staff, employees, and management of the hospital.

As discussed above, integration and conversion of health care providers may have serious tax implications. The provision of certain medical services may, however, occasion some of the most serious conflicts affecting members of the communities served by these providers. Conflicts involving maintenance of religious integrity and the provision of access to certain medical services can often result in the elimination of options for some patients. Due to the various and constantly changing demographics of many communities, it is not possible to delineate the consequences of a specific merger without examining the community and health care institutions involved. It is possible within the

---

111. Mission Statement, Baptist Hospital, Nashville, Tenn. (available through Baptist Hospital's General Council's office).

112. For example, the mission statement of Glendale Adventist Medical Center in California states:

> Glendale Adventist Medical Center is caring people...
> Working together with our community to promote healing, health and wellness for the whole person.
> Committed to Servanthood as exemplified by the life of Christ.
> For our guests, this means that the management, medical staff and employees of Glendale Adventist Medical Center will:
> Place the needs of patients first,
> Respect and protect their rights,
> Allocate and use resources effectively for their benefit,
> Provide service with the highest level of competency and caring.

http://www.adventisthealthsocal.com.

113. For examples of mission statements, visit the following websites: http://www.njc.org/markethtml/NJCmre.html; http://www.sfhs.edu/mission.html; http://www.adventisthealthsocal.com/AHSC/1about.html.

scope of this discussion, however, to provide a limited examination of the extent to which various religious philosophies differ with regard to the provision of patient care or to specific medical treatments or practices.

It should be clear that economic pressures and demand for medical services have forced many nonprofit health care providers to seek out associations with other health care entities, whether they be nonprofit or for-profit institutions, in order to stay in business.[114] Although such consolidation of costs and sharing of resources and revenues often appears to have beneficial economic consequences for the community being served, it can also result in some medical services being limited or even eliminated.[115]

Reproductive health issues

When health care entities consider a merger, the provision of reproductive services can be a very controversial topic. Given the large numbers of Roman Catholic-affiliated health care providers, as described above, the teachings of the Catholic church often become an issue in any attempt to merge a Roman Catholic-affiliated entity (most often a hospital) with another health care provider.[116] The Ethical and Religious Directives for Health Care Services created by the National Conference of Catholic Bishops serve as a guide for bishops to follow in overseeing the operation of Catholic hospitals within their dioceses.[117] Although each bishop is encouraged to follow these directives, guidelines have had different interpretations and applications depending on the particular bishop or hospital board involved.[118] Differences among dioceses may reflect personal predilections of the officials involved, but more likely are a result of "geograph[ic], population and economic market realities."[119]

Since the directives are simply an attempt to "give moral direction to what [the bishops] see as an intensely moral enterprise," in many areas they are often vague, open to interpretation, or in need of a definition of terms.[120] On the issue of abortion and assisted suicide, the directives appear quite clear, but the document does not address fully such issues as the "morning-after pill," sterilization, or contraception.[121] The directives strictly forbid any action directly intended to terminate a pregnancy or destroy a viable fetus, because such action "infringes" on "natural" reproductive events.[122] This ban on "infringement" also appears to apply to reproductive-assistance measures, such as in-vitro fertilization, as well as to permanent or temporary contraceptive practices.[123]

---

114. See generally Jane Hochberg, Comment, The Sacred Heart Story: Hospital Mergers and Their Effects on Reproductive Rights, 75 Or. L. Rev. 945, 949 (1996).

115. See id.

116. See id.

117. See Carol Bayley, Address at the National Health Lawyers' Association Conference, Mergers and Acquisitions 2000: Tomorrow's Deals Today (Jan. 16, 1998).

118. See Hochberg, supra note 114, at 949.

119. Bayley supra note 117.

120. Id.

121. See id.

122. See Hochberg, supra note 114; U.S. Bishops' Meeting, Ethical and Religious Directives for Catholic Health Care Services 45 (1994) [hereinafter Religious Directives].

123. See Hochberg, supra note 114, at 951–55.

Under Jewish law, abortion or contraception may be used when required to protect the life of the mother.[124] According to Jewish medical ethicists, the actions taken for the protection of life may come at any time in the woman's lifetime. Thus, "before the fact, [women] must protect themselves by contraception or, after the fact [women may protect their lives] by abortion, because protection of [a mother's life] comes first."[125] Jewish law emphasizes *pikkuah nefesh*, the need to protect women "against any threat to their health before or after the event, and to give necessary healing at all times."[126] Unlike the Roman Catholic view, Judaism welcomes the option of in-vitro fertilization as an alternative way to fulfill the *mitzvah* of giving birth. According to the position taken by Jewish ethicists, reproductive technologies are merely a means to assist a couple in their roles as partners with the divine in creation of new life.[127] If needed, multi-fetal pregnancy reduction is permitted under Jewish law, but only when it maximizes the chances of survival for the mother and minimizes the risks to the other fetuses.[128]

The Lutheran Church, Missouri Synod takes a view comparable to that of Roman Catholics, holding that abortion is contrary to divine law and is an option only when necessary to save the life of the mother.[129] By contrast, the United Methodist Church and the Presbyterian Church do not prohibit the practice of abortion. The United Methodist Church recognizes a woman's rights to terminate pregnancy, and encourages and coordinates support for safeguarding the legal option of abortion.[130] The Presbyterian Church has not determined exactly when human life begins, and thus has been unable to give moral guidance on the issue of abortion, leaving the moral decision in the hands of each woman.[131] The Presbyterian Church suggests, however, that the decision to abort a fetus be the choice of last resort.

Right to die

Both the Roman Catholic church and the Evangelical Lutheran Church in America (ELCA) accept that patients have the right to refuse burdensome treatment when its benefits do not significantly outweigh the risks of further suffering.[132] Along similar lines, the ELCA does not require physicians and other health care providers to administer all available methods of medical treatment when they will not "contribute to an improvement in the patient's underlying condition or prevent death from that condi-

---

124. *See* Daniel Eisenberg, Abortion and Halacha, Institute for Jewish Medical Ethics, eisenber@oasis.rad.upenn.edu.

125. *Id.*

126. *Id.*

127. *See* Speech by Rabbi Dr. David Feldman, Symposium on Ethical Dilemmas Regarding HIV Patients and Care-givers, Nov. 27, 1994 at Touro Law Center, http://www.law.touro.edu/Publications.

128. *See* Daniel Eisenberg, Multifetal Pregnancy in Halacha, Institute for Jewish Medical Ethics, eisenber@oasis.rad.upenn.edu.

129. *See* Lutheran Church Missouri Synod, Frequently Asked Questions—Abortion, http://www.lcms.org/cic/abortion.html.

130. *See* Bible Believers' Resource Page, Methodist Church: The United Methodist Church and Abortion, http://www.tcsn.net/kcongron/kjcethd.htm.

131. *See* Presbyterians Pro-Life, Presbyterians and Abortion: A Look at Our Church's Past, http://www.ppl.org.lookpast.html.

132. *See* Evangelical Lutheran Church in America, A Message on…End-of-Life Decisions, http://www.elca.org/dcs/dying.html [hereinafter ELCA].

tion."[133] These churches, like the law courts, recognize the importance of patient autonomy over hospital and physician interests in the refusal of futile treatment.[134] It should be understood that even those religiously affiliated hospitals that have protocols prohibiting the withholding or withdrawal of treatment may be constrained in applying their policies when patients lawfully refuse treatment. For example, in *Bartling v. Superior Court*,[135] the California appellate court held that the right of a competent adult patient to refuse medical treatment is constitutionally guaranteed.[136] In order to preserve the patient's right to self-determination, the court stated that if a patient requests treatment or services contrary to the hospital's mission, the hospital may seek to transfer the patient to another health care facility willing to comply with the patient's desires.[137] However, if the transfer cannot occur immediately, the hospital must grant the patient or his/her agent the authority to refuse treatment.

Physician-assisted suicide

While only Oregon currently has legislation providing for physician-assisted suicide, this issue is likely to provide the basis for future conflicts between religiously affiliated providers and their patients if additional states follow the apparent suggestion of the United States Supreme Court and adopt legislation recognizing the practice.[138] As in the right-to-die issue, physician-assisted suicide may also require the balancing of patient autonomy with the rights of religiously affiliated heath care providers to determine which treatments and services are compatible with their beliefs and policies. Although many religions do not require the use of extraordinary measures to prolong a patient's life, most religions do "object to the active hastening of death."[139] The Roman Catholic church, for example, grants patients the right to refuse treatment when there is no hope for recovery, but it directly opposes all suicides no matter how extreme the patient's suffering.[140] It strictly prohibits patients from requesting physician-assisted suicide, and believes that no authority may "legitimately recommend or permit such action."[141] According to the Union of Orthodox Jewish Congregations of America, Jewish law forbids assisting in a suicide, even for a terminally ill patient, since such assistance is deemed to undermine the sanctity of human life.[142]

Many religions' views on assisted suicide correspond with the Catholic and Jewish teachings; for example, the ELCA believes physicians and other health care providers are obliged to relieve suffering through the "aggressive management of pain, even when

---

133. *Id.*

134. *See* Boozang, *supra* note 1, at 1461 n.168 (discussing Religious Directives, *supra* note 122; American Dietetic Association, Position of the American Dietetic Association: Legal and Ethical Issues in Feeding Permanently Unconscious Patients, http://www.eatright.org/alegal.html.

135. 209 Cal. Rptr. 220 (Ct. App.1984).

136. *See* Boozang, *supra* note 1, at 1456 (citing *Bartling*, 209 Cal. Rptr. at 225).

137. *See Bartling*, 209 Cal. Rptr. at 220.

138. Washington v. Glucksberg, 521 U.S. 702 (1997), and Vacco v. Quill, 521 U.S. 793 (1997).

139. Boozang, *supra* note 1, at 1463.

140. *See* American Dietetic Association, *supra* note 134 (citing Committee for Prolife Activities, National Conference of Catholic Bishops, Nutrition and Hydration: Moral and Pastoral Reflections, No. 516-X (1992)).

141. Administrative Committee National Conference of Catholic Bishops, Euthanasia, http://www.euthanasia.com/bishops/html.

142. *See id.*

it may result in an earlier death."[143] However, the ELCA prohibits any "deliberate action of a physician to take the life of a patient, even when this is the patient's wish."[144]

Organ donation and transplantation

Although many religions have not discouraged organ donation, most faiths maintain it is a matter of personal choice.[145] Even so, it should be noted that less than ten percent of Americans are aware that their religions clearly encourage the practice and even urge it.[146]

For example, the Catholic church takes the position that dead bodies should always be treated respectfully; for many years it discouraged the practice of cremation.[147] However, current Roman Catholic doctrine views organ donation as "meritorious."[148] Catholics view organ donation as an act of charity, fraternal love, and self-sacrifice, and regard transplants as morally and ethically acceptable. Similarly, the Jewish faith believes people are "partners with God in creating and maintaining life. What is ordinarily problematic and prohibited not only becomes permissible, it's encouraged." Thus, Judaism teaches that if needed to save or maintain life, a dead body should be harvested for any usable organs.[149] Judaism teaches that saving a human life takes precedence over maintaining the sanctity of the human body.

Like Catholicism and Judaism, most religions support organ donation and transplantation.[150] Members of the Amish community will consent to transplantation if it is for the health and welfare of the recipient. Buddhists treat organ donation as a matter of individual conscience. Hindus are not prohibited by religious law from donating. Muslims were formerly barred by the Moslem Religious Council from receiving donated organs, but the council has recently ruled that transplantations may be allowed as long as donors provide consent in advance. Jehovah's Witnesses do not encourage organ donation, but neither do they strictly forbid it so long as all organs and tissue are completely drained of blood before transplantation. Most Protestant sects encourage and endorse organ donation, so long as those procuring organ donation give proper respect to the potential donor's conscience and the right to make decisions regarding his or her own body.

Religious Beliefs and Provision of Health Care Services

Issues involving organ donation and transplantation, women's reproductive health, the right to die, and physician-assisted suicide are examples of the potential clash be-

143. ELCA, *supra* note 132.
144. *Id.*
145. *See* Bill Briggs, Church Organs, Denver Post, Nov. 16, 1997, at F01.
146. *See id.* (discussing the results of a 1997 Gallup poll).
147. *See id.*
148. *Id.*
149. *See id.*
150. *Id.*

tween patient demand for medical services and the restrictions on providing them that arise in religiously affiliated health institutions.[151] These conflicts become more complex in mergers between nonprofit and for-profit entities, or between nonprofit hospitals with different religious affiliations. To ensure patient access to quality health care services, religious institutions seeking to merge or convert will increasingly need to strike a balance between patient demands for specific services and the rules of sponsoring religious institutions that prohibit such services. One commentator has stated the bottom line in this area: "To the extent...religious health providers see no possibility of compromise, they must either seek an exemption from civil authorities or withdraw from their health care ministry."[152]

Actions taken by a religiously affiliated health care provider, whether to provide or not provide certain services, directly affect patient care and autonomy in medical decision making. Limiting the options available to patients implicates not only their philosophical notions of autonomy and personal choice, but also their common law right to informed consent.

Religiously affiliated hospitals and their sponsoring organizations must determine the extent to which they are "morally able to compromise" their philosophical positions in order to adapt to the evolving health care market through the process of integration with other providers or participation in managed-care plans.[153] In addition, health care policy makers and legislators must assess the extent to which the health care system will accommodate the beliefs of the sectarian provider and the limits on services stipulated by those beliefs.[154] It is clear that all parties involved must work at providing health care that allows for access to the highest level of patient care while preserving the religious integrity of the sectarian providers.[155]

There is no simple approach to determining the terms of a merger between a religiously affiliated health care provider and another religiously affiliated, secular nonprofit, or for-profit entity. The merging parties must remain sensitive to the needs of the communities they serve. If the community mandates services that are disagreeable to either party, the parties should consider seeking different partners with which to merge. Certain practical commitments to the provision of specific services must be shared in order for the merger to be appropriate.[156]

The constant changes in the health care market will continue to make it increasingly difficult for health care organizations to accommodate both sectarian and secular interests.[157] As the difficulties persist, conflicts will undoubtedly occur.[158] Many analysts and health care institutions remain hopeful that mergers or other similar transactions involving secular and sectarian facilities will "satisfy the competing needs of theology and economics."[159]

Regardless of the arrangement, it is important to remember that religious institutions seek to enter the health care market fundamentally to provide charitable care to

---

151. *See* Boozang, *supra* note 1, at 1474.
152. *Id.* at 1475.
153. *Id.* at 1441.
154. *See id.*
155. *See id.*
156. *See* Bayley, *supra* note 117.
157. *See* Boozang, *supra* note 1, at 1441.
158. *See id.*
159. *Id.* at 1440.

their communities. Religiously affiliated hospitals have contributed greatly to the success of our current health care system, and now they must explore ways in which they can continue providing their much-needed assistance in the new century.

Section V

Constitutional Coherence and the Legal Structures of American Churches

William P. Marshall

In his chapter "Religious Structures Under the Federal Constitution," Thomas C. Berg sets forth the current state of the constitutional law governing church structures. He notes that the state of the law is unsettled.[1] This observation is, of course, exactly correct.[2] Religion Clause doctrine has been marked by confusion and contradiction virtually from its inception.[3] After all, in what other area has the Supreme Court been forced to admit its own "internal inconsistence"[4] or explicitly concede that "it has sacrifice[d] clarity and predictability for flexibility"?[5]

This lack of stability in the constitutional law of the Religion Clauses should raise concerns for those interested in the legal issues surrounding church structures, since constitutional concerns lurk in the background of nearly every matter that affects the relationship of church and state. Some of the legal issues discussed in this book, for example, such as employment and intrachurch property-dispute resolution, already have a strong constitutional component. Other topics may give rise to constitutional concerns as doctrinal development proceeds.

Even the stated purpose of this volume—the development of a law of religious structures from the perspective of religious self-understanding—has constitutional overtones. James A. Serritella argues in his Prologue that "any civil law treatment of religion that does not respect [religion's] self-understanding is suspect and most likely flies in the face of our constitutional guarantees of religious freedom."[6] But the opposite

---

1. Thomas C. Berg, "Religious Structures Under the Federal Constitution," in this volume.
2. Berg is not alone in his appraisal of the lack of structure underlying Religion Clause doctrine. The condemnation of Religion Clause jurisprudence as confused and unpredictable is universal. *See, e.g.*, Kent Greenawalt, *Quo Vadis*: The Status and Prospects of "Tests" Under the Religion Clauses, 1995 Sup. Ct. Rev. 323 (the tests that the Court employs in its Religion Clause inquiries are in "total disarray").
3. *See, e.g.*, William P. Marshall, "We Know It When We See It," The Supreme Court and Establishment, 59 S. Cal. L. Rev. 495 (1986).
4. Walz v. Tax Comm'n, 397 U.S. 664, 668 (1970).
5. Committee for Public Educ. and Religious Liberty v. Regan, 444 U.S. 646, 662 (1980).
6. James A. Serritella, Prologue to this volume.

may be true as well; a civil law that defers too much to religion's self-understanding may also offend constitutional standards.

This chapter will not recapitulate Berg's excellent account of existing constitutional doctrine. It will, however, attempt to set forth some of the reasons underlying the doctrinal chaos that pervades the jurisprudence, and examine some constitutional concerns that may arise regarding efforts to develop a set of rules governing church structure that proceed from religion's self-understanding. The first part offers an introductory prologue—a short account of the first Supreme Court case that addressed religious freedom issues. The second part briefly reviews the doctrinal tumult that currently exists in the jurisprudence. The third part canvasses some of the tensions inherent in church/state issues. The fourth part discusses the merits and weaknesses of a "religious self-understanding" approach as it pertains to the constitutional issues implicated by the legal structures of American churches.

Terrett v. Taylor

The first Supreme Court case addressing church/state issues involved the legal structure of an American church. In 1801 the Virginia legislature attempted to assert title to property owned by the Episcopal Church. It based this attempt upon its understanding of religious freedom. As the state saw it, two of its previous statutes—one of which had incorporated the church and the other of which had granted the church title to the property—transgressed the appropriate boundaries of the relationship between church and state. Accordingly, the state believed it necessary to rescind those statutes and claim title.

The federal Supreme Court eventually came to the Episcopal Church's rescue in a case entitled *Terrett v. Taylor*.[7] In *Terrett*, Justice Story, writing for the Court, maintained that principles of religious freedom did not prohibit churches from receiving the benefits of state incorporation and property law. Rather, Story suggested that there was a wealth of state benefits that could be granted to churches without violating religious freedom. As he stated: "[T]he free exercise of religion cannot be justly deemed to be restrained, by aiding with equal attention the votaries of every sect to perform their own religious duties, or by establishing funds for the support of ministers [or] for the endowment of churches."[8]

As the first Supreme Court case on the subject, one might suppose that *Terrett* would have a major impact in framing freedom-of-religion issues. Despite its standing, however, *Terrett*'s precedential effect on freedom-of-religion issues has been limited at best. The decision did not interpret or discuss the First Amendment, and the actual basis of the Court's holding involved a matter wholly separate from religious freedom concerns. (The Court held that Virginia no longer exercised authority over the specific land in question because by 1801 the property had become a part of the District of Columbia.)[9] Nevertheless, important lessons may be learned from the *Terrett* decision. The first is that it shows there was no general consensus in the founding generation as to the rules

---

7. 13 U.S. (9 Cranch) 43 (1815).
8. *Id.* at 49.
9. *See id.* at 55.

of church and state. History does not provide clear guideposts as to how contemporary religious freedom issues are to be resolved.[10] As the first Supreme Court discussion of the subject, *Terrett* clearly has significance. But it is also of some consequence that the state—Virginia—most schooled on matters of church/state relations, and upon whose view of religious freedom the First Amendment was based,[11] believed that principles of religious freedom demanded that a state could not even so much as incorporate a religious body.

Second, the case reflects the wide range of legitimate disagreement that exists in the area of church/state relations. The theories of Justice Story and of the Virginia legislature appear to be diametrically opposed, yet both are based upon the common goal of fostering religious freedom. *Terrett* thus dramatically evinces that there is no obvious single mechanism for achieving this goal. It also demonstrates that the difficulties and contradictions that pervade church/state issues are not solely the function of the emergence of the modern secular state. The wide disparities in approaches to church/state issues stem not from recent innovations in modern constitutional law, but from the very beginning of the Republic.[12]

Third, the case illustrates the inevitability of church/state interaction. Churches may deal with non-temporal issues, but they exist in a temporal sphere. *Terrett* involved a church's title to real property—but as this book attests, the contacts between church and state are not limited to property issues, but concern a wide range of matters. The frequency of these contacts, moreover, is increasing. On the one side, the regulatory role of the state has of course expanded dramatically in the last century, and now governs everything affecting churches from charitable solicitations to historical preservation. At the same time, churches also have significantly broadened their range of activities: churches operate schools, offer countless varieties of social services, provide transportation, engage in social and political activism, and run commercial enterprises of every conceivable description. They hire employees, enter into contracts, own property, receive bequests, are injured by the negligent acts of others, and occasionally injure others by their own negligent acts. There are few areas of modern life in which churches do not participate, and few areas of law that do not potentially affect church activity. The challenge faced by the Virginia legislature and by Justice Story was to create a rule that furthered the values of religious freedom while accounting for the reality of the church's temporal presence. As the chapters in this book amply demonstrate, that challenge has not abated.

---

10. *See also* Carol Weisbrod, On Evidences and Intentions: The More Proof, the More Doubt, 18 Conn. L. Rev. 803 (1986).

11. *See* Everson v. Board of Educ., 330 U.S. 1 (1947). Two of the most important historical documents used as guides for interpreting the Religion Clauses-Thomas Jefferson's Bill of Establishing Religious Freedom and James Madison's Memorial and Remonstrance Against Religious Assessment-stem from the Virginia experience. *See* Thomas Jefferson, A Bill for Establishing Religious Freedom, in 2 The Papers of Thomas Jefferson 545 (Julian P. Boyd ed., 1950) and James Madison, Memorial and Remonstrance Against Religious Assessments, in 8 The Papers of James Madison 295 (Robert A. Rutland et al. eds. (1973)).

12. Actually, the historical debate runs even deeper. As Mark DeWolfe Howe has explained, there were two views of religious liberty that informed the founding generation. The first, associated with Thomas Jefferson, asserted that the state must be protected from the dominance and incursion of religion in order to assure individual liberty. The second, derived from Roger Williams, contended that religion must be separated from the state in order to protect religion. To Williams, a church dependent upon state favor "cannot be true to its better self." *See* Mark DeWolfe Howe, The Garden and the Wilderness 7–8 (1965).

The Current Doctrinal Quagmire

To any observer, Religion Clause doctrine does not appear to be in a healthy state. The Court's establishment test, originally set forth in *Lemon v. Kurtzman*,[13] has been under constant attack[14] and its current condition can, at best, only be described as seriously weakened.[15] The test is so anemic that in a recent case the Court took the unprecedented step of overruling a decision it had reached under *Lemon*,[16] doing so on the grounds that its original holding had been undercut by later cases.[17] The Court took this step, ironically, while adhering to *Lemon* as still providing the applicable law. Justice Scalia may then not be far off when he analogizes *Lemon* to "a ghoul in a late-night horror movie that repeatedly sits up in its grave and shuffles abroad, after being repeatedly killed and buried."[18]

Establishment Clause chaos, moreover, is not a new development. The Court's establishment approach, for example, has led it to conclude that there is a constitutional difference between the state providing tax deductions to the parents of parochial school children and the state providing tax credits to the parents of those children,[19] and that the constitutionality of state-sponsored nativity scenes at city halls depends on whether the displays are accompanied by secular symbols or are free-standing.[20] Similar distinctions pervade the jurisprudence.

The confusion may be traced to the first modern Establishment Clause case, *Everson v. Board of Education*.[21] In *Everson* the Court was faced with a constitutional challenge to a state program that provided bus transportation for children attending parochial schools at taxpayer expense. The Court's decision began with a rhetorical flourish.

> The 'establishment of religion' clause of the First Amendment means at least this: Neither a state nor the Federal Government can set up a church. Neither can pass laws which aid one religion, aid all religions, or prefer one religion over another.... No tax in any amount, large or small, can be levied to support

---

13. 403 U.S. 602 (1971). The *Lemon* test requires that in order to survive Establishment Clause scrutiny, a challenged enactment must (1) have a secular purpose, (2) have a primary effect that neither advances nor inhibits religion, and (3) not foster excessive government entanglement with religion.

14. *See* Ira C. Lupu, The Lingering Death of Separationism, 62 Geo. Wash. L. Rev. 230 (1994); Michael S. Paulsen, Lemon is Dead, 43 Case W. Res. L. Rev. 795 (1993); Timothy V. Franklin, Squeezing the Juice Out of the Lemon Test, 72 Educ. L. Rep. 1 (1992).

15. Kent Greenawalt states, for example, that "*Lemon* has ceased to operate as a general Establishment Clause test." Greenawalt, *supra* note 2, at 359.

16. *See* Aguilar v. Felton, 473 U.S. 402 (1985), *overruled by* Agostini v. Felton, 521 U.S. 203 (1997).

17. *See* Agostini v. Felton, 521 U.S. 203, 237 (1997).

18. Lamb's Chapel v. Center Moriches Union Free Sch. Dist., 508 U.S. 384, 398–99 (1993) (Scalia, J., dissenting).

19. The former, according to the Court, are permissible while the latter are not. *See* Mueller v. Allen, 463 U.S. 388 (1983) (upholding a tax deduction program for parochial school students); Committee for Public Education v. Nyquist, 413 U.S. 756 (1973) (striking down a tax credit for parents of parochial school students).

20. This distinction has been referred to as "the two-reindeer rule." Richard S. Myers, Reflections on the Teaching of Civic Virtue in the Public Schools, 74 U. Det. Mercy L. Rev. 63 (1996).

21. 330 U.S. 1 (1947).

any religious activities or institutions, whatever they may be called, or whatever form they may adopt to teach or practice religion. Neither a state nor the Federal Government can, openly or secretly, participate in the affairs of any religious organization or groups and vice versa. In the words of Jefferson, the clause against establishment of religion by law was intended to erect 'a wall of separation between Church and State.'[22]

This language notwithstanding, the Court upheld the state program, leading the dissenting Justice Jackson to conclude that the Court actions were similar to those of Byron's Julia who, in the act of not consenting, consented.[23]

The Free Exercise Clause has fared somewhat better in promoting consistent results; the Court has denied most free exercise challenges that it has faced. Nevertheless, free exercise jurisprudence has also had more than its fair share of tumult. In 1980, for example, the Court overruled its free exercise test and replaced it with an entirely different methodology.[24] In addition, even when the Court has not been refashioning standards, there has often been an incongruence between the test it has announced and the results that it has reached. For many years, the Court held that burdens on free exercise rights could be justified only if the state's actions were supported by a compelling state interest[25]—a test that, when applied in other contexts such as free speech, has virtually guaranteed that the constitutional claimant would prevail.[26] When the test was applied in free exercise cases, however, the Court found compelling interests in such relatively minor concerns as the government's administration of its tax laws[27] and its interest in uniform military dress.[28] The Court's abandonment of the compelling interest test, moreover, has not led to doctrinal clarity. As part of abandoning the test as applied to free exercise challenges, the Court held that religious exercise interests might be entitled to greater constitutional protection when presented as part of a "hybrid right" with another constitutional interest.[29] The notion that the constitution has "hybrid rights" is itself impenetrable, and the prediction of when such rights might be found is simply anyone's guess.[30]

---

22. *Id.* at 15–16.

23. *See id.* at 19 (Jackson, J., dissenting).

24. *See* Employment Div. v. Smith, 494 U.S. 872 (1990) (holding that the compelling interest test initially set forth in *Sherbert v. Verner*, 374 U.S. 398 (1963), would no longer be utilized in assessing free exercise challenges to neutrally applicable laws and would be replaced by minimal scrutiny except in cases involving "hybrid rights" and situations in which the state has in place a system of individualized exemptions and refuses to consider religious hardship as eligibility for the exemption).

25. *See Sherbert*, 374 U.S. at 398.

26. As Gerald Gunther has written, the application of a compelling interest test (or strict scrutiny) generally means that the review of the challenged provision will be "fatal in fact." Gerald Gunther, In Search of Evolving Doctrine on a Changing Court: A Model for a Newer Equal Protection, 86 Harv. L. Rev. 1, 8 (1972). *But see* Ashutosh Bhagwat, Hard Cases and the (D)Evolution of Constitutional Doctrine, 30 Conn. L. Rev. 961, 965 (1998) (arguing that strict scrutiny review has been significantly softened to the extent that, even under this heightened review, courts have been willing "to uphold governmental actions which impinge upon even central protections granted by the Constitution").

27. *See* United States v. Lee, 455 U.S. 252 (1982).

28. *See* Goldman v. Weinberger, 475 U.S. 503 (1986).

29. *See Smith*, 494 U.S. at 881–82.

30. For a telling critique of the concept of hybrid rights as used in *Smith*, see James D. Gordon III, Free Exercise on the Mountaintop, 79 Cal. L. Rev. 91, 98–99 (1991).

The Challenges to Constructing a Coherent Constitutional Approach to Issues of Church Structures

While it is easy to criticize Supreme Court doctrine, it nevertheless remains true that the challenges to constructing an intelligible Religion Clause jurisprudence pertaining to church structure are formidable. The area is beset by internal contradiction and paradox, and efforts to proceed in one direction invariably lead to problems raised by another. This section will briefly canvass some of these concerns.

Text

In understanding the dilemmas raised by Religion Clause analysis, one need begin only with the text. The First Amendment provides that "Congress shall make no law respecting an establishment of religion, or prohibiting the free exercise thereof."[31] Literally, this language may be read as simultaneously requiring that government must not favor religion (the Establishment Clause) and that it must provide special deference to religion (the Free Exercise Clause). The tension between the two clauses has been apparent in the case law. For example, in *Sherbert v. Verner* the Court held that the Free Exercise Clause required that a claimant for unemployment compensation could not be denied benefits because her religious commitment to resting on the sabbath made her unavailable for work.[32] According to the Court, the religious believer could not be forced to choose between forgoing the benefits for the sake of her religious beliefs and accepting employment that violated those beliefs. This result in *Sherbert*, however, as its dissent noted, is troubling for Establishment Clause reasons.[33] Taxpayers, in effect, were required by the holding to subsidize Mrs. Sherbert. As such, the decision presumably is antagonistic to Establishment Clause policies.[34]

The tension also works in reverse. Stringent application of the Establishment Clause may offend free exercise concerns. Numerous Establishment Clause decisions, for example, prevent aid to children attending parochial school—even though similar benefits are provided to students attending public schools. The Court's rationale underlying its parochial school decisions is consistent with antiestablishment policies—citizens should not be taxed to support the inculcation of religious beliefs.[35] However, the resulting regime arguably offends free exercise concerns. If the right to raise a child according to one's religious beliefs is constitutionally protected,[36] then parents should ar-

---

31. U.S. Const. amend. I.

32. *See* Sherbert v. Verner, 374 U.S. 398 (1963).

33. *See id.* at 418–23 (Harlan, J., dissenting).

34. The result in *Sherbert* was not overturned in *Smith*. The Court held that the compelling interest would continue to apply in cases such as those in which "the State has in place a system of individualized exemptions" and does not extend that system to cases of "religious hardship." *Smith*, 494 U.S. at 884.

35. *See* James Madison, Memorial and Remonstrance, *in* 2 Writings of James Madison, 183 (1900) *cited in Everson*, 330 U.S. at 12.

36. *See* Wisconsin v. Yoder, 406 U.S. 205 (1972). *Yoder* itself was left untouched by the *Smith* decision. According to the Court, the interest in raising a child according to one's religious beliefs was

guably not be forced to choose between sending their children to religious schools and foregoing state-provided benefits by sending their children to secular schools that do not further their religious mission.[37]

Definitional concerns

The need to define religion also compounds the difficulty of the constitutional enterprise. A jurisprudence that allows granting special benefits to religious organizations (whether the granting of those benefits is seen as a constitutional requirement or as a permissible statutory option) obviously would insert courts and administrative agencies into the business of defining religion in order to determine eligibility. But as many have noted, defining religion creates its own set of Religion Clause concerns.[38] There are free exercise issues if the religious claimant is improperly adjudicated to be nonreligious, and there are establishment concerns created by a court's or state's improperly granting or denying an "official" imprimatur of theological legitimacy.

Sincerity

Even when the definitional issues are clear, Religion Clause inquiries may raise problems because of the need to determine sincerity. This is especially true if a constitutional regime is created in which religious institutions are entitled to benefits (such as tax exemptions) not available to other entities. In such circumstances, the possibility is manifest that organizations may fraudulently attempt to claim religious status in order to qualify for the benefit.[39] Yet how are courts to resolve the sincerity issue?

The impossibility of the sincerity task is well illustrated by the Supreme Court's only foray into the subject in *United States v. Ballard*.[40] This case involved a federal prosecution for mail fraud against members of the so-called "I am" sect, which claimed that its leader, Guy Ballard, was a "divine messenger" from Saint Germain who had, "by reason of supernatural attainments, the power to heal persons of ailments and diseases" including those classified by the medical profession as incurable.[41] In reviewing the constitutionality of the jury charge offered at trial, the Court held that the First

---

a hybrid right between free exercise and substantive due process that continued to demand strict scrutiny.

37. *See* Michael W. McConnell, The Selective Funding Problem: Abortions and Religious Schools, 104 Harv. L. Rev. 989 (1991).

38. *E.g.*, Ira C. Lupu, Where Rights Begin: The Problem of Burdens on the Free Exercise of Religion, 102 Harv. L. Rev. 933, 953–60 (1989).

39. *See, e.g.,* Ecclesiastical Order of Ism of Am, Inc. v. Commissioner, 80 T.C. 833 (1983) (tax court denied exemption to organization on the ground that the purpose of the Ism of Am was nothing more than a commercial tax service devoted to counseling its local chapters on the tax benefits of religious tax exemptions), *aff'd*, 740 F.2d 967 (6th Cir. 1984); Hansen v. Commissioner, 820 F.2d 1464 (9th Cir. 1987) (Ninth Circuit upheld sanctions assessed against appellant when the two-person Church of Man gave a $300,000 award to appellant's wife for her devotion to the Church); Smith v. Commissioner, 800 F.2d 930 (9th Cir. 1986) (sanctions upheld as earnings from the Denali Universal Life Church were improperly used by appellants to pay off mortgages, car loans, and telephone bills).

40. 322 U.S. 78 (1944).

41. *Id.* at 80.

Amendment demanded that the jury could not decide that a fraud had occurred on the basis of its own disbelief in the truth of the defendants' religious claims. The Court reasoned that allowing judicial fact finders to engage in the determination of religious bona fides would threaten the abilities of persons to believe what they choose—no matter how implausible those beliefs may seem to others.[42] According to the Court, the trier of fact could find fraud only if it believed that the religious claims of the defendants were being made insincerely. The problem with this resolution, however, as Justice Jackson argued in dissent, is that sincerity is impossible to determine without some inquiry into believability.[43] *Ballard* means, in short, that the requisite claim of religious sincerity demanded by allocating benefits to a category based upon religious belief is unintelligible.

Cultural heritage

A fourth difficulty within Religion Clause jurisprudence is that Religion Clause policies often come into conflict with imbedded historical practices. When this occurs, the Court is placed in the unenviable position of having either to declare a traditional part of the culture unconstitutional or, in the alternative, to bend its rules to accommodate the challenged practice. Generally, these issues arise in relation to governmental practices that have religious vestiges, such as Sunday closing laws[44] or Christmas celebrations.[45] The Court's response to the establishment issues that arise in these cases reflects the intractability of the enterprise. The Court has dealt with such issues, for example, by suggesting that obviously religious practices have become "secularized"[46]—a conclusion that satisfies neither those within the particular religious tradition (because it demeans their religious faith)[47] nor those outside it (who find the practices a symbol of the second-class status of their own particular religion).[48]

The problem of historical acceptance may also arise in relation to issues affecting church structure. For example, in *Walz v. Tax Commission*[49] the Court was faced with a legislative measure that one might consider to be at the heart of the antiestablishment prohibition—namely, financial aid to religion in the form of a property tax exemption.[50] Understandably, however, the Court was reluctant to declare tax exemptions un-

---

42. *See id.* at 86–87.

43. *See id.* at 92–95 (Jackson, J., dissenting).

44. *See* McGowan v. Maryland, 366 U.S. 420 (1961).

45. *See* Lynch v. Donnelly, 465 U.S. 668 (1984); County of Allegheny v. ACLU, 492 U.S. 573 (1989).

46. *Lynch*, 465 U.S. at 685; *McGowan*, 366 U.S. at 448. The secularization claim was particularly hard to maintain in *McGowan* given the decidedly religious bent present in the statute itself, which described the Sunday law as being designed to not profane "the Lord's Day." *McGowan*, 366 U.S. at 448.

47. *See Lynch*, 465 U.S. at 727 (Blackmun, J., dissenting).

48. *See County of Allegheny*, 492 U.S. at 626 (O'Connor, J., concurring and dissenting).

In *Marsh v. Chambers*, 463 U.S. 783 (1983), the Court tried to have it both ways. At issue in *Marsh* was the constitutionality of a state-paid chaplain leading a prayer at the opening of the legislative session. The Court upheld the practice without applying constitutional doctrine at all. Rather, the Court simply concluded that because the practice of legislative prayer had been around in the First Congress, it should be found constitutional.

49. 397 U.S. 664 (1970).

50. *See id.* at 690–91 (Brennan, J., concurring).

constitutional considering their historical pedigree and the fact that such exemptions for religious institutions were present in all fifty states.[51] Accordingly, the exemption was upheld despite its being a subsidy.[52]

Religion as politics

The difficulty in fashioning a coherent Religion Clause jurisprudence also pertains to the political role that religion has in society. Sometimes this role is direct and explicit. Religion often gets directly involved in the public debate over issues of national importance. During the 1960s, for example, religion was extremely active in promoting racial equality and in opposing the war in Vietnam. More recently, it has been active in the pro-life movements and in efforts to oppose the death penalty.

Religion may also become involved in expressly partisan politics. Jesse Jackson, a minister, has sought the Democratic nomination for president of the United States.[53] Pat Robertson, also a minister, has in turn sought the Republican nomination.[54] Meanwhile organizations like the Christian Coalition have been actively involved in furthering the agenda of the Republican party, while many inner-city churches have promoted the electoral interests of the Democrats.[55]

Religion, in short, is not insular. Nor can it be. Religious values and beliefs compose an important part of the social fabric that underlies political choice. Religious belief and religious morality provide much of the background against which political decisions are made. Religion is also not static. Religious beliefs, like political beliefs, are often in the process of change and, like other types of value systems, are in competition with each other and with secular belief systems for the hearts and minds of adherents.[56]

The recognition of this activist side of religion compounds Religion Clause inquiry. On one hand it makes it problematic to favor religious belief, because to do so would empower religious principles vis-a-vis other forms of belief that compete for adherents in the marketplace of ideas. On the other, disenfranchising religion by means of Establishment Clause restrictions would weaken it relative to other types of ideology and therefore potentially distort the marketplace against religious beliefs.[57]

---

51. *See id.* at 685.

52. *See id.* at 695 (Harlan, J., concurring).

53. *See* Gaylord Shaw, Jackson Says He Will Seek '88 Nomination, L.A. Times, Sept. 8, 1987, at A1.

54. *See* Pat Robertson; Evangelist Joins Race in a Flurry of Petitions, N.Y. Times, Sept. 20, 1987, at D05.

55. *See* Randy Lee, When a King Speaks of God; When God Speaks to a King: Faith, Politics, and the Constitution in the Clinton Administration, 63 Law & Contemp. Probs. 391 (2000) (manuscript at 12–13, on file with author).

56. *See* Stephen J. Stein, Religion/Religions in the United States: Changing Perspectives and Prospects, 75 Ind. L.J. 37 (discussing the flourishing of multiple religions in the United States and the migration of believers between religious sects and denominations) (2000); *see also* Mary Rourke, Redefining Religion in America, L.A. Times, June 21, 1998, at A1 (reporting that at least fifty percent of people in America do not die in the religion in which they were born).

57. *See* Widmar v. Vincent, 454 U.S. 263 (1981) (holding that the government may not impermissibly disadvantage religious speech); Rosenberger v. Rector of Univ. of Va., 515 U.S. 819 (1995) (same).

Religion as economics

Constructing a Religion Clause jurisprudence is also troublesome because religion does not exist in an insular economic sphere. Consider, for example, the case of *Tony and Susan Alamo Foundation v. Secretary of Labor*.[58] In *Alamo* the Court was faced with a free exercise challenge to wage, overtime, and recordkeeping of provisions of the Fair Labor Standards Act. The Tony and Susan Alamo Foundation operated a number of commercial establishments and employed a number of its members in its operations. It reimbursed its employees by providing them with food, clothing, shelter, and other benefits rather than wages or cash salaries. This arrangement was apparently acceptable to the employees because the receipt of wages purportedly conflicted with their religious beliefs and the beliefs of the Alamo organization.

How should the Religion Clauses address this issue? On the one hand, it could be argued that "if members of the Alamo religious movement are inspired to work for the glory of God for long hours at no pay, their neighbors are not injured and the government has no legitimate right to intervene."[59] On the other, however, the claim of insularity cannot be easily maintained. First, the business competitors of the Alamo Foundation's enterprises would be unfavorably disadvantaged because of the foundation's reduced labor costs. Similarly, workers outside the foundation might be harmed by the resulting "downward pressure on wages in competing industries."[60] Finally, the society at large may be harmed if Alamo's workers need to seek medical or welfare assistance because of their own lack of financial resources. Religious organizations, in short, have pervasive economic impact on the rest of society. Accordingly, carving out a separate sphere of regulation for religious organizations may not be as easy as some might believe.[61]

Religion's Self-Understanding and Constitutional Law

The preceding section explains why the coherent development of Religion Clause doctrine has proved so elusive. There are tensions and contradictions inherent in the jurisprudence that inhibit the construction of a clear and linear doctrine. Creating a jurisprudence in which the legal structures of American churches were based solely upon religion's own self-understanding would not remove these conflicts. To begin with, it would not reach the problems raised by the presence of religious vestiges in our cultural heritage. Those issues, after all, depend upon cultural and not religious perspectives. The conclusion that Christmas has been secularized,[62] for example, is not the product of a religious point of view.

The self-understanding approach, moreover, if applied in other areas of Religion Clause tension, could exacerbate rather than alleviate constitutional concerns. *Alamo* is

---

58. 471 U.S. 290 (1985).

59. Michael W. McConnell, Free Exercise Revisionism and the Smith Decision, 57 U. Chi. L. Rev., 1109, 1145 (1990).

60. *Alamo Found.*, 471 U.S. at 299.

61. I have made this argument previously in William P. Marshall, In Defense of Smith and Free Exercise Revisionism, 58 U. Chi. L. Rev. 308, 314–15 (1991).

62. *See* Lynch v. Donnelly, 465 U.S. 668 (1984).

a case in point. As noted previously, in *Alamo* the self-understanding of the religious institution was that its adherents were engaging in the furtherance of a religious mission in their work in the foundation's enterprises. To the Tony and Susan Alamo Foundation, the resulting relationship was not that of an employer and employee, but that of a religious leader and follower. Yet, as the *Alamo* case attests, deferring to the religious institution's self-understanding would give religious structures unfair competitive advantages in the economic marketplace. Such a result, in addition to undercutting the purpose of the challenged regulatory provision, might also offend antiestablishment policies.[63]

Similar concerns would develop in other contexts. Churches that involve themselves in partisan political contests, for example, often construe their behavior as a part of their religious mission and not as political campaigning or candidate advocacy in the secular sense.[64] In these circumstances the church, according to its self-understanding, should not be subject to regulations, such as tax-exempt status limitations or campaign finance restrictions, that would otherwise apply to political activity. Exempting the religious organization from these requirements based on its self-understanding would, however, place it at a relative advantage vis-à-vis nonreligious organizations engaging in, or desiring to engage in, similar activities. The resulting favoring of religion in the political marketplace could raise substantial free speech, equal protection, and establishment concerns.[65]

Finally, even with respect to the definition and sincerity inquiries, relying on a religious institution's self-understanding is troublesome. Permitting organizations to define themselves as "religious" or as "sincere" would provide cover for fraud and abuse and debase the value and integrity of the meaning of "church" and of "religion."

Perhaps a constitutional regime that defers to religion could be constructed nevertheless. Carl H. Esbeck, for example, advocates such an approach in his chapter in this book.[66] As Esbeck notes, however, even this approach can create its own conflicts. This is because the religious understanding of the appropriate parameters of the relationship between church and state is also beset by opposing positions.

On the one side is the prophetic model, which counsels against a religious organization's acceptance of government aid. Under this model, religion should not allow itself to receive state aid because to do so would compromise the religious mission and foster an ill-advised dependence on government beneficence, processes, and regulations. On the other side is the priestly model, which posits that it is permissible for religion to accept state benefits to help further its worldly mission, and that fears of excessive state intrusion into religious affairs are unsubstantiated. Esbeck's solution is to allow the religious institution to follow whichever model it chooses. He would defer to the

---

63. *See* Estate of Thornton v. Caldor, Inc., 472 U.S. 703 (1985) (establishment violation found where challenged provision imposed hardship on third parties).

64. *See* Branch Ministries, Inc. v. Rossotti, 40 F. Supp. 2d 15 (D.D.C. 1999). The Branch Ministries Church sponsored a full-page advertisement in the Washington Times and USA Today four days prior to the 1992 presidential election, warning Christians not to vote for Bill Clinton. Citing Clinton's purported support of abortion, homosexuality, and condom distribution in public schools, the advertisement concluded that "Bill Clinton is promoting policies that are in rebellion to God's laws." *Id.* at 17.

65. *See* Texas Monthly, Inc. v. Bullock, 489 U.S. 1 (1989) (sales tax exemption for religious publications struck down because it favored those seeking to disseminate a religious message).

66. Carl H. Esbeck, "Regulation of Religious Organizations via Governmental Financial Assistance," in this volume.

self-understanding of the potential recipient in outlining the appropriate church/state boundaries for its own organization.[67]

Not acceptable to Esbeck, however, is a system in which the constitutional relationship between church and state is constructed upon a purportedly secular point of view which asserts that the purpose of constitutional protections is freedom *from* religion. As he states, "there are those who stand outside these [the prophetic and priestly] models and want no aid to religion—not because they care about church autonomy but because they care about freedom from religion, or because they are from that quarter of liberal modernity that rejects any public role for religion."[68] This view, according to Esbeck, should be discounted in favor of deference to the religious organizations' self-understanding. As he states, "If there must be losers, those unsympathetic to religious free exercise and church autonomy are appropriate candidates."[69]

Powerful arguments can be advanced in favor of the religion-deferential position. Religion is a supremely important aspect of human existence. It raises and responds to the most fundamental questions regarding the meaning of life and the limits of human understanding. Protecting the institutions that house religious belief and practice should therefore be of the highest constitutional priority.

Second, protecting religion is critical because it furthers pluralism. Religious institutions form intermediary institutions that shield the individual from government.[70] They foster a sense of community responsibility[71] and they enrich the culture. Supporting the institutions that further these values should not be controversial.

Third, religion often provides the conscience of the community and the society. Religion teaches that there are values beyond only the individual's self-interests and moral obligations beyond one's own self-fulfillment.[72] Religion fosters important understandings of right and wrong and good and evil. Accordingly, the institutions that address these fundamental and requisite aspects of human society should be entitled to stringent constitutional protection.

Fourth, religion provides solace to persons in their times of greatest need. Churches comfort grieving mourners, provide social services to the poor and disenfranchised, and offer a place to turn for those who feel spiritually desolate and alone. Accordingly, the value of religion in American life is immeasurable, and constructing a constitutional jurisprudence that fosters this value by especially protecting religion should seem entirely straightforward.

Straightforward, however, it is not. To begin with, many of the benefits noted above are not unique to religion. The fostering of human understanding, pluralism, community, morality, and comfort is not solely a religious enterprise. Each of these matters may be advanced by organizations and belief systems not based on religious views. Deference to religious organizations solely because of the role they play in promoting these values may therefore not be justified.

---

67. *Id.*
68. *Id.*
69. *Id.*
70. *See* Roberts v. United States Jaycees, 468 U.S. 609, 619 (1984); *see also* Frederick M. Gedicks, Toward a Constitutional Jurisprudence of Religious Group Rights, 1989 Wis. L. Rev. 99.
71. *See* Timothy Hall, Religion and Civic Virtue: A Justification of Free Exercise, 67 Tul. L. Rev. 87 (1992).
72. *See generally* Frank I. Michelman, The Supreme Court, 1985 Term: Foreword: Traces of Self-Government, 100 Harv. L. Rev. 4, 17–36 (1986).

But the more fundamental problem with a religion-deferential approach is that it treats religion as an unequivocal and undifferentiated force for good.[73] Religion, however, is far more complex. To begin with, it is not always an unequivocal force for good. It is often intolerant, despotic, and oppressive, and the recognition of this "dark side" of religion is at the core of our constitutional understanding. Thomas Jefferson, for example, understood that religion could be a source of "inextinguishable hatred"[74] as well as a source of truth.[75] James Madison, in turn, was well aware of religion's power to destroy, rather than foster, a sense of community.[76] The understanding of religion's complexity is what explains why the First Amendment has both the Free Exercise Clause and the Establishment Clause. Given world events,[77] this understanding is also pertinent to our approach to church/state issues today.

Religion is also not monolithic. It is composed of a multitude of sects and denominations that often stand in deep and abiding opposition to each other, competing for adherents and arguing over the truth of religious claims. Such division may lead to serious social upheaval and worse. Theological disputes are the frequent causes of wars, persecutions, and religious subjugation.

Religious divisions may also lead to lesser but equally serious harms. The original call by Madison and others to prohibit taxing the citizenry to promote religious establishments was based on the realistic appraisal that subsidized religion might use the provided monies to attack and demean the tenets and beliefs of other faiths.[78] It was not based upon the need to protect the government from religion.

The position of many who argue against aid to religion is not, as the religious apologists maintain, based upon a misguided preference for an antiseptic secularism. Nor is it based upon some ill-conceived view of the primacy of secular values. Rather, it is based upon the need to protect religion from religion—a fear that history and current events have established to be all too justified. A government that opens its doors too widely to religious influence is one that invites sectarian divisions and sectarian strife.

All of this, of course, does not mean that the rules governing the legal structures of American churches cannot, or should not, ever be informed by religious understanding. Nor does it mean, as the state of Virginia believed in *Terrett v. Taylor,* that the absolute division between church and state must be maintained at all costs. Rather, it suggests that the inquiry into the legal structures surrounding churches will allow no easy

---

73. Marci A. Hamilton, Religion and the Law in the Clinton Era: An Anti-Madisonian Legacy, 63 Law & Contemp. Probs. 359 (2000) (manuscript at 5, on file with author).

74. As Jefferson wrote, "I have never permitted [myself] to meditate a specific creed. These formulas have been the bane and ruin of the Christian church, which, through so many ages, made of Christendom a slaughter-house and at this day divides it into castes of inextinguishable hatred to one another." 15 The Writings of Thomas Jefferson 374 (A. Bergh ed., 1903) (letter to Reverend Thomas Whittemore).

75. Thomas Jefferson, A Bill For Establishing Religious Freedom, *supra*, note 11 (noting the importance of freedom of religion in the search for truth).

76. James Madison was equally distrustful of institutional religion. *See* Hamilton, *supra* note 73, at 361–3 (noting Madison's skeptical views towards organized religion); Arlin M. Adams & Charles J. Emmerich, A Nation Dedicated to Religious Liberty 25 (1990) (same).

77. Northern Ireland, Indonesia, the former Yugoslavia, the Middle East, and Northern India are but some examples. The United States also is not immune from religious hate and fanaticism. *See, e.g.,* Hamilton, *supra* note 73, at 389 (discussing the growth and proliferation of religiously-defined hate groups and militias in the United States); Kevin Sack, Hate Groups in U.S. Are Growing, N.Y. Times, Mar. 3, 1998, at A10.

78. *See Everson,* 330 U.S. at 12.

or unitary solution. The prophetic, priestly, and secular models of church/state relations all inform our understanding of the complex relationship between church and state. They all should be relied upon to inform our constitutional understanding.

The resulting constitutional law governing the legal structure of American churches is thus unlikely to become a model of clarity. The jurisprudence will remain besieged by conflicting policies and impulses. In the end, however, a constitutional law that properly takes into account all the competing forces in this great debate may be the one that best assures religious liberty.

Full and Free Exercise of Religion

Edward McGlynn Gaffney, Jr.

Can the exercise of religion be full and free? James Madison thought so. A full month before the birth of the American nation in Philadelphia in July of 1776, the Commonwealth of Virginia declared its independence from Great Britain and issued a Declaration of Rights proclaiming that all persons "are equally entitled to the full and free exercise of [religion] according to the dictates of Conscience."[1] The language is Madison's. As a delegate to the Virginia Convention, Madison urged an important revision of the draft prepared by George Mason. Where Mason had written the Lockean term "toleration,"[2] Madison argued for substituting the language cited above.

In the words of John Courtney Murray, intolerance can be a terrible vice, but toleration is not much of a virtue.[3] Toleration implies a tolerator putting up with a toleratee. Condescension of this sort quickly identifies the limits of toleration. Thus John Locke, the principal proponent of toleration in the late seventeenth century, was unwilling to extend it to Jews, Catholics, Muslims, or atheists.[4] The Act of Toleration[5] that Locke inspired acknowledged religious diversity to the extent of allowing dissenting Protestants to worship as they pleased, but it still retained the establishment of the Church of England and imposed civil penalties on nonmembers of that preferred community. Only Anglicans, for example, could hold political office.[6] And the act did not extend to Roman Catholics or non-Christians. Historian Thomas Curry notes that the

---

1. William T. Hutchinson and William M. E. Rachal, eds., 1 The Papers of James Madison 174 (1962). The texts of Mason's proposal and Madison's revision are reprinted in John T. Noonan, Jr., and Edward McGlynn Gaffney, Jr., Religious Freedom: History, Cases, and Other Materials on the Interaction of Religion and Government 162–63 (2001); for a discussion of this event, see John T. Noonan, Jr., The Lustre of Our Country: The American Experience of Religious Freedom 67–70 (1998).

2. *See* John Locke, A Letter Concerning Toleration (1688), *reprinted in* Noonan and Gaffney, Religious Freedom, *supra* note 1, at 137–55.

3. Cited in Noonan and Gaffney, Religious Freedom, *supra* note 1, at xix.

4. John Locke, A Letter Concerning Toleration (1688), *reprinted in* Noonan and Gaffney, Religious Freedom, *supra* note 1, at 153–55.

5. An Act for Exempting Their Majesties' Protestant Subjects Dissenting from the Church of England from the Penalties of Certain Laws (Act of Toleration), 1689, 1 W. & M., c. 181; printed in Andrew Browning, ed., English Historical Documents, 1660–1714, 400–403 (1953).

6. *See* Thomas J. Curry, Farewell to Christendom: The Future of Church and State in America 24–25 (2001).

act "brought about a high degree of religious harmony in the American colonies,"[7] but that was because the overwhelming majority of Americans were dissenting Protestants. Neither in the founding period nor in the present does the term "toleration" have as strong a resonance as "full and free exercise of religion."

The law of free exercise did not allow complete freedom in religious matters. For example, the New York Constitution of 1777 provided: "[T]he free exercise and enjoyment of religious profession and worship, without discrimination or preference, shall forever hereafter be allowed, within this State, to all mankind: Provided, That the liberty of conscience, hereby granted, shall not be so construed as to excuse acts of licentiousness, or justify practices inconsistent with the peace or safety of this State."[8] The state constitutional provisions of the founding generation allowed the government, in effect, to set some limits on free exercise of religion, but the state could do so only by defining the secular good of protecting the public order and public safety. Throughout America the government was removed from the business of defining religious orthodoxy and could no longer define or control religious beliefs and practices. The self-understanding of religious communities was given primacy of place in our constitutional order. Anglicans could define the way they would worship and be governed, and so could Presbyterians. Baptists, likewise, did not have to seek a license from the government to be able to announce the Gospel in the way they wished.

Can the judiciary protect religious freedom more vigorously than legislatures can? Once again, Madison provides an answer as different from the views of Locke as his view of full and free exercise of religion was from Locke's idea of toleration. Locke had advanced the concept of sovereignty beyond the power of the monarch to the power of the Parliament, but he could not imagine a judiciary with independent power to set aside enactments of the Parliament. As Locke put it, "there is no judge upon earth between the supreme magistrate and the people."[9] "In the absence of such a mediator," Michael McConnell notes, "individual conscience could be compelled to yield to government in the event of a conflict."[10] A century after Locke, Madison and the founding generation introduced into American politics and jurisprudence the idea of judicial review.[11] Hence Madison could argue in the debate over the Bill of Rights in the First Congress: "If [the provisions of the Bill of Rights] are incorporated into the constitution, independent tribunals of justice will consider themselves in a peculiar manner the guardians of those rights; they will be an impenetrable bulwark against every assumption of power in the legislative or executive; they will be naturally led to resist every en-

---

7. *Id.* at 25; *see also* 110 ("the Act of Toleration...introduced into America a degree of religious liberty unknown before that time").

8. N.Y. Const. of 1777, art. XXXVIII, *reprinted in* 2 Federal and State Constitutions, Colonial Charters, and Other Organic Laws of the United States 1338 (B. Poore 2d ed. 1878). Compare this provision with an example of toleration of dissenting Protestants enacted by the colony of New York in 1683, providing that those professing "faith in God by Jesus Christ" should not be molested "for any difference in opinion or matter of religious concernment" if they did not "actually disturb the civill peace of the Province," Hugh Hastings, 2 Ecclesiastical Records of the State of New York 864 (1901). Michael McConnell cites the New York provision and similar provisions in the constitutions of New Hampshire and Georgia; Michael W. McConnell, The Origins and Historical Understanding of Free Exercise of Religion, 103 Harv. L. Rev. 1409, 1456–57 (1990).

9. John Locke, A Letter concerning Toleration, in Noonan and Gaffney, Religious Freedom, *supra* note 1, at 153.

10. McConnell, *supra* note 8, at 1444.

11. *See, e.g.,* David Currie, The Constitution in the Supreme Court: The First Hundred Years, 1789–1888 (1985) (framers and ratifiers intended courts to engage in constitutional judicial review).

croachment upon rights expressly stipulated for in the constitution by the declaration of rights."[12]

As McConnell argues, "An independent judiciary could define religious liberty affirmatively, in terms of what religious liberty requires, and not merely what the legislature concedes."[13] The impulse is laudable, but judges should focus on limiting intrusion by the political branches into religious matters, not on "defining religious liberty," which is generally not within their competence. It is especially obnoxious when judges define religious liberty negatively, in the sense of invalidating provisions in which the political branch has indicated that it does not have a strong interest in universal application of a norm with no exceptions.

In the previous chapter, Professor Marshall is only half a Madisonian. He accepts, of course, the institution of judicial review. His chapter is focused almost entirely on judicial decisions on religious freedom. By and large, however, the case law that Marshall reports is suffused with judicial toleration (and occasional intolerance), not the more robust sense of freedom for which Madison argued. And these cases frequently involve judicial decisions not about secular values such as public safety, but about the very thing that Madison and the founding generation denied to government (including judges): decisions about religious matters beyond their ken. Marshall also does not point out that in recent years the political branches of government have often been more protective of religious freedom than the independent judiciary.[14]

Marshall underscores the general incoherence in the Court's discussion of the Religion Clause of the First Amendment. Like him and many other scholars,[15] I think the Court's jurisprudence on our first freedom is confusing. Unlike him, I do not think the confusion can be overcome simply by subsuming religious freedom within the other civil liberties secured in the First Amendment, such as freedom of speech or of the press.[16] In the language of the Williamsburg Charter, a bicentennial document celebrating religious freedom, "Far from being a sub-category of free speech or a constitutional redundancy, religious liberty is distinct and foundational."[17] Or as Judge John T. Noonan has put it: "If Free Speech could be substituted for Free Exercise, the first of our First Amendment freedoms would be otiose, a fossil preserved without a purpose....

12. 1 Annals of Cong. 457 (J. Gales ed. 1834) (June 8, 1789).

13. McConnell, *supra* note 8, at 1445.

14. *See* note 143 below.

15. *See, e.g.*, Jesse Choper, The Religion Clauses of the First Amendment: Reconciling the Conflict, 41 U. Pitt. L. Rev. 673, 680–81 (1980); Antonin Scalia, On Getting It Wrong By Making It Look Easy, in Edward McGlynn Gaffney, Jr., ed., Private Schools and the Public Good: Policy Alternatives for the Eighties 174 (1981); Michael J. Paulsen, Religion, Equality, and the Constitution: An Equal Protection Approach to Establishment Clause Adjudication, 61 Notre Dame L. Rev. 311, 315–17 (1986); John Garvey, Another Way of Looking at School Aid, 1985 Supreme Court Rev. 61, 67; Phillip E. Johnson, Concepts and Compromises in First Amendment Religious Doctrine, 72 Cal. L. Rev. 817, 825–31 (1984); Note, The Supreme Court, Effect Inquiry, and Aid to Parochial Education, 37 Stan. L. Rev. 219, 234 (1984); and Leonard W. Levy, The Establishment Clause: Religion and the First Amendment 128–29 (1986).

16. *See, e.g.*, William P. Marshall, In Defense of the Search for Truth as a First Amendment Justification, 30 Ga. L. Rev. 1 (1995); William P. Marshall, The Religious Freedom Restoration Act: Establishment, Equal Protection and Free Speech Concerns, 56 Mont. L. Rev. 227 (1995); William P. Marshall, In Defense of Smith and Free Exercise Revisionism, 58 U. Chi. L. Rev. 308 (1991); William P. Marshall, Solving the Free Exercise Dilemma: Free Exercise as Expression, 67 Minn. L. Rev. 545 (1983).

17. The Williamsburg Charter, 8 J.L. & Relig. 1, 17 (1990).

Our first freedom...is more spacious than Free Speech. It is more fundamental and more precious."[18]

The purpose of this chapter is to enlarge the context within which readers may assess the various contributions to the volume, and to encourage readers toward deeper commitment to the necessity of protecting the self-understanding of religious communities and their members about their religious beliefs and practices.

The cases that Marshall sets forth are marked by three principal mistakes about the Religion Clause. First, they assume that there are two conflicting clauses dealing with religion in the First Amendment: an Establishment Clause that empowers courts to determine the effect of legislation on religious communities, and a Free Exercise Clause that empowers courts to extend protection occasionally to the exercise of religious practices that courts agree to tolerate. Second, these cases are often based on a contextual and highly selective reading of historical evidence. Third, these cases proceed on a false understanding both of human nature—upon which the founders of the Republic and the framers of the Fourteenth Amendment grounded the protection of religious freedom—and of religious experience, which is typically connected with religious communities.

Since there is a recurrent difficulty in the use of history to address the meaning of the Religion Clause, this chapter explores general considerations about the use of history as a tool of interpretation. It offers an analogy between the task of constitutional interpretation and the quest for the historical figures central to Judaism and Christianity, Moses and Jesus. As in any analogy, differences between the tasks of biblical and constitutional interpretation should be obvious. The central point of similarity is that serious historical investigation leads in both instances not to despair about retrieval of the insights of the founders, but to modest yet important discoveries about the meaning that infuses religious and constitutional thinking in our own era.[19]

The chapter sketches a working hypothesis for what the two provisions of the Religion Clause—nonestablishment and free exercise—meant in late eighteenth-century American history, informed by its colonial background. It argues that nonestablishment and free exercise of religion are not competing goals but complementary values. It illus-

---

18. John T. Noonan, Jr., Religious Liberty at the Stake, 84 Va. L. Rev. 459, 467 (1998). Both religious opinions and their expression were protected under early state constitutional provisions relating to religion, but so were religious practices. For example, Maryland, prohibited punishment of any person "on account of his religious persuasion or profession, or for his religious practice." Md. Declaration of Rights of 1776, art. XXXIII, *reprinted in* 1 Federal and State Constitutions, *supra* note 8, at 817, 819; *see* McConnell, *supra* note 8, at 1459–60.

19. *See, e.g.,* Antonin Scalia, A Matter of Interpretation: Federal Courts and the Law (1997); for samples of originalist writing about the Religion Clause, see McConnell, *supra* note 8; Walter Berns, The First Amendment and the Future of American Democracy (1976); and Michael J. Malbin, Religion and Politics: The Intentions of the Authors of the First Amendment (1978); for a general critique of this enterprise, see H. Jefferson Powell, The Original Understanding of Original Intent, 98 Harv. L. Rev. 885, 887–88 (1985) (concluding from the historical evidence that reliance on "original intent" emerged as a dominant interpretive strategy after 1800 and that this strategy in turn differed significantly from modern versions of originalism); for a critique of the application of originalism to the Religion Clause, see Philip A. Hamburger, A Constitutional Right of Religious Exemption: An Historical Perspective, 60 Geo. Wash. L. Rev. 915 (1992); Gerald V. Bradley, Beguilded: Free Exercise Exemptions and the Siren Song of Liberalism, 20 Hofstra L. Rev. 245 (1991); Daan Braveman, The Establishment Clause and the Course of Religious Neutrality, 45 Md. L. Rev. 352, 373 (1986) (a "literal quest for the Framers' intent... [is] both futile and misdirected"); Mark V. Tushnet, The Constitution of Religion, 18 Conn. L. Rev. 701, 706–708 (1986).

trates how the purpose of the First Amendment was not to enlarge the power of courts to help religion, but to deny the power of government to define religion and in this way to leave the exercise of religion—in Madison's phrase—"full and free." It notes briefly that nineteenth-century American history sheds light on the meaning of the Fourteenth Amendment. It surveys some of the case law to see how it measures up to the historical points made above. And it concludes with an argument that religious exercise cannot be free in any meaningful sense unless this freedom is understood to protect religious communities.

General Reflections on Historical Method

In the two chapters in this volume on exemption of religious bodies from federal and state taxation, I rely extensively on history as a tool for understanding. So do several other contributors to this volume. There is much to be said for testing the legitimacy of current practices—such as tax exemption of religious communities—against the historical experience of the republic, including the teachings of the founders. In making this claim, however, I do not imagine that the study of an idealized golden era can provide the objective meaning of the Constitution in simple clarity for all to behold save those who do not wish to see. On the contrary, all interpretation is just that: interpretation. As the Canadian philosopher Bernard Lonergan has demonstrated, human subjects attain to objectivity or correct judgment only when they ask relevant questions, formulate reasonable hypotheses to guide their inquiry, and satisfy the quest for understanding by explaining the data with the fewest possible assumptions (especially gratuitous ones).[20]

The search for historical meaning as a means of informing the present generation is always an arduous task. There is so much to recall that we forget a lot of important historical materials. There are so many apparently conflicting strands of evidence that we either throw up our hands in despair or artfully select the things we wish to recall and try to avoid the inconvenient bits that do not support our hypotheses. But the difficulty of the historical task does not counsel against the effort to find appropriate links between past and present. The path to our common future as a nation would be obscured if we fell prey to collective amnesia or intentional ignorance of relevant experience. To be isolated from our ancestors and our heritage turns out not to be liberating, but more like being cast into a dark future with neither map nor compass. What counts as "the American heritage" is, in short, a matter for contention. We must contend about our history, even to achieve disagreement about principles of the highest order.[21]

In one sense it is inevitable that American history will be used in constitutional debate. How else than by reference to long national experience can we assess the meaning of the twin values of nonestablishment and free exercise of religion? The issue is not, as some commentators imagine,[22] whether recourse may be had to history in the interpre-

---

20. *See* Bernard J.F. Lonergan, Insight: A Study of Human Understanding 46–53, 56–59 (1958).
21. *See* George Weigel, Achieving Disagreement: From Indifference to Pluralism, 8 J.L. & Relig. 175 (1990).
22. *See* John E. Nowak and Ronald D. Rotunda, Constitutional Law 1310 (6th ed. 2000) (dismissing the "irresistible impulse to appeal to history when analyzing issues under the religion clauses" as "unfortunate because there is no clear history as to the meaning of the clauses").

tation of the Religion Clause, but whether history will be used skillfully. To resolve that issue, a brief discussion of common concerns in historical method is in order at the outset.

It is an epistemological commonplace that interpretation is always undertaken by conscious human subjects and is in that sense "subjective." As Steven Smith has noted, there is no "singular and even objective ideal that in some sense exists independently of people's opinions *about* religious freedom."[23] But it does not follow that we are free to ignore the meaning of the past in our search for the constitutional legitimacy of controversial practices such as those explored in this volume.

The Supreme Court has frequently recommended the use of history in understanding the application of the Religion Clause of the First Amendment[24] to cases and controversies of the modern period. The justices have even written historical essays from time to time to bolster their conclusions on a variety of contested matters involving the Religion Clause.[25] The justices who commend the use of history sometimes give the impression that retrieving historical meaning is easy, or at least straightforward. Thus Chief Justice Burger could write in *Lynch v. Donnelly* that interpretation of the Religion Clause should "compor[t] with what history reveals was the contemporaneous understanding of its guarantees."[26] Chief Justice Rehnquist (then an associate justice) could write in *Wallace v. Jaffree*: "The true meaning of the Establishment Clause can only be seen in its history.... As drafters of our Bill of Rights, the Framers inscribed the principles that control today. Any deviation from their intentions frustrates the permanence of that Charter and will only lead to the type of unprincipled decisionmaking that has plagued our Establishment Clause cases since *Everson*."[27]

It is easy to sympathize with the thrust of both comments. The disarray of the Court's Religion Clause jurisprudence is a phenomenon noted by commentators of all stripes.[28] It must be especially frustrating for those most directly engaged in the task, the justices.[29] But there are several difficulties with the approach to history assumed by Chief Justices Burger and Rehnquist. First, the supposed ease with which the lessons of the past will unravel for all to behold is belied by the very fact that the justices disagree with one another frequently about what the founders meant.[30] Even more disturbing than their disagreements with one another is the misunderstanding of how memory and the retrieval of the past functions in society or in a particular individual. Burger's

---

23. Steven D. Smith, Foreordained Failure: The Quest for a Constitutional Principle of Religious Freedom 7 (1995).

24. "Congress shall make no law respecting an establishment of religion nor prohibiting the free exercise thereof." U.S. Const., Amend. I.

25. *See, e.g.,* Lynch v. Donnelly, 465 U.S. 668, 678 (1984); Marsh v. Chambers, 463 U.S. 783, 787 (1983); Walz v. Tax Comm'n of City of New York, 397 U.S. 664, 671 (1970) (Brennan, J., concurring); School Dist. of Abington Township v. Schempp, 374 U.S. 203, 226 (1963) (Brennan, J., concurring).

26. 465 U.S. 668, 673 (1984).

27. Wallace v. Jaffree, 472 U.S. 38, 113 (1985) (Rehnquist, J., dissenting).

28. *See* note 15, *supra.*

29. *See, e.g.,* Committee for Public Education and Religious Liberty v. Regan, 444 U.S. 646, 662 (1980) (the Court's construction of establishment "sacrifices clarity and predictability for flexibility").

30. *See, e.g.,* the conflict of opinions between Chief Justice Burger and Justice Brennan in *Marsh v. Chambers*, 463 U.S. 783 (1983). For Burger, the issue was settled by referring to a practice that was "deeply embedded in the history and tradition of this country." *Id.* at 786. Justice Brennan wrote in dissent: "the Court's focus here on a narrow piece of history is, in a fundamental sense, a betrayal of history." *Id.* at 817 (Brennan, J., dissenting).

confidence that "history reveals" things is like thinking that "texts speak." Texts do not speak; they are read by finite minds capable of as much common nonsense as common sense. History does not reveal things; inquiring minds discover relevant truths by paying close attention to things said or done in the past. Or sometimes we fail to discover things because we overlook an item of history that is truly important but does not impinge upon our consciousness.

Second, there is the difficulty of anachronism, expecting to find answers extant before the question had been asked. As suggested above, some commentators cherish the myth of a golden era. If such a period ever existed, it cannot be discovered by looking only in one place in America. As important as Virginia was to the development of a commitment to nonestablishment and free exercise, a full account—which I do not attempt in this chapter—must include the experience of religious freedom in many other settings as well. For example, Pennsylvania served as a model for religious freedom.[31] As Curry notes, it "provided liberty of worship to all who believed in God and required that all religions be supported solely by voluntary offerings.... William Penn... founded...a large commonwealth that did not establish a church or a government-supported religion."[32] And at the dawn of the republic Pennsylvania provided the critical support for the adoption of the principle that the government lacks power in religious matters.

It cannot, moreover, be assumed that the founders all agreed about the application of general principles to specific arrangements involving the support of religion. Thus Professor Smith notes:

> [A]ll Americans could accept phraseology protecting the "rights of conscience" or banning the imposition of "articles of faith" or the "establishment of one sect in preference to another." They disagreed, however, over the substantive meaning of such terms. A majority of Virginians, for example, had clearly demonstrated that in their view a general assessment violated the "rights of conscience" while a majority of the inhabitants of Massachusetts obviously felt it did not. Both states proclaimed equal devotion to the term "rights of conscience," but because all believed that such matters pertained to the states, and that they were making explicit the fact that the federal government had nothing to do with religion, no collision of their differing views as to what constituted a violation of "rights of conscience" took place.[33]

Neither can a golden era be discovered by looking only at one moment in the past. For example, some lawyers, judges, and commentators are fond of looking at the founding period to unravel the meaning of the Religion Clause. Later in this chapter I discuss the importance of understanding nineteenth-century history as well, since it sheds light on the meaning of the Fourteenth Amendment.

Third, there is the problem of relevance. Even if a student of history unlocks the door to a golden era, the discovery will not resolve current issues without resolute commitment to a rigorous process of critical thinking and analogical reasoning. Otherwise, we are left with non sequiturs and non-fits between historical evidence and current practice.

---

31. *See, e.g.,* Merrill Jensen et al., eds., 2 The Documentary History of the Ratification of the Constitution 288, 386, 392, 399–400, 467, 514, 597, 623 (1976).

32. Curry, *supra* note 6, at 27.

33. Thomas J. Curry, The First Freedoms: Church and State in America to the Passage of the First Amendment 202 (1986); for a careful discussion of the church/state arrangements in New England, *see id.* at 134–92; *see also* Curry, *supra* note 6, at 30–32, 38–39, 41–42.

Fourth, there is the danger of determinism,[34] or being bound by a particular interpretation of the significance of an original moment when that moment may just as easily be regarded as having set in motion a process of liberation on that very matter.[35] Tax exemption of religious communities is a classic instance of this phenomenon. Some who support the practice maintain that things were ever so and therefore must remain so. Others who oppose the practice see it as having been locked into established religion at the founding moment and worthy of repudiation today for that very reason.

Fifth, as the last example illustrates, there is the problem of scotosis or bias.[36] There are none so blind as those who do not want to see. Too frequently lawyers and constitutional commentators engage in history with what one might call an "attitude." For example, I once advocated nonpreferentialism as an acceptable standard in the adjudication of cases involving financial assistance to parents of children attending religious schools.[37] The hope is that bias or blindness can be overcome by openness and insight. The danger is that people interested in a particular outcome may resist such change, remaining content to cite favorite passages from the past and to ignore conflicting evidence. Curry is blunt about this, accusing both sides of the current struggle over the Religion Clause of "determined exercise of selective memory...wholesale subversion of history...refusal to accept overwhelming evidence...and utter misinterpretation of evidence."[38]

Thus strict separationists invoke the metaphor of a wall of separation in Thomas Jefferson's letter to the Danbury Baptists, citing as paradigmatic Justice Black's reiteration of this theme in *Everson v. Board of Education*,[39] whose rhetoric if not logic[40] they applaud. For them, the wall—one that is "high and impregnable"[41]—is the primary metaphor for understanding the relation between the government and religious communities. The very choice of metaphor can lead to a rigidity and inflexibility that does not inquire, as did the farmer in Robert Frost's poem, about what is being walled in or out.[42] Madison, on the other hand, employed the metaphor of a line rather than a

---

34. *See* Isaiah Berlin, Historical Inevitability (1954).

35. *See* Powell, *supra* note 19 above.

36. *See* Lonergan, Insight, *supra* note 20, at 191–96 ("Just as insight can be desired, so too can it be used when unwanted").

37. *See* Mueller v. Allen, 463 U.S. 388 (1983), Brief Amicus Curiae of Council of American Private Education. Shortly afterwards, I read Curry, The First Freedoms, *supra* note 33, and Douglas Laycock, "Nonpreferential" Aid to Religion: A False Claim About Original Intent, 27 Wm. & Mary L. Rev. 875 (1986). Both persuaded me that I was wrong about this point, and I have not intentionally misled the Court or my students on it since then.

38. Curry, *supra* note 6, at 109.

39. 330 U.S. 1 (1947).

40. Justice Black allowed the State of New Jersey to fund the transportation of children to religious schools. In dissent, Justice Robert Jackson wrote that "the undertones of the opinion, advocating complete and uncompromising separation...seem utterly discordant with its conclusion. The case which irresistibly comes to mind as the most fitting precedent is that of Julia who according to Byron's reports 'whispering "I will ne'er consent"—consented.'" *Id.* at 19 (Jackson, J., dissenting).

41. *Id.* at 18.

42. Justice Frankfurter concluded his concurring opinion in *Illinois ex rel. McCollum v. Board of Educ.,* 333 U.S. 203 (1948) with five words—"Good fences make good neighbors"—borrowed from a famous poem, "Mending Wall," by Robert Frost. The Complete Poems of Robert Frost 39 (1995). Frankfurter did not refer to the text of the poem, which he must have assumed his readers to know by heart. Because I cannot make the same assumption, I include some comment on the poem, which Frankfurter badly misread. The poem begins: "Something there is that doesn't love a wall." In the poem, two New England farmers annually rebuild a stone wall that nature and the work of hunters have eroded each winter. One farmer is quite content to engage in this springtime ritual. The other farmer quietly wonders whether this annual wall-building is worth the bother. He,

wall,[43] thus urging a flexibility close to Holmes's maxim that "the life of the law is experience not logic."[44]

On the other side of the wall or line, ardent accommodationists search through records of the founding period in the hope of finding evidence of governmental spending for religion, which they imagine is inoffensive if distributed on an evenhanded basis. For example, they invoke the financing of religious activities in the Northwest Territory by Congress in the early period of the republic as proof that it is permissible for the government to support the advancement of religion.[45] For them, a locus classicus among judicial opinions is Justice Rehnquist's dissenting opinion in *Wallace v. Jafree,* which they recall especially for the following summary of the nonestablishment provision:

> The Framers intended the Establishment Clause to prohibit the designation of any church as a 'national' one. The Clause was also designed to stop the Federal Government from asserting a preference for one religious denomination or sect over others. Given the 'incorporation' of the Establishment Clause as against the States via the Fourteenth Amendment in *Everson,* States are prohibited as well from establishing a religion or discriminating between sects. As its history abundantly shows, however, nothing in the Establishment Clause requires government to be strictly neutral between religion and irreligion, nor does that Clause prohibit Congress or the States from pursuing legitimate secular ends through nondiscriminatory sectarian means.[46]

Or they would love to see Christmas crèches on government property so long as Jews can also prominently display some symbol of their faith, such as a menorah, on government property too. So they invoke the historical practice of allowing a national holiday

---

at least, stops to ask: "Why do they make good neighbors?" Before rebuilding or fortifying a wall, this farmer would "ask to know / What I was walling in or walling out." Frost gives several generous hermeneutical clues about which farmer reflects his own views on wall building. For example, unedited by Frankfurter, the full line of the poem reads: "*He only says,* 'Good fences make good neighbors'" (emphasis added). At the conclusion of the poem, Frost notes that the unreflective farmer cited by Frankfurter "will not go behind his father's saying, / And he likes having thought of it so well / He says again, 'Good fences make good neighbors.'"

43. Madison suggested not a wall, but a line differentiating "the rights of religion and the Civil Authority." Letter of James Madison to the Reverend Jasper Adams, 1832, 9 The Writings of James Madison 484 (1910), reprinted in John F. Wilson and Donald L. Drakeman, eds., Church and State in American History 80–82 (2d ed. 1987). Historian Sidney E. Mead noted that Madison's metaphor, unlike Jefferson's, "does not conjure up the image of a solid and unchanging structure built by the founders, but rather 'the path of a moving point, thought of as having length but not breadth.'" Mead, Neither Church nor State: Reflections on James Madison's "Line of Separation," 10 J. Ch. & St. 349, 350 (1968).

44. Oliver Wendell Holmes, Jr., The Common Law 1 (1881).

45. *See, e.g.,* Robert L. Cord, Separation of Church and State: Fact and Fiction (1982); Cord, Church-State Separation: Restoring the "No Preference" Doctrine of the First Amendment, 9 Harv. J. L. & Pub. Pol'y 129 (1986); *see also* Chester James Antieau et al., Freedom from Federal Establishment: Formation and Early History of the First Amendment Religious Clauses (1964); Daniel L. Dreisbach, Real Threat and Mere Shadow: Religious Liberty and the First Amendment (1987); John G. West, Jr., The Politics of Revelation and Reason: Religion and Civic Life in the New Nation 11–78 (1996). *But see* Leonard Levy, The Establishment Clause: Religion and the First Amendment 112–45 (2d ed. 1994) (arguing that the founders meant to prohibit all aid — even nondifferentiated aid — to religion); Laycock, *supra* note 37.

46. Wallace, 472 U.S. at 99 (Rehnquist, J., dissenting). As I argue below, no constitutionally sound approach to the formation of tax policy can expect legislators to be indifferent to the claim that religious believers may not enjoy special tax benefits that are not available to nonbelievers.

on Christmas day, and they cherish Justice Kennedy's dissenting opinion in *County of Allegheny v. ACLU, Greater Pittsburgh Chapter*.[47] Their favorite metaphor is the Naked Public Square.[48] This metaphor, too, can lead to rigidity. If misused as a slogan for governmental "help" of religion, it can serve as a poor excuse for not thinking carefully about who is doing what and to whom.

This sort of bias also shows up in litigation as "law office history," an uncomplimentary term coined by Alfred Kelly, a prominent legal historian who was sharply critical of the misuse of the past in the adversarial climate of litigation.[49] Although no one—whether a lawyer or historian—can see everything, all should try to avoid intentional selective reading of the past.

An Analogy from Biblical Interpretation: The Quests for the Historical Moses and Jesus

Constitutional interpretation might learn something from the turmoil that has surrounded biblical interpretation in its quests for historical understanding of its central figures, Moses and Jesus. The interpretive moves made by scripture scholars are relevant to the search for coherent principles of constitutional interpretation grounded in history.

The problem of whether much could be known about the historical Moses arose in nineteenth-century Germany, more or less at the same time that history was taking its place in the academy as a separate discipline. At that place and time there was considerable fascination with the possibility that historians would be able to narrate past events with precision and without much fear of bias. In von Ranke's famous phrase, the goal of history was to be able to describe the past exactly as it happened (*wie es eigentlich gewesen*).

Historians should strive for accuracy in reporting events of the past, but it is naive to imagine that they can describe things exactly as they happened. For one thing, this view underestimates both the perspective of the observer and the obscurity of the observed. As for the objects of the historical gaze—our ancient ancestors—it was soon discovered that they had been generally less concerned with preserving details for the sake of accuracy than with constructing a grand narrative that would bind listeners together, a

---

47. 492 U.S. 573, 655 (1989) (Kennedy, J., dissenting).

48. *See* Richard John Neuhaus, The Naked Public Square: Religion and Democracy in America (1984). Some disciples of Neuhaus have so overused his powerful expression that he may live to regret that he coined the phrase. He intended it as a challenge to regnant secularist ideology, not as an invitation for more "benign" government intervention in favor of religion.

49. Alfred Kelly, Clio and the Court: An Illicit Love Affair, 1965 Sup. Ct. Rev. 119. Philip Kurland also criticized " 'law office history,' written the way brief writers write briefs, by picking and choosing statement and events favorable to the client's cause." Philip B. Kurland, The Origins of the Religion Clauses of the Constitution, 27 Wm. & Mary L. Rev. 839, 842 (1986). *See also* Gerard V. Bradley, Church-State Relationships in America (1987); Mark DeWolfe Howe, The Garden and the Wilderness (1965); Charles Miller, The Supreme Court and the Uses of History (1969); and William Wiecek, Clio as Hostage: The United States Supreme Court and the Uses of History, 24 Cal. W. L. Rev. 227 (1988). Even Homer nods. Kelly omitted to mention that he assisted the NAACP in writing a brief in the Brown case that did not forthrightly address the issue on which the Court sought guidance: did the framers of the Fourteenth Amendment intend to end racial discrimination in education?

story that would identify them as members of a particular community. To achieve that goal, storytellers felt free to employ a wide variety of literary forms that had little, if anything, to do with facticity and everything to do with communal meaning. As for the subjects of historical interpretation, many nineteenth-century historians had a remarkable lack of self-awareness about the intensely value-laden assumptions—for example, their naive trust in Hegelian dialectics or in the myth of the inevitability of progress—they brought to their enterprise.

Just as secular historians became increasingly aware of the cultural complexity of the formation of traditions, biblical theologians became willing to apply to the study of the Bible the same tools of literary criticism that their colleagues in history were employing.[50] Within a single book of the Bible, scholars identified two or sometimes three passages describing a particular theme in various distinct ways. This discovery led them to posit a hypothesis that various passages in the first five books of the Bible were written at different times by different authors. Torah was not a continuous narrative flowing from the stylus of Moses. It was a collection of fragmented blocks of materials, confidently labeled as belonging either to a southern tradition called J (because it used the word "Jahveh" as the designation of God) or to a northern tradition called E (because it instead used the word "Elohim"). With the fall of the northern tribes to the Assyrians in 721 B.C.E., the hypothesis ran, J and E were merged into a JE tradition, which was sustained in Jerusalem. Then—as might be imagined in a tidy Hegelian universe in which things keep improving—along came D, the chunk of materials that stretches from Deuteronomy to the Deuteronomistic books constructed in a similar style (Joshua, Judges, 1 and 2 Samuel, 1 and 2 Kings). Finally, more or less in the period of the exile of the Judeans to Babylon (586–535 B.C.E.), a group of priests put together a consecutive narrative, called P to mark it as the contribution of the priestly authors. By the time the people returned to Jerusalem to build the second Temple, they had a collection of writings that fused the traditions into a consecutive narrative known as Torah, but identified by the higher critics as JEDP.

More than a century later, the documentary hypothesis sketched above no longer commands the broad support among scholars that it used to enjoy. The shattering of consensus on particular details of the hypothesis, however, has not meant that scholars now imagine that Moses wrote everything in Torah from the first two chapters of Genesis (with their distinct creation narratives) to the last chapter of Deuteronomy (with its description of the death of Moses). It is still legitimate, even important, to inquire whether we can know much about what Moses actually said or did from the five books of Torah, which were written, long after Moses died, by believers for the sake of their fellow believers.

Before long a similar question shook the Christian world. How can we know much about what Jesus actually said or did from the four Gospels, which were written by believers for the sake of other believers? The beginning of the twentieth century saw a flurry of activity among exegetes who sought to expose how little we could know about the historical Jesus from the text of the Gospels. This period stretched from Albert Schweitzer[51] at the turn of the century to Rudolf Bultmann[52] at midcentury.

---

50. *See, e.g.,* Joseph Blenkinsopp, The Pentateuch: An Introduction to the First Five Books of the Bible (1992).

51. *See, e.g.,* Albert Schweitzer, The Quest of the Historical Jesus: A Critical Study of Its Progress from Reimarus to Wrede (1956); The Kingdom of God and Primitive Christianity (1968).

52. *See* Rudolf Bultmann, The History of the Synoptic Tradition (1963); Form Criticism: Two Essays on New Testament Research (1962).

Later came a "new quest,"[53] as it was called, undertaken primarily by some of Bult-mann's disciples,[54] who attempted to steer the question in a more useful direction. They did not deny the validity of the earlier question, but instead reframed it in such a way as to focus more clearly on the distinct role of each Gospel writer as an editor or redactor of the materials.[55] This matter had been overlooked in the earlier dissection of the Gospels into tiny isolated fragments. Similarly, in the "new quest" for the historical Moses, scholars are inclined much less to divide Torah into isolated fragments than to understand the formation of the canon as a communal process that preserved distinct traditions within the community of Israel.[56]

Without belaboring the analogy between scriptural and constitutional interpreta-tion, I note a strong similarity between these two interpretive tasks. Both are efforts to comprehend development, to integrate continuity with change. There can be no strong sense of continuity if the new quest can only achieve a vague awareness that something important happened in the past. That was the focus of the older quest, which left the seeker with disaggregated fragments of information and not much of a big picture. In the newer search for meaning in the Hebrew Bible and the New Testa-ment, the emphasis has been on connecting the past with the present moment of the interpreter. This method candidly acknowledges the centrality of the inquiring mind in the present, while understanding the past as having been mediated to us through other inquiring minds. The result is not the debunking of stories of origins, but a fuller appreciation of the process by which these traditions have been formed, as well as of the contributions that various authors and editors have made in the production of the scriptural texts.

In each context the hermeneutical task—the search for meaning in prior texts—is complicated but unavoidable. It is complicated because we can no longer proceed with naive confidence in our ability to know exactly what transpired in the biblical founding period. It is unavoidable because any community that purports to remain in continuity with its founders may not assume that the current generation can simply define itself in any way it wishes, without any regard for how it relates to its central story of origins. Similarly, with constitutional interpretation the task is also complicated but unavoid-able. It is complicated because the claims made about a "central narrative" in the founding period are themselves contentious, and also because exaggerated law office history that argues in a one-sided manner for a particular outcome is not acceptable method. It is unavoidable because without any mooring in a national narrative that in-cludes both nonestablishment and free exercise of religion, the current generation will be free to choose results, and then to rationalize them, more or less at whim.

---

53. *See* James McConkey Robinson, A New Quest of the Historical Jesus (1959).

54. *See, e.g.,* Raymond E. Brown, After Bultmann, What?: An introduction to the Post Bultman-nians, Cath. Bib. Q. 26 (1964) 1–30. The primary works canvassed in Brown's article were Günther Bornkamm, Jesus of Nazareth (1960), Günther Bornkamm, Gerhard Barth, and Heinz Joachim Held, Tradition and Interpretation in Matthew (1963); Willi Marxsen, Mark the Evangelist: Studies on the Redaction History of the Gospel (1969); and Hans Conzelmann, The Theology of St. Luke (1961).

55. *See, e.g.,* Norman Perrin, What is Redaction Criticism? (1969); Perrin, Rediscovering the Teaching of Jesus (1967).

56. *See, e.g.,* Hans Walter Wolff, The Kerygma of the Yahwist, Walter Brueggemann, Wolff's Kerygmatic Methodology, in Walter Brueggemann and Hans Walter Wolff, eds. The Vitality of Old Testament Traditions (1982); Norbert Lohfink, The Christian Meaning of the Old Testament (1968); Joseph Blenkinsopp, Prophecy and Canon: A Contribution to the Study of Jewish Origins (1977).

Informed by the newer quest in biblical interpretation, the effort to identify a central narrative in the history of religious freedom should be careful and modest about what it can prove. But that does not mean that the entire enterprise of searching for meaning in the origins of American constitutionalism is doomed to failure, any more than the careful study of Judaism and Christianity within the historical contexts in which these religions arose leads to the conclusion that these religious faiths are devoid of meaning or value.

The Central Meaning of the Religion Clause

The history of the struggle for religious freedom culminated in eighteenth-century America with an astonishing repudiation of governmental power. "Congress shall make no law" is a precise negative parallel to Article I, section 8: "Congress shall have the power to..."[57] The First Amendment Religion Clause denied to the federal government the power to define and control religion.

There are many themes in current discourse about the Religion Clause. Four stand out as dominant in the case law and scholarly commentary on nonestablishment: substantive neutrality, nondiscrimination, nonendorsement, and nonentanglement of government with religion. These themes are overlapping and complementary. Even when taken together, however, these ways of thinking about nonestablishment are not as clear as the insight that the First Amendment Religion Clause is about the government's lack of power.

This central historical insight has been obscured by more than a half century of sloppy history written for the most part not by historians but by lawyers untrained in the discipline, or by judges relying on briefs containing law office history, in which lawyers artfully select portions of source documents and blithely ignore conflicting evidence. "Thinking like a lawyer" has come to mean that attorneys may draw any large conclusion they like from bits and pieces of evidence they deem interesting. Although many of these conclusions are erroneous, the errors go unchallenged by the commentators, who generally assume that the judges know what they are talking about. Hence historical mistakes take on an aura of respectability and even of authority simply because they have been uttered by judges. The process comes full circle when lawyers recycle judicial errors in their briefs.

Several contributors to this volume have avoided this regrettable practice. They rely instead on reputable historians such as Thomas Curry, who has contributed a solid account of religion in the colonial and early republican period.[58] Now a Catholic bishop, Curry has recently published an extended essay entitled *Farewell to Christendom*,[59] in which he argues that the First Amendment is a limiting, self-denying ordinance restraining government, a mandate that the state will exercise no power in religious questions and that "Congress shall make no law..." in that domain of human experience. Curry writes:

> Religious freedom proceeds from government's leaving people alone to decide on their own religious beliefs and practices. Some would, with the best of

---

57. When the first five words of the First Amendment are contrasted with the first words of Article I, § 8: "Congress shall have the power to..." the First Amendment appears clearly as a denial of power. Akhil Reed Amar, Anti-Federalists, The Federalist Papers, and the Big Argument for Union, 16 Harv. J.L. & Pub. Policy 111, 115 (1993).

58. Curry, *supra* note 33.

59. Curry, *supra* note 6.

intentions for society, now have government return to the practice of sponsoring and promoting religious beliefs and observances. Others, equally well-intentioned, would guard against the abuses of the established religions of the past by endowing government with power to corral religion, to locate the Church behind a wall or barrier of the State's making.

In reality, the First Amendment is about government's lack of power. It is no more a mandate to promote religion than it is one to create a boundary defining the sphere and activity of religion. Rather, it embodies a new way of arranging government, the full understanding of which is still emerging. The gravitational force of Christendom, built up over more than fifteen hundred years, remains strong. The silence of those empty spaces created by the disappearance of established churches can still disturb or even terrify even those who are not religious. Nevertheless, the great American experiment still challenges religious believers to realize that the denial of government power over the Church resulted not from a depreciation of religious belief, but from a profound appreciation that religion was too important to be left to politicians, too precious and necessary to a vibrant society to be made the tool of government manipulation.[60]

Curry deplores the misplaced focus among some commentators on what the government can do to "help" religion, because this inevitably brings government into making religious decisions. The purpose of the Religion Clause is to acknowledge and allow the natural right to religious liberty without government interference. It is freedom from government power. Identifying the free exercise of religion merely with the absence of government compulsion is to equate it with religious toleration—a mistake that Madison corrected with his famous revision of George Mason's draft of the Virginia Declaration of Rights in 1776.[61]

The Complementarity of Nonestablishment and Free Exercise

Are nonestablishment and free exercise competing values that effectively nullify one another? The cases canvassed by Professor Marshall generally proceed on the assumption that the First Amendment contains two provisions on religion that are at odds with each other. This view is widely shared, but it is not required by the text of the amendment or by the history leading to its adoption. The problem of the imagined tension between these provisions is the result of judges "thinking like lawyers," logically rather than historically. The Court has repeatedly bifurcated the provisions on religion, even suggesting that one provision commands one result and the other requires the opposite.

In this view, nonestablishment and free exercise are not merely distinguishable modes of discourse but contradictory and mutually exclusive terms. The two provisions on religion in the First Amendment are viewed as separate "clauses" pulling in opposite

---

60. *Id.* at 5.

61. *See* Noonan, *supra* note 1, at 69–70; the source materials are gathered in Noonan and Gaffney, Religious Freedom, *supra* note 1, at 162–63. *See also* Noonan, Religious Liberty at the Stake, *supra* note 18, at 461.

directions in some grand tug-of-war. Positing such a conflict within the Religion Clause is about as plausible as believing that the Free Press Clause was intended both to foster greater dissemination of opinions and to repress any thought the government finds offensive.

When the Court writes in this way, it shows little regard for the experience that Justice Holmes described as being "the life of the law."[62] Metaphors employed by the justices to describe the relation between the two provisions do not help matters. The starkest of these was offered by Chief Justice (then Associate Justice) Rehnquist, who suggested that the terms nonestablishment and free exercise are like the twin monsters from the ancient world, Scylla and Charybdis,[63] that meant extreme peril for mariners.[64]

Chief Justice Burger was fond of mixing his metaphors. For example, he imagined the rival religion clauses (plural) to be on a collision course, one tending to swallow up the other. In another Burger metaphor, the two provisions were "in tension" with one another.[65] Tension, of course, can be a positive, even a necessary thing. For example, a sailor who leans out of a boat provides balanced counterforce to a strong wind, thus enabling the boat to stay afloat and move forward. But Burger did not intend any such positive connotation. He meant the sort of unhealthy tension between rival forces that tends to be destructive if left unchecked. Rarely is it asked who put the tension there in the first place. The answer is not Madison or the people who ratified the First Amendment, but the Court and commentators, fairly recently in our nation's history. The "tension" judges and scholars perceive in the relationship between disestablishment and free exercise is of their own making.

When Burger offered yet another image—judges walking a tightrope—someone should have sent it to *The New Yorker* as a "Block that Metaphor!" item. These mixed and misplaced metaphors do not provide a solid explanation for the Court's elaborate and confusing jurisprudence, which is based on a misreading of the text of the First and Fourteenth amendments and their surrounding history.

When mistakes abound in the understanding of American history, is it any wonder that thoughtful commentators like Smith despair of the Court ever providing us with a coherent understanding of the Religion Clause?[66] There is, of course, no single unified

---

62. Holmes, The Common Law, *supra* note 44, at 1.

63. *See* Thomas v. Review Board, 450 U.S. 707, 720 (Rehnquist, J. dissenting) (1981).

64. Scylla was a dangerous rock on the southern tip of Italy; Charybdis was a nearby whirlpool in the narrow Straits of Messina between Sicily and the Italian mainland. These navigational perils were represented as female monsters in ancient mythology. In The Odyssey, Homer describes Scylla as a "horrible monster" past whom "no crew can boast that they ever sailed without loss, since from every passing vessel she snatches a man with each of her [six] heads and so bears off her prey." Homer, The Odyssey 191 (E.V. Rieu trans. 1946). Charybdis is depicted as a "dread monster" who "sucks the dark waters down three times a day, and spews them up three times." Odysseus's divine guide, Circe, prays that heaven will keep him and his crew from this spot "when she is at her work, for not even the Earthshaker [Poseidon] could save you from disaster." *Id.* 191–92. The metaphor adopted by Rehnquist and later by Justice Scalia in his dissent in *Texas Monthly, Inc. v. Bullock*, 489 U.S. 1, 29 (Scalia, J. dissenting), implies a negative connotation for both parts of the Religion Clause. These justices imagine nonestablishment and free exercise not as related manifestations of an identical principle of freedom, but as twin perils or dangers, neither of which can be evaded without risking the other. Both Rehnquist and Scalia frequently invoke "those who framed and adopted the First Amendment," but none of the framers of the Religion Clause advanced the strange view that one portion of the clause imperiled the other.

65. *Walz*, 397 U.S. at 668–69.

66. Smith, *supra* note 23; *but see* Thomas C. Berg, Religion Clause Anti-Theories, 72 Notre Dame L. Rev. 693 (1997) (arguing that the way out of bad theory is better theory, not anti-theory);

understanding of religious experience. But that is the very fact that grounds the American approach to religious freedom, in which nonestablishment removes the government from evaluating and approving or disapproving of religion, and free exercise secures both individual conscience and the independence of religious communities. The two values of the Religion Clause are not contradictions in terms. They are complementary and harmonious. As Curry puts it, "There is no conflict in the First Amendment, because it was designed for the single purpose of keeping the government from interfering in religious matters or from sponsoring religious beliefs and practises."[67]

In a variety of ways, several scholars have for decades been urging a unitary approach to the Religion Clause. The first was Philip Kurland, who in 1961 proposed a "strict neutrality" approach that would allow the government to neither impose a burden nor confer a benefit because of religion.[68] Six years later, Donald Giannella asserted that the framers had found no tension between the two provisions, but suggested that this had been a failure on their part to comprehend what they had done.[69] In 1978, Gail Merel noted that on the surface Kurland appeared to advocate a neutral principle of equal treatment of religion under both provisions, but that in effect he had tilted decidedly in favor of the nonestablishment principle "at a cost of almost total emasculation of the free exercise provision."[70] Merel proposed that the need was less to imagine the two provisions as opposite ends of a tug-of-war than to untie the doctrinal knots that had unnecessarily caused the perception of tension in the first place. Kurland acknowledged with candor that his position "met with almost uniform rejection" and that "the Supreme Court refused to have anything to do with it."[71] Two years later Leo Pfeffer, a veteran litigator in church/state cases who urged a strict separationist view on the Court, wrote that "the religion clauses of the first amendment encompass a unitary guaranty of separation and freedom."[72]

In 1986 Curry adduced extensive evidence in the records of late eighteenth-century America that nonestablishment and free exercise were practically interchangeable cate-

---

David Steinberg, Gardening at Night: Religion and Choice, (Book Review of Smith, Foreordained Failure) 74 Notre Dame L. Rev. 987 (1999); Smith, The Religion Clauses in Constitutional Scholarship, (Reply to Steinberg's review) 74 Notre Dame L. Rev. 1033 (1999).

67. *See* Curry, *supra* note 6, at 106; *see also* at 21, 44–45, 68, 71, 93, 104.

68. *See* Philip B. Kurland, Of Church and State and the Supreme Court, 29 U. Chi. L. Rev. 1 (1961).

69. *See* Donald A. Giannella, Religious Liberty, Nonestablishment, and Doctrinal Development, Part I: The Religious Liberty Guarantee, 80 Harv. L. Rev. 1381, 1389 (1967). Note the equation of free exercise with religious liberty.

70. Gail Merel, The Protection of Individual Choice: A Consistent Understanding of Religion Under the First Amendment, 45 U. Chi. L. Rev. 805, 808 (1978).

71. Philip Kurland, The Irrelevance of the Constitution: the Religion Clauses of the First Amendment and the Supreme Court, 24 Vill. L. Rev. 3, 24 (1978). John Witte appears to follow Kurland's approach in a comment he makes about the irreconcilability of the provisions of the Religion Clause: "The disestablishment clause forbids government from imparting special benefits to religious groups. The free exercise clause forbids government from imposing special burdens on religious groups. Neither the exemption nor the taxation of religious property appears to satisfy the mandates of both clauses. To exempt religious property, while taxing that of other nonreligious groups, appears to violate the 'no special benefit' mandate of the disestablishment clause. To tax religious property, while exempting that of other nonprofit groups, appears to violate the 'no special burden' mandate of the free exercise clause. The controversy thus seems to fall within the *terra incognita* between the First Amendment religion clauses." John Witte, Jr., Tax Exemption of Religious Property, in Religion and the American Constitutional Experiment: Essential Rights and Liberties 186 (2000).

72. Leo Pfeffer, Freedom and/or Separation: The Constitutional Dilemma of the First Amendment, 64 Minn. L. Rev. 561, 564 (1980).

gories in the founding period.[73] Several other scholars wrote on this point in the same year in which Curry's book appeared. Michael Paulsen wrote that "it makes little textual or historical sense to read the two clauses as conflicting in the first place"; instead, "the religion clauses of the first amendment encompass a unitary guaranty of separation and freedom."[74] Similarly, Thomas McCoy and Gary Kurtz argued that the clauses should be treated as a single conceptual unit.[75]

In a lecture delivered in 1988, Richard John Neuhaus took the argument a step further, suggesting that the current incoherence of Religion Clause jurisprudence is a corollary of the commonplace view of the clause as containing two provisions that are mutually opposed:

> The conventional wisdom is that there are two religion clauses that must somehow be "balanced," one against the other. But these provisions of the First Amendment are not against each other. Each is in the service of the other. More precisely, there is one religion clause, not two. The meaning of a "clause," apart from the narrowly grammatical, is that it is an article or stipulation. The two-part religion clause of the First Amendment stipulates that there must be no law respecting an establishment of religion. The reason for this is to avoid any infringement of the free exercise of religion. Non-establishment is not a good in itself, it does not stand on its own feet. The positive good is free exercise, to which non-establishment is instrumental.[76]

Dean Kelley, who served for more than thirty years as counselor in religious liberty for the National Council of Churches of Christ in the U.S.A., took issue with this approach. Kelley thought that Neuhaus was downplaying either the historical or the contemporary significance of the prohibition against an established religion. I read Neuhaus simply to be reminding us that the reason for the prohibition of an established religion—both at the time of the framing and now—is to promote religious liberty. Nonestablishment is "instrumental" in this sense, but "instrumental" is not a term of derision; it identifies the means through which a goal is reached. Understood in this way, both values expressed in the Religion Clause are interrelated to one another as means to end.

Both Neuhaus and Kelley served on the drafting committee that produced an important bicentennial document on religious freedom known as the Williamsburg Charter. They obviously reached consensus on the text of this document, which states:

> Both parts [of the First Amendment Religion Clause] No establishment and Free exercise, are to be comprehensively understood as being in the service of religious liberty as a positive good. At the heart of the Establishment clause is the prohibition of state sponsorship of religion and at the heart of Free Exercise clause is the prohibition of state interference with religious liberty. No

---

73. *See* Curry, *supra* note 33, at 192.

74. Michael A. Paulsen, Religion, Equality, and the Constitution: An Equal Protection Approach to Establishment Clause Adjudication, 61 Notre Dame L. Rev. 311, 324 (1986).

75. *See* Thomas McCoy and Gary Kurtz, A Unifying Theory for the Religion Clauses of the First Amendment, 39 Vand. L. Rev. 249, 253 (1986).

76. Richard John Neuhaus, Contending for the Future: Overcoming the Pfefferian Inversion, 8 J.L. & Religion 115, 115–116 (1990); *see also* Neuhaus, A New Order of Religious Freedom, 60 Geo. Wash. L. Rev. 620, 627 (1992) ("[T]here is no conflict, no tension, no required 'balancing' between free exercise and establishment. There are not two religion clauses. There is but one Religion Clause").

sponsorship means that the state must leave to the free citizenry the public expression of ultimate beliefs, religious or otherwise, providing only that no expression is excluded from, and none governmentally favored, in the continuing democratic discourse. No interference means the assurance of voluntary religious expression free from governmental intervention. This includes placing religious expression on an equal footing with all other forms of expression in genuinely public forums.[77]

McConnell argued in 1985 that the task of differentiating permissible and impermissible accommodation of religion is governed by both provisions of the Religion Clause.[78] In 1992 he emphasized that shifting judicial interpretations of these provisions have made it difficult to see them as harmonious:

> One might expect that these two provisions, which form a single grammatical unit and reflect a common history, would be interpreted complementarily. This rarely has been true. Until recently, the Free Exercise Clause was interpreted in a manner favorable to accommodation, while the Establishment Clause was interpreted to create obstacles to accommodation. This led to a jurisprudence in which judicial discretion was maximized and the results appeared to be at war with one another. The current trend in the Court is the reverse: [since *Employment Division v. Smith*] the Free Exercise Clause no longer is interpreted to require accommodation in most instances, but the Establishment Clause no longer is interpreted to interfere with them, in most instances. This leads to a jurisprudence in which legislative discretion is maximized and the Clauses, since they are rarely applied, rarely conflict.... The goal of harmonizing the two Religion Clauses appears as distant as ever.[79]

In 1991 Mary Ann Glendon and her co-author Raul Yanes also treated both provisions of the Religion Clause as parts of a single whole, arguing that this approach would eliminate artificial distinctions between establishment and free exercise.[80]

In his magisterial treatise on American constitutional law Laurence Tribe fell in with those who imagine a conflict between the two Religion Clauses, resolving it in favor of the Free Exercise Clause by fashioning one of his famous two-tiered definitions. With no warrant for his view either in the text of the First Amendment or in the history surrounding its adoption, Tribe suggested that religion be given an expansive meaning for purposes of accommodating free exercise claims and a narrow understanding for purposes of Establishment Clause analysis.[81]

In a lecture delivered in 1992 Judge John Noonan took a dim view of this approach:

> Current usage, I am afraid, refers to 'the religion clauses'—an unfortunate usage that I think Justice Black was responsible for, at least introducing it into decisions of the Supreme Court [citing *Everson*]. There are no clauses in the constitutional provision. Clauses have a subject and predicate. This provision has a single subject, a single verb, and two prepositional phrases. It is a shabby and inadmissible technique to put the two prepositional phrases dealing with

---

77. The Williamsburg Charter, 8 J.L. & Relig. 1, 15 (1990).

78. *See* Michael W. McConnell, Accommodation of Religion, 1985 Sup. Ct. Rev. 1.

79. Michael W. McConnell, Accommodation of Religion: An Update and a Response to the Critics, 60 Geo. Wash. L. Rev. 685, 695–96, 742 (1992).

80. *See* Mary Ann Glendon and Raul F. Yanes, Structural Free Exercise, 90 Mich. L. Rev. 477, 536–37 (1991).

81. *See* Laurence Tribe, American Constitutional Law § 14-6, at 1179–88 (2d ed. 1988).

religion into conflict with each other as a statement that with any fidelity to the text should be read as one.[82]

In the epilogue to his recent volume on religious freedom in America, Judge Noonan offered ten commandments about the interpretation of these matters. One of them has commentators like Tribe in mind: "You shall respect the content and the context of the sixteen words creating religious freedom in the Constitution, and you shall not artfully divide the words from one another, nor omit any of them, nor impose two meanings on a single word."[83]

The common note struck among most of these very diverse authors—Curry, Glendon, Kurtz, McConnell, McCoy, Merel, Neuhaus, Noonan, Pfeffer, and Yanes—is a repudiation of the widely held view that the two First Amendment provisions on religion have meanings so different that they need to be reconciled, or worse, are virtually irreconcilable.[84]

To assert a harmonious interrelationship between these provisions does not end thoughtful inquiry about church/state relationships, which were different in different states, but by the time the First Amendment was ratified, there were no official state establishments in America:

> Rhode Island, Pennsylvania, New Jersey, and Delaware had never established a religion. New York, the Carolinas, and Virginia had abandoned the establishments they had inherited. Maryland allowed for a general assessment type of support, of the kind that Virginia had proposed, but the majority of the people of the state decisively defeated its implementation. Georgia provided for a similar arrangement, but this was never implemented either. Massachusetts, Connecticut, and New Hampshire did not legislate establishments of religion, and the supporters of the Church-State systems there would have vigorously denied that they constitute an establishment of religion. The First Amendment was not intended to protect the establishments in the states because in the understanding of Americans at the time, there were no state establishments to protect.[85]

---

82. John T. Noonan, Jr., The End of Free Exercise?, 42 DePaul L. Rev. 567 (1992).

83. Noonan, *supra* note 1, at 357.

84. For example, Jesse Choper sees the relationship between the provisions as one of logically irreconcilable theses: "On the one hand, the Court has read the establishment clause as saying that if a law's purpose is to aid religion, it is unconstitutional. On the other hand, the Court has read the free exercise clause as saying that, under certain circumstances, the state must aid religion. Logically, the two theses are irreconcilable." Jesse H. Choper, The Free Exercise Clause: A Structural Overview and an Appraisal of Recent Developments, 27 Wm. & Mary L. Rev. 943, 947–48 (1986). Choper proposed to "reconcile" the clauses as follows: "Government action should be held to violate the Establishment Clause if it meets two criteria: first, if its purpose is to aid religion; and second, if it significantly endangers religious liberty in some way by coercing, compromising, or influencing religious beliefs." *Id.* at 948; *see also* Suzanna Sherry, *Lee v. Weisman*: Paradox Redux, 1992 Sup. Ct. Rev. 123, 147, 149 ("it is not possible simultaneously to implement the core values of both religion clauses.... The time has come to admit the conflict and to make an honest choice"). Her "honest choice" is to subordinate free exercise to nonestablishment; see Suzanna Sherry, Enlightening the Religion Clauses, 7 J. Contemp. Legal Issues 473 (1996).

85. Curry, *supra* note 6, at 41. Professor Akhil Amar suggests that the First Amendment was aimed at preventing the disestablishment of religion in six states which he views as having an establishment at the time of the amendment's ratification (New Hampshire, Massachusetts, Connecticut, Maryland, South Carolina, and Georgia). Amar omits discussion of contemporary views on disestablishment after the revolution. Akhil Reed Amar, The Bill of Rights: Creation and Reconstruction 32–45 (1998). *See also* Smith, *supra* note 23.

The approach one takes to the grammar and meaning of the Religion Clause is not a purely theoretical matter; it can also have far-reaching practical consequences. The net effect of viewing the nonestablishment principle as antireligious is that secularism wins out normally or even normatively, and that free exercise claims prevail only rarely and grudgingly. It is not clear whether Bruce Ackerman,[86] Suzanna Sherry,[87] or Kathleen Sullivan[88] would say precisely that,[89] but it seems a reasonable inference from their calls for a version of neutrality that brackets religious convictions (Ackerman), that subordinates free exercise to nonestablishment so as to subordinate religion to reason (Sherry), and that understands the Constitution to command a secular public order (Sullivan).

In sharp contrast, McConnell, who has explored how the two provisions of the Religion Clause can be viewed as harmonious, arrives at quite a different conclusion:

> Let there be no doubt: The Establishment Clause was a deliberate choice to allow all sects and modes of belief, religious as well as secular, to compete for the allegiance of the people, without official preference. The attempt to press the Religion Clauses into service as an instrument for "collective relativism," or

---

86. *See, e.g.*, Bruce A. Ackerman, Social Justice in the Liberal State 11 (1980) (in political decision-making, no citizen may assert "that his conception of the good is better than that asserted by any of his fellow citizens"); and Ackerman, We the People: Foundations 160 (1991). I wrote in 1992: "Among academics [there] seems to be an uncritical sociological assumption that America is a firmly secular nation." Edward McGlynn Gaffney, Jr., Hostility to Religion America Style, 42 DePaul L. Rev. 263, 268 (1992). Nothing in the intervening decade has led me to change my view. In 1990 I offered several historical examples of religion in American public life that challenged Ackerman's sense of what he called "neutrality" and that supported the basic approach to this issue taken by Michael J. Perry, Morality, Politics, and Law: A Bicentennial Essay (1988); Edward McGlynn Gaffney, Jr., Politics Without Brackets on Religious Convictions: Michael Perry and Bruce Ackerman on Neutrality, 64 Tul. L. Rev. 1143 (1990). Since then, Perry has written several books sustaining the argument that the Constitution does not command a secular public order in the sense that religious convictions may never play a role in the formation of public policy. *See, e.g.*, Michael J. Perry, Love and Power: The Role of Religion and Morality in American Politics 8–29 (1991) (criticizing the view that "disputed beliefs about human good should play no or at most a marginal role in political justification"); Perry, Religion in Politics: Constitutional and Moral Perspectives (1997).

87. *See* Suzanna Sherry, Enlightening the Religion Clauses, 7 J. Contemp. Legal Issues 473 (1996) (free exercise is subordinate to nonestablishment, the purpose of which is to subordinate religion to reason).

88. *See* Kathleen M. Sullivan, Religion and Liberal Democracy, 59 U. Chi. L. Rev. 195, 197–99 (1992). *See also* Kyron Huigens, Science, Freedom of Conscience, and the Establishment Clause, 13 U. Puget Sound L. Rev. 65, 104 (1989); Robert Audi, The Separation of Church and State and the Obligations of Citizenship, 18 Phil. & Pub. Affairs 259, 274–96 (1989); Edward B. Foley, Political Liberalism and Establishment Clause Jurisprudence, 43 Case W. Res. L. Rev. 963 (1993).

89. Smith writes of Sullivan: "Whether Kathleen Sullivan understands her position in this way is unclear. She introduces her view that the Constitution commands a secular public order in a vaguely historical way—she sometimes uses the past tense, and she alludes to a social contract that was ostensibly made at some point in time—but offers no historical evidence to support her claim or to dispel the suspicion that her social contract, like other familiar social contracts, is a convenient historical fiction.... Hence, when Sullivan asserts that the Constitution establishes a secular public order, I cannot confidently say whether she means (a) that the framers intended this, (b) that the Supreme Court has construed the religion clauses to mean this, (c) that Sullivan herself likes this view and therefore attributes it to the Constitution by employing a helpful fiction, or (d) something else." Smith, *supra* note 23, at 150. Reviewers regard Smith's project as "anti-theory"; *see* Christopher L. Eisgruber & Lawrence G. Sager, Review Essay: Unthinking Religious Freedom, 74 Tex. L. Rev. 577, 578 (1996); Thomas Berg, *supra* note 66.

any other official orthodoxy, must be condemned in the strongest possible terms.[90]

McConnell has also written: "Some argue for a totally secular public sphere...on the ground that the First Amendment committed the United States to a certain public philosophy: a liberal, democratic, secular 'civil religion'.... As an historical assertion about the meaning of the First Amendment, however, this position is plainly false."[91] In a similar vein, Frederick Mark Gedicks and Roger Hendix have written: "Much as those who influence American political and cultural institutions may want to insist that ours is a secular state..., Americans remain avowedly religious, with all of the unrational and unempirical—and spiritual and transcendent—conceptions of reality which that term implies. Insistence upon exclusively secular constructions of reality today is as undemocratic as social darwinism was in 1906."[92] There is no contradiction between a government cabined to the secular and a society that is openly and strongly religious. The one generates the other.

Claiming that a position is linked with the American heritage can be controversial, but if we do not contend vigorously about this matter we may forget which country we live in and which constitution we are exploring. In the Soviet Union, state-imposed atheism held sway for nearly seventy-five years. In revolutionary France, anticlericalism and antireligiosity were confused with liberty, fraternity, and equality. But whenever Americans have conformed to a model of disestablishment that entailed hostility towards religion, it has been not normative but aberrational.[93]

One shrewd observer of America, Alexis de Tocqueville, was fully aware of the antireligious excesses in his own country. Perhaps for that very reason, he was astonished to see the degree to which religion played so vital a role in mid-nineteenth-century American life. He wrote: "Religion—which with the Americans never mixes directly in the government of the society—must be considered as the foremost of their political institutions."[94] No one familiar with Tocqueville's argument would make the mistake that he thought religion was still established in the United States. On the contrary, it was precisely because of nonestablishment that he found free exercise of religion so evident as to rank as "the foremost" of the institutions that equip one for ruling and being ruled.

The commonplace bifurcation of the Religion Clause into two separate competing clauses has deeply affected the Court's jurisprudence on religion. It is mistaken. So are the tons of commentary in which scholars repeat the same error, which has no basis in the text of the First Amendment or in the history surrounding its adoption.

---

90. McConnell, *supra* note 79, at 740.

91. Michael W. McConnell, Religious Freedom at a Crossroads, 59 U. Chi. L. Rev. 115, 190–191 (1992); *see also* John H. Garvey, The Pope's Submarine, 30 San Diego L. Rev. 849, 872 (1993) (nonestablishment principle does not forbid "public officials to act on beliefs [with] religious origins" and free exercise principle "positively encourages it"); Garvey, A Comment on Religious Convictions and Lawmaking, 84 Mich. L. Rev. 1288 (1986).

92. Frederick Mark Gedicks & Roger Hendix, Democracy, Autonomy, and Values: Some Thoughts on Religion and Law in Modern America, 60 S. Cal. L. Rev. 1579, 1618 (1987); *see also* Richard John Neuhaus, ed., Unsecular America (1986).

93. *See* Gaffney, Hostility to Religion, *supra* note 86.

94. Tocqueville, Democracy in America (1845), *reprinted in* Noonan and Gaffney, Religious Freedom, *supra* note 1, at 244–53.

The Relevance of Nineteenth-Century
History to Free Exercise of Religion

Much of this volume refers to practices of state and local government. The concluding comments of this chapter urge religious leaders and government lawyers to identify the common ground between them in an effort to avoid expensive litigation. When such litigation becomes necessary, the standard legal tool relied upon in courts to resolve such conflicts assumes that the twin values of nonestablishment and free exercise, discussed above, are binding on the states as part of the liberty secured against state action by the Due Process Clause of the Fourteenth Amendment.

In 1940 the Court decided to apply the Religion Clause of the First Amendment to the laws and customs of the several states. It held the liberty secured by the Fourteenth Amendment Due Process Clause ("No State shall...deprive any person of...liberty... without due process of law") to include the religious liberty protected by the First Amendment. The tool used to justify this result is known as substantive due process. John Hart Ely famously compared the oddness of the term — blending substance and process — to "green pastel redness."[95] So familiar, however, is this category in constitutional law that little attention is paid to its curiousness.

One advantage of paying attention to the nineteenth-century context of the framing of the Fourteenth Amendment would be a reassessment of the Privileges and Immunities Clause at the beginning of the text: "No State shall make or enforce any law which shall abridge the privileges or immunities of the citizens of the United States." This text is a much more likely vehicle for protecting religious freedom against infringement by the states than the Due Process Clause, which — as Ely correctly notes — is really about process. As I noted in the chapter on exemption of religious communities from federal taxation, the rich concept of privileges and immunities has deep roots in Roman law, where it was used for centuries to secure the religious freedom of Jews.[96] Amar has focused attention on the Privileges or Immunities provision as a better vehicle for achieving incorporation of the Bill of Rights against the states.[97] He notes, for example, that Congressman John Bingham, who drafted section 1 of the amendment, explained that he began the text "No State shall" in conscious imitation of the framers of Article I, section 9, which also begins "No State shall."[98] Bingham also expressly linked the privileges and immunities of national citizens with the first eight amendments of the Bill of Rights, including the Religion Clause.[99]

---

95. John Hart Ely, Democracy and Distrust 18 (1980).

96. Edward McGlynn Gaffney, Jr., "Exemption of Religious Communities from Federal Taxation," in this volume.

97. Amar, *supra* note 85, at 169–71, 181–86

98. Cong. Globe, 42d Cong., 1st Sess. 84 app. (1871), *citing* Chief Justice Marshall in *Barron v. Baltimore*, 32 U.S. 243 (1833), *cited in* Amar, *supra* note 85, at 164–65. The headline in the Congressional Globe for Bingham's speech on Feb. 28, 1866, reads: "In Support of the Proposed Amendment to Enforce the Bill of Rights."

99. Cong. Globe, 42d Cong., 1st Sess. 84 app. (1871), *cited in* Amar, *supra* note 85, at 183. Amar rightly wonders why "some scholars, most notably Charles Fairman and Raoul Berger, have suggested that when Bingham invoked 'the bill of rights,' he didn't mean what he said." *Id.*

Since this amendment was added to the Constitution as part of the movement to re-build or reconstruct the nation after the Civil War, it is imperative that scholars focus on that setting as the context within which the provisions of the Bill of Rights, including the Religion Clause, took on new meaning. Kurt Lash has contributed two articles, one on nonestablishment and one on free exercise, setting out the salient points of nineteenth-century history, including the vigorous role of religion in the abolitionist movement,[100] leading up to the adoption of the Fourteenth Amendment.[101] Lash notes that the framers of the Fourteenth Amendment were well aware that state legislatures could prevent the exercise of religion by the slaves from being full and free simply by making it a crime to teach blacks to read.[102] He concludes that since the framers saw through the "neutrality" of such laws, they intended the Fourteenth Amendment to serve as a bulwark against such state enactments, whether they took direct aim at the free exercise of religion or achieved the same result through "generally applicable" norms that on their face did not mention religion.[103] Lash also notes that for all the intensity of the Reconstruction Re-publicans' commitment to ending racial segregation, they respected the autonomy of re-ligious communities enough to exempt them from a general ban on segregation in pub-lic places, including cemeteries.[104] Several decades after the dismantling of Jim Crow laws, this exemption may seem a curious way of honoring religious freedom, but it illus-trates once again that the framers of our Constitution understood that they lack power to define or to control religious beliefs and practices.

Smith comments on Lash's work as follows:

> From *Everson* on, the extensive historical efforts in this field have focused on the colonial and founding periods; the critical evidence has included Jefferson's Virginia Statute for Religious Freedom, Madison's "Memorial and Remon-strance," and the discussions in the First Congress. If Lash is right, all these sources recede in relevance; Madison and Jefferson, Isaac Backus and John Le-land, would be displaced as definers of constitutional religious freedom by John Bingham, Thaddeus Stevens, Charles Sumner, and their contemporaries. Originalist scholars and judges would look to discern the views about the rela-

---

100. *See* materials in Noonan and Gaffney, Religious Freedom, *supra* note 1, at 254–87.

101. *See* Kurt T. Lash, The Second Adoption of the Establishment Clause: The Rise of the Non-establishment Principle, 27 Ariz. St. L.J. 1085 (1995); Lash, The Second Adoption of the Free Exer-cise Clause: Religious Exemptions under the Fourteenth Amendment, 88 Nw. U. L. Rev. 1106 (1994).

102. Lash, Second Adoption of Free Exercise, note 101 above, 88 Nw. U. L. Rev., at 1135–37 (1994) ("laws preventing blacks from learning to read the Bible were no less violations of religious liberty because the abridgement was the result of a religiously neutral law").

103. *Id.* at 1155. For example, Matthew Carpenter stated: "It cannot be doubted that they...in-tended to, and thought they had, carefully excluded the whole subject of religion from federal con-trol or interference." Cong. Globe, 42d Cong., 2d Sess. (1872), *excerpted in* The Reconstruction Amendments' Debates 600 (Va. Comm'n on Constitutional Gov't ed., 1967). And Senator Henry Anthony stated: "I am very anxious indeed to vote to give to the colored people all their legal rights, but I shall not vote to give any person any religious rights, or to take from any person any religious rights. If there are white men so foolish as to believe that it is not right for negroes to worship with them, I pity them, but I shall not vote to deprive them of their undoubted right to worship so.... I shall not vote for any bill that contains any provision which interferes with religious worship, even if it compels me to vote against the amnesty bill, which I should regret very much." *Id.* at 610. When Senator Sumner removed the provision purporting to regulate churches, his legislation was passed.

104. Lash, Religious Exemptions Under the Fourteenth Amendment, *supra* note 101, at 1151 n. 202, 1154–55.

tionship between government and religion that prevailed, not in the founding period, but rather in the post-Civil War reconstruction era.[105]

The comment is curious. Why the hesitation to acknowledge that Lash is right? Is it not obvious that in the search for the meaning of any text, attention should be paid to its authors and supporters? And why the needless conclusion that Madison and other founders should recede in relevance or should be displaced as definers of constitutional religious freedom? Lash did not argue that we should ignore the founding period, but that we must also pay attention to the views about religious freedom that led the framers of the Fourteenth Amendment to reaffirm the core principles of the Bill of Rights and apply them to the several states. This is not a case of either/or, but of both/and.

A Short Digest of the Case Law on the Religion Clause

Have the federal courts performed the role that Madison and the founders imagined they would?[106] The first judicial decision concerning an act of Congress challenged as a violation of free exercise involved the Church of Jesus Christ Latter-day Saints. In 1862 President Lincoln signed "An Act to punish and prevent the Practice of Polygamy in the Territories of the United States."[107] The Mormons claimed that statutes punishing polygamy unconstitutionally burdened the beliefs that underlie their practice of plural marriage. In *Reynolds v. United States*[108] the Court upheld a criminal conviction of George Reynolds, secretary to Brigham Young, for polygamy, adopting not only Jefferson's metaphor of a "wall of separation,"[109] but also Jefferson's distinction between belief

---

105. Smith, *supra* note 23, at 53. Amar does seem as welcoming of Lash's work as it deserves. He writes: "If, as Lash claims, 'freedom of religion' in the 1860s meant libertarian autonomy from government intrusion...." Amar, *supra* note 85, at 256. Why "if?"

106. This question is limited to what federal courts made of the First and Fourteenth Amendments. For a discussion of the treatment of religion in state constitutions, see Craig B. Mousin, "State Constitutions and Religious Liberty," in this volume.

107. 12 Stat. 501–502 (1862).

108. 98 U.S. 145 (1878).

109. *Id.* at 164. The wall metaphor was coined by Thomas Jefferson in his letter to the Danbury Baptists on Jan. 1, 1802. Noonan and Gaffney, Religious Freedom, *supra* note 1, 205–206. In the modern period it made its appearance in *Everson v. Bd. of Education*, 330 U.S. 1, 16 (1947). The justices have not agreed about the dimensions or composition of the wall. For Justice Black in Everson the wall was meant to be "high and impregnable." Justice Jackson lamented in *State of Ill., ex rel. McCollum v. Board of Ed. School Dist. No. 71, Champaign County, Ill.*, 333 U.S. 203, 238 (1948), that the wall was as "winding as the famous serpentine wall designed by Mr. Jefferson" at the University of Virginia. For Chief Justice Burger in *Lemon v. Kurtzmann*, 403 U.S. 602, 614 (1971) "the line of separation, far from being a 'wall,' is a blurred, indistinct, and variable barrier depending on all the circumstances of a particular relationship." Why, especially after the tearing down of the Berlin Wall as a symbolic moment signaling both the deep yearning for human freedom and the end of Cold War tensions, are Americans so enamored of the wall metaphor to describe the relationship between religious believers and the government? Disestablishment of an official religion is an important American achievement that differentiates competences. But that does not mean that the separation between these realms is best imaged by a wall. At least it might help to inquire, in the language of one of the farmers in Robert Frost's famous poem, "Mending Wall," what one is "walling in and walling out." The Collected Poems of Robert Frost 39 (1995), *supra* note 42. James Madison suggested not a wall but a line differentiating "the rights of religion and the Civil Authority." Letter of James Madison to the Reverend Jasper Adams, 1832, 9 The Writings of James Madison 484 (Putnam's, 1910),

and practice. This distinction had no basis whatever in the state constitutional provisions on free exercise, which manifestly included practices as well as beliefs.

The distinction between belief and action was ignored in *Davis v. Beason*,[110] the second Mormon case, which imposed on a Mormon the civil penalty associated with the regime of "toleration"—political disenfranchisement—merely for his beliefs in the doctrine of plural marriage. During this period Mormons were also excluded from jury service on the same basis.

Finally, in *The Late Corp. of the Church of Jesus Christ of Latter-day Saints v. United States*,[111] the Court sustained an act of Congress revoking the charter of the Mormon Church and confiscating its property. The president of the church, Wilford Woodruff, then issued the Mormon Manifesto, acknowledging: "Inasmuch as laws have been enacted by Congress forbidding plural marriages, which laws have been pronounced constitutional by the court of last resort, I hereby declare my intention to submit to those laws, and to use any influence with the members of the Church over which I preside to have them do likewise."[112] Without conceding a change in belief, Woodruff acknowledged that circumstances no longer made the practice applicable. No matter how the church explained the shift to its members, it is difficult to refrain from characterizing it as a change of belief that had come to pass because of federal law applied directly against a church.

For several decades the Court declined to honor the claims of conscience for exemptions from laws. In 1929 it refused citizenship to a Hungarian woman already past the age of military service, solely because of her refusal to declare that she would participate in the military.[113] It upheld the expulsion from the University of California at Berkeley of two Methodist students who took seriously the teaching of their church in 1928: "We renounce war as an instrument of national policy." Asserting a religious belief "that war, training for war, and military training are immoral," the students were suspended for

---

reprinted in John F. Wilson and Donald L. Drakeman, eds., Church and State in American History 80–82 (2d ed. 1987). Historian Sidney E. Mead notes that Madison's metaphor of a line, unlike Jefferson's wall, "does not conjure up the image of a solid and unchanging structure built by the founders, but rather 'the path of a moving point, thought of as having length but not breadth.'" Mead, Neither Church nor State: Reflections on James Madison's "Line of Separation," 10 J. Ch. & St. 349, 350 (1968). For comment on *Everson* within the context of the attempt of the French Revolution to eliminate religion in French public life, see Curry, *supra* note 6, at 46–53.

110. 133 U.S. 333 (1890), upholding anti-Mormon test oath, Rev. Statutes of Territory of Idaho, § 501, requiring voters to take an oath that they are not members of an organization that teaches polygamy; Noonan and Gaffney, Religious Freedom, *supra* note 1, at 299.

111. 136 U.S. 1 (1890).

112. *Id.* Noonan and Gaffney, *supra* note 1, at 306. For a discussion of the Mormon cases, see Sarah Barringer Gordon, The Mormon Problem: Religion, Marriage, and Constitutional Conflict in Nineteenth-Century America (2001).

113. United States v. Schwimmer, 279 U.S. 644 (1929). Rosika Schwimmer, a forty-nine-year-old Hungarian immigrant applying for naturalization, declared, "I am not willing to bear arms." The reason she offered for this position was: "My 'cosmic consciousness of belonging to the human family' is shared by all those who believe that all human beings are the children of God." The Court upheld denial of her naturalization application on the ground that the duty of citizens to defend their government by arms was a "fundamental principle of the Constitution." *See also* United States v. Macintosh, 283 U.S. 605 (1931). Douglas Clyde Macintosh, a Canadian, applied for naturalization. He was a Baptist minister who had served as chaplain at the front in World War I; he was now Dwight Professor of Theology at Yale. He declared he would not support the United States "right or wrong" or promise to take up arms in its defense. He "could not put allegiance to the government of any country before allegiance to the will of God." He, too, was denied citizenship. *But see* Girouard v. United States, 328 U.S. 61 (1946).

failing to take a required course in military training at a time when no war was being waged and when America's isolationism rendered war unlikely.[114] And it upheld a state's refusal to admit to the bar an otherwise qualified applicant who declined to take an oath to support the Illinois constitution, which required all able-bodied persons to bear arms in time of war.[115]

The government could not have sustained the Vietnam War without military conscription. The draft law exempted from military service persons whose opposition was not merely personal or sociological, but was grounded in belief in a Supreme Being.

The Court invoked Paul Tillich's concept of the Ground of Being to extend the exemption to those who did not maintain a belief in God in a traditional sense.[116] Congress revised the draft law, eliminating the reference to a Supreme Being and extending exempt status to those who "by virtue of religious training or belief [were] opposed to war in any form."[117] The Court defined "religious training or belief" in a creative way that extended exempt status to persons who diverged from traditional religious belief in God,[118] but it defined "war in any form" in a rigid way that denied exempt status to a Catholic who was willing to serve in the military but opposed the Vietnam War[119] on the ground that it did not conform to the teaching of his church in the Second Vatican Council: "Any act of war aimed indiscriminately at the destruction of entire cities or of extensive areas along with their population is a crime against God and man himself. It merits unequivocal and unhesitating condemnation."[120]

The Court refused to allow Jehovah's Witnesses to involve their children in the distribution of religious literature in violation of child labor laws.[121] A federal circuit court required a Witness to have a blood transfusion.[122] The Supreme Court held that states could enforce Sunday closing laws—grounded in colonial blue laws—that put observant Jews and other sabbatarians at a distinct economic disadvantage,[123] and it sustained the application of minimum wage laws to unpaid volunteers in a religious community.[124] Many of these results are justifiable, but none is correct where judges engage in deciding religious matters.

The Madisonian expectation of vigorous judicial enforcement of the Bill of Rights did not emerge until well after the creation of the modern welfare state, with its pervasive regulation of nearly every dimension of the economy. Two cases in the 1940s illus-

---

114. Hamilton v. Regents of the Univ. of Cal., 293 U.S. 245 (1934).

115. *In re* Summers, 325 U.S. 561 (1945).

116. United States v. Seeger, 380 U.S. 163 (1965); on his application for exempt status, Seeger indicated that his "skepticism or disbelief in the existence of God" did "not necessarily mean lack of faith in anything whatsoever"; that he maintained a "belief in and devotion to goodness and virtue for their own sakes, and a religious faith in a purely ethical creed." He cited such personages as Plato, Aristotle, and Spinoza for support of his ethical belief in intellectual and moral integrity "without belief in God, except in the remotest sense."

117. Selective Service Act of 1967, 81 Stat. 104, 50 U.S.C. App. § 456(j).

118. Welsh v. United States, 398 U.S. 333 (1970).

119. Negre v. Larsen, 401 U.S. 437 (1971).

120. Pastoral Constitution on the Church in the Modern World, Par. 80, Walter Abbott, ed., The Documents of Vatican II 294 (1966).

121. Prince v. Massachusetts, 321 U.S. 158 (1944).

122. *In re* President and Directors of Georgetown College, 331 F.2d 1000 (D.C. Cir.), *cert. denied*, 377 U.S. 978 (1964); *see also* John F. Kennedy Memorial Hosp. v. Heston, 58 N.J. 576, 279 A.2d 670 (1971).

123. Braunfeld v. Brown, 366 U.S. 599 (1961).

124. Tony and Susan Alamo Found. v. Secretary of Labor, 471 U.S. 290 (1985).

trate the contrast between Locke and Madison on toleration and free exercise, and on the role of the judiciary in protecting civil liberties. In the first case, *Minersville School District v. Gobitis*[125] the Witnesses had been told that they had no free exercise right to an exemption from saluting the flag. Although the Court was nearly unanimous in *Gobitis*, few of its decisions in modern times have met with such across-the-board intellectual rejection.[126]

Much of what people do when they are exercising their religious convictions involve some form of communication or expressive activity—listening, speaking, singing, waiting quietly, marching in procession. Thus it is possible to characterize a free exercise claim under the rubric of free speech.[127] The Court did so in the second flag salute case, *West Virginia State Board of Education v. Barnette*.[128] On Flag Day in 1943, the Court announced that school officials could not require Jehovah's Witnesses to salute the flag. The ground for this decision was that the government may not compel a person to say things they did not believe. If someone were to say years later that these two results can be harmonized on the ground that the 1940 decision was a free exercise case and the 1943 decision was a free speech case, would that be reasonable?

One way to decide would be to ask the Witnesses about the basis for their refusal to salute the flag. In both instances, they would tell us, it was manifestly a religious matter based squarely upon their interpretation of the second commandment prohibiting worship of graven images.[129] None of the justices in 1943, including the dissenters, were in the slightest doubt that *Gobitis* still stood on solid ground; all understood clearly that the 1940 decision had been reversed. The *Barnette* court expressly overruled *Gobitis*—a point duly noted by Justice Frankfurter, the author of *Gobitis*, who dissented in *Barnette*.

The Court reached this starkly different result within a short period of three years, in part because of the eruption of outrageous violence[130] against the Witnesses after the

---

125. 310 U.S. 586 (1940).

126. The *Gobitis* opinion was repudiated roundly in many journals of opinion. The *New Republic*, which Frankfurter had helped found, said the Court had come "dangerously close" to being the victim of war hysteria. *Christian Century*, a liberal Protestant magazine, said, "Courts that will not protect even Jehovah's Witnesses will not long protect anybody." *America*, a Jesuit journal, said that the Court had permitted destruction of "one of the most precious rights under the Federal and our State Constitutions." The *Harvard Educational Review* said the decision subordinated the civil liberties of minorities to "the will of the majority." Thirty-nine law reviews discussed the decision, thirty-one of them critically. David R. Manwaring, Render unto Caesar: The Flag-Salute Controversy 149–57 (1962).

127. Characterizing free exercise as free speech is no guarantee that the religious speech will be protected. Sometimes it has been. Wooley v. Maynard, 430 U.S. 705 (1977); Widmar v. Vincent, 454 U.S. 263 (1981); Lamb's Chapel v. Ctr. Moriches Union Free Sch. Dist., 508 U.S. 384 (1993); Rosenberger v. Rector and Visitors of the Univ. of Virginia, 515 U.S. 819 (1995). Sometimes it has not. Heffron v. International Soc'y for Krishna Consciousness, 452 U.S. 640 (1981); International Soc'y for Krishna Consciousness v. Lee, 505 U.S. 672 (1992).

128. 319 U.S. 624 (1943).

129. Exod. 20:3–4; Deut. 5:7–9.

130. The Witnesses were already unpopular. Before the *Gobitis* decision came down on June 3, 1940, they had been victims of several incidents of mob violence in Texas. After the decision, individual Witnesses were attacked in Maine (beatings, burning of the Kingdom Hall in Kennebunk); West Virginia (forced drinking of castor oil); Wyoming (tarring and feathering); Nebraska (castration); Arkansas (shooting); Illinois, Indiana, Maryland, Mississippi, Oregon (mob attacks). Forty percent of the incidents occurred in two states, Oklahoma and Texas. Small towns, intolerant of outsiders, were the usual sites. Manwaring, *supra* note 125, at 163–73.

first decision, and in part because of the events unfolding after the United States entered the war against Nazi Germany, where the nation-state was deified and absolute allegiance to the Führer was demanded, with special prominence given to the swastika flag at mass rallies planned as pagan liturgical rituals.[131]

Whatever the reasons for the result in *Barnette*, the two cases represent profoundly differing approaches to judicial protection of religious minorities. Justice Jackson wrote in *Barnette*:

> The very purpose of a Bill of Rights was to withdraw certain subjects from the vicissitudes of political controversy, to place them beyond the reach of majorities and officials and to establish them as legal principles to be applied by the courts. One's right to life, liberty, and property, to free speech, a free press, *freedom of worship* and assembly, and other fundamental rights may not be submitted to vote; they depend on the outcome of no elections."[132]

Frankfurter wrote in his dissent:

> The constitutional protection of religious freedom terminated disabilities, it did not create new privileges. It gave religious equality, not civil immunity. Its essence is freedom from conformity to religious dogma, not freedom from conformity to law because of religious dogma.... Otherwise each individual could set up his own censor against obedience to laws conscientiously deemed for the public good by those whose business it is to make laws."[133]

Writing shortly after the Court's opinion in *Smith*, which embraced the spirit of the dissent in *Barnette*, McConnell concludes his masterful article on the historical origins of free exercise with a comment on the Frankfurter dissent:

> Justice Frankfurter overlooked the unique American contribution to church-state relations and embraced instead the Enlightenment ideal of Locke and Jefferson. Locke and Jefferson may well have been animated, in Justice Frankfurter's words, by the "freedom from conformity to religious dogma." But that is not what the Baptists, Quakers, Lutherans, and Presbyterians who provided the political muscle for religious freedom in America had in mind. To them, the freedom to follow religious dogma was one of this nation's foremost blessings, and the willingness of the nation to respect the claims of a higher authority than "those whose business it is to make laws" was one of the surest signs of its liberality.[134]

---

131. This was not an abstract theoretical matter for the Witnesses. "From 1933 to 1945, the Nazis imprisoned 10,000 Jehovah's Witnesses, executing more than 200 for refusing military service. As many as 5000 died in concentration camps. Despite persecution, Witnesses clung fervently to their religious beliefs, which did not allow the bearing of arms, and steadfastly refused to swear allegiance to the Nazi state." Marilyn Harran et al., The Holocaust Chronicle 171 (2000). *See also* Falk Pingel, "Jehovah's Witnesses," in Israel Gutman, ed, 2 Encyclopedia of the Holocaust 742–43 (1990); Hans Hesse, Persecution and Resistance of Jehovah's Witnesses during the Nazi Regime, 1933–1945 (2001); and The Jehovah's Witnesses and the Nazis: Persecution, Deporatation, and Murder, 1933–1945 (2001).

132. *Barnette*, 319 U.S. at 638 (emphasis added).

133. *Id.* at 653 (Frankfurter, J., dissenting).

134. McConnell, *supra* note 8, at 1517.

In *Sherbert v. Verner,*[135] *Wisconsin v. Yoder,*[136] and *Thomas v. Review Board,*[137] the Court adopted a methodology that required government lawyers to demonstrate the compelling character of the government's interest in a regulation burdening the exercise of religion, and to show an effort to accommodate the exercise of religion through a less burdensome means. This arrangement allows the government to prevail over a religious claim, not by attacking the claim but by demonstrating the paramount importance of the government's legitimate secular interest and its inability to achieve that interest in any way other than by burdening religious exercise.

Is this methodology required by the First Amendment Religion Clause? To put the question that way is misleading. It assumes that the founders could have foreseen the development of a vast regulatory apparatus and could have provided for a balancing mechanism to keep excessive governmental power in check. As Curry writes, "studies of the [first] amendment often treat it as a statement intended to provide answers at the time to specific questions in a distant future, rather than as a proclamation of principle by a people unable to envisage its application beyond the limits of their own experience."[138] But Curry also argues that "[i]n the absence of direct historical evidence, the issue of exemptions for the sake of conscience must be debated within the context of what is most compatible with the spirit and purpose of the First Amendment,... [which] was enacted to deprive the government of power in religious matters."[139] Curry concludes, as I do, that exempting religious claimants from a law in which the government does not have a compelling interest is "more in harmony with the original purpose of the amendment than...the 'secular rule' that if laws are valid secular laws, they admit of no exemption apart from what the legislatures choose to provide."[140]

Whether or not the Court's methodology in *Sherbert,* *Yoder,* and *Thomas* is consistent with the spirit and purpose of the First Amendment, it must be acknowledged that this method of protecting religious freedom had become ineffective by the 1980s, when the Court repeatedly trivialized the free exercise of religion,[141] or at least made it pretty

---

135. 374 U.S. 398 (1963).

136. 406 U.S. 205 (1972).

137. 450 U.S. 707 (1981).

138. Curry, *supra* note 6, at 4; *see also* Curry, *supra* note 33, at 221 ("Except in a few instances [the founders] passed to subsequent generations the task of working out the consequences of the principle that the state had no competence in religious matters in a society wherein customs, mores, laws, and religion intertwined and wherein the majority equated religion with Protestantism").

139. Curry, *supra* note 6, at 97.

140. *Id.* at 98. Curry notes three difficulties with the "secular rule." First, it "assumes that a law is not aimed at the restriction of religious belief or practice," placing "assessment of a religious matter in the hands of secular judges." Second, it "assigns the vindication of religious liberty to the political process, even though the purpose of the Bill of Rights is to withdraw certain rights from that political process, to proclaim them as inalienable, anterior to government, and not dependent on the will of the majority." Third, it is "ineffective as a rule of law in that it proposes relief for majorities who have no need of it and voids relief for minorities who do." *Id.* at 98–99.

141. *See, e.g.,* Goldman v. Weinberger, 475 U.S. 503 (1986) (rabbi in armed forces required to remove yarmulke lest it "detract from the uniformity sought by the dress regulations"); O'Lone v. Estate of Shabazz, 482 U.S. 342 (1987) (sustaining prison regulations failing to accommodate sincerely held religious beliefs of Muslims to take part in Jumu'ah, weekly communal prayer service); Lyng v. Northwest Indian Cemetery Protective Association, 485 U.S. 439 (1988) (allowing construction of road for private logging interests through federally owned land, despite Court's acknowledgement that it would have "devastating effects on traditional Indian religious practices" and despite agency finding that reasonable alternative existed).

easy for government lawyers to prevail by exaggerating the importance of the interest they presented to courts as "compelling."[142] In many of these instances, Congress provided legislative relief that was more sensitive to religious liberty than the Court had been.[143]

In *Employment Division v. Smith*,[144] the Court relied upon the first flag salute case without mentioning that *Gobitis* had been overruled in *Barnette*. It adopted the Lockean regime of toleration, not the Madisonian vision of full and free exercise of religion. It viewed the judicial function in the self-restraint that is consistent with the Lockean notion that "there is no judge upon earth between the supreme magistrate and the people,"[145] not the Madisonian promise that "independent tribunals of justice will consider themselves in a peculiar manner the guardians of [the] rights"[146] secured in the First Amendment. But it suggested at least that the political branches might surround religious exercise with greater freedom than they deemed required by the Constitution: "Values that are protected against government interference through enshrinement in the Bill of Rights are not thereby banished from the political process."[147] Most significantly, the *Smith* Court undermined the methodology of *Sherbert-Yoder-Thomas*, shifting the burden of proof to the religious claimant, who would now be required to demonstrate that the government intended to single out his or her religious beliefs for intentional mischief, or that the statute or custom under question took direct aim at a religious belief or practice.

The Court promptly docketed a case of that sort and ruled in *Church of Lukumi Babalu Aye, Inc. v. City of Hialeah, Florida*[148] that it meant business when it ruled in *Smith* that intentional discrimination against a religious community—"persecution," as Justice Kennedy called it—was constitutionally impermissible. Although it is some comfort to learn that the justices have pledged themselves to guard against persecution, since when is full-blown persecution of a religious community the measure of the value of religious freedom? The Court once again had substituted something less robust than the full and free exercise of religion that Madison advocated.

---

142. In *United States v. Lee*, 455 U.S. 252 (1982) the Court imposed social security tax payments on the Amish, despite their view that it is sinful to receive social security benefits or to pay the tax. Chief Justice Burger suggested that the rationale for this conclusion was that uniform collection of the tax—even from persons who would never draw any benefits from the system—was essential for the survival of the social security system.

143. In response to *Goldman v. Weinberger*, relying upon its power to spend and to regulate the army and navy, Congress enacted legislation providing that members of the armed forces may wear items of religious apparel whole in uniform, except where the Secretary of Defense determines that donning such apparel would interfere with the performance of military duties. National Defense Authorization Act for Fiscal Year 1988 and 1989, 101 Stat. 1019, 1086–87, 10 U.S.C. §774. In response to *O'Lone v. Estate of Shabaz*, Congress enacted the Religious Land Use and Institutionalized Persons Act of 2000, Pub. L. 106-274, 114 Stat 803. Within months after *Lyng v. Northwest Indian Cemetery Protective Association*, Congress withheld authorization from the Secretary of the Interior to build the proposed road. Amendments to Department of the Interior and Related Agencies Appropriations Act, Pub. L. 100-446, 102 Stat. 1826 (Sept. 27, 1988); *see* H.R. Rep. No. 713, 100th Cong., 2d Sess. 72 (1988). In response to *United States v. Lee*, Congress afforded relief to the Amish in the tax code.

144. 494 U.S. 872 (1990).

145. John Locke, A Letter concerning Toleration, in Noonan & Gaffney, Religious Freedom, *supra* note 1, at 153.

146. 1 Annals of Cong. 457 (J. Gales ed. 1834) (June 8, 1789).

147. *Smith*, 494 U.S. 872, 890 (1990).

148. 508 U.S. 520 (1993).

What remained to be seen was whether the Court also meant what it said when it announced in *Smith* that aggrieved parties could always turn to the political branches for redress of grievances. A broad coalition of religious communities persuaded their representatives in Congress to act. The Judiciary Committees of the House and Senate held hearings and found that religious freedom had suffered because of this shift in judicial attitude. The House approved the bill unanimously, and the Senate adopted the legislation by a vote of 97–3. On November 16, 1993, President Clinton signed the Religious Freedom Restoration Act (RFRA),[149] providing a remedy to religious claimants that shifted the burden of proof on these matters back to the government.

In *City of Boerne v. Flores*,[150] under the power to landmark historical sites, a city in Texas had decided that a church could not tear down a structure and build a newer church to accommodate the needs of a growing congregation. The result of this decision was to deny to many Catholics every Sunday the opportunity to take part in the Mass. On any of the views explored below—substantive neutrality, nondiscrimination, and nonentanglement of government with religion—the church should have emerged with freedom to enlarge its space of worship. But this conflict became the vehicle for testing the constitutionality of RFRA. Sometimes the Court gets involved in an interbranch conflict to inform Congress that it may not invade the prerogatives of the executive branch.[151] In *Boerne* the emphasis was on shoring up the authority of the judiciary. Justice Kennedy cited *Marbury v. Madison*[152] for the proposition that "When the Court has interpreted the Constitution, it has acted within the province of the Judicial Branch, which embraces the duty to say what the law is."[153] The Court invalidated RFRA as applied to the states, characterizing the remedy devised by Congress as a "substantive" determination, a matter left for judges alone to resolve. And the Court made powerful inroads on the enforcement power of the Fourteenth Amendment,[154] which refers to Congress, not the judiciary, and which had been the power source for civil rights laws

---

149. 42 U.S.C. § 2000bb-1 et seq.; *see* Douglas Laycock & Oliver S. Thomas, Interpreting the Religious Freedom Restoration Act, 73 Tex. L. Rev. 209 (1994), and Thomas C. Berg, What Hath Congress Wrought? An Interpretive Guide to the Religious Freedom Restoration Act, 39 Vill. L. Rev. 1 (1994).

150. 521 U.S. 507 (1997).

151. *See, e.g.,* Buckley v. Valeo, 424 U.S. 1 (1976) (Congress does not have power to appoint member of Executive branch); *but see* Morrison v. Olson, 487 U.S. 654 (1988) (judges may appoint prosecutors, who may spend public funds without an authorization of funds from Congress!).

152. 1 Cranch (5 U.S.) 137, 177 (1803) ("It is emphatically the province and duty of the judicial department to say what the law is"); see also Federalist No. 78 (Hamilton), The Federalist Papers 492 (1966) ("The interpretation of the laws is the proper and peculiar province of the courts").

153. 521 U.S. 507, 536 (1997).

154. Section 5 of the Fourteenth Amendment provides: "The Congress shall have power to enforce, by appropriate legislation, the provisions of this article." *See* Article I, §8: "The Congress shall have Power...to make all Laws which shall be necessary and proper for carrying into Execution the foregoing Powers." A conflict arose over the interpretation of the necessary and proper clause in the Washington administration. Alexander Hamilton, secretary of the treasury, urged a broad interpretation that favored legislation setting up a national bank. Thomas Jefferson, secretary of state, urged a strict construction opposing the bank. Opinion on the Constitutionality of the Bill Establishing a National Bank (Feb. 15, 1791), 19 The Papers of Thomas Jefferson 275 (J. Boyd ed. 1974). Attorney General Edmund Randolph argued against the constitutionality of the bank bill. See Walter Dellinger and H. Jefferson Powell, The Constitutionality of the Bank Bill: The Attorney General's First Constitutional Law Opinions, 44 Duke L.J. 110 (1994). President Washington sided with Hamilton. Chief Justice Marshall articulated the classical judicial view of the necessary and proper clause in *McCulloch v. Maryland*, 17 U.S. (4 Wheat.) 316 (1819) (unanimously sustaining power of Congress to charter the Second Bank of the United States).

that transformed the country in the 1960s. To what end? To reinstate Lockean toleration, or the view of Mason before Madison won him over. As noted above, this view is rife with problems of who will do the tolerating and the limits of what will be tolerated.

Although Professor Marshall has defended *Employment Division v. Smith*[155] and I continue to regard it as mistaken, the scope of this chapter is much larger than the scholarly debate over *Smith* and RFRA.[156] It is about different understandings of religious life. In the Lockean version of our constitution, religious exercise is confined to what the government will tolerate. In the Madisonian version, religion flourishes—as it has throughout the American centuries—not because it is helped or sponsored by the government, but because it has claimed as a natural right the freedom to thrive and to prosper with God's gracious help.

Free Exercise and the Protection
of Religious Communities

In one way or another, all of the essays in this volume reinforce a single common theme, that the self-understanding of religious communities is worthy of respect in our republic. Douglas Laycock argues that the right to church autonomy includes not simply "the bare freedom to carry on religious activities," but also "the right of churches to conduct these activities autonomously: to select their own leaders, define their own doctrines, resolve their own disputes, and run their own institutions."[157] Why so? Because, Laycock notes, "[r]eligion includes important communal elements for most believers. They exercise their religion through religious organizations, and these organizations must be protected...."[158] In a similar vein, Tribe acknowledges: "Any attempt to constitutionalize the relationship of the state to religion must address the fact that much of religious life is inherently associational...."[159] For example, Perry Dane describes the

---

155. *See* William P. Marshall, In Defense of Smith and Free Exercise Revisionism, 58 U. Chi. L. Rev. 308 (1991).

156. *See, e.g.,* Michael McConnell, Free Exercise Revisionism and the Smith Decision, 57 U. Chi. L. Rev. 1109 (1990); Douglas Laycock, The Remnants of Free Exercise, 1990 Sup. Ct. Rev. 1; James Gordon, Free Exercise at the Mountaintop, 79 Cal. L. Rev. 91 (1991); for scholarly views opposed to the permissibility of RFRA, see Eugene Gressman and Angela C. Carmella, The RFRA Revision of the Free Exercise Clause, 57 Ohio St. L.J. 65 (1996 ("The RFRA is a congressional arrow aimed directly at the heart of the independent judicial function of constitutional interpretation"); William W. Van Alstyne, The Failure of the Religious Freedom Restoration Act Under Section 5 of the Fourteenth Amendment, 46 Duke L.J. 291 (1996); Christopher L. Eisgruber and Lawrence G. Sager, Why the Religious Freedom Restoration Act Is Unconstitutional, 69 N.Y.U. L. Rev. 437 (1994); and Marci Hamilton, The Religious Freedom Restoration Act: Letting the Fox into the Henhouse Under Cover of Section 5 of the Fourteenth Amendment, 16 Cardozo L. Rev. 357 (1994).

157. Douglas Laycock, Toward a General Theory of the Religion Clauses: The Case of Church Labor Relations and the Right to Church Autonomy, 81 Colum. L. Rev. 1373, 1389 (1981). It is possible to read this duty of safeguarding free exercise of religion either as a governmental guarantee or as a warning against governmental intermeddling in religious beliefs that the people retain as a matter of natural right. Curry has shown that the second view is the original perspective of the framers of the First Amendment.

158. *Id.*

159. Tribe, *supra* note 81, §14-1, at 1155.

dimensions of communal life that must exist in order that Judaism be exercised freely: Jews need access not only to a synagogue where a minyan can pray, but also to kosher slaughtering and to a cemetery in which their dead may be buried according to the rituals observed by their community.[160] Analogous points could be made about the ways in which other faiths entail communal obligations or have associational dimensions.

The handling of intrachurch disputes by the courts is a good barometer of whether free exercise or toleration is the dominant mode of constitutional interpretation. Tribe notes: "The doctrine of judicial deference to a religion's internal decision-making organs...has deep historical roots."[161] Justice Miller articulated the classic statement of this view *in Watson v. Jones*,[162] an 1871 decision resolving a dispute among Presbyterians in Louisville, Kentucky, over whether the General Assembly of the church possessed authority to determine which of two factions was in conformity with the church's teaching on slavery and insurrection. The Court clearly recognized that it had no power to determine church teaching, since "[t]he law knows no heresy, and is committed to the support of no dogma, the establishment of no sect."[163] Instead, the Court adopted the rule of judicial deference to each religious community. If a church is governed in a congregational polity, then the local community could determine by a majority vote whether or not to remain in connection with the national denomination. But if a church is governed in a hierarchical manner, then the courts are bound to accept the judgment of the judicatory of that denomination. As Justice Miller put it: "whenever the questions of discipline, or of faith, or ecclesiastical rule, custom, or law have been decided by the highest of these church judicatories to which the matter has been carried, the legal tribunals must accept such decisions as final, and as binding on them."[164] The record indicated that the General Assembly had "the power of deciding in all controversies respecting doctrine and discipline; of reproving, warning, or hearing testimony against any error in doctrine or immorality in practice, in any Church, Presbytery, or Synod;...of superintending the concerns of the whole church;...of suppressing schismatical contentions and disputations; and, in general, of recommending and attempting reformation of manners, and the promotion of charity, truth, and holiness through all the churches under their care."[165] Hence the Court ruled in favor of the faction that the General Assembly had determined was the legitimate owner of the church property.

The Court did not determine which group had the better view of the morality of slavery, or the more correct view of Presbyterian polity. On the contrary, it correctly noted that it had no power to do so. Instead, the Court expressly repudiated the "departure from doctrine" approach, according to which courts determined which religious body should retain property donated with an implied trust, the body more closely maintaining the doctrine espoused by the donor, or the body that had departed from that doctrine or teaching. It is precisely this judicial involvement in religious matters that Justice Miller rejected in *Watson*. Nearly a century later, the Court reached the same conclusion — not as a matter of federal common law but as a matter of constitutional interpretation in *Presbyterian Church in the United States v. Mary Elizabeth Blue*

---

160. Perry Dane, The Varieties of Religious Autonomy, in Gerhard Robbers, ed. Church Autonomy: A Comparative Survey 117 (2001).

161. Tribe, *supra* note 81, §14-1, at 1155.

162. Watson v. Jones, 80 U.S. 679, 728–29 (1871).

163. *Id.* at 728.

164. *Id.* at 727.

165. *Id.* at 682.

Hull Memorial Presbyterian Church.[166] These decisions are exemplary illustrations of the claim above that the central purpose of the First Amendment Religion Clause was to deny to the government any power to decide religious matters.

Unfortunately, Tribe overstates the current situation when he writes: "Especially in the area of religion, courts in this country have been reluctant to interfere with the internal affairs of private groups."[167] Tribe wrote this appraisal after the Court had departed significantly from the sensible approach it had adopted in *Watson v. Jones* and confirmed in *Blue Hull*. In *Jones v. Wolf*,[168] the Court adopted a new approach that promised to limit judicial inquiry into religious doctrine,[169] but has in fact created a field day for judicial intermeddling in religious matters, creating not simply a few conflicts among the states but utter chaos for religious communities. In a single footnote an appellate court describes the chaos that has been generated by *Jones v. Wolf:* "Most courts faced with a post-*Jones* church property dispute did not have to choose between the polity approach and the neutral principles approach without precedential guidance. They simply noted that prior case law or statutes in their state required or suggested that one or the other approach be utilized."[170] As a result of this confusion in the lower courts, three Christian communities that clearly maintain a hierarchical polity—Epis-

---

166. 393 U.S. 440, 441 (1969) (question presented is "whether the restraints of the First Amendment, as applied to the States through the Fourteenth Amendment, permit a civil court to award church property on the basis of the interpretation and significance the civil court assigns to aspects of church doctrine").

167. Tribe, *supra* note 81, §14-1, at 1155.

168. 443 U.S. 595 (1979).

169. At several points in his commentary Tribe approves of the approach taken by the majority in *Jones v. Wolf*. Tribe, *supra* note 81, §14-6, at 1181, n. 4 (*Jones v. Wolf* limits judicial inquiry into religious doctrine in church property cases); §14-7, at 1190 (in construing deeds or wills, courts have consistently refused to interpret and apply religious terms; the fear has been that the judicial inquiry traditional as to nonreligious terms would cut too deeply into the autonomy of religious institutions); §14-11, at 1238–39 (neutral principles approach is "best understood as a way to reduce the entanglement that may result from judicial fact-finding").

170. Bishop of Colorado v. Mote, 716 P.2d 85, 96 n. 10 (Colo. 1986), *citing* Harris v. Apostolic Overcoming Holy Church of God, Inc., 457 So.2d 385, 387 (Ala. 1984) (neutral principles); Protestant Episcopal Church in the Diocese of Los Angeles v. Barker, 171 Cal. Rptr. 541, 548–49, *cert. denied*, 454 U.S. 864 (1981) (neutral principles); New York Annual Conference of the United Methodist Church v. Fisher, 438 A.2d 62, 68 (Conn. 1980) (polity approach); Grutka v. Clifford, 445 N.E.2d 1015, 1019 (Ind. App. 1983), *cert. denied*, 465 U.S. 1006 (1984) (neutral principles); Fluker Community Church v. Hitchens, 419 So.2d 445, 447–48 (La.1982) (neutral principles); Graffam v. Wray, 437 A.2d 627, 634 (Me.1981) (neutral principles); Babcock Memorial Presbyterian Church v. Presbytery of Baltimore, 464 A.2d 1008, 1016 (Md. 1983), *cert. denied*, 465 U.S. 1027 (1984) (neutral principles); Antioch Temple, Inc. v. Parekh, 422 N.E.2d 1337, 1340–42 (Mass. 1981) (polity); Bennison v. Sharp, 329 N.W. 2d 466, 474 (Mich. App. Ct. 1982) (polity); Piletich v. Deretich, 328 N.W. 2d 696, 701–02 (Minn.1982) (neutral principles); Protestant Episcopal Church v. Graves, 417 A.2d 19, 23–24 (N.J. 1980), *cert. denied sub nom.* Moore v. Protestant Episcopal Church, 449 U.S. 1131 (1981) (polity); Southside Tabernacle v. Pentecostal Church of God, 650 P.2d 231, 235 (Wash. App. Ct. 1982) (polity); Church of God of Madison v. Noel, 318 S.E. 2d 920, 923–24 (W. Va. 1984) (polity). A few courts chose a neutral principles approach after deciding not to follow more or less explicit polity precedents. *E.g.,*York v. First Presbyterian Church of Anna, 474 N.E. 2d 716 (Ill. App. Ct. 1984), *cert. denied*, 474 U.S. 864 (1985); Presbytery of Elijah Parish Lovejoy v. Jaeggi, 682 S.W. 2d 465 (Mo. 1984), *cert. denied*, 471 U.S. 1117 (1985); Presbytery of Beaver-Butler v. Middlesex Presbyterian Church, 489 A.2d 1317 (Pa. 1974), *cert. denied*, 474 U.S. 887 (1985); Foss v. Dykstra, 319 N.W. 2d 499 (S.D. 1982). And in *Fonken v. Community Church of Kamrar*, 339 N.W. 2d 810 (Iowa 1983), the Iowa Supreme Court had no precedent requiring the selection of one approach over the other, but the court avoided the issue by applying both polity and neutral principles (reaching the same result) without expressing a preference for either one.

copalians,[171] Presbyterians,[172] and Russian Orthodox Christians[173]—have all been held to be congregational in polity, with the consequence that a majority of those voting at the local level of these churches, called a parish, were awarded the church's property when they decided to leave the church.

Curry writes of *Jones v. Wolf*:

> In this case, the Court took a long step toward imposing a secularist approach on churches. It assumed that essentially religious documents can be read in purely secular terms and that the Court is the judge of religious doctrine because it has the power to decree when "doctrinal controversy" is not involved.[174]

It is perfectly acceptable for secular judges not to know much about the polity of religious organizations. Their competence is supposed to be in secular matters, not in theology or in canon law.[175] What is completely unacceptable is for judges to act as though they are empowered to translate their ignorance of the hierarchical structure of Episcopalians, Presbyterians, and Orthodox Christians into judicial decrees that have the effect of transforming hierarchically governed churches into Congregationalists or Baptists. That is an arrogation of the power that the First Amendment sought to deny to government, including judges. It is the replacement of full and free exercise of religion with a pale substitute, toleration, that turns quickly into ill-disguised intolerance or hostility. It is the disrespect or contempt for religious difference that is destructive of authentic pluralism.

This point brings us back to the importance of characterization stressed by James A. Serritella in his Prologue to this volume. A religious community and a civil corporation share some things in common. For example, after the demise of charitable immunity, both are regarded as legal "persons" who may sue and be sued. As Justice Miller wrote

---

171. The polity of the Protestant Episcopal Church in the United States is viewed as episcopal in Michigan and as congregational in Kentucky. *Compare* Bennison v. Sharp, 329 N.W. 2d 466 (Mich. Ct. App. 1982) *with* Bjorkman and St. John's Protestant Episcopal Church of Bellevue v. The Protestant Episcopal Church in the United States of America of the Diocese of Lexington, 759 S.W. 2d 583 (Ky. 1988).

172. The polity of the Presbyterian Church (U.S.A.) was viewed as hierarchical in Maryland and as congregational in Pennsylvania. *Compare* Babcock Memorial Presbyterian Church v. Presbytery of Baltimore, 464 A.2d 1008, 1016 (Md. 1983), *cert. denied*, 465 U.S. 1027 (1984) *with* Presbytery of Beaver-Butler v. Middlesex Presbyterian Church, 489 A.2d 1317 (Pa. 1986), *cert. denied*, 474 U.S. 887 (1985).

173. Primate and Bishops' Synod of the Russian Orthodox Church Outside of Russia v. Russian Orthodox Church of the Holy Resurrection, Inc., 636 N.E. 2d 211 (Mass. 1994), *cert. denied*, 513 U.S. 1121 (1995). I represented the petitioner in this matter. No justice voted to hear this case, which seems clearly inconsistent with the Court's teaching in the Russian Orthodox cases decided at the height of the Cold War, when the leadership of the church in Moscow was regarded as tainted by connection with the Communist regime of the Soviet Union. *See* Kedroff v. Saint Nicholas Cathedral of the Russian Orthodox Church in North America, 344 U.S. 94 (1952); *see* Mark DeWolfe Howe, Foreword: Political Theory and the Nature of Liberty, The Supreme Court, 1952 Term, 67 Harvard L. Rev. 91–95 (1953) (celebrating Court's recognition that the freedom of religious exercise could reside in a church as well as in an individual, and linking "liberty of self-government" of a church with authentic pluralism). *See also* St. Nicoholas Cathedral v. Kreshik, 164 N.E. 2d 687 (N.Y. 1959), *summarily reversed per curiam*, Kreshik v. St. Nicholas Cathedral, 363 U.S. 190 (1960) (repudiating judicial decision that "rests on the same premises which were found to have underlain the enactment of the statute struck down in Kedroff").

174. Curry, *supra* note 6, at 74–75.

175. *See, e.g.*, Thomas v. Review Board, 450 U.S. 707, 715 (1981) ("Intrafaith differences...are not uncommon among followers of a particular creed, and the judicial process is singularly ill equipped to resolve such differences").

in *Watson*: "Religious organizations come before us in the same attitude as other volun- tary associations for benevolent or charitable purposes, and their rights of property, or of contract, are equally under the protection of the law, and the actions of their mem- bers subject to its restraints."[176] As several chapters in this book illustrate, moreover, re- ligious organizations may, like commercial corporations, be subject to governmental regulation under some circumstances.[177] But a church is not the same thing as General Motors or some other Fortune 500 company. To treat religious organizations as if they were simply the same as commercial corporations in every respect would be to render the exercise of religion in this country neither full nor free.

Conclusion: Sensible Compromises and Resolute Resistance to Governmental Interference with Religion

I conclude this chapter with a story of compromise, one that might seem obvious but was surprisingly hard to come by. The case is unreported, but it is regrettably not a law school hypothetical. In real life, protracted negotiations were unavailing, and the church had to take a city to court before a settlement was reached. The conflict began with a demand by the fire department of Anderson Township in Hamilton County, Ohio, issued to a Catholic church that it refrain from allowing worshippers to hold lit candles during the midnight Mass on Christmas. Accepting the government's order would have had profound effects on the liturgical life of many Christian communities that use fire at a religious service known as the Paschal vigil;[178] and it would set a terrible precedent for the government to define and control the worship of any religious com- munity. At the outset of the negotiations, the city asserted that its interest in fire pre- vention trumped any other consideration. Christians were free to pray or to sing at this service, but not to engage in conduct—such as lighting the Paschal fire—that con- tained a risk to the safety of the community. Note the exaggeration of the governmental interest.

After *Sherbert, Yoder,* and *Thomas,* this case should have been easy—not because the governmental interest was insignificant, but because the government could easily have accommodated or respected the concerns of the religious community while safeguard- ing its own interest.[179] This approach takes seriously the least restrictive alternative stan- dard announced in *Sherbert, Yoder,* and *Thomas.* Instead, the Cincinnati case dragged on and threatened to escalate into a full-blown confrontation. Why so? I offer two pos- sible explanations. First, *Sherbert* got government attorneys used to exaggerating the na- ture of governmental interests—in this case, by pretending that a small controlled fire could burn the whole city—and it may have gotten church lawyers rusty at seeking the

---

176. Watson v. Jones, 80 U.S. at 714.

177. *See, e.g.,* Patrick J. Schiltz and Douglas Laycock, "Employment in Religious Organizations," and Thomas C. Berg, "Religiously Affiliated Education," in this volume.

178. For a fuller description of this issue, see Edward McGlynn Gaffney, Jr. Curious Chiasma: Rising and Falling Protection of Religious Freedom and Gender Equality, 4 U. Pa. J. Const. L. 394, 444–47 (2002).

179. *See* McConnell, *supra* note 78.

common ground. Second, *Smith* and *Boerne* withdrew from governmental attorneys any serious motivation to be respectful of religious communities, which they aggregate too readily within the scope of their legitimate secular concerns.

To return to the facts in the Ohio case, my suggestion to the church lawyers seeking my counsel was that the case didn't involve a stark either/or alternative but had plenty of room for both sides to get what they needed. I urged the church lawyers to keep driving the government lawyers to the common ground in the hope that they could eventually see the point that a win/win solution was desirable. Would it impress the authorities if the church took seriously the Gospel injunction to walk a second mile with an adversary compelling you to walk one mile?[180] In these circumstances it might not only mean having doors easily opened from the inside or fire extinguishers installed throughout the church. It might also mean having a firefighter train ushers in the use of such equipment, or providing the ushers with cell phones for emergency use.

But there is one thing it cannot mean. That is allowing municipal authorities to tell Lutherans, Catholics, Episcopalians, and other liturgical Christians that celebrating the spark of light piercing the darkness in the way they have done for centuries—by lighting a fire—is a violation of neutral, generally applicable laws governing public safety. When pressed to that kind of obedience, the church might fortify itself by remembering the teaching of Jesus that they should not give to Caesar what belongs to God, even if Caesar demands it.[181]

The likelihood that government attorneys would give up their excessive demands upon hearing a sermonette on this text is slim. Perhaps the only word that would be communicative under such circumstances is the one famously uttered by Colonel Anthony McAuliffe when the Nazis demanded that he surrender his troops in an engagement during World War II: "Nuts!"[182] In many instances in the present moment of our history, that single word sadly contains the best hope of this volume. For when sensible compromise with the government becomes impossible, then resolute resistance may become a religious duty.

To draw an intelligent line between the obligation to obey the civil authority and the obligation to obey a higher power, religious communities need to know their own traditions well. They must also be aware of the central role of religious freedom in our nation's history. The contributors to this volume have described many points of intersection between law and religion in which both kinds of knowledge are necessary. If a profound understanding of the teachings and traditions of one's religious community is conjoined with a deep awareness of the history of religious freedom in America, we

---

180. Matt. 5:41.

181. Mark 12:13–17. The saying of Jesus to give to the emperor what is the emperor's and to God what is God's occurs at the end of a story in which the Pharisees and Herodians mean to trap Jesus into a denial of Roman power over Jews. The question of financial tribute by believers to the state (the exact reverse of the American question of financial support by the state for believers) is crucial. Jesus's answer is on the surface neutral, but structured so that the emphasis is on giving what is God's to God. J. Duncan M. Derrett, Law in the New Testament (1970) 313–38; and Derrett, Luke's Perspective on Tribute to Caesar, in Richard Cassidy and Philip Scharper, eds., Political Issues in Luke-Acts 38–48 (1983).

182. One of the most famous lines of World War II history was written in December 1944 by Anthony McAuliffe, the acting commander of the 101st Airborne Division and other attached troops during the siege of Bastogne, Belgium. When the Germans surrounded this unit and demanded their surrender, McAuliffe sent back a one-word reply: "Nuts!" Obituary of Anthony McAuliffe, N.Y. Times, Aug. 14, 1975, at 34.

should be able to emerge from the present state of confusion about the relation of law and religion.

In an era when the courts behave under the guidance of Locke's view that "there is no judge upon earth between the supreme magistrate and the people," it is necessary for religious communities to submit to legislatures petitions for the redress of their grievances, for legislatures appear to be more sensitive than courts to the need to secure our first freedom. At a moment in our history when courts have forgotten that their function is to protect religious freedom more vigorously than legislatures—not by defining religions and intermeddling in their affairs, but by curbing all attempts of government to exercise power in religious matters—religious communities must remind judges of Madison's promise that "independent tribunals of justice will consider themselves in a peculiar manner the guardians of those rights; they will be an impenetrable bulwark against every assumption of power in the legislative or executive; they will be naturally led to resist every encroachment upon rights expressly stipulated for in the constitution by the declaration of rights."

If religious communities persist in the memory of their own traditions and the history of our country, we may again be guided by the vision of the framers of the First and the Fourteenth Amendments. In such a climate, it should again be possible for Americans to exercise their various religious commitments vigorously, for persons of all faiths and of none are "equally entitled to the full and free exercise of [religion] according to the dictates of Conscience."[183]

---

183. 1 The Papers of James Madison 174 (1962), *reprinted in* Noonan and Gaffney, Religious Freedom, *supra* note 1, at 162–63.

Epilogue

James A. Serritella

Oliver Wendell Holmes wrote that "the life of the law is not logic but experience." Our law relating to commercial organizations is rich with experience. It is vivid, real, and nuanced because our understanding of these organizations is vivid, real, and nuanced. Our law relating to religious organizations is, unfortunately, also infused with our understanding of commercial organizations. Too often it is blurred, artificial, and primitive because our understanding of religious organizations is flawed by weak or nonexistent analogies to commercial organizations and commercial concepts. Constitutional guarantees of religious freedom are applied to this flawed understanding with very mixed results, and religious freedom is often compromised.

We look to commercial organizations' self-understanding to learn about them. Often scholars, lawyers, courts, and legislatures also turn to commercial organizations to learn about religious organizations, probably because we tend to look to what we know to help us understand what we do not know. Too frequently, however, this approach involves projecting commercial interpretations onto religious phenomena. As a result, our understanding of religious organizations often misses the mark.

It would be better to try to understand such organizations on their own merits. Their self-understanding would seem to be an obvious starting point. Some will throw up their hands and say this approach will not work because religious organizations and religious issues are too inscrutable ever to be understood. But this view would condemn our jurisprudence to Plato's cave where we could see nothing but shadows. Our law's understanding of religious organizations is confused by a history of viewing them through commercial-law lenses; our constitutional guarantees of religious freedom require that we try to view things in a more appropriate way.

There are also those who caution that the Constitution includes protection from religious excesses. Religious freedom, however, is not the only liberty that presents the risk of abuse or excesses. These risks are a reason not to abandon the quest for freedom but to search out limits that preserve freedom. Good order and good citizenship cannot exist without limits and concern for the common good. In our legal system, we work toward the common good by trying to strike a balance between sound limits and freedom. Focusing on a religious organization's self-understanding is likely to make it easier for us to strike that balance and sort out limits that protect both religious freedom and good order.

Our Constitution not only guarantees religious freedom, it challenges us to achieve it. Religious organizations should take up this challenge and insist that their attorneys present their self-understanding sensitively and accurately. Courts, legislatures, and government officials should be sensitive to this self-understanding and fashion their rulings to honor it. The constitutional guarantees themselves emanate from the Founding Fathers' view of man and society. Religion is central to that view, and so our motivation to take up the challenge goes much deeper than the law or jurisprudence; it goes to the quick of human existence. We hope that this volume in some small measure enhances efforts to meet this challenge.

About the Authors

Thomas C. Berg is a Professor of Law at the University of Saint Thomas in Minneapolis. He was a Rhodes Scholar at Oxford University and has degrees with honors from Northwestern University, Oxford, and the University of Chicago in both law and religious studies. Professor Berg has written more than thirty-five articles about religious freedom, constitutional law, and the role of religion in American society. He is also the author of *The State and Religion in a Nutshell* and, with Michael McConnell and John Garvey, the casebook *Religion and the Constitution*. He has testified before Congress several times in support of religious freedom, and has written more than twenty briefs in religious freedom cases in the United States Supreme Court and lower courts. In recognition of his work he received the Religious Liberty Defender of the Year Award from the Christian Legal Society in 1996. He was the program coordinator for DePaul University's Center for Church/State Studies from 1991 to 1992, and has served on its Legal Scholars Advisory Board since 1994. He has also served as a member of the Religious Liberty Advisory Commission for the National Council of Churches since 1998.

Patricia B. Carlson has been a director at the law firm of Burke, Warren, MacKay & Serritella, P.C., in Chicago since 1997. She specializes in corporate law, tax law, and trusts and estates, and has lectured and published articles on these topics. Her article "Illinois Law Concerning Nonprofit Organizations" was published in *The Exempt Organization Tax Review* in 1998. Ms. Carlson has served as a consultant for the Catholic Charities Housing Development Corporation in Chicago, and as an assistant research coordinator for DePaul University's Center for Church/State Studies. She received her A.B. with honors from Princeton University, her M.A. in Public Affairs from the University of Minnesota, and her J.D. with honors from Northwestern University.

Angela C. Carmella is a Professor of Law at Seton Hall University, where she teaches property law and courses focusing on religion and the First Amendment. She has published extensively in the field of law and religion, and spent a sabbatical as a visiting lecturer and scholar at Harvard University's divinity school. Professor Carmella serves on the editorial council of the *Journal of Church and State*, on the Legal Scholars Advisory Board of DePaul University's Center for Church/State Studies, and on the Religious Liberty Committee of the National Council of Churches. She is a member of the Catholic Commission on Intellectual and Cultural Affairs, and was named a fellow at Harvard's Center for the Study of Values in Public Life. She received her A.B. summa cum laude from Princeton University, her J.D. cum laude from Harvard Law School, and an M.T.S. degree in theology from Harvard's divinity school. She practiced law in Boston before entering academia.

Mark E. Chopko is general counsel for the United States Conference of Catholic Bishops. He is the chief civil law advisor to the national organizations chartered by the Roman Catholic bishops to represent their public and church policy interests. He is an attorney and counselor to these organizations and to their management, staff, directors, and officers. Mr. Chopko assists a national association of diocesan legal counsel and also serves as director of legal staff, offering comprehensive corporate, tax, litigation, intellectual property, employment, and specialty services to these organizations and to diocese and state Catholic conferences. He serves as a confidential advisor to other national Catholic groups in areas of church finance, education, and religious life. Mr. Chopko is an author and lecturer specializing in constitutional law with an emphasis on church/state relations, biomedical issues, and education. He serves on the Religious Liberty Committee for the National Council of Churches, is a member of the executive committee of the Nonprofit and Association Committee of the American Corporate Counsel Association, and is a member of the Legal Scholars Advisory Board of DePaul University's Center for Church/State Studies. He received his B.S. in Chemistry summa cum laude from the University of Scranton, and his J.D. cum laude from Cornell University.

W. Cole Durham is the Susa Young Gates University Professor of Law at Brigham Young University and the director of the BYU International Center for Law and Religion Studies. He is the author of numerous scholarly articles on church/state issues and, with Noel B. Reynolds, was co-editor of *Religious Liberty in Western Thought*. Professor Durham has been particularly active in matters involving religious freedom and church/state relations. He has testified before Congress in hearings on religious intolerance in Europe and on the proposed Religious Liberty Protection Act. He is a member of the executive committee of the International Academy for Freedom of Religion and Belief, and serves as an advisory member of church/state centers at DePaul and Baylor universities. He is also a member of the board of the International Religious Liberty Association, and of the International Advisory Board of the Oslo Coalition on Freedom of Religion or Belief. He has been actively involved in consultations on laws dealing with religious freedom and religious associations in Russia, Ukraine, Albania, Azerbaijan, Bulgaria, the Czech Republic, Estonia, Georgia, Hungary, Romania, Latvia, Lithuania, and Slovakia, and has also been heavily involved in work on a law for not-for-profit organizations in Bulgaria. He served as a public member of the U.S. delegation to the Organization for Security and Cooperation in Europe's Human Dimension Seminar on Constitutional, Legal, and Administrative Aspects of the Freedom of Religion, which was held in Warsaw, Poland, from April 16 to 19, 1996. He has served since then on the Advisory Panel of Experts on Freedom of Religion or Belief advising the OSCE's Office of Democratic Institutions and Human Rights on religion matters. Until June 1999, he was chairman of the board of the International Center for Not-for-Profit Law in Washington, D.C. He received both his A.B. and his J.D. from Harvard University, where he was a note editor for the *Harvard Law Review* and managing editor of the *Harvard International Law Journal*.

Carl H. Esbeck is the Isabella Wade & Paul C. Lyda Professor of Law at the University of Missouri at Columbia. He previously served as director of the Center for Law and Religious Freedom, a division of the Christian Legal Society, in Washington, D.C. In 1995 he received the Blackwell Sanders Award from the MU School of Law for distinguished achievement in teaching, as well as the 1995 recipient of the Defender of Religious Freedom award from the Center for Law and Religious Freedom. Professor Esbeck received the Lloyd E. Roberts Memorial Prize in the Administration of Justice awarded by the MU School of Law alumni in 1993 for his work on amici curiae briefs filed in religious liberty cases. He has the authored numerous scholarly articles on church/state and religious freedom issues. He is a member of the Legal Scholars Advisory Board of DePaul University's Center for Church/State Studies, and of the Advisory Committee for the *Journal of Law and Religion*. He received his B.S. from Iowa State University of Science and Technology, and his J.D. from Cornell University.

Edward McGlynn Gaffney, Jr. is a Professor of Law at Valparaiso University. He served as the director of content for the National Constitution Center in Philadelphia, and as the associate director for the Committee on Ecumenical and Interreligious Affairs for the United States Conference of Catholic Bishops. He is the author of several books on church/state issues, including *Religious Freedom: History, Cases, and Other Materials on the Interaction of Government & Religion* (with John T. Noonan, Jr.), 2001; *Government & Campus: Federal Regulation of Religious Affiliated Higher Education* (with Philip Moots), 1983; *State & Campus: State and Regulation of Religious Affiliated Higher Education* (with Fernand Dutile), 1984; and *Ascending Liability in Religious and Other Nonprofit Organizations* (with Philip Sorensen), 1984. He has participated in appellate advocacy and in congressional testimony on issues concerning religious freedom for more than twenty years, and was given the Champion of Justice award for his work on behalf of religious freedom. He has served on the editorial board of the *Journal of Law and Religion*, and on the Legal Scholars Advisory Board of DePaul University's Center for Church/State Studies, since their inception. Professor Gaffney served as dean of the Valparaiso University School of Law from 1990 to 1997, has taught at Notre Dame and Loyola Universities, and has been a visiting scholar at Stanford and Pepperdine Universities, and the University of Pennsylvania. Professor Gaffney received his S.T.L. from Gregorian University in Rome, his J.D. and M.A. from Catholic University, and his LL.M. from Harvard University.

Patty Gerstenblith is a Professor of Law at DePaul University, where she teaches courses in cultural property, intellectual property, law and the arts, property, wills and trusts, and law of not-for-profit organizations. She has taught and published widely in the areas of law and the arts, cultural heritage, and nonprofit organizations. Her most recent articles include "The Public Interest in Restitution of Cultural Objects," published in the *Connecticut Journal of International Law* in 2001, and "Protection of Cultural Heritage Found on Private Land: The Paradigm of the Miami Circle and Regulatory Takings Doctrine after Lucas," published in the *Saint Thomas Law Review* in 2000. She is the editor in chief of the *International Journal of Cultural Property* and was appointed to the President's Cultural Property Advisory Committee by President Clinton in 2000. She is also a member of the executive committee of the Art and Law Section of the American Association of Law Schools, and a member of the steering committee of the International Cultural Property Committee of the American Bar Association. Professor Gerstenblith is the 1998 recipient of the John Courtney Murray Award from DePaul University's Center for Church/State Studies. She received her A.B. from Bryn Mawr College, her J.D. cum laude from Northwestern University as a member of the Order of the Coif, and her Ph.D. in Fine Arts and Anthropology from Harvard University.

H. Reese Hansen is dean and Professor of Law at the J. Reuben Clark Law School at Brigham Young University. He is the author of the *Bogart, Oaks, Hansen, and Neeleman Casebook on Trusts* as well as a judicial reference book, law practice manuals, and several legal articles. He has served as a member of the board of trustees of the Law School Admissions Council, director of law school admissions services, the founding chair of the section for law school deans of the Association of American Law Schools, a member of the American Bar Association Foreign Law Initiative Law School Advisory Committee, and director of the Association of Religiously Affiliated Law Schools. In 1996 he received the first "Award for Illustrious Civility in the Law" from the board of bar commissioners of the Utah State Bar, in recognition of his exemplary public service. Professor Hansen received his B.S. in Business Administration from Utah State University and his J.D. from the University of Utah, where he was research and note editor of the *Utah*

Law Review and was named to the Order of the Coif. Prior to becoming a professor, he practiced law in Salt Lake City.

Donald H. J. Hermann is a Professor of Law and Philosophy at DePaul University. He is also the founder and director of DePaul's Health Law Institute. He has written numerous articles on health law and is author or co-author of several books on the subject, including *AIDS Law in a Nutshell*, *Legal Aspects of AIDS*, *Mental Health and Disability Law in a Nutshell*, and *The Insanity Defense: Philosophical, Historical, and Legal Perspectives.* Professor Hermann served as a United States Supreme Court Judicial Fellow during Chief Justice Berger's term, and was appointed a Law and Humanities Fellow at Harvard University, and a Law and Economics Fellow at the University of Chicago. He is a member of the Legal Scholars Advisory Board for DePaul University's Center for Church/State Studies. He received his A.B. from Stanford University, his J.D. from Columbia University, and his LL.M. from Harvard. Professor Hermann also holds a Ph.D. in Philosophy from Northwestern University, an M.A.A.H. degree from the School of the Art Institute of Chicago, and an M.L.A. from the University of Chicago.

Douglas Laycock holds the Alice McKean Young Regents Chair in Law and is the associate dean for research at the University of Texas. He has written extensively on the topic of religious liberty and other legal issues, and is the author of two books on the law of remedies. He is a fellow of the American Academy of Arts and Sciences. Professor Laycock served as appellate counsel for the churches in *Church of the Lukumi Babalu Aye v. City of Hialeah*, the last successful free exercise claim before the Supreme Court, and in *City of Boerne v. Flores*, defending the validity of the Religious Freedom Restoration Act as applied to state and local governments. In *Santa Fe Independent School District v. Doe*, he was counsel for parents objecting to prayer at high school football games. He has also filed friend of the court briefs in many other religious liberty cases in the Supreme Court. He received his B.A. with high honor from Michigan State University, and his J.D. cum laude from the University of Chicago.

William P. Marshall is a Professor of Law at the University of North Carolina School of Law. He has previously served as the Galen J. Roush Professor of Law at Case Western Reserve University, and has been a visiting professor at Northwestern University, the University of Connecticut, and William and Mary University. Professor Marshall has published many articles on constitutional topics, with a special emphasis on the Establishment Clause and free exercise of religion. He served with the Minnesota attorney general from 1977 to 1981, as associate counsel for the White House from 1997 to 1998, and as deputy White House counsel from 1999 to 2001. As a litigator he represented the state of Minnesota in three United States Supreme Court cases regarding religious issues, including *Mueller v. Allen*, *Larson v. Valente*, and *ISKCON v. Heffron*. Professor Marshall received his B.A. from the University of Pennsylvania and his J.D. from the University of Chicago.

Martin E. Marty is the Fairfax M. Cone Distinguished Service Professor Emeritus at the University of Chicago, where he received his Ph.D. He is the author of more than fifty books, including the three-volume *Modern American Religion*, and is the editor of the five-volume *The Fundamentalism Project*. He is a contributing editor of the weekly publication *Christian Century*. Professor Marty was the recipient of the National Book Award in 1972, the National Humanities Medal in 1977, and the Medal of the American Academy of Arts and Sciences in 1995. He served as a Lutheran pastor for ten years before joining the University of Chicago faculty in 1963.

John P.N. Massad is a professional anthropologist who specializes in research design and implementation, applying anthropological analysis to program evaluation and policy development. Dr. Massad has served as research director of DePaul University's Center for Church/State Studies, furthering research into the impact of constitutional law on religious free exercise and regulatory policy from a multidisciplinary perspective. He is currently a senior research associate and project director with LTG Associates, Inc., a minority-owned anthropological consulting firm specializing in evaluation and program design for health programs designed to reach historically underserved populations. He has also served as project director for a landmark study in the Episcopal Diocese of Washington, D.C., in support of the development of a diocese-wide communications plan. Dr. Massad earned his M.A. in Cultural Anthropology from the University of Kansas, and his Ph.D. from Northwestern University.

Craig B. Mousin is the DePaul University Ombudsperson. He served as executive director of DePaul University's Center for Church/State Studies from 1990 to 2001. He was also co-coordinator of the DePaul College of Law Asylum and Immigration Clinic from 1995 to 2003. He received his B.S. cum laude from Johns Hopkins University, his J.D. with honors from the University of Illinois, and his M.Div. from Chicago Theological Seminary. He is an ordained minister at the Wellington Avenue United Church of Christ.

Stephen J. Pope is an associate professor at Boston College, where he teaches courses on social ethics and theological ethics. He has also taught at the University of Saint Thomas, and was a visiting professor at the University of Notre Dame. Professor Pope participates in a faculty summer seminar at Oxford University on the relationship between science and Christianity, and has participated in numerous lectures and seminars sponsored by the Society of Christian Ethics, the American Association for the Advancement of Science, and the American Academy of Religion, among others. He has published several scholarly works including the books *The Evolution of Altruism and the Ordering of Love* and *The Ethics of Aquinas*, and is currently working on a book entitled *Human Evolution and Christian Ethics*. Professor Pope received his B.A. in Philosophy and History from Gonzaga University, his M.A. from the University of Chicago, and his Ph.D. in Theological Ethics from the University of Chicago.

Patrick J. Schiltz taught law for five years at the University of Notre Dame before leaving to accept an appointment as the founding associate dean of the University of Saint Thomas School of Law in Minnesota. After serving as a law clerk to United States Supreme Court Justice Antonin Scalia, Professor Schiltz practiced law in Minneapolis with the law firm of Faegre & Benson. As a litigator, he represented more than a dozen religious denominations in several hundred matters throughout the United States. He received his B.A. summa cum laude from the College of Saint Scholastica and his J.D. magna cum laude from Harvard University. Professor Schiltz also served on the board of editors for the *Harvard Law Review*.

James A. Serritella is a partner at the law firm of Burke, Warren, MacKay & Serritella, P.C., and has represented numerous organizations of many religious traditions over three decades. He is the founder of DePaul University's Center for Church/State Studies and serves as the chair of its Legal Scholars Advisory Committee. Mr. Serritella has lectured extensively both in the United States and abroad on religious freedom, and has published numerous scholarly articles on church/state issues. He is a member of the executive committee of the Diocesan Attorneys Association, the board of directors of the International Academy of Religious Freedom, the Canon Law Society of America, the board of governors of the Catholic Lawyers Guild, and the Chicago Bar Association's Interfaith Law Committee. He was presented the Outstanding Leaders Award from the Carmelite Order in 1979, the John Courtney Murray Award from the DePaul Center for

Church/State Studies in 1988, the Pax et Bonum Award from the Franciscan Friars in 1992, and the Rerum Novarum Award from Saint Joseph Seminary in 1999. He received an Honorary Doctor of Laws Degree from the North Park College and Theological Seminary in 1996. Mr. Serritella received his B.A. from State University of New York, a second B.A. from the Pontifical Gregorian University in Rome, and an M.A. and J.D. from the University of Chicago.

Elizabeth A. Sewell is the associate director of the Brigham Young University International Center for Law and Religion Studies. Prior to joining the center, she was an associate in the Washington, D.C., firm of Mayer, Brown & Platt, where she was a member of the Appellate and Supreme Court Litigation Group. She has briefed a variety of constitutional issues in federal and state courts of appeals and in the United State Supreme Court. Ms. Sewell also clerked for Judge J. Clifford Wallace of the U.S. Court of Appeals for the Ninth Circuit. Drawing on her fluency in Russian, Czech, German, and French, she has been active in writing and lecturing on church/state and comparative law topics and has testified before Congress on religious freedom issues. Ms. Sewell graduated summa cum laude from the J. Reuben Clark Law School where she was editor in chief of the *Brigham Young University Law Review*.

Rhys H. Williams is a Professor of Sociology and department head at the University of Cincinnati. He is the author of numerous articles on the intersection of religion, culture, social movements, and politics in the United States, and has coauthored a book on the subject, entitled *A Bridging of Faiths: Religion and Politics in a New England City*. He is member of the editorial council of the *Journal of Church and State*. In 2000 he received the Distinguished Article Award in the Sociology of Religion from the American Sociological Association for his article "Visions of the Good Society and the Religious Roots of American Political Culture," which appeared in *Sociology of Religion* in 1999. Professor Williams received his Ph.D. from the University of Massachusetts.

Index

Justices of Supreme Court

Black, Hugo, 780

Brennan, William, 98, 133, 164, 430, 457, 685

Burger, Warren, 368, 406, 410, 430, 431, 432, 440, 452, 778, 787

Frankfurter, Felix, 679

Ginsburg, Ruth Bader, 133

Holmes, Oliver Wendell, 17, 781, 787

Jackson, Robert, 53, 59, 83, 475, 763, 766, 800

Kennedy, Anthony, 133, 396, 491, 501, 569, 570, 571, 782, 802, 803

Marshall, John, 81, 82, 207, 406, 407, 464, 511

Marshall, Thurgood, 486, 490

O'Connor, Sandra Day, 151, 430, 712

Powell, Lewis, 151, 396, 397, 398, 399, 401, 453, 681

Rehnquist, William, 133, 171, 320, 778, 781, 787

Scalia, Antonin, 133, 246, 249, 396, 551, 762

Souter, David, 133

Story, Joseph, 760

Thomas, Clarence, 133, 396, 712, 714

Other Persons

Adams, Arlin, 25

Alexander III, 423

Ambrose, 417

Antiochus IV Epiphanes, 413, 414

Ballard, Guy, 765

Backus, Isaac, 428

Bakker, Jim, 444

Bakker, Tammy Faye, 444

Baus, Karl, 418

Becker, Mary, 453, 454

Becket, Thomas, 423, 424

Bennett, Wallace, 455

Berg, Thomas C., 168, 184, 185, 197, 672, 759, 760, 813

Bultmann, Rudolf, 783, 784

Calvin, John, 19, 424

Campbell, Peter, 260

Carlson, Patricia B., 217, 218, 226, 406, 813

Carmella, Angela, 158, 159, 194, 218, 405, 406, 648, 700, 701, 813

Catherine of Aragon, 424

Charles I, 426

Charles II, 424

Choper, Jesse H., 15, 16, 18, 19, 20, 24

Chopko, Mark, 406, 633, 636, 646, 813

Couser, Richard, 273

Cleopatra, 414

Clinton, Bill, 354, 391, 410. 803, 815

Constantine, 416

Curry, Thomas, 429, 467, 468, 773, 779, 780, 785, 786, 788, 789, 791, 801, 807

Cyrus the Persian, 413

Dane, Perry, 31, 32, 33, 46, 48, 79, 220, 804

David, 412

Devins, Neal, 690

Diocletian, 416

Durkheim, Emile, 10

Dutile, 705, 815

Eliade, Mircea, 9

Elizabeth I, 425

Ellman, Ira, 147, 149, 342

Esbeck, Carl H., 11, 14, 47, 48, 82, 130, 221, 222, 498, 708, 716, 769, 814

Falwell, Jerry, 711

Fletcher, George, 21, 22

Freeman, George, 24, 26, 27

Frost, Robert, 780

Gaffney, Jr., Edward McGlynn, 71, 168, 705, 815

Geertz, Clifford, 11, 64

Geoghan, John, 640

Gerstenblith, Patty, 217, 219, 220, 221, 253, 262, 301, 303, 304, 565, 815

Giannella, Donald, 484, 788

Greenawalt, Kurt, 15, 19, 20, 24, 25, 26, 27, 29, 30, 44

Gregory I, 422

Gregory XII, 422

Groome, Thomas, 648

Han, Thich Nhat, 635

Hansen, H. Reese, 219, 220, 221, 226, 254, 320, 321, 323, 815

Harrison, Paul, 126

Harrod, Allen, 634

Hatch, Nathan, 180

Hensley, Kirby, 445

Henry II, 423

Henry VIII, 424

Hermann, Donald H.J., 672, 673, 816

Hobbes, Thomas, 43, 44

Hopkins, Bruce, 434, 435, 436

Horsmann, Henry, 216

Howe, Mark DeWolfe, 179

Hull, Cordell, 410, 484

Hunter, James Davison, 675

Ingber, Stanley, 14, 15, 18, 19, 20, 24, 26, 39, 30

Jackson, Jesse, 451, 767

James I, 426

Jefferson, Thomas, 240, 430, 462, 512, 513, 763, 771, 780, 795, 796, 800

Johnson, Lyndon B., 448

Julian, 417

Kennedy, John F., 451, 483

Kelly, Alfred, 782

Kelly, Dean, 789

King, Jr., Martin Luther, 451

Koresh, David, 634

Kurland, Philip, 28, 29, 788

Kurtz, Gary, 789

Kurtz, Lester, 96, 97

Law, Bernard, 648

Laycock, Douglas, 46, 47, 135, 136, 405, 489, 497, 498, 499, 500, 502, 532, 535, 688, 690, 692, 804, 816

Linde, Hans, 187

Locke, John, 40, 44, 58, 508, 773, 774, 799, 800, 810

Lonergan, Bernard, 411, 432, 505, 777

Lovin, Robin, 206

Luther, Martin, 424

Lutz, Donald, 177

Madison, James, 65, 135, 138, 240, 430, 460, 462, 463, 466, 477, 479, 491, 506, 512, 513, 771, 773, 774, 775, 777, 795, 796, 799, 802, 804, 810

Malinowski, Branislaw, 10

Merel, Gail, 788

Marett, R. R., 8, 17, 20

Mark Anthony, 414

Mason, George, 773, 786, 804

Marshall, William P., 168, 185, 775, 776, 786, 804, 816

Marty, Martin E., 510, 511, 661

Mattei, Hugo, 216

Massad, John P.N., 79, 169, 217, 218, 816, 817

McCoy, Thomas, 789, 791

McConnell, Michael, 711, 774, 775, 790, 791, 792, 793, 800, 813

McLaughlin, Philip, 655

Mead, Sidney, 85

Melton, J. Gordon, 116

Miller, Perry, 178

Moon, Sun Myung, 444

Mosk, Stanley, 191

Murray, John Courtney, 207, 773, 791

Neuhaus, Richard John, 510, 789

Niebuhr, H. Richard, 86, 87, 177, 178, 180

Noonan, John T., 419, 465, 775, 790, 791, 815

Nussbaum, J. Martin, 640

Oaks, Dallin, 286, 289, 310

O'Brien, Thomas, 655

Oleck, Howard, 273

Otto, Rudolph, 9

Paine, Tom, 428, 508

Paschal II, 422

Paulsen, Michael, 789

Penn, William, 427, 779

Pfeffer, Leo, 788, 791

Pope, Steven J., 406

Robertson, Pat, 451, 767

Rousseau, Jean-Jacques, 41

Schiltz, Patrick J., 405, 532, 536, 642, 643, 817

Schleiermacher, Friedrich, 9

Schweitzer, Albert, 727, 783

Scott, Austin, 259

Serritella, James A., 81, 82, 168, 169, 405, 459, 473, 474, 494, 566, 661, 759, 801, 811, 817, 818

Smart, Ninian, 12

Smith, Steven, 497, 778, 779, 787

Smith, Wilfred Cantwell, 9

Solomon, 412

Sweeney, Constance, 651, 653

Tarr, Alan, 179, 195, 196

Tillich, Paul, 10, 11, 13, 22, 23, 24, 89, 798

Theodosius, 417, 418

Tocqueville, Alexis de, 409, 410, 510, 681, 793

Tribe, Laurence H. 14, 15, 320, 790, 791, 804, 805, 806

Troeltsch, Ernst, 123

Tylor, E.B., 8, 17

Urban II, 422

Valentinian, 418

Von Ranke, Otto, 782

Warner, Carolyn, 655

Warner, Stephen, 169, 208

Washington, James, 179

Weber, Max, 123

Weiss, Jonathan, 28, 29, 30

William I, 425

Williams, Rhys H., 169, 217, 818

Williams, Roger, 427

Wittgenstein, Ludwig, 8, 12, 24

Wood, Gordon, 179

Wrightington, Sydney, 261

Wuthnow, Robert, 111, 205

Zollman, Carl, 180

Definition of Religion (Durham & Sewell)

definition of religion, legal approaches to, 13-32

    communitarian approach to definition of religion, 21-22

    family resemblance or analogical definitions of religion, 24-27

    multi-factor tests, 25-26

    functional definitions of religion, 22-24

        criticism of, 23-24

    interjurisdictional respect approach to the definition of religion, 31-32

    neutrality-based abstention principle as a means of protecting religious freedom, 27-29

    reductionist approach to definition of religion, 29-30

    total deference to the believer's definition of religion, 30, 34-35

    substantive definitions of religion, 17-20

        criteria for defining religion under the Free Exercise Clause, 18-20

        modern, 18-20

        traditional, 17

    unitary or dual definitions of religion, 14-16

        tension between the two religion clauses, 14-16

definition of religion, problems of, 3-8

    definition of religion, as act of religious autonomy, 5-6

    definition of religion, relation to distinction between church and state, 5

definition of religion, social science approaches, 8-13

    essentialist definitions of religion, 9

    family resemblance or analogical definitions of religion, 12-13

    functionalist definitions of religion, 10-11

    substantive definitions of religion, 8

limited deference approach to definition of religion, 33-57

    effect of context and purpose on definition of religion, 39

    limited conception of the state, 41-44

    limited deference approach as a means of protecting religious freedom, 36-38, 45-49, 70

    interjurisdictional respect approach, interrelation between order of the state and independent order of religion, 33, 40-45

limited deference approach, explanatory value of, 66-69

Definition of Religion, *continued*
limited deference approach, grounds for
   limiting state deference to definitions
   of religion, 49-56
   constraints upon the exercise of state
      power: necessity, 56
   constraints upon the exercise of state
      power: neutrality and equal treat-
      ment, 56
   limitations based on grounds overrid-
      ing religious freedom: independent
      overriding state interests, 55
   limitations inherent in religious free-
      dom: fraud, 52-54
   limitations inherent in religious free-
      dom: sincerity, 50-52
limited deference approach, relevance to
   difficulties of defining religion, 57-65
   difficulty of drawing boundary be-
      tween order of the state and order
      of religion, 58
   difficulty of drawing boundary be-
      tween religion and commerce, 60
   difficulty of drawing boundary be-
      tween religion and culture, 62
   difficulty of drawing boundary be-
      tween religion and fraud, 59
   difficulty of drawing boundary be-
      tween religious and personal beliefs,
      61
   difficulty of the secularization of reli-
      gious beliefs and practices, 63-65
   difficulty of underbreadth or over-
      breadth of definition of religion, 57,
      69
other problematic definitions of religion,
   71-81
   application of limited deference ap-
      proach to problematic definitions,
      80
   definition of clergy for the purpose of
      exemption from child-abuse report-
      ing statutes, 73-79
   definition or religious instruction or
      proselytization, 72
   definition of the terms church, reli-
      gious organization, denomination,
      71-72

Religious Polity (Marty & Serritella)
religious denomination, definition of, 85
religious community and culture, relation
   between, 86-87
religious polity and civil law, constitutional approaches, 89-102
   implied trust, 91
   neutral principles approach, 90, 97-
      102
      difficulties, 99-102
   polity approach, 89-90, 91-97
      legal determination of a church's
         polity, 92-97
      forms of polity, 93-95
religious polity and civil law, relation between, 87-88
religious polity, definition of, 85-86
religious polity, recognition of "New Religious Movements," 103
religious polity, suggestions for advancement of free exercise, to religious
   groups, 104-106
religious polity, suggestions for advancement of free exercise, to legislatures,
   107-108
religious polity, suggestions for advancement of free exercise, to courts, 106-
   107

**Religious Diversity, Civil Law, and Insti-
   tutional Isomorphism** (Williams &
   Massad)
church and state, history of, 112-114
institutional isomorphism, 112
legal structure, definition of religious organization's, 111-112
religious structure, as articulation of
   group identity, 114
religious structure, definition of religious
   organization's, 111-112
religious and legal structure, disarticulation between, 112, 127
1994 Survey of religious organizations at
   the national level, 115-123
   Survey findings, 117-123
      church/sect typology, 123
      coercive isomorphism, 124-125
      diversity of religious structures,
         119-120

institutional isomorphism, 124
mimetic isomorphism, 125
rise of national bureaucratic structures, 126
standardization of legal structures, 120-121
size and time since incorporation, 122-123
Survey method, 116-117
Survey population, 116

Religious Structures under the Federal Constitution (Berg)
definition of religious structure or organization, 130, 155
broader concept of structure, 130, 155
formal legal status, 130, 155, 158
for profit vs. not-for-profit, 163
Establishment Clause, 129, 134, 137
Lemon test, 137
non-entanglement test, 138-139
free exercise of religion, 129, 133-136
burden upon religious practice, 133-135
church autonomy, church governance, 135
church autonomy, faith and doctrine, 135
church autonomy, freedom of worship and conduct, 133
equal treatment, 132, 135
Memorial and Remonstrance Assessment Against Religious Assessments, 135
nondiscrimination, 134
separation, 131, 133, 134
substantive freedom (church autonomy), 134, 135
general Religion Clause approaches
equal treatment approach, 132, 153, 160
deference to government approach, 132, 133
Lemon v. Kurtzman, 131
separationist approach, 131-132, 153, 154
internal church disputes, 145-150, 153
church property, 145
deference to church polity, 146, 153
discipline, 145

employment, 145, 149
gap-filling rules, 146-150
neutral principles approach, 146, 150-151, 153
policy based rules, 147-150
legislative accommodations to religion, 141-145, 157
Federal Unemployment Tax Exemption (FUTA), 161-162, 167
multifactor analysis, 158-160
"pervasively" religious, 156-158
Religious Freedom Restoration Act, 141-145, 158
standard of scrutiny, "compelling government interest," 142

State Constitutions and Religious Liberty (Mousin)
Blaine Amendment, 182, 203, 206
disestablishment of religion, 179-181
education funding, history of, 180
factor analysis, 173
funding of religious institutions under state constitutions, 197-204
education funding, 197-198
vouchers and tax credits, 198-203
land use regulation, 189
religious autonomy, impact of state constitutions on, 168-169
state constitutional and common law history, 176-184
state constitutions, models of interpretation
compelling interest and least restrictive means test, 190
deference, 191
dual sovereignty, 172, 201
failure to develop independent interpretative frameworks, 186-191, 195, 208
legislative accommodation, 191
Lemon test, 202
lockstep, 172, 185, 200
neutral principles, 192
primacy, 172, 185, 187-188, 202-204
trends favoring influence of interpretations of federal constitutions, 204-208
uncertainty of federal law, 193-195

State Constitutions and Religious Liberty,
continued
state constitutions, relation to federal
    constitutions, 170-171
    distinctive protections, 173-174
    Supremacy Clause, 170-171, 172
structural differences between state and
    federal constitutions, 184
    enumerated powers, 184
    federalism, 184, 208
    state sovereignty, 184
taxing religious organizations, 188
textual differences between federal and
    state constitutions, 173-176
unemployment compensation, 188

**Legal Structuring of Religious Institu-
    tions** (Durham)
deference approach, 220
charitable choice, 222
"institutional isomorphism," 218
internal disputes, 219
legal structures as facilitators of religious
    autonomy, 214
neutral principles approach, 220
  distinction from "neutral, generally ap-
    plicable laws," 221
relationship of legal structure to free exer-
    cise of religion, 213-214
religious corporation as facilitator of reli-
    gious autonomy, 218
trust as facilitator of religious autonomy,
    216

**Associational Structures of Religious Or-
    ganizations** (Gerstenblith)
choice of structural forms within a state,
    242-243
corporation sole, 234-239
corporate structures designed for reli-
    gious organizations, 230
    denominational statutes, 232-234
    general religious incorporation laws,
    231
foreign corporations, 243-244
legal structures, history and background
    of, 223-226
    business corporations, 223
    general incorporation statutes, 223

legal structure, definition of, 223
    mutual benefit organization, 225
    1994 Report on the Survey of Religious
        Organizations at the National Level,
        225
    "non-distribution constraint," 225
    not-for-profit corporations, 223
    public benefit organization, 225
    special charter system, 223
    state law as governing the formation of
        legal structures, 224
not-for-profit corporation, incorporation
    as specific type, 228-230
not-for-profit corporation with religious
    purpose, 226
relationship between legal structure and
    the Religion Clauses, 244-251
    accountability of religious organiza-
        tions for conduct, 245, 251
    Establishment Clause, excessive entan-
        glement test, 248
    Establishment Clause, whether special
        exemptions violates, 245
    free exercise of religion, distinction be-
        tween institutional and individual
        aspects, 250-251
    legislative exemptions from regulation
        of specific religious practices, 249
    neutral principles of law approach, 245
    Religious Freedom Restoration Act of
        1993, 247-248
states that prohibit incorporation of reli-
    gious organizations, 239-242

**Unincorporated Associations and Chari-
    table Trusts** (Carlson)
charitable trusts, 253-260
    constructive trusts, 253
    express trusts, 253
    implied trusts, 253
    resulting trusts, 253
charitable trusts, use of by religious orga-
    nizations, 254-260
    change of charitable purpose, 256
    method of advancing religion, 257
    protection of retirement assets of reli-
        gious orders, 258-260
    purpose of the charitable trust, 255
    tax-qualified retirement plans, 258-260

1994 Report on the Survey of Religious Organizations at the National Level, 254, 262
unincorporated associations, 261-278
    assets on dissolution of association, 268
    capacity to file suit, 270
    formation of corporation, 264
    member ability to sue unincorporated association, 270
    member liability for acts, 270
    merger, ability to enter into, 269
    property, holding of title, 263
    property disputes, adjudication of, 268
    recommendations, 272-278
    Roman Catholic religious orders, 262
    Uniform Unincorporated Nonprofit Association Act (UUNA Act), 263, 273, 274
    unincorporated associations, definition of, 261

Religious Organizations and the Law of Trusts (Hansen)
church property disputes, internal, 279, 282
church polity
    church polity, determination of, 302-303
    congregational church polity, 284-285
    hierarchical or episcopal church polity, 284-285
    presbyterial church polity, 284-285
charitable trust doctrine, 279
    constructive trusts, 282-284
    express trusts, 282-283
    implied trust doctrine, 280, 284
        deference to church polity, 284, 287
        departure-from-doctrine, 284, 286-287
        history of, 285-290
    resulting trusts, 282-284
constitutional approaches.
    combined deference and neutral principles approach, 297-300, 302
    criticism of strict neutral principles approach, 301-304
    neutral principles of law approach, 280, 288, 289, 313

nondeterminist approach, 289
    presumption of majority rule of corporation in neutral principles approach, 295
    strict deference approach, 289, 291-293
    strict neutral principles approach, 289, 293-296
    two-step analysis, 290, 291, 293, 294
legal structure of religious organizations, 304-312
    corporation sole, 306, 308
    cy pres, doctrine of, 312
    enforcement of charitable trusts by attorney general, 309-311
    language of conveyances of property, 312
    membership corporation model, 306
    not-for-profit corporation, 304-308
    regulation of religious not-for-profit corporations, 306, 307
    trust, 304, 308
    trustee corporation, 306
    unincorporated association, 304
state statutes, influence on legal structure of religious organizations, 312-313

Civil Court Resolution of Property Disputes among Religious Organizations (Gerstenblith)
religious property disputes, historical and constitutional background
    civil courts, authority to settle internal disputes, 324, 326
    compulsory deference approach, 321
    "departure-from-doctrine" approach, 325, 326
    Free Exercise and Establishment clauses, relation of, 319-321
    hybrid approaches, 322-323
    neutral principles of law approach, 319-321, 326
    "polity" approach, 325, 326
neutral legal principles, sources of
    contract and corporate law, contract principle, 342-346
    express trusts, 330-331
    formal title doctrine, 327-329
    implied trusts, 331-333, 335

Civil Court Resolution of Property Disputes among Religious Organizations, *continued*
    actual intent, 338
    amendment of church constitutions to create express trusts, 339
    constructive trust, 331-333
    "compulsory deference" approach, 334
    "departure-from-doctrine" approach, 333-334
    Free Exercise and Establishment clauses, tension between, 342
    "hybrid" approach, 335
    "implied consent," 336
    resulting trust, 331-333
    strict standard of intent, 337
    transference of church property through estoppel, 340-341
  neutral principles of law approach, as guarantee of free exercise, 347
  neutral principles of law approach, definition of, 317
  state incorporation law, 345
  trust and property law, 327

Regulation of Religious Organizations via Governmental Financial Assistance (Esbeck)
conditions of governmental assistance, 356-357
  fiscal accountability as a condition of governmental assistance, 356
conditions of governmental assistance affecting church polity, curriculum, self-definition, 363-368
  accreditation of post-secondary schools, 364-366
  impact of government aid upon self-definition of religious community, 366-368
  regulation of curriculum, 364
conditions of governmental assistance based on requirement of separation of church and state, 358-363
  prohibition against use of funds for religious instruction or worship, 358
  prohibition against use of funds for training or education for religious vocation, 358, 361-362
  prohibitions on services rendered in facilities decorated with religious symbols, 358-360
  prohibitions on use of funds for improvement of sectarian-use real estate, 358
  requirement to form a separate non-profit organization, 358, 360
conditions restricting lobbying and partisan political activity, 377-378
  Lobbying Disclosure Act, lobbying registration and reporting requirements, 378
  prohibition on religious organizations' involvement in political campaigns, 377
  prohibition on religious organizations lobbying for legislation, 378
constitutional questions
  exemption of religious institutions from regulation, 385
  financial assistance regulations that violate Establishment Clause, 384
  financial assistance regulations that violate Free Exercise Clause, 383
  receipt of government assistance as "state action," 385-387
division within the religious community over appropriateness of receiving government assistance, 387-390
factors affecting government regulation of church-based charitable activities, 354-356
  degree of connection between charitable activity and central religious body, 355
  direct or indirect government aid, 356
  means by which government assistance is delivered, 355-356
  multiple levels of government involvement in a given program, 356
  nature of organization, 354-355
government-mandated disclosure of information, 376-377
government-mandated due process requirements, 376
government-mandated employment benefits, 377
health and safety requirements, 378-380

history of relation of government to church-based charitable activities, 351-354

nondiscrimination requirements of civil rights legislation, 368

Age Discrimination Act of 1975, 371

Civil Rights Restoration Act of 1987, 372-375

"federally assisted nondiscrimination acts," 372

section 504 of Rehabilitation Act of 1973, 372

Title VI of Civil Rights Act of 1964, 371

Title IX of Educational Amendments of 1972, 372

remedies for noncompliance with federal regulations, 380-382

remedies for noncompliance with state and municipal regulations, 382

Appendix: Charitable Choice and the Critics (Esbeck)

Community Services Block Grant of 1998, 391

free exercise rights of the beneficiaries of aid, protection of, 392

nondiscrimination against religious providers of social services, 391

diversion of aid for religious purposes as violation of Establishment Clause, 398

Lemon v. Kurtzman test, 397-399

neutral direct government aid, 396

neutral indirect government aid, 396

neutrality doctrine, 396-400

pervasively sectarian doctrine, constitutionality of, 397-399

religious autonomy of faith-based providers, protection of, 392

direct subsidy of religion as violation of Establishment Clause, 395

employment of staff according to religious faith, 393, 394

receipt of federal aid by faith-based organizations, 394

federal civil rights laws, applicability to hiring/employment, 393

"internal governance," protection of right of, 393

employment of staff according to religious faith, criticisms of, 394

Substance Abuse and Mental Health Services Administration of 2000, 391

Welfare Reform Act of 1996, 391

Exemption of Religious Organizations from Federal Taxation (Gaffney)

civil society, role of religion in, 409

consequences of nondiscrimination principle for the structures of religious organizations, 457-458

exemption of nonprofit organizations from taxation, 409

exemption of religion from taxation, general statutory principles

operational test, 436

organizational test, 433-436

exemption of religion from taxation, history of, 411-432

based in principle of religious freedom, 411-412

constitutional roots of tax exemption, 431-432

in colonial America, 426-429

in Hebrew Bible, 412-414

in medieval England, 419-424

in New Testament, 415

in Roman law, 414-415

in Roman law, exemptions for Christianity, 416

in the American republic, 429-431

in the English Reformation, 424-426

regulation of religious bodies as a result of tax-exempt status, 438-456

abortion, Roman Catholic Church on, 450

ban on electioneering, 443, 448-451

church autonomy to select leaders, 454

conformity of religious organizations to public policy, 451-454

definition of religion by government, 443

definition of religious organizations' social ministry by government, 454-457

fraudulent evasion of tax laws: Jim and Tammy Faye Bakker, 444

Exemption of Religious Organizations from Federal Taxation, *continued*

gender discrimination, 453-454

improper classification of ministries as nonreligious, 455

Internal Revenue Service exemption: "integrated auxiliary of a church," 455-457

Internal Revenue Service guidelines for prohibited electioneering activity, 449

Internal Revenue Service guidelines for determining whether organization is religious, 445-446

legislation, limits on the influencing of, 443, 447-448

prohibition against personal benefit, 444

racial discrimination, 451-453

specific provisions in Internal Revenue Code relating to religious organizations, 438-442

Church Audit Procedure Act, 441-442

exemption from FICA, 439

exemption from FUTA, 439

federal employment taxes, 438

Social Security Act: Federal Insurance Contributions Act (FICA) and Federal Unemployment Tax Act (FUTA), 438

Exemption of Religious Communities from State and Local Taxation (Gaffney)

basic principles in constitutional law

nondiscrimination or nonendorsement, 461, 467, 494

nonentanglement, 461, 467, 494

substantive neutrality, 461, 467, 494

civil society, role of religion in, 509-512

Free Exercise and Establishment clause, relationship of

complementarity of, 468, 489-490, 495-496

tension between, 469-470, 477, 489-490, 495-496

tax exemption and the principle of substantive neutrality, 497-499

neutrality and separation, distinction between, 498

substantive neutrality, definition of, 498

substantive neutrality and formal neutrality, distinction between, 498

tax exemption and direct subsidy, distinction between, 499

tax expenditure theory, 499

tax exemption and the principle of nondiscrimination, 501-502

tax exemption and the principle of nonentanglement, 503-505

governmental definition of religion for the purpose of determining exemption from taxation, 504

Supreme Court on religious exemption from state and local taxation, *Murdock v. Pennsylvania* (1943) and *Follett v. McCormick* (1943), 470-477

definition of religious activity as commercial by the government, 472-473

flag salute, 471-472, 474-475

free exercise of religion, 477

incorporation of Free Exercise Clause into the Fourteenth Amendment, 471

invalidation of laws enacted under New Deal by judicial review (substantive due process), 470

Jehovah's Witnesses, 471-475

judicial review (substantive due process), 470

relation of Religion Clause to other First Amendment rights, 476

tax exemption as economic benefit, 476

taxation as means to discriminate against religion, 472

taxation of religious literature, 471-475

Supreme Court on religious exemption from state and local taxation, *Texas Monthly v. Bullock* (1989) and *Jimmy Swaggart Ministries* (1990)

inclusiveness of beneficiary class, 488

nondiscrimination or nonendorsement, 489-490

secular benefit requirement of tax exemption, 488

substantive neutrality, 489-490, 494

tax exemption as economic benefit, 487

tax exemption as establishment of religion, 487

Supreme Court on religious exemption from state and local taxation, *Walz v. Tax Commission of New York* (1970)

definition of religious activity by the government, 483

distinction between tax exemption of religion and direct subsidy to religion, 484-486

government aid to primary and secondary schools, 479

inclusiveness of beneficiary class, 480

Lemon test (excessive entanglement test), 480

relation of Religion Clause to other First Amendment rights, 479

relation of secular benefit requirement to nondiscrimination, 482

secular benefit requirement of tax exemption, 481-482

tax exemption as economic benefit, 478, 483-486

tax exemption as establishment of religion, 479

tax exemption as substantively neutral, 479

tax exemption based upon conformity with public policy or harmony with the public interest, 483

"unbroken" history of tax exemption, 479

Williamsburg Charter, 481

Supreme Court's use of *Walz v. Tax Commission of the City of New York* as legal history, 461-469

definition of religion by government as a form of excessive entanglement, 467

tax exemption embedded in the national culture, 461

Free Exercise Clause and Establishment Clause, complementarity of, 468

"law-office history," use of *Walz* as, 461

political divisiveness test, 463-465

promotion of free exercise of religion, 461

Religion Clause as self-denying ordinance, 467-468

tax exemption as economic benefit, 463

tax exemption as privilege of "established religion," 463-464

tax exemption as substantively neutral, 467

"unbroken" history of tax exemption, 461

universality of exemption by state legislatures, 461

state and local legislators as protectors of religious tax exemption, 505-509

Employment in Religious Organizations (Schiltz & Laycock)

advice to religious organizations, 559-563

employment disputes, 561

First Amendment defenses, 562

nature of institution, 559

nature of employment and employment contracts, 559-560

nature of conduct, 560

constitutional protection of religious employment decisions, 528

Establishment Clause, 528

Free Exercise Clause, compelling state interest (*Sherbert v. Verner*), 528, 542-549

Free Exercise Clause, "generally applicable law" (*Employment Division v. Smith*), 528, 549-552

neutral principles of law, 536-537

religious autonomy, 537, 539-540

rule of compulsory deference. 529, 536-537

employment relations and policies, 691-700

collective bargaining, 698

employment discrimination laws: race and sex, 697

employees, teachers and others, 678, 692-693

Fair Labor Standards Act (minimum wage and equal pay), 691, 697

federal and state unemployment compensation laws, 691, 699-700

National Labor Relations Board, 691

Employment in Religious Organizations,
continued
religious preferences in employment,
694-696, 701
Establishment Clause, 552-558
character and purpose of the institution, 553-556
excessive entanglement, 552, 556-558
Lemon test, 552-558
nature of aid, 556
internal church disputes, 145, 149
legislative accommodations, Federal Unemployment Tax Act exception
(FUTA), 161, 162, 167
Sherbert understanding of Free Exercise
Clause, 542-549
governmental regulation of employment, 544-545
"pretext inquiry," 545-547
Sherbert test, 543
Smith understanding of Free Exercise
Clause, 549-552
"equality right," 549
"hybrid cases," 551
neutral principles, 549
"substantive right," 549
Watson line of cases (*Watson v. Jones*),
528, 529-542
application in religious employment
cases, 538-542
church doctrine, excessive entanglement in, 540
"ministerial exception" cases, 539

Land Use Regulation of Churches
(Carmella)
land use regulation, constitutional approaches, 567-572, 590
equality approach, 568
liberty approach, 568
land use regulation, definition of, 565
land use regulation, impact upon religious structure, 565
land use regulation, legislative exemptions
and accommodations, 570
impermissible accommodations, 570
mandatory accommodations, 570
permissible accommodations, 570
land use regulation, zoning, 572-579

accessory uses, 577-578
church location, 572-574
dimensional regulations, 575-577
environmental regulation, 585-587
nonworship religious buildings, 578
preservation ordinances, 579-585
private restrictions, 579
secondary effects, 572
takings, 587-588
1994 Report on the Survey of Religious Organizations at the National Level, 566
Religious Freedom Restoration Act, 569,
571, 577-578, 582
Religious Land Use and Institutionalized
Persons Act of 2000, 571
religious structure and property use, 566-
567
accessory uses, 567, 577-578
nonworship religious buildings, 578
religious structure, definition of, 565
religious structure, relation to legal structure, 588-590

Derivative Liability (Chopko)
definition of, 591-593
risk-spreading considerations, 593
social reform, as a means of, 593, 620-
625
denominational defenses against, 626-630
organizational liability, particular areas
of, 604-607
accident cases, 605
agent or employee, 606
contracts and indebtedness, 606-608
counseling, 611-614
discipline, defamation, and other torts,
614
doctrine of "imputed negligence," 608
"ecclesial agency," 607
respondeat superior, 605
torts, 605
undue influence, duress, and fraud,
618-620
principles governing imposition of responsibility, 598
denominational responsibility, 600-603
situational responsibility, 603-604
statutory or corporate responsibility,
598-600

scope of duties or employment, 608-610
    abuse of minors, 609-610
    counseling sessions, 611
    sexual misconduct arising from unauthorized activities, 609

How the Legal System's Treatment of Clerical Sexual Misconduct with Minors Affects Religious Freedom (Pope & Carlson)
condemnation of clergy sexual abuse by most religious traditions, 634-635
contingency fees, 644-645
court's authority to treat clergy sexual abuse, 640-641
    deference to church autonomy, 641
        exceptions based on fraud and collusion, 641
    neutral principles of law approach, 641
derivative liability, 657-664
    agency theory, 657-658
    higher church body directly negligent, 659-661
    conspiracy and RICO, 661-664
individual liability of clergy, 634-636
just claim of victim for compensation, 644
liability of churches for clergy misconduct, theories of liability
    respondeat superior, 637, 645-646
    breach of fiduciary duty, 638, 645-646
    negligent hiring and supervision, 640, 646-647
    state statutes governing unlicensed mental health professionals, 652
relation between forgiveness and justice, 648-649
religious freedom
    definition of religious freedom, 634, 643
    impact on religious freedom, bankruptcy, 664-665
    impact on religious freedom, financial burden of liability, 643-645
    impact on religious freedom, legal treatment of clergy sexual abuse, 634
    impact on religious freedom, liability for negligent hiring, 646-647
    impact on religious freedom, liability for negligent supervision, 647-651
    impact on religious freedom, mandated remedies by the court, 655-656
    impact on religious freedom, respondeat superior and breach of fiduciary claims, 645-646
    protection of clergy sexual abuse by religious freedom, 634-636
religious autonomy, church polity, 665-666
religious autonomy, discipline of clergy, 666
review of church records in court proceedings, 652-655
statutory reporting of child sexual abuse, 656-657

Religiously Affiliated Education (Berg)
academic freedom, 696-697
admissions, 678, 704
    discrimination: race and sex, 704-705
    religious preferences in admissions, 705-707
    Title IX, 691, 694-695, 705
curriculum and campus life, 678
curriculum and teacher certification, 688-691
discipline and code of conduct, 678, 696-697, 704
employment relations and policies, 691-700
    collective bargaining, 698
    employment discrimination laws: race and sex, 697
    employees, teachers, and others, 678, 692-693
    Fair Labor Standards Act (minimum wage and equal pay), 691, 697
    federal and state unemployment compensation laws, 691, 699-700
    National Labor Relations Board, 691
    religious preferences in employment, 694-696, 701
government financial assistance to religious schools, 707-717
    Civil Rights Restoration Act of 1987, 717

Religiously Affiliated Education, *continued*
conditions restricting the religious
character of schools, 708-716
direct aid, 712
educational assistance to students and
parents, 713
Establishment Clause restrictions, 709-
710
excessive entanglement (*Lemon* test),
710
equal aid, 711
equal "indirect aid" to colleges, 713-
714
equal "indirect aid" to elementary and
secondary schools, 714
nondiscrimination requirements, 717
pervasively religious character of
schools, 710, 713
school voucher programs, 714
state constitutional provisions, restrictions, 714
legal approaches to religious schools, 679-
686
common school model, 679-681
deference to the political branches,
684-686
equality paradigm, 684-686
"hybrid" claims, 684
plurality of institutions model, 681-
683
separation of religion and state model,
683
strict standard of scrutiny, 684
"pervasively sectarian" character, 678
religious autonomy, factors affecting the
rights to, 688
religious organizations, structure of, 676
definition of, 676
formal legal structure, 676
broader conception of structure, 676

**Appendix - The Supreme Court's
Voucher Decision (***Zelman v. Simmons-Harris***) (Berg)**
school voucher programs, Establishment
Clause questions, 720-722
criteria for constitutionality of, 720-
722
direct aid, 720

direct aid, restrictions to secular uses,
720
indirect aid, 720
neutrality, class of beneficiaries, 720
neutrality, class of eligible institutions,
720
parental choice, 720-721
criteria for determining genuineness
of, 721-722
school voucher programs, regulations imposed upon religious schools, 723-725
employment discrimination laws, 723
exemptions to regulation, 724-725
deference to government, 724
endorsement or promotion of religion, 725
equality rationale, 724
First Amendment right to freedom
of expression and association,
724
"hybrid" claims, 724-725
removal of significant government
burden upon religious exercise,
725
religious preferences in employment,
725
school voucher programs, state constitutional restrictions, 722-723
Free Exercise or Equal Protection
clause challenges to state constitutional restrictions, 723
prohibition against use of state funds
for private schools, 722
prohibition against use of state funds
for religious schools, 722
prohibition against use of state funds
to religious worship or instruction,
722-723

**Religiously Affiliated Health Care
Providers: Legal Structures and Transformations (Hermann)**
legal structures of religious health care
providers
changes in health care environment,
729
charitable trust status, 734-735
corporate charter, 728
governing structure, 728

history of the health care system, 731-732

managed care, 730

tax-exempt status, 733-734

tests to determine charitable status, 734

conversions of religiously affiliated hospitals, 730-749

antitrust concerns, 739-740

"alienation of property," 745-746

availability of care for the uninsured and indigent, 737

"carve outs," 749

conversion of Roman Catholic-sponsored hospital, 745

cy pres, doctrine of, 740

Ethical and Religious Directives (ERDs) by National Council of Catholic Bishops, 747, 751

federal and state legislation and guidelines, 730, 741-744

Internal Revenue Service guidelines for maintenance of not-for-profit status, 741

joint venture, 737

merger as a result of duress, 749

process of combining forces, 737

sale of all assets, 737

tax and antitrust implications, 730, 740-741

ethical conflicts and issues, 750-754

"Commentary on: Reply of the Sacred Congregation for the Doctrine of Faith on Sterilization in Catholic Hospitals," 748

Jewish tradition, 751-752

organ donation and transplantation, 754

reproductive health issues, 747, 751

right-to-die, 752-753

Roman Catholic tradition, 751

physician-assisted suicide, 753

Presbyterian Church, 752

sterilization, 747, 749-750

sterilization, canon law, 747-750

"Sterilization in Catholic Hospitals," 747

United Methodist Church, 752

Constitutional Coherence and the Legal Structures of American Churches (Marshall)

biblical interpretation, comparison of constitutional interpretation to, 782

definition of religion, 765

secularization of religious practices, 766

sincerity of believer, 765-766

Establishment Clause, 762-763

Lemon v. Kurtzman test, 762

free exercise of religion, 763, 773-787

distinction of free exercise from toleration, 785

freedom from religion approach (secularization model), 770

"full and free exercise," 773, 776-777

"hybrid" rights, 763

limiting ordinance, 785

nondiscrimination, 785

nonendorsement, 785

nonentanglement, 785

religious self-understanding approach (deference model), 760-771

religious self-understanding approach (deference model), difficulties with, 768-771

substantive neutrality, 785

tension between the Establishment and Free Exercise clauses, 761, 764, 786-787

history as guide in interpretation, 776

history as precedent, 761

religion and economics, 768

Fair Labor Standards Act, 768

religion and politics, 767

unitary approaches, 788

complementarity of Free Exercise Clause and Establishment Clause, 776-777, 788

separation, 788

strict neutrality, 788

Full and Free Exercise of Religion (Gaffney)

accommodations to religious exercise (exemptions from generally applicable laws), 785

Act of Toleration, 773-774

Full and Free Exercise of Religion, *continued*

history as guide in interpretation of the Religion Clause, 776, 777-782, 794-795
  comparison to theories of biblical interpretation, 782-785
  history as guide in interpretation, difficulties of, 778-782
  nineteenth-century history as guide in interpretation, 794-795
  Supreme Court decisions on the Religion Clause, 796-804
free exercise of religion, 773-774, 776-777, 785-793
  belief and action, distinction between, 797, 808
  exemption from military service, 797-798
  flag salute, 799-801
  Free Exercise Clause, relation to Establishment Clause, 776, 786-793
  Free Exercise Clause, tension with Establishment Clause, 786-787
  "full and free exercise," 773-774, 776-777
    distinction from toleration, 774, 785

limiting ordinance, 785
incorporation into the Fourteenth Amendment, 794-795
institutional autonomy of religious organizations, 804-807
judicial review, 774-775
subsumption of religious freedom under other civil liberties, 775
toleration, 773-774
unitary approaches to the Religion Clause
  complementarity of Free Exercise Clause and Establishment Clause, 776-777, 786-793
  strict neutrality approach, 788
  strict separationist approach, 788
ways of thinking about Religion Clause
  as freedom from government power (full and free exercise), 786-787
  complementarity of Free Exercise Clause and Establishment Clause, 776-777, 786-793
  nondiscrimination, 785
  nonendorsement, 785
  nonentanglement, 785
  substantive neutrality, 785
Williamsburg Charter, 775, 789-790